Adolescence

Eleventh Edition

Adolescence

Laurence Steinberg

Temple University

McGraw Hill Education

ADOLESCENCE, ELEVENTH EDITION

5 6 7 8 9 10 LWI 21 20 19 18

ISBN   978-1-259-56782-7

MHID 1-259-56782-6

Senior Vice President, Products & Markets: *Kurt L. Strand*
Vice President, General Manager, Products & Markets: *Michael Ryan*
Vice President, Content Design & Delivery: *Kimberly Meriwether David*
Managing Director: *William Glass*
Director: *Krista Bettino*
Director, Product Development: *Meghan Campbell*
Lead Product Developer: *Dawn Groundwater*
Product Developer: *Bruce Cantley*
Marketing Manager: *Christina Yu*
Director, Content Design & Delivery: *Terri Schiesl*
Program Manager: *Debra Hash*
Content Project Manager (Core): *Sheila M. Frank*
Content Project Manager (Assessment): *Jodi Banowetz*
Buyer: *Susan K. Culbertson*
Design: *Matt Backhaus*
Content Licensing Specialist (Image): *Shawntel Schmitt*
Content Licensing Specialist (Text): *Jacob Sullivan*
Cover Image: © *Sean Justice/Getty Images*
Compositor: *SPi Global*
Printer: *LSC Communications*

Library of Congress Cataloging-in-Publication Data

Names: Steinberg, Laurence D., 1952- author.
Title: Adolescence / Laurence Steinberg, Temple University.
Description: Eleventh Edition. | New York : McGraw-Hill Education, 2016. |
    2017 | Revised edition of the author's Adolescence, 2014.
Identifiers: LCCN 2015040572 | ISBN 9781259567827 (alk. paper)
Subjects: LCSH: Adolescent psychology—Textbooks.
Classification: LCC BF724 .S75 2016 | DDC 305.235—dc23
LC record available at http://lccn.loc.gov/2015040572

mheducation.com/highered

For Wendy and Ben

About the Author

© Axel Griesch

LAURENCE STEINBERG, Ph.D., is the Distinguished University Professor and Laura H. Carnell Professor of Psychology at Temple University. He graduated from Vassar College in 1974 and from Cornell University in 1977, where he received his Ph.D. in human development and family studies. He is a Fellow of the American Psychological Association, the Association for Psychological Science, and the American Academy of Arts and Sciences and former President of the Society for Research on Adolescence and the Division of Developmental Psychology of the American Psychological Association. Dr. Steinberg has been on the editorial boards of many major journals, including *Developmental Psychology* and *Child Development,* where he served as Associate Editor. He chaired the National Academies' Committee on the Science of Adolescence and has been a frequent consultant to state and federal agencies and lawmakers on child labor, secondary education, and juvenile justice policy. His work was cited numerous times by the U.S. Supreme Court in its landmark decisions that abolished the juvenile death penalty and mandatory sentences of life without parole for juveniles.

Dr. Steinberg is one of the most highly cited scholars in the field of developmental psychology. His own research has focused on a range of topics in the study of contemporary adolescence, including parent–adolescent relationships, risk taking and decision making, mental health, adolescent brain development, school-year employment, academic achievement, and juvenile crime and justice. He has been the recipient of numerous honors, including the John P. Hill Award for Outstanding Contributions to the Study of Adolescence, given by the Society for Research on Adolescence; the Society for Adolescent Medicine's Gallagher Lectureship; and, from the American Psychological Association, the Urie Bronfenbrenner Award for Lifetime Contribution to Developmental Psychology in the Service of Science and Society, the Award for Distinguished Contributions to Research in Public Policy, and the APA Presidential Citation. In 2009, he was named as the first recipient of the Klaus J. Jacobs Research Prize for Productive Youth Development.

Dr. Steinberg also has been recognized for excellence in research and teaching by the University of California, the University of Wisconsin, and Temple University, where he was honored in 1994 as one of that university's Great Teachers. He has taught undergraduate and graduate courses in adolescence for nearly 40 years and has served as the doctoral advisor to more than 35 students, many of whom have gone on to become influential scholars in their own right in the field of adolescence. In 2013, he received the Elizabeth Hurlock Beckman Award, a national prize given to college professors who have "inspired their former students to achieve greatness."

In addition to *Adolescence,* Dr. Steinberg is the author or co-author of approximately 400 scholarly articles on growth and development during the teenage years, as well as the books *You and Your Adolescent; When Teenagers Work: The Psychological and Social Costs of Adolescent Employment* (with Ellen Greenberger); *Crossing Paths: How Your Child's Adolescence Triggers Your Own Crisis* (with Wendy Steinberg); *Beyond the Classroom: Why School Reform Has Failed and What Parents Need to Do* (with B. Bradford Brown and Sanford Dornbusch); *The 10 Basic Principles of Good Parenting* (which has been published in 10 languages); *Rethinking Juvenile Justice* (with Elizabeth Scott); and *Age of Opportunity: Lessons From the New Science of Adolescence.* He is co-editor of *Studying Minority Adolescents: Conceptual, Methodological, and Theoretical Issues* (with Vonnie McLoyd) and the *Handbook of Adolescent Psychology* (with Richard Lerner).

Brief Contents

About the Author   vi
A Note from the Author   xiv
Preface   xv

Introduction The Study of Adolescent Development   1

PART 1

The Fundamental Changes of Adolescence   13

1 Biological Transitions   13
2 Cognitive Transitions   42
3 Social Transitions   69

PART 2

The Contexts of Adolescence   95

4 Families   95
5 Peer Groups   122
6 Schools   152
7 Work, Leisure, and Media   181

PART 3

Psychosocial Development During Adolescence   208

8 Identity   208
9 Autonomy   235
10 Intimacy   260
11 Sexuality   290
12 Achievement   320
13 Psychosocial Problems in Adolescence   347

Mc Graw Hill Education **connect®**

McGraw-Hill Education Psychology's APA Documentation Style Guide

Glossary   G1
References   R1
Name Index   I1
Subject Index   I24

Contents

About the Author vi
A Note from the Author xiv
Preface xv

Introduction
The Study of Adolescent Development   1

The Boundaries of Adolescence   3

Early, Middle, and Late Adolescence   4

A Framework for Studying Adolescent Development   4

The Fundamental Changes of Adolescence   4

The Contexts of Adolescence   5

Psychosocial Development in Adolescence   7

Theoretical Perspectives on Adolescence   8

Biosocial Theories   8

Organismic Theories   9

Learning Theories   9

Sociological Theories   10

Historical and Anthropological Theories   11

Stereotypes Versus Scientific Study   11

PART 1

The Fundamental Changes of Adolescence   13

Chapter 1
Biological Transitions   13

Puberty: An Overview   14

The Endocrine System   14

What Triggers Puberty?   16

How Hormones Influence Adolescent Development   17

Somatic Development   18

Changes in Stature and the Dimensions of the Body   18

Sexual Maturation   19

The Timing and Tempo of Puberty   21

Variations in the Timing and Tempo of Puberty   22

Genetic and Environmental Influences on Pubertal Timing   23

The Psychological and Social Impact of Puberty   26

The Immediate Impact of Puberty   26

The Impact of Specific Pubertal Events   30

The Impact of Early or Late Maturation   30

Obesity and Eating Disorders   34

Obesity   34

Anorexia Nervosa, Bulimia, and Binge Eating Disorder   36

Physical Health and Health Care in Adolescence   40

The Paradox of Adolescent Health   40

Causes of Mortality in Adolescence   40

Promoting Adolescent Health   41

Chapter 2
Cognitive Transitions   42

Changes in Cognition   43

Thinking About Possibilities   43

Thinking About Abstract Concepts   45

Thinking About Thinking   45

Thinking in Multiple Dimensions   46

Adolescent Relativism   47

Theoretical Perspectives on Adolescent Thinking   47

The Piagetian View of Adolescent Thinking   47

The Information-Processing View of Adolescent Thinking   48

The Adolescent Brain   51

How Your Brain Works   52

The Age of Opportunity   54

What Changes in Adolescence?   55

Implications for Adolescent Behavior   60

Individual Differences in Intelligence in Adolescence   60

> The Measurement of IQ   60
>
> Types of Intelligence   61
>
> Culture and Intelligence   61

Adolescent Thinking in Context   62

> Social Cognition in Adolescence   62
>
> Adolescent Risk Taking   64

Chapter 3
Social Transitions   69

Social Redefinition and Psychosocial Development   70

The Elongation of Adolescence   71

Adolescence as a Social Invention   72

> The "Invention" of Adolescence   73
>
> Emerging Adulthood: A New Stage of Life or a Luxury of the Middle Class?   74

Changes in Status During Adolescence   77

> Drawing a Legal Boundary   77
>
> Inconsistencies in Adolescents' Legal Status   78

The Process of Social Redefinition   79

> Common Practices in the Process of Social Redefinition   79

Variations in Social Transitions   80

> Variations in Clarity   81
>
> Variations in Continuity   84

The Transition into Adulthood in Contemporary Society   87

> Special Transitional Problems of Poor and Minority Youth   88
>
> The Effects of Poverty on the Transition into Adulthood   89
>
> What Can Be Done to Ease the Transition?   89

The Influence of Neighborhood Conditions on Adolescent Development   90

> Processes of Neighborhood Influences   92

PART 2
The Contexts of Adolescence   95

Chapter 4
Families   95

Is Conflict Between Teenagers and Parents Inevitable?   96

> The Generation Gap: Fact and Fiction   96
>
> What Do Adolescents and Parents Usually Fight About?   97

Family Relationships at Adolescence   98

> A Time of Reorganization and Change   98
>
> The Adolescent's Parents at Midlife   99
>
> Changes in Family Needs and Functions   100
>
> Transformations in Family Relations   101
>
> Sex Differences in Family Relationships   103

Family Relationships and Adolescent Development   104

> Parenting Styles and Their Effects   105
>
> Ethnic Differences in Parenting Practices   108
>
> Autonomy and Attachment in the Adolescent's Family   109
>
> Adolescents' Relationships with Siblings   109

Behavioral Genetics and Adolescent Development   110

> Genetic and Environmental Influences on Adolescent Development   111
>
> Why Are Siblings Often So Different?   111

The Adolescent's Family in a Changing Society   112

> The Changed and Changing Nature of Family Life   112
>
> Adolescents and Divorce   114
>
> The Specific Impact of Marital Conflict   115
>
> The Longer-Term Effects of Divorce   116
>
> Custody, Contact, and Conflict following Divorce   116
>
> Remarriage   117
>
> Economic Stress and Poverty   118
>
> Special Family Forms   120

The Importance of the Family in Adolescent Development   121

Chapter 5
Peer Groups   122

The Origins of Adolescent Peer Groups in Contemporary Society   124

Changes in the Size of the Youth Population   124

Is There a Separate Youth Culture?   125

The Nature of Adolescent Peer Groups   127

Changes in Peer Groups during Adolescence   127

Cliques and Crowds   128

Changes in Clique and Crowd Structure Over Time   130

Adolescents and Their Crowds   133

The Social Map of Adolescence   133

Crowds as Reference Groups   133

Adolescents and Their Cliques   135

Similarity among Clique Members   135

Common Interests among Friends   137

Similarity between Friends: Selection or Socialization?   140

Popularity and Rejection in Adolescent Peer Groups   142

Determinants of Popularity and Rejection   142

Relational Aggression   145

Victimization and Harassment   147

The Peer Group and Psychosocial Development   151

Chapter 6
Schools   152

The Broader Context of U.S. Secondary Education   154

The Origins of Secondary Education   154

School Reform: Past and Present   155

What Should Schools Teach?   157

Education in the Inner Cities   158

The Social Organization of Schools   158

School Size and Class Size   158

Age Grouping and School Transitions   160

Tracking   163

Ethnic Composition   167

Alternatives to Public Schools   167

Classroom Climate   169

The Best Classroom Climate for Adolescents   169

Teacher Expectations and Student Performance   170

The Importance of Student Engagement   171

School Violence   174

Beyond High School   176

The College-Bound   176

The Non-College-Bound   178

Schools and Adolescent Development   179

Characteristics of Good Schools   179

The Effects of School on Adolescent Development   179

Chapter 7
Work, Leisure, and Media   181

Adolescents' Free Time in Contemporary Society   182

Patterns of Time Use in Contemporary America   182

Patterns of Time Use in Other Countries   183

Adolescents and Work   184

The Rise and Fall of the Student Worker   184

Teenage Employment in Other Nations   185

The Adolescent Workplace Today   186

Employment and Adolescent Development   186

Youth Unemployment   189

Adolescents and Leisure   190

Adolescents' Free Time and Their Moods   190

Structured Leisure Activities   191

Unstructured Leisure Time   193

Promoting Positive Youth Development   195

Adolescents, Media, and the Internet   196

Patterns of Media Use   196

Theories of Media Influence and Use   198

Adolescents' Exposure to Controversial Media Content   200

Electronic Media and Adolescent Development   203

Mass Media and Adolescent Girls' Body Image   206

The Adolescent Consumer   206

Free Time and Adolescent Development   207

PART 3

Psychosocial Development During Adolescence 208

Chapter 8
Identity 208

Identity as an Adolescent Issue 209

Changes in Self-Conceptions 210

Changes in the Content and Structure of Self-Conceptions 210

Dimensions of Personality in Adolescence 212

Changes in Self-Esteem 213

Stability and Changes in Self-Esteem 213

Group Differences in Self-Esteem 215

Antecedents and Consequences of High Self-Esteem 218

The Adolescent Identity Crisis 219

Erikson's Theoretical Framework 219

Identity Versus Identity Diffusion 219

The Social Context of Identity Development 220

Resolving the Identity Crisis 221

Problems in Identity Development 221

Research on Identity Development 223

Determining an Adolescent's Identity Status 223

Studying Identity Development Over Time 224

Identity and Ethnicity 225

The Development of Ethnic Identity 226

Discrimination and Its Effects 228

Multiethnic Adolescents 230

Identity and Gender 231

Gender-Role Development 232

Gender-Role Socialization During Adolescence 232

Masculinity and Femininity 233

Chapter 9
Autonomy 235

Autonomy as an Adolescent Issue 237

The Development of Emotional Autonomy 238

Emotional Autonomy and Detachment 238

Emotional Autonomy and Individuation 239

Research on Emotional Autonomy 239

Emotional Autonomy and Parenting Practices 241

The Development of Behavioral Autonomy 243

Changes in Decision-Making Abilities 243

When Do Adolescents Make Decisions as Well as Adults? 244

Changes in Susceptibility to Influence 245

Ethnic and Cultural Differences in Expectations for Autonomy 248

The Development of Cognitive Autonomy 249

Moral Development During Adolescence 249

Prosocial Reasoning, Prosocial Behavior, and Volunteerism 252

Political Thinking During Adolescence 255

Religious Beliefs During Adolescence 256

Chapter 10
Intimacy 260

Intimacy as an Adolescent Issue 262

Theoretical Perspectives on Adolescent Intimacy 262

Sullivan's Theory of Interpersonal Development 263

Interpersonal Development during Adolescence 263

Attachment in Adolescence 264

The Development of Intimacy in Adolescence 268

Changes in the Nature of Friendship 268

Changes in the Display of Intimacy 269

Sex Differences in Intimacy 271

Changes in the Targets of Intimacy 273

Friendships with the Other Sex 277

Dating and Romantic Relationships 279

Dating and the Development of Intimacy 280

The Development of Dating Relationships 282

The Impact of Dating on Adolescent Development 284

Intimacy and Psychosocial Development 288

Chapter 11
Sexuality   290

Sexuality as an Adolescent Issue   291

Sexual Activity During Adolescence   292

Stages of Sexual Activity   293

Sexual Intercourse During Adolescence   293

Changes in Sexual Activity Over Time   296

The Sexually Active Adolescent   297

Psychological and Social Characteristics of Sexually Active Adolescents   297

Hormonal and Contextual Influences on Sexual Activity   299

Parental and Peer Influences on Sexual Activity   300

Sex Differences in the Meaning of Sex   304

Sexual Orientation   305

Sexual Harassment, Rape, and Sexual Abuse During Adolescence   306

Risky Sex and its Prevention   309

Contraceptive Use   309

AIDS and Other Sexually Transmitted Diseases   311

Teen Pregnancy   312

Adolescent Parenthood   315

Sex Education   318

Chapter 12
Achievement   320

Achievement as an Adolescent Issue   321

The Importance of Noncognitive Factors   323

Achievement Motivation   323

Beliefs About Success and Failure   324

Environmental Influences on Achievement   328

The Influence of the Home Environment   329

The Influence of Friends   331

Educational Achievement   333

The Importance of Socioeconomic Status   334

Ethnic Differences in Educational Achievement   335

Changes in Educational Achievement Over Time   338

Dropping Out of High School   340

Occupational Achievement   342

The Development of Occupational Plans   342

Influences on Occupational Choices   343

Chapter 13
Psychosocial Problems in Adolescence   347

Some General Principles about Problems in Adolescence   348

Psychosocial Problems: Their Nature and Covariation   350

Comorbidity of Externalizing Problems   350

Comorbidity of Internalizing Problems   352

Substance Use and Abuse   352

Prevalence of Substance Use and Abuse   353

Causes and Consequences of Substance Use and Abuse   357

Drugs and the Adolescent Brain   360

Prevention and Treatment of Substance Use and Abuse   361

Externalizing Problems   362

Categories of Externalizing Problems   362

Developmental Progression of Antisocial Behavior   364

Changes in Juvenile Offending Over Time   365

Causes of Antisocial Behavior   367

Prevention and Treatment of Externalizing Problems   371

Internalizing Problems   371

The Nature and Prevalence of Depression   372

Sex Differences in Depression   373

Suicide and Non-Suicidal Self-Injury   375

Causes of Depression and Internalizing Disorders   377

Treatment and Prevention of Internalizing Problems   378

Stress and Coping   378

connect McGraw-Hill Education
Psychology's APA Documentation Style Guide

Glossary   G1

References   R1

Name Index   I1

Subject Index   I24

A Note from the Author

Two psychopathic killers persuaded me to abandon my dreams to someday become a comedy writer and study psychology instead. I did not enter college intending to become either a psychologist or a professor. I majored in English, hoping to study creative writing. I became interested in psychology during the second semester of my freshman year, because of an introductory course in personality theory. My professor had assigned the book *In Cold Blood,* and our task was to analyze the personalities of Dick and Perry, the two murderers. I was hooked. I followed this interest in personality development to graduate school in developmental psychology, where I learned that if you really wanted to understand how we develop into the people we ultimately become, you have got to know something about adolescence. That was more than 40 years ago, and I'm still as passionate about studying this period of life as I was then.

I hope that this book gets you more excited about adolescence, too.

One reason I like teaching and writing about adolescence is that most students find it inherently interesting, in part because pretty much everyone has such vivid recollections of what it was like to be a teenager. In fact, researchers have discovered that people actually remember events from adolescence more intensely than events from other times, something that has been referred to as the "reminiscence bump."

The reminiscence bump makes teaching adolescence both fun and frustrating. Fun, because it isn't hard to get students interested in the topic. Frustrating, though, because it's a challenge to get students to look at adolescence from a scientific, as well as personal, perspective. That, above all, is my goal for this book. I don't want you to forget or set aside your own experience as an adolescent. (I couldn't make that happen, anyway.) But what I hope I can do is to help you understand adolescence—your own adolescence as well as the adolescence that is experienced by others around the world—more deeply and more intelligently, by introducing you to the latest science on the subject. I still maintain a very active program of research of my own, and that necessitates staying on top of the field's most recent and important developments. There is a lot of exciting work being done on adolescence these days (one of my interests is the adolescent brain), and I want to share this excitement with you. Who knows, maybe you'll become hooked, too.

I've tried to do my best at covering the most important topics and writing about them in a way that is not only informative, but fun and interesting to read. If there's something I could have done better, please let me know.

Laurence Steinberg
Temple University
laurence.steinberg@temple.edu

Preface

Steinberg . . . Cutting-edge science, personalized for today's students

As a well-respected researcher, Laurence Steinberg connects current research with real-world application, helping students see the similarities and differences in adolescent development across different social, economic, and cultural backgrounds.

Through an integrated, personalized digital learning program, students gain the insight they need to study smarter, stay focused, and improve their performance.

Personalized Study, Better Data, Improved Results

SmartBook is now available for *Adolescence*!

McGraw-Hill Education's SmartBook® is an adaptive learning program designed to help students stay focused and maximize their study time. Based on metacognition, and powered by McGraw-Hill LearnSmart®, SmartBook's adaptive capabilities provide students with a personalized reading and learning experience that helps them identify the concepts they know, and more importantly, the concepts they *don't* know.

SmartBook is the first and only adaptive reading experience currently available.

- **Make It Effective.** SmartBook™ creates a personalized reading experience by highlighting the most impactful concepts a student needs to learn at that moment in time. This ensures that every minute spent with SmartBook™ is returned to the student as the most value-added minute possible.
- **Make It Informed.** The reading experience continuously adapts by highlighting content based on what the student knows and doesn't know. Real-time reports quickly identify the concepts that require more attention from individual students—or the entire class. SmartBook™ detects the content a student is most likely to forget and brings it back to improve long-term knowledge retention.

Real People, Real World, Real Life

McGraw-Hill Education's Milestones is a powerful video-based learning tool that allows students to experience life as it unfolds, from infancy through emerging adulthood. A limited number of Milestones videos are now available for viewing within the McGraw-Hill Connect Media Bank for Steinberg's *Adolescence,* 11e.

Studying Adolescence in Context

The primary goal of *Adolescence* is to help students understand how the context in which adolescents come of age shapes the way in which they develop. Adolescent development cannot be understood apart from the context in which young people live and grow up—families, peer groups, schools, neighborhoods, and work and leisure settings. Perhaps the greatest expansion of knowledge during the past two decades has been about adolescents from ethnic minority groups, from families that have recently immigrated to a new culture from parts of the world other than North America, and from studies conducted by scholars outside the United States. The eleventh edition of *Adolescence* integrates discussions of ethnicity and culture throughout every chapter, focusing not only on ethnic differences in development but also on similarities that cut across adolescents from different social, economic, and cultural backgrounds.

Thinking Critically to Make Connections

Four sets of questions interspersed throughout the text ask students to think more deeply about particular research findings. "**Making the Cultural Connection**" asks students to contemplate how particular findings might (or might not) change if the research were carried out in a different cultural context. "**Making the Personal Connection**" asks students to think about their own adolescent experience in the context of the research. "**Making the Scientific Connection**" asks students to consider a finding's scientific implications. "**Making the Practical Connection**" challenges students to think about how a finding might inform policy or practice. Many instructors may want to use these questions as a launching pad for class discussions or as essay questions on examinations.

Analyzing the Latest Research

Adolescence strives to provide students with the most current, most thorough coverage of the scientific literature on adolescent development. The material in each chapter has been thoroughly updated. The eleventh edition includes more than 1,000 new studies from over 60 scientific journals from the fields of psychology, education, neuroscience, sociology, psychiatry, criminology, economics, law, medicine, and public health. I've tried to emphasize studies that break new ground (like studies of brain development), change the way the field thinks (like studies of why aggressive adolescents are often popular), or update existing findings with more recent samples or newer methods (like studies of Internet use) in order to give students the opportunity to review and analyze the latest information the field has to offer.

Content Changes

The overall organization of *Adolescence* has not changed since the previous edition. Specifically, the chapters about psychosocial development during adolescence are separate from those about the contexts of adolescence. In this way, the psychosocial concerns of adolescence—identity, autonomy, intimacy, sexuality, and achievement—are presented as central developmental concerns that surface across, and are affected by, different settings.

In response to feedback from some instructors that the text had become wordy, I devoted special attention in this edition to the quality of the writing. Each chapter has been shortened somewhat without dropping coverage of any major areas of research. I did this by doing what I teach my students about good writing: To follow Strunk and White's famous dictum, from *The Elements of Style*, to "Omit needless words."

This book contains an Introduction and 13 chapters, which are grouped into three parts: the fundamental biological, cognitive, and social changes of the period (Part 1); the contexts of adolescence (Part 2); and psychosocial development during the adolescent years (Part 3). The Introduction presents a model for studying adolescence that serves as both the organizational framework for the text and an overview of some of the basic disciplinary perspectives on the period. I have found the framework to be extremely helpful in teaching adolescent development, and I highly recommend using it. However, if the model does not fit with your course outline or your own perspective on adolescence, it is possible to use the text without using the framework. Each chapter is self-contained, and so it is not necessary to assign chapters in the sequence in which they are ordered in the text. Most users assign the chapters in the order in which they appear, but some assign the chapters in a sequence that pairs an aspect of psychosocial development with the context that most influences it (for example, "Schools" with "Achievement," or "Peer Groups" with "Intimacy"), and that has worked well for them.

Theory and Methods

Although the Introduction reviews how different disciplines (such as psychology, neuroscience, sociology, anthropology, and history) approach the study of adolescence, it does not provide detailed examinations of particular theories or research methods. My preference is to integrate material on theory and methods when it is most relevant, in a way that shows students how research and theory are related. At the beginning of the chapter on intimacy, for instance, several perspectives on close relationships (for example, attachment theory and Sullivan's perspective on psychosocial development) are presented, and then the relevant research is examined. Similarly, the research methods and tools employed in the study of adolescence are discussed in the context of specific studies that illustrate the powers—or pitfalls—of certain strategies.

Chapter-By-Chapter Changes

The eleventh edition of *Adolescence* features updated and expanded coverage of key issues in development in every chapter. Below is a complete list of changes in each chapter:

Chapter 1

- Thorough update of all content (more than 80 new citations)
- Expanded discussion of causes of the decline in the age of puberty
- Expanded discussion of adolescent sleep
- Expanded discussion of adolescent obesity
- Expanded discussion of eating disorders
- Expanded discussion of the impact of puberty on brain development

Chapter 2

- Thorough update of all content (more than 90 new citations)
- Expanded discussion of memory during adolescence and the "reminiscence bump"
- Expanded material on the basics of brain development
- Greatly expanded discussion of structural and functional changes in the adolescent brain
- Added discussion of brain plasticity in adolescence
- Expansion of material on "the social brain"
- Expanded discussion of risk taking in adolescence

Chapter 3

- Thorough update of all content (more than 50 new citations)
- Addition of discussion of the elongation of adolescence
- Expanded discussion of mental health problems among emerging adults
- Added discussion of the adverse consequences of growing up in affluent communities
- Expanded discussion of impact of neighborhood poverty

Chapter 4

- Thorough update of all content (more than 70 new citations)
- Added discussion of dangers of parental overcontrol
- Expanded discussion of closeness between adolescents and parents
- Revised discussion of sibling relationships
- Updated statistics on household composition

Chapter 5

- Thorough update of all content (more than 100 new citations)
- Expanded discussion of unsupervised time with peers
- Dropped dated material on study of "nerds to normals"
- Added discussion of parental role in managing cross-ethnic friendships
- Expanded discussion of relationship between popularity and deviance
- Expanded discussion of bullying and victimization
- Expanded discussion of cyberbullying

Chapter 6

- Thorough update of all content (more than 50 new citations)
- Updated discussion of big fish-little pond effect
- Added material on homeschooling
- Expanded discussion of student engagement and its measurement
- Expanded discussion of differential treatment of minority adolescents in schools
- Updated material on ADHD and medication for the condition

Chapter 7

- Thorough update of all content (more than 90 new citations)
- Condensed discussion of part-time employment
- Added discussion of stress associated with organized sports participation
- Updating of statistics on Internet use
- Updated discussion of the impact of the Internet on adolescent development
- Updated discussion of the impact of social networking sites

Chapter 8

- Thorough update of all content (more than 80 new citations)
- Integrated new information on brain science and self-conceptions
- Updated material on ethnic identity development and discrimination
- Added discussion of differences among sexual identity, sexual orientation, and gender roles
- Added discussion of the development of sexual identity, including transgender youth

Chapter 9

- Thorough update of all content (more than 80 new citations)
- Revised discussion of emotional autonomy
- Replaced discussion of self-reliance with discussion of self-regulation
- Updated discussion of the brain science of peer influence
- Added discussion of adolescents' beliefs about the causes of poverty and affluence
- Added material on cohort differences in civic engagement

Chapter 10

- Thorough update of all content (more than 70 new citations)
- Added material on the development of the social brain and implications for adolescent relationships

Chapter 11

- Thorough update of all content (more than 90 new citations)
- Expanded discussion of sex differences in emotional reactions to sexual debut
- Expanded discussion of sexual harassment, especially of LGBTQ youth
- Moved material on sexual identity to chapter 8 (Identity)
- Added discussion of long-acting reversible contraceptive use among adolescents

Chapter 12

- Thorough update of all content (more than 70 new citations)
- New discussion of noncognitive contributors to academic success
- Expanded discussion of importance of parental expectations
- Updated statistics on U.S. high school achievement

Chapter 13

- Thorough update of all content (more than 130 new citations)
- Expanded discussion of comorbidity of internalizing and externalizing problems
- Expanded discussion of mental health problems in adolescence and young adulthood
- New discussion of suicide contagion among adolescents
- Expanded discussion of the relationship between experimentation with substances and adolescent adjustment
- Updated discussion of drugs and the adolescent brain
- Updated all statistics on prevalence and demographic differences in substance abuse, crime, and depression
- Rewritten all diagnostic criteria tables to be consistent with the DSM-5
- Added discussion of abuse of prescription drugs

Supplements

For the Instructor

The supplements for the eleventh edition have been carefully revised and updated. The instructor resources for the new edition include an Instructor's Manual, Test Bank, and PowerPoint presentations for each chapter.

Acknowledgments

Revising *Adolescence* at a time when so much new information is available is a challenge that requires much assistance. Over the years, my students (as well as many who have written to me from other institutions) have suggested numerous ways in which the text might be improved, and I have learned a great deal from listening to them. I am especially grateful to Karol Silva, who ably tracked down and organized much of the new research published in the three years between editions.

I also wish to thank my colleagues at McGraw-Hill Education, including William Glass, Managing Director; Krista Bettino, Brand Manager; Dawn Groundwater, Lead Product Developer; Carly Britton, Editorial Coordinator; Sheila Frank, Content Project Manager; Christina Yu, Marketing Manager; and Bruce Cantley, Product Developer.

In addition, I am grateful to the many colleagues and students across the country who took the time during the past 30 years to send me comments and suggestions based on their firsthand experiences using *Adolescence* in the classroom. They have improved the text with each edition.

Laurence Steinberg

The Study of Adolescent Development

The Boundaries of Adolescence
   Early, Middle, and Late Adolescence

A Framework for Studying Adolescent Development
   The Fundamental Changes of Adolescence
   The Contexts of Adolescence
   Psychosocial Development of Adolescence

Theoretical Perspectives on Adolescence
   Biosocial Theories
   Organismic Theories
   Learning Theories
   Sociological Theories
   Historical and Anthropological Theories

Stereotypes Versus Scientific Study

© Eric Audras/PhotoAlto/Getty Images RF

1

In the spring of 2015, the world watched closely as a young man named Dzhokhar Tsarnaev went on trial for the Boston Marathon bombing. The question before the jury was not whether Tsarnaev had committed this horrific crime—he had admitted as much—but whether he should receive a sentence of life in prison or the death penalty.

Tsarnaev was 19 when the bombing took place. Among the witnesses called by Tsarnaev's defense team was Jay Giedd, a prominent expert in adolescent brain development. Giedd testified that recent studies showed that the brain was still maturing during the late teens and early 20s. Building on Giedd's testimony, Tsarnaev's attorneys argued that people this age lacked the ability to stand up to a more powerful peer, like an older brother, and that this immaturity made Tsarnaev less than fully responsible for his behavior and, accordingly, less deserving of capital punishment.

Defense attorneys for Dzhokhar Tsarnaev, the admitted Boston Marathon bomber, used adolescent brain science to argue that he should be spared the death penalty. The jury disagreed.
© FBI/Handout/Getty Images News/Getty Images

The jury rejected this argument. On May 15, 2015, Dzhokhar Tsarnaev was sentenced to death. It is almost certain that his defense attorneys will appeal this decision.

Although advances in adolescent brain science did not sway the jury in the Boston Marathon bombing case, the science of adolescent development is changing the way in which we think about this stage of life (Steinberg, 2014). Historically, and pretty much around the world, we have drawn a legal boundary between adolescence and adulthood at age 18 (even though in the United States there are some things people are permitted to do at an earlier age, like driving, and others that are prohibited until several years later, like purchasing alcohol). But what if the brain is still maturing in the early 20s? What if things like impulse control or the ability to fully think through the future consequences of one's decisions are still developing into the mid-20s? Should this change how we define adulthood under the law?

This question is one that I have been studying and writing about for the past 20 years, and I still don't have a simple answer. If science is our guide, where should we draw the line between adolescence and adulthood? It's not just an abstract, academic exercise. How we answer this question has far-reaching ramifications for society and, of course, for teenagers. At what age should a pregnant adolescent be able to obtain an abortion without her parents' permission? How old should individuals have to be to see a psychologist or have cosmetic surgery without their parents knowing? Have we picked the right ages in deciding who can drive, see R-rated movies, or buy cigarettes? And how should we respond to young offenders? "Do the adult crime, do the adult time" may sound fair from the perspective of crime victims, but does it make sense in light of what we know about adolescent development? When he committed the Boston Marathon bombing, was Dzhokhar Tsarnaev an adolescent or an adult?

making the practical connection

Studies of adolescent brain development have revealed that the brain continues to mature well into the mid-20s. This research was used in several U.S. Supreme Court cases, where the Court ruled that adolescents should not be as punished as severely as adults, even when they have been convicted of the same crimes. But some advocates for youth have worried that this same research can be used to limit what teenagers are allowed to do, such as drive or seek an abortion without their parents' knowledge. How would you respond to someone who, on the basis of this research, says that if adolescents are too young to be punished like adults, they are too young to be treated like adults in other ways as well?

What is the nature of adolescents' identity development in a changing world? How should society deal with problems of youth unemployment, underage drinking, teenage pregnancy, and juvenile crime? What is the best way to prepare young people for adulthood?

Answering these questions requires a thorough understanding of adolescents' psychological development, and in this book we will examine how—and why—people's hopes and plans, fears and anxieties, and questions and concerns change as they develop from childhood to adulthood.

Answering these difficult questions requires more than an understanding of the ways in which individuals change psychologically as they move through adolescence, though. It also requires knowledge of how they develop physically, how their brain matures, how their relationships with others change, how as a group they are viewed and treated by society, how adolescence in our society differs from adolescence in other cultures, and how the nature of adolescence itself has changed over the years. In other words, a complete understanding of adolescence in contemporary society depends on being familiar with biological, social, sociological, cultural, and historical perspectives on the period (Dahl & Hariri, 2005).

The Boundaries of Adolescence

The word *adolescence* is derived from the Latin *adolescere,* which means "to grow into adulthood" (R. Lerner & Steinberg, 2009). In all societies, adolescence is a time of growing up, of moving from the immaturity of childhood into the maturity of adulthood, of preparation for the future (Larson, Wilson, & Rickman, 2009; Schlegel, 2009). **Adolescence** is a period of transitions: biological, psychological, social, economic. During adolescence, individuals become interested in sex and biologically capable of having children. They become wiser, more sophisticated, and better able to make their own decisions. They become more self-aware, more independent, and more concerned about what the future holds. Over time, they are permitted to work, to get married, to drive, and to vote. Think for a moment about how much you changed between when you finished elementary school and when you graduated from high school. I'm sure you'll agree that the changes you went through were remarkable.

adolescence
The stage of development that begins with puberty and ends when individuals make the transition into adult roles, roughly speaking, from about 10 until the early 20s.

As you can see in Table 1, there are a variety of boundaries we might draw between childhood and adolescence, and between adolescence and adulthood. Whereas a biologist would place a great deal of emphasis on the attainment and completion of puberty, an attorney would look instead at important age breaks designated by law, and an educator might draw attention to differences between students enrolled in different grades in school. Is a biologically mature fifth-grader an adolescent or a child? Is a 20-year-old college student who lives at home an adolescent or an adult? There are no right or wrong answers to these questions. It all depends on the boundaries we use to define the period. Determining the beginning and ending of adolescence is more a matter of opinion than of absolute fact.

Rather than argue about which boundaries are the correct ones, it makes more sense to think of development during adolescence as involving a *series* of transitions from immaturity into maturity (Howard & Galambos, 2011; Settersten et al., 2005; Trejos-Castillo & Vazsonyi, 2011). Some of these passages are long and some are short; some are smooth and others are rough.

Table 1 The boundaries of adolescence. Here are some examples of the ways in which adolescence has been distinguished from childhood and adulthood that we examine in this book. Which boundaries make the most sense to you?

Perspective	When Adolescence Begins	When Adolescence Ends
Biological	Onset of puberty	Becoming capable of sexual reproduction
Emotional	Beginning of detachment from parents	Attainment of separate sense identity
Cognitive	Emergence of more advanced reasoning abilities	Consolidation of advanced reasoning abilities
Interpersonal	Beginning of shift in interest from parental to peer relations	Development of capacity for intimacy with peers
Social	Beginning of training for adult work, family, and citizen roles	Full attainment of adult status and privileges
Educational	Entrance into junior high school	Completion of formal schooling
Legal	Attainment of juvenile status	Attainment of majority status
Chronological	Attainment of designated age of adolescence (e.g., 10 years)	Attainment of designated age of adulthood (e.g., 21 years)
Cultural	Entrance into period of training for ceremonial rite of passage	Completion of ceremonial rite of passage

early adolescence
The period spanning roughly ages 10–13, corresponding roughly to the junior high or middle school years.

middle adolescence
The period spanning roughly ages 14–17, corresponding to the high school years.

late adolescence
The period spanning roughly ages 18–21, corresponding approximately to the college years.

emerging adulthood
The period spanning roughly ages 18–25, during which individuals make the transition from adolescence to adulthood.

puberty
The biological changes of adolescence.

And not all of them occur at the same time. Consequently, it is quite possible—and perhaps even likely—that an individual will mature in some respects before he or she matures in others. The various aspects of adolescence have different beginnings and different endings for every individual. An individual can be a child in some ways, an adolescent in other ways, and an adult in still others.

For the purposes of this book, we'll define adolescence as beginning with puberty and ending when individuals make the transition into adult roles, roughly from age 10 until the early 20s. Although at one time "adolescence" may have been synonymous with the teenage years (from 13 to 19), the adolescent period has lengthened considerably in the past 100 years, both because physical maturation occurs earlier and because so many individuals delay entering into work and marriage until their mid-20s (Steinberg, 2014).

Early, Middle, and Late Adolescence

Because so much psychological and social growth takes place during adolescence, most social scientists and practitioners view adolescence as composed of a series of phases rather than one single stage (Samela-Aro, 2011). The 11-year-old whose time and energy is wrapped up in hip-hop, Facebook, and baseball, for example, has little in common with the 21-year-old who is involved in a serious romance, worried about pressures at work, and looking for an affordable apartment.

Social scientists who study adolescence differentiate among **early adolescence** (about ages 10–13), **middle adolescence** (about ages 14–17), and **late adolescence** (about ages 18–21). In discussing development during adolescence, we'll need to be sensitive not only to differences between adolescence and childhood, or between adolescence and adulthood, but also to differences among the various phases of adolescence itself. Some writers also have suggested that a new phase of life, called **emerging adulthood** (Arnett, 2004), characterizes the early and mid-20s. However, despite the popularity of this idea in the mass media, there is little evidence that "emerging adulthood" is a universal stage or that the majority of young people in their

mid-20s are in some sort of psychological or social limbo (Côté & Bynner, 2008; Kloep & Hendry, 2014). Indeed, what is most striking about the transition from adolescence to adulthood today is just how many different pathways there are. Some individuals spend their 20s single, dependent on their parents, and bouncing from job to job, while others leave adolescence and go straight into marriage, full-time employment, and economic independence (Osgood, Ruth, Eccles, Jacobs, & Barber, 2005).

A Framework for Studying Adolescent Development

This book uses a framework for studying adolescence that is based on a model originally suggested by John Hill (1983). The model has three basic components: (1) the fundamental changes of adolescence, (2) the contexts of adolescence, and (3) the psychosocial developments of adolescence.

The Fundamental Changes of Adolescence

What, if anything, is distinctive about adolescence as a period in development? According to Hill, three features of adolescent development give the period its special flavor and significance: (1) the onset of puberty, (2) the emergence of more advanced thinking abilities, and (3) the transition into new roles in society. These three sets of changes—biological, cognitive, and social—are the *fundamental changes* of adolescence. Importantly, they are universal changes; virtually without exception, all adolescents in every society go through them.

Biological Transitions The chief elements of the biological changes of adolescence—which collectively are referred to as **puberty**—involve changes in the young person's physical appearance (including breast development in girls, the growth of facial hair in boys, and a dramatic increase in height for both sexes) and the development of the ability to conceive children (Bogin, 2011).

We'll look at the biological changes that occur in early adolescence and examine how puberty affects the adolescent's psychological development and social relationships.

Cognitive Transitions The word *cognitive* refers to the processes that underlie how people think. Changes in thinking abilities make up the second of the three fundamental changes of adolescence. Compared with children, adolescents are much better able to think about hypothetical situations (that is, things that have not yet happened but might, or things that may not happen but could) and about abstract concepts, such as friendship, democracy, or morality (Keating, 2011). As you'll read, groundbreaking research on brain development is beginning to shed light on the ways in which these and other changes in thinking during adolescence result from the maturation of various brain regions and systems (Engle, 2013).

making the cultural connection

In contemporary industrialized society, we do not have formal ceremonies that designate when a person has become an "adult." Do we have more informal ways to let individuals know when they have made the transition? What were the most important events in your life that signaled your entrance into adulthood?

Social Transitions All societies distinguish between individuals who are viewed as children and those who are seen as ready to become adults. Our society, for example, distinguishes between people who are "underage," or minors, and people who have reached the age of majority. Not until adolescence are individuals permitted to drive, marry, and vote. Such changes in rights, privileges, and responsibilities constitute the third set of fundamental changes that occur at adolescence: social changes. In some cultures, the social changes of adolescence are marked by a formal ceremony—a **rite of passage.** In most contemporary industrialized societies, the transition is less clearly marked, but a change in social status is a universal feature of adolescence (Markstrom, 2011b).

The Contexts of Adolescence

Although all adolescents experience the biological, cognitive, and social transitions of the period, the *effects* of these changes are not uniform for all young people. Puberty makes some adolescents feel attractive and self-assured, but it makes others feel ugly and self-conscious. Being able to think in hypothetical terms makes some teenagers thankful that they grew up with the parents they have, but it prompts others to run away from home. Reaching 18 prompts some teenagers to enlist in the military or apply for a marriage license, but for others, becoming an adult is frightening and unsettling.

If the fundamental changes of adolescence are universal, why are their effects so varied? Why isn't everyone affected in the same ways by puberty, by advanced thinking abilities, and by changes in legal status? The answer is that the psychological impact of the biological, cognitive, and social changes of adolescence is shaped by the environment in which the changes take place. In

The implications of the cognitive changes of adolescence are far-reaching. © Fuse/Getty Images RF

other words, psychological development during adolescence is a product of the interplay between a set of three very basic, universal changes and the context in which these changes are experienced.

Consider, for example, two 14-year-old girls growing up in neighboring communities. When Ashley went through puberty, around age 13, her parents' first reaction was to restrict her social life. They were afraid she would become too involved with boys and neglect her schoolwork. Ashley thought her parents were being ridiculous. She rarely had a chance to meet anyone she wanted to date, because all the older boys went to the high school across town. Even though she was in the eighth grade, she was still going to school with fifth-graders. Ashley reacted by pulling away from parents she felt were overprotective.

Kayla's adolescence was very different. When she had her first period, her parents did not panic about her developing sexuality. Instead, they took her aside and discussed sex and pregnancy with her. They explained how different contraceptives worked and made an appointment for Kayla to see a gynecologist in case she ever needed to discuss something with a doctor. This made perfect sense. Although she was still only 14, Kayla would probably begin dating soon, because in her community, the junior and senior high schools had been combined into one large school, and the older boys frequently showed interest in the younger girls. Puberty brought Kayla closer to her parents, not more distant.

Two teenage girls. Each goes through puberty, each grows intellectually, and each moves closer in age to adulthood. Yet each grows up under very different circumstances: in

rite of passage A ceremony or ritual marking an individual's transition from one social status to another, especially marking the young person's transition to adulthood.

ecological perspective on human development
A perspective on development that emphasizes the broader context in which development occurs.

different families, in different schools, with different groups of peers, and in different communities. Both are adolescents, but their adolescent experiences are markedly different. And, as a result, each girl's psychological development will follow a different course.

Imagine how different your adolescence would have been if you had grown up a century ago and, instead of going to high school, had been expected to work full-time from the age of 15. Imagine how different it might be to grow up 100 years from today. And imagine how different adolescence is for a teenager from a very poor family than for one whose family is wealthy. It is impossible to generalize about the nature of adolescence without taking into account the surroundings and circumstances in which young people grow up.

For this reason, the second component of our framework is the *context* of adolescence. According to the **ecological perspective on human development,** whose main proponent was Urie Bronfenbrenner (1979), we cannot understand development without examining the environment in which it occurs. In modern societies, there are four main contexts in which young people spend time: families, peer groups, schools, and work and leisure settings.

Of course, these settings themselves are located within neighborhoods, which influence how they are structured and what takes place in them. It would be naive, for example, to discuss the impact that "school" has on adolescent development without recognizing that a school in an affluent suburb is likely very different from one in the inner city or in a remote rural area. And the community in which these settings are located is itself embedded in a broader context that is shaped by culture, geography, and history (Bronfenbrenner, 1979).

Although young people growing up in modern America share some experiences with young people all over the world, their development is different in many ways from that of young people in other societies, especially those in less affluent and less industrialized ones, because their families, peer groups, schools, work and leisure settings, and neighborhoods are different (Larson et al., 2009). In other words, the contexts of adolescence are themselves shaped and defined by the larger society in which young people live. In this book, we'll be especially interested in the contexts of adolescence in contemporary industrialized society and the ways in which they affect young people's development. Key contexts include the following:

Families Adolescence is a time of dramatic change in family relationships (Cox, Wang, & Gustafsson, 2011; Martin, Bascoe, & Davies, 2011). In addition, many changes in what constitutes a "family" have taken place over the past several decades, leading to tremendous diversity in family forms and household composition in modern society. It's important to understand how changes within the family, and in the broader context of family life, affect young people's psychological development.

Peer Groups Over the past 100 years, the peer group has come to play an increasingly important role in the socialization and development of teenagers (Dijkstra & Veenstra, 2011). But has the rise of peer groups in contemporary society been a positive or negative influence on young people's development? This is one of the many questions that has interested researchers who study the nature and function of adolescent peer groups and their effects on teenagers' psychological development.

Schools Contemporary society depends on schools to occupy, socialize, and educate adolescents. But how good a job are schools doing? What should schools do to help prepare adolescents for adulthood? And how should schools for adolescents be structured (Cortina & Arel, 2011)?

Work, Leisure, and the Mass Media Some of the most important influences on adolescent development are found outside of home and school: part-time jobs (Stone, 2011), extracurricular activities (Zarrett & Mahoney, 2011), and the mass media (Brown & Bobkowski, 2011a), including the Internet (Uhls, Espinoza, Greenfield, Subrahmanyam, & Šmahel, 2011). To what extent do these forces influence adolescents' attitudes, beliefs, and behavior?

One of the most important contexts for adolescent development is the peer group. © SW Productions/Getty Images RF

Psychosocial Development in Adolescence

The third, and final, component of our framework concerns the major *psychosocial developments* of adolescence—identity, autonomy, intimacy, sexuality, and achievement—as well as certain psychosocial problems that may arise in adolescence. Social scientists use the word **psychosocial** to describe aspects of development that are both psychological and social in nature. Sexuality, for instance, is a psychosocial issue because it involves both psychological change (that is, changes in the individual's emotions, motivations, and behavior) and changes in the individual's relationships.

Of course, it is not only during the adolescent years that concerns about identity, autonomy, intimacy, sexuality, and achievement arise, and psychological or social problems can and do occur during all periods of the life cycle. These psychosocial issues are present throughout the life span, from infancy through late adulthood. They represent basic developmental challenges that we face as we grow and change: (1) discovering and understanding who we are as individuals—**identity;** (2) establishing a healthy sense of independence—**autonomy;** (3) forming close and caring relationships with other people—**intimacy;** (4) expressing sexual feelings and enjoying physical contact with others—**sexuality;** and (5) being successful and competent members of society—**achievement.**

Although these concerns are not unique to adolescence, development in each of these areas takes a special turn during this stage. Understanding how and why such psychosocial developments take place during adolescence is a major interest of scientists who study this age period. We know that individuals form close relationships before adolescence, for example, but why is it that romantic relationships first develop during adolescence? We know that toddlers struggle with learning how to be independent, but why during adolescence do individuals need to be more on their own and make some decisions apart from their parents? We know that children fantasize about what they will be when they grow up, but why don't these fantasies become serious concerns until adolescence?

Identity   In adolescence, a variety of important changes in the realm of identity occur (Harter, 2011; Thomaes, Poorthuis, & Nelemans, 2011). The adolescent may wonder, "Who am I, and what kind of life will I have?" Coming to terms with these questions may involve a period of experimentation—a time of trying on different personalities in an attempt to discover one's true self. The adolescent's quest for identity is not only a quest for a personal sense of self but also for recognition from others that he or she is a special, unique individual. Some of the most important changes of adolescence take place in the realms of identity, self-esteem, and self-conceptions.

Autonomy   Adolescents' struggle to establish themselves as independent, self-governing individuals—in their own eyes and in the eyes of others—is a long and occasionally difficult process, not only for young people but also for those around them, especially their parents (Zimmer-Gembeck, Ducat, & Collins, 2011). Three aspects of autonomy are of special importance during adolescence: becoming less emotionally dependent on parents (McElhaney, Allen, Stephenson, & Hare, 2009), learning to function independently (Steinberg, 2014), and establishing a personal code of values and morals (Morris, Eisenberg, & Houltberg, 2011).

Intimacy   During adolescence, important changes take place in the individual's capacity to be intimate with others, especially with peers. During adolescence, friendships emerge that involve openness, honesty, loyalty, and exchange of confidences, rather than simply a sharing of activities and interests (B. Brown & Larson, 2009; W. Collins & Steinberg, 2006). Dating takes on increased importance, and as a consequence, so does the

---

psychosocial
Referring to aspects of development that are both psychological and social in nature, such as developing a sense of identity or sexuality.

identity
The domain of psychosocial development involving self-conceptions, self-esteem, and the sense of who one is.

autonomy
The psychosocial domain concerning the development and expression of independence.

intimacy
The psychosocial domain concerning the formation, maintenance, and termination of close relationships.

sexuality
The psychosocial domain concerning the development and expression of sexual feelings.

achievement
The psychosocial domain concerning behaviors and feelings in evaluative situations.

Sexuality is a central psychosocial issue of adolescence.
© Patrick Sheandell/Photo Alto/Fotosearch RF

capacity to form romantic relationships that are trusting and loving (Shulman, Connolly, & McIssac, 2011).

Sexuality Sexual activity usually begins during the adolescent years (Diamond & Savin-Williams, 2011). Becoming sexual is an important aspect of development during adolescence—not only because it transforms the nature of relationships between adolescents and their peers but also because it raises a range of difficult questions for the young person. These concerns include efforts to incorporate sexuality into a still-developing sense of self, the need to resolve questions about sexual values and morals, and coming to terms with the sorts of relationships into which the adolescent is prepared—or not prepared—to enter.

Achievement Adolescence is a time of important changes in individuals' educational and vocational behavior and plans. Crucial decisions—many with long-term consequences—about schooling and careers are made during adolescence. Many of these decisions depend on adolescents' achievement in school, on their evaluations of their own competencies and capabilities, on their aspirations and expectations for the future, and on the direction and advice they receive from parents, teachers, and friends (Wigfield, Ho, & Mason-Singh, 2011).

Psychosocial Problems Although most adolescents move through the period without experiencing major psychological upheaval, this stage of life is the most common time for the first appearance of serious psychological difficulties (Kessler et al., 2005; Olfson Druss, & Marcus, 2015). Three sets of problems are often associated with adolescence: drug and alcohol use and abuse (Chassin, Hussong, & Beltran, 2009), delinquency and other "externalizing problems" (Farrington, 2009), and depression and other "internalizing problems" (Graber & Sontag, 2009). In each case, we examine the prevalence of the problem, the factors believed to contribute to its development, and approaches to prevention and intervention.

Theoretical Perspectives on Adolescence

The study of adolescence is based not just on empirical research but also on theories of development (Newman & Newman, 2011b). You will read more about different theories of adolescence throughout this book, but an overview of the major ones may be helpful.

It's useful to organize theoretical perspectives on adolescence around a question that has long dominated discussions of human development more generally: How much is due to "nature," or biology, and how much is due to "nurture," or the environment? Some theories of adolescence emphasize biology, others emphasize the environment, and still others fall somewhere between the two extremes (see Figure 1). We'll begin with a look at the most extreme biological perspectives and work our way across a continuum toward the other extreme—perspectives that stress the role of the environment.

Biosocial Theories

The fact that biological change during adolescence is noteworthy is not a matter of dispute—how could it be, when puberty is such an obvious part of adolescence? But experts on adolescence disagree about how important this biological change is in defining the psychosocial issues of the period. Theorists who have taken a biological or, more accurately, "biosocial" view of adolescence stress the hormonal and physical changes of puberty as driving forces. The most important biosocial theorist was G. Stanley Hall (1904), considered the "father" of the scientific study of adolescence.

Hall's Theory of Recapitulation G. Stanley Hall, who was very much influenced by Charles Darwin, the author of the theory of evolution, believed that the development of the individual paralleled the development of the human species, a notion referred to as his theory of recapitulation. Infancy, in his view, was equivalent to the time during our evolution when we were primitive, like animals. Adolescence, in contrast, was seen as a time that paralleled the evolution of our species into civilization. For Hall, the development of the individual through these stages was determined primarily by instinct—by biological and genetic forces within the person—and hardly influenced by the environment.

The most important legacy of Hall's view of adolescence is the notion that it is inevitably a period of "storm and stress." He believed that the hormonal changes of puberty cause upheaval, both for the individual and for those around him or her. Because this turbulence is

Theoretical Perspectives on Adolescence

Extremely biological —— Extremely environmental

Biosocial (e.g., Hall, Dual Systems) — Organismic (e.g., Piaget, Erikson) — Learning (e.g., Bandura) — Sociological (e.g., Mannheim, Lewin) — Historical/Anthropological (e.g., Benedict)

Figure 1 Theories of adolescence range from the extremely biological, like that of G. Stanley Hall, to the extremely environmental, like that of Ruth Benedict.

biologically determined, it is unavoidable. The best that society can do is to find ways of managing the young person whose "raging hormones" invariably cause difficulties.

Although scientists no longer believe that adolescence is inherently problematic or that pubertal hormones themselves cause emotional problems, much contemporary work continues to emphasize the role that biological factors play in shaping the adolescent experience. More than 100 years ago, in fact, Hall speculated about brain maturation, hormonal influences on behavior, and changes in patterns of sleep during adolescence—all very hot topics in the study of adolescence today (Dahl & Hariri, 2005). Current work in the biosocial tradition, also influenced by Hall and his followers, explores the genetic bases of individual differences in adolescence and the evolutionary bases of adolescent behavior (Hollenstein & Lougheed, 2013).

Dual Systems Theories   Recent advances in brain science have given rise to an alternative biosocial account of adolescent development, one that stresses changes in the anatomy and activity of the brain. Among the most prominent of these theories are so-called "dual systems" theories, which stress the simultaneous development of two different brain systems—one that governs the ways in which the brain processes rewards, punishments, and social and emotional information, and another that regulates self-control and advanced thinking abilities, like planning or logical reasoning (Steinberg, 2010). The arousal of this first system takes place early in adolescence, while the second system is still maturing. This creates a "maturational imbalance" (Casey et al., 2011), which has been compared to starting a car without having a good braking system in place. The main challenge of adolescence, according to this view, is to develop better self-regulation, so that this imbalance doesn't result in problems (Steinberg, 2014).

Organismic Theories

Our next stop on the continuum is what are called "organismic" theorists. Like biosocial theorists, organismic theorists recognize the importance of the biological changes of adolescence. But unlike their biosocial counterparts, organismic theories also take into account the ways in which contextual forces interact with and modify these biological forces.

If you have had previous course work in developmental psychology, you have undoubtedly encountered the major organismic theorists, for they have long dominated the study of human development. Three of these theorists, in particular, have had a great influence on the study of adolescence: Sigmund Freud (1938), Erik Erikson (1968), and Jean Piaget (Inhelder & Piaget, 1958). Although these theorists share in common an organismic orientation, the theories they developed emphasize different aspects of individual growth and development.

Freudian Theory   For Freud, development was best understood in terms of the psychosexual conflicts that arise at different points in development. Like Hall, Freud saw adolescence as a time of upheaval. According to Freud, puberty temporarily throws the adolescent into a period of psychological crisis, by reviving old conflicts over uncomfortable sexual urges that had been buried in the unconscious (including feelings toward one's parents).

Sigmund Freud himself actually had very little to say specifically about adolescence. But his daughter, Anna Freud (1958), extended much of her father's thinking to the study of development during the second decade of life, emphasizing the need for adolescents to break away, or "detach," from their parents in order to develop normally. This work was carried on by neo-Freudians such as Peter Blos (1979).

Eriksonian Theory   Erik Erikson, whose work built on Freud's, also believed that internal, biological developments moved the individual from one developmental stage to the next. But unlike Freud, Erikson stressed the psychosocial, rather than the psychosexual, conflicts faced by the individual at each point in time. Erikson proposed eight stages in psychosocial development, each characterized by a specific "crisis" that arises at that point in development because of the interplay between the internal forces of biology and the demands of society. In Erikson's theory, development in adolescence revolves around the identity crisis. According to Erikson, the challenge of adolescence is to resolve the identity crisis and to emerge with a coherent sense of who one is and where one is headed.

Piagetian Theory   For Jean Piaget development could best be understood by examining changes in the nature of thinking. Piaget believed that, as children mature, they pass through distinct stages of cognitive development.

In Piaget's theory, adolescence marks the transition from concrete to abstract thought. Adolescence is the period in which individuals become capable of thinking in hypothetical terms, a development that permits a broad expansion of logical capabilities. The development of abstract thinking in adolescence is influenced both by the internal biological changes of the developmental period and by changes in the intellectual environment encountered by the individual.

Learning Theories

As we move across the theoretical continuum from extreme biological views to extreme environmental ones, we encounter a group of theories that shift the emphasis from biological forces to environmental ones. Whereas organismic theorists emphasize the interaction between biological change and environmental demands, learning theorists stress the context in which behavior takes place. The capacity of the individual to learn from experience is assumed to be a biological given that is in place long before adolescence. What is of interest to learning theorists is the content of what is learned.

Learning theorists are not especially developmental in their approach and, as a consequence, have little to say specifically about adolescence as a developmental period. Indeed, for learning theorists, the basic processes of human behavior are the same during adolescence as during other periods of the life span. But learning theorists have been extremely influential in the study of adolescent development because they have helped us understand how the specific environment in which an adolescent lives shapes his or her behavior.

Behaviorism There are two general categories of learning theorists. One group, known as behaviorists, emphasizes the processes of reinforcement and punishment as the main influences on adolescent behavior. The main proponent of this view was B. F. Skinner (1953), whose theory of operant conditioning has had a tremendous impact on the entire field of psychology. Within an operant conditioning framework, reinforcement is the process through which a behavior is made more likely to occur again, whereas punishment is the process through which a behavior is made less likely to occur again. From this vantage point, adolescent behavior is nothing more or less than the product of the various reinforcements and punishments to which the individual has been exposed. An adolescent who strives to do well in school, for example, does so because in the past she or he has been reinforced for this behavior or has been punished for not behaving this way. Similarly, a teenager who continues to experiment with risky behavior is being reinforced for this sort of activity or punished for being especially cautious.

Social Learning Theory A related approach is taken by social learning theorists such as Albert Bandura (Bandura & Walters, 1959). Social learning theorists also emphasize the ways in which adolescents learn how to behave, but in contrast to behaviorists, they place more weight on the processes of modeling and observational learning. According to these theorists, adolescents learn how to behave not simply by being reinforced and punished by forces in the environment but also by watching and imitating those around them. Social learning approaches to adolescence have been very influential in explaining how adolescents learn by watching the behavior of those around them, especially parents, peers, and figures in the mass media, like celebrities. From this vantage point, an adolescent who strives to do well in school or who takes a lot of risks is probably imitating family members, friends, or actors portrayed in the mass media.

Sociological Theories

The emphasis of biosocial, organismic, and learning theories is mainly on forces within an individual, or within that individual's environment, that shape development and behavior. In contrast, sociological theories of adolescence attempt to understand how adolescents, *as a group,* come of age in society. Instead of emphasizing differences among individuals in their biological makeups or their experiences in the world, sociological theorists focus on the factors that all adolescents or groups of adolescents have in common by virtue of their age.

Adolescent Marginality Sociological theories of adolescence often have focused on relations between the generations and have tended to emphasize the difficulties young people have in making the transition from adolescence to adulthood, especially in industrialized society. Two themes have dominated these discussions. One theme, concerning the marginality of young people, emphasizes the difference in power that exists between the adult and the adolescent generations. Two important thinkers in this vein are Kurt Lewin (1951) and Edgar Friedenberg (1959). Contemporary applications of this viewpoint stress the fact that many adolescents are prohibited from occupying

According to social learning theory, a lot of adolescent behavior is learned by observing peers and other significant role models. © Brand X Pictures/ Punchstock RF

meaningful roles in society and therefore experience frustration and restlessness. Some writers have claimed that many of the problems we associate with adolescence have been created, in part, by the way in which we have structured the adolescent experience, treating adolescents as if they are more immature than they actually are and isolating young people from adults (Epstein, 2007).

Intergenerational Conflict The other theme in sociological theories of adolescence concerns conflict between the generations. Theorists such as Karl Mannheim (1952) and James Coleman (1961) stressed the fact that adolescents and adults grow up under different social circumstances and therefore develop different sets of attitudes, values, and beliefs. As a consequence, there is inevitable tension between the adolescent and the adult generations. Some writers, like Coleman, have gone so far as to argue that adolescents develop a different cultural viewpoint—a counterculture—that may be hostile to the values or beliefs of adult society.

Historical and Anthropological Theories

Historians and anthropologists who study adolescence share with sociologists an interest in the broader context in which young people come of age, but they take a much more relativistic stance. Historical perspectives, such as those offered by Glen Elder (1980), Joseph Kett (1977), and Thomas Hine (1999), stress the fact that adolescence as a developmental period has varied considerably from one historical era to another. As a consequence, it is impossible to generalize about such issues as the degree to which adolescence is stressful, the developmental tasks of the period, or the nature of intergenerational relations. Historians would say that these issues all depend on the social, political, and economic forces present at a given time. Even something as basic to our view of adolescence as the "identity crisis," they say, is a social invention that arose because of industrialization and the prolongation of schooling. Prior to the Industrial Revolution, when most adolescents followed in their parents' occupation, people didn't have "crises" over who they were or what they were going to do in life.

Adolescence as an Invention One group of theorists has taken this viewpoint to its extreme, arguing that adolescence is *entirely* a social invention (Bakan, 1972). They believe that the way in which we divide the life cycle into stages—drawing a boundary between childhood and adolescence, for example—is nothing more than a reflection of the political, economic, and social circumstances in which we live. They point out that, although puberty has always been a feature of

human development, it was not until the rise of compulsory education that we began treating adolescents as a special and distinct group. In other words, social conditions, not biological givens, define the nature of adolescent development. We noted earlier that contemporary writers debate whether a new phase of life, "emerging adulthood," actually exists. Writers who believe that different stages of life are social inventions would say that if emerging adulthood has become a stage in development, it only has because society has made it so, not because people have really changed in any fundamental way.

Anthropological Perspectives A similar theme is echoed by anthropologists who study adolescence, the most important of whom were Ruth Benedict (1934) and Margaret Mead (1928/1978). Benedict and Mead pointed out that societies vary considerably in the ways in which they view and structure adolescence. As a consequence, these thinkers viewed adolescence as a culturally defined experience—stressful and difficult in societies that saw it this way, but calm and peaceful in societies that had an alternative vision. Benedict, in particular, drew a distinction between nonindustrialized societies, where the transition from adolescence to adulthood is generally gradual and peaceful, and modern industrialized societies, where transition to adulthood is abrupt and difficult.

making the scientific connection

Some writers have argued that the stage of life we call adolescence is a social invention. What do they mean by this? Could you say this about other periods of development? Is infancy a social invention? Is middle age? What about "emerging adulthood"?

Stereotypes Versus Scientific Study

One of the oldest debates in the study of adolescence is whether adolescence is an inherently stressful time for individuals. As we noted earlier, G. Stanley Hall, who is generally acknowledged as the father of the modern study of adolescence, likened adolescence to the turbulent, transitional period in the evolution of the human species from savagery into civilization.

This portrayal of teenagers as passionate, troubled, and unpredictable persists today. One 12-year-old girl I was counseling told me that her mother had been telling her that she would go through a difficult time when she turned 14—as if some magical, internal alarm clock was set to trigger storm and stress on schedule.

The girl's mother wasn't alone in her view of adolescence. Sometime this week pay attention to how teenagers are depicted in popular media. If they are not portrayed as troublemakers—the usual role in which they are cast—adolescents are sex-crazed idiots (if they are male), giggling fools or "mean girls" (if they are female), or tormented lost souls, searching for their place in a strange, cruel world (if they aren't delinquent, sex-crazed, giggling, or gossiping). It's not only fictionalized portrayals of teenagers that are stereotyped. Scholars, too, have been influenced by this viewpoint—a disproportionate number of scientific studies of adolescents have focused on young people's problems rather than their normative development (Steinberg, 2014).

Stereotypes of adolescents as troubling, and troubled, have important implications for how teenagers are treated—by teachers, by salespersons, and by parents. One study, for example, measured mothers' general beliefs about adolescence to see how well these preconceptions predicted how their teenager behaved (Buchanan & Hughes, 2009). The more likely a mother was to believe that teenagers are risk taking and rebellious, the more likely it was that her teenager actually behaved this way one year later, perhaps because the mother's expectations led her to behave in a way that brought out the worst in her adolescent. Parent–teenager relations are influenced by the expectations they have about each other. For example, one study found that when mothers believed that their teenagers were likely to use alcohol this actually lead to increases in their child's drinking (Madon, Willard, Guyll, Trudeau, & Spoth, 2006).

Fortunately, the tremendous growth of the scientific literature on adolescence over the past three decades has led to more accurate views of normal adolescence among practitioners who work with young people, although a trip to the "Parenting" section of your local bookstore will quickly reveal that the storm-and-stress stereotype is still alive and well, where most books are "survival guides" (Steinberg, 2014). (I once saw a book titled *Surviving Your Dog's Adolescence*!) Today, most experts do not dismiss the storm-and-stress viewpoint as entirely incorrect but see the difficulties that some adolescents have as due largely to the context within which they grow up.

You probably have many preconceptions of your own about adolescence. These beliefs are based in part on your own experiences as a teenager and in part on the images of adolescents that you have been exposed to over the years—in books, on film, and on television. As several writers have pointed out, scholars' descriptions of teenagers are influenced by the time during which they are writing. To the extent that we *want* to see adolescents as different from adults, writers exaggerate the differences between teenagers and their elders and portray young people as "out of control due to hormonal storms" (Lesko, 1996, p. 157). During periods of economic downturn, for instance, when jobs are scarce, adolescents are depicted as immature, unstable, and incompetent, whereas during periods of war, they are portrayed as mature, responsible, and capable (Enright, Levy, Harris, & Lapsley, 1987). Presumably, these characterizations serve a hidden agenda—during depressions, there are fewer jobs to go around, and adults may need to see adolescents as incapable of working, whereas the reverse is true during wartime, when adolescents are needed to take on jobs and serve in the military.

making the personal connection

If someone were to make generalizations about the nature of adolescence by analyzing *your* experiences as a teenager, how would the period be portrayed?

Adolescence, like any other developmental stage, has both positive and negative elements (Siegel & Scovill, 2000). Young people's willingness to challenge authority, for instance, is both refreshing (when we agree with them) and annoying (when we do not). Their propensity to take risks is both admirable and frightening. Their energy and exuberance is both exciting and unsettling.

One of the goals of this book is to provide you with a more realistic understanding of adolescent development in contemporary society—an understanding that reflects the best and most up-to-date scientific knowledge. As you read the material, think about your personal experiences as an adolescent, but try to look beyond them and be willing to question the "truths" about teenagers that you have grown accustomed to over the years. This does not mean that your experiences were not valid, or your recollections inaccurate. (In fact, studies show that we remember things that happen during adolescence more vividly than any other time [Steinberg, 2014]). But remember that your experiences as a teenager were the product of a unique set of forces that have made who you are today. The person who sits next to you in class—or the person who right now, in some distant region of the world, is thinking back to his or her adolescence—was probably exposed to different forces than you were and probably had a different set of adolescent experiences as a consequence.

Biological Transitions

© Comstock Images RF

Puberty: An Overview

The Endocrine System

What Triggers Puberty?

How Hormones Influence Adolescent Development

Somatic Development

Changes in Stature and the Dimensions of the Body

Sexual Maturation

The Timing and Tempo of Puberty

Variations in the Timing and Tempo of Puberty

Genetic and Environmental Influences on Pubertal Timing

The Psychological and Social Impact of Puberty

The Immediate Impact of Puberty

The Impact of Specific Pubertal Events

The Impact of Early or Late Maturation

Obesity and Eating Disorders

Obesity

Anorexia Nervosa, Bulimia, and Binge Eating Disorder

Physical Health and Health Care in Adolescence

The Paradox of Adolescent Health

Causes of Mortality in Adolescence

Promoting Adolescent Health

According to an old joke, there are only two things in life that one can be sure of—death and taxes. To this brief list, we might add puberty—the physical changes of adolescence. Not all adolescents experience identity crises, rebel against their parents, or fall madly in love, but virtually all go through puberty, the biological changes that change our appearance and ultimately make us capable of sexual reproduction.

Puberty, however, is greatly affected by the context in which it occurs. Physical development is influenced by a host of environmental factors, and the timing and rate of pubertal growth vary across regions of the world, socioeconomic classes, ethnic groups, and historical eras. Today, in contemporary America, the average girl has her first period at about age 12. At the turn of the 20th century, she was around 14½.

Physical and sexual maturation profoundly affect the ways in which adolescents view themselves and are viewed and treated by others. But the social environment exerts a tremendous impact on the psychological and social consequences of going through puberty (Skoog & Stattin, 2014). In some societies, pubertal maturation brings with it a series of public initiation rites that mark the passage of the young person into adulthood, socially as well as physically. In other societies, recognition of the physical transformation from child into adult takes more subtle forms. Parents may merely remark, "Our little boy has become a man," when they discover that he needs to shave, or "Our little girl has grown up," when they learn that she has gotten her first period. Early or late maturation may be cause for celebration or cause for concern, depending on what is admired or made fun of in a given peer group at a given point in time. The fifth-grader who is developing breasts might be embarrassed, but the ninth-grader who has not developed breasts might be equally self-conscious.

In sum, even the most universal aspect of adolescence—puberty—is hardly universal in its impact on the young person. In this chapter, we examine just how and why the environment in which adolescents develop exerts its influence even on something as fundamental as puberty. As you will learn, the adolescent's social environment even affects the age at which puberty begins.

Puberty: An Overview

Puberty derives from the Latin word *pubertas,* which means "adult." Technically, the term refers to the period during which an individual becomes capable of sexual reproduction. More broadly, however, puberty encompasses all the physical changes that occur in adolescents as they pass from childhood into adulthood (Dorn & Biro, 2011).

Puberty has three chief physical manifestations:

1. A rapid acceleration in growth, resulting in dramatic increases in height and weight.

2. The development of primary sex characteristics, including the further development of the gonads (sex glands), which results in a series of hormonal changes.

3. The development of secondary sex characteristics, including changes in the genitals and breasts, and the growth of pubic, facial, and body hair.

Each of these sets of changes is the result of developments in the endocrine and central nervous systems, many of which begin years before the signs of puberty are evident—some actually occur at conception (Susman & Dorn, 2009). No new hormones are produced at puberty. Rather, the levels of some hormones that have been present since before birth increase, whereas others decline.

The Endocrine System

The **endocrine system** produces, circulates, and regulates levels of hormones. **Hormones** are highly specialized substances that are secreted by one or more endocrine glands and then enter the bloodstream and travel throughout the body. **Glands** are organs that stimulate particular parts of the body to respond in specific ways. Many of the hormones that play important roles at puberty carry their instructions by activating certain neurons in the brain, called **gonadotropin-releasing hormone (GnRH) neurons** (Bogin, 2011; Novaira et al., 2011).

The Hormonal Feedback Loop   The endocrine system receives its instructions to increase or decrease circulating levels of particular hormones from the central nervous system, mainly through the firing of GnRH neurons in the brain. The system works like a thermostat. Hormonal levels are "set" at a certain point, which may differ depending on the stage of development, just as you might set a thermostat at a certain temperature (and

endocrine system
The system of the body that produces, circulates, and regulates hormones.

hormones
Highly specialized substances secreted by one or more endocrine glands.

glands
Organs that stimulate particular parts of the body to respond in specific ways to particular hormones.

gonadotropin-releasing hormone (GnRH) neurons
Specialized neurons that are activated by certain pubertal hormones.

use different settings during different seasons or different times of the day). By setting your room's thermostat at 60°F, you are instructing your heating system to go into action when the room becomes colder than that. Similarly, when a particular hormonal level in your body dips below the endocrine system's **set point** for that hormone, secretion of the hormone increases; when the level reaches the set point, secretion temporarily stops. And, as is the case with a thermostat, the setting level, or set point, for a particular hormone can be adjusted up or down, depending on environmental or internal bodily conditions.

Such a **feedback loop** becomes increasingly important at the onset of puberty. Long before adolescence—in fact, before birth—a feedback loop develops involving three structures: the **pituitary gland** (which controls hormone levels in general), the **hypothalamus** (the part of the brain that controls the pituitary gland, and where there is a concentration of GnRH neurons), and the **gonads** (in males, the **testes**; in females, the **ovaries**), which release the "sex" hormones—**androgens** and **estrogens**. This feedback loop is known as the **HPG axis** (for **H**ypothalamus, **P**ituitary, **G**onads) (see Figure 1). Although you may think of androgens as "male" hormones and estrogens as "female" hormones, both types of hormones are produced by each sex, and both are present in males and females at birth. During adolescence, however, the average male produces more androgens than estrogens, and the average female produces more estrogens than androgens (Susman & Dorn, 2009).

Your HPG axis is set to maintain certain levels of androgens and estrogens. When these levels fall below the set points, the hypothalamus no longer inhibits the pituitary, permitting it to stimulate the release of sex hormones by the gonads, and other puberty-related hormones by the adrenal gland. When hormone levels reach the set point, the hypothalamus responds by inhibiting its stimulation of the pituitary gland. Just as you might change the setting on your heating thermostat automatically every November 1, or when your utility bill has become too expensive, your brain is constantly monitoring a variety of signals and adjusting your hormonal set points in response. Puberty begins when several different signals—genetic as well as environmental—instruct the brain to change the set point (Sisk & Foster, 2004).

Adrenarche Just before puberty, the pituitary begins to secrete hormones that act on the thyroid and on the adrenal gland as well as hormones that stimulate overall bodily growth. The release of these substances is also under the control of the hypothalamus. The thyroid and adrenal gland, in turn, secrete hormones that cause various bodily changes to take place. Most individuals, in America and around the world, report that their first sexual attraction took place at the "magical age of 10," before they went through puberty. These early sexual feelings may be stimulated by maturation of the adrenal glands, called **adrenarche** (Herdt & McClintock, 2000), which also contributes to the development of body odor, signaling the beginning of sexual maturation to others (Campbell, 2011).

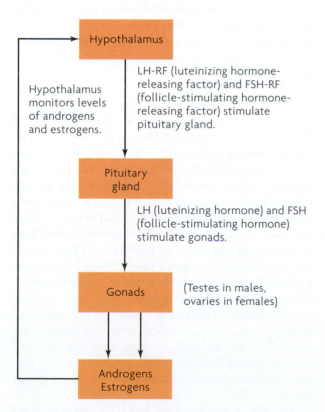

Hypothalamus monitors levels of androgens and estrogens.

LH-RF (luteinizing hormone-releasing factor) and FSH-RF (follicle-stimulating hormone-releasing factor) stimulate pituitary gland.

LH (luteinizing hormone) and FSH (follicle-stimulating hormone) stimulate gonads.

(Testes in males, ovaries in females)

Figure 1 **Levels of sex hormones are regulated by a feedback system (the HPG axis) composed of the hypothalamus, pituitary gland, and gonads.**
(Grumbach, Roth, Kaplan, & Kelch, 1974)

set point
A physiological level or setting (e.g., of a specific hormone) that the body attempts to maintain through a self-regulating system.

feedback loop
A cycle through which two or more bodily functions respond to and regulate each other, such as that formed by the hypothalamus, the pituitary gland, and the gonads.

pituitary gland
One of the chief glands responsible for regulating levels of hormones in the body.

hypothalamus
A part of the brain that controls the functioning of the pituitary gland.

gonads
The glands that secrete sex hormones: in males, the testes; in females, the ovaries.

testes
The male gonads.

ovaries
The female gonads.

androgens
A class of sex hormones secreted by the gonads, found in both sexes, but in higher levels among males than females following puberty.

estrogens
A class of sex hormones secreted by the gonads, found in both sexes, but in higher levels among females than males following puberty.

HPG (hypothalamic-pituitary-gonadal) axis
The neurophysiological pathway that involves the hypothalamus, the pituitary gland, and the gonads.

adrenarche
The maturation of the adrenal glands that takes place during adolescence.

Early feelings of sexual attraction to others are stimulated by adrenarche, the maturation of the adrenal glands, which takes place before the outward signs of puberty are evident.
© Glow Images RF

cortisol
A hormone produced when a person is exposed to stress.

kisspeptin
A brain chemical believed to trigger the onset of puberty.

leptin
A protein produced by the fat cells that may play a role in the onset of puberty through its impact on kisspeptin.

melatonin
A hormone secreted by the brain that contributes to sleepiness and that triggers the onset of puberty through its impact on kisspeptin.

Changes at puberty in the brain system that regulates the adrenal gland are also important because this is the brain system that controls how we respond to stress (Del Giudice, Angeleri, & Manera, 2009). One reason adolescence is a period of great vulnerability for the onset of many serious mental disorders is that the hormonal changes of puberty make us more responsive to stress (Monahan, Guyer, Silk, Fitzwater, & Steinberg, 2016; Romeo, 2013; Stroud et al., 2009; Trépanier et al., 2013; Worthman, 2011). This leads to excessive secretion of the stress hormone **cortisol,** a substance that at high and chronic levels can cause brain cells to die (Carrion & Wong, 2012; Gunnar, Wewerka, Frenn, Long, & Griggs, 2009). Keep in mind that there is a difference between saying that adolescence is an inherently stressful time (which it is not) and saying that adolescence is a time of heightened vulnerability to stress (which it is).

making the personal connection

Do you remember your first feelings of sexual attraction for someone? How old were you?

What Triggers Puberty?

Although the HPG axis is active before birth, it is relatively quiet during childhood. Something happens during middle childhood, though, that reawakens the HPG axis and signals it that the body is ready for puberty (see Figure 2). Some of this is due to a clock whose "puberty alarm" is set very early in life by information coded in the genes (the age at which someone goes through puberty is largely inherited). But some of the reawakening of the HPG axis at puberty is due to multiple signals that tell the brain it is time to "get the childbearing show on the road." These signals indicate whether there are sexually mature mating partners in the environment, whether there are sufficient nutritional resources to support a pregnancy, and whether the individual is physically mature and healthy enough to begin reproducing.

The onset of puberty is stimulated by an increase in a brain chemical called **kisspeptin** (Roseweir & Millar, 2009) (so named because it was discovered in Hershey, Pennsylvania, the birthplace of chocolate kisses). The production of kisspeptin in the brain is affected by other chemicals, most importantly **leptin,** which stimulates it, and **melatonin,** which suppresses it. Leptin is a protein produced by fat cells, and which exists in our body in levels proportionate to our amount of body fat. It plays a critical role in the regulation of hunger and appetite, by suppressing our desire to eat when we're full. In some senses, leptin serves to signal the brain not just that we are full enough, but that we are "fat enough." Melatonin is a hormone that helps regulate the sleep cycle, which we'll discuss later in this chapter.

Your genes predispose you to go through puberty around a particular age, but the more fat cells you have, and the more light to which you have been exposed during childhood, the more likely it is that you will go through puberty on the early side of your inherited propensity. Someone with the same genes, but who is thin and doesn't get as much light exposure, will go through puberty later (Lomniczi et al., 2013). This is why puberty starts earlier among obese children and among children who grow up closer to the equator. Obese children have more body fat and therefore produce a lot more leptin, which stimulates kisspeptin production. Children who live near the equator are exposed to relatively more sunlight each year, and they have lower melatonin levels as a result, so their kisspeptin production is not suppressed as much as it is among children who live closer to the poles. Exposure to artificial light, especially the kind of light emitted from electronic gadgets, can also suppress melatonin levels and hasten puberty (Greenspan & Deardorff, 2014).

The reason that body fat and light exposure affect the timing of puberty is found in our evolutionary history. Humans evolved when resources were scarce, and it was adaptive to conceive and bear as many offspring

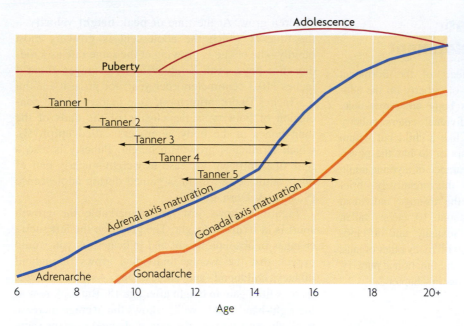

Figure 2 The biological changes we associate with adolescence actually unfold over a long period of time, beginning with the maturation of the adrenal axis during childhood and ending with the maturation of the gonadal axis in the early 20s. Tanner 1, 2, 3, 4, and 5 refer to different stages of pubertal maturation (see page 20). (Adapted from Dorn et al., 2006)

as possible, since not all of them would survive. If the ultimate goal is to bear as many children as possible, once someone has developed enough fat and senses that the season is right for gathering food, it is time to start maturing physically. Our genes don't know that we no longer live in a resource-scarce world and can store food in our cupboards and refrigerators so that we have plenty to eat in the dark of winter. Although conditions have changed, our brains evolve much more slowly, and the timing of puberty is still affected by our brain's circulating levels of leptin and melatonin.

How Hormones Influence Adolescent Development

Most people understandably think that changes in behavior at puberty result from changes in hormones at that time. But this is only partially correct. Long before adolescence—in fact, before birth—hormones organize the brain in ways that may not be manifested in behavior until childhood or even adolescence (Sisk & Foster, 2004). Generally, until about eight weeks after conception, the human brain is "feminine" unless and until it is exposed to certain "masculinizing" hormones, like testosterone. Because levels of testosterone are higher among males than females while the brain is developing, males usually end up with a more "masculinized" brain than females. This sex difference in brain organization predetermines certain patterns of behavior, many of which may not actually appear until much later (Collaer & Hines, 1995). Studies of sex differences in aggression, for example, show that even though some of these differences may not appear until adolescence, they likely result from the impact of prenatal hormones, rather than from hormonal changes at puberty.

In other words, the presence or absence of certain hormones early in life "program" the brain and the central nervous system to develop in certain ways and according to a certain timetable (Sisk & Foster, 2004). Because we may not see the resulting changes in behavior until adolescence, it is easy to mistakenly conclude that the behaviors result from hormonal changes that take place at the time of puberty. In reality, however, exposure to certain hormones before birth may set a sort of alarm clock that does not go off until adolescence. Just because the alarm clock rings at the same time that puberty begins does not mean that puberty *caused* the alarm to go off.

Many changes in behavior at adolescence do occur because of changes in hormone levels at puberty, however. For instance, the increase in certain hormones at puberty is thought to stimulate the development of secondary sex characteristics, such as the growth of pubic hair. There is also growing evidence that puberty affects the brain in ways that increase adolescents' emotional arousal and desire for highly rewarding, exciting activities, which may make some teenagers more prone to emotional and behavioral problems (Castellanos-Ryan, Parent, Vitaro, Tremblay, & Séguin, 2013; Forbes & Dahl, 2010; LeMoult, Colich, Sherdell, Hamilton, & Gotlib, 2015; Op de Macks et al., 2011; Speilberg et al., 2015).

Still other changes during puberty are likely to be results of an interaction between prenatal and pubertal hormones (Collaer & Hines, 1995). Hormones that are present during the development of the fetus may organize a certain set of behaviors (for example, our brains may be set up to have us later engage in sexual behavior), but certain changes in those hormones at puberty may be needed to activate the pattern; that is, individuals may not become motivated to engage in sex until puberty.

adolescent growth spurt
The dramatic increase in height and weight that occurs during puberty.

peak height velocity
The point at which the adolescent is growing most rapidly.

epiphysis
The closing of the ends of the bones, which terminates growth after the adolescent growth spurt has been completed.

Somatic Development

The effects of the hormonal changes of puberty on the adolescent's body are remarkable. The individual enters puberty looking like a child but within four years or so has the physical appearance of a young adult. During this relatively brief period, the average individual grows about 10 inches taller, matures sexually, and develops an adult-proportioned body. Along with many other organs, the brain changes in size, structure, and function at puberty, a series of developments we'll discuss in Chapter 2.

Changes in Stature and the Dimensions of the Body

The Adolescent Growth Spurt   The simultaneous release of growth hormones, thyroid hormones, and androgens stimulates rapid acceleration in height and weight. This dramatic increase in stature is called the **adolescent growth spurt.** What is most incredible about the adolescent growth spurt is not so much the absolute gain of height and weight that typically occurs but the speed with which the increases take place. Think for a moment of how quickly very young children grow. At the time of **peak height velocity**—the time at which the adolescent is growing most rapidly—he or she is growing at the same rate as a toddler. For boys, peak height velocity averages about 4 inches (10.3 centimeters) per year; for girls, it's about 3.5 inches (9.0 centimeters). One marker of the conclusion of puberty is the closing of the ends of the long bones in the body, a process called **epiphysis,** which terminates growth in height. Puberty is also a time of significant increase in weight—nearly half of one's adult body weight is gained during adolescence (Susman & Dorn, 2009).

Figure 3 shows just how remarkable the growth spurt is in terms of height. The graph on the left shows changes in absolute height and indicates, as you would expect, that the average individual grows throughout infancy, childhood, and adolescence. As you can see, there is little gain in height after age 18. But look now at the right-hand graph, which shows the average increase in height per year (i.e., the *rate* of change) over the same age span. Here you can see the acceleration in height at the time of peak height velocity.

Figure 3 also indicates that the growth spurt occurs, on average, about two years earlier among girls than boys. In general, as you can see by comparing the two graphs, boys tend to be somewhat taller than girls before age 11; then girls tend to be taller than boys between ages 11 and 13; and finally, boys tend to be taller than girls from about age 14 on. You may remember what this was like during the fifth and sixth grades. Sex differences

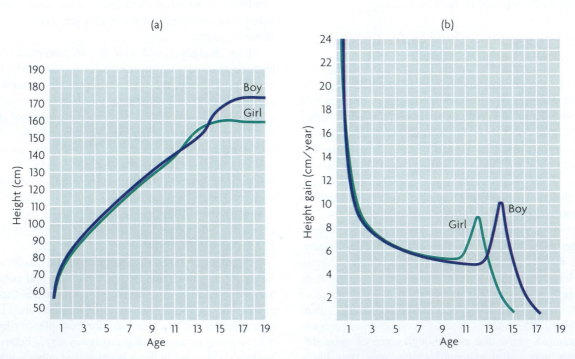

Figure 3   (a) Height (in centimeters) at different ages for the average male and female youngster. (b) Gain in height per year (in centimeters) for the average male and female youngster. Note the adolescent growth spurt. (Adapted from Marshall, 1978)

in height can be a concern for many young adolescents when they begin socializing with members of the opposite sex, especially if they are tall, early-maturing girls or short, late-maturing boys.

Much of the height gain during puberty results from an increase in the length of the torso rather than the legs. The sequence in which various parts of the body grow is fairly regular. Extremities—the head, hands, and feet—are the first to accelerate in growth. Accelerated growth occurs next in the arms and legs, followed by torso and shoulder growth.

Young adolescents often appear to be out of proportion physically—as though their nose or legs were growing faster than the rest of them. This is because different parts of the body do not all grow at the same rate or at the same time during puberty. This can lead to an appearance of awkwardness or gawkiness in the young adolescent, who may be embarrassed by the disproportionate growth of different body parts. It is probably little consolation for the someone going through the awkward phase to be told that an attractive balance probably will be restored within a few years, but, fortunately, this is what usually happens.

Sex Differences in Muscle and Fat The spurt in height during adolescence is accompanied by an increase in weight that results from an increase in both muscle and fat, but there are important sex differences in adolescent body composition. Before puberty, there are relatively few sex differences in muscle development and only slight sex differences in body fat. In both sexes, muscular development is rapid during puberty, but muscle tissue grows faster in boys than girls (Bogin, 2011). In contrast, body fat increases for both sexes during puberty, but more so for females than for males, especially during the years just before puberty. (For boys, there is actually a slight decline in body fat just before puberty.) The end result of these sex differences is that boys finish adolescence with a muscle-to-fat ratio of about 3 to 1, but the comparable ratio for girls is approximately 5 to 4. This has important implications for understanding why sex differences in strength and athletic ability often appear for the first time during adolescence. According to one estimate, about half of the sex difference in athletic performance during early adolescence results simply from the difference in body fat (Smoll & Schutz, 1990).

It is tempting to attribute sex differences in athletic performance to changes in body fat and to hormonal factors, because androgens, which increase during puberty in males at a much faster rate than in females, are closely linked to growth in aspects of the body that influence athletic ability. But with age, environmental factors like diet and exercise become increasingly important influences on sex differences in physical performance (Smoll & Schutz, 1990). There are strong social pressures on

girls to curtail "masculine" activities—including some forms of exercise—at adolescence, and studies show that girls are more likely than boys to markedly reduce their physical activity in preadolescence. Moreover, adolescent girls' diets, especially those of Black girls, are generally less adequate nutritionally than the diets of boys, particularly in important minerals like iron (Johnson, Johnson, Wang, Smiciklas-Wright, & Guthrie, 1994). Both factors could result in sex differences in exercise tolerance. In other words, sex differences in physical ability are influenced by a variety of factors, of which hormonal differences are but one part of a complex picture.

Body Dissatisfaction Among Adolescent Girls The rapid increase in body fat among females in early adolescence frequently prompts girls to become overly concerned about their weight—even when their weight is within the normal range for their height and age (Calzo et al., 2012). As you will read later in this chapter, adolescence is the period of greatest risk for the development of eating disorders such as anorexia and bulimia.

Although the majority of girls diet unnecessarily during this time in response to the increase in body fat, the girls who are most susceptible to feelings of dissatisfaction with their bodies during this phase of development are those who mature early and begin dating early (Smolak et al., 1993). Girls who spend a lot of time talking about their looks with their friends, who are teased about their weight, or who are pressured to be thin are especially vulnerable to feelings of body dissatisfaction (Webb & Zimmer-Gembeck, 2014). In fact, for girls, it is comparing themselves with their friends, and not just being exposed to media portrayals of thinness, that leads to dissatisfaction (Ferguson, Muñoz, Garza, & Galdino, 2014). In contrast, boys' feelings about how they look revolve around how muscular they are and do not seem to be affected by comparisons with peers. There are also important ethnic and cross-cultural differences in the ways in which adolescent girls feel about their changing bodies. In many parts of the world, including North and South America, Europe, and Asia, there is strong pressure on girls to be thin (Jones & Smolak, 2011). Black adolescents seem less vulnerable to these feelings of body dissatisfaction than other girls (Ali, Rizzo, & Heiland, 2013; Jung & Forbes, 2013; Nishina, Ammon, Bellmore, & Graham, 2006), and consequently they are less likely to diet, in part because of ethnic differences in conceptions of the ideal body type (Granberg, Simons, & Simons, 2009).

Sexual Maturation

Puberty brings with it a series of developments associated with sexual maturation. In both boys and girls, the

secondary sex characteristics
The manifestations of sexual maturity at puberty, including the development of breasts, the growth of facial and body hair, and changes in the voice.

Tanner stages
A widely used system that describes the five stages of pubertal development.

development of the **secondary sex characteristics** is typically divided into five stages, often called **Tanner stages,** after the British pediatrician who devised the categorization system.

Sexual Maturation in Boys

The sequence of developments in secondary sex characteristics among boys is fairly orderly (see Table 1). Generally, the first stages of puberty involve growth of the testes and scrotum, accompanied by the first appearance of pubic hair. Approximately 1 year later, the growth spurt in height begins, accompanied by growth of the penis and further development of pubic hair—now coarser and darker. The five Tanner stages of penis and pubic hair growth in boys are shown in Figure 4.

The emergence of facial and body hair are relatively late developments. The same is true for the deepening of the voice, which is gradual and generally does not occur until very late adolescence. During puberty, there are changes in the skin as well. The skin becomes rougher, especially around the upper arms and thighs, and there is increased development of the sweat glands, which often gives rise to acne, pimples, and increased oiliness of the skin.

During puberty, there are slight changes in the male breast—to the embarrassment of many boys. Breast development is largely influenced by estrogens. As noted earlier, both estrogens and androgens are present in both sexes and increase in both sexes at puberty, although in differing amounts. In the male adolescent, the areola (the area around the nipple) increases in size, and the nipple becomes more prominent. Some boys show a slight enlargement of the breast, although in the majority of cases this is temporary.

Other, internal changes occur that are important elements of sexual maturation. At the time that the penis develops, the seminal vesicles, the prostate, and the bulbourethral glands also enlarge and develop. The first ejaculation of seminal fluid generally occurs about one year after the beginning of accelerated penis growth, although this is often determined culturally rather than biologically, since for many boys first ejaculation occurs as a result of masturbation (J. Tanner, 1972). One interesting observation about the timing and sequence of pubertal changes in boys is that boys are generally fertile (i.e., capable of fathering a child) before they have developed an adultlike appearance (Bogin, 2011). As you will read in the next section, the opposite is true for girls.

Sexual Maturation in Girls   The sequence of development of secondary sex characteristics among girls (shown in Table 1) is less regular than it is among boys. Generally, the first sign of sexual maturation in girls is the elevation of the breast—the emergence of the "breast bud." In about one-third of all adolescent girls, however, the appearance of pubic hair precedes breast development. The development of pubic hair in females follows a sequence similar to that in males—generally, from sparse, downy, light-colored hair to denser, curlier, coarser, darker hair. Breast development often occurs concurrently and generally proceeds through several stages. In the bud stage, the areola widens, and the breast and nipple are elevated as a small mound. In the middle stages, the areola and nipple become distinct from the breast and project beyond the breast contour. In the final stages, the areola is recessed to the contour of the breast, and only the nipple is elevated. The female breast undergoes these changes at puberty regardless of changes in breast size. For this reason, changes in the shape and definition of the areola and nipple are far better indicators of sexual maturation among adolescent girls than is breast size alone. The five Tanner stages of breast and pubic hair growth in girls are shown in Figure 5.

Table 1 The sequence of physical changes at puberty

Girls		Boys	
Age of First Appearance (Years)	**Characteristic**	**Age of First Appearance (Years)**	**Characteristic**
1. 7–13	Growth of breasts	1. 10–13½	Growth of testes, scrotal sac
2. 7–14	Growth of pubic hair	2. 10–15	Growth of pubic hair
3. 9½–14½	Body growth	3. 10½–16	Body growth
4. 10–16½	Menarche	4. 11–14½	Growth of penis
5. About two years after pubic hair	Underarm hair	5. About the same time as penis growth	Change in voice (growth of larynx)
6. About same time as underarm hair	Oil- and sweat-producing glands	6. About two years after pubic hair appears	Facial and underarm hair
		7. About same time as underarm hair	Oil- and sweat-producing glands, acne

Source: B. Goldstein, 1976.

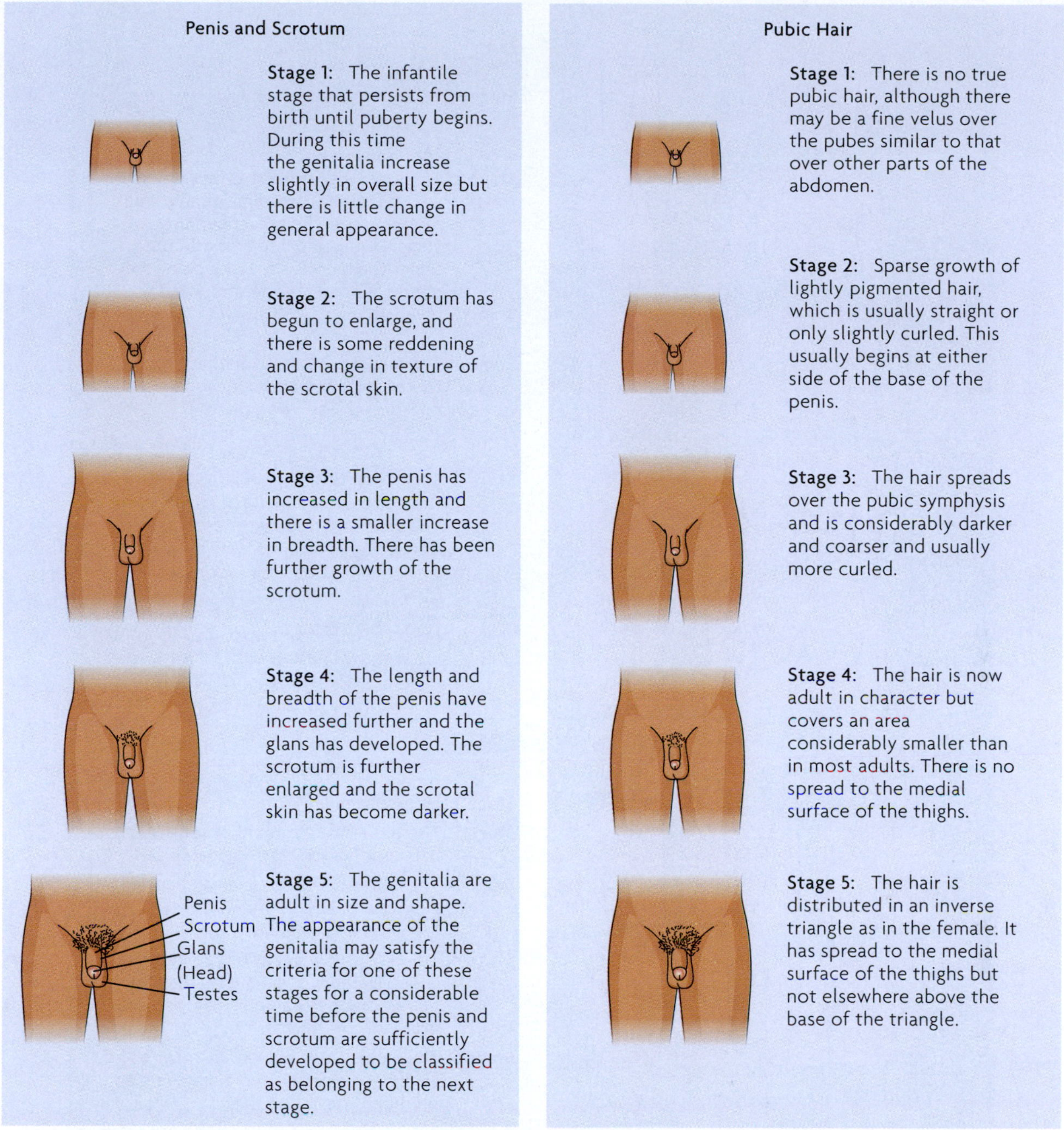

Penis and Scrotum

Stage 1: The infantile stage that persists from birth until puberty begins. During this time the genitalia increase slightly in overall size but there is little change in general appearance.

Stage 2: The scrotum has begun to enlarge, and there is some reddening and change in texture of the scrotal skin.

Stage 3: The penis has increased in length and there is a smaller increase in breadth. There has been further growth of the scrotum.

Stage 4: The length and breadth of the penis have increased further and the glans has developed. The scrotum is further enlarged and the scrotal skin has become darker.

Penis
Scrotum
Glans
(Head)
Testes

Stage 5: The genitalia are adult in size and shape. The appearance of the genitalia may satisfy the criteria for one of these stages for a considerable time before the penis and scrotum are sufficiently developed to be classified as belonging to the next stage.

Pubic Hair

Stage 1: There is no true pubic hair, although there may be a fine velus over the pubes similar to that over other parts of the abdomen.

Stage 2: Sparse growth of lightly pigmented hair, which is usually straight or only slightly curled. This usually begins at either side of the base of the penis.

Stage 3: The hair spreads over the pubic symphysis and is considerably darker and coarser and usually more curled.

Stage 4: The hair is now adult in character but covers an area considerably smaller than in most adults. There is no spread to the medial surface of the thighs.

Stage 5: The hair is distributed in an inverse triangle as in the female. It has spread to the medial surface of the thighs but not elsewhere above the base of the triangle.

Figure 4 **The five pubertal stages for penile and pubic hair growth.** (From Morris & Udry, 1980)

As is the case for boys, puberty brings important internal changes for adolescent girls that are associated with the development of reproductive capacity. In girls, these changes involve development and growth of the uterus, vagina, and other aspects of the reproductive system. In addition, there is enlargement of the labia and clitoris.

As is apparent in Table 1, the growth spurt is likely to occur during the early and middle stages of breast and pubic hair development. **Menarche,** the beginning of menstruation, is a relatively late development. Generally, full reproductive function does not occur until several years after menarche, and regular ovulation follows menarche by about two years (Bogin, 2011; Hochberg, Gawlik, & Walker, 2011). Unlike boys, therefore, girls generally appear physically mature before they are fertile.

menarche
The time of first menstruation, one of the most important changes to occur among females during puberty.

The Timing and Tempo of Puberty

Thus far, no mention has been made of the "normal" ages at which various pubertal changes are likely to take place. This is because variations in the timing of

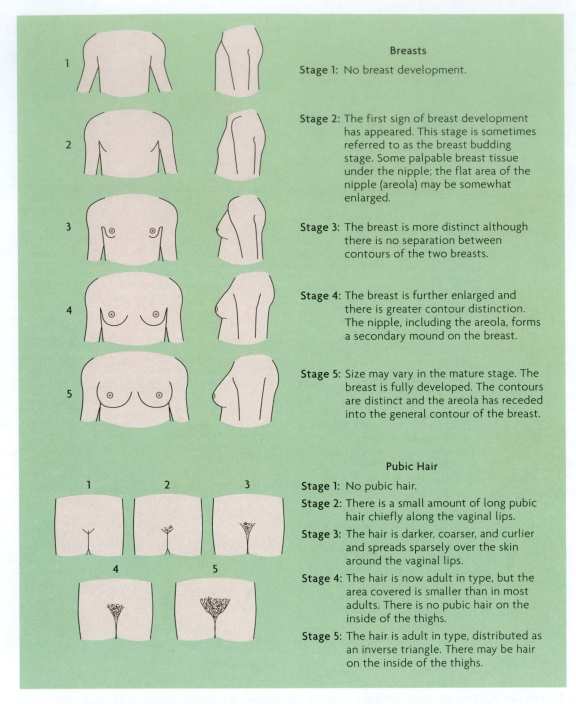

Breasts

Stage 1: No breast development.

Stage 2: The first sign of breast development has appeared. This stage is sometimes referred to as the breast budding stage. Some palpable breast tissue under the nipple; the flat area of the nipple (areola) may be somewhat enlarged.

Stage 3: The breast is more distinct although there is no separation between contours of the two breasts.

Stage 4: The breast is further enlarged and there is greater contour distinction. The nipple, including the areola, forms a secondary mound on the breast.

Stage 5: Size may vary in the mature stage. The breast is fully developed. The contours are distinct and the areola has receded into the general contour of the breast.

Pubic Hair

Stage 1: No pubic hair.

Stage 2: There is a small amount of long pubic hair chiefly along the vaginal lips.

Stage 3: The hair is darker, coarser, and curlier and spreads sparsely over the skin around the vaginal lips.

Stage 4: The hair is now adult in type, but the area covered is smaller than in most adults. There is no pubic hair on the inside of the thighs.

Stage 5: The hair is adult in type, distributed as an inverse triangle. There may be hair on the inside of the thighs.

Figure 5   **The five pubertal stages for breast and pubic hair growth.** (From Marshall & Tanner, 1969)

puberty (the age at which puberty begins) and in the tempo of puberty (the rate at which maturation occurs) are so great that it is misleading to talk even about average ages. Importantly, differences among adolescents in when and how quickly they go through puberty, how synchronized the different changes on puberty are, and how adolescents perceive their own pace of development all have important mental health implications (Mendle, 2014).

Variations in the Timing and Tempo of Puberty

The onset of puberty can occur as early as age 5 in girls and 6½ in boys, or as late as age 13 in girls and 13½ in boys. In girls, the interval between the first sign of puberty and complete physical maturation can be as short as a year and a half or as long as 6 years. In boys, the comparable interval ranges from about 2 to 5 years

(J. Tanner, 1972). Think about it: Within a totally normal population of young adolescents, some individuals will have completed the entire sequence of pubertal changes before others have even begun. In more concrete terms, it is possible for an early-maturing, fast-maturing youngster to complete pubertal maturation by age 10—3 years before a late-maturing youngster has even begun puberty, and 8 years before a late-maturing, slow-maturing youngster has matured completely!

There is no relation between the age at which puberty begins and the rate at which pubertal development proceeds. The timing of puberty may have a small effect on one's ultimate height or weight, however, with late maturers, on average, being taller than early maturers as adults, and early maturers, on average, being somewhat heavier—at least among females (St. George, Williams, & Silva, 1994). Adult height and weight are far more strongly correlated with height and weight during childhood than with the timing of puberty, however (Pietiläinen et al., 2001).

Within the United States, there are ethnic differences in the timing and rate of pubertal maturation. Several large-scale studies of U.S. youngsters indicate that Black girls mature significantly earlier than Mexican American girls, who, in turn, mature earlier than White girls (Chumlea et al., 2003; Herman-Giddens et al., 1997). Although the reasons for this ethnic difference are not known, it does not appear to be due to ethnic differences in income, weight, or area of residence (S. E. Anderson, Dallal, & Must, 2003). One possible explanation for the earlier maturation of non-White girls is that they may be more frequently exposed to chemicals in the environment that stimulate earlier puberty, such as those contained in certain hair care products and cosmetics (Susman & Dorn, 2009).

Individuals vary considerably in when puberty begins and the rate with which it progresses. © Peathegee Inc/Getty Images RF

Genetic and Environmental Influences on Pubertal Timing

Why do some individuals mature relatively early and others relatively late? Researchers who study variability in the onset and timing of puberty approach the issue in two ways. One strategy involves the study of differences among individuals (i.e., studying why one individual matures earlier or faster than another). The other involves the study of differences among groups of adolescents (i.e., studying why puberty occurs earlier or more rapidly in certain populations than in others). Both sets of studies point to both genetic and environmental factors (Ge, Natsuaki, Neiderhiser, & Reiss, 2007).

Individual Differences in Pubertal Maturation

Differences in the timing and rate of puberty among individuals growing up in the same general environment result chiefly, but not exclusively, from genetic factors.

Comparisons between identical twins and individuals who are not genetically identical indicate that the timing and tempo of an individual's pubertal maturation are largely inherited (Mustanski, Viken, Kaprio, Pulkkinen, & Rose, 2004). A specific region on chromosome 6 has been identified as one of the markers for pubertal timing in both boys and girls (Bogin, 2011).

Despite this powerful influence of genetic factors, the environment plays an important role. In all likelihood, every individual inherits a predisposition to develop at a certain rate and to begin pubertal maturation at a certain time. But this predisposition is best thought of as an upper and lower age limit, not a fixed absolute. Whether the genetic predisposition that each person has to mature around a given age is actually realized, and when within the predisposed age boundaries she or he actually goes through puberty, is subject to the influence of many external factors. In other words, the timing and tempo of pubertal maturation are the product of an interaction between nature and nurture.

By far the two most important environmental influences on pubertal maturation are nutrition and health. Puberty occurs earlier among individuals who are better nourished and grow more throughout their prenatal, infant, and childhood years (Terry, Ferris, Tehranifar, Wei, & Flom, 2009). Not surprisingly, girls who are taller or heavier than their peers mature earlier (St. George et al., 1994), whereas delayed puberty is more likely to occur among individuals with a history of protein and/or caloric deficiency. Chronic illness during childhood and adolescence is also associated with delayed puberty, as is excessive exercise. Generally, then, after genetic factors, the most important determinant of the timing of puberty is the overall physical well-being of the individual from conception through preadolescence (Susman & Dorn, 2009).

Familial Influences on Pubertal Timing   A number of studies suggest that social factors in the home environment may influence the onset of maturation, especially in girls. Puberty occurs somewhat earlier among girls who grew up in father-absent families, in less cohesive or more conflict-ridden households, or with a stepfather (Ellis, 2004); early puberty is also more common among girls who were sexually abused during childhood (Boynton-Jarrett et al., 2013; Mendle, Leve, Van Ryzin, & Natsuaki, 2014; Mendle, Ryan, & McKone, 2015; Negriff, Blankson, & Trickett, 2014). One explanation for the finding that family conflict may accelerate pubertal maturation is that tension in the family may induce stress, which, in turn, may affect hormonal secretions in the adolescent (Arim, Tramonte, Shapka, Dahinten, & Willms, 2011; Belsky, Steinberg, Houts, & Halpern-Felsher, 2010; Belsky et al., 2007), especially among girls who are genetically susceptible to this influence (Ellis, Shirtcliff, Boyce, Deardorff, & Essex, 2011; Hartman, Widaman, & Belsky, 2014; Manuck, Craig, Flory, Halder, & Ferrell, 2011).

pheromones
A class of chemicals secreted by animals that stimulate certain behaviors in other members of the species.

Scientists have expressed concern about the continuing decline in the age when puberty begins, because pubertal hormones affect the developing brain in ways that increase sensation seeking.
© Ingram Publishing RF

In addition, the presence of a stepfather may expose the adolescent girl to **pheromones** (a class of chemicals secreted by animals that stimulate certain behaviors in other members of the species) that stimulate pubertal maturation. In general, among humans and other mammals, living in proximity to one's close biological relatives appears to slow the process of pubertal maturation, whereas exposure to unrelated members of the other sex may accelerate it.

Although it may seem surprising that something as biological as puberty can be influenced by factors in the social environment, scientists have long known that our social relationships can indeed affect our biological functioning. One of the best-known examples of this is that women who live together—such as dormitory roommates—find that their menstrual periods begin to synchronize over time (C. Graham, 1991; McClintock, 1980).

Group Differences in Pubertal Maturation   Researchers typically study group differences in puberty by comparing average ages of menarche in different regions. Most of these studies have indicated that genetic factors play an extremely small role in determining group differences in pubertal maturation (Eveleth & Tanner, 1990). Differences among countries in the average rate and timing of puberty are more likely to reflect differences in their environments than differences in their populations' gene pools (Bogin, 2011).

The influence of the broader environment on the timing and tempo of puberty can be seen in more concrete terms by looking at two sets of findings: (1) comparisons of the average age of menarche across countries and (2) changes in the average age of menarche over time. Although menarche does not signal the onset of puberty, researchers often use the average age of menarche when comparing the timing of puberty across different groups or regions, because it can be measured more reliably than other indicators. And while the age of menarche doesn't directly reflect when males in that same group are going through puberty, it does so indirectly, because in places where girls mature early, boys mature early, too (Steinberg, 2014).

First, consider variations in the age of menarche across different regions of the world. Menarche generally is earlier in countries where individuals are less likely to be malnourished or to suffer from chronic disease (Bogin, 2011). For example, in western Europe and in the United States, the median age of menarche ranges from about 12 to 13½ years. In Africa, however, the median age ranges from about 14 to 17 years. The range is much wider across Africa because of the greater variation in environmental conditions there.

The Secular Trend   We can also examine environmental influences on the timing of puberty by looking at changes in the average age of menarche over the past two

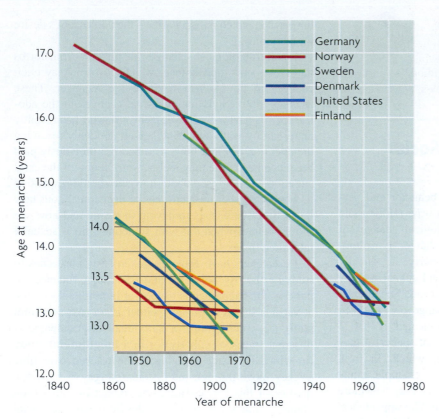

Figure 6 The age at menarche has declined considerably over the past 150 years. This decline is known as the secular trend.
(Adapted from Eveleth & Tanner, 1990)

centuries. Because nutritional conditions have improved during the past 150 years, we would expect to find a decline in the average age at menarche over time. This is indeed the case, as can be seen in Figure 6. This pattern, known as the **secular trend,** is attributable not only to improved nutrition but also to better sanitation and better control of infectious diseases. In most European countries, maturation has become earlier by about 3 to 4 months per decade. For example, in Norway 150 years ago, the average age of menarche may have been about 17 years. Today, it is between 12 and 13 years. Similar declines have been observed over the same period in other industrialized nations and, more recently, in developing countries as well (Ma et al., 2009).

The secular trend is less well documented among boys, in part because there is no easily measured marker of puberty, like menarche. One unusual factoid that is consistent with the decline in the age of puberty among boys over many centuries, though, is the observation that the average age at which boys experience their voice breaking (a sign of male pubertal development), based on reports from European children's choirs, dropped from about 18 in the mid-1700s to around 10½ today (Mendle & Ferrero, 2012). The drop in the age of male puberty appears to be continuing, and has fallen during the past three decades (Herman-Giddens et al., 2012). Interestingly, although puberty is starting earlier, there is some evidence that it taking longer to complete, meaning that children are spending more time in the midst of puberty than ever before (Mendle, 2014).

The average age of puberty among American adolescents has continued to decline, most probably because of increased rates of obesity, which affects leptin levels (Currie et al., 2012); exposure to certain man-made chemicals in cosmetics, food, and the environment that affect development by mimicking actual pubertal hormones (Hochberg et al., 2011); and increased exposure to artificial light, which affects melatonin secretion (Greenspan & Deardorff, 2014).

One reason scientists have expressed concern about the continuing decline in the age when puberty begins is that pubertal hormones affect the developing brain in ways that make adolescents more inclined to engage in sensation seeking (Steinberg, 2014). Brain systems that govern self-regulation are less influenced by puberty, so the secular trend has not affected the age at which the maturation of impulse control takes place. If the increase in sensation seeking is taking place before children are able to regulate urges to do exciting things, it may lead to increases in risky and reckless behavior, especially when the risk taking is impulsive (Kjurana et al., 2012). The end result is that, as the age of puberty has dropped, the amount of time elapsed between the arousal of sensation seeking and the maturation of self control has grown, creating a larger window of vulnerability to risky behavior (Steinberg, 2014). Consistent with this, as the age of puberty has fallen, rates of adolescent mortality have risen (Mendle, 2014).

secular trend
The tendency, over the past two centuries, for individuals to be larger in stature and to reach puberty earlier, primarily because of improvements in health and nutrition.

making the scientific connection

Some studies indicate that the secular trend has been more dramatic among females than males. Why might this be the case?

The Psychological and Social Impact of Puberty

Puberty can affect the adolescent's behavior and psychological functioning in a number of ways (Hollenstein & Lougheed, 2013). First, the biological changes of puberty can have a direct effect on behavior. For example, increases in testosterone at puberty are directly linked to an increase in sex drive and sexual activity among adolescent boys (Halpern, Udry, & Suchindran, 1996). (The impact of hormonal change on girls' sex drive and sexual activity is more complicated.)

Second, the biological changes of puberty may change the adolescent's self-image, which, in turn, may affect how he or she behaves. For example, a boy who has recently gone through puberty may feel more grown up as a result of his more adultlike appearance. This, in turn, may make him seek more independence from his parents. He may ask for a later curfew, a larger allowance, or the right to make decisions about things that previously were decided by his parents. As we will see later in this chapter, the physical changes of puberty often spark conflict between teenagers and their parents, in part because of

cross-sectional study
A study that compares two or more groups of individuals at one point in time.

longitudinal study
A study that follows the same group of individuals over time.

Contrary to widespread belief, there is little evidence that the hormonal changes of puberty contribute in a dramatic way to adolescent moodiness. © Westend61/Getty Images RF

the ways in which puberty affects the adolescent's desire for autonomy.

Finally, biological change at puberty transforms the adolescent's appearance, which, in turn, may elicit changes in how *others* react to the teenager. These changes in reactions may provoke changes in the adolescent's behavior. An adolescent girl who has recently matured physically may find herself suddenly receiving the attention of older boys who had not previously paid her much heed. She may feel nervous about all the extra attention and confused about how she should respond to it. Moreover, she must now make decisions about how much time she wishes to devote to dating and how she should behave when out with someone who is sexually interested in her.

Researchers have generally taken two approaches to studying the psychological and social consequences of puberty. One approach is to look at individuals who are at various stages of puberty, either in a **cross-sectional study** (in which groups of individuals are compared at different stages of puberty) or in a **longitudinal study** (in which the same individuals are tracked over time as they move through the different stages of puberty). Studies of this sort examine the impact of puberty on young people's psychological development and social relations. Researchers might ask, for example, whether youngsters' self-esteem is higher or lower during puberty than before or after.

A second approach compares the psychological development of early and late maturers. Because there is large variation in pubertal timing, individuals of the same chronological age and who are in the same grade in school may be at very different stages of puberty. How does being early or late to mature affect the adolescent's psychological development? Here, a typical question might be whether early maturers are more popular in the peer group than are late maturers.

The Immediate Impact of Puberty

Studies of the psychological and social impacts of puberty indicate that physical maturation, regardless of whether it occurs early or late, affects the adolescent's self-image, mood, and relationships with parents.

Puberty and Self-Esteem   Although puberty can be a potential stressor with temporary adverse psychological consequences, this is true only when it is coupled with other changes that necessitate adjustment. In this respect, the impact of puberty on adolescents' psychological functioning is to a great extent shaped by the social context in which puberty takes place (Susman & Dorn, 2009).

The impact of puberty on self-esteem varies by gender and across ethnic groups, with girls more adversely affected than boys, and with White girls, in particular, at greatest risk for developing a poor body image (J. Siegel, Yancey, Aneshensel, & Schuler, 1999). Given the premium in contemporary American society placed on thinness, the increase in body dissatisfaction among White girls that takes place at puberty is, not surprisingly, linked to specific concerns that girls have about their hips, thighs, waist, and weight (Rosenblum & Lewis, 1999). Interestingly, the way adolescents feel about their physical appearance when they begin adolescence remains remarkably stable over time, regardless of whether their actual attractiveness changes (Rosenblum & Lewis, 1999).

Puberty and Adolescent Moodiness Although an adolescent's self-image can be expected to change during a time of dramatic physical development, self-esteem or self-image is reasonably stable over time, with long and sturdy roots reaching back to childhood. For this reason, some researchers have turned their attention to the impact of puberty on more transient states, such as mood. One reason for this focus is that adolescents are thought to be moodier, on average, than either children or adults. One classic study, in which adolescents' moods were monitored repeatedly by electronic pagers, for example, showed that their moods fluctuate during the course of the day more than do the moods of adults (Csikszentmihalyi & Larson, 1984).

Many adults assume that adolescent moodiness is directly related to the hormonal changes of puberty (C. Buchanan, Eccles, & Becker, 1992). Is there any scientific evidence that the hormonal changes of puberty cause adolescents to be moody or, for that matter, that these hormonal changes affect the adolescent's psychological functioning or behavior at all?

According to several comprehensive reviews of research on hormones and adolescent mood and behavior, the direct connection between hormones and mood is not very strong (C. Buchanan et al., 1992; Duke, Balzer, & Steinbeck, 2014). When studies do find a connection between hormonal changes at puberty and adolescent mood or behavior, the effects are strongest early in puberty, when the process is being "turned on" and when hormonal levels are highly variable. Pubertal hormones affect brain systems responsible for emotional arousal in ways that make adolescents more responsive to what is going on around them (Forbes, Phillips, Silk, Ryan, & Dahl, 2011; Masten et al., 2011). For example, *rapid* increases in many of the hormones associated with puberty—such as testosterone, estrogen, and various adrenal androgens—may be associated with increased irritability, impulsivity, aggression (in boys) and depression (in girls), especially when the increases take place very early in adolescence. One interpretation of these findings is that it is not so much the absolute increases in these hormones during puberty but their rapid fluctuation early in puberty that may affect adolescents' moods. Once the

hormone levels stabilize at higher levels, later in puberty, their negative effects wane (C. Buchanan et al., 1992).

Although rapid increases in hormones early in puberty are associated with depressed mood in girls, it turns out that stressful life events, such as problems in the family, in school, or with friends, play a far greater role in the development of depression than do hormonal changes (Brooks-Gunn, Graber, & Paikoff, 1994). Similarly, while high levels of testosterone have been associated with impulsivity and aggression and low levels with depression, these associations are weaker among adolescents who have positive family relationships (A. Booth et al., 2003).

In other words, there is there little evidence that adolescents' moodiness results exclusively from the storm and stress of raging hormones. Over the course of a day, a teenager may shift from elation to boredom, back to happiness, and then to anger. But these shifts in mood appear to have more to do with shifts in activities—elated when seeing a girlfriend, bored in social studies class, happy when having lunch with friends, and angry when assigned extra work at the fast-food restaurant—than with internal, biological changes (Schneiders et al., 2006).

Puberty and Changes in Patterns of Sleep Many parents complain that their teenage children go to bed too late in the evening and sleep in too late in the morning, a pattern that begins to emerge in early adolescence (see Figure 7). It now appears that the emergence of this pattern—called a **delayed phase preference**—is driven by the biological changes of puberty, and it is seen not only in humans, but in other mammals as well (Carskadon, 2011).

Falling asleep is caused by a combination of biological and

> **delayed phase preference**
> A pattern of sleep characterized by later sleep and wake times, which usually emerges during puberty.

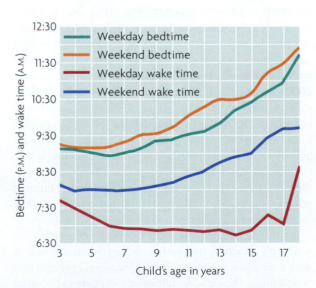

Figure 7 **Children's weekday and weekend bedtimes and wake times, by age.** (Adapted from Snell et al., 2007)

Important changes in the sleep cycle take place after puberty. This "delayed phase preference" causes adolescents to want to stay up later at night and makes them feel more tired in the early morning hours. © Randy Faris/Corbis/age fotostock RF

environmental factors. One of the most important is the secretion of melatonin, which, as you know, plays a role in triggering puberty. Melatonin levels change naturally over the course of the 24-hour day, mainly in response to the amount of light in the environment. Feelings of sleepiness increase and decrease with melatonin levels—as melatonin rises, we feel sleepier, and as it falls, we feel more awake. Over the course of the day, we follow a sleep–wake cycle that is calibrated to changes in light and regulated by melatonin secretion.

During puberty, the time of night at which melatonin levels begin to rise changes, becoming later and later as individuals mature physically. In fact, the nighttime increase in melatonin starts about 2 hours later among adolescents who have completed puberty than among those who have not yet begun (Carskadon & Acebo, 2002). As a result of this shift, individuals become able to stay up later before feeling sleepy. In fact, when allowed to regulate their own sleep schedules (as on weekends), most teenagers will stay up until around 1:00 a.m. and sleep until about 10:00 a.m. Because the whole cycle of melatonin secretion is shifted later at puberty, this also means that once adolescents have gone through puberty, they are more sleepy early in the morning than they were before puberty.

Falling asleep is affected by the environment as well—it's much easier to fall asleep when a room is dark than when it's bright. When preadolescents get into bed at night, they tend to fall asleep very quickly—even if there is something that they want to stay up for—because their melatonin levels are already high. After

going through puberty, though, because of the delayed timing of the increase in melatonin, it is easier for individuals to stay up later, so that if there is something more exciting to do—search the Internet, stream a YouTube, text a friend—it is not difficult to remain awake (Taylor, Jenni, Acebo, & Carskadon, 2005). Some scientists believe that many adolescents' sleep deprivation stems directly from overuse of computers and cell phones (Punamäki, Wallenius, Nygård, Saarni, & Rimpelä, 2007), although the notion that adolescents' lack of sleep is due to over-stimulation at bedtime is more than 100 years old (Matricciani, Olds, Blunden, Rigney, & Williams, 2012). Thus, the tendency for adolescents to stay up late is due to the inter-action of biology (which delays the onset of sleepiness) and the environment (which provides an impetus to stay up). This shift in sleep preferences, to a later bedtime and a later wake time, begins to reverse around age 20, at a slightly earlier age among females than males (Frey, Balu, Greusing, Rothen, & Cajochen, 2009; Roenneberg et al., 2004). The end result is that there is a marked decline in the amount of sleep people get each night during adolescence followed by an increase during the early 20s (Maslowsky & Ozer, 2014) (see Figure 8).

If getting up early the next day were not an issue, staying up late would not be a problem. Unfortunately, most teenagers need to get up early on school days, and the

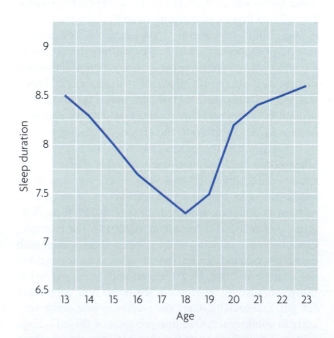

Figure 8 Over the course of adolescence, the average number of hours slept per night declines until the late teens and then begins to increase. (Maslowsky & Ozer, 2014)

combination of staying up late and getting up early leads to sleep deprivation and daytime sleepiness. The shift in the timing of the melatonin cycle contributes to this; when teenagers get out of bed early in the morning, their melatonin levels are relatively higher than they are at the same time of day for preadolescents. Indeed, adolescents are least alert between the hours of 8:00 and 9:00 a.m. (when most schools start) and most alert after 3.00 p.m., when the school day is over (R. Allen & Mirabell, 1990). Sleep researchers estimate that, because of early school start times, adolescents get two fewer hours of sleep per night when the school year begins than they did during the preceding summer months (Hansen, Janssen, Schiff, Zee, & Dubocovich, 2005). This has prompted many experts to call for communities to delay their school starting times (Adolescent Sleep Working Group, 2014a).

The tendency for individuals to go to bed later as they become teenagers has become stronger over the past 30 years (Iglowstein, Jenni, Molinari, & Largo, 2003), perhaps because the availability of television, the Internet, and other electronic media during late-night and early-morning hours has increased (Adolescent Sleep Working Group, 2014b). This suggests that the late-night hours kept by many adolescents are voluntary, but made easier by the changes in the sleep centers of the brain. There is also evidence that exposure to light depresses melatonin secretion, so that staying up late with the lights on or staring at computer, smartphone, tablet, or TV screens will delay the rise in melatonin even more; using eyeglasses that block the blue-wavelength light emitted by these screens can help reduce the adverse effects of screen light on sleep (van der Lely et al., 2015). It has also been suggested that the demands of school and extracurricular activities are taking their toll on adolescents' sleep by keeping them busy into the late hours (Keyes, Maslowsky, Hamilton, & Schulenberg, 2015). Whatever the reason, because teenagers' wake time has not changed, but their bedtime has gotten later, today's teenagers get significantly less sleep than their counterparts did several decades ago. In the early 1990s, one-third of American 15-year-olds reported getting adequate sleep most nights; today fewer than 25% do (Keyes et al., 2015).

Although individuals' preferred bedtime gets later as they move from childhood into adolescence, the amount of sleep they need each night remains constant, at around nine hours. There is now a consensus among scientists that most teenagers are not getting enough sleep, and that inadequate sleep in adolescence leads to all sorts of problems, including depression (Alvaro, Roberts, & Harris, 2013; Pieters et al., 2015), poor self-control (Meldrum, Barnes, & Hay, 2015), delinquency (McGlinchey & Harvey, 2014), alcohol and drug use (Pasch, Latimer, Cance, Moe, & Lytle, 2012), obesity (Mitchell, Rodriguez, Schmitz, & Audrain-McGovern,

2013), cognitive impairment (Potkin & Bunney, 2012; Rossa, Smith, Allan, & Sullivan, 2014; Thomas, Monahan, Lukowski, & Cauffman, 2015), and poor school performance (Lin & Yi, 2014). The good news is that getting just one additional hour of sleep each night has been shown to significantly improve adolescents' well-being (Winsler, Deutsch, Vorona, Payne, & Szklo-Coxe, 2015).

Despite many adolescents' belief that catching up on sleep on weekends will make up for sleep deprivation during the week, having markedly different bedtimes on weekends versus weekdays actually contributes to further sleep-related problems (Wolfson & Carskadon, 1998). (The best thing teenagers can do to avoid problems waking up on school days is to force themselves to get up at the same time on the weekend as on school days, regardless of how late they have stayed up.) Not surprisingly, sleep-related difficulties among teenagers are also linked to the consumption of caffeine (Pollack & Bright, 2003) and tobacco (Patten, Choi, Gillin, & Pierce, 2000), both of which are stimulants. About 10% of teenagers report chronic insomnia (E. Johnson, Roth, Schultz, & Breslau, 2006), which increases the risk of other psychological problems (R. Roberts, Roberts, & Duong, 2008) as well as sleep difficulties in adulthood (Dregan & Armstrong, 2010).

Puberty and Family Relationships Research into the impact of puberty on family relationships has found that puberty appears to increase conflict and distance between parents and children, although the "distancing" effect of puberty on adolescent–parent relationships is not as consistently observed in ethnic minority families (Molina & Chassin, 1996; Sagrestano, McCormick, Paikoff, & Holmbeck, 1999). In White families, however, as youngsters mature from childhood toward the middle of puberty, emotional distance between them and their parents increases, and conflict intensifies, especially between adolescents and mothers (Laursen, Coy, & Collins, 1998; Ogletree, Jones, & Coyl, 2002). The change that takes place is reflected in an increase in "negatives" (e.g., conflict, complaining, anger) and, to a lesser extent, a decrease in "positives" (e.g., support, smiling, laughter) (e.g., Flannery et al., 1994). Although negative interchanges may diminish after the adolescent growth spurt, adolescents and their parents do not immediately become as close as they were before the adolescents entered puberty. Interestingly, puberty also increases distance between children and their parents in most species of monkeys and apes, and some writers have suggested that the pattern seen in human adolescents may have some evolutionary basis—it helps ensure that once they mature sexually, adolescents will leave home and mate outside the family (Steinberg & Belsky, 1996).

This connection between pubertal maturation and parent-child distance is not affected by the age at which the adolescent goes through puberty—the pattern is seen among early as well as late maturers. To date, we do not know whether this effect results from the hormonal changes of puberty (which may make young adolescents more testy), from changes in the adolescent's physical appearance (which may change the way parents treat their adolescent), or from changes in other aspects of adolescents' psychological functioning that are affected by puberty and, in turn, affect family relationships (like newfound interest in dating).

Pubertal Maturation and Peer Relationships Puberty may have an effect on relationships in the peer group, too. Boys and girls who are physically mature are more likely than their less mature peers to be involved in cross-sex romantic activities such as having a boyfriend or girlfriend or going out on dates (Compian, Gowen, & Hayward, 2004), although this depends on the social norms of the adolescent's peer group and the prevailing expectations about the age at which teenagers should begin dating (Gargiulo, Attie, Brooks-Gunn, & Warren, 1987). Pubertal maturation is *not* associated with having platonic relationships with other-sex peers, however (Compian et al., 2004).

The Impact of Specific Pubertal Events

Several studies have focused specifically on adolescents' attitudes toward and reactions to particular events at puberty, such as girls' reactions to menarche or breast development and boys' reactions to their first ejaculation.

In general, most adolescents react positively to the biological changes associated with puberty, especially those associated with the development of secondary sex characteristics. One study of adolescent girls' attitudes toward breast development, for example, found that the majority of girls greeted this change positively (Brooks-Gunn, Newman, Holderness, & Warren, 1994).

Adolescent girls' attitudes toward menarche are less negative today than they appear to have been in the past (J. Lee, 2008), a change that may be attributable to the increase in information about menstruation provided in schools and in the media (Merskin, 1999). Among today's adolescent girls, menarche is typically accompanied by gains in social maturity, peer prestige, and self-esteem—as well as by increased self-consciousness (Brooks-Gunn & Reiter, 1990). Nevertheless, many young women have developed a negative image of menstruation before reaching adolescence, and they enter puberty with a mixture of excitement and fear (S. Moore, 1995). Girls whose mothers are helpful and matter-of-fact in their response to menarche report the most positive memories of the experience (J. Lee, 2008).

Menstrual symptoms are reported to be more severe among women who expect menstruation to be uncomfortable, among girls whose mothers lead them to believe that menstruation will be unpleasant or uncomfortable, and in cultures that label menstruation as an important event. In Mexico and in China, for example, where attitudes toward menarche are especially ambivalent, menarche may have an adverse effect on girls' mental health, an effect not generally observed in the United States (Benjet & Hernandez-Guzman, 2002; Tang, Yeung, & Lee, 2003). In addition, girls who experience menarche early and who are unprepared for puberty report more negative reactions to the event (Koff & Rierdan, 1996; Tang, Yeung, & Lee, 2004).

Far less is known about boys' reactions to their first ejaculation, an experience that is analogous to menarche in girls. Although most boys are not very well prepared for this event by their parents or other adults, first ejaculation does not appear to cause undue anxiety, embarrassment, or fear. In contrast to girls, who generally tell their mothers shortly after they have begun menstruating and tell their girlfriends soon thereafter, boys, at least in the United States, do not discuss their first ejaculation with either parents or friends (J. Stein & Reiser, 1994). Cultural differences in boys' responses to their first ejaculation are likely related to differences in how cultures view masturbation. As is the case with girls and menarche, boys' reactions to their first ejaculation are more positive when they have been prepared for the event (J. Stein & Reiser, 1994).

The Impact of Early or Late Maturation

Adolescents who mature relatively early or relatively late stand apart from their peers physically and may elicit different sorts of reactions and expectations from those around them. Adolescents often are all too aware of whether they are early or late relative to their classmates, and their feelings about themselves are likely to be influenced by their comparisons. One study found that early-maturing adolescents were more likely to be "pseudomature"—wishing they were older, hanging around with older peers, less involved in school, and more oriented toward their peers (Galambos, Barker, & Tilton-Weaver, 2003). Indeed, adolescents' *perceptions* of whether they are an early or a late maturer are often more strongly related to how they feel about and are affected by puberty than whether they actually are early or late (Kretsch, Mendle, & Harden, 2014; Moore, Harden, & Mendle, 2014; Reynolds & Juvonen, 2012). Further, adolescents' behavior is related to how old they feel, not simply to how physically mature they are (Galambos, Kolaric, Sears, & Maggs, 1999). Nevertheless, early and late maturers are often treated differently by others and view themselves differently, and as a result, they may behave differently. As we shall see, early and late maturation have different consequences at puberty than in the long run, different consequences in different contexts, and, most important, different consequences for boys and girls.

Early Versus Late Maturation Among Boys   Over the past 60 years, research on boys' pubertal timing has usually found that early-maturing boys feel better about themselves and are more popular than their late-maturing peers, although a few studies have found elevated rates of depression and anxiety among early-maturing boys relative to their on-time peers (Mendle & Ferrero, 2012; Negriff & Susman, 2011) and among boys who go through puberty especially rapidly (Mendle, Harden, Brooks-Gunn, & Graber, 2010). Interestingly, although all adolescents are adversely affected by being bullied by their peers, the impact of victimization is greater for early maturers, perhaps because being picked on when one is larger than average is all the more embarrassing (Nadeem & Graham, 2005).

Although findings on the emotional effects of early maturation on boys are mixed, it is well established that early-maturing boys are more likely than their peers to get involved in antisocial or deviant activities, including truancy, minor delinquency, and problems at school (Negriff & Susman, 2011). They are also more likely to use drugs and alcohol and engage in other risky activities (Baams, Dubas, Overbeek, & van Aken, 2015; Drapela, Gebelt, & McRee, 2006; Kaltiala-Heino, Koivisto, Martutunen, & Fröjd, 2011), even as young adults (Biehl, Natsuaki, & Ge, 2007). One explanation for this is that boys who are more physically mature are less closely supervised by adults and spend more time hanging out in settings in which delinquent behavior is more likely to occur, like parts of neighborhoods where there are few adults around (Kretschmer, Oliver, & Maughan, 2014; Schelleman-Offermans, Knibbe, & Kuntsche, 2013). It is also likely that older-looking boys develop friendships with older peers, who lead them into activities that are problematic for the younger boys (Negriff, Ji, & Trickett, 2011a). Once involved with these older peer groups, the early maturers' higher rate of delinquency and substance use increases over time through their social contacts (Silbereisen et al., 1989).

Early-maturing boys enjoy some psychological advantages over late maturers with respect to self-esteem and admiration from peers during early adolescence, when some boys have matured physically but others have not. But what about later during adolescence, when the late maturers have caught up? It turns out that there may be some interesting advantages for late-maturing boys, despite their initially lower popularity. Although early and late maturers exhibit similar psychological profiles before adolescence, during puberty and one year later, late maturers show significantly higher ratings on measures of intellectual curiosity, exploratory behavior, and social initiative. While they are in the midst of puberty, early maturers experience more frequent and more

Early maturing boys are more likely to be involved in problem behavior than adolescents who are the same age but slower to mature. © BananaStock/Getty Images RF

intense temper tantrums and depression (Ge, Brody, Conger, Simons, & Murry, 2002; Ge et al., 2003).

Early Versus Late Maturation in Girls   In contrast to the mixed impact that early maturation has on the emotional well-being of boys, considerable research shows that early-maturing girls have more emotional difficulties than their peers, including poorer self-image and higher rates of depression, anxiety, eating disorders, and panic attacks (Greenspan & Deardorff, 2014; Negriff & Susman, 2011). These difficulties seem to have less to do with the direct effects of hormones and more to do with the ways in which looking different from their peers affects girls' feelings about their appearance and social relationships with other adolescents (Mendle et al., 2007; Conley, Rudolph, & Bryant, 2012). For example, the impact of early maturation is worse on girls who are heavier than on their thinner peers (Tanner-Smith, 2010). There is also evidence that early maturation in girls is associated with higher emotional arousal (Graber, Brooks-Gunn, & Warren, 2006). It is not clear, however, whether the effects of early puberty on depression are limited to adolescence or persist into adulthood (Gaysina, Richards, & Hardy, 2015).

Given the role of social factors in linking early maturation and girls' psychological distress, it is no surprise that the ultimate impact of early maturation on the young girl's feelings about herself appears to depend on the broader context in which maturation takes place. Studies of American girls generally find that early-maturing girls have lower self-esteem and a poorer self-image, because of our cultural preference for thinness and our ambivalence about adolescent sexuality. The negative effects of early maturation on girls' mental health vary across ethnic groups, however, with more adverse consequences seen among White girls than their Black or Hispanic peers, presumably because puberty is more likely to lead to body dissatisfaction among White girls (Negriff & Susman, 2011). Girls who are prone to ruminate or cope poorly when they have problems seem especially vulnerable to the stress of maturing early (Crockett, Carlo, Wolff, & Hope, 2013; Hamilton, Hamlat et al., 2014; Hamilton, Stange et al., 2014). Context matters, though: One recent study of both boys and girls found that the adverse consequences of early puberty were limited to adolescents who came from high-risk households, consistent with the idea that puberty itself isn't inherently stressful but can intensify the effects of other stressors (Lynne-Landsman, Graber, & Andrews, 2010b).

Although some early-maturing girls have self-image difficulties, their popularity with peers is not jeopardized. Early maturers are more popular than other girls, especially, as you would expect, when the index of popularity includes popularity with boys (Simmons, Blyth, & McKinney, 1983). However, early-maturing girls not only enjoy more popularity with boys, but are often the victims of rumors and gossip (Reynolds & Juvonen, 2011; Sontag, Graber, & Clemans, 2011) and are more likely to suffer from social anxiety (Blumenthal et al., 2011). Ironically, then, it may be in part because the early maturer is more popular with boys that she reports more emotional upset: Early pressure to date and, perhaps, to be involved in a sexual relationship may take its toll on girls' mental health. Consistent with this, research indicates that early-maturing girls are more vulnerable to emotional distress when they have relatively more friendships with boys (Ge, Best, Conger, & Simons, 1996) and when they are in schools with older peers (for

example, sixth-graders who are in a school that has seventh and eighth-graders, too) (Blyth, Simmons, & Zakin, 1985). Perhaps the problem isn't early maturation as much as it is the way that older boys react to it.

There are several theories explaining why early maturation is harder on girls than boys (Negriff & Susman, 2011; Rudolph, Troop-Gordon, Lambert, & Natsuaki, 2014). One explanation is the "maturational deviance" hypothesis. Simply put, youngsters who stand far apart from their peers—in physical appearance, for instance—may experience more psychological distress than adolescents who blend in more easily. Because girls on average mature earlier than boys, early-maturing girls mature earlier than both their male and female peers. This makes them really stand out at a time when they would rather fit in and, as a result, may make them more vulnerable to emotional distress. This explanation would also account for the lower self-esteem of late-maturing boys, who deviate toward the other extreme.

A second explanation for the sex difference in the impact of early maturation focuses on "developmental readiness." If puberty is a challenge that requires psychological adaptation by the adolescent, perhaps younger adolescents are less ready to cope with the challenge than older ones. Because puberty occurs quite early among early-maturing girls, it may tax their psychological resources. Early maturation among boys, because it occurs at a later age, would pose less of a problem. This also helps to explain why late-maturing boys seem better able than early maturers to control their temper and their impulses when they are going through puberty: They are relatively older and psychologically more mature. If the developmental readiness hypothesis is true, both girls and boys should experience more difficulty if they are early maturers than if they are on time or late, but the difficulty should be temporary. This appears to be the case among boys (for whom the negative effects of early puberty occur during puberty itself, but then fade), but not for girls (for whom the negative effects of early puberty persist) (Ge et al., 2003).

A final explanation for the relatively greater disadvantage of early maturation for girls concerns the cultural desirability of different body types (Petersen, 1988). Early maturation for girls means leaving behind the culturally admired state of thinness. Many girls are distressed when they mature because they gain weight. Early maturers experience this weight gain at a time when most of their peers are still girlishly thin. One interesting study showed that in ballet companies—where thinness is even more important than in the culture at large—late maturers, who can retain the "ideal" shape much longer than earlier maturers, have fewer psychological problems than even on-time girls (Brooks-Gunn & Warren, 1985). In contrast, at puberty, boys move from a culturally undesirable state for males (short and scrawny) to a culturally admired one (tall and muscular). Early

Although they are often more popular than their peers, early maturing girls are at greater risk for a wide range of emotional and behavioral problems. © Klaus Tiedge/ Fancy Collection/SuperStock RF

maturers enjoy the advantage of being tall and muscular before their peers—a special benefit in a society that values males' athletic prowess—and therefore are more likely to react well to puberty. The fact that the effects of early maturation on girls' self-esteem vary across cultures suggests that contextual factors need to be taken into account in explaining this pattern of sex differences.

Whatever the explanation, it's important for parents and school counselors to bear in mind that early-maturing girls are at heightened risk for psychological problems. Unfortunately, as long as our culture overvalues thinness and encourages the view that females should be judged on the basis of their physical appearance rather than their abilities, values, or personality, the risks of early puberty will probably endure. Adults can help by being supportive, by helping the early-maturing girl recognize her strengths and positive features—physical and nonphysical alike—and by preparing her for puberty before it takes place.

Like their male counterparts, early-maturing girls are also more likely to become involved in problem behavior, including delinquency, drinking, and drug use; to have school problems; and to experience early sexual intercourse (Boden, Fergusson, & Horwood, 2011; Negriff & Susman, 2011; Verhoef, van den Eijnden, Koning, & Vollebergh, 2013) (see Figure 9). This is true in Europe and the United States (Silbereisen et al., 1989) and across ethnic groups within the United States (Baams et al., 2015; Deardorff, Gonzales, Christopher, Roosa, & Millsap, 2005). These problems appear to arise because early-maturing girls, like early-maturing boys, are more likely to spend time unsupervised (Kretschmer et al., 2014), hanging out with older adolescents, especially older adolescent boys, who initiate them into activities that might otherwise be delayed (Haynie, 2003; Negriff

et al., 2011b). Other explanations for the link between early maturation and girls' problem behavior have also been proposed: One recent study suggests that association may be partly due to common genetic influences (i.e., genes that influence both the timing of puberty and involvement in delinquency) (Harden & Mendle, 2012). Another found that early maturation leads to early sexual activity, which in turn leads to delinquency (Negriff, Susman, & Trickett, 2011b).

Again, however, it is important to consider the role of context in interaction with pubertal change. Although early-maturing girls are more likely to engage in delinquent behavior than late maturers, this may hold true only for girls who attend coeducational high schools (Caspi, Lynam, Moffitt, & Silva, 1993). Early-maturing girls in all-female schools are no more likely than late maturers to be involved in delinquent activities, presumably because there are far fewer opportunities for delinquency in same-sex schools. Thus, while early puberty may predispose girls toward more frequent and earlier deviance, this predisposition may be realized only in an environment that permits the behavior—such as a school or out-of-school setting that places early-maturing girls in close contact with older boys (Stattin, Kerr, & Skoog, 2011). Similarly, among both boys and girls, the impact of early maturation on problem behavior or depression is accentuated when adolescents have many stressful life events, have harsh and inconsistent parents, or live in disadvantaged urban neighborhoods (Benoit, Lacourse, & Claes, 2013; Deardorff et al., 2013; Obeidallah, Brennan, Brooks-Gunn, & Earls, 2004). This helps explain why the impact of early maturation on problem behavior is relatively greater among minority adolescents, who are more likely to live in poor communities (Negriff & Susman, 2011), because early maturation

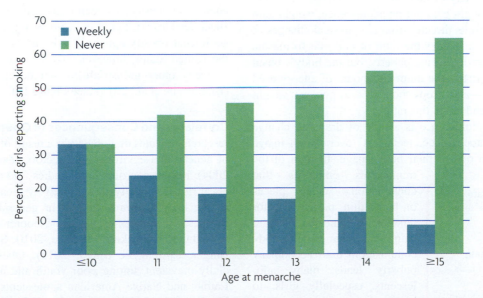

Figure 9   Early-maturing girls are more likely to use tobacco, alcohol, and other drugs than girls who mature on time or late. (From Dick et al., 2000)

does not have especially adverse effects on Black girls who don't live in poor neighborhoods (Carter, Caldwell, Matusko, Antoinucci, & Jackson, 2011; DeRose, Shiyko, Foster, & Brooks-Gunn, 2011).

The earlier involvement of early-maturing girls in problem behavior may adversely affect their long-term educational achievement and mental health. In one study of Swedish girls, the school problems of early-maturing girls persisted over time, leading to the development of negative attitudes toward school and lower educational aspirations. In young adulthood, there were marked differences between early and late-maturing girls' levels of education; the late-maturing girls were twice as likely as early-maturing girls to continue beyond the compulsory minimum number of years of high school (Magnusson et al., 1986). In a different study, of American girls, researchers found that women who had been early maturers reported higher levels of psychological distress and were more likely than others to have experienced a serious mental disorder at some point in adolescence or young adulthood (Graber, Seeley, Brooks-Gunn, & Lewinsohn, 2004).

making the cultural connection

Consider the research on the psychological consequences of early versus late maturation in males and females. Most of this research has been done in the United States. Are the effects of being early, on time, or late likely to be similar in different parts of the world?

Obesity and Eating Disorders

Although a variety of nutritional and behavioral factors can lead to weight gain during adolescence, weight gain sometimes results directly from the physical changes of puberty. Not only does the ratio of body fat to muscle increase markedly during puberty, but the body's **basal metabolism rate**—the minimal amount of energy used when resting—also drops about 15%. A person's weight is partly dependent on this rate.

Because adolescence is a time of dramatic change in physical appearance, teenagers' overall self-image is very much tied to their body image. In light of the tremendous emphasis that contemporary society places on being thin, particularly for females, the normal weight gain and change in body composition that accompany puberty leads many adolescents, especially girls, to become extremely concerned about their weight.

basal metabolism rate
The minimal amount of energy used by the body during a resting state.

body mass index (BMI)
A measure of an individual's body fat, the ratio of weight to height; used to gauge overweight and obesity.

Obesity

Many adolescents, of course, have legitimate concerns about being overweight. The easiest way to determine whether someone is overweight is to calculate his or her **body mass index (BMI),** which is done by dividing the person's weight, measured in kilograms, by the square of the person's height, measured in meters. Individuals are considered obese if their BMI is at or above the 95th percentile for people of the same age and gender, at great risk for obesity if their BMI is at or above the 90th percentile, and overweight if their BMI is at or above the 85th percentile (Zametkin, Zoon, Klein, & Munson, 2004). (Charts showing the BMI cutoffs for males and females of different ages can be found at www.cdc.gov/growthcharts.) Using this definition, more than one-sixth of adolescents in the United States are obese (Ogden, Carroll, & Flegal, 2008), and another 15% are at great risk for obesity, a rate that increased substantially between 1970 and 2000 but has since leveled off (Spruijt-Metz, 2011). Compared to their peers in the mid-1960s, the average 15-year-old boy today is 15 pounds heavier, and the average 15-year-old girl is 10 pounds heavier—increases that are far greater than could possibly be due to changes in height. Obesity is now considered the single most serious public health problem afflicting American teenagers. Fortunately, there is some evidence that the situation may be getting better; since 2001, rates of exercise among adolescents have increased whereas consumption of sweets and sugary soft drinks has declined (Iannotti & Wang, 2013).

By some estimates, the adolescent obesity epidemic will cost the United States more than $250 billion as a result of obese individuals' lost productivity and direct medical costs in adulthood (Lightwood, Bibbins-Domingo, Coxson, Wang et al., 2009). The increase in adolescent obesity has been especially dramatic among Black females (H. Lee, Lee, Guo, & Harris, 2011). The adolescent obesity epidemic is by no means limited to the United States, however, and has been documented in many other industrialized and developing nations (Braithwaite et al., 2013) (see Figure 10).

Correlates and Consequences of Obesity   Current research indicates that obesity is a result of the interplay of genetic and environmental factors (Zametkin et al., 2004). Recent neuroimaging studies find that individuals at risk for obesity show relatively greater activation of the brain's reward centers in general, heightened responses to images of food, and poorer impulse control (Batterink, Yokum, & Stice, 2010; Stice, Yokum, Burger, Epstein, & Small, 2011). Obesity is especially prevalent among poor youth and among Black, Latino, and Native American adolescents (Burdette & Needham, 2012; Huh, Stice, Shaw, & Boutelle, 2012; Miech et al., 2006; K. A. T. Wickrama, Wickrama, &

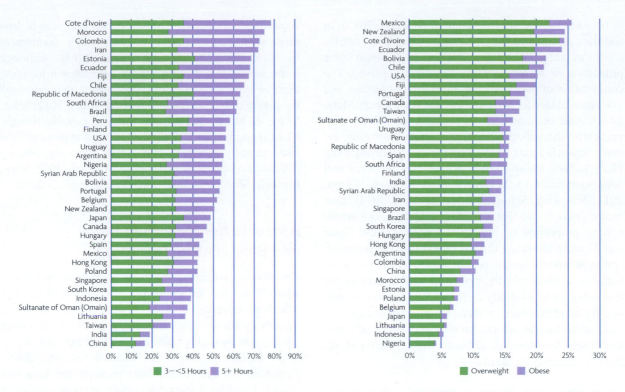

Figure 10 The adolescent obesity epidemic is by no means limited to the United States. Television viewing is likely to be a contributor (Braithwaite et al., 2013). This figure shows the proportions of teens who watch either few or many hours of television each day (left) and the proportions who are overweight or obese (right).

Bryant, 2006). There is also worrisome evidence that, with each successive generation born in the United States, Latino youth show increasingly poorer nutrition (M. L. Allen et al., 2007).

Research on the psychological consequences of obesity has not led to consistent conclusions, in part because the psychological correlates of being overweight vary across ethnic groups, with more adverse correlates seen among White and Hispanic than Black adolescents (BeLue, Francis, & Colaco, 2009; Leech & Dias, 2012). While some studies show higher levels of psychological distress among obese individuals (such as depression and low self-esteem), many studies show no such effect, and some research indicates that depression leads to obesity, rather than vice versa (Zametkin et al., 2004). In addition, the long-term psychological consequences of obesity in adolescence appear to be greater for females than males, perhaps because overweight girls are teased more than overweight boys (Lampard, MacLehose, Eisenberg, Neumark-Sztainer, & Davison, 2014). This harassment, like other forms of bullying, can disrupt adolescents' academic performance and attainment (Crosnoe, 2007; Echeverria, Velez-Valle, Janevic, & Prytowsky, 2014). Additionally, because nearly 80% of obese adolescents will be obese adults, obesity during adolescence places the individual at much higher risk for other health problems, including hypertension (high blood pressure), high cholesterol levels, diabetes, and premature death (Institute of Medicine, 2006; Ma,

Flanders, Ward, & Jemal, 2011). The good news is that the long-term health consequences of adolescent obesity disappear among individuals who are not obese as adults (Juonala, Magnussen, & Berenson, 2011). Other benefits of increasing one's physical activity in adolescence include improved academic performance (Bezold et al., 2014; Srikanth, Petrie, Greenleaf, & Martin, 2014) and diminished risk for depression (McPhie & Rawana, 2015).

Genetic factors are important contributors to obesity, but the condition also has strong environmental causes. Although rates of obesity may differ from country to country, the factors that contribute to obesity are similar in different parts of the world (Bratihwaite et al., 2013). Too many adolescents eat too much high-calorie, low-fiber food (drinking far too many sugary soft drinks and consuming too much junk food), and too few are physically active, spending excessive amounts of time with television, video games, and electronic media, and not enough time exercising or playing sports (Braithwaite et al., 2013). There is a pronounced increase in sedentary behavior between childhood and adolescence (Nader, Bradley, Houts, McRitchie, & O'Brien, 2008; Ortega et al., 2013). In one recent study of American adolescents, only one-fourth reported a lifestyle characterized by high levels of physical activity and diets high in fruits and vegetables; another quarter reported lots of time watching TV or on the computer, and diets high in sweets, soft drinks, and chips; and the remaining half fell somewhere in between these extremes (Iannotti & Wang, 2013). In addition, as noted earlier, inadequate sleep also contributes to weight gain, and there has been an increase in the proportion of adolescents who are sleep-deprived. The combination of poor nutrition, insufficient exercise, and inadequate sleep is a recipe for obesity (Spruijt-Metz, 2011). And because adolescents tend to affiliate with peers who share their tastes and interests (including, literally, tastes in food), obese teenagers are relatively more likely to have obese friends, which may reinforce bad behavioral habits (de la Haye, Robins, Mohr, & Wilson, 2013; Simpkins, Schaefer, Price, & Vest, 2013). One recent study found that attending a high school where a large proportion of juniors and seniors were obese significantly increased the likelihood that the freshmen and sophomores would be obese, too (Leatherdale & Papadakis, 2011). Finally, numerous studies have shown that exposure to adversity early in life is associated with obesity in adolescence, perhaps because stress exposure can undermine the subsequent development of self control (Bae, Wickrama, & O'Neal, 2014; Hanson et al., 2013; Lumeng et al., 2013).

Preventing and Treating Obesity Much recent attention has focused on the availability of unhealthy foods and beverages in and near American schools (Hoyt et al., 2014). Manufacturers of high-calorie and high-fat foods have been criticized for marketing these products to younger children, because food preferences are known to develop largely during early childhood (Institute of Medicine, 2006). Of course, although schools and advertisers undoubtedly influence what children and adolescents eat and drink, the bulk of what children and adolescents put into their mouths comes from their own homes. Obesity is less likely to develop among adolescents who have good relationships with their parents, probably because they are more likely to share family meals where healthy food is served (Berge, Wall, Loth, & Neumark-Sztainer, 2010; Hammons & Fiese, 2011). In addition, the availability of parks and recreational facilities is linked to lower rates of obesity, as is parental encouragement of exercise (Nesbit, Kolobe, Sisson, & Ghement, 2014; Spruijt-Metz, 2011). Taken together, these studies indicate that preventing obesity will require multifaceted efforts involving parents, the mass media, food and beverage manufacturers, restaurants, schools, and communities.

Research has also evaluated a variety of approaches to individual weight loss, including behavioral therapy designed to gradually alter patterns of diet and exercise and medications designed to promote weight loss. Adolescents can be taught to successfully regulate their cravings for food (Silvers et al., 2014). Several evaluations indicate that the

disordered eating
Mild, moderate, or severe disturbance in eating habits and attitudes.

combination of behavior modification and weight loss medication is more effective than either component by itself (Kirschenbaum & Gierut, 2013). Although some weight-loss programs have been shown to work, there is wide variability in success rates, depending on the nature of the program (Sarwer & Dilks, 2012; Stice, Shaw, & Marti, 2006). One thing is certain, though: Radical approaches to weight control—fad diets and the like—actually increase, rather than decrease, obesity (Neumark-Sztainer, Wall, Story, & Standish, 2012; Stice, Presnell, Shaw, & Rohde, 2005; Zhang et al., 2011a).

Anorexia Nervosa, Bulimia, and Binge Eating Disorder

Health care professionals are concerned not only about adolescents who are obese but also about adolescents who have unhealthy attitudes toward eating and toward their body image. Only about one-fourth of American adolescents are highly satisfied with their body (A. Kelly, Wall, Eisenberg, Story, & Neumark-Sztainer, 2005). Egged on by advertisers, who promote the idea that "thin is beautiful," many adolescents respond to normal bodily changes at puberty by dieting, often unnecessarily. More than half of all adolescent girls consider themselves overweight and have attempted to diet (M. Fisher et al., 1995). One study found that 14% of female college undergraduates were so concerned about eating that they were embarrassed at buying a chocolate bar in public (Rozin, Bauer, & Catanese, 2003)! Gender differences in concerns about weight emerge long before adolescence (Phares, Steinberg, & Thompson, 2004).

Disordered Eating Experts today think about **disordered eating** on a continuum, ranging from dieting that may be perfectly sensible and healthy, to disordered eating that is unhealthy but not at a level requiring treatment, to full-blown clinical disorders (Tyrka, Graber, & Brooks-Gunn, 2000). Disordered eating is associated with a range of stress-related psychological problems, including poor body image, depression, alcohol and tobacco use, and poor interpersonal relationships (Eichen, Conner, Daly, & Fauber, 2012; Neumark-Sztainer, Story, Dixon, & Murray, 1998). It is not clear, however, whether these problems precede or follow from the eating disorder (Leon, Fulkerson, Perry, Keel, & Klump, 1999).

Studies of magazines aimed at women and adolescent girls reveal clear and consistent messages implying that women cannot be beautiful without being slim and promoting a range of weight loss products (Davison & McCabe, 2011). Between 1970 and 1990, moreover, images presented in these magazines' advertisements changed, with the "ideal" body shape becoming slimmer and less curvaceous (Guillen & Barr, 1994). Exposure to commercials containing images of females with idealized thin bodies increases girls' dissatisfaction with their own bodies (Rodgers, McLean, & Paxton, 2015). Interestingly, among Hispanic girls in the United States, those who are more Americanized are significantly more likely to develop disordered eating than those who are less acculturated (Gowen, Hayward, Killen, Robinson, & Taylor, 1999). Girls whose mothers have body image problems are especially likely to engage in extreme weight loss behaviors (Ogle & Damhorst, 2003), as are those who report more negative relationships with their parents (Archibald, Graber, & Brooks-Gunn, 1999).

Some young women become so concerned about gaining weight that they take drastic—and dangerous—measures to remain thin. In the more severe cases, young women who suffer from an eating disorder called **anorexia nervosa** actually starve themselves in an effort to keep their weight down. Others go on eating binges and then force themselves to vomit or take laxatives to avoid gaining weight, a pattern associated with an eating disorder called **bulimia.** Adolescents with these sorts of eating disorders have an extremely disturbed body image: They see themselves as overweight when they are actually underweight. Some anorexic youngsters may lose between 25% and 50% of their body weight. As you might expect, bulimia and anorexia, if untreated, lead to a variety of serious physical problems. Nearly 20% of anorexic teenagers inadvertently starve themselves to death.

A newly identified disorder, called **binge eating disorder,** has recently been recognized by clinicians (Stice, Shaw, & Ochner, 2011). Individuals with this disorder binge eat and feel distressed about doing so, but do not try to compensate for their binges through extreme weight loss measures. As a consequence, individuals with binge eating disorder are at high risk for obesity. Because this disorder has only been defined recently, there is very little research on its causes, correlates, or treatment.

Anorexia and bulimia each began to receive a great deal of popular attention during the 1980s because of their dramatic nature and their frequent association in the mass media with celebrities. Perhaps because of this attention, initial reports characterized these eating disorders as being of epidemic proportion. Although unhealthy eating and unnecessary dieting are prevalent among teenagers, the incidence of clinically defined anorexia and bulimia is small. Fewer than 1% of female adolescents are anorexic, and only about 3% are bulimic (Stice & Rohde, 2013). Rates among females are substantially higher than among males—anorexia and bulimia are 10 times more prevalent among adolescent girls than boys (Stice et al., 2011), although the female-to-male ratio is substantially smaller for less severe forms of these disorders (Muise, Stein, & Arbess,

2003; Ricciardelli & McCabe, 2004). Unlike anorexia and bulimia, binge eating disorder is only slightly more prevalent among females than males, which suggests that it may have an entirely different etiology. Although it is widely believed that eating disorders are especially common among affluent, suburban, White, and Asian American girls, systematic studies do not support this contention. Disordered eating and body dissatisfaction have been reported among poor as well as affluent teenagers and among Black and Hispanic as well as Asian and White youngsters (Jacobi et al., 2004; Lee et al., 2013; Olvera et al., 2014).

Body Dissatisfaction Although the incidence of anorexia and bulimia is small, the proportion of adolescents who are unhappy with their body shape or weight is not. In one study, more than a third of girls whose weight

anorexia nervosa
An eating disorder found chiefly among young women, characterized by dramatic and severe self-induced weight loss.

bulimia
An eating disorder found primarily among young women, characterized by a pattern of binge eating and extreme weight loss measures, including self-induced vomiting.

binge eating disorder
An eating disorder characterized by a pattern of binge eating that is not accompanied by drastic attempts to lose weight.

Body dissatisfaction during adolescence can lead to disordered eating. © Preappy/Getty Images RF

was considered normal by medical and health standards believed that they were overweight—including 5% who actually were *underweight* by medical criteria. (In contrast, fewer than 7% of normal-weight boys and no under-weight boys described themselves as being overweight.) More than 70% of the girls reported that they would like to be thinner than they are (as opposed to one-third of the boys), and more than 80% said that being thinner would make them happier, more successful, and more popular (Paxton et al., 1991). Dissatisfaction with body shape and weight is likely to lead to the development of eating problems (Boone, Soenens, & Luyten, 2014; Francisco et al., 2015), depression (Stice & Bearman, 2001; Stice, Hayward, Cameron, Killen, & Taylor, 2000), and the initiation of smoking (Austin & Gortmaker, 2001; Fulkerson & French, 2003; Stice & Shaw, 2003). More than half of high school girls have engaged in some form of unhealthy behavior (e.g., fasting, smoking, vomiting after eating, using diet pills) in order to lose weight (Croll, Neumark-Sztainer, Story, & Ireland, 2002), although there is evidence that this practice has waned somewhat in recent years (Park, Scott, Adams, Brindis, & Irwin, 2014).

Unfortunately, many girls gain weight during puberty, and for early adolescent girls, being overweight is highly correlated with being seen as unattractive by others (Rosenblum & Lewis, 1999). Despite adults' wishes that girls not place so much emphasis on being thin, research indicates that the widespread belief among adolescent girls that being slim will increase their popularity, especially with boys, is in fact based in reality (Halpern, Udry, Campbell, & Suchindran, 1999). That is, the pressure girls feel to be thin in order to attract boys does not just come from television, movies, and magazines—it comes from their actual experience. Indeed, one analysis found that, regardless of a girl's

ethnicity, each 1-point increase in a young woman's BMI (an index of the degree to which she is overweight) was associated with a 6% decrease in the probability of her being in a romantic relationship (Halpern, King, Oslak, & Udry, 2005). In that study, a 5-foot 3-inch girl who weighed 110 pounds was twice as likely to date as a girl of the same height and level of pubertal maturity who weighed 126 pounds.

Fewer studies have examined body dissatisfaction among adolescent boys, although it is clear that there is an idealized, muscular, male body type that many boys aspire to. As is the case with girls, boys who do not fit this image report more body dissatisfaction, but the relation between appearance and body dissatisfaction among males is somewhat more complicated than it is among females. Whereas being heavy is the main source of dissatisfaction among girls, being heavy or being thin are both sources of dissatisfaction among boys (Calzo et al., 2012) (see Figure 11). In fact, boys are more likely to be teased for being underweight (and underdeveloped) than for being overweight. As is the case among girls, being teased by peers about one's body is a significant source of distress for boys (Lawler & Nixon, 2011).

Prevalence and Causes of Anorexia and Bulimia
Historical and cross-cultural trends in the prevalence of anorexia and bulimia point to important differences between the two disorders (Keel & Klump, 2003). Whereas anorexia has been observed all over the world, bulimia has been reported almost exclusively in Western cultures or in cultures exposed to strong Western influences. And whereas anorexia has increased in prevalence steadily over time, the prevalence of bulimia increased significantly between 1970 and 1990 but has declined somewhat since then, paralleling trends in females' reported body dissatisfaction, which also peaked in the

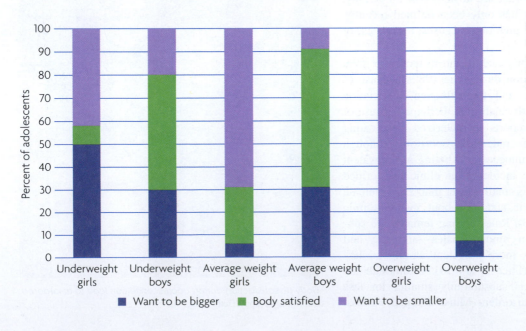

Figure 11   Body dissatisfaction by BMI classification for girls and boys. (Lawler & Nixon, 2011)

early 1990s (despite the fact that individuals' BMI continued to increase) (Cash, Morrow, Hrabosky, & Perry, 2004). This suggests that bulimia is a much more culturally determined disorder than is anorexia. Consistent with this, the degree to which anorexia is an inherited disorder is far more comparable from one culture to another than is the case for bulimia.

Today, experts view eating disorders as part of a more general syndrome of psychological distress. Many studies have found links between eating disorders and other serious mental health problems, such as depression, obsessive-compulsive disorder, or substance abuse; many adolescents with eating disorders display such psychological problems (Ferreiro, Seoane, & Senra, 2014; Granillo, Grogan-Kaylor, Delva, & Castillo, 2011; Rodgers, Paxton, & McLean, 2013); and depression sometimes precedes the development of an eating disorder, rather than the reverse (Ferreiro, Wichstrøm, Seoane, & Senra, 2014). These studies suggest that anorexia and bulimia may be best understood as particular manifestations of a more general underlying psychological problem—called "internalized distress"—that can be displayed in a variety of ways (Allen, Byrne, Oddy, & Crosby, 2013). In support of this view, some evidence suggests that the same medications that are successful in treating depression and obsessive-compulsive disorder are useful in treating bulimia (but, interestingly, not anorexia) (B. Walsh et al., 2006).

Given that anorexia and bulimia are 10 times more common in females than males, broader social forces are probably a main factor in the development of these eating disorders (Keel & Klump, 2003). Research indicates that girls who are early maturers and early daters are likely to report greater dissatisfaction with their body and to be at greater risk for disordered eating (Cauffman & Steinberg, 1996; Smolak, Levine, & Gralen, 1993; Swarr & Richards, 1996); that girls who perceive that they are under pressure to be thin or who have accepted thinness as an ideal toward which to strive are more susceptible to eating disorders (Francisco et al., 2015; Sonneville et al., 2015); and that girls who turn to popular magazines for information about dieting and appearance are more likely to have a high drive for thinness, low body satisfaction, and disturbed patterns of eating (D. C. Jones, Vigfusdottir, & Lee, 2004; M. Levine, Smolack, & Hayden, 1994).

Adolescents' beliefs about ideal body types are also shaped by the people they spend time with. Girls' attitudes toward eating and dieting are influenced by the attitudes of their parents (especially their mothers) and friends (Eisenberg, & Neumark-Sztainer, 2010; Hutchinson, Rapee, & Taylor, 2010; E. R. Mackey & La Greca, 2008; Neumark-Sztainer, Bauer, Friend, Hannan, Story, & Berge, 2010; Salafia & Gondoli, 2011). Being teased about one's weight is especially likely to lead to disordered eating, as well as symptoms of depression (M. Eisenberg, Neumark-Sztainer, Haines, & Wall, 2006; Haines, Neumark-Sztainer, Eisenberg, & Hannan, 2006).

Just because cultural conditions contribute to the development of disordered eating doesn't mean that individual characteristics do not play a role as well. Cultural conditions may predispose females more than males toward anorexia and bulimia, and girls and young women who have certain genetic vulnerabilities (eating disorders are partly heritable), psychological traits (such as proneness to depression or low self-esteem), physical characteristics (such as early pubertal maturation), familial characteristics (such as strained relations with parents), or social concerns (such as a strong interest in dating) may be more likely to develop problems (e.g., Cauffman & Steinberg, 1996; S. Frank & Jackson, 1996; Ricciardelli & McCabe, 2001). The onset of eating disorders, like so many aspects of adolescent development, is likely the product of a complex interaction between individual and contextual factors.

Less is known about the causes and consequences of body dissatisfaction among adolescent males than among females, but many contemporary adolescent boys feel pressure to be especially muscular, and some engage in unhealthy behaviors, such as anabolic steroid use, in order to develop an appearance that is more similar to the idealized male body type (Ricciardelli & McCabe, 2004). Moreover, body dissatisfaction is predictive of dieting, unhealthy weight control behaviors, and binge eating among males as well as females, regardless of whether they are actually overweight (Crow, Eisenberg, Story, & Neumark-Sztainer, 2006; Neumark-Sztainer, Paxton, Hannan, Haines, & Story, 2006). Recent studies of male adolescents in China have found similar patterns (Jackson & Chen, 2014).

A variety of therapeutic approaches have been employed successfully in the treatment of anorexia and bulimia, including individual psychotherapy and cognitive behavioral therapy, group therapy, family therapy, and antidepressant medications (Stice et al., 2011). The treatment of anorexia often requires hospitalization initially in order to ensure that starvation does not progress to fatal or near-fatal levels. The treatment of bulimia, especially with cognitive behavioral therapy, has proven far more successful than the treatment of anorexia.

making the practical connection

What might be done to counter the impact of cultural pressures that encourage the development of eating disorders among young women? Is the spread of Western media around the world likely to contribute to rising rates of eating disorders in other countries?

Physical Health and Health Care in Adolescence

Although puberty is undoubtedly the most important biological development of adolescence, concerns about the physical health and well-being of young people are far broader than those involving sexual maturation. In the past two decades, the field of **adolescent health care** has grown rapidly, as health educators and practitioners have come to better understand that the many of the health care needs of adolescents differ from those of children and adults (P. Williams, Holmbeck, & Greenley, 2002).

The Paradox of Adolescent Health

Adolescence is a paradox as far as physical health is concerned. On the one hand, it is one of the healthiest periods in the life span, characterized by a relatively low incidence of disabling or chronic illnesses (such as asthma or cancer), fewer short-term hospital stays, and fewer days in which individuals stay home sick. Nonetheless, in the United States, nearly 1 in 15 adolescents has at least one disabling chronic illness, with the main causes of disability being mental disorders such as depression, respiratory illnesses such as asthma, and muscular and skeletal disorders such as arthritis (Ozer & Irwin, 2009). Fortunately, in the past 50 years, rates of death and disability resulting from illness and disease during adolescence have decreased substantially, and new medical technologies and better health care delivery have improved the physical well-being of children, especially those with chronic illnesses and disabling medical conditions (Quittner, Romero, Kimberg, Blackwell, & Cruz, 2011). Adolescents are far less likely than individuals of any other age to seek and receive medical care through traditional office visits to practitioners, however, and there are large socioeconomic and ethnic disparities in adolescents' access to health care, with poor and ethnic minority youth far less likely to have adequate health insurance and access to health care than affluent or White youths (Ozer & Irwin, 2009).

Still, the most virulent threat to adolescent health comes not from disease or illness but from unhealthy behaviors (such as drug use), violence (both self-inflicted and inflicted by others), and risky activity (such as unprotected sexual intercourse or reckless driving) (P. Williams et al., 2002). In some senses, then, many of the improvements in preventing and treating the traditional medical problems of the period—those having to do with chronic illnesses—have

adolescent health care
A field of study and health care devoted to understanding the health care needs of individuals during the second decade of life.

graduated driver licensing
A licensing system in which full adult driving privileges are not granted all at once to teen drivers, but phased in over time.

been offset by what some scientists call the "new morbidity and mortality" of adolescence. Contributors to this new morbidity and mortality include accidents (especially automobile accidents), suicide, homicide, substance abuse (including tobacco and alcohol use), and sexually transmitted diseases (including AIDS).

Although some progress in reducing the rates of chronic illness and behavioral health problems among adolescents was made during the late 1990s, the situation has improved very little since then. Motor vehicle deaths, the use of diet pills, and smoking have continued to decline, but rates of homicide, suicide, binge drinking, depression, and risky sex have not changed in the past two decades. Health among people in their early 20s is even worse than it is among adolescents (Park et al., 2014). Unfortunately, recent reviews of the effectiveness of educational programs designed to reduce adolescents' health risk behaviors have not been encouraging (Hale, Fotzgerald-Yau, & Viner, 2014). Some experts have called for a complete rethinking about how to reduce adolescent risk taking, by focusing on changing the contexts in which adolescents live, rather than trying to change adolescents' attitudes of beliefs (Steinberg, 2016).

Causes of Mortality in Adolescence

The contrast between the old and new mortalities of adolescence is readily apparent. Fifty years ago, illness and disease accounted for more than twice as many deaths among teenagers as violence or injury, but the reverse is true today. Unintentional injuries are the leading cause of death worldwide, followed by AIDS, infectious disease, homicide, and suicide, in that order (Blum & Nelson-Mmari, 2004). Approximately 45% of all teenage deaths in the United States result from car accidents and other unintentional injuries, and another 27% are a result of homicide or suicide (Ozer & Irwin, 2009). Adolescents are involved in more driving accidents than adults, primarily because they are less experienced behind the wheel (at any age, new drivers are more likely to have accidents than seasoned drivers), but also because they are more likely to take chances while driving (Cvijanovich, Cook, Mann, & Dean, 2001; Dee & Evans, 2001; Harré, 2000). Two of the most important contributors to serious car accidents involving teenage drivers are driving at night and driving with other teenagers in the car (Simons-Morton, Hartos, Leaf, & Preusser, 2005). This finding has led many states to implement **graduated driver licensing** programs, which place restrictions on when and with whom teenagers can drive until they have gained sufficient experience; these programs have reduced automobile fatalities (Simons-Morton, 2011).

Unlike some other periods of the life span (such as infancy or old age), when we are more vulnerable to disease and illness, in adolescence most health problems are preventable. Moreover, patterns of diet, drug use, and exercise established during adolescence persist into adulthood (P. Williams et al., 2002). As a result of this recognition, the focus in the field of adolescent health has shifted away from traditional medical models (in which the emphasis is on the assessment, diagnosis, and treatment of disease) and toward more community-oriented approaches (in which the emphasis is on the prevention of illness and injury and the promotion of good health) (National Research Council and Institute of Medicine, 2009).

Promoting Adolescent Health

As many experts point out, health behavior is influenced by a number of factors, of which knowledge is only one component (e.g., H. Leventhal & Keeshan, 1993). Changes in the context in which adolescents live (such as the accessibility of handguns or the availability of tobacco, alcohol, and illicit drugs) must accompany changes in adolescents' knowledge and understanding if lasting health promotion is to be accomplished (Nation et al., 2003). For example, investigations of the impact of changing one element of the broader context of adolescent health—the legal drinking age—have found that raising the age led to a significant decline in accidental death rates among young automobile drivers and pedestrians, as well as in the rates of unintentional injuries not involving cars and homicides (Institute of Medicine, 2015). Similarly, the single most effective policy for reducing teen smoking has been raising the price of cigarettes (Gruber & Zinman, 2001), and the prevalence of adolescent smoking is a direct function of the number of retail outlets selling tobacco in their immediate neighborhood (Novak, Reardon, Raudenbush, & Buka, 2006). Experts believe that one way to further diminish rates of adolescent smoking would be to raise the minimum legal purchase age for tobacco to 21, so that cigarettes would be kept out of the social networks of high school students (Institute of Medicine, 2015).

Improving the health of young people is an especially important concern among those working with adolescents who are poor or from ethnic minority groups, because these youngsters are at greater risk for many of the old *and* new morbidities and mortalities of adolescence (Ozer & Irwin, 2009). Non-White youngsters, for example, are relatively more likely than White youngsters to suffer from a chronic illness (Ozer & Irwin, 2009), to be obese or to have high blood pressure or high cholesterol levels (National Heart, Lung, and Blood Institute Growth and Health Study Research Group, 1992), to be physically inactive (Wolf et al., 1993), to be victims of violent crimes (Earls, Cairns, & Mercy, 1993), to contract AIDS (Sells & Blum, 1996), to die from drowning (Warneke & Cooper, 1994), and to be murdered (Sorenson, Richardson, & Peterson, 1993). Homicide is the leading cause of death for Black adolescents, accounting for almost half of all deaths among Black youth. American Indian/Alaska Native males have a suicide rate higher than that of any other racial/ethnic group. Yet, despite their generally poorer health, minority youngsters are less likely to have access to sources of medical care, less likely to visit the doctor when ill, and less likely to have health insurance (Ozer & Irwin, 2009).

The combination of poor health and limited access to health care is even more concentrated among the sizable proportion of adolescents who live in poverty, a disproportionate number of whom are from ethnic minority backgrounds (Yoshikawa, Aber, & Beardslee, 2012). There is now convincing evidence that the links between health and socioeconomic status are strong and pervasive across different sorts of health problems, with physical and mental health problems increasing linearly as one moves down the socioeconomic ladder (Keating & Hertzman, 2000). Because increases in the size of the adolescent population over the next several decades worldwide will be concentrated among poor and minority youth (Fussell & Greene, 2002), the most daunting challenge facing health care providers and policymakers will be finding ways of minimizing or even eliminating the socioeconomic and ethnic disparities in health and health care that currently exist around the world (Ozer & Irwin, 2009).

2 Cognitive Transitions

Changes in Cognition

Thinking About Possibilities
Thinking About Abstract Concepts
Thinking About Thinking
Thinking in Multiple Dimensions
Adolescent Relativism

Theoretical Perspectives on Adolescent Thinking

The Piagetian View of Adolescent Thinking
The Information-Processing View of
  Adolescent Thinking

The Adolescent Brain

How Your Brain Works
The Age of Opportunity
What Changes in Adolescence?
Implications for Adolescent Behavior

Individual Differences in Intelligence in Adolescence

The Measurement of IQ
Types of Intelligence
Culture and Intelligence

Adolescent Thinking in Context

Social Cognition in Adolescence
Adolescent Risk Taking

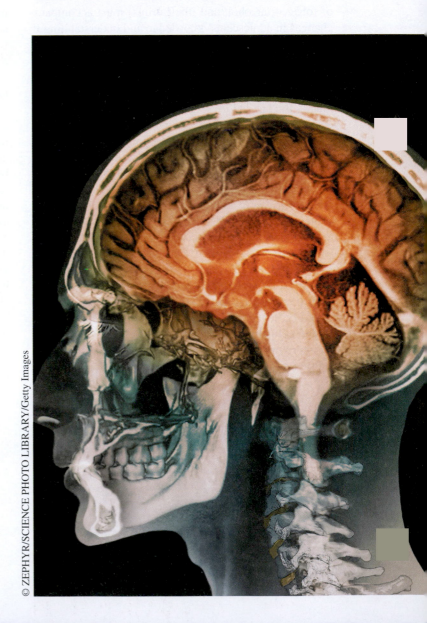

© ZEPHYR/SCIENCE PHOTO LIBRARY/Getty Images

Changes in cognition, or thinking, represent the second of three fundamental changes that occur during adolescence—in addition to puberty and the transition into new social roles. Like developments in the other two domains, the cognitive transitions of adolescence have far-reaching implications for the young person's psychological development and social relations. Indeed, the expansion of thought during adolescence represents as significant an event and as important an influence on the adolescent's development and behavior as puberty.

During the last two decades, scientists have made tremendous gains in understanding brain maturation during adolescence through the use of imaging techniques that permit us to look inside the adolescent brain, just as an X-ray permits physicians to look directly at bones. We now have a good idea of how the brain changes during the adolescent years and the implications of these changes for behavioral, emotional, and, of course, cognitive development. Later in this chapter, we'll look at brain maturation in adolescence in detail. But let's begin by simply describing how adolescents think and, more importantly, how their thinking differs from that of children and adults.

Changes in Cognition

Most people would agree that adolescents are "smarter" than children. Teenagers clearly *know* more than children—after all, the longer we live, the more opportunities we have to acquire new information. But adolescents also *think* in ways that are more advanced, more efficient, and generally more effective than children (Keating, 2011; Kuhn, 2009). Compared to children:

- Adolescents are better at thinking about what is possible, instead of limiting their thought to what is real.
- Adolescents are better at thinking about abstract things.
- Adolescents think more often about the process of thinking itself.
- Adolescents' thinking is more often multidimensional, rather than limited to a single issue.
- Adolescents are more likely to see things as relative, rather than as absolute.

Let's look at each of these advantages—and some of their implications for adolescents' behavior—in greater detail.

Thinking About Possibilities

Children's thinking is oriented to the here and now—to things and events that they can observe directly. But adolescents are able to consider what they observe against a backdrop of what is possible. Put another way, for the child, what is possible is what is real; for the adolescent, what is real is just a subset of what is possible. This allows adolescents to think "counterfactually"—to think not only about how things actually are, but to think about what might have been (Beck & Riggs, 2014).

Consider how individuals think about themselves. Children don't wonder, the way adolescents often do, about how their personalities might change in the future, or how they might have been different had they grown up under different circumstances. When you are a child,

you simply are who you are. In adolescence, who you are is just one possibility of who you could be.

This does not mean that children are incapable of imagination or fantasy. Nor does it mean that children are unable to conceive of things being different from what they observe. But adolescents are able to move easily between the specific and the abstract, to generate alternative possibilities and explanations systematically, and to compare what they actually observe with what they believe is possible.

The adolescent's ability to reason systematically in terms of what is possible comes in handy when learning math and science. The study of mathematics in junior and senior high school (algebra, geometry, and trigonometry) often requires that you begin with an abstract or theoretical formulation—for example, "the square of a right triangle's hypotenuse is equal to the sum of the squares of the other two sides" (the Pythagorean theorem). This

Although many parents believe that their children become more argumentative during adolescence, what is more likely going on is that the cognitive changes of the period enable them to be better arguers. © Tetra Images/Getty Images RF

theorem is a proposition about all *possible* right triangles, not just triangles that you might actually observe. In mathematics, you learn how to apply these theorems to concrete examples (that is, real triangles). Scientific experimentation also involves the ability to generate possibilities systematically. In a chemistry experiment in which you are trying to identify an unknown substance by performing various tests, you must first be able to imagine alternative possibilities for the substance's identity in order to know what tests to conduct.

The adolescent's use of this sort of thinking is not limited to scientific problem solving. We see it in the types of arguments adolescents employ, in which they are better able than children to envision and anticipate the possible responses of an opponent and to have one or more counterarguments handy. Many parents believe that their children become more argumentative during adolescence. What probably happens, though, is that their children become *better arguers* (Steinberg, 2011). Adolescents don't accept other people's points of view unquestioningly—including their parents' viewpoints. They evaluate them against other theoretically possible beliefs. This improvement in the adolescent's intellectual ability likely contributes to the bickering and squabbling that often occur between teenagers and their parents (Smetana, 1989).

making the practical connection

In what ways did your high school classes take advantage of the advanced thinking abilities that develop in adolescence? In what ways were opportunities to do this missed? What might teachers do to stimulate more advanced thinking?

Deductive Reasoning One manifestation of the adolescent's increased facility with thinking about possibilities is the development of **deductive reasoning.** Deductive reasoning is a type of logical reasoning in which you draw logically necessary conclusions from a general set of premises, or givens. Consider the following problem:

> All hockey players wear mouth guards.
> Kim is a hockey player.
> Does Kim wear a mouth guard?

deductive reasoning
A type of logical reasoning in which one draws logically necessary conclusions from a general set of premises, or givens.

Individuals who reason deductively understand that the correct conclusion (Kim wears a mouth guard) necessarily follows from the first two statements. No additional knowledge about hockey or about Kim is necessary to reach the correct answer. Deductive reasoning is seldom used before adolescence, and its development is one of the major intellectual accomplishments of the period (Morris & Sloutsky, 2001).

Adolescents are also better able than children to recognize when a logical problem does not provide sufficient information and to respond by saying that the question can't be answered with any certainty. Suppose we were to change the problem to this:

> All hockey players wear mouth guards.
> Kim is wearing a mouth guard.
> Is Kim a hockey player?

If you answer this type of question quickly, without thinking it through, you might say that Kim is indeed a hockey player. But, in fact, this isn't necessarily the case. Whereas children are easily fooled by such problems, adolescents are more likely to say that there is no way of knowing whether Kim plays hockey, because we are not told that the *only* people who wear mouth guards are hockey players.

One reason for their superior performance on these sorts of problems is that adolescents are better able to catch themselves before they incorrectly answer the question and pause a moment before responding (Daniel & Klaczynski, 2006). As you will read later in this chapter, the ability to stop yourself before acting automatically (and perhaps incorrectly) is controlled by a region of the brain that has been shown to mature during adolescence (Casey & Caudle, 2013; Luna, Paulsen, Padmanabhan, & Geier, 2013).

Hypothetical Thinking Related to the development of deductive reasoning is the emergence of hypothetical, or "if-then," thinking. In order to think hypothetically, you need to see beyond what is directly observable and apply logical reasoning to anticipate what might be possible. Being able to plan ahead, to see the future consequences of an action, and to provide alternative explanations of events all require being able to think hypothetically.

Thinking hypothetically also permits us to suspend our beliefs about something in order to argue in the abstract. Being capable of assuming a hypothetical stance is important when it comes to debating, because doing so permits us to understand the logic behind another person's argument without necessarily agreeing with it. Playing devil's advocate, for example—when you formulate a position contrary to what you really believe in order to challenge someone else's reasoning—requires hypothetical thinking.

Hypothetical thinking also has implications for the adolescent's social behavior. Taking the perspective of others enables the adolescent to think through what someone else might be thinking or feeling ("If I were in her situation, I would feel pretty angry"). This helps in formulating and arguing a viewpoint, because it allows adolescents to think a step ahead of the opposition—a cognitive tool that comes in handy when dealing with parents ("If they come back with 'You have to stay home and clean up the garage,' then I'll remind them about the time they let my sister go out when *she* had chores to do"). And hypothetical thinking plays an important role in decision making, because it permits one to plan ahead and foresee the consequences of choosing one alternative over another ("If I go out for the soccer team, then I am going to have to give up my part-time job").

Thinking About Abstract Concepts

The appearance of more systematic, abstract thinking is a second notable aspect of cognitive development during adolescence. We noted earlier that children's thinking is more concrete and more bound to observable events and objects than is that of adolescents. This difference is clear when we consider the ability to deal with abstract concepts—things that cannot be experienced directly through the senses.

Abstract thinking is clearly seen in adolescents' ability to think in more advanced ways about interpersonal relationships, politics, philosophy, religion, and morality—topics that involve such abstract concepts as friendship, faith, democracy, fairness, and honesty. The growth of social thinking during adolescence is directly related to the young person's improving ability to think abstractly. Later in this chapter, we will examine the ways in which social thinking—generally referred to as "social cognition"—improves in adolescence.

Thinking About Thinking

A third gain in cognitive ability during adolescence involves thinking about thinking itself, a process sometimes referred to as **metacognition.** Metacognition often involves monitoring your own cognitive activity during the thinking process—for example, when you consciously use a strategy for remembering something (such as *Every Good Boy Deserves Fun,* for the notes of the treble clef in music notation) or when you make sure you've understood something you're reading before going on to the next paragraph. Interventions designed to improve adolescents' metacognitive skills have been shown to enhance reading, writing, test taking, and performance on homework (W. Williams et al., 2002).

Not only do adolescents "manage" their thinking more than children do, but they also are better able to explain how they do it. When asked, adolescents can explain not only *what* they know but *why* knowing what they know enables them to think differently and solve problems more effectively (Reich, Oser, & Valentin, 1994). In addition, adolescents are much better able than children to understand that people do not have complete

control over their mental activity. Adolescents and adults are much more likely than children to understand that it is impossible to go for a long period of time without thinking about anything, that we often have thoughts that we don't want to have, and that the unwanted thoughts we try to get rid of often return (Flavell, Green, & Flavell, 1998).

Another interesting way in which thinking about thinking becomes more apparent during adolescence is in increased introspection and self-consciousness. When we are introspective, we are thinking about our own emotions. When we are self-conscious, we are thinking about how others think about us. These processes permit the sorts of self-examination and exploration that are important tools for establishing a coherent sense of identity.

Adolescent Egocentrism   The ability to think about thinking sometimes results in problems for young adolescents, before they adjust to having such powerful cognitive tools. Being able to introspect, for instance, may lead to periods of extreme self-absorption—referred to as "adolescent egocentrism" (Elkind, 1967). Adolescent egocentrism results in two distinct problems in thinking that help to explain some of the seemingly odd beliefs and behaviors of teenagers (Goossens, Seiffge-Krenke, & Marcoen, 1992).

The first, the **imaginary audience,** comes from having such a heightened sense of self-consciousness that you imagine that your behavior is the focus of everyone else's attention. For example, a teenager who is going to a concert with 10,000 other people may worry about dressing the right way because "everybody will notice." Given the cognitive limitations of adolescent egocentrism, it is hard to persuade young adolescents that the "audience" is not all that concerned with their behavior or appearance. Recent studies of brain maturation suggest that the parts of the brain that process social information—such as perceptions of what others are thinking—undergo significant change during early adolescence, just when self-consciousness is increasing (Burnett, Sebastian, Kadosh, & Blakemore, 2011; Mills, Lalonde, Clasen, Giedd, & Blakemore, 2014; Pfeifer & Blakemore, 2012; Pfeifer et al., 2013; Somerville et al., 2013). In fact, brain imaging studies indicate that adolescents' self-perceptions rely more than adults' on what they believe others think of them (Pfeifer, Masten, Borofsky, Dapretto, Fuligni et al., 2009).

A second problem resulting from adolescent egocentrism is called the **personal fable.** The personal

metacognition
The process of thinking about thinking itself.

imaginary audience
The belief, often brought on by the heightened self-consciousness of early adolescence, that everyone is watching and evaluating one's behavior.

personal fable
An adolescent's belief that he or she is unique and therefore not subject to the rules that govern other people's behavior.

fable revolves around the adolescent's egocentric (and erroneous) belief that his or her experiences are unique. For instance, an adolescent teenager whose relationship with a girlfriend has just ended might tell his sympathetic mother that she could not possibly understand what it feels like to break up with someone—even though breaking up is something that most people experience plenty of times in life. Maintaining a personal fable of uniqueness has some benefits, in that it enhances adolescents' self-esteem and feelings of self-importance. But holding on to a personal fable also can be dangerous: think about a sexually active adolescent who believes that pregnancy simply won't happen to her, or a reckless driver who believes that he will defy the laws of nature by taking hairpin turns at breakneck speed.

Although it was once thought that the reason was due to their heightened susceptibility to the personal fable, researchers have found it difficult to confirm that egocentrism actually peaks in early adolescence. In fact, certain aspects of adolescent egocentrism, such as the personal fable, persist through the adult years (Frankenberger, 2000; Quadrel, Fischhoff, & Davis, 1993). Ask any *adult* cigarette smoker if she or he is aware of the scientific evidence linking cigarette smoking with heart and lung disease, and you'll see that the personal fable is quite common among many individuals who have long since left adolescence.

making the personal connection

Think back to your own adolescence. Can you recall times when you experienced an imaginary audience? How about more recently? Do you think this happened more when you were younger than it does now?

Thinking in Multiple Dimensions

A fourth way in which thinking changes during adolescence involves the ability to think about things in multiple dimensions (Kuhn, 2009). Whereas children tend to think about things one aspect at a time, adolescents can see things through more complicated lenses. For instance, when a certain hitter comes up to the plate in a baseball game, a preadolescent who knows that the hitter has a good home-run record might exclaim that the batter will hit the ball out of the stadium. An adolescent, however, would consider the hitter's record in relation to the specific pitcher on the mound and would weigh both factors, or dimensions, before making a prediction (perhaps this player often hits homers against left-handed pitchers but frequently strikes out against righties).

The ability to think in multidimensional terms is evident in a variety of situations. Adolescents can give much more complicated answers than children to questions such as "Why did the Civil War begin?" or "How did Jane Austen's novels reflect the changing position of women in European society?" Thorough answers to these sorts of questions require thinking about several dimensions simultaneously, because many factors led to the Civil War, just as many factors affected the way in which people reacted to Austen's work.

The development of a more sophisticated understanding of probability is also made possible by an improved ability to think in multiple dimensions. Suppose I give you a set of blue and yellow beads. I ask you to divide them into two containers so that the containers have different numbers of beads overall but that the probability of reaching into a container and picking a blue bead is the same for each. In order to do so, you would have to vary the number of blue beads *and* the number of yellow beads between the two containers, because the probability of drawing a blue bead is a function of both the number of blue beads and the number of yellow beads. It is not until early adolescence that individuals can solve this sort of problem successfully (Falk & Wilkening, 1998).

As is the case with other gains in cognitive ability, the ability of individuals to think in multiple dimensions also has consequences outside of school. Adolescents describe themselves and others in more complicated terms ("I'm both shy and extroverted") and find it easier to look at problems from multiple perspectives ("I know that's the way you see it, but try to look at it from her point of view"). Understanding that people's personalities are not one-sided, or that social situations can have different interpretations, permits the adolescent to have far more sophisticated—and far more complicated—self-conceptions and relationships.

Sarcasm and *South Park* Adolescents' ability to look at things in multiple dimensions also enables their understanding of sarcasm. As an adult, you know that the meaning of a speaker's statement is communicated by a combination of what is said, how it is said, and the context in which it is said. If I turned to you during a boring lecture, rolled my eyes, and said, in an exaggeratedly earnest tone, "This is the most interesting lecture I've ever heard," you'd know that I actually meant just the opposite. But you'd know this only if you paid attention to my inflection and to the context, as well as the content, of my statement. Only by attending simultaneously to multiple dimensions of speech can we distinguish between the sincere and the sarcastic. It's no surprise that our ability to use and detect sarcasm and irony improves during preadolescence and adolescence (Glenwright & Pexman, 2010).

Why do young adolescents laugh hysterically when characters in movies aimed at their age group say things like "He said 'erector set'"? Adolescents' ability to think

The development of advanced thinking abilities allows adolescents to appreciate sarcasm, irony, and satire, such as that used in shows like "South Park." © Hulton Archive/Getty Images

in multiple dimensions also permits them to appreciate satire, metaphor, and the ways in which language can be used to convey multiple messages. Teenagers' ability to use and appreciate sarcasm, irony, and satire helps to explain why shows like *The Simpsons, South Park,* and *Family Guy* have always had such strong appeal in this age group. (Not to mention that they are often pretty funny to adults, too. Our son's school once summoned his class's parents to watch an "offensive" episode of *South Park* to show us how our children were being harmed by television; the demonstration ended prematurely, though, because we parents were laughing too hard.)

Adolescent Relativism

A final aspect of cognition that changes during adolescence concerns a shift from seeing things in absolute terms—in black and white—to seeing things as relative. Compared to children, adolescents are more likely to question others' assertions and less likely to accept "facts" as absolute truths.

This increase in relativism can be exasperating to parents, who may feel as though their teenagers question everything just for the sake of argument. Difficulties often arise, for example, when adolescents begin seeing parents' values that they had previously considered absolutely correct ("Moral people do not have sex before they are married") as completely relative ("Welcome to the twenty-first century, Dad").

Theoretical Perspectives on Adolescent Thinking

Although there is general agreement that adolescents' thinking is more advanced than children's, there is far less consensus about the processes underlying this advantage. Part of the lack of agreement stems from the fact that no one single factor distinguishes thinking during adolescence from thinking during childhood (Keating, 2011). And part stems from the different points of view that theorists have taken toward cognitive development in general. Because researchers working from different theoretical perspectives have posed different research questions, used different tasks to measure thinking, and emphasized different aspects of cognitive activity, their studies provide different, but nevertheless compatible, pictures of mental development during adolescence.

Two theoretical viewpoints that have been especially important are the Piagetian perspective and the information-processing perspective. Although these two views of adolescent thinking begin from different assumptions about the nature of cognitive development in general, they each provide valuable insight into why thinking changes during adolescence (Kuhn, 2009).

The Piagetian View of Adolescent Thinking

Piaget's Theory of Cognitive Development   Theorists who adopt a Piagetian perspective take a **cognitive-developmental view** of intellectual development. They argue that cognitive development proceeds through a fixed sequence of qualitatively distinct stages, that adolescent thinking is fundamentally different from the type of thinking employed by children, and that during adolescence, individuals develop a special type of thinking that they use across a variety of situations.

According to Piaget, cognitive development proceeds through four stages: (1) the **sensorimotor period** (from birth until about age 2), (2) the **preoperational period** (from about age 2 until about age 5), (3) the period of **concrete operations** (from about age 6 until early adolescence), and (4) the period of **formal operations** (from adolescence through adulthood). Each stage is characterized by a particular type of thinking, with earlier stages of thinking being incorporated into new, more advanced, and more adaptive forms of reasoning. According to Piaget, transitions into higher stages of reasoning are most likely to occur when the child is biologically

cognitive-developmental view
A perspective on development, based on the work of Piaget, that takes a qualitative, stage-theory approach.

sensorimotor period
The first stage of cognitive development, according to Piaget, spanning the period roughly between birth and age 2.

preoperational period
The second stage of cognitive development, according to Piaget, spanning roughly ages 2–5.

concrete operations
The third stage of cognitive development, according to Piaget, spanning the period roughly between age 6 and early adolescence.

formal operations
The fourth stage of cognitive development, according to Piaget, spanning the period from early adolescence through adulthood.

ready for the transition and the environment demands more advanced thinking. Piagetian theorists believe that abstract logical reasoning is the chief feature that differentiates adolescent thinking from that of children (Keating, 2011).

We noted that adolescents' thinking can be distinguished from the thinking of children in several respects—among them, being able to think hypothetically, multidimensionally, and abstractly. The connection between these skills and the development of formal operations is clear: In order to think about alternatives to what really exists, to think in multidimensional terms, and to systematically think about concepts that aren't directly observable, you need a system of reasoning that works just as well in abstract, imagined, and complicated situations as it does in concrete ones.

Not all adolescents (or, for that matter, all adults) develop formal-operational thinking or employ it regularly and in a variety of situations. Some research has found that adolescents who have been taught how to use deductive reasoning are more likely to display formal thinking, which suggests that the development of advanced reasoning abilities can be facilitated by training (Morris & Sloutsky, 1998).

There is a difference, of course, between what adolescents are capable of doing and what they actually do. Gaps between people's reasoning abilities and how logically they think in everyday situations are huge, and everyday decision making is fraught with logical errors that cannot be explained by cognitive incompetence (Kahneman, 2011). This is true for adults as well as adolescents. For example, if asked whether they would rather try to pull a lucky lottery ticket from an envelope of 10 tickets, of which only 1 is lucky, versus an envelope of 100 tickets, of which 10 are lucky, most people select the second option—even if they know that the mathematical odds of pulling a lucky ticket are identical in the two scenarios.

Although its influence has waned considerably over the past four decades, the Piagetian perspective on cognitive development during adolescence has stimulated a great deal of research on how young people think (Keating, 2011). Where the perspective falls short is in its claim that cognitive development proceeds in a stage-like fashion and that the stage of formal operations is the stage of cognitive development characteristic of adolescence (Keating, 2011; Kuhn, 2009). In fact, very little research supports this view. Rather,

advanced reasoning capabilities develop gradually and continuously from childhood through adolescence and beyond, in more of a steady fashion than was proposed by Piaget (that is, more like a ramp than like a staircase). Rather than talking about a distinct stage of cognitive activity characteristic of adolescence, it is more accurate to depict these advanced reasoning capabilities as skills that are employed by older children more often than by younger ones, by some adolescents more often than by others, and by individuals when they are in certain situations (especially familiar ones) more often than when they are in other ones (Kuhn, 2009).

The Information-Processing View of Adolescent Thinking

Piaget attempted to describe adolescent thinking as a whole, and to use one overarching concept—formal operations—to characterize the period. Other scientists have tried to identify the specific abilities that improve as individuals move from childhood into adolescence and beyond. Just what is it about the ways adolescents think about things that makes them better problem solvers than children? This question has been the focus of researchers working from a second vantage point: the **information-processing perspective.**

Studies of changes in specific components of information processing have focused on five areas in which improvement occurs during adolescence: attention, memory, processing speed, organization, and metacognition. All of these skills improve as individuals move from childhood through adolescence, mainly during the first half of the adolescent decade (Keating, 2004). These gains help to explain why adolescents are better than children at abstract, multidimensional, and hypothetical thinking.

Attention During adolescence, we become better at paying attention. Improvements take place both in **selective attention,** in which adolescents must focus on one stimulus (a reading assignment) and tune out another (the electronic beeping of a younger brother's video game), and in **divided attention,** in which adolescents must pay attention to two sets of stimuli at the same time (such as studying while texting with a friend) (Memmert, 2014; Mizuno et al., 2011). Improvements in attention mean that adolescents are better able than children to concentrate and stay focused on complicated tasks, such as reading and comprehending difficult material. There also is considerable evidence that the ability to inhibit an unwanted response (for instance, stopping yourself from looking up at a commercial that suddenly appears on the television in the corner of the room while you are reading) improves during early and middle adolescence (Kuhn, 2009). This improvement is likely linked to maturation of brain systems that govern impulse control (Casey & Caudle, 2013).

information-processing perspective
A perspective on cognition that derives from the study of artificial intelligence and attempts to explain cognitive development in terms of the growth of specific components of the thinking process (such as memory).

selective attention
The process by which we focus on one stimulus while tuning out another.

divided attention
The process of paying attention to two or more stimuli at the same time.

Improvements in selective attention and divided attention enable adolescents to tune out interference and focus on the task at hand.
© John Giustina /Photodisc/Getty Images RF, © Tim Pannell/Corbis RF/Corbis

Memory   Second, memory abilities improve during adolescence. This is reflected both in **working memory,** which involves the ability to remember something for a brief period of time, such as 30 seconds, and in **long-term memory,** which involves being able to recall something from a long time ago (Keating, 2004). Studies of adolescents' ability to remember personally meaningful events from earlier in life, an aspect of long-term memory called **autobiographical memory,** find that our earliest memories, some of which we lose during childhood, stabilize sometime during early adolescence, when most people can remember back to when they were about two and a half years old, but not much earlier than this (Reese, Jack, & White, 2010).

Adults generally remember details about the people, places, and events they encountered during adolescence better than those from other years, a phenomenon called the **reminiscence bump** (Rubin, 1986). The reminiscence bump does not appear to result from better memory, because basic memory abilities remain strong until midlife. Nor is it due to the fact that so many important events happen for the first time during adolescence (e.g., first love, first job, first time living away from parents). Even mundane events that took place during adolescence are recalled better than those that happened at other ages. Moreover, we tend to remember other, less personal things from adolescence better, too—things like movies, books, music, and current events (Janssen, Chessa, & Murre, 2007).

Something is different about how everyday experiences are encoded during adolescence, as if the brain's "recording device" is calibrated to be hypersensitive at this age. When certain chemicals in the brain are released at the same time an event is experienced, the event is more easily remembered than when levels of these chemicals are not as high. These chemicals are released when we experience something that elicits strong negative or positive feelings. As we'll see, brain regions responsible for strong emotions are especially sensitive during adolescence. As a result, the adolescent brain is chemically primed to encode memories more deeply (Knutson & Adcock, 2005). As you'll read later in this chapter, brain systems that govern emotion undergo dramatic change in adolescence. The reminiscence bump doesn't exist because more emotional events take place in adolescence, but because ordinary events trigger stronger emotions.

When we think of the importance of memory in problem solving, we typically think of having to retrieve facts that we deliberately have memorized—one aspect of long-term memory. But working memory may be even more important than long-term memory for the sort of problem solving likely encountered in adolescence (Amso, Haas, McShane, & Badre, 2014). For example, in order to answer multiple-choice questions, you need to be able to remember each option long enough to compare it with the other choices as you read them. Think for a moment of how frustrating it would be to try to solve a multiple-choice problem if, by the time you had read the final potential answer, you had forgotten the first one!

Working memory skills increase between childhood and adolescence and over the course of adolescence (Sprondel, Kipp, & Mecklinger, 2011). Improvements in

working memory
That aspect of memory in which information is held for a short time while a problem is being solved.

long-term memory
The ability to recall something from a long time ago.

autobiographical memory
The recall of personally meaningful past events.

reminiscence bump
The fact that experiences from adolescence are generally recalled more than experiences from other stages of life.

working memory coincide with the continued maturation of brain regions during adolescence that are responsible for this aspect of cognition (Conklin, Luciana, Hooper, & Yarger, 2007; Hanson et al., 2012; Jolles, Kleibeuker, Rombouts, & Crone, 2011). More specifically, advances in working memory during adolescence are linked to the ways in which these areas of the brain are organized and connected, which permits more efficient and powerful information processing (Finn, Sheridan, Kam, Hinshaw, & D'Esposito, 2010; Ghetti, DeMaster, Yonelinas, & Bunge, 2010). And because these brain regions are still developing in early adolescence, it is possible to improve individuals' basic cognitive abilities through training (Schmiedak, Lovden, & Lindenberger, 2014).

Speed A third component of information processing related to the observed improvements in thinking in adolescence is an increase in the sheer speed of information processing (Kail & Ferrer, 2007). Regardless of the task employed, older adolescents process the information necessary to solve the problem faster than early adolescents, who, in turn, process information faster than preadolescents. This increase in the speed of information processing occurs mainly in early adolescence; the difference in speed between a 9-year-old and a 12-year-old is greater than that between a 12-year-old and a 15-year-old, which, in turn, is greater than that between a 15-year-old and an 18-year-old (see Figure 1) (Kail & Ferrer, 2007). Processing speed does not change very much between middle adolescence and young adulthood (Brahmbhatt, McAuley, & Barch, 2008).

Organization A fourth information-processing gain in adolescence involves improvements in organizational strategies (Siegler, 2006). Adolescents are more planful than children—they are more likely to approach a problem with an appropriate strategy in mind and are more flexible in their ability to use different strategies in different situations (Albert & Steinberg, 2011a). The use of mnemonic devices (such as using HOMES to remember the names of the Great Lakes—Huron, Ontario, Michigan, Erie, and Superior) and other organizational strategies helps to account for differences in the performance of older and younger children on academic tasks requiring memory (Siegler, 2006).

For instance, think for a moment about how you approach learning the information in a new textbook chapter. After years of studying, you are probably well aware of particular strategies that work well for you (underlining, highlighting, taking notes, writing in the margins), and you begin a reading assignment with these strategies in mind. Because children are not as planful as adolescents, their learning is not as efficient. Developmental differences in levels of planning during childhood and adolescence can be seen quite readily by comparing individuals' approaches to the guessing game 20 Questions. With age, individuals' strategies become increasingly more efficient—when guessing the name of a person, an adolescent might begin by asking whether the person is dead or alive, then male or female, and so forth, whereas a young child might just start randomly throwing out the names of specific people (Drumm & Jackson, 1996).

Metacognition We noted earlier that one of the most important gains in adolescence is in the realm of metacognition—thinking about thinking. Adolescents are more likely than children to think about their own thoughts—a tendency, as we saw, that helps to explain their greater self-consciousness. One explanation for this emphasizes adolescents' greater sensitivity to social information, which, as you will read later in this chapter, is linked to specific changes in the brain that occur during puberty (Somerville, 2013). But from an information-processing perspective, adolescents' heightened self-consciousness results from advances in basic cognitive abilities. For the first time, the adolescent is capable of "thinking about thinking about thinking," a process that places demands on working memory. Once you begin thinking about what other people might think you are thinking, it is hard to avoid becoming self-conscious.

Advances in metacognition have benefits as well. Because adolescents are better at thinking about their own thoughts, they are much better at monitoring their own learning (Crone, Somsen, Zanolie, & Van der Molen, 2006; Kuhn, 2009). While studying, adolescents are able to step back and assess how well they are learning the material. Doing this enables them to pace their studying accordingly—to speed up and skim the material if they feel that they are learning it easily or to slow down and repeat a section if they are having a hard time. Brain systems that are active when individuals are monitoring their own performance continue to mature throughout adolescence and early adulthood, which may help the development of metacognition (Ladouceur, Dahl, & Carter, 2007).

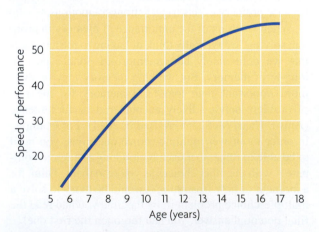

Figure 1 Speed of information processing increases markedly between ages 5 and 15 and then begins to level off. (Adapted from Kail & Ferrer, 2007)

By the time they have turned 15, adolescents are just as proficient as adults in basic cognitive abilities. Working memory, attention, and logical reasoning abilities increase throughout childhood and early adolescence and then level off around this age (Gathercole, Pickering, Ambridge, & Wearing, 2004; Luciana, Conklin, Hooper, & Yarger, 2005). However, at this age people are still developing more sophisticated cognitive skills, such as thinking creatively, planning ahead or judging the relative costs and benefits of a risky decision (Kleibeuker, Koolschijn, Jolles, De Dreu, & Crone, 2013; Albert & Steinberg, 2011b), and in the coordination of cognition and emotion, when feelings might interfere with logical reasoning (for example, when you have to make a decision when you are angry or when faced with peer pressure) (Albert, Chein, & Steinberg, 2013). In fact, much of what we have learned about brain maturation in adolescence—the subject of the next section—helps explain why the development of these advanced abilities may not be complete until individuals reach their mid-20s.

contribution to our understanding of what takes place in the brain during adolescence has come from studies using various imaging techniques, especially **functional magnetic resonance imaging (fMRI)** and **diffusion tensor imaging (DTI)**. These techniques allow researchers to take pictures of individuals' brains and compare their anatomy and activity. Some aspects of brain development in adolescence are reflected in changes in **brain structure** (for instance, certain parts of the brain are relatively smaller in childhood than adolescence, while others are relatively larger), whereas others are reflected not so much in the brain's structure but in changes in **brain function** (for instance, adolescents may use

functional magnetic resonance imaging (fMRI)
A technique used to produce images of the brain, often while the subject is performing some sort of mental task.

diffusion tensor imaging (DTI)
A technique used to produce images of the brain that shows connections among different regions.

brain structure
The physical form and organization of the brain.

brain function
Patterns of brain activity.

The Adolescent Brain

It was once believed that improved intellectual functioning in adolescence would be reflected in larger brain size. But the brain reaches its adult size by age 10, making it impossible that changes in thinking during adolescence are due to sheer increases in the size of the brain (Paus, 2009). For many years, scientists could not find links between physical changes in the brain and improvements in cognitive functioning during adolescence.

All this changed a little more than 15 years ago. Since 2000, there has been an explosion in research on adolescent brain development, and the speed with which our understanding of adolescent brain development has grown has been absolutely breathtaking (Engle, 2013).

Improvements in the methods used to study brain maturation—including studies of brain growth and development in other animals (because all mammals go through puberty, it is possible to study "adolescent" brain development in other species), studies of changes in brain chemistry, and postmortem studies of brain anatomy—have advanced the field in important ways (Paus, 2009; Spear, 2010). But the major

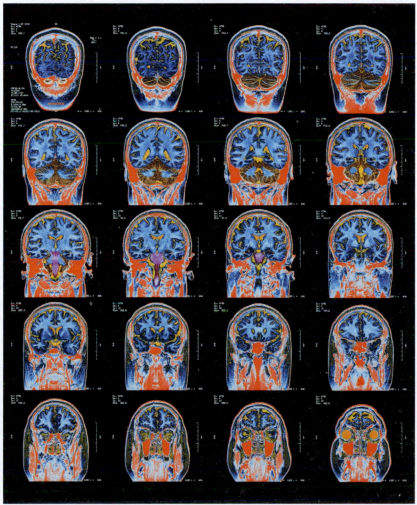

Advances in brain-imaging technology have contributed to our understanding of how the brain changes at adolescence. These images are created through a process known as functional magnetic resonance imaging, or fMRI. © Science Photo Library/Getty Images RF

different parts of the brain than children when performing the same task) (e.g., Dosenbach et al., 2010; O'Hare, Lu, Houston, Bookheimer, & Sowell, 2008; Wang, Huettel, & De Bellis, 2008).

Using DTI, scientists are able to see the ways in which various regions of the brain are connected and compare patterns of interconnections among people at different ages (e.g., Klingberg, 2006). This allows us to better understand how "communication" patterns linking different regions of the brain change with development. Researchers use fMRI to examine patterns of activity in various regions of the brain while individuals are performing a different tasks (for example, recalling a list of words, viewing photos of friends, or listening to music).

Participants in an fMRI study are asked to perform tasks on a computer while they are lying inside a brain scanner. With this setup, it is possible to study both how patterns of brain activity differ during different tasks (for example, when we are actively reading versus being read to) and whether people of different ages show different patterns of brain activity while performing the very same task. In our lab, for instance, my collaborators and I are studying how patterns of brain activity vary when individuals perform tasks either alone or with their friends watching them, and whether the ways in which the presence of friends affects brain activity differ between teenagers and adults (e.g., Smith, Steinberg, Strang, & Chein, 2015).

Scientists have also studied age differences in patterns of brain activity using **electroencephalography (EEG),** which measures electrical activity at different locations on the scalp. EEG can be used to examine changes in electrical activity—called **event-related potentials (ERPs)**—in response to different stimuli or events (Segalowitz & Davies, 2004). Scientists often compare ERPs between people of different ages to determine when, if at all, patterns of brain activity undergo developmental change (e.g., Bishop, Hardiman, Uwer, & von Suchodoletz, 2007; Feinberg & Campbell, 2010).

Are Male and Female Brains Different? Many popular books claim that there are important differences between the brains of adolescent boys and girls (and, for that matter, adult men and women). Research indicates, however, that differences between the genders in brain structure and function are very small and unlikely to explain differences between males and females in the way they behave or think (Paus, 2009; Spear, 2010). In general, male brains are about 10% larger than female brains (even accounting for the fact that

electroencephalography (EEG)
A technique for measuring electrical activity at different locations on the scalp.

event-related potentials (ERPs)
Changes in electrical activity in areas of the brain in response to specific stimuli or events.

neurons
Nerve cells.

male bodies, on average, are bigger than females'), but as noted above, there is no relation between sheer brain size and intellectual functioning, so it is unlikely that this small difference in size has any practical significance. In addition, there are few consistent sex differences in the size of specific brain regions or structures—some parts of the brain are slightly larger among females, and some are slightly larger among males (Ardekani, Figarsky, & Sidtis, 2013; Dennison et al., 2013; Blakemore, 2011; Koolschijn & Crone, 2013).

Several studies have looked specifically for connections between pubertal hormone and brain development, since male and female brains are exposed to different levels of testosterone and estrogen (Bramen et al., 2012; Hertig, Maxwell, Irvine, & Nagel, 2012). It is clear that the structure of the brain is changed by exposure to sex hormones, but the ways in which the brains of adolescent boys and girls differ as a result of sex hormones is enormously complicated (Cédric, Koolschijn, Peper, & Crone, 2014). Some studies also show different patterns of connections between brain regions in males and females (Lopez-Larson, Anderson, Ferguson, & Yurgelun-Todd, 2011; Raznahan et al., 2011; Tomasi & Volkow, 2012), although the importance of these changes for understanding sex differences in behavior or cognition is not known. By and large, however, the similarities between males and females in brain structure and function—before, during, and after adolescence—are far more striking than the differences. Most experts agree that differences between how males and females think are too small to be of practical significance and do not justify educational curricula or teaching techniques that have been specially geared for boys or girls (Miller & Halpern, 2014). There may be other reasons to prefer single-sex schools over coeducational ones, but sex differences in brain development isn't one of them.

How Your Brain Works

The brain functions by transmitting electrical signals across circuits that are composed of interconnected cells, called **neurons.** Each neuron has three parts—a cell body; a longish projection called an axon, which terminates in many small tips; and thousands of tiny, antennae-like branches, called dendrites, which themselves split off into smaller and smaller spines, like a plant's root system. In the adult brain, each neuron has about 10,000 connections. Collectively, neurons and the projections that connect them are called "gray matter."

When electrical impulses travel along a neural circuit, they leave one neuron through its axon and enter the next one through one of the receiving neuron's dendrites. The transmission of current from one neuron to another can be thought of as the passage of information along that particular pathway, like runners on a track team passing a baton during a relay race. Everything we think, perceive, feel, or do depends on the flow of electrical impulses across the brain's circuits.

The axon of one neuron is not actually connected to the dendrites of another, though, the way an electrical wire in your home is connected to a light switch, or the way the prongs of an appliance plug touch the active contacts inside an outlet. There is a tiny gap, called a **synapse,** between the tip of one neuron's axon and another neuron's dendrite. In order for an impulse to be relayed to a neighboring neuron, the electrical charge has to "jump" across this gap. How does this happen?

The transfer of current across the synapse when a neuron fires is enabled by the release of chemicals called **neurotransmitters.** You've probably heard of some of the most important neurotransmitters, like dopamine or serotonin. Many of the most widely prescribed antidepressants work, for instance, by altering the amount of serotonin in brain circuits that control mood.

When neurotransmitters are released from the "sending" neuron and come into contact with the receptors on the dendrites of the "receiving" neuron, a chemical reaction occurs on the other side of the synapse which triggers a new electrical impulse, which travels on its way to the next neuron in the circuit, jumping across the next synapse with the help of neurotransmitters. This process is repeated whenever information travels through the brain's elaborate circuitry.

Each neurotransmitter has a specific molecular structure that fits into a receptor for which it is precisely designed, the way a key fits into a lock. An impulse that stimulates a neuron to release dopamine will trigger a response in a neuron that has dopamine receptors, but not in one that only has receptors for a different neurotransmitter. This enables the brain to stay organized—if any time a neuron fired it activated every other neuron in the neighborhood, all helter-skelter, it would be impossible to maintain well-defined brain circuits—an enormous challenge in an organ that packs one hundred billion neurons, each with ten thousand connections, into the space inside your skull. This way, when a neuron that is part of a circuit that regulates mood fires, it affects how you feel, not whether you move your big toe.

A key process in early brain development is the development of billions and billions of synapses—the connections between neurons. The formation of some of these synapses is genetically programmed, but others are formed through experience. The rate of synapse formation peaks at about age 1 and slows down in early childhood, but the development of new synapses continues throughout life as we learn new skills, build memories, acquire knowledge, and adapt to changing circumstances. The more a synapse is used, the stronger its electrical pathway becomes.

Gray Matter Initially the brain produces many more connections among cells than it will use. At 1 year of

age, the number of synapses in the infant brain is about *twice* the number in the adult brain (Couperus & Nelson, 2006). However, soon after birth unused and unnecessary synapses start to be eliminated, a process called **synaptic pruning.** As a general rule, we tend to assume that "more is better," but that's not the case here. Imagine a meadow between two patches of forest. Hundreds of lightly trodden paths connect one side to the other (the unpruned brain). Over time people discover that one path is more direct than others. More people begin using this path more often, so it becomes wider and deeper. Because the other paths are no longer used, the grass grows back and those paths disappear. That's what synaptic pruning is like—the "paths" we use repeatedly become more and more ingrained, whereas those we do not use disappear. Synaptic pruning results in a decrease in the amount of gray matter in the brain, which is often manifested in a thinning of the areas that have been pruned (Brain Development Cooperative Group, 2012).

Synaptic pruning continues through adolescence and is normal and necessary to development and functioning. Just as pruning a rose bush—cutting off weak and misshapen branches—produces a healthier plant with larger flowers, so synaptic pruning enhances the brain's functioning. Synaptic pruning makes the brain more efficient by transforming an unwieldy network of small pathways into a better organized system of "superhighways."

> **synapse**
> The gap in space between neurons, across which neurotransmitters carry electrical impulses.
>
> **neurotransmitters**
> Specialized chemicals that carry electrical impulses between neurons.
>
> **synaptic pruning**
> The process through which unnecessary connections between neurons are eliminated, improving the efficiency of information processing.

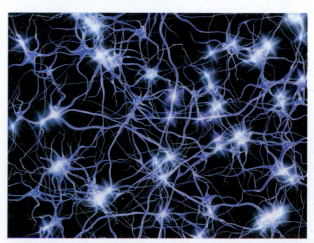

During infancy and childhood, the brain produces more connections between neurons, called synapses, than is necessary. Adolescence is a time when many of these unnecessary synapses are eliminated, a process called "pruning." © Science Photo Library—PASIEKA/Getty Images RF

Generally, the development of synapses is characterized by a period of growth (when more and more synapses are created) followed by a period of decline (when more and more synapses are eliminated). When we plot the density of synapses over time, we see a ∩-shaped curve—or, more accurately, a series of ∩-shaped curves that peak at different ages, depending on the specific region of the brain (Tanaka, Matsui, Uematsu, Noguchi, & Miyawaki, 2012). That is, although synaptic pruning takes place throughout infancy, childhood, and adolescence, different regions of the brain are pruned at different points in development. As a rule, the brain regions in which pruning is taking place at a particular point in development are the regions associated with the greatest changes in cognitive functioning during that stage, because as a particular pathway of neural transmission becomes more efficient, the specific cognitive process it supports improves. For example, synaptic pruning in the brain's visual system is most dramatic early in infancy, when our visual abilities are improving the most.

White Matter Cells other than neurons also play a role in transmitting electrical impulses along brain circuits. These cells, known as "white matter," provide support and protection for neurons and compose a fatty substance, called myelin, that surrounds the axons of certain neurons, like the plastic sheath around electrical wires. Myelin insulates brain circuits, keeping the impulses flowing along their intended pathways rather than leaking out. Circuits that are coated in myelin carry impulses about a hundred times faster than circuits that are not myelinated, making them much more efficient, especially if the circuits cover a large territory.

myelination
The process through which brain circuits are insulated with myelin, which improves the efficiency of information processing.

plasticity
The capacity of the brain to change in response to experience.

developmental plasticity
Extensive remodeling of the brain's circuitry in response to experiences during childhood and adolescence, while the brain is still maturing.

adult plasticity
Relatively minor changes in brain circuits as a result of experiences during adulthood, after the brain has matured.

The growth of myelin, called **myelination,** occurs in waves, beginning before birth and continuing into young adulthood (Paus, 2009). Unlike synapses, with their ∩-shaped pattern of growth, white matter increases throughout childhood and adolescence, well into adulthood, although at different rates in different regions of the brain at different points in development (Brain Development Cooperative Group, 2012). As with synaptic pruning, examining *where* myelination is occurring most dramatically at a particular point in development provides clues about the aspects of cognitive functioning that are changing most at that stage.

The Age of Opportunity

One of the most exciting new discoveries in neuroscience is that some areas of the brain may be especially malleable, or "plastic," in adolescence—it is more easily shaped, for better or for worse, by experience during adolescence than at any time other than the first few years of life (Lillard & Erisir, 2011; Selemon, 2013; Zelazo & Carlson, 2012). That's why adolescence has been described as an "age of opportunity" (Steinberg, 2014).

Scientists have known for some time now that the brain is particularly malleable during the first 3 years after birth. But the discovery that adolescence is a second period of heightened brain **plasticity** is a relatively recent development (Selemon, 2013). Plasticity refers to the capacity of the brain to change in response to experience. It's the process through which the outside world gets inside us and changes us. The brain's remarkable malleability in response to experience enables us to learn and strengthen abilities, from very basic ones (like memory) to very advanced ones (like planning ahead). This is at the heart of brain plasticity. It's not only "use it or lose it." It's also "use it and improve it." This is true at all ages, but it is much more easily and reliably accomplished before adulthood, when the brain is much more plastic.

Why It's Hard for Old Dogs to Learn New Tricks
There are two types of brain plasticity. **Developmental plasticity** refers to the malleability of the brain during periods in which the brain is being built, when its anatomy is still changing in profound ways, as is the case in adolescence. Some of these changes involve the development or loss of brain cells, but the most important changes involve the brain's "wiring"—that is, how its one hundred billion neurons are interconnected.

The other type of plasticity is **adult plasticity.** Because every time we learn or remember something there must be some enduring biological change in the brain, the brain must possess a certain degree of plasticity at all ages. If this weren't true, it would be impossible to acquire new knowledge or abilities in adulthood. Because we can always learn new things, however, there is always some amount of plasticity in the brain, no matter how old we are. But the two kinds of plasticity differ significantly.

First, adult plasticity doesn't fundamentally alter the neural structure of the brain, whereas developmental plasticity does. Developmental plasticity involves the growth of new brain cells and the formation of new brain circuits. Adult plasticity mainly involves fairly minor modifications to existing circuits. It's like the difference between learning how to read (which is a life-altering change) and reading a new book (which usually is not).

Second, brain systems are far less malleable during periods of adult plasticity than they are during periods of developmental plasticity. In fact, the developing brain is chemically predisposed to be modified by experiences, like clay when it is still soft, whereas the adult brain is predisposed to resist modification—like that same clay once it has hardened (Spear, 2013). This is the reason we don't become better at seeing or hearing after we have matured beyond infancy, or why we have so much more trouble learning to ski or surf as adults than as children. By the time we are adults, the brain systems that regulate vision, hearing, and coordination have hardened. This is also why it is far easier to learn a foreign language before adolescence than after—brain systems responsible for language acquisition have matured by then.

Finally, because the developing brain is so much more malleable, it can be influenced by a far wider range of experiences than can the mature brain. When the brain is developing, it is shaped by experiences that we aren't even aware of. Once the brain has matured, we need to pay attention to and give meaning to our experiences in order to be affected by them in an enduring way.

The developing brain is sculpted both by passive exposure and by active experience. That means that before our brain has fully matured, we can be affected, in potentially permanent ways, by *every* experience, whether it's positive or negative, whether we understand it or not—in fact, whether or not we're even aware of it. It's not surprising, then, that we recall things from adolescence more easily than we do from adulthood.

Because plasticity is what allows us to learn from experience, it enables us to adapt to the environment. Without it, our ancestors couldn't have remembered which contexts were safe and desirable, because they supplied food or water, for example, and which were to be avoided, because they were dangerous. The malleability of our brains greatly benefits us because it allows us to acquire new information and abilities. Periods of heightened plasticity, like infancy or adolescence, are therefore good times to intervene in order to promote positive development.

But this malleability is a risk as well, because during these times of heightened sensitivity, the brain is also more vulnerable to damage from physical harms, like drugs or environmental toxins, or psychological ones, like trauma and stress (Romeo, 2013). The plasticity of the adolescent brain is why the adverse effects of using recreational drugs during adolescence (and during early adolescence, in particular) are more lasting than those associated with using the same drugs in adulthood.

making the scientific connection

Advances in neuroscience have revealed that adolescence is a second period of heightened brain plasticity. Why might this be evolutionarily adaptive? What is it about adolescence that might make it an important time for the brain to be malleable?

What Changes in Adolescence?

Changes in Brain Structure During Adolescence

During adolescence, the brain is "remodeled" through synaptic pruning and myelination in particular brain regions (Spear, 2013) (see Figure 2). One part of the brain that is pruned dramatically in adolescence is the **prefrontal cortex,** the region of the brain most important for sophisticated thinking abilities, such as planning, thinking ahead, weighing risks and rewards, and controlling impulses (Casey, Tottenham, Liston, & Durston, 2005). Pruning also takes place in other parts of the cortex in adolescence (Blakemore, 2011).

There is also continued myelination of the cortex throughout adolescence, which also leads to many cognitive advances (Ferrer et al., 2013; Ordaz, Foran, Velanova, & Luna, 2013). Myelination is stimulated by puberty (Menzies, Goddings, Whitaker, Blakemore, & Viner, 2015), but also by experiences such as education (Noble, Korgaonkar, Grieve, & Brickman, 2013) and exercise (Herting, Colby, Sowell, & Nagel, 2014).

Although scientists initially focused on the thinning of gray matter as the main feature of structural change in the brain at adolescence, there has been increasing interest in the importance of the increase in white matter, which improves the efficiency of connections within and across brain regions (Ferrer et al., 2013; Spear, 2013). Better connectivity between different parts of the cortex allows us to think faster. Better connectivity between the prefrontal cortex and the **limbic system,** an area of the brain involved in the processing of emotions, social information, and reward and punishment, leads to improvements in our ability to regulate our emotions and coordinate our thoughts and feelings (Dwyer et al., 2014; Ladouceur, Peper, Crone, & Dahl, 2012; Smith, Steinberg, & Chein, 2014). Structural maturation of the prefrontal cortex is not complete until the mid-20s (Casey et al., 2005; Hooper, Luciana, Conklin, & Yarger, 2004; Paus, 2009).

Changes in Brain Function During Adolescence

The two most important changes in brain function involving the prefrontal cortex in adolescence both lead to greater efficiency in information processing (Spear, 2010). First, patterns of activation *within* the prefrontal cortex generally become more focused. For instance, in experiments in which participants are presented with a rapid succession of images and asked to push a button when a certain image appears, but refrain from pushing it when a different image appears (a process known as

prefrontal cortex
The region of the brain most important for sophisticated thinking abilities, such as planning, thinking ahead, weighing risks and rewards, and controlling impulses.

limbic system
An area of the brain that plays an important role in the processing of emotional experience, social information, and reward and punishment.

Figure 2   Synaptic pruning (reflected in the thinking of the cortex) and myelination (reflected in increases in white matter) take place in many brain regions during adolescence, including the parietal, temporal, and frontal lobes. (Tamnes et al., 2010)

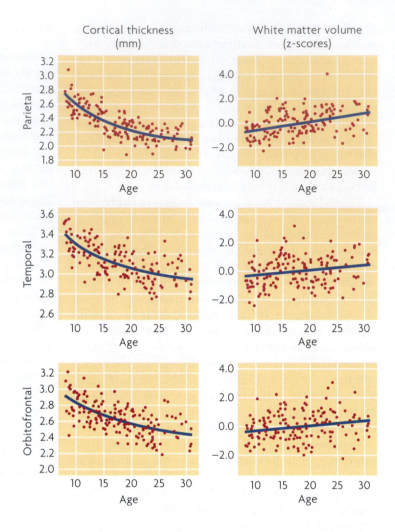

response inhibition), adolescents are less likely than children to activate prefrontal regions that are not relevant to performing the task well. As adolescents grow into adulthood and these brain systems further mature, self-control improves, as does performance on tests that measure other aspects of advanced thinking, often referred to as **executive function** (Andrews-Hanna, Seghete, Claus, Burgess, Ruzic, & Banich, 2011; Zelazo & Carlson, 2012) (see Figure 3).

Second, over the course of adolescence, individuals become more likely to use multiple parts of the brain simultaneously and coordinate activity *between* prefrontal regions and other areas, including other portions of the cortex and areas of the limbic system (Christakou, Brammer, & Rubia, 2011; Strang, Pruessner, & Pollak, 2011; Thomas et al., 2011). This is especially important on difficult tasks, where the task demands may overtax the prefrontal cortex working alone, and especially on tasks that require self-control, where it

response inhibition
The suppression of a behavior that is inappropriate or no longer required.

executive function
More advanced thinking abilities, enabled chiefly by the maturation of the prefrontal cortex, especially in early adolescence.

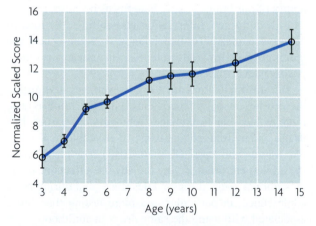

Figure 3   Performance on measures of advanced thinking, or "executive function," improves steadily during the first part of adolescence. (Zelazo & Carlson, 2012)

is necessary to coordinate thinking and feeling (Albert & Steinberg, 2011b). In fact, when adolescents who are tested for self-control are told that they will be rewarded for controlling themselves, they perform better than when no such rewards are offered (Geier & Luna, 2012; Strang & Pollak, 2014; Teslovich et al., 2014).

This simultaneous recruitment of multiple brain regions working as a "team," referred to as **functional connectivity,** is made possible by the increase in physical connections between brain regions (Dosenbach et al., 2013). Children's brains are characterized by a large number of relatively "local" connections (i.e., connections between nearby brain regions), but as individuals mature through adolescence and into adulthood, more distant regions become increasingly interconnected (Hwang, Hallquist, & Luna, 2013; Sherman et al., 2014). This is seen even when individuals are lying still, just resting (Jaeger, Selmeczy, O'Connor, Diaz, & Dobbins, 2012; Power, Fair, Schlaggar, & Petersen, 2010). The maturation of functional connectivity is more or less complete by age 22 (see Figure 4).

Risk and Reward A different type of functional change results from changes, especially in the limbic system, in the ways in which the brain is affected by certain neurotransmitters, including **dopamine** (which plays an important role in our experience of reward) and **serotonin** (which plays an important role in the experience of different moods). These changes, which are partly caused by puberty, make adolescents more emotional, more responsive to stress, more sensitive to rewards, and more likely to engage in reward seeking and sensation seeking than either children or adults (Braams, van Duijvenvoorde, Peper, & Crone, 2015; Bjork, Lynne-Landsman, Sirocco, & Boyce, 2012;

Galvan, 2013; Luciana & Collins, 2012). They are also thought to increase individuals' vulnerability to substance abuse, because they seek higher levels of reward; depression, because of their increased vulnerability to stress; and other mental health problems, because of their easily aroused emotions, including anger and sadness (see Figure 5) (Churchwell, Carey, Ferrett, Stein, & Yurgelun-Todd, 2012; Forbes et al., 2010; Luciana, 2013). One other negative consequence of this increase in emotional reactivity is an increase in adolescents' sensitivity to feeling threatened, which may prompt some adolescents to lash out at others and others to deliberately seek out experiences that are frightening (Dreyfuss et al., 2014; Spielberg, Olino, Forbes, & Dahl, 2014). As adolescents mature toward adulthood, these trends begin to reverse, and individuals become less easily aroused by positive or negative stimuli.

These changes in the functioning of the limbic system occur relatively early in adolescence, in contrast to developments in the prefrontal cortex, which are still ongoing in early adulthood (Blakemore & Robbins, 2012; Luciana, 2013; Mills, Goddings, Clasen, Giedd, & Blakemore, 2014).

functional connectivity
The extent to which multiple brain regions function at the same time, which improves during adolescence.

dopamine
A neurotransmitter especially important in the brain circuits that regulate the experience of reward.

serotonin
A neurotransmitter that is especially important for the experience of different moods.

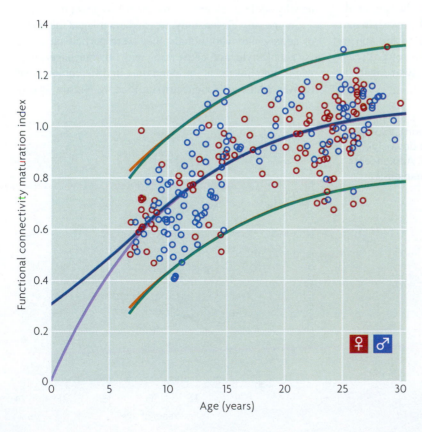

Figure 4 The maturation of functional connectivity is more or less complete by age 22. (Dosenbach et al., 2010)

Figure 5   The age of onset of most common psychiatric disorders is somewhere between the ages of 10 and 20. New research on adolescent brain development helps explain why this is the case. (Paus, Keshavan, & Giedd, 2008)

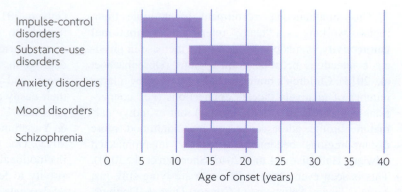

This relatively late maturation of the prefrontal cortex, particularly compared to the changes that take place in the limbic system at puberty, has been the subject of much discussion among those interested in risk taking and behavioral problems in adolescence, because this gap in timing may help explain the dramatic increase in risky behavior that takes place between childhood and adolescence, as well as the decline in risk taking that occurs as individuals mature into adulthood (Casey et al., 2011; Steinberg, 2008). In essence, the brain changes in ways that may provoke individuals to seek novelty, reward, and stimulation several years before the complete maturation of the brain systems that regulate judgment, decision making, and impulse control (Galvan, 2010; Padmanabhan, Geier, Ordaz, Teslovich, & Luna, 2011; Van Leijenhorst et al., 2010). In the words of one team of writers, it's like "starting the engines with an unskilled driver" (C. Nelson et al., 2002, p. 515). As the "braking system" improves, in part because of maturation of the prefrontal cortex and its connections to other brain regions, and as reward seeking declines, individuals become less likely to engage in risky behavior.

The Social Brain   Yet another important change in the brain in adolescence involves a network of regions referred to as the "social brain" (Mills, Lalonde, Clasen, Giedd, & Blakemore, 2014).

In most species of mammals, individuals become more social around the time of puberty, which makes perfect sense, given that adolescence evolved as a stage of development designed to prepare individuals for mating and reproduction (De Lorme, Bell, & Sisk, 2013). Changes in the social brain in early adolescence, which increase the brain's sensitivity to social cues, like other people's facial expressions and behavior, intensify adolescents' sensitivity to social evaluation, which is why adolescents are more prone to feel embarrassed than either children or adults (see Figure 6) (Guyer, Choate, Pine, & Nelson, 2012; Silk et al., 2012; Somerville, 2013; van den Bos, de Rooij, Miers, Bokhorst, & Westenberg, 2014). This may be why adolescents are so susceptible to peer pressure.

In one very clever study, researchers imaged the brains of adolescents who thought they were participating in a Facebook-style task, networking with other teenagers who were being imaged at the same time in different locations (Guyer, McClure-Tone, Shiffrin, Pine, & Nelson, 2009).

Figure 6   Changes in the social brain during adolescence have both costs and benefits. One downside is that people become more self-conscious. Adolescents report feeling embarrassed more often than either children or adults. (Somerville, 2013)

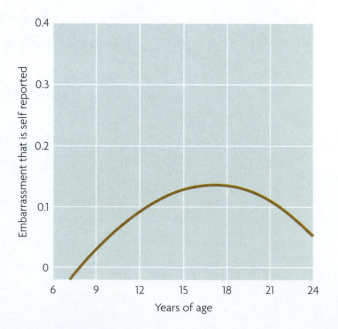

(Inside the fMRI equipment was a computer screen, on which the researchers could show any images of their choosing.) While being imaged, the adolescents were shown pictures of the other teenagers and asked to rate how interested they were in chatting with them online. The adolescents, who were told that their own photograph was posted online, received what they thought was feedback from the other teenagers. In reality, though, no other teenagers were connected to the network, and the feedback the adolescents received was rigged to be positive (interested in chatting) half the time and negative (not interested in chatting) half the time. When the adolescents were told that other teenagers were interested in them, areas of their brain known to be sensitive to rewards like food and money were activated, suggesting that social rewards may be processed during adolescence in ways similar to the ways in which we process other types of rewards. Other studies have identified regions of the brain that are activated when adolescents are made to feel excluded, and have shown that teenagers who show stronger activation of these regions when made to feel rejected are at greater risk for depression (Masten et al., 2011).

Other research indicates that sensitivity to others' mental states increases during adolescence, a change that is reflected in changes in patterns of brain activity when individuals witness others (Burnett et al., 2011; Masten, Eisenberger, Pfeifer, & Dapretto, 2013; Pfeifer & Blakemore, 2012). For instance, individuals' ability to recognize subtle changes in others' facial expressions improves during adolescence (Garcia & Scherf, 2015; Kragel, Zucker, Covington, & LaBar, 2015). The increase in sex hormones at puberty appears to play a role in influencing this increase in sensitivity to others' facial

expressions (Goodings, Heyes, Bird, Viner, & Blakemore, 2012; Moore et al., 2012; Scherf, Behrmann, & Dahl, 2012), which makes perfect sense. If you're interested in finding a willing sex partner, it probably helps to pay attention to other peoples' facial expressions.

Although this increased attentiveness to other people's mental states likely has a number of benefits (it may make teenagers more socially skilled, for example), it also makes adolescents more easily distracted by others' emotional expressions (Cohen-Gilbert & Thomas, 2013). An important implication of this for parents is that yelling at a teenager in an angry voice may not be an especially effective means of getting the adolescent to listen, because the teenager may end up paying more attention to the angry emotion than to the content of what is being said. Indeed, when adolescents listen to recordings of their mother being critical, this increases activity in emotional regions of the brain, but dampens activity in regions that govern self-regulation and logical reasoning (Lee, Siegle, Dahl, Hooley, & Silk, 2014).

making the cultural connection

New research shows that brain systems governing things like impulse control, planning ahead, and balancing risk and reward are still maturing during late adolescence. Yet, rates of adolescents' risky behavior, such as experimentation with drugs or unprotected sex, vary considerably around the world. If these sorts of behaviors are more common in adolescence because of the way the brain is changing, shouldn't they be more universal?

Changes in a region referred to as "the social brain" make adolescents more sensitive to other people's emotional states. © I love images/city break/Alamy RF

Implications for Adolescent Behavior

Correlation Is Not Causation Evidence of a correlation between changes in brain structure or function and changes in adolescent behavior does not necessarily mean that the first is necessarily causing the second (Kuhn, 2009; Paus, 2009).

We know that adolescents' behavior affects their brain development. An obvious illustration of this relationship involves the impact of alcohol and other drugs on the brain, but there are other, more subtle examples as well. As mentioned earlier, the process of synaptic pruning is influenced by experience: Repeated activation of a specific collection of neurons as a result of engaging in a particular behavior will actually result in structural changes that strengthen the connections among those neurons, which in turn will make them function more efficiently. For example, practicing the same task over and over again makes it easier and easier to perform the task each time. Scientists have grown increasingly interested in seeing whether different sorts of training programs or interventions can improve adolescents' self-control (Crone, 2009) or reduce their tendencies toward sensation seeking (Romer et al., 2011), both of which may reduce risky behavior.

One question I'm often asked is when adolescents start to think like adults, or at what age the adolescent brain becomes the adult brain. As you now know, the answer depends on which aspects of thinking or brain development one is concerned about. When it comes to relatively more sophisticated cognitive abilities, such as thinking ahead, envisioning the future consequences of a decision, balancing risks and rewards, or controlling impulses—all of which are governed mainly by the prefrontal cortex—research on brain maturation certainly suggests that these capabilities are still developing well after individuals enter their 20s. But when it comes to more basic abilities, such as those involving memory, attention, and logical reasoning, especially under optimal conditions, brain and behavioral studies indicate that the average 15-year-old performs no worse than the average adult. Where we draw the boundary between adolescence and adulthood—at least as far as cognitive development is concerned—should probably depend on why the boundary is being drawn and on what specific abilities are relevant to the behavior in question (Steinberg, Cauffman, Woolard, Graham, & Banich, 2009).

Individual Differences in Intelligence in Adolescence

For the most part, theorists who have studied adolescent cognitive development from either a Piagetian or an information-processing framework, or through brain research, have focused on the universals in adolescent intellectual growth. These theorists ask, How does thinking change as individuals move into adolescence? What processes drive cognitive development as children become teenagers? What cognitive competencies do all adolescents share?

In contrast, other theorists have been more interested in studying individual differences in intellectual abilities. They ask, How can we account for different patterns of intellectual growth within the adolescent population? How large are individual differences in intelligence in adolescence? Are some adolescents brighter than others? If so, why, and in what ways?

The Measurement of IQ

To answer questions about the relative intelligence of individuals, psychologists have had to devise ways of assessing intelligence—no easy feat given the considerable disagreement over what "intelligence" really is. Today, the most widely used measures are intelligence tests, or IQ (for "intelligence quotient") tests. Among these tests are the Stanford-Binet, the Wechsler Intelligence Scale for Children (WISC-IV), and the Wechsler Adult Intelligence Scale (WAIS-III). An individual's IQ is computed by dividing his or her mental age by his or her chronological age and then multiplying the result by 100. A score of 100 is used to designate the midway point. An IQ score below 100 indicates a poorer test performance than the average person of the same age; a score above 100 indicates a better performance than average.

Although someone's score on an intelligence test is often reported in terms of her or his overall IQ, intelligence tests actually comprise a series of tests, and it is usually possible to look at performance in different areas independently. The WISC-IV and the WAIS-III, for example, each contain two groups of tests: verbal tests, which include measures of vocabulary, general information, comprehension, and arithmetic abilities, and performance tests, which include measures of memory, perceptual reasoning, and picture completion.

Changes in specific aspects of IQ performance during adolescence are correlated with synaptic pruning in brain regions known to play a role in those specific types of learning (Ramsden, Richardson, Josse, Thomas, & Ellis, 2011; van den Bos, Crone, & Güroğlu, 2012). And there is a link between intelligence and brain development. More intelligent adolescents have a more dramatic and longer period of production of synapses before adolescence and a more dramatic pruning of them after (P. Shaw et al., 2006), more connections between the prefrontal cortex and other brain regions (Cole, Yarkoni, Repovš, Anticevic, & Braver, 2012), and a longer period of brain plasticity (van den Bos, Crone, & Güroğlu, 2012).

Mental abilities assessed by conventional IQ tests increase dramatically through childhood and adolescence, reaching a plateau sometime in mid-to-late adolescence. (It is no coincidence that this plateau occurs at around the same age as that for information processing, because IQ test performance depends a lot on information-processing abilities.) This argues strongly in favor of educational interventions prior to mid-adolescence; interventions in early childhood, especially, have been shown to improve intellectual performance during adolescence (B. C. Campbell, Pungello, Miller-Johnson, Burchinal, & Ramey, 2001). In addition, research shows that extended schooling during adolescence itself enhances individuals' performance on standardized tests of intelligence (Ceci & Williams, 1999). Whereas individuals who had dropped out of school early showed unchanging—and relatively lower—scores on intelligence tests during adolescence, students who remained in school, especially those in the more advanced tracks, showed impressive gains in verbal ability over time.

Types of Intelligence

The IQ test represents only one of many ways of assessing intelligence in adolescence. Indeed, many theorists have argued that its exclusive focus on "school smarts"—the sorts of abilities that are related to scholastic success—yields a one-sided picture of what it means to be an intelligent person. Two of the better-known attempts to expand on this narrow definition come from the work of Robert Sternberg (1988) and Howard Gardner (1983). Many of Sternberg and Gardner's ideas formed the basis for the best-selling book *Emotional Intelligence,* by journalist Daniel Goleman (1995).

Sternberg's "Triarchic" Theory Sternberg proposed a triarchic, or three-part, theory of intelligence. He argued that a thorough assessment of an individual's intellectual capabilities requires that we look at three distinct but interrelated types of intelligence: (1) componential intelligence, which involves our abilities to acquire, store, and process information; (2) experiential intelligence, which involves our abilities to use insight and creativity; and (3) contextual intelligence, which involves our ability to think practically. Componential intelligence is closest to the type of intelligence measured on traditional intelligence tests. Experiential intelligence is closest to what we call "creativity." And contextual intelligence is closest to what we might call "street smarts." Everyone has all three types of intelligence, but some individuals are stronger in one respect than in others. You probably can think of individuals who are good test takers but who are not particularly creative or sensible. According to Sternberg's model, these individuals would be high in componential intelligence but low in experiential and contextual intelligence.

More importantly, Sternberg's view forces us to look at individuals who are not good test takers but who are creative or street smart as being just as intelligent as individuals who score high on IQ tests—they're just intelligent in a different way. Sternberg argued that society needs individuals with all types of intelligence and that it is time we started assessing—and encouraging—experiential and contextual intelligence as much as we do componential intelligence.

Gardner's Theory of Multiple Intelligences Howard Gardner's theory of multiple intelligences also stresses that there is more to being smart than being "book smart." Gardner proposed that there are seven types of intelligence: verbal, mathematical, spatial, kinesthetic (having to do with movement), self-reflective, interpersonal, and musical. According to his view, for example, outstanding athletes such as basketball great LeBron James or soccer legend Mia Hamm have a well-developed kinesthetic intelligence, which allows them to control their bodies and process the movements of others in extraordinary ways. Although conventional tests of intelligence emphasize verbal and mathematical abilities, these are not the only types of intelligence that we possess—nor are they the only types that we should value.

Culture and Intelligence

Vygotsky's Perspective Much of our current thinking about the nature of intelligence has been influenced by the work of the Russian psychologist Lev Vygotsky (1930/1978), who emphasized the broader context in which intellectual development occurs. According to this view, it is essential that we understand the nature of the environment in which an adolescent develops in terms of its demands for intelligent behavior and its opportunities for learning. Individuals develop and use intellectual skills not simply as a function of their cognitive maturation but also in response to the everyday problems they are expected to solve. The very same children who perform poorly on school-based tests of knowledge may excel when faced with an equally challenging test of competence in the real world—such as figuring out the most efficient route between school and home through a dangerous neighborhood.

Vygotsky argued that children and adolescents learn best in everyday situations when they encounter tasks that are neither too simple nor too advanced, but just slightly more challenging than their abilities permit them to solve on their own. Within this **zone of proximal development,** young people, through close collaboration with a more experienced instructor (whether an adult or another child),

zone of proximal development

In Vygotsky's theory, the level of challenge that is still within the individual's reach but that forces an individual to develop more advanced skills.

are stimulated to "reach" for the more advanced level of performance. The role of the instructor is to help structure the learning situation so that it is within the reach of the student—a structuring process called **scaffolding.** If you watch good parents, teachers, or coaches at work, you will probably observe a great deal of scaffolding.

Adolescent Thinking in Context

Just as it is important to ask how the broader context influences adolescents' cognitive development, it is also important to ask how their cognitive development influences their interactions with their environment. Most of the thinking adolescents do occurs in everyday situations, not just when they are taking tests designed to see how smart they are.

As our understanding of adolescent thinking has expanded, researchers have begun to look beyond laboratory experiments and standardized tests to examine how the cognitive changes of adolescence actually affect teenagers' day-to-day thoughts and actions. Do advances in deductive reasoning or information-processing abilities make a difference in the real world? How do the brain changes that take place in adolescence play out in everyday experiences? To answer these questions, psychologists

scaffolding
Structuring a learning situation so that it is just within the reach of the student.

social cognition
The aspect of cognition that concerns thinking about other people, about interpersonal relations, and about social institutions.

mentalizing
The ability to understand someone else's mental state.

theory of mind
The ability to understand that others have beliefs, intentions, and knowledge that may be different from one's own.

Improvements in social cognition during adolescence lead adolescents to think in more sophisticated ways about themselves and their relationships. © Inti St Clair/Getty Images RF

have studied the practical side of adolescent thinking with respect to how people think about social situations and how they think about risk.

Social Cognition in Adolescence

Social cognition involves such cognitive activities as thinking about people, social relationships, and social institutions (Smetana & Villalobos, 2009). Compared with those of children, adolescents' conceptions of interpersonal relationships, their understanding of human behavior, their ideas about social institutions and organizations, and their ability to figure out what other people are thinking is far more developed. Gains in the area of social cognition help account for many of the psychosocial advances typically associated with adolescence—advances in the realms of identity, autonomy, intimacy, sexuality, and achievement. Individual differences in social cognitive abilities also help explain why some adolescents have more social problems than others (Dodge, Coie, & Lynam, 2006; Fontaine, Yang, Dodge, Bates, & Pettit, 2008).

Research on social cognition during adolescence includes many topics, but four of the most often studied concern (1) theory of mind; (2) thinking about social relationships; (3) understanding social conventions; and (4) conceptions of laws, civil liberties, and rights (Rote & Smetana, 2011; Smetana & Villalobos, 2009).

Theory of Mind During preadolescence and adolescence, individuals develop a more nuanced understanding of other people's personalities and psychological states, enabled in part by brain maturation in systems that support what is called **mentalizing**—the ability to understand someone else's mental state (Burnett et al., 2011; C. Harenski, K. Harenski, Shane, & Kiehl, 2012; Pfeifer & Peake, 2012). As they develop a more sophisticated **theory of mind,** the ability to understand that others have beliefs, intentions, and knowledge that may be different from one's own, adolescents are better able to interpret the feelings of others and to infer their motives and feelings, even when specific information of this sort is not directly observable (Choudhury, Blakemore, & Charman, 2006; Dumontheil, Apperly, & Blakemore, 2010). Adolescents also become better at lying as a result of these improvements in social cognition (Evans & Lee, 2011).

Not only are adolescents more capable of discerning another person's perspective on some issue or event, they are also better able to understand that person's perspective on their own point of view. Ultimately, adolescents' improvements in their ability to figure out what others are thinking lead to improvements in communication, because they become more capable of formulating arguments in terms that are more likely to be understood by someone whose opinion is different. This gain in perspective taking may change the dynamics of adolescents' relationships with their parents—for better (because adolescents are able to see more things from their parents' point of view) and for worse (because adolescents may use these advanced social cognitive abilities to challenge their parents' authority) (Smetana & Villalobos, 2009).

Thinking About Relationships Improvements in mentalizing lead to changes in the way that adolescents think about relationships with peers and parents. One topic that researchers have been especially interested in concerns adolescents' beliefs about peer exclusion (Leets & Sunwolf, 2005). All other things equal, children believe that it is wrong to exclude peers from social activities (i.e., whether to invite the whole class or just one's close friends to a birthday party). With age, however, as adolescents' understanding of group dynamics becomes more sophisticated, they begin to take into account other considerations, like personality ("she's not open-minded . . . we all feel weird around her"), the activity context ("we thought he wasn't good enough to play basketball"), and the reason for excluding some individuals but not others ("[The party] was a team thing") (Recchia, Brehl, & Wainryb, 2012, p. 198). On the other hand, adolescents become more likely, with age, to believe that social exclusion on the basis of gender orientation, nationality, or ethnicity is wrong (Brenick & Killen, 2014; Malti, Killen, & Gasser, 2012).

Changes in adolescents' understanding of social relationships also transform their beliefs about authority, which has important implications for their relationships with parents and other adults (Smetana & Villalobos, 2009). With age, adolescents increasingly distinguish between moral issues (such as whether it is acceptable to steal from someone else) and conventional ones (such as whether one eats dessert before or after the main course) (Lahat, Helwig, & Zelazo, 2013). Although the stereotype of adolescents is that they invariably come to reject the authority of adults, research shows that what happens instead is that adolescents increasingly distinguish between issues that authority figures have the right to regulate and issues that are their own personal choices.

As adolescents begin to make these distinctions, they often question their parents' authority. Issues that had been viewed as matters of right and wrong start to seem like matters of personal choice and, as such, beyond the bounds of parental authority (Cumsille, Darling, Flaherty, & Martínez, 2009). For example, parents' rules about things like the cleanliness of the adolescent's bedroom or bedtimes on school nights, which had been accepted as matters of right and wrong, start to seem like arbitrary conventions that are open to debate. Here's how one girl described it:

> In the beginning their word was law I guess. Whatever they decided together was what we would do regardless of what. . . . Now I will push back if I don't think it's fair. . . . I won't maybe give in as easily which can be good and bad (Parkin & Kuczynski, 2012, p. 649).

One main source of conflict between adolescents and their parents involves which issues parents have legitimate authority over and which they do not. An adolescent boy explained how he handled it:

> I don't enjoy that they ask me questions all the time and nag me about going out and stuff. . . . I'll give them answers but they're discreet answers. I'll give them little parts of things just to make it sound good, I guess (Parkin & Kuczynski, 2012, p. 649).

Similar changes occur in adolescents' beliefs about their teachers' authority (Smetana & Bitz, 1996) and the authority of groups to dictate how individuals should behave (Helwig, Yang, Tan, Liu, & Shao, 2011). For instance, adolescents understand that teachers have the right to demand that students show up for class on time and sit quietly if asked, but believe that students should be able to decide where they sit in class or during lunch.

Social Conventions The realization that individuals' perspectives vary, and that their opinions may differ as a result, leads to changes in the ways that adolescents approach issues regarding social conventions (Smetana & Villalobos, 2009). During middle childhood, **social conventions**—the social norms that guide day-to-day behavior, such as waiting in line to buy movie tickets—are seen as arbitrary and changeable, but adherence to them is not; compliance with such conventions is based on rules and on the dictates of authority. When you were 7 years old, you might not have understood why people had to wait in line to buy movie tickets, but when your parents told you to wait in line, you waited. By early adolescence, however, conventions often are seen as arbitrary social expectations. As an adolescent, you begin to realize that people wait in line because they are expected to, not because they are forced to. Indeed, young adolescents often see social conventions as *nothing but* social expectations and, consequently, as insufficient reasons for compliance. You can probably imagine youngsters in their midteens saying something like this: "Why wait in a ticket line simply because other people are lined up? There isn't a *law* that forces you to wait in line, is there?"

Gradually, however, adolescents begin to see social conventions as the means by which society regulates people's behavior. Conventions may be arbitrary, but we follow them because we share an understanding of how people are expected to behave in various situations. We wait in line for theater tickets not because we want to comply with any rule, but because it is something we are accustomed to doing.

Ultimately, individuals come to see that social conventions help to coordinate interactions among people. Social norms and expectations are derived from and maintained by individuals having a common

social conventions
The norms that govern everyday behavior in social situations.

perspective and agreeing that, in given situations, certain behaviors are more desirable than others, because such behaviors help society and its institutions function more smoothly. Without the convention of waiting in line to buy movie tickets, the pushiest people would always get tickets first. Older adolescents can see that waiting in line not only benefits the theater by keeping order but also preserves everyone's right to a fair chance to buy tickets. In other words, we wait in line patiently because we all agree that it is better if tickets are distributed fairly.

Laws, Civil Liberties, and Rights As is the case with individuals' developing understanding of relationships between people, over the course of adolescence individuals also become more nuanced in the way they think about the relationship between the individual and society. Most research on adolescents' beliefs about rights and civil liberties comes from studies of Western, middle-class youth, and it is important to be cautious about generalizing the findings of these studies to young people from other cultures. Nevertheless, even in collectivist cultures that place less emphasis on the rights of the individual, adolescents become increasingly likely to believe that there are some freedoms—like freedom of speech and freedom of religion—that should not be restricted (Smetana & Villalobos, 2009). That said, research also finds that, with age, teenagers come to believe that there are situations in which it may be legitimate to restrict individual rights to serve the benefit of the community.

Researchers have also looked at changes in adolescents' beliefs about their rights to be taken care of (called "nurturance rights") and their rights to make their own decisions (called "self-determination rights") (Ruck, Abramovich, & Keating, 1998). In general, there are few changes in individuals' endorsement of nurturance rights as they get older—adolescents are just as likely as children to believe that parents have an obligation to provide food, clothing, and other types of support. But support for self-determination rights (e.g., the right to keep a private diary) increases markedly over the course of adolescence. As is the case with support for basic individual rights, like the right to free speech or religion, the growth in support for self-determination rights is seen among adolescents from a diverse array of Western and non-Western cultures (Cherney & Shing, 2008).

Several themes cut across the research findings from studies of different aspects of social cognition—the way we think about people, relationships, conventions, and rights. First, as individuals move into and through adolescence they become better able to step outside themselves and see things from other vantage points. Second, adolescents are better able to see that the social "rules" we follow (in the family, at school, and in broader society) are not absolute and are therefore subject to debate and questioning. Third, with age, adolescents develop a more differentiated, more nuanced understanding of social norms. Yes, individuals are entitled to certain rights, but there are some situations under which it might be appropriate to curtail them. Yes, it is generally wrong to exclude others, but sometimes social exclusion is justifiable (Killen, Rutland, Abrams, Mulvey, & Hitti, 2013).

These gains in social cognition help to account for gains in social competence during adolescence. Adolescents who have more sophisticated social cognitive abilities actually behave in more socially competent ways (N. Eisenberg, Morris, McDaniel, & Spinrad, 2009). Although there is more to social competence than social cognition, being able to understand social relationships is an important component of social maturity.

Adolescent Risk Taking

A second practical application of research into adolescent thinking involves the study of adolescent risk taking. The main health problems of adolescence are the result of behaviors that can be prevented—behaviors such as substance abuse, reckless driving, and unprotected sex. In the real world (IOM and NRC, 2011a), and on many laboratory tasks of risky decision making (Burnett, Bault, Coricelli, & Blakemore, 2010; Defoe, Dubas, Figner, & van Aken, 2015; Shulman & Cauffman, 2014; Steinberg et al., 2009), adolescents take more risks than adults.

The Centers for Disease Control and Prevention, a federal agency that monitors the health of Americans, surveys American teenagers annually and asks whether they had engaged in various behaviors during the previous 30 days (Centers for Disease Control and Prevention, 2014). Risk taking is common among adolescents. More than 40% of teen drivers report having texted while driving, one-fifth had ridden with an intoxicated driver, and one-tenth themselves have driven after drinking. Among teenagers who ride bicycles, 88% report rarely or never wearing a helmet (Centers for Disease Control and Prevention, 2014).

Behavioral Decision Theory A number of writers have looked at adolescent risk taking from a perspective called **behavioral decision theory** (Kahneman, 2011). In this perspective, which draws heavily on economics, decision making is a rational process in which individuals calculate the costs and benefits of alternative courses of action and behave in ways that maximize the benefits and minimize the costs. According to this theory, all behaviors, including risky ones, can be analyzed as the outcome of a process involving five steps: (1) identifying alternative choices, (2) identifying the consequences

behavioral decision theory An approach to understanding adolescent risk taking, in which behaviors are seen as the outcome of systematic decision-making processes.

that might follow from each choice, (3) evaluating the costs and benefits of each possible consequence, (4) assessing the likelihood of each possible consequence, and (5) combining all this information according to some decision rule (Beyth-Marom, Austin, Fischhoff, Palmgren, & Jacobs-Quadrel, 1993).

So, for example, an adolescent girl who is trying to decide whether to accept a ride home from a party with friends who have been drinking will (1) identify the choices (to accept the ride or not), (2) identify the consequences ("If I accept the ride, and we get into an accident, I could be seriously hurt, but if I don't accept the ride, my friends will make fun of me for being a 'loser'"), (3) evaluate the desirability of each consequence ("Appearing like a 'loser' to my friends is bad, but being in an accident would be terrible"), (4) assess the likelihood of each consequence ("My friends probably won't really change their opinion of me just because I turn down the ride, and my friend who is driving is so drunk that he really might get into an accident"), and (5) combine all the information according to some decision rule ("All things considered, I think I won't take the ride").

From the perspective of behavioral decision theory, then, it is important to ask whether adolescents use different processes than adults in identifying, estimating, and evaluating behavioral options and consequences. If risky decisions are the result of faulty information processing—in attention, memory, metacognition, or organization, for example—perhaps it would make sense to train adolescents in these basic cognitive abilities as a means of lessening their risk taking.

As we have seen, however, adolescents, at least by the time they are 15 or so, have the same basic cognitive abilities as adults (Beyth-Marom et al., 1993; Furbey & Beyth-Marom, 1992). This is true even for issues as complicated as deciding whether to abort a pregnancy (Steinberg, 2014). The major gains in the cognitive skills that affect decision making appear to occur between childhood and adolescence, rather than between adolescence and adulthood. Thus, educating adolescents in how to make "better" decisions is not likely to reduce risk taking (Steinberg, 2015).

Do Adolescents Really Feel Invulnerable? A second possibility that is often suggested is that adolescents are more likely to feel invulnerable—more likely, that is, to subscribe to the personal fable that they will not be harmed by potentially harmful activities. However, as you read earlier, there is no evidence for the widely held belief that adolescents are more likely to subscribe to personal fables than are adults. More importantly, studies indicate that young adolescents are *less* likely than young adults to see themselves as invulnerable—if anything, young adolescents *overestimate* the risks involved in potentially harmful behavior (Fischhoff, de Bruin, Perker, Millstein, & Halpern-Felsher, 2010). There is

Recent research on cognitive development in adolescence has been aimed at understanding the thinking behind adolescent risk taking. © RubberBall Productions/Getty Images RF

no evidence, for example, that adolescents are worse at perceiving risks than adults are (Ivers et al., 2009; Van Leijenhorst, Westenberg, & Crone, 2008). However, research indicates that adolescents vary far more than adults in how they interpret words and phrases used to describe risk—words like "probably," "likely," or "a very low chance"—suggesting that health educators and practitioners should not take for granted that an adolescent's understanding of a message about risk is what the educator thinks it is (Mills, Reyna, & Estrada, 2008). Similarly, just because an adolescent says that she knows that having "safe sex" can protect her against sexually transmitted diseases doesn't necessarily mean that she knows the specific behaviors that constitute safe sex (Reyna & Farley, 2006).

Age Differences in Values and Priorities If adolescents use the same decision-making processes as adults, and if adolescents are no more likely than adults to think of themselves as invulnerable, why, then, are adolescents more likely to engage in risky behavior? One answer may involve the different values and priorities that adolescents and adults have. For example, an individual's decision to try cocaine at a party may involve evaluating a number of different consequences, including the legal and health risks, the pleasure the drug may induce, and the way in which he or she will be judged (both positively and negatively) by the other people present. An adult and an adolescent may both consider all these consequences, but the adult may place relatively more weight on the health risks of trying the drug, while the adolescent may place relatively more weight on the social consequences of not trying it. Although an adult may see an adolescent's decision to value peer acceptance more than health as irrational, an adolescent may see the adult's decision as equally incomprehensible. Behavioral decision theory reminds us that many decisions—even risky ones—can be seen as rational once we understand how an individual estimates and evaluates the consequences of various courses of action.

One very important difference between adolescents and adults is that, when weighing the costs and benefits of engaging in a risky behavior, adolescents are more attuned to the potential rewards than are adults (Ben-Zur & Reshef-Kfir, 2003; Cauffman et al., 2010). This difference is consistent with changes that are taking place in the limbic system around the time of puberty, which we discussed earlier in this chapter. One study of delinquents found, for instance, that adolescents' criminal activity was more strongly related to their beliefs about the potential rewards of the activity (for example, being seen as "cool") than to their perceptions of the activity's riskiness (for example, the chances of being arrested) (Matsueda, Kreager, & Huizinga, 2006). As several writers have pointed out, this has important implications for the prevention of risky behavior among adolescents. It may be more important to convince adolescents that the rewards of a risky activity are small (for example, that few people will actually look up to someone for being violent) than to persuade them that the costs are large (for example, that being incarcerated will be terrible).

In all likelihood, of course, neither adolescents' nor adults' decisions are always made in as straightforward or rational a way, as suggested by behavioral decision theory. Nevertheless, this approach has opened up a new way of thinking about adolescent risk taking. Instead of viewing risky activities as the result of irrational or faulty judgment, experts are now trying to understand where and how adolescents obtain the information they use in reaching their conclusions, and how accurate the information is. If, for example, adolescents underestimate the likelihood of getting pregnant following unprotected sex, sex education efforts might focus on teaching teenagers the actual probability. (Of course, this presumes that adolescents' decisions about whether to have sex are made rationally, which may not be the case [P. Levine, 2001].)

sensation seeking
The pursuit of experiences that are novel or exciting.

Emotional and Contextual Influences on Risk Taking
We should also keep in mind that emotional and contextual

factors, as well as cognitive ones, contribute to adolescent risk taking (Dahl, 2008; Rivers, Reyna, & Mills, 2008; Steinberg, 2010). Several researchers have noted that adolescents may differ from adults in important ways that are not captured by measures of logical reasoning, such as susceptibility to peer pressure, impulsivity, orientation to the present rather than the future, or reward seeking (Cauffman et al., 2010; de Water, Cillessen, & Scheres, 2014; Steinberg et al., 2008; Steinberg et al., 2009). A number of studies have shown that adolescents' decision making is as good as adults' when individuals are tested under calm conditions, but that the quality of adolescents' decision making declines more than adults' when they are emotionally aroused (Figner & Weber, 2011; van Duijvenvoorde, Jansen, Visser, & Huizenga, 2010).

With respect to emotional factors, for example, studies show that individuals who are high in reward seeking and **sensation seeking**—that is, who seek out novel and intense experiences—are more likely to engage in various types of risky behaviors than their peers (C. A. Johnson et al., 2008; D. Miller & Byrnes, 1997), and that both reward seeking and sensation seeking are higher during adolescence than childhood or adulthood (Cauffman et al., 2010; Shulman & Cauffman, 2013; Steinberg et al., 2008). Similarly, adolescents who are especially impulsive are also more likely to engage in risky behavior (Quinn & Harden, 2013). One reason that middle adolescence is a period of heightened risk taking is that it is a period characterized by a combination of high sensation seeking and high impulsivity (Harden & Tucker-Drob, 2011; Smith, Xiao, & Bechara, 2012), especially among boys (Shulman, Harden, Chein, & Steinberg, 2014) (see Figure 7).

The context in which individuals spend time matters, too (Boyer, 2006). A good deal of adolescents' risk taking takes place in contexts in which they are emotionally aroused (either very positively or very negatively), unsupervised by adults, and with their peers (Albert & Steinberg, 2001; Kretsch & Harden, 2014). For example, one recent study found that adolescents with mothers who worked nights were more likely to take risks, in part because the parents were less likely to know their teen's whereabouts (Han, Miller, & Waldfogel, 2010). As noted earlier, individuals' susceptibility to peer pressure is higher during early and middle adolescence than later, suggesting that one reason for teenagers' greater risk taking is the fact that they spend so much time in the peer group (Steinberg & Monahan, 2007). Most adolescent risk taking, including delinquency, drinking, and reckless behavior, occurs when other teenagers are present, and adolescents are more likely to take risks when their friends are around (Steinberg, 2014). Although adolescent drivers, on average, take more chances than adults, how adolescents drive depends on who is in the car; adolescents drive much more safely when their parents

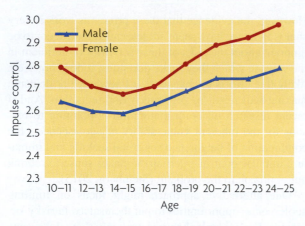
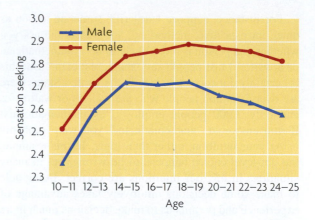

Figure 7 Adolescence is a time of heightened sensation seeking and still developing self-control, especially among males. (Shulman et al., 2014)

are passengers than when they are driving alone or with their friends (Simons-Morton et al., 2011; Telzer, Ichien, & Qu, 2015).

The effect of peers on adolescent risk taking is clearly evident in studies of driving crashes. As Figure 8 shows, having multiple passengers in the car increases the risk of crashes dramatically among 16- and 17-year-old drivers, significantly among 18- and 19-year-old drivers, and not at all among adults. This is both because adolescent passengers can be distracting to new drivers and because adolescents are simply more likely to take risks in the presence of peers (Centifanti, Modecki, MacLellan, & Gowling, 2014; Foss & Goodwin, 2014; Pradhan et al., 2014). Consistent with this, in one experiment, in which adolescents, college undergraduates, and adults who were either alone or in a room with their friends played a video driving game that permitted risky driving—for instance, driving through an intersection after a traffic light had turned yellow—found that the mere fact of having friends watching their performance increased risk taking among adolescents and undergraduates, but not adults (M. Gardner & Steinberg, 2005). In a subsequent study, in which the researchers imaged the teens' brains while they played a similar video driving game,

the results indicated that the brain regions associated with the experience of reward were much more likely to be activated when the teenagers were observed by their friends than when they were alone, and that risky driving was correlated with heightened activity in the brain's reward areas. Thus, in the presence of their peers, adolescents may pay more attention to the potential rewards of a risky decision than they do when they are alone (O'Brien, Albert, Chein, & Steinberg, 2011; Smith, Steinberg, Strang, & Chein, 2015).

Logic and Intuition More recently, several theorists have proposed models of adolescent risk taking that consider the ways in which two different thinking systems—one that is deliberative and logical, and one that is intuitive and gut-level—interact to influence behavior (Reyna & Brainerd, 2011). According to these perspectives, the heightened risk taking seen during adolescence, and the drop in risk taking in adulthood, can't be entirely due to deficiencies in logical reasoning, because adults themselves do not always act logically. As the Nobel Prize–winning psychologist Daniel Kahneman has pointed out (2011), we all often behave in ways that defy logic.

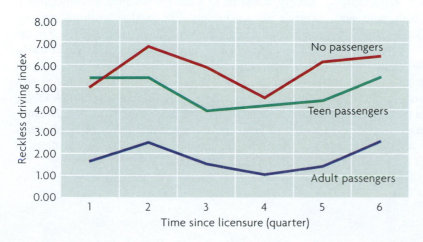

Figure 8 Although adolescents on average are riskier drivers than adults, who is in the car makes a big difference. Teens drive more recklessly when they are alone or with peers than when they have adult passengers. (Simons-Mortin et al., 2011)

For instance, suppose I describe someone to you as quiet, introspective, methodical, and nerdy, and ask you whether that person is more likely to be a mathematician or a waiter. Most people say "mathematician." But this is certainly not correct—since in the United States there are over 7 million people who are waiters or waitresses and only 3,000 people employed as mathematicians! If you answered "mathematician," you were probably using your intuition, rather than logic. In this example, the gut-level choice happens to be wrong, but in many situations in life, our intuitions are correct. Being able to make some decisions intuitively takes advantage of experience and permits us to make decisions much more quickly than we would be able to do if we had to reason everything out.

Although the development of logical thinking may differentiate adolescents from children, the main change to take place between adolescence and adulthood is not the further development of logical decision making (as you read earlier, this is pretty much completed by age 15 or so), but the continued development of intuitive decision making that is based on experience. What stops adults from taking a lot of risks is not that they are good at systematically analyzing the probabilities of various outcomes, but because they get a gut-level feeling that keeps them away from the risky act. If I am standing on a cliff overlooking a dark body of water that I can't see into, the reason I don't jump is not that I've logically assessed my chances of getting hurt and decided that the odds are not in my favor. I don't jump because something inside me immediately tells me that it is a dumb thing to do. I don't even have to think about it. In one study in which adolescents and adults were asked whether some obviously risky things (e.g., "setting your hair on fire," "swimming with sharks,") were bad things to do while their brain was scanned, the researchers found that the adolescents took longer to respond and were more likely than adults to activate brain regions that are involved in deliberative thinking; adults, in contrast, were more likely than adolescents to activate regions that reflect gut-level responding (Baird, Fugelsang, & Bennett, 2005). One other study has found that improvements in deliberative decision-making abilities are associated with more, not less, risk taking (Wolff & Crockett, 2011).

Reducing Adolescent Risk Taking   Generally speaking, the most common approach to reducing adolescent risk taking is through classroom-based education programs designed to teach adolescents about the dangers of various activities (e.g., smoking, unprotected sex, drinking and driving), about making better decisions, and about resisting peer pressure to engage in risky activity.

However, the evidence that these programs work is very shaky. If, as we have seen, adolescents do not seem to be ignorant about the risks of these activities or deficient in the ways in which they make decisions, it does not seem likely that efforts to change their knowledge or decision making will result in very much risk reduction. And if recent research on brain maturation is pointing to reasons for the inherent vulnerability of adolescence—the combination of heightened sensation seeking and immature impulse control—perhaps it makes sense to rethink our approach to the problem (Steinberg, 2015).

One alternative approach might focus on limiting adolescents' opportunities to put themselves in risky situations. For example, because we know that adolescents are more likely to have automobile accidents when they have teenage passengers in the car or drive at night, limiting the situations under which teenagers are permitted to drive, especially after they are newly licensed, would give adolescents that coveted driver's license but limit risky driving. Many states have found that graduated driver licensing, which phases adolescent drivers into full unrestricted driving privileges over time, lowers the incidence of fatal crashes involving 16-year-old drivers, although it appears to increase the incidence of crashes among 18-year-olds (Masten, Foss, & Marshall, 2011b).

It is also possible to reduce adolescent risk taking through economic policies. For example, although anti-tobacco education has met with only limited success, increases in the cost of cigarettes have dramatically reduced the rate of teen smoking. Thus, raising the price of tobacco or alcohol would likely diminish adolescents' use of these products, because adolescents generally do not have a great deal of money and would therefore be sensitive to increases in the cost of smoking or drinking (Chaloupka, 2004). Another possibility would be to make risky substances harder for adolescents to obtain, by more strictly enforcing policies that prohibit stores from selling tobacco and alcohol to minors, limiting the supply of illegal drugs, or enforcing laws that limit adolescents' access to firearms (Rowland, Toumbourou, & Livingston, 2015; Smith et al., 2013). Yet a third possibility would be to make the penalties for engaging in certain risky behaviors, like reckless or drunk driving, more severe, and in so doing increase the salience of the potential costs of engaging in the risky behavior. Finally, to the extent that sensation seeking may be a normal part of adolescence, perhaps we can figure out how to provide safe outlets for this motivation. Not all risk taking is bad, after all. The challenge for parents, educators, and policymakers is to find ways to permit adolescents to take risks without putting themselves in situations in which they can hurt themselves.

Social Transitions

3

Social Redefinition and Psychosocial Development

The Elongation of Adolescence

Adolescence as a Social Invention
  The "Invention" of Adolescence
  Emerging Adulthood: A New Stage of Life or a Luxury of the Middle Class?

Changes in Status During Adolescence
  Drawing a Legal Boundary
  Inconsistencies in Adolescents' Legal Status

The Process of Social Redefinition
  Common Practices in the Process of Social Redefinition

Variations in Social Transitions
  Variations in Clarity
  Variations in Continuity

The Transition into Adulthood in Contemporary Society
  Special Transitional Problems of Poor and Minority Youth
  The Effects of Poverty on the Transition Into Adulthood
  What Can Be Done to Ease the Transition?

The Influence of Neighborhood Conditions on Adolescent Development
  Processes of Neighborhood Influences

© Ariel Skelley/Getty Images RF

What events in your life told you—and others around you—that you were no longer a child and had finally become an adolescent? Was it when you turned 13? Finished elementary school? Went to your first boy–girl party? Were allowed to be out at the mall without an adult?

And what signaled, or will signal, that you are an adult? Turning 18? Turning 21? Getting your first full-time job? Getting your driver's license? Graduating from college? Getting your first apartment? Getting married?

Each of these social transitions is not just an event. Each is also a source of information—to the person and those in his or her life—about the person's stage of development. Parents may treat their children differently once they start high school, even if their appearance and behavior haven't changed. Neighbors might look at a child who has grown up next door differently once they see him or her driving. Adolescents may feel differently about themselves once they have started working at a "real" job.

In all societies, adolescence is a period of social transition for the individual. Over the course of these years, people cease to be viewed by society as children and come to be recognized as adults. This chapter is about the ways in which individuals are redefined during adolescence and the implications of this process for psychological development. Although the specific elements of this social passage from childhood into adulthood vary across time and place, the recognition that the individual's status has changed—a **social redefinition** of the individual—is universal.

In this chapter, we will look at a third fundamental feature of adolescence—changes in the way in which society defines who that person is and determines what rights and responsibilities she or he has as a consequence. Along with the biological changes of puberty and changes in thinking abilities, changes in social roles and social status constitute yet another universal feature of development during adolescence. As you will read, some theorists have argued that the nature of adolescent development is far more influenced by the way in which society defines the economic and social roles of young people than by the biological or cognitive changes of the period.

The study of social transitions in adolescence provides an interesting vehicle through which to compare adolescence across different cultures and historical epochs. Puberty, after all, is pretty much the same everywhere (although its timing and meaning may vary from place to place). Abstract thinking and logical reasoning don't differ from one society to the next (although *what* people think and reason about certainly does). The social transitions of adolescence are not the same, however. Although the existence of a social passage from childhood into adulthood is universal, huge differences exist between the processes of social redefinition in industrialized society and those in the developing world. In examining some of these differences, you will come to understand better how the way in which society structures the transition of adolescents into adult roles influences the nature of psychosocial development during the period.

Social Redefinition and Psychosocial Development

Like the biological and cognitive transitions of adolescence, the social transitions have important consequences for the young person's psychosocial development. In the realm of identity, for example, attainment of adult status may transform a young woman's self-concept, causing her to feel more mature and to think more seriously about future work and family roles. Similarly, an individual may feel older and more mature the first time he reports to work, goes into a bar, drives without an adult in the car, or votes. In turn, these new activities and opportunities may prompt self-evaluation and introspection.

Becoming an adult member of society, accompanied as it is by increases in responsibilities and freedom, also has an impact on the development of autonomy, or independence. In contrast to the child, the adolescent-turned-adult faces a wider range of

social redefinition
The process through which an individual's position or status is redefined by society.

decisions that may have serious long-term consequences (Woolard & Scott, 2009). An individual who has reached the drinking age, for example, must decide how to handle this new privilege. Should he go along with the crowd and drink every weekend night, follow his parents' example and abstain from drinking, or chart a middle ground? And in return for the privileges that come with adult status, the adolescent-turned-adult is expected to behave in a more responsible fashion. For example, receiving a driver's license carries with it the obligation of driving safely. The attainment of adult status provides chances for the young person to exercise autonomy and to develop a greater sense of independence.

Changes in social definition often bring with them changes in relationships with others. Social redefinition at adolescence is therefore likely to raise new questions and concerns for the young person about intimacy—including such matters as dating and marriage. Many parents prohibit their children from dating until they have reached an "appropriate" age, and not until the

age of majority (the legal age for adult status) are individuals allowed to marry without first gaining their parents' permission. In certain societies, young people may even be *required* to marry when they reach adulthood, entering into a marriage that may have been arranged while they were children (Schlegel, 2009).

Changes in status at adolescence also may affect sexual development. In contemporary society, for example, laws governing sexual behavior (such as the definition of **statutory rape**) typically differentiate between individuals who have and have not attained adult status. One problem continuing to face contemporary society is whether sexually active individuals who are not yet legal adults should be able to make independent decisions about such matters as abortion and contraception (Woolard & Scott, 2009).

Finally, reaching adulthood often has important implications in the realm of achievement. In contemporary society, people can hold informal jobs, like babysitting, when they are still young, but it is not until adult work status is attained (typically at age 15 or 16 in the United States) that young people can enter the labor force as full-time employees. And not until young people have reached a designated age are they permitted to leave school of their own volition. In less industrialized societies, becoming an adult typically entails entrance into the productive activities of the community. Together, these shifts are likely to prompt changes in the young person's skills, aspirations, and expectations.

The Elongation of Adolescence

Adolescence is longer today than it has ever been in human history.

Deciding how we define a stage of life—when it begins and when it ends—is inherently subjective. Experts use puberty to mark the beginning of adolescence because it's easy to measure, has obvious consequences (like sexual maturation), and is universal. In societies that have formal rites of passage, puberty has long been used to indicate when people are no longer children.

We may lack formal initiation ceremonies in modern society, but we still use puberty to mark the passage into adolescence. Getting consensus on when the period ends is harder. Although there are a few objective biological boundaries between adolescence and adulthood—for instance, the point at which people stop growing taller or when they can bear children—these somehow just don't feel right. Some people finish their growth spurts when they're as young as 12 or 13, and some can even become a parent at this age, but few of us, at least in today's world, feel comfortable labeling a 13-year-old as an "adult." That's why we tend to use some sort of social indicator to draw the line between adolescence and adulthood, like attaining the age of legal majority, starting a full-time job, or moving out of one's parents' home.

Reasonable people may disagree about *which* social indicator makes the most sense, but they would probably agree that a cultural marker of adulthood makes more sense than a biological one.

This is why experts define adolescence as *beginning in biology and ending in culture.*

Of all the possible markers of the beginning and end of adolescence, menstruation and marriage are probably the best ones to use in order to see if adolescence actually has gotten longer. Both are widely experienced, and we can date both of them accurately. For most women, menarche is a memorable event, and one whose date is regularly recorded in doctors' files. Scientists in the Western world have been keeping track of the average age of girls' first menstruation since about 1840, and we have a very good idea of how the advent of puberty has changed since then. There is no comparable pubertal event for boys that screams, "I am a man," but the ages at which males and females within the same society go through puberty are highly correlated. Even though girls typically go through puberty a year or two before boys, in societies in which puberty is early for girls, it comes early for boys, too.

The age at which people marry is even more reliably documented than the age of menarche. Government officials have long noted how old people are when they take their wedding vows, and as a consequence we have accurate statistics about marriage that go back for centuries. This is certainly not to say that one must be

age of majority
The designated age at which an individual is recognized as an adult.

statutory rape
Sex between two individuals, even when it is consensual, when at least one of the persons is below the legal age of consent; in the United States, the specific age of consent varies from state to state.

The stage of adolescence has been lengthened by an increase in the age at which people make the transition into adult roles. The age of marriage has risen steadily over the past 50 years.
© Studio Zanello/Streetstock Images/Getty Images RF

inventionists
Theorists who argue that the period of adolescence is mainly a social invention.

married in order to be an adult, only that changes in the average age of marriage are useful for tracking historical trends. Trends in the age at which people complete their schooling, begin their careers, or set up independent households would also be fine ways to track historical changes in the transition into adulthood, but we haven't kept very good official records of these for nearly as long we've been recording marriages. And although getting married, leaving school, starting a career, or setting up a home do not all take place at the same age, they tend to move in lockstep from one generation to the next. When the average age for getting married rises over time, so do the others.

In the middle of the nineteenth century, adolescence lasted around 5 years—that's how long it took girls to go from menarche to marriage in the mid-1800s. At the turn of the twentieth century, the average American woman got her first period between fourteen and fifteen and married when she was just under 22. In 1900, adolescence lasted a little less than 7 years.

During the first half of the twentieth century, people began getting married at a younger age, but the age of puberty continued to decline. This froze the length of adolescence at about 7 years. In 1950, for example, the average American female went through menarche at around 13-1/2 and married at 20.

From 1950 on, though, things changed. The drop in the age of puberty continued, but people started marrying later and later. Each decade, the average age of menarche dropped by about 3 or 4 months, whereas the average age at marriage rose by about a year. By 2010, it took 15 years for the average girl to go from menarche to marriage (Steinberg, 2014).

As we shall see, the passage from adolescence into adulthood today is especially difficult for young people growing up in poverty, in part because social institutions that once enabled poor youth to make a successful transition into adulthood no longer provide sufficient support (Settersten, Furstenberg, & Rumbaut, 2005). In today's economy, making a smooth and successful transition into adult work and family roles is challenging enough for individuals who graduate from college, but it has become incredibly difficult for those who only complete high school and almost impossible for those without a high school diploma.

The lengthening of adolescence as a developmental period has had important implications for how young people see themselves, relate to others, and develop psychologically. Consider just a few examples:

- Parents used to "launch" their children from home very close to the age of puberty. As a consequence, individuals spent very little time living under the same roof with their parents once they had become sexual beings. In contemporary society, however, individuals live with their parents long after they have become sexually mature. What impact might this have on parent–child relationships?

- Adolescents today probably aren't any less emotionally mature than they were 100 years ago—if anything, growing up under many of the pressures that people face today may have made them more mature at a younger age. But because the financial cost of living independently has increased so rapidly, adolescents' economic "maturity" (that is, their ability to support themselves without help from their parents) lags far behind their psychological maturity (that is, their ability to behave responsibly). What implications does this have? How does it feel to be an adult psychologically but a child financially?

- One of the main reasons that adolescence has been lengthened is that much more formal education is now necessary in order to make a successful transition into adult work roles. School, however, is not something that all individuals enjoy equally. How might forcing all adolescents to follow the same pathway into adulthood benefit some but not others?

Adolescence as a Social Invention

Many writers, often referred to as **inventionists,** have argued that adolescence, as a period in the life cycle, is mainly a social invention (e.g., Fasick, 1994). They point out that, although the biological and cognitive changes characteristic of the period are important in their own right, adolescence is defined primarily by the ways in which society recognizes (or does not recognize) the period as distinct from childhood or adulthood.

Our images of adolescence are influenced by the fact that society draws lines between adolescence and childhood (for instance, the boundary between elementary and secondary school) and between adolescence and adulthood (for instance, the age at which someone can vote). Inventionists stress that it is only because we see adolescence as distinct that it exists as such. They point to other cultures and other historical periods in which adolescence has been viewed very differently.

Many of these theorists view the behaviors and problems characteristic of adolescence in contemporary society, such as delinquency, as a consequence of the way that adolescence is defined and young people are treated, rather than the result of the biological or cognitive givens of the period. As you know, this is an entirely different view from that espoused by writers such as G. Stanley Hall, who saw the psychological changes of adolescence as driven by puberty and, as a result, by biological destiny.

The "Invention" of Adolescence

Have there always been adolescents? Although this may seem like a simple question with an obvious answer, it is actually a very complicated issue. Naturally, there have always been individuals between the ages of 10 and 20, or who just passed through puberty, or whose frontal lobes were still maturing. But according to the inventionist view, adolescence as we know it in contemporary society did not really exist until the Industrial Revolution of the mid-nineteenth century (Fasick, 1994). In the agricultural world of the sixteenth or seventeenth century, children were treated primarily as miniature adults, and people did not make precise distinctions among children of different ages ("child" referred to anyone under the age of 18 or even 21). Children provided important labor to their families, and they learned early in their development the roles they were expected to fill later in life. The main distinction between children and adults was based not on their age or their abilities but on whether they owned property (Modell & Goodman, 1990). As a consequence, there was little reason to label some youngsters as "children" and others as "adolescents"—in fact, the term *adolescent* was not widely used prior to the nineteenth century.

The Impact of Industrialization   With industrialization came new patterns of work, education, and family life. Adolescents were among those most dramatically affected by these changes. First, because the economy was changing so rapidly, away from the simple and predictable life known in agrarian society, the connection between what individuals learned in childhood and what they would need to know in adulthood became increasingly uncertain. Although a man may have been a farmer, his son would not necessarily follow in his footsteps. One response to this uncertainty was that parents, especially in middle-class families, encouraged adolescents to spend time in school, preparing for adulthood. Instead of working side by side with their parents and other adults at home, as was the case before industrialization, adolescents became increasingly more likely to spend their days with peers, being educated or trained for the future. This led to the increased importance of peer groups and youth culture, defining characteristics of modern adolescence we take for granted today that were not prominent until the early twentieth century.

Inventionists point out that the redefinition of adolescence as a time of preparation rather than participation also suited society's changing economic needs (Fasick, 1994). One initial outcome of industrialization was a shortage of job opportunities, because machines were replacing workers. Although adolescents provided inexpensive labor, they were now competing with adults for a limited number of jobs. One way of protecting adults' jobs was to remove adolescents from the labor force, by turning them into full-time students. To accomplish this, society needed to begin discriminating between individuals who were "ready" for work and those who were not. Although there was little factual basis for the distinction, society began to view adolescents as less capable and more in need of guidance and training—legitimizing what was little more than age discrimination. Individuals who earlier in the century would have been working next to adults were now seen as too immature or too unskilled to carry out similar tasks—even though the individuals themselves hadn't changed in any meaningful way.

A less cynical view of the events of the late nineteenth century emphasizes the genuine motivation of some adults to protect adolescents from the dangers of the new workplace, rather than the selfish desire to protect adults' jobs from teenagers. Industrialization brought with it worrisome changes in community life, especially in the cities. Many factories were dangerous working environments, filled with new and unfamiliar machinery. The disruption of small farming communities and the growth of large urban areas was accompanied by increases in crime and "moral degeneracy." **Child protectionists** argued that young people needed to be kept away from the labor force for their own good. In addition to the rise of schools during this time, the early twentieth century saw the growth of many organizations aimed at protecting young people, such as the Boy Scouts and other adult-supervised youth clubs (Modell & Goodman, 1990).

The Origins of Adolescence as We Know It Today
It was not until the late nineteenth century—little more than 100 years ago—that adolescence came to be viewed as it is today: a lengthy period of preparation for adulthood, in which young people, in need of guidance and supervision, remain economically dependent on their elders. This view started within the middle class—where parents had more to gain by keeping their children out of the labor force and educating them for a better adulthood—but it spread quickly throughout society. Because the workplace has continued to change in ways that make the future uncertain, the idea of adolescence as a distinctive period of preparation for adulthood has remained intact. Adolescence, as a transitional stage between childhood and adulthood, now exists in virtually all societies around the world (Larson et al., 2009).

Two other modifications of the definition of adolescence also gave rise to new terminology and ideas. The first of these is the introduction of the term **teenager,** which was not employed until about 70 years ago. In contrast to "adolescent," "teenager" suggested a less serious age, during which individuals concern themselves

child protectionists
Individuals who argued, early in the twentieth century, that adolescents needed to be kept out of the labor force in order to protect them from the hazards of the workplace.

teenager
A term popularized about 50 years ago to refer to young people; it connoted a more frivolous and lighthearted image than did "adolescent."

Although adolescence was invented during the late 19th century, it was not until the middle of the 20th century that our present-day image of the teenager was created. Making an important contribution to this image were the mass media—magazines such as Seventeen cultivated the picture of the happy-go-lucky teenager as a way of targeting advertisements toward an increasingly lucrative adolescent market. © Francesco Scavullo/Seventeen Magazine

with cars, clothes, and cosmetics. An important social change that led to the development of the concept of teenager was the increased affluence and economic freedom enjoyed by American adolescents during the late 1940s and early 1950s (Fasick, 1994; Hine, 1999). Advertisers recognized that teenagers represented an important consumer group and, with the help of new publications such as *Seventeen* magazine, began cultivating the image of the happy-go-lucky teenager as a means of targeting ad campaigns toward the lucrative adolescent market (Osgerby, 2008; Palladino, 1996). Interestingly, although the image of the American teenager—fun-loving, irresponsible, and independent—now appears all over the world, in some societies it is viewed favorably (because it is evidence that the society has reached a level of affluence to be able to afford it), while in others it is held up as an example of what adults do *not* want their children to become (Larson et al., 2009).

A second term whose acceptance grew as a result of social change is **youth,** which was used long before "adolescent." But, prior to industrialization, youth had a vague, imprecise meaning and could refer to someone as young as 12 or as old as 24 (Modell & Goodman, 1990). Gradually,

youth
Today, a term used to refer to individuals ages 18 to 22; it once referred to individuals ages 12 to 24.

and during the 1960s in particular, the growth of the college population and the rise in student activism focused attention on individuals who were somewhere between adolescence and young adulthood—those from 18 to 22. Many adults referred to the changes they saw in attitudes and values among college students as the "youth movement." One theorist went so far as to argue that youth is a separate stage in the life cycle, psychologically as well as chronologically distinct from adolescence and adulthood (Keniston, 1970), an idea that is similar to the concept of "emerging adulthood," which we will examine later in this chapter. Many college students today are unsure about whether they are adolescents or adults, since they may feel mature in some respects (keeping up an apartment or being involved in a serious relationship) but immature in others (having to depend on parents for economic support or having to have an advisor approve class schedules). Although it may strike you as odd to think of 22-year-olds as adolescents, the lengthening of formal schooling in contemporary society has altered the way we define adolescence, because the majority of young people continue their education past high school and are forced to delay their transition into many adult work and family roles (Steinberg, 2014). By this definition, many 22-year-olds (and many individuals who are even older) are still not yet adults—a situation that often perplexes parents as much as their adult children.

making the personal connection

Think for a moment about how your parents' adolescence differed from yours. What changes have taken place in society since then that might have contributed to this?

Emerging Adulthood: A New Stage of Life or a Luxury of the Middle Class?

The transition to adulthood has become so delayed in many industrialized societies that some have argued that there is a new stage in life—emerging adulthood—that may last for some individuals until their mid-20s (Arnett, 2009). Proponents of this idea contend that the period from ages 18 to 25 is neither adolescence nor adulthood, but a unique developmental period in its own right, characterized by five main features:

- the exploration of possible identities before making enduring choices;
- instability in work, romantic relationships, and living arrangements;
- a focus on oneself and, in particular, on functioning as an independent person;

- the feeling of being between adolescence and adulthood; and
- the sense that life holds many possibilities.

Is Emerging Adulthood Universal? This profile certainly describes many young people in contemporary society, particularly those whose parents can foot the bill while their "emerging adults" are figuring out what they want to do with their lives. As many writers have pointed out (e.g., Arnett, 2009), however, emerging adulthood does not exist in all cultures—in fact, it exists in very few (the United States, Canada, Australia, New Zealand, Japan, and the more affluent nations of Western Europe). And even within countries in which there are significant numbers of emerging adults, the majority of individuals cannot afford to delay the transition from adolescence into full-fledged adulthood for a half decade. Several recent analyses indicate that there is a great deal of variability among people in their mid-20s with respect to the dimensions of emerging adulthood (Côté, 2014).

It is also important to note that the existence of emerging adulthood is not entirely an economic phenomenon. Many emerging adults live the way they do because the economy forces them to, but many simply do it by choice—they want to take some time before assuming full adult responsibilities. Expectations about the age at which one gets married appear to be especially important to this decision (J. S. Carroll et al., 2007). The existence of emerging adulthood may have a lot to do with values and priorities, and not just the economy.

Psychological Well-Being in Emerging Adulthood
Very little research has examined psychological development and functioning during emerging adulthood. The profile initially described by some writers suggests both a potentially difficult time, characterized by floundering and financial instability, and a time of carefree optimism and independence. There is evidence for both

views. Several studies show that for the majority of people, emerging adulthood is generally one of positive and improving mental health (see Figure 1). At the same time, however, the period between 18 and 25 is a time during which a substantial number of people report serious mental health problems, like depression or substance abuse. In any given year, nearly one-fifth of people this age suffer from some sort of mental illness, and, despite the media attention given to teen suicide, the suicide rate among young adults is twice what it is among teenagers (Institute of Medicine, 2015).

One study of mental health during this age period followed a national sample of American youths from age 18 to their mid-20s. The researchers compared four groups: (1) those who reported positive well-being across the entire interval, (2) those who reported negative well-being across the entire interval, (3) those whose well-being started low but increased, and (4) those whose well-being started high but decreased (Schulenberg, Bryant, & O'Malley, 2004). (There also was a large group whose well-being was average to begin with and stayed that way.) They then looked to see whether these patterns of well-being over time were related to indicators of individual functioning, by rating whether individuals had been succeeding, maintaining, or stalling as they moved into adulthood (see Table 1, on page 76). Three main findings emerged. First, over 80% of the sample showed great stability in their well-being over the period, consistent with findings from many other studies indicating that psychological functioning in childhood and adolescence is highly predictive of success later in life (e.g., M. J. Shanahan & Bauer, 2004). This is because success in one stage (doing well in high school) usually leads to success in the next stage (getting into a good college), and some basic "resources" predict success throughout the life span—as the old joke goes, if you want to succeed in life, make sure you have a high IQ, money, and good parents (e.g., K. Burt, Obradović, Long, & Masten, 2008). Second, for more than a sixth

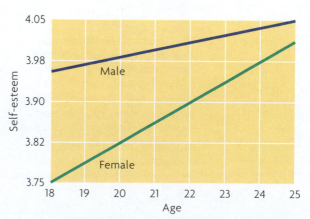

Figure 1 For some, early adulthood is a time of improved mental health, as indicated by decreases in depression and increases in self-esteem. (Galambos et al., 2006)

of the sample, this period was one of substantial change in mental health—about 7% of the sample were well-functioning adolescents whose mental health declined, and another 10% were troubled adolescents who became "exemplary" young adults. Finally, experiences in the domains of work, romance, and citizenship—but not in the domains of school or finances—were especially linked to changes in well-being. Other studies also have found that success in the worlds of work and romance are related to well-being during this time (Galambos et al., 2006).

Has a new stage of life actually arisen? How widespread does a pattern of behavior have to be for us to conclude that a new stage of development has emerged? Does emerging adulthood exist if it is common in Boston or Berkeley, but not in Biloxi, Baghdad, or Beijing? It is hard to say. "Midlife" is a stage that we take for granted in contemporary America but that doesn't exist

Table 1   Descriptions of developmental task domains

Domain	Succeeding	Maintaining	Stalling
Peer involvement	• Goes out two or more times a week for fun and recreation at age 22 and age 26	• Neither succeeding nor stalling	• Goes out one or fewer times a week for fun and recreation at age 22 and age 26
Education	• Graduated from 4-year college by age 26, or • Expected to graduate from 2-year college and received 2-year degree	• Expected to graduate from 4-year college and received 2-year degree, or • Did not expect 2- or 4-year degree and did not receive either degree, or • Expected 2-year degree and did not receive 2-year degree by age 26	• Expected 4-year college degree and did not receive either 2- or 4-year degree by age 26
Work	• No unemployment at age 22 or 26, and • Working 10+ months/year at full-time job by age 26, and • High job confidence at age 26	• Neither succeeding not stalling (e.g., homemaker or otherwise not working and not looking for work outside home)	• Some unemployment at age 22 and/or 26, and • Low job confidence at age 26
Substance abuse avoidance (healthy coping/ lifestyle)	• No substance use at any age (18, 22, 26) [Four indicators of substance use; cigarettes (current use), binge drinking (in past 2 weeks), marijuana (current use), and other illicit drugs (in past 12 months)]	• Some substance use, but less than stalling	• Use of two or more substances at all three ages (18, 22, 26), and/or • Use of three or more substances at age 26
Romantic involvement	• At age 26, married or engaged (with or without cohabitation), and • No divorce history	• At age 26, cohabiting, or • Dating more than once a month, and/or • Divorced, but remarried	• At age 26, not married, not engaged not cohabiting, and • Dating once a month or less
Citizenship	• Three indicators reported at age 22 and age 26: social conscience, charity, and awareness of social/ political events • Measures indicate at least one strong connection at age 22 and at least two strong connections at age 26	• Measures indicate some strong connections but not as frequent as at succeeding level	• Measures indicate no strong connections at age 26
Financial autonomy	• Self and/or spouse providing all resources at age 26	• Some resources come from other than self or spouse (and not stalling)	• At age 26, less than half of support is from self and/or spouse, and/or • Live with parents and receive some financial help (>20%) from them

Source: Schulenberg et al., 2004.

everywhere, or at least, not as we think of it (Schweder, 1998). Nevertheless, the notion that people go through a distinct and unique set of psychological transitions during middle age has become widely accepted (if perhaps less supported by hard evidence than in popular media portrayals).

Clearly, in some parts of the world, and in some segments of society, the transition between adolescence and adulthood has been lengthened—that much is indisputable. More individuals attend college than in previous eras, which delays their entrance into the world of work, and more postpone getting married, which delays their settling into a more stable lifestyle. But whether this means that the psychological functioning of 23-year-olds who follow this pattern of a delayed and prolonged transition is significantly different from that of 23-year-olds who transition from college directly into full-time employment and marriage is anyone's guess, because it hasn't been studied. In other words, whether a *psychological* stage of emerging adulthood really exists has yet to be established (Côté, 2014).

For example, even though the transition into adult work and family roles has been delayed in many segments of society, there is no evidence that this has been accompanied by a comparable prolongation into adulthood of problem behaviors typically associated with late adolescence, such as crime or substance abuse (Hayford & Furstenberg, 2008). In other words, it is entirely possible that economic forces have delayed the transition into *social* adulthood (i.e., the roles that people occupy) but have not affected the transition into *psychological* adulthood.

Changes in Status During Adolescence

Changes in social definition at adolescence typically involve a two-sided modification in the individual's status. On the one hand, the adolescent is given certain privileges and rights that are typically reserved for the society's adult members. On the other hand, this increased power and freedom generally are accompanied by increased expectations for self-management, personal responsibility, and social participation.

Drawing a Legal Boundary

With the attainment of adult status, the young person is often permitted more extensive participation in the community's decision making. In many American Indian groups, such as the Navajo or Apache, it is only after a formal **initiation ceremony** that adolescents are granted adult status (Markstrom, 2011a). In contemporary America, attaining the age of majority brings the right to vote. But along with this increased power usually come new obligations. In most societies, young adults are expected to serve their communities in cases of emergency or need, and in many cultures, training for warfare is often demanded of young people once they attain adult status (Benedict, 1934). On the other hand, in most societies, it is not until adult status is attained that individuals are permitted to participate in certain activities that are reserved for adults. Gambling, purchasing alcoholic beverages, and seeing X-rated films are but three of the many privileges we reserve in America for individuals who have reached the legal age of adulthood.

Once an adolescent is designated as an adult, she or he is also subject to a new set of laws. In some instances, attaining adult status brings with it greater leniency under the law, whereas in others, it is associated with harsher treatment. In the United States, for example, certain activities that are permissible among adults are violations of the law when they are committed by young people. (We use the term **status offense** to refer to a behavior that is problematic because of the young person's *status* as a juvenile.) As a college student, you cannot be legally punished for not showing up for class, as would have been the case if you didn't show up for high school. If you decide you don't want to return home when you are on a break, you don't have to, at least not as far as the law is concerned; in contrast, running away from home during adolescence is against the law in many jurisdictions. Certain crimes, when committed by a minor, are adjudicated in a separate **juvenile justice system,** which operates under different rules and principles than the **criminal justice system** that applies to adults. Although being tried in the juvenile justice system usually results in a less severe sanction than being found guilty of the same crime in adult court, this is not always the case (Kurlychek & Johnson, 2010).

The legal regulation of adolescent behavior in the United States has been quite controversial in recent years. Part of the problem is that development during adolescence is so rapid and so variable between individuals that it is difficult to know at what chronological age a line should be drawn between legally viewing someone as an adult and viewing him or her as a child (Cauffman, Shulman, Bechtold, & Steinberg, 2015). This problem is compounded by the fact that we draw the boundary at different places for different purposes (for example, driving at 16, voting at 18, buying alcohol

initiation ceremony
The formal induction of a young person into adulthood.

status offense
A violation of the law that pertains to minors but not adults.

juvenile justice system
A separate system of courts and related institutions developed to handle juvenile crime and delinquency.

criminal justice system
The system of courts and related institutions developed to handle adult crime.

In the United States, there are many inconsistencies under the law with respect to the treatment of adolescents. Some rulings have viewed young people as having the same rights as adults, whereas others have not. © Cass Gilbert/Image Source RF

at 21, and so on). This inconsistency makes it hard to point to any specific age and say with certainty that there is consensus about where the legal boundary should be drawn. One current controversy is whether new findings from studies of adolescent brain development should influence where we draw these legal lines (Steinberg, 2014).

making the practical connection

At what age do you think we should draw the line between legal adolescence and legal adulthood? Should this age be the same for all activities, or should different activities have different age boundaries?

Adolescents as Criminal Defendants There is especially great disagreement about how we should view and treat young people who commit serious violent offenses (E. Scott & Steinberg, 2008). Are juveniles who commit crimes less blameworthy than adults because they are less able to foresee the consequences of their actions or resist the pressure of others to engage in antisocial activity? Or should we hold adolescents and adults to the same standards of criminal responsibility? If a youngster has committed a violent crime, should he or she be treated as a child (and processed by the legal system as a delinquent) or tried as an adult (and processed as a criminal)? Should young teenagers and adults who are convicted of the same crime receive the same penalties? In 2005, the U.S. Supreme Court raised the age at which individuals can be exposed to the death penalty from 16 to 18 (*Roper v. Simmons,* 2005), and several more recent cases have asked whether it is constitutional to sentence juveniles to life without parole (Cauffman et al., 2015).

One issue that arises in cases in which a juvenile might be tried as an adult is whether the adolescent is competent to stand trial. In the United States, it is not permissible to try someone in a criminal proceeding if the individual does not understand the charges, does not understand the nature of the trial, or is unable to make reasoned decisions about the case (for example, whether to take the stand in his or her own defense). Historically, questions about a defendant's competence to stand trial have been raised only in cases in which the individual is mentally ill or mentally retarded. Now that more and more juveniles are being tried as adults at younger and younger ages, however, experts have asked whether some young defendants may be incompetent to stand trial simply because of cognitive or emotional immaturity (Viljoen, McLachlan, Wingrove, & Penner, 2010). One study of this issue found that about one-third of those aged 13 and younger, and one-fifth of 14- and 15-year-olds, were as impaired in their abilities to serve as a competent defendant as were mentally ill adults who had been found not competent to stand trial (Grisso et al., 2003). Research also indicates that juveniles, even those who are relatively mature, are less likely than adults to understand their rights when being questioned by the police, more likely to confess to a crime than remain silent, and less likely to discuss disagreements about their defense with their attorneys (Redlich, Silverman, & Steiner, 2003; Rogers et al., 2014; Viljoen, Klaver, & Roesch, 2005).

Inconsistencies in Adolescents' Legal Status

Many other issues surrounding the legal status of adolescents in the United States remain vague and confusing (Cauffman et al., 2015). Two U.S. Supreme Court cases indicate just how inconsistent our views of adolescents' status are. In one case, *Hazelwood v. Kuhlmeier,* the Court ruled that a public high school can censor articles written by students for their school newspaper, on the grounds that adolescents are so immature that they need the protection of wiser adults. Yet the same Court also ruled, in *Board of Education v. Mergens,* that students who wanted to form a Bible study group had the right to meet on campus because high school students are mature enough to understand that a school can permit the expression of ideas that it does not necessarily endorse. Similarly, in *Hodgson v. Minnesota,* the Court ruled that, because of their maturity, adolescents do not need to obtain parental consent to get an abortion. Yet the Court also ruled, in *Roper v. Simmons,* that adolescents should not be subject to the death penalty, because their immaturity makes them less responsible for their criminal behavior (and therefore less "punishable") (Cauffman et al., 2015).

There are many other examples of this sort of inconsistency. For example, courts have ruled that teenagers have the right to obtain contraceptives or purchase violent video games without their parents' approval. But they also have upheld laws forbidding adolescents access to cigarettes or to magazines that, although vulgar, are not considered so obscene that they are outlawed among adults (Zimring, 1982). As you know, the age at which adolescents are permitted to engage in various adult behaviors—driving, voting, drinking, viewing R-rated movies, smoking—varies considerably from one domain to the next. Is there a pattern to this inconsistency? In general, legal decisions tend to set the age boundary high when the behavior in question is viewed as potentially damaging to the young person (for example, buying alcohol), but have set the boundary low when the behavior is thought to have potential benefit (for example, having access to contraceptives) (E. Scott & Steinberg, 2008).

The Process of Social Redefinition

Social redefinition during adolescence is not a single event but, like puberty or cognitive maturation, a series of events that often occur over a relatively long time. In contemporary America, the process of redefinition typically begins at age 15 or 16, when people are first permitted to drive and work in the formal labor force. But in most states, the social redefinition of the adolescent continues well into young adulthood. Some privileges of adulthood, such as voting, are not conferred until the age of 18, and others, such as purchasing alcoholic beverages, don't come until the age of 21, 5 or 6 years after the redefinition process begins. Even in societies that mark the social redefinition of the young person with a dramatic and elaborate initiation ceremony, the social transformation from child into adult may span many years, and the initiation ceremony may represent just one element of the process (Markstrom, 2011b). In fact, the initiation ceremony usually marks the beginning of a long period of training and preparation for adulthood, not the adolescent's final passage into adult status.

In many cultures, the social redefinition of young people occurs in groups. The young people of a community are grouped with peers of approximately the same age—a **cohort**—and move through the series of status transitions together. One of the results of such age grouping is that very strong bonds are formed among people who have shared certain rituals. In many American high schools, for example, attempts are made to create class spirit or class unity by fostering bonds among students who will graduate together. In many Latino communities, adolescent girls participate together in an elaborate sort of "coming-out" celebration, called the **quinceañera.** On college campuses, fraternities and sororities may conduct group initiations that involve

Formal rites of passage from adolescence to adulthood are rare in contemporary society. Certain cultural ceremonies—like the quinceañera, a coming-of-age celebration for young women in some Latino communities—are about as close as we come in today's society. © Michael Dwyer/Alamy

difficult or unpleasant tasks, and special ties may be forged between "brothers" or "sisters" who have pledged together.

Common Practices in the Process of Social Redefinition

Although the specific ceremonies, signs, and timetables of social redefinition during adolescence vary from one culture to another, several general themes characterize the process in all societies.

Real or Symbolic Separation from Parents First, social redefinition usually entails the real or symbolic separation of young persons from their parents (Markstrom, 2011b). During late childhood, children in some societies are expected to begin sleeping in households other than their own. Youngsters may spend the day with their parents but spend the night with friends of the family, with relatives, or in a separate residence reserved for preadolescents. In America, during earlier times, it was customary for adolescents to leave home temporarily and live with other families in the community, either to learn specific occupational skills as apprentices or to work as domestic servants (Kett, 1977). In contemporary societies, the separation of adolescents from their parents takes somewhat different forms. They are sent to summer camps, to boarding schools, or, as is more common, to college.

cohort
A group of individuals born during the same general historical era.

quinceañera
An elaborate sort of "coming-out" celebration for adolescent girls that is practiced in many Latino communities.

An Emphasis on Differences Between the Sexes

A second aspect of social redefinition during adolescence entails the accentuation of physical and social differences between males and females (Schlegel & Barry, 1991). This accentuation of differences occurs partly because of the physical changes of puberty and partly because in many cultures adult work and family roles are often highly sex-differentiated. Many societies separate males and females during religious ceremonies, have individuals begin wearing sex-specific articles of clothing (rather than clothing permissible for either gender), and keep males and females apart during initiation ceremonies.

In many non-Western societies today, the privileges extended to males and females once they have reached puberty are so different that adolescence often is an entirely different phenomenon for boys and girls (Larson et al., 2009). Examples of the differential treatment of adolescent boys and girls in non-Western cultures abound, but in general, girls' behavior is more subject to the control of adults, whereas boys are given more freedom and autonomy (Markstrom, 2011b). Girls are expected to remain virgins until marriage, for example, whereas boys' premarital sexual activity is tolerated. Girls are expected to spend time preparing for domestic roles, whereas boys are expected to acquire vocational skills for employment outside the home. And formal schooling is far less available to girls than to boys, especially in rural societies.

The separation of males and females in adolescence is not limited to non-Western societies, though. In earlier times in America (and to a certain extent in many other industrialized societies today), during adolescence, males and females were separated in educational institutions, either by excluding adolescent girls from secondary and higher education, grouping males and females in different schools or different classrooms, or having males and females follow different curricula. In present-day America, many of these practices have been discontinued because of legal rulings prohibiting sex discrimination, but some elements of accentuated sex differentiation and sex segregation during adolescence still exist—for example, in residential arrangements, styles of dress, athletic activities, and household chores. And many contemporary ceremonies designed to recognize the young person's passage into adulthood differentiate between males and females (for example, the **Bar Mitzvah** and the **Bas Mitzvah** ceremonies for Jewish males and females, respectively).

Bar (Bas) Mitzvah
In Judaism, the religious ceremony marking the young person's transition to adulthood.

scarification
The intentional creation of scars on some part or parts of the body, often done as part of an initiation ceremony.

Passing on Information from the Older Generation

A third aspect of social redefinition during adolescence typically entails passing on cultural, historical, and practical information from the adult generation to the newly inducted cohort of young people. This information may concern (1) matters thought to be important to adults but of limited utility to children (for example, information about the performance of certain adult work tasks), (2) matters thought to be necessary for adults but unfit for children (for example, information regarding sex), or (3) matters concerning the history or rituals of the family or community (for example, how to perform certain ceremonies). In traditional societies, initiates are often sent to some sort of "school" in which they are instructed in the productive activities of the community (hunting, fishing, or farming). Following puberty, boys and girls receive instruction about sexual relations, moral behavior, and societal lore (M. Fried & Fried, 1980; N. Miller, 1928).

In contemporary society, too, adolescence is a time of instruction in preparation for adulthood. Elementary school students, for example, are generally not taught a great deal about sexuality, work, or financial matters; such course work is typically reserved for high school students. We also restrict entrance into certain "adult" activities (such as sexually explicit movies) until adolescents are believed old enough to be exposed to them.

Because formal initiation ceremonies are neither very common nor very meaningful in modern society, students sometimes overlook important similarities between the processes of social redefinition in traditional and contemporary societies. Practices like separating children from their parents or **scarification**—the intentional creation of scars on some part or parts of the body, often done as part of an initiation ceremony—may seem alien to us. But if we look beneath the surface, at the meaning and significance of each culture's practices, we find many common threads. In contemporary society, for example, although we do not practice anything as "alien" as scarification, we do have our share of body rituals, many of which are not seen until adolescence and which might seem equally alien to someone unfamiliar with our society: the punching of holes in earlobes or other parts of the body (ear or body piercing), the scraping of hair from faces or legs (shaving), the permanent decoration of skin (tattoos), and the application of brightly colored paints to lips, eyes, and cheeks (putting on makeup).

Variations in Social Transitions

Although the presence of social redefinition in a general sense is a universal feature of adolescent development, there is considerable diversity in the nature of the transition. Examining social redefinition from cross-cultural and historical perspectives provides a valuable means of contrasting the nature of adolescence in different social contexts. Two very important dimensions along which societies differ in the process of social redefinition are in the explicitness, or *clarity,* of the transition and in the smoothness, or *continuity,* of the passage.

Variations in Clarity

Because initiation ceremonies are in many ways religious ceremonies, they are most often found in societies in which a shared religious belief unites the community and structures individuals' daily experiences. Universal, formal initiation ceremonies therefore have never been prevalent in U.S. society, largely because of the cultural diversity of the population and the general separation of religious experience from everyday affairs.

There are, however, factors other than the presence of formal rites of passage that determine how clear the transition into adult status is to young persons and to society. One such factor concerns the extent to which various aspects of the transition to adulthood occur at about the same time for individuals and during the same general period for adolescents growing up together (Elder, 1980). When transitions into adult work, family, and citizenship roles occur close in time, and when most members of a cohort experience these transitions at about the same age, the passage into adulthood has greater clarity. If all young people were to graduate from high school, enter the labor force, and marry at the age of 18, this age would be an implicit boundary between adolescence and adulthood, even without a formal ceremony. When different aspects of the passage occur at different times, and when adolescents growing up in a similar environment experience these transitions in different order and along different schedules, the boundary between adolescence and adulthood is cloudier.

The Clarity of Social Redefinition in Contemporary Society   When did you become an adolescent? When did you (or when will you) become an adult? If you are like most individuals in contemporary society, your answers to these questions will not be clear-cut. In one study of Danish youth, for example, when asked if they felt like adults, most 17- to 24-year-olds and nearly half of 25- to 29-year-olds answered that they were adults in some ways but not in others (Arnett & Padilla-Walker, 2015). In modern society, we have no formal ceremonies marking the transition from childhood into adolescence, nor do we have any way to mark the passage from adolescence into adulthood. Although in many religious, cultural, and social groups, the young American adolescent may undergo an initiation ceremony of sorts—the confirmation, the Bar or Bas Mitzvah, and the quinceañera are some examples—rarely does such a rite have much significance outside the youngster's family, circle of friends, or religious community. School graduation ceremonies perhaps come the closest to universal rites of passage in contemporary society, but school graduation

There are very few formal rites of passage in modern society, although in many religions, there are ceremonies that signify coming of age, like the Bar or Bas Mitzvah ceremony in Judiasm. © Comstock Images RF

doesn't bring with it many meaningful or universal changes in social status, responsibilities, or privileges.

As a result, social redefinition in contemporary society does not give adolescents any clear indication of when their responsibilities and privileges as an adult begin. As we noted earlier, laws governing the age at which individuals can and cannot do "adult" activities are inconsistent (Steinberg, 2014). In many states, for example, the age for starting employment is 15; for driving, 16; for attending restricted (R-rated) movies without parents, 17; for voting, 18; and for drinking, 21. In some states, the age at which someone can be tried as an adult for a serious violent crime is as low as 10 (Hartney, 2006).

In short, we have few universal markers of adulthood—adolescents are treated as adults at different times by different people in different contexts. A young person may be legally old enough to drive, but his parents may feel that 16 is too early and may refuse to let him use the family car. Another may be treated like an adult at work, where she works side by side with people three times her age, but be treated like a child at home. A third may be viewed as an adult by her mother but as a child by her father. The same young person whom we send into combat is not permitted to buy beer, even though combat is far more dangerous than drinking. It is little wonder, in light of the mixed and sometimes contradictory expectations facing young people, that for many adolescents the transition into adult roles is sometimes a confusing passage.

Adolescents' Views of Themselves   Because contemporary society does not send clear or consistent messages to young people about when adolescence ends and adulthood begins, young people living within the same society can have widely varying views of their own social status and beliefs about age-appropriate behavior. For this reason, it is instructive to ask people what they think defines the transition to adulthood, as a way of gauging the way in which adult status is conceptualized by the broader society. Studies of how people define adulthood in contemporary society indicate three interesting trends (Arnett, 1998).

First, in modern society, at least in the United States and Canada, adolescents place relatively less emphasis than they do in traditional societies on attaining specific roles (for example, worker, spouse, parent) as defining characteristics of adulthood and relatively more on the development of various character traits indicative of self-reliance (for example, being responsible, independent, or self-controlled) (Kenyon, Rankin, Koerner, & Dennison, 2007). Parents of young people similarly emphasize psychosocial maturity as the defining feature of reaching adulthood (E. Nelson et al., 2007).

Consistent with this, in one study of individuals ages 17 to 29, the best predictor of subjective age—that is, what age they *felt* they were, regardless of how old they actually were—was their level of psychosocial maturity (Galambos, Turner, & Tilton-Weaver, 2005). Among contemporary American youths, for instance, "accepting responsibility for one's self" is the most frequently mentioned criterion for being an adult. Of the role-related transitions viewed as important among contemporary youth, being able to support oneself financially is the most important defining criterion of adulthood (Arnett, 1998). Perhaps for this reason, less than one-third of college undergraduates see themselves unambiguously as adults.

Second, over time, there has been a striking decline in the importance of family roles—marriage and parenthood—as defining features of what it means to be an adult. In early American society, the role of head of household was an especially important indicator of adult status for males, and taking on the roles of wife and mother defined adulthood for females. In surveys of contemporary youth, though, when they are asked whether certain accomplishments are necessary for an individual to be considered an adult, only 17% of the respondents say that being married is necessary, and just 14% say that it is necessary to become a parent (Arnett, 1998).

Finally, the defining criteria of adulthood have become more or less the same for males and females in contemporary industrialized society, unlike the case in traditional societies or during previous eras. In nonindustrialized cultures, the requirements for male adulthood were to be able to "provide, protect, and procreate," whereas for females, the requirements for adulthood were to care for children and run a household (Markstrom, 2011b). Contemporary youth, in contrast, view the various indicators of adult status as equally important (or equally unimportant) for males and females (Arnett, 1998).

Given the absence of clear criteria that define adult status in contemporary societies, it is not surprising that, among people of the same age, some may feel older than their peers, while others may feel younger. How old an adolescent feels affects his or her behavior. Adolescents who feel older spend more time with other-sex peers, feel more autonomous, and engage in more problem behavior (Galambos, Kolaric, Sears, & Maggs, 1999). Psychologists have been interested in changes in individuals' subjective age and, more specifically, in when individuals make the transition from feeling older than they really are (as most teenagers do), to feeling younger than they really are (as most adults do) (Galambos et al., 2005). Studies of North American youth have found that this shift takes place around age 25, among both males and females.

The Clarity of Social Redefinition in Traditional Cultures Unlike the case in contemporary society, social redefinition during adolescence is very clear in most traditional cultures. Typically, the passage from childhood into adolescence is marked by a formal initiation ceremony, which publicly proclaims the young person's assumption of a new position in the community (Markstrom, 2011b). For boys, such ceremonies may take place at puberty, at a designated chronological age, or at a time when the community decides that the individual is ready for the status change. For girls, initiation is more often linked to puberty and, in particular, to the onset of menstruation. In both cases, the initiation ceremony serves to ritualize the passing of the young person out of childhood and, if not directly into adulthood, into a period of training for it.

In many initiation ceremonies, the adolescent's physical appearance is changed, so that other members of the community can distinguish between initiated and uninitiated young people. For example, new types of clothing may be worn following initiation, or some sort of surgical operation or scarification may be performed to create a permanent means of marking the individual's adult status. Unlike the case in contemporary society, where we often can't tell who is a juvenile and who is an adult by physical appearance alone (and where adults are often upset by images of preadolescents that are too adultlike), in most traditional societies, there is no mistaking which individuals are adults and which are still children. In most modern industrialized societies, we have grown accustomed to seeing teenagers who try to dress like adults, and adults who try to dress like teenagers, but such a state of affairs would be highly uncommon in traditional cultures.

The Circumcision Controversy One practice involving the physical transformation of the adolescent that has generated a great deal of controversy is circumcision. **Circumcision** is a procedure in which some part of the genitals is cut and permanently altered. There are important differences between male and female circumcision. In the United States, male circumcision, in which the foreskin around the penis is removed during infancy, is very common and is performed both for religious reasons (mainly among Jews) and for health reasons, because male circumcision is associated with decreased risk of urinary tract infections and sexually transmitted diseases, including HIV infection. There is no evidence that men are harmed emotionally by being circumcised, and complications from the procedure are minimal and far fewer than the health risks associated with not being circumcised (Tobian et al., 2009).

Female circumcision, or **female genital mutilation,** which involves the cutting or removal of the clitoris and, often, the labia, is rarely practiced outside of North Africa (where, in some countries, such as Mali, Somalia, and Egypt, virtually all women have been circumcised, usually during childhood or preadolescence). Unlike male circumcision, female circumcision has no associated health benefits and carries many risks, including infection and chronic pain during urination, menstruation, and intercourse. After circumcision, it is virtually impossible for a woman to achieve an orgasm during sex (Althaus, 1997). Many international groups, citing female circumcision as a human rights violation, have called for a worldwide prohibition against the practice.

The Clarity of Social Redefinition in Previous Eras

What is the transition to adulthood like today? Well, compared to what? We often use the **baby boom** generation—individuals who were adolescents in the late 1950s and 1960s—as an implicit point of comparison when characterizing today's young people, perhaps because the baby boom generation has provided the basis for so many of the images of modern family life that are deeply embedded in our cultural psyche. (How often

have you heard someone use the television show *Leave It to Beaver,* which ran from 1957 to 1963, as a comparison point in discussions of family life?) But the baby boomers' transition to adulthood was highly unusual in many respects. Let's compare life today with life in 1960, during the middle of *Leave It to Beaver*'s run on television, as an example:

- In 1960, the average age of marriage was 20 for women and 22 for men; today, it is 27 and 29, respectively (U.S. Census Bureau, 2014).

- In 1960, fewer than 10% of young adults between the ages of 25 and 34 lived with their parents; in 2014, close to 15% did (U.S. Census Bureau, 2014) (see Figure 2). Within this age group, living with one's parents is more common among younger, less educated, and non-White individuals (Hallquist, Cuthbertson, Killeya-Jones, Halpern, & Harris, 2011).

- In 1960, a very high proportion of adolescents went directly from high school into full-time employment or the military, and only one-third of American high school graduates went directly to college; today, about two-thirds of high school graduates go directly to college (National Center for Education Statistics, 2015).

In other words, in 1960, three key elements of the transition to adulthood—getting married, moving out of the parents' home, and completing one's education—all occurred relatively early compared to today, and all took place within a fairly constricted time frame. By that standard, today's transition to adulthood looks excessively long and vaguely defined. Indeed, one recent

circumcision
A procedure in which some part of the genitals is cut and permanently altered.

female genital mutilation
The cutting or removal of the clitoris, performed in some cultures as part of the initiation of female adolescents.

baby boom
The period following World War II, during which the number of infants born was extremely large.

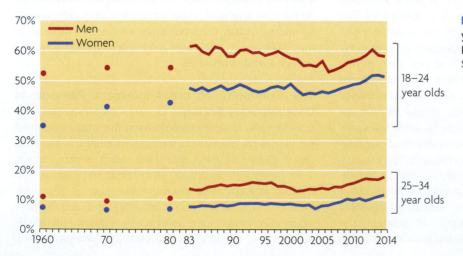

Figure 2   **The proportion of young adults who live at home has continued to increase.**
Source: United States Census Bureau

Contrasts are often drawn between adolescence today and adolescence in the 1950s, as portrayed in shows like Leave it to Beaver. *This is probably not the best point of comparison, though, because the 1950s was a very unusual time. The long passage into adulthood characteristic of adolescence today actually shares much in common with adolescence at the beginning of the twentieth century.* © PF1 WENN Photos/Newscom

study of patterns of schooling, work, romance, and residence during emerging adulthood found that individuals frequently move back and forth between periods of independence and dependence. This suggests that the progression from adolescence to adulthood today not only is long but also occurs in fits and starts (P. K. Cohen, Chen, Hartmark, & Gordon, 2003). It's little wonder that 60% of people in their mid-20s today don't know whether they are adolescents or adults.

Compared to the situation 50 or 60 years ago, then, today's transition to adulthood is long and rocky. But the transition into adulthood was just as disorderly and prolonged during the nineteenth century as it is today (Kett, 1977). Many young people at that time moved back and forth between school, where they were viewed as children, and work, where they were viewed as adults.

Moreover, timetables for the assumption of adult roles varied considerably from one individual to the next, because they were highly dependent on family and household needs rather than on generally accepted age patterns of school, family, and work transitions. An adolescent might have been working and living away from home, but if his family needed him—because, let's say, someone became ill—he would leave his job and move back in with his parents. During the middle of the nineteenth century, in fact, many young people were neither enrolled in school nor working, occupying a halfway stage that was not quite childhood but not quite adulthood, either (M. Katz, 1975).

At the beginning of the twentieth century, the transition to adulthood actually was very drawn out. Age at first marriage was just about the same among males at the turn of the twentieth century (26) as it is today (29), although age at first marriage among females is much older today (27) than it was a century ago (22) (U.S. Census Bureau, 2014). And the proportion of 25- to 34-year-olds living at home was much higher early in the twentieth century than it was during the 1950s (Parker, 2012). At least in industrialized societies, the brief and clear transition into adulthood experienced by many baby boomers in the mid–twentieth century was the exception, not the rule. It's important not to lose sight of that. Although the notion of "emerging adulthood" may ring true today, it is by no means a new phenomenon. The label didn't exist 150 years ago, but young people then shared a great deal in common with today's emerging adults.

Variations in Continuity

The process of social redefinition also varies across cultural and historical contexts along the dimension of *continuity*—the extent to which the adolescent's transition into adulthood is gradual or abrupt. Gradual transitions, in which the adolescent assumes the roles and status of adulthood bit by bit, are referred to as **continuous transitions.**

Transitions that are not so smooth, in which the young person's entrance into adulthood is more sudden, are referred to as **discontinuous transitions.** For example, children who grow up working on the family farm and continue this work as adults have a continuous transition into adult work roles. In contrast, children who do not have any work experience while they are growing up and who enter the labor force for the first time when they graduate from college have a discontinuous transition into adult work roles.

The Continuity of the Adolescent Passage in Contemporary Society In contemporary society, we tend to exclude young people from the world of adults; we give them little direct training for adult life and then thrust them abruptly into total adult independence. Transitions into adulthood in contemporary industrialized society are more discontinuous than in other cultural or historical contexts. Consider, for example, three of the most important roles of adulthood that individuals are expected to carry out successfully—worker, parent,

continuous transitions
Passages into adulthood in which adult roles and statuses are entered into gradually.

discontinuous transitions
Passages into adulthood in which adult roles and statuses are entered into abruptly.

and citizen. Adolescents in contemporary society receive little prior preparation for any of these positions.

For instance, young people are segregated from the workplace throughout most of their childhood and early adolescent years, and they receive little direct training in school relevant to the work roles they will likely find themselves in as adults. The sorts of jobs available to teenagers today, such as working the counter of a fast-food restaurant, bear little resemblance to the jobs most of them will hold as adults. The transition into adult work roles, therefore, is fairly discontinuous for most young people in industrialized society, and, according to many employers, a high proportion of young people leave school without adequate preparation for the workplace.

The transition into adult family roles is even more abrupt than the transition into work roles. Before actually becoming parents, most young people have little training in child rearing or other related matters. Families are relatively small today, and youngsters are likely to be close in age to their siblings; as a result, few opportunities exist for participating in child care activities at home. Schools generally offer little, if any, instruction in family relationships and domestic activities. And with childbirth generally taking place in hospitals rather than at home, few young people today have the opportunity of observing a younger sibling's birth.

Passage into adult citizenship and decision-making roles is also highly discontinuous in contemporary Western society. Adolescents are permitted few opportunities for independence and autonomy in school and are segregated from most of society's political institutions until they complete their formal education. Young people are permitted to vote once they turn 18, but they receive little preparation for participation in government and community roles prior to this time. In the United States, for example, we require foreigners who wish to become citizens to understand the workings of the American government, but no such familiarity is required of individuals in order to graduate from high school.

Instead of being gradually socialized into work, family, and citizenship roles, adolescents in modern society typically are segregated from activities in these arenas during most of their childhood and youth. Yet young people are expected to perform these roles capably when they become adults. With little experience in meaningful work, adolescents are expected to find, get, and keep a job immediately after completing their schooling. With essentially no training for marriage or parenting, they are expected to form their own families, manage their own households, and raise their own children soon after they reach adulthood. And without any previous involvement in community activities, they are expected on reaching the age of majority to vote, file their taxes, and behave as responsible citizens.

The Continuity of the Adolescent Passage in Traditional Cultures   The high level of discontinuity found in contemporary America is not characteristic of adolescence in traditional societies. Consider the socialization of young people in Samoa, described in detail by the late anthropologist Margaret Mead in her classic book *Coming of Age in Samoa* (1928/1978). From early childhood on, the Samoan youngsters she observed were involved in work tasks that have a meaningful connection to the work they will perform as adults. They participated in the care of younger children, in the planting and harvesting of crops, and in the gathering and preparation of food. Their entrance into adult work roles was gradual and continuous, with work tasks being graded to their skills and intelligence. They were charged with the socialization of their infant brothers and sisters, particularly during middle childhood, when they are not yet strong enough to make a substantial contribution to the community's fishing and farming. Gradually, they were taught the fundamentals of weaving, boating, fishing, building, and farming. By the time they reached late adolescence, Samoan youngsters were well trained in the tasks they would need to perform as adults.

Such continuity is generally the case in societies in which hunting, fishing, and farming are the chief work activities. As Mead observed, the emphasis in these societies is on informal education in context rather than on formal education in schools. Children are typically not isolated in separate educational institutions, and they accompany the adult members of their community in daily activities. Adolescents' preparation for adulthood, therefore, comes largely from observation and hands-on experience in the same tasks that they will carry out as adults. Typically, boys learn the tasks performed by adult men, and girls learn those performed by adult women. When work activities take adults out of the community, it is not uncommon for children to accompany their parents on these expeditions (N. Miller, 1928).

As several writers have pointed out, modernization and globalization have made the transition from adolescence to adulthood longer and increasingly more discontinuous all over the world (Larson et al., 2009; Tomasik & Silbereisen, 2011). As successful participation in the workforce increasingly has come to require formal education, parents have become less able to provide their children with advice on how best to prepare for adulthood. Increasingly, school, rather than hands-on experience in the workplace, is how individuals all over the world are expected to prepare for adult work (National Research Council, 2005). How these changes are affecting the psychological development of young people in developing countries is a question that researchers are only now beginning to examine. It is very likely, however, that many of the familiar psychological struggles that have up until now been characteristic of adolescence in modern, industrialized societies—developing a sense of identity, choosing among occupational alternatives, stressing out over getting into a good college, and renegotiating relationships with one's parents, to name just three—are becoming more common among young people all over the world. Ironically, then, at the same time that cross-cultural research on adolescents has expanded dramatically, the nature of adolescence has become more and more similar around the world. In research my colleagues and I have been conducting in a diverse array of countries in Europe, Asia, Africa, and the Americas, we have been surprised at how similar patterns of development are across these very different cultural contexts (Steinberg, 2014).

making the cultural connection

Globalization is changing the face of adolescence all over the world, but many experts believe that it has been a mixed blessing for many developing countries. With respect to young people, what are some of the pros and cons of the increasing integration of various countries and cultures into a more global society?

The Continuity of the Adolescent Passage in Previous Eras During earlier periods in American history, the transition into adult roles and responsibilities began at a younger age and proceeded along a more continuous path than it is today. This is especially true with regard to work. During the eighteenth and the early nineteenth century, when many families were engaged in farming, many adolescents were expected to work on the family farm and learn the skills necessary to carry on the enterprise after their parents became elderly. Boys often accompanied their fathers on business trips, learning the nuances of salesmanship and commerce (Kett, 1977)—a pattern reminiscent of that found in many traditional societies.

Many other young people left home relatively early— some as early as age 12—to work for nonfamilial adults in the community or in nearby villages (M. Katz, 1975; Kett, 1977). In the mid-nineteenth century, young adolescents commonly worked as apprentices, learning skills and trades; others left home temporarily to work as servants or to learn domestic skills. The average nineteenth-century youngster in Europe or America left school well before the age of 15 (Chisholm & Hurrelmann, 1995; Modell, Furstenberg, & Hershberg, 1976).

Although adolescents of 100 years ago took on full-time employment earlier in life than they typically do today, they were likely to live under adult supervision for a longer period than today's youth. Although the transition into work roles may have occurred at a younger age in the nineteenth century than in the twentieth, this transition was made in the context of semi-independence rather than complete emancipation (M. Katz, 1975; Kett, 1977; Modell & Goodman, 1990). This semi-independent period—which for many young people lasted from about 12 to 22, and often beyond—may have increased the degree of continuity of the passage into adulthood by providing a time during which young people could assume certain adult responsibilities gradually (M. Katz, 1975). By 1900, the semi-independence characteristic of adolescence in the nineteenth century had largely disappeared (Modell & Goodman, 1990). Despite the complaints today of many social commentators (and many college graduates) about the increasing prevalence of unpaid internships as a bridge between college and full-time paid employment (e.g., Kamenetz, 2006), this transitional pathway into the world of adult work today is actually pretty similar to what existed in the nineteenth century.

Socialization for family and citizenship roles may also have been more continuous in previous eras. Living at home during the late-adolescent and early-adult years, particularly in the larger families characteristic of households 100 years ago, contributed to the preparation of young people for future family life. It was common for the children in a family to span a wide age range, and remaining at home undoubtedly placed the older adolescent from time to time in child-rearing roles. As opposed to today's adolescents, who typically have little experience with infants, adolescents 100 years ago were more likely to have fed, dressed, and cared for their younger siblings. They were also expected to assist their parents in maintaining the household (Modell et al., 1976), which no doubt benefited young people when they eventually established a home separate from their parents.

Current Trends in Home Leaving Recent reports of trends in home leaving suggest that this aspect of the transition into adulthood may be changing in many industrialized countries. On average, individuals are living with their parents longer today than in recent years. More than 55% of all Americans ages 18 to 24 (about 60% of males, and about 50% of females) either live with or are supported by their parents (U.S. Census Bureau, 2014). Most experts attribute this to the increased costs of housing and transportation, which make it difficult for individuals to move out of their parents' home (or give up their parents' financial support) and establish a separate residence and the increase in the proportion of high school graduates who attend college (and rely on their parents' support for this). A similar trend is evident in Europe, although the proportion of young adults who live with their parents varies considerably from country to country (Eurostat, 2010). One potentially positive consequence of the increase in young adults living at home is that the usual rise in alcohol and drug use seen when adolescents go off to college (Fromme, Corbin, & Kruse, 2008) is not nearly as great when individuals continue to live with their parents (White, Fleming,

Changes in the economy have led many young adults to move back in with their parents. © Matelly/Getty Images RF

Kim, Catalano, & McMorris, 2008) (see Figure 3). The presence of parents tends to put a damper on partying.

How living with their parents in late adolescence affects psychological development and mental health likely depends on the extent to which this experience is seen as normative. But even in the United States, where a premium is placed on becoming independent from one's parents, about half of all young adults living at home report that it has not affected their relationships with their parents one way or the other, and one-quarter actually say that their relationship has improved (Parker, 2012). One study of European youth found that those who lived at home longer remained closer to their parents throughout adulthood (Leopold, 2012). Among Asian and Hispanic young adults in particular, who are more likely to have been raised in a culture that places special importance on family obligations, living with one's parents in late adolescence and early adulthood may be characterized by especially positive feelings and close family relationships (Fuligni & Pedersen, 2002).

The impact of the economy on adolescents' home leaving reaffirms the importance of looking at the broader context in defining what "normal" adolescence is. In 1960, because it was the exception for adolescents to live

at home past high school, we tended to view individuals who did so as being less independent or less mature than their peers. But now that living at home has become the norm, we no longer view it as a sign of immaturity. Above all, we need to keep in mind that, because adolescence is in part defined by society, its nature changes along with society (Tomasik & Silbereisen, 2012).

Historic events, such as the Great Recession in the first decade of this century, the 2003 war in Iraq, and Hurricane Katrina, may temporarily alter the nature of the adolescent passage. For instance, studies show that adolescents who were exposed to Hurricane Katrina showed symptoms of exposure to stress that persisted significantly longer than is usually the case (McLaughlin et al., 2010; Robertson, Stein, & Schaefer-Rohleder, 2010; Rowe, La Greca, & Alexandersson, 2010; Weems, Taylor, Cannon, Marino et al., 2010). It will be interesting to see how the dramatic economic downturn that took place in 2009 altered the nature of the transition into adulthood and, if so, whether this affected adolescents' psychological development. It is not yet clear whether this crisis forced young people to grow up faster (because their families needed their help) or, alternatively, actually slowed their development (because economic conditions limited opportunities to enter the labor force and establish independent residences).

The Transition Into Adulthood in Contemporary Society

We do not know for certain whether today's prolonged and discontinuous passage into adulthood impedes or

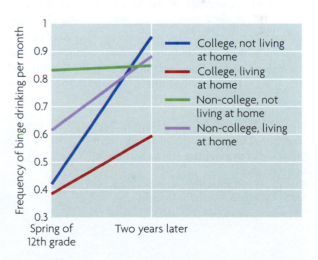

Figure 3 The frequency of binge drinking more than doubles when high school seniors go off to college and move out of their parents' home. In contrast, there is very little change in binge drinking after high school graduation among non-college youth or among college students who continue to live with their parents. (White et al., 2008)

enhances adolescents' psychosocial development. Much probably depends on whether the adolescent has access to the resources necessary for such a protracted transition, especially when jobs are scarce and the cost of housing is high. Indeed, many commentators have noted that there is not one transition into adulthood in contemporary America, but three very different transitions: one for the "haves," one for the "have-nots," and one for those who are somewhere in between (Furstenberg, 2006). Growing income inequality, not only in the United States, but around the world, is furthering this trend (Steinberg, 2014).

As we look to the future, we can point to two specific societal trends that are reshaping the nature of the transition from adolescence to adulthood (Mortimer & Larson, 2002). First, as I have noted throughout this chapter, the length of the transitional period is increasing. As the labor force continues to shift toward jobs that demand more and more formal education, the amount of time individuals need to spend as economically dependent students will increase, which will delay their assumption of all sorts of adult roles, including family roles. One of the reasons that individuals are marrying at a later age today is that it takes longer to accumulate enough wealth to establish a separate residence or start a family. Another is that the progress made by young women in higher education and in the labor force has encouraged more of them to delay getting married to devote attention to their careers before starting a family. The continuing decline in the age of puberty is also lengthening adolescence. Today, the transition between childhood and adulthood takes longer than it did in the past century. Tomorrow, it will take even longer.

Second, as success in the labor force comes to be more and more dependent on formal education, the division between the "haves"—those who have access to money, schools, and information technology—and "have-nots"—those who are poor, less well educated, and cut off from important resources, will grow. This division

will be seen not only between wealthy and poor countries but, increasingly, between the affluent and the poor within countries, because globalization, for all its potentially positive features, contributes to income inequality (Tomasik & Silbereisen, 2011). As the economies of developing countries improve, the importance of formal education increases, which then further separates the life conditions of the educated and the uneducated, a pattern seen vividly today in countries like China and India.

One extremely important international trend concerns different birthrates in different parts of the world: Because the birthrate in poor and developing countries is so much higher than it is in wealthy nations, the distribution of the world's adolescents is changing dramatically. As we move further into the twenty-first century, relatively fewer and fewer of the world's teenagers will come from affluent parts of the world, and relatively more and more will live in impoverished countries (Larson et al., 2009) (Figure 4).

Special Transitional Problems of Poor and Minority Youth

No discussion of the transitional problems of young people in America today would be complete without noting that youngsters from some minority groups—Black, Hispanic, and American Indian youth, in particular—have more trouble negotiating the transition into adulthood than do their White and Asian counterparts. This is due to many factors, including poverty, discrimination, segregation, and disproportionate involvement with the justice system (Iselin, Mulvey, Loughran, Chung, & Mulvey, 2012; Neblett, Gaskin, Lee, & Carter, 2011; McLoyd et al., 2009).

Youngsters from minority backgrounds make up a substantial and growing portion of the adolescent population in America. At the beginning of this century, about two-thirds of American adolescents were White. Today,

Figure 4   The projected growth of the world's adolescent population will occur primarily in developing and in less developed nations.
Source: United Nations, Department of Economic and Social Affairs, Population Division

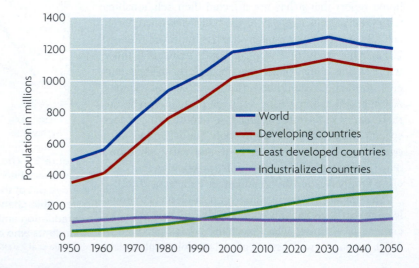

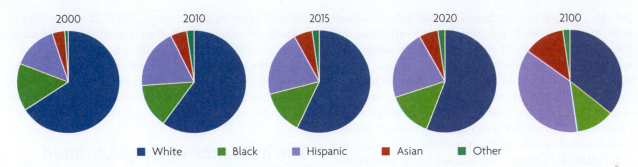

| 2000 | 2010 | 2015 | 2020 | 2100 |

■ White ■ Black ■ Hispanic ■ Asian ■ Other

Figure 5 The ethnic composition of the United States will continue to change dramatically over the twenty-first century. (Federal Interagency Forum on Child and Family Statistics, 2005)

about 22% of American adolescents are Hispanic, 14% Black, 6% Asian or Pacific Islanders, 3% biethnic youth, and 1% American Indian and Native Alaskan youth. In other words, about 45% of American adolescents are from ethnic minority groups. By the end of this century, the U.S. Census Bureau estimates that nearly two-thirds of American adolescents will be non-White and that Hispanic adolescents will be the largest ethnic group in the country (see Figure 5).

Many American adolescents were not born in the United States, of course. One curiosity within studies of ethnic minority youth and the transition to adulthood concerns the better-than-expected mental health and school performance of immigrant adolescents in the United States. For reasons not entirely understood, foreign-born adolescent immigrants generally have better mental health, exhibit less problem behavior, and perform better in school than do adolescents from the same ethnic group who are native-born Americans (Fuligni, Hughes, & Way, 2009; Lansford, 2011). Indeed, one of the most interesting findings to emerge from research on immigrant adolescents is that their "Americanization" appears to be associated with worse, not better, outcomes.

The Effects of Poverty on the Transition Into Adulthood

Of all the factors that may impair youngsters' ability to move easily from adolescence into adulthood, poverty is at the top of the list (Yoshikawa, Aber, & Beardslee, 2012). Poverty is associated with failure in school, unemployment, delinquency, and teen pregnancy, all of which contribute to transitional difficulties (Guldi, Page, & Stevens, 2007; McLoyd et al., 2009). Because minority youngsters are more likely than other teenagers to grow up in poverty, they are also more likely to encounter transitional problems during middle and late adolescence.

Experiencing poverty during adolescence has an especially negative effect on adolescents' school achievement (Kendig, Mattingly, & Bianchi, 2014; McLoyd et al., 2009). Poverty impedes the transition to adulthood

among all teenagers, regardless of race, of course; but because minority youth are more likely to grow up poor, they are also more likely to have transition problems. As you will see in later chapters, school dropout rates are much higher among Hispanic and American Indian teenagers than among other groups, and college enrollment is lower among Black, Hispanic, and American Indian youth. In addition, unemployment is much higher among Black, Hispanic, and American Indian teenagers; Black and Hispanic youth are more likely to be victimized by crime and exposed to violence; and rates of out-of-wedlock births are higher among Black and Hispanic teenagers than among White teenagers. All these factors disrupt the transition into adulthood by limiting individuals' economic and occupational success.

What Can be Done to Ease the Transition?

A variety of suggestions have been offered for making the transition into adulthood smoother for all young

A variety of psychological and social problems are more common among adolescents who grow up amidst poverty.
© Tyrone Turner/Getty Images

people, including restructuring secondary education, expanding work and volunteer opportunities, and improving the quality of community life for adolescents and their parents. Some have suggested that adolescents be encouraged to spend time in voluntary, nonmilitary service activities—such as staffing day care centers, working with the elderly, or cleaning up the environment—for a few years after high school graduation so that they can learn responsibility and adult roles (McLellan & Youniss, 2003; Sherrod & Lauckhardt, 2009). Still others have pointed out that adolescents cannot come of age successfully without the help of adults, and that programs are needed to strengthen families and communities and to bring adolescents into contact with adult mentors (Burt & Paysnick, 2012; Farruggia, Bullen, & Davidson, 2013). Overall, most experts agree that a comprehensive approach to the problem is needed and that such an approach must simultaneously address the educational, employment, interpersonal, and health needs of adolescents from all walks of life (Balsano, Theokas, & Bobek, 2009).

Mentoring There has been growing interest in mentoring programs for at-risk adolescents, many of whom have few relationships with positive adult role models (Hurd, Varner, & Rowley, 2012; Rhodes, 2004). Adolescents who lack positive adult role models are more likely to have psychological and behavioral problems (Bryant & Zimmerman, 2003; K. F. Parker & Reckdenwald, 2008).

Mentoring programs seek to pair adults with young people through community or school-based efforts designed to facilitate positive youth development, improve academic achievement, and deter antisocial behavior. Evaluations of mentoring programs indicate that they have a small, positive effect on youth development. Adolescents who have been mentored are less likely to have problems in school and at home, less likely to use drugs and alcohol, and less likely to get into trouble with the law (Hurd, Sánchez, Zimmerman, & Caldwell, 2012; Rhodes & Lowe, 2009). Not surprisingly, the impact of mentoring varies as a function of characteristics of the mentor, the young person, and their relationship (Fruiht & Wray-Lake, 2013; Rhodes & Lowe, 2009). Mentoring appears to have the most beneficial effects on adolescents whose other relationships are good, but not great (perhaps because the ones with great other relationships didn't need the mentoring as much and because the ones with poor ones did not have the social skills to profit from the mentoring) (Schwartz, Rhodes, Chan, & Herrera, 2011). In general, mentoring tends to be more successful when the mentor maintains a steady presence in the youth's life over an extended period (at least 2 years), has frequent contact with the youngster, and involves the adolescent in a wide range of recreational, social, and practical activities (Schwartz,

Rhodes, Spencer, & Grossman, 2013). It is important to note, however, that although mentoring may benefit adolescents, other influences in their lives are also important, and mentoring alone is not sufficient to meet the needs of at-risk youth (DuBois & Silverthorn, 2005). One potentially important influence, to which we now turn, is the neighborhood in which the adolescent lives.

The Influence of Neighborhood Conditions on Adolescent Development

One factor contributing to the especially worrisome situation of poor and minority youth in the United States is that poverty has become much more concentrated over the past 40 years, with greater and greater clustering of poor families into economically and racially segregated communities. In response to this, a number of researchers have studied the ways in which neighborhoods influence adolescent development (T. Leventhal, Dupéré, & Brooks-Gunn, 2009). Although other characteristics of neighborhoods in addition to poverty potentially can affect adolescents' development (for example, the ethnic composition, crime rate, or availability of social service programs), far more is known about the effects of poverty than about any other neighborhood factor. Exposure to neighborhood poverty is an especially prevalent problem among non-White adolescents (Chauhan, Reppucci, & Turkheimer, 2009; Gudiño, Nadeem, Kataoka, & Lau, 2011).

Studying neighborhood influences on adolescent development is tricky business. We know that growing up in a very poor household increases adolescents' risks for all sorts of problems. But because poor families tend to live in poor neighborhoods, it is not always easy to separate the effects of *neighborhood* disadvantage from the effects of *family* disadvantage. To do this, researchers compare adolescents whose family situations are similar, but who live in very different types of neighborhoods. This is not always easy to do—as you can imagine, few affluent families live in poor neighborhoods, and few poor families live in affluent ones.

There is also the problem of cause and effect. If families in a good neighborhood seem to be functioning better than families in a poor one, it might simply reflect the fact that better-functioning families choose to live in better neighborhoods (rather than indicate that the neighborhood actually influenced family functioning) (Boyle, Georgiades, Racine, & Mustard, 2007). There have been a few experiments in which the researchers took this into account, by randomly assigning families from poor neighborhoods to either remain where they were living or be relocated into more advantaged neighborhoods, and then tracking the psychological development and behavior of adolescents in the two groups. These studies

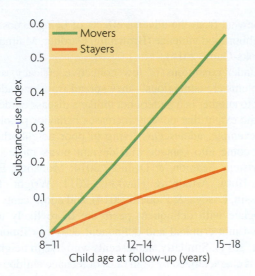

Figure 6 Contrary to expectation, in an experiment designed to study neighborhood effects, poor adolescents whose families were moved to more affluent neighborhoods increased their use of alcohol and illicit drugs. (Fauth et al., 2007)

have found mixed effects of relocation, with some studies showing positive effects, others showing no effect, and some actually showing negative effects (J. R. Kling, Ludwig, & Katz, 2005; T. Leventhal, Fauth, & Brooks-Gunn, 2005; Osypuk et al., 2012; Sharkey & Sampson, 2010) (see Figure 6). To complicate things further, some of these experiments have found that moving to a more affluent neighborhood tends to have a more positive effect on girls than boys (Clampet-Lundquist, Edin, Kling, & Duncan, 2011). Other studies have found similarly puzzling results. For example, one analysis of changes in the level of neighborhood poverty found that adolescents in high-poverty neighborhoods that changed for the better over time were *more* likely to show increases in problems than those whose neighborhoods did not, but that the opposite pattern held for adolescents in moderate-poverty neighborhoods, where change for the better led to improvements in boys' well-being (Leventhal & Brooks-Gunn, 2011) Evaluations of the adolescent outcomes of other anti-poverty experiments have shown similarly mixed results (Snell et al., 2013).

How can we account for the finding that relocating poor families to more affluent neighborhoods sometimes has negative effects on adolescents' behavior? There are several possible explanations (Fauth, Leventhal, & Brooks-Gunn, 2007). First, adolescents from poor families that moved may have encountered more discrimination in the new neighborhoods than in their old ones. Second, although it is generally true that advantaged communities have more resources than disadvantaged ones, it is possible that poor families who moved to more affluent neighborhoods actually may have had less access to community resources than they did in their old neighborhoods. Third, adolescents who moved to more

advantaged neighborhoods may have ended up feeling more disadvantaged than their peers who remained in poor communities because the adolescents who moved compared their life circumstances to those of their more affluent peers. Finally, there is some evidence that parents in poor neighborhoods may monitor their children relatively more vigilantly because they worry about crime and other dangers; adolescents who are more closely monitored tend to have fewer problems.

The Price of Privilege Although poverty has a wide range of adverse consequences for adolescents' development, there is accumulating evidence that growing up in an extremely affluent neighborhood may carry its own risks. Compared to teenagers in middle-class communities, boys in wealthy neighborhoods report higher levels of delinquency and girls report more anxiety and depression (Lund & Dearing, 2013). This is consistent with several studies that have documented the surprisingly high prevalence of psychological and behavioral problems among teenagers in affluent suburban communities (Levine, 2008; Luthar, Barkin, & Crossman, 2013). The higher incidence of problems among adolescents from wealthy communities appears to emerge in early adolescence, when teenagers begin experimenting with alcohol and illegal drugs, which may be fueled by pressure to excel in school and extracurricular activities and enabled by parents who are either too preoccupied to notice or simply choose to look the other way. Affluent adolescents' substance use, in turn, leads to all sorts of troubles, among them delinquency, depression, and precocious sex.

Impact of Poverty on Adolescent Development
Although there are problems associated with growing up amid wealth, there is clear evidence that growing up in a poor neighborhood has devastating effects on adolescent behavior, achievement, and mental health, and that these effects are above and beyond those attributable to growing up in a poor family or attending a financially strapped school (Foster & Brooks-Gunn, 2013; T. Leventhal et al., 2009; McBride, Berkel, Gaylord-Harden, Copeland-Linder, & Nation, 2011). Adolescents growing up in impoverished urban communities are more likely than their peers from equally poor households but better neighborhoods to be sexually active at an earlier age, to bear children as teenagers, to become involved in criminal activity, and to achieve less in, or even drop out of, high school—factors that seriously interfere with the successful transition into adulthood (Carlson, McNulty, Bellair, & Watts, 2013; Dupéré, Lacourse, Willms, Leventhal, & Tremblay, 2008; Wodtke, Harding, & Elwert, 2011). Interestingly, it is the absence of affluent neighbors, rather than the presence of poor ones, that seems to place adolescents in impoverished communities at greatest risk (T. Leventhal & Brooks-Gunn,

2004). Although virtually all neighborhood research has focused on urban adolescents, studies find that growing up in poor rural communities also places adolescents at risk (Farmer et al., 2003; Reijneveld et al., 2010).

Processes of Neighborhood Influences

How might neighborhood conditions affect the behavior and development of adolescents? Three different mechanisms have been suggested (T. Leventhal et al., 2009) (see Figure 7).

Collective Efficacy First, neighborhood conditions shape the norms that guide individuals' values and behaviors. Poverty in neighborhoods breeds social isolation and social disorganization, undermining a neighborhood's sense of **collective efficacy**—the extent to which neighbors trust each other, share common values, and count on each other to monitor the activities of youth in the community (Sampson, Raudenbusch, & Earls, 1997). As a consequence, it is easier for deviant peer groups to form and to influence the behavior of adolescents in these communities (Maimon & Browning, 2010; Trucco, Colder, Wieczorek, Lengua, & Hawk, 2014). Rates of teen pregnancy, school failure, mental health problems, and antisocial behavior are all higher in neighborhoods that have low levels of collective efficacy (Caughy et al., 2012; Hurd, Stoddard, & Zimmerman, 2013; Karriker-Jaffe, Foshee, Ennett, & Suchindran, 2008). Living in a neighborhood high in collective efficacy—where adults monitor the behavior of all adolescents, not just their own—is especially important for adolescents whose parents are themselves not very vigilant (Kirk, 2009). In addition, it appears that collective efficacy encourages adolescents to form a deeper emotional bond with their community, which in turn makes them feel safer, a finding that has been replicated in many countries (Dallago et al., 2009; Lenzi, Vieno, Santinello, & Perkins, 2013). This connection also protects adolescents

collective efficacy
A community's social capital, derived from its members' common values and goals.

somewhat from the adverse effects of being exposed to neighborhood violence (Browning, Gardner, Maimon, & Brooks-Gunn. 2014).

Under conditions of low collective efficacy, social problems are contagious—they spread from one adolescent to another in a pattern not unlike a disease epidemic. To the extent that poverty increases behavior problems, for example, adolescents living in poor neighborhoods will come into contact with deviant peers more often (Gartstein, Seamon, & Dishion, 2014; Monahan, Egan, Van Horn, Arthur, & Hawkins, 2011; Wright, Kim, Chassin, Losoya, & Piquero, 2014), and adolescents who associate with delinquent peers are more likely to be drawn into criminal and delinquent activity (Simons & Burt, 2011). Similarly, adolescents who live in neighborhoods characterized by high rates of teenage childbearing grow up exposed to large numbers of peers who are relatively more tolerant of this behavior, which affects their own attitudes toward premarital childbearing (Baumer & South, 2001). Adolescents who see nothing but poverty and unemployment in their communities have little reason to be hopeful about their own future, and they may feel that they have little to lose by having a baby, dropping out of school, or becoming involved in criminal activity (Kingston, Huizinga, & Elliott, 2009; McLoyd, Kaplan, Purtell, & Huston, 2011; Ramos, Victor, Seidl-de-Moura, & Daly, 2013). Neighborhood poverty also has an impact on adolescents' sexual behavior and decisions about whether to abort a pregnancy—with those living in poor neighborhoods more likely to be sexually active at an early age and to have the baby—but not on their likelihood of getting pregnant or using contraception (Cubbin, Santelli, Brindis, & Braveman, 2005; South & Baumer, 2001). The impact of living amid low collective efficacy is especially bad among individuals who are impulsive or insensitive to the feelings of others (Dupéré, Lacourse, Willms, Vitaro, & Tremblay, 2007; M. Meier, Slutske, Arndt, & Cadoret, 2008).

The Impact of Stress Second, the stresses associated with poverty undermine the quality of people's relationships with each other. Poverty interferes with parents'

Figure 7 Neighborhood conditions influence adolescents' development by shaping the norms to which adolescents are exposed; by influencing the quality of the relationships they have with others, including their parents; and by facilitating or limiting adolescents' and families' access to economic and institutional resources.

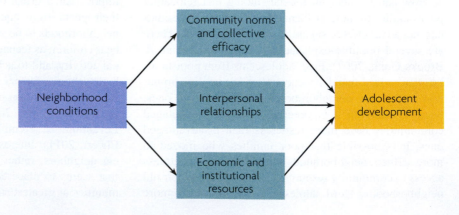

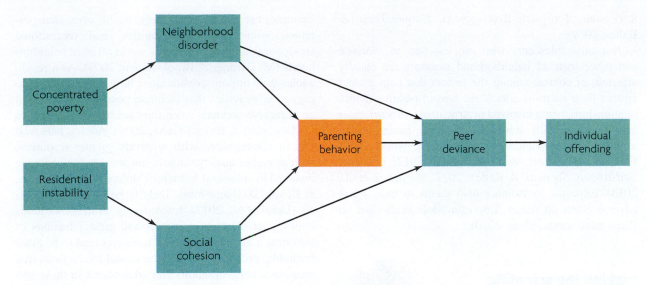

Figure 8 Neighborhood disadvantage diminishes parental effectiveness, which leads adolescents to affiliate with deviant peers and get involved in crime and delinquency. (Chung & Steinberg, 2006)

ability to be effective parents (White, Liu, Nair, & Tein, 2015). Across all ethnic groups, poverty is associated with harsh, inconsistent, and punitive parenting, and these factors, in turn, are linked to adolescent misbehavior (Coley, Leventhal, Lynch, & Kull, 2013; Deutsch, Crockett, Wolff, & Russell, 2012; McLoyd et al., 2009; White & Roosa, 2012). When parents are not effective in supervising and monitoring their teenagers, for example, and when teenagers have little social support from parents or other adults, the teenagers are more likely to associate with antisocial peers and get into trouble (see Figure 8) (Chung & Steinberg, 2006; Odgers et al., 2012).

The link between family poverty and delinquency is even stronger among poor families living in poor neighborhoods (Hay, Fortson, Hollist, Altheimer, & Schaible, 2007). Consistent with this, the harmful effects of exposure to negligent or harsh parenting are even more pronounced in disadvantaged neighborhoods (Browning, Leventhal, & Brooks-Gunn, 2005; Knoester & Haynie, 2005; Roche, Ensminger, & Cherlin, 2007). Studies of whether the impact of good parenting is affected by neighborhood conditions have not yielded consistent results, however. Some studies show that positive family relationships are more effective in good neighborhoods (e.g., Cleveland, Feinberg, & Greenberg, 2010), while others show the reverse (e.g., Salzinger, Feldman, Rosario, & Ng-Mak, 2011).

The impact of poverty on levels of neighborhood violence is especially devastating. Adolescents who grow up in poor neighborhoods are far more likely than other youth to be exposed to chronic community violence, and repeated exposure to violence and other types of stress increases the risk of behavioral, emotional, and even physical health problems (Brenner, Zimmerman, Bauermeister, & Caldwell, 2012, 2013;

Copeland-Linder, Lambert, Chen, & Ialongo, 2011; Evans & Kim, 2013; Farrell, Mehari, & Goncy, 2014). They are more likely to interpret ambiguous situations as threatening, to have poor self-control, and to show increases in blood pressure and heart rate as a consequence, placing them at risk for heart disease (E. Chen, Langer, Raphaelson, & Matthews, 2004). There is even evidence that growing up in violence-ridden neighborhoods affects brain development in ways that interfere with the development of self-control (Bogdan & Hariri, 2012; Thomason et al., 2015). When tested in laboratory experiments, adolescents who have grown up in disordered neighborhoods show a relatively greater tendency to take risks (Furr-Holden, Milam, Reynolds, MacPherson, & Lejuez, 2012).

Adolescents who themselves have been exposed to violence are more likely to engage in violent behavior, to think about killing themselves, and to report symptoms of depression, posttraumatic stress disorder, hopelessness, callousness, precocious sex, and substance abuse (Howard, Kimonis, Muñoz, & Frick, 2012; Monahan, King, Shulman, Cauffman, & Chassin, in press; Swisher & Warner, 2013; Voisin, Hotton, & Neilands, 2014). One study found that witnessing gun violence *doubles* an adolescent's risk for committing violence in the future (Bingenheimer, 2005). The adverse effects of exposure to violence have been documented in hundreds of studies, not only of urban youth in the United States (where most of these studies have been conducted), but in other parts of the world as well, such as Northern Ireland (McAloney, McCrystal, Percy, & McCartan, 2009) and the Middle East (Klodnick, Guterman, Haj, & Leshem, 2014). Generally speaking, being the victim of violence has more consistent harmful effects than witnessing it, which, in turn, is more harmful than simply hearing about it (Fowler, Tompsett, Braciszewski, Jacques-Tiura, & Baltes, 2009).

Not all adolescents who are exposed to violence and other sorts of neighborhood stressors are equally affected, of course; among the factors that help protect against their harmful effects are having positive family relationships, being involved in structured extracurricular activities, especially among Black youth, having strong religious beliefs (Hardaway, McLoyd, & Wood, 2012; Francois, Overstreet, & Cunningham, 2012; LeBlanc, Self-Brown, Shepard, & Kelley, 2011; McMahon et al., 2013). Exposure to violence also seems to have a less adverse effect on Asian American adolescents than on Black adolescents (Chen, 2010).

making the scientific connection

Inner-city neighborhoods typically come to mind when we think of adolescents growing up in poverty, but many poor adolescents live in rural, not urban, areas. In what ways is poverty different for urban versus rural youth? How might this affect the nature of adolescence in each type of community?

Limited Access to Resources   Third, adolescents who grow up in poor neighborhoods have access to fewer resources than do those who grow up in more advantaged communities. In poor neighborhoods, for example, the quality of schools, health care, transportation, employment opportunities, and recreational services are all lower than they are in affluent neighborhoods (M. Gardner & Brooks-Gunn, 2009). As a result, adolescents in poor communities have fewer chances to engage in activities that facilitate positive development or to receive services when they are having difficulties (T. Leventhal & Brooks-Gunn, 2004). Adolescents who live in communities with relatively greater resources, such as higher-quality schools, are less likely to become involved in antisocial behavior (Molnar, Cerda, Roberts, & Buka, 2008) and more likely to be kind toward others (Lenzi et al., 2012). Interestingly, in neighborhoods with higher levels of resources and greater feelings of cohesion, adults' beliefs about teenagers tend to be more favorable, probably because the casual interactions that take place between adults and adolescents in these settings are more positive (Zeldin & Topitzes, 2002). The presence of institutional resources, then, often goes hand in hand with the presence of positive social relationships.

Most of the effects of neighborhoods on adolescent development are indirect, transmitted through the impact of the neighborhood on the more immediate settings in which adolescents spend time (Riina, Martin, Gardner, & Brooks-Gunn, 2012). For example, neighborhood disorder affects the way that parents behave, and this, in turn, affects adolescents' development and mental health. Neighborhoods influence individuals by transforming what takes place within the more immediate contexts that are embedded in them.

Families

4

Is Conflict Between Teenagers and Parents Inevitable?

The Generation Gap: Fact and Fiction

What Do Adolescents and Parents Usually Fight About?

Family Relationships at Adolescence

A Time of Reorganization and Change

The Adolescent's Parents at Midlife

Changes in Family Needs and Functions

Transformations in Family Relations

Sex Differences in Family Relationships

Family Relationships and Adolescent Development

Parenting Styles and Their Effects

Ethnic Differences in Parenting Practices

Autonomy and Attachment in the Adolescent's Family

Adolescents' Relationships with Siblings

Behavioral Genetics and Adolescent Development

Genetic and Environmental Influences on Adolescent Development

Why Are Siblings Often So Different?

The Adolescent's Family in a Changing Society

The Changed and Changing Nature of Family Life

Adolescents and Divorce

The Specific Impact of Marital Conflict

The Longer-Term Effects of Divorce

Custody, Contact, and Conflict Following Divorce

Remarriage

Economic Stress and Poverty

Special Family Forms

The Importance of the Family in Adolescent Development

© Marc Romanelli/Blend Images LLC RF

The next time you are in a bookstore, take a look at the books in the section on parent–adolescent relationships. Judging from the number of "survival guides"—ones like *Why Do They Act That Way?*; *Get Out of My Life, But First, Could You Drive Me and Cheryl to the Mall?*; *How to Survive the Coming Years of Change*; *Yes, Your Teen Is Crazy*; and even *Yes, Your Parents Are Crazy*—you'd think that stress and strain between teenagers and parents is commonplace, even normal. Unlike advice books on infancy, which emphasize normative development, books for parents of teenagers tend to focus on problems (Steinberg, 2011). This is unfortunate, for two reasons. First, the stereotype presented in these writings isn't true. And second, the more parents believe in the stereotype of adolescents as difficult, the more they expect their own child to conform to it, and the worse their relationship with their teenager becomes (Jacobs, Chin, & Shaver, 2005). In other words, parents' beliefs that they are going to have a difficult time with their child once he or she enters adolescence can become what psychologists call a **self-fulfilling prophecy**—an expectation that is realized because we act in ways that make it happen.

In truth, scientific studies indicate that, on average, there is very little emotional distance between young people and their parents (Laursen & Collins, 2009). Although some families have serious problems, the overwhelming majority of adolescents feel close to their parents, respect their judgment, feel that they love and care about them, and have a lot of respect for them as individuals (Steinberg, 2001).

Sure, there are times when adolescents and parents have their problems. But there are times when younger children and their parents have problems, and when adults and their parents do, too. Family problems are no more likely to occur during adolescence than at other times in the life span. Moreover, among teenagers and parents who report having problems, the great majority had troubled relations during childhood (Laursen & Collins, 2009), and declines in the quality of family relationships in adolescence are greatest in families where relationships were less close to begin with (Laursen, DeLay, & Adams, 2010). Only a very small percentage of families who enjoy positive relations during childhood develop serious problems during adolescence.

In this chapter, we'll look at the family as a context for adolescent development, with three broad questions in mind. First, how do family relationships change during adolescence—that is, what is the effect of adolescence on the family? Second, how are adolescents affected by their experiences in the family—in other words, what is the effect of the family on adolescents? And third, how have changes in family life over the past half century affected the adolescent experience?

Is Conflict Between Teenagers and Parents Inevitable?

It is impossible to discuss adolescents' relationships with their parents without talking about parent–adolescent conflict, a topic that not only dominates popular writings on this stage of life but also has been the focus of decades of research by scholars (Laursen & Collins, 2009).

The Generation Gap: Fact and Fiction

Most people believe that adolescents and adults hold different values and attitudes, but this is not the case. Teenagers and their parents usually have surprisingly similar beliefs about such things as the importance of hard work, educational and occupational ambitions, and the personal characteristics and attributes that they think are important and desirable (Knafo & Schwartz, 2003). Indeed, when it comes to basic, core values—concerning religion, work, education, and so on—diversity *within* the adolescent population is much more striking than are differences between the generations. Why is this so? Because adolescents and their parents share a common social, regional, and cultural background, and these are the factors that shape our central beliefs.

Although there isn't much of a gap between the generations when it comes to basic values, there is often one between teenagers and adults in matters of personal taste, most clearly evident in styles of dress, preferences in music, and leisure activities (Laursen & Collins, 2009). Unlike basic values, which develop gradually over time and are shaped from an early age, preferences and tastes for things like clothing, music, and recreational pursuits are far more likely to change with fads and fashions. Adolescents are more likely to be influenced by their friends than by their parents in these matters, and as a consequence, parents and teenagers often disagree about them. Because adolescents spend a great deal of time with their friends (and because much of that time is spent in activities in which taste in clothes, music, and so on is important), teenagers' preferences are likely to be shaped to a large measure by forces outside the family. This also means that the size of the generation gap will fluctuate from one historical epoch to the next. For example, a study of nearly 200,000 European adolescents from 16 nations found, for example, that the percentage of adolescents who perceive communication with their

self-fulfilling prophecy
The idea that individuals' behavior is influenced by others' expectations for them.

parents as difficult increased during the mid 1990s and declined between the late 1990s and the mid 2000s (see Figure 1) (Tabak et al., 2012). Moreover, although the countries varied in their economic, political, and cultural climates, the pattern of change was similar across the countries studied.

What Do Adolescents and Parents Usually Fight About?

If parents and teenagers typically don't argue over "big" issues, what do they fight about? They squabble about things like curfews, leisure time activities, clothing, and the cleanliness of bedrooms. These have been the major sources of disagreement in families with teenagers for at least as long as scientists have been studying the issue (Laursen & DeLay, 2011; Martin, Bascoe, & Davies, 2011). And, although conflict between adolescents and parents over these mundane matters is generally less frequent in ethnic minority than in White families, the topics of disagreement are similar across ethnic groups and cultures (Smetana, Daddis, & Chuang, 2003). A study of adolescents in the People's Republic of China and Hong Kong, for example, found that the most common sources of conflict between adolescents and parents were everyday issues, such as time spent on schoolwork, household chores, and choice of friends (Yau & Smetana, 2003).

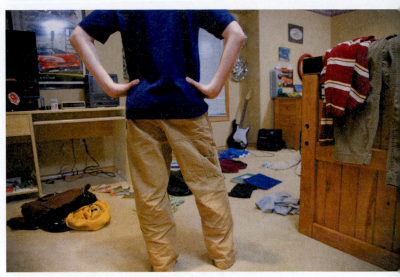

One source of conflict between parents and teenagers involves differences in the way they define issues. Making sure that the adolescent's bedroom is tidy is seen by parents as an area over which parents should have jurisdiction. Teenagers, however, tend to see their bedroom as their own private space and decisions about neatness as matters of personal choice.
© Fuse/Getty Images RF

Why do parents and teenagers argue over such mundane things? According to several studies, a major contributor to adolescent–parent bickering is the fact that teenagers and their parents define the issues of contention very differently—a finding that has been replicated across many cultural and ethnic groups (Chen-Gaddini, 2012; Smetana & Villalobos, 2009). Parents view many issues as matters of right and wrong—not necessarily in a moral sense, but as matters of custom or convention. Adolescents, in contrast, are likely to define these same issues as matters of personal choice (Martin, Bascoe, & Davies, 2011). A mother who disapproves of her daughter's clothing says, "People just don't dress that way to go to school." The daughter responds, "Maybe *you* wouldn't dress this way, but *I* do."

Rebels With a Cause   Contrary to stereotype, though, adolescents rarely rebel against their parents just for the sake of rebelling (Darling, Cumsille, & Martínez, 2007). In fact, they are willing to accept their parents' rules as legitimate when they agree that the issue is a moral one (whether it is permissible to cheat on a school test) or one involving safety (whether it is permissible to drink and drive), but they are less inclined to accept their parents' authority when they view the issue as personal (what clothes to wear to a party) (Jackson, 2002; Smetana & Daddis, 2002). In other words, rather than resisting all of their parents' attempts to make and enforce rules (the stereotype that many people have of teenagers), adolescents distinguish between rules they think their parents have a right to make (for instance, having to let their parents know what time they'll be home after going out)

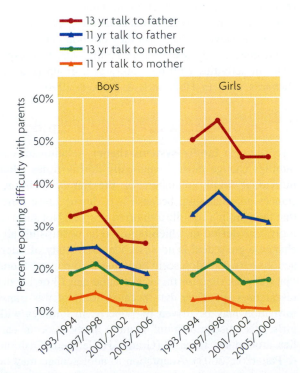

Figure 1 In a study of 200,000 European adolescents, the quality of parent-adolescent relationships fluctuated across historical epochs. (Tabak et al., 2012)

and rules that they think are out of bounds (for example, having to keep their bedroom orderly), a distinction that in many ways is quite understandable (Kuhn, Phan, & Laird, 2013; Smetana & Villalobos, 2009). Of course, there are differences among adolescents in the extent to which they believe their parents have the authority to regulate various sorts of decisions; adolescents who see parents as having more legitimate authority have fewer behavior problems (Cumsille et al., 2009; Kuhn & Laird, 2011; Trinkner, Cohn, Rebellon, & Van Gundy, 2012). Not surprisingly, adolescents who are less likely to believe that their parents have a right to know how they spend their time are more likely to conceal their activities from them (Keijsers & Laird, 2014; Rote & Smetana, 2015; Tilton-Weaver, 2014).

As you'll read, conflict between parents and children increases during early adolescence. One reason for this is that adolescents come to see more and more issues that they previously saw as legitimate for their parents to regulate (for example, how late they can stay up on school nights) as matters of personal choice—a finding that has been replicated in numerous parts of the world, including North America, South America, and Asia, and among both White and Black adolescents in the United States (e.g., Hasebe, Nucci, & Nucci, 2004; Milnitsky-Sapiro, Turiel, & Nucci, 2006; Smetana, 2005). When parents attempt to regulate what adolescents believe are personal issues, teens are likely to describe their parents as being overly controlling. Perhaps because of this, the effects of feeling psychologically controlled by their parents, which has a negative impact on adolescents' mental health, are very different from the effects of feeling that their parents simply want to know where they go and what they do, which has a positive impact (Loukas, 2009; Padilla-Walker, 2008; Smetana, Campione-Barr, & Daddis, 2004). Adolescents who think their parents are overcontrolling are likely to become oppositional (Van Petegem, Soenens, Vansteenkiste, & Beyers, 2015). How parents get their information also matters: Snooping, as opposed to asking, is likely to lead to problems (Hawk, Becht, & Branje, 2015), as does close parental monitoring in the absence of a warm parent–adolescent relationship (Lippold, Greenberg, Graham, & Feinberg, 2014).

In other words, teenagers and their parents often clash more over the definition of the issue (e.g., whether something is a matter of safety rather than a matter of personal choice) than over the specific details. The struggle, then, is over who has the authority—and whose jurisdiction the issue falls into. Because early adolescence is a time when adolescents' reasoning abilities are changing, the ways that individuals understand family rules and regulations change as well. As a consequence of normal cognitive development,

family systems theory
A perspective on family functioning that emphasizes interconnections among different family relationships (such as marital, parent–child, sibling).

a 9-year-old child who is willing to accept his parents' views—who doesn't question his mother when she says, "We do not leave clothes on the floor"—grows into an adolescent who understands that some issues are matters of personal choice, rather than social convention ("It's my room, so why should it bother you?").

One manifestation of this change in perspective is an increase, with age, in adolescents' willingness to lie to their parents. In one study (S. A. Perkins & Turiel, 2007), in which adolescents were presented with hypothetical situations and asked whether it was acceptable to lie to one's parents about a personal matter (e.g., dating someone your parents dislike), about half of the younger adolescents (12- to 14-year-olds) said it was acceptable to lie, whereas more than 80% of the older adolescents (15- to 17-year-olds) did. Partial disclosures—"lies of omission"—are especially common. As one 14-year-old explained:

> I just tell [my mother] where we be going and stuff. And if we're going to stay out late and stuff like that, I don't tell her none of that stuff. . . . Like if we're going to the mall and stuff, I just don't tell her that we're going to go to parties. (Bakken & Brown, 2010, p. 374)

Family Relationships at Adolescence

Although it is incorrect to characterize adolescence as a time of high conflict in most families, it is important to keep in mind that adolescence is nevertheless a period of change and reorganization in family relationships and daily interactions (Laursen & DeLay, 2011; Martin, Bascoe, & Davies, 2011). As they develop, adolescents spend increasingly less time in family activities, especially in activities with the family as a group (Larson, Richards, Moneta, Holmbeck, & Duckett, 1996).

A Time of Reorganization and Change

According to **family systems theory,** relationships in families change most dramatically during times when individual family members or the family's circumstances are changing, because it is during these times that the family's equilibrium often is upset. Not surprisingly, one period in which family relationships usually change a great deal is adolescence. One study of interactions between adolescent boys and their parents found that the peak time for this was around age 13 or 14; the researchers speculate that, because some of this transformation may be driven by puberty, in families with girls, this "disequilibrium" is more likely to occur earlier, around age 11 or 12 (Granic, Hollenstein, Dishion, & Patterson, 2003). Adaptation to adolescence may be especially difficult when the teenager is emotionally rigid (Lichtwarck-Aschoff, Kunnen, & van Geert, 2009) or temperamentally difficult (Trentacosta et al., 2011).

The specific concerns and issues characteristic of families at adolescence arise not just because of the changing needs and concerns of the young person but also because of changes in the adolescent's parents and in the needs and functions of the family. You already have an understanding of the biological, cognitive, and social changes adolescents go through, and how these may affect the family system. But to fully understand family relationships during the adolescent years, we need to take into account characteristics of the adolescent's parents and of families at this stage as well.

The Adolescent's Parents at Midlife

Because people typically have their first child around age 30, most parents are in their early 40s when the first child enters early adolescence. This age can be a potentially difficult time for many adults, whether they have children or not. Some theorists have gone so far as to describe it as a time of **midlife crisis** (Lachman, 2004).

Midlife Meets Adolescence   If we look at the nature of the midlife crises in some detail, we see that the developmental concerns of parents and adolescents are complementary (Steinberg & Steinberg, 1994). Consider the issue of biological change. At the same time that adolescents are entering into a period of rapid physical growth, sexual maturation, and, ultimately, the period of the life span that society has labeled one of the most physically attractive, their parents are beginning to feel increased concern about their own bodies, about their physical attractiveness, and about their sexual appeal (Banister, 1999). One mother of an early-adolescent girl once remarked, in an interview with my research staff, that it was jarring to realize that when she and her daughter walked down the street, men now looked at her daughter, and not at her.

A second overlap of crises concerns perceptions of time and the future. At the same time that adolescents are developing the capability to think systematically about the future and do, in fact, start looking ahead, their parents are beginning to feel that possibilities for changing their own lives are limited. Before midlife, individuals tend to measure time in terms of how long they have been alive; after midlife, they are more likely to see things in terms of how much longer they have to live (Lang & Carstensen, 2002). One reason for this shift may be that at midlife adults are reminded of their mortality because they see their own parents aging. Whatever the reason, the naive optimism of adolescence may clash with the hardened pragmatism of middle age.

Finally, consider the issue of power, status, and entrance into the roles of adulthood. Adolescence is the time when individuals are on the threshold of gaining a great deal of status. Their careers and marriages lie ahead of them, and choices may seem limitless. For their

For many adults, their child's adolescence coincides with their own passage through midlife. Not all adults experience a "midlife crisis," but for many, this is a time of heightened introspection and self-doubt. The collision of adolescence and midlife may make the period an especially challenging one in some families. © Bob Thomas/ Photodisc/Getty Images RF

parents many choices have already been made—some successfully, others perhaps less so. Most adults reach their "occupational plateau"—the point at which they can tell how successful they are likely to be—during midlife, and many must deal with whatever gap exists between their early aspirations and their actual achievements (Lachman, 2004). In sum, for adolescents, this phase in the family life cycle is a time of boundless horizons; for their parents, it means coming to terms with choices made when they were younger.

This overlap of crises is likely to have an impact on family relationships (Steinberg & Steinberg, 1994). A father who is worried about his own physical health may suddenly feel uncomfortable about playing one-on-one basketball games with his growing son, as they did for years when the boy was younger. An adolescent girl with big plans for the future may find it difficult to understand why her father seems so cautious and narrow-minded when she asks him for advice.

midlife crisis
A psychological crisis over identity believed to occur between the ages of 35 and 45, the age range of most adolescents' parents.

An adolescent boy may find his mother's constant attention annoying; he doesn't see that, to her, his interest in independence signifies the end of an important stage in her career as a parent. The adolescent's desire for independence appears to be especially stressful for parents (Steinberg & Steinberg, 1994).

This generalization about the collision of adolescence and midlife must be tempered, though. The average age at marriage has increased, and proportionately more couples today are delaying childbearing until they have become established in their careers (Gregory, 2007). As a consequence, adults tend to be older today when their children reach adolescence than was the case two decades ago. How being an older parent affects relationships during adolescence hasn't been adequately studied.

The Mental Health of Parents In families with middle-aged adults, adjusting to adolescence may take more of a toll on the mental health of parents than their adolescents (Steinberg & Steinberg, 1994). Nearly two-thirds of mothers and fathers describe adolescence as the most difficult stage of parenting (Pasley & Gecas, 1984), and this period is the low point in parents' marital and life satisfaction (Gecas & Seff, 1990). Parents who are deeply involved in work outside the home or who have an especially happy marriage may be buffered against some of these negative consequences, however, whereas single mothers may be especially vulnerable to them (Silverberg, Marczak, & Gondoli, 1996; Steinberg & Steinberg, 1994). In fact, a strained relationship between a midlife parent and his or her adolescent child may drive the parent to devote relatively more time to work (Fortner, Crouter, & McHale, 2004). At the same time, studies show that parents' mental health problems affect the way they interact with their adolescents, which in turn adversely affects the teenagers (Yap, Schwartz, Byrne, Simmons, & Allen, 2010).

The notion that parents' mental health declines when they enter the "empty nest" stage is a myth, especially among mothers. Parents' mental health is worse when their teenage children are living at home than it is once they have moved out, and when children leave home, it is fathers, not mothers, who typically feel the greatest sense of loss (Steinberg & Steinberg, 1994).

....

making the scientific connection

Many studies have found that marital satisfaction is lower when parents' firstborn child is a teenager than at any other point in the marriage. Why do you think this might be?

Changes in Family Needs and Functions

It is not only individual family members who undergo change during the family's adolescent years. The family as a unit changes as well in its economic circumstances, its relationship to other social institutions, and its functions.

Family finances are often strained during adolescence. Children grow rapidly during puberty, and clothing for adolescents is expensive. Keeping up with the "must-haves" of the peer culture—designer clothes, smartphones, and so forth, not to mention car expenses—may push a family budget to the limit. Many families also begin saving money for large anticipated expenditures, such as the adolescent's college education. And in some families, parents may find themselves having to help support their own parents when their children are still economically dependent. The financial demands placed on parents in the "sandwich generation" (that is, sandwiched between their adolescent children and their aging parents) require considerable adjustment.

The adolescent's family also must cope with the increasing importance of the peer group (Laursen & DeLay, 2011). During elementary school, the child's social world is fairly narrow. The family is the central setting. During late childhood and early adolescence, however, the peer group becomes a setting in which close ties are forged, and parents and adolescents often argue about the teenager's reluctance to give up time with friends for family activities.

How adolescents and parents adjust to this shift in orientation varies across ethnic groups, since certain cultures are more likely to stress family obligations—like helping with household chores—than others (Hardway & Fuligni, 2006; Kiang, Andrews, Stein, Supple, & Gonzalez, 2013). Many immigrant families place an

Different expectations between immigrant parents and teenagers are a significant source of stress for adolescents and parents alike, especially when the adolescent is more Americanized and the parents are less so, a phenomenon known as generational dissonance. © Bonnie Kamin / PhotoEdit

especially high value on **familism,** an orientation toward life in which the needs of one's family take precedence over the needs of the individual (Germán, Gonzales, & Dumka, 2009). Adolescents who value familism and assist their families are less likely to get depressed and less likely to get involved with antisocial peer groups, which lessens their chances of drinking or using illicit drugs (Roosa et al., 2011; Telzer, Gonzales, & Fuligni, 2013; Telzer, Tsai, Gonzales, & Fuligni, 2015). But sometimes parents' ideas about family responsibilities clash with the more individualistic orientation characteristic of many mainstream American families.

Different expectations between immigrant parents and teenagers are a significant source of stress for adolescents and parents alike, especially when the adolescent is more Americanized and the parents are less so, a phenomenon known as **generational dissonance** (Cordova, Ciofu, & Cervantes, 2014; Schwartz, 2013; Wang, Kim, Anderson, Chen, & Yan, 2011; Wu & Chao, 2011). Studies of Mexican American families, for example, have found that stress and family conflict are higher in Latino families with relatively more acculturated adolescents (Gonzales, Deardoff, Formoso, Barr, & Barrera, Jr., 2006; C. R. Martinez, Jr., 2006). Different expectations about the adolescent's social life can cause problems between newly arrived immigrants and their teenagers, as this Chinese mother of a 15-year-old girl explains:

> Sometimes some of her male friends called. After she hung up the phone I often asked her, "Who is he?" She then answered, "My male classmates." I asked her, "Why is he calling you every night?" then she said I was overpowering her and even intruding into her privacy. I said "I'm just asking. Is there any problem?" I asked her, "Are you dating? He does not have to call and ask you about homework every night, does he?" She then said, "We are just chatting." I said, "If you guys are having casual conversations, does he have to call her every night?" Since then, her male friends dared not call her. (Qin, 2008, p. 27)

Important changes in family functions also take place during adolescence. During infancy and childhood, the functions and responsibilities of the family are clear: nurturance, protection, and socialization. While all of these are still important during adolescence, adolescents are in need of support more than nurturance, of guidance more than protection, and of direction more than socialization. Making the transition from the family functions of childhood to the family functions of adolescence is not necessarily easy, especially in contemporary society, where preparation for adulthood—one of the chief tasks of adolescence that was once carried out primarily by the family—is increasingly performed by other institutions, such as the school. Many parents feel at a loss to figure out just what their role during adolescence is. It's important that they know that having close family relationships is just as important in adolescence as it was in childhood (Steinberg, 2011).

Transformations in Family Relations

Together, the biological, cognitive, and social transitions of adolescence; the changes experienced by adults at midlife; and the changes undergone by the family during this stage set in motion a series of transformations in family relationships. There is a movement away from patterns of influence and interaction that are asymmetrical and imbalanced toward ones in which parents and adolescents are on a more equal footing. Early adolescence—when this shift toward more egalitarian relationships first begins—may be a time of temporary disruption in family relationships.

Changes in the Balance of Power   During early adolescence young people begin to try to play a more forceful role in the family, but parents may not yet acknowledge adolescents' input. Young adolescents may interrupt their parents more often but have little impact. By middle adolescence, however, teenagers act and are treated much more like adults. They have more influence over family decisions, but they do not need to assert their opinions through interruptions and similarly immature behavior (Grotevant, 1997).

Increases in the assertiveness and influence of adolescents as they get older reflect their changing needs and capabilities. To adapt to the changes triggered by the child's entrance into adolescence, family members must have some shared sense of what they are experiencing and how they are changing. Yet parents and teenagers often live in "separate realities," perceiving their day-to-day experiences in very different ways (Laursen & DeLay, 2011). A mother and son, for example, may have a conversation about schoolwork. She may experience the conversation as simply a serious discussion; he may perceive it as an argument. One study of Black families, in which mothers, teenagers, and researchers all rated a videotape of the mother and teenager having a discussion, found that the teenagers rated their mother's behavior far more negatively than did either the mother or the researcher (Campione-Barr & Smetana, 2004). One interesting finding to emerge from recent research on brain maturation in adolescence is that young adolescents may be especially sensitive—perhaps even overreact—to the emotional signals given off by others (Pfeifer & Blakemore, 2012). A parent may speak to an adolescent in a serious voice, but the adolescent may experience it as anger (E. Nelson, Leibenluft, McClure, & Pine, 2005).

The Role of Puberty   The adolescent's biological and cognitive maturation likely plays a role in unbalancing the family system during early

---

familism
An orientation toward life in which the needs of one's family take precedence over the needs of the individual.

generational dissonance
Divergence of views between adolescents and parents that is common in families of immigrant parents and American-born adolescents.

Conflict between parents and adolescents can play a very important and positive role in the adolescent's social and cognitive development, so long as family relationships are warm.
© digitalskillet/Getty Images RF

adolescence. Family relationships change during puberty, with adolescents and their parents bickering more frequently and feeling less close (De Goede, Branje, & Meeus, 2009; Marceau, Ram, & Susman, 2014).

Although puberty seems to distance adolescents from their parents, it is not associated with familial "storm and stress." Rates of outright conflict between parents and children are not dramatically higher during adolescence than before or after (Laursen & DeLay, 2011). Rather, disputes between parents and teenagers are typical of the sorts of arguments people have when a more powerful person (the parent) is trying to get a less powerful one (the adolescent) to do something (Adams & Laursen, 2001). Similarly, the diminished closeness is more likely to be manifested in increased privacy on the part of the adolescent and less physical affection between teenagers and parents, rather than any serious loss of love or respect between them (Keijsers, Branje, Frijns, Finkenauer, & Meeus, 2010; Laursen & Collins, 2009). The distancing that takes place between parents and teenagers in early and middle adolescence is temporary. Parent–child relationships tend to become less conflicted and more intimate during late adolescence and show no decline in closeness as the adolescent enters young adulthood. If anything,

identifying with and feeling responsible for one's family increases during the early 20s (see Figure 2) (Tsai, Telzer, & Fuligni, 2013). Nevertheless, the bickering can take a toll on parents' and teenagers' mental health (Steinberg, 2001). Some studies have found that individuals who reported more conflict with their parents during adolescence had more problems both later in adolescence and in young adulthood (Herrenkohl, Kosterman, Hawkins, & Mason, 2009; Klahr, McGue, Iacono, & Burt, 2011a). Although it is certainly possible that adolescents who have problems are more likely to provoke conflict with their parents, studies that have been able to separate cause and effect have found that family conflict actually leads to the development of mental health problems (Klahr, Rueter, McGue, Iacono, & Burt, 2011b) and emotional distress, regardless of ethnicity (Chung, Flook, & Fuligni, 2009). Conflict at home spills over into the adolescents' school life and relationships with friends, causing problems and emotional distress (Chung, Flook, & Fuligni, 2011; Timmons & Margolin, 2015). In some families, adolescents and parents even disagree about what they argue about (Ehrlich, Richards, Lejuez, & Cassidy, 2015)!

Patterns of conflict and closeness in the family at adolescence vary across ethnic groups. In Asian households, there is an increase in conflict, as in non-Asian families, but not until later in adolescence (Greenberger & Chen, 1996). Another study, comparing Black families with White families, found that White parents tended to give adolescents relatively more autonomy over decisions, although opportunities for adolescent decision making increased in both ethnic groups over time (see Figure 3) (Gutman & Eccles, 2007).

Because the disagreements parents and adolescents have typically revolve around issues of parental control, patterns of squabbling and bickering may vary across cultural groups whose timetables for adolescent independence differ. Patterns of conflict and closeness in immigrant families often differ as a function of the family's degree of acculturation. One study of Mexican American families found lower rates of parent–adolescent cohesion

Figure 2   As adolescents mature into young adulthood, their identification with their family grows stronger.
(Tsai, Telzer, & Fuligni, 2013)

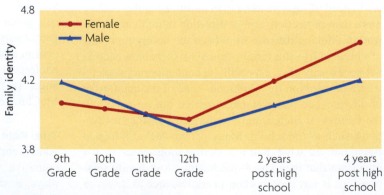

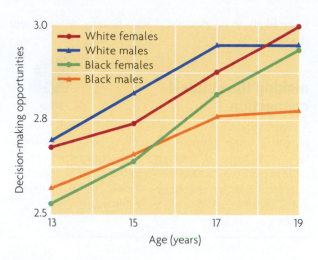

Figure 3 Parents generally give adolescents greater opportunity to make decisions as they get older, although the pattern of change varies by race and gender. (Gutman & Eccles, 2007)

during mid-adolescence among more highly acculturated families than in less Americanized ones, probably because in traditional Mexican families, adolescents are less likely to challenge their parents (Baer & Schmitz, 2007). Similarly, conflict is less frequent, and cohesion higher, in households where teenagers and their parents communicate in their native language (Tseng & Fuligni, 2000). Parental monitoring appears to be more important in ethnic minority families in which the adolescent has a weaker ethnic identity, consistent with the idea that adolescents who are more Americanized may need more vigilant parents to keep them out of trouble (Nagoshi, Marsiglia, Parsai, & Castro, 2011).

In any case, the first half of adolescence may be a more strained and distant time for the family than earlier or later, although this may be more true in the case of firstborns than in the case of later-borns, perhaps because parents may learn from experience (L. Shanahan, McHale, Osgood, & Crouter, 2007). Part of the problem is that conflicts between teenagers and parents tend to be resolved not through compromise but through one party giving in or walking away, neither of which enhances the quality of the relationship or contributes to anyone's well-being (C. Tucker, McHale, & Crouter, 2003b). As relationships between parents and adolescents become more egalitarian, they get better at resolving conflicts (Van Doorn, Branje, & Meuss, 2011).

Violations of Expectations Several researchers have studied changes in adolescents' cognitive abilities and how these changes may reverberate throughout the family. We noted that changes in the ways adolescents view family rules and regulations may contribute to increased conflict between them and their parents (Laursen & DeLay, 2011). Early adolescence is also a time of changes in youngsters' views of family relationships and

in family members' expectations of each other (Lanz, Scabini, Vermulst, & Gerris, 2001).

A child may enter adolescence expecting that it will be a time of great freedom, whereas the parents may view the same period as one in which tighter reins are necessary. Another child, perhaps influenced by television sitcoms portraying nothing but happy families, may imagine that adolescence will be a time of increased closeness and shared activities in the family, only to find that his or her parents have been looking forward to having time to themselves. It is easy to see how differences in expectations can escalate into arguments and misunderstandings. When questioned about whether adolescents were expected to disclose secrets to their parents, for example, adolescents' expectations for secrecy were much greater than parents' (Smetana, Metzger, Gettman, & Campione-Barr, 2006).

Sex Differences in Family Relationships

Differences between the family relations of sons and daughters are minimal. Although there are occasional exceptions to the rule, sons and daughters report comparable degrees of closeness to their parents, amounts of conflict, types of rules (and disagreements about those rules), and patterns of activity. Observational studies of interactions between parents and adolescents indicate that sons and daughters interact with their parents in remarkably similar ways (Steinberg & Silk, 2002).

Teenagers relate very differently to mothers and fathers, though. Across many ethnic groups and cultures, adolescents tend to be closer to their mothers, to spend more time alone with their mothers, and to feel more comfortable talking to their mothers about problems and other emotional matters; as a consequence, mothers tend

Adolescents' relationships with their mothers and fathers are very different. © Don Hammond/Design Pics RF

to be more involved than fathers in their adolescents' lives (Updegraff, McHale, Crouter, & Kupanoff, 2001; S. K. Williams & Kelly, 2005). Fathers often rely on mothers for information about their adolescent's activities, but mothers rarely rely on fathers for this (Crouter, Bumpus, Davis, & McHale, 2005; Waizenhofer, Buchanan, & Jackson-Newsom, 2004). Fathers are more likely to be perceived as relatively distant authority figures to be consulted for objective information (such as help with homework) but not for emotional support (such as help with problems with a boyfriend or girlfriend) (Crockett, Brown, Russell, & Shen, 2007). Interestingly, adolescents also fight more often with their mothers than with their fathers and perceive mothers as more controlling, but this does not appear to jeopardize the closeness of the mother–adolescent relationship (Shek, 2007). Although adolescents spend about twice as much time with their mothers as with their fathers, time spent with fathers—perhaps because it is a relative rarity—is more predictive of adolescents' social competence and feelings of self-worth (Figure 4) (Lam, McHale, & Crouter, 2012).

Family Relationships and Adolescent Development

Thus far, we have looked at the sorts of issues and concerns faced by most families during the adolescent years. In our focus on the experiences that families have in common, we have not discussed how relationships differ from family to family, and whether these differences have consequences for the adolescent. Some parents are stricter than others. Some adolescents are given a great deal of affection, while others are treated more distantly. In some households, decisions are made through open discussion and verbal give-and-take; in others, parents lay down the rules, and children are expected to follow them. Are different patterns of family relationships associated with different patterns of adolescent development? Are some styles of parenting

more likely to be associated with healthy development than others?

Before we try to answer these questions, several cautions are in order. Although we tend to see children's behavior as the result of their parents' behavior, socialization is a two-way street (W. A. Collins, Maccoby, Steinberg, Hetherington, & Bornstein, 2000). Just as parents affect their adolescents' behavior, adolescents affect how their parents behave (Coley, Votruba-Drzal, & Schindler, 2009; Wang, Dishion, Stoirmshak, & Willet, 2011; Willoughby & Hamza, 2011). Harsh discipline leads to increases in adolescent behavior problems, but when adolescents behave badly, parents respond by becoming more punitive, overcontrolling, or detached (Moilanen, Rasmussen, & Padilla-Walker, 2014; Murray, Haynie, Howard, Cheng, & Simons-Morton, 2013; Roche, Ghazarian, Little, & Leventhal, 2011; Wang & Kenny, 2014). This interplay between parenting and adolescent development is so strong that it even contributes to the transmission of parenting styles across generations (Deater-Deckard, 2014; Kerr, Capaldi, Pears, & Owen, 2009).

In addition, various types of parenting affect different adolescents differently. For example, although adolescents whose parents are hostile or aloof are more likely to exhibit antisocial behavior (e.g., Dobkin, Tremblay, & Sacchitelle, 1997), the link between negative parenting and adolescent problem behavior is stronger among teenagers

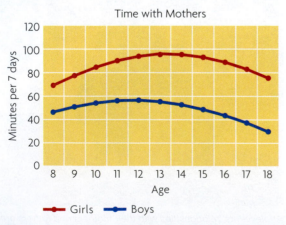

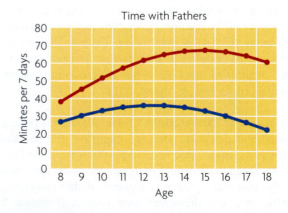

Figure 4 Age Differences in Time Spent with Mothers and Fathers.

who are temperamentally more impulsive; among adolescents who are more timid, the same sort of parenting leads to anxiety and depression (Chen & Jacobson, 2013; Williams et al., 2009). Furthermore, adolescents who have a greater genetic risk for developing problems (by virtue of their family history) are more likely to evoke from their parents the sort of behavior that has been shown to lead to the development of problems (O'Connor, Deater-Deckard, Fulker, Rutter, & Plomin, 1998).

Parenting Styles and Their Effects

There are a variety of ways to characterize parents' behavior toward their children. One of the most useful approaches derives from the work of psychologist Diana Baumrind (1978). According to her, two aspects of the parent's behavior toward the adolescent are critical: parental responsiveness and parental "demandingness" (Maccoby & Martin, 1983). **Parental responsiveness** is the degree to which the parent responds to the child's needs in an accepting, supportive manner. **Parental demandingness** is the extent to which the parent expects and demands mature, responsible behavior. Parents vary on each of these dimensions. Some are warm and accepting, while others are unresponsive and rejecting; some are demanding and expect a great deal, while others are permissive and demand very little.

Four Styles of Parenting Because parental responsiveness and demandingness are more or less independent of each other—that is, it is possible for a parent to be demanding without being responsive, and vice versa—it is possible to look at various combinations of these two dimensions (see Figure 5). Many studies of parents and children indicate that the fourfold classification scheme presented in Figure 5 is very important in understanding the impact of parents' behavior on the child, and psychologists have given labels to the four different prototypes presented in the figure (Crockett & Hayes, 2011; Martin, Bascoe, & Davies, 2011).

Parents who are both responsive and demanding are authoritative. **Authoritative parents** are warm but firm. They set standards for the child's conduct but form expectations consistent with the child's needs and capabilities. They value the development of autonomy and self-direction but assume the ultimate responsibility for their child's behavior. Authoritative parents deal with their child in a rational, issue-oriented manner, frequently engaging in discussion over matters of discipline. Authoritative parents strive to raise a child who is self-reliant, with a strong sense of initiative.

parental responsiveness One of the two important dimensions of parenting; responsiveness refers to the degree to which the parent responds to the child's needs in an accepting, supportive manner.

parental demandingness One of two important dimensions of parenting; demandingness refers to the degree to which the parent expects and insists on mature, responsible behavior from the child.

authoritative parents Parents who use warmth, firm control, and rational, issue-oriented discipline, in which emphasis is placed on the development of self-direction.

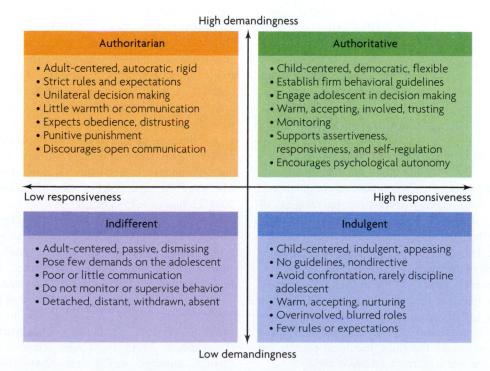

Figure 5 **A typological conceptualization of parenting styles based on the dimensions of responsiveness and demandingness.** (Adapted from Martin, Bascoe, & Davies, 2011)

Adolescents fare better when their parents are warm and firm, a style known as authoritative parenting. © Ryan McVay/ Photodisc/Getty Images RF

authoritarian parents
Parents who use punitive, absolute, and forceful discipline, and who place a premium on obedience and conformity.

indulgent parents
Parents who are characterized by responsiveness but low demandingness, and who are mainly concerned with the child's happiness.

indifferent parents
Parents who are characterized by low levels of both responsiveness and demandingness.

Parents who are very demanding but not responsive are authoritarian. **Authoritarian parents** value obedience and conformity. They tend to favor more punitive, absolute, and forceful discipline. Verbal give-and-take is not common, because authoritarian parents believe that children should accept their parents' rules and standards without question. They don't encourage independent behavior and, instead, place a good deal of importance on restricting the child's autonomy. Authoritarian parents place a premium on compliance.

A parent who is very responsive but not at all demanding is indulgent. **Indulgent parents** behave in an accepting, benign, and more passive way in matters of discipline. They demand very little, giving the child a high degree of freedom to act as he or she wishes. Indulgent parents believe that control is an infringement on children's freedom that may interfere with healthy development. Instead of actively shaping their child's behavior, indulgent parents are more likely to view themselves as resources for the child. Indulgent parents are especially concerned with raising a happy child.

Parents who are neither demanding nor responsive are indifferent. **Indifferent parents** do whatever is

necessary to minimize the time and energy they must devote to interacting with their child. In extreme cases, indifferent parents may be neglectful. They know little about their child's activities and whereabouts, show little interest in their child's experiences at school or with friends, rarely converse with their child, and rarely consider their child's opinion. Rather than raising their child according to a set of beliefs about what is good for the child's development (as do the other three parent types), indifferent parents structure their home life primarily around their own needs and interests.

making the personal connection

Where would you place your parents in the four-way model of parenting styles? Would your parents agree?

The Power of Authoritative Parenting   Few areas of research in the field of adolescent development have received as much attention as the link between what parents do and how adolescents turn out, and the findings of this body of work are amazingly consistent (W. A. Collins & Steinberg, 2006). Young people who have been raised in authoritative households are more psychosocially mature than peers who have been raised in authoritarian, indulgent, or indifferent homes. Adolescents raised in authoritative homes are more responsible, self-assured, creative, intellectually curious, socially skilled, and academically successful. Adolescents raised in authoritarian homes, in contrast, are more dependent, more passive, less socially adept, less self-assured, and less curious. Adolescents raised in indulgent households are less mature, less responsible, and more conforming to their peers. Adolescents raised in indifferent homes are often impulsive and more likely to be involved in delinquent behavior and in precocious experimentation with sex, drugs, and alcohol. Although it generally is not a good thing for parents to disagree about how they raise their teenagers, studies show that it is better to have at least one authoritative parent than two nonauthoritative ones who share the same point of view (McKinney & Renk, 2008; L. Simons & Conger, 2007).

The link between authoritative parenting and healthy adolescent development has been found in studies of a wide range of ethnicities, social classes, and family structures, not only within the United States (e.g., Bean, Barber, & Crane, 2006; Cleveland, Gibbons, Gerrard, Pomery, & Brody, 2005; Luthar & Latendresse, 2005; Simpkins et al., 2009) but also in parts of the world as diverse as Iceland (Adalbjarnardottir & Hafsteinsson, 2001), the Czech Republic (Dmitrieva, Chen, Greenberger, & Gil-Rivas, 2004), India (Carson, Chowdhury, Perry, & Pati, 1999), China (Pilgrim, Luo, Urberg, & Fang, 1999), Israel (Mayseless, Scharf, &

Sholt, 2003), Switzerland (Vazsonyi, Hibbert, & Black, 2003), and Palestine (Punamäki, Qouta, & Sarraj, 1997). The evidence favoring authoritative parenting is so strong that some experts have suggested that the question of which type of parenting benefits teenagers the most need not be studied anymore (see Table 1) (Steinberg, 2001). Educational programs designed to teach parents how to be more responsive and more demanding have been shown to foster healthy adolescent development and behavior (e.g., Brody et al., 2006; Connell & Dishion, 2008; Herrenkohl, Hill, Hawkins, Chung, & Nagin, 2006).

At the other extreme, parenting that is indifferent, neglectful, hostile, or abusive has harmful effects on adolescents' mental health and development, leading to depression and a variety of behavior problems (Coley, Medeiros, & Schindler, 2008; Hoeve et al., 2008). Severe psychological abuse (excessive criticism, rejection, or emotional harshness) appears to have the most deleterious effects (Dube et al., 2003).

How Authoritative Parenting Works Why is authoritative parenting so consistently associated with healthy adolescent development? First, authoritative parents provide an appropriate balance between restrictiveness and autonomy, giving the adolescent opportunities to develop self-reliance while providing the standards, limits, and guidelines that teenagers still need (Martin, Bascoe, & Davies, 2011; Padilla-Walker, Fraser, & Harper, 2012). Authoritative parents are more likely to give children more independence gradually as they get older, which helps children develop self-reliance and self-assurance. Because of this, authoritative parenting

Table 1 The 10 Basic Principles of Good Parenting

Several years ago, after reviewing decades of research on parenting and child development, I came to the conclusion that we really did know what sort of parenting is most likely to help children and adolescents grow up in healthy ways. I summarized this evidence in a book titled *The 10 Basic Principles of Good Parenting* (Steinberg, 2005b). Here's what all parents, regardless of their child's age, should keep in mind:

1. What You Do Matters
2. You Can Not Be Too Loving
3. Be Involved in Your Child's Life
4. Adapt Your Parenting to Fit Your Child
5. Establish Rules and Set Limits
6. Help Foster Your Child's Independence
7. Be Consistent
8. Avoid Harsh Discipline
9. Explain Your Rules and Decisions
10. Treat Your Child With Respect

Source: Steinberg, 2005b.

promotes the development of adolescents' competence and enhances their ability to withstand a variety of potentially negative influences, including stress (Hazel, Oppenheimer, Technow, Young, & Hankin, 2014; Pearce, Jones, Schwab-Stone, & Ruchkin, 2003) and exposure to antisocial peers (Flamm & Grolnick, 2013; Hazel, Oppenheimer, Technow, Young, & Hankin, 2014; Tilton-Weaver, Burk, Kerr, & Stattin, 2013).

Second, because authoritative parents are more likely to engage their children in verbal give-and-take, they are likely to promote the sort of intellectual development that provides an important foundation for the development of psychosocial maturity (Smetana, Crean, & Daddis, 2002). Authoritative parents are less likely than other parents to assert their authority by turning adolescents' personal decisions (such as over what type of music they listen to) into moral issues (Smetana, 1995b). Family discussions in which decisions, rules, and expectations are explained help the child understand social systems and social relationships. This understanding plays an important role in the development of reasoning abilities, theory of mind, moral judgment, and empathy (N. Eisenberg, Morris, McDaniel, & Spinrad, 2009; Miklikowska, Duriez, & Soenens, 2011).

Third, because authoritative parenting is based on a warm parent–child relationship, adolescents are more likely to identify with, admire, and form strong attachments to their parents, which makes them more open to their parents' influence (Darling & Steinberg, 1993). Having regular family meals appears to have a strong protective effect, although it is the quality of the parent–adolescent relationship, rather than the frequency with which families eat together, that matters (Meier & Musick, 2014; Miller, Waldfogel, & Han, 2012; Skeer & Ballard, 2013). Adolescents who are raised by nonauthoritative parents often end up having friends their parents disapprove of, including those involved in problem behavior (Knoester, Haynie, & Stephens, 2006). And adolescents who are forced to spend time with parents they don't get along with do not benefit from joint activities (Offer, 2013).

Finally, the child's own behavior, temperament, and personality shape parenting practices (Albrecht, Galambos, & Jansson, 2007; Beaver & Wright, 2007; Denissen, van Aken, & Dubas, 2009). Children who are responsible, self-directed, curious, and self-assured elicit warmth, flexible guidance, and verbal give-and-take. In contrast, children who are irritable, aggressive, dependent, or immature may provoke behavior that is excessively harsh, passive, or distant (de Haan, Prinzie, & Deković, 2012; Lansford et al., 2011; Roche et al., 2011). Parents enjoy being around children who are responsible, independent, and willing to tell them about their activities and whereabouts, and they treat them more warmly as a result. Although parental monitoring does deter adolescent problem behavior (Coley,

Although parenting practices vary across cultures, the ways in which adolescents are affected by different types of parenting generally do not. © Michael DeLeon/Getty Images RF

Votruba-Drzal, & Schindler, 2008; Gartstein, Seamon, & Dishion, 2014; Laird, Marrero, & Sentse, 2010; Poulin & Denault, 2012), some of what often appears to be effective parental monitoring may actually be the end result of a warm parent–adolescent relationship in which the adolescent willingly discloses information (Garthe, Sullivan, & Kliewer, 2014; Hare, Marston, & Allen, 2011; Hunter, Barber, Olsen, McNeely, & Bose, 2011; Kerr & Stattin, 2012).

In contrast, children who are continually acting up make their parents short-tempered, impatient, or distant. When parents have little knowledge of their adolescent's behavior, this leads to an increase in delinquency. Increases in delinquency, in turn, lead to decreases in parental knowledge, perhaps because delinquency often goes hand in hand with secrecy (Laird, Pettit, Bates, & Dodge, 2003) (see Figure 6).

In other words, the relationship between adolescent competence and authoritative parenting may be the result of a reciprocal cycle in which the child's psychosocial maturity leads to authoritative parenting, which, in turn, leads to the further development of maturity

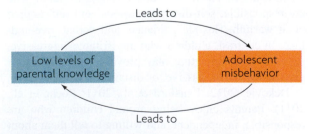

Figure 6 The relation between parenting and adolescent behavior is often reciprocal. (Adapted from Laird et al., 2003)

(Repetti, 1996). In contrast, nonauthoritative parenting may lead to the development of emotional and behavioral problems, which may lead parents to disengage even more (Burke, Pardini, & Loeber, 2008; Dishion, Nelson, & Bullock, 2004).

Ethnic Differences in Parenting Practices

A number of researchers have asked whether parents from different ethnic groups vary in their child rearing, and whether the relation between parenting styles and adolescent outcomes is the same across different ethnic groups. These are two different questions: The first concerns average differences between groups in their approaches to parenting (for example, whether Asian parents are stricter than White parents), whereas the second concerns the correlation between parenting practices and adolescent adjustment in different groups (for example, whether the effect of strictness is the same in Hispanic families as it is in Black families).

In general, authoritative parenting is less prevalent among Black, Asian, or Hispanic families than among White families, no doubt because parenting practices are often linked to cultural values and beliefs (Qu, Pomerantz, & Deng, 2014; Smetana & Chuang, 2001). Nevertheless, even though authoritative parenting is less common in ethnic minority families, its effects on adolescent adjustment are beneficial in all ethnic groups (Simons, Simons, & Su, 2012; Vazsonyi & Belliston, 2006). In other words, ethnic minority youngsters benefit from parenting that is responsive and demanding, just as their nonminority peers do.

Ethnic minority parents are also more demanding than White parents, even after taking ethnic differences in socioeconomic status into account (Chao & Otsuki-Clutter, 2011), an approach exemplified (some might say, caricatured) by a type of parent described as a "Tiger Mother" (Chua, 2011). As opposed to research on authoritative parenting, however, showing similar effects across ethnic groups, research on parental control indicates that the adverse effects of this style of parenting may be greater among White youngsters than among their ethnic minority counterparts (Morrison Gutman, Sameroff, & Eccles, 2002; Ruiz, Roosa, & Gonzales, 2002). There are several explanations for this.

First, because ethnic minority families are more likely to live in dangerous communities, authoritarian parenting, with its emphasis on control, may not be as harmful and may even offer some benefits (Richman & Mandara, 2013). Second, definitions of parental control don't always make sense when applied to parents from different cultures (Chao & Otsuki-Clutter, 2011). Because most of the research on parenting and adolescent development has been conducted by White researchers, other groups' approaches to child rearing (which appear very controlling, but which are neither aloof nor hostile) may be mislabeled as authoritarian when they are actually better understood as protective (Halgunseth, Ispa, & Rudy, 2006; Jackson-Newsom, Buchanan, & McDonald, 2008). Nevertheless, it is important to keep in mind that the conclusion to be drawn from these studies is not that overly controlling parenting is better than authoritative parenting for ethnic minority adolescents, but that it is not as harmful in these groups as it has been shown to be among White adolescents (W. A. Collins & Steinberg, 2006).

Autonomy and Attachment in the Adolescent's Family

Several studies of conversations between adolescents and their parents have examined factors in the nature of parent–adolescent communication that contribute to healthy adolescent development. In these studies, families are asked to discuss a problem together, and their interaction is videotaped and later analyzed.

Families with psychologically competent teenagers interact in ways that permit family members to express their autonomy and individuality while remaining emotionally connected to other family members (McElhaney, Allen, Stephenson, & Hare, 2009). Verbal give-and-take is the norm, and people are encouraged to express their own opinions, even when this leads to disagreements. The importance of maintaining close relationships in the family is emphasized, however, and adolescents are encouraged to consider how their actions may affect others. Adolescents who are permitted to assert their own opinions within a family context that is secure and loving develop higher self-esteem and more mature coping abilities. Adolescents whose autonomy is squelched are at risk for developing feelings of depression and low self-esteem, whereas those who do not feel connected are more likely than their peers to develop behavior problems (Bender et al., 2007; McElhaney et al., 2009).

In other words, adolescents appear to do best when they grow up in a family atmosphere that permits the development of individuality against a backdrop of close family ties (Grolnick, Kurowski, Dunlap, & Hevey, 2000; Walsh, Shulman, Bar-On, & Tsur, 2006). In these families, conflict between parents and adolescents can play a very important and positive role in the adolescent's social and cognitive development, because individuals are encouraged to express their opinions in an atmosphere that does not risk severing the emotional attachment (McElhaney et al., 2009). Perhaps for this reason, adolescents whose perceptions of their family differ a little bit from those of their parents are better adjusted than those whose views are either identical to their parents' or extremely divergent (Guion, Mrug, & Windle, 2009).

Because siblings live in close proximity to each other, they have added opportunities for both positive and negative interactions. © Mike Harrington/Getty Images

Adolescents' Relationships with Siblings

The Nature of Sibling Relationships in Adolescence

Sibling relationships during adolescence have characteristics that set them apart both from relationships with parents and relationships with friends (East, 2009; Kramer & Conger, 2011). Adolescents rate their sibling relationships similarly to those with their parents in companionship and importance, but more like friendships with respect to power, assistance, and their satisfaction with the relationship (Furman & Buhrmester, 1985).

Young adolescents often have emotionally charged relationships with siblings that are marked by conflict and rivalry, but also by nurturance and support (Campione-Barr & Smetana, 2010). As children mature from childhood to early adolescence, sibling conflict increases (Brody, Stoneman, & McCoy, 1994), with adolescents reporting more negativity in their sibling relationships than in their relationships with peers (Buhrmester & Furman 1990) and less effective conflict resolution than with their parents (C. Tucker, McHale, & Crouter, 2003a). Adolescents see aggression toward siblings as more acceptable than aggression toward friends, which sometimes leads to behavior between siblings that is absolutely ruthless. Consider this 16-year-old girl's account of her behavior toward her younger sister:

> I'm kind of mean to her just 'cause she's my sister, you know? . . . Sometimes I tell her like, "oh just because you don't have any friends, that doesn't mean you can come and hang out with my friends" because that's something that usually gets to her, so you tend to lean towards that, to make her go away. . . . One time . . . she kept on trying to play with me and my friend, and we were yelling at her . . . We hurt her a little bit and she started crying. . . . I wish it

didn't happen. . . . We were really mad at her, and I don't know why, and she just really wanted someone to play with. (Reccchia, Wainryb, & Pasupathi, 2013)

Over the course of adolescence, adolescents' relationships with siblings, and especially with younger siblings, become more egalitarian but also more distant and less emotionally intense (Tucker, Updegraff, & Baril, 2010), although patterns of change in sibling relationships differ between same-sex and mixed-sex dyads (see Figure 7). In same-sex dyads, intimacy increases between preadolescence and middle adolescence, and then declines somewhat. In mixed-sex dyads, the pattern is the opposite: intimacy drops between preadolescence and mid-adolescence, and then increases. In fact, by late adolescence, brothers and sisters are closer than are same-sex siblings, although both types of relationships become closer as individuals leave home and move into young adulthood (Scharf, Shulman, & Avigad-Spitz, 2005; Whiteman, McHale, & Crouter, 2011). Despite these changes over time, though, there is considerable stability in the quality of sibling relationships between childhood and adolescence. Siblings who are relatively closer during middle childhood are relatively closer as adolescents (J. Dunn, Slomkowski, & Beardsall, 1994).

A Network of Relationships The adolescent's interpersonal world is a web of interconnected relationships. The quality of the parent–adolescent relationship influences the quality of relations among brothers and sisters (e.g., East & Khoo, 2005). Harmony and cohesiveness in the parent–adolescent relationship are associated with less sibling conflict and a more positive sibling relationship (East, 2009). In contrast, adolescents who experience maternal rejection and negativity are more aggressive with siblings.

By the same token, children and adolescents learn much about social relationships from

behavioral genetics
The scientific study of genetic influences on behavior.

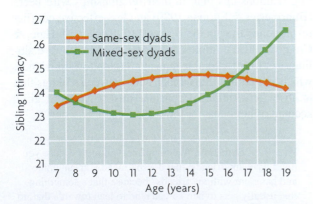

Figure 7 Patterns of change in intimacy between siblings differ between same-sex and mixed-sex dyads. (Kim et al., 2006)

sibling interactions, and they bring this knowledge and experience to friendships outside the family (East, 2009; Harper, Padilla-Walker, & Jensen, 2014). In poorly functioning families, aggressive interchanges between unsupervised siblings often provide a training ground within which adolescents learn, practice, and perfect antisocial and aggressive behavior (Criss & Shaw, 2005; J. Snyder, Bank, & Burraston, 2005). The reverse is true as well—the quality of adolescents' relationships with their friends influences how they interact with their siblings (Kramer & Kowal, 2005).

The quality of the sibling relationship also affects adolescents' psychological well-being (Bascoe, Davies, & Cummings, 2012; McHale, Updegraff, & Whiteman, 2012; Solmeyer, McHale, & Crouter, 2014). Positive sibling relationships contribute to adolescents' academic competence, sociability, health, autonomy, and self-worth (McHale et al., 2012). Having a close sibling relationship can partially ameliorate the negative effects of family stress (Waite, Shanahan, Calkins, Keane, & O'Brien, 2011) and of not having friends in school (East, 2009), and siblings can serve as sources of advice and guidance (Kolburn Kowal & Blinn-Pike, 2004). Of course, siblings can influence the development of problems, too (Bank, Burraston, & Snyder, 2004)! Younger sisters of adolescent mothers are relatively more likely to engage in early sexual activity and to become pregnant during adolescence (East, Reyes, & Horn, 2007). Siblings also influence each other's drug use and antisocial behavior (Low, Shortt, & Snyder, 2012; Samek, McGue, Keyes, & Iacono, 2014; Whiteman, Jensen, & Maggs, 2013).

Behavioral Genetics and Adolescent Development

One topic of interest to researchers who study adolescents and their siblings concerns how closely siblings resemble each other in characteristics such as intelligence, personality, and interests. Recent advances in the study of **behavioral genetics** have provided new insights into this issue, as well as a host of others concerning the joint impact of genes and the environment on development.

Researchers examine this issue in three main ways: (1) studying adolescents who are twins, to see whether identical twins are more similar than fraternal twins (e.g., McGue, Elkins, Walden, & Iacono, 2005); (2) studying adolescents who have been adopted, to see whether adopted adolescents are more like their biological parents than like their adoptive parents (e.g., Abrahamson, Baker, & Caspi, 2002); and (3) studying adolescents and their siblings in stepfamilies, to see whether similarity between siblings varies with their biological relatedness (e.g., Neiderhiser et al., 2004). In addition to examining whether and how much given traits are genetically versus environmentally determined, researchers also ask how these two sets of factors interact (for example, whether the same environment affects people with different genetic makeups in different ways, or whether people with different genetic makeups evoke different reactions from others) (W. A. Collins, Maccoby, Steinberg, Hetherington, & Bornstein, 2000).

Genetic and Environmental Influences on Adolescent Development

In studies of genetic and environmental influences on adolescent development, researchers distinguish between two types of environmental influences. **Shared environmental influences** are factors in the environment that individuals, such as siblings, have in common and that make the individuals similar in personality and behavior. **Nonshared environmental influences** are factors in the environments of individuals that are not similar and that, as a consequence, make the individuals different from one another (Turkheimer & Waldron, 2000).

Studies indicate that both genetic and nonshared environmental influences, such as differential parental treatment, peer relations, and school experiences, are particularly strong in adolescence. In contrast, shared environmental factors, such as family socioeconomic status or the neighborhood in which two siblings live, are less influential (McGue, Sharma, & Benson, 1996; Pike et al., 1996). In studies of siblings, nonshared environmental influences can include factors within the family as well as outside of it. For example, if two siblings are treated very differently by their parents, this would be considered a nonshared environmental influence. This sort of nonshared environment—that is, the nonshared environment that results from people having different experiences within what would appear to be the same context—seems to be the most important (Turkheimer & Waldron, 2000).

Genetic factors strongly influence many qualities that previously had been assumed to be shaped mainly by the environment. Aggressive behavior is especially driven by genetics, although shared and nonshared environmental influences on adolescents' antisocial behavior, including aggression, also have been found (S. A. Burt, McGue, Kreuger, & Iacono, 2007). Genetic factors also have been linked to various emotional and behavioral problems, such as risk for suicide and depression (Jacobson & Rowe, 1999) and alcohol dependence (Dick, 2011). Research also has found strong genetic influences on adolescent competence, self-image, and self-conceptions (S. McGuire et al., 1999).

Intelligence in adolescence (as indexed by IQ) is also under strong genetic control, with genetic influences compounding over time and ultimately becoming more influential than the family environment (Briley &

Tucker-Drob, 2013; Tucker-Drob, Briley, & Harden, 2013). The maturation of brain regions associated with complex reasoning also becomes increasingly under genetic control over time (Lenroot & Giedd, 2008). Genetic influences on school performance, in contrast to intelligence, are more modest (Loehlin, Neiderhiser, & Reiss, 2005).

> **shared environmental influences** Nongenetic influences that make individuals living in the same family similar to each other.
>
> **nonshared environmental influences** The nongenetic influences in individuals' lives that make them different from people they live with.

Many studies have shown that adolescents with the same genetic predispositions (such as genes associated with risk for depression) develop differently if they grow up in different environments (e.g., Brody et al., 2012; Li, Berk, & Lee, 2013). For instance, genetic influences on antisocial behavior are stronger among adolescents who have delinquent peers (Beaver, DeLisi, Wright, & Vaughn, 2009; Latendresse et al., 2011) and weaker among those who do well in school (Johnson, McGue, & Iacono, 2009). Genetic influences on intelligence are stronger in families with highly educated parents, because the influence of genes on intelligence is stronger in environments that provide more learning opportunities, allowing children to benefit from their genetic advantages (Tucker-Drob & Harden, 2012). In other words, genes may shape *tendencies,* but whether these tendencies are actualized often depends on the environment.

Why Are Siblings Often So Different?

If the family is an important influence on development, how can we explain the fact that siblings who grow up in the same family often turn out to be very different from one another? One answer is that siblings actually may have very different family experiences, because they have been treated differently by their parents, they perceive similar experiences in different ways, or because they grew up in the same household at different times in the family's life (C. Tucker, McHale, & Crouter, 2003b; Ellis, Schlomer, Tilley, & Butler, 2012). One brother may describe his family as close-knit, while another may have experienced it as distant. One girl may describe her family life as plagued with argument and conflict, while her sister describes it as peaceful and agreeable. Even though we may assume that children growing up in the same family have shared the same environment, this is not necessarily the case.

As you might expect, unequal treatment from mothers or fathers often creates conflict among siblings and is linked to a variety of problems, such as depression, antisocial behavior, and early pregnancy (East & Jacobson, 2003; Reiss et al., 1995). Studies also show that differences in siblings' real and perceived family experiences are related to different patterns of development (Barrett-Singer & Weinstein, 2000; Mekos, Hetherington, & Reiss, 1996). Better-adjusted adolescents are more likely than their siblings to report that they had close relationships with their parents, that their relations with brothers or sisters were friendly, that they were involved in family decision making, and that they were given a high level of responsibility around the house (L. Shanahan, McHale, Crouter, & Osgood, 2008). As they get older, adolescents appreciate the reasons for parents treating siblings differently. Sibling relationships are strained only when this differential treatment is perceived as unfair (Feinberg, Neiderhiser, Simmens, Reiss, & Hetherington, 2000; Kowal & Kramer, 1997).

Treating siblings differently may actually be a good thing for parents to do, so long as each sibling is treated well. When siblings are treated differently by their parents, they get along better—presumably because this differential treatment makes them feel unique and lessens **sibling rivalry** (Feinberg, McHale, Crouter, & Cumsille, 2003). Perhaps you have a brother or sister whom you resemble more than you'd like—so much, in fact, that you've had a hard time establishing your own personality. When siblings feel this way, they often deliberately try to be different from each other—a phenomenon known as **sibling deidentification.** An adolescent whose brother or sister is a star athlete, for instance, may shun sports and focus on cultivating other types of talents, perhaps in academics or in the arts, in order to diminish feelings of competition. Similarly, although having an older sibling who is academically successful seems to promote younger adolescents' achievement, too much academic support from an older sibling may actually undermine a younger adolescent's success in school (Bouchey, Shoulberg, Jodl, & Eccles, 2010).

sibling rivalry
Competition between siblings, often for parental attention.

sibling deidentification
The process through which siblings deliberately try to be different from each other.

In addition to having different experiences inside the family, siblings also may have very different experiences outside the family—at school, with friends, in the neighborhood. These contexts provide yet another source of nonshared environmental influence. Because factors other than the family environment shape adolescent development and behavior, siblings may turn out very different if they have divergent experiences outside the home.

The Adolescent's Family in a Changing Society

In America and in many other industrialized countries, the family has undergone a series of profound changes during the past half century that have diversified its form and, as a result, adolescents' daily experiences. Increased rates of divorce and childbearing outside of marriage, as well as a changing international economy, have dramatically altered the world in which children and adolescents grow up. Although some of the most striking trends in family life slowed during the early 1990s, they did not reverse by any means. The divorce rate and proportion of single-parent families, which skyrocketed during the 1970s and 1980s, stabilized at their historically high levels at the beginning of the 1990s and have changed relatively little since then (U.S. Census Bureau, 2012). Diversity in family forms is also reflected in the sizable numbers of adolescents who are raised by adoptive parents, lesbian and gay parents, and foster parents.

The Changed and Changing Nature of Family Life

Divorce The U.S. divorce rate increased markedly beginning in the 1960s, rising steadily, and at times rapidly, until 1980. Although this rate declined during the 1990s, it has leveled off, and it is now estimated that about 40% of all first marriages end in divorce. More than 40% of all American children will experience their parents' divorce (Emery, Beam, & Rowen, 2011). Because most divorces occur early in a marriage, adolescents are more likely than children to grow up in a divorced family than to actually experience their parents' divorce. It is important to keep in mind, however, that the divorce rate varies considerably among people with different levels of education—divorce is much less common among college graduates than nongraduates (Hurley, 2005).

Single Parenthood In addition to adolescents who live in a single-parent household as a consequence of

One reason adolescents with divorced parents are more likely to have problems than their peers is that divorce often exposes children to marital conflict, which adversely affects their mental health. © Zoey/Image Source/PunchStock RF

their parents' divorce, a sizable percentage of youngsters will spend time in a single-parent household from birth; indeed, today, 40% of all children are born outside of marriage, only half of whom are born to a cohabiting couple (Emery et al., 2011). Keep in mind, though, that a substantial number of adolescents who are classified as living in single-parent households actually live with more than one adult, often with the unmarried partner of the child's parent (Fields, 2003). When youngsters live with only one of their biological parents, either in single-parent or in two-parent households, it is usually with the mother; only about 15% of children who live with one parent live with their father (U.S. Census Bureau, 2012).

There are important racial and ethnic differences in these patterns of family life. Whereas close to 85% of all Asian children, 75% of all White children, and 60% of all Hispanic children live with two parents, only 33% of Black children do (U.S. Census Bureau, 2012). Black youngsters are far more likely to experience parental divorce and to be born outside of marriage, but they are far less likely to experience their parents' remarriage. As a consequence, Black adolescents spend longer periods of time in single-parent households.

Remarriage Because more than three-fourths of divorced men and two-thirds of divorced women remarry, the majority of youngsters whose parents separate also live in a stepfamily at some time. And, because the divorce rate is higher for second marriages than for first ones, the majority of youth whose parents remarry will experience a *second* divorce. Because divorces generally occur faster in remarriages—one-fourth happen within 5 years—many children confront a second divorce before they have finished adapting to having a stepparent.

Poverty Approximately 20% of all adolescents in the United States grow up in abject poverty, and an additional 40% grow up in low-income families (National Center for Children in Poverty, 2015) (see Figure 8). Perhaps more importantly, the gap between the very poor and the very

Poverty often diminishes the quality of parenting in a household, which adversely affects adolescent development. © John Moore/ Getty Images News/Getty Images

wealthy is at an all-time high (White, 2014). Poverty is much more likely to touch the lives of non-White adolescents; approximately 35% of Black and 30% of Hispanic children grow up in poverty (National Center for Children in Poverty, 2015). One reason for the large disparity in poverty rates between White and non-White children is the racial disparity in rates of single parenthood: Because non-White children are more likely to be raised in single-parent homes, they are more likely to be poor.

To what extent has the changed nature of the American family changed the nature of adolescent development? How do divorce, single parenthood, remarriage, poverty, and new family forms affect adolescents' development?

Many individuals are certain that the answer to these questions is, "For the worse." But before we jump to this conclusion, it is important to raise two considerations. First, although increases in adolescents' problems between 1950 and 1980—as indexed by such indicators

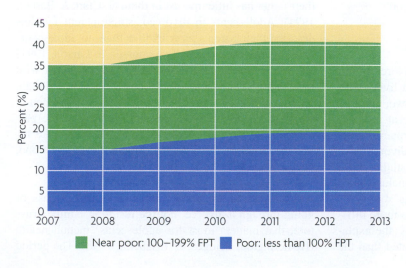

Near poor: 100–199% FPT   Poor: less than 100% FPT

Figure 8 **The proportion of adolescents growing up in poverty has increased during the last decades.** (National Center for Children in Poverty, 2010)

Note: FPT refers to the "federal poverty threshold."

as drug use, suicide, and poor school achievement, for example—occurred alongside many of these shifts in family life, it is difficult to say that the family changes *caused* the changes in adolescent behavior. Adolescents' psychological and behavioral well-being took a turn for the better in the early 1980s, despite the continued "demise" of the family (Furstenberg, 1990). Moreover, the one group of young people whose psychological and behavioral profile has improved most markedly in the past 25 years—poor, minority youngsters—experienced the most dramatic "decline" in family life during this time.

Second, because the conditions under which divorce, single parenthood, and remarriage take place vary tremendously from family to family, it is hard to generalize about their effects. (In contrast, it is relatively easy to generalize about the effects of poverty on adolescents, which are almost always negative.) For some young people, divorce may bring a welcome end to family conflict and tension; for others, it may be extremely disruptive. Some young people living with only their mother actually see their father more often than do their peers who live in homes where the father ostensibly is present (D. N. Hawkins, Amato, & King, 2006).

It is also the case that broad categories of family structures (e.g., "intact," "single-parent," etc.) often combine types of households that are very different in other respects (Apel & Kaukinen, 2008). Adolescents whose biological parents are cohabiting have a rate of antisocial behavior that is 40% higher than those whose biological parents are married and a rate of antisocial behavior that is about the same as adolescents who live in households with a biological mother and no other adult. Similarly, adolescents from "intact" families who live with both biological parents in families where one or both of the parents has a child from a prior marriage generally have a fairly high rate of problems, despite their living with both biological parents (Halpern-Meekin & Tach, 2008). In other words, variations *within* different family structures are likely to be more important than the differences among them. This is readily apparent when we look at how adolescents are affected by parental divorce.

Adolescents and Divorce

At one time, research on adolescents and divorce would likely have started with the assumption that living with one parent was not as good as living with two, and that children whose parents divorced would be at a disadvantage relative to those whose parents remained married. Over time, researchers' ideas about divorce have changed dramatically, as new and better studies have challenged, clarified, and tempered the conclusions of past research. While most social scientists still agree that adolescents from divorced homes have more difficulties than those from nondivorced homes, the explanation for this finding is far more complicated than the

conventional wisdom that "Two parents are better than one" or "All children need a mother and a father." Five sets of findings have questioned these simple assertions.

The Effect of Divorce Is Small in Magnitude First, although divorce clearly diminishes youngsters' well-being, the impact of divorce itself is small (Amato & Anthony, 2014). Although there are differences between children from divorced and nondivorced homes in school achievement, behavior problems, psychosocial adjustment, and family relations—all favoring individuals from nondivorced homes—the differences are seldom substantial. In general, the effects of divorce tend to be stronger among school-aged individuals than preschoolers or college students. One especially intriguing finding is that the effects of divorce are smaller among youngsters from the United States than from other countries. The explanation: Divorce is more common in the United States, and American children from divorced homes are less likely to be stigmatized and more likely to have access to psychological services, such as counseling.

Quality Matters Second, the quality of the relationships the young person has with the important adults in her or his life matters more than the number of parents present in the home (Mandara & Murray, 2000). Adolescents from stepfamilies have as many, if not more, problems than those from single-parent homes, even though adolescents in stepfamilies have two parents in the home (J. P. Hoffman, 2002). In addition, youngsters from single-parent families that have not experienced divorce (for example, youngsters who have lost a parent through death, or youngsters with a single mother who never married) have fewer difficulties than their counterparts from divorced or remarried homes (Demo & Acock, 1996). Finally, adolescents in two-parent homes do not always have warm and close relationships with their parents. Indeed, adolescents living in father-absent homes have higher self-esteem than adolescents who live in two-parent homes but who feel that their father has little interest in them (J. Clark & Barber, 1994). Adolescents in divorced, single-parent families describe their parents as friendlier than do adolescents whose parents are married (Asmussen & Larson, 1991) and are in a relatively more positive mood when with their family than when with friends (Larson & Gillman, 1996). Adolescents and their parents argue less often in single-parent households, perhaps because single parents tend to be more permissive, which may make for less parent-adolescent conflict (Smetana, Yau, Restrepo, & Braeges, 1991).

Adaptation to Divorce Third, it is the process of going through a divorce, not the resulting family structure, that matters most for adolescents' mental health (Hetherington, Bridges, & Insabella, 1998). The period of greatest difficulty for most adolescents is right around the time of the divorce (Jeynes, 2001). Although many young people show signs of difficulty immediately after their parents split up—problems in school, behavior problems, and increased anxiety—two years later, the majority have adjusted to the change and behave comparably to teens whose biological parents have remained married (Hetherington et al., 1998). Although adolescents whose parents have divorced have more problems than those whose parents remain married, the vast majority of individuals with divorced parents do not have significant problems (Hetherington et al., 1998).

Conflict and Stress   Fourth, research has linked the adverse consequences of divorce to a number of factors not specifically due to having a single parent (Crosnoe & Cavanaugh, 2010). These include the exposure of the children to marital conflict (Amato & Cheadle, 2008), disorganized or disrupted parenting (Linver, Brooks-Gunn, & Kohen, 2002), and increased stress in the household, often due to loss of income (Pong & Ju, 2000; Sun & Li, 2002). Adolescents living in two-parent families in which no divorce has occurred are also harmed by marital conflict, suboptimal parenting (especially parenting that is too lenient, too harsh, or inconsistent), and loss of income. In other words, the adverse, and usually temporary, effects of divorce or remarriage on adolescent well-being usually reflect the heightened conflict, disorganization, and stress surrounding the event, not the divorce or remarriage per se. The most important pathway through which divorce may adversely affect adolescent adjustment is via its disruptive impact on parenting (Amato & Sobolewski, 2001; Jeong & Chun, 2010).

Genetic Influences   Finally, although some of the apparent effects of parental divorce are the result of exposure to such stressors as marital conflict or disorganized parenting (S. A. Burt, Barnes, McGue, & Iacono, 2008; Frisco, Muller, & Frank, 2007), genetic differences between adolescents whose parents have divorced and those whose parents have not may account for part of this. Adults who divorce are different from those who do not with respect to many traits that have strong genetic origins—such as predispositions to different sorts of emotional and behavioral problems, like depression or substance abuse—and these traits are passed on from parents to children (D'Onofrio et al., 2006). One reason that adolescents from divorced homes have more problems than their peers is that they have inherited from their divorced parents some of the same traits that may have influenced their parents' decision to get divorced in the first place (O'Connor, Caspi, DeFries, & Plomin, 2000).

Individual Differences in the Effects of Divorce   There also are differences among children in how vulnerable they are to the short-term effects of divorce. In general, immediate problems are relatively more common among boys, younger children, children with a difficult temperament, children who do not have supportive relationships with adults outside the family, and youngsters whose parents divorce during the transition into adolescence (Saxbe, Margolin, Shapiro, & Baucom, 2012). Because early adolescence is a time during which individuals seem to be especially sensitive to stress, parental divorce at this time may have a relatively stronger impact (Ivanova, Mills, & Veenstra, 2011).

Social support from others may be an especially important resource for inner-city children growing up in single-parent homes (Lamborn & Nguyen, 2004; Pallock & Lamborn, 2006). Support from kin appears to increase single parents' effectiveness in child rearing, and this, in turn, tends to limit adolescents' misbehavior. Studies of Black youngsters have found that children growing up in home environments that include a grandparent as well as a parent fare significantly better than those growing up in single-parent homes or in stepfamilies. These studies, as well as others, remind us that relatives other than parents may play an extremely important role in adolescents' lives (Henderson, Hayslip, Sanders, & Louden, 2009; Richardson, 2009), especially within ethnic groups that historically have placed a great deal of importance on maintaining close ties to extended family members. This helps explain why the impact of divorce on adolescent adjustment is weaker among Black adolescents than among adolescents from other backgrounds (Heard, 2007; Kowaleski-Jones & Dunifon, 2006).

The Specific Impact of Marital Conflict

Although divorce is generally associated with short-term difficulties for the adolescent, at least some of the differences between adolescents from divorced versus nondivorced homes were present before the parents divorced (Sun, 2001). One explanation for this is that children in the households that later divorced were exposed to higher levels of marital unhappiness and conflict and strained parent–child relationships, both of which are known to disrupt parenting and increase children's difficulties (Amato & Booth, 1996; Forehand, Neighbors, Devine, & Armistead, 1994) (see Figure 9). Children's maladjustment, in turn, adversely affects the quality of their parents' marriage, creating a vicious cycle (Cui, Donnellan, & Conger, 2007).

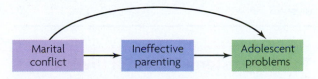

Figure 9 The effects of exposure to marital conflict are both direct and indirect through its negative impact on parenting.

The recognition that exposure to marital conflict, apart from and in addition to divorce itself, has harmful effects on children's development has prompted many researchers to study how the quality of the adolescent's parents' marriage affects teenagers' mental health and behavior (e.g., Cui, Conger, & Lorenz, 2005; Cummings, Cheung, Koss, & Davies, 2014). Several conclusions have emerged from this research. First, children are more adversely affected by marital conflict when they are aware of it than when it is more covert (Harold & Conger, 1997). Marital conflict is particularly harmful when it is especially hostile, physically violent, or frightening. Exposure to overt marital conflict and domestic violence has been linked to a wide range of adolescent problems, including depression, aggression, and delinquency (Choe & Zimmerman, 2014; Fosco & Feinberg, 2014; Goeke-Morey, Papp, & Cummings, 2013; Su, Simons, & Simons, 2011).

Second, children are more negatively affected when the marital conflict leads to feelings of insecurity or self-blame (Cummings, George, McCoy, & Davies, 2012; Davies, Martin, & Cicchetti, 2012; Schwartz, Stutz, & Lederman, 2012; Siffert, Schwartz, & Stutz, 2011). Adolescents who blame themselves for their parents' conflict, whose feelings of security are challenged, or who are drawn into their parents' arguments are more likely to feel anxious, depressed, and distressed (Buehler, Franck, & Cook, 2009; Grych, Raynor, & Fosco, 2004).

Finally, marital conflict more adversely affects the adolescent when the conflict disrupts the quality of the parent–child relationship (Amato & Sobolewski, 2001). Adolescents are directly affected by exposure to their parents' conflict, to be sure, but several studies have found as well that tension between spouses spills over into the parent–child relationship, making mothers and fathers more hostile, more irritable, and less effective as parents (Bradford, Vaughn, & Barber, 2008; Buehler, Benson, & Gerard, 2006; Cui & Conger, 2008; T. Schofield et al., 2009). Adolescents who perceive their parents as hostile or uncaring are more likely to report a wide range of emotional and behavioral problems than are their peers.

making the practical connection

Based on the available research, what advice would you give to parents of teenagers who are considering divorce?

The Longer-Term Effects of Divorce

Individuals whose parents divorce during preadolescence and adolescence often demonstrate adjustment difficulties later, even after 2 or 3 years (e.g., Hetherington, 1993).

Some research indicates that individuals whose parents divorced during childhood or adolescence continue to have adjustment problems well into their 30s (Cherlin, Chase-Lansdale, & McRae, 1998). These effects do not appear to be ameliorated by parental remarriage; adolescents from stepfamilies score similarly, or worse, on measures of longer-term adjustment, as do adolescents from single-parent, divorced homes (Hetherington et al., 1998).

Sleeper Effects   To what can we attribute these "sleeper" effects—effects of divorce that may not be apparent until much later in the child's development? Two possible explanations come to mind. The first is that the ways in which adjustment difficulties might be expressed may not surface until adolescence. For example, social scientists believe that increased drug use and higher rates of early pregnancy are consequences of the lower level of parental monitoring in divorced homes (M. R. Moore & Chase-Lansdale, 2001). But because younger children are unlikely to use drugs or be sexually active, no matter what their family background, the effect of the poor monitoring is not seen until adolescence, when individuals might begin using drugs and having sex.

A second explanation concerns the particular developmental challenges of adolescence (S. J. Steinberg, Davila, & Fincham, 2006). Adolescence is a time when individuals first begin experimenting with intimate sexual relationships. If having one's parents divorce or being exposed to marital conflict affects one's conceptions of relationships or views of romantic commitment (Shulman, Zlotnik, Shachar-Shapira, Connolly, & Bohr, 2012), it makes sense that some of the effects of early parental divorce will not be manifested until the adolescent begins dating and gets seriously involved in romantic relationships (Donahue et al., 2010).

Custody, Contact, and Conflict Following Divorce

After a divorce, do adolescents fare better or worse in different kinds of living arrangements? Does contact with the nonresidential parent contribute to the adolescent's well-being?

The nature of the relationship between the adolescent's divorced parents, and not which one he or she lives with, is the key factor (Booth, Scott, & King, 2010). In the years immediately following a divorce, children may fare a bit better in the custody of the parent of the same sex, but these effects are not long-lasting; over time, both male and female adolescents fare equally well either in dual custody or in sole custody (C. Buchanan et al., 1996), a finding that was replicated in a study of lesbian couples who have separated (Gartrell, Bos, Peyser, Deck, & Rodas, 2011). More important, especially for adolescents who have dual residences, are two factors: whether the ex-spouses continue to fight and place the child between them, and whether the adolescent's discipline is consistent across the two households. Adolescents whose parents have a congenial, cooperative relationship and who receive consistent and appropriate discipline from both homes report less emotional difficulty and fewer behavioral problems (C. Buchanan et al., 1996; Coiro & Emery, 1996).

Adolescents whose parents have divorced also vary in the extent to which they have contact with the parent they no longer live with, typically their father. Contact between adolescents and their father following a divorce usually diminishes very quickly after the father moves out and continues to decline over time, especially among men who remarry or enter into a new romantic relationship (Stephens, 1996). Generally speaking, adolescents who have regular postdivorce contact with their father have fewer problems (e.g., Booth et al., 2010; Coley & Medeiros, 2007; Mitchell, Booth, & King, 2009), but not all studies have reached this conclusion, and some have concluded that it is healthy adolescent functioning that influences fathers' involvement, rather than the reverse (D. N. Hawkins, Amato, & King, 2007). More important than the father's involvement is the level of conflict between the divorced parents and the nature of the adolescent's relationship with the father before and after the divorce (Bastaits, Ponnet, & Mortelmans, 2012; Karre & Mounts, 2012). Adolescents benefit from contact with their nonresidential parent when conflict between their parents is minimal, but suffer from such contact when parental conflict is intense. Similarly, adolescents benefit when they have frequent contact with a nonresidential parent with whom they had a close relationship when their parents were married, but suffer from contact with one with whom they didn't get along prior to the divorce. One consistent finding, though, is that financial support from fathers is associated with less problem behavior and higher academic achievement (Menning, 2002).

What Divorced Parents Tell Their Teenagers

Researchers have examined the sorts of disclosure that take place between recently divorced mothers and their children (Koerner, Jacobs, & Raymond, 2000; Koerner, Wallace, Lehman, Lee, & Escalante, 2004). Mothers were equally likely to talk to sons and daughters, and their conversations were similar, consistent with a point made earlier—namely, that for the most part adolescent males and females are treated similarly by their parents. Two topics of conversation, in particular, have piqued researchers' interest: complaints about and anger toward the ex-husband and worries about finances, both of which are common concerns among recently divorced women. Among mothers who disclose these sorts of feelings, an important motive for doing so is not the mother's need for a confidante, but her desire to shape her daughter's impression of her and the circumstances surrounding the divorce. Here's one example:

I talk to her about anything. Complaints I have about her father. [Alison] thinks the divorce is all my fault. Her Dad has been absent for two years. He called on occasion and sent presents on Christmas and b-Days. While he was gone Alison turned him into some sort of God in her mind. Now that he has returned to the area he wants little or nothing to do with his kids. When Alison complains, I make statements like, "Alison, you're starting to see the side of your Dad that I was married to" or "He never gave me any time either." (Koerner et al., 2000, p. 305)

Not all mothers share their feelings about these topics with their child. As one put it:

I try really hard not to say anything negative about my ex-husband to my children. We agreed when we got divorced to always do what was best for our children. So far, so good. (Koerner et al., 2000, p. 305)

Consistent with other research indicating that adolescents fare worse when they are drawn into their divorced parents' conflict, adolescents whose mothers complain to them about their ex-husbands or discuss their financial concerns report more psychological distress, in the form of anxiety, depression, tension, and psychosomatic complaints. Adolescents are especially likely to worry about family finances and the impact of the divorce on their future (Koerner, Korn, Dennison, & Witthoft, 2011). As several adolescents explained:

I was thinking, my gosh, my dad doesn't care about me—he's not paying it [child support]! I felt like going and calling my dad and yelling at him because I think he doesn't care about it. (11-year-old daughter, quoted in Koerner et al., 2004, p. 52)

My mom constantly rags on and on about how my dad is such a jerk and won't pay her as much as she thinks he should. It disturbs me incredibly because my dad is very kind when I visit him and I don't think my mom is fair. (15-year-old son, quoted in Koerner et al., 2004, p. 52)

My mom talks to me about how we don't have extra money. I don't really like to hear how little money we have. . . . I feel sad and kinda angry when we talk about money cause before the divorce this topic never, really came up to talk about. . . . (13-year-old daughter, quoted in Koerner et al., 2004, p. 52)

Remarriage

Adolescents growing up in stepfamilies—especially if the remarriage occurred during early adolescence rather than childhood—often have more problems than their peers, a finding that holds regardless of whether the stepparents are legally married or cohabiting (S. Brown & Rinelli, 2010; Harcourt, Adler-Baeder, Erath, & Petit, 2015). Youngsters growing up in single-parent homes are more likely than those in intact homes to be involved in delinquent activity, but adolescents in stepfamilies are even more at risk for this sort of problem behavior than are adolescents in single-parent families. This results, in part, because they are exposed to a "double dose" of marital conflict—normal, everyday conflict between the parent and stepparent and additional conflict between ex-spouses (T. Hanson, McLanahan, & Thomson, 1996; MacDonald & DeMaris, 1995)—and because they are exposed to a new set of potentially difficult issues that arise from the blending of children from two different marriages (Hetherington et al., 1999).

Like the short-term effects of divorce, the short-term effects of remarriage vary among children, although not necessarily in the same ways. In general, girls have more difficulty in adjusting to remarriage than boys, and older children have more difficulty than younger ones (Hetherington, 1993; V. Lee, Burkham, Zimiles, & Ladewski, 1994). One explanation for this is that both boys and younger children have more to gain from their mother's remarriage than do girls or older children, who may have become accustomed to having a single mother (Hetherington, 1991). Over time, gender differences in adjustment to remarriage disappear, and in remarriages that last more than 5 years, the adjustment of male and female children is similar (Hetherington et al., 1999). One interesting finding, especially in light of the growing number of young adults who depend on their parents' financial support, is that remarried parents and stepparents are less inclined than other parents to provide money to their children over the transition to adulthood (Aquilino, 2005).

Difficulties Adjusting to Parental Remarriage

Remarriage during the adolescent years is extremely stressful when families are unable to accommodate the new stepparent relationship. Given what we know about family reorganization and change during adolescence, having to integrate a new type of relationship into a family that is already undergoing a great deal of change may be more than some families can cope with. Many adolescents find it difficult to adjust to a new authority figure moving into the household, especially if that person has different ideas about rules and discipline, and particularly if the new authority figure is not legally married to the child's biological parent (Hetherington et al., 1999). This is especially true when the adolescent is already vulnerable, either because of previous psychological problems or because of a recent divorce or other stressful event.

By the same token, many stepparents find it difficult to join a family and not be accepted immediately by the children as the new parent. Stepparents may wonder why love is not forthcoming from their stepchildren, who often act critical, resistant, and sulky. Although many stepfathers and their adolescent stepchildren establish positive relationships, the lack of a biological connection between stepparent and stepchild—coupled with the stresses associated with divorce and remarriage—make this relationship especially vulnerable to problems. Adolescents in remarried households fare better when their stepparent can establish a consistent, supportive, authoritative style of discipline (Hetherington et al., 1999).

This research underscores the need—particularly as remarriage has become a more common part of American family life—to understand the special problems that may arise in the course of family reorganization (Crosnoe & Cavanaugh, 2010). Several studies indicate that children's adjustment declines somewhat each time they must cope with a change in their family's household composition (e.g., Barnett, Rowley, Zimmerman, Vansadia, & Caldwell, 2011; Fomby & Bosick, 2013; Hernandez, Pressler, Dorius, & Mitchell, 2014), in part because parenting may become less effective during each family transition (Forgatch, DeGarmo, & Knutson, 1994; Kurdek & Fine, 1993). Given the fact that the benefits of authoritative parenting are just as strong in divorced and remarried families as they are in other homes, experts believe that clinicians who work with families that have undergone marital transitions should help parents learn and adopt this parenting style.

One factor that seems to make a big difference in the adjustment of children in stepfamilies is the nature of the relationship they have with their noncustodial parent—the biological parent with whom they no longer live. Children fare better when there is consistency in discipline between their custodial and noncustodial parents and when they have a good relationship with the noncustodial parent, especially in the years immediately following the remarriage (Gunnoe, 1994). Having a close relationship with the noncustodial parent does not appear to undermine the relationship with the custodial parent (C. Buchanan & Maccoby, 1993), nor does it undermine the relationship between the adolescent and the stepparent (Yuan & Hamilton, 2006). Indeed, studies find that adolescents who feel close to *both* their father and stepfather have better outcomes than those who feel close to one but not the other (V. King, 2006; Risch, Jodl, & Eccles, 2004).

Economic Stress and Poverty

In recent years, and in light of the economic downturn of the last decade, there has been an upsurge in interest in the ways in which adolescents' mental health is affected by changes in their family's financial situation. To date, the studies of family income loss and adolescent adjustment suggest a number of parallels with the research on divorce and remarriage.

The Effects of Financial Strain

Like divorce, income loss is associated with disruptions in parenting, which, in turn, lead to increases in adolescent difficulties, including a diminished sense of mastery, increased emotional distress, academic and interpersonal problems, and delinquency. According to the Family Stress Model (Conger, Ge, Elder, Lorenz, & Simons, 1994), financial strain increases mothers' and fathers' feelings of depression and anxiety, worsens marriages, and causes conflicts between parents and adolescents (Hardaway & Cornelius, 2013; Ponnet, Van Leeuwen, Wouters, & Mortelmans, 2014; Uçanok & Güre, 2014; White, Liu, Nair, & Tein, 2015). These consequences, in turn, make parents more irritable, which adversely affects the quality of their parenting (see Figure 10). These patterns have been observed in countries around the world. In contrast, parents who are able to maintain a more positive outlook through the difficult time are more likely to protect their adolescents from the psychological harm associated with financial strain (Neppi, Shinyoung, Schofield, & Donnellan, 2015).

The family climate created by economic strain puts adolescents at risk for a variety of problems. When adolescents are repeatedly exposed to marital conflict—especially when it is not resolved—they are more likely to become aggressive and depressed. And when adolescents themselves are the recipients of aggressive parenting, they are likely to imitate this behavior in their relationships with siblings (K. Conger, Conger, & Elder, 1994) and peers (S. T. Williams, Conger, & Blozis, 2007), and, later, in their own marriage (Straus & Yodanis, 1996) and with their children (R. Simons, Whitbeck, Conger, & Chyi-In, 1991).

The Impact of Chronic Poverty Researchers have also studied the impact on adolescents of growing up amid chronic economic disadvantage (McLoyd et al.,

2009; Yoshikawa, Aber, & Beardslee, 2012). Persistent poverty, like temporary economic strain, undermines parental effectiveness, making mothers and fathers harsher, more depressed, less vigilant, less consistent, and more embroiled in conflict. These consequences all have negative effects on adolescent adjustment, which are manifested in increases in anxiety and depression, more frequent conduct problems, diminished school performance, and less prosocial behavior (Benner & Kim, 2010; Burrell & Roosa, 2009; Carlo, Padilla-Walker, & Day, 2011b; Lee, Wickrama, & Simons, 2012).

Growing up poor affects adolescents' mental health in a variety of ways. Poor adolescents are more likely to be exposed to violence, to feel more alienated from school, and to be exposed to high levels of stress. Homeless adolescents share many of the same problems with other youth who experience chronic poverty, including higher rates of depression and suicidal thoughts, academic difficulties, and behavior problems (Unger, Kipke, Simon, Montgomery, & Johnson, 1997; Whitbeck, Hoyt, & Bao, 2000). There are nearly 2 million homeless children and adolescents in the United States, the majority of whom are adolescents (National Coalition for the Homeless, 2007).

Studies of families living in poverty also tell us what parents living in poor neighborhoods can do to help protect their children from the adverse consequences of growing up in poor inner-city or rural neighborhoods (Brody, Stoneman, & Flor, 1996). Families fare better when they have adequate sources of social support (R. Taylor & Roberts, 1995) and when they have strong ties to religious institutions (Brody et al., 1996). Two specific sets of family management strategies employed by parents in poor neighborhoods seem to work: those that attempt to strengthen the adolescent's competence through effective

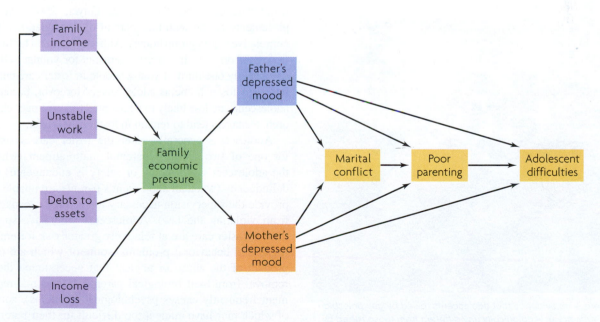

Figure 10 Economic strain affects adolescent adjustment via several pathways. (Conger et al. 1994)

child rearing within the home environment or through involving the child in positive activities outside the home, and those that attempt to minimize the child's exposure to dangers in the neighborhood (Crosnoe, Mistry, & Elder, 2002). Although adolescents in poor neighborhoods benefit from consistent parental monitoring—perhaps even from monitoring that is more vigilant than that used by families in more advantaged communities—they do not thrive when their parents exercise excessive control (McCarthy, Lord, Eccles, Kalil, & Furstenberg, 1992).

Special Family Forms

Adolescents and Adoption Studies of the psychological development of adolescents who have been adopted have yielded mixed and often contradictory results. On average, adopted individuals show relatively higher rates of delinquency, substance use, precocious sexual activity, psychological difficulties, and poorer school performance, but the magnitude of the difference between adopted and nonadopted adolescents is small, especially when other factors, like family resources or pubertal timing, are taken into account (Brooker, Berenbaum, Bricker, Corley, & Wadsworth, 2012). One reason for the mixed results and relatively modest effects is that there is a good deal of variability among adopted adolescents in their adjustment and in their feelings about being adopted. Adopted adolescents who are preoccupied with having been adopted are relatively more alienated from and mistrustful of their adoptive parents (J. K. Kohler, Grotevant, & McRoy, 2002).

foster care
A placement in a temporary living arrangement when a child's parents are not able to provide care, nurturance, or safety.

There is no evidence that adolescents raised by gay or lesbian parents are psychologically any different from those raised by straight parents. © Laura Doss/Getty Images RF

Adolescents with Lesbian or Gay Parents Several well-designed studies have looked at the psychological consequences of growing up with lesbian or gay parents. Although the right of same-sex couples to legally marry is now guaranteed under U.S. law, in many states a parent's sexual orientation may be a consideration in adoption, custody, and parental visitation decisions, in part because of concerns about the impact of living with a lesbian or gay parent. These concerns are unwarranted. There is no evidence whatsoever that children or adolescents with lesbian or gay parents are psychologically different from those with straight parents, a finding that has now been replicated numerous times, across many different domains of psychological development, including gender identity and sexual orientation (e.g., Gelderen, Bos, & Gartell, 2015). In the words of one expert:

> More than 25 years of research on the offspring of nonheterosexual parents has yielded results of remarkable clarity. Regardless of whether researchers have studied the offspring of divorced lesbian and gay parents or those born to lesbian and gay parents, their findings have been similar. Regardless of whether researchers have studied children or adolescents, they have reported similar results. Regardless of whether investigators have examined sexual identity, self-esteem, adjustment, or qualities of social relationships, the results have been remarkably consistent. In study after study, the offspring of lesbian and gay parents have been found to be at least as well adjusted overall as those of other parents. (Patterson, 2009, p. 732)

Adolescents in Foster Care According to recent estimates, about 175,000 teenagers are in foster care. **Foster care** is a broad term that refers to a placement in a temporary living arrangement when the adolescent's parents are not able to provide care, nurturance, or safety (Pinderhughes, Jones Harden, & Guyer, 2007). Such placements can be with members of the extended family, nonrelatives, or in group homes. Although we tend to think of foster homes as living arrangements for younger children, nearly one-third of young people in foster care enter into their foster home as adolescents. Moreover, because adolescents are less likely to be adopted than younger children, teenagers tend to remain in foster care longer.

Adolescents generally enter the foster care system for one of two reasons: parental maltreatment (when the adolescent's well-being or safety is endangered) or delinquency (when an adolescent's parents are unable to provide the supervision necessary to keep their teenager from violating the law). Adolescents who have spent time in foster care are at relatively greater risk for emotional and behavioral problems, some of which are the product of the abuse or neglect that necessitated their removal from their biological parents' home (maltreatment frequently causes psychological problems), some of which may have made it too difficult for their parents to adequately care for them (in which case the adolescent may be placed in a therapeutic environment designed for teenagers with psychological problems), and some of which may actually result from the foster care placement itself (for example, placement in a group home increases the adolescent's risk for delinquency (Ryan, Marshall, Herz, & Hernandez, 2008). Many adolescents move in and out of different placements, back and forth between their parents' home and a foster care placement, or between different foster care arrangements; frequent disruptions in living arrangements can lead to behavioral problems (Fisher, Stoolmiller, Mannering, Takahashi, & Chamberlain, 2011; Proctor, Skriner, Roesch, & Litrownik, 2010). After a period of time in foster care, adolescents are either reunified with their biological parents or adopted by someone other than their parents, or, if they are old enough, declared independent. As you can imagine, making the transition to independent adulthood—already a challenge for many youth who grew up in stable and supportive family environments— is even more difficult for adolescents whose lives have been so disrupted and who do not have parents on whom they can rely for support. Adolescents who have been in foster care are at higher risk for homelessness than other youth (Fowler, Toro, & Miles, 2009).

The Importance of the Family in Adolescent Development

As you have seen, there is considerable diversity among families with adolescents—diversity in background, in income, in parenting style, and in household composition. Yet no factor seems to influence adolescent adjustment more than the quality of relationships at home (Kaminski, Puddy, Hall, Cashman, Crosby et al., 2010). As one team of experts concluded on the basis of a comprehensive study of the lives, behavior, and health of 90,000 American teenagers:

> Across all of the health outcomes examined, the results point to the importance of family and the home environment for protecting adolescents from harm. What emerges

most consistently as protective is the teenager's feeling of connectedness with parents and family. Feeling loved and cared for by parents matters in a big way. (Blum & Rinehart, 2000, p. 31)

Study after study finds that adolescents who believe their parents or guardians are there for them—caring, involved, and accepting—are healthier, happier, and more competent than their peers, however health, happiness, or competence is assessed. This conclusion holds true regardless of the adolescent's age, sex, ethnicity, social class, or country, and across all types of families, whether married or divorced, single-parent or two-parent, rich or poor (Dornbusch, Erickson, Laird, & Wong, 2001; Schwarz et al., 2012). This has led many psychologists, including myself, to call for widespread efforts to increase the quality of parenting that children and adolescents receive as a way of preventing emotional and behavioral problems and promoting healthy development (Kumpfer & Alvarado, 2003). As I have written elsewhere, we know what the basic principles of good parenting are (Steinberg, 2005b). The challenge facing us is to figure out how best to disseminate this information to the people who need it most—parents.

Despite the tremendous growth and psychological development that take place as individuals leave childhood on the road toward adulthood, despite society's pressures on young people to grow up fast, despite all the technological and social innovations that have transformed family life, and contrary to claims that parents don't really make a difference (that by adolescence, parents' influence is overshadowed by the peer group or the mass media), adolescents continue to need the love, support, and guidance of adults who genuinely care about their development and well-being. Being raised in the presence of caring and committed adults is one of the most important advantages a young person can have in life. Although parental love may be expressed in different ways in different parts of the world, its importance for healthy adolescent development is unquestionable, regardless of cultural context (McNeely & Barber, 2010).

5 Peer Groups

The Origins of Adolescent Peer Groups in Contemporary Society

Changes in the Size of the Youth Population

Is There a Separate Youth Culture?

The Nature of Adolescent Peer Groups

Changes in Peer Groups During Adolescence

Cliques and Crowds

Changes in Clique and Crowd Structure Over Time

Adolescents and Their Crowds

The Social Map of Adolescence

Crowds as Reference Groups

Adolescents and Their Cliques

Similarity Among Clique Members

Common Interests Among Friends

Similarity Between Friends: Selection or Socialization?

Popularity and Rejection in Adolescent Peer Groups

Determinants of Popularity and Rejection

Relational Aggression

Victimization and Harassment

The Peer Group and Psychosocial Development

It is about 8:00 A.M. A group of teenagers congregates in the hallway in front of their first-period classroom, discussing their plans for the weekend. As the first-period bell sounds, they enter the classroom and take their seats. For the next 4 hours (until there is a break in their schedule for lunch), they will attend class in groups of about 25 adolescents to 1 adult.

At lunch, the group meets again to talk about the weekend. They have about 45 minutes until the first afternoon period begins. After lunch, they spend another 2 hours in class—again, in groups of about 25 adolescents and 1 adult. The school day ends, the group convenes yet again, and they go to someone's house to hang out for the rest of the day. Everyone's parents are working; they are on their own. At about 6:00 P.M., they disperse and head home for dinner. Some have plans to meet up later that night. Several will talk on the phone. Virtually all of them will text. And they will see one another first thing the next morning.

Adolescents in modern society spend a remarkable amount of time with people their own age. High school students in the United States and Europe spend twice as much of their time each week with peers as with parents or other adults—not even counting time in class (B. Brown & Larson, 2009; Dijkstra & Veenstra, 2011). Virtually all adolescents spend most of each weekday with their peers while at school, and the vast majority see or talk to their friends in the late afternoon, in the evening, and over the weekend (Larson & Verma, 1999). Time spent with peers increases steadily over the course of adolescence (Lam, McHale, & Crouter, 2014). It's easy to see why: Adolescents' moods are most positive when they are with their friends, time spent with friends becomes more rewarding

peer groups
Groups of individuals of approximately the same age.

over the course of adolescence, and, as Figure 1 illustrates, teenagers' moods become more positive over the course of the week, as the weekend approaches (Larson & Richards, 1998).

American society is highly age segregated. From the time youngsters stop spending their full day at home—certainly by age 5, but for many of those in day care, as early as the first year of life—until they graduate from high school at age 18 or so, they are grouped with children their own age. Other than relatives, they have little extended contact with older or younger people. Age grouping carries over into after-school, weekend, and vacation activities. In contemporary society, **peer groups**—groups of people who are roughly the same age—are one of the most important contexts in which adolescents spend time. The significance of peer groups gives adolescence in contemporary society some of its most distinctive features.

Understanding how adolescent peer groups form and what takes place within their boundaries is critical to understanding adolescent development. No discussion of adolescent identity development is complete without examining how and why teenagers derive part of their identity from the group they spend time with. No discussion of the development of autonomy is complete without considering how adolescents learn to make independent decisions when they are with their friends. No discussion of intimacy can ignore understanding teenagers' friendship groups and how they are formed. No discussion of adolescent sexuality is complete without talking about how, when, and why peer groups change from same-sex groups to mixed-sex groups. And no discussion of the development of achievement in adolescence can ignore the role that friends play in influencing each other's attitudes toward school.

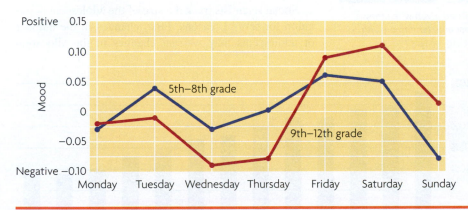

Positive 0.15
0.10
0.05
Mood
0
−0.05
Negative −0.10

Monday   Tuesday   Wednesday   Thursday   Friday   Saturday   Sunday

5th–8th grade

9th–12th grade

Figure 1   **As the weekend approaches and adolescents anticipate spending more time with their friends, their mood takes a marked turn for the better.** (Larson & Richards, 1998)

The Origins of Adolescent Peer Groups in Contemporary Society

Contact between adolescents and their peers is found in all cultures, of course. But not all societies have peer groups that are as narrowly defined and age segregated as those in contemporary society (B. Brown, 2004; Larson & Verma, 1999).

The spread of compulsory education was a major factor in the development of peer groups as we know them today. Educators first developed the idea of free public education, with students grouped by age—a practice known as **age grading**—in the middle of the nineteenth century. In doing so, they established an arrangement that would encourage the development and maintenance of age-segregated peer groups. It was not until the second quarter of the twentieth century, however,

age grading
The process of grouping individuals within social institutions on the basis of age.

baby boom
The period following World War II, during which the number of infants born was extremely large.

that most adolescents were directly affected by educational age grouping. Attending elementary school was common before 1900, but until 1930 or so, high school was a luxury available only to the affluent. Adolescent peer groups based on friendships formed in school were not prevalent until well into the twentieth century.

Changes in the Size of the Youth Population

Perhaps the most important factor influencing the rise of adolescent peer groups in contemporary society was the rapid growth of the teenage population between 1955 and 1975. Following the end of World War II, many parents wanted to have children as soon as possible, creating what has been called the postwar **baby boom.** The products of this baby boom became adolescents during the 1960s and early 1970s, creating an "adolescent boom" for about 15 years. The size of the population ages 15–19 nearly doubled between 1955 and 1975 and, more importantly, rose from less than 7% of the total population to well over 10%. During the mid-1970s more than 1 out of every 6 Americans was a teenager.

This trend turned downward in 1975. The relative size of the adolescent population decreased until 1995. But during the last decade of the twentieth century—when the products of the baby boom began raising adolescents of their own—the size of the teenage population began increasing once again. In the year 2000, there were 20 million 15- to 19-year-olds in the United States, and an additional 20 million people were between 10 and 14. In other words, as we entered the twenty-first century, approximately 1 in 7 Americans were adolescents. The proportion of the U.S. population that is adolescent is estimated to remain at about this level through the next half century (U.S. Census Bureau, 2000). Keep in mind, though, that patterns of change in the size of the adolescent population vary considerably around the world, mainly because of different birthrates (see Figure 2).

Social scientists track the size of the adolescent population for several reasons. First, changes in the number of adolescents may warrant changes in the allocation

Contemporary society is very age-graded. Even when they are in activities outside school, adolescents tend to be with same-aged peers. © Bernard Jaubert/Getty Images

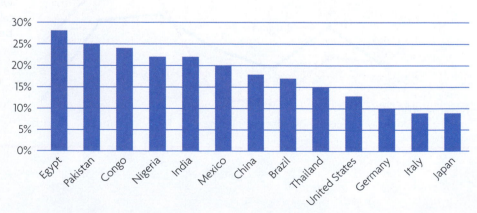

Figure 2 The proportion of the population that is adolescent varies around the world—it is highest in developing countries, especially in the Arab world, and lowest in highly industrialized countries, like Japan.
(United Nations, 2010)

of funds for social services, educational programs, and health care, since adolescents' needs are not the same as those of children or adults. Second, changes in the size of the adolescent population have implications for understanding the behavior of cohorts. A cohort is a group of individuals born during a particular period, such as the baby boomers (born in the late 1940s and early to mid-1950s), "Gen X" (born in the early 1970s), the "Millennials" (the adolescent children of the baby boomers, born in the 1980s and early 1990s, also known as "Generation Y"), or "Generation Z" (born during the 1990s, and sometimes referred to as the iGeneration, because of the growth of the Internet during their time) (see Table 1). Baby boomers, for example, were members of a very crowded cohort. During their adolescence, they encountered a lot of competition for places in college, jobs, and so on. The size of this cohort also meant that it could attract a great deal of public attention, from politicians to advertisers. In contrast, members of Gen X, who were adolescents in the late 1980s and early 1990s, were members of a much smaller cohort, with less competition among individuals but far less clout. Because the Gen Z cohort, today's teenagers, is considerably larger than Gen X, it will likely be much more influential.

Is the rise of peer groups in modern society necessarily a bad thing? This question has sparked some of the hottest debates in the study of adolescence over the past 30 years (B. Brown & Larson, 2009). There are those who claim that age segregation has led to the development of a separate youth culture, in which young people maintain attitudes and values that are different from—even contrary to—those of adults. But some argue that industrialization and modernization have made peer groups more important, that adults alone can no longer prepare young people for the future, and that peer groups play a vital role in the socialization of adolescents for adulthood (J. Harris, 1995).

Is There a Separate Youth Culture?

The belief that age segregation has fueled the development of a separate—and troublesome—youth culture was first expressed more than 50 years ago, in *The Adolescent Society,* an extensive study of the social worlds of 10 American high schools (Coleman, 1961). According to the study, adolescents lived in a social world where academic success was frowned on, where doing well in school did not earn the admiration of peers, and where wealth, athletic ability (for boys), and good looks (for girls) mattered most.

Sound familiar? When adults today complain about the questionable morals and poor character of today's young people, they are saying nothing different from what adults were asserting in the middle of the twentieth century (and what adults said about them, when *they* were teenagers). Frankly, there probably hasn't been a generation of adults that didn't complain about young people.

About 10 years ago, a team of researchers wanted to see just how much had changed since *The Adolescent Society* was published (Garner, Bootcheck, Lorr, & Rauch, 2006). They assessed the social climate of seven schools that varied in size, the ethnic and socioeconomic composition of the student body, and whether they were inner-city, suburban, or semirural.

There were both similarities and differences between what they found and the adolescent society of the 1960s. The combination of physical attractiveness, athletic ability, and money was still associated with popularity. Academic success was valued, but an atmosphere of anti-intellectualism prevailed, and doing well in school clearly was not a pathway to popularity.

Other things were different, though, especially in communities that were not composed mainly of White, middle-class families. In these schools, the student body was fragmented into crowds defined largely by ethnicity and social class. There was often tension among crowds as well as strong opposition to middle-class culture in some segments of the schools. In some senses, then, the diversification of American society also diversified the adolescent society. An important lesson here is that the world of adolescents usually reflects the broader context at that time.

Do Adolescents Inhabit a Separate World? According to some observers, age segregation has so strengthened the power of the peer group that American adolescents have become alienated from and unfamiliar with the values of adults. In this view, problems such as youth unemployment, teenage suicide, juvenile delinquency, drug and alcohol use, and teen pregnancy can be attributed to the rise of peer groups and the isolation of adolescents from adults. Many observers

Adults have long worried whether there is a distinct youth culture that is counter to mainstream values. © terry harris just greece photo library / Alamy RF

Table 1 Cohorts, periods, and ages

Cohort Name	Became Young Adults (16–30)	Key Events at That Time	in Census Year											
			1900	1910	1920	1930	1940	1950	1960	1970	1980	1990	2000	2010
Generation Z	2002–2005	Internet explosion												16–24
Millennials	1992–2015	Information era: economic growth and global politics											16–24	25–30
Gen X	1982–2005	Reagan era: economic polarization, political conservatism										16–24	25–30	
Late baby boomers	1972–95	Watergate era: economic recession, employment restructuring									16–24	25–30		
Early baby boomers	1962–85	Hippies: social movements, campus revolts								16–24	25–30			
Happy days generation	1952–75	Family and conformity: baby boom and Cold War/McCarthy era							16–24	25–30				
Happy days/greatest generation	1942–65	Family and conformity: baby boom and Cold War/McCarthy era						16–24	25–30					
Greatest generation/children of Great Depression	1932–55	Hard times: economic depression and World War II					16–24	25–30						
Children of Great Depression	1922–45	Hard times: economic depression and World War II				16–24	25–30							
Lost Generation	1912–35	World War I and Roaring Twenties, Prohibition			16–24	25–30								
…	1902–25	Age of invention and World War I		16–24	25–30									
…	1892–1915	Age of invention, urbanization	16–24	25–30										

of the adolescent scene note that all these problems have increased dramatically since the 1940s, as peer groups have become more prominent and age segregation has become more prevalent. Their argument is that the increase in adolescents' problems can be directly linked to the rise in the power of adolescent peer groups.

Has the Youth Culture Harmed Adolescents? Has the rise of adolescent peer groups really caused so many problems?

This question is hard to answer. Age segregation certainly has increased over the past 60 years, but society has changed in other ways during this same time—ways that may also have contributed to increases in such problems as crime and drug use. The world is a more stressful and uncertain place to grow up in now than it was in the past. Adolescents experience enormous pressures from parents, peers, and the mass media. More important, even though society has continued to become increasingly age segregated, the rates of many adolescent problem behaviors— crime and drug use are good examples—have fluctuated considerably over the past three decades. If age segregation were the "true" cause of adolescents' problems, this would not be the case. There have been periods when adolescent problem behaviors have declined despite the fact that age segregation has remained high.

To be sure, contemporary adolescents spend more time in peer groups than in past eras. But there is no evidence that today's young people are more susceptible to the influence of their friends than their counterparts were previously, nor has it been shown that teenagers are any worse off because peer groups have come to play a more prominent role. More important, it is simply incorrect to describe the peer group as a universally negative influence; adolescents exert both positive and negative influences on each other (Piehler, 2011). Some peers influence each other to use drugs and spend time partying rather than studying, but other peer groups discourage drug use and value academic achievement. In other words, although peers continue to remain highly influential, the directions in which they influence each other are highly variable.

making the cultural connection

Do you think the values of the adolescent "society" differ in different parts of the world, or is it more likely that athletic ability, good looks, and money contribute to popularity everywhere? If you have classmates who grew up somewhere other than the United States, ask them what made people popular in their high school.

The Nature of Adolescent Peer Groups

Changes in Peer Groups During Adolescence

When you look at a typical elementary school playground, it's clear that peer groups are an important feature of the social world of childhood. But even though peer groups exist well before adolescence, during the teenage years they change in significance and structure. Four specific developments stand out (B. Brown, 1990; B. Brown & Larson, 2009).

In What Ways Do Peer Groups Change? First, there is a sharp increase during adolescence in the sheer amount of time individuals spend with their peers and in the relative time they spend in the company of peers versus adults. If we count school as a setting in which adolescents are mainly with people their age, well over half of the typical American adolescent's waking hours are spent with peers, as opposed to only 15% with adults— including their parents (most of the remaining time is spent alone or with a combination of adults and peers). Indeed, during the transition into adolescence, there is a dramatic drop in the amount of time adolescents spend with parents; for boys, this is mainly replaced by time spent alone, whereas for girls, it is replaced by time alone and time with friends (Dijkstra & Veenstra, 2011).

Second, during adolescence, peer groups function much more often without adult supervision than they do during childhood, partly because adolescents are more mobile and partly because they seek, and are granted, more independence (Dijkstra & Veenstra, 2011). As you can see from Figure 3, both supervised and unsupervised time with peers, and, especially, with opposite-sex peers, increase steadily throughout adolescence (Lam, McHale, & Crouter, 2014). Groups of younger children typically play in the presence of adults or in activities organized or supervised by adults (for example, organized sports), whereas adolescents are granted far more independence. A group of teenagers may go off to the mall or the movies on their own or hang out at the home of someone whose parents are absent.

Third, during adolescence, increasingly more contact with peers is between males and females (Lam et al., 2014). During childhood, peer groups are highly sex segregated. This is especially true of peer activities of children in school and other settings organized by adults, although somewhat less so of their more informal activities, such as neighborhood play. During adolescence, however, an increasingly larger proportion of an individual's significant others are peers of the other sex (Dijkstra & Veenstra, 2011; Mehta & Strough,

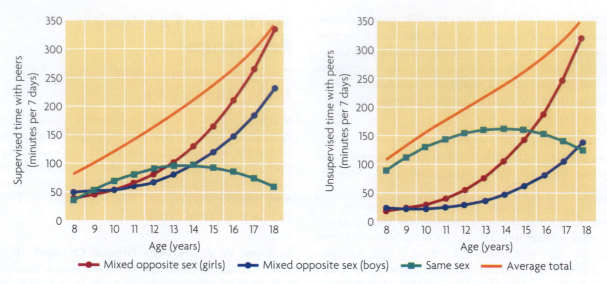

Figure 3 Both supervised (left) and unsupervised (right) time with peers increase during adolescence. The increase in the amount of time that girls spend with peers is especially steep. (Lam et al., 2014)

2009). The shift from same-sex peer groups to mixed-sex groups tends to occur around the beginning of high school (Lam et al., 2014).

Finally, whereas children's peer relationships are limited mainly to relatively small groups—at most, three or four children at a time—adolescence marks the emergence of larger collectives of peers, called crowds (Brown & Larson, 2009). In junior high school cafeterias, for example, the "popular" crowd sits in one section of the room, the "brains" in another, and the "jocks" in a third. These crowds typically develop their own minicultures, characterized by particular styles of dressing, talking, and behaving (Chen, 2012). Not until early adolescence can individuals accurately list the various crowds in their schools and reliably describe the stereotypes that distinguish the crowds from one another (B. Brown, Mory, & Kinney, 1994).

What Causes Peer Groups to Change? These changes in peer relations have their origins in the biological, cognitive, and social transitions of adolescence (Dijkstra & Veenstra, 2011). Puberty stimulates adolescents' interest in romantic relationships and distances them from their parents, which helps to explain why adolescents' social networks increasingly include more other-sex peers and fewer adults. The cognitive changes of adolescence permit a more sophisticated understanding of social relationships, which allows the sort of abstract categorization that leads to grouping individuals into crowds. And changes in social definition may stimulate changes in peer relations as a sort of adaptive response: The larger, more anonymous social setting of the secondary school forces

cliques
Small, tightly knit groups of between 2 and 12 friends, generally of the same sex and age.

adolescents to seek out individuals whom they perceive as having common interests and values, perhaps as a way of re-creating the smaller, more intimate groups of childhood (B. Brown, 2004). Instead of floundering in a large, impersonal high school cafeteria, someone who belongs to the cheerleader crowd, or even someone who is one of the "nerds," may head directly for a place at a familiar table.

Cliques and Crowds

Adolescents' peer groups are organized around two related, but different, structures (B. Brown & Larson, 2009). **Cliques** are small groups of between 2 and 12 individuals—the average is about 5 or 6—generally of the same sex and, of course, the same age. Cliques can be defined by common activities (for example, the football players, or a group of students who study together regularly) or simply by friendship (e.g., a group of girls who have lunch together every day, or a group of boys who have grown up together). The clique provides the main social context in which adolescents interact with one another. It's the social setting in which adolescents hang out, talk to each other, and form close friendships. Some cliques are more open to outsiders than others (that is, the members are less "cliquish"), but virtually all cliques are small enough that the members feel they know each other well and appreciate each other more than people outside the clique do (B. Brown & Larson, 2009).

How Cliques Structure Social Networks A study of the structure, prevalence, and stability of cliques among 9th-graders in five different high schools within a large American school district illustrates the ways in which cliques structure adolescents' friendship networks

(Ennett & Bauman, 1996). Based on interviews with students over a 1-year period, the researchers categorized adolescents as *clique members* (individuals who have most of their interactions with the same small group of people), *liaisons* (individuals who interact with two or more adolescents who are members of cliques, but who themselves are not part of a clique), and *isolates* (individuals who have few or no links to others in the network).

Three interesting patterns emerged. First, despite the popular image of adolescents as "cliquish," fewer than half the adolescents in any school were members of cliques. Second, girls were more likely than boys to be members of cliques, whereas boys were more likely than girls to be isolates. Finally, adolescents' positions in their school's social network were relatively stable over time: Adolescents who were members of cliques in the 9th grade were clique members in 10th grade; 9th-grade isolates remained, for the most part, isolates 1 year later. This does not mean that the membership of specific cliques is stable—typically, it isn't—only that individuals who were members of a clique at one point of time were members of a clique 1 year later. In other words, there is stability in adolescents' tendency to join cliques, but not in the makeup of particular groups (B. Brown, 2004). In another study, about 75% of 7th-graders were members of cliques and about 15% were isolates; very few were liaisons or connected to just one other adolescent in a dyad

(A. M. Ryan, 2001). Not surprisingly, the more recently a student has arrived at a school, the less well connected he or she is likely to be; developing a social network is especially hard on students whose families move frequently (South & Haynie, 2004).

> **crowds**
> Large, loosely organized groups of young people, composed of several cliques and typically organized around a common shared activity.

How Adolescents Sort Into Crowds   Cliques are quite different in structure and purpose from crowds. **Crowds** are based on "the identification of adolescents who share a similar image or reputation among peers, or who have a common feature such as ethnicity or neighborhood, even if they do not consider each other friends or spend much time interacting with each other" (B. Brown, 2004). In contemporary American high schools, typical crowds include "jocks," "brains," "nerds," "populars," and "druggies." The labels for these crowds may vary from school to school ("nerds" versus "geeks," "populars" versus "preps"), but their generic presence is commonplace around the world, and you can probably recognize these different types of crowds from your own school experience (Arnett, 2002; Delsing, ter Bogt, Engels, & Meeus, 2007; Sim & Yeo, 2012). (A major exception is "jocks," a crowd that is seldom found in non-American schools. In Europe and Asia, adolescents' athletic events are typically organized around clubs

Adolescents usually belong to at least one clique, a close group of about a half dozen friends, usually of the same age and sex.
© Angela Hampton/Angela Hampton Picture Library / Alamy

located in the community rather than school teams.) Unlike cliques, crowds are not settings for adolescents' intimate interactions or friendships, but instead serve three broad purposes: to locate adolescents (to themselves and to others) within the social structure of the school, to channel adolescents toward some peers and away from others, and to provide contexts that reward certain lifestyles and disparage others (B. Brown & Larson, 2009).

The key point is that membership in a crowd is based mainly on reputation and stereotype, rather than on actual friendship or social interaction. This is very different from membership in a clique, which, by definition, hinges on shared activity and friendship. In concrete terms, and perhaps ironically, an adolescent does not have to actually have "brains" as friends, or hang around with "brainy" students, to be one of the "brains." If he dresses like a "brain," acts like a "brain," and takes honors courses, then he is a "brain" as far as his crowd membership goes.

The fact that crowd membership is based on reputation and stereotype has important implications. It can be very difficult for adolescents, who—if they don't change their reputation early on in high school—may find themselves stuck, at least in the eyes of others, in a crowd they don't want to belong to or even see themselves as a part of (B. Brown, Von Bank, & Steinberg, 2008). Plus, some individuals can be members of more than one crowd simultaneously, if their reputation is such that they fit into them (B. Brown, 2004). According to some estimates, close to half of high school students are associated with one crowd, about one-third are associated with two or more crowds, and about one-sixth do not clearly fit into any crowd (B. Brown, 2004). Although an adolescent's closest friends are almost always members

Early adolescence is often marked by the transition from same-sex peer groups to mixed-sex peer groups. © Pamela Moore/Getty Images RF

of the same clique, some of them may belong to a different crowd, especially when one crowd is close in lifestyle to the other (Urberg, Değirmencioğlu, Tolson, & Halliday-Scher, 1995). For example, a "brain" will have some friends who are also "brains" and some who are "nerds" but few, if any, who are "druggies" (B. Brown et al., 1994).

More importantly, crowds are not simply clusters of cliques; the two different structures serve entirely different purposes. Because the clique is based on activity and friendship, it is the peer setting in which adolescents learn social skills—how to be a good friend, how to communicate effectively, how to be a leader, how to enjoy someone else's company, or how to break off a friendship that is no longer satisfying. In contrast, because crowds are based more on reputation and stereotype than on interaction, they probably contribute more to the adolescent's sense of identity and self-conception—for better and for worse—than to his or her actual social development.

Changes in Clique and Crowd Structure Over Time

There are important changes in the structure of cliques and crowds during the adolescent years, driven in large measure by the increased importance of romantic relationships (Connolly, Furman, & Konarski, 2000; Kuttler & La Greca, 2004).

How Romance Changes the Peer Group   During early adolescence, adolescents' activities revolve around same-sex cliques. They are not yet involved in partying and typically spend their leisure time with a small group of friends, playing sports, talking, or simply hanging out.

Somewhat later, as boys and girls become more interested in one another romantically—but before romantic relationships actually begin—boys' and girls' cliques come together. This is clearly a transitional stage. Boys and girls may go to parties or hang out, but the time they spend together mainly involves interaction with peers of the same sex. When young teenagers are still uncomfortable about dealing with members of the other sex, this context provides an opportunity in which they can learn more about peers of the other sex without having to be intimate or risk losing face. It is not unusual, for example, at young adolescents' first mixed-sex parties, for groups of boys and girls to position themselves at other sides of a room, watching each other but seldom interacting.

As some adolescents become interested in romantic relationships, part of the group begins to split off into mixed-sex cliques, while other individuals remain in the group but in same-sex cliques. This shift is usually led by the clique leaders, with other clique members following along. For instance, a clique of boys whose main activity is playing basketball may discover that one of the guys they look up to has become more interested in going to mixed-sex parties Saturday nights than in hanging out and playing video games with the guys. Over time, they will begin to follow his lead, and their all-male activities will become more infrequent. A study of middle school dances over the course of the academic year found that the integration of boys' and girls' peer groups increased over time, but that this occurred mainly among physically attractive adolescents (no surprise, because being good-looking contributes to status in the peer group) (see Figure 4) (Pellegrini & Long, 2007).

During middle adolescence, mixed-sex and mixed-age cliques become more prevalent (Molloy, Gest, Feinberg, & Osgood, 2014), and in time, the peer group becomes composed entirely of mixed-sex cliques (Cooksey, Mott, & Neubauer, 2002). One clique might consist of the drama students—male and female students who know each other from school plays. Another might be composed of four girls and four boys who like to get high. Preppies—male and female—might make up a third. Interestingly, the transition from same-sex groups to mixed-sex groups is associated with an increase in alcohol and drug use among females, and in alcohol use among males, most likely because the activities that draw males and females together often involve socializing (Poulin, Denault, & Pedersen, 2011).

Finally, during late adolescence, peer crowds begin to disintegrate. Pairs of adolescents who see themselves as couples begin to split off from the activities of the larger group. The larger peer group is replaced by loosely associated sets of couples. Adolescents begin to shift some of their attention away from friends and toward romantic partners (Kuttler & La Greca, 2004). Groups of couples may go out together from time to time, but the feeling of being in a crowd has disappeared. This pattern—in which the couple becomes the focus of social activity—persists into adulthood.

When viewed from a structural point of view, the peer group's role in the development of intimacy is clear.

Over time, the structure of the peer group changes, in keeping with adolescents' changing needs and interests. The adolescent's capacity for close relationships develops first through friendships with peers of the same sex, and only later does intimacy enter into other-sex relationships. Thus, the structure of the peer group changes during adolescence in a way that parallels the adolescent's development of intimacy: As the adolescent develops increasing facility in intimate relationships, the peer group moves from the familiarity of same-sex activities to contact with other-sex peers, but mainly in the safety of the larger group. It is only after adolescents have been slowly socialized into dating roles—primarily by modeling their higher-status peers—that the safety of numbers is no longer needed and adolescents begin pairing off.

Changes in Crowds   There also are changes in peer crowds during this time. Many of these changes reflect the growing cognitive sophistication of the adolescent. For example, as adolescents mature intellectually, they come to define crowds more in terms of abstract, global characteristics ("preppies," "nerds," "jocks") than in terms of concrete, behavioral features ("the ballet crowd," "the Mass Effect crowd," "the kids who play basketball on 114th Street") (Dijkstra & Veenstra, 2011). As you know, this shift from concrete to abstract is a general feature of cognitive development in adolescence. In addition, as adolescents become more cognitively capable, they become more consciously aware of the crowd structure of their school and their place in it (B. Brown, 2004). Over the course of adolescence, the crowd structure also becomes more differentiated, more permeable, and less hierarchical, which allows adolescents more freedom to change crowds and enhance their status (B. Brown, 2004; Horn, 2003). In early adolescence, a school may have only two broad crowds (e.g., "normals" and "losers"). By high school, there may be several different ways to be "normal" ("populars," "jocks," "average") and several different ways to be a "loser" ("brains," "nerds," "burnouts").

The Transformation of the Nerds   In one fascinating study of the day-to-day experiences of "nerds" and their interactions with other students was based on an **ethnography** of the social interaction and peer culture in a high school in a small Midwestern city. In contrast to survey or experimental research, which is typically quantitative in nature (that is, the data collected can be quantified), ethnographic research is qualitative. The researcher spends a considerable amount of time observing interactions within the setting, interviewing many adolescents, and writing up field notes, much as an anthropologist would do in studying a foreign culture. Ethnographic approaches can be extremely useful in studying social relationships, because they provide rich, descriptive data.

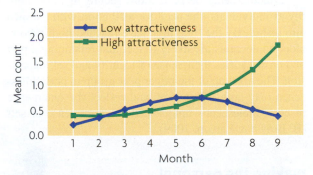

Figure 4   Intermingling of boys' and girls' peer groups increases during early adolescence, but it starts first among physically attractive adolescents, who often are clique leaders. Mean count refers to the mean number of interactions with other-sex peer groups.
(Pellegrini & Long, 2007)

ethnography
A type of research in which individuals are observed in their natural settings.

Peer crowds play an important role in defining the adolescent's place within the social hierarchy of the school. © Fuse/Getty Images RF

The study found that many individuals managed to transform themselves from "nerds" into "normals" during high school. For some, this was accomplished because the high school peer structure was more differentiated and permeable. As opposed to middle school, where there were only two groups—the popular and the unpopular—in high school, there were more socially acceptable groups. For others, the transition to "normal" came about through gains in self-assurance that came with physical and social development. And for still others, the transformation was facilitated by a more sophisticated, confident view of the social hierarchy—one that permitted them to reject the premise that whatever the popular kids valued was necessarily desirable.

In essence, the transformation of "nerds" to "normals" was enabled by a combination of factors both within the context (the increasing differentiation and permeability of the peer crowd system) and within the adolescent (the physical, cognitive, and social maturation of the individual) (B. Brown, 1996). This study, as well as other ethnographies of adolescent peer groups, reminds us of the potential for growth and change during the adolescent years, even for individuals who begin the period at a social disadvantage.

The Waxing and Waning of Crowds As crowds become more salient influences on adolescents' view of their social world, they come to play an increasingly important role in structuring adolescents' social behavior (B. Brown & Larson, 2009). By 9th grade, there is nearly universal agreement among students about their school's crowd structure, and the strength of peer group influence is very high. Between 9th and 12th grades, however, the significance of the crowd structure begins to decline, and the salience of peer pressure wanes.

In one study, students were presented with several scenarios asking if it was all right to exclude someone from a school activity (cheerleading, basketball, student council) because the person was a member of a certain crowd ("jock," "gothic," "preppie") (Horn, 2003). They were also asked whether it was acceptable to deny individuals resources (for example, a scholarship) on the basis of their crowd membership. Consistent with the decline in the salience of peer crowds between middle and late adolescence, 9th-graders were more likely than older students to say that excluding someone from an activity on the basis of his or her crowd was all right. Students of all ages agreed that it was less acceptable to deny students resources because of crowd membership (which virtually all students viewed as immoral) than to exclude them from an activity (which was less often seen as a moral issue).

This pattern of a decline in the salience of peer crowds parallels developmental changes in adolescents' susceptibility to peer pressure (Steinberg & Monahan, 2007). As crowds become less important, between middle and late adolescence, their influence over the individual's behavior weakens (B. Brown, 2004). Most probably, the interplay between changes in the importance of the crowd and changes in adolescent's susceptibility to peer influence is reciprocal.

Just as the changes in the structure of cliques play a role in the development of intimacy, changes in the salience of crowds play an important role in adolescent identity development. Adolescence is frequently a time for experimentation with different roles and identities. During the early adolescent years, before adolescents have "found" themselves, the crowd provides an important basis for self-definition (B. Newman & Newman, 2001a). By locating themselves within the crowd structure of their school—through clothing, language, or choice of hangouts—adolescents wear "badges" that say "This is who I am." At a time when adolescents may not actually know just who they are, associating with a crowd provides them with a rudimentary sense of identity.

As adolescents become more secure in their identity as individuals, the need for affiliation with a crowd diminishes. By the time they have reached high school, older adolescents are likely to feel that remaining a part of a crowd stifles their sense of identity and self expression. The breakup of the larger peer group in late adolescence may both foreshadow and reflect the emergence of each adolescent's unique and coherent sense of self (B. Brown & Larson, 2009).

making the personal connection

Think back to your own high school experience. What were the major crowds in your school? What common characteristics did you share with the people who were in your clique?

Adolescents and Their Crowds

The Social Map of Adolescence

Although we often hear people talk about a universal "youth culture," most ethnographic studies of high schools indicate that the social world of adolescents is far more multifaceted than this. One helpful scheme for mapping the social world of adolescence classifies crowds along two dimensions: how involved they are in the institutions controlled by adults, such as school and extracurricular activities, and how involved they are in the informal, peer culture (Brown, 1990) (see Figure 5).

"Jocks" and "populars," for example, are very involved in the peer culture, but they are also very involved in the institutions valued by adults (sports and school organizations, for example). "Brains" and "nerds," in contrast, are also involved in adult-controlled organizations (in their case, academics), but they tend to be less involved in the peer culture. "Partyers" are on the opposite side of the map from "nerds": These adolescents are very involved in the peer culture but are less so in adult institutions. "Burnouts" and adolescents who are members of delinquent gangs are not involved in either the peer culture or adult institutions. Other crowds, such as "normals" or "druggies," fall somewhere between these extremes.

Crowds as Reference Groups

Knowing where an adolescent fits into the social system of the school can tell us a lot about the person's behavior and values. This is because crowds contribute to the definition of norms and standards for such things as clothing, leisure, and tastes in music. Being a "jock" means more than simply being involved in athletics; it means wearing certain types of clothes, listening to certain types of music, spending Saturday nights in certain spots, and using a particular slang.

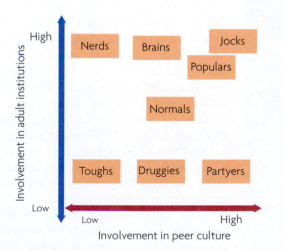

Figure 5   A model for mapping the social world of adolescent peer groups. (From Brown, 1990)

Another way of putting this is that adolescents' crowds serve as **reference groups.** They provide their members with an identity in the eyes of others. Adolescents judge one another on the basis of the company they keep, and they become branded on the basis of whom they hang out with. Such labels as "jocks," "brains," "populars," "druggies," and "skaters" serve as shorthand notations—accurate or inaccurate— to describe what someone is like as a person, what he or she holds as important, and how he or she spends time. Individuals who are members of more unconventional crowds (e.g., "Hip Hoppers," "Metalheads") engage in more problem behavior, whereas those who are in more conventional ones (e.g., "Normals," "Jocks") report less (Doornwaard, Branje, Meeus, & ter Bogt, 2012).

> **reference groups**
> A group against which an individual compares him or herself.

Crowd Membership and Adolescent Identity   Crowd membership is important not only because crowds are used by adolescents when talking about one another but also because membership in a crowd is often the basis for an adolescent's own identity (B. Brown & Larson, 2009). A girl who hangs out with the "preppies" identifies herself as such by wearing their "uniform," shopping in their stores, and speaking their language. After a while, preppiness becomes part of her own self-concept; she wouldn't think of dressing or talking any other way. Or consider the boys whose clique is held together by a dislike of school. Since this attitude toward school is continuously reinforced by the clique, each boy's feelings about school become strengthened, and not liking school becomes part of each boy's identity. Even if something very positive happens at school, it becomes difficult for someone in the clique to admit that it makes him feel good about himself. Doing well on a test or receiving a compliment from a teacher is likely to be dismissed as unimportant.

Because the adolescent's peer group plays such an important role as a reference group and a source of identity, the nature of the crowd with which an adolescent affiliates is likely to have an important influence on his or her behavior, activities, and self-conceptions (Birkeland, Breivik, & Wold, 2014; Brechwald & Prinstein, 2011; Dijkstra & Veenstra, 2011). Although most adolescents feel pressure from their friends to behave in ways that are consistent with their crowd's values and goals, the specific pressure varies from one crowd to another. "Druggies" report much more peer pressure to misbehave, for example, than "jocks" (Clasen & Brown, 1985). Crowd membership can also affect the way adolescents feel about themselves. Adolescents' self-esteem is higher among students who are identified with peer groups that have relatively more status in their school (B. Brown, Von Bank, & Steinberg, 2008). Over the course of adolescence, symptoms of psychological distress decline among the "populars" and "jocks" but increase among the "brains" (Doornwaard et al., 2012; Prinstein & La Greca, 2002).

Not surprisingly, adolescents whose peers identify them as members of low-status crowds fare better psychologically when they don't see themselves this way, but the opposite is true for adolescents whose peers label them as members of high-status crowds, where denying one's affiliation with the crowd is associated with worse mental health (B. Brown, Von Bank, & Steinberg, 2008). Of course, the longer-term consequences of crowd membership during adolescence are not necessarily the same as their immediate impact. One study that examined the young-adult outcomes of high school crowd membership found that both "brains" and "jocks" showed the most favorable patterns of psychological adjustment over time (Barber, Eccles, & Stone, 2001). Individuals who had been members of antisocial peer groups fared the worst.

Adolescents' behavior is affected by their crowd membership in several ways (Brechwald & Prinstein, 2011). First, adolescents often imitate the behavior of high-status peers—the crowd leaders. The socially popular girls, for example, may dress in a certain way, and the less popular ones (the "wannabes"), who want to be associated with them, follow suit. Popular students receive far more attention from others, especially from those who themselves are popular (Lansu, Cillessen, & Karremans, 2014).

Second, crowds establish social norms—values and expectations—that members strive to follow. That is, even lower-status members of a crowd influence each other by behaving in ways that identify them as members (e.g., using certain expressions when speaking), and

other adolescents who want to be accepted by them conform to these standards.

Third, when crowd members behave in ways that are consistent with these norms, they are reinforced for doing so. An adolescent who dresses in a way that is consistent with a crowd's expectation may be complimented ("nice shoes, Sophie") whereas one who does not may be ignored, or even made fun of ("I can't believe you're wearing those!").

Finally, when adolescents are reinforced for following a crowd's norms, they feel better about themselves and further incorporate their crowd membership into their identity. After being praised many times for her clothes by one of the popular crowd's members, for example, a girl will start to think of herself as a member of that crowd and begin to derive her identity in part from it.

Ethnicity and Crowd Membership Many of the basic distinctions among crowds that have been found in studies of predominantly White high schools (for example, academically oriented crowds, partying crowds, deviant crowds, trendy crowds) also exist among adolescents from ethnic minority groups (B. Brown & Mounts, 1989). There is evidence, however, that in multiethnic high schools adolescents first divide across ethnic lines and then form into the more familiar adolescent crowds within ethnic groups. In a large multiethnic high school, there may be separate groups of Black "jocks" and White "jocks," of Hispanic "populars" and Black "populars," and so on (Hardie & Tyson, 2013). In multiethnic schools, adolescents from one ethnic group are less likely to see crowd distinctions within other ethnic groups than they are within their own group. Thus, to White students, all Asian adolescents are part of the "Asian" crowd, whereas the Asian students see themselves as divided into "brains," "populars," and other groups (B. Brown & Mounts, 1989).

The meaning associated with belonging to different crowds also may differ across ethnic and socioeconomic groups, although this varies considerably from school to school (Knifsend & Juvonen, 2014; Tyson, Darity, & Castellino, 2005). Although one widely cited study reported that high-achieving Black students are ostracized for "acting White" (Fordham & Ogbu, 1986), many studies do not find this to be typical (e.g., Horvat & Lewis, 2003; Tyson et al., 2005). In fact, in many schools, *all* students who are highly committed to school, regardless of their ethnicity, are teased or excluded for being "nerds" or "brains," or simply for doing well in school (Schwartz, Kelly, & Duong, 2013). Similarly, in some schools it may be admirable to be a "jock," while in others it may

In multiethnic high schools, peer groups often divide along ethnic lines.
© Ababsolutum/Getty Images RF

be frowned upon. The values we associate with being in one crowd as opposed to aren't the same across all school contexts.

Adolescents and Their Cliques

What draws adolescents into one clique and not another? Because cliques serve as a basis for adolescents' friendships and play an important role in their social development, many researchers have studied the determinants of clique composition.

Similarity Among Clique Members

The most important influence on the composition of cliques is similarity. Adolescents' cliques typically are composed of people who are of the same age, ethnicity, and—at least during early and middle adolescence—the same sex (Ennett & Bauman, 1996).

Age Segregation Although many adolescents have friends who are one school grade ahead or behind (Bowker & Spencer, 2010), age grouping in junior and senior high schools makes it unlikely that an individual will have friends who are substantially older or younger. A 10th-grader who is enrolled in 10th-grade English, 10th-grade math, 10th-grade history, and 10th-grade science simply does not have many opportunities to meet adolescents who are in different grades. Age segregation in adolescents' cliques appears to result mostly from the structure of schools. By way of comparison, adolescents' online friends are less similar in age than the friends they make in school (Mesch & Talmud, 2007).

Sex Segregation During early and middle adolescence, cliques also tend to be composed of adolescents of the same sex (Ennett & Bauman, 1996). This sex segregation begins in childhood and continues through most of adolescence, although it is stronger among White students than among Black students (Filardo, 1996), and it weakens later in adolescence (Mehta & Strough, 2009).

The causes of sex segregation in adolescents' cliques are more interesting than the causes of age segregation, because schools seldom separate boys and girls into different classes. Why, then, do adolescent males and females separate themselves into different cliques? Social scientists who study gender and development have suggested several reasons (Maccoby, 1990).

First, cliques are formed largely on the basis of shared activities and interests. Preadolescent and early adolescent boys and girls are interested in different things (Mehta & Strough, 2009). Not until adolescents begin dating do boys' cliques and girls' cliques mix, presumably because dating provides a basis for common activity. Consistent with this, one study of adolescents' social networks found that the proportion of other-sex friends more than doubles between 6th and 10th grades (Poulin & Pedersen, 2007). And, in keeping with the notion that this coincides with the onset of dating, the increase is especially notable among early-maturing girls, whose networks increasingly include somewhat older boys that they know outside of school. Even so, by 10th grade, most adolescents' networks are still dominated by same-sex friends, who make up about three-quarters of the average social network.

A second reason for sex segregation in adolescent peer groups concerns young adolescents' sensitivity about sex roles. Over the course of childhood, boys and girls become increasingly concerned about behaving in ways judged to be sex-appropriate. When little boys show an interest in dolls, they are often told either explicitly (by parents, friends, and teachers) or implicitly (by television, books, and other mass media), "Boys don't play with dolls—those are for girls." And when girls start wrestling or roughhousing, they are often similarly reprimanded.

As a consequence of these continual reminders that there are boys' activities and girls' activities, early adolescents—who are trying to establish a sense of identity—are very concerned about acting in sex-appropriate ways, although this is more true of boys than girls (Galambos, Berenbaum, & McHale, 2009). This makes it very difficult for an adolescent boy to be a part of a girls' clique, in which activities are likely to revolve around clothing and talking about boys, or a girl to be part of a boys' clique, in which activities are likely to be dominated by athletics and other physical pursuits (Mehta & Strough, 2009). Adolescents who go against prevailing sex-role norms by forming friendships with members of the other sex may be teased about being "fags" or may be ostracized by their peers because they are "girly" (Oransky & Marecek, 2009). (Interestingly, gay male adolescents typically have more other-sex friendships than same-sex friendships [Diamond & Dubé, 2002].) Ironically, once dating becomes the norm, adolescents who *don't* have relationships with peers of the other sex become the objects of equally strong suspicion and social rejection.

Ethnic Segregation Ethnicity is not a strong determinant of clique composition during childhood, but it becomes increasingly powerful as youngsters get older (Raabe & Beelman, 2011). By middle and late adolescence, adolescents' peer groups typically are ethnically segregated, with very few ethnically mixed cliques in most high schools (Ennett & Bauman, 1996). This appears to be the case, although somewhat less so, even within schools that have been desegregated. One study of a multiethnic New York City public high school found, for example, that nearly three-quarters of the Latino students, two-thirds of the Black students, and 85% of the Asian students had friends who were predominantly from the same ethnic group (Way & Chen, 2000). In fact, cross-ethnic friendships are less common in ethnically diverse schools than in schools where one ethnic group predominates (Moody, 2001; Quillian & Campbell, 2003).

An analysis of data from a large, nationally representative sample of adolescents found that ethnicity continues to be an enormously powerful determinant of friendship patterns—far more powerful than socioeconomic status (Quillian & Campbell, 2003). The rift between Black students and students from all other ethnic groups, especially Whites and Asians, is especially strong. Although Asian students report the highest degree of discrimination by peers, Black students' reports of being discriminated against by other students increase over time (see Figure 6) (Cooc & Gee, 2014; Greene, Way, & Pahl, 2006; Qin, Way, & Mukherjee, 2008).

Ethnicity is such a strong determinant of adolescents' cliques that adolescents are more likely to have friends of the same ethnicity who come from the opposite end of the socioeconomic spectrum than to have friends from the same social class but a different ethnic group. Studies of whether cross-ethnic friendships are more common among Asian and Hispanic adolescents who are American born than among their peers who are immigrants have found that immigrants are less likely to have cross-ethnic friendships, perhaps because of language barriers (Hamm, Brown, & Heck, 2005; Kiang, Peterson, & Thompson, 2011; Titzman, 2014). But even among ethnic minority youth whose families have been in the United States for generations, there is a strong preference for same-ethnicity friends (Quillian & Campbell, 2003). Parents appear to influence this preference, as indicated by a study of Mexican American adolescents, which found that adolescents were more likely to have non-Mexican friends when their parents were themselves more strongly oriented toward Anglo culture (Updegraff, McHale, Whiteman, Thayer, & Crouter,

2006). The social climate of the school likely matters as well: Feelings of discrimination often drive ethnic minority students into peer crowds that are defined by ethnicity (B. Brown, Herman, Hamm, & Heck, 2008).

It is difficult to know why such strong ethnic segregation persists in adolescents' friendship selection. Ethnic segregation in adolescents' cliques is only partly due to residential segregation (Mouw & Entwisle, 2006). One possibility is that some ethnic segregation in friendship patterns is due to differential levels of academic achievement of adolescents from different ethnic groups (Graham, Munniksma, & Juvonen, 2014). On average, White and Asian adolescents get significantly higher grades in school than Black or Hispanic adolescents. As you'll read, friends usually have similar attitudes toward school, educational aspirations, and grades (B. Brown, 2004). Ethnic differences in school achievement therefore may lead to ethnic separation in adolescent peer groups (Hallinan & Williams, 1989). Cross-ethnic friendships are more rare in schools that frequently separate students into different academic tracks (Stearns, 2004).

A second reason for ethnically segregated peer groups—according to one study of adolescents in a recently desegregated school—is attitudinal. In this school, the White adolescents perceived their Black peers as aggressive, threatening, and hostile. The Black students, in turn, saw the White students as conceited, prejudiced, and unwilling to be friends with them. These perceptions, which fed on each other, made the formation of interracial peer groups unlikely. The more the White students believed that the Black students were hostile, the more the White students acted distant and kept to themselves. But the more the White students acted this way, the more likely the Black students were to feel rejected, and the more hostile they became. In general, White students are less apt to initiate contact with Black students and to select them as friends than vice versa (Quillian

Figure 6 Black students report increasingly more discrimination by other students over time, whereas it declines among Latino students. Asian American students report the highest level of peer discrimination. (Greene et al., 2006)

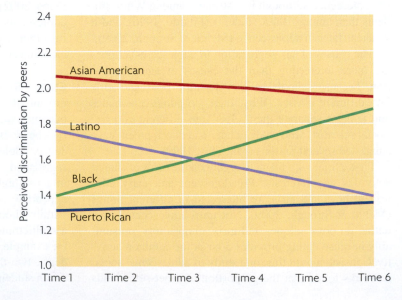

Adolescents are more likely to have friends from the same ethnic group than from the same socioeconomic background.
© Imagebroker/Alamy RF

& Campbell, 2003). Asian students are especially unlikely to have Black friends (Chen & Graham, 2015). One way out of this cycle of misunderstanding is to bring youngsters from different backgrounds together from an early age, before they have had time to build up prejudices and lock on to stereotypes, which tend to develop prior to adolescence (Raabe & Beelman, 2011). Same-ethnic and cross-ethnic friends have different advantages: the former increase students' ethnic pride, but in ethnically diverse classrooms, the latter make students feel safer and less vulnerable (Graham et al., 2014).

Parents' attitudes about the value of having friends from different ethnic groups makes a difference. Whereas some parents actively encourage their teenagers to have friends from other ethnic groups, others discourage it, and still others are content to have their children make their own choices, although they may have mixed feelings about them. Compare these three parents' responses to interview questions about their children's friendships (from Mounts, Karre, & Kim, 2013):

> I just remembered, one of the reasons why I like this community and one of the reasons why I wanted Rose to also go to that church is because they talk about all races being one community. I want each of my children to, and this is

really important to me, to get to know people from different races. . . . And I was hoping that she could meet people who had that mindset that all races are created equal and all races are valuable. (p. 319)

> I don't want her to be around, especially Palestinians. God! Especially if they're Muslims and they just (trails off). I guess that shouldn't be fair, but you know, the whole covering thing, you know, no, no, no, no, no. (p. 317)

> Well, it doesn't matter to me what ethnic background David's friends are, whether they are Black or Spanish or White or Chinese, you know, uh. As long [as] these people don't hurt or, if their, or, I don't, I don't want him going and making friends with, um, with a Mexican that, that may be related to a gang or a Black, you know. Or White, it doesn't matter, you know. (p. 316)

The broader context matters, too. Ethnic segregation in adolescent peer relationships is far less common in Canada than in the United States (Maharaj & Connolly, 1994). The cultural context in Canada is more supportive of multicultural tolerance and more aggressive in its approach to multicultural education and ethnic integration. And context continues to influence friendship choices as individuals move from high school to college: Students who live in dorms where there is a lot of contact between ethnic groups are relatively more likely to develop cross-ethnic friendships (Stearns, Buchmann, & Bonneau, 2009).

Common Interests Among Friends

Thus far, we have seen that adolescents' cliques are usually composed of individuals who are the same age, in the same grade, and of the same ethnicity. But what about factors beyond these? Do adolescents who associate with one another also share certain interests and activities? Generally, they do. Three factors appear to be especially important in determining adolescent clique membership and friendship patterns: orientation toward school, orientation toward the teen culture, and involvement in antisocial activity (Crosnoe & Needham, 2004).

Orientation Toward School Adolescents and their friends tend to be similar in their attitudes toward school, their school achievement, and their educational plans (Flashman, 2012; Kiuru et al., 2012), although this tends to be more true among White and Asian adolescents than among Black adolescents (Hamm, 2000). Adolescents who earn high grades, study a great deal, and plan to go on to college usually have friends who share these characteristics and aspirations. One reason for this is that how much time students devote to schoolwork affects their involvement in other activities. A second is that parents who stress achievement may insist that their teens only spend time with peers who do well in school (Zhao & Gao, 2014). Yet another is that students' friendships are often drawn from the peers with whom they have

Adolescents and their friends usually share common interests, in everything from academics to antisocial behavior. © BananaStock/ PunchStock RF

classes, and if schools track students on the basis of their academic achievement, their friends will be more likely to have similar records of school performance (Crosnoe, 2002). Someone who is always studying will not have many friends who stay out late partying, because the two activities conflict. By the same token, someone who wants to spend afternoons and evenings out having fun will find it difficult to remain friends with someone who prefers to stay home and study. When adolescents' academic performance change (for better or for worse), they tend to change their friendships in the same direction (Flashman, 2012).

Students also influence each other's academic performance (Shin & Ryan, 2014). For instance, girls' decisions about whether to take advanced math classes are significantly influenced by the course-taking decisions of their friends (K. A. Frank et al., 2008). Friends exert a similar influence on GPA: Given two students with similar records of past achievement, the student whose friends do better in school is likely to get better grades than the one whose friends do worse (Véronneau & Dishion, 2011). Indeed, of all the characteristics of friends that influence adolescents' behavior, their friends' school performance has the greatest impact, not only on their own academic achievement, but also on their involvement in problem behavior and drug use (T. Cook, Deng, & Morgano, 2007). Perhaps not

surprisingly, students whose friends tend to come from school have higher GPAs than those whose friends tend to come from other contexts, such as the neighborhood (Witkow & Fuligni, 2010).

Orientation Toward the Teen Culture Adolescents and their friends generally listen to the same type of music, dress alike, spend their leisure time in similar types of activities, and share patterns of drug use (B. Brown & Larson, 2009). It would be very unlikely, for example, for a "jock" and a "druggie" to be part of the same clique, because their interests and attitudes are so different. In most high schools, it is fairly easy to see the split between cliques—in how people dress, where they eat lunch, how much they participate in the school's activities, and how they spend their time outside of school. Similarity in patterns of substance use is such a strong influence that it often serves as the basis for forming cross-ethnic group friendships, which, as we noted earlier, are not common (Hamm, 2000).

Involvement in Antisocial Activity A number of studies, involving both boys and girls from different ethnic groups, indicate that antisocial, aggressive adolescents often gravitate toward each other, forming deviant peer groups (Espelage, Holt, & Henkel, 2003; Kiesner & Pastore, 2005; Laursen, Hafen, Kerr, & Stattin, 2012). Contrary to the popular belief that antisocial adolescents do not have friends, or that they are interpersonally inept, these youngsters do have friends, but their friends tend to be antisocial as well. Although adolescents with deviant friends show some of the same emotional problems as adolescents without friends, even those with deviant friends are less lonely than their friendless peers (Brendgen, Vitaro, & Bukowski, 2000). As you might expect, adolescents with more antisocial friends are more likely to engage in antisocial activity, but some adolescents have personalities that make them especially susceptible to the influence of antisocial peers (Allen, Chango, Szwedo, Schad, & Marston, 2012; Falk et al., 2014; Molano, Jones, Brown, & Aber, 2013; Mrug, Madan, & Windle, 2012; Thomas & McGloin, 2013). Adolescents are influenced by the antisocial behavior of their classmates, as well, even if the classmates are not actually friends (Muller, Hoffman, Fleischli, & Studer, 2015). Even within facilities for juvenile delinquents, the relatively more antisocial adolescents tend to gravitate together and influence each other toward more antisocial activity (Bayer, Hjalmarsson, & Pozen, 2009; B. Lee & Thompson, 2009).

Although we would not necessarily want to call all of these antisocial peer groups "delinquent," since they are not always involved in criminal activity, understanding the processes through which antisocial peer groups are formed provides some insight into the development of delinquent peer groups, or gangs (Gilman, Hill, Hawkins, Howell, & Kosterman, 2014; Melde & Esbensen, 2011).

Gangs are antisocial peer groups that can be identi-fied by name (often denoting a neighborhood or part of the city) and common symbols ("colors," tattoos, hand signs, jewelry, etc.). Adolescents who belong to gangs are at greater risk for many types of problems in addi-tion to antisocial behavior, including elevated levels of psychological distress, impulsivity, psychopathic ten-dencies, exposure to violence, and violent victimization (Dmitrieva, Gibson, Steinberg, Piquero, & Fagan, 2014; Gordon et al., 2014; Melde, Taylor, & Esbensen, 2009; Pyrooz, 2014). This is also true for female adolescents who hang around with male gangs, which increases their involvement in high-risk sexual behavior, drug use, and crime (Yarnell, Pasch, Brown, Perry, & Komro, 2014). Adolescents who are gang members also are more likely to have behavioral and mental health problems in adult-hood (Augustyn, Thornberryt, & Krohn, 2014; Gilman, Hill, & Hawkins, 2014).

Adolescent gangs both resemble and differ from other sorts of peer groups. On the one hand, gangs look much like other types of cliques and crowds, in that they are groups of adolescents who are similar in background and orientation, share common interests and activities, and use the group to derive a sense of identity (M. Harris, 1994). One study of Latino youth in Southern California found that it was especially important to differentiate between gangs, which were organized and had long his-tories of involvement in serious antisocial behavior, and "crews," which also engaged in fighting, tagging, and partying, but which did not engage in serious violence (Lopez, Wishard, Gallimore, & Rivera, 2006). This distinction has important legal ramifications, because anti-gang laws that mandate tougher penalties for crimes committed by gangs may be incorrectly applied to ado-lescents who commit delinquent acts with their friends (or crew) but who are not members of gangs.

The processes that lead adolescents to join gangs are not the same as those that lead to membership in crews and other sorts of peer groups, though. Gang members tend to be more isolated from their family, have more emotional and behavioral problems, and have poorer self-conceptions than other adolescents, including those who are involved in antisocial activity but who are not gang members (Esbensen, Deschenes, & Winfree, 1999; Harper & Robinson, 1999). The relationships that anti-social adolescents have with their clique-mates are often less satisfying than are those between other adolescents and their friends (Pabon, Rodriguez, & Gurin, 1992). This finding has implications for the design of interven-tions aimed at controlling delinquency by involving anti-social peer groups in positive activities; in the absence of their shared interest in antisocial activities, delinquent peers may have little reason to maintain their friendship.

The Role of Parents The process of antisocial peer group formation in adolescence begins in the home, during childhood (Tolan, Gorman-Smith, & Henry, 2003). Problematic parent-child relationships—ones that are coercive and hostile—lead to the development of an antisocial disposition in the child, and this disposition con-tributes, in elementary school, to both school failure and rejection by classmates (Pardini, Loeber, & Stouthamer-Loeber, 2005). Rejected by the bulk of their classmates, aggressive boys "shop" for friends and are accepted only by other aggressive boys. Once these friendships are formed, the boys, like any other clique, reward each other for participating in a shared activity—in this case, antiso-cial behavior. Improvements in parenting during adoles-cence reduce teenagers' association with antisocial peers, which, in turn, reduces problem behavior (R. Simons, Chao, Conger, & Elder, 2001).

gangs
Organized peer groups of anti-social individuals.

The family and peer contexts are connected through other processes as well (Brown & Bakken, 2011; Schroeder & Mowen, 2014). Parents often "manage" their adolescent's friendships by monitoring the indi-viduals their child spends time with, guiding their child toward peers they like, prohibiting contact with peers they dislike, and supporting friendships they approve of (Mounts, 2007; Updegraff, Kim, Killoren, & Thayer, 2010). Parents also act as "consultants," helping their teenagers work out problems with their friends (Mounts, 2011). Adolescents whose parents act as consultants in this way are less likely to be involved in drug use and delinquent activity and report more positive relationships with their friends (Mounts, 2004). On the other hand, excessive attempts to control an adolescent's choice of friends may backfire; when parents forbid adolescents from associating with peers the parents disapprove of, they may inadvertently drive adolescents to become closer to those peers, perhaps in defiance of these restrictions on their independence (Keijsers et al., 2012; Tilton-Weaver, Burk, Kerr, & Stattin, 2013). Rather than viewing the family and peer contexts as separate worlds, it is important to keep in mind that what takes place in one setting often has an impact on what occurs in others.

The role of the family in friendship choice has also been described in studies of crowds (B. Brown, Mounts, Lamborn, & Steinberg, 1993; C. Mason, Cauce, Gonzales, & Hiraga, 1996). One of the factors that influences the crowd an adolescent belongs to is her or his upbringing. Parents play a role in socializing certain traits in their children, and these orientations, whether toward aggression or academic achievement, predispose adolescents toward choosing certain friends or crowds with which to affiliate. Once in these cliques or crowds, adolescents are rewarded for the traits that led them there in the first place, and these traits are strengthened.

One problem with accounts of adolescent develop-ment that posit the peer group as more important than the family (e.g., J. R. Harris, 1998) is that they fail to take into account the fact that the family has a strong effect on adolescents' choice of peers. For example, a child who is raised to value academics will perform well in school and will likely select friends who share this orientation. Over time, these friends will reinforce the youngster's academic orientation and strengthen his or her school performance. By the same token, antisocial adolescents, who are drawn toward other antisocial peers, become more antisocial over time as a result (Benson & Buehler, 2012). Even when adolescents have relatively more antisocial friends, having better relationships at home and a stronger attachment to school will make them less susceptible to their friends' negative influence—even in the context of a gang (Crosnoe, Erickson, & Dornbusch, 2002; Walker-Barnes & Mason, 2004; Trudeau, Mason, Randall, Spoth, & Ralston, 2012).

The finding that adolescents become more antisocial when they spend time with antisocial peers has prompted some experts to question the wisdom of group-based interventions for adolescents with conduct problems (Dishion, McCord, & Poulin, 1999). Several studies of programs designed to reduce adolescents' delinquency or aggression, for example, have found that, instead of having the desired effect, the programs actually increase participants' problem behavior. They have what scientists call **iatrogenic effects** (Mahoney, Stattin, & Lord, 2004).

Iatrogenic effects are the undesirable consequences of well-intentioned treatments—for example, when the side effects of a medication are far worse than the problem it is intended to treat. When antisocial adolescents spend time with like-minded peers, they frequently teach each other how to be "more effective" delinquents and reward each other for misbehavior. One observational study of adolescent friends talking to each other on camera (Piehler & Dishion, 2014) found that individuals who had a history of involvement in antisocial behavior engaged in more spontaneous conversation about antisocial activities and rewarded each other in the way they responded (e.g., "We were so wasted last Friday." "Oh, yeah, that was insane!" "Remember the time we stole that vodka?" "That was so awesome!"). Several writers have described this process as "deviancy training" (e.g., Dishion, Nelson, Winter, & Bullock, 2004). Knowing that group treatments for antisocial behavior have iatrogenic effects is obviously important for the design of programs for delinquent and aggressive youth.

Other approaches to violence reduction that make sense intuitively have frequently proven ineffective, if not exactly harmful. For instance, some researchers have found that trying to teach adolescents to use nonviolent forms of conflict resolution are often unsuccessful because such behaviors are perceived by adolescents as being weak or even inviting retaliation (Farrell et al., 2010).

iatrogenic effects
Unintended adverse consequences of a treatment or intervention.

Here are some typical responses from urban Black students when asked why using nonviolent means of settling arguments was unpopular (Farrell et al., 2010, p. 11):

> They [other students] want to see a fight. They want to see chaos. They want to see people go at each other, so it's like a big show or something. They like fighting. They'll try to egg them on.

> If you don't fight, people gonna say stuff about you. If you do fight, they still will, but you know that you won . . . you don't want everybody to think you a punk or nothing.

> Other people think you're scared or something, so you just go ahead and fight him, try to show off, try to prove that you're better or . . . that you're not scared.

Similarity Between Friends: Selection Or Socialization?

Because antisocial activities are such a strong determinant of clique composition, many adults have expressed concern over the influence of peers in promoting delinquent activity and drug and alcohol use. Parents often feel that if their teenager runs with the wrong crowd, he or she will acquire undesirable interests and attitudes. They worry, for instance, when their child starts spending time with peers who seem to be less interested in school or more involved with drugs. But which comes first—joining a clique or being interested in a clique's activities? Do adolescents develop interests and attitudes because their friends influence them, or is it more that people with similar interests and tastes are likely to become friends?

This question has been examined in many studies that have tracked adolescents and their friendships over time. By tracing patterns of attitudinal and behavioral change, and comparing these shifts with patterns of friendship formation and change, researchers can determine whether adolescents are attracted to one another because of their initial similarity (what social scientists refer to as *selection*), become similar because friends influence each other (referred to as *socialization*), or a combination of the two (Brechwald & Prinstein, 2011).

In general, studies indicate that both selection and socialization are at work (see Figure 7) across a variety of attitudinal and behavioral domains, including school

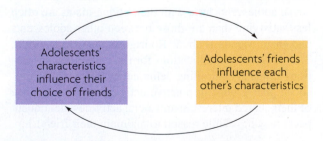

Figure 7 Adolescents' choice of friends both influences and is influenced by their traits and interests.

achievement, happiness, drug use, mental health, and delinquency (Light, Greenan, Rusby, Nies, & Snijders, 2013; Parker et al., 2015; Rayner, Schniering, Rapee, Taylor, & Hutchinson, 2013; Schaefer, Haas, & Bishop, 2012; van Workum, Scholte, Cillessen, Lodder, & Giletta, 2013), and in romantic relationships as well as friendships (Simon, Aikins, & Prinstein, 2008). Adolescents who use alcohol or tobacco, for example, are more likely to choose other alcohol or tobacco users as friends (Osgood et al., 2013), especially when they attend schools with a large number of substance-using students (an example of selection). By the same token, spending time with friends who use these substances increases the adolescents' own use as well (an example of socialization) (Ennett et al., 2006; Fujimoto, Unger, & Valente, 2012). The more substance-using friends an adolescent has, and the closer he or she feels to them, the more the adolescent is likely to use alcohol and drugs (McGloin, Sullivan, & Thomas, 2014). Even dating someone whose friends are substance users has similar effects (Haynie, Doogan, & Soller, 2014; Kreager & Haynie, 2011).

Similarly, adolescents who are bullies or who sexually harass others are more likely to have friends who behave similarly (Jewell, Bron, & Perry, 2014; Low, Polanin, & Espelage, 2013; Sentse, Kiuru, Veenstra, & Salmivalli, 2014; Sijtsema, Rambaran, Caravita, & Gini, 2014). Conversely, antisocial adolescents who have few friends, and few aggressive friends in particular, are likely to become less antisocial over time (Adams, Bukowski, & Bagwell, 2005; Botvin & Vitaro, 1995), whereas those with antisocial friends who become even more antisocial themselves become more delinquent (Monahan, Steinberg, & Cauffman, 2009; Weerman, 2011). In general, adolescents' level of antisocial behavior tends to become more similar to that of their friends over time; interestingly, the larger the initial discrepancy between friends in their levels of delinquency, the more likely they are to become similar (McGloin, 2009). This process is not limited to antisocial behavior: Adolescents who report more depressive symptoms are likely to choose other depressed adolescents as friends, which, in turn, negatively affects their own mood and that of their other friends (Brendgen, Lamarche, Wanner, & Vitaro, 2010; Goodwin, Mrug, Borch, & Cillessen, 2012; Kiuru, Burk, Laursen, Nurmi, & Salmela-Aro, 2012). Adolescents who are overweight are likely to have other overweight adolescents as friends, largely because they are rejected by their nonoverweight classmates (Schaefer & Simpkins, 2014).

How much of adolescents' similarity to their friends is due to selection and how much is due to socialization? The answer depends on what behavior or attitude is being studied. Socialization is far stronger over day-to-day preferences in things like clothing or music than over many of the behaviors that adults worry about, such as binge drinking or risky sex (Jaccard, Blanton, & Dodge, 2005; Knecht, Burk, Weesie, & Steglich, 2011), or even obesity

(de la Haye, Robins, Mohr, & Wilson, 2011). Although parents don't want to hear it, selection is a stronger factor than socialization when it comes to problem behavior and drug use (de la Haye, Green, Kennedy, Plooard, & Tucker, 2013; DeLay, Laursen, Kiuru, Salmela-Aro, & Nurmi, 2013; Fortuin, van Geel, & Vedder, 2014). That is, adolescents who use drugs or engage in delinquency are more likely to select friends with these tastes than to be corrupted by them.

One analysis of data from a large, nationally representative sample of adolescents found that adolescents' friendship groups fell into one of four profiles: high functioning (a network of high-achieving friends who were involved in school-based extracurricular activities and who reported low use of alcohol and few symptoms of depression), maladjusted (friends showed the opposite pattern), disengaged (friends were not engaged in much of anything, including drinking), and engaged (friends were engaged in school, achieved decent grades, and neither abstained from nor abused alcohol) (Crosnoe & Needham, 2004). More important, an individual adolescent's behavior could be predicted on the basis of her or his friendship group's profile. Adolescents' socioeconomic background and family situation were strongly related to characteristics of their friendship network, with teenagers from more educated, two-parent families more likely to fall into the high-functioning and engaged groups.

Stability of Adolescent Friendships   Adolescents' cliques show only moderate stability over the course of the school year—with some members staying in the clique, others leaving, and new ones joining—although cliques become more stable later in high school (Poulin & Chan, 2010). Although the actual composition of adolescents' cliques may shift over time, the defining characteristics of their cliques or their best friends do not (Hogue & Steinberg, 1995; Luo, Urberg, & Rao, 1995). That is, even though some members of an adolescent's clique may leave and be replaced by others, the new members are likely to have attitudes and values that are quite similar to the former members' (B. Brown, 2004).

Even "best friendships" are likely to change during the school year. Only about one-third of students who name a best friend in the fall of a school year rename the same person as their best friend in the spring (that person was typically listed as a friend, but not the best friend) (Değirmencioğlu, Urberg, Tolson, & Richard, 1998). Instability is also the case in best friendships in which adolescents name each other as their best friend. Only half of all reciprocated best friendships that exist at the beginning of a school year exist at the end; surprisingly, remaining friends over the course of a school year has nothing to do with the quality of the friendship (Bowker, 2004). Same-sex friendships tend to be more stable than opposite-sex friendships, and boys' friendships trend to be more stable than girls'. Generally

sociometric popularity
How well-liked an individual is.

perceived popularity
How much status or prestige an individual has.

speaking, friendship stability is higher among well-adjusted adolescents than their more troubled peers, although it isn't clear whether this is because stability contributes to adjustment, because better-adjusted adolescents are better at maintaining friendships, or, most likely, a combination of both (Poulin & Chan, 2010). The most common causes of broken friendships are jealousy, incompatibility, violations of intimacy, and aggression (Casper & Card, 2010) (see Table 2).

Popularity and Rejection in Adolescent Peer Groups

Thus far, our discussion has focused on how and why crowds and cliques serve as the basis for adolescents' social activities and attitudes. But what about the internal structure of peer groups? Within a clique or a crowd, what determines which adolescents are popular and which are not?

Determinants of Popularity and Rejection

In recent years, psychologists have changed their thinking about what it is that leads to popularity during adolescence. Although it is widely agreed that popular adolescents are generally more socially skilled than their unpopular peers, there is surprising variability among popular teenagers with respect to other characteristics. One reason for this is that there are two forms of popularity, and they don't always go hand in hand (B. Brown & Larson, 2009). One form, **sociometric popularity,** refers to how well-liked someone is. The other form, **perceived popularity,** refers to how much status, or prestige, someone has (Litwack, Aikins, & Cillessen, 2012). So, for example, a leader of the "preppie" crowd who is snobby might be very high in perceived popularity but not in sociometric popularity. Conversely, a member of a crowd that has less prestige who happens to be a really nice person with a good sense of humor may be high in sociometric popularity but low in perceived popularity. By the time they are 14, adolescents understand the difference between the two (van den Berg, Burk, & Cillessen, 2014). If you think back to your own high school days, you can probably remember people of each type.

Whereas sociometric popularity is determined mainly by social skills, friendliness, sense of humor, and so forth, which are valued by people of all ages and backgrounds, the determinants of perceived popularity are highly variable. Because the determinants of status can easily differ between schools, or even among groups within the same school, it is hard to predict which adolescents will be popular without knowing what is valued in that adolescent's social context (Jonkmann, Trautwein, & Lüdtke, 2009; Kreager, 2007b). For example, among White and

Table 2   Summary of broad categories of features that led to dislike

Category	Exemplar Quotes
Jealousy	"She stole my boyfriend and my closest friends. Then got angry when she found out I slept with him."
	"This person disliked my boyfriend/date I was going to bring to the prom, which led me to going to the prom with my boyfriend only. I felt that she had ruined my senior life in high school."
Incompatibility	"An argument started when my friend would just make really loud noises for no reason, and when I would ask her to stop she would just continue."
	"This person was loud, annoying, and really had no point of talking because her argument made no sense."
	"We stopped talking and hanging out for no apparent reason. All of a sudden it just ended."
Intimacy-rule Violations	"We were best friends, but I couldn't trust her because she lied to me too many times."
	"In the beginning she seemed like an awesome friend but then, after I started getting close to her, I saw her true colors revealed. She had a very evil way of trying to hurt people and put them down. She was also very untrustworthy."
Aggression	"She spread rumors about me because the guy she liked, liked me."
	"She was with a boy at our senior BBQ and was taking her time when we were in a rush. She and the boy went home with someone else instead of me and didn't tell me. The next day I confronted her and we got into a fight and suspended from school. That's when she started spreading rumors."

Latino teenagers, drinking is associated with status, but this is not the case among Black adolescents (Choukas-Bradley, Giletta, Neblett, & Prinstein, 2015).

Although there is one main pathway to sociometric popularity (having good social skills), the determinants of perceived popularity are variable and ever changing. Having a boyfriend or girlfriend, for example, may have little to do with perceived popularity in 5th grade, but may be highly correlated with it in 9th grade. Within the very same school, some adolescents are highly regarded by their peers because they are good-looking and athletic (the conventional image of the popular teenager), whereas others are equally admired because they are rebellious, delinquent, and aggressive (B. E. Becker & Luthar, 2007; Jonkmann et al., 2009). Moreover, whereas many of the things that *lead to* popularity also make adolescents more likeable (e.g., athletic ability, physical attractiveness, social skills), some of the things that help to *maintain* popularity once it is established may actually make adolescents less likeable (e.g., using gossip to control or manipulate others) (Dijkstra, Cillessen, Lindenberg, & Veenstra, 2010b; Lansu & Cillessen, 2011; Neal, 2010). In general, adolescents tend to affiliate with peers who have a similar level of popularity within their school (Dijkstra, Cillessen, & Borch, 2013; Logis, Rodkin, Gest, & Ahn, 2013), mainly because the more popular kids reject the less popular ones (Berger & Dikjstra, 2013).

Predicting perceived popularity is further complicated by the fact that peer norms change, and socially competent adolescents are skilled at figuring them out, adjusting their behavior in response to them, and even influencing them. If smoking marijuana becomes something that is valued by the peer group, popular adolescents will start getting high more regularly (Allen, Porter, McFarland, Marsh, & McElhaney, 2005). And when popular adolescents start to engage in a particular behavior, that behavior often becomes more admired. Indeed, one of the reasons it is hard to persuade adolescents to "just say no" to drinking, smoking, and sex is that these activities are often associated with being popular (Balsa, Homer, French, & Norton, 2011; Lansford, Killeya-Jones, Miller, & Costanzo, 2009; Mayeux, Sandstrom, & Cillessen, 2008). Even things like fighting, bullying or carrying a weapon, which most adolescents do not approve of, become more acceptable when popular adolescents start to do these things (Bellmore, Villarreal, & Ho, 2011; Dijkstra, Lindenberg, & Veenstra, 2008; Dijkstra et al., 2010).

Adolescents are easily swayed by the opinions of high-status peers to endorse activities that they might otherwise reject and to run the other way from activities endorsed by low-status peers, even if they secretly enjoy them (G. L. Cohen & Prinstein, 2006). Adolescents often behave in ways they believe popular students act, although these perceptions are not always accurate. For

Researchers distinguish between "sociometric" popularity—how well-liked someone is—and "perceived" popularity—how much prestige someone has. They don't always go hand in hand.
© David Grossman/Alamy

instance, popular kids are often thought to engage in more substance use than they actually do (Helms et al., 2014).

Popularity and Aggression Although psychologists used to believe that aggressive and antisocial adolescents are likely to be rejected by their classmates, it turns out that some of these teenagers are quite popular (de Bruyn, Cillessen, & Wissink, 2010; Rullison, Gest, & Lokem, 2013; Fanti, Brookmeyer, Henrich, & Kuperminc, 2009; Waasdorp, Baker, Paskewich, & Leff, 2013), although their popularity tends to wane as adolescents get older and antisocial behavior is no longer something that teenagers admire (Young, 2014). Nor do these traits continue to have the same effects on one's social life: One recent study, entitled "What Ever Happened to the 'Cool' Kids?" found that adolescents whose early popularity came from impressing their peers with delinquent and "pseudomature" behavior (like precocious sex) had more interpersonal and behavioral problems as young adults (Allen, Schad, Oudekerk, & Chango, 2014).

Studies have identified two distinct types of popular boys (Rodkin, Farmer, Pearl, & Van Acker, 2000). One group has characteristics typically identified in studies of popular youth: They are physically and academically competent, friendly, and neither shy nor aggressive. A second group, however, is extremely aggressive, physically competent, and average or below average in friendliness, academic competence, and shyness. Similarly, one study of girls found two distinctly different groups of popular adolescents: girls who were prosocial and good students, and girls who were antisocial and antiacademic, some of whom actually were even bullies (de Bruyn & Cillessen, 2006).

How can we explain this? Wouldn't we expect adolescents who are antisocial or aggressive toward others

instrumental aggression
Aggressive behavior that is deliberate and planned.

reactive aggression
Aggressive behavior that is unplanned and impulsive.

to be *unpopular?* Evidently, it is not aggression alone, but the combination of aggression and difficulty controlling emotions or a lack of social skills, that leads to problems with peers (Dijkstra, Lindenberg, Verhulst, Ormel, & Veenstra, 2009; Wolters, Knoors, Cillessen, & Verhoeven, 2014). Consistent with this, aggressive adolescents who use their aggression strategically—what is referred to as **instrumental aggression**—are much more popular than aggressive adolescents whose aggression is unplanned— what is referred to as **reactive aggression** (Prinstein & Cillessen, 2003). It's also important to distinguish between aggression, which may increase adolescents' popularity, and delinquency, which tends to diminish it (Rulison, Kreager, & Osgood, 2014).

The Dynamics of Popularity   Two ethnographies of early adolescent girls provide insight into the dynamics of popularity. In a classic study, the researcher (Eder, 1985) spent 2 years in a middle school observing interactions among early adolescent girls in various extracurricular and informal settings (in the cafeteria, in the hallway, at school dances). Although the study is more than 30 years old, many of the researcher's observations still ring true today.

In this school, the cheerleaders were considered the elite crowd, and girls who made the cheerleading squad were immediately accorded social status. Other girls then attempted to befriend the cheerleaders as a means of increasing their own perceived popularity. This, in turn, increased the cheerleaders' prestige within the school, as they became the most sought-after friends. Girls who were successful in cultivating friendships with the cheerleaders became a part of this high-status group and more popular. But because even popular adolescents can only maintain a finite number of friendships, they ended up snubbing other classmates who wanted to be their friends. Ironically, this often leads to popular adolescents becoming disliked (Mayeux et al., 2008). Thus, adolescents who hang out with popular adolescents may themselves become perceived as more popular over time but they may also become less well-liked, because they are seen as snobby status-seekers, especially by their less popular peers (Dijkstra, Cillessen, Lindenberg, & Veenstra, 2010b; Lansu, Cillessen, & Karremans, 2012).

In another ethnography, the researcher spent time observing and interviewing a group described by teachers as the "dirty dozen" (D. Merten, 1997). This group of girls, "considered 'cool,' 'popular,' and 'mean,'" were "a combination of cute, talented, affluent, conceited, and powerful" (1997, p. 178). The researcher was interested in understanding "why a clique of girls that was popular and socially sophisticated was also renowned for its meanness" (1997, p. 188).

The answer, he discovered, was that meanness was one of the ways that the clique ensured that no one member became stuck-up as a result of her popularity in the eyes of her classmates. Thus, while it was important for clique members to maintain their popular image, if any clique member appeared to become too popular, the other members would turn on her, undermining her standing with other girls by gossiping, starting rumors, and deliberately attempting to disrupt her friendships. The following quote, from a girl whose friends turned on her, will sound all too familiar:

> Gretchen was starting to get really mad at me. I talked to her about it and I asked her what was wrong. She just said, "Oh, I heard something you said about me." But I didn't say anything about her. Sara was mad at me. I don't know why. She started being mad at me and then she started making things up that [she said] I said. Sara told Brenda and Gretchen so that they would get mad at me, too. So now I guess Gretchen has made up something and told Wellesley. They are all mad at me and laughing and everything. (D. Merten, 1997, p. 182)

Ironically, then, one of the potential costs of being popular in adolescence is that if you become too popular, you face the very real possibility of being the object of other classmates' meanness.

Although popularity clearly has some costs, the advantages of being popular far outweigh the disadvantages. Being popular is not the same as having close and intimate friendships, but the two often go hand in hand (Asher, Parker, & Walker, 1996). Compared with their less popular peers, popular adolescents are more likely to have close and intimate friendships, have an active social life, take part in extracurricular activities, and receive more social recognition (such as being selected as leaders of school organizations) ((Franzoi, Davis, & Vasquez-Suson, 1994). Part of the overlap between popularity and friendship stems from the fact that many of the characteristics that make adolescents popular are the same ones that make them sought after as friends—chief among them, having good social skills. Actually, adolescents who see themselves as well-liked and socially competent fare well over time, regardless of whether they are genuinely popular among their classmates (McElhaney, Antonishak, & Allen, 2008).

Some adolescents who are not especially popular in school may have a well-developed network of friends outside of school. Because most research on adolescents' peer networks has been limited to school-based friendships, we know relatively little about the nature or effects of nonschool friendships. But we do know that many adolescents have a social life outside of school— at church, in the neighborhood, in nonschool extracurricular activities—that is quite different from their life in school. Studies that examine the impact of friends on adolescent development may miss important information if they do not include information about the number and characteristics of the adolescent's nonschool friends. Having friends outside school can buffer the harmful consequences of having few friends in school (Kiesner, Poulin, & Nicotra, 2003).

Rejected Adolescents Just as there are different reasons for being popular, there are also different reasons for being rejected. It's important to distinguish among three types of disliked adolescents, though (Bierman & Wargo, 1995; Coie, Terry, Lenox, Lochman, & Hyman, 1995; D. French, Conrad, & Turner, 1995). One set of unpopular adolescents comprises teenagers who have trouble controlling their aggression. Withdrawn adolescents make up a second unpopular set; these adolescents are shy, anxious, and inhibited and boys of this sort are frequently victims of bullying (Coplan et al., 2013; Erath, Flanagan, & Bierman, 2007). A third group is both aggressive and withdrawn. These adolescents have problems controlling their hostility, but like other withdrawn children, they tend to be nervous about initiating friendships with other adolescents.

The origins of peer rejection in adolescence can frequently be traced to earlier periods of development. Often, adolescents who are rejected by their peers had experienced peer rejection during middle childhood, and this rejection, in turn, was the consequence of behavioral and emotional difficulties apparent in early elementary school (Ettekal & Ladd, 2015; Pedersen, Vitaro, Barker, & Borge, 2007; Monahan & Booth-LaForce, 2015). Others are rejected in adolescence mainly because they've been rejected in the past (Ladd, Ettekal, Kochenderfer-Ladd, Rudolph, & Andrews, 2014).

Regardless of its causes, rejection by peers is a significant source of stress for adolescents, who show greater brain activation to rejection than children do, as well as a stronger biological stress response to it (Bolling et al., 2011; Stroud et al., 2009). During adolescence there are important changes in the brain that lead individuals to become more sensitive to the emotions, expressions, and opinions of others. One fascinating study of adolescents' ratings of music imaged participants' brains while they were listening to songs with or without the songs' popularity revealed. Changing one's evaluation of a song after being told whether it was popular or not was correlated with brain activity in regions known to reflect anxiety, suggesting that feeling anxious about whether one's tastes in music are "correct" may lead teenagers to conform to others (Berns, Capra, Moore, & Noussair, 2010).

Relational Aggression

Most studies of the peer relations of aggressive children have focused on children who are overtly aggressive (either physically or verbally). This has led researchers to pay relatively more attention to the social relationships of aggressive boys than girls, because boys exhibit

more overt aggression (Card, Stucky, Sawalani, & Little, 2008). Girls also act aggressively toward peers, but their aggression is often social, not physical (Crick, 1996). They engage in **relational aggression**—aggression intended to harm other adolescents through deliberate manipulation of their social standing and relationships.

> **relational aggression**
> Acts intended to harm another through the manipulation of his or her relationships with others, as in malicious gossip.

Individuals use relational aggression to hurt others by excluding them from social activities, damaging their reputations with others, or withdrawing attention and friendship. Physical and relational aggression follow similar developmental trajectories during adolescence, increasing during early adolescence and then declining from mid-adolescence on, and are correlated (individuals who are highly aggressive in one way are also aggressive in the other, and individuals who are frequent victims of physical aggression are also frequent victims of relational aggression) (Card et al., 2008; Karriker-Jaffe, Foshee, Ennett, & Suchindran, 2009; Nylund, Bellmore, Nishina, & Graham, 2007). Like physical aggression, the roots of relational aggression are often

Although boys are more physically aggressive than girls, girls often engage in what has been called relational aggression— an attempt to harm someone by ruining his or her reputation or disrupting his or her friendships. © Image Source/Alamy RF

found in the family: Adolescents who use a lot of relational aggression frequently have parents who are harsh or controlling (Kawabata, Alink, Tseng, van IJzendoorn, & Crick, 2011).

"Mean Girls"   Although relational aggression was first noticed in observations of girls, studies show that both genders employ it (Juvonen, Wang, & Espinoza, 2012), but that girls are more aware of it, more distressed by it, and more often the victims of it (Card et al., 2008; Pronk & Zimmer-Gembeck, 2010; Sullivan, Farrell, & Kliewer, 2006). Girls are more likely than boys to say that it is morally wrong to exclude someone simply on the basis of the crowd to which he or she belongs (Horn, 2003). Adolescents whose aggression is atypical for their gender (that is, girls who are highly physically aggressive and boys who are highly relationally aggressive) show more maladjustment than their peers whose aggression is more gender-stereotypic (Crick, 1997).

Girls' use of relational aggression has attracted a great deal of popular attention, as reflected in the best-selling books *Odd Girl Out* (Simmons, 2003) and *Queen Bees and Wannabees* (Wiseman, 2003), which served as the basis for the movie *Mean Girls*. Perhaps in response, educators have expressed concerns about "meanness" in school environments, noting that teachers have devoted far more attention to preventing overt physical fighting than relational aggression—despite the fact that victims of relational aggression also suffer as a result (Desjardins & Leadbeater, 2011; Siegel, La Greca, & Harrison, 2009). Some have called for educational programs designed to help teachers understand, assess, prevent, and respond to the problem when it arises in their classroom, as well as schoolwide programs designed to teach tolerance and acceptance and encourage students to disapprove of relational aggression when they see it. Changing students' attitudes about relational aggression—which many adolescents see as fine, even if they object to physical aggression—is important, because adolescents' attitudes about the acceptability of relational aggression (for example, agreeing with the statement "In general, it is OK to not let someone sit with your group of friends at the lunch table") predict their use of it (Werner & Nixon, 2005). In the opinion of most experts, middle schools ought to be the focus of such interventions (Yoon, Barton, & Taiarol, 2004).

making the scientific connection

Is relational aggression something that is more common in adolescence than adulthood? If so, why might this be? If not, is it expressed differently among adults?

Preventing relational aggression is easier said than done (A. J. Rose, Swenson, & Waller, 2004). Adolescents who use relational aggression often are more popular than their peers (Dawes & Xie, 2014). In some ways, this is hardly surprising, because the whole *point* of using relational aggression is to maintain one's status and popularity, and because the same social skills that make one popular (learning how to "read" other people, being able to adjust one's behavior to maintain one's status, having a good sense of humor, etc.) are useful when one is spreading rumors, gossiping, or trying to undermine someone else's reputation (Bowker & Etkin, 2014). The reason some physically aggressive boys are often more popular than their peers is that physical aggression and relational aggression may go hand in hand, and it is their relational aggression, not their physical aggression, that contributes to their popularity. Many programs designed to reduce relational aggression may be ineffective because adolescents are reluctant to stop doing something that maintains their popularity, or even improves their friendships, even if it is at the expense of someone else (Banny, Heilbron, Ames, & Prinstein, 2011; A. J. Rose & Swenson, 2009).

Consequences of Rejection   Being unpopular has negative consequences for adolescents' mental health and psychological development—peer rejection and friendlessness are associated with subsequent depression, behavior problems, and academic difficulties (Bellmore, 2011). But studies show that the specific consequences of peer rejection may differ for rejected youth who are aggressive versus those who are withdrawn. Aggressive individuals who are rejected are at risk for conduct problems and involvement in antisocial activity as adolescents, not just as a direct result of their rejection, but because the underlying causes of their aggression (for instance, poor self-control) also contribute to later conduct problems (Laird, Pettit, Dodge, & Bates, 2005). In contrast, withdrawn children who are rejected are likely to feel lonely and are at risk for low self-esteem, depression, and diminished social competence—again, both as a result of being rejected and in part because the underlying causes of their timidity (for instance, high anxiety) also contribute to later emotional problems (Card & Hodges, 2008; Pedersen et al., 2007). Rejection is especially likely to lead to depression in adolescents who place a lot of importance on their standing in the peer group and who believe that they, rather than the peers who reject them, are at fault (Prinstein & Aikins, 2004). Adolescents who are both aggressive and withdrawn are at the greatest risk of all (Rubin, LeMare, & Lollis, 1990).

Many psychologists believe that unpopular youngsters lack some of the social skills and social understanding necessary to be popular with peers. Unpopular aggressive children are more likely than their peers to think that other children's behavior is deliberately hostile, even when it is not. When accidentally pushed while waiting in line, for instance, many unpopular aggressive children are likely to retaliate because they believe that the person who did the pushing did it on purpose. This so-called **hostile attributional bias** plays a central role in the aggressive behavior of rejected adolescents (Crick & Dodge, 1994). Adolescents who are prone to make hostile attributions tend to have friends who view the world through a similar lens (Halligan & Phillips, 2010). Interventions aimed at changing the way aggressive adolescents view their peers have been successful in reducing rates of aggression (Dodge, Godwin, & The Conduct Problems Prevention Group, 2013; Yeager, Miu, Powers, & Dweck, 2013; Yaeger, Trzesniewski, & Dweck, 2013).

Victimization and Harassment

What about unpopular withdrawn children? What are their social skills deficits? In general, unpopular withdrawn children are excessively anxious and uncertain around other children, often hovering around the group without knowing how to break into a conversation or activity (Rubin et al., 1990). Their hesitancy, low self-esteem, and lack of confidence make other children feel uncomfortable, and their submissiveness makes them easy targets for bullying (Olweus, 1993; Salmivalli, 1998). Many of these youngsters are especially sensitive to being rejected, a feeling that increases in adolescence as brain regions that monitor social information become more easily aroused (Falk et al., 2014; Moor, Marieke, Crone, & van der Molen, 2014; Zimmer-Gembeck et al., 2013; Zimmer-Gembeck, Trevaskis, Nesdale, & Downey, 2013). Some are depressed, and their depression leads them to behave in ways that make them targets of harassment (generally speaking, people of all ages don't like to hang around with depressed individuals) (Kochel, Ladd, & Rudolph, 2012). Unfortunately, the more these children are teased, rejected, and victimized, the more anxious and hesitant they feel, and the more they blame themselves for their victimization, which only compounds their problem—creating a sort of cycle of victimization (see Figure 8) (Chen & Graham, 2012; Harper, 2012; Mathieson, Klimes-Dougan, & Crick, 2014; Siegel et al., 2009).

One of the most pernicious effects of victimization is that it undermines feelings of academic competence, academic performance, and school engagement, which has cascading effects well beyond adolescence—even after taking into account background factors, victimization during adolescence is associated with lower educational attainment, and, as a consequence, diminished earnings in adulthood (Cornell, Gregory, Huang, & Fan, 2013; Espinoza, Gonzales, & Fuligni, 2013).

Not all rejected students are bullied, though. Children who are victimized but who have supportive friends are less likely to be caught in this vicious cycle than those who are don't (Kendrick, Jutengren, & Stattin, 2012). It also helps to be good-looking and wealthy, as well as a good athlete or student; rejected adolescents with any of these traits are less likely to be actively picked on than other rejected teens (Knack, Tsar, Vaillancourt, Hymel, & McDougall, 2012).

> **hostile attributional bias**
> The tendency to interpret ambiguous interactions with others as deliberately hostile.

making the practical connection

What can be done to reduce victimization in schools? If you were asked to design an intervention, what would it entail?

Peer harassment is something that students can be exposed to both directly (when they are the victims) or indirectly (when they witness harassment but aren't themselves victimized). These two different types of experience have both similar and dissimilar effects (Janosz et al., 2008; Nishina & Juvonen, 2005). Being victimized or witnessing the harassment of others makes students anxious, but, oddly enough, witnessing the harassment of others appears to buffer some of the harmful effects of being victimized. Adolescents who are victims of harassment but who do not see anyone else being victimized are more likely to feel humiliated and angry than those who are both victims and witnesses. Presumably, being singled out for harassment feels worse than being just one of many who are picked on (Brendgen et al., 2013). For this reason, some studies find that in ethnically diverse schools, victimized students whose ethnic group is in the minority are not as harmed psychologically as are victimized students whose ethnic group is in the majority, who are less able to attribute their victimization to their ethnicity and more likely to blame it on their own shortcomings (Graham, Bellmore, Nishina, & Juvonen, 2009). Other studies have found that the adverse effects of being bullied are pretty much the same regardless of a school's ethnic makeup, however (Mehari & Farrell, 2015).

Figure 8   **Anxious adolescents are frequently harassed and picked on by others, which leads them to be rejected by their peers and more anxious as a result.** (Kochel et al., 2012)

Bullies and Victims   Although relationships between adolescents who dislike each other have not been studied extensively, such mutual antipathies are not uncommon (Abecassis, Hartup, Haselager, Scholte, & Van Lieshout, 2002). These relationships frequently involve bullies and victims, often with an antisocial adolescent repeatedly harassing a withdrawn classmate (Güroğlu, Haselager, van Lieshout, Cornelis, & Scholte, 2009). Adolescents who are bullies are also likely to assist and reinforce other bullies and, like the bullies they support, are also more likely to have conduct problems and be callous and indifferent to the problems of others (Crapanzano, Frick, Childs, & Terranova, 2011; Fanti & Kimonis, 2012; van Noorden, Haselager, Cillessen, & Bukowski, 2015).

Studies of American and European youth indicate that about one-third of students report having been bullied at some time during the past year, although in some studies, the percentage of students who report having been victimized has been considerably higher (Haynie et al., 2001; Nansel et al., 2001; Williford, Brisson, Bender, Jenson, & Forrest-Bank, 2011). Rates of victimization vary considerably from country to country, although around the world, adolescents who come from less affluent families are more likely to be bullied (Analitis et al., 2009).

Interestingly, the prevalence of bullying is higher in schools and in countries characterized by greater income inequality (Due et al., 2009; Menzer & Torney-Purta, 2012). For example, bullying is far less prevalent in Sweden, where the gap between rich and poor is very small, than in Russia, where income inequality is much greater (see Figure 9). Apparently, it is more acceptable for the strong to victimize the weak in countries where

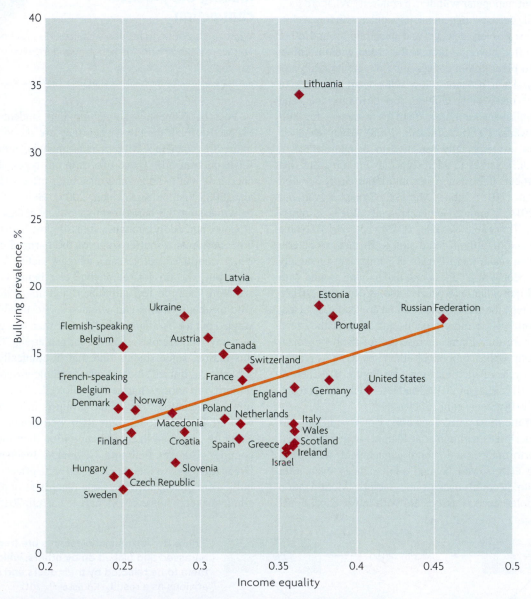

Figure 9   Rates of bullying vary considerably from country to country. Bullying is more prevalent in countries with greater income inequality. (Due et al., 2009)

having a wide gap between the economically "strong" and economically "weak" is also more widely tolerated.

Cyberbullying   Researchers are just now beginning to systematically study **cyberbullying** (e.g., bullying that occurs over the Internet or via cell phones). Despite the attention it receives in the popular media, in part because of a few very high-profile cases, online harassment is far less common than most people think, and, more importantly, less common than in-person harassment (either verbal or physical).

Rates of different types of bullying vary considerably from study to study, in part because researchers define bullying in different ways, which is why it is important to draw estimates from multiple studies rather than depend on a single one (Patton et al., 2014). According to a recent comprehensive review, physical bullying is about twice as common (nearly 35% of students have been either the perpetrator or victim of physical bullying) as electronic bullying (which has involved about 15% of students as bullies or victims) (Modecki, Minchin, Harbaugh, Buerra, & Runions, 2014). Rates of bullying and victimization have both declined in the United States (see Figure 10) (Perlus, Brooks-Russell, Wang, & Iannotti, 2014). Even still, cyberbullying is common, and it affects victims in ways that are similar to physical bullying (Bonanno & Hymel, 2013).

Adolescents who engage in traditional bullying also frequently engage in cyberbullying, and adolescents who are frequent victims of traditional bullying are also the victims of electronic harassment (Fletcher et al., 2014; Jose, Kljakovic, Scheib, & Notter, 2012; Modecki et al., 2014; Waasdorp & Bradshaw, 2015). Contrary to popular belief, most Internet bullying is not anonymous, and most victims of online bullying suspect a friend or someone else from their school (Juvonen & Gross, 2008; Waasdorp & Bradshaw, 2015). Not surprisingly, bullies who "specialize" in cyberbullying, which takes a bit of planning, tend to be less reactive in their aggression and more instrumental, often using electronic bullying to enhance their own social status (Badaly, Kelly, Schwartz, & Dabney-Lieras, 2012; Sontag, Clemans, Graber, & Lyndon, 2011). They are also less likely to view cyberbullying as wrong (Talwar, Gomez-Garibello, & Shariff, 2014). Interestingly, whereas conventional bullying tends to make adolescents less popular, cyberbullying tends to have the opposite affect (Wegge, Vendebosch, Eggermont, & Pabian, 2014). Adolescents are more

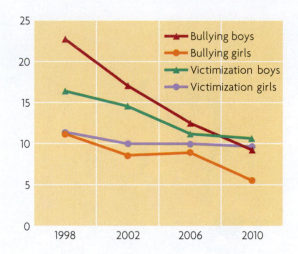

Figure 10   **Trends in bullying and victimization over time among U.S. students in grades six through ten.** (Perlus et al., 2014)

likely to engage in cyberbullying if they believe that their friends are, too (Hinduja & Patchin, 2013).

> **cyberbullying**
> Bullying that occurs over the Internet or via cell phones.

Students who are harassed by their classmates, whether in person or electronically, report a range of adjustment problems, including low self-esteem, depression, suicidal ideation, and academic difficulties, as well as problems in social skills and difficulties in controlling negative emotions, such as anger and aggression (Cole et al., 2014; Fredstrom, Adams, & Gilman, 2011; Juvonen, Wang, & Espinoza, 2011; Herts, McLaughlin, & Hatzenbuehler, 2012; Plaisier & Konijn, 2013; Zwierzynska, Wolke, & Lereya, 2013). Some adolescents who are victimized become alienated and disengaged from school, and, ultimately, form bonds with antisocial peers, which draws the previously victimized teenagers into antisocial activity (Rudolph et al., 2014; Tortura, Karver, & Gesten, 2013) (see Figure 11).

Although being bullied has adverse consequences regardless of whether other students witness it, public victimization, especially when other students watch but don't offer any assistance, is particularly humiliating (Nishina, 2012). Sadly, the effects of being harassed in middle school are still observed in high school (Rusby, Forrester, Biglan, & Metzler, 2005) and later in adulthood (Wolke, Copeland, Angold, & Costello, 2013).

Many adolescents who report having been victimized also report bullying others. These adolescents have the

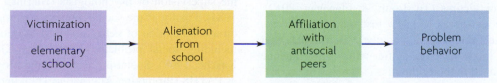

Figure 11   **Victimization in elementary school can lead to alienation, which may drive victimized students into deviant peer groups. This then increases problem behavior.** (Rudolph et al., 2014)

Although cyberbullying receives a lot of media attention, it is only about half as common as face-to-face bullying. © Andrey Shadrin/ Getty Images RF

greatest adjustment problems, just as children who are both aggressive and withdrawn are typically the most disturbed (Bradshaw, Waasdorp, Goldweber, & Johnson, 2012; Copeland, Wolke, Angold, & Costello, 2013; Winsper, Lereya, Zanari, & Wolke, 2012). One reason that bullying and victimization are often seen in the same children is that some adolescents react to victimization by becoming more aggressive and bullying other children. (Victims are more likely to become bullies than the reverse [Haltigan & Vaillancourt, 2014].) Another may be that certain elements of the broader context—the climate of the school, for instance—may increase or decrease the likelihood of aggression between classmates (Ferráns & Selman, 2014). Teachers and principals may be able to make changes in their school's climate that will reduce aggression between students (Aceves, Hinshaw, Mendoza-Denton, & Page-Gould, 2010; Guerra, Williams, & Sadek, 2011; Hektner & Swenson, 2012; Veenstra, Lindenberg, Huitsing, & Salmivalli, 2014).

What about students who see their classmates bullied? One study of bystanders found that onlookers were more likely to intervene and defend the victim in schools in which doing so was expected—not so much by teachers but by other students (Pozzoli, Gini, & Vieno, 2012). This has important implications for intervention, because it suggests that reducing the incidence of bullying in schools should focus on all students, and not just the bullies or victims (Tu, Erath, & Flanagan, 2012). It's hard for witnesses to know just how to intervene, though. Here's one student's advice, when asked what another girl might have done after witnessing someone being victimized in their school:

> I don't think she should say, "What you're doing is really inhuman, guys," because that would just make it so that

they don't want to talk to her. . . . But at the same time, I don't think she should egg it on as something good. She should suggest something that doesn't completely separate her from the group, like, "Maybe you should be a little bit nicer." Kind of subtle. . . . Something so that you get their attention, but that you're not insulting them. (Ferráns, Selman, & Feigenberg, 2012, p. 459)

It is important to note, however, that a significant amount of bullying occurs outside of school—according to one national survey, in fact, more high school students reported being victimized *outside* school than at school (Turner, Finkelhor, Hamby, Shattuck, & Ormrod, 2011).

Adolescents' responses to being bullied vary. One recent study found that there were four categories of victims: those who were mainly passive (e.g., ignoring the bully or walking away), those who were mainly aggressive (e.g., fighting back, either physically or verbally), those who were support-seeking (e.g., telling a parent), and those who did a little of everything. (Support-seeking was reported by middle school students but was rarely seen in high school, perhaps because at this age, asking an adult for help in responding to a bully is seen as immature and weak.) Interestingly, victims who used passive strategies reported fewer emotional or behavioral problems than those who fought back, sought help, or used a mixture of approaches (Waasdorp & Bradshaw, 2011), although feeling supported by parents or teachers (if not directly asking for their help) seems to have a protective effect against the adverse effects of victimization (Yeung & Leadbeater, 2013). Other studies find that victims who avoid blaming themselves for having been bullied and respond by behaving proactively (avoiding the bully), rather than retaliating, fare better (Singh & Bussey, 2011). Although it is hard to persuade adolescents that these are the most effective responses, it helps to explain that bullies do what they do in order to get attention, and that when they are ignored, they are likely to seek other targets (Steinberg, 2011).

Helping Unpopular Teens Psychologists have experimented with different sorts of interventions designed to improve the social skills of unpopular adolescents. These social competence training programs have focused on three different strategies. One type of program has been designed to teach social skills—self-expression, leadership, and how to converse (Repinski & Leffert, 1994). A second approach has been to have unpopular adolescents participate in group activities with popular ones under the supervision of psychologists (Bierman & Furman, 1984). Finally, some social competence programs focus on a combination of behavioral and cognitive abilities, including social problem solving (e.g., Greenberg & Kusche, 1998). Social-problem-solving programs, such as PATHS (Promoting Alternative Thinking Strategies), are designed to improve individuals' abilities to judge social situations and figure out acceptable ways of behaving. Adolescents are taught to calm down and think before they react, to decide what the problem is, to figure out what their goal is, and to think of positive approaches toward reaching that goal. Instead of lashing out at a classmate who grabbed the last basketball from a gym closet, for example, a hot-tempered boy who had been through this sort of program might calm himself down, tell himself that his goal is to play basketball rather than get into a fight, and approach another student to ask if he can get into a game. PATHS has been shown to effectively reduce behavioral problems among elementary school children (Conduct Problems Prevention Research Group, 1999).

The Peer Group and Psychosocial Development

Regardless of the structure or norms of a particular peer group, peers play an extremely important role in the psychological development of adolescents. Problematic peer relationships are associated with a range of serious psychological and behavior problems during adolescence and adulthood. Individuals who are unpopular or who have poor peer relationships during adolescence are more likely than their socially accepted peers to be low achievers in school, drop out of high school, show higher rates of delinquent behavior, and suffer from an array of emotional and mental health problems as adults. Although it is likely that poorly adjusted individuals have difficulty making friends, psychological problems result from—as well as cause—problems with peers (Marion, Laursen, Zettergren, & Bergman, 2013; Witvliet, Brendgen, van Lier, Koot, & Vitaro, 2010; Woodward & Fergusson, 1999).

Adolescents consider the time they spend with their peers to be among the most enjoyable parts of the day (Csikszentmihalyi & Larson, 1984). One reason is that activities with friends are typically organized around having a good time, in contrast to activities with parents, which are more likely to be organized around household chores or the enforcement of parental rules (Larson, 1983). Rather than being competing institutions, the family and peer group mainly provide contrasting opportunities for adolescent activities and behaviors. The family is organized around work and other tasks, and it may be important in the socialization of responsibility and achievement. The peer group provides more frequent opportunities for interaction and leisure, which contributes to the development of intimacy and enhances the adolescent's mood and psychological well-being.

6 Schools

The Broader Context of U.S. Secondary Education

The Origins of Secondary Education

School Reform: Past and Present

What Should Schools Teach?

Education in the Inner Cities

The Social Organization of Schools

School Size and Class Size

Age Grouping and School Transitions

Tracking

Ethnic Composition

Alternatives to Public Schools

Classroom Climate

The Best Classroom Climate for Adolescents

Teacher Expectations and Student Performance

The Importance of Student Engagement

School Violence

Beyond High School

The College-Bound

The Non-College-Bound

Schools and Adolescent Development

Characteristics of Good Schools

The Effects of School on Adolescent Development

© Pgiam/Getty Images RF

Because of the important and multifaceted role it has come to play in modern society, the **secondary educational system**—middle schools, junior high schools, and high schools—has been the target of a remarkable amount of criticism, scrutiny, and social science research.

Secondary school touches the lives of all adolescents in industrialized societies, as well as an increasingly larger proportion of the population in the developing world. Virtually all American adolescents under the age of 17 and nearly all 17- and 18-year-olds are enrolled in school. In most developing countries, attending high school is much more common among children of the wealthy, often because poor families need their adolescents to work. But even in the poorest parts of the world—sub-Saharan Africa, for example—close to two-thirds of 10- to 14-year-olds and 40–50% of 15- to 19-year-olds are enrolled in school (National Research Council, 2005), although rates around the world vary considerably from country to country (United Nations, 2012) (see Figure 1). With the exception of a few countries, such as Afghanistan, rates of enrollment in secondary school are comparable for males and females.

Schooling is as time-consuming as it is pervasive. During most of the year, the typical American student spends more than one-third of his or her waking hours each week in school or in school-related activities (Larson & Verma, 1999). Between ages 11 and 18, the typical American student will spend about 7,000 hours in school—not even counting time on homework and school-related activities outside of school (Elmore, 2009).

secondary educational system
The system of middle schools, junior high schools, and high schools.

Not only are schools the chief educational arena for adolescents, but they also play an extremely important role in defining the young person's social world and in shaping psychosocial development. Naturally, the development of achievement—motivation, aspirations, and expectations—is profoundly affected by the adolescent's experiences in school. (Think about the differences between going to a good school and going to a bad one.) But schools influence psychosocial development far beyond the domain of achievement. How adolescents do in school influences their academic self-conceptions and occupational choices, shaping their identity. The way in which a school is organized affects the adolescent's sense of independence, and the way a classroom is run affects the extent to which the adolescent learns to *think* independently. Schools often define adolescents' social networks, thereby influencing the development of interpersonal relationships. And the majority of adolescents, at least in the United States, learn about sexuality in school and are influenced by their classmates' norms for sexual behavior. You simply cannot understand adolescence as a developmental period without understanding the ways in which schools shape the adolescent experience.

In this chapter, we examine the organization and workings of secondary schools at multiple levels of analysis. Perhaps your first inclination is to think about what takes place in the classroom. While this is important, a thorough understanding of schooling and its impact on adolescent development requires going beyond the classroom (Eccles & Roeser, 2011). What takes place in the classroom is influenced by the way in which the school is organized,

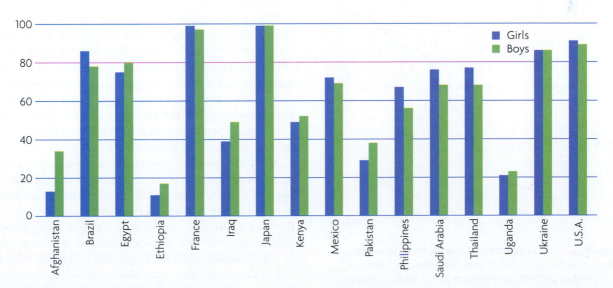

Figure 1 The proportion of male and female adolescents in selected countries who are enrolled in secondary school. (United Nations, 2012)

and the way in which the school is organized, in turn, is influenced by the needs and demands of the community and of society. Unlike the family or peer group, whose structure is not under the direct or deliberate control of society, schools are environments created to serve

specific purposes (Elmore, 2009). In many respects, the schools we have today—for all their strengths and weaknesses—are the schools we designed. This is abundantly clear when we look at the history of secondary education in America.

The Broader Context of U.S. Secondary Education

Today in the United States, virtually all young people ages 14–17 are enrolled in school. In 1930, only about half of this age group were students, and at the turn of the twentieth century, only 1 in 10 were (see Figure 2) (D. Tanner, 1972; William T. Grant Foundation, 1988).

Not only are there considerably more youngsters enrolled in school today than there were 50 years ago, but today's students also spend more days per year in school. In 1920, for example, the average school term was 162 days, and the average student attended for only 121 days, or 75% of the term. By 1968, however, the school term had been lengthened to nearly 180 days, which remains the national average, and the typical student today attends more than 90% of the term (National Center for Education Statistics, 2013).

Adolescents also remain in school for more years now than they did in previous eras. In 1924, fewer than 33% of all youngsters entering the 5th grade eventually graduated from high school; today, more than 80% of all high school students graduate on time, and a substantial number of those who do not eventually get their

diploma, either by completing high school at a later date or through equivalency programs or continuation schools (National Center for Education Statistics, 2015).

The Origins of Secondary Education

The rise of secondary education in America was the result of several historical and social trends that converged at the turn of the twentieth century. Most important were industrialization, urbanization, and immigration.

Following widespread industrialization during the late nineteenth century, the role of children and young adolescents in the workplace changed dramatically. As productivity became more dependent on workers' use of machines, employers recognized that they needed employees who were more skilled than youngsters ordinarily were. In addition, the few unskilled jobs that remained after industrialization required strength beyond the capacity of many youth (Church, 1976). Social reformers expressed concerns about the dangers children faced working in factories, and labor unions—an increasingly powerful force in the early 1900s—sought to protect not only the welfare of children but their own job security. New child labor laws narrowed and limited the employment of minors (Bakan, 1972). Together, these changes kept many youngsters out of the labor force.

Life in American cities was changing markedly. Industrialization brought with it urbanization and, along with several waves of immigrants, new problems. The effects of a rapidly expanding economy were seen in the tenements and slums of America's cities: poor housing, overcrowded neighborhoods, crime. Eager to improve living conditions for the masses, social reformers envisioned education as a means of improving the lives of the poor and working classes.

Many also saw compulsory secondary education as a means of social control. High schools would take thousands of idle young people off the streets and place them in an environment where they could be supervised and kept out of trouble. Anxious to see that foreign-born immigrants were well socialized into the American way of life, reformers presented universal secondary education as a necessary part of the process of Americanization (Church, 1976; D. Tanner, 1972). By 1915, the idea of universal compulsory education for adolescents had gained widespread acceptance.

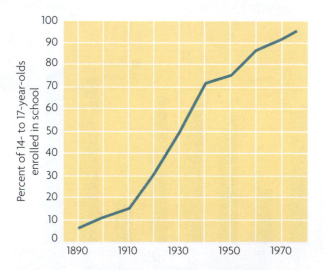

Figure 2   The proportion of the 14- to 17-year-old population enrolled in school increased dramatically between 1910 and 1940, continued to increase until 1970, and then leveled off. Today, nearly 95% of individuals this age are in school. (D. Tanner, 1972; William T. Grant Foundation, 1988)

Prior to the early twentieth century, high schools were for the elite. In curriculum, staff, and student composition, they were similar to the colleges of the day, with the emphasis mainly on classical liberal arts instruction (Church, 1976; D. Tanner, 1972). By 1920, educators saw a need for curricular reform. Now that secondary education was aimed at the masses, schooling was not just a means of intellectual training but also a way of preparing youth for life in modern society. It was argued that education should be more practical and include preparation for work and citizenship.

The 1920s marked the birth in the United States of what came to be known as the **comprehensive high school,** an educational institution that promised to meet the needs of a diverse and growing population of young people. Classes in general education, college preparation, and vocational education were all housed under one roof. This was also a time of tremendous change in the high school curriculum. New courses were added in music, art, family life, health, physical education, and other subjects designed to prepare adolescents for family and leisure as well as work.

By the middle of the twentieth century, the high school had come a long way from its exclusive focus at the turn of the century on the intellectual development of the elite. Its concern had broadened to include the social and intellectual development of all young people. And today, despite continuing questioning and criticism, the comprehensive high school remains the cornerstone of American secondary education. It is, however, not the exemplar to which all countries aspire—few other countries attempt to educate such a diverse group of young people under one roof. Most separate the college-bound from the non-college-bound into separate schools. The comprehensive "high school" is a distinctively American institution.

The proportion of American adolescents enrolled in high school grew dramatically between 1920 and 1940. © The Granger Collection, NYC

unfamiliar with the world of work, schools were asked to provide opportunities for work-study programs and classes in career education (President's Science Advisory Committee, 1974). In the 1990s, as society grappled with a broad array of social problems affecting and involving youth—problems such as violence, AIDS, and drug abuse—we once again looked to schools for assistance, asking schools to implement an array of preventive interventions (Dryfoos, 1993). One reason that schools today are asked to do so much more than educate adolescents is that new demands are placed on schools every time a different social problem involving adolescents receives widespread attention.

> **comprehensive high school**
> An educational institution that evolved during the first half of the twentieth century, offering a varied curriculum and designed to meet the needs of a diverse population of adolescents.

School Reform: Past and Present

Although we naturally think of schools as institutions whose primary goal is education, they are much more than this. Schools are also potentially important tools of social intervention, because it is through schools that the greatest number of young people can most easily be reached. For this reason, the study of schools is extremely important to social scientists and policy makers who are interested in influencing adolescent development. In fact, one way to understand the ways in which adults want adolescents to change is to look at the ways that schools have been reformed over the years.

Here are three examples of what I mean: During the 1950s, politicians felt that the United States had lost its scientific edge to the former Soviet Union. As a consequence, schools were asked to offer more courses in math and science (Conant, 1959). In the 1970s, when social scientists felt that adolescents were growing up

No Child Left Behind   Toward the end of the 1990s, concerns that inner-city schools were not producing graduates who could compete for high-skills jobs grew. In response to a public increasingly interested in alternatives to conventional public education, such as charter schools or home schooling, schools were called upon to raise standards for all students (e.g., Ravitch, 2001). In January 2002, President George W. Bush signed into law the No Child Left Behind Act, a sweeping and controversial piece of legislation mandating that states ensure that all students, regardless of their economic circumstances, achieve academic proficiency (U.S. Department of Education, 2006). No Child Left Behind (NCLB) required that schools create and enforce academic standards by annually testing all students and by reporting the results of students' performance to the public. Underperforming schools—schools where students' test scores did not improve—would be given an opportunity to do a better job the following year, by providing

social promotion
The practice of promoting students from one grade to the next automatically, regardless of their school performance.

critical thinking
Thinking that involves analyzing, evaluating, and interpreting information, rather than simply memorizing it.

additional instruction, tutoring, or special services for students who needed them. But schools that continued to fail eventually would have funding taken away and might be forced to close.

On the face of it, NCLB sounds reasonable enough. Today, a huge proportion of American students do not meet even minimal standards for academic performance, and poor performance is disproportionately seen among disadvantaged, Black, Hispanic, and Native American students. Many commentators had criticized the practice of **social promotion**—moving students from one grade to the next regardless of their academic performance—arguing that poor and ethnic minority youth especially were being cheated out of a good education and graduated without the skills necessary to succeed in college or the labor force (Steinberg, 1996). Forcing schools to regularly assess student progress and publicize how students were faring would give parents and the community the information they needed to put pressure on

Assessing student achievement has been the focus of American education policy for the past two decades. Critics have complained that too much time is being spent testing students.
© Radius Images/Corbis RF

schools to do better. No one could disagree with the basic idea that all students—regardless of their background—deserve a high-quality public education (Borkowski & Sneed, 2006).

Although NCLB sounded good in principle, it was problematic in practice and met with tremendous resistance from the start (Darling-Hammond, 2006). States complained that they did not have the resources to conduct the mandated assessments or to respond to failing students' poor performance. Teachers and parents complained that the focus on standardized testing adversely affects what takes place in the classroom—if a school's financial future depends only on test scores, why should teachers do anything other than teach to the test? (Be honest—how much effort do *you* devote to learning material that you know you won't be tested on?) Some critics worried that the shift in focus to standardized testing would discourage schools from using assignments that improve important capacities like self-control, persistence, and determination—which are critical for success but more likely influenced through working on longer-term projects than studying for tests (Duckworth, Quinn, & Tsukama, 2012).

Many questions about NCLB were raised: What happens to subjects that will not appear on the test, like current events, or to the teaching of skills that are impossible to assess through standardized exams, such as **critical thinking?** Who determines how tough the tests are or what level of achievement is acceptable? And, with millions of dollars at stake, what was to stop schools from manipulating their scores, by encouraging poor-performing students to be absent on testing days or by helping students cheat on the tests, which some schools did (S. Levitt & Dubner, 2005)? Some critics of NCLB argued that it was having the opposite effect of what was intended, providing incentives for schools to push low-achieving students out (Darling-Hammond, 2006). Nevertheless, the movement toward performance-based accountability—holding teachers, schools, school districts, and states accountable for the achievement of their students—has been the most important change in the world of American education in the past 20 years (Elmore, 2009).

No Child Left Behind remained in place after President Barack Obama took office in 2009, although his administration sought to fix many of the problems that had developed during the policy's early years: that schools were "gaming the system," by setting their standards especially low, so that they could report that a high proportion of their students were making passing grades; that teachers were teaching to the test, in order to avoid being punished if their students tested poorly; and that school districts were reporting school-wide average scores without revealing that there were huge achievement gaps between the low- and high-performing students. President Obama's education secretary stressed the need to have high standards for all students and, just as important, a set of *common* standards across all

50 states (U.S. Department of Education, 2009). (One of the problems with NCLB as originally implemented is that it permitted individual states to set their own standards, which resulted in markedly different estimates of "proficiency" from one state to another.)

The administration also tried to build more flexibility into NCLB by encouraging schools to experiment with different approaches to raising student achievement, through a competition called "Race to the Top." As new research began to demonstrate the importance of having high-quality teachers, schools were encouraged to develop better ways of evaluating their teachers, helping teachers improve their classroom skills, and replacing poor teachers with better ones. Unfortunately, "Race to the Top" didn't change high school student achievement any more than NCLB did (Steinberg, 2014). Debates about how to turn America's high schools around continue.

What Should Schools Teach?

Suppose you are asked to list the things you think young people need to know in order to be competent, responsible, satisfied adults. Which items on your list should be the responsibility of high schools? Should high school curricula be limited to traditional academic subjects, or should schools play a broader role in preparing young people for adulthood by providing instruction more directly relevant to work, family, leisure, and citizenship? Should students receive instruction only in English, mathematics, science, and social studies, or should they take courses as well in "general education"—in subjects such as art, home economics, health, sex education, driver education, and personal finance? Which courses should be required, and which should be left as electives? If you were to discuss this with your classmates, you'd probably find plenty of disagreement.

Standards-Based Reform The past three decades have been dominated by what is called **standards-based reform,** which focuses on policies designed to improve achievement by holding schools and students to a predetermined set of benchmarks measured by achievement tests. This gave rise to proposals that American schools adopt the **Common Core,** a set of standards in English language arts and mathematics that schools across the country would be expected to use to evaluate whether their students were learning what they ought to learn in each grade. Although states were given wide flexibility in how they would implement the standards (they would have control over the curriculum and instructional methods they would use), the Common Core continues to be controversial. Many states that signed on to the plan initially have since broken from it.

Like NCLB, standards-based reform sounds good in principle, but implementing this change has been more difficult than you might think. Educators haven't been able to agree on the body of knowledge and skills that comprise what high school graduates should know and be able to do. And as states soon discovered, large numbers of their students did not fully acquire the knowledge and capabilities assessed on standardized graduation examinations. It is all well and good to propose that all high school seniors must pass a graduation test in order to earn a diploma, but what happens when one-third or one-half of a state's high school seniors fail the test? The economic, social, and political costs of holding back such large numbers of students because they could not pass these "exit exams" was simply too great. This created a huge incentive for states to develop exams with very low requirements for passing, which, of course, defeats the whole purpose of standards-based reform.

Amid widespread disappointment over the state of public education in America, increasing numbers of parents began to look at other options—among them, **charter schools** (public schools that are given more freedom to set their own curricula), schools that are run by private corporations rather than local school boards, home schooling, and government-subsidized **school vouchers** (which can be used for private school tuition). Although all of these alternatives gained popularity during the late 1990s, research on their costs and benefits has been inconclusive (Steinberg, 2014). There is considerable variability among charter, for-profit, and private schools, as well as homeschooling environments, just as there is among public schools. The bottom line is that what takes place within a school is probably more important than the nature of its funding and oversight. This idea has led many experts to argue that we should focus on the ways in which we train, certify, place, and compensate teachers (Darling-Hammond, 2006).

standards-based reform
Policies designed to improve achievement by holding schools and students to a pre-determined set of standards measured by achievement tests.

Common Core
A proposed set of standards in language arts and mathematics that all American schools would be expected to use.

charter schools
Public schools that have been given the autonomy to establish their own curricula and teaching practices.

school vouchers
Government-subsidized vouchers that can be used for private school tuition.

making the cultural connection

The United States is one of the only industrialized countries in the world that does not have national graduation examinations that are administered to all students, regardless of where they go to school. Do you think having national exams is a good or bad idea? Why do you think this practice is not as popular in the United States as it is elsewhere?

Education in the Inner Cities

Some commentators have argued that the problem of low student achievement is not an across-the-board problem, but one that is concentrated mainly among poor and minority youngsters living in inner cities (Berliner & Biddle, 1995). Although other critics (e.g., Stedman, 1998; Steinberg, 1996) have noted that poor achievement is a problem in all segments of American society, virtually all social scientists concur that the education crisis, and its implications for the future of the labor force, is especially urgent within inner-city public schools. Indeed, the achievement gap between White and non-White youngsters, which had been closing for some time, grew wider during the 1990s, especially in large urban school districts. It narrowed again toward the end of the twentieth century, but has remained substantial since (Barton & Coley, 2010).

Although there are occasional success stories, such as the Harlem Children's Zone (Tough, 2008) or KIPP (www.kipp.org), a system of charter schools that creates a culture of achievement, maintains high expectations for all students, and emphasizes character development as well as academics, inner-city schools in America continue to have tremendous problems. Just 10% of the high schools in the United States produce *half* of the country's dropouts, and one-third of Black and Latino students attend one of these "drop-out factories" (Sparks, 2015). And, although there have been modest improvements in some subjects at some grade levels, the gap in achievement between Black and Hispanic students, on the one hand, and White and Asian students, on the other, remains very wide. Among 8th-graders, for example, 60% of Asian students and 45% of White students are proficient in math, compared to 21% of Hispanic students and 14% of Black students. Huge gaps exist in

reading as well, with 52% of Asian students and 46% of White students proficient, compared to 22% of Hispanic students and 17% of Black students (National Center for Education Statistics, 2013). In the nation's large inner-city public schools, only one-sixth of students are judged proficient in science, a fact that has enormous implications for these adolescents' chances at success in an increasingly high-tech economy (National Center for Education Statistics, 2011a).

Why has school reform failed in so many urban schools? Experts point to several factors. First, the concentration of poverty in many inner-city communities has produced a population of students with an array of personal and situational problems—problems that few schools are equipped or able to address (Farrell et al., 2007). Recent surveys of American high school students indicate that so many are afraid of being victimized that nearly one-fifth of high school students across the country regularly carry a gun, knife, or club, with even higher percentages doing so in some inner-city neighborhoods (Centers for Disease Control and Prevention, 2014a). Many urban school districts are burdened by huge administrative bureaucracies that impede reform and hinder educational innovation. Students in urban schools report less of a sense of "belonging" to their school, which leads to disengagement and poor achievement (Anderman, 2002). And the erosion of job opportunities in inner-city communities has left many students with little incentive to remain in school or to devote a great deal of effort to academic pursuits (Kantor & Brenzel, 1992). Many reformers now believe that to fix the problems of urban education, we must change the entire context in which inner-city children live, not merely what goes on in their schools (Tough, 2008).

The Social Organization of Schools

In addition to debating curricular issues, social scientists interested in school reform have discussed the ways in which secondary schools should be organized. Because the organization of a school affects students' day-to-day experiences, variations in school organization can have profound effects on adolescents' development and behavior. In this section, we examine the research on five key aspects of school organization: (1) school and classroom size, (2) different approaches to age grouping, (3) tracking, or the grouping of students in classes according to their academic abilities, (4) the ethnic composition of schools, and (5) public versus private schools.

School Size and Class Size

As the idea of the comprehensive high school gained widespread acceptance, educators attempted to deliver a wider range of courses and services under a single

Just ten percent of America's high schools account for half of the country's dropouts. Almost all of them are located in inner-city neighborhoods. © Andrew Burton/Getty Images

roof. As a consequence, schools became larger and larger over the course of the twentieth century. By the end of the 1990s, in many metropolitan areas, students attended enormous schools, with enrollments of several thousand students.

Is Bigger Better?   One advantage enjoyed by larger schools is that they can offer a more varied curriculum—a large high school, for instance, may be able to offer many specialized courses that a small school is unable to staff. But is bigger necessarily better?

A fair amount of research conducted over the past 40 years says, "No." Indeed, one of the most consistent conclusions to emerge from recent evaluations of school reform efforts is that student performance and interest in school improve when their schools are made less bureaucratic and more intimate. Numerous studies indicate that students achieve more when they attend schools that create a cohesive sense of community (V. Lee, Smith, & Croninger, 1997; Ready, Lee, & Welner, 2004). Students' attachment to school is weaker in larger schools, particularly when the number of students in a grade exceeds 400 (Holas & Huston, 2011; Weiss, Carolan, & Baker-Smith, 2010).

While school size may affect academic outcomes, it does not necessarily affect students' emotional attachment to the institution (Anderman, 2002) or their mental health (T. T. Watt, 2003). Contrary to widespread opinion, there is no evidence that rates of student victimization are higher in larger schools, although victimization is less likely in schools where the student-teacher ratio is lower, perhaps because it is easier for schools to establish and enforce norms about how to behave (Gottfredson & DiPietro, 2011; Klein & Cornell, 2010). In addition, many large schools are divided into **schools within schools.** Although few such transformations have been studied systematically, the existing research indicates both advantages and disadvantages to this approach. On the positive side, creating schools within schools leads to the development of a more positive social environment; on the negative side, though, if not done carefully, schools may inadvertently create "schools" within one school that vary considerably in their educational quality.

Some of the most interesting findings of research on school size concern participation in extracurricular activities rather than classroom achievement. You might expect that, in addition to providing a more varied curriculum, large schools are able to offer more diverse extracurricular activities to their students—and indeed they do. Large schools can support more athletic teams, after-school clubs, and student organizations. But because large schools also contain so many more students, actual rates of participation in different activities are only half as high in large schools as in smaller ones. As a result, in larger schools, students tend more often to be observers than participants in school activities. For instance, during the fall, a small school and a large school might each field teams in football, soccer, and cross-country running, together requiring a total of 100 students. An individual's chances of being 1 of those 100 students are greater in a school that has only 500 students than in a school with an enrollment of 4,000.

The Strengths of Small Schools   Because students in small schools are more likely than students in large schools to be active in a wider range of activities, they are more likely to report doing things that help them develop their skills and abilities, allow them to work closely with others, and make them feel needed and important. In a small school, chances are, sooner or later, most students will find themselves on a team, in the student government, or in an extracurricular organization. Students in small schools also are more likely to be placed in positions of leadership and responsibility, and they more often report having done things that made them feel confident and diligent. School size especially affects the participation of students whose grades are not very good. In large schools, academically marginal students often feel like outsiders and rarely get involved in school activities. In small schools, however, these students feel a sense of involvement and obligation equal to that of more academically successful students. The ideal size of a high school is between 600 and 900 students (V. Lee & Smith, 1997).

In short, although large schools may be able to offer more diverse curricula and provide greater material resources to their students, the toll that school size may take on student learning and engagement appears to exceed the benefits of being bigger (V. Lee & Smith, 1995). Evidence also suggests that there is more inequality in students' educational experiences in larger schools, where students may be sorted into tracks of differing quality. In small schools, in contrast, it is more likely that all students are exposed to the same curriculum, if only because the school cannot afford to offer more than one.

Variations in Class Size   Policy makers do not always implement social science findings in ways that accurately reflect the research evidence. Encouraged by the results of research on smaller *schools,* many politicians have called for smaller *classes.* However, in contrast to studies of schools, studies of classrooms indicate that variations within the typical range of classroom sizes—from 20 to 40 students—do not affect students' scholastic achievement once they have reached adolescence. Small classes benefit young elementary school children (up until third grade), who may need more individualized instruction (Finn, Gerber, & Boyd-Zaharias, 2005), but adolescents in classes with 40 students learn

schools within schools
Subdivisions of the student body within large schools created to foster feelings of belongingness.

junior high school
An educational institution designed during the early era of public secondary education, in which young adolescents are schooled separately from older adolescents.

middle school
An educational institution housing 7th- and 8th-grade students along with adolescents who are 1 or 2 years younger.

just as much as those in classes with 20 (Mosteller, Light, & Sachs, 1996).

An important exception to this finding involves situations that call for highly individualized instruction or tutoring, where smaller classes are more effective. For example, in remedial classes, where teachers must give a great deal of attention to each student, small classes are valuable. One implication of these findings is that it may be profitable for schools that maintain regular class sizes of 25–30 students to increase the sizes of these classes a bit and cut down on the number of classrooms in order to free some instructors, and to trim the sizes of classes for students who need specialized, small-group instruction.

The Problem of Overcrowding   One certain impediment to delivering high-quality education, especially in large metropolitan school districts, is overcrowding (Ready et al., 2004). Nearly 15% of U.S. secondary schools are overcrowded—that is, the size of the student body is at least 6% larger than the school was designed to house—and an additional 8% are "severely overcrowded," with the student body 25% above capacity. Schools with more than 50% ethnic minority students are especially likely to be overcrowded. Achievement is lower in overcrowded schools because of stress on both students and teachers, the use of facilities for instruction

that were not designed to serve as classrooms (such as gyms), and inadequate resources.

Educators have attempted to reduce the adverse effects of overcrowding through a variety of measures—some successful, others not. Many school districts use temporary structures, such as trailers, to provide additional classroom space. Unfortunately, many such portable units, especially older ones, are constructed with materials that are harmful to students' physical health, and the tight quarters and poor ventilation common in these structures can create toxic environments (Ready et al., 2004). Other districts—most famously, Los Angeles—have created multitrack programs, whereby schools are used year-round, and students are organized into groups, with one group on vacation at any given point in time. Evaluations of this approach have been mixed.

Age Grouping and School Transitions

A second issue that social scientists have examined in the study of school organization concerns the ways in which schools group students of different ages and the frequency with which students are expected to change schools.

Early in the twentieth century, most school districts separated youngsters into an elementary school (which had either six or eight grades) and a secondary school (which had either four or six grades). Students changed schools once (after either 6th or 8th grade). However, many educators felt that the two-school system was unable to meet the special needs of young adolescents, whose intellectual and emotional maturity was greater than that expected in elementary school, but not yet at the level necessary for high school. During the early years of compulsory secondary education, the establishment of separate schools for young adolescents began, and the **junior high school** (which contained the 7th, 8th, and sometimes 9th grades) was born (Hechinger, 1993). Toward the end of the twentieth century, the **middle school**—a three- or four-year school housing the 7th and 8th grades with one or more younger grades—gained in popularity, replacing the junior high school in many districts (Elmore, 2009).

In more recent years, school districts have moved away from housing young adolescents separately and are returning to a two-school model (usually K–8 and 9–12), in light of many studies showing that students demonstrate higher achievement and fewer behavioral problems under this arrangement (Weiss & Baker-Smith, 2010). It is important to note, however, that the particular grade configuration of a school is less important than the school's educational climate and quality of instruction (Elmore, 2009; Holas & Huston, 2012). In one study, 6th-grade girls attending elementary school, where they were the oldest students, reported more fighting and more suicidal thoughts than their counterparts who were in middle school (Gunter & Bakken, 2010), and in another, which was conducted in small,

Researchers have studied whether young adolescents fare better or worse in middle schools or junior high schools that separate them from children and older adolescents. Many districts are eliminating these schools and returning to a model that has just an elementary school and a high school.
© Maskot/Corbis RF

rural communities, there was more bullying in K–8 and K–12 schools than in districts that had separate elementary and secondary schools (Farmer, Hamm, Leung, Lambert, & Gravelle, 2011).

making the scientific connection

In light of what you know about development during early adolescence, are you surprised by the results of the study that found higher rates of problems among 6th-grade girls attending elementary school than among those in middle school? Can you speculate on why this may have been the case?

The Transition into Secondary School   Many studies find that students' academic motivation and school grades drop as they move from elementary into middle or junior high school (Dotterer, McHale, & Crouter, 2009). Scores on standardized achievement tests don't decline during this same time, though, suggesting that the drop in grades may be more a reflection of changes in grading practices and student motivation than in students' knowledge (Eccles, 2004).

Researchers also have examined how transitioning to a new school affects student achievement and behavior. In many of these studies, researchers compare school arrangements in which students remain in elementary school until 8th grade—that is, where they change schools once—with arrangements in which they move from elementary school, to middle or junior high school, and then to high school—where they change schools twice. In general, school transitions, whenever they occur, temporarily disrupt the academic performance, behavior, and self-image of adolescents; more frequent school changes are associated with lower achievement, as well as higher rates of emotional and behavioral problems (Herbers, Reynolds, & Chen, 2013). Over time, though, most youngsters adapt successfully to changing schools, especially when other aspects of their life—family and peer relations, for example—remain stable and supportive, and when the new school environment is well suited for adolescents (Seidman, Lambert, Allen, & Aber, 2003).

Researchers do not agree about whether the drop in academic motivation and achievement that occurs after elementary school is due to the school transition itself (that is, whether students suffer *whenever* they have to change schools) or to the nature of the difference between elementary school, on the one hand, and middle or junior high school, on the other. Some experts believe that the poor performance of middle and junior high schools is due primarily to their failure to meet the particular developmental needs of young adolescents (Booth & Gerard, 2014; Eccles & Roeser, 2009). Between 6th and 8th grade, for example, students report declines in how supportive their teachers and classmates are, how much autonomy students have, and how clear and fair school rules are (Way, Reddy, & Rhodes, 2007). Because adolescence is a time during which relationships with peers and nonfamilial adults become more important, independence becomes more desirable, and rules and regulations are increasingly scrutinized, these changes in school climate create a mismatch between what adolescents need and what their schools provide. This leads many young adolescents to disengage from school (Eccles & Roeser, 2009; Hughes, Im, Kwok, Cham, & West, 2014). Unfortunately, disengaging from school increases the risk of developing behavior problems, whereas remaining connected to school protects against some of the harmful effects of poor family relationships (Loukas, Roalson, & Herrera, 2010; Oelsner, Lippold, & Greenberg, 2011; Wang, Brinkworth, & Eccles, 2013).

How Secondary Schools Differ from Elementary Schools   The classroom environment in the typical middle school or junior high school is quite different from that in the typical elementary school (Eccles, Lord, & Roeser, 1996). Not only are junior high schools larger and less personal, but middle and junior high school teachers hold different beliefs about students than do elementary school teachers—even when they teach students of the same chronological age (Midgley, Berman, & Hicks, 1995). Teachers in junior high schools are less likely to trust their students and more likely to emphasize discipline, which creates a mismatch between what students at this age desire (more independence) and what their teachers provide (more control). Teachers in junior high schools also tend to be more likely to believe that students' abilities are fixed and not easily modified through instruction—a belief that interferes with student achievement. In addition, teachers in junior high or middle schools are less likely than other teachers to feel confident about their teaching ability (Eccles & Roeser, 2009).

It is hardly surprising that students experience a drop in achievement motivation when they enter middle or junior high school, given the change in environments they experience and the mismatch between what adolescents need developmentally and what the typical school context provides. The issue is not that the adolescents must make a transition; it is the *nature* of the transition they must make. Although students' self-esteem drops during the transition into middle or junior high school, it increases during the early high school years, so changing schools in and of itself isn't the problem. Consistent with this, middle school students attending more personal, less departmentalized schools, or schools where they are more involved, do better than their peers in more rigid and more anonymous schools (V. Lee & Smith, 1993; Wang & Holcombe, 2010). Not surprisingly, changing schools is easier on students who move into small rather than large institutions (Russell, Elder, & Conger, 1997).

Why do junior high school teachers differ from those who teach elementary school? The answer isn't clear-cut. People who choose to become junior high teachers do not differ all that much from those who choose to teach younger grades. Rather, it may be that the organization and anonymity of junior high schools have a negative effect on the teachers who work in them, which affects the way they interact with students. There is a lot of evidence that students are more engaged in school when their teachers are more engaged in their work (Louis & Smith, 1992).

Cultural stereotypes about adolescence also have a negative influence on teachers' beliefs. Many adults believe that adolescence is an inevitably difficult time—not only for teenagers themselves but also for those who work with them. To the extent that teachers come into the junior high classroom with negative images of adolescence—that teenagers are inherently unruly, unteachable, or perplexing—their preconceptions may interfere with their work as educators (Midgley, Feldlaufer, & Eccles, 1988). (This same sort of process affects parents who hold negative stereotypes about adolescence.) As we'll see in a later section of this chapter, one of the most important influences on the adolescent's experience in school is the climate of the classroom.

Individual Differences in the Extent of Transitional Problems Although some aspects of the transition into secondary school may be difficult for students to negotiate, not all students experience the same degree of stress (Fenzel, 2001). Students who have more academic and psychosocial problems before making a school transition cope less successfully with it (S. A. Little & Garber, 2004; Murdock et al., 2000; Roeser, Eccles, & Freedman-Doan, 1999). Often there are cascading effects, with academic and behavioral problems in elementary school leading to more problems during the transition into middle school (Moilanen, Shaw, & Maxwell, 2010b). Cascades can work in the opposite direction as well; students scoring high in social competence before the transition into

a new school become even more competent over the course of the change. In the face of the challenges posed by changing schools, "the psychosocially rich become richer, while the psychologically poor become poorer" (Monahan & Steinberg, 2011, p. 576).

Factors other than students' prior record also influence their transition to middle or high school. Adolescents who have close friends before and during the transition adapt more successfully to the new school environment (Wentzel, Barry, & Caldwell, 2004), although the benefits of staying with their friends accrue only to students who had been doing well previously. Students who had been doing poorly actually adjust better if they enroll in a different school than their friends, perhaps because their friends were contributing to their poor performance (Schiller, 1999).

In short, the transition into secondary school does not have uniform effects on all students (Jackson & Schulenberg, 2013; Li & Lerner, 2011). More vulnerable adolescents, adolescents with fewer sources of social support, and adolescents moving into more impersonal schools are more susceptible to the adverse consequences of this transition than their peers are. Not surprisingly, studies of poor, inner-city youngsters, who often are coping with problems associated with economic stress and neighborhood disadvantage, find especially significant negative effects of the school transition on these students' self-esteem, achievement, perceptions of the school environment, reports of social support, and participation in extracurricular activities (Eccles, 2004).

Generally speaking, boys, ethnic minority students, and students from poor families are more likely to become disengaged from school during early adolescence (Li & Lerner, 2011). Among Black and Latino students, transitioning to a school where the proportion of students from the same ethnic background is lower than it had been at their previous school is associated with greater disengagement from school, lower grades, and more frequent absences (see Figure 3) (Benner & Graham, 2009).

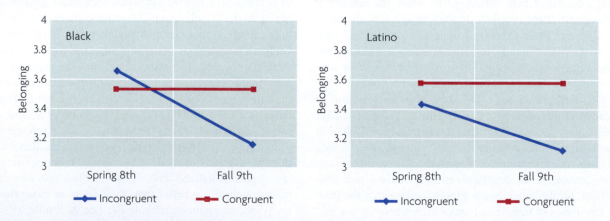

Figure 3 Transitioning into secondary school may lead to feelings of disengagement when there are fewer students of the same ethnic background. *Congruent* refers to whether the student's ethnicity is the same as that of the majority of students in the school. (Benner & Graham, 2009)

Parental support and involvement are associated with better adolescent adjustment during school transitions (Isakson & Jarvis, 1999). One study of low-income Black students found that students who fare best during the transition not only have parents who are involved in their education, but supportive teachers as well (Gutman & Midgley, 2000). It is therefore possible to enhance low-income students' adjustment to middle school through interventions targeted at their parents. One program had parents participate in an 11-week program designed to increase their understanding of adolescent development and their effectiveness as parents (Bronstein et al., 1998). Children whose parents participated in the program were functioning better psychologically and behaviorally, both immediately after the program and 1 year later, than were those whose parents did not participate. Moreover, the children whose parents participated did not show the decline in functioning that often is associated with the transition into middle school.

Research on tracking suggests that it has positive effects on the achievement of students in the more advanced tracks but negative effects on students in the lower tracks.
© EyeWire/Photodisc/Getty Images RF

Tracking

In some schools, students with different academic abilities and interests do not attend classes together. Some classes are designated as more challenging and more rigorous, and are reserved for students identified as especially capable. Other classes in the same subject area are designated as average classes and are taken by most students. Still others are designated as remedial classes and are reserved for students having academic difficulties. The process of separating students into different levels of classes within the same school is called ability grouping, or **tracking.** Not all high schools track students. In some schools, students with different abilities take all their classes together.

Even among schools that use tracking, there are important differences in how tracking is done (J. Jones, Vanfossen, & Ensminger, 1995). Some schools are more inclusive in their tracking, permitting a relatively high proportion of students into the highest track (including some students whose abilities do not warrant such placement). Other schools are more exclusive, limiting the places in the highest track to a privileged few (even if this means placing some high-ability students in the lower tracks). And still other schools are "meritocratic," placing students in tracks that accurately match their abilities.

Pros and Cons of Tracking   Educators have debated the pros and cons of tracking for years, but research

provides no definitive answers about its overall effects (Eccles & Roeser, 2009). Proponents of tracking note that ability grouping allows teachers to design class lessons that are more finely tuned to students' abilities. Tracking may be especially useful in high school, where students must master certain basic skills before they can learn such specialized subjects as science, math, or foreign languages. Critics of tracking point out, however, that students in the remedial track receive not just a different education, but one that's worse than that provided to those in more advanced tracks (Darling-Hammond, 1997). Moreover, the effects of tracking are not limited to academic outcomes. Schools play an important role in influencing adolescents' friendship choices. When students are tracked, they tend to socialize only with peers from the same academic group. Tracking can polarize the student body into different subcultures that are often hostile toward each other (Eccles & Roeser, 2009).

Critics of tracking also point out that decisions about track placements often discriminate against poor and ethnic minority students and may hinder rather than enhance their academic progress (Oakes, 1995). Some school counselors may assume that ethnic minority or poor youngsters are not capable of handling the work in advanced classes and may automatically assign them to average or remedial classes, where less material is covered and the work is less challenging. One analysis of national data found that Black students were especially likely to be

tracking
The practice of separating students into ability groups, so that they take classes with peers at the same skill level.

enrolled in lower-track math classes in schools in which Blacks are in the minority, even after taking into account students' qualifications (S. Kelly, 2009).

Not all research indicates that track placements are biased. Other studies have found that students' ability has a stronger influence than their background on initial track placement (Dauber, Alexander, & Entwisle, 1996), but that middle-class and White students initially placed in lower tracks are more likely to be moved into higher ones, in part because their parents frequently succeed in "lobbying" their child's school for a higher track placement (Hallinan, 1996; Wells & Serna, 1996). Adolescents from well-off families more frequently consult with their parents about what courses to take than do less affluent adolescents, which leads more affluent students to take more (and more advanced) math and science classes (Crosnoe & Huston, 2007).

On the Wrong Track   Early track placements set in motion an educational trajectory that is often difficult to change without the deliberate intervention of the student's parents (Dauber, Alexander, & Entwisle, 1996; Hallinan, 1996; D. Stevenson, Schiller, & Schneider, 1994). And the ways in which students' schedules are arranged may lead students to be tracked in several different subject areas simply because they are tracked in one class, which makes the effects of tracking even more substantial (Heck, Price, & Thomas, 2004). If the only class period during which advanced math is offered is the same as the class period during which remedial English is taught, a student who is assigned to remedial English will not be able to take advanced math (Lucas & Berends, 2002).

Students in different tracks have markedly different opportunities to learn (Gamoran, 1996). Those in the more advanced tracks receive more challenging instruction and better teaching, and they are more likely to engage in classroom activities that emphasize critical thinking rather than rote memorization (Darling-Hammond, 1997). As a result, being placed in a more advanced track has a positive influence on school achievement (how much the student actually learns over time), on subsequent course selection (what curriculum the student is exposed to), and on ultimate educational attainment (how many years of schooling the student completes). To the extent that a student's family background influences his or her track placement, tracking has the effect of maintaining income inequality (Oakes, 2005).

Because students are assigned to different tracks on the basis of test scores and other indicators of aptitude, and because students in the lower tracks receive an inferior education (which leads to lower test scores), the net effect of tracking over time is to increase preexisting academic differences among students. Students who need the most help are assigned to the tracks in which the quality of instruction is the poorest; not surprisingly, studies find that students in lower tracks exert less effort, which also limits their learning (Callahan, 2005; Carbonaro, 2005). Although students in the lower tracks usually get the short end of the educational stick, there are some exceptions—for example, schools in which classes in the lower tracks are taught by strong teachers who insist on maintaining high standards (Gamoran, 1993; Hallinan, 1996).

The Effects of Tracking on Student Achievement
Hundreds of studies have looked at the impact of tracking on student achievement (Hallinan, 1996). Unfortunately, this research suggests both positive and negative effects and, more importantly, different effects on students in different tracks. Tracking has positive effects on the achievement of high-track students, negative effects on low-track students, and negligible effects on students in the middle (Hallinan, 1996). Because of this, decisions about whether to implement tracking in nontracked schools, or whether to "detrack" schools that use tracking, are often controversial. Parents of students in the higher tracks favor the practice, while parents of students in the lower tracks oppose it (Wells & Serna, 1996).

Even in schools that do not have formal tracking, teachers may group students within the same class into ability groups. In such an arrangement, students may have a wider range of peers with whom to compare themselves than they would in separate tracks, since their classes are more diverse in composition. The impact of this comparison on both students and teachers is quite interesting. For high-ability students, within-classroom ability grouping raises their expectations for achievement and raises their teachers' evaluations of them; for low-ability students, the opposite is true: They have lowered expectations and get worse grades from their teachers (Reuman, 1989). In classes with mixed ability groups, the high-ability students look better, and the low-ability students look worse, than they would in a conventionally tracked school or in a school in which ability grouping is not used (H. Marsh, Chessor, Craven, & Roche, 1995). As is the case with tracking, within-classroom ability grouping also exposes students in different groups to different levels of educational quality, with students in the high-ability groups receiving more challenging instruction and more engaging learning experiences (Catsambis, 1992).

Students at the Extremes   Related to the issue of tracking are questions concerning the placement of individuals who are considered **gifted students** and of those who have a **learning disability.** Adolescents who

gifted students
Students who are unusually talented in some aspect of intellectual performance.

learning disability
A difficulty with academic tasks that cannot be traced to an emotional problem or sensory dysfunction.

score 130 or higher on an intelligence test are considered gifted. Adolescents with a learning disability are those whose actual performance is significantly poorer than their expected performance (based on intelligence or aptitude tests, for example) and whose difficulty with academic tasks cannot be traced to an emotional problem, such as coping with a parental divorce, or a sensory dysfunction, such as a visual or hearing impairment.

Most learning disabilities are neurological in origin (Berninger & Miller, 2011; Shaywitz, Gruen, & Shaywitz, 2007). Common types of specific learning disabilities include **dyslexia** (impaired ability in reading or spelling), **dysgraphia** (impaired ability in handwriting), and **dyscalculia** (impaired ability in arithmetic). Learning disabilities are common—about one in five school-age children and youth is at risk for a learning disability, with rates of learning disabilities significantly more common among boys than girls (Berninger & Miller, 2011).

Educators have debated whether gifted students and those with learning disabilities are best served by instruction in separate classes (for example, in enriched classes for gifted students or in special education classes for students with a learning disability) or by **mainstreaming,** the integration of all students with special needs into regular classrooms. Pros and cons of each approach have been identified. On the one hand, separate special education programs can be tailored to meet the specific needs of students and can target educational and professional resources in a cost-effective way. On the other hand, segregating students on the basis of academic ability may foster social isolation and stigmatization—either for being "stupid" or for being a "brainiac."

Generally, educators favor mainstreaming over separate classrooms for adolescents with special needs. (In the case of adolescents with disabilities, mainstreaming, whenever possible, is required by law in the United States.) Proponents of mainstreaming argue that the psychological costs of separating adolescents with special academic needs from their peers outweigh the potential academic benefits. Studies of gifted youngsters have found, for example, that those who are integrated into regular classrooms have more positive academic self-conceptions than those assigned to special classes (H. Marsh et al., 1995), and that these effects persist even after graduating (H. Marsh, Trautwein, Lüdtke, Baumert, & Köller, 2007).

One downside to being placed with students of high academic ability is that when students compare themselves to their high-achieving classmates, they don't feel as competent as they would if their point of comparison were students who were not so smart (Becker et al., 2014; Thijs, Verkuyten, & Helmond, 2010). This phenomenon, called the **big fish–little pond effect,** has been documented around the world (H. Marsh & Hau, 2003). The effect seems to be limited to what goes on

in students' regular schools; students who participate in summer programs for the academically talented don't seem to suffer psychologically as a consequence (Makel, Lee, Olszewski-Kubilius, & Putallaz, 2012).

Being a big fish in a little pond is also helpful for admission to college. One study of some 45,000 applications to three elite universities found that applicants' chances of being accepted are greater when they come from high schools with a relatively lower proportion of other high-achieving students than when applicants with the same credentials come from high schools with many other high achievers (Espenshade, Hale, & Chung, 2005). In addition, high-ability students who attend schools where the student body is more diverse also have higher career aspirations, in part because they feel better about themselves in comparison to their peers (Nagengast & Marsh, 2012). There's a catch, though: Although high-ability students who attend schools with peers who are less talented feel better about themselves, they may actually learn less (Wouters, De Fraine, Colpin, Van Damme, & Verschuren, 2012).

Whereas the big fish–little pond effect suggests that gifted students might not be better off psychologically in classes restricted to high-achieving students—and argues in favor of mainstreaming them—it poses a dilemma for those who favor mainstreaming students with learning disabilities. Low-achieving students, when mainstreamed, end up comparing themselves to students whose performance is better, and may end up feeling worse about themselves than had they been separated into special classes with comparably achieving peers (H. Marsh & Hau, 2003). Perhaps because of this, even with mainstreaming, adolescents who have learning disabilities may suffer psychological consequences related to their problems in school. Compared with average-achieving students, adolescents with learning disabilities report more social and behavioral difficulties and more problems coping with school. They are also more likely than other adolescents to have poor peer relations, are less likely to participate in school-based extracurricular activities, and are more likely to drop out of school (Berninger & Miller, 2011). Given the tremendous importance society places on school success, it is not difficult to see why students who have difficulties learning would suffer psychological as well as scholastic problems.

Experts recommend that adolescents with learning disabilities receive extra instruction in study skills, time management,

dyslexia
Impaired ability in reading or spelling.

dysgraphia
Impaired ability in handwriting.

dyscalculia
Impaired ability in arithmetic.

mainstreaming
The integration of adolescents who have educational handicaps into regular classrooms.

big fish–little pond effect
The reason that individuals who attend high school with high-achieving peers feel worse about themselves than comparably successful individuals with lower-achieving peers.

organization skills, note-taking, and proofreading. In addition, they may need help in increasing motivation, dealing with social and emotional difficulties resulting from problematic peer relationships, overcoming their reluctance to participate in class or seek assistance from teachers, and coping with fears that they are not as intelligent as other students (which is not the case) or that they will be failures as adults (Berninger & Miller, 2011).

Attention Deficit/Hyperactivity Disorder   Although it is not technically a learning disability, adolescents who have **attention deficit/hyperactivity disorder (ADHD)** frequently have academic difficulties that can be traced to this problem. ADHD is usually diagnosed during childhood, but the condition persists into adolescence in 50 to 70% of cases, and into adulthood in about half of all children with the diagnosis (Antshel & Barkley, 2011).

ADHD is defined by persistent and impairing symptoms of inattention, impulsivity, and/or hyperactivity, although the defining feature of ADHD in adolescence (as opposed to childhood) is generally inattention, rather than impulsivity or hyperactivity (Sibley et al., 2012). Adolescents with ADHD are classified into one of three subtypes: predominantly inattentive (about 30 to 40% of all cases), predominantly hyperactive/impulsive (fewer than 5% of all cases, and rarely seen during adolescence), or combined (between 50 and 60% of all cases). One reason the prevalence of ADHD declines with age is that some individuals develop better attention and impulse control as they mature from childhood into adolescence and adulthood. In addition to being at risk for academic difficulties, individuals with ADHD are also at risk for a wide range of nonscholastic problems, including substance abuse, difficulties in delay of gratification, anxiety, problematic peer relations, obesity, and depression (Demurie, Roeyers, Baeyens, & Sonuga-Barke, 2012; Khalife et al., 2014; Seymour et al., 2012; Tseng, Kawabata, Gau, & Crick, 2014). ADHD also is present in many cases of serious juvenile delinquency.

ADHD is a biological disorder with a strong genetic component (Chang, Lichtenstein, & Larsson, 2012; Zheng, Lichtenstein, Asherson, & Larsson, 2013). In addition, it can be caused by damage to the brain either prenatally (sometimes caused by maternal smoking or drinking during pregnancy) or shortly after birth (as the result of birth complications or low birth weight). Recent studies of brain development during adolescence point to delays or deficiencies in the development of regions that are known to be associated with self-regulation, such as the prefrontal cortex; synaptic pruning of this region occurs at a slower pace among individuals with ADHD than among those without the

disorder. Interestingly, individuals who do not have ADHD, but who are more hyperactive and impulsive than their peers, show patterns of brain development that are somewhere between those seen in adolescents with ADHD and adolescents who have very good impulse control, which suggests that ADHD may be an extreme point on a continuum rather than a qualitatively distinct category (Shaw et al., 2011).

ADHD is frequently treated with some sort of stimulant medication, such as methylphenidate (Ritalin) or a combination of amphetamines (e.g., Adderall). Stimulant medication is helpful in about 70 percent of cases. Certain types of antidepressants, such as bupropion (Wellbutrin) have also been shown to be effective, especially with adolescents who have both ADHD and some sort of mood disorder, such as anxiety or depression. Psychological therapies for ADHD also are widely used, often in conjunction with medication, although such therapies are more commonly used with children than adolescents (Antshel & Barkley, 2011).

One concern about the wide use of stimulant medication by adolescents with ADHD is that many individuals who receive such medication share it with their nonafflicted friends, who may use the medication recreationally or for help with studying (stimulant medication improves attention in most individuals, regardless of whether they have ADHD). In addition, students who attend high-pressure schools may use ADHD medication selectively to improve their test performance, going on medication during the school year but going off it during the summer, a practice seen much more in affluent communities than in poorer ones (King, Jennings, & Fletcher, 2014).

Adolescents with attention deficit/hyperactivity disorder (ADHD) are frequently prescribed stimulant medication, such as Ritalin or Adderall. These medicines are effective in about 70 percent of cases. © Chris Gallagher/Science Source

Ethnic Composition

Following the landmark U.S. Supreme Court rulings in *Brown v. Board of Education of Topeka* (1954, 1955), in which the Court found that it was unconstitutional to maintain separate schools for children on the basis of race, many school districts adopted measures designed to make schools more diverse. They did this either by assigning students to schools in a way that would create ethnic diversity or by encouraging voluntary desegregation, through measures like having "magnet" schools that would create diversity by drawing students from different neighborhoods (for instance, by having citywide schools specializing in the performing arts). Although the Supreme Court ruled in 2007 that school districts may no longer use race as a factor in deciding how to assign students to schools (R. Barnes, 2007), efforts to create ethnic and racial diversity through voluntary measures are still in use in many cities.

Effects of Desegregation   Studies of the short-term effects of desegregation on high school students have been mixed. On the one hand, research indicates that desegregation has surprisingly little impact on the achievement levels of either minority or White youngsters (Entwisle, 1990). In addition, some evidence suggests that minority youngsters' self-esteem is higher when they attend schools in which they are in the majority. In general, students fare better psychologically when the cultural environment of their neighborhood is consonant with the cultural environment of their school (Goldsmith, 2004; Seaton & Yip, 2009). In schools that mix students from low- and high-income neighborhoods, students from low-income neighborhoods actually do worse than they do when they attend schools that are less socioeconomically diverse, especially if they are Black or Hispanic (Crosnoe, 2009; Owens, 2010).

Consistent with this, students who have been bused to school out of their neighborhood report weaker feelings of attachment to their school than do students whose schools draw directly from the local community (Anderman, 2002). Students' attachment to school also is higher when they attend schools where relatively more of their classmates are from the same ethnic group (Georgiades, Boyle, & Fife, 2013; M. Johnston, Crosnoe, & Elder, 2001). Students feel safer, less lonely, and less harassed in relatively more diverse multiethnic schools (i.e., where the proportions of students from different ethnic groups are similar) than in multiethnic schools that are less balanced (Juvonen, Nishina, & Graham, 2006). In general, though, research suggests that being in the minority in one's school is hard on students.

Male and female students from ethnic minority groups often have different experiences with peers when they attend schools in which they are a small minority. Cross-ethnic friendships are more common among male than

female students, in part because males are more likely to be involved in athletics, which provides opportunities for White and minority students to interact (Holland, 2012). In addition, in suburban schools to which inner-city students are bussed, the view that Black boys are cool and tough leads them to be admired by White boys and included in social activities, whereas the stereotypes of Black girls as loud and assertive are off-putting to White girls, who aren't interested in socializing with them (Ispa-Landa, 2013).

Being in the Minority   The difficulties associated with attending school where one is in a distinct minority are well documented (Phelan, Yu, & Davidson, 1994). Consider these excerpts from the researchers' interviews with students:

> Ivonne, Mexican American female: Well, I kind of feel uncomfortable. Not many Mexicans and Hispanics are in [my] classes. They [other students] probably think of me as weird, because they probably have this view that most Hispanics are dumb or something. They have that opinion, you know, [Hispanics] get bad grades. So, I don't know why I feel uncomfortable. I just . . . it means you're not really with any other . . . many people. Maybe by the end of the year they will realize that I belong. (p. 425)

> Trinh, Vietnamese American female: [Because I'm Vietnamese] I notice the little things more often than other people. Just like, I don't really get noticed by all the popular people. OK, everyone in the class, I know their names and everything. . . . Like being Vietnamese . . . like they have a lot of Americans in here. That there are more of them, and when you're alone, you're nervous over little things. (p. 425)

> Sonia, Mexican American female: Yeah, it's weird, 'cause most teachers, you know—White teachers—some of them are kind of prejudiced. . . . It's probably the way they look at you, the way they talk, you know when they're talking about something—about something like when they talk about the people who are going to drop out, and they . . . look around, look around [at you]. . . . And then Mr. Kula, when he's talking about teenage pregnancy or something like that. He turns around and he looks at us. It's like—he tries to look around the whole room, so we won't notice but like he mostly like tries to tell us, tries to get it through our heads, you know. Sometimes I think he's prejudiced. And sometimes I think he's trying to help us. (p. 431)

Alternatives to Public Schools

Although the vast majority of students attending secondary school in America are enrolled in conventional public schools, a substantial minority attend private schools, either parochial (i.e., with a religious affiliation) or independent, or specially created public schools, like charter schools or magnet schools. In the past, researchers cared little about studying differences between public schools

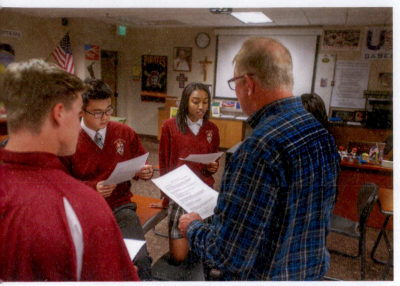

Although social scientists disagree over their interpretation, studies have shown that adolescents who attend parochial schools generally achieve at a higher rate than those attending public schools. © Marmaduke St. John/Alamy

and their alternatives. But during the late 1980s and 1990s, many policy makers suggested that one way to improve schools would be to give parents more choice in determining where their child was enrolled, to force schools to compete for the best students. There is some evidence to support this: When information about school test scores is provided to parents, parents choose to send their children to higher-performing schools, which in turn increases the students' achievement (Hastings & Weinstein, 2008).

One concrete suggestion in this spirit was that states provide parents with school vouchers that could be used to "purchase" education at a school of their choosing—private or public. Another suggestion was that states permit the development of charter schools—independent public schools that are freer to operate as they wish, without some of the constraints imposed by the state's education bureaucracy. In light of these suggestions, researchers became interested in whether some types of schools produced more high-achieving students than others.

making the practical connection

Providing parents with vouchers that they can use to send their children to private schools has been recommended as a way of improving the quality of schools, by creating a "marketplace" in which schools must compete with each other. Critics of voucher programs argue that vouchers will encourage the families of the most talented students,

with the most involved parents, to leave public schools, and that public schools need good students and engaged parents to function effectively. Is there a way to resolve this conflict?

Are alternatives to public schools better than public schools? Although some studies have found that students' test scores are higher in private schools (especially Catholic schools), this appears to be due more to the characteristics of the students who attend them than to the private schools themselves (Braun, Jenkins, & Grigg, 2006; Hallinan & Kubitschek, 2012; Lubienski & Lubienski, 2006), although some studies have found genuine advantages for Catholic school students, especially among poor, inner-city, minority youth (Jeynes, 2002). Students who attend private school may also be encouraged (or required) to take more advanced courses than students in public schools, which contributes to their superior performance on achievement tests (Carbonaro & Covay, 2010). There is less research on adolescents who are homeschooled, who account for about 3% of American adolescents, but it appears to be important to distinguish between homeschoolers who have strong religious ties and those who don't. Homeschooling for adolescents with strong religious ties doesn't seem to be a problem as far as achievement is concerned. But compared to teens with similar backgrounds who attend traditional schools, homeschooled adolescents with weak religious ties are three times more likely to be behind their expected grade level on achievement tests, and only half as likely to participate in extracurricular activities (Green-Hennessy, 2014).

These studies, as well as a large body of research, indicate that students' family background is a far more powerful influence on their achievement than is the quality of the schools they attend. Similarly, evaluations of the impact of charter schools and voucher programs on student achievement, once students' background characteristics are taken into account, have not produced consistent results; at the very least, research indicates that these are not likely to be "silver bullets" in the effort to raise American student achievement (Loveless, 2002). This is also true in disadvantaged urban areas, where it had been hoped that charter schools might be the solution to the many problems that plague education in the inner city. One additional concern is that in urban areas, the availability of private schools contributes to racial segregation, because many White students who would otherwise attend their neighborhood public school attend private school instead (Saporito & Sohoni, 2006).

The climate of public and private schools, especially Catholic schools, is often very different. As many writers have pointed out, a Catholic school is a community in which parents, teachers, and students all share similar values and attitudes. Strong communities, whether based in neighborhoods or schools, generate what has been called **social capital**—interpersonal resources that, like financial capital, give "richer" students advantages over "poorer" ones. Students profit from the social capital associated with attending a Catholic school, because the lessons taught in school are reinforced at home, at church, and in the neighborhood, and because the links between home and school are stronger (Teachman et al., 1996). In addition, private schools typically assign more homework and are more orderly and disciplined (an important element of the climate in good schools) (Coleman, Hoffer, & Kilgore, 1982). Students who attend private schools (Catholic or otherwise) are substantially less likely to report feeling unsafe, being exposed to gangs, or witnessing fighting between ethnic groups (National Center for Education Statistics, 2002).

Classroom Climate

We have seen that certain elements of the school's social organization—size, age grouping, tracking, and so forth—can affect students' motivation, behavior, and achievement. But these factors have relatively modest effects on students, and they are important mainly because they influence what takes place in classrooms and in other school settings. Ultimately, the most important school-related influence on learning and psychosocial development during adolescence is what takes place in the classroom.

Various aspects of the school climate have important effects on youngsters' learning and achievement (Eccles & Roeser, 2011). How teachers interact with students, how classroom time is used, and what sorts of standards and expectations teachers hold for their students are all more important than the size of the school, its ethnic composition, its approach to ability grouping, or the way age groups are combined.

The Best Classroom Climate for Adolescents

What sort of climate brings out the best in students? The same factors that influence positive adolescent adjustment at home are important at school. Students achieve and are engaged more in school when they attend schools that are responsive and demanding. Moreover, academic functioning and psychological adjustment affect each other, so that a positive school climate—where relationships between students and teachers are positive, and teachers are both supportive and demanding—enhances adolescents' psychological well-being as well as their achievement (Eccles, 2004; Gutierrez, 2000; Kalil & Ziol-Guest, 2008; Reddy, Rhodes, & Mulhall, 2003), mainly by strengthening their engagement in

class (Dotterer & Lowe, 2011; Reyes, Brackett, Rivers, White, & Salovey, 2012).

social capital
The interpersonal resources available to an adolescent or family.

Students and teachers are more satisfied in classes that combine a moderate degree of structure with high student involvement and high teacher support, a finding that has emerged in studies of students from various socioeconomic backgrounds, ethnic groups, and countries (Jia et al., 2009; Vieno, Perkins, Smith, & Santinello, 2005; Way & Robinson, 2003). In these classes, teachers encourage students' participation but do not let the class get out of control. Classes that are too task oriented—particularly those that also emphasize teacher control—make students anxious, uninterested, and unhappy (Moos, 1978). Students do best when their teachers spend a high proportion of time on lessons (rather than on setting up equipment or dealing with discipline problems), begin and end lessons on time, provide clear feedback to students about what is expected of them, and give ample praise to students when they perform well (Eccles & Roeser, 2011). Students also demonstrate higher achievement when the classroom climate promotes cooperation between students, rather than competition (Roseth, Johnson, & Johnson, 2008).

One of the strongest influences on how much students enjoy going to school is the extent to which they feel their teachers respect and care about them (Hallinan, 2008). Students in schools in which teachers are supportive but firm and maintain high, well-defined standards for behavior and academic work have stronger bonds to their school and more positive achievement motives; these beliefs and emotions, in turn, lead to fewer problems, even in the face of stress, as well as better attendance, lower rates of delinquency, more supportive friendships, and higher test scores (Eccles, 2004; Li & Lerner, 2011; Loukas, Ripperger-Suhler, & Horton, 2009; Rudasill, Sawyer, Spence, & Bjerg).

There are many similarities between good teachers and good parents (Wentzel, 2002). The pattern of classroom variables associated with positive student behavior and attitudes is similar to the authoritative family environment (Pellerin, 2005). Similarly, an overemphasis on control in the classroom in the absence of support is reminiscent of the authoritarian family, whereas a lack of clarity and organization is reminiscent of both the indulgent family and the indifferent family—and these styles in the classroom appear to affect adolescents detrimentally, just as they do at home. A recent evaluation of a program designed to improve the ways in which teachers interact with students found significant improvements in student achievement (Allen, Pianta, Gregory, Mikami, & Lun, 2011) (see Figure 4). The combination of positive student-teacher relationships in the context of an orderly and well-managed classroom and school not only facilitates academic achievement, but also reduces behavior problems (Gregory et al., 2010; Wang, Selman, Dishion,

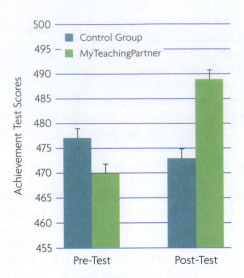

FIGURE 4 A recent evaluation of a program designed to improve the ways in which teachers interact with students found significant improvements in student achievement. (Allen et al., 2011)

& Stormshak, 2010). Schools that provide both structure and support have lower rates of suspension than other schools (Gregory, Cornell, & Fan, 2011).

Teacher Expectations and Student Performance

There is a strong correlation between teacher expectations and student performance. This is both because teachers' expectations are often accurate reflections of their students' ability, and because teacher expectations actually create "self-fulfilling prophecies" that ultimately influence how their students behave (Jussim,

Student performance influences, and is influenced by, teacher expectations. © Hero images/Glow Images RF

Eccles & Madon, 1996). Teacher expectations have a cumulative long-term impact on student achievement, lowering the performance of students whose teachers perceive them as less capable than they actually are (de Boer, Bosker, & van der Werf, 2010). Children from poor families are particularly vulnerable to the effects of teacher expectations, benefiting when expectations are high but suffering when they are low (Sorhagen, 2013).

Which pathway is more powerful—the impact of student performance on teacher expectations, or the impact of teacher expectations on student performance? It appears that about 80% of the connection between teacher expectations and student achievement results from teachers having accurate perceptions, and about 20% is an effect of the self-fulfilling prophecy. Even though the self-fulfilling prophecy effect during any given school year is relatively small, it can be sizable when accumulated over years of schooling.

Because teachers' expectations influence students' performance, it is important to understand where these expectations come from. Unfortunately, teachers are likely to base their expectations in part on students' ethnic and socioeconomic background. In much the same way that these factors sometimes influence tracking decisions, they may consciously and unconsciously shape teachers' expectations. Teachers may call on poor or minority students less often than they call on affluent or White students—conveying a not-so-subtle message about whose responses the teacher believes are more worthy of class attention (Eccles & Roeser, 2011).

Several studies report that Black and Latino students perceive their teachers as having low expectations and holding stereotypes about their likelihood of misbehaving (M. B. Spencer, 2005). White teachers rate the misbehavior of Black students more harshly than do Black teachers (D. Downey & Pribesh, 2004), and this leads to Black students receiving harsher discipline and more severe punishments than their peers receive for the same infractions. Not all minority students are perceived negatively by White teachers, however: Asian students are actually viewed more positively than White students, and White teachers' perceptions of Latino students don't differ from their perceptions of White students (McGrady & Reynolds, 2013).

There is also evidence that teachers are more likely to give undeserved positive feedback to students who have done poor work when the students are Black or Latino than when they are White, which undermines minority students' achievement by lowering the standards to which they are held (Harber et al., 2012). It's not difficult to see how years of exposure to this sort of treatment can adversely affect students' self-concepts and interest in school. Imagine confronting the situation described by this Black high school junior:

> So I had this um teacher where she taught basically all my subjects, and um she would give, I noticed my math for instance, I noticed that she would be giving the

Caucasian students different math work than me. So she just assumed like I didn't have the ability to do what they were doing. . . . I was like the only person who had different work and I would work so hard in her class, like I did everything I was suppose to do. (Hope, Skoog, & Jagers, 2014, p. 97)

Teachers' biases against lower-class or minority adolescents may make it difficult for students from these groups to attain a level of academic accomplishment that permits upward mobility. In addition, biased treatment by teachers—having low expectations for some ethnic groups and high expectations for others—can increase student alienation and feelings of hostility between students from different ethnic groups (Debnam, Johnson, Waasdorp, & Bradshaw, 2014; Rosenbloom & Way, 2004).

Parents also play an important role in the links between teacher expectations and student achievement. One recent study of Latino students found that how involved a student's parents were in school influenced their high school children's achievement directly (adolescents whose parents are involved in school perform better than their peers) but also affected teachers' expectations for their child's achievement, which, in turn, led to better student performance (see Figure 5) (Kuperminc, Darnell, & Alvarez-Jiminez, 2008). Other research has found that one factor that helps protect low-income students against the impact of low teacher expectations is having high expectations for achievement from their parents (Benner & Mistry, 2007).

The Importance of Student Engagement

It is important to keep in mind that students, as well as teachers, influence the classroom climate. In much the same way that the relationship between parents and

One reason so many teenagers complain of boredom in school is that few school hours are spent in activities that engage them intellectually or encourage critical thinking. © David Lassman/Syracuse Newspapers/The Image Works

adolescents is reciprocal—parents influence how their teenagers develop, but teenagers influence what their parents do—so is the relationship between teachers and their students. Effective teachers can engage and excite their students, and engaged and excited students can motivate their teachers to be more effective. Students who are engaged in school profit more than just academically from it: It enhances their mental health and protects them against the harmful effects of family problems, stress, and victimization (Crespo, Jose, Kielpikowski, & Pryor, 2013; Debnam et al., 2014; Loukas & Pasch, 2013; Wang & Peck, 2013; Wood et al., 2012). Year-to-year fluctuations in high school students' connection to school are correlated with year-to-year fluctuations in how much they say they that they believe school is interesting and valuable (Gillen-O'Neal & Fuligni, 2013).

According to national surveys, levels of **student engagement** and excitement in American schools are low. Many students are just going through the motions when they are in school, and high school teachers often confront a roomful of students who are physically present but psychologically absent (Steinberg, 1996). This is a shame, because engaging students in school is also good for their overall mental health: Students who are disengaged from school are more likely to misbehave and engage in substance use, both because doing poorly in school leads to problem behavior and because students who engage in problem behavior are evaluated more negatively by their teachers (G. C. Patton et al., 2006; Payne, 2009; Zimmerman, Schute, Taskinen, and Koller, 2013).

Disengagement in school comes in different forms (see

student engagement
The extent to which students are psychologically committed to learning and mastering the material rather than simply completing the assigned work.

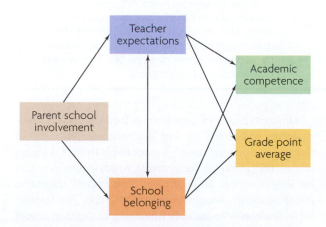

Figure 5 **Parent involvement in school influences their high school children's achievement, both directly and indirectly, by raising teachers' expectations for their child's performance.** (Kuperminc et al., 2008)

Table 1   Typology of engagement

Engagement type	Enjoy Affective	Put in effort Behavioral	See value Cognitive	Example
Purposefully engaged		√	√	A student studies hard for a calculus test because he knows that understanding the material and doing well on the test are important to achieving his future goals; he does not enjoy the studying however.
Fully engaged	√	√	√	A student enjoys creating a documentary film project with her peers because she cares deeply about the topic, and she sees the assignment as a worthwhile use of her time. She spends a lot of time and effort working on this project.
Rationally engaged			√	A student sees the importance of learning about global warming in Earth Science class, but he is not willing to exert effort required to concentrate and take notes because he finds the teachers' lecture to be excruciatingly boring.
Busily engaged		√		A student works hard to get her homework completed accurately, though she does not particularly care about the material or the questions. Nor does she see their relevance to her interests and aspirations. She finds the prefabricated worksheets she must complete to be boring and monotonous.
Pleasurably engaged	√			A student enjoys listening to his teacher relay stories about World War I; however, he does not value this topic or see it as relevant. He does not take notes, he does not concentrate on the details the teacher shares, and he allows his mind to wander occasionally.
Mentally engaged	√		√	A student enjoys working on her project in art class and she cares about mastering the technique; however, it is the day before spring break and she is not putting a lot of thought or effort into her project. She is just trying to get it done quickly so the class can have a party.
Recreationally engaged	√	√		A student works hard to help his group-mates score more points than any other group during a game in class; he is thinking hard and reviewing his notes carefully to find the correct answers, and he is having fun with his peers, enjoying the game and the friendly competition; however, when asked if he values either the material the class is reviewing or the skills he may be developing by playing the game, he says, "No. They are not connected to my larger goals."

Table 1). Some disengaged students show their lack of interest in school through their behavior, by not showing up regularly or failing to complete assignments. Others disengage emotionally, losing interest in school and feeling that school is depressing or an unsafe place. Still others disengage cognitively, checking out mentally when they are in class and devoting little effort to their schoolwork (Wang & Peck, 2012). In one study, about one-sixth of students were disengaged behaviorally, cognitively, and emotionally ("minimally engaged"), whereas an equal proportion were engaged in all three ways (see Figure 6).

Different forms of engagement feed on each other—someone who starts to feel disconnected from school (emotional disengagement) is more likely to start skipping school (behavioral disengagement), which in turn increases the likelihood that he or she will lose interest (cognitive disengagement) (Wang & Fredericks, 2014). Not surprisingly, students who are only minimally engaged in school in 9th grade were more likely to drop out before graduating, less likely to enroll in college, and more likely to be depressed (although students who were just emotionally disengaged reported the highest rates of depression).

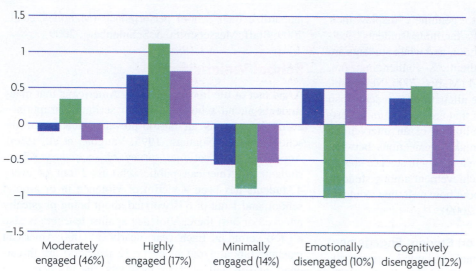

Figure 6 Only about one-sixth of students are highly engaged in high school. About one-third are disengaged either behaviorally, emotionally, or cognitively. (Wang & Peck, 2012)

Boring Classes, Bored Students In view of this, several writers have suggested that if we want to understand the impact of classroom climate on student achievement, we need to better understand how to enhance student engagement—the extent to which students are psychologically committed to learning and mastering the material rather than simply completing the assigned work (Steinberg, 2014). Students frequently say they are bored while in school—especially high school students, who find school far more boring than do middle school students. As you can see in Figure 7, students are bored for most of the time on weekdays between 8:00 A.M. and 3:00 P.M., and the improvement in their mood seems to have more to do with the school day ending than with any special activity that takes place in the evening. The make-work, routinized, rigid structure of most classrooms, in which teachers lecture at students rather than engage them in discussion, alienates many adolescents from school and undermines their desire to achieve.

The notion that many students feel disengaged from school—unchallenged and bored—has been borne out in numerous studies of contemporary American students (Steinberg, 2014). Even in high-achieving schools, about two-thirds of students are not fully engaged; they work hard, but they don't enjoy their schoolwork or find it valuable. And this lack of engagement is associated with more frequent reports of school stress, cheating, and a variety of stress-related disorders, including depression, aggression, and psychosomatic problems, such as headaches and exhaustion (Conner & Pope, 2013).

Here's a sobering account from a researcher who spent more than 500 hours observing classes in 20 different high schools (Fine, 2014, p. 3):

> Most of these schools were . . . fairly bleak places to spend time in. The tone of the teaching . . . seemed to reflect an uneasy truce between the adults and their charges. Most classrooms were places to passively sit and listen. Most work was comprised of tasks that asked students to recall or minimally apply what they had been told. At best, being in high school seemed to represent an investment in building an arsenal of facts and skills that might pave the way for interesting work in college and beyond; at worst, it was a way to wait out the four years before becoming a legal adult.

Think back to your own high school experience. What distinguished the good classes from the tedious ones? Students are engaged when teachers provide

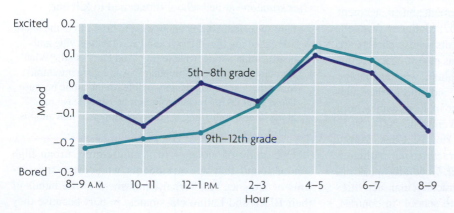

Figure 7 Studies of fluctuations in adolescents' mood over the course of the day show that students—especially high school students—feel bored most of the time they are in school. (Larson & Richards, 1998)

opportunities for students to genuinely display their competencies, when schools facilitate students' feelings of belonging to their school, and when students are assigned work that is "authentic"—challenging, fun, and relevant to the real world (Marks, 2000; Newmann, 1992). There is nothing more alienating to students than being asked to perform tasks that are boring, uninteresting, and irrelevant. One evaluation of an intervention designed to help students make connections between their lives and what they were learning in science classes improved engagement and achievement among students who had low expectations about how well they would do (Hulleman & Harackiewicz, 2009).

Out-of-School Influences on Student Engagement

Teachers and school personnel, of course, are not the only influences on adolescents' behavior in school. The peer group's support, values, and norms also exert an important influence, especially in high school (Wang & Eccles, 2012). Adolescents with friends who support academic achievement are more likely to feel connected to their school. Those with antisocial friends are more likely to feel alienated.

High schools vary a great deal in the extent to which the prevailing peer culture emphasizes academic success as a route toward status and popularity. In schools in which academic success is not valued, students are less likely to achieve grades that match their ability. A bright student who attends a school in which getting good grades is frowned upon by other students will actually get lower grades than he or she would in a school in which scholastic success is generally admired. Even within the same school, cliques and crowds differ enormously in the extent to which they encourage or discourage academic success. Some peer groups (for instance, the "brains") place a great deal of pressure on their members to succeed in school and may engage in behaviors (such as studying together) that promote academic success. Other groups, in contrast, may actively discourage scholastic efforts and disparage success.

Other researchers have focused on adolescents' experiences outside of school—at home, at work, and in extracurricular activities—and on the impact of those experiences on their school achievement and engagement (Dotterer, McHale, & Crouter, 2007; Mahoney, Vandell, Simpkins, & Zarrett, 2009). Students whose parents are involved in school activities (such as parent–teacher conferences and "back-to-school" nights), who encourage and emphasize academic success, and who use authoritative parenting practices do better in secondary school than their peers (A. Gregory & Weinstein, 2004; N. E. Hill & Tyson, 2009; Simons-Morton & Chen, 2009). After-school employment and extracurricular participation also affect school achievement. Generally speaking, involvement in school-based extracurricular activities strengthens students' attachment to school. In contrast, students who overextend themselves on the job may

jeopardize their school performance (Mahoney et al., 2009; Staff, Messersmith, & Schulenberg, 2009).

School Violence

A sad fact of life in contemporary America is that many students attend schools in which serious disruption—even violence—is an all-too-prevalent feature of the school climate (Noguera, 1995; Vaughan et al., 1996). According to a national survey of secondary school students in American public schools, 1 out of every 4 students has been a victim of violence in or around school, and 1 out of 6 is worried about being physically attacked or hurt there. Violence against teachers is also all too common. Each year, nearly 300,000 American teachers (about 1 out of every 12 teachers) are threatened, and in half of these incidents, the teachers have been physically attacked (Espelage et al., 2013).

These problems are especially common in middle schools (Nolle, Guerino, & Dinkes, 2007). One study found that nearly half of all middle schoolers had been threatened at school (Flannery, Weseter, & Singer, 2004). In another study, of 6th-graders attending a multiethnic school in Los Angeles, half the students surveyed reported having been verbally harassed during the previous 2 weeks, and about one-fifth said they had been physically victimized (Nishina & Juvonen, 2005). Generally speaking, victimization is less common in more ethnically diverse schools, but within such schools, students who are in the smallest minority are the most likely to be victimized (Felix & You, 2011). Violence is more common in overcrowded schools located in poor urban neighborhoods (Khoury-Kassabri, Benbenishty, Astor, & Zeira, 2004).

Interviews with students who live in communities where violence is common illuminate the ways in which these youngsters manage their day-to-day activities to avoid exposing themselves to harm (Irwin, 2004). Some make sure that they steer clear of students who have reputations for violent behavior and go out of their way to act friendly if they can't avoid them. Others learn which parts of town to avoid. Still others befriend peers who can serve as protectors, as this 16-year-old Latina did after someone at her school threatened to kill her:

> I got so scared. I didn't know what to do. I ran in the house and called my friend Daryl and I was really crying and [said] "I don't know what to do." And Daryl's all, "What's his number? What's his number?" And I gave it to him. Since that day, that same guy will leave me alone because Daryl went up to him and told him he better leave me alone or else something is going to happen to him and his family. (Irwin, 2004, pp. 467–468)

One study of violence in a multiethnic, urban high school found that Asian students were often the victims of violence and verbal harassment at the hands of their Black and Latino classmates, in part because they believed that teachers favored Asians and discriminated against their non-Asian classmates (Rosenbloom & Way, 2004). According to the researchers:

> Students reported random "slappings" by male and female peers as they walked through the hallways. Slappings are quick, pop shots, often to the head or body as students passed one another in the hall or anywhere else. Asian students described them as unnerving, randomly occurring, and humiliating violations that are particularly harrowing for the boys when girls slap them. . . . Along with the slappings, Asian American students were observed and reported being pushed, punched, teased, and mocked by their non-Asian American peers. (Rosenbloom & Way, 2004, p. 433)

Experts disagree about how best to respond to violence in schools. Some educators have suggested that schools should refer aggressive students to law enforcement, and many schools have police officers on duty to deter assaults and arrest students who cause trouble. But some writers contend that the new, get-tough approach to violence prevention in schools—referred to as **zero tolerance**—has not helped. Suspending or expelling students from school *increases* their likelihood of getting into further trouble (Monahan, VanDerhei, Bechtold, & Cauffman, 2014). School violence is more effectively reduced through programs that attempt to create a more humane climate (American Psychological Association [APA] Zero Tolerance Task Force, 2008). One unintended consequence of zero-tolerance policies is that many students end up with arrest records and contact with the justice system for acts that in the past would have been treated as disciplinary infractions by school officials (Casella, 2003). This has a disproportionate impact on Black students, who are more likely than others to report that school rules are unfair and inconsistently enforced, and to be suspended or expelled, even though they are no more likely to commit the sorts of acts that would warrant these responses (APA Zero Tolerance Task Force, 2008; Kupchik & Ellis, 2008). Here's how one ethnic minority girl described the situation at her high school, as recounted by two researchers who were doing field work there (Hardie & Tyson, 2013):

zero tolerance
A get-tough approach to adolescent misbehavior that responds seriously or excessively to the first infraction.

> [T]he student … spontaneously remarked that she thought the school was racist. She explained that she had six tardies from her homeroom teacher but that when she was there on time, she would see white students come in late and not get tardies. She insisted that black students received tardies even if they walked into the room as the bell was sounding. (p. 96)

Another student described something similar:

> Like, if we [Black students], one of us say anything, it don't even have to be a cussword, anything like that, it's automatically you're suspended or something like that. But I know one of my friends took somebody to the office because they was cussing and acting a fool to her, who was—he was a white student, my friend was black. And he didn't get into trouble. It was like [the administrator thought], "I knew he wouldn't do that." (p. 97)

Among the many recommendations offered by a task force of the American Psychological Association, after a careful review of the research evidence, are that schools define infractions carefully and train staff in how to respond appropriately, reserve suspension or expulsion for only the most serious disruptive behavior, require school police officers to have training in adolescent development, and implement preventive measures to improve school climate and increase students' attachment to school. Students who are at risk for misbehavior in school are less likely to get into trouble in schools where students generally feel more connected to school than in schools where students are more alienated (see Figure 8) (Vogel & Barton, 2013). Of course, one of the ways to do this would be to reduce the number of disruptive students,

Figure 8 Impulsive adolescents are more likely to be violent in school, but the degree to which the student body feels connected makes a big difference. In this study, impulsive students were twice as likely to carry a gun in schools with alienated students than in schools with more attached ones.
(Vogel & Barton, 2011)

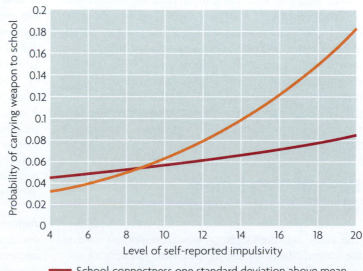

─── School connectness one standard deviation above mean

─── School connectedness one standard deviation below mean

by intervening to change their behavior at an earlier age (LeBlanc, Swisher, Vitaro, & Tremblay, 2008).

Lethal School Violence A series of widely publicized school shootings in the United States—such as the school shootings at Columbine High School or Sandy Hook Elementary School—has drawn national attention to the problem of lethal school violence (M. Moore, Petrie, Braga, & McLaughlin, 2003). As with many topics that generate a great deal of attention in the media, much of what was asserted about school shootings has turned out not to be the case. Although violence in schools is indeed a significant problem, lethal school shootings are extremely rare events, especially when you consider the number of schools and students in the United States (there are about 50 million schoolchildren in the United States, and fewer than 20 students are killed in American schools each year) (Centers for Disease Control and Prevention, 2014b).

Far more children and adolescents are killed at home or in the community than in or around school; indeed, schools are among the *safest* places for adolescents to be (Mulvey & Cauffman, 2001). In fact, an American adolescent is 4 times more likely to be struck by lightning than to be shot in school (Steinberg, 2001)! In addition, although the school shootings that garnered public attention generally involved White youth, a disproportionate number of homicides in schools involve non-White youth, both as perpetrators and victims (M. Anderson et al., 2001). Perhaps most importantly, it is virtually impossible to predict which students will commit acts of lethal violence (Mulvey & Cauffman, 2001). Boys, students with mental health problems, and adolescents who have easy access to guns are more likely than others to be involved in school shootings (M. Moore et al., 2003), but identifying the specific students with these characteristics who will commit lethal crimes in school is a different matter altogether. Most experts believe that, in the absence of a proven means of identifying in advance adolescents who will commit acts of lethal violence in school, the most effective policy involves limiting adolescents' access to guns and identifying and treating young people with mental health problems (M. Moore et al., 2003). It is also essential to create a school climate in which students feel responsible for one another and are willing to take action if they hear a peer talking about "doing something dangerous" (Flanagan & Stout, 2010; Syvertsen, Flanagan, & Stout, 2009).

Beyond High School

The College-Bound

The early twentieth century was an important time in the United States for the development not only of secondary schools but higher education as well. Although colleges and, to a lesser extent, universities had existed for some time previously, not until the latter part of the nineteenth century did diversity in institutions of higher education begin to develop. Early postsecondary institutions were typically small, private, liberal arts academies, often with a strong theological emphasis. But during a relatively brief period bridging the nineteenth and twentieth centuries, these colleges were joined by a host of other types of institutions, including large private universities, technical colleges, professional schools, publicly financed state universities, land grant colleges, urban universities, and two-year community colleges (Brubacher & Rudy, 1976).

The Growth of College Enrollment Although postsecondary educational institutions multiplied and became more varied during the early twentieth century, enrollment in college was still a privilege enjoyed by very few young people until the 1960s. In 1900, only 4% of the 18- to 21-year-old population was enrolled in college, and by 1930, the proportion had grown only to 12%. Even as recently as 1950, fewer than 1 in 5 young people were enrolled in college (Church, 1976). During the first half of the twentieth century, then, colleges and universities were not prominent in the lives of most American youth.

Postsecondary education grew dramatically between 1950 and 1970, paralleling the rise of secondary education between 1920 and 1940. By 1960, one-third of all young people were entering college directly from high school. Today, more than two-thirds of high school graduates enroll in college immediately after graduation (National Center for Education Statistics, 2015). The increase in enrollments has been especially dramatic among women. In 1970, close to 70% of undergraduates were male; by the end of this decade, it is estimated that about 60% of all college students will be female (National Center for Education Statistics, 2012). Although there were large increases in the enrollment of minority youth in higher education during the 1970s, the proportion fell during the early 1980s, primarily because of reductions in the availability of financial aid (Baker & Velez, 1996). Today, among high school graduates, 80% of Asian American students, two-thirds of White and Hispanic students, and nearly 60% of Black students go directly into college (see Figure 9). Youth from immigrant families, despite the fact that their parents typically did not attend American colleges themselves, and despite often having to support their family financially, are just as likely to enroll in and succeed in college as are American-born youth (Fuligni & Witkow, 2004).

American Postsecondary Education If there are two dominant characteristics that distinguish the development of postsecondary education in contemporary America from that in other parts of the world, they

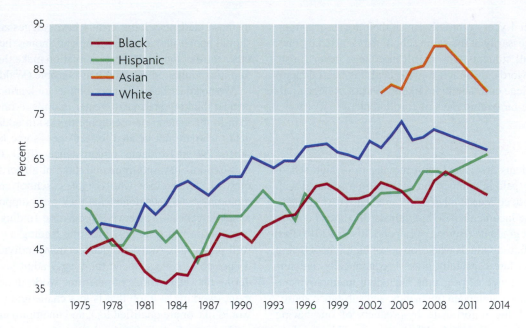

Figure 9 Rates of college enrollment immediately after high school have risen over time. (Data were not separated out for Asian American students prior to 2003.) (National Center for Education Statistics, 2015)

are diversity and accessibility (Brubacher & Rudy, 1976). In countries other than the United States, post-secondary education is likely to be monopolized by monolithic public universities. Individuals are often separated into college and non-college-bound tracks early in adolescence, typically on the basis of standardized national examinations. In fact, rather than housing all high school students in comprehensive high schools such as those found in the United States, most other industrialized nations separate students during early or middle adolescence into schools for college-bound youngsters and schools designed to provide vocational and technical education. In the United States, the post-secondary education system is composed of a wide variety of public and private two- and four-year institutions, some emphasizing a liberal arts education and others focusing more on technical, vocational, and pre-professional training.

The goals of students attending college in the United States also vary greatly. The population of individuals enrolled in community college, which tends to be older than that attending four-year institutions, includes highly committed students who intend to transfer to a four-year college or are working toward a specific associate's degree or certificate (together, about half of all community college students). But it also includes students who are less committed and not sure why they are going to school (and whose attendance is sporadic), as well as some who are just taking a course here or there out of interest in the subject matter. Similar variability in commitment and goals likely characterizes the population of students enrolled in four-year colleges and universities.

The Transition from High School to College In some respects, the transition from high school to college parallels the transition from elementary to secondary school. For many students, going to college means entering an even larger, more formidable, and more impersonal environment. For some, the transition may coincide with other life changes, such as leaving home, breaking off or beginning an important romantic relationship, or having to manage their own residence or finances for the first time. Many Latino students report that family obligations and financial responsibilities, in combination with commitments to school and work, can make the transition to college especially stressful, particularly for second-generation students, who may feel caught between the challenges of adapting to the university environment and the demands placed on them by their parents (Nuñez, 2009).

As a consequence of all these factors, although many more American adolescents enroll in college today than in previous years, a very large number do not graduate. The United States has the lowest college completion rate in the industrialized world (Steinberg, 2014). Fewer than 60% of all students who enroll in a four-year college complete their degree within 6 years; at private, for-profit schools, this figure is less than 25% (National Center for Education Statistics, 2014). Perhaps as a consequence of increasing accessibility, poor matching, and a lack of "consumer" knowledge among college applicants, rates of college attrition are extremely high: Nearly one-third of students who enter a full-time, two-year college program drop out after just 1 year, as do about one-fifth of students who enter a four-year college (Steinberg, 2014). And while many of the students who leave after 1 year eventually finish their degree program, if not necessarily at the same school they started in, one-third of all students who enroll in college never finish. In other words, although a great deal has been done to make college entrance more likely, rates of college graduation lag far behind rates of enrollment.

The Non-College-Bound

The problems associated with moving from high school to college pale in comparison with those associated with not going to college at all. College graduates earn substantially more income than do individuals who attend college but do not graduate (Bureau of Labor Statistics, 2015) (see Figure 10). Individuals who drop out of high school before graduation fare especially poorly economically and suffer a wide range of problems, including unemployment, delinquency, unintended pregnancy, and substance abuse.

One of the unfortunate by-products of our having made postsecondary education so accessible—and so expected—is that we have turned our backs on individuals who do not go directly to college, even though they compose *one-third* of the adolescent population. Our secondary schools are geared almost exclusively toward college-bound youngsters (Krei & Rosenbaum, 2001). In most contemporary American high schools, counseling is geared toward helping college-bound students continue their education. Billions of dollars, in the form of financial aid and subsidized public college tuition, are given

to these students. Some critics have suggested that we should spend just as much time and money helping the other third of the adolescent population make their transition into adulthood as smooth as possible (Wald, 2005).

We noted earlier that opportunities for learning and for critical thinking are much greater in college-prep classes than in the general or vocational tracks. In addition, students who are not headed for college—some by choice, others by unavoidable circumstance—find that their high schools have not prepared them at all for the world of work. Even those who complete school and earn a diploma—who have done what they were supposed to do as adolescents—may have a hard time finding employment and a nearly impossible time finding a satisfying, well-paying job. As a consequence, many individuals who do not go to college spend their early adult years floundering between periods of part-time work, underemployment (working at a job that is less challenging than they would like or are qualified for), and unemployment.

As manufacturing jobs began to be replaced by minimum-wage service jobs, the chances of making a decent living without a college degree has worsened appreciably. Today, young adults without college experience often must try to make ends meet on minimum-wage jobs, which offer little in the way of promotion or advancement. The economic problems faced by non-college-bound youth have been compounded by the escalating costs of such essentials as housing and health care. It's not surprising that rates of depression

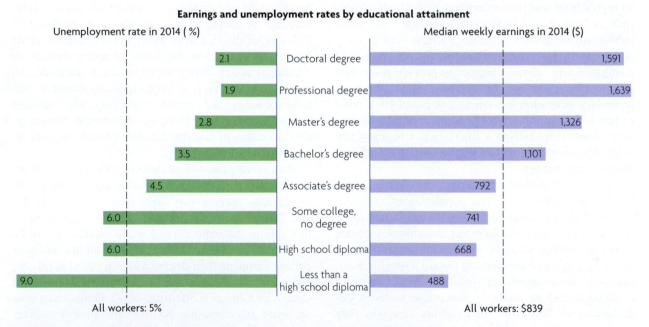

Earnings and unemployment rates by educational attainment

Unemployment rate in 2014 (%)	Educational attainment	Median weekly earnings in 2014 ($)
2.1	Doctoral degree	1,591
1.9	Professional degree	1,639
2.8	Master's degree	1,326
3.5	Bachelor's degree	1,101
4.5	Associate's degree	792
6.0	Some college, no degree	741
6.0	High school diploma	668
9.0	Less than a high school diploma	488

All workers: 5%   All workers: $839

Figure 10   Individuals with more years of education earn more and are more likely to be employed. One important change that has taken place in recent years is a decline in the value of going to college but not finishing. Completing a few years of college without getting a degree provides little advantage over just graduating from high school. (Bureau of Labor Statistics, 2015)

Note: Data are for persons age 25 and over. Earnings are for full-time wage and salary workers.
Source: Current Population Survey, U.S. Bureau of Labor Statistics, U.S. Department of Labor.

are significantly higher among young adults who are not in school than among those who are, and they are especially high among individuals who are neither in school nor steadily employed (Aseltine & Gore, 2005).

Schools and Adolescent Development

Characteristics of Good Schools

Despite all the debate about how secondary schools ought to be organized and reformed, there is a fair degree of consensus among experts about the characteristics of good schools for adolescents (Eccles & Roeser, 2011), at least as far as student achievement is concerned. First and foremost, good schools emphasize intellectual activities (Ravitch, 2000). They create this atmosphere in different ways, depending on the nature and size of the student body, but in these good schools, a common purpose—quality education—is valued and shared by students, teachers, administrators, and parents (V. Lee, Smith, & Croninger, 1994). Learning is more important to students than athletics or extracurricular activities, and seeing that students learn is more important to teachers and administrators than seeing that they graduate. All students are expected to learn, and all students are taught by teachers who use proven instructional methods.

Second, good schools have teachers who are committed to their students and who are given freedom and autonomy by administrators in the way that they express this commitment in the classroom (V. Lee & Smith, 1996; V. Lee et al., 1997). In all schools, of course, teachers have curricular requirements that they must fulfill. But in good schools, teachers are given relatively more authority to decide how their lessons are planned and how their classes are conducted. When teachers are given a say in school governance, they find it easier to commit to the shared values of the institution.

Third, good schools are well integrated into the communities they serve (Eccles & Roeser, 2009). Active attempts are made to involve parents in education, which is an important influence on student achievement and a deterrent against dropping out (Rumberger & Palardy, 2005). Links are forged between the high school and local colleges and universities, so that advanced students may take more challenging and more stimulating courses for high school credit. Bridges are built between the high school and local employers, so that students begin to see the relevance of their high school education to their occupational futures.

Fourth, good schools are composed of good classrooms, where students are active participants in the process of education, not passive recipients of lecture material. The atmosphere is orderly but not oppressive.

Innovative projects replace rote memorization as a way of encouraging learning. Students are challenged to think critically and to debate important issues, rather than being asked simply to regurgitate yesterday's lessons (Eccles & Roeser, 2011).

Finally, good schools for adolescents are staffed by teachers who are well-qualified and who have received specific training in teaching adolescents. Studies conducted in many different countries find that students who attend schools with a high proportion of teachers who are certified, who majored in the subject they are teaching, and who are experienced achieve more and are more likely to graduate than their peers in schools with less qualified teachers. Unfortunately, schools that serve the most needy students—from poor families or with limited language skills—are least likely to have qualified teachers (Eccles & Roeser, 2011).

making the personal connection

Based on the criteria of good schools discussed in this chapter, how would you rate the high school that you attended?

The Effects of School on Adolescent Development

Whatever the shortcomings of schools, staying in school is preferable to dropping out, not only in terms of future earnings but in terms of intellectual development as well. When Norway some years ago increased the number of years of schooling it required adolescents to complete, the average IQ of the young adult population increased significantly (Brinch & Galloway, 2012). In general, though, schooling affects adolescents' achievement scores more than their performance on tests of cognitive skills, such as memory, suggesting that the impact of school may be primarily through students' acquisition of new information, rather than improved information processing abilities (Finn et al., 2014).

Although evidence on the impact of schooling on information processing abilities is limited, research on the effects of schooling on tests of achievement is not. One study contrasted the performance of dropouts and graduates on a battery of standardized tests of achievement administered during late adolescence (Alexander, Natriello, & Pallas, 1985). The study took into account differences in achievement levels that existed before the dropouts had left school (2 years before the assessment was conducted), because dropouts are more likely than graduates to show achievement problems early in their education. Compared with the dropouts, adolescents who stayed in school gained far more intellectually over the 2-year interval in a variety of content areas. More importantly, the results showed that the adverse effects of dropping out were most intense among socioeconomically disadvantaged youth. Paradoxically, then, those students who are most likely to leave school prior to graduation are the most harmed by doing so.

One other way of assessing the contribution of schools to adolescents' intellectual development is by comparing changes in knowledge during the school year with changes during the summer. Several studies have done just this (e.g., H. Cooper, Charlton, Valentine, & Muhlenbruck, 2000). Using information about the academic progress of students measured at three points in time—the beginning of the school year, the end of the school year, and the beginning of the next school year—researchers were able to see how the academic progress of students during the summer compared with their academic progress during the school session. Among higher socioeconomic status (SES) students, academic progress during the school year was comparable to that during the summer, in large measure because their parents encouraged them to continue at least some intellectual pursuits over summer vacation. Among disadvantaged students, however, the pattern was different. Although their rates of progress during the school year were more or less equal to those of higher-SES students, during the summer months, disadvantaged students' scores declined. In other words, if it were not for the effects of school on cognitive development, the discrepancy between affluent and poor youngsters' achievement scores would be much greater than it currently is. One benefit of summer school for disadvantaged students is that it diminishes the decline in achievement that would otherwise occur between the spring and fall semesters (H. Cooper et al., 2000).

Far less is known about the impact of schools on psychosocial development. Most schools are not structured to promote psychosocial development, given their excessive focus on conformity and obedience and their lack of encouragement for creativity, independence, and self-reliance (Friedenberg, 1967). This certainly comes through loud and clear when adolescents are asked about their classroom experiences. But there are many good schools in which students not only learn the academic material taught in classes but also learn about themselves, their relationships with others, and society. Attending a school that has a positive climate can even help protect against some of the adverse effects of exposure to the sort of family environment or peer group that increases the risk of alcohol and drug use (Mayberry, Espelage, & Koenig, 2009).

It is also important to recognize that despite adults' intentions and objectives, students do not view school solely in terms of its academic agenda. Adults may evaluate schools in terms of their contribution to adolescents' cognitive and career development, but for the typical adolescent, school is a primary setting for socializing. Students' happiness in school is most influenced by their relationships with their peers (M. Z. Booth & Sheehan, 2008). When we ask about the consequences of leaving school early, then, we must take into account the impact this may have on the individual's social, as well as cognitive, development.

Studies also show that students' experiences within a school can vary widely according to their track, their peer group, and their extracurricular activities. Academically talented and economically advantaged students have a more positive experience in school than their less capable or less affluent counterparts do—positive not only with respect to what they learn in class but also with respect to the impact of school on their feelings about themselves as individuals. They receive more attention from their teachers, are more likely to hold positions of leadership in extracurricular organizations, and are more likely to experience classes that are engaging and challenging. In other words, the structure of a school—its size, its tracking policy, its curricula—provides different intellectual and psychosocial opportunities for students who occupy different places within that structure. The best answer to the question "How do schools affect adolescent development?" is another question: "Which schools, which adolescents, and in what ways?"

Work, Leisure, and Media

7

© Moxie Productions/Getty Images RF

Adolescents' Free Time in Contemporary Society

Patterns of Time Use in Contemporary America

Patterns of Time Use in Other Countries

Adolescents and Work

The Rise and Fall of the Student Worker

Teenage Employment in Other Nations

The Adolescent Workplace Today

Employment and Adolescent Development

Youth Unemployment

Adolescents and Leisure

Adolescents' Free Time and Their Moods

Structured Leisure Activities

Unstructured Leisure Time

Promoting Positive Youth Development

Adolescents, Media, and the Internet

Patterns of Media Use

Theories of Media Influence and Use

Adolescents' Exposure to Controversial Media Content

Electronic Media and Adolescent Development

Mass Media and Adolescent Girls' Body Image

The Adolescent Consumer

Free Time and Adolescent Development

One of the hallmarks of teenage life in industrialized society is that adolescents have considerable amounts of time to spend at their discretion. Today's teenagers spend more time in leisure activities than they do in school, more time alone than with members of their family, more time each week on a part-time job than on homework, and considerably more time listening to music, online, using social media, or watching television than in the classroom (D. Roberts et al., 2009; Staff et al., 2009). In this chapter, we look at these other important contexts of adolescence—the contexts of work, leisure, and the mass media, including the Internet.

Adolescents' Free Time in Contemporary Society

The abundance of free time in the lives of contemporary adolescents has several origins. Ironically, one of the most important contributors was the development of compulsory schooling. Prior to this, adolescents were expected to work full-time, and most maintained schedules comparable to those of adults, working long hours each week. With the spread of secondary schools during the early decades of the twentieth century, however, adolescents were in effect barred from the labor force: The part-time jobs held by teenagers that are familiar to us today—working behind fast-food counters or in supermarkets, for instance—did not exist in large numbers, making opportunities for after-school employment rare.

One indirect effect of compulsory high school, then, was to increase the amount of free time available to young people—time that previously would have been occupied by work. At the turn of the twentieth century, adults were so worried about the free time available to adolescents that they began to establish various youth clubs and activities—such as the Boy Scouts and organized sports—in order to occupy teenagers' "idle hands" (Hine, 1999). Organized leisure became an institutionalized part of adolescence as a supplement to school and a replacement for full-time employment.

A second influence on the rise of free time for adolescents in contemporary society was the increased affluence of Americans following World War II. The invention of the "teenager"—and, more important, the discovery of the teenager by those in advertising and marketing—changed the nature of adolescence. As adolescents gained more autonomy, they became consumers with plenty of discretionary income (Osgerby, 2008). This week, notice the commercials and advertisements aimed at teenagers on television, in magazines, or online. You'll see that much of the advertising concerns leisure expenditures: Music, movies, restaurants, electronic gadgets, cosmetics, athletic equipment, and so on.

Patterns of Time Use in Contemporary America

How do adolescents spend their free time? Figure 1 presents the results of two American time-use surveys of 15- to 17-year-olds, one conducted in the late 1970s, and the other conducted about 15 years ago (Zick, 2010). Among both girls and boys, there was a significant decline in the proportion of time devoted to paid jobs and a significant increase in time devoted to leisure; time devoted to housework also dropped among boys, but not among girls.

Figure 2 further breaks down adolescents' leisure time for the sample studied more recently. In that survey,

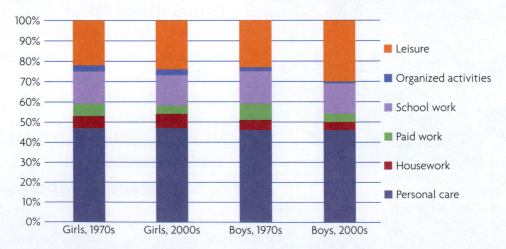

Figure 1 In recent decades, there has been a decline in the amount of time adolescents spend in paid jobs and an increase in the amount of time they devote to leisure activities. (Zick, 2010)

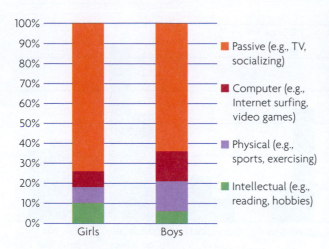

Figure 2   Adolescents' leisure time is dominated by passive activities, such as watching TV or talking to friends. Far less time is spent in activities thought to be beneficial to intellectual or physical development. (Zick, 2010)

One important feature of adolescence in contemporary society is the tremendous amount of time teenagers have for leisure activities.
© Digital Vision RF

the average teenage girl reported spending more than 6 hours a day in leisure activity, and the average boy reported spending more than 7 hours daily. But as you can see, both girls and boys spend a huge amount of free time in passive activities, like watching TV, talking on the phone, and relaxing. In fact, more than one-third of all girls and nearly one-fourth of all boys reported spending *all* of their leisure time in passive activities—on average, more than 4 hours per day. In contrast, only about 30 minutes a day are spent in activities thought to be mentally challenging, such as reading or playing a musical instrument, or physically beneficial (also about 30 minutes a day), such as sports or exercise (Zick, 2010).

Group averages can be deceptive, however. In one study, which tracked adolescents' time use over high school, the researchers identified several distinct groups of students (M. J. Shanahan & Flaherty, 2001). One especially busy group—about one-third of the students—spent considerable time in a range of pursuits, including extracurricular activities, paid work, schoolwork, time with friends, and household chores. A second group, about one-fourth of the sample, was similarly busy but did not hold a paying job. A third group, whose numbers increased from about 12% in the 9th grade to 20% in the 12th grade, devoted substantial time to a paying job but spent little time on other activities. A fourth group spent no time in work or extracurricular activities, but a substantial amount of time hanging around with friends.

Although the study found that adolescents' time use patterns changed a bit with age (as adolescents got older, they were more likely to spend at least some of their free time in a paid job), teenagers who were busy 9th-graders were likely to be busy throughout high school. Overall, the results suggest that adolescents' free time is not best thought of as a "zero sum" phenomenon, where

involvement in one activity displaces involvement in another. Rather, there are well-rounded adolescents who have substantial time commitments across many different activities, adolescents who tend to focus on one type of activity (usually sports), and adolescents who don't do much of anything outside of school (see Figure 3) (A. F. Feldman & Matjasko, 2007). Similar patterns of adolescent time use have been observed in many countries (Ferrar, Chang, Li, & Olds, 2013).

Most studies find that relatively busier adolescents are better adjusted and more accomplished than their classmates, but whether their better adjustment is a cause or consequence of their busy schedules isn't clear (Nelson & Gastic, 2009). In one study of low-income minority youth, some forms of engagement were associated with positive outcomes when combined with a second type of activity (for example, athletics and academics), but with negative outcomes if it was the only activity an adolescent was involved in (athletics alone) (Pedersen et al., 2005). Other studies of more representative populations also find that a "mixed" extracurricular portfolio may be better for adolescents' development than one that only includes sports (Kort-Butler & Hagewen, 2011; Viau & Poulin, 2014).

Patterns of Time Use in Other Countries

Patterns of adolescents time use differ considerably around the world. Teenagers in the United States spend far more time on leisure, and far less time in productive activities, than their counterparts in other countries. American students' use of their free time for school-related activities is especially low, and, as you would expect, it is particularly low among lower-achieving students (Witkow, 2009). For instance, the average American

Figure 3 Studies of extracurricular participation generally find that there are large numbers of students who participate in multiple activities, large numbers who participate only in sports, and large numbers who are nonparticipants. (Feldman & Matjasko, 2007)

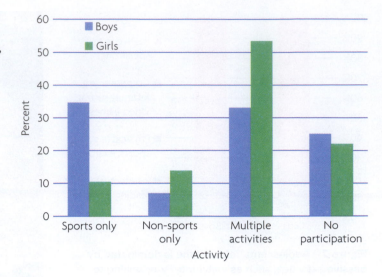

high school student spends fewer than 5 hours per week on homework; in Asian countries such as India, Taiwan, and Japan, the average is between 4 and 5 hours *per day* (Larson & Verma, 1999). And European and Asian adolescents spend almost 3 times as many hours each week reading for pleasure as do American adolescents (Larson & Verma, 1999). In contrast, American teenagers spend relatively more time playing sports, socializing with friends, caring for their physical appearance, and working at after-school jobs (Larson & Seepersad, 2003).

What is the effect of all this free time on adolescents' behavior and development? Are they learning about the real world from their part-time jobs? Are extracurricular activities beneficial? Are teenagers driven toward sex and violence by the mass media? Are they really affected by the music they listen to, videos on YouTube, or violent video games? Has the increase in time that they spend online adversely affected their ability to relate to others in person? Are concerns about adolescents' exposure to pornography and sexual predators on the Internet legitimate, or are they overstated? These are some of the questions we will address in this chapter. We begin by examining how teenagers are affected by after-school jobs.

Adolescents and Work

The majority of American high school students will have worked in an after-school job before graduating (Staff et al., 2009). Although working while attending high school is currently common in the United States, part-time employment did not become widespread until the 1980s, when about half of all high school students—and nearly three-quarters of all high school seniors—held jobs during the school year. School-year employment became less popular at the beginning of the twenty-first century, and today, the proportion of high school students who work during the school year is at its lowest level in recent history (Morisi, 2008; Stone, 2011). The

pattern of rise and fall in student employment tells an interesting story about the nature of adolescence in modern society.

The Rise and Fall of the Student Worker

Prior to 1925, teenagers from all but the most affluent families left school between the ages of 12 and 15 to become full-time workers (Horan and Hargis, 1991). Depending on their social class, adolescents were either students or workers, but not both.

As secondary education became more widespread, more young people remained in school well into middle and late adolescence, and fewer dropped out to work. Compulsory education laws were passed in most states that required individuals to stay in school until at least turning 16, child labor laws restricting adolescents' employment were enacted, and part-time jobs were not plentiful (Kett, 1977). As a result of these social and legislative changes, the employment of American teenagers declined steadily during the first four decades of the twentieth century. It's hard to imagine, given the presence of teenagers behind cash registers and fast-food counters today, but in 1940, only about 3% of high school students worked during the school year (U.S. Department of Commerce, 1940).

The situation began to change during the second half of the twentieth century, with the growth of the retail and service sectors of the economy. Employers needed people who were willing to work part-time for relatively low wages and short work shifts. Many businesses looked to teenagers to fill these jobs—and, in the mid-1970s teenagers were plentiful. The proportion of American high school students holding part-time jobs rose dramatically during the 1970s. Working during the school year became a way of life.

This trend began to reverse itself about 20 years ago, for several reasons (Morisi, 2008). Policymakers began calling for tougher standards in high schools. Schools began requiring more from their students, and many implemented graduation requirements. As more and more students sought college admission, a higher proportion of them began taking Advanced Placement (AP) courses, which had homework requirements that placed demands on students when they were out of school.

Second, just as adolescent workers became increasingly in demand as the service economy expanded during the last half of the twentieth century, the retraction of the economy during the first decade of the twenty-first century increased competition for the same jobs that teenagers could have just for the asking a couple of decades before. As the recession worsened and many adults lost their jobs, stores and restaurants began hiring unemployed adults instead of high school students (a pattern reminiscent of the early twentieth century, when competition for factory jobs prevented many teenagers from working). Immigration also brought to the United States many adults who were willing to take the part-time, minimum-wage jobs that had been the mainstays of the student employment. If you had walked into a fast-food restaurant in the 1980s, you would have been struck by the number of teenagers behind the counter. Today, many fast-food restaurants still employ a lot of adolescents, but they work side by side with people two, three, and even four times their age.

Finally, the growth of new technologies during the first part of the twenty-first century expanded leisure opportunities for many teenagers, many of who simply preferred to spend their free time online than behind a cash register. Over the past three decades there has been a significant increase in the proportion of adolescents who, when asked what they want out of a job, report that having time for leisure is important, and a decline in the proportion who say they would work even if they had enough money (Wray-Lake, Syvertsen, Briddell, Osgood, & Flanagan, 2011). The amount of time adolescents devoted to paid employment shrank as the amount they spent on leisure increased. Studies of student workers conducted during the 1980s and 1990s indicated that the vast majority of student workers were middle-class youth who were working because they wanted to, not because they had to—to earn money for extras, rather than for necessities. During the recession, teenagers' hourly wages did not keep pace with increases in the price of the things they were interested in purchasing (Zick, 2010). As more and more attractive (and relatively inexpensive) leisure options became available, and as the economic benefits of working declined, teenagers saw less reason to take on after-school jobs (see Figure 4).

Teenage Employment in Other Nations

The extent and nature of teenage employment vary considerably around the world (Stone, 2011; Verma &

Larson, 2003). In developing nations where industrialization is still in a relatively early stage and a large percentage of the population is poor, most adolescents leave school early—at least by American standards. The majority enter into full-time employment by age 15 or 16, in jobs similar to the ones they will hold as adults. Very often, adolescents work for their families. The pattern in these countries closely resembles that in America 100 years ago: school for adolescents of the extremely affluent, and work for the rest (Larson & Verma, 1999). The trade-off between school and work is changing in the developing world, however. As more and more adolescents from developing nations have stayed in school, the number of adolescents in these countries' labor force has declined at about the same rate. In China, where educational opportunities have expanded rapidly in recent decades, about half of all 16-year-olds were employed in the late 1980s, but fewer than one-quarter were employed just 10 years later (National Research Council, 2005).

Student employment in other comparably industrialized countries, where social and economic conditions are more similar to those in the United States, also vary considerably from country to country (Stone, 2011). School year employment is common in Canada and Australia, where about half of all students hold jobs, but it is nearly unheard of in Japan or Korea, where schoolwork is more demanding of teenagers' afternoons, evenings, and weekends. The proportion of employed students in Western Europe generally falls somewhere between these two extremes, but it varies considerably from country to country—school-year employment is rare in France, Italy, and Spain, but common in Great Britain, the Netherlands, and Sweden.

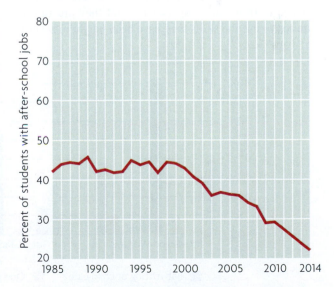

Figure 4 **A smaller proportion of adolescents have after-school jobs today than at any time in recent history. A bad economy, more demands from schools, and an expanding universe of leisure activities have all been factors.** (Bureau of Labor Statistics, 2015)

making the cultural connection

Student employment during the school year is more common in the United States, Canada, and Australia than elsewhere. How might this make the nature of adolescence different in these countries than in other parts of the world?

The Adolescent Workplace Today

Common Adolescent Jobs Today, the majority of teenagers are employed in the retail and service industries. In general, older students are more likely to hold formal jobs (for example, retail or restaurant work) than are younger students, who are more likely to hold informal jobs (such as babysitting or yard work) (see Figure 5) (Staff et al., 2009). As expected, working teenagers in rural areas are more likely to be employed in agricultural occupations than are their urban or suburban counterparts.

As you also can see from Figure 5, a small number of jobs accounts for a very large proportion of today's student workers. About 60% of employed 8th-graders work in just one of two jobs: babysitting or yard work. Job opportunities are nearly as restricted for older teenagers: Restaurant work (such as a counter worker in a fast-food restaurant) and retail sales work (such as a cashier in a clothing store) account for more than half of all working students' jobs. Very few teenagers are employed on farms or in factories anymore (Staff et al., 2009).

The Adolescent Work Environment Most teenagers' jobs are pretty dreary. Few permit adolescents to behave independently or make decisions; they receive little instruction from their supervisors, and they are rarely required to use the skills they have been taught in school

(Greenberger & Steinberg, 1986). With occasional exceptions, most teenagers' jobs are repetitive, monotonous, and intellectually unchallenging. Some are even highly stressful, requiring that youngsters work under intense time pressure without much letup and exposing them to potential injury and accidents (National Research Council, 1998). Not all jobs are this tedious or dangerous, of course, and some researchers have argued that adolescents in better jobs, in which they can learn genuinely useful skills, benefit from employment (Mortimer, Pimentel, Ryu, Nash, & Lee, 1996). While this may be true in theory, only a small proportion of adolescents hold jobs where there is ample opportunity to learn new or higher-level skills.

This characterization of adolescents' jobs as tedious is not something that teenagers themselves report. The majority of adolescent workers describe their jobs favorably, saying that they learned things, liked the people with whom they worked, had opportunities to exercise responsibility, and were satisfied with their pay. Perhaps compared to school, where adolescents are frequently bored and seldom challenged, even menial jobs are comparatively satisfying. And perhaps there is something about earning money and having some responsibility, regardless of how modest, that makes adolescents feel better about themselves and translates into a positive description of their work experience. As you will see in a later section of this chapter, when adolescents are placed in positions of responsibility, they come to feel more responsible.

Employment and Adolescent Development

The impact of employment on the psychological development of adolescents has been the focus of numerous

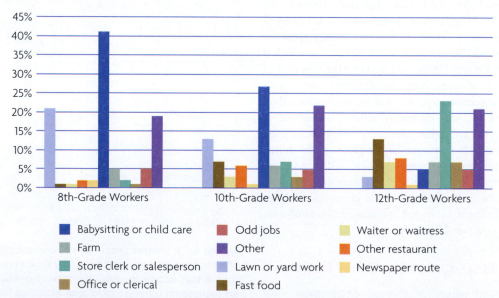

Figure 5 As adolescents age, they become less likely to work in informal jobs, like babysitting, and more likely to enter the formal labor force, mainly in retail stores and restaurants. (Staff et al., 2009)

studies (Staff et al., 2009). Researchers have asked three broad questions: whether working helps adolescents develop a sense of responsibility; whether working interferes with other activities, such as school; and whether working promotes the development of undesirable behaviors, such as drug and alcohol use.

The Development of Responsibility   Most people believe that working builds character, teaches adolescents about the real world, and helps them prepare for adulthood, but these assumptions are not generally supported by research. There is surprisingly little evidence that holding a job makes adolescents more responsible (Monahan, Lee, & Steinberg, 2011; Mortimer & Johnson, 1998). Moreover, some research has found high rates of misconduct on the job among adolescent workers (for example, stealing from employers, lying about the number of hours worked), especially those whose work is not closely supervised by adults (Staff et al., 2009).

One specific aspect of responsibility that working is believed to affect is money management. Because a high school senior who holds a minimum-wage job for 20 hours a week—a common pattern among high school seniors—earns more than $500 per month, holding a job may provide many opportunities for learning how to budget, save, and spend money wisely. Few teenagers exercise a great deal of responsibility when it comes to managing their earnings, though. The majority of adolescent workers spend most of their earnings on personal expenses, like clothes or cars. Fewer than 10% of adolescents who work save most of their income for future education, and even fewer use their earnings to help their families with household expenses (National Center for Education Statistics, 2005).

Many working teenagers may develop **premature affluence**—which results from getting used to having a relatively luxurious standard of living before having any serious financial responsibilities, like rent, food, or utility bills. Perhaps as a consequence, adolescents who have earned (and spent) a lot from their jobs while in high school are less satisfied with their financial situations as young adults, because they had become accustomed to living in an unrealistic world in which they had a large amount of discretionary income and few obligations (Bachman, 1983). Ironically, the very experience that many adults believe builds character may teach adolescents unrealistic lessons about the meaning of money.

Peoples' recollections of what they learned from working as teenagers are far more positive than many studies of adolescent work indicate (Mortimer, 2003). Many adults say that their jobs as teenagers helped them learn things like punctuality, ways to deal effectively with strangers, and even cope with work one didn't necessarily want to do. Here's how one adult put it, looking back on his job at a carwash:

> It was a brainless job. . . . The hardest part was fighting off the boredom, and we would get creative about how to do this, usually while getting high. But it was an important

Many adolescents hold part-time jobs during the school year. Research has questioned whether working is good or bad for adolescent development.
© Randy Faris/Corbis RF

experience—I saw what it was like to work, got more independent, and made some friends I still know. The money helped me get my first car and first real girlfriend. (Staff et al., 2009, p. 270)

The most reasonable conclusion we can draw about the impact of working on psychological development is that it depends on the nature of the job, just as the impact of schooling depends on the nature of the school (Rauscher, Wegman, Wooding, Davis, & Junkin, 2013). In jobs in which adolescents are given genuine responsibility, make important decisions, and perform challenging tasks, they are more likely to come away feeling more mature, competent, and dependable. In jobs in which the work is repetitive, stressful, or unchallenging, they probably will gain very little from the experience. But given what we know about employment opportunities for teenagers, it seems reasonable to say that while it is *possible* for an adolescent to benefit psychologically from working, it is not *probable*. According to one recent analysis, the most common adolescent jobs—in fast-food restaurants or retail stores, for

premature affluence
Having more income than one can manage maturely, especially during adolescence.

Working long hours takes its toll on performance in school. Employed students often protect their grades by cutting corners, taking easier classes, and cheating.
© Antonio_Diaz/Getty Images RF

example—ranked highest in stress and in interference with other parts of life, and lowest in their likelihood of providing skills or leading to a career (Staff et al., 2009).

The Impact on Schooling A second question that has received a fair amount of research attention concerns the impact of working on adolescents' involvement in other activities, most notably, schooling. Here, studies indicate that the issue is not whether a teenager works, but how much (Stone, 2011).

Working more than 20 hours a week jeopardizes adolescents' school performance and engagement (Nagengast, Marsh, Chiorri, & Hau, 2014). Youngsters who work long hours are absent from school more often, are less likely to participate in extracurricular activities, report enjoying school less, spend less time on their homework, and earn slightly lower grades. These results occur both because teenagers who are less interested in school choose to work longer hours, and because working long hours leads to disengagement from school (Monahan et al., 2011; Safron, Sy, & Schulenberg, 2003). Working long hours takes an especially bad toll on achievement among White and Asian students from middle-class families (Bachman, Staff, O'Malley, & Freedman-Doan, 2013).

Intensive involvement in a part-time job may even increase the likelihood of dropping out of school (Staff et al., 2009). Students who spend a lot of time on the job have less ambitious plans for further education (H. Marsh & Kleitman, 2005), and they complete fewer years of college, in part because students with low aspirations for the future choose to work longer hours than their peers (Bachman, Staff, O'Malley, Schulenberg, & Freedman-Doan, 2011; Staff et al., 2009). It is important to stress, however, that working fewer than 20 hours

per week does not appear to have these adverse effects (Staff et al., 2009). Indeed, some studies find that a large number of students are able to manage school and work effectively, as long as they keep their work hours in check. Many benefit from learning how to manage their time effectively (M. J. Shanahan & Flaherty, 2001).

The impact of working on students' actual grades and achievement test scores is small (Staff et al., 2009), but extensive employment during the school year may take its toll on school performance in ways that are not revealed by looking only at grade point averages or test scores. Students who work a great deal pay less attention in class and exert less effort on their studies (Monahan et al., 2011). When students work a great deal, they often develop strategies for protecting their grades. These strategies include taking easier courses, cutting corners on assignments, copying homework from friends, and cheating (Steinberg & Dornbusch, 1991). Teachers express concern about the excessive involvement of students in after-school jobs (Bills, Helms, & Ozcan, 1995). Some teachers have responded by lowering classroom expectations, assigning less homework, and using class time for students to complete assignments that otherwise would be done outside of school (Bills et al., 1995). When large numbers of students in a school are employed, even those who don't have jobs can be affected indirectly. There is no evidence that summer employment, though, even for long hours, affects school performance, suggesting that the negative impact of working on school performance is probably due to the time demands of having a job while being a student (Oettinger, 1999).

The Promotion of Problem Behavior Many people think that keeping teenagers busy with work keeps them out of trouble. Contrary to popular belief, however, employment during adolescence does not deter delinquent activity (Monahan, Steinberg, & Cauffman, 2013). Indeed, several studies suggest that working long hours may actually be associated with *increases* in aggression, school misconduct, minor delinquency, and precocious sexual activity (Monahan et al., 2011; Rich & Kim, 2002; Staff, VanEseltine, Silver, & Vurrington, 2012). Many studies also have found that rates of smoking, drinking, and drug use are higher among teenage workers than nonworkers, especially among students who work long hours (Monahan et al., 2011; Ramchand, Ialongo, & Chilcoat, 2007).

The extent to which working actually *causes* these problems isn't clear—remember, correlation is not causation. Working long hours clearly creates problems for some students. But the higher rate of delinquency among working adolescents is also because delinquent youth are simply more likely than their peers to choose to work long hours (Staff, Osgood, Schulenberg, Bachman, & Messersmith, 2010). Similarly, working long hours leads to increases in substance use, but students who smoke, drink, and use other drugs also are more likely to want to work long hours (Bachman et al., 2011; Monahan et al., 2011).

A variety of explanations have been proposed for the impact of extensive employment on problem behavior. The impact of working on drug and alcohol use probably reflects the fact that adolescents who work long hours have more discretionary income and, hence, greater opportunity to purchase cigarettes, alcohol, and other drugs. In addition, drug and alcohol use are more common among adolescents who work under conditions of high job stress than among their peers who work for comparable amounts of time and money but under less stressful conditions—and many adolescents work in stressful work settings, like fast-food restaurants (Staff et al., 2009). It may also be that working long hours disrupts adolescents' relationships with their parents, which, in turn, leads to problem behavior (Longest & Shanahan, 2007; Roisman, 2002). Whatever the reason, the impact of school-year employment on drug and alcohol use persists over time: People who worked long hours as teenagers drink and use drugs more in their late 20s than their peers who worked less or not at all (Mihalic & Elliott, 1997).

Possible Benefits for Poor Youth   One point of debate among researchers who study adolescent employment concerns the differential impact of working on middle-class versus poor youth. Some researchers have found that working, even in the sorts of jobs available to teenagers, has special benefits for inner-city adolescents from single-parent families, from poor families, with poor school records, or with histories of delinquency (Monahan et al., 2013; Purtell & McLoyd, 2013; Rocheleau & Swisher, 2012). The age at which inner-city teenagers begin working makes a difference, though. Working during junior high school or the early high school years increases the chances that poor minority youth will drop out of school and engage in problem behavior, whereas working later in high school does not (Entwisle, Alexander, & Olson, 2005; Olatunji, 2005). Working early in adolescence may make school seem less important, whereas working in later adolescence, when making the transition to adult work roles is more imminent, may make school seem more important. It is important, therefore, that working complement, rather than take the place of, school. One recent study of juvenile delinquents found that working during high school was only beneficial if the adolescent was also attending school regularly (Monahan et al., 2013).

In sum, although teenagers generally enjoy working, there is little evidence, with the exception of disadvantaged inner-city youth, that doing so contributes in significant ways to their psychosocial development. Studies of work and adolescent development point to a complicated pattern of cause and effect that unfolds

over time. Adolescents who are less attached and committed to school, and who are more involved in problem behavior, are more likely to choose to work long hours. Working long hours, in turn, leads to more disengagement from school and increased problem behavior. In other words, intensive employment during the school year most threatens the school performance and psychological well-being of those students who can least afford to suffer the consequences of overcommitment to a job.

making the personal connection

Think back to your own work experiences as an adolescent, during either the summer or the school year. What were the best jobs you had? Which ones were the worst? Why?

Youth Unemployment

Although the employment of teenagers has become commonplace in contemporary America, some young people who wish to work are unable to find jobs. However, except for summer months, youth unemployment is not a pervasive problem, once the proportion of young people who are in school is taken into account. For example, in 2015, 82% of all 16- to 19-year-olds were enrolled in school (either in high school or college); of the remaining 18% who were not in school, about 53% were employed, and about 12% were looking for full- or part-time work (the other 35% were neither working nor looking for work) (Bureau of Labor Statistics, 2015b). Overall, then, only a small percentage of 16- to 19-year-olds—about 2%—were out of school and looking for work (see Figure 6).

As you might expect, unemployment is especially likely among adolescents who have dropped out of high

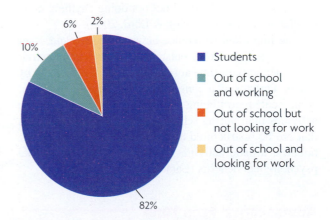

Figure 6   Most 16- to 19-year-olds are students. The percentage of young people who are not in school, unemployed, and looking for work is very small. (Bureau of Labor Statistics, 2015b)

experience sampling method (ESM) A method of collecting data about adolescents' emotional states, in which individuals are signaled and asked to report on their mood and activity.

school. You may be surprised to find out, though, that the unemployment rate among recent high school graduates who have not gone on to college is not all that different from that of high school dropouts (in 2014, 29% of recent high school graduates who were not in college were unemployed, compared with 30% of high school dropouts) (Bureau of Labor Statistics, 2015b). In contrast, just 10 years ago, the unemployment rate among dropouts was *twice as high* as it was among recent high school graduates who were not in college.

Unemployment has been a problem among high school dropouts for decades, but the high rate of unemployment among high school graduates who do not go to college is a recent phenomenon. Unfortunately, many experts worry that this state of affairs may not reverse itself after the current recession lifts, because success in the labor force increasingly requires at least some college education, if not a college degree. It was once believed that we should focus our efforts on finding ways to help high school dropouts and those with just a high school diploma make the transition from high school into the world of work. In view of the changed and changing labor market, with its demands for well-educated workers, it makes more sense to reform schools so that all students graduate with enough academic skill to enroll in college.

Adolescents and Leisure

Adolescents in the United States and other Western countries spend nearly half their waking hours in leisure activities, such as socializing with friends, either in person, by phone, or electronically; watching television and listening to music; searching the Internet and playing video games; playing sports, practicing a musical instrument, or working on hobbies; and sometimes not doing anything at all (J. Mahoney, Larson, Eccles, & Lord, 2005).

One important difference between leisure and other activities is that adolescents choose their leisure activities, whereas their time at school and work is dictated by others. Perhaps as a consequence, and not surprisingly, adolescents report being in a better mood during leisure activities than during school or work. Leisure activities that are both structured and voluntary—such as sports, hobbies, artistic activities, and clubs—provide special psychological benefits (Larson, 2000).

Adolescents' Free Time and Their Moods

Researchers have been interested in how adolescents' moods change when they are involved in leisure activities, but studying adolescents' emotional states is tricky, because individuals' emotions change during the day, and a researcher's assessment at a specific point in time may not reflect their moods at other points in the day. Suppose a researcher wanted to know how adolescents' moods were affected by various activities—such as attending school, watching television, or having dinner with the family. Although it would be possible to interview respondents at some later point and ask them to recall their moods at different points in the day, we can't be sure whether their recollections would be entirely accurate.

The Experience Sampling Method One of the most interesting innovations in the study of adolescence was designed to overcome this problem. Using a technique called the **experience sampling method (ESM),** researchers collect much more detailed information about adolescents' experiences over the course of the day. Adolescents carry electronic devices, such as smartphones, and, when they are signaled, report whom they are with, what they are doing, and how they are feeling. The ESM has been used to chart adolescents' moods, monitor their social relationships, and catalog their activities in far greater detail than has been previously available.

In one early ESM study (Larson & Richards, 1991), before there were smartphones, nearly 500 adolescents ages 9–15 carried pagers and booklets of self-report forms for one week and filled out a survey each time they were signaled. The form contained a series of questions about companionship ("Who were you with [or talking to on the phone]?"), location ("Where were you?"), activity ("What were you doing?"), and mood (the adolescents used a checklist to report their feelings). The adolescents were beeped seven times each day, once during every 2-hour block between 7:30 A.M. and 9:30 P.M. The researchers charted changes in activities, companionship, and mood over the course of the week.

Adolescents' moods are most positive when they are with their friends and least positive when they are alone; their moods when with their family fall somewhere in between. Between grades 5 and 9, adolescents' moods while with friends become more positive, whereas their moods while with their family become more negative between elementary and middle school (between grades 5 and 7) and then rise between middle school and high school (between grades 8 and 9). This dip parallels findings from other research on family relations that point to early adolescence as a time of heightened strain in the parent–child relationship (Laursen & Collins, 2009).

When adolescents are in school, they report moderate levels of concentration but very low levels of motivation or interest in what they are doing. When they are with friends, teenagers report moderate levels of motivation and interest but low levels of concentration. It is only when adolescents are playing sports or involved in the arts, a hobby, or an extracurricular organization that they report high levels of both concentration and interest. This combination produces what some psychologists have referred to as a **flow experience** (Csikszentmihalyi, 1990). You've probably experienced this sensation when you were deeply involved in an activity that was both enjoyable and absorbing.

One ESM study of after-school programs found that the positive combination of high motivation, concentration, and engagement was most commonly observed when young adolescents were involved in sports or arts enrichment (Shernoff & Vandell, 2007). While adolescents are in unstructured leisure activities, like watching TV, they tend to show the same pattern of moderate interest but low concentration as when they are socializing with friends. Participation in structured extracurricular activities, such as hobbies or sports, has been shown to be the most positive way for adolescents to spend free time, in terms of their current and future psychological development (McHale, Crouter, & Tucker, 2001; Zaff, Moore, Papillo, & Williams, 2003).

Structured Leisure Activities

School-sponsored extracurricular activities provide the context for much of adolescents' leisure activity (Farb & Matjasko, 2012; J. Mahoney et al., 2009). According to recent surveys, about two-thirds of American high school students participate in one or more extracurricular activities, although participation rates vary greatly from school to school. The most popular extracurricular activity in the United States is athletics, in which about half of all adolescents participate; it is also the extracurricular activity that has been most extensively studied (Theokas, 2009). The other two main extracurricular activities are those related to music (about one-fifth of adolescents are members of a school band, chorus, orchestra, or glee club) and those related to academic or occupational interests (about one-fifth are members of clubs devoted to science, foreign languages, or certain careers).

Extracurricular participation is influenced by a number of factors (Fredericks & Simpkins, 2012; Lenzi et al., 2012; J. Mahoney et al., 2009). It is more prevalent among adolescents from more affluent families, among students who earn better grades, and among students from smaller schools and smaller, more rural communities, where school activities often play a relatively more central role in the lives of adults and adolescents alike (for example, where an entire community may turn out for Friday night football). Middle-class parents encourage their children to participate in extracurricular activities primarily as a means of self-improvement (often, with the child's future in mind), whereas working-class families are more likely to do so as a way of keeping their teens safe and out of trouble during after-school hours (Bennett, Lutz, & Jayaram, 2012). Adolescents whose parents are involved in the community or who reinforce their children's

For many adolescents around the world, school-sponsored extracurricular activities provide the context for much of their leisure activity.
© John Flournoy/The McGraw-Hill Education

interests are also more likely to participate (Persson, Kerr, & Stattin, 2007). Extracurricular participation is stable over time—students who are highly involved in these activities at the beginning of high school are likely to stay highly involved through graduation (Denault & Poulin, 2009).

> **flow experience**
> The experience of high levels of both concentration and interest at the same time.

The Impact of Extracurricular Participation on Development   Extracurricular participation has many benefits. It improves students' performance in school and reduces the likelihood of dropping out. It deters delinquency, drug use, and other types of risk taking. And it enhances students' psychological well-being and social status (Agans et al., 2014; Brand et al., 2010; Farb & Matjasko, 2012; Fredericks & Eccles, 2010; Jewett et al., 2014; Knifsend & Graham, 2011). Participation in organized community-based activities also protects adolescents in disadvantaged neighborhoods from exposure to violence, by keeping them in safer settings after school (Gardner & Brooks-Gunn, 2009; Gardner, Browning, & Brooks-Gunn, 2012). Despite concerns that the extracurricular overscheduling of youth, especially in affluent communities, creates pressures that compromise adolescents' mental health, several studies have found no such effect (Farb & Matjasko, 2012; Luthar & Barkin, 2012; Mahoney & Vest, 2012; Randall, Bohnert, & Travers, 2015).

The one exception to this uniformly positive picture is that involvement in team sports, which is associated with many psychological benefits, such as better mental health, better sleep, and higher school achievement, is also associated with increased alcohol use and delinquency. This latter consequence is seen especially among boys who have a strong "jock" identity and who participate in school-sponsored, male-dominated sports, like football (Gardner, Roth, & Brooks-Gunn, 2008; Mays & Thompson, 2009; Viau & Poulin, 2014).

Extracurricular participation in high school is correlated with participation in college and with community involvement in adulthood. Youngsters who are participants as 9th-graders are likely to be similarly busy throughout high school, and people who are "do-ers" during adolescence tend to remain so in young and middle adulthood. Along similar lines, individuals who participate in sports during adolescence are likely to continue athletic activities in adulthood (D. Perkins, Jacobs, Barber, & Eccles, 2003).

Studies have found benefits of participating in structured extracurricular activities as many as 8 years after high school graduation, especially among individuals whose extracurricular participation lasted at least 2 years and occupied a relatively high number of hours each week. These benefits were seen only among individuals whose activities were school-sponsored, however, perhaps because this helps strengthen students' attachment to school, which in turn contributes to their future educational success (M. Gardner, Roth, & Brooks-Gunn, 2008; Knifsend & Graham, 2011). This "spillover effect" is especially strong among adolescents who are less able students and among those who go to schools in poor communities (Guest & Schneider, 2003; J. Mahoney & Cairns, 1997).

One study of a high school theater production also found that the experience contributed in important ways to adolescents' emotional development. Through the course of preparing for their performance, students learned how to better manage their emotions, better understand others' feelings, and learn how to deal more effectively with anger, frustration, and stress. Although these opportunities

arise in all sorts of situations, the atmosphere cultivated by the activity's advisors appears to be crucial for making the experience a positive one (Gaudreau, Amiot, & Vallerand, 2009; Larson & Brown, 2007). The quality of relationships adolescents develop with the adults they encounter in extracurricular activities is an especially important influence on the overall impact of the experience (Crean, 2012; Scales, Benson, & Mannes, 2006).

Researchers speculate that extracurricular activities have positive effects because they increase students' contact with teachers and other school personnel who reinforce the value of school (as when a coach or advisor counsels a student about plans for college) and because participation itself may improve students' self-confidence and self-esteem. Some educators believe that extracurricular participation also helps bond students to their school, especially in the case of adolescents who are not achieving academically; for many of them, their extracurricular activity is what keeps them coming to school each day (Blomfield & Barber, 2011; Dotterer, McHale, & Crouter, 2007; J. Mahoney et al., 2009). Adolescents who combine participation in sports with other sorts of extracurricular activities, and who therefore have multiple points of "attachment" to their school, fare better than those who are solely involved in athletics (Linver, Roth, & Brooks-Gunn, 2009; Zarrett et al., 2009).

Some of the positive effects of extracurricular participation also stem from the fact that these activities bring adolescents into contact with peers who influence them in beneficial ways; extracurricular activities often lead to new friendships (Ntoumanis, Taylor, & Thøgersen-Ntoumanis, 2012; Schaefer, Simpkins, Vest, & Price, 2011; Simpkins, Eccles, & Becnel, 2008). When the activity strengthens membership in a peer group involved in prosocial activities that revolve around the school, participation can be beneficial to the adolescent's development and achievement (J. Mahoney, 2000).

Not all activities revolve around prosocial endeavors, though, and participation in certain sports can increase adolescents' involvement in problem behavior (Crean, 2012). One study of male football players and wrestlers found that they were relatively more likely to get into serious fights (similar effects were not found for boys who played other sports) and that violence was most common among football players whose friends also played football (Kreager, 2007a). Another found similar effects of sports participation on delinquency—boys who participated in organized sports were more likely to spend their free time hanging out with their friends, and this led them to be involved in more antisocial (although not necessarily violent) behavior (Gardner & Brooks-Gunn, 2009). (As you will read in a moment, during adolescence, spending unstructured, unsupervised time with friends is a recipe for trouble.)

Several additional cautions have been raised about adolescents' participation in athletics (Steinberg, 2014b). As

Participation in school-sponsored extracurricular activities, like athletics, leads to better school achievement.
© Image Source/Isadora Getty Buyou /Image Source RF

extracurricular sports have become more competitive, the number of young people injured during these activities has risen substantially. According to some estimates, more than half of all adolescents who play organized sports have played while injured. Half of all coaches say they've been aware that one of their players was playing with an injury, sometimes with a serious sprain or broken bones. One-third of all adolescent athletes say they've been deliberately injured by an opponent. Each year, well over 1 million adolescent athletes are treated in emergency rooms.

In addition, many adolescents feel anxious and tense within the competitive atmosphere that has come to dominate after-school sports in many communities. Nearly three-quarters of all student athletes have been screamed at by a coach, and 40% of these adolescents say they wanted to quit the team as a result. Thus, while competitive athletics are a source of considerable pleasure for some adolescents, they are a source of equally considerable stress for others (Larson, Hansen, & Moneta, 2006; Scanlan, Babkes, & Scanlan, 2005). This is why having a coach who understands and looks out for these potential problems is so important.

making the scientific connection

Why are the apparent effects of participation in extra-curricular activities different from those associated with part-time employment? How might these two sets of experiences differ?

Unstructured Leisure Time

One important distinction is between structured and supervised leisure activities, like school- or community-sponsored extracurricular activities, and unstructured leisure activities, such as hanging out with friends without any organized activity in mind. Participation in structured leisure activities tends to have positive effects on adolescent development. Time spent in unstructured leisure activities does the reverse (Siennick & Osgood, 2012).

Routine Activity Theory

> **routine activity theory**
> A perspective on adolescence that views unstructured, unsu-pervised time with peers as a main cause of misbehavior.

Several writers have argued that the combination of a lack of structure, socializing with peers, and the absence of adult supervision encourages delinquency and other problem behaviors. According to **routine activity theory,** "the less structured an activity, the more likely a person is to encounter opportunities for problem behavior in the simple sense that he or she is not occupied doing something else" (Osgood et al., 2005, p. 51). Because adolescence is a time of heightened peer pressure and heightened susceptibility to peer influence, and because one of the strongest deterrents against problem behavior is the presence of an adult, it is hardly surprising that unstructured peer activity without adult supervision is associated with all sorts of problems—depression, delinquency, drug and alcohol use, violence, and precocious sexual activity (A. Anderson & Hughes, 2009; Ham, McHale, & Crouter, 2014; Maimon & Browning, 2010; McHale, Updegraff, Kim, & Cansier, 2009; Miller, 2013).

Even something as positive sounding as spending time at a community recreation center can increase adolescents' problem behavior if their time is unstructured and minimally supervised (J. Mahoney, Stattin, & Lord, 2004). Hanging out with friends in the absence of adult supervision at night, in particular, substantially increases the likelihood of problem behavior. Adolescents who spend five or more evenings out in an average week are at least 4 times more likely to be involved in antisocial activity than those who go out less than twice a week (Gage, Overpeck, Nansel, & Kogan, 2005). As one team of writers wryly put it, "Whether you like or dislike your father, it will be more convenient to smoke marijuana when he isn't around" (Osgood, Wilson, O'Malley, Bachman, & Johnston, 1996, p. 640).

Time After School   A prime time for unstructured and unsupervised leisure is during the afternoon on school days—after school has let out but before parents have returned home from work. As Figure 7 indicates,

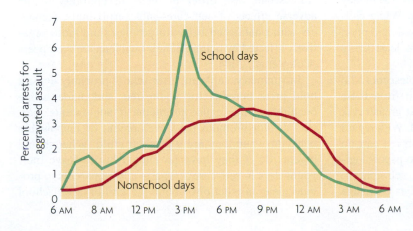

Figure 7   **More arrests occur during school afternoons than at any other time, presumably because this is the time when adolescents are least likely to be supervised.** (Osgood et al., 2005)

Many teenagers spend time after school unsupervised.
© Jose Luis Pelaez Inc./Getty Images RF

for instance, delinquency is more common on weekday afternoons than at any other time (Osgood et al., 2005).

In 2014, nearly 75% of mothers with children between ages 6 and 17, and more than 90% of fathers with children this age, were employed (Bureau of Labor Statistics, 2015d). While some youngsters whose parents are at work during the afternoon are involved in school- or community-based programs that provide adult supervision, others spend their after-school hours away from adults, in their homes, with friends, or simply hanging out in neighborhoods and shopping malls (Mahoney & Parente, 2009). Affluent, suburban, and White children are most likely to be home unsupervised, and poor, minority, and urban and rural children are least likely (J. Mahoney et al., 2009).

Psychologists have debated whether adolescents who take care of themselves after school profit from these opportunities for self-management or are at greater risk for problems because they aren't supervised. With regard to the first, most studies show that children in self-care do not differ from their peers when it comes to psychological development, school achievement, or self-conceptions (J. Mahoney et al., 2009). These studies challenge

the idea that having to care for oneself contributes to the development of self-reliance or responsibility—similar to studies of part-time employment. With regard to the second, self-care after school is associated with a wide range of adverse outcomes. Compared to young people who are supervised after school, those who aren't feel more socially isolated and depressed, and are more likely to have school problems, use drugs and alcohol, be involved in antisocial behavior, and be sexually active at earlier ages (D. Cohen, Farley, Taylor, Martin, & Schuster, 2002; Mahoney & Parente, 2009; Shumow, Smith, & Smith, 2009).

One limitation of studies of youth in self-care is that they typically lump together all children who take care of themselves after school, even though there are important differences in their after-school arrangements (J. Mahoney et al., 2009). Adolescents who go straight home after school are far less likely to engage in problem behavior than are those who go to a friend's house or who just hang out (Mahoney & Parente, 2009). In addition, youngsters in self-care who are raised by authoritative parents and who are monitored by their parents from a distance—via telephone check-ins, for example—are no more susceptible to problem behavior than are children whose parents are home with them after school (Galambos & Maggs, 1991; Vandell & Ramanan, 1991).

Spending time after school with friends in unsupervised settings is more problematic under some circumstances than others. It's not simply spending unsupervised time with peers that increases an adolescent's likelihood of alcohol and drug use; it's the combination of lacking supervision, having friends who like to party and use drugs, and being especially susceptible to peer pressure (L. Caldwell & Darling, 1999). The harmful effects of low parental monitoring are especially bad in neighborhoods where other adults are unlikely to provide supervision if parents aren't around (Coley, Morris, & Hernandez, 2004). The negative effects of low parental monitoring and unsupervised peer group activity are especially pronounced in unsafe neighborhoods (Pettit, Bates, Dodge, & Meece, 1999). Adolescents also differ in their susceptibility to the adverse effects of self-care—not surprisingly, teenagers with established behavior problems are more negatively affected by being on their own than are their peers (Coley et al., 2004).

In summary, self-care after school probably doesn't hold great benefits for youngsters and, under some conditions, may cause problems if adolescents' parents do not promote the development of responsible behavior when they are with their child. What should parents do if they have no choice but to leave their youngsters in self-care? Experts advise parents to provide clear instructions about the child's after-school activities and whereabouts, ask the child to check in with an adult as soon as he or she gets home, and teach the child how to handle any emergencies that arise (Steinberg, 2011).

Promoting Positive Youth Development

In light of evidence that certain types of extracurricular activities appear to benefit adolescents, and in view of the potential dangers of leaving adolescents unsupervised after school, experts have called for better and more readily available after-school programming for adolescents. They argue that well-designed programs not only will deter problem behavior by providing adolescents with adult supervision but can also promote **positive youth development** (Bowers, Geldhof, Johnson, J. Lerner, & R. Lerner; Ramey & Rose-Krasnor, 2012; Yohalem & Wilson-Ahlstrom, 2010).

Although the label "positive youth development" is relatively new, the concept is not. Indeed, the goals espoused by proponents of positive youth development programs today bear a striking resemblance to the stated goals of youth programs that have been around for ages, like the YMCA (founded in London in 1844 and transported to the United States in 1851), the Boys and Girls Clubs of America (founded in 1860), 4-H clubs (founded at the turn of the twentieth century), and scouting (founded in 1910). In 1866, the YMCA of New York City announced that its purpose was "the improvement of the spiritual, mental, social and physical condition of young men" (YMCA, 2006).

Experts' interest in helping young people develop strengths, rather than simply preventing them from getting into trouble, has burgeoned in recent years (e.g., Lerner, von Eye, Lerner, Lewin-Bizan, & Bowers, 2010; Lewin-Bizan, Bowers, & Lerner, 2010). There are many different models of positive youth development, but they all are very similar (J. Lerner et al., 2009; J. Mahoney et al., 2009). One of the most widely cited emphasizes the Five C's of positive youth development: Competence, Confidence, Connection, Character, and Caring/Compassion (see Table 1) (Bowers, et al., 2014). Another model, the EPOCH model of positive adolescent psychology, stresses similar attributes: Engagement, Perseverance, Optimism, Connectedness, and Happiness (Kern, Benson, Steinberg, & Steinberg, in press). These characteristics, in one form or another, are often the focus of contemporary community-based programming for youth, including programs emphasizing community service, volunteer activity, mentoring, and skill building.

What makes a positive youth development program successful? A key component to program success is the extent to which participants volunteer their commitment, are placed in demanding roles, are encouraged to meet high expectations, are expected to take responsibility for their behavior, and are helped to understand the consequences of failing to fulfill their obligations (Dawes & Larson, 2011). Researchers have described a multistep process through which program participation contributes to the development of responsibility (Salusky et al., 2014). First, adolescents voluntarily take on new roles and obligations. As an adolescent stage manager in a theater company described it:

> I'm the person that people are relying on to keep the show moving, like, I have to monitor the stage while the music is happening and if something goes wrong, it's my job to like, whatever it takes, . . . like problem solving, but quickly to keep the show going. (p. 422)

Second, adolescents must stick with their job, even in the face of challenges. Many volunteers experience

positive youth development The goal of programs designed to facilitate healthy psychosocial development and not simply to deter problematic development.

Table 1 The Five C's of positive youth development

Competence	A positive view of one's actions in domain-specific areas, including social, academic, cognitive, and vocational. Social competence pertains to interpersonal skills (e.g., conflict resolution). Cognitive competence pertains to cognitive abilities (e.g., decision making). School grades, attendance, and test scores are part of academic competence. Vocational competence involves work habits and career choice explorations.
Confidence	An internal sense of overall positive self-worth and self-efficacy; one's global self-regard, as opposed to domain-specific beliefs.
Connection	Positive bonds with people and institutions that are reflected in bidirectional exchanges between the individual and peers, family, school, and community in which both parties contribute to the relationship.
Character	Respect for societal and cultural rules, possession of standards for correct behaviors, a sense of right and wrong (morality), and integrity.
Caring/compassion	A sense of sympathy and empathy for others.

Source: R. Lerner et al., 2005.

frustration during the initial phases of their participation; sometimes the work is too hard, sometimes it was too boring; sometimes it is just overwhelming. It is important to hang in through difficult periods.

Third, youth benefit most when they persevere and derive a sense of accomplishment from their success, Many attribute this to the expectations and support of the program leaders:

> You feel that you owe it to them to do things right and to do them the way they are expected to be done . . . not because necessarily they are always hounding you about it, but just because you want to do it. (p. 423)

Ultimately, this leads to changes in adolescents' self-conceptions—they come to see themselves as more dependable and mature, which affects how they behave outside the program as well.

In other words, expecting adolescents to behave responsibly helps them develop a sense of responsibility (Coatsworth & Conroy, 2009; Larson & Angus, 2011). This, in turn, often leads parents to see their teens as more self-reliant, which may increase parental autonomy-granting, further contributing to the development of independence (Larson, Pearce, Sullivan, & Jarrett, 2007). Parents frequently report that their teenagers had become more attentive and considerate after having been in a well-run program (Salusky et al., 2014).

Adolescents, Media, and the Internet

Patterns of Media Use

In 2009, a Los Angeles high school teacher asked her 10th-grade class to unplug themselves for a week—to go entirely without electronic media for that whole time (Lopez, 2009). Here's one student's report. It's typical of what others wrote:

> For me, the hardest media to break away from for 7 days was the 46-inch TV in the living room, plus all of the other TVs in the house. I watch TV almost every day. When it is on, I cannot resist watching. I thought being without media was hard at the beginning, but while it went on, it got harder and harder, even in the same day. The first day was the hardest. I was left in silence, with everything gone and disconnected. I think that part was the hardest. Thinking about other things. Usually I like hearing my thoughts, but that day, they kind of got annoying. I didn't want to listen to myself anymore.

new media
Digital media typically accessed via computers, smart-phones, or other Internet-based devices.

Mass media have become so much a part of the typical adolescent's life that for many, staying "connected" starts to take on qualities of an addiction. Another student in the study wrote, "Being without media was harder than I ever realized. I thought it was going to be a cake walk, but it turned into a hell. I found myself thinking that I should just give up, and I kept talking to myself." Many students reported sleeping much more than usual as a way of coping; adolescents frequently use media to distract themselves from negative thoughts and emotions (Larson, 1995). At the end of the week, most said that the experience was interesting, in that it taught them how dependent on these media they were, but that they could not wait to return to their smartphones, computers, and televisions.

Until the last 20 years or so, most research on the impact of the media on adolescent development focused on television, movies, and recorded music. During the past two decades, though, there has been an explosion in adolescents' use of **new media,** in part because access to electronic media has expanded so rapidly. Adolescents not only access music and video content through conventional sources, such as televisions, but on computers and, increasingly, on smartphones. The sheer amount of media content that is created and distributed today is incredibly vast (D. Roberts et al., 2009).

Many of the questions adults have asked about new media focus on their assumed negative effects, just as with prior research on older media, when adults asked whether rock music promotes drug use, whether television viewing "rots your brain," whether video games encourage violence, and so on. It's an age-old inquiry: Consider the following passage, taken from a the report of a U.S. Senate committee hearing on juvenile delinquency:

> The child today in the process of growing up is constantly exposed to sights and sounds of a kind and quality undreamed of in previous generations. As these sights and sounds can be a powerful force for good, so too can they be a powerful [force for] evil. Their very quantity makes them a factor to be reckoned with in determining the total climate encountered by today's children during their formative years.

The Senate hearing, held in 1955, was about the contribution of comic books to adolescent crime (U.S. Senate Committee on the Judiciary, 1955, p. 1). Hard as it may be to believe, in the late 1800s, parents voiced similar concerns about the corrupting influence of the "questionable" content contained in mass-market novels by authors like Jane Austen (Uhls, 2015)!

Research on new media and adolescent development is similarly slanted (Adachi & Willoughby, 2012). Among the questions asked are whether exposure to online sexual content encourages sexual activity, whether using social networking sites exposes adolescents to Internet predators, whether online gaming increases aggression, whether the growing use of electronic forms of communication is hampering the development of social skills, and whether some adolescents have actually become addicted to the Internet. We'll take a look at these and other questions about the media's impact on adolescent development, but before we do, let's look at how widespread media use is among today's adolescents.

Media Saturation   By any measure, the availability of media in young people's lives is remarkable—today's adolescents live in a world that is not simply "media-rich" but absolutely "media-saturated" (J. Brown & Bobkowski, 2011a). Virtually all American households have at least one television (and half subscribe to premium channels, like HBO), and close to half of adolescents live in a household that has a TV screen in the family car. Computers and Internet access are present in virtually all homes, regardless of family income. More than 90% of American teens go online daily, and about 25% report being online "almost constantly," often using social media (girls) or playing video games (boys) (see Figure 8). The most popular social media sites among adolescents are Facebook, Instagram, and Snapchat (Lenhart, 2015).

Almost three-fourths of all adolescents have their own smartphone, or access to one, and they spend less time on their phones talking to other people than they do on other activities (Lenhart, 2015; Rideout, Foeher & Roberts, 2010). According to some surveys, the average teenagers sends about 70 text messages each day; nearly one-fifth send more than 200 texts daily (Lenhart, 2012; 2015). One problem that has received a great deal of attention is the high prevalence of texting while driving among teenagers—a dangerous practice that half of all American teenagers do monthly (Olson, Shults, & Eaton, 2013).

Adolescents' total media exposure—the amount of time they spend each day using one of the mass media—is extremely high, and substantially higher than it was 20 years ago. The average adolescent spends nearly 8 hours each day using one or more media, and this includes time spent using different media simultaneously (that is, where

Adults have worried about teenagers' exposure to mass media for centuries. Today it's the Internet. In the 1950s, it was comic books. © Mary Evans/National Archives/The Image Works

1 hour watching TV while on the Internet and talking on a cell phone would be recorded as only 1 hour of media use, even though it technically is 3 hours of exposure). Although adolescents' time spent viewing television programs at their regularly scheduled times has declined, the availability of recorded programs and television content on other devices (like computers) has led to an overall increase in time spent viewing video content. When media multitasking is taken into account, the amount of

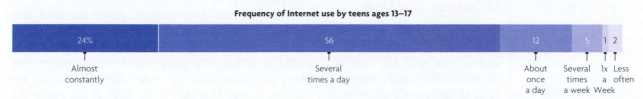

Frequency of Internet use by teens ages 13–17

24%	56	12	5	1	2
Almost constantly	Several times a day	About once a day	Several times a week	1x a Week	Less often Week

Figure 8   Virtually all American teens are online daily. One-fourth report being online "almost constantly."
(Lenhart, 2015)

time teenagers are *exposed* to media each day is close to 11 hours. The highest levels of media use are reported by early adolescents, and by Black and Hispanic teenagers (Rideout et al., 2010). The only type of media use that has not increased in the past decade is reading print materials. In 2009, adolescents spent only an average of 20 minutes a day reading words on a printed page.

There has been an enormous increase in the last decade in the amount of time adolescents spend on the Internet, in part because of easier access due to smartphones and in part because the Internet is now used to deliver content that had been delivered some other way in the past (e.g., watching television programs on Hulu rather than on a television, playing video games online rather than with an Xbox or PlayStation (Rideout et al., 2010). There is some research indicating that close to 10% of preadolescents and adolescents devote so much energy to playing video games that their behavior is "pathological" (Gentile et al., 2011; van den Eijnden, Spijkerman, Vermulst, van Rooij, & Engels, 2010). On some experimental tests of attention and self-control, individuals who report that their devotion to online gaming is a problem appear similar to individuals with other types of addiction (van Holst et al., 2012).

Online gaming appears particularly likely to be associated with compulsive Internet use (van Rooij, Schoenmakers, van den Eijnden, & van de Mheen, 2010). Given that most of these games involve violence (Strasburger, Jordan, & Donnerstein, 2010), it is not surprising that pathological video gaming is correlated with self-reported aggressive behavior (Ko, Yen, Liu, Huang, & Yen, 2009; Willoughby, Adachi, & Good, 2012), although, as you will read, in many media studies, it is hard to determine cause and effect (i.e., aggressive teenagers may be more drawn to aggressive games). The issue is further complicated by the fact that the impact of gaming on psychological development depends on the adolescent's motives for playing: Playing for fun decreases negative consequences, whereas playing to escape increases them (Hellström, Nilsson, Leppert, & Aslind, 2012). Plus, playing prosocial games can lead to increases in empathy, which may increase adolescents' inclinations to help others (Prot et al., 2013).

cultivation theory
A perspective on media use that emphasizes the impact media exposure has on individuals.

uses and gratification approach
A perspective on media use that emphasizes the active role users play in selecting the media to which they are exposed.

Theories of Media Influence and Use

The impact of the media on teenagers' behavior and development has been the subject of much debate and disagreement (J. Brown & Bobkowski, 2011b; Strasburger et al., 2010). It is extremely difficult to disentangle cause and effect, because adolescents choose which mass media they are exposed to and how much exposure they have (D. Roberts et al., 2009). Although it has been speculated that violent film images provoke aggression, for example, it is just as likely, if not more so, that aggressive adolescents are more prone to choose to watch violent images (Roe, 1995). Similarly, sexual behavior may be correlated with listening to "sexy" music or watching television programs with a lot of sexual content, but it is impossible to say which causes which (Steinberg & Monahan, 2011). And, although several major studies of media use (D. Roberts, Foehr, & Rideout, 2005; Rideout et al., 2010) have found that adolescents who report a lot of media use are significantly more troubled (bored, unhappy, in trouble at home or school) than adolescents who use these media less often, it is not known whether large doses of mass media cause problems, whether adolescents with more problems spend more time online, as a way of distracting themselves from their troubles or alleviating boredom, or both (Pea et al., 2012; Szwedo, Mikami, & Allen, 2011). It is important to keep in mind, too, that not all media exposure is the same, and that not all exposure is bad. Some adolescents use the Internet to stay up on the news (Lin, Cheong, Kim, & Jung, 2010). Mass media have been used successfully to communicate information about safe sex, dissuade teenagers from using tobacco and illicit drugs, and help chronically ill adolescents comply with their medication regimens (J. Brown & Bobkowski, 2011b; Strasburger et al., 2010).

There are three basic schools of thought concerning the media's impact (or lack thereof) on adolescent development. One argues that adolescents' knowledge about the world, attitudes and values, and behavior are influenced by the content to which they are exposed. You've no doubt heard contentions like these hundreds of times: Playing violent video games makes adolescents aggressive, watching sexy movies makes adolescents sex-crazed, being exposed to Internet pornography affects the ways that adolescents think about gender roles, listening to rap lyrics encourages adolescents to engage in violence and crime, viewing beer commercials during the Super Bowl makes adolescents drink beer, and so on. According to this view, the media shape adolescents' interests, motives, and beliefs about the world—a view known as **cultivation theory** (Gerbner, Gross, Morgan, & Signorelli, 1994).

A second school of thought, called the **uses and gratifications approach** (E. Katz, Blumler, & Gurevitch, 1974), stresses that adolescents choose the media to which they are exposed. According to this view, any correlation between what adolescents are exposed to and what they do or think is due not to the influence of the media, but to the fact that individuals with particular inclinations choose media that are consistent with their interests. Adolescents aren't randomly assigned to be exposed to various media, after all. They deliberately choose the media they use, either for entertainment, information, bonding with others, or developing a sense of identity. Aggressive adolescents are more likely to purchase violent video games because they enjoy being aggressive; teenagers who are interested in sex are more likely to look for pornography on the Internet because they want to masturbate or feel sexually aroused; adolescents who are involved with drugs like to listen to music that glorifies drug use; and beer-drinking adolescents are more likely to watch football and to be exposed to beer commercials (which, after all, is why beer companies advertise during football games and not on the Animal Planet network). According to this view, adolescents' preexisting interests and motives shape their media choices, rather than the other way around.

According to the third school of thought, adolescents' preferences and their media exposure affect each other. Moreover, adolescents not only choose what they are exposed to, but *interpret* the media in ways that shape their impact. This view is referred to as the **media practice model** (Steele & Brown, 1995).

Imagine two adolescents who accidentally stumble onto a sexually explicit website on the Internet. One, a sexually experienced teenager who is curious about pornography, views the website with interest—perhaps it even makes him feel aroused. The other, who isn't interested in sex, sees the very same content and feels repulsed. Not only is the experience not arousing, but it also makes him even less interested in having sex than he was before landing on the site. One 13-year-old sees a beer commercial and thinks, "That's how I'm going to party when I'm old enough to drink." Another sees the exact same images and thinks, "What idiots those people are—look how stupid beer makes you act." Two adolescents are flipping through television channels—one, who collects rap music, sees a flash of a Kendrick Lamar music video that grabs her interest and stops flipping channels to watch. The other, who is into country music, doesn't even notice the clip. According to the media practive model, the ways in which media do (or do not) affect adolescents depend on the ways in which the media are experienced and interpreted.

These problems in distinguishing among **correlation** (when two things go hand in hand), **causation** (when one thing actually causes another), **reverse causation** (when the correlation between two things is due not to the first thing causing the second, but to the reverse), and **spurious causation** (when the correlation between two things is due to the fact that each of them is correlated with some third factor) make it almost impossible to say for sure whether media exposure genuinely affects adolescent development (see Figure 9).

The only sure way to demonstrate cause and effect where media influence is concerned is to conduct an experiment in which people are randomly assigned to be (or not be) exposed to the medium to see how it affects them. But experiments of this are difficult to do well. Even the most ardent believers in the power of media influence acknowledge that one exposure to a commercial, movie, song, or Internet site is unlikely to change someone's behavior. If the impact of media exposure is incremental and cumulative—perhaps taking years of exposure to have an effect—it may be quite powerful but impossible to demonstrate in a brief experiment. All of this is to say that you should view any claims about the presence—or absence—of media influence on adolescent development with caution.

media practice model
A perspective on media use that emphasizes the fact that adolescents not only choose what media they are exposed to but also interpret the media in ways that shape their impact.

correlation
The extent to which two things vary systematically with each other.

causation
The correlation between two things attributable to the effect one thing has on the other.

reverse causation
Relationship in which the correlation between two things is due not to the first thing causing the second, but to the second causing the first.

spurious causation
Relationship in which the correlation between two things is due to the fact that each of them is correlated with some third factor.

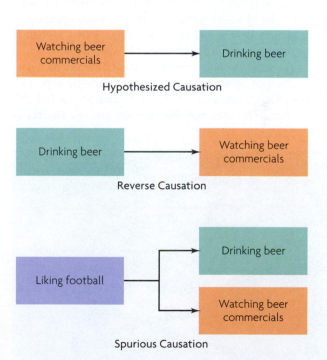

Figure 9   Two things can be correlated because the first causes the second (the hypothesized correlation), or some third factor causes both of them (spurious causation). Research on media "effects" on adolescent development has a hard time separating the three.

Adolescents' Exposure to Controversial Media Content

These chicken-and-egg problems notwithstanding, a few generalizations about media usage and adolescent development have enough supporting evidence, however indirect, to generate some consensus among experts. The bulk of the research has focused on the three topics about which adults are most concerned (some might say obsessed): sex, violence, and drugs.

Sex Sexual themes are ubiquitous on television, with more than 70% of all shows popular among teenagers containing sexual content, and with an average of nearly seven sexual scenes per hour (Kunkel, Eyal, Finnerty, Biely, & Donnerstein, 2005). Sexual content is found across virtually all television genres, so teenagers are exposed to sex on television whether their tastes run toward comedies, action shows, or dramas, although the context in which sex is depicted varies across different categories (Schooler, Sorsoli, Kim, & Tolman, 2009). Actually, the prevalence of sexual content in shows favored by adolescents declined a bit since 2000, most likely because of the increase in popularity of reality shows like *American Idol,* which have displaced shows with more sexual content (usually dramas) on the list of programs most watched by teenagers. Most sexual content on prime-time TV does not contain graphic images of individuals having sex, but instead is made up of humorous and suggestive comments. On daytime television, however, a lot of sexual imagery is of individuals engaging in passionate kissing and erotic touching. Sexual content is also common in music videos (L. M. Ward, 2003).

The most common sexual messages involve men seeing women as sex objects, sex as a defining aspect of masculinity, sex as a competition, and sex as fun and exciting. The message that women are sex objects is

Research on the impact of adolescents' exposure to sex on TV or in movies is controversial. © Mondadori/Getty Images

one that teenagers seem especially susceptible to (Ward, Vandenbosch, & Eggermont, 2015). Similar messages are carried in many music videos, in which men are shown as aggressive and dominant, and women are seen as the subservient objects of men's sexual advances (D. Roberts et al., 2009). One issue that has concerned many sex educators is the relative absence of messages concerning the possible physical consequences of sex (for example, pregnancy and STDs), although these messages have become more common now than in the past, in part because the entertainment industry has tried to respond more responsibly to concerns about the way sex has been portrayed (Kunkel et al., 2005). There are cross-cultural differences in the ways in which these messages are expressed, though: One study found that both losing one's virginity and becoming pregnant were depicted more positively in the Netherlands (where attitudes toward teen sex are more liberal) than in the United States (Joshi, Peter, & Valkenburg, 2014). There is plenty of sexual content in new media as well, and the content is typically more explicit than that in older media. Half of all adolescents have seen pornography on the Internet (J. Brown and Bobkowski, 2011b).

Whether and in what ways exposure to sexual media content affects adolescents' sexual development is controversial. Some studies have concluded that exposure to sex on television or online accelerates adolescents' sexual behavior, leading them to start having sex at an earlier age (Chandra et al., 2008; O'Hara, Gibbons, Gerrard, Li, & Sargent, 2012; R. L. Collins, Martino, Elliott & Miu, 2011). Others have found that adolescents who are interested in sex choose to expose themselves to more sexual content but are not affected by it (Steinberg & Monahan, 2011). Still others find evidence for both (Bleakley, Hennessy, Fishbein, & Jordan, 2008), or different effects on different adolescents. One recent study found that exposure to sexually explicit websites increased the likelihood of sexual activity among adolescents who had just entered puberty, but decreased it among those who were sexually mature (Vandenbosch & Eggermont, 2012).

Although questions remain about whether exposure to sexual media content alters adolescents' sexual *behavior,* many studies demonstrate that repeated exposure affects adolescents' attitudes, beliefs, and intentions (L'Engle, Brown, & Kenneavy, 2006; D. Roberts et al., 2009; L. M. Ward, 2003). For example, adolescents who watch a lot of music videos have more tolerant attitudes toward sexual harassment and more sex-stereotyped attitudes about sexual relationships (L. M. Ward, Hansbrough, & Walker, 2005). Other studies have found that exposure to explicit sex on the Internet is associated with having more permissive attitudes about sex and greater willingness to engage in sexual harassment (J. Brown & Bobkowski, 2011b; J. Brown & L'Engle, 2009). Whether such exposure affects adolescents' attitudes and behaviors because it changes their beliefs about what is normative, or whether it works by actually making adolescents more sexually aroused, is not known.

making the practical connection

Politicians often argue that the mass media adversely affects adolescents' development, and regularly propose legislation that would restrict adolescents' access to media content they believe is dangerous. What do you think about this? What policies, if any, do you support that would affect adolescents' access to mass media?

Violence Adolescents are also exposed to a great deal of violent imagery on television, in movies, in certain music genres, and in video games (J. Brown & Bobkowski, 2011a; D. Roberts et al., 2009). More than 60% of TV programming contains violence. Young people see about 10,000 acts of media violence each year, and more than one-fourth of all violent incidents on TV involve guns. By the age of 18, the typical adolescent will have seen about 200,000 violent acts just on television alone (Strasburger et al., 2010). The amount of violence in popular films has been on the rise (Figure 10) (Bleakley, Jamieson, & Romer, 2012).

Precise estimates of the amount of violent imagery in the most popular video games or other visual media are not available, but frequent concerns have been raised over the impact of violent video games on young people (Ivory, 2008; Strasburger et al., 2010). Adolescents who spend a lot of time playing violent video games get into more fights and arguments than their peers (Krahé, Busching, & Möller, 2012), but it is difficult to know whether playing such games makes adolescents more hostile or impulsive, whether adolescents who are more aggressive and impulsive to begin with are simply more likely to want to play violent games, or both (Adachi & Willoughby, 2013a; Gentile, Swing, Lim, & Khoo, 2012).

Moreover, how adolescents respond to video games varies as a function of whom they play them with; one study found that when adolescents played violent video games with their parents, they reported *declines* in aggression (Coyne, Padilla-Walker, Stockdale, & Day, 2011).

Experimental research on the effects of video games on adolescent behavior are inconclusive, with some studies finding small effects and others none at all (Ferguson, Garza, Jerabeck, Ramos, & Galindo, 2012), even among adolescents with mental health problems (Ferguson & Olson, 2014). Although controlled experiments have shown that exposure to the lyrics of violent songs increases individuals' aggressive thoughts (C. A. Anderson, Carnagey, & Eubanks, 2003; Coyne & Padilla-Walker, 2015), many experts doubt that playing violent video games or listening to music with violent lyrics causes adolescents to engage in the sorts of serious violent acts that alarmists have raised concerns about, such

Research has questioned the widespread belief that playing violent video games makes teenagers more aggressive.
© James Woodson/Digital Vision/Getty Images RF

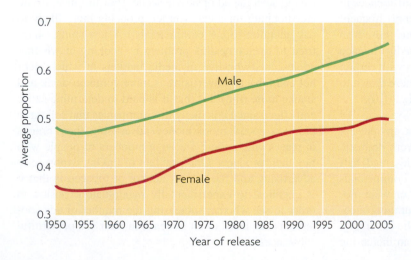

Figure 10 The proportion of male and female characters who engage in violence in top-grossing films has been increasing. (Bleakley et al., 2012)

as lethal school shootings. Indeed, careful studies of the impact of playing violent video games find that they do not make adolescents more aggressive (Ferguson, 2011; Ferguson & Kilburn, 2009), a point that was noted by a prominent group of social scientists in a brief submitted to the U.S. Supreme Court in *Brown v. Entertainment Merchants,* a 2010 case in which the Court ruled that a California law banning the sale of violent video games to minors was unconstitutional (Ferguson, 2013). As some have noted, given the millions of copies of violent games that have been sold, if playing video games had a significant impact on real-world violence, we'd likely be in the midst of a violence epidemic—yet juvenile violence has declined substantially since peaking in the early 1990s, despite the proliferation of violent video games (Reichhardt, 2003). In fact, one analysis indicated that the proliferation of violent video games has led to a *drop* in violent crime (Markey, Markey, & French, 2014). Nor is it clear that putting labels on games to alert adolescents and their parents to violent content is an effective strategy, anyway—this sort of labeling makes the games more, not less, attractive to teenagers (Bijvank, Konijn, Bushman, & Roelofsma, 2009).

In contrast to studies of video games, numerous studies have shown that repeated exposure to violent imagery on television leads to aggressive behavior in children and youth, especially among those who have prior histories of aggression (Robertson, McAnally, & Hancox, 2013). It is important to note, however, that other factors, such as experiences in the family or community, are likely far greater influences on adolescent violence than media exposure (Strasburger & Donnerstein, 1999). Nevertheless, it is now well established that exposure to TV violence in childhood is linked to aggressive behavior toward others in adolescence and adulthood, a heightened tolerance of violence, and greater desensitization to the effects of violence on others, although some of this effect is likely due to the tendency for people with aggressive tendencies to choose to watch violent programming (Huesmann, 2007; D. Roberts et al., 2009). For instance, although studies have found differences in brain anatomy between adolescents who report frequent exposure to television and movie violence and those who do not, it is not clear whether exposure to media violence causes brain changes or whether individuals with certain patterns of brain structure or function are more drawn to certain types of stimulation (Strenziok et al., 2010).

Drugs Alcohol, tobacco, or illicit drugs are present in nearly three-quarters of prime-time network dramatic programs, virtually all top-grossing movies, and half of all music videos. Nearly 10% of the commercials that young people see on TV are for beer or wine. For every public service announcement discouraging alcohol use, teenagers see 25–50 ads for alcoholic beverages. Plus, alcohol and tobacco companies have an increasing presence on the Internet (Jenssen, Klein, Salazar, Daluga, & DiClemente, 2009; Strasburger et al., 2010).

Adolescents are also exposed to alcohol and tobacco through films, which frequently depict actors smoking and drinking, a concern because teenagers are more likely to smoke if their favorite film star is a smoker (D. Roberts et al., 2009). Importantly, the effects of seeing smoking in movies are strongest among adolescents who are initially less inclined to take up smoking, which argues against the notion that adolescents' desire to smoke leads to their exposure to smoking in movies and suggests instead that exposure to smoking in movies may actually influence adolescents to start smoking. As a consequence of this research, movie distributors are now putting antismoking ads on DVDs of movies that contain scenes with smoking (Heatherton & Sargent, 2009).

Studies of exposure to ads for alcohol and tobacco, as well as antismoking commercial messages, have shown that they are effective in changing teenagers' attitudes about drinking and smoking, both positively and negatively (D. Roberts et al., 2009; Grenard, Dent, & Stacy, 2013; Scull, Kupersmidt, & Erausquin, 2013). Evaluations of media campaigns designed to reduce adolescent smoking, drinking, and drug use show that certain types of messaging may be more effective than others. Whereas emphasizing the questionable motives of the tobacco industry (as in the "Truth" campaign) has proven to be effective, repeated exposure to other kinds of antidrug messaging can lead adolescents to believe that drug use is more common than it actually is, inadvertently stimulating adolescents' interest in using drugs.

It is very hard to know whether changing adolescents' exposure to messages about drinking and smoking actually changes their behavior. Although adolescents who report having seen ads for alcohol or tobacco are more likely to drink and smoke, this correlation could be due to the fact that people who use and enjoy a product are simply more likely to attend to depictions of that product being used and are therefore more likely to report having seen the ad or movie scene. (For instance, if you are shopping for a car, you are probably more likely to pay attention to car commercials.) A few studies have tried to overcome this problem by looking at whether adolescents who live in media markets in which alcohol and tobacco advertising is more common drink and smoke more (they do), but it is hard to determine cause and effect, since it is likely that companies that sell these products spend more money advertising their brands in places where there are large numbers of people who buy their products. One problem in linking exposure to advertising and the use of alcohol or tobacco is that it is unethical to experimentally manipulate exposure in order to see whether increasing the number of ads adolescents see leads to an increase in their use of harmful substances.

Electronic Media and Adolescent Development

The increased availability of electronic communication has undoubtedly influenced the way that adolescents socialize. According to recent estimates, 80% of teens who are online (and virtually all adolescents are online) use social media. In keeping with the general notion that the main purposes of adolescents' media use, in addition to communication, are entertainment and information seeking, other sites that draw many teenage visitors are YouTube (for entertainment) and Google (for information).

The impact of Internet socializing on adolescents' behavior and development is interesting, poorly understood, and controversial. Among the main concerns that have been raised are whether communicating with friends and acquaintances electronically rather than in person is adversely affecting adolescents' development and whether strangers who might wish to harm young people, such as sexual predators, could use publicly posted information to establish relationships and initiate sexual contact with them.

Although many adults worry that the increased use of electronic communication has had an adverse impact on adolescents' social development, this does not seem to be the case.
© Blend Images - JGI/Jamie Grill/ Brand X Pictures/ Getty Images RF

Adolescent Development and the Internet Many parents are concerned that the large amount of time that teenagers spend on the Internet has had a negative effect on their social development and relationships. Some worry that electronic interactions have replaced face-to-face ones, to the detriment of the development of social skills. Still others worry that adolescents are forming relationships with strangers and that these may take time away from intimacy with "real" friends. And, of course, many simply worry that the sheer amount of time adolescents spend online is unhealthy because it has displaced other, more valuable activities.

Has adolescents' extensive use of the Internet affected their development and mental health? As the title of one book on the subject aptly conveys, "It's complicated" (Boyd, 2014). Many unanswered questions remain, but it looks as if the effects of Internet use—whether positive or negative—are much smaller than its proponents or detractors have claimed (Jackson, 2008).

We can safely assume that, to the extent that time on the Internet is displacing time spent in physical activity, it is having a detrimental impact on adolescents' physical health. Many adolescents suffer from sleep difficulties as a result of their late-night media use (Lemola, Perkinson-Gloor, Brand, Dewald-Kaufmann, & Grob, 2014). And the amount of time adolescents spend watching TV and playing video games is inversely linked to the amount of time they spend in physical activity (Motl, McAuley, Birnbaum, & Lytle, 2006). On average, the typical American 15-year-old spends at least 8 hours each day sitting in front of one sort of screen or another, but less than an hour in moderate physical activity (Nader, Bradley, Houts, McRitchie, & O'Brien, 2008;

Rideout et al., 2010). Health experts are concerned that the vast amounts of time teenagers spend on the Internet is sedentary, which is associated with obesity, high blood pressure, and other indicators of poor health (Goldfield et al., 2011; Mitchell, Pates, Beets, & Nader, 2013; Rosen et al., 2014). Most experts believe that the high rate of obesity among American teenagers is due, in part, to the large amount of time—estimated to be close to 60 hours a week—young people spend watching TV, playing video games, or online. Keep in mind, though, that while some of the time adolescents spend on the Internet displaces physical activity, a fair amount simply replaces time that would have been spent watching television, which is also correlated with obesity (Braithwaite et al., 2013).

Researchers have also asked whether adolescents use the Internet to acquire information that can improve their health or understanding of the world. To the extent that the Internet is used by adolescents to acquire accurate information, it can be a positive force. This may be especially true with respect to educating adolescents about healthy behavior, such as safe sex, in developing countries, where it is often difficult to reach a large audience of adolescents through classrooms (Borzekowski, Fobil, & Asante, 2006).

The ultimate value of the Internet as an educational tool depends on the quality and content of the information conveyed, as two studies of eating disorders illustrate. Whereas one study found that an Internet-based intervention was effective in reducing binge eating (M. Jones et al., 2008), another found that many adolescents with eating disorders visit websites that actually promote disordered eating (J. L. Wilson, Peebles, Hardy, & Litt, 2006). Similarly, whereas some message

Internet addiction
A disorder in which an individual's use of the Internet is pathological, defined by six symptoms: salience, mood change, tolerance, withdrawal, conflict, and relapse and reinstatement.

boards on the Internet devoted to self-injurious behavior, like cutting, can provide valuable social support to adolescents who compulsively injure themselves, others encourage the behavior and provide instructions on various cutting techniques (Mitchell, Wells, Priebe, & Ybarra, 2014). One study of race-related exchanges among adolescents on the Internet found plenty of examples of both hostile racist comments and civil discussions of racial tolerance (Tynes, 2007). Obviously, it is hard to generalize about the effects of spending time online without examining the content of the information that is exchanged.

Social communication on the Internet, like social communication face-to-face or over the phone, creates both positive and negative experiences (Szwedo, Mikami, & Allen, 2012). We hear a lot about things like cyberbullying, but two-thirds of adolescents report that things have happened through social networking that have made them feel better about themselves, and nearly 60% say that social networking has made them feel closer to someone. On the other hand, 25% of adolescents report that something that happened online led to a face-to-face argument with someone, and nearly that percent reported that something online led to the end of a friendship. Almost all adolescents report having seen someone post something mean about someone, but 85% have said that they had told someone posting mean things to stop (Lenhart et al., 2011).

Although many adults worry that adolescents' online friends will displace the friendships they maintain in person, this fear appears to be unfounded (Valkenburg & Peter, 2011). Using a social network site does not seem to amount to all that much more than finding an efficient way to stay in touch with friends (Reich, 2010). Most adolescents use the Internet to communicate with people they see in person, too (Underwood, Ehrenreich, More, Solis, & Brinkley, 2015). Similarly, although adolescents' media use can cut into time with their family, many families report that shared media use brings them closer. Shared media viewing plays a role in many families' rituals (e.g., watching the same shows or movies together on holidays) (Coyne, Padilla-Walker, Fraser, Fellows, & Day, 2014). And sharing time together, even time watching TV, provides opportunities for parents to learn more about their teenagers' activities. As one parent explained:

> See, my son's the type you have to drag things out of him as far as what happened in school or, you know, what's going on. He never says anything. Now, if we're watching a show or something and something comes up, you know, he may mention, oh, that happened, you know, the other day. So it kind of keeps me abreast of what's going on with that age group (Strasburger, Wilson, & Jordan, 2009, p. 499).

Even among those adolescents with both online and face-to-face friends, most maintain a balance of contact with each. But for a small proportion of teenagers (fewer than 5 percent), things get out of hand, and they develop what has been termed **Internet addiction** (Adiele & Olatokun, 2014; Kuss, van Rooij, Shorter, Griffiths, & van de Mheen, 2013; Smahel, Brown, & Blinka, 2012). Internet addiction is defined by six symptoms: *salience* (being online is the most important thing in life), *mood change* (one's mood fluctuates as a function of Internet experiences), *tolerance* (needing more and more Internet time to feel satisfied), *withdrawal* (experiencing negative feelings when prevented from being online), *conflict* (the Internet has caused problems in one's relationships or some other aspect of life), and *relapse and reinstatement* (returning to addictive Internet behavior after getting it under control).

A certain proportion of teenagers become so addicted to maintaining their online relationships that they may develop what has been nicknamed "Facebook depression," which is thought to be the result of spending too much time obsessing about one's online relationships (O'Keefe, Clarke-Pearson, & Council on Communications and Media, 2011). Frequent instant messaging, especially with acquaintances who are not close friends, can become compulsive and lead to feelings of depression (van den Eijnden, Meerkerk, Vermulst, Spijkerman, & Engels, 2008). Of course, it is not known whether these adolescents were especially prone to depression or would have developed these feelings as a result of ruminating about their offline friendships, and there is some evidence that compulsive Internet users are more introverted, less agreeable, and less emotionally stable (van der Aa et al., 2009). Not surprisingly, the impact of social media on adolescents' moods depends on what they learn when they check their accounts: When adolescents seek and find social support, they feel better; when they seek it but don't get it, they feel worse (Frison & Eggermont, 2015).

Studies find that more frequent online communication brings friends closer, perhaps because online communication facilitates self-disclosure. Communicating over the Internet with friends may be especially important for socially anxious adolescents, who may find it easier to interact online than in person (Antheunis, Schouten, & Krahmer, 2014; Dolev-Cohen & Barak, 2013; Forest & Wood, 2012). However, these same studies find that spending a lot of time in other online activities (e.g., watching videos) leads to *lower* quality relationships with one's close friends, presumably because the activities take time away from interacting with them. The Internet can help strengthen adolescents' close relationships if it is used to communicate with one's existing friends (and in this sense, using the Internet to stay in touch is probably not all that different from spending time with one's friends on the phone) (Ranney & Troop-Gordon, 2012), but has the potential to weaken friendships if it occupies the adolescent in activities that aren't shared, or cause adolescents to stress out if it leads friends to ruminate about their problems with each other (Murdock, Gorman, & Robbins, 2015).

As with other research in media "effects," studies of online behavior have difficulty separating cause and effect, and these problems are compounded when the research is actually conducted over the Internet, as much of it has been, since the samples in these studies are bound to be individuals who are online more frequently. Some evidence suggests that adolescents with relatively more psychological problems and poorer family relationships are more likely than their peers to form close online relationships with strangers, but we do not know whether having these sorts of online relationships leads to or follows from maladjustment (Szwedo, Mikami, & Allen, 2011; Wolak, Mitchell, & Finkelhor, 2003; Ybarra, Alexander, & Mitchell, 2005). It is quite plausible that adolescents who have problems simply are more likely to seek out relationships with people over the Internet (M. Gould, Munfakh, Lubell, Kleinman, & Parker, 2002). Despite the considerable media attention given to the topic, evidence linking psychological problems to excessive Internet use is inconsistent, with some studies linking high Internet use to insomnia, depression, social isolation, and missed school, but others finding no such effects (Israelashvili, Kim, & Bukobza, 2012; Jackson, 2008).

The Internet and Cognitive Development   Very few studies have looked at the impact of Internet or video game use on cognitive development, despite hopes that adolescents will benefit from having increased access to a world of information, and fears that the Internet will distract teenagers from more stimulating pursuits, like reading (an odd fear, given the fact that even before computers were so widespread, reading outside of school had been pretty much displaced by television). To date, research suggests that both the hopes and the fears are probably exaggerated (Hofferth & Moon, 2012). According to a study of more than 190,000 students from 22 countries, there is no evidence that adolescents' school performance is either helped or harmed by playing video games (Drummond & Sauer, 2014). A few studies show that playing video games may enhance visual skills, reaction time, hand-eye coordination, information-processing skills, and problem solving abilities (Adachi & Willoughby, 2013b; Buelow, Okdie, & Cooper, 2015; Ivory, 2008; Jackson, 2008). And, despite concerns about the impact of Internet use on brain development, credible scientific research on the topic is virtually nonexistent (Mills, 2014).

Sexual Predators, Pornography, and "Sexting"
Some parents are anxious about the ways in which the anonymity of the Internet may expose their teenagers to individuals who wish to harm them in some way, like sexual predators and cyberbullies. Despite the attention devoted to it in popular media, Internet bullying is a far less prevalent problem than is face-to-face bullying, and most cyberbullying is very mild, taking the form of ignoring or disrespecting the victim (Jackson, 2008). Is the same true for sexual predators on the Internet? Has this problem been exaggerated by media coverage as well? Yes it has.

According to the most recent Youth Internet Safety Survey, conducted by the U.S. Department of Justice, about 9% of young people received an unwanted sexual solicitation online in 2010, down from 19% in 2000 and 13% in 2005 (L. Jones, Mitchell, & Finkelhor, 2011a). The 50% decline during this 10-year period could be due to several factors, including successful efforts to teach adolescents Internet safety, publicity about the criminal prosecution of predators, and, most likely, the shift in online socializing from public chat rooms to social networking sites, which permit adolescents to limit their online contact to people they choose.

Although adults often express concerns about adolescents using the Internet to view pornography, much of the pornographic material on the Internet to which adolescents are exposed is unwanted rather than actively sought. In 2010, 15% of all adolescents reported receiving unwanted sexual material, although fewer than half said that they had received material that upset them (L. Jones et al., 2011a). The incidence of "sexting"— sending sexually explicit pictures over the Internet, usually by smartphone—is similarly exaggerated in the popular press. According to systematic surveys, only 1% of adolescents had sent or appeared in photos that showed naked breasts, genitals, or buttocks (K. Mitchell, Finkelhor, Jones, & Wolak, 2012). Evidently, those who are sending the pictures are sending them to multiple recipients, though—6% of adolescents reported having *received* a sexually explicit photo. (Adolescents who receive such photos rarely distribute them.) Rather than viewing sexting as having unique correlates, it makes more sense to view it as a specific instance of risk taking more generally. Teenagers who engage in sexting are more prone to other sorts of risky activity, including risky sex (Delevi & Weisskirch, 2013; Dir, Cyders, & Coskunpinar, 2013; Temple et al., 2014; Ybarra & Mitchell, 2014). Nor is it common for law enforcement officials to arrest adolescents for sexting; in most cases in which police take action, an adult has been involved (Wolak, Finkelhor, & Mitchell, 2012).

Despite adults' concern about the dangers the Internet poses to adolescents, the vast majority of teenagers use the Internet in ways that are not only benign, but similar to their parents: to stay in touch with friends, to download and enjoy popular entertainment, and to keep up with the world around them.

Mass Media and Adolescent Girls' Body Image

Several commentators have raised concerns about the messages to which young women are exposed in magazines aimed at them, especially in light of widespread body dissatisfaction among adolescent girls. The majority of articles in these magazines focus on dating and heterosexual relationships, and most emphasize the importance of physical attractiveness and thinness.

According to researchers, articles and advertisements in these magazines convey a clear message that attracting males by being physically beautiful is the road to true happiness for women. Adolescent girls who frequently read fashion magazines are more dissatisfied with their bodies than are girls who do not, and controlled experiments have indicated that showing girls images of thin models increases their body dissatisfaction (D. Roberts et al., 2009). Moreover, frequently reading magazine articles about dieting or weight loss leads to increases in unhealthy weight control behaviors, such as intentional vomiting and inappropriate use of laxatives (van den Berg, Neumark-Sztainer, Hannan, & Haines, 2007). There is also evidence that spending a lot of time on social networking sites can increase girls' body image concerns (Tiggemann & Slater, 2014). This is consistent with other research suggesting that adolescents' body image concerns are more strongly influenced by comparing themselves with people they know than with media figures (Ferguson, Muñoz, Garza, & Galindo, 2014).

Similar results are reported in studies of girls' responses to appearance-related commercials on television and websites, which, like ads in fashion magazines, typically feature attractive, thin models (Harrison & Hefner, 2008; Slater, Tiggemann, Hawkins, & Werchon, 2012), as well

as reality TV shows about cosmetic surgery (Ashikali, Dittmar, & Ayers, 2014; C. Markey & P. Markey, 2012). Although very few studies have examined the media's impact on males' body image, boys and men are more dissatisfied with their body after seeing advertising or music videos featuring muscular male models (Agliata & Tantleff-Dunn, 2004; Mulgrew, Volcevski-Kostas, & Rendell, 2013). Ironically, the same media that implicitly encourage adolescent girls to be thin and adolescent boys to be muscular devote considerable time and resources to encouraging adolescents to eat, and to eat unhealthy food, at that! More than one-quarter of the television advertisements seen by American adolescents are for food, beverages, or restaurants, with ads for candy, snacks, cereals, and fast food among the most frequent (J. Brown & Bobkowski, 2011b).

The Adolescent Consumer

A final, and very important, aspect of adolescent media use is economic. The size of the adolescent population, the prevalence of student employment, and the fact that adolescents save less than any other age group make young people an attractive target for a variety of businesses (Osgerby, 2008). Teenagers spend more than $90 billion per year, and the total amount of money spent by and for adolescents between 12 and 17 exceeds $200 billion annually (Packaged Facts, 2007). Although there has been a worldwide recession since 2008, 75% of teenagers report that they are receiving as much or more spending money than they did the previous year (Dolliver, 2010). Not surprisingly, much of adolescents' money is spent on discretionary purchases related to leisure activities. And, unfortunately, many adolescents spend money on alcohol and cigarettes—according to one estimate, underage drinkers account for about one-sixth of the $100 billion dollars spent each year on alcohol (Horner, Jamieson, & Romer, 2008).

We can certainly debate the merits of cultivating such strong consumer urges among the young and impressionable. Some critics contend that advertising aimed at teenagers takes advantage of the fact that they are more impulsive and self-conscious than adults (see Pechmann, Levine, Loughlin, & Leslie, 2005). On the other hand, America's economy is driven by consumer spending, and the segments of our economy that are devoted to leisure and recreation depend on the adolescent market. Among the most important industries are those connected with movies, music, sports, and television. Teenagers make up a large, and therefore influential, segment of the consumers of these products—as a glance at the local movie listings or a few minutes of channel-surfing will readily attest.

Adolescents' use of the Internet has led to the development of a wide variety of new strategies aimed at marketing products to this age group. These include targeted ads placed on social media websites like YouTube or

More than $200 billion is spent each year by or for teenagers.
© Purestock/PunchStock RF

Instagram, embedding promotional content into Twitter feeds or Facebook posts, branded websites (websites that are devoted to specific products), "advergaming" (placing advertisements within online games), online TV ads, branded apps for mobile devices, and **viral marketing,** a strategy that encourages people to pass on a marketing message to others (Common Sense Media, 2014). Because adolescents are likely to use technologies that can easily and instantly connect them to thousands of other teenagers, using young people to spread the word about new products is highly effective (Montgomery, Chester, Grier, & Dorfman, 2012).

The influence of the adolescent market extends well beyond the youth cohort, however—as evidenced by the uncanny predictability with which adult tastes in clothing and music often follow those of teenagers, albeit in a toned-down fashion. Teenagers often have considerable influence over their parents' purchases, which gives added incentive for advertisers to market products with young people's tastes in mind (Zollo, 2004).

Free Time and Adolescent Development

Adults have mixed feelings about adolescents' activities outside of school. On the positive side, adults take pride in watching their children's sports teams and creative activities, and they believe that these productive uses of leisure time help build character and teach important skills, such as teamwork and perseverance. (Think about all the movies you have seen about the character-building benefits of team sports.) Similarly, most adults view holding a part-time job as a worthwhile activity that provides opportunities for learning and the development of responsibility.

On the other hand, adults view many adolescent leisure activities as wasted time or, worse, as preludes to trouble. They worry about groups of teenagers cruising the mall; they cringe at images of adolescents riveted to their smartphones; they worry about adolescents' exposure to sex and violence on television, in film, in music, and on the Internet. Although we might wish for the "good old days" before the advent of smartphones, Facebook, Instagram, and video streaming, those good old days are long gone. And keep in mind that even during those supposed good old days, adults worried about how adolescents spent their idle time and about the corrupting influence of such evils as rock 'n' roll, dime-store romances, television, and comic books.

This mixed view of adolescents' free time reflects an interesting paradox about the nature of adolescence in modern society. Because industrialized society has "given" adolescents a good deal of free time, adults expect them to use it productively. But by definition, free time is supposed to be time that can be used for purposes other than being productive. Some theorists believe that

the existence of large blocks of uncommitted time is one feature of adolescence in modern society that has the potential to contribute in positive ways to young people's development. One potential benefit of participation in leisure activities is that it helps adolescents feel happier, more competent, and more connected to others (DesRoches & Willoughby, 2013; Leversen, Danielsen, Birkeland, & Samdal, 2012).

> **viral marketing**
> A way of promoting products or services by encouraging individuals to pass information on to others.

Many misconceptions about the pros and cons of various uses of free time abound. Most adults view participation in structured extracurricular activities as a good thing, and this seems to be the case. But most people are equally sure that working is good for teenagers, even though studies show that the costs of intensive involvement in part-time work during the school year outweigh the benefits. And, although adults believe that the mass media have a uniformly negative effect on adolescents' behavior, studies show that adolescents' interests affect their media use more than vice-versa.

The impact of the mass media on adolescent development has become especially controversial as the role of technology in adolescents' lives has expanded. Most adults, especially parents, are absolutely certain that nothing good comes from adolescents' exposure to video games, social media, and the Internet, and they often blame the mass media for a wide array of adolescents' problems—despite the fact that parents themselves exert a far greater influence on adolescent development than do any of the media about which they are often so alarmed. Moreover, because adolescents choose the media to which they are exposed, it is very difficult to demonstrate that adolescents are actually affected by what they see and hear. This is not to say that the media have no impact on adolescents' behavior and well-being. But we should be careful not to confuse cause and effect or overstate the strength of the media's influence. It is also important to keep in mind that the mass media can be used to promote positive behavior and healthy development, to provide information about a rapidly changing world, and to facilitate communication with others.

By valuing adolescents' free time only when it is used productively, adults may misunderstand the important functions that leisure time serves in the psychosocial development of young people. Free time plays an important role in helping young people develop a sense of themselves, explore their relationships with each other, and learn about the society around them (Coatsworth et al., 2005). A moderate amount of solitude (during which daydreaming is a central activity) is positively related to high school students' psychological well-being (Larson, 1997). And, for better or for worse, the mass media are globalizing adolescence, contributing to the development of a common culture that gives adolescents all over the world much to share.

Part 3 Psychosocial Development During Adolescence

8 Identity **9** Autonomy **10** Intimacy **11** Sexuality **12** Achievement **13** Psychosocial Problems in Adolescence

8 Identity

Identity as an Adolescent Issue

Changes in Self-Conceptions

Changes in the Content and Structure of Self-Conceptions

Dimensions of Personality in Adolescence

Changes in Self-Esteem

Stability and Changes in Self-Esteem

Group Differences in Self-Esteem

Antecedents and Consequences of High Self-Esteem

The Adolescent Identity Crisis

Erikson's Theoretical Framework

Identity Versus Identity Diffusion

The Social Context of Identity Development

Resolving the Identity Crisis

Problems in Identity Development

Research on Identity Development

Determining an Adolescent's Identity Status

Studying Identity Development Over Time

Identity and Ethnicity

The Development of Ethnic Identity

Discrimination and Its Effects

Multiethnic Adolescents

Identity and Gender

Gender-Role Development

Gender-Role Socialization during Adolescence

Masculinity and Femininity

What am I like as a person? You're probably not going to understand. I'm complicated! With my really close friends, I am very tolerant. I mean, I'm understanding and caring. With a group of friends, I'm rowdier. I'm also usually friendly and cheerful but I can get pretty obnoxious and intolerant if I don't like how they're acting. I'd like to be friendly and tolerant all of the time, that's the kind of person I want to be, and I'm disappointed when I'm not. At school, I'm serious, even studious every now and then, but on the other hand I'm a goof-off too, because if you're too studious, you won't be popular. So I go back and forth, which means I don't do all that well in terms of my grades. But that causes problems at home, where I'm pretty anxious when I'm around my parents. They expect me to get all A's, and get pretty annoyed with me when report cards come out. I care what they think about me, and so then I get down on myself, but it's not fair! I mean, I worry about how I probably should get better grades, but I'd be mortified in the eyes of my friends if I did too well. So I'm usually pretty stressed out at home, or sarcastic, since my parents are always on my case. But I really don't understand how I can switch so fast. I mean, how can I be cheerful with my friends, then coming home and feeling anxious, and then getting frustrated and sarcastic with my parents. Which one is the real me? (15-year-old girl, quoted in Harter, 2011, p. 311)

Because changes take place during adolescence in the ways people view and feel about themselves, the study of identity development has been a major focus of research and theory on adolescents (Harter, 2011). In this chapter, we examine why adolescence is a time of major changes in identity, why individuals differ in their patterns of identity development, and how the course of adolescent identity development is shaped by the nature of life in contemporary society.

Identity as an Adolescent Issue

Changes in the way we view and feel about ourselves occur throughout life. You have probably heard and read about the so-called midlife crisis—which is thought to occur during middle age. And certainly, important changes in self-conceptions and in self-image take place throughout childhood. When 4-year-olds and 10-year-olds are asked to describe themselves, the older children provide a far more complex self-portrait. Whereas young children restrict their descriptions to lists of what they own or like to do, older children are more likely to tell you about their personality as well.

If changes in identity occur throughout the life cycle, why have researchers who are interested in identity development paid so much attention to adolescence? One reason is that the changes in identity that take place during adolescence involve the first substantial reorganization and restructuring of the individual's sense of self at a time when he or she has the intellectual capability to appreciate fully just how significant the changes are. Although important changes in identity certainly occur during childhood, adolescents are far more self-conscious about these changes and feel them much more acutely.

Puberty and Identity Development Another reason for the attention that researchers and theorists have given the study of identity development during adolescence concerns the fundamental biological, cognitive, and social changes characteristic of the period. It is not hard to see why puberty plays an important role in provoking identity development during adolescence. When you change the way you look—for example, when you have your hair colored or cut in a different way, lose a great deal of weight, or dramatically change how you dress—you sometimes

Adolescence is often a time when individuals ask questions about who they are and where they are headed. Concerns with physical appearance often intensify. © Corbis RF/Corbis

feel as though your personality has changed, too. During puberty, when adolescents are changing so dramatically on the outside, they understandably have questions about changes that are taking place on the inside. Undergoing the physical changes of puberty may prompt fluctuations in one's self-esteem and self-conceptions.

Cognitive Change and Identity Development Just as the broadening of intellectual capabilities during early adolescence provides new ways of thinking about problems, values, and interpersonal relationships, it also permits adolescents to think about themselves in new ways. It is not until adolescence that people are able to think

possible selves
The various identities an adolescent might imagine for him- or herself.

future orientation
The extent to which an individual is able and inclined to think about the potential consequences of decisions and choices.

self-conceptions
The collection of traits and attributes that individuals use to describe or characterize themselves.

self-esteem
The degree to which individuals feel positively or negatively about themselves.

sense of identity
The extent to which individuals feel secure about who they are and who they are becoming.

in systematic ways about hypothetical and future events. This is manifested in two specific ways that have implications for identity development. First, adolescents become much more able to imagine their **possible selves**—the various alternative identities that they may adopt (Markus & Nurius, 1986). This may be related to the heightened self-consciousness characteristic of early adolescence. Brain-imaging studies find that patterns of brain activity during tasks in which individuals are asked to think about themselves differ significantly between adolescents and adults (Burnett et al., 2011; Pfeifer & Blakemore, 2012; Sebastian, Burnett, & Blakemore, 2008).

Second is an impressive increase in **future orientation**—the ability and tendency to consider the long-term consequences of one's decisions and imagine what one's life might be like in the years to come (Nurmi, 2004; Steinberg et al., 2009). It is not until adolescence that individuals typically begin to wonder, "Who will I become?" or "What am I really like?" Because the preadolescent child's thinking is concrete, it is difficult to think seriously about being a different person. But the changes in thinking that take place during adolescence open up a whole new world of alternatives.

Social Roles and Identity Development Finally, changes in social roles at adolescence open up a new array of choices and decisions. In contemporary society, adolescence is a time of important decisions about school, work, relationships, and the future. Facing these decisions about their place in society does more than provoke adolescents to ask questions about who they are and where they are headed—it *necessitates* asking them. At this point in life, young people must make important choices about their education and their commitments to other people, and thinking about these questions prompts them to ask more questions about themselves: "What do I really want out of life?" "What things are important to me?" "What kind of person would I really like to be?" Questions about the future, which inevitably arise as the adolescent prepares for adulthood, raise questions about identity (Côté, 2009).

Identity development is better understood as a series of interrelated developments—rather than one single development—that involve changes in the way we view ourselves in relation to others and in relation to the broader society in which we live. Generally, researchers and theorists have taken three different approaches to the question of how the individual's sense of identity changes during adolescence.

The first approach emphasizes changes in **self-conceptions**—the traits and attributes individuals see in themselves. A second approach focuses on adolescents' **self-esteem,** or self-image—how positively or negatively they feel about themselves. Finally, a third approach emphasizes changes in one's **sense of identity**—who one is, where one has come from, and where one is going.

Changes in Self-Conceptions

As individuals mature intellectually and undergo the sorts of cognitive changes characteristic of adolescence, they come to conceive of themselves in more sophisticated and more differentiated ways. Adolescents are much more capable than children of thinking about abstract concepts and considerably more proficient in processing large amounts of information. These intellectual capabilities affect the way in which individuals characterize themselves. Compared with children, who tend to describe themselves in relatively simple, concrete terms, adolescents are more likely to employ complex, abstract, and psychological self-characterizations (Harter, 2011). In addition, with development comes greater consistency between how individuals describe themselves and how they actually behave (Davis-Kean et al., 2008). There is also evidence that adolescents' ideas about the sort of person they would like to be (their "ideal self") become more stable over time (Zentner & Renaud, 2007).

Changes in the Content and Structure of Self-Conceptions

Self-conceptions change in structure and content during the transition from childhood into and through adolescence. They become more differentiated and better organized (Byrne & Shavelson, 1996). Let's first consider the idea that self-conceptions become more differentiated.

Differentiation of the Self-Concept In answer to the question "Who am I?" adolescents are more likely than children to link traits and attributes that describe themselves to specific situations, rather than using them as global characterizations. Whereas a preadolescent might say "I'm nice" or "I'm friendly," but not specify when or under what conditions, an adolescent is more likely to say "I'm nice if I'm in a good mood" or "I'm friendly when I am with people I've met before." The realization that their personality is expressed in different ways in different situations is one example of the increased differentiation that characterizes self-conceptions as adolescents mature toward adulthood.

There is another way in which self-conceptions become more differentiated at adolescence. Unlike characterizations provided by children, adolescents' self-descriptions take into account who is doing the describing (Harter, 2011). Teenagers distinguish between their own opinions of themselves and the views of others.

Suppose you ask people to describe how they behave when they are with others. Instead of saying, "I'm shy" or "I'm outgoing," an adolescent might say something more complicated, such as "People don't think I'm shy, but most of the time, I'm really nervous about meeting other kids for the first time." Adolescents also recognize that they may come across differently to different people, another type of differentiation in self-conceptions that does not appear until this age—for example, "My parents think I'm quiet, but my friends know I really like to party a lot." Neuroimaging studies show that adolescents' self-conceptions may be particularly sensitive to the opinions of others (Pfeifer et al., 2009).

Organization and Integration of the Self-Concept

With this shift toward increased differentiation in self-conceptions comes better organization and integration (Harter, 2011). When children are asked to describe themselves, the traits and attributes they list are often disorganized. Adolescents, in contrast, are likely to organize and integrate different aspects of their self-concept into a more logical, coherent whole. Whereas a younger child may list a sequence of several traits that appear to be contradictory ("I am friendly, and I am shy"), an adolescent will attempt to organize apparently discrepant bits of information into more highly organized statements ("I am shy when I first meet people, but after I get to know them, I'm usually pretty friendly").

Self-conceptions continue to become more psychological well into the high school years. The increased psychological complexity of self-conceptions may present some difficulties, though, when adolescents become able to recognize—but not yet quite understand or reconcile—inconsistencies and contradictions in their personality. The proportion of adolescents who give opposite traits in self-descriptions, who feel conflicts over such discrepancies, and who feel confused over such discrepancies increases markedly between 7th and 9th grades and then declines somewhat (Harter & Monsour, 1992). When asked to reflect on contradictions in their personalities, early, middle, and late adolescents respond in very different ways, as the following examples illustrate (Harter, 1990, p. 358):

> I guess I just think about one thing about myself at a time and don't think about the other until the next day. (11–12 years old)

> I really think I am a happy person and I want to be that way with everyone, but I get depressed with my family and it really bugs me because that's not what I want to be like. (14–15 years old)

> You can be shy on a date, and then outgoing with friends because you are just different with different people; you can't always be the same person and probably shouldn't be. (17–18 years old)

Although the recognition that one's personality is multifaceted—even contradictory—may initially cause some distress, it has a number of advantages in the long run. Some psychologists have suggested that the development of a more complicated view of the self is one way that individuals cope with the recognition of their faults and weaknesses, a recognition that comes with increased self-awareness ("I'm not really a nasty person, I just act mean when people tease me"). Consistent with this, adolescents who have more complex and clearer self-conceptions are less likely to become depressed or anxious (Van Dijk et al., 2014).

Another advantage of having a more differentiated self-concept is the ability to distinguish among one's self (who one really is), ideal self (who one would like to be), and feared self (who one most dreads becoming). An important aspect of having a healthy self-concept is having an ideal self to balance a feared self. Delinquent adolescents are less likely than nondelinquent youth to have this sort of balanced view; although delinquent adolescents might dread becoming criminals, for instance, they may not have a positive ideal self (for example, being successfully employed) to balance this fear (Oyserman & Markus, 1990).

False-Self Behavior   Another interesting consequence of adolescents' recognition that they are not always consistent in their personality concerns their ability to distinguish between their true and false selves (that is, their authentic and inauthentic selves). Adolescents are most likely to behave inauthentically in romantic

Adolescence is a time during which individuals begin to knowingly present themselves to others in ways that are inauthentic.
© Ken Karp/The McGraw-Hill Education Inc.

false-self behavior
Behavior that intentionally presents a false impression to others.

five-factor model
The theory that there are five basic dimensions to personality: extraversion, agreeableness, conscientiousness, neuroticism, and openness to experience.

and dating situations and with classmates, and they are least likely to put on a false front with close friends. **False-self behavior**—acting in a way one knows is inauthentic—occurs less often with parents than with dates, but more often with parents than with close friends (Harter, 2011). Although adolescents sometimes say that they dislike false-self behavior, they also say that sometimes it is acceptable, such as when trying to impress another person or hide an aspect of their personality that others do not like. You can easily imagine how the ability to put on a false front would come in handy when meeting someone for the first time.

Adolescents differ in the degree to which they present false fronts and in their reasons for doing so. In general, adolescents who report less emotional support from parents and peers, who have low self-esteem, and who are relatively more depressed and hopeless are more likely to engage in false-self behavior (Impett, Sorsoli, Schooler, Henson, & Tolman, 2008). The connection between false-self behavior and low self-esteem runs in both directions; some adolescents engage in false-self behavior because they have low self-esteem, whereas others experience a drop in self-esteem because they knowingly put on a false front. Depression and hopelessness are highest among adolescents who engage in false-self behavior because they genuinely devalue their true self, in contrast to those who put on a false front because they want to please others, or because they are experimenting with different personalities (Harter, Marold, Whitesell, & Cobbs, 1996).

making the personal connection

When was the last time you put on a false self? What was your motivation? How did you feel afterward?

Understanding how self-conceptions change during adolescence helps to explain why issues of identity begin to take on so much importance at this stage. As self-conceptions become more abstract, and as young people become more able to see themselves in psychological terms, they become more interested in understanding their own personalities and motivations. The distress caused by recognizing one's inconsistencies may spur identity development. You may recall having wondered as a teenager about your personality development, the influences that shaped your character, and how your personality had changed over time: "Am I more like my father or like my mother? Why do my sister and I seem so

different? Will I always be so nervous?" Although these sorts of questions may seem commonplace to you now, in all likelihood, you did not think about these things until adolescence, when your own self-conceptions became more abstract and more sophisticated.

Dimensions of Personality in Adolescence

While many researchers have studied adolescent personality development by examining young people's self-conceptions, others have used standardized inventories designed to assess important aspects of personality. Most researchers who study personality use the **five-factor model** (McCrae & John, 1992). According to this model, there are five critical personality dimensions, often referred to as the "big five": *extraversion* (how outgoing and energetic someone is), *agreeableness* (how kind or sympathetic), *conscientiousness* (how responsible and organized), *neuroticism* (how anxious or tense), and *openness to experience* (how curious and imaginative). Although the five-factor model was developed through research on adults, it has been successfully applied to adolescents, too (Caspi, 1997; McCrae et al., 2002). For example, delinquent adolescents are more likely than their peers to score high in extraversion and low in agreeableness and conscientiousness, whereas adolescents who are high achievers in school score high in conscientiousness and openness (John, Caspi, Robins, Moffitt, & Stouthamer-Loeber, 1994). The five-factor model applies equally well across groups of adolescents from different ethnic backgrounds (Markstrom-Adams & Adams, 1995; Rowe, Vazsonyi, & Flannery, 1994).

There are both genetic and environmental influences on personality, although the environment becomes somewhat more important as people age (Kandler, 2012). Individuals may inherit temperamental predispositions (such as a high activity level or an inclination to be sociable), which are observable early in life, and these predispositions may "harden" and become organized into personality traits partially in response to the environment (Caspi, 2000; Gest, 1997). An active and sociable child who enjoys interacting with others may be rewarded for doing so and, over time, become extraverted. Both temperament and personality become increasingly stable as we grow older, in part because we tend to spend time in environments that reward and reinforce the traits that draw us to these settings (B. Roberts & DelVecchio, 2000). As a result, we become more like ourselves every day!

Between childhood and mid-adolescence, people become less extraverted, perhaps as they become more self-conscious, and less conscientious, perhaps as they begin to become more emotionally autonomous from their parents (Van den Akker, Deković, Asscher, & Prinzie, 2014). The rate of change in personality begins to slow during the early 20s (Syed & Seiffge-Krenke, 2013). Between adolescence and young adulthood, individuals continue to become less extraverted, but as they mature, they become more conscientious, more agreeable, more resilient, and more emotionally stable (Meeus, Van de Schoot, Klimstra, & Branje, 2011; Van den Akker et al., 2014). Girls mature earlier than boys emotionally, but boys catch up over time, so that by the end of adolescence, there are few gender differences in maturity (De Bolle et al., 2015; Klimstra, Hale, Raaijmakers, Branje, & Meeus, 2009).

In sum, many core personality traits, such as impulsivity or timidity, are stable between childhood and adolescence and between adolescence and young adulthood (McCrae et al., 2002; Specht, Luhmann, & Geiser, 2014; van Aken, Hutteman, & Denissen, 2011). Although the external manifestations of these traits may change with age (for example, anxiety may appear as bed-wetting in early childhood but as nervous talkativeness in adolescence), our basic, underlying traits turn out to be remarkably unchanging. For example, individuals who displayed relatively higher levels of aggression in preadolescence, temper tantrums during childhood, or negative emotions during infancy are more likely to behave aggressively as adolescents (Caspi, Henry, McGee, Moffitt, & Silva, 1995; Hart, Hofman, Edelstein, & Keller, 1997). Similarly, individuals who had difficulty controlling their impulses as preschoolers are more likely to be rash, aggressive, and sensation seeking as adolescents and young adults, whereas individuals who were inhibited as young children tend to be relatively more timid, anxious, and shy. Not surprisingly, individuals who are well-adjusted in early and middle childhood tend to be resilient and competent in adolescence (Gest, 1997; Hart et al., 1997; Shiner, Masten, & Tellegen, 2002). Despite popular stereotypes about adolescence as a time of "rebirth," research does not show that adolescence is a time of tumultuous upheaval in personality.

Changes in Self-Esteem

It's long been believed that the "storm and stress" of adolescence creates problems in self-esteem—how adolescents evaluate themselves. This turns out not to be true. But although there isn't a dramatic drop in self-esteem at this age, adolescents' feelings about themselves fluctuate from day to day, particularly during the early adolescent years. From about age 14 on, self-esteem is highly stable (Birkeland, Melkevik, Holsen, & Wold, 2012). And, despite commentary in the popular press about the excessively high self-esteem characteristic of today's teenagers, careful statistical analyses show that there has been no appreciable increase in American adolescents' self-esteem during the past several decades (Trzesniewski & Donnellan, 2009).

Stability and Changes in Self-Esteem

The stability of a trait (like intelligence or self-esteem) has nothing to do with the degree to which people change with age, because stability merely refers to the extent to which individuals' relative ranking within a group stays more or less the same over time. Height, for instance, is a stable trait (tall children tend to become tall adults) that nevertheless changes a great deal with age (individuals grow taller between childhood and adulthood). Asking whether self-esteem changes during adolescence (whether people's view of themselves becomes more positive or negative) is not the same as asking whether self-esteem is stable during this period (whether individuals with high self-esteem as children are likely to have high self-esteem as adolescents).

Self-esteem becomes increasingly more stable between childhood and early adulthood, suggesting that adolescents' feelings about themselves gradually consolidate over time, becoming less likely to fluctuate in response to different experiences (Erol & Orth, 2011; Trzesniewski, Donnellan, & Robins, 2003) (see Figure 1). Day-to-day fluctuations in mood tend to become smaller between early adolescence and late adolescence (Larson, Moneta, Richards, & Wilson, 2002).

Studies of *changes* in self-esteem as individuals move through adolescence have not yielded consistent findings, partly because researchers have focused on different aspects of individuals' self-image. Some studies find that individuals' feelings about themselves become more

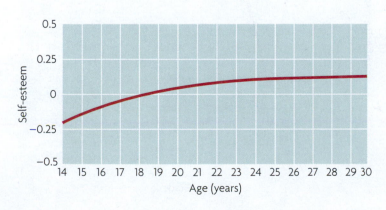

Figure 1 Self-esteem increases during adolescence but begins to level off as individuals enter young adulthood. (Erol & Orth, 2011)

Self-esteem (y-axis: −0.5, −0.25, 0, 0.25, 0.5)
Age (years) (x-axis: 14 15 16 17 18 19 20 21 22 23 24 25 26 27 28 29 30)

negative over the course of adolescence (Jacobs, Lanza, Osgood, Eccles, & Wigfield, 2002), but others find that they become more positive (Orth & Robins, 2014). In general, however, changes in self-perceptions (whether positive or negative) are greater during early adolescence than during middle or late adolescence (Liu & Xin, 2014) (see Figure 2). From middle adolescence through young adulthood, self-esteem either remains at about the same level or increases (Chung et al., 2014; Côté, 2009; Orth & Schmitt, 2015). Although there is a general trend for individuals' average mood to become less positive over the course of adolescence (children are usually in a more positive mood than young adolescents, who are generally in a better mood than older adolescents), this trend begins to level off around age 16 (Larson et al., 2002). Teenagers who experience frequent fluctuations in mood also report higher levels of anxiety and depression (Maciejewski et al., 2014).

Although adolescence is not a time of storm and stress, problems in self-image may arise for a brief period during early adolescence. To fully understand why, it is necessary to distinguish among three aspects of adolescents' self-image: their self-esteem (how positively or negatively they feel about themselves), their **self-consciousness** (how much they worry about their self-image), and their **self-image stability** (how much their self-image changes from day to day) (Simmons, Rosenberg, & Rosenberg, 1973).

Fluctuations in adolescents' self-image are most likely to occur between the ages of 12 and 14. This is a time of major changes in brain systems that regulate how we think about ourselves and others (Pfeifer & Peake, 2012). Interestingly, the brains of adolescents with relatively higher self-esteem tend to have stronger connections between areas of the brain that regulate how we think about ourselves and areas that control feelings of reward (Chavez & Heatherton, 2015). Compared with preadolescents or older adolescents, young adolescents have lower self-esteem, are more self-conscious, and have a more unstable self-image. Generally, the differences between preadolescents and early adolescents are greater than those between younger and older adolescents, which indicates that the most marked fluctuations in self-image occur during the transition into adolescence, rather than over the course of adolescence itself (Thomaes, Poorthuis, & Nelemans, 2011).

The extent to which an individual's self-esteem is volatile is itself a stable trait. Young adolescents whose self-image fluctuates a lot from moment to moment are likely to develop into older adolescents who experience the same thing (Savin-Williams & Demo, 1983). Young adolescents with the most volatile self-image report the highest levels of anxiety, tension, and adjustment problems (Molloy, Ram, & Gest, 2011; Rosenberg, 1986). This is especially likely among adolescents who have a great deal of stress in their day-to-day lives (Tevendale, DuBois, Lopez, & Prindiville, 1997). Having a volatile self-image may make individuals especially vulnerable to the effects of stress.

Fluctuations in self-image during early adolescence probably are due to several interrelated factors. First, the sort of egocentrism that is common in early adolescence may make young adolescents painfully aware of others' reactions to their behavior. Second, as individuals become more socially active, they begin to learn that people play games when they interact, and they learn that it is not always possible to tell what others are thinking on the basis of how they act or what they say. This ambiguity may leave young adolescents— who are relatively unskilled at this sort of "impression management"—puzzled and uncomfortable about how they are really viewed by others. Finally, because

self-consciousness
The degree to which an individual is preoccupied with his or her self-image.

self-image stability
The degree to which an individual's self-image changes from day to day.

Figure 2 Changes in self-esteem are greater in early adolescence than during middle adolescence. This graph shows levels of self-esteem averaged across more than 35,000 students drawn from many studies of Chinese adolescents. (Liu & Xin, 2014)

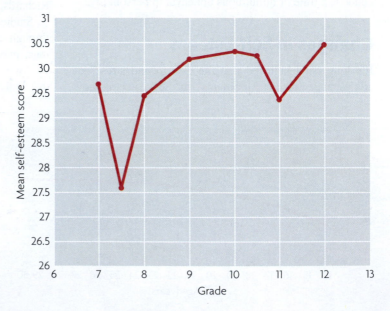

of the increased importance of peers, young adolescents are especially interested in their peers' opinions of them. For the first time, they may have to come to terms with contradictions between the messages they get from their parents ("That haircut you just got makes you even prettier—you look great with short hair") and the messages they get from their friends ("You'd better wear a hat until your hair grows back!"). Hearing contradictory messages can create uncertainty about oneself (Rosenberg, 1986).

The Wrong Question? Studies of age differences in self-esteem often hide substantial differences among people of the same age. Some adolescents have very stable self-esteem over time, whereas others do not (Birkeland et al., 2012; Morin, Maïano, Marsh, Nagengast, & Janosz, 2013). Not surprisingly, adolescents with better family and peer relationships are more likely than their peers to maintain positive self-esteem or develop enhanced self-esteem over time (Diehl et al., 1997). Similar variability in patterns of life satisfaction has also been reported (Tolan & Larsen, 2014) (see Figure 3).

Some critics of studies of the stability of self-esteem in adolescence also question the validity of examining self-esteem in such a general sense. Although most research on adolescent self-esteem has focused on teenagers' overall feelings about themselves, young people evaluate themselves both globally, which may be a good indicator of general psychological well-being, but also along several distinct dimensions, such as academics, athletics, appearance, social relationships, and moral conduct (Côté, 2009). As a consequence, it is possible for an adolescent to have high self-esteem when it comes to academic abilities, low self-esteem when it comes to athletics, and

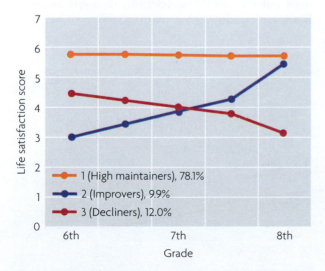

Figure 3 Life satisfaction over the middle school years. Nearly 80% of middle school students report consistently high satisfaction with life. Only about 10% reported a drop in life satisfaction between grades 6 and 8 (adapted from Tolan & Larsen, 2014).

moderate self-esteem when it comes to physical appearance, social relationships, or moral behavior.

Components of Self-Esteem Within broad domains of self-esteem (for example, academics, athletics, or social relationships), adolescents often have quite differentiated views of themselves. For example, adolescents' evaluations of their social competence within the context of their relationships with their parents may be very different from the way they see themselves in the context of their relationships with teachers, which in turn may differ from their evaluations of themselves in the peer group (Harter, Waters, & Whitesell, 1998). Even within the realm of peer relationships, adolescents' social self-esteem may vary depending on whether they are thinking about their friendships or their romantic relationships (Connolly & Konarski, 1994). Therefore, it may be misleading to characterize an adolescent's "social self-esteem" as low or high without specifying the relationship being referred to. The same goes for academic self-esteem: Because students evaluate their abilities in specific subject areas both in comparison to other students ("I am terrible at math compared to everyone else in this class") and relative to their abilities in other subject areas ("I am so much better at math than I am at history"), making sweeping statements about an adolescent's overall academic self-image is often unwise (Arens, Yeung, Craven, & Hasselhorn, 2011; Marsh & Hau, 2004).

Do some aspects of self-esteem contribute more to an adolescent's overall self-image than others? Yes, they do. Adolescents' physical self-esteem—how they feel about their appearance—is the most important predictor of overall self-esteem, followed by self-esteem about relationships with peers (Harter, 1999). Less important are self-esteem about academic ability, athletic ability, or moral conduct. Interestingly, although researchers find that adolescents' physical self-esteem is the best predictor of their overall self-esteem, adolescents, when asked, say that their physical appearance is one of the least important contributors to how they feel about themselves. In other words, adolescents are often unaware of the degree to which their self-worth is based on their feelings about their appearance (DuBois, Tevendale, Burk-Braxton, Swenson, & Hardesty, 2000). Physical self-esteem is a more important influence on overall self-esteem among girls than boys, although both genders' self-esteem is linked to how they feel about their appearance (Kistler, Rodgers, Power, Austin, & Hill, 2010; Thomaes et al., 2011; van den Berg, Mond, Eisenberg, Ackard, & Neumark-Sztainer, 2010). These findings help to explain why girls are more likely than boys to experience self-image difficulties and depression.

Group Differences in Self-Esteem

Sex Differences Early adolescent girls are more vulnerable to disturbances in their self-image than any other

Early adolescent girls' self-esteem is lower, their degree of self-consciousness is higher, and their self-image is shakier than is the case for boys. © Paul/Getty Images RF

group of youngsters. Compared to early adolescent boys, early adolescent girls' self-esteem is lower, their degree of self-consciousness is higher, and their self-image is shakier. Girls also are more likely than boys to say negative things about themselves, to feel insecure about their abilities, and to worry whether other people like being with them. Sex differences in adolescents' self-perceptions become smaller over the course of adolescence (Fredricks & Eccles, 2002).

Sex differences in self-esteem are most pronounced among White adolescents. Similar patterns have been found among Hispanic adolescents but not, for the most part, among Black adolescents (Erkut, Szalacha, Garcia Coll, & Alarcon, 2000; van den Berg et al., 2010). Studies

of Black girls do not find the same sort of self-esteem vulnerability as is found in studies of White girls, in part because Black girls do not experience the same drop in body image during puberty (K. Brown et al., 1998) (see Figure 4).

Why would girls have greater self-esteem problems during early adolescence than boys? The answer may be related to the special significance of physical appearance and acceptance by peers in determining self-esteem. Because young girls are more concerned than boys about physical attractiveness, dating, and peer acceptance, they may experience a greater number of self-image problems. Because Black girls do not feel as negatively about their appearance as White or Hispanic girls, they have higher overall self-esteem and show less of a decline in self-esteem over adolescence (Gray-Little & Hafdahl, 2000; Malanchuk & Eccles, 1999).

Ethnic Differences   Black adolescents on average have higher self-esteem than White adolescents, who, in turn, tend to have higher self-esteem than Hispanic, Asian, or Native American youth (Biro, Striegel-Moore, Franko, Padgett, & Bean, 2006; Twenge & Crocker, 2002). Several studies indicate that Asian American adolescents have particularly low self-esteem relative to their peers (e.g., Herman, 2004), a finding that some researchers have attributed to higher rates of peer rejection (Niwa, Way, & Hughes, 2014).

A number of researchers have asked why Black adolescents have such high self-esteem, given the prevalence of prejudice in American society and the generally disadvantaged position of Black individuals in the workplace and school, two institutions where individuals' performance influences their self-image. There are three main explanations for the relatively high self-esteem of Black adolescents.

Figure 4   **Race differences in patterns of change in girls' physical self-esteem.**
(K. Brown et al., 1998)

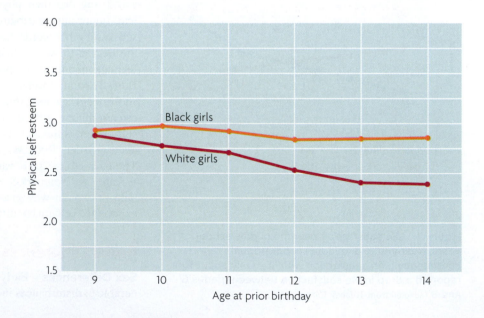

First, despite their encounters with racism and prejudice, Black teenagers often benefit from the support and positive feedback of adults in the Black community, especially in the family (Gaylord-Harden, Ragsdale, Mandara, Richards, & Petersen, 2007). This is not surprising, given the wealth of research showing that the approval of significant others is an especially powerful influence on adolescents' self-esteem—much more so than the opinion of the broader society (e.g., Gray-Little & Hafdahl, 2000; Whitesell, Mitchell, Kaufman, & Spicer, 2006).

Second, all teenagers—minority and otherwise—tend to shift their priorities over time so that they come to value those activities at which they excel or that are valued within the context in which they live. The self-esteem of adolescents who grow up in more "collectivistic" cultures, where getting along with others is especially important, is more tied to their social competence than is the case among teenagers in more individualistic societies (Santo et al., 2013). Adolescents are able to protect their self-esteem by focusing on some traits rather than others. A boy who is an outstanding student but who feels physically unattractive and does not do well in sports will likely derive positive self-esteem from his school achievement and not restrict his self-evaluation to his looks or performance on the playing field. One way that Black adolescents may respond to their relatively poorer school performance is to change their feelings about the importance of doing well in school, which weakens the connection between academic success and self-esteem. (Minimizing the importance of doing well in school may protect one's self-esteem, which is good, but it leads to poorer school achievement, which is not.)

Adolescents who attend schools in which they are in the ethnic minority may suffer greater self-esteem problems than their peers who attend schools in which they are in the majority. Although desegregation may have a positive impact on minority adolescents' academic achievement, this benefit may be counterbalanced by the apparently negative impact of desegregation on minority students' self-image. © Thinkstock/Comstock Images/Getty Images RF

Finally, the very strong sense of ethnic identity that exists among Black adolescents enhances their overall self-esteem (DuBois, Burk-Braxton, Swenson, Tevendale, & Hardesty, 2002; Gaylord-Harden et al., 2007). Ethnic differences in self-esteem, favoring Black adolescents, have increased over the past 25 years (perhaps because ethnic identity has become a more relevant issue in society) and are greater during adolescence than childhood (perhaps because ethnic identity is a more salient issue during adolescence than before) (Twenge & Crocker, 2002).

Ethnic differences also exist in patterns of change in self-esteem during adolescence. In one study of Black, Latino, and Asian urban adolescents, Black students and biracial students (mainly Black/Latino) had higher self-esteem in early adolescence, and this remained high throughout the adolescent years. In contrast, Latino students had relatively lower self-esteem early in adolescence, but caught up with their Black peers by the end of high school. Asian students began with the lowest self-esteem, and it remained lower than that of other groups over time (see Figure 5). Similar patterns were found in a large national sample of American youth (Erol & Orth, 2011). In contrast to studies of White adolescents, there were no sex differences in levels or patterns of change in self-esteem in this sample of ethnic minority adolescents.

The ethnic diversity of the context in which adolescents develop has a substantial impact on their self-image. High school students who live in a social environment or go to a school in which their ethnic or socioeconomic group is in the minority are more likely to have

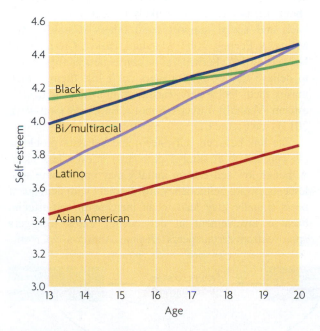

Figure 5 Ethnic differences in patterns of self-esteem over time. (Greene & Way, 2005)

self-image problems than those who are in the majority (Rosenberg, 1975). This seems to be true with regard to religion, socioeconomic status, ethnicity, and household composition. Black teenagers, for example, have a higher opinion of themselves when they go to schools in which Black students are a majority than when they attend predominantly White schools, where they may feel out of place and under pressure to play down their cultural heritage. By the same token, Jewish adolescents have higher self-esteem in schools in which there are many other Jewish students than in schools in which Jews compose a small minority of the student body. Similarly, levels of maladjustment are higher among both Hispanic and non-Hispanic youngsters when they are in the minority in their school (Kaufman, Gregory, & Stephan, 1990).

Antecedents and Consequences of High Self-Esteem

Several researchers have examined the link between self-esteem and adolescent behavior in an attempt to see whether certain sorts of experiences contribute—either positively or negatively—to adolescents' feelings about themselves. Others have posed the question in reverse: Does having high (or low) self-esteem lead adolescents to behave in particular ways?

Influences on Self-Esteem Self-esteem is enhanced by having the approval of others, especially parents and peers, and by succeeding in school (Birkeland, Bfreivik, & Wold, 2014; Chung et al., 2014; Ojanen & Perry, 2007). These correlates of high self-esteem have been found in virtually all ethnic and cultural groups, although the self-esteem of Asian youngsters seems especially influenced by their academic success (e.g., Szesulski, Martinez, & Reyes, 1994). Thus, even though there are ethnic differences in average levels of self-esteem, the correlates of self-esteem are similar in different ethnic groups (Rowe et al., 1994). Being close to one's parents and feeling like a good son or daughter are also associated with higher self-esteem, but it isn't clear which one leads to the other (Harris et al., 2015; Kiang, 2012).

Adolescents whose self-esteem is too wrapped up in the approval of others—especially the approval of peers—may be at risk for developing self-image problems, since peer acceptance may fluctuate over time (Harter, Stocker, & Robinson, 1996). Adolescents who derive their self-esteem relatively more from peers than from teachers or parents show more behavioral problems

and poorer school achievement (DuBois, Felner, Brand, & George, 1999). One explanation for the increase in problem behavior that takes place over the course of adolescence is that adolescents tend to look relatively more to their peers for social support as they get older (DuBois, Burk-Braxton et al., 2002).

Consequences of High or Low Self-Esteem Although it once was believed that enhanced self-esteem leads to school success, there actually is little evidence for this, and a lot of evidence that things go in the opposite direction (e.g., J. Schmidt & Padilla, 2003). Academic success leads to improvements in how adolescents feel about themselves, not the other way around. These findings cast doubt on the logic behind programs designed to raise teenagers' school performance by increasing their self-esteem. High self-esteem during adolescence does enhance adolescents' well-being, however, whereas low self-esteem may lead to mental health problems, both in the short run (Orth & Robins, 2013) and well into adulthood (Trzesniewski et al., 2006), although this may be due to the fact that many of the same factors that contribute to high self-esteem in adolescence (such as achievement) are themselves stable over time and correlated with self-esteem at later ages (Boden, Fergusson, & Horwood, 2008).

The relationship between low self-esteem and emotional and behavioral problems is complicated (Gerard & Buehler, 2004; Tram & Cole, 2000). Low self-esteem is one of several symptoms of depression, but it appears that low self-esteem is more likely to lead to depression than the reverse (Orth, Robins, Widaman, & Conger, 2014). One reason that low self-esteem may lead to depression is that adolescents with negative feelings about themselves are less likely to seek positive feedback and social support from others (Cassidy, Ziv, Mehta, & Feeney, 2003; Marshall, Parker, Ciarrochi, & Heaven, 2014). Perhaps as a consequence, they come to believe that other teenagers don't like them, which makes them feel lonely, further diminishing their self-esteem (Vanhalst, Luyckx, Scholte, Engels, & Goossens, 2013) (see Figure 6).

The link between self-esteem and behavior problems (as opposed to emotional problems) is even less clear. Although low self-esteem initially may impel some adolescents toward delinquency, involvement with delinquent peers actually may lead to an increase in self-esteem, because involvement in delinquency earns teenagers approval from certain peers (Dishion, Andrews, & Crosby,

Figure 6 Low self-esteem often discourages adolescents from seeking out social support from others, which can lead to feelings of loneliness.

1995; W. Mason, 2001). Furthermore, adolescents with high self-esteem are more likely to experiment with alcohol than are those with low self-esteem (Scheier, Botvin, Griffin, & Diaz, 2000), most probably because high self-esteem is associated with being in the more popular social crowds, in which drinking is more common.

The Adolescent Identity Crisis

Many of literature's most important novels, from classics like *Jane Eyre, Portrait of the Artist as a Young Man,* and *The Catcher in the Rye* to more contemporary stories like *The Fault in Our Stars, The House on Mango Street, The God of Animals,* and *The Perks of Being a Wallflower,* revolve around an adolescent's identity crisis. The coming-of-age novel is a classic literary genre.

If you were asked to write a novel about your own identity development, what would you mention? Perhaps you would talk about developing a sense of purpose, or clarifying long-term plans and values, or becoming more confident about who you really are and where you are headed (Hill, Burrow, & Summer, 2013). If these are the sorts of things that come to mind when you think about identity development in adolescence, you are thinking about an aspect of development that psychologists refer to as the sense of identity. The dominant view in the study of adolescent identity development emphasizes precisely these aspects of psychosocial development, and the theorist whose work has been most influential in this area is Erik Erikson.

Erikson's Theoretical Framework

Erikson's (1959, 1963, 1968) theory developed out of his clinical and cross-cultural observations of young people at various stages of development. He viewed the developing person as moving through a series of eight psychosocial crises over the course of the life span. Each crisis, although present in one form or another at all ages, takes on special significance at a given period of the life cycle because biological and social forces interact to bring the crisis into prominence.

Erikson believed that the establishment of a coherent sense of identity—what he called the crisis of **identity versus identity diffusion**—is the chief psychosocial crisis of adolescence. The maturational and social forces that converge at adolescence force young people to reflect on their place in society, on the ways that others view them, and on their options for the future.

Identity Versus Identity Diffusion

Prior to adolescence, the child's identity is like patches of fabric that have not yet been sewn together. But by the end of adolescence, these pieces of cloth will have been woven into a unique patchwork quilt.

Achieving a balanced and coherent sense of identity is intellectually and emotionally taxing. According to Erikson, it is not until adolescence that one even has the mental or emotional capacity to tackle this task. He believed that the key to resolving the crisis of identity versus identity diffusion lies in the adolescent's interactions with others. By responding to the reactions of people who matter, the adolescent selects and chooses from among the many elements that could conceivably become a part of his or her identity. The other people with whom the young person interacts serve as a mirror that reflects back information about who he or she is and ought to be. As such, the responses of significant others shape the adolescent's developing sense of identity. Through others' reactions, adolescents learn whether they are competent or inept, attractive or ugly, socially adept or awkward. Perhaps more importantly—especially during periods when their sense of identity is still forming—adolescents learn from others what they do that they ought to keep doing, and what they do that they ought to stop.

One process through which this occurs is via the sharing of important memories with others (McLean, Syed, Yoder, & Greenhoot, 2014). When we tell stories to friends or family members about our previous experiences, we do so for a variety of reasons, one of which is to help ourselves understand who we are and how we were changed by the experience. In one study of college undergraduates (McLean, 2005), students were asked to describe occasions in the past year in which they shared an important memory with another person. One participant described the following event, which took place when he was in high school:

> I was at my friend's house one night with my main group of friends. They were all smoking marijuana and drinking. I did not feel comfortable with trying marijuana. They tried hard to get me to try it, but I chose not to. One of my friends (my best) supported my choice. *I learned who my real friends were. But more important, I learned that I can be strong with my decisions if I choose to, regardless of the outside influence.*

He then described telling his college friends about the event:

> The subject of drugs came up and so I explained the above story to them. They seemed to enjoy the story and applauded me on my resiliency. Now, my friends here [at college] will ask me if I want to do anything and they will not harass me about it, regardless of my answer. *It pays to be strong when you want to.* (McLean, 2005, p. 687, italics in original)

Increasingly, adolescents use social media, like Facebook, to accomplish this (Davis, 2013; Jordán-Conde,

identity versus identity diffusion
According to Erikson, the normative crisis characteristic of the fifth stage of psychosocial development, predominant during adolescence.

psychosocial moratorium
A period during which individuals are free from excessive obligations and responsibilities and can therefore experiment with different roles and personalities.

Mennecke, & Townsend, 2014). The key point is that developing an identity is a social as well as mental process. Erikson placed a great deal of weight on the role of others (and, especially, on those individuals who have influence over the adolescent) in shaping the adolescent's sense of self. The adolescent's identity is the result of a mutual recognition between the young person and society: The adolescent forges an identity, but, at the same time, society identifies the adolescent.

The Social Context of Identity Development

The social context in which the adolescent attempts to establish a sense of identity exerts a tremendous impact on the nature and outcome of the process. If the adolescent's identity is forged out of a recognition on the part of society, society will play an important role in determining which sorts of identities are possible alternatives. And of those identities that are genuine options, society will influence which are desirable and which aren't. As a consequence,

the course of identity development varies over different historical eras, in different cultures, and among different subcultures within the same society (Kroger, 1993).

The social context also influences whether the search for self-definition will be a full-blown crisis or a more manageable challenge. The more alternatives available to the young person and the more arenas in which decisions must be made, the more difficult establishing a sense of identity will be. Growing up in contemporary America, where adolescents have a range of careers to decide among, for example, is far more likely to provoke an occupational identity crisis than is growing up in a small agrarian community in which each young person continues farming the family's land.

The rapid rate of social change in most of the world has raised new and more complex sets of questions for young people to consider—questions not only about occupational plans but also about values, lifestyles, and commitments to other people. Today, even in some countries where until recently individuals had little choice about the life they would lead, adolescents must ask themselves what sort of work they want to do; if they want to remain single, live with someone, or marry; and if and when they want to have children. The likelihood of going through a prolonged and difficult identity crisis is probably greater today, and more prevalent around the world, than it has ever been.

making the cultural connection

During the past 10 years, there have been dramatic political changes in much of the Arab world. Do you think that changes in these societies' "identity" will lead to changes in patterns of adolescent identity development?

The Psychosocial Moratorium   According to Erikson, the complications inherent in identity development in modern society have created the need for a **psychosocial moratorium**—a "time out" during adolescence from excessive responsibilities and obligations that might restrict the pursuit of self-discovery. Adolescents in contemporary America are given a moratorium of sorts by being encouraged to remain in school for a long time, where they can think seriously about their plans for the future without making irrevocable decisions. For adolescents who can tolerate not knowing where they are headed and who use this time to gather information and explore a variety of options, the moratorium can be an exhilarating experience. For others, though, the moratorium is a period of uncomfortable and anxious indecision (Meeus, van de Schoot, Keijsers, & Branje, 2012).

During the psychosocial moratorium, the adolescent can experiment with different roles and identities in a context that permits and encourages exploration. The

Role experimentation during adolescence often involves trying on different looks, images, and patterns of behavior. According to theorists such as Erik Erikson, having the time and freedom to experiment with different roles is an important prelude to establishing a coherent sense of identity. © SW Productions/Brand X Pictures/ Getty Images RF

experimentation involves trying on different postures, personalities, and ways of behaving—sometimes to the consternation of the adolescent's parents, who may wonder why their child's personality seems so changeable. One week, an adolescent girl will spend hours putting on makeup; the next week, she will insist to her parents that she is tired of caring so much about the way she looks. An adolescent boy will come home one day with a shaved head and piercings, and a few weeks later he will discard this image for that of a preppie. Although many parents worry about their teenage children going through these sorts of phases, much of this behavior is normal experimentation.

Having the time to experiment with roles is an important prelude to establishing a coherent sense of identity. But role experimentation can take place only in an environment that allows and encourages it (Côté, 2009). Without a moratorium, a full and thorough exploration of the options and available alternatives cannot occur, and identity development will be impeded. According to Erikson, adolescents must grow into an adult identity, rather than be forced into one prematurely.

It is clear that the sort of moratorium Erikson described is an ideal; indeed, some might even consider it to be a luxury of the affluent. Many young people—perhaps even most—do not have the economic freedom to enjoy a long delay before taking on the responsibilities of adult life. For many youngsters, alternatives do not exist in any realistic sense, and introspection only interferes with the more pressing task of survival. Does the 17-year-old who has to drop out of school to work a full-time job go through life without a sense of identity? Do youngsters who cannot afford a psychosocial moratorium fail to resolve the identity crisis?

Certainly not. But from Erikson's perspective, the absence of a psychosocial moratorium in some adolescents' lives—either because of restrictions they place on themselves, restrictions placed on them by others, or their life circumstances—is truly regrettable. The price these youngsters pay is not the failure to develop a sense of identity but lost potential. You may know people whose parents forced them into prematurely choosing a certain career or who had to drop out of college and take a job they really did not want because of financial pressures. Without a chance to explore, to experiment, and to choose among options for the future, these adolescents may not realize all that they are capable of becoming. It is easy to see how the broader context in which adolescents grow up affects this. Think, for example, of how individuals' plans for the future may have had to change during the Great Recession that began in 2008.

Resolving the Identity Crisis

Is establishing a sense of identity something that is conscious? According to Erikson, it is. It is experienced as a sense of well-being, a feeling of "being at home in one's body," a sense of knowing where one is going, and an inner assuredness of recognition from those who count. It is a sense of sameness through time—a feeling of continuity between the past and the future.

Establishing a coherent sense of identity takes a long time. Most writers on adolescence and youth believe that identity exploration continues well into young adulthood. But rather than thinking of the adolescent as going through a single identity crisis, it probably makes more sense to view the phenomenon as a series of crises that may concern different aspects of the young person's identity and that may surface—and resurface—at different points in time throughout the adolescent and young-adult years. During adolescence, the feeling of well-being associated with establishing a sense of identity is often fleeting. Ultimately, however, the identity crisis of adolescence, when successfully resolved, culminates in a series of basic life commitments: occupational, ideological, social, religious, ethical, and sexual (Côté, 2009).

Problems in Identity Development

Given the wide variations in developmental histories that individuals bring to adolescence and the wide variations in the environments in which they develop, it is not surprising to find differences in the ways in which individuals approach and resolve the identity crisis. Problems in identity development can result when someone has not successfully resolved earlier crises, or when the adolescent is in an environment that does not provide the necessary period of moratorium. Three sorts of problems received special attention from Erikson: identity diffusion, identity foreclosure, and negative identity.

Identity Diffusion   **Identity diffusion** is characterized by an incoherent, disjointed, incomplete sense of self. It can vary in degree from a mild state of not quite knowing who one is while in the midst of an identity crisis to a more severe, psychopathological condition that persists beyond a normal period of exploration. Identity diffusion is marked by disruptions in the individual's sense of time (some things seem to happen much faster than they really do, while others seem to take forever); excessive self-consciousness, to the point that it is difficult to make decisions; problems in work and school; difficulties in forming intimate relationships with others; and concerns over sexuality. In other words, identity diffusion is reflected not only in problems of identity but also in the areas of autonomy, intimacy, sexuality, and achievement.

A classic example of an adolescent in the throes of identity diffusion is Holden Caulfield in the novel *The Catcher in the Rye*. He has flunked out of

identity diffusion
The incoherent, disjointed, incomplete sense of self characteristic of not having resolved the crisis of identity.

Some adolescents fail to thoroughly engage in the process of identity exploration because their parents have selected an identity for them. Erikson called this "identity foreclosure."
© JGI/Jamie Grill/Blend (RM)/Corbis

identity foreclosure
The premature establishment of a sense of identity, before sufficient role experimentation has occurred.

negative identity
The selection of an identity that is obviously undesirable in the eyes of significant others and the broader community.

several prep schools, has severed most of his friendships, and has no sense of where he is headed. At one point, walking up Fifth Avenue in New York City, Holden says, "Every time I came to the end of a block and stepped off the goddam curb, I had this feeling that I'd never get to the other side of the street. I thought I'd just go down, down, down, and nobody'd ever see me again. Boy, did it scare me" (Salinger, 1951/1964, pp. 197–198).

Identity Foreclosure   Some young people bypass—either willingly or unwillingly—the period of exploration and experimentation that precedes the establishment of a healthy sense of identity. Instead of considering a range of alternatives, these adolescents prematurely commit themselves to a role, or series of roles, and settle upon a certain identification as a final identity. In essence, these individuals are not given—or do not take advantage of—a psychosocial moratorium. A college freshman who made up her mind about becoming a doctor at the age of 13 may enroll in a rigid premed curriculum without considering other career possibilities. The circumvention of the identity crisis is called **identity foreclosure.**

Typically, the roles adopted in the process of identity foreclosure revolve around the goals set for the young person by parents or other authority figures. The adolescent may be led into these roles directly or may be forced into them indirectly, by being denied a true psychosocial moratorium. Perhaps the parents of the would-be doctor have arranged their child's school schedule and summer vacations so that all of her spare time is spent taking extra science courses. No time is left for role experimentation or introspection. Individuals who have bypassed the identity crisis have made commitments, but they have not gone through a period of experimentation before making them. Identity foreclosure is an interruption of the identity development process, one that interferes with the individual's discovery of his or her full range of potentials.

Negative Identity   Adolescents sometimes appear to select identities that are obviously undesirable to their parents and their community. The examples are familiar: the daughter of the local district attorney who repeatedly gets into trouble with the law, the son of prestigious and successful parents who refuses to go to college, the child of a devoutly religious family who insists that he or she is a confirmed atheist. Because the establishment of a healthy sense of identity is so intimately tied to the recognition of the adolescent by those who matter, the adoption of a so-called **negative identity** is a sign of problems in identity development. The adolescent who adopts a negative identity is recognized by those around him or her, but not in a way that fosters healthy development.

Selecting a negative identity usually represents an attempt to forge some sense of self-definition in an environment that has made it difficult to establish an acceptable identity. This appears to be especially likely when, after repeatedly trying and failing to receive positive recognition from those who are important in their lives, adolescents turn to a different, perhaps more successful, route to being noticed. Consider this example: The son of successful parents is a good student but not quite good enough to please his excessively demanding parents. He feels he is a nobody in his parents' eyes, so he drops out of school to play guitar in a band—something his parents vehemently oppose. As Erikson pointed out, most adolescents would rather be somebody "bad" than nobody at all.

making the practical connection

Are there any aspects of today's environment that might make the resolution of the identity crisis especially difficult? Can you think of anything that might be done to help facilitate healthy identity development?

Research on Identity Development

The term *identity status* refers to the point in the identity development process that characterizes an adolescent at a given time. In order to determine an individual's identity status, most researchers have used an approach that focuses on the processes of exploration (experimenting with different ideas about occupations, values, relationships, and so forth) and commitment (making choices among various alternatives) (Marcia, 1966). Some theorists (e.g., Luyckx, Goossens, & Soenens, 2006) distinguish between two different stages: exploration in "depth" (making a commitment to an identity and then exploring one's options) and exploration in "breadth" (exploring one's options and then making a further commitment). Others (e.g., Meeus, 2011) see identity development as a more dynamic process, with individuals moving back and forth between commitment and exploration over time. In all of these frameworks, the important point is that healthy identity involvement requires experimentation and exploration before finalizing one's choices about work, love, and lifestyle.

Determining an Adolescent's Identity Status

In identity status research, based on their responses to an interview or questionnaire, individuals are assigned to one of four identity states ("state" is the right word, because research shows that individuals move from state to state, and not necessarily in an orderly fashion): (1) identity achievement (the individual has established a coherent sense of identity—that is, has made commitments after a period of exploration), (2) moratorium (the individual is in the midst of a period of exploration), (3) identity foreclosure (the individual has made commitments but without a period of exploration), or (4) identity diffusion (the individual does not have firm commitments and is not currently trying to make them).

Research employing this approach has supported many aspects of Erikson's theory (Meeus, 2011; Meeus et al., 2012). The strongest support comes from studies that show a pattern of correlations between various traits and the different identity statuses that are consistent with predictions based on Erikson's model. For example, individuals who are in a state of identity achievement are psychologically healthier than others on a variety of measures: They score highest on measures of achievement motivation, moral reasoning, intimacy with peers, and career maturity. Individuals in the midst of a moratorium score highest on measures of anxiety, show the highest levels of conflict over issues of authority, and are themselves the least rigid and least authoritarian. Individuals classified as being in the foreclosure status have been shown to be the most authoritarian and most prejudiced and to have the highest need for social approval, the lowest level of autonomy,

and the greatest closeness to their parents. Individuals in a state of identity diffusion display the highest level of psychological, behavioral, and interpersonal problems: They are the most socially withdrawn and most likely to engage in antisocial behavior and show the lowest level of intimacy with peers (Crocetti, Klimstra, Hale, Koot, & Meeus, 2013; Meeus, 2011).

Ways of Resolving the Identity Crisis Several researchers have also described the ways in which different individuals resolve the identity crisis (e.g., Berzonsky, 2004). It is possible to differentiate among individuals who tend to actively seek information and approach identity-related decisions with an open mind (having an "informational" orientation), those who attempt to conform to family and other social expectations and try to get identity-related decisions over as quickly as possible (a "normative" orientation), and those who tend to procrastinate and avoid making identity-related decisions (a "diffuse/avoidant" orientation). The informational orientation is more characteristic of identity achievers, the normative orientation is more characteristic of individuals who are identity foreclosed, and the diffuse/avoidant orientation is more characteristic of individuals who exhibit identity diffusion.

More evidence of this sort comes from a study that attempted to link classifications based on a measure of identity development with scores on the personality dimensions tapped within the five-factor model of personality (Clancy & Dollinger, 1993). Adolescents who were classified as identity achievers were higher in extraversion and less neurotic than other adolescents; foreclosed adolescents were less open; and diffused adolescents were more neurotic, less open, and less agreeable. It was not clear from this study whether different personality constellations led to different patterns of identity development or, alternatively, whether different patterns of identity development influenced subsequent personality. Given what we know about the childhood antecedents of personality traits, the former explanation (that personality affects identity development) seems more likely than the latter (Klimstra, 2013; Luyckx, Teppers, Klimstra, & Rassart, 2014).

One of the defining characteristics of individuals who have achieved a coherent sense of identity, at least in contemporary American society, is that they approach life's decisions with a strong sense of **agency**—they take responsibility for themselves, feel in control of their decisions, and have confidence that they will be able to overcome obstacles along the way (Côté, 2000). Studies of college students from different ethnic groups have shown that a strong sense of personal agency is predictive of identity achievement across ethnic and socioeconomic groups (e.g., Schwartz, Côté, & Arnett, 2005). Being "in charge" of one's life may be especially important in contemporary industrialized society, where the transition to adulthood is prolonged and individuals are faced with a tremendous number of identity-related decisions. Individuals in their

Most research indicates that the chief period for identity development is in late adolescence, when many individuals are enrolled in college. © Robert Daly/Caia Image/Glow Images RF

agency
The sense that one has an impact on one's world.

late teens or early 20s who, when asked whether they are adolescents or adults, say they are not sure, are less likely to have achieved a sense of identity than are those who are certain that they have reached adulthood (L. J. Nelson & Barry, 2005). It is not clear whether having a coherent sense of identity leads one to think of oneself as an adult or, instead, whether seeing oneself as an adult leads one to have a more coherent sense of identity. But it does seem that becoming an adult, at least in industrialized society, is a psychological transition as well as one characterized by entering the formal roles of adulthood.

What sorts of parenting practices are associated with different identity statuses? Generally, individuals whose identity development is healthy are more likely to have had authoritative homes characterized by warm, but not excessively constraining relations (Berzonsky, 2004; W. Beyers & Goossens, 2008; Dumas, Lawford, Tieu, & Pratt, 2009). People who grow up in these environments are encouraged to assert their individuality but remain connected to their families. Typically, the absence of parental warmth is associated with problems in making commitments—the most extreme case being identity diffusion—whereas the absence of parental encouragement of individuality is associated with difficulties exploration (Côté, 2009).

Studying Identity Development Over Time

In order to examine the development of a sense of identity, researchers have done both cross-sectional studies (comparing individuals of different ages) and longitudinal studies (following the same individuals over a period of time). Many of these studies have challenged some widely held beliefs about the nature of identity development in adolescence (Côté, 2009; Meeus, 2011).

First, studies show that a coherent sense of identity generally is not established before age 18, let alone earlier in adolescence, as originally theorized (Côté, 2009). This is especially true among boys, who tend to lag behind girls in identity development in early and middle adolescence but catch up by late adolescence (as is the case with emotional maturity more generally) (Klimstra Hale, Raaijmakers, Branje, & Meeus, 2010). There is clearly a decline with age in the proportion of individuals who are in a state of moratorium or diffusion (Klimstra et al. 2010; Meeus, Van de Schoot, Keijsers, Schwartz, & Branje, 2010). But the proportion of individuals who are in a state of identity achievement before late adolescence is low. In general, when comparisons are made among groups of individuals of different ages over the span from 12 to 24, differences in identity status are most frequently observed between groups in the 18- to 21-year-old range. Few consistent differences emerge in comparisons of teenagers in the middle adolescent years. Although self-examination may take place throughout adolescence, the consolidation of a coherent sense of identity does not begin until very late in the period (Côté, 2009). The late teens and early 20s appear to be the critical times for a sense of identity to crystallize (Nurmi, 2004; Schwartz, Côté, & Arnett, 2005). Although individuals engage in more of this sophisticated self-reflection as they mature through adolescence, attempts to speed up this process, by training individuals to think more about how specific life events had played a role in their development, are not effective (Habermas & de Silveira, 2008).

Second, changes in identity status are less systematic than originally had been hypothesized. Although we might expect that individuals move from a state of diffusion to a state of foreclosure or moratorium, and then either remain foreclosed or move to a state of identity achievement, not all individuals follow this pattern. In one study of Dutch youth, nearly 60% of the individuals classified as in a state of identity diffusion were no longer classified that way 4 years later, and nearly 75% of individuals who were in the midst of a moratorium at the beginning of the study were no longer in this category at the later assessment (Meeus, Iedema, & Vollebergh, 1999). But two-thirds of individuals who looked like they had foreclosed the identity development process were in the midst of an identity crisis 4 years later, suggesting that foreclosure may be a temporary stage rather than a permanent one, at least for some adolescents. Other studies have come to similar conclusions (Côté, 2009).

Moreover, in these same studies, a large proportion of individuals who were at one point classified as "identity achieved" status later shifted status over the course of the study, indicating that "achievement," like "foreclosure," may be temporary (Meeus et al., 2010). In the

Dutch study, for example, half of the adolescents who were classified as identity achieved at the first assessment were not classified this way 4 years later.

How could some individuals who at one point had apparently resolved their identity crisis actually not have resolved it—at least, not in any final sense? According to some writers, these sorts of regressions to a less mature identity status are part of the normal process of identity development (Kroger, 2003). The achievement of a sense of identity in adolescence is not a final state, but a step on a long route toward the establishment of a mature sense of self.

Finally, many individuals who show signs of identity diffusion early on remain in this state, as do many individuals who spend time in a state of moratorium. In other words, there are some individuals who are perpetually confused (at least during adolescence and young adulthood) about who they are, as well as others who seem to be always exploring and experimenting with new identities (Meeus et al., 2010). Individuals who are high in anxiety have an especially difficult time (Crocetti, Klimstra, Keijsers, Hale, & Meeus, 2009).

The factors associated with changing from one identity status to another are not well understood (Kroger & Green, 1996; LaVoie, 1994). Psychologists have been much better at describing the various stages that adolescents move through over the course of their identity development than at explaining why or how individuals' sense of identity changes when it does. The little research that has been done on this subject indicates that turning points in the development of a sense of identity are provoked both by internal factors—discontent with one's life, for example—and by specific life events or changes in life circumstances, such as making the transition out of high school (Kalakoski & Nurmi, 1998; Kroger & Green, 1996). Individuals are able to "make meaning" out of these turning points, using the event to come to a better understanding of themselves (Kang, Okazaki, Abelmann, Kim-Prieto & Lan, 2010; McLean, Breen, & Fournier, 2010; Tavernier & Willoughby, 2012). When adults look back on their life and attempt to tell a story that makes sense, they tend to put more weight on events that took place during adolescence and young adulthood, a phenomenon that has been described as a "reminiscence bump" (Thorne, 2000).

making the scientific connection

Adults tend to refer back to adolescence more than other periods when creating a narrative about their life. Do you think this is because events during adolescence *are* more important in shaping one's life, because events during adolescence are simply remembered more clearly, because adolescence is the first time that individuals begin creating a life story, or for some other reason?

Because college provides a psychosocial moratorium for many people, researchers have asked whether college attendance facilitates identity development (Côté, 2009). This has proven to be a difficult question to answer. While studies have found that the proportion of college students who are classified as identity achieved increases from around 20% during freshman year to as many as 40% by senior year, whether this development can be attributed to the college experience is hard to say, since this increase might have taken place just as a result of maturation (Pascarella & Terenzini, 2005). Although in theory one could test this by comparing identity development among college students with late adolescents who are not enrolled in college, in practice this is not easy to do. One problem (in addition to the difficulty researchers find in recruiting samples of noncollege individuals to participate in research studies) is that people are not randomly assigned to go to college or not. Thus, even if one were to find that college students showed relatively greater identity development than nonstudents, this could be due to factors that differentiate people who go to college from those who do not.

Identity and Ethnicity

For individuals who are not part of the majority culture, integrating a sense of **ethnic identity** into their overall sense of personal identity is often an important task of late adolescence, perhaps just as important as establishing a coherent occupational, ideological, or interpersonal identity (Chao & Otsuki-Clutter, 2011; Fuligni, Hughes, & Way, 2009; Seaton & Gilbert, 2011). An extensive literature has been amassed on the process through which ethnic identity develops and on the implications of having a strong versus weak sense of ethnic identity for adolescent adjustment and behavior. Ethnic identity has been studied in samples of Black, Hispanic, Native American, Asian, and White youth (Fuligni et al., 2009; M. D. Jones & Galliher, 2007; Markstrom, 2011a; D. L. Newman, 2005). In America, White youth generally have a weaker sense of ethnic identity than their non-White peers, but many White adolescents, especially those from more working-class backgrounds, identify strongly with a particular ethnic group (such as German, Irish, Italian) and derive part of their overall sense of self from this identification (J. M. Grossman & Charmaraman, 2009; R. Roberts et al., 1999). Nevertheless, if given a list of labels to identify their own ethnic background, White adolescents in America are less likely than ethnic minority adolescents to choose labels based on their specific heritage (for example, "German," "Italian American," "Jewish") and more likely to use generic

ethnic identity
The aspect of individuals' sense of identity concerning ancestry or racial group membership.

"panethnic" labels (for example, "White") or simply to identify themselves as "American" (Fuligni, Witkow, & Garcia, 2005).

Among immigrant adolescents, there is considerable vacillation between identifying oneself as a member of a broad ethnic category (e.g., Latino, Asian) and identifying oneself as a member of a group defined by one's country of origin (e.g., Mexican, Chinese) (Fuligni, Kiang, Witkow, & Baldelomar, 2008), as well as variability in definitions of how best to maintain an identity that merges being a member of one's ethnic group and being a member of the country into which the family has immigrated (Ko & Perreira, 2010; Li, 2009; Nguyen & Brown, 2010; Qin, 2009). Language and style of dress are often used by immigrant youth to make a statement about their identity, as these Hmong girls explain:

> Kandi: A lot of people aren't proud of being Hmong and if you speak Hmong with them they'll be like, "Why are you speaking Hmong, that's stupid, speak English. Hello, you're in America, speak English."

> Eve: I just hate when they tell you that. Like, I can speak as much as I want. (Nguyen & Brown, 2010, p. 857)

The Development of Ethnic Identity

The process of ethnic identity development is similar to the process of identity development more generally, with an unquestioning view of oneself often being displaced or upset by a crisis (Yip, 2014). Often, but not always, the precipitating event involves an experience during which the individual encounters prejudice, becomes aware of his or her group's underrepresentation in some activity or setting, or suddenly feels different from adolescents from other backgrounds (Syed & Azmitia, 2006). Here's how one Asian American woman described her "awakening":

> I was on the computer chatting with my friend, and he was telling me he has plans to go to Japan to visit for vacation. Then I told him I would like to visit China, and he said to me, "China sounds so shady, but you dirty chink would totally fit in anyway." I told him immediately I was offended by his comment, but he thought I was joking about my emotions. I told him to take that comment back because I didn't find it funny. I felt very offended; I was thinking to myself, "Is that how others view Chinese people?" (Syed & Azmitia, 2006, p. 1019)

Following the crisis, individuals engage in a period of exploration, during which they may immerse themselves in learning about their ethnic heritage. (Increasingly, a good deal of this exploration occurs online, as is the

Having a strong sense of ethnic pride is associated with a wide range of psychological benefits.
© Lee Snider/The Image Works

case for identity exploration more generally [Davis, 2013; Tynes, 2007]). This process of exploration leads to increases in self-esteem (Corenblum, 2014; Umaña-Taylor, Gonzales-Backen, & Guimond, 2009). Eventually, as the value of having a strong ethnic identity becomes clear, the individual establishes a more coherent sense of personal identity that includes this ethnic identity (Seaton, Yip, & Sellers, 2009; Whitehead, Ainsworth, Wittig, & Gadino, 2009). Adolescents' feelings about their own ethnic group become more positive during both early and middle adolescence (when ethnic identity first becomes salient and individuals become immersed in their own culture), although actual identity exploration does not really begin until middle adolescence (S. E. French, Seidman, Allen, & Aber, 2006). Between middle and late adolescence, exploration declines, as individuals begin to develop a more consolidated identity (Pahl & Way, 2006). Adolescents with a strong sense of ethnic identity have better mental health than those whose sense of ethnic identity is more diffuse (Gartner, Kiang, & Supple, 2014; Seaton, Scottham, & Sellers, 2006; Yip, Seaton, & Sellers, 2006). One reason for this is that a strong ethnic identity helps to foster a sense of meaning in life, which has been shown to be related to overall adjustment (Kiang & Fuligni, 2010).

The development of ethnic identity is profoundly affected by the context in which adolescents live (Tsai & Fuligni, 2012; Williams, Tolan, Durkee, Francois, & Anderson, 2012). For instance, patterns of ethnic identity development are affected by the ethnic composition of the adolescent's school, the adolescent's immediate peer group, and the extent to which the adolescent has contact with other teenagers from the same or different backgrounds (Douglas, Yip, & Shelton, 2014; Kiang, Witkow, Baldelomar, & Fuligni, 2010; Nishina, Bellmore, Witkow, & Nylund-Gibson, 2010; Yip, Seaton, & Sellers, 2010).

Moving through the early stages of ethnic identity development may be speeded up somewhat when parents take a more deliberate approach to the socialization of an ethnic identity (Hernandez, Conger, Robins, Bacher, & Widamun, 2014; McHale et al., 2006; Umaña-Taylor, Alfaro, Bámaca, & Guimond, 2009). **Ethnic socialization** (also referred to as "racial socialization") is the process parents use to attempt to teach their children about their ethnic or racial identity and about the special experiences they may encounter within the broader society as a result of their ethnic background (Evans et al., 2012). Having a strong ethnic identity and sense of ethnic pride is consistently associated with higher self-esteem, stronger self-efficacy, and better mental health (Rivas-Drake et al., 2014; Smokowski, Evans, Cotter, & Webber, 2014).

Ethnic socialization in minority families typically focuses on at least three themes: understanding and valuing one's culture, dealing with racism, and succeeding in mainstream society (Chao & Otsuki-Clutter, 2011; Moua & Lamborn, 2010; Varner & Mandara, 2013). Ethnic socialization also occurs indirectly, for example, when parents stress the importance of family obligations (Kiang & Fuligni, 2009; Umaña-Taylor, Alfaro, Bámaca, & Guimond, 2009; Tsai, Telzer, Gonzales, & Fuligni, 2015).

Ethnic socialization by parents encourages adolescents to think positively about their ethnic heritage, which may lead to a stronger sense of ethnic identity (Rivas-Drake, Hughes, & Way, 2009; Umaña-Taylor & Guimond, 2010). But more ethnic socialization isn't necessarily better; in one study, the best-adjusted Black adolescents came from homes in which their mothers provided a moderate number of racial socialization messages, rather than many or few (Frabutt, Walker, & MacKinnon-Lewis, 2002). In fact, when parents and other caregivers describe their own experiences of discrimination, this adversely affects their adolescents' mental health (Ford, Hurd, Jagers, & Sellers, 2013). Occasional communication of highly positive messages may be most effective approach for parents to take (Neblett, Smalls, Ford, Nguyên, & Sellers, 2009).

Frequent contact with peers from the same ethnic group leads adolescents to develop stronger positive feelings about their ethnicity (Yip, Douglass, & Shelton, 2013). But having positive attitudes about one's own ethnic group also is correlated with having positive attitudes about adolescents from other ethnic groups, suggesting that ethnic socialization may enhance, rather than upset, interracial relations (Phinney, Ferguson, & Tate, 1997). In fact, many adolescents with a strong ethnic identity are members of peer crowds for which ethnicity is *not* a defining feature (B. Brown, Herman, Hamm, & Heck, 2008).

The mental health of ethnic minority youth is also affected by their orientation to the mainstream culture. In general, positive mental health among ethnic minority adolescents is associated with biculturalism—having a strong, positive ethnic identity and a healthy awareness of the potential for discrimination, while maintaining involvement in the mainstream culture (Reitz, Motti-Stefanidi, & Asendorpf, 2014; Roche, Ghazarian, & Fernandez-Esquer, 2012; Umaña-Taylor et al., 2014; Unger, 2014). For example, among ethnic minority youth, academic achievement is highest when adolescents feel connected to their ethnic group, are aware of racism, and believe that it is important to the people in their life to be academically successful within mainstream society (McGill, Hughes, Alicea, & Way, 2012). Being aware of potential racism and mistrusting others are not the same thing, however; awareness of racism is associated with better achievement, but mistrust is associated with doing more poorly in school (Huynh & Fuligni, 2008).

ethnic socialization
The process through which individuals develop an understanding of their ethnic or racial background, also referred to as racial socialization.

Recent Immigrants   Several researchers have focused on the special situation of ethnic minority youth who are recent immigrants to a new culture (e.g., Fuligni, Hughes, & Way, 2009; Gonzales, 2011). Despite the fact that adolescents who are recent immigrants frequently report high levels of academic, familial, social, and economic stress (Cervantes & Cordova, 2011), foreign-born ethnic minority adolescents tend to express more positive feelings about mainstream American ideals than do their counterparts whose families have been in the United States longer. In addition, in the United States, foreign-born and first-generation ethnic minority youth (i.e., adolescents whose parents were born in a different country) perform better in school and are less likely to be involved in delinquent behavior or have physical, emotional, and behavioral problems than adolescents from the same ethnic group whose parents were born in America (Clotfelter, Ladd, & Vigdor, 2012; Hao & Woo, 2012; Guarini, Marks, Patton, & Garcia Coll, 2015; Killoren & Deutsch, 2013; Prado et al., 2009), a phenomenon that is known as the **immigrant paradox** (Marks, Ejesi, & Garcia Coll, 2014). (The immigrant paradox is not always seen in countries outside the United States, however [Vaquera & Kao, 2012].) One explanation for this is that ethnic minority immigrants arrive in their new country idealistic about their prospects, but the longer their family lives in the new context, the more likely they are to become both Americanized and disillusioned (Tartakovsky, 2009). One recent study of Mexican-American youth also found that over the course of adolescence, there was a decline in teenagers' orientation to traditional Mexican family values, which was associated with increases in risky behavior (Updegraff, Umaña-Taylor, McHale, Wheeler, & Perez-Brena, 2012). Another explanation for the higher achievement and better mental health of immigrant adolescents is that newly arrived immigrant parents provide more effective supervision of their children (Chao & Otsuki-Clutter, 2011; Marsiglia, Nagoshi, Parsani, Booth, & Castro, 2014; Schwartz et al., 2013).

The process of identity development among adolescents from recent immigrant families also depends on the context in which the family lives, as a study of Vietnamese adolescents from Southern California illustrates (Vo-Jutabha, Dinh, McHale, & Valsiner, 2009). In this study, the researchers compared the identity development of adolescents living in a Vietnamese enclave ("Little Saigon") with those who lived nearby, but in a more diverse community. For adolescents living inside the enclave, pressures on them to adopt a strong Vietnamese identity had both

immigrant paradox
The fact that on many measures of psychological functioning and mental health, adolescents who have immigrated more recently to the United States score higher on measures of adjustment than adolescents from the same ethnic group whose family has lived in the United States for several generations.

helped focus their identity development but also constrained it, frustrating those teenagers whose behavior conflicted with the expectations of adults in the community. As one girl from Little Saigon noted:

> You want to do what makes you feel happy or comfortable but they put you in this little ethnicity box. Especially here. Going to church you wear *ao dai* [traditional Vietnamese dress]. I'm not rebelling but I don't want to be another Asian girl in an American crowd. I want to be myself. I'm not going against my parents or tradition. I want to make my own morals and traditions and it makes me happy. (p. 682)

Adolescents living outside the enclave had more opportunities to explore a wider range of alternatives, but were more passive in their identity exploration and often actively fought attempts by their parents to encourage a strong Vietnamese identity. As one boy put it:

> My parents expect me to speak Vietnamese consistently. Every now and then they just say that I forgot it and that I don't know how to speak it anymore. . . . Of course, I understand it and my parents expect me to be in a Viet Club or something. But I mean c'mon, really c'mon. (pp. 683–684)

Discrimination and Its Effects

The task of developing a coherent sense of identity is much more complicated for minority adolescents than for their majority counterparts (Gray-Little & Hafdahl, 2000; H. Stevenson, Reed, Bodison, & Bishop, 1997). Because identity development is profoundly influenced by the social context in which the adolescent lives, the development of minority adolescents must be understood in relation to the specific context that they face in contemporary society (Byrd & Chavous, 2011; Chao & Otsuki-Clutter, 2011; Markstrom, 2011a; Rivas-Drake et al., 2009). All too often, this context includes racial stereotypes, discrimination, and mixed messages about the costs and benefits of identifying too closely with the majority culture (see Figure 7).

The adverse effects of discrimination are especially intense among American ethnic minority youth with a strong attachment to the mainstream culture (Derlan et al., 2014) and for those whose parents were born in the United States (Sirin et al., 2015). Immigrant adolescents who speak with an accent are stereotyped as "perpetual foreigners," which can lead to discrimination and victimization (S. Kim, Wang, Deng, Alvarez, & Li, 2011; Özdemir & Stattin, 2014). One recent study of American adolescents of Iranian descent revealed that many of these teenagers identified themselves as Persian, rather than Iranian, because of the negative portrayals of Iranian individuals in the media (Daha, 2011). Similarly, it is impossible to fully understand the process of ethnic identity development among American Indian adolescents without taking

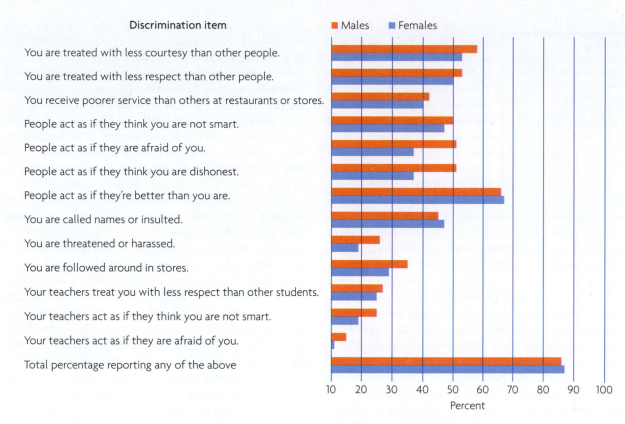

Figure 7   **The experience of discrimination is common among Black adolescents.** (Seaton et al., 2008)

into account the particular history of American Indians in the United States (Markstrom, 2011a).

It is well established that individuals—from any group—who report experiencing high levels of discrimination suffer psychologically as a result. Adolescents' psychological well-being, including their self-esteem, is adversely affected by discrimination and prejudice. Adolescents who report frequent experiences of being insulted, excluded, and teased about their race or ethnicity have relatively more psychological problems than do their peers who face no discrimination (C. H. Caldwell, Kohn-Wood, Schmeelk-Cone, Chavous, & Zimmerman, 2004; Huynh & Fuligni, 2010; Sellers, Copeland-Linder, Martin, & Lewis, 2006).

Many studies of Asian, Black, and Latino youth have found that feeling discriminated against is predictive of subsequent conduct problems, depression, and lower achievement in school (Benner & Graham, 2011; Bogart et al., 2013; Brody, Kogan, & Chen, 2012; English, Lambert, & Ialongo, 2014; Hurd, Varner, Caldwell, & Zimmerman, 2014; Huynh, 2012; Seaton, Caldwell, Sellers, & Jackson, 2010). The source of the

discrimination matters: Feeling discriminated against by teachers leads to poorer school performance, whereas peer discrimination adversely affects mental health (Benner & Graham, 2013; Niwa et al., 2014).

There are many reasons that feeling discriminated against may be harmful to one's mental health, but one important process derives from the effect of discrimination on adolescents' feelings of control: Adolescents who feel discriminated against in school report feeling less control over their academic achievement, which leads to feelings of depression (Smith-Bynum, Lambert, English, & Ialongo, 2014). Another possibility is that the experience of discrimination leads to depression and alienation, which, in turn, leads adolescents to affiliate with deviant peers, increasing the likelihood that they will engage in risky and antisocial behavior (M. Roberts et al., 2012) (see Figure 8). Growing up in a racially isolated, poor neighborhood especially intensifies feelings of discrimination, which increases adolescents' involvement in violence (Martin et al., 2011).

Individuals vary both in the extent to which they feel discriminated against and in the extent to which they are

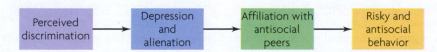

Figure 8   **One pathway linking perceived discrimination to antisocial behavior is through the impact of discrimination on depression and alienation, which leads adolescents to affiliate with antisocial peers.** (Adapted from M. Roberts et al., 2012)

multidimensional model of racial identity

A perspective on ethnic identity that emphasizes three different phenomena: racial centrality (how important race is in defining individuals' identity), private regard (how individuals feel about being a member of their race), and public regard (how individuals think others feel about their race).

adversely affected by it, and it appears that ethnic identity is an important factor (Riina & McHale, 2012; Umaña-Taylor, Tynes, Toomey, Williams, & Mitchell, 2015). The **multidimensional model of racial identity** has been used to help make sense out of a complex web of findings (Seaton, Upton, Gilbert, & Volpe, 2014; Sellers et al., 2006). According to this model, we need to take into account three different aspects of racial identity: racial centrality (how important race is in defining individuals' identity), private regard (how individuals feel about being a member of their race), and public regard (how individuals think others view their race). Generally speaking, during adolescence racial centrality increases and private regard tends to remain stable, but changes in public regard differ among adolescents from different backgrounds (Rivas-Drake & Witherspoon, 2013; Rogers, Scott, & Way, 2015). In one study of New York City middle school students, public regard increased among Chinese American adolescents, but it declined among Black, Puerto Rican, and Dominican youth (Hughes, Way, & Rivas-Drake, 2011). One possible explanation for this is that Black and Latino students report that their teachers have more negative attitudes toward them than do Asian youth, whose teachers generally see them in a more favorable light.

Adolescents who have experienced discrimination firsthand are more likely to believe that the public has low regard for their ethnic group (Seaton et al., 2009). However, individuals who believe that the public has low regard for their ethnic group are more sensitive to racial cues, which, in turn, may heighten their experience of discrimination; this process may be accentuated in families where parents engage in relatively more ethnic socialization (Rivas-Drake et al., 2009; Wang & Huguley, 2012). This is not to say that individuals with heightened sensitivity to discrimination are simply imagining it; rather, individuals with heightened sensitivity may be better at perceiving more subtle signs of genuine racial bias. One recent study found that the experience of feeling discriminated against adversely affects adolescents' mental health regardless of what they attribute the discrimination to (e.g., ethnicity, gender, physical appearance, etc.) (Seaton, Caldwell, Sellers, & Jackson, 2010).

How all of this works together to affect adolescents' mental health is tricky. Having positive feelings about one's race is positively linked to psychological well-being and protects against the harmful effects of stress and discrimination (Benner & Kim, 2009; Galliher, Jones, & Dahl, 2011; Umaña-Taylor, Wong, Gonzales, & Dumka, 2012; Williams, Aiyer, Durkee, & Tolan, 2014).

Consistent with this, adolescents whose parents have emphasized the positive aspects of ethnic socialization (e.g., having pride in one's ethnic group) and who have more positive family relationships fare better in the face of discrimination than those whose parents have emphasized the negative (e.g., the need to be wary about potential racism) (Berkel et al., 2009; Delgado, Updegraff, Roosa, & Umaña-Taylor, 2011; Juang & Alvarez, 2010; Smokowski et al., 2009). Having a strong ethnic identity is also protective against the harmful effects of online discrimination (Tynes, Umaña-Taylor, Rose, Lin, & Anderson, 2012).

However, the impact of having race as a central part of one's identity (which is not the same thing as having high private regard for one's ethnic group) is complicated: It makes adolescents more sensitive to discrimination (which hurts their mental health), but some studies show that it makes them more able to cope with it (which helps) (Berkel et al., 2010; C. S. Brown, Alabi, Huynh, & Masten, 2011; Chavous, Rivas-Drake, Smalls, Griffin, & Cogburn, 2008; Kiang, Peterson, & Thompson, 2011; Thomas et al., 2009), although not all studies find this (e.g., Deng, Kim, Vaughan, & Li, 2010; Seaton, Neblett, Upton, Hammond, & Sellers, 2011). Believing that the public has high regard for one's ethnic group lifts adolescents' school performance, but believing that the public has a positive view of one's race also intensifies the effects of discrimination—perhaps because people feel especially wounded when they don't expect to encounter it (Hughes, Way, & Rivas-Drake, 2011; Sellers, Copeland-Linder, Martin, & Lewis, 2006).

Multiethnic Adolescents

One understudied group of adolescents for whom developing a sense of ethnic identity may be especially challenging consists of **multiethnic** youth—adolescents whose parents are not from the same ethnic or racial group. Understanding psychological development among multiethnic adolescents has taken on increased importance as their numbers have grown (Chao & Otsuki-Clutter, 2011; Fisher, Reynolds, Hsu, Barnes, & Tyler, 2014). In 2010, 17% of all infants with a Black parent were born to one Black parent and one White parent, and 34% of all infants with an Asian parent were born to one Asian parent and one White parent (Frey, 2012).

Developing a consistent ethnic identity is challenging for biracial adolescents, especially during early adolescence (Marks, Patton, & Coll, 2011). Many biracial adolescents change their racial identity over time, switching between adolescence and young adulthood from being biracial to being "monoracial" (identifying oneself with just one ethnic group); in one study of Black, White, and biracial Black/White adolescents, nearly three-quarters of the biracial group changed their self-identification over a 4-year period, which may reflect the ways in which the cultural desirability of being seen as a member of one ethnic group or another fluctuates over time (Terry & Winston, 2010). Although this switching has been observed in all ethnic groups, in one study it was especially common among adolescents who identified as Native Americans, either exclusively or in combination with a White self-identification (Hitlin, Brown, & Elder, Jr., 2006). The majority of individuals who had identified themselves as both White and Native American when they were adolescents identified themselves only as White when they were young adults. However, a large number of adolescents who identified themselves only as White identified themselves as both White and Native American several years later. Similar patterns of change were seen among other multiracial individuals, but not nearly as often.

Identity and Gender

Identity and gender are linked in several different ways. **Gender identity** refers to one's sense of oneself as male, female, or transgender, which refers to individuals whose gender identity does not match the sex they were designated at birth, usually based on their external sex organs. **Sexual orientation** refers to the extent to which someone is romantically and sexually attracted to members of the same sex (homosexual, which includes gay men or lesbians), members of the other sex (heterosexual, or "straight"), or both (i.e., bisexual). **Gender-role behavior** refers to the extent to which an individual behaves in traditionally "masculine" or "feminine" ways.

A great deal of confusion stems from the fact that these three concepts are not related. For example, there is no connection between sexual orientation and sex-role behavior or gender identity. Individuals with strong, or even exclusive, homosexual attractions exhibit the same range of masculine and feminine behaviors that is seen among individuals with strong or exclusive heterosexual interests. In other words, exclusively gay men (like exclusively heterosexual men) may act in very masculine, very feminine, or both masculine and feminine ways. The same holds true for exclusively lesbian and exclusively heterosexual women, as well as bisexual men and women. Along similar lines, individuals with homosexual or bisexual interests are generally not confused about their gender identity—or, at least, they are no more confused than are individuals with heterosexual interests.

Several writers have described the process through which gay, lesbian, and bisexual individuals discover, come to terms with, and disclose their sexual orientation (Diamond, 2008; Savin-Williams & Ream, 2007). Although the traditional model of this progression— feeling different as a child, engaging in gender-atypical behavior, being attracted to members of the same sex and uninterested in those of the other sex, realizing one's sexual attraction to others of the same sex, and consciously questioning one's sexual orientation—describes the experience of many sexual-minority adolescents, it by

Research on adolescents who have two parents from different ethnic groups has not kept up with the growth of the multiethnic population. © Mike Kemp/Rubberball/Getty Images RF

no means is universal. Indeed, some writers have suggested that this may be more applicable to the development of White gay men than to lesbians, bisexual adolescents, or ethnic minority gay men (Diamond, 1998; Dubé & Savin-Williams, 1999). For example, there is evidence that females' sexual orientation may be more fluid than males', with many more bisexual or lesbian adolescents changing sexual orientation during young adulthood than heterosexual individuals or gay males (Diamond, 2008; Saewyc, 2011; Savin-Williams, Joyner, & Rieger, 2012).

Society's prejudice and ignorance about homosexuality likely cause significant psychological distress for sexual-minority adolescents, especially if they encounter hostility from those around them (Saewyc, 2011; T. E. Smith & Leaper, 2006). The developmental tasks in the domains of identity, intimacy, and sexuality present formidable challenges for many teenagers. These challenges may be exacerbated for sexual-minority adolescents, who are forced to resolve these issues without the same degree of social support as their heterosexual peers (Diamond & Lucas, 2004). Gay, lesbian, and bisexual adolescents who believe that their sexual orientation is a burden to people in their lives are at greater risk for depression and suicidal thoughts (Baams, Grossman, & Russell, 2015).

multiethnic
Having two parents of different ethnic or racial backgrounds.

gender identity
One's sense of oneself as male, female, or transgender.

sexual orientation
Whether one is sexually attracted to individuals of the same sex, other sex, or both.

gender-role behavior
The extent to which an individual behaves in traditionally "masculine" or "feminine" ways.

Although adolescents who describe themselves as transgender are often grouped for purposes of discussion with lesbian, gay, and bisexual youth, transgender individuals report the same variety of sexual orientations as do other individuals. Information on the size of the transgender population, either in adolescence or adulthood, is scant. One recent report estimates that about 1 in 100,000 American adults are transsexual women (individuals who identify themselves as women but who were labeled as male at birth) and 1 in 400,000 are transsexual men (individuals who identify themselves as men but who were labeled as female at birth) (IOM and NRC, 2011b).

Many experts believe that we should view gender identity, sexual orientation, and gender-role behavior as fluid rather than fixed, and as points along continua rather than absolute categories (Savin-Williams & Vrangalova, 2013). A young man may go through a period during which he is sexually attracted to other men and wonder if he is gay, only to find at a later age that he is exclusively interested in women. Another may think of himself as "mostly heterosexual." An adolescent girl who expressed traditionally feminine interests as a child may discover that she actually enjoys a mix of activities that include some stereotypically masculine ones and some stereotypically feminine ones. Someone who spent her childhood and adolescence identified as male may realize that she is more comfortable identifying as a woman.

Gender-Role Development

Popular books proclaim that men and women are fundamentally different; that men and women come from different "planets"; that males and females learn, speak, and navigate the world in different ways; and that adolescent boys and girls need to be schooled and raised in different ways. But the fact of the matter is that, apart from some obvious physical differences, adolescent males and females actually aren't all that different (Perry & Pauletti, 2011; Priess & Hyde, 2011). I'm sorry to disappoint you (if I have), but scientific studies of the sexes simply do not support the claims of those who argue that males and females have brains that are wired in differently, have different perspectives on morality, or learn in fundamentally dissimilar ways.

Whether large sex differences in adolescent behavior had existed in the past but have disappeared (certainly a possibility, given the fact that men and women faced different expectations and opportunities in past generations) or whether they were just assumed to be larger than they were isn't known. But differences *within* groups of males or females are far more substantial than differences between them. Throughout this book, I've noted when studies have found meaningful sex differences in the ways in which adolescents develop or function. If I

gender intensification hypothesis
The idea that pressures to behave in sex-appropriate ways intensify during adolescence.

haven't mentioned them, it's either because they weren't reported or weren't observed.

Apart from differences in strength, adolescent males and females do not differ in their abilities, and although girls are more "people-oriented" and boys are more "things-oriented," the magnitude of sex differences in interests and attitudes is smaller than most people think (Priess & Hyde, 2011). The most consistent sex differences are seen in the ways adolescent boys and girls express aggression (males are generally more physically aggressive than females, who tend to use social or verbal aggression) and intimacy (females are more likely to express intimacy verbally, whereas males express it mainly through shared activities), and in the extent to which males and females are prone to low self-esteem and depression (females are more prone to both). There are few, if any, sex differences in patterns of family relationships, performance on achievement tests, or in the correlates of competence, popularity with peers, and healthy psychological development.

Gender-Role Socialization During Adolescence

Despite the fact that psychological differences between the sexes are trivial or nonexistent, many individuals continue to hold strong beliefs about what is "normal" for males and for females, and psychologists have been interested in the consequences of behaving or not behaving in ways that are stereotypically masculine or feminine. Some studies have found that pressures to behave in sex-stereotypic ways appear to increase temporarily during middle adolescence, something referred to as the **gender intensification hypothesis** (Galambos, Berenbaum, & McHale, 2009; Lobel, Nov-Krispin, Schiller, Lobel, & Feldman, 2004). Individuals' *beliefs* about gender roles become more flexible as they move through adolescence, largely as a result of the cognitive changes of the period, but social pressures may drive teenagers toward more gender-stereotypic *behavior;* indeed, the impact of environmental factors on gender-role behavior is much stronger than the impact of the hormonal changes of puberty (Galambos et al., 2009). As teenagers begin to date, for example, it may become more important for them to act in ways that are consistent with gender-role expectations and that meet with approval in the peer group. Boys who do not act masculine enough and girls who do not act feminine enough may be less popular with and less accepted by their same- and other-sex peers (T. E. Smith & Leaper, 2006). Adolescents are more intolerant about peers behaving in gender-atypical ways than they are about variations in sexual orientation (Horn, 2007; Toomey, Ryan, Diaz, Card, & Russell, 2010).

Not all studies find an increase in gender-stereotyped behavior in middle adolescence (e.g., Jacobs et al., 2002; McHale, Kim, Whiteman, & Crouter, 2004) or in pressure to conform to traditional gender roles (Priess, Lindberg, & Hyde, 2009). One reason for discrepancies between studies is that the extent to which gender-stereotypic

Pressures to behave in sex-stereotypic ways may temporarily intensify during middle adolescence. © Syracuse Newspapers/Li-Hau Lan/ The Image Works

behavior becomes more pronounced or demanded in adolescence likely depends on the realm of behavior studied, the developmental history of the adolescent, and the broader context in which the adolescent lives (Daniels & Leaper, 2011; Galambos, Berenbaum, & McHale, 2009; McHale, Shanahan, Updegraff, Crouter, & Booth, 2004). For instance, although people tend to become more traditional in their attitudes about gender roles between early and middle adolescence, this pattern is not universal. One study of changes in gender role attitudes broke the sample down by sex, birth order, and the sorts of attitudes the parents had. Whereas firstborn boys with brothers and parents with traditional attitudes about gender become more traditional in their own attitudes over time, second-born girls with brothers and less traditional parents did not (Crouter, Whiteman, McHale, & Osgood, 2007).

Masculinity and Femininity

Individuals vary in their degrees of masculinity and femininity. Some are decidedly more masculine than feminine, and others are decidedly more feminine than masculine. And some people have a high degree of both masculinity and femininity; they might be both highly

ambitious (a trait usually considered masculine) and highly sensitive (a trait usually considered feminine).

Generally speaking, individuals' degree of masculinity or femininity is highly stable over time. In one study that tracked people from preschool through adolescence, girls who had been rated as relatively more masculine as preschoolers felt less similar to other girls when they were 13, were less content being girls, and had a stronger preference for traditionally male activities, whereas those who had been rated as more feminine had stronger preferences for traditionally female activities. Similarly, boys who had been rated as more feminine when they were preschoolers felt less similar to other boys when they were adolescents and were not especially drawn to traditionally male activities (Golombok, Rust, Zervoulis, Golding, & Hines, 2012).

If expectations to conform to traditional gender stereotypes intensify during adolescence, we would expect that boys who are especially masculine and girls who are especially feminine would fare better psychologically than their peers who behave in gender-atypical ways. Do more feminine girls and more masculine boys feel better about themselves?

The answer to this question may differ for males and females (Galambos, Berenbaum, & McHale, 2009). Although boys and girls who behave in gender-typical ways are more accepted than their peers whose behavior does not conform with gender-role stereotypes (Kochel, Miller, Updegraff, Ladd, & Kochenderfer-Ladd, 2012), and feel better about themselves as a result of this (Menon, 2011), the costs of being gender-atypical are greater for boys than girls (T. E. Smith & Leaper, 2006). It is not surprising, therefore, to find that during adolescence boys are likely to cut back on the display of stereotypically feminine traits, such as being emotionally expressive, whereas neither boys nor girls reduce the display of traditionally masculine traits, such as instrumentality (McHale, Kim, Dotterer, Crouter, & Booth, 2009) (see Figure 9).

By the time they have reached early adolescence, teenagers understand that it is easier for girls to sometimes behave in masculine ways than it is for boys to occasionally act in feminine ways (Mulvey & Killen, 2015). Consistent with research on younger children, adolescent males who do not conform to traditionally masculine gender-role norms have lower self-esteem, are judged more deviant, and are more likely to be bullied than are females whose behavior departs from exclusively feminine roles (Gupta et al., 2013; Roberts, Rosario, Slopen, Calzo, & Austin, 2013). Boys who have a more traditionally masculine orientation, while higher in self-acceptance than other boys, are more likely to be involved in various types of problem behavior—perhaps because part of being masculine in contemporary society involves being "man enough" to experiment with delinquency, drugs and alcohol, and unprotected sex (Kulis, Marsiglia, & Hurdle, 2003), or because boys who live in difficult environments, where problem behavior is prevalent, adopt a more "macho" posture to survive in the community (Cunningham, 1999). Conversely, girls who have a more traditionally feminine gender-role orientation are more likely to develop more traditionally feminine sorts of psychological problems, such as disordered eating (McHale, Corneal, Crouter, & Birch, 2001). Girls who believe that women's worth comes primarily from their sexual appeal

earn lower grades and score worse on achievement tests than their peers. In one clever experiment, in which adolescent girls were asked to prepare and videotape a mock newscast, ostensibly to measure their aptitude for journalism, the researchers found that girls who were more "sexualized" (i.e., who had internalized the idea that being attractive to men is an important part of one's identity) spent more time putting on make-up and less time going over the newscast script than girls who were less sexualized (McKenney & Bigler, 2014).

Given that pressures to conform with gender-role norms affect both girls and boys during adolescence, why is it that boys suffer greater self-image problems when they deviate from what is viewed as appropriate behavior for their sex? The answer is that although girls may be pressured to adopt (or maintain) certain feminine traits during adolescence, they are not necessarily pressured to relinquish all elements of masculinity. In contrast, boys are socialized from a very early age not to adopt feminine traits and are judged deviant if they show any signs of femininity. Boys are more likely to see themselves as "typical males" than girls are to see themselves as "typical females," more likely to be content to be male than girls are to be female, and more pressured to act in stereotypically male ways than girls are to act in stereotypically female ways (Egan & Perry, 2001).

In other words, girls can be highly pressured during adolescence to behave in feminine ways without necessarily being punished or labeled deviant for exhibiting some masculine traits at the same time; thus, for girls, having a mixture of masculine and feminine traits is a viable alternative to exclusive femininity. Girls may feel increasingly pressured to dress nicely and to wear makeup when they reach adolescence, but they are not pressured to give up athletics or other typically masculine interests. Boys, however, from childhood on, are pressured not to behave in feminine ways. Their gender-role socialization does not intensify during adolescence as much as it does for girls because it is so intense to begin with.

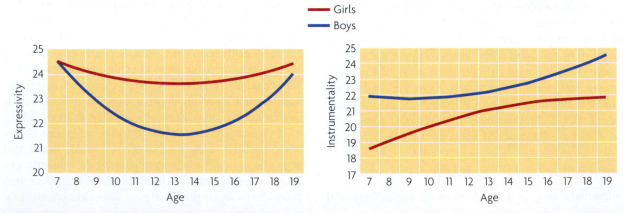

Figure 9 During adolescence, boys increasingly avoid displaying stereotypically feminine traits, but comparable pressure on girls to avoid stereotypically masculine traits is much milder. As a consequence, boys show a drop in emotional expressiveness, but girls do not show a similar decline in instrumentality. (McHale, Kim, Dotterer, Crouter, & Booth, 2009)

Autonomy

Autonomy as an Adolescent Issue

The Development of Emotional Autonomy
Emotional Autonomy and Detachment
Emotional Autonomy and Individuation
Research on Emotional Autonomy
Emotional Autonomy and Parenting Practices

The Development of Behavioral Autonomy
Changes in Decision-Making Abilities
When Do Adolescents Make Decisions as Well
as Adults?

Changes in Susceptibility to Influence
Ethnic and Cultural Differences in
Expectations for Autonomy

**The Development of Cognitive
Autonomy**
Moral Development during Adolescence
Prosocial Reasoning, Prosocial Behavior, and
Volunteerism
Political Thinking During Adolescence
Religious Beliefs During Adolescence

© Jupiterimages/Getty Images RF

When I got my driver's license, I looked at it as freedom, getting out from my parents, going places you couldn't get to before because you had to have your parent's permission . . . not having to be worried about being dropped off and being picked up. Going to the library even or a dance club or a party and not having to worry about, I don't know, your parents having to come pick you up. Not necessarily, it wasn't embarrassment for me, it was more, just like okay, I make my own choices I can leave when I want to, you know, I made this decision to come here you know I'll drop you off. I felt more like an adult but um, I don't know, I went to the beach, to people's houses, friends' houses, the movies. (Best, 2006, p. 63)

For most adolescents, establishing a sense of autonomy is as important a part of becoming an adult as is establishing a sense of identity. Becoming an autonomous person—a self-governing person—is one of the fundamental developmental tasks of adolescence.

Although we often use the words *autonomy* and *independence* interchangeably, in the study of adolescence, they mean slightly different things. Independence refers to individuals' capacity to behave on their own. The growth of independence is surely a part of becoming autonomous during adolescence, but autonomy has emotional and cognitive as well as behavioral components. In other words, autonomy is not just about acting independently—it is also about feeling independent and thinking for oneself.

During adolescence, there is a movement away from the dependency typical of childhood and toward the autonomy typical of adulthood—not only among human adolescents, but among mammals more generally (all mammals go through puberty and therefore experience something analogous to human adolescence) (Casey, Duhoux, & Cohen, 2010). But the growth of autonomy during adolescence is frequently misunderstood. Autonomy is often confused with rebellion, and becoming an independent person is often equated with breaking away from the family. This perspective on autonomy goes hand in hand with the idea that adolescence is inevitably a time of stress and turmoil.

Just as the view that adolescence is a period of storm and stress has been questioned repeatedly by scientific research, experts on adolescence have changed the way they think about the development of autonomy. Rather than viewing autonomy in adolescence as an abrupt rebellion against parental authority, researchers now see it as gradual, progressive, and—although important—relatively undramatic (McElhaney, Allen, Stephenson, & Hare, 2009;

Zimmer-Gembeck, Ducat, & Collins, 2011). Many writers have pointed to the adaptive nature of adolescents' desire for autonomy, arguing that the adolescents' need to distance themselves from their parents has an evolutionary basis, sparking an increase in novelty-seeking and exploration that facilitates reproduction outside of the family (Casey et al., 2010; Steinberg, 2010).

Because today's adolescents spend so much time away from the supervision of adults, either by themselves or with their peers, learning how to govern their own behavior in a responsible fashion is crucial. Given the large numbers of single-parent and two-career households in many industrialized countries, many young people are expected to care for themselves for a good part of the day. Many feel pressured—by parents, by friends, and by the media—to grow up quickly and to act like adults at an earlier age. Many adolescents who grow up in poverty feel a different sort of pressure to grow up—they are expected to take on adult responsibilities to assist their families during times of need (Burton, 2007).

There is a curious paradox in all of this, though. Although adolescents have been asked to become more autonomous psychologically and socially, they have become less autonomous economically. Because of the extension of schooling well into the 20s for most people, and the difficulty many young adults have had finding employment during the recent recession, financial independence may not come until long after psychological independence. Many young people who are emotionally independent from their parents find it frustrating to have to abide by their rules as long as their parents are supporting them economically. They may believe that the ability to make their own decisions has nothing to do with financial dependence. An 18-year-old college freshman who has a part-time job, a full load of classes, and a serious relationship with his girlfriend may be independent in these respects, but he may still be living at home because he can't afford to do otherwise. His parents may feel that as long as their son lives in their home, they should decide how late he can stay out at night. But he may feel that his parents have no right to tell him when he can come and go. This sort of difference of opinion can be a source of problems and confusion for teenagers and their parents, particularly when they have difficulty agreeing on an appropriate level of independence for the adolescent (Steinberg, 2011). Disagreements over autonomy-related concerns are at the top of the list of things that provoke quarrels between adolescents and parents (Laursen & Collins, 2009).

Autonomy as an Adolescent Issue

Like identity, autonomy is a psychosocial concern that surfaces and resurfaces during the entire life cycle. The development of independent behavior begins long before puberty. Toddlers try to establish an initial sense of autonomy when they begin to explore their surroundings on their own and assert their desire to do as they please—a stage of development so frustrating to parents that it is often called "the terrible twos." The toddler who insists on saying "No!" and the young adolescent who insists on keeping her whereabouts secret are both demonstrating their growing sense of independence and autonomy. And just as psychologists see toddlers' oppositional behavior as normal, they also see adolescents' interest in privacy as normal, too—however frustrating that might be to parents (McElhaney et al., 2009).

Although early childhood and adolescence are important periods for the development of autonomy, issues of autonomy are not resolved once and for all upon reaching young adulthood. Questions about being able to function independently arise whenever individuals find themselves in positions that demand a new degree of self-reliance. Following a divorce, someone who has depended on a spouse for economic support, guidance, or nurturance must find a way to function more independently. During late adulthood, autonomy may become a significant concern of someone who, after losing a spouse, suddenly finds it necessary to depend on others for assistance and support.

If establishing and maintaining a healthy sense of autonomy is a lifelong concern, why has it attracted so much attention among scholars interested in adolescence? When we look at the development of autonomy in relation to the biological, cognitive, and social changes of adolescence, it's easy to see why.

Puberty and the Development of Autonomy Some theorists have suggested that puberty triggers changes in the young person's emotional relationships at home (Laursen & Collins, 2009; Zimmer-Gembeck, Ducat, & Collins, 2011). Adolescents' interest in turning away from parents and toward peers for emotional support—part of establishing adult independence—may be stimulated by their emerging interest in sexual relationships and concerns over dating and intimate friendships. From an evolutionary perspective, adolescent independence-seeking is a natural consequence of sexual and physical maturation, and "leaving the home" after puberty is something that is observed not just in humans, but in other primates as well (Casey et al., 2010; Steinberg, 2014). Puberty drives the adolescent away from exclusive emotional dependence on the family. In addition, changes in stature and physical appearance at puberty may provoke changes in how much autonomy the young person is granted by parents and teachers. Children may be given more responsibility simply because they look older.

Leaving home and establishing independence at puberty is seen not just in humans, but in most primates and many other mammals. © JeannetteKatzir/Getty Images RF

Cognitive Change and the Development of Autonomy
The cognitive changes of adolescence also play an important role in the development of autonomy (Albert & Steinberg, 2011; Zimmer-Gembeck, Ducat, & Collins, 2011). Part of being autonomous involves being able to make independent decisions. When individuals turn to others for advice, they often receive conflicting opinions; if you are trying to decide between staying home to study for an exam and going out to a party, your professor and the person throwing the party will probably give you different advice. As an adult, you are able to see that each individual's perspective influences his or her advice. The ability to see this, however, calls for a level of intellectual abstraction that is not available until adolescence. Being able to take other people's perspectives into account, to reason in more sophisticated ways, and to foresee the future consequences of alternative courses of action all help the adolescent weigh the opinions and suggestions of others more effectively and reach independent decisions. The cognitive changes of adolescence also provide the logical foundation for changes in thinking about social, moral, and ethical problems. These changes in thinking are important prerequisites to the development of a system of values based on one's own sense of right and wrong, and not merely on rules and regulations handed down by parents or other authority figures (N. Eisenberg et al., 2009; Morris et al., 2011; Smetana & Villalobos, 2009).

Social Roles and the Development of Autonomy
Finally, changes in social roles and activities during adolescence are bound to raise concerns related to independence, as the adolescent moves into new positions that demand increasing degrees of responsibility and self-reliance (Coatsworth & Conroy, 2009; Halpern-Felsher, 2011).

emotional autonomy
The establishment of more adultlike and less childish close relationships with family members and peers.

behavioral autonomy
The capacity to make independent decisions and to follow through with them.

cognitive autonomy
The establishment of an independent set of values, opinions, and beliefs.

Becoming involved in new roles and taking on new responsibilities, such as having a job or a driver's license, place the adolescent in situations that require and stimulate the development of independent decision making. A teenager might not really think much about the responsibilities associated with taking a job until she actually ends up in one (D. Wood, Larson, & Brown, 2009). Choosing whether to drink does not become an important question until the adolescent begins to approach the legal drinking age. And deciding what his political beliefs are becomes a more pressing concern when the young person realizes that he will soon have the right to vote.

making the scientific connection

Many psychologists contend that the two periods of life during which autonomy is an especially salient issue are early adolescence and toddlerhood. What do these periods share in common that might account for the importance of autonomy during each?

Three Types of Autonomy Psychologists have described autonomy in three ways (McElhaney et al., 2009; Zimmer-Gembeck, Ducat, & Collins, 2011). The first is **emotional autonomy**—that aspect of independence related to changes in the individual's close

relationships, especially with parents. The second is **behavioral autonomy**—the capacity to make independent decisions and follow through on them. And the third is **cognitive autonomy** (sometimes called "value autonomy"), which involves having independent values, opinions, and beliefs.

The Development of Emotional Autonomy

The relationship between children and their parents changes repeatedly over the life cycle. Changes in the expression of affection, the distribution of power, and patterns of verbal interaction, to give a few examples, are likely to occur whenever important transformations take place in the child's or parents' competencies, concerns, and social roles.

By the end of adolescence, people are far less emotionally dependent on their parents than they were as children. We can see this in several ways. First, older adolescents do not generally rush to their parents when they are upset, worried, or in need of assistance. Second, they do not see their parents as all-knowing or all-powerful. Third, they often have a great deal of emotional energy wrapped up in relationships outside the family; they may feel more attached to a boyfriend or girlfriend than to their parents. And finally, older adolescents are able to see and interact with their parents as people— not just as their parents. Many parents find that they can confide in their adolescent children, which was not possible when their children were younger, or that their adolescent children can sympathize with them when they have had a hard day at work. These sorts of changes in the adolescent-parent relationship all reflect the development of emotional autonomy (McElhaney et al., 2009; Zimmer-Gembeck, Ducat, & Collins, 2011).

Emotional Autonomy and Detachment

Psychoanalytic Theory and Detachment Early writings about emotional autonomy were influenced by psychoanalytic thinkers such as Anna Freud (1958), who argued that the physical changes of puberty cause disruption and conflict inside the family. Freud believed that intrapsychic conflicts that had been repressed since early childhood are reawakened at early adolescence by resurgent sexual impulses. (These conflicts revolve around the young child's unconscious attraction toward the parent of the other sex and ambivalent feelings toward the parent of the same sex.) The reawakened conflicts are expressed as increased tension, arguments, and discomfort in the family. As a consequence, early adolescents are driven to separate themselves from their parents emotionally, and they turn their emotional energies to relationships with peers— in particular, peers of the opposite sex. Psychoanalytic

Being able to drive greatly increases adolescents' autonomy from parental control. © BananaStock/BananaStock/PunchStock RF

theorists call this process of separation **detachment,** because to them it appears as though the adolescent is attempting to sever the attachments that were formed during infancy and strengthened throughout childhood.

Freud and her followers viewed detachment and the accompanying storm and stress inside the family as normal, healthy, and inevitable aspects of emotional development during adolescence. In fact, Freud believed that the absence of conflict between an adolescent and his or her parents signified that the young person was having problems growing up.

Research on Detachment   Studies of adolescents' family relationships have not supported Freud's view. In contrast to predictions that high levels of adolescent-parent tension are the norm, that adolescents detach themselves from relationships with their parents, and that adolescents are driven out of the household by unbearable levels of family conflict, every major study done to date of teenagers' relations with their parents has shown that most families get along well during the adolescent years (McElhaney et al., 2009; Zimmer-Gembeck, Ducat, & Collins, 2011). Although parents and adolescents may bicker more often than they did during earlier periods of development, there is no evidence that this bickering significantly diminishes closeness between them in any lasting way (W. A. Collins & Steinberg, 2006; Laursen & Collins, 2009). Most individuals report becoming closer to their parents in late adolescence, especially after they have made the transition into college (Lefkowitz, 2005; McElhaney et al., 2009).

In other words, although teenagers and their parents modify their relationships during adolescence, their emotional bonds aren't severed. Emotional autonomy during adolescence involves a *transformation,* not a breaking off, of family relationships; adolescents can become emotionally autonomous from their parents without becoming detached from them (Laursen & Collins, 2009; McElhaney et al., 2009; Van Petegem, Vansteenkiste, & Beyers, 2012), although achieving this balance can be more difficult in cultural contexts in which individualism is not as strongly valued as it is in many Western cultures (Yu, 2011). Adolescents who are better able to balance autonomy and connectedness in their relationships with their parents are also better able to balance autonomy and intimacy in their friendships and romantic relationships (Oudekirk, Allen, Hessel, & Molloy, 2015; Taradash, Connolly, Pepler, Craig, & Costa, 2001).

Emotional Autonomy and Individuation

As an alternative to the classic psychoanalytic perspective on adolescent detachment, some theorists have suggested that we view the development of emotional autonomy in terms of the adolescent's developing sense of **individuation** (Blos, 1967). Individuation, which begins during infancy and continues into late adolescence, involves a

In contrast to the view that tension between adolescents and their parents is the norm, every major study done to date of family relations in adolescence has shown that most teenagers and their parents get along quite well. © Image Source/Getty Images RF

gradual, progressive sharpening of one's sense of self as autonomous, competent, and separate from one's parents.

Individuation does not involve stress and turmoil. Rather, it entails relinquishing childish dependencies on parents in favor of a more mature, more responsible, and less dependent relationship (McElhaney et al., 2009; Zimmer-Gembeck, Ducat, & Collins, 2011). Adolescents who establish a healthy sense of autonomy accept responsibility for their choices and actions (Van Petegem, Beyers, Vansteenkiste, & Soenens, 2012). Rather than rebelling against her parents' midnight curfew by deliberately staying out later, a girl who has a healthy sense of individuation might take her parents aside before going out and say, "This party tonight is going to go later than midnight. If it does, I'd like to stay a bit longer. Why don't I call you at eleven and let you know when I'll be home?"

Research on Emotional Autonomy

The development of emotional autonomy is a long process, beginning early in adolescence and continuing into young adulthood (McElhaney et al., 2009). There are many indicators of this. Adolescents start to see their parents' flaws. They depend less on them to fix things that have gone wrong. As they individuate, teenagers realize that there are things about themselves that their parents aren't aware of (Steinberg & Silverberg, 1986). There often is a drop in the number of their

detachment
In psychoanalytic theory, the process through which adolescents sever emotional attachments to their parents or other authority figures.

individuation
The progressive sharpening of an individual's sense of being an autonomous, independent person.

friends whom their parents know, reflecting an increase in the size of teenagers' social networks and in their need for privacy (Feiring & Lewis, 1993). Adolescents' willingness to express negative emotions in front of their parents, such as anger or sadness, is lower during early adolescence than before or after, perhaps because keeping some emotional distance from one's parents is a part of the individuation process (Zeman & Shipman, 1997).

Adolescents become less likely to say that they have the same opinions as their parents, or that they always agree with them (McElhaney et al., 2009; Zhang & Fuligni, 2006). This, in turn, is associated with changes in adolescents' beliefs about their parents' authority over them. Adolescents become increasingly likely to draw distinctions between aspects of their life that their parents have the right to regulate and those that they think are not really their parents' business (Darling, Cumsille, & Martinez, 2008; Laird & Marrero, 2011; Nucci, Smetana, Araki, Nakaue, & Comer, 2014; S. A. Perkins & Turiel, 2007).

De-Idealization   Children place their parents on a pedestal; adolescents knock them off it. Psychologists believe that this "de-idealization" of parents may be one of the first aspects of emotional autonomy to develop, because adolescents shed their childish images of their parents before replacing them with more mature ones. Even during the high school years, adolescents have some difficulty in

As adolescents develop emotional autonomy, they often begin to question and challenge their parents more frequently.
© BananaStock/PunchStock RF

seeing their parents as individuals beyond their roles as parents. This aspect of emotional autonomy may not develop until much later—perhaps not until young adulthood (Smollar & Youniss, 1985). Seeing one's parents as people typically develops later in adolescents' relations with their fathers than with their mothers, because fathers interact less often with their adolescents in ways that permit them to be seen as individuals (Smollar & Youniss, 1985).

The Importance of Maintaining the Connection   In contrast to the old view that adolescents need to sever their ties with their parents in order to grow up healthily, a number of studies find that the development of emotional autonomy, and individuation in particular, may have different psychological effects on adolescents depending on whether the parent-child relationship is a close one. Adolescents who become emotionally autonomous, but who also feel distant or detached from their parents, score poorly on measures of psychological adjustment, whereas adolescents who demonstrate the same degree of emotional autonomy, but who still feel close and attached to their parents, are psychologically healthier than their peers (J. Allen, Porter, McFarland, McElhaney, & Marsh, 2007). These studies remind us that it is important to distinguish between separating from one's parents in a way that nevertheless maintains emotional closeness in the relationship (which is healthy) and breaking away from one's parents in a fashion that involves alienation, conflict, and hostility (which is not) (Jager, Yuen, Putnick, Hendricks, & Bornstein, 2015; Parra, Oliva, & Sánchez-Queija, 2015). Lying to one's parents and concealing undesirable things from them, which may be more an indicator of detachment than healthy individuation, is associated with psychological problems (Ahmad, Smetana, & Klimstra, 2014; Laird, Marrero, Melching, & Kuhn, 2013; Rote & Smetana, 2014; Tilton-Weaver, 2013). As individuals make the transition from adolescence into adulthood and work through much of the individuation process, they increasingly see lying to their parents as unacceptable (Jensen, Arnett, Feldman, & Cauffman, 2004).

What Triggers Individuation?   What triggers individuation? Two different models have been suggested (Laursen & Collins, 2009). According to several researchers, puberty is the main catalyst (e.g., Holmbeck, 1996; Steinberg, 2000). Changes in the adolescent's physical appearance provoke changes in the way that adolescents are viewed—by themselves and by their parents—which, in turn, provoke changes in parent-child interaction. Shortly after puberty, most families experience an increase in bickering and squabbling. Adolescents' feelings of connectedness to their parents often decline in early adolescence, when bickering is more frequent, but increase in late adolescence after this temporary period of heightened squabbling is over (Pinquart & Silbereisen, 2002).

Other authors believe that adolescents' movement toward higher levels of individuation is stimulated by their cognitive development (W. A. Collins, 1990; Smetana, 1995a). The development of emotional autonomy in adolescence may be provoked by young people's development of more sophisticated understandings of themselves and their parents. Prior to adolescence, individuals accept their parents' views of themselves as accurate ("My parents think I am a good girl, so I must be"). But as individuals develop more differentiated self-conceptions in early and middle adolescence, they come to see that their parents' view is but one of many—and one that may not be entirely correct ("My parents think I am a good girl, but they don't know what I am really like"). By late adolescence, individuals are able to see that these apparent discrepancies between their self-conceptions and their parents' views are perfectly understandable ("There are sides of me that my parents know and sides of me that they don't") (Harter, 2011).

Separating from one's parents is not as turbulent as was once believed, but it nevertheless has its difficult moments. Even though the images children have of their parents as all-knowing and all-powerful may be naive, these idealized pictures still provide emotional comfort. Leaving such images behind can be both liberating and frightening, for parents as well as teenagers. The development of emotional autonomy is associated not only with insecurity among adolescents, but also with increased feelings of anxiety and rejection among parents (Hock, Eberly, Bartle-Haring, Ellwanger, & Widaman, 2001). Difficulties in the process of individuation also arise when adolescents push for independence at an earlier age than parents are willing to grant it. Adolescents usually believe that teenagers should be granted autonomy earlier than parents do (Ruck, Peterson-Badali, & Day, 2002).

Emotional Autonomy and Parenting Practices

Whether provoked by puberty or by the development of more advanced cognitive skills, and whether approached with confidence or trepidation, one fact is certain: Healthy individuation and positive mental health are fostered by close, not distant, family relationships (McElhaney et al., 2009). Tense family relationships during adolescence indicate problems, not positive development. The adolescents who feel the most autonomous—those who are most likely to feel that they have been granted enough freedom by their parents—are not the ones who have severed relationships at home. In fact, just the opposite is true: Autonomous adolescents are close to their parents, enjoy doing things with them, have few conflicts with them, feel free to turn to them for advice, and say they would like to be like them (McElhaney et al., 2009; Qin & Pomerantz, 2013). Rebellion, negativism, and excessive involvement in the peer group are more common among psychologically immature adolescents than among mature ones (Steinberg, 1990). Even during college, students who live away from home (which is in its own way a type of autonomy)—as opposed to remaining in their parents' home and commuting to school—report more affection for their parents, better communication, and higher levels of satisfaction with the relationship (Holmbeck, Durbin, & Kung, 1995). In other words, strained family relationships appear to be associated with a *lack* of autonomy during adolescence, rather than with its presence (Bomar & Sabatelli, 1996).

In Asian and Western countries alike, adolescents whose parents impede the individuation process are more likely to show signs of psychological distress (Campione-Barr, Greer, & Kruse, 2013; Helwig, To, Q. Wang, Liu, & Pomerantz, 2014; Kouros & Garber, 2014). Adolescents who do not feel good about themselves and who have very intrusive parents are especially vulnerable to depression (Pomerantz, 2001). In contrast, around the world, adolescents whose parents provide support for their growing interest in autonomy report better mental health than those whose parents do not (see Figure 1) (Chueng, Pomerantz, & Dong, 2013; Ferguson, Kasser, & Jahng, 2011; Lekes, Gingras, Philippe, Koestner, & Fang, 2010).

Adolescents whose parents are emotionally close to the point of being intrusive or overprotective—parents

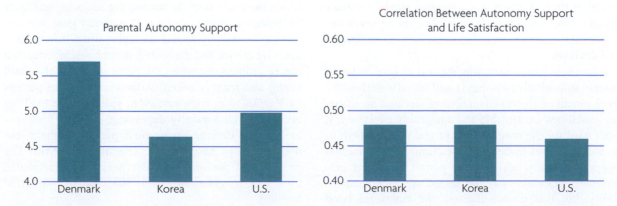

Figure 1 Although adolescents in different cultures receive different degrees of parental support for becoming autonomous, the correlation between autonomy support from parents and adolescents' life satisfaction is similar in different cultural contexts. (Ferguson, Kasser, & Jahng, 2011)

psychological control
Parenting that attempts to control the adolescent's emotions and opinions.

who use a lot of **psychological control**—may have difficulty individuating from them, which may lead to depression, anxiety, aggression, and feelings of incompetence and dependence (Hare, Szwedo, Schad, & Allen, 2014; Kuppens, Laurent, Heyvart, & Onghena, 2013; Lansford, Laird, Pettit, Bates, & Dodge, 2014). In some families, adolescents respond to excessive parental control by actively rebelling (Van Petegem, Soenens, Vansteenkiste, & Beyers, 2015).

Keep in mind, of course, that parents are also influenced by their teenagers: Adolescents who are bullied, and who presumably become more anxious and timid as a result, are more likely to elicit psychological control from their parents (Ma & Bellmore, 2012). Similarly, adolescents with psychological problems are more likely to provoke conflict with their parents, which makes some parents more controlling (Steeger & Gondoli, 2013).

Emotional Autonomy and Parenting Style Independence, responsibility, and self-esteem are all fostered by parents who are authoritative (friendly, fair, and firm) rather than authoritarian (excessively harsh), indulgent (excessively lenient), or indifferent (aloof to the point of being neglectful). As a result, the development of emotional autonomy follows different patterns in different types of households.

In authoritative families, guidelines are established for the adolescent's behavior, and standards are upheld, but they are flexible and open to discussion. Although parents may have the final say when it comes to their child's behavior, the decision that is reached usually comes after consultation and discussion—with the child included (Benish-Weisman, Levy, & Knafo, 2013; Mauras, Grolnick, & Friendly, 2013). In discussing an adolescent's curfew, for example, authoritative parents will sit down with their child and explain how they arrived at their decision and why they picked the hour they did. They will also ask the adolescent for his or her suggestions and consider them carefully in making a final decision.

It is not difficult to see why the sort of give-and-take found in authoritative families is well suited to the healthy development of emotional autonomy. Because standards and guidelines are flexible and adequately explained, it is not hard for the family to adjust and modify them as the child matures (Smetana & Asquith, 1994). Gradual changes in family relations that permit the young person more independence and encourage more responsibility, but that do not threaten the emotional bond between parent and child—in other words, changes that promote increasing emotional autonomy—are relatively

easy to make in a family that has been flexible all along (Vuchinich, Angeletti, & Gatherum, 1996). Plus, having a close relationship with one parent protects against the adverse effects of the other parent's psychological control (Murray, Dwyer, Rubin, Knighton-Wisor, & Booth-LaForce, 2013).

In authoritarian households, where rules are rigidly enforced and seldom explained, adjusting to adolescence is more difficult. Authoritarian parents see the child's emotional independence as rebellious or disrespectful, and they resist their adolescent's growing need for independence, rather than accepting it. Seeing that their daughter is becoming interested in boys, an authoritarian parent may implement a rigid curfew in order to restrict the teenager's social life. Authoritarian parents may inadvertently maintain the dependencies of childhood by failing to give their children sufficient practice in making decisions and being responsible for their actions. In essence, authoritarian parenting may interfere with adolescent individuation.

When closeness, as well as support for autonomy, is absent, the problems are compounded. In families in which excessive parental control is accompanied by extreme coldness and punitiveness, adolescents may rebel against their parents' standards explicitly, in an attempt to assert their independence in a visible and demonstrable fashion (Kakihara, Tilton-Weaver, Kerr, & Stattin, 2010). Adolescents were more likely to "act out"—to misbehave—when their parents are overreactive or intrusive (van den Akker, Deković, & Prinzie, 2010); one study found that the more frequently parents called their adolescent's cell phone, the more dishonest the adolescent was (Weisskirch, 2009). Such rebellion is not indicative of genuine emotional autonomy—it's a demonstration of the adolescent's frustration with his or her parents' rigidity and lack of understanding.

In both indulgent and indifferent families, a different sort of problem arises. These parents do not provide sufficient guidance for their children, and as a result, the youngsters do not acquire adequate standards for behavior. In the absence of parental guidance and rules, permissively reared teenagers often turn to their peers for advice and emotional support—a practice that can be problematic when the peers are themselves still young and inexperienced. Adolescents whose parents have failed to provide sufficient guidance are likely to become psychologically dependent on their friends—emotionally detached from their parents, perhaps, but not genuinely autonomous (Steinberg, 1990). The problems of parental permissiveness are exacerbated by a lack of closeness, as is the case in indifferent families.

Some parents who have raised their children permissively until adolescence are caught off guard by the consequences of not having been stricter earlier on. The greater orientation toward the peer group of permissively raised adolescents may involve the young person in behavior that his or her parents disapprove of. As a consequence, some parents who have been permissive throughout a youngster's childhood shift gears when he or she enters adolescence, becoming autocratic in an attempt to control a youngster over whom they feel they have lost their authority. Parents who have never placed any restrictions on their child's out-of-school activities during elementary school may suddenly begin monitoring her social life once she enters junior high school. Shifts like these can be extremely hard on adolescents—just at the time when they are seeking greater autonomy, their parents become more restrictive. Having become accustomed to relative leniency, adolescents whose parents change the rules in the middle of the game may find it difficult to accept standards that are being strictly enforced for the first time.

The Development of Behavioral Autonomy

Whereas the development of emotional autonomy is played out mainly in adolescents' relationships with their parents, the development of behavioral autonomy—the ability to act independently—is seen both inside and outside the family, in relationships with peers as well as parents. Broadly speaking, behavioral autonomy refers to the capacity for independent decision making. Researchers who have studied behavioral autonomy have looked at changes in *decision-making abilities* and in *susceptibility to the influence of others*.

Changes in Decision-Making Abilities

The more sophisticated reasoning processes used by adolescents permit them to hold multiple viewpoints in mind simultaneously, allowing them to compare people's different perspectives, which is crucial for weighing the opinions and advice of others. Because adolescents are better able than children to think in hypothetical terms, they also are more likely to contemplate the long-term consequences of each choice. Moreover, the enhanced role-taking capabilities of adolescence permit teenagers to consider another person's opinion while taking into account that person's point of view. This is important in determining whether someone who has given advice has special areas of expertise, particular biases, or vested interests that the teenager should keep in mind. Taken together, these cognitive changes result in improved decision-making skills and,

consequently, in the individual's enhanced ability to behave independently.

Improvements in Self-Regulation   Many studies have documented important improvements in decision-making abilities during middle and late adolescence that are linked to gains in self-regulation (Christakopu, 2014). With age, adolescents become more likely to consider both the risks and benefits associated with the decisions they make and more likely to weigh the long-term consequences of their choices, not just the immediate ones (Crone & van der Molen, 2007; Steinberg, Graham et al., 2009). Across many different cultural contexts, strong self-regulation is one of the most robust predictors of success in life, whereas weak self-regulation is linked to all sorts of emotional and behavioral problems (Denissen, van Aken, Penke, & Wood, 2013; Evans & Fuller-Rowell, 2013; Roper, Vecera, & Vaidya, 2014; Steinberg, 2014; Trommsdorff, 2012).

Improvements in self-regulation appear to be due to two separate, but related developments (Shulman, Harden, Chein, & Steinberg, 2014). First, there is a decline over the course of adolescence in the extent to which decisions are influenced by their potential immediate rewards (de Water, Cillessen, & Scheres, 2014). Most situations in which we have to decide among alternative choices (Should I stay home and study or go out with my friends? Should we sneak into the movie theater or stand in line and pay for tickets? Should I sleep with my girlfriend right now or wait until tomorrow night, when I'll make sure to have a condom?) present a combination of potential rewards and potential costs. What we decide

The brain's pleasure centers are more easily aroused during early adolescence than in childhood or adulthood, which makes adolescent decision making more influenced by the prospect of immediate rewards. © ERproductions Ltd/Blend Images RF

to do is often the result of how strong those rewards and costs are. Someone who is just thinking about having fun with his friends, saving money by seeing the movie for free, or how good unprotected sex is going to feel will act differently than someone who is thinking about the grade he might get on a test he didn't study for, what would happen if he got caught sneaking into the theater, or the possibility of getting his girlfriend pregnant.

During early adolescence, individuals are much more drawn to the potential benefits of a decision than the potential costs. As they mature, the relative balance of reward and cost changes, so that by late adolescence, these factors are weighed about evenly (Cauffman et al., 2010). Psychologists have now mapped this development onto changes in patterns of brain activation, showing that the regions of the brain that are especially sensitive to reward are more intensely activated during early and middle adolescence than childhood or adulthood, especially when rewards are being anticipated, as they might be when adolescents are thinking about how much fun they are going to have before they head out for an evening (Galvan, 2013; Van Leijenhorst, Zanolie et al., 2010). Some of the heightened "reward sensitivity" seen among adolescents is not even conscious (Cauffman et al., 2010). Adolescents are just as consciously aware as adults of the potential rewards and costs of a decision—they are just influenced more by the anticipated rewards (Van Leijenhorst, Westenberg, & Crone, 2008).

Not only are younger adolescents more drawn to rewards than are adults, but they also seem especially drawn to *immediate* rewards (Steinberg, 2008). Consider the following question: Would you rather have $200 tomorrow or $1,000 a year from now? How about $600 tomorrow versus $1,000 a year from now? Individuals who are willing to settle for a smaller amount in order to get it sooner are more drawn to immediate rewards. Figure 2 shows the amount of money individuals of different ages would settle for if they received it tomorrow rather than waiting a year (Steinberg, Graham et al., 2009). As you can see, preadolescents and early adolescents are much more willing to settle for less, as long as they can get it sooner.

A second influence on changes in decision making concerns individuals' ability to control their impulses (Steinberg, Albert et al., 2008; van Duijvenvoorde,

Jansen, Bredman, & Huizenga, 2012; Weiser & Reynolds, 2011). Regions of the brain that govern self-regulation are still developing during adolescence and early adulthood, as are connections between brain regions that control impulses and those that respond to rewards (Luna, Paulsen, Padmanabhan, & Geier, 2013; Peper et al., 2013; van den Bos, Rodriguez, Schweitzer, & McClure, 2015). This improvement in self-control has important implications for decision making. With age, individuals are better at thinking ahead, imagining and analyzing the consequences of their decisions, seeking and evaluating the advice of others, and making decisions that aren't hasty or excessively influenced by their emotions (Munakata, Snyder, & Chatham, 2012). The combination of heightened reward sensitivity and immature impulse control may lead adolescents to make a lot of risky—even dangerous—decisions. Some writers have suggested that one way to diminish adolescent risk taking is to encourage them to do things like mindfulness meditation, which has been shown to increase self regulation (Steinberg, 2014).

When Do Adolescents Make Decisions as Well as Adults?

The recognition that individuals' decision-making skills improve over the course of adolescence has prompted numerous debates about young people's abilities to make decisions in the real world—for example, with regard to having access to medical care without their parents' approval or functioning as competent defendants in court. Many such debates revolve around where we should draw the legal boundary between adolescence and adulthood for things like driving, purchasing alcohol or cigarettes, or being tried in adult court (Steinberg, 2012).

One relevant line of research has examined adolescents' legal decision making (Grisso et al., 2003; Kambam & Thompson, 2009; M. G. Schmidt, Reppucci, & Woolard, 2003). In the typical study, adolescents and adults are presented with vignettes involving an individual who had gotten into trouble with the law and asked how the individual should handle different situations—being interrogated by the police, consulting with an attorney, deciding whether to plead guilty in return for a lesser sentence

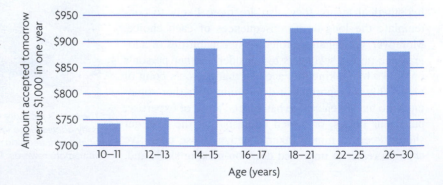

Figure 2 Younger adolescents are especially drawn to immediate rewards. This graph shows age differences in the amount of money individuals would settle for if they could have it immediately, versus waiting one year for $1,000. (Steinberg, Graham, et al., 2009)

versus going to trial, or taking her or his chances on the outcome. In these studies, adolescents are less likely than adults to think about the long-term implications of their decisions, more likely to focus on the immediate consequences, and less able to understand the ways in which other people's positions might bias their interests. For example, when asked what a guilty individual should do when being interrogated by the police, younger adolescents are more likely than adults to say that they should confess (which is not what most attorneys would recommend) rather than remain silent (the most advisable thing to do). Younger adolescents are more inclined to think about the immediate consequences of their actions ("If I tell the police the truth, they'll let me go home"), not the longer-term implications ("If I confess, this information can be used against me in court").

One difficulty in making decisions about where to draw lines between adolescents and adults is that mature decision making is the product of both cognitive abilities (such as being able to reason logically) and emotional factors (such as being able to control one's impulses), which are aspects of development that proceed along somewhat different timetables (Steinberg, Cauffman et al., 2009). The maturation of basic cognitive abilities is complete at around age 16. Many writers have argued that older adolescents should therefore have the right to seek health care services (including abortions and contraception) without parental knowledge or consent. But because there are improvements in things like impulse control, planning ahead, and risk assessment well into early adulthood, there is a period during which adolescents may *think* like adults but *behave* in a much more immature way. Individuals who are opposed to trying juvenile offenders as adults use this evidence to argue in favor of treating juveniles who have committed crimes less harshly than adults because of their immature judgment (Modecki, 2008; Owen-Kostelnik, Reppucci, & Meyer, 2006; E. Scott & Steinberg, 2008).

One way of resolving this problem is to make sure our treatment of adolescents is consistent with what we know about psychological development in ways that are specific to the legal matters in question (Steinberg, Cauffman et al. 2009). In other words, if the skills necessary for making one type of decision mature earlier than those necessary for another, it would make sense to have a different age boundary for each.

making the practical connection

Based on what you have read about changes in decision-making abilities in adolescence, should adolescents be treated like adults under the law? If you were a lawmaker, where would you draw the line for issues concerning access to health care? For responses to violations of the law?

Changes in Susceptibility to Influence

As adolescents come to spend more time outside the family, the opinions and advice of others—not only peers but adults as well—become more important. A variety of situations arise in which adolescents may feel that their parents' advice may be less valid than the opinions of others. Adolescents might seek the advice of friends, rather than their parents, about how to dress. They may turn to a teacher or guidance counselor for advice about what courses to take in school. Or they might talk something over with more than one person. A teenage girl who is trying to decide whether to take a part-time job after school might discuss the pros and cons with her parents but also ask friends for their advice. When different "advisors" disagree, adolescents must reconcile the differences of opinion and reach their own independent conclusions.

In situations in which parents and peers give conflicting advice, do teenagers tend to follow one group more often than the other? Adolescents are often portrayed as being extremely susceptible to the influence of peer pressure—more so than children or young adults—and as being stubbornly resistant to the influence of their parents. But is peer pressure really more potent during adolescence than at other times?

The Influence of Parents and Peers   Researchers have studied conformity and peer pressure during adolescence by putting adolescents in situations in which they must choose between the wishes of their parents and those of their peers, or between their own wishes and those of others—typically, parents or friends. An adolescent might be told to imagine that he and his friends discover the answer sheet to an upcoming test on the floor outside the teachers' lounge. His friends tell him that they should keep it a secret. But the adolescent tells his mother about it, and she advises him to tell the teacher. He then would be asked by the researcher to say what he would do.

Adolescents turn for advice to different people in different situations (Finken & Jacobs, 1996; Halpern-Felsher, 2011). In some situations, peers' opinions are more influential, but in others, parents' views are more powerful. Adolescents are more likely to conform to peers' opinions when it comes to short-term, day-to-day, and social matters—styles of dress, tastes in music, choices among leisure activities, and so on. This is particularly true during the junior high school and early high school years. When it comes to long-term questions concerning educational or occupational plans, however, or to issues concerning values, religious beliefs, or ethics, teenagers are primarily influenced by their parents (W. A. Collins & Steinberg, 2006). When adolescents' problems center on a relationship with a friend, they usually turn to a peer, a preference that becomes stronger with age. But adolescents' willingness to turn to an adult for advice with problems—especially those that involve getting along with their parents—remains very strong and increases as individuals move toward late adolescence (Morrison, Laughlin, Miguel, Smith, & Widaman, 1997).

Responding to Peer Pressure Studies that contrast the influence of peers and adults do not really reveal all there is to know about peer pressure. Most peer pressure operates when adults are absent—when adolescents are at a party, driving home from school, or hanging out with their friends. To get closer to this issue, researchers have studied how adolescents respond when they must choose between the pressure of their friends and their own opinions of what to do. For example, an adolescent might be asked whether he would go along with his friends' pressure to vandalize some property even though he did not want to do so (e.g., Bámaca & Umaña-Taylor, 2006).

Most studies using this approach show that conformity to peers is higher during middle adolescence than later (Steinberg & Monahan, 2007). Some studies find that conformity to peers increases between early and middle adolescence, peaking around age 14, whereas others find no change during this time (T. Sim & Koh, 2003) or that preadolescents are even more susceptible to peer influence than teenagers (Steinberg & Monahan, 2007). The especially heightened susceptibility to peer pressure around age 14 is most often seen when the behavior in question is antisocial—such as cheating, stealing, or trespassing—especially in studies of boys (Erickson, Crosnoe, & Dornbusch, 2000). These findings are in line with studies of delinquency, which are often committed by boys in groups, often during middle adolescence (Farrington, 2009). Adolescents who are more susceptible to peer pressure to engage in delinquent activity actually are more likely to misbehave (J. Allen, Porter, & McFarland, 2006; Monahan, Steinberg, Cauffman, & Mulvey, 2009). Susceptibility to antisocial peer pressure is also higher among relatively more acculturated Latino adolescents than their less acculturated peers, and higher among Latino adolescents who were born in the United States than those who were born abroad, consistent with research showing higher rates of delinquency among more acculturated adolescents (Bámaca & Umaña-Taylor, 2006; Umaña-Taylor & Bámaca-Gómez, 2003; Wall, Power, & Arbona, 1993).

The consequences of being especially susceptible to one's peers depend on who those peers are. For instance, whereas high susceptibility to peer influence predicts adolescents' antisocial behavior if their friends are antisocial, the same level of susceptibility is not predictive of problem behavior if their friends are not (Monahan, Steinberg, & Cauffman, 2009; Paternoster, McGloin, Nguyen, & Thomas, 2013). And, of course, many adolescents have friends who pressure them *not* to get involved in questionable, illegal, or risky activities (Kam & Wang, 2014).

Although we know that conformity to peer pressure is high during early adolescence, it isn't clear why. One possibility is that young adolescents are more susceptible to peer influence because of their heightened orientation toward social stimuli (Nelson, Lau, & Jarcho, 2014; Somerville, 2013). Another is that individuals' susceptibility to peer pressure doesn't change, but that peer pressure may be especially strong around the time individuals are 14. In other words, adolescent peer groups may exert more pressure on their members to conform than do groups of younger or older individuals, and the pressure may be strong enough to make even the most autonomous teenagers comply.

Yet a third account is that being around other teenagers changes the way the adolescent brain functions. During adolescence the mere presence of friends activates brain regions associated with the experience of reward, but that no such effect is found when adolescents are with their parents, or when adults are with *their* friends, as shown in Figure 3 (Chein, Albert, O'Brien, Uckert, & Steinberg, 2011; Smith, Steinberg, Strang, & Chein, 2015; Telzer, Ichien, & Qu, 2015). Even adolescent mice show an increase in sensitivity to rewards

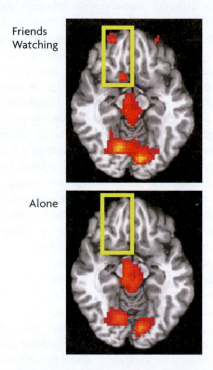

Figure 3 Adolescents are more susceptible to peer influence than adults are. This figure shows two brain scans, one taken while adolescents were playing a driving game when their friends were watching, and the other taken when the adolescents were playing alone. The area surrounded by the yellow rectangle is a part of the brain that is activated when we experience reward. One reason adolescents may behave more recklessly when they are with their friends is that the presence of peers may make them pay more attention to the potential rewards of a risky choice. (Chein et al., 2011)
© Photos courtesy of Laurence Steinberg

when with their "peers," something that isn't seen in adult mice (Logue, Chein, Gould, Holliday, & Steinberg, 2014). When adolescents are with their friends, they may be especially likely to pay attention to the potential rewards of a risky choice, and less likely to notice the potential costs (Habib et al., 2015; Haddad, Harrison, Norman, & Lau, 2014; Smith, Chein, & Steinberg, 2014; Weigard, Chein, Albert, Smith, & Steinberg, 2014).

Because adolescents experience pleasure when they are with their peers, they are more likely to go along with the crowd to avoid being rejected (W. A. Collins & Steinberg, 2006). Adolescents who are led to believe they are interacting in a chat room with either high-status or low-status peers (which is manipulated by the experimenters in the way the peers are described) about the acceptability of various illegal or risky behaviors are more influenced by the opinions of high-status peers, an effect that is especially strong among adolescents who are particularly susceptible to peer influence (Choukas-Bradley, Giletta, Widman, Cohen, & Prinstein, 2014). This creates a dilemma: Teenagers must strike a balance between asserting their independence and fitting in (Allen, Chango, & Szwedo, 2014). One of the challenges of adolescence is that being popular with peers often requires a willingness to engage in behaviors that adults disapprove of, like drinking.

Individual Differences in Susceptibility to Peer Influence

Within a group of teenagers who are the same age, some are highly autonomous, others are easily influenced by their peers, others are oriented toward their parents, and still others are swayed by both peers and parents, depending on the situation (Prinstein, Brechwald, & Cohen, 2011). Girls are less susceptible to peer pressure than boys, as are Black adolescents in comparison to adolescents from other ethnic groups. Asian American adolescents, in contrast, seem especially susceptible to peer pressure, perhaps consistent with the greater emphasis placed on the importance of the group over the individual in Asian cultures (Steinberg & Monahan, 2007). Adolescents from single-parent families, as well as those with less supportive or more controlling parents, appear especially susceptible to peer pressure (S. Chan & K. Chan, 2013; C. Wong, Crosnoe, Laird, & Dornbusch, 2003).

Studies of adolescent brain development are adding to our growing understanding of differences among adolescents in their susceptibility to peer influence (Brechwald & Prinstein, 2011). Individuals who show a pattern of brain activity indicating heightened sensitivity to social evaluation are less able to resist peer influence (Buck, Kretsch, & Harden, 2013; Falk et al., 2014; Guyer et al., 2014; Sebastian et al., 2011), as are adolescents who are in the midst of puberty, perhaps because pubertal hormones make adolescents more sensitive to social influence (Kretsch & Harden, 2014), as well as those who are

Peers have a powerful influence over adolescents' tastes in clothes, hairstyles, and other day-to-day decisions. © Reed Kaestner/Corbis RF/Corbis

high in sensation seeking (Segalowitz et al., 2012). Being able to resist peer pressure is associated with stronger connections between areas of the brain active during decision making and other regions, perhaps because individuals who are more likely to stand up to their friends are better able to better control the impulsive, emotional decision making that often occurs in the peer group (Grosbras et al., 2007; Paus et al., 2008). Similarly, adolescents whose neural activity is indicative of better emotion regulation also report more resistance to peer influence (Pfeifer, Masten, Moore, & Oswald, 2011). This brain research is consistent with the idea that a key aspect of positive development in adolescence involves the development of self-regulation (Gestdóttir & Lerner, 2007; Monahan, Steinberg, Cauffman, & Mulvey, 2009).

Parenting and Behavioral Autonomy

Like emotional autonomy, behavioral autonomy appears to be associated with authoritative rather than permissive, authoritarian, or neglectful parenting (W. A. Collins & Steinberg, 2006). The sexual behavior of adolescents who have discussed sex with their parents is less influenced by peer pressure than is the behavior of adolescents who have not done so (Whitaker & Miller, 2000), and adolescents whose parents strongly disapprove of smoking are less likely to be influenced by their friends' smoking than are adolescents whose parents haven't voiced their disapproval (Sargent & Dalton, 2001). Other research finds that impulsive adolescents are less likely to consult with their parents before making decisions (Romich, Lundberg, & Tsang, 2009).

The situation is a bit more complicated, however. The impact of having authoritative parents on adolescents' susceptibility to peer pressure depends on the nature of the peer pressure. Adolescents from authoritative homes

Parents from different ethnic groups have different ideas about the appropriate age at which to grant adolescents autonomy.
© Ashok Sinha/Getty Images

are less susceptible to antisocial peer pressure, but they may be *more* susceptible to the influence of positive peers. Adolescents from authoritative homes are less likely to be influenced by having drug-using friends, but they are more likely to be influenced by having friends who perform well in school (Mounts & Steinberg, 1995). It is also important to distinguish between adolescents who are excessively dependent on their peers (and who forgo their parents' rules and pay less attention to their schoolwork for the sake of being popular with peers) and those who turn to peers for counsel but do not ignore their parents' guidance (Fuligni, Eccles, Barber, & Clements, 2001). Substituting peers for parents leads to problem behavior; adding peers to the list of persons one turns to for advice, so long as that list includes parents, does not. In other words, it is detachment from parents, rather than attachment to peers, that is potentially harmful.

The ways in which parents and adolescents negotiate changes in behavioral autonomy have implications for adolescents' adjustment (Chen-Gaddini, 2012; S. Goldstein, Davis-Kean, & Eccles, 2005; Roche et al., 2014). Adolescents who have less positive relationships with their parents are more likely to be especially peer oriented, to affiliate with antisocial peers, and to spend time with friends in unsupervised settings, all of which heighten the risk for problem behavior. But parents need to maintain a healthy balance between asserting control and granting autonomy. Granting too much autonomy before adolescents are ready for it or granting too little autonomy once adolescents are mature enough to handle it creates adolescents who are the most strongly peer oriented. Adolescents whose parents become more authoritarian over time (stricter and less likely to permit the adolescent to make decisions) are the most peer oriented of all.

Although many parents clamp down on their teenagers' independence out of fear that not doing so will allow the youngsters to fall under the "evil" influence of the peer group, this strategy often backfires. Having parents limit their autonomy at just the time when more independence is desired and expected makes adolescents turn away from the family and toward their friends.

Ethnic and Cultural Differences in Expectations for Autonomy

The development of behavioral autonomy varies across cultures because of differences in the age expectations that adolescents and parents have for independent behavior. Adolescents' mental health is best when their desire for autonomy matches their expectations for what their parents are willing to grant (Juang, Lerner, McKinney, & von Eye, 1999). For example, White adolescents and their parents have earlier expectations for adolescent autonomy than do Asian adolescents and parents from the same countries (Rosenthal & Feldman, 1990). Because of this, Asian adolescents may be less likely to seek autonomy from their parents than White adolescents, and White adolescents are less likely than Asian adolescents to define themselves in terms of their relationship with their parents (Pomerantz, Qin, Wang, & Chen, 2009). Perhaps because of this, increased autonomy is strongly associated with better emotional functioning among American youth (where being an independent person is highly valued), but less so among Asian adolescents (Qin, Pomerantz, & Wang, 2009).

Sex and birth order differences in behavioral autonomy tend to be very small and are often inconsistent—contrary to the popular beliefs that boys are granted more autonomy than girls or that later-born adolescents are granted earlier freedom because their older siblings have paved the way (Wray-Lake, Crouter, & McHale, 2010). Some studies find sex and birth order differences in the extent to which parents grant autonomy, but the pattern varies depending on the particular constellation of sons and daughters in the household and on the parents' attitudes toward sex roles (more traditionally minded parents grant more autonomy to sons than daughters, but more educated parents grant more autonomy to daughters than sons [Bumpus, Crouter, & McHale, 2001; Wray-Lake et al., 2010]). Sex differences in the extent to which adolescents are granted independence appear to be especially pronounced within Black households, where boys are given substantially more freedom then girls (Daddis & Smetana, 2005).

In families that have immigrated to a new culture, parents and adolescents often have different expectations about granting autonomy (Romo, Mireles-Rios, & Lopez-Tello, 2014). As a rule, because adolescents generally acculturate more quickly to a new culture than do parents, a family that has moved from a culture in which it is normal to grant autonomy relatively later in adolescence (as in most Asian countries) to one in which it is normal to grant autonomy relatively earlier (as in the United States) may experience conflict as a result of differences in the expectations of adolescents and parents (Bámaca-Colbert, Umaña-Taylor, Espinosa-Hernández, & Brown, 2012). Adolescents' expectations for autonomy are shaped to a great extent by their perceptions of how much independence their friends have (Daddis, 2011).

The Development of Cognitive Autonomy

The development of cognitive autonomy entails changes in the adolescent's beliefs, opinions, and values. It has been studied mainly by looking at how adolescents think about moral, political, and religious issues.

Three trends in the development of cognitive autonomy are especially noteworthy. First, adolescents become increasingly abstract in the way they think about moral, political, and religious issues. This leads to more complicated decisions about how to act when one's beliefs about one issue conflict with one's beliefs about another. Consider an 18-year-old who is deciding whether to participate in a deliberately disruptive demonstration against policies he believes support the interests of environmental polluters. Instead of looking at the situation only in terms of the environmental issues, he might also think about the implications of knowingly violating the law by being disruptive. Second, during adolescence, beliefs become increasingly rooted in general principles. An 18-year-old might say that demonstrating against pollution is acceptable because protecting the environment is more important than living in accord with the law, and so breaking a law is legitimate when the status quo leads to environmental degradation. Finally, beliefs become increasingly founded in the young person's own values, not merely in a system of values passed on by parents or other authority figures. Thus, an 18-year-old may look at the issue of environmental protection in terms of what he himself believes, rather than in terms of what his parents have told him to think.

Much of the growth in cognitive autonomy can be traced to the cognitive changes characteristic of the period. With adolescents' enhanced reasoning capabilities and the further development of hypothetical thinking come a heightened interest in ideological and philosophical matters and a more sophisticated way of looking at them. The ability to consider alternate possibilities and to engage in thinking about thinking allows for the exploration of differing value systems, political ideologies, personal ethics, and religious beliefs.

The growth of cognitive autonomy follows and is encouraged by the development of emotional and behavioral autonomy, which typically take place earlier in adolescence (W. A. Collins & Steinberg, 2006). The establishment of emotional autonomy provides adolescents with the ability to look at their parents more objectively. When adolescents

no longer see their parents as omnipotent and infallible, they may reevaluate the ideas and values that they accepted without question as children.

> **prosocial behavior**
> Behaviors intended to help others.

As adolescents begin to test the waters of independence behaviorally, they may experience a variety of cognitive conflicts caused by having to compare the advice of parents and friends and having to deal with competing pressures to behave in different ways. These conflicts may prompt young people to consider in more serious and thoughtful terms what they really believe. For example, during adolescence, individuals become increasingly likely to say that it is permissible to lie to one's parents about disobeying them when they think their parents' advice is immoral (for instance, if the parents had forbidden their teenager to date someone from another race) (S. A. Perkins & Turiel, 2007). This struggle to clarify values, provoked in part by the exercise of behavioral autonomy, is a key component of the process of developing a sense of cognitive autonomy.

Moral Development During Adolescence

Moral development has been the most widely studied aspect of cognitive autonomy during adolescence. The study of moral development involves both reasoning (how individuals think about moral dilemmas) and behavior (how they behave in situations that call for moral judgments). Related to this is the study of **prosocial behavior,** acts people engage in to help others (Morris et al., 2011).

Assessing Moral Reasoning   The dominant theoretical viewpoint in the study of moral reasoning is grounded in Piaget's theory of cognitive development. Theories of morality that stem from this viewpoint emphasize shifts in the type of reasoning that individuals use in making moral decisions, rather than changes in the content of the decisions they reach or the actions they take as a result (N. Eisenberg et al., 2009; Smetana & Villalobos, 2009).

Researchers assess individuals' moral reasoning by examining their responses to hypothetical dilemmas about difficult, real-world situations, such as these (Gibbs, Basinger, Grime, & Snarney, 2007):

> Judy was a 12-year-old girl. Her mother promised her that she could go to a special rock concert coming to their town if she saved up from babysitting and lunch money to buy a ticket to the concert. She managed to save up the $15 the ticket cost plus another $5. But then her mother changed her mind and told Judy that she had to spend the money on new clothes for school. Judy was disappointed and decided to go to the concert anyway. She bought a ticket and told her mother that she had only been able to save $5. That

preconventional moral reasoning
The first level of moral reasoning, which is typical of children and is characterized by reasoning that is based on rewards and punishments associated with different courses of action.

conventional moral reasoning
The second level of moral development, which occurs during late childhood and early adolescence and is characterized by reasoning that is based on the rules and conventions of society.

postconventional moral reasoning
The level of moral reasoning during which society's rules and conventions are seen as relative and subjective rather than as authoritative; also called principled moral reasoning.

Saturday she went to the performance and told her mother that she was spending the day with a friend. A week passed without her mother finding out. Judy then told her older sister, Louise, that she had gone to the performance and had lied to her mother about it. Louise wonders whether to tell their mother what Judy did. *Should Louise, the older sister, tell their mother that Judy lied about the money, or should she keep quiet?*

Two young men, brothers, had got into serious trouble. They were secretly leaving town in a hurry and needed money. Karl, the older one, broke into a store and stole $1,000. Bob, the younger one, went to a retired old man who was known to help people in town. He told the man that he was very sick and that he needed $1,000 to pay for an operation. Bob asked the old man to lend him the money and promised that he would pay him back when he recovered. Really, Bob wasn't sick at all, and he had no intention of paying the man back. Although the old man didn't know Bob very well, he lent him the money. So Bob and Karl skipped town, each with $1,000. *Which is worse, stealing like Karl or cheating like Bob?*

Perhaps the best-known dilemma used by researchers who study moral reasoning involves a man who had to choose between stealing a drug to save his wife or letting his wife remain mortally ill:

In Europe, a woman was near death from a very bad disease, a special kind of cancer. There was one drug that the doctors thought might save her. It was a form of radium that a druggist in the same town had recently discovered. The drug was expensive to make, but the druggist was charging 10 times what the drug cost him to make. He paid $200 for the radium and charged $2,000 for a small dose of the drug. The sick woman's husband, Heinz, went to everyone he knew to borrow the money, but he could only get together about $1,000, which was half of what it cost. He told the druggist that his wife was dying, and asked him to sell it cheaper or let him pay later. But the druggist said, "No, I discovered the drug and I'm going to make money from it." Heinz got desperate and broke into the man's store to steal the drug for his wife. *Should the husband have done that? Was it right or wrong?*

Stages of Moral Reasoning Whether or not you think that Heinz should have stolen the drug, or that Louise should tell her mother, or that cheating someone is worse than stealing from a store is less important than the reasoning behind your answers. According to this perspective, there are three levels of moral reasoning: **preconventional moral reasoning,** which is dominant during most

of childhood; **conventional moral reasoning,** which is usually dominant during late childhood and early adolescence; and **postconventional moral reasoning** (sometimes called principled moral reasoning), which emerges sometime during the adolescent or young adult years.

Preconventional thinking is characterized by reference to external and physical events. Preconventional moral decisions are not based on society's standards, rules, or conventions (hence the label *pre*conventional). Children at this stage approach moral dilemmas in ways that focus on the rewards and punishments associated with different courses of action. One preconventional child might say that Heinz should not have stolen the drug because he could have been caught and sent to jail. Another might say that Heinz was right to steal the drug because people would have been angry with him if he had let his wife die. In either case, the chief concern to the preconventional thinker is what would happen to Heinz as a result of his choice.

Conventional thinking about moral issues focuses not so much on tangible rewards and punishments as on how an individual's behavior will be judged by others. In conventional moral reasoning, special importance is given to the roles people are expected to play and to society's rules, institutions, and conventions. Individuals behave properly because, in so doing, they receive the approval of others and help to maintain the social order. The correctness of society's rules is not questioned, however—individuals do their duty by upholding and respecting the social order. A conventional thinker might say that Heinz should not have stolen the drug because stealing is against the law. But another might counter that Heinz was right to steal the drug because it is what a good husband is expected to do. According to most studies of moral reasoning, the majority of adolescents and adults think primarily in conventional terms—they evaluate moral decisions in terms of a set of socially accepted rules that people are expected to abide by.

Postconventional reasoning is relatively rare. At this level of reasoning, society's rules and conventions are seen as relative and subjective rather than as absolute and definitive. Individuals may have a moral duty to abide by society's standards for behavior—but only insofar as those standards support and serve moral ends. Occasions arise in which conventions ought to be questioned and when more important principles—such as justice, fairness, or the sanctity of human life—take precedence over established social norms. For instance, a postconventional response might be that Heinz should not have stolen the drug because in doing so he violated an implicit agreement among members of society—an agreement that gives each person the freedom to pursue his or her livelihood. However, another principled thinker might respond that Heinz was right to steal the drug because someone's life was at stake and because preserving human life is more important than respecting individual freedoms. Whereas conventional thinking is oriented toward society's rules, postconventional thinking is founded on more broadly based, abstract principles. For this reason, the development of postconventional reasoning is especially relevant to the discussion of cognitive autonomy.

Moral reasoning becomes more principled over the course of childhood and adolescence (N. Eisenberg et al., 2009). Preconventional reasoning dominates the responses of children; conventional responses begin to appear during preadolescence and continue into middle adolescence; and postconventional reasoning does not appear until late adolescence, if at all. Movement into higher stages of moral reasoning occurs when children are developmentally "ready"—when their reasoning is predominantly at one stage but partially at the next higher one—and when they are exposed to the more advanced type of reasoning by other people, such as parents or peers (N. Eisenberg et al., 2009). The development of moral reasoning tends to follow a pattern in which individuals move from periods of consolidation (in which their reasoning is consistently at a particular stage of development), into periods of transition (in which there is more variability in their stages of reasoning), into new periods of consolidation (in which their reasoning is consistent, but at a higher stage than during the previous period of consolidation) (L. Walker, Gustafson, & Hennig, 2001). These gains in moral reasoning are accompanied by changes in brain systems that permit us to become less selfish (Crone, 2013).

Although not all individuals enter a stage of postconventional thinking during adolescence, many begin to place greater emphasis on abstract values and moral principles (Rest et al., 1999). Moreover, if individuals of different ages are presented with other peoples' moral arguments, older individuals are more often persuaded by justifications that are more advanced. Thus, the appeal of postconventional moral reasoning increases over the course of adolescence, while the appeals of preconventional and of conventional reasoning both decline. The appeal of postconventional thinking appears to increase both with age and with schooling; most adults reach a plateau in moral reasoning after completing their formal education. Although for many years psychologists debated whether there were sex differences in the way that individuals approach moral problems, and many popular books were based on the idea that men and women think differently about ethical issues, studies have not found this to be true (Smetana & Villalobos, 2009).

Moral Reasoning and Moral Behavior It is one thing to reason about hypothetical moral problems in an advanced way; it is quite another to behave consistently with one's reasoning. After all, it is common for people to say one thing (cheating on a test is immoral) but do another (sneak a peek at a classmate's test when running out of time during an exam).

Although individuals do not always behave in ways that are absolutely consistent with their moral reasoning, on average, people who reason at higher stages behave in more moral ways (N. Eisenberg et al., 2009). Adolescents who are capable of reasoning at higher stages are less likely to commit antisocial acts, less likely to cheat, and less likely to bow to the pressures of others, as well as more tolerant, more likely to engage in political protests, more likely to volunteer their time, and more likely to assist others in need of help. They are also more likely to be influential over their friends in group decisions about moral problems (Gummerum, Keller, Takezawa, & Mata, 2008). Conversely, those who reason at lower stages of moral thought are more aggressive, delinquent, accepting of violence, and tolerant of others' misbehavior (N. Eisenberg et al., 2009; Stams et al., 2006).

Moral behavior and moral reasoning do not always go hand in hand. Most of us have found ourselves in situations in which we behaved less morally than we would have liked to. Accordingly, we should not expect moral behavior to follow exactly from moral reasoning, because other factors complicate moral decision making. For example, you probably realize in the abstract that complying with highway speed limits is important because such limits prevent accidents, and you likely obey these limits most of the time. But you may have found yourself in a situation in which you weighed your need to get somewhere in a hurry (maybe you were late for an appointment) against your belief in the importance of obeying speeding laws, and you decided that in this instance you would behave in a way inconsistent with your belief. Situational factors influence moral choices, and they also influence moral reasoning. When

The ways in which individuals think about moral dilemmas change during adolescence. © Eric Audras/PhotoAlto/Veer RF

moral disengagement
Rationalizing immoral behavior as legitimate, as a way of justifying one's own bad acts.

individuals perceive that they will be severely hurt by behaving in a morally advanced way (for example, if standing up for someone might get you injured), they are less likely to reason at a higher moral level (Sobesky, 1983).

The correlation between adolescents' moral reasoning and their moral behavior is especially likely to break down when they define issues as personal choices rather than ethical dilemmas (for instance, when using drugs is seen as a personal matter rather than a moral issue). This helps explain why adolescents' moral reasoning and risk taking are unrelated; people can be very advanced in their reasoning but still engage in risky behavior (N. Eisenberg et al., 2009). If people consider various risky behaviors (for example, experimenting with drugs, having unprotected sex) to be personal decisions rather than ethical ones, their moral reasoning will be relatively unimportant in predicting how they will act.

Individuals are more likely to engage in risky behavior (even if it is unethical) when they see the behavior as a matter of personal taste rather than a question of right and wrong. It is not clear, however, whether viewing risk taking as a personal choice is likely to lead to more risk taking, or whether individuals who've engaged in a risky activity are likely to redefine the issue as a personal rather than moral one, as a way of justifying their behavior after the fact. In either case, this suggests that interventions designed to stimulate moral reasoning will have little impact on adolescents' risk taking if they fail to convince adolescents that the behavior in question involves a moral and not just a personal choice. This is why delinquency and aggression are more common among adolescents who score higher on measures of **moral disengagement** (the tendency to rationalize immoral behavior as legitimate, as when one justifies stealing from someone as a way of retaliating) (Paciello, Fida, Tramontano, Lupinetti, & Caprara, 2008).

Prosocial Reasoning, Prosocial Behavior, and Volunteerism

Changes in Prosocial Reasoning Although most research on the development of morality has focused on what adolescents do under circumstances in which a law might be broken or a rule violated, researchers have increasingly turned their attention to the study of reasoning and behavior in prosocial situations. In general, the ways in which individuals think about prosocial phenomena, such as honesty or kindness, become more sophisticated during late adolescence, just like their moral reasoning (Morris et al., 2011). Over the course of adolescence, individuals come to devalue prosocial acts that are done for self-serving reasons (to receive a reward, return a favor, or improve their image) and value those

that are done out of genuine empathy, a pattern that has been observed across a variety of cultures (N. Eisenberg et al., 2009). During late adolescence, prosocial reasoning continues to become more advanced, leveling off sometime in the early 20s (N. Eisenberg, Cumberland, Guthrie, Murphy, & Shepard, 2005). Some research connects these changes in reasoning to developments in regions of the brain that govern our ability to look at things from other people's perspectives (Crone, 2013).

making the personal connection

Did you grow up in a family that engaged in the sorts of discussions thought to promote more advanced levels of moral reasoning? What are some examples of the ways in which your family did (or did not) do this?

Generally, the same type of parenting that facilitates the growth of healthy emotional autonomy also contributes to the development of moral and prosocial reasoning. Adolescents whose parents engage them in discussion, elicit their point of view, and practice authoritative parenting display more advanced reasoning than their peers (N. Eisenberg et al., 2009; Padilla-Walker, Carlo, Christensen, & Yorgason, 2012; Recchia, Wainryb, Bourne, & Pasupathi, 2014). It appears that this type of parenting makes adolescents more likely to feel sympathy toward others, which in turn prompts prosocial behavior (Eisenberg, VanSchyndel, & Hofer, 2015; Shen, Carlo, & Knight, 2013). Growing up in a home that stresses familism (the importance of fulfilling one's obligations to the family) leads adolescents to become more prosocial toward others (Knight, Carlo, Basillo, & Jacobson, 2014). In addition, positive parenting helps facilitate the development of empathy and emotion regulation, both of which contribute to prosocial development (see Figure 4) (Padilla-Walker & Christensen, 2011; Wray-Lake & Flanagan, 2012).

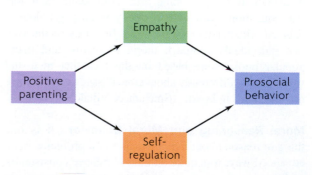

Figure 4 **Positive parenting promotes prosocial behavior by increasing adolescents' abilities to regulate their emotions and empathize with others.** (Padilla-Walker & Christensen, 2011)

Prosocial Reasoning and Prosocial Behavior

Adolescents who show more advanced prosocial reasoning and who place a high value on prosocial behavior behave in ways that are consistent with this (Hardy, Carlo, & Roesch, 2010). Adolescents who have volunteered considerable amounts of time in service activities score higher on measures of moral reasoning than their peers, are more committed to the betterment of society, and, as children, were made aware of the suffering of those who are less fortunate (Hart & Fegley, 1995; Matsuba & Walker, 2005; Yates & Youniss, 1996). Individuals who score high on measures of prosocial moral reasoning also have been shown to be more sympathetic and empathic (N. Eisenberg, Carlo, Murphy, & Van Court, 1995), to engage in more prosocial behavior (N. Eisenberg, Zhou, & Koller, 2001), and to be less likely to behave violently after having witnessed violence themselves (Brookmeyer, Henrich, & Schwab-Stone, 2005). In general, female adolescents score higher on measures of prosocial moral reasoning than do male adolescents, as do both males and females who are relatively more feminine (Carlo, Koller, Eisenberg, Da Silva, & Frohlich, 1996; N. Eisenberg et al., 2001; Morris et al., 2011).

Although prosocial reasoning becomes more advanced over the course of adolescence, changes in prosocial *behavior* during adolescence are not as consistent. Some studies find that individuals become more empathic, sympathetic, and helpful as they move into and through adolescence (Padilla-Walker, Dyer, Yorgason, Fraser, & Coyne, 2015), but many do not (N. Eisenberg et al., 2009), and some even have found that adolescents become *less* helpful toward others over the high school years (Carlo, Crockett, Randall, & Roesch, 2007). In experiments in which individuals are given money and must choose between keeping it all for themselves or giving half to an anonymous peer, older teenagers are *less* likely to share things equitably (see Figure 5) (Meuwese, Crone, de Rooij, & Güroğlu, 2015). However, with age there is an increase in adolescents' willingness to compensate peers who have been victimized by others (Will, Crone, van den Bos, & Güroğlu, 2013).

More consistent are research findings indicating that prosocial behavior is fairly stable with age (prosocial children grow up to be prosocial teenagers) and across different contexts (adolescents who are helpful to classmates in school are more likely than their less prosocial peers to also be helpful to strangers in the mall). Also, girls are generally more caring and prosocial than boys, perhaps because parents emphasize prosocial development more in raising daughters than sons (N. Eisenberg et al., 2009). Encouraging adolescents to spend time thinking about what's important to them seems to increase their tendency to act prosocially (Thomaes, Bushman, de Castro, & Reijntjes, 2012). And having prosocial friends and higher-quality friendships leads to more prosocial behavior (Barry & Wentzel, 2006; Monahan & Booth-LaForce, 2015; van Hoorn, van Dijk, Meuwese, Rieffe, & Crone, 2014).

Civic Engagement One of the most obvious ways in which adolescents can demonstrate prosocial behavior is through various types of civic engagement (Flanagan & Wray-Lake, 2011; Sherrod & Lauckhardt, 2009). **Civic engagement** is a broad term for a category of activities that reflect involvement in political and community affairs, including staying knowledgeable about politics and current affairs, participating in conventional political activities (e.g., contacting a political representative about an issue, campaigning for a candidate, or voting in an election), participating in alternative political activities (e.g., being part of a demonstration or a boycott), and engaging in community service.

Because the minimum age for voting in most countries is 18 or older, little research has been conducted on adolescents' involvement in political activities, although a number of surveys have been conducted to measure students' knowledge and attitudes on a range of political issues. Most of these studies have found that only a small proportion of young people are politically engaged, not just in the United States, but around the world. Nor does this change once people become old enough to vote. In the United States, election turnouts continue to be lower among young people than among adults, and, with the exception of a temporary spark in interest following major political and world events (such as the 9/11 terrorist attack), adolescents' interest in, and knowledge

> **civic engagement**
> Involvement in political and community affairs, as reflected in knowledge about politics and current affairs, participation in conventional and alternative political activities, and engaging in community service.

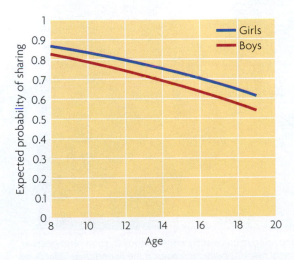

Figure 5 With age, adolescence become less likely to share equally with others, especially when doing so may be costly to oneself. (Meuwese et al., 2015)

service learning
The process of learning through involvement in community service.

of, political issues is meager (Sherrod & Lauckhardt, 2009). Experts attribute this in part to the widespread absence of civics education in American high schools and to the tendency of adolescents to focus their civic energies on organizations that they are more directly involved with, such as schools, religious institutions, and extracurricular clubs.

Most research on civic engagement in adolescence has focused on community service. Volunteering in community service activities, sometimes referred to as **service learning,** is more common in the United States than in most other countries. Researchers have been interested in both the antecedents of volunteering (what leads adolescents to become involved in volunteer activities) and its consequences (how adolescents are affected by volunteering). Several conclusions have emerged from this work. First, apart from attending a school in which some sort of community service is required, the best predictors of volunteerism in adolescence are being actively involved in religion (most probably because many volunteer activities are organized through religious institutions) and having parents who are active as volunteers in the community (Lenzi, Vieno, Santinello, Nation, & Voight, 2014; van Goethem, van Hoof, van Aken, de Castro, & Raaijmakers, 2014). Volunteers also tend to be female, more socially mature, more extraverted, and more altruistic (N. Eisenberg et al., 2009).

It has been difficult to document the effects of volunteering on adolescent development because individuals who choose to volunteer are different to begin with from their peers who do not (Atkins, Hart, &

Donnelly, 2005; Schmidt, Shumow, & Kackar, 2012). Nevertheless, studies of volunteering that follow adolescents over time indicate that engaging in community service leads to short-term gains in social responsibility, increases in the importance individuals place on helping others, and increased commitment to tolerance, equal opportunity, and cultural diversity (N. Eisenberg et al., 2009; Flanagan, Kim, Collura, & Kopish, 2014; Reinders & Youniss, 2006). There also is some evidence that volunteering in adolescence predicts volunteering in adulthood (Chan, Ou, & Reynolds, 2014; Hart, Donnelly, Youniss, & Atkins, 2007). The extent to which these effects persist over time depends, in part, on how long the volunteer activity lasts; the shorter the activity, the more short-lived the effects (Horn, 2012).

During the past several decades, many school districts began requiring, or considering requiring, community service of all students. This suggestion has been met with both praise and criticism. Proponents argue that service activities help develop concern for the community and facilitate adolescents' prosocial development. Opponents counter that forcing adolescents to do something they don't want to do will make them even *more* negative about community service and less likely to volunteer at later ages. Some worry that turning an activity that adolescents may want to do into a school requirement makes the activity less intrinsically rewarding.

Several studies have compared students who have volunteered for community service with those who have had it forced on them. It does not seem that requiring community service makes students develop negative attitudes about volunteering, regardless of whether they had been volunteers previously. But the evidence is mixed with regard to whether the effects are different between adolescents who willingly participate and those who do it only because it is a requirement. Some studies find that participating in community service activities has positive effects regardless of whether the participation is voluntary or required (Hart et al., 2007; J. Schmidt, Shumow, & Kackar, 2007), but others do not (Horn, 2011), and still others find that participation has little effect regardless of whether it is mandatory or voluntary (Henderson, Brown, Pancer, & Ellis-Hale, 2007).

One reason for these discrepancies is that students' volunteer experiences vary considerably in quality, ranging from ones that engage adolescents in helping others directly to those that occupy them in tedious clerical work (Ferreira, Azevedo, & Menezes, 2012; Henderson, Pancer, & Brown, 2014). Another is that community service only may be beneficial if adolescents are required to reflect on their experience (van Goethem, van Hoof, de Castro, Van Aken, & Hart, 2014). One important difference between students who are forced into community service and those who volunteer is that volunteers are more likely to continue their service work after graduation. In other words, whatever the positive

Engaging in community service leads to short-term gains in social responsibility, increases in the importance individuals place on helping others, and increased commitment to tolerance, equal opportunity, and cultural diversity. © Hero Images/ Getty Images RF

effects of participation, they are not enough to turn adolescents who aren't especially interested in community work into adults who are (Planty, Bozick, & Regnier, 2006). Perhaps the most reasonable conclusion one can draw from these studies is that the potential benefits to the *recipients* of the adolescents' service (the children they tutor, the elderly they visit, or the neighborhoods whose parks they clean up) may be greater than those to the volunteers.

There has been much discussion about whether contemporary generations of adolescents are more or less community-oriented than previous ones were. Generally speaking, there have been few significant changes over time in adolescents' degree of concern for others, with no changes since the mid-1960s in the extent to which American adolescents' believe that it is important to "make a contribution to society," feel empathy for people from other backgrounds, do things to help others, or correct inequalities. In fact, there have been significant increases in the proportion of youth who say that it is important to be well-off financially and have a great deal of money, and decreases in the proportion who say that it is important to develop "a meaningful philosophy of life" (see Figure 6) (Twenge, Campbell, & Freeman, 2012).

Political Thinking During Adolescence

Less is known about the development of political thinking during adolescence than about moral development, but political thinking, like moral reasoning, becomes more principled, more abstract, and more independent during the adolescent years. This pattern is linked both to the general cognitive developments of adolescence and to the growth of specific expertise, as the adolescent is exposed to more political information and ideas (Flanagan, 2004).

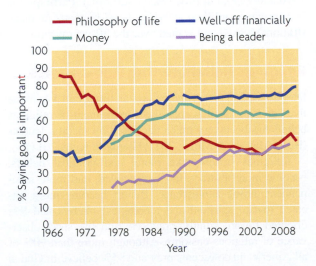

Figure 6 Changes in the proportion of American adolescents who describe various life goals as important. (Twenge et al., 2012)

Changes in Political Thinking Political thinking changes during adolescence in several important ways (Flanagan, 2004). First, it becomes more abstract. In response to the question "What is the purpose of laws?" for example, 12- and 13-year-olds are likely to reply with concrete answers—"So people don't kill or steal," "So people don't get hurt," and so on. Older adolescents are likely to respond with more abstract and more general statements—"To ensure safety and enforce the government" or "They are basically guidelines for people. I mean, like this is wrong and this is right and to help them understand" (Adelson, 1972, p. 108). Individuals' understanding of various rights—for example, their beliefs about whether children and adolescents have the right to have some control over their lives—also becomes more abstract with age (Ruck, Abramovitch, & Keating, 1998). With age, individuals are more likely to judge the appropriateness of having certain rights (e.g., freedom of speech) in light of characteristics of the individual (e.g., whether the individual is mature enough to act responsibly) and the context within which the right is expressed (e.g., whether the authority who is regulating speech is a parent or a government official) (Helwig, 1997; Tenenbaum & Ruck, 2012). There is strong support among adolescents for fundamental democratic principles such as representation and majority rule, even in countries whose governments do not operate on these principles (Helwig, Arnold, Tan, & Boyd, 2007; Smetana & Villalobos, 2009).

Second, political thinking during adolescence becomes less authoritarian and less rigid (Flanagan & Galay, 1995). Young adolescents are inclined toward obedience, authority, and an uncritical, trusting, and acquiescent stance toward government. For example, when asked what might be done in response to a law that is not working out as planned, an older teenager may suggest that the law needs to be reexamined and perhaps amended. A young adolescent will "propose that it be enforced more rigorously." In contrast to older adolescents, younger adolescents are "more likely to favor one-man rule as [opposed to] representative democracy," show "little sensitivity to individual or minority rights"; and are "indifferent to the claims of personal freedom" (Adelson, 1972, p. 108). Living under the rule of a young adolescent would be unpleasant.

Finally, during late adolescence people often develop a roughly coherent and consistent set of attitudes—a sort of ideology—that does not appear before this point and that is based on a set of overarching principles. These principles may concern a wide range of issues, including civil liberties, freedom of speech, and social equality (Flanagan & Galay, 1995; Helwig, 1995). As is the case among adults, adolescents' views about political matters—the causes of unemployment, poverty, or homelessness, for example—are strongly linked to their social

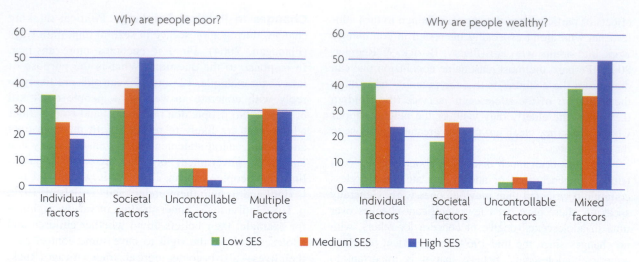

Figure 7 Socioeconomic differences in adolescents' explanations for poverty and wealth.

upbringing. Adolescents from higher social classes tend to attribute unemployment, poverty, and homelessness to societal factors ("People are poor because not everyone receives the same skills or training and encouragement when they are young"), whereas adolescents from lower-class backgrounds are more likely to attribute these problems to individual factors ("People are poor because they are lazy and don't want to work hard"). Socioeconomic differences in explanations of why some people are wealthy are not as striking, but they follow a similar pattern, with adolescents from lower-class backgrounds more likely to favor individual explanations ("People are rich because they stayed in school") than societal ones ("Some people are rich because they inherited money or a big business"). Adolescents' explanations of wealth tend to be more multifaceted than their explanations of poverty (see Figure 7) (Flanagan et al., 2014).

Shifts in all three of these directions—increasing abstraction, decreasing authoritarianism, and increasing use of principles—are similar to the shifts observed in studies of moral development, and consistent with the idea that cognitive autonomy emerges during late adolescence. The movement away from authoritarianism, obedience, and unquestioning acceptance of the rulings of authority indicates that an important psychological concern for older adolescents involves questioning the values and beliefs emanating from parents and other authority figures, as they begin to establish their own priorities.

Political Thinking and Political Behavior As is the case with moral development, there often are gaps between adolescents' political thinking in hypothetical situations and their actual attitudes and behavior. The most important influence on the political behavior of young people tends to be the social context in which they grow up (Flanagan, 2004; Kirshner & Ginwright, 2012). This context includes both the immediate community and the larger social and historical environment. Minority adolescents, especially those living in environments in which there are limited economic opportunities, tend to be more cynical about politics than their White counterparts.

The importance of context can be clearly seen when adolescents' civic engagement and political participation are tracked over time. One analysis of 30 years of data from a large, nationally representative sample of American high school seniors identified several important trends (Syvertsen, Wray-Lake, Flanagan, Osgood, & Briddell, 2011). As you can see in Figure 8, since 1990 there has been a steady increase in the proportion of young people who report engaging in community service (perhaps because there was an increase during this time in the number of schools that required it). The increase was especially notable among college-bound seniors. The figure also shows that there was a drop in participation in "conventional" civic activities (e.g., voting, contacting elected officials) between 1976 and 1990, but little change after that. Participation in alternative political activities (e.g., boycotts, demonstrations) waxed and waned over the 30-year period.

Religious Beliefs During Adolescence

Despite the fact that religion plays an important role in the lives of many adolescents, the development of religious beliefs has been very much neglected by social scientists (Burg, Mayers, & Miller, 2011; Clardy & King, 2011).

Religious beliefs, like moral and political beliefs, become more abstract, more principled, and more independent during adolescence. Beliefs become more oriented toward spiritual and ideological matters and less oriented toward rituals, practices, and the strict observance of religious customs. Although more than 90% of all American adolescents pray and 95% believe in God, a substantial proportion of young people say that organized religion does not play a very important role in their lives (Gallup & Bezilla, 1992; Holder et al., 2000; Wallace,

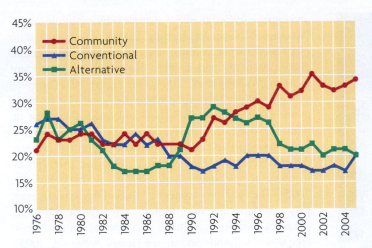

Figure 8 Changes over time in adolescents' involvement in conventional political activities (e.g., voting), alternative political activities (e.g., demonstrations), and community service (Syvertsen et al., 2011)

Forman, Caldwell, & Willis, 2003). Compared with children, adolescents place more emphasis on the internal aspects of religious commitment (such as what an individual believes) and less on the external manifestations (such as whether an individual goes to church) (Lopez, Huynh, & Fuligni, 2011). Adolescence is an important time for "spiritual questioning, doubting, and creating" (P. King & Roeser, 2009, p. 447). There are enormous differences around the world in the extent to which adolescents say that God is important in their life (see Figure 9).

making the cultural connection

As shown in Figure 9, there is wide cultural variability around the world in the significance of religion in adolescents' lives. To what extent do you think this affects the nature of adolescence more generally? Is the experience of adolescence as a developmental period likely to be different for young people who grow up in a context where religion is important compared to those who grow up in one where it plays less of a role?

Studies of the development of religious beliefs indicate many parallels with the development of moral and political reasoning. During late adolescence, individuals enter into a stage in which they begin to form a system of personal religious beliefs, rather than relying solely on the teachings of their parents (P. King & Roeser, 2009), which is similar to adolescents' transition to principled moral reasoning or to the development in late adolescence of a coherent political ideology. Developments in all three domains—moral, political, and religious—reflect the underlying growth of cognitive abilities and the shift from concrete to abstract reasoning that characterizes the adolescent transition. This fundamental shift in cognitive ability affects adolescents' thinking across a wide variety of topics.

Religious development has two main components: **religiosity** (the religious practices one engages in) and **spirituality** (one's personal quest for answers to questions about God and the meaning of life) (P. King, Ramos, & Clardy, 2013). Although both can be part of the process of psychosocial development, religiosity may be more important for identity development, since it involves the identification of oneself with a particular religious group

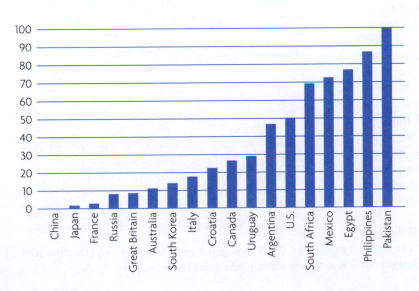

Figure 9 The proportion of adolescents from different countries who report that God is very important in their life. (Based on Clardy & King, 2011)

During adolescence, religious beliefs become more oriented toward spiritual and ideological matters and less oriented toward rituals, practices, and the strict observance of religious customs.
© Morey Milbradt, SW Productions/Brand X Pictures/Punchstock RF

and its practices and beliefs (not unlike identifying oneself with a particular ethnic group), whereas spirituality may be more closely linked to the development of cognitive autonomy, since it involves the development of a personal meaning system, self-awareness, and certain values. For most religious adolescents, religiosity and spirituality are deeply interconnected (D. C. French, Eisenberg, Vaughan, Purwono, & Suryanti, 2008). But there are substantial numbers of adolescents who practice religion without giving much thought to its spiritual aspects (for instance, adolescents who attend religious services each week or celebrate religious holidays either because their parents expect them to or because they enjoy the familiarity and routine of regular observance), as well as many who devote a great deal of time and energy to thinking about spiritual matters but who don't identify with an organized religion or practice customary religious rituals.

religiosity
The degree to which one engages in religious practices, like attending services.

spirituality
The degree to which one places importance on the quest for answers to questions about God and the meaning of life.

Patterns of Religious Involvement The stated importance of religion—

and especially religiosity—declines during adolescence (Koenig, McGue, & Iacono, 2008). Compared with older adolescents, younger ones are more likely to attend church regularly and to state that religion is important to them (Wallace et al., 2003) (see Figure 10). The early years of college are a time when many individuals reexamine and reevaluate the beliefs and values they grew up with. For some, this involves a decline in regular participation in organized religious activities (perhaps because the college environment doesn't encourage this) but an increase in spirituality and religious faith (Lefkowitz, 2005). The religious context of the college environment plays an important role, though; religious commitment often becomes stronger among students who attend a college with a religious orientation (Barry & Nelson, 2005).

Although some parents interpret the adolescent decline in religiosity as indicating rebellion against the family's values, the development of religious thinking during late adolescence is better understood as part of the overall development of cognitive autonomy. As adolescents develop a stronger sense of independence, they may leave behind the unquestioning conventionality of their younger years as a first step toward finding a truly personal faith. Adolescents who continue to comply with their parents' religious beliefs without ever questioning them may actually be showing signs of immature conformity or identity foreclosure, not spiritual maturity.

Individual Differences in Religiosity Although individuals usually become less involved in formal religion during adolescence, adolescents differ in their degree of religiosity (Dollahite, Layton, Bahr, Walker, & Thatcher, 2009; Good, Willoughby, & Busseri, 2011). According to U.S. surveys, about 85% of American adolescents

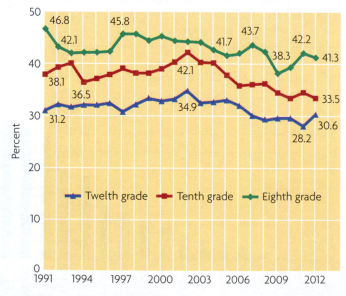

Figure 10 Weekly religious attendance among U.S. 8th-, 10th-, and 12th-graders. (Child Trends Databank, 2014)

report an affiliation with a religious group; of the remaining 15%, about 10% report not being religious, 3% say they are uncertain, and another 3% describe themselves as atheist or agnostic (King et al., 2013).

About half of all American adolescents say that formal religious participation is important in their life (P. King & Roeser, 2009). Approximately one-third report weekly attendance at religious services, one-sixth attend once or twice per month, and about 45% rarely or never attend services; regular attendance at religious services drops over the course of high school. Adolescent religious attendance declined gradually during the 1980s and 1990s but has changed very little since then.

About half of U.S. adolescents identify themselves as Protestant (and close to half of Protestants identify themselves as conservative Christians), and about one-fifth as Catholic. Adolescent girls are slightly more likely to be religious than adolescent boys (this sex difference is found among adults, too). In general, Black and Latino adolescents are more religious than youth from other ethnic backgrounds, as are adolescents who live in the South or Midwest (P. King & Roeser, 2009; C. Smith & Denton, 2005; Wallace et al., 2003). Rates of adolescents' religious participation are considerably higher in the United States than other parts of the world. In contrast to the 41.9% of American youth who participate in an organization sponsored by a religious group, the figures are 14.4% in Western Europe, 27.6% in Southern Europe, 19.9% in Asia/Pacific regions, 13.1% in Northern Europe, and 10.3% in Eastern Europe (King et al., 2013).

The Impact of Religious Involvement on Development

Religious adolescents are better adjusted and less depressed than other adolescents, less likely to have premarital sex, less likely to use drugs, and less likely to engage in delinquency (Kim-Spoon, McCullough, Bickel, Farley, & Longo, 2014; P. King, Carr, & Boiter, 2011; Ludden, 2011; Yonker, Schnabelrauch, & DeHaan, 2012). Although some of the apparent beneficial effects of religious involvement are because adolescents who are involved in religion often have other positive influences in their life that promote positive development and prevent problem behavior, like supportive parents, prosocial peers, or adults outside the immediate family who care about them (French, Purwono, & Triwahyuni, 2011; Spilman, Neppi, Donnellan, Schofield, & Conger, 2013), being religious in and of itself appears to deter problem behavior and delay the onset of sexual activity (Good & Willoughby, 2011; R. K. Jones, Darroch, & Singh, 2005; Steinman & Zimmerman, 2004). Religious involvement may play an especially important role in buffering inner-city Black adolescents against the harmful effects of neighborhood disorganization and exposure to violence (Benhorin & McMahon, 2008; Fowler et al., 2008; S. T. Li, Rosario et al., 2008; Rose, Joe, Shields, & Caldwell, 2014), and there also is evidence that religious involvement may help protect against the adverse effects of family conflict (K. A. Davis & Epkins, 2009). There is more consistent evidence for the role that religion plays in preventing problem behavior than for its role in promoting positive development. Although studies show that religious adolescents are more involved in the community, more altruistic, and more prosocial, other research finds that rates of identity foreclosure are higher among religious adolescents (P. King & Roeser, 2009).

Some clues to the reasons that religious involvement may protect against involvement in problem behavior come from the finding that religiosity, rather than spirituality, is the stronger predictor of staying out of trouble (Good & Willoughby, 2014; Jang & Franzen, 2013; Kim-Spoon, Farley, Holms, Longo, & McCullough, 2014; Salas-Wright, Vaughn, Hodge, & Perron, 2012). Moreover, it does not appear to be attending religious services that matters—it is being a part of a community of individuals who share similar values and engage in similar activities (French, Christ, Lu, & Purwono, 2014; French, Purwono, & Rodkin, 2012). In one study of churchgoing rural youth, adolescents frequently mentioned participating in youth groups and the relationships they formed with youth group leaders as important influences on their behavior and development (M. Good & Willoughby, 2007). Seen in this light, the connection between religious participation and lower problem behavior is not surprising, since some of the strongest predictors of adolescents' involvement in sex, drugs, and delinquency are the behavior and attitudes of their peers.

10 Intimacy

Intimacy as an Adolescent Issue

Theoretical Perspectives on Adolescent Intimacy

Sullivan's Theory of Interpersonal Development

Interpersonal Development During Adolescence

Attachment in Adolescence

The Development of Intimacy in Adolescence

Changes in the Nature of Friendship

Changes in the Display of Intimacy

Sex Differences in Intimacy

Changes in the Targets of Intimacy

Friendships with the Other Sex

Dating and Romantic Relationships

Dating and the Development of Intimacy

The Development of Dating Relationships

The Impact of Dating on Adolescent Development

Intimacy and Psychosocial Development

© The McGraw-Hill Companies, Inc./Erin Melloy

260

My boyfriend and I fell asleep together one night at my house [when I was 15]. We were curled up facing each other. I fell asleep looking at his face. I had a dream that night where I was falling. . . . I looked into his eyes and I knew that we were having the same dream. We immediately hugged each other and we both knew what had happened simply by looking in each other's eyes.

(A 21-year-old's response when asked to recall "a vivid, highly memorable, personally important memory that 'conveys powerfully how you have come to be the person you currently are.'") (McLean & Thorne, 2003, p. 641).

One of the most remarkable things about adolescence is the way close relationships change during these years. Think about the friendships you had as a child and compare them with those you had as a teenager. Think about the boyfriends or girlfriends that children have and the boyfriends or girlfriends adolescents have. And think about relationships between parents and their children and about how these relationships change during adolescence. In all three cases, adolescents' relationships are closer, more personal, more involved, and more emotionally charged than children's. During adolescence, in short, relationships become more intimate. In this chapter, we examine how and why this occurs.

To begin with, we need to draw a distinction between intimacy and sexuality. The concept of intimacy—at least as it is used in the study of adolescence—does not have a sexual or physical connotation. Rather, an intimate relationship is an emotional attachment between two people that is characterized by concern for each other's well-being; a willingness to disclose private, and occasionally sensitive, topics; and a sharing of common interests and activities. (An easy way to

remember this is "caring," "daring," and "sharing.") Two individuals can have an intimate relationship without having a sexual one. And, by the same token, two people can have a sexual relationship without being especially intimate.

Although the development of intimacy during adolescence is almost always studied in relation to friendships and romantic relationships with peers, adolescents' intimate relationships aren't limited to other teenagers. Parents often have intimate relationships with their adolescent children, especially when the children have reached a sufficient level of maturity. Siblings, even with many years between them, are often close confidants. Sometimes, young people form intimate relationships with adults who are not in their immediate family.

Obviously, one of the central issues in the study of intimacy during adolescence is the onset of dating. Although the young person's initiation into romantic relationships is undoubtedly important, it is not the only noteworthy change that occurs in close relationships during adolescence. Adolescence is also an important time for changes in what individuals look for in friends, in their capacity to be intimate with friends of both sexes, and in the way they express closeness to others. When college students were asked what the most important criteria are for deciding when someone is ready to get married, the capacity for intimacy with another person is the most consistently mentioned indicator, among both males and females (Carroll et al., 2009) (see Table 1). Interestingly, in this sample of nearly 800 American college students from around the country, who averaged 20 years in age, only 9% of the men and just 5% of the women said they were ready for marriage, whereas 60% of men and 67% of women said they weren't. The rest were ambivalent.

Table 1 **When is someone ready to get married?**

Criterion	Percent of American college students who say this is necessary
Be able to express feelings in close relationships	98
Be able to listen to others in an understanding way	98
Be able to discuss personal problems with others	98
Be respectful of others when dealing with differences	98
Accept responsibility for the consequencess of your actions	97
Committed to a long-term love relationship	96
Avoid aggressive and violent behavior	95
Become less self-oriented, develop greater consideration for others	95
Financially independent from parents and others	91
For a man, become capable of supporting a family financially	91
For a woman, become capable of running a household	91

Source: Carroll et al., 2009.

Intimacy as an Adolescent Issue

Intimacy is an important concern throughout most of the life span. During childhood, not having friends is associated with a wide range of psychological and social problems (Rubin, Bukowski, & Parker, 2006). And during adulthood, having at least one intimate friendship is beneficial to an individual's health: People who have others to turn to for emotional support are less likely to suffer from psychological and physical disorders (Myers, Lindentthal, & Pepper, 1975). Without question, close relationships are extremely important to people of all ages. Why, then, is the development of intimacy especially important during adolescence?

One reason is that it is not until adolescence that truly intimate relationships—relationships characterized by openness, honesty, self-disclosure, and trust—emerge. Although children certainly have important friendships, their relationships are different from those formed during adolescence. Children's friendships are activity oriented; they are built around games and shared activities. To a child, a friend is someone who likes to do the same things he or she does. But teenagers' close friendships are more likely to have a strong emotional foundation; they are built on the sorts of bonds that form between people who care about and know and understand each other in a special way (Kobak & Madsen, 2011).

Another reason for the importance of intimacy during adolescence concerns the changing nature of the adolescent's social world—during early adolescence, the increasing importance of peers in general, and during middle and late adolescence, the increasing importance of other-sex peers in particular (Furman, Brown, & Feiring, 1999). In this chapter, we look at changes in adolescent peer relations again, but in a different light—as part of the development of intimacy. Although experiences in the family are important for the initial development of social skills, experiences in friendships, especially during adolescence, contribute above and beyond the benefits of good parenting to the development of social competence (Glick & Rose, 2011).

Puberty and the Development of Intimacy Why do such important changes take place in close relationships during adolescence? Several theorists point to significant links between the development of intimacy during adolescence and the biological, cognitive, and social changes of the period (Savin-Williams & Berndt, 1990). Naturally, changes in sexual impulses at puberty provoke interest in sex, which leads to the development of romantic relationships. With puberty and sexuality come new issues and concerns requiring serious, intimate discussions. Some young people feel hesitant to discuss sex and dating with their parents and turn instead to relationships outside the family. And some of the most intimate conversations adolescents have with their friends involve their relationships with actual or potential romantic partners. These concerns may also prompt the development of intimate friendships with other-sex peers, perhaps for the first time.

Cognitive Change and the Development of Intimacy
Advances in thinking—especially in the realm of social cognition—are also related to the development of intimacy (Rote & Smetana, 2011). Compared to children, adolescents have more sophisticated conceptions of social relationships and better communication skills. These developments permit adolescents to establish and maintain relationships with greater empathy, self-disclosure, and sensitivity; they also contribute to adolescents' feelings of loneliness if they perceive themselves as socially isolated (Laursen & Hartl, 2013). Limitations in preadolescents' ability to look at things from another person's point of view may make intimate interpersonal relationships a cognitive impossibility, because it is hard to be an intimate friend to someone with whom you are unable to empathize.

Changes in Social Roles and the Development of Intimacy We can also point to changes in the adolescent's social roles as potentially affecting the development of intimacy. The behavioral independence that often accompanies the transition into adolescence provides greater opportunities for adolescents to be alone with their friends, engaged in intimate discussion. Adolescents spend more time in conversation with their friends than in any other activity (Dijkstra & Veenstra, 2011). Moreover, the recognition of adolescents as "near adults" may prompt their parents and other adults to confide in them and turn to them for support. Shared experiences such as working, as well as the development of emotional autonomy, may help give young people and their parents more of a basis for friendship and communication (Youniss & Smollar, 1985). Finally, changes in the structure of schools during early adolescence—often giving younger teenagers more contact with older ones—may promote new types of peer relationships (Eccles & Roeser, 2009).

During the course of preadolescence and adolescence, relationships are gradually transformed from the friendly but activity-oriented friendships of childhood to the more self-conscious, analytical, and intimate relationships of adulthood. In the next section, we examine why and how this transformation occurs.

Theoretical Perspectives on Adolescent Intimacy

The most important theoretical perspectives on the development of intimacy during adolescence are those of Harry Stack Sullivan (1953a) and various writers who have studied attachment relationships in adolescence

(Kobak & Madsen, 2011; McElhaney, Allen, Stephenson, & Hare, 2009). Let's look at each of these views in turn.

Sullivan's Theory of Interpersonal Development

Sullivan took a far less biological view of development than other thinkers who have written about adolescence. Instead, he emphasized the social aspects of growth, suggesting that psychological development can be best understood by looking at our relationships with others. In his view, the challenges of adolescence (actually, of the entire life cycle) revolve around trying to satisfy changing interpersonal needs (Buhrmester, 1996).

Stages of Interpersonal Needs Sullivan's perspective starts from the premise that, as children develop, different interpersonal needs surface that lead either to feelings of security (when the needs are satisfied) or feelings of anxiety (when the needs are frustrated). Sullivan charted a developmental progression of needs, beginning in infancy and continuing through adolescence (see Table 2) (Sullivan, 1953b). These changing interpersonal needs define the course of interpersonal development through different phases of the life span. During middle childhood, for example, youngsters need to be accepted into peer groups, or else they feel rejected and ostracized.

In Sullivan's view, the security that is derived from having satisfying relationships with others is the glue that holds one's sense of self together. Identity and self-esteem are gradually built up through interpersonal relationships. Sullivan viewed psychosocial development as cumulative: The frustrations and satisfactions individuals experience during earlier periods affect their later relationships and developing sense of identity. The child who as an infant has her need for contact or tenderness frustrated will approach interpersonal relationships at subsequent ages with greater anxiety, a more intense need for security, and a shakier sense of self. In contrast, the infant who has his interpersonal needs met will approach later relationships with confidence and optimism.

When important interpersonal transitions arise (for example, during childhood, when the social world is broadened to include significant relationships with peers), having a solid foundation of security in past relationships aids in the successful negotiation of the transition. An individual who is nervous about forming relationships with others is likely to have trouble forming new types of relationships, because they threaten an already tentative sense of security. A child who does not have a strong sense of security may have many friends in elementary school but be too afraid to form intimate friendships upon reaching preadolescence. She may try to maintain friendships like those of childhood—friendships that focus on playing games, for example, rather than talking—long after friends have outgrown getting together to "play." As a result, that youngster may be rejected by peers and come to feel lonely and isolated.

Interpersonal Development During Adolescence

Looking back at the progression of interpersonal needs that Sullivan mapped out, we can see that he distinguished between intimacy and sexuality; perhaps more importantly, he suggested that the need for intimacy—which surfaces during preadolescence—precedes the development of romantic or sexual relationships, which do not emerge until adolescence. In other words, Sullivan believed that the capacity for intimacy first develops prior to adolescence and in the context of same-sex, not other-sex, relationships. This turns out to be one of the most important observations in Sullivan's theory, because as you will read, the quality of individuals' same-sex friendships is predictive of the quality of their later romantic relationships. One of the main challenges of adolescence, according to Sullivan, is making the transition from the nonsexual, intimate, same-sex friendships of preadolescence to the sexual, intimate, other-sex friendships of late adolescence.

Table 2 Interpersonal needs associated with different developmental eras: Sullivan's theory

Developmental Epochs	Interpersonal Needs
Infancy (0 to 2–3 yrs)	Need for contact with people, need for tenderness from mothering one
Early childhood (2–3 to 6–7 yrs)	Need for adult participation in child's play
Middle childhood (6–7 to 8–10 yrs)	Need for peer playmates, need for acceptance into peer society groups
Preadolescence (8–10 to 12–14 yrs)	Need for intimacy and consensual validation in same-sex chumships
Early adolescence (12–14 to 17–18 yrs)	Need for sexual contact, need for intimacy with other-sex partner
Late adolescence (17–18 yrs to adult)	Need for integration into adult society

Source: H. S. Sullivan, 1953a.

As adolescents' needs for intimacy increase, so does the emphasis they place on intimacy as an important component of friendship.
© Dragon Images/Shutterstock.com RF

Not all youngsters feel secure enough as preadolescents to forge these more mature, intimate friendships. Their feelings of insecurity are so strong that anxiety holds them back. Some youngsters never fully develop the capacity to be intimate with others, a limitation that takes its toll on relationships throughout adolescence and adulthood. Sullivan felt that forming intimate friendships during preadolescence is a necessary precondition to forming close relationships as an adolescent or young adult.

According to Sullivan, preadolescence comes to an end with the onset of puberty. Early adolescence is marked by the emergence of sexuality, in the form of a powerful, biological sex drive. As a consequence of this development, the preferred "target" of the adolescent's need for intimacy changes. He or she must begin to make the shift from intimate relationships with members of the same sex to intimate relationships with members of the other sex. During the historical epoch when Sullivan was writing, homosexuality was considered abnormal, and like other writers of his era, Sullivan equated normal sexual development with the development of heterosexual relationships. Social scientists no longer hold this view, however, and most would say that the crucial interpersonal challenge for the young adolescent is not the movement from same-sex to other-sex friendships, but the transition from nonromantic to romantic relationships.

Like all interpersonal transitions, the movement from nonromantic to romantic relationships can be fraught with anxiety. For adolescents who do not have a healthy sense of security, it can be scary to leave the safety of

nonsexual friendships and venture into the world of dating and sexuality. Socially anxious adolescents are less likely to have satisfying friendships, which makes them less able to develop satisfying cross-sex friendships and romantic relationships (Hebert, Fales, Nangle, Papadakis, & Grover, 2013).

The overarching challenge of adolescence, according to Sullivan, is to integrate an established need for intimacy with an emerging need for sexual contact in a way that does not lead to excessive anxiety. Sullivan saw adolescence as a time of experimentation with different types of relationships. Some adolescents choose to date many different people to try to find out what they are looking for in a relationship. Others get involved very deeply with a boyfriend or girlfriend in a relationship that lasts throughout their entire adolescence. Others may have a series of serious relationships. Still others keep intimacy and sexuality separate. They may develop close **platonic relationships** (nonsexual relationships) with other-sex peers, for example, or they may have sexual relationships without getting very intimate with their sex partners. Sullivan viewed the adolescent's experimentation with different types of relationships as a normal way of handling new feelings, new fears, and new interpersonal needs. For many young people, experimentation with sex and intimacy continues well into late adolescence. If the interpersonal tasks of adolescence have been negotiated successfully, we enter late adolescence able to be intimate, able to enjoy sex, and, most critically, able to experience intimacy and sexuality in the same relationship.

Attachment in Adolescence

Today, a different theoretical perspective guides the study of intimate relationships in adolescence, one that draws on theories of the development of the attachment relationship during infancy (Kobak & Madsen, 2011). In many ways, the basic ideas developed by Sullivan (namely, that early relationships set the stage for later ones) were maintained, but a different perspective and vocabulary have come to dominate contemporary theory and research on adolescents' intimate relationships. In order to understand how attachment theory is applied to the study of adolescence, we need to look first at how the concept of "attachment" has been used to understand development in infancy.

Attachment in Infancy   In writings on infant development, an **attachment** is defined as a strong and enduring emotional bond. Virtually all infants form attachment relationships with their mother (and most do so with their father and other caregivers as well), but not all infants have attachment relationships of the same quality. Psychologists differentiate among four types of infant attachment: secure, anxious-avoidant, anxious-resistant,

platonic relationships
Nonsexual relationships with individuals who might otherwise be romantic partners.

attachment
The strong affectional bond that develops between an infant and a caregiver.

and disorganized. A **secure attachment** between infant and caregiver is characterized by trust; an **anxious-avoidant attachment** is characterized by indifference on the part of the infant toward the caregiver; an **anxious-resistant attachment** is characterized by ambivalence. Children who develop a disorganized attachment, which is characterized by extremely problematic behavior, such as uncontrollable crying, are most at risk for psychological problems (Kerns & Brumarlu, 2014). The security of the early attachment relationship is important, because studies show that infants who have had a secure attachment are more likely to grow into psychologically healthy and socially skilled children (Matas, Arend, & Sroufe, 1978).

Attachment theory has given rise to two different, but related, questions about adolescent development. First, is there a link between the quality of attachment formed in infancy and mental health or behavior in adolescence? And, second, can the same three-category framework used to characterize interpersonal relationships in infancy—secure, anxious-avoidant, anxious-resistant—be used to characterize interpersonal relationships in adolescence?

Does Infant Attachment Predict Adolescent Intimacy? Many theorists who study adolescent development believe that the nature of individuals' attachment to caregivers during infancy continues to have an influence on their capacity to form satisfying intimate relationships during adolescence and adulthood, for two reasons (McElhaney et al., 2009). First, some theorists have argued that the initial attachment relationship forms the basis for the model of interpersonal relationships we employ throughout life (Bowlby, 1969). This **internal working model** determines to a large measure whether people feel trusting or apprehensive in relationships with others and whether they see themselves as worthy of others' affection. An internal working model is a set of beliefs and expectations people draw on in forming close relationships with others—whether they go into relationships expecting acceptance or anticipating rejection. According to the theory, individuals who enjoyed a secure attachment relationship during infancy will have a more positive and healthy internal working model of relationships during adolescence, whereas individuals who were anxiously attached as infants will have a less positive one (Dykas, Woodhouse, Jones, & Cassidy, 2014; Kobak & Madsen, 2011; McElhaney et al., 2009).

Several studies have found that adolescents' working models for their relationships with parents are similar to their working models of relationships with friends, and that adolescents' working models of relationships with friends are similar to their working models of relationships with romantic partners (e.g., Furman, Simon, Shaffer, & Bouchey, 2002). In addition, a number of writers have suggested that individuals who emerge from

infancy with an insecure attachment are more sensitive to being rejected by others in later romantic encounters, a trait that psychologists call **rejection sensitivity** (N. L. Collins & Feeney, 2004; Norona, Salvatore, Welsh, & Darling, 2014). Individuals who are high in rejection sensitivity and emotional insecurity are more likely to develop symptoms of depression and anxiety, which in turn, lead to further increases in rejection sensitivity (Chango, McElhaney, Allen, Schad, & Marston, 2012; Davies, Sturge-Apple, Bascoe, & Cummings, 2014; Hafen, Spilker, Marston, & Allen, 2014).

In recent years, several teams of neuroscientists have studied adolescents' neural responses to rejection by imaging their brain activity while playing an online game called "Cyberball" (K. Williams, Yeager, Cheung, & Choi, 2012; White, Wu, Borelli, Mayes, & Crowley, 2013). Participants are told that they will be playing a ball-tossing game via the Internet with two other adolescents in other scanners (in actuality, there are no other players). On a screen inside the scanner, adolescents see cartoon images representing the other players, as well as a cartoon image of their own "hand" (see Figure 1). The ball is thrown back and forth among the three players, with the participant choosing which person to throw to, and the throws of the other two "players" determined by the computer. At the beginning of the game, the computerized players are equally likely to throw the ball to the participant or the other player. However, as the task progresses, the other players stop

secure attachment
A healthy attachment between infant and caregiver, characterized by trust.

anxious-avoidant attachment
An insecure attachment between infant and caregiver, characterized by indifference on the part of the infant toward the caregiver.

anxious-resistant attachment
An insecure attachment between infant and caregiver, characterized by distress at separation and anger at reunion.

internal working model
The implicit model of interpersonal relationships that an individual employs throughout life, believed to be shaped by early attachment experiences.

rejection sensitivity
Heightened vulnerability to being rejected by others.

You can throw the ball by clicking on the name or picture of another player

Kimberly   Josh

You

Figure 1 Using a computer game called "Cyberball," researchers scan adolescents' brains in order to better understand their responses to social exclusion.
(K. Williams et al., 2012)

Attachment theory, which has been used mainly in the study of infancy, has influenced the study of close relationships in adolescence. © JGI/Blend Images LLC RF

throwing to the participant. The researchers then compare participants' brain activity when they are excluded to that when they are included. Adolescents high in rejection sensitivity actually show a different pattern of brain activity in response to exclusion, and those who do so are more likely to develop symptoms of depression (Masten et al., 2011). As young adults, adolescents who spent a lot of time with their friends in adolescence show patterns of brain activity that indicate less sensitivity to rejection (Masten, Telzer, Fuligni, Lieberman, & Eisenberger, 2012).

making the personal connection

Think about your own internal working model of relationships. Are there consistencies in the ways in which you approach close relationships with different people? Would you say that you are high or low in "rejection sensitivity"?

A second reason for the continued importance of early attachment relationships during adolescence is that interpersonal development is cumulative: What happens during infancy affects what happens in early childhood, which affects what happens in middle childhood, and so on (Boyer & Nelson, 2015; Kerns, 1996). In other words, individuals who leave infancy with a secure attachment may be on a different interpersonal trajectory than those who leave infancy insecure. (Here's where you can see similarities between this perspective and Sullivan's.) The only way to examine this proposition is to follow individuals over time and trace their interpersonal development.

Numerous studies that have done this show that insecure infants are more likely to develop psychological and social problems during childhood and adolescence, including poor peer relationships (e.g., Weinfield, Ogawa, & Sroufe, 1997) and poor self-regulation (Farley & Kim-Spoon, 2014; Schwarz, Stutz, & Ledermann, 2012). It is thought that these problems in peer relations during childhood affect the development of social competence during adolescence—in essence, forming a link between early experience and later relationships (Fraley, Roisman, Booth-LaForce, Owen, & Holland, 2013; Jaffari-Bimmel, Juffer, van IJzendoorn, Bakermans-Kranenburg, & Mooijaart, 2006). In contrast, secure infants are more likely to grow into socially competent teenagers and young adults (Raby, Roisman, Fraley, & Simpson, 2015). The benefits of positive relations with peers also extend beyond adolescence: People who establish healthy intimate relationships with age-mates during adolescence are psychologically healthier and more satisfied with their lives as adults (Raudino, Fergussson, & Horwood, 2013).

Of course, it is possible for interpersonal development to be cumulative without the root cause of this continuity being the individual's internal working model. Individuals who have positive peer relationships in childhood may simply learn how to get along better with others, and this may lead to more positive peer relationships in adolescence, which, in turn, may lead to better relationships in adulthood (Lansford, Yu, Pettit, Bates, & Dodge, 2014). One study that followed individuals from birth through midlife found a cascade of interpersonal connections over time: low-quality parent-child relationships were linked to low-quality parent-adolescent relationships, which predicted low-quality romantic relationships in young adulthood and dissatisfaction with life in middle age (Overbeek, Stattin, Vermulst, Ha, & Engels, 2007). Individuals with more negative views of themselves disengage from peers, which may lead to poorer-quality peer relationships and peer rejection, thereby intensifying their negative self-image (M. S. Caldwell, Rudolph, Troop-Gordon, & Kim, 2004). Adolescents who have high-quality relationships with their parents are more likely to develop high self-esteem, which in turn facilitates the development of better romantic relationships in young adulthood (Johnson & Galambos, 2014).

How strong is the *specific* link between infant attachment and the quality of interpersonal relationships in adolescence and young adulthood? Do individuals who were securely attached as infants have more positive working models of relationships as adolescents or young adults? Studies that have followed individuals from infancy all the way through adolescence and beyond have yielded conflicting results. Some have shown considerable continuity from infancy through adolescence (e.g., C. Hamilton, 2000; Waters, Merrick, Treboux, Crowell, &

Albersheim, 2000), but others have shown no continuity whatsoever (M. Lewis, Feiring, & Rosenthal, 2000; Weinfield, Sroufe, & Egeland, 2000). Some researchers have suggested that individuals' security of attachment remains stable only in the absence of major life events that could upset the course of interpersonal development (such as the loss of a parent or parental divorce), and that the lack of continuity observed in some studies is due to the importance of intervening events (Beckwith, Cohen, & Hamilton, 1999; Waters et al., 2000; Weinfield et al., 2000). Others, however, argue that the significance of early attachment for later relationships is far outweighed by the importance of the experiences the individual has in childhood and the context in which he or she lives as an adolescent (M. Lewis et al., 2000).

Attachment in Adolescence   In addition to employing the four-way attachment classification scheme to study the links among infancy, childhood, and adolescence, attachment theorists have applied similar classifications to the study of adolescents' attachments to others (e.g., McElhaney et al., 2009; Obsuth, Henninghausen, Brumariu, & Lyons-Ruth, 2014), as well as to adolescents' internal working models (e.g., Kobak, Cole, Ferenz-Gillies, Fleming, & Gamble, 1993). In some of these studies, adolescents' current relationships with parents and peers are assessed; in others, adolescents are asked to recount their childhood experiences through the use of a procedure called the **Adult Attachment Interview** (Main, Kaplan, & Cassidy, 1985). The interview focuses on individuals' recollections of their early attachment experiences and obtains information on the ways in which the individual recounts his or her childhood history. A variety of schemes for coding responses to the interview have been devised, but most categorize individuals as "secure," "dismissing," or "preoccupied."

Many researchers have found that adolescents in different attachment categories differ in predictable ways (McElhaney et al., 2009). Compared with dismissing or preoccupied adolescents, secure adolescents interact with their mothers with less unhealthy anger and more appropriate assertiveness, suggesting fewer difficulties in establishing emotional autonomy (Kobak et al., 1993). Individuals with dismissive or preoccupied attachment profiles are more likely to show a range of emotional and behavior problems in adolescence, including depression, maladaptive coping, anxiety, eating disorders, conduct problems, and delinquency (e.g., J. Allen, Porter, McFarland, McElhaney, & Marsh, 2007; Kobak, Zajac, & Smith, 2009; Seiffge-Krenke & Beyers, 2005). They are more likely to recall negative aspects of their interactions with others (Dykas, Woodhgouse, Ehrlich, & Cassidy, 2012). Not surprisingly, adolescents who are judged to have had a secure infant attachment have more stable romantic relationships than their insecure counterparts (K. Davis & Kirkpatrick, 1994). People's security of attachment in infancy predicts social competence in childhood, security of attachment to close friends in adolescence, and positive romantic relationships in adulthood (Nosko, Tieu, Lawford, & Pratt, 2011; Simpson, Collins, Tran, & Haydon, 2007) (Figure 2). Of course, it is hard to say whether social competence leads to healthier attachments or vice versa (most probably, both are true).

Numerous studies also have looked at the quality of adolescents' current attachments to parents and peers (Chango, Allen, Szwedo, & Schad, 2014; McElhaney et al., 2009; Vandevivere, Braet, & Bosmans, 2015). Individuals who have secure attachments during adolescence are more socially competent, more successful in school, less likely to engage in substance use, and better adjusted than their insecure peers (J. Allen et al., 2007; Branstetter, Furman, & Cottrell, 2009; Çuhadaroğlu Çetin, Tüzün, Pehlivantürk, Ünal, & Gökler, 2010; Gorrese & Ruggieri, 2012; Granot & Mayseless, 2012). There is also some evidence that adolescents' attachment to their mother is

Adult Attachment Interview
A structured interview used to assess an individual's past attachment history and "internal working model" of relationships.

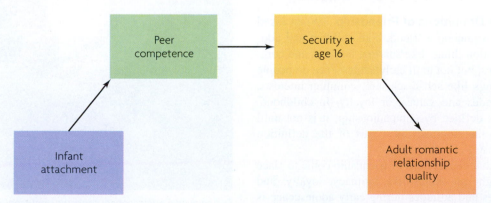

Figure 2   The quality of infant attachment is linked to adult romantic relationships through effects on social development in childhood and adolescence. (Simpson et al., 2007)

typically more secure and more important, and attachment to their father less so, over the entire adolescent period (Doyle, Lawford, & Markiewicz, 2009; Markiewicz, Lawford, Doyle, & Haggart, 2006). One recent study of the ways in which adolescents' multiple attachments varied in importance found that individuals whose attachment to their father ranked very low—lower even than attachments to people outside the family—were at relatively greater risk for emotional and behavioral problems (Rosenthal & Kobak, 2010). Security of attachment also predicts whether and at what age adolescents "leave the nest": Insecurely attached adolescents are more likely to delay moving out or to return to their parents' home than their more securely attached peers (Seiffge-Krenke, 2006).

Although attachment security is generally very stable over adolescence, it can change if adolescents are living in dysfunctional family situations or under a lot of stress (J. Allen, McElhaney, Kuperminc, & Jodl, 2004). In other words, early attachment security is not an "inoculation" that protects individuals from psychological problems forever, but rather a psychological advantage that increases the probability of developing in healthy ways. In general, attachments to parents become more secure over the course of adolescence (Ruhl, Dolan, & Buhrmester, 2014).

By the same token, the degree of security in an adolescent's attachment style interacts with other experiences to shape mental health and behavior: Positive experiences (like having an authoritative parent) have even more positive effects among adolescents with a secure style, whereas negative experiences are not as harmful (J. Allen, Hauser, O'Connor, & Bell, 2002). Among adolescents with an insecure attachment style, negative experiences (like having excessively intrusive parents) have an even worse effect than they would otherwise (P. Marsh, McFarland, & Allen, 2003).

The Development of Intimacy in Adolescence

Changes in the Nature of Friendship

Changes in Definitions of Friendship When asked what makes someone a friend, both children and adolescents mention things like sharing, helping, and common activities, but not until early adolescence do people mention things like self-disclosure, common interests, similar attitudes and values, or loyalty. In childhood, friendship is defined by companionship; it is not until adolescence that intimacy is a part of the definition (Buhrmester & Furman, 1987).

The fact that conceptions of friendship come to place greater weight on things like intimacy, loyalty, and shared values and attitudes during early adolescence is consistent with Sullivan's theory. As adolescents' needs for intimacy increase, so does the emphasis they place on intimacy as an important component of friendship. The findings are also consistent with what we know about other cognitive changes during early adolescence. Compared to children, adolescents are better at thinking about abstract concepts such as intimacy and loyalty, and their judgments of others are more sophisticated, more psychological, and less tied to concrete attributes like how they look or the things they own.

Jealousy The importance of intimacy as a defining feature of close friendship continues to increase throughout early and middle adolescence (McNelles & Connolly, 1999; Phillipsen, 1999). But an interesting pattern of change occurs around age 14. During middle adolescence (between ages 13 and 15), particularly among girls, concerns about loyalty and anxieties over rejection become more pronounced and may temporarily overshadow concerns about intimate self-disclosure (Berndt & Perry, 1990). Adolescents who keep a lot of secrets from their friends report higher levels of depression (Laird, Bridges, & Marsee, 2013).

The sorts of conflicts adolescents have with their friends change during this time. Whereas older adolescents'

During middle adolescence, concerns about jealousy often surface in adolescent girls' friendships. © Thinkstock/Comstock Images/Getty Images RF

making the cultural connection

Images of jealous adolescent girls pervade American movies and television shows that feature teenagers. Do you think this is a common phenomenon around the world? Or is it less likely to be found in cultures where dating is delayed until early adulthood?

conflicts are typically over private matters, younger adolescents' conflicts are often over perceived public disrespect (Shulman & Laursen, 2002). Adolescents who report high levels of peer conflict and low levels of peer support are more likely to engage in risky behavior, perhaps as a response to the stress caused by problems with their friends (Telzer, Fuligni, Lieberman, Miernicki, & Galván, 2015).

Girls show a pronounced increase in jealousy over their friends' friends during early adolescence (J. Parker, Low, Walker, & Gamm, 2005). Girls who have low self-esteem and are high in rejection sensitivity are especially likely to become jealous of their friends' relationships with other girls. In some senses, then, intimate friendship is a mixed blessing for young adolescent girls—they get the benefits of having confidantes with whom they can easily talk about their problems, but their friendships are more fragile and more easily disrupted by feelings of betrayal. As a consequence, girls' friendships on average do not last as long as boys' do (Benenson & Christakos, 2003).

How might Sullivan have explained this pattern? Why might loyalty become such a pressing concern for girls during the middle adolescent years? One possibility is that at this age, girls may start to feel more nervous about their relationships with friends because they are beginning to make the transition into other-sex relationships. As Sullivan noted, these transitions can make individuals feel insecure. Anxiety over dating and heightened feelings of insecurity can cause adolescent girls to especially value the trust and loyalty of their close friends. Indeed, close friends who have highly intimate and exclusive relationships with each other often behave more aggressively with friends than they do toward peers who are not their close friends (Grotpeter & Crick, 1996).

Adolescents' close friendships also are distinguished from their casual friendships in the types of conflicts they have and the ways in which disagreements are resolved (Laursen, 1995, 1996; Raffaelli, 1997). Although conflicts between adolescents and their close friends are less frequent than they are between adolescents and less intimate peers, arguments with close friends are more emotional with lots of anger and hurt feelings. Conflict between close friends is more likely to provoke efforts to restore the relationship than is conflict between casual friends. Nonetheless, some best friendships don't survive, and others are "downgraded" from best friend to "good friend" (Bowker, 2011).

Changes in the Display of Intimacy

In addition to placing greater emphasis on intimacy and loyalty in defining friendship than children do, teenagers are also more likely to *display* intimacy in their relationships, in what they know about their friends, how responsive they are, how empathic they are, and how they resolve disagreements.

Knowing Who Their Friends Are As individuals move into and through adolescence, they gain knowledge about more intimate aspects of their friends' lives. Although preadolescents and adolescents have comparable degrees of knowledge about characteristics of their best friends that are not especially personal (such as the friend's telephone number or birthday), adolescents know significantly more things about their friends that are intimate (such as what their friends worry about or what they are proud of) (Savin-Williams & Berndt, 1990). Between the end of elementary school and the end of high school, increasingly more adolescents agree with such statements as "I know how [my friend] feels about things without his [or her] telling me" and "I feel free to talk to [my friend] about almost everything" (Sharabany, Gershoni, & Hofman, 1981).

Over the course of adolescence, adolescents' reports of friendship quality increase steadily. These improvements in friendship quality lead to gains in social competence, which in turn lead to further improvements in the quality of adolescents' friendships (Glick & Rose, 2011). Although there are ethnic differences in average levels of friendship quality—Asian American adolescents report more dissatisfaction with their friendships than do other adolescents—the rate of improvement in friendship quality over time is the same (Way & Greene, 2006). And, despite fears that spending time socializing over the Internet will undermine adolescents' social competence, the people adolescents interact with online are mainly the same people they interact with offline (Reich, Subrahmanyam, & Espinosa, 2012) (see Figure 3). Actually, adolescents who use the Internet a lot for social networking are *less* socially isolated than their peers (Smahel et al., 2012).

Caring and Concern People also become more responsive to close friends, less controlling, and more tolerant of their friends' individuality during adolescence (Berndt & Perry, 1990; Keller, Edelstein, Schmid, Fang, & Fang, 1998; Shulman, Laursen, Kalman, & Karpovsky, 1997). Before preadolescence, children are actually less likely to help and share with their friends than with other classmates (perhaps because children are more competitive with their friends than with other youngsters and do not want to feel inferior). By about age 9, children treat their friends and other classmates similarly when it comes to sharing and cooperation. But by

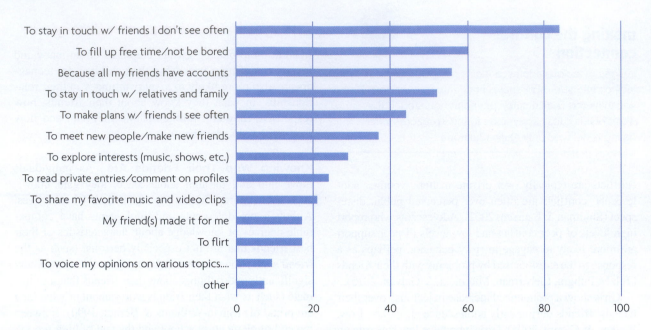

Figure 3 Adolescents use social networking sites primarily to communicate with people they have offline relationships with. (Reich et al., 2012)

the time they have reached early adolescence, friends are more helpful and generous toward each other than toward other classmates. Experiments in which individuals play computer games with an anonymous partner find increases with age in both trust and reciprocity (see Figure 4) (van den Bos, Westenberg, van Dijk, & Crone, 2010).

Adolescents are also physically and physiologically responsive to their friends: Studies show that the behaviors and emotional states of pairs of friends are more frequently synchronized, or "on the same wavelength," than are those of acquaintances, even when the friends and acquaintances are engaged in the same task (Field et al., 1992). Perhaps because of this, adolescents show greater levels of empathy and social understanding in situations in which they are helping or comforting others. Compared with children, adolescents are more likely to understand and acknowledge how their friends feel when those friends are having problems. Over the course of adolescence, attempts to help friends with personal problems

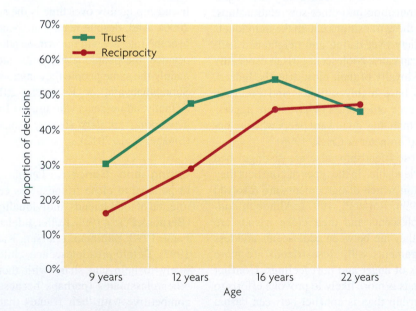

Figure 4 Experiments in which individuals play computer games with an anonymous partner find increases with age in both trust and reciprocity. (van den Bos, Westenberg, van Dijk, & Crone, 2010)

become more centered on providing support and less aimed at distracting them from their troubles (Denton & Zarbatany, 1996).

Conflict Resolution   The ways in which close friends resolve conflict also change. As individuals move from childhood into adolescence, and from adolescence into young adulthood, they become more likely to end their disagreements by negotiation (trying to compromise or find a solution that is acceptable to both friends) or disengagement (walking away from the situation) and less likely to end them with one person coercing or overpowering the other and getting his or her way; across cultures, negotiation is the main way that adolescents cope with conflicts they have with friends (see Figure 5) (Seiffge-Krenke et al., 2013). Negotiation is also more common between romantic partners than between friends and more common between close friends than between acquaintances (Laursen, Finkelstein, & Betts, 2001).

Sex Differences in Intimacy

How Females Are More Intimate   There are striking sex differences in intimacy during adolescence. When asked to name the people who are most important to them,

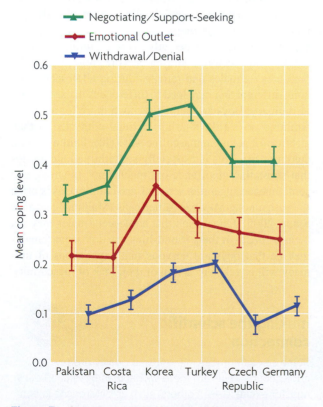

Figure 5   **Across countries in very different parts of the world, negotiation is the most common tactic adolescents use to resolve conflict they have with friends.** (Seiffge-Krenke et al., 2013)

adolescent girls—particularly in the middle adolescent years—list more friends than boys do, and girls are more likely to mention intimacy as a defining aspect of close friendship. In interviews, adolescent girls express greater interest in their close friendships, talk more frequently about their intimate conversations with friends, express greater concern about their friends' faithfulness and greater anxiety over rejection, and place greater emphasis on emotional closeness in their evaluation of romantic partners (Feiring, 1999; J. Parker, Low, Walker, & Gamm, 2005). Girls are more likely than boys to make distinctions in the way they treat intimate and nonintimate friends and to fight about relationships; girls prefer to keep their friendships more exclusive and are less willing to include other classmates in their cliques' activities (Bukowski, Sippola, Gauze, Hoza, & Newcomb, 1993; Raffaelli, 1997). In conversations, girls are more collaborative, whereas boys are more controlling (Strough & Berg, 2000).

When self-disclosure is used as the measure of intimacy, boys' friendships with other boys aren't comparable to girls' friendships with other girls until late in adolescence, if at all (McNelles & Connolly, 1999; Radmacher & Azmitia, 2006; Shulman et al., 1997). And girls are more sensitive and empathic than boys, especially in knowing when their friends are depressed or comforting them when they are distressed (Swenson & Rose, 2003; Van der Graaff et al., 2014). One reason girls are more likely than boys to confide in friends is that girls expect that self-disclosure will make them feel better, whereas boys expect it to be a waste of time that will make them feel "weird" (Rose et al., 2012). In these very numerous—and very important—respects, the expression of intimacy is more advanced among adolescent girls than among boys (Buhrmester, 1996).

Although this carries many advantages for girls, it also carries some liabilities. Girls' mental health is more positively affected than boys' when things are going well with their friends, but girls suffer more when things are going poorly (Flook, 2011). Girls also are more likely than boys to spend excessive time discussing each other's problems—something called **co-rumination** (A. J. Rose, 2002; Rose, Schwartz-Mette, Glick, Smith, & Luebbe, 2014). Co-rumination, often done in the context of discussing problems with romantic relationships, turns out to be a double-edged sword, especially for girls—it brings friends closer, but it also contributes to depression and anxiety (Dirghangi et al., 2015; Starr & Davila, 2009; Stone & Gibb, 2015; Waller, Silk, Stone, & Dahl, 2014). In fact, co-rumination makes anxiety and depression "contagious," transmitting symptoms between the pair of individuals, either because listening to someone's problems is itself distressing (Smith & Rose, 2011) or through "emotional mimicry," where one person unconsciously takes

co-rumination
Excessive talking with another about problems.

on the feelings of another (Schwartz-Mette & Rose, 2012). Among boys, co-rumination also improves friendships, but does not increase depression or anxiety as much or as consistently as it does among girls (A. J. Rose, Carlson, & Waller, 2007), because girls are more likely to get upset when they hear that their friends are having problems (Smith & Rose, 2011). This doesn't mean that adolescents should avoid talking to friends about their feelings and problems—they just need to keep it in check. Adolescents also have to be careful not to engage in too much "negative feedback seeking" (asking other people to verify their flaws, as in, "My voice is so annoying, right?"). Too much of this leads to rejection by others, which then only makes people feel even worse (Borelli & Prinstein, 2006).

There also are interesting sex differences in the nature of conflicts between close friends during adolescence. Boys' conflicts are briefer, typically over issues of power and control (such as whose turn it is in a game), more likely to escalate into physical aggression, and usually resolved without any explicit effort to do so, often by just "letting things slide." Girls' conflicts, in contrast, are longer, typically about some form of betrayal in the relationship (such as breaking a confidence or ignoring the other person), and only resolved when one of the friends apologizes (Noakes & Rinaldi, 2006; Raffaelli, 1997). When friendships end, girls are more adversely affected by the loss of the relationship (Bakker, Ormel, Verhulst, & Oldehinkel, 2010).

And How They Aren't On some measures of friendship, adolescent boys and girls show similar degrees of intimacy. Although girls are more likely to mention self-disclosure when asked to define close friendship and report more self-disclosure in their friendships, boys and girls have equivalent degrees of intimate knowledge about their best friends (McNelles & Connolly, 1999; Shulman et al., 1997). When boys are with their friends, they are just as likely as girls to share each other's emotional state (McNelles & Connolly, 1999). Although girls are generally more considerate, sex differences in helpfulness are very small (N. Eisenberg et al., 2009).

There's no question that intimacy is a more conscious concern for adolescent girls than it is for adolescent boys. But this doesn't mean that intimacy is *absent* from boys' relationships or unimportant for their mental health (Way, 2013). Rather, they express intimacy in different ways. Boys' friendships are more oriented toward shared activities than toward the explicit satisfaction of emotional needs, as is often the case in girls' friendships. The development of intimacy between adolescent males may be more subtle, reflected more in shared activities than in self-disclosure, even in young adulthood (McNelles & Connolly, 1999; Radmacher & Azmitia, 2006) and even in online communication (Valkenburg & Peter, 2007). Another possibility is that the development of close friendships among males starts at a later age than it does among females. There are substantial sex differences in friendship quality at age 13,

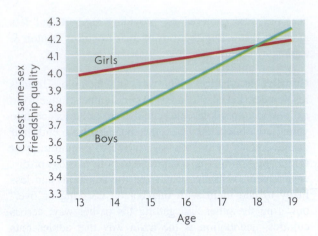

Figure 6 Changes in friendship quality over time. (Way & Greene, 2006)

but by age 18 these are gone (see Figure 6) (Way & Greene, 2006). It's a familiar pattern: During early and middle adolescence, girls are more emotionally and socially mature than boys, but by late adolescence, boys have caught up. (I know that many female readers are shaking their heads at this, but that's what the research says.)

The Origins of Sex Differences Many theorists have suggested that sex differences in intimacy are the result of different patterns of socialization. From an early age, females are more strongly encouraged to develop and express intimacy—especially verbal intimacy—than males. Other factors could be at work, however. Social pressures on males and females during adolescence are quite different and may lead to differences in expressions of intimacy. Boys are punished much more for acting in feminine ways (like sharing feelings with others) than girls are for acting in masculine ways (like holding strong emotions in). This is especially so within ethnic groups that stress the importance of "machismo" (a strong and sometimes exaggerated sense of masculinity), as is often the case among Mexican Americans (Stanton-Salazar & Spina, 2005). One reason that adolescent males may not be as intimate in their friendships as adolescent females may be that boys are nervous that expressions of intimacy will be taken as a sign of their lack of masculinity.

making the scientific connection

Some sex differences in friendship quality predate adolescence—girls are more verbal than boys at an early age, for example—but others, such as differences in conflict resolution or in feelings of jealousy, do not seem to emerge until this developmental period. What aspects of the transition into adolescence differ for girls and boys that might account for sex differences in intimacy?

Although much research has concluded that girls experience more intimacy in their relationships than boys do (Buhrmester, 1996; Maccoby, 1990), these studies have been based mainly on samples of White youngsters. Several studies of non-White youth find that there may *not* be similar patterns of sex differences in intimacy in some ethnic groups (DuBois & Hirsch, 1990; D. Jones, Costin, & Ricard, 1994). One study of Black, Asian American, and Latino adolescents found no sex differences in support between friends among African American teenagers; slight sex differences among Latino teenagers, with girls reporting more friendship support than boys; and large sex differences among Asian American teenagers, but with boys reporting more support than girls (Way & Chen, 2000). Sanctions against intimate disclosure may be stronger among White males than among their minority counterparts.

Changes in the Targets of Intimacy

Adolescence is a time of noteworthy changes in the "targets" of intimate behavior. During preadolescence and early adolescence, intimacy with peers is hypothesized to replace intimacy with parents, and during late adolescence, intimacy with peers of the other sex is thought to take the place of intimacy with same-sex friends. Actually, this view appears to be only somewhat accurate. As we'll see, new targets of intimacy do not *replace* old ones. Rather, new targets are *added to* old ones.

Parents and Peers as Targets of Intimacy Two conclusions emerge repeatedly in studies of adolescents' intimacy with parents and peers. First, from early adolescence on, teenagers describe their relationships with their best friends and romantic partners as more intimate and less stressful than those with their mother or father (Persike & Seiffge-Krenke, 2014). Second, although there may be a slight drop in intimacy between adolescents and parents sometime during adolescence, the

By virtually any measure, girls display more intimacy in their friendships than do boys. © Blend Images/Shutterstock.com RF

decline reverses as young people move toward young adulthood (see Figure 7) (Keijers & Poulin, 2013).

Intimacy between individuals and their parents declines between the 5th and 10th grades, but increases between 10th grade and young adulthood. Time spent in family activities declines throughout preadolescence and adolescence, but the amount of time adolescents spend alone with their mother or father follows a curvilinear pattern, increasing between preadolescence and middle adolescence, and then declining (Lam, McHale, & Crouter, 2012). Intimacy with friends increases steadily throughout adolescence, although most dramatically during the early adolescent years. Intimacy with romantic partners also increases steadily throughout adolescence, but in this case, the most dramatic increase takes place during the late high school years (Buhrmester, 1996).

In other words, while peers become relatively more important during adolescence as confidants and sources

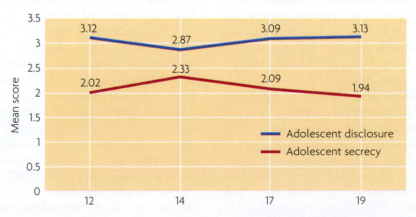

Figure 7 Intimacy between teenagers and parents declines during the early part of adolescence, but then rebounds. (Keijers & Poulin, 2013)

of emotional support, by no means do parents become unimportant (De Goede, Branje, Delsing, & Meeus, 2009). When adolescents are asked to list the important people in their lives—people they care about, go to for advice, or do things with—the number of peers listed increases over the course of adolescence. At the same time, however, there are no changes over adolescence in the percentage of individuals listing their mother or father. More importantly, studies indicate that adolescents who spend a good deal of time with their parents also spend a good deal of time with their friends. Thus, rather than drawing distinctions between parent-oriented and peer-oriented adolescents, it makes more sense to distinguish between adolescents who have a lot of social contact and enjoy a great deal of support from others (both family and friends) and those who are socially isolated or lonely (Fallon & Bowles, 1997; Scholte, van Lieshout, & van Aken, 2001).

One of the most consistent findings to emerge from studies of adolescents' peer and family relationships is that the qualities of these relationships are closely linked. In other words, we can see features of adolescents' relationships with their parents and their parents' marital relationship—how close they are, how much they tolerate independence, how they deal with conflict, how much control they assert over their children's friends, and so forth—in their relationships with their friends and romantic partners (Ackerman et al., 2013; Connolly & McIsaac, 2009; Cook, Buehler, & Blair, 2013; Rodriguez, Perez-Brena, Updegraff, & Umaña-Taylor, 2014; Trifan & Stattin, 2014). On a theoretical level, this provides support for both social learning and attachment-based views of adolescent intimacy, in that it suggests that the lessons young people learn in close relationships at home provide a template for the close relationships they form with others. Teenagers whose relationships with parents are emotionally close but not very individuated tend to stay longer in romantic relationships, even when the relationships are not very good, suggesting that difficulties in establishing healthy autonomy at home may carry over to romantic relationships (Smetana & Gettmen, 2006). These findings suggest that one approach to improving the peer relationships of adolescents who are having difficulties might be to focus on improving the quality of their relationships at home (Updegraff, Madden-Derdich, Estrada, Sales, & Leonard, 2002).

Studies of adolescents' preferences for social support similarly show that the likelihood of turning to a peer during a time of trouble increases during adolescence, but that the likelihood of turning to a parent remains constant. Between ages 7 and 14, the amount of support children receive from their immediate family remains fairly constant, while the amount of support received from friends increases (M. Levitt, Guacci-Franci, & Levitt, 1993). In other words, even though adolescents begin to see their friends as increasingly important sources of emotional support, they do not cease needing or using their parents for the same purpose. What seems to occur, instead, is that adolescents develop preferences for social support that vary as a function of the specific issue.

Adolescents typically feel freer to express anger during arguments with family members than during arguments with friends, presumably because anger may lead to the end of a friendship but not to the end of a family relationship (Laursen, 1993). Perhaps because of this, adolescents report more angry feelings after conflicts with their parents than after conflicts with their friends (Adams & Laursen, 2001). And when asked to recall key events in their past that contributed to their sense of identity, college students' reminiscences of their relationships with their parents more often emphasize conflict and separation, whereas their recollections of their relationships with their friends more often emphasize closeness (McLean & Thorne, 2003).

Ethnic differences in the expression of intimacy between adolescents and parents are fairly modest (Fuligni, Hughes, & Way, 2009). Ethnic minority American adolescents are more likely to say that it is important to respect, assist, and support their family than are White adolescents (Fuligni, Tseng, & Lam, 1999), but ethnic differences in adolescents' beliefs and expectations appear to be more substantial than ethnic differences in how adolescents and their parents actually interact. Indeed, with the exception of families who are very recent immigrants to the United States, relations between American adolescents and their parents look surprisingly similar across ethnic groups (Fuligni, 1998).

There are important differences between adolescents' relationships with mothers versus fathers, however. In general, adolescents interact much more often with, are closer to, and argue more with their mother than with their father, a pattern seen among males as well as females and across a variety of cultures (Fuligni, 1998). Of their two parents, adolescents see their mother as being more understanding, more accepting, and more willing to negotiate, and as less judgmental, less guarded, and less defensive (see Figure 8). The difference between perceptions of mothers and fathers is especially large among girls: As a rule, the mother-daughter relationship tends to be the closest, and the father-daughter relationship the least intimate, with mother-son and father-son relationships falling in between (Monck, 1991; Noller & Callan, 1990; K. Rice & Mulkeen, 1995).

In summary, an important transition in intimate relationships takes place during early adolescence. Peers become the most important source of companionship and intimate self-disclosure, surpassing parents and siblings (Buhrmester & Furman, 1987; Larson & Richards, 1991). Peers become increasingly important targets of intimacy not simply because they are similar in age but because they grow up in a different family. As adolescents begin the process of individuation, they often need

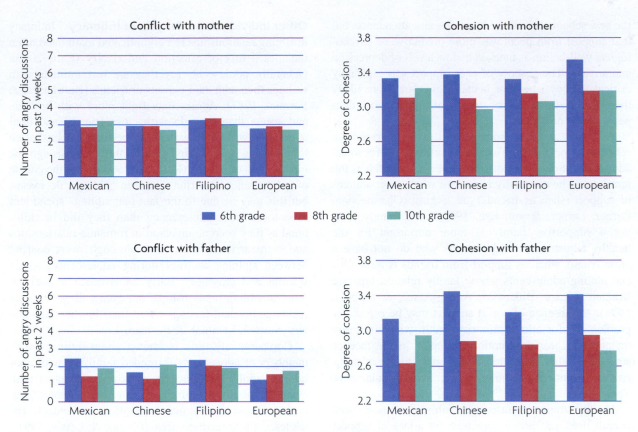

Figure 8   Adolescents' reports of conflict and cohesion with mothers and fathers in four ethnic groups. (Fuligni, 1998)

to seek intimacy outside the family as a means of establishing an identity beyond their family role. Although this shift in intimacy is normative, a shift in primary attachment figures at this age is not: Adolescents who report that their strongest attachment is to a friend or romantic partner are more likely to have insecure attachments with their parents (Freeman & Brown, 2001).

The Different Roles of Parents and Peers   dolescents have very different sorts of intimate relationships with parents and peers, and these differences point to different ways in which mothers, fathers, and friends contribute to social development. Even in close families, parent-adolescent relations are characterized by an imbalance of power. Parents are nurturers, advice givers, and explainers whom adolescents turn to for their experience and expertise. Adolescents' interactions with their friends are more mutual, more balanced, and more likely to provide them with opportunities to express alternative views and engage in an equal exchange of feelings and beliefs. Conflicts between adolescents and their parents are relatively more likely to end with a "winner" and a "loser," whereas conflicts between adolescents and their friends are relatively more likely to end in compromise or, at least, equal outcomes (Adams & Laursen, 2001).

Rather than viewing one type of relationship as more or less intimate than the other, it is more accurate to say

that both types of intimacy are important. Each influences a different aspect of the adolescent's developing character in important ways. Intimacy with parents provides opportunities to learn from those older and wiser; intimacy with friends provides opportunities to share experiences with individuals who have a similar perspective and degree of expertise. Adolescents who have strong attachments to both parents and peers are better adjusted than those who have strong attachments in one type of relationship but not the other (Laible, Carlo, & Raffaelli, 2000). In addition, the positive impact of having supportive friends in adolescence is greater when an adolescent also has supportive parents (Helsen, Vollebergh, & Meeus, 2000).

The different functions of intimacy with parents and peers are nicely illustrated in a study of social support during a transition into a new school (S. Dunn, Putallaz, Sheppard, & Lindstrom, 1987). Changing schools during adolescence can sometimes be stressful, and **social support**—emotional or instrumental assistance from others—can help buffer adolescents against the potential negative effects of stress (Hauser & Bowlds, 1990). The study found that support from family members was more predictive of adaptation to the demands of

social support
The extent to which an individual receives emotional or instrumental assistance from his or her social network.

the new school, as indexed by grades and attendance, but that support from peers was more predictive of psychological well-being, as indexed by low levels of depression and anxiety. The absence of peer support was especially critical for boys, perhaps because girls are more likely than boys to seek out other sources of support when their peers do not provide it.

A lack of support from parents or from friends in school is associated with low self-worth and poorer social adjustment. Social support from one source (such as the family) can be especially important when other sources of support (such as friends) are lacking (Ohannessian, Lerner, Lerner, & von Eye, 1994). Accordingly, having a supportive family is more important for the healthy adjustment of adolescents who do not have a close friend, whereas support from friends is more crucial among adolescents whose family relationships are strained (Gauze, Bukowski, Aquan-Assee, & Sippola, 1996). An absence of social support may be especially problematic for ethnic minority youth, who often rely on peers to provide emotional support in the face of stress and other difficulties inherent in living in high-risk environments (Benner, 2011; Stanton-Salazar & Spina, 2005).

Having support from parents, siblings, or nonschool friends does not fully compensate for a lack of support from classmates, though, and having support from siblings, classmates, or others does not fully compensate for a lack of support from parents (East & Rook, 1992; Gore & Aseltine, 1995). In other words, optimal social development during adolescence may require healthy relationships with *both* parents and peers (Jose, Pyan, & Pryor, 2012; Vaughan, Foshee, & Ennett, 2010; Walters, Lester, & Cross, 2014). Family relationships and peer relationships influence, rather than compete with, each other (Fallon & Bowles, 1997; Gavin & Furman, 1996).

Although the importance of peer relationships undoubtedly increases during adolescence, the significance of family relationships does not decline so much as it narrows in focus. Parents do not cease to be important sources of influence or targets of intimacy. Throughout adolescence, parents and teenagers remain close, parents (especially mothers) remain important confidants, and both mothers and fathers continue to be significant influences on the adolescent's behavior and decisions. Having a supportive relationship with one parent can compensate somewhat from a less close relationship with the other (Rueger, Chen, Jenkins, & Choe, 2014). Even in adolescence, being close to one's parents has a more positive impact on psychological health than being close to one's friends (Greenberg, Siegel, & Leitch, 1983). That said, peers take on an increasingly important role in the individual's social life over the course of adolescence (B. Brown & Larson, 2009). Although peers do not replace parents, they make unique and influential contributions to the adolescent's social development.

Other Individuals as Targets of Intimacy Intimacy in sibling relationships is a complicated matter and often includes a mix of affection and rivalry (East, 2009). Generally, adolescents say they are less intimate with siblings than with their parents or friends (Buhrmester & Furman, 1987). Adolescents fight more with brothers and sisters than they do with close friends, and their arguments with siblings tend to be resolved less often by giving in or by letting things slide than through the intervention of parents (Raffaelli, 1997). Over the course of adolescence, conflict between siblings decreases, but this may be due to the fact that siblings spend less time together in adolescence than they did in childhood as they become involved in romantic relationships and extracurricular activities. Although overt conflict between siblings declines during adolescence, so do warmth and closeness. Early adolescence is the low point in sibling relationships, but even college students report ambivalent feelings about their brothers and sisters (Stocker, Lanthier, & Furman, 1997).

Comparatively little is known about intimacy with members of adolescents' extended family or with non-familial adults like teachers or coaches. Contact with extended family is infrequent for many adolescents, because those family members often live outside the adolescent's immediate area (Feiring & Lewis, 1991). There is a slight increase in intimacy with extended family members during childhood, but an especially steep drop-off in intimacy with grandparents and other extended family members between childhood and adolescence (Buhrmester & Furman, 1987; Creasey & Kaliher, 1994; M. Levitt et al., 1993). Nevertheless, adolescents benefit from having grandparents involved in their life (Yorgason, Padilla-Walker, & Jackson, 2011).

Although a decline in intimacy with grandparents is often observed during adolescence, this is not as common among adolescents who are living with a single, divorced mother (Dunifon, 2013). Divorce is associated with increased contact between adolescents and their grandparents, especially between the adolescent and his or her maternal grandfather. Ties to grandmothers are especially strong among Black adolescents, particularly among girls from divorced households (Hirsch, Mickus, & Boerger, 2002). Puberty seems to increase intimacy between adolescent boys from divorced homes and their grandfathers (perhaps to compensate for diminished contact with their father), whereas it seems to distance adolescent girls from their grandfathers (perhaps because of discomfort with the girl's sexuality).

Researchers also have asked whether relationships between adolescents and nonfamilial adults in schools, workplaces, or neighborhoods can play a significant role in teenagers' lives (Greenberger, Chen, & Beam, 1998; Munsch, Liang, & DeSecottier, 1996). Indeed, studies suggest that the development of relationships with non-familial adults is a normative part of adolescence, not a sign of difficulties at home (Beam, Chen, & Greenberger, 2002; Rhodes & Lowe, 2009), and that relationships with positive role models outside the family contribute to healthy development above and beyond the contribution of family relationships and well into late adolescence (Chang, Greenberger, Chen, Heckhausen, & Farruggia, 2010; Haddad, Chen, & Greenberger, 2011). Close friendships may develop naturally between adolescents and their teachers or work supervisors or can be cultivated through community organizations, such as Big Brothers/Big Sisters, or similar programs designed to pair young people—especially those under stress—with supportive and caring adults. Linking an adolescent with a mentor is one of the most important components of successful youth programs (Theokas & Lerner, 2006). The benefits of having a Big Brother or Big Sister are especially great among adolescents with more difficulties at home, such as those living in foster care (Rhodes, Haight, & Briggs, 1999). Not all close relationships with nonparental adults benefit adolescents' development, however: Adolescent boys who have close friendships with young adult men are more likely to engage in antisocial behavior when they perceive their older friends as likely to condone or commit antisocial acts themselves (Greenberger et al., 1998).

Friendships with the Other Sex

Not until late adolescence do intimate friendships with other-sex peers begin to be important. Studies of preadolescents and young teenagers point to very strong sex segregation in adolescents' friendships, with boys rarely reporting friendships with girls, and girls rarely reporting friendships with boys, at least until middle adolescence (Galambos, Berenbaum, & McHale, 2009).

Origins of the "Sex Cleavage" The schism between boys and girls during early adolescence results from various factors. First, despite whatever changes may have taken place in American society in sex-role socialization during the past 50 years, it is still the case that preadolescent and early adolescent boys and girls have different interests, engage in different sorts of peer activities, and perceive themselves to be different from each other (Galambos, Berenbaum, & McHale, 2009). The sex cleavage in adolescent friendships results more from adolescents' preferring members of the same sex—and the activities they engage in—than from their actually disliking members of the other sex. Boys express more positive feelings about their female classmates than vice versa (Bukowski, Sippola, & Hoza, 1999).

The transitional period—between same-sex nonsexual relationships and other-sex sexual ones—can be a trying time for adolescents. This period usually coincides with the peer group's shift from same-sex cliques to mixed-sex crowds. The interpersonal strains and anxieties inherent in the transition show up in the teasing, joking around, and overt discomfort that young adolescents so often display in situations that are a little too close to being romantic or sexual. One reason for the mutual physical playfulness that boys and girls engage in is that it satisfies normal curiosity about sexual feelings while being ambiguous enough to be denied as motivated by romantic interest. Whereas rough play—play fighting—between boys is typically done to show who is dominant, the same behavior between boys and girls is often semisexual in nature—what some have labeled "poke and push courtship" (Pellegrini, 2003).

These observations support the claim that intimacy between adolescent boys and girls is relatively slow to develop and generally is tinged with an air of sexuality. Contrary to the idea that cross-sex intimacy comes to replace intimacy with peers of the same sex, however, intimate friendships between adolescents of the same sex are not displaced by the emergence of intimacy between adolescent males and females (Connolly & Johnson, 1993). Although the likelihood of other-sex peers appearing on adolescents' lists of people who are important to them increases during early and middle adolescence, and although the amount of time adolescents spend with other-sex peers increases as well, the number of same-sex peers listed also increases or remains constant, and time spent with same-sex peers does not decline (Richards, Crowe, Larson, & Swarr, 1998; Zimmer-Gembeck, 1999). However, there are substantial individual differences in patterns of time allocation to same- and other-sex relationships. Some adolescents shift their energy from same-sex friends to other-sex relationships early and abruptly, others do so gradually over the course of high school, and still others do not shift their focus at all (Zimmer-Gembeck, 1999).

As cross-sex relationships begin to develop, adolescents may mask their anxieties by teasing and joking around with members of the other sex. © Hammond HSN/Design Pics RF

Although intimacy between the sexes increases during early adolescence (Buhrmester & Furman, 1987), many adolescents do not list a single other-sex peer as a significant person in their lives. In middle school, only 8% of adolescents' friendships are with members of the other sex; by high school, this figure has risen only to 13% (Değirmencioğlu & Urberg, 1994). One exception to this general trend is seen among gay male adolescents, who tend to have more female than male friends (Diamond & Dubé, 2002).

When females do include other-sex peers on their list of important people, the boys they mention are often older and often from another school; when boys list girls as important friends, they generally are of the same age or younger (Poulin & Pedersen, 2007). Consequently, the increase in time spent with other-sex peers that occurs in adolescence takes place much earlier among girls than boys—by the time they are in 11th grade, girls are spending 10 hours each week alone with a boy, compared to only 5 hours per week spent by boys alone with a girl. Young adolescents of both sexes spend a lot of time thinking about the other sex, but relatively little time with them. As adolescents get older, the time they spend thinking about the other sex tends to be increasingly associated with negative moods, perhaps because the fantasies about the other sex experienced in early adolescence come to be replaced by unrequited longings for romantic companionship (Richards et al., 1998).

Some Functions of Other-Sex Friendships Although the emergence of close other-sex friendships in early adolescence is not explicitly in the context of romance, it sets the stage for later romantic experiences (Connolly & McIsaac, 2009). In early and middle

adolescence, age differences in other-sex friendships are similar to those seen between dating partners, with boys generally older than their female friends, rather than the reverse (Montgomery & Sorell, 1998). In addition, adolescents who have more other-sex friends than their peers early in adolescence tend to enter into romantic relationships at an earlier age and tend to have longer romantic relationships (Feiring, 1999). This could be due to many factors, including the adolescent's use of the pool of other-sex friends to "rehearse" for later romantic relationships (Kreager, Molloy, Moody, & Feinberg, 2015) or to develop a social network that is used to meet potential dates later on (Connolly, Furman, & Konarski, 2000). In any case, even preadolescents as young as nine differentiate between cross-sex relationships that are platonic and those that are romantic (Connolly, Craig, Goldberg, & Pepler, 1999).

Not all relationships between males and females in adolescence are romantic, of course, and having close, other-sex friendships is a common experience (Connolly & McIsaac, 2009; Kuttler, La Greca, & Prinstein, 1999; Stanton-Salazar & Spina, 2005). Two very different types of adolescents appear to have close other-sex friends—adolescents who are socially competent and highly popular with same-sex peers, and adolescents who are socially incompetent and highly unpopular with same-sex peers (Bukowski, Sippola, & Hoza, 1999). Among boys, having an other-sex friend compensates for not having same-sex friends, leading to more positive mental health than is seen among boys without any friends at all. Among girls, however, the results are mixed. Although some studies have found that for girls "there is no advantage, or perhaps there is even a disadvantage, to having a friendship with a boy" (Bukowski et al., 1999, p. 457), others have found that, among less sexually advanced girls, having platonic friendships with boys is associated with a more positive body image—perhaps because these friendships permit girls to feel that boys like them for themselves, without the added cost of feeling pressured to have sex (Compian, Gowen, & Hayward, 2004). The downside is that having male friends increases girls' likelihood of being involved in antisocial behavior (Arndorfer & Stormshak, 2008; Mrug, Borch, & Cillessen, 2011; Poulin, Denalt, & Pedersen, 2011), especially if their male friends are antisocial (Cauffman, Farruggia, & Goldweber, 2008). (One of the ways through which parental monitoring deters adolescent girls' substance use is by limiting their friendships with boys [Poulin & Denault, 2012].) Another potential cost is that many cross-sex friendships draw females into traditional caregiving roles, reinforcing traditional sex-role stereotypes.

All things considered, boys have more to gain from friendships with girls than vice versa. Having an intimate relationship with an other-sex peer is more strongly related to boys' general level of interpersonal intimacy

Platonic friendships between adolescent males and females often prepare the adolescent for the transition into romantic relationships. © Monkey Business Images/Shutterstock.com RF

than it is to girls' (Buhrmester & Furman, 1987). Whereas boys report that their friendships with girls are more rewarding than their friendships with other boys, girls do not describe their friendships with boys as more rewarding than their friendships with other girls (J. Thomas & Daubman, 2001). These findings are not surprising, given that adolescents' friendships with girls (regardless of whether they themselves are male or female) tend to be more intimate and supportive than their friendships with boys (Kuttler et al., 1999).

Dating and Romantic Relationships

Dating plays a very different role in adolescents' lives today than it did in previous times (Connolly & McIsaac, 2009). In earlier eras, dating was not so much a recreational activity (as it is today) as a part of the process of courtship and mate selection. Individuals would date in order to ready themselves for marriage, and unmarried individuals would play the field—under the watchful eyes of chaperones—for a relatively long period before settling down (Montgomery, 1996). At the turn of the twentieth century, most individuals did not marry until their mid-20s (U.S. Census Bureau, 2009b). The first half of the twentieth century saw a gradual decline in the average age of marriage, however, and as a result, individuals began dating more seriously at an earlier age. By the mid-1950s, the average age at first marriage in the United States had fallen to 20 among women and 22 among men—which means that substantial numbers of individuals were in premarital relationships during high school and marrying during their late adolescent years.

The function of adolescent dating changed as individuals began to marry later and later—a trend that began in the mid-1950s and continues today (see Figure 9). Now, the average age at which people marry is considerably later than it was 50 years ago—about age 27 for women and 29 for men, although the age at which couples begin living together has not changed (Manning, Brown, & Payne, 2014; U.S. Census Bureau, 2014). This, of course, gives high school dating a whole new meaning, because today it is clearly divorced from its function in mate selection. Adults continue to regulate and monitor adolescent dating in order to prevent rash or impulsive commitments to early marriage (Laursen &

Figure 9 The median age at marriage in the United States declined from 1900 through the mid-1950s but rose markedly during the second half of the twentieth century. (U.S. Census Bureau, 2014)

Jensen-Campbell, 1999), but in the minds of most young people, high school dating has little to do with finding a potential spouse. Nor do today's adolescents see cohabitation (living together) as a substitute for marriage (Manning, Longmore, & Giordano, 2007).

Romantic relationships during adolescence are very common: One-fourth of American 12-year-olds, one-half of 15-year-olds, and more than two-thirds of 18-year-olds report having had a romantic relationship in the past 18 months. The average American adolescent begins dating around age 13 or 14, although nearly half of all adolescents have at least one date before they turn 12. By age 16, more than 90% of adolescents of both sexes have had at least one date, and during the later years of high school, more than half of all students average one or more dates weekly. Only 15% of high school students date less than once a month (Feiring, 1993). By age 18, virtually all adolescents have dated once, and three-fourths have had at least one steady relationship (Neemann, Hubbard, & Masten, 1995).

As is the case with platonic friendships, girls tend to become romantically involved with boys who are slightly older, whereas boys tend to become involved with girls who are the same age or younger. Because the average duration of romantic relationships during the middle high school years is about 6 months, most adolescents report having experienced a breakup during the last year. Perhaps as a way of protecting themselves from more pain than is necessary, most teenagers say that they were in control of the breakup (either alone or by mutual agreement) (Connolly & McIsaac, 2009). Nevertheless, as you will read later in this chapter, the breakup of a romantic relationship is a significant source of distress for many adolescents, and, as you read earlier, the ups and downs of romantic life often dominate conversations between friends.

Dating and the Development of Intimacy

Contemporary discussions of adolescent romance draw on Sullivan's theory of interpersonal development, attachment theory, and ecological perspectives on development (Connolly & McIsaac, 2009). From Sullivan comes the idea that there is a developmental progression in individuals' capacity for intimacy, with the emergence of romantic relationships occurring after individuals have experienced emotional closeness within same-sex friendships. From attachment theory comes the idea that individuals differ in the quality of their romantic relationships and that these differences are paralleled by differences in the relationships individuals have with parents and peers. And from the ecological perspective comes the idea that romantic relationships, like all relationships, need to be viewed within the social context in which they occur.

The Nature and Significance of Romance The capacity for intimacy, which initially develops out of same-sex friendships, eventually is brought into romantic relationships, which for the vast majority of adolescents are with members of the other sex. In this sense, relationships between romantic partners are better thought of as a context in which intimacy is expressed rather than where it is learned. Consistent with this, the quality of adolescents' friendships is predictive of the quality of their subsequent romantic relationships, whereas the reverse is not true (Connolly et al., 2000).

Romantic relationships play a different role in the development of intimacy for females than for males (Feiring, 1999). In many cultures, boys are not encouraged to develop the capacity to be emotionally expressive, particularly in their relationships with other males. During middle adolescence, girls are better than boys at self-disclosure and interpersonal understanding, so that when adolescents first start having serious romantic relationships, girls generally are better at being intimate. Early sexual relationships are far more likely to revolve around love, emotional involvement, and intimacy for girls than for boys (Montgomery, 2005; Shulman & Scharf, 2000). This is very important, because for girls romantic relationships provide a context for the further *expression* of intimacy, whereas for boys they provide a context for the further *development* of intimacy. Relationships with the other sex therefore play a more important role in the development of intimacy among boys than among girls, who, on average, develop and experience intimacy earlier with same-sex friends than boys do (Buhrmester & Furman, 1987). The way a girl interacts with her boyfriend is more strongly related to the girl's internal working model of relationships than the boy's, perhaps because girls' greater prior experience with intimacy has led them to better align how they behave with how they really feel (Furman & Simon, 2006).

Although boys' capacity for intimacy may lag behind girls', it is important not to confuse ability with aspiration. In the past, much was made of the different meanings of romantic relationships to adolescent males and females, but today it appears that the sexes are more similar than different in how their romantic relationships develop (Connolly & McIsaac, 2009). The stereotype of the emotionally stunted but swaggering boy who enters into a romantic relationship purely for sex and uses his power and influence to get it no longer appears accurate, although adolescent couples are more likely to have intercourse when the girl reports that her boyfriend holds the power in the relationship (Giordano, Manning, & Longmore, 2010). Boys are often more awkward and less confident than the girls they are dating and just as eager to be emotionally close. Here's a 17-year-old talking about his girlfriend:

> She kept insisting I wasn't going to work out and I kept insisting I wanted to try it and one night, and like I said I couldn't sleep, and I wrote her a letter, front and back,

crying the whole time and then I handed the letter to her the next morning. . . . It was really emotional, like how she hurt me and how it wasn't right. (Giordano, Longmore, & Manning, 2006, p. 277)

Or how about this 18-year-old young man:

I guess she was more mature than I was and I guess I wasn't on her level you know because she wanted to do it [have sex] more than I did. . . . she said that I wasn't mature enough and you know all that stuff. . . . I was too young, I was scared, I didn't know what I was doing I wasn't ready for it. I think I felt like I was too young. . . . she was my girlfriend and that's what she wanted. (Giordano et al., 2006, p. 281)

There are also important cultural differences in how adolescents approach dating: In one study, Hispanic adolescents were more likely to emphasize romantic aspects of the relationship and were more willing to accept traditional views of the roles of males and females in relationships, whereas Black adolescents were more pragmatic and egalitarian in their attitudes (Milbrath, Ohlson, & Eyre, 2009). Compare, for instance, these very different perspectives on relationships:

. . . girls are more into the fairytale kin' a love, you know. An' the happy endings and . . . ROSES! They want roses once-in-a-while, too. I mean . . . a red rose, one red rose, it wouldn't hurt. And to make it like a surprise. You know, like to leave it in their locker. . . . an' the girl opens it up an' like, "Oh My God!" (Hispanic, 18-year-old female) (Milbrath et al., 2009, p. 338)

Well, he has . . . to tell her how much he care about her an' how much he doesn't want to hurt her an' how he doesn't care about them, an' how he'll lie to them, an', "I'm telling' you this an' I'm tryin' to let chyou know that I'm gonna cheat on you becuz I care about chyou an' I don't wanna lie to you." . . . he has to have a lot of game. (Black, 16-year-old female) (Milbrath et al., 2009, p. 341)

The Role of Context   The age at which dating begins is influenced by the norms and expectations in the adolescent's community. Romantic relationships are more common at a younger age in other industrialized countries than in North America, but by late adolescence, rates of dating are similar. Within the United States and in Canada, Asian adolescents are less likely than other adolescents to date, whereas the prevalence of dating is very similar among Black, Hispanic, Native American, and White adolescents, although some studies find that Hispanic girls start dating at a later age than either Black or White girls (Connolly & McIsaac, 2009). Westernization is leading many adolescents from Asian cultures to develop interests in dating at an earlier age than is typical within their culture (Dhariwal & Connolly, 2013). In one study, a high proportion of Asian adolescents hid the fact that they were dating from their parents, because they did not want their parents to worry about their school performance:

They know I have a guy that I spend a lot of time with, but I don't think they really know how serious it is, because I really don't want them to know, because if something ever happened with me in school, if I failed a class, I know that they would blame him, even though it would probably be my fault because he is really supportive and it's not like I am always with him, but they would think that. They would think that he is a bad influence on me. (18-year-old Asian female) (Lau, Markhan, Lin, Flores, & Chacko, 2009, p. 104)

Although early maturers begin dating somewhat earlier than late maturers (Lam, Shi, Ho, Stewart, & Fan, 2002; Neemann et al., 1995), age norms within the adolescent's school and peer group are more important in determining the age at which dating begins than is the adolescent's physical maturity. A physically immature 14-year-old who goes to school where it is expected that 14-year-olds will date is more likely to date than is a physically mature 14-year-old who lives in a community where dating is typically delayed until age 16. Early maturers whose peers are dating are especially likely to date early (Friedlander, Connolly, Pepler, & Craig, 2007). Dating also begins earlier among adolescents who have older siblings, who are less close to their parents, and who live with single mothers, especially if the mother is sexually active herself (de Graaf, de Schoot, Woertman, Hawk, & Meeus, 2012; Longmore, Manning, & Giordano, 2001; Tyrell, Wheeler, Gonzales, Dumka, & Millsap, 2014). Family instability (changes in parents' marital status through divorce or remarriage) is associated with dating, especially among boys, with adolescents from more unstable families more likely to date and more likely to have multiple romantic partners (Valle & Tillman, 2014). Whether this is due to less vigilant parental monitoring, a desire on the part of the adolescent to escape a difficult home environment, or both is not known (Cavanagh, Crissey, & Raley, 2008).

Patterns of Dating   "Dating" can mean a variety of different things, from group activities that bring males and females together (without much actual contact between the sexes), to group dates in which a group of boys and girls go out jointly (and spend part of the time in couples and part of the time in the larger group), to casual dating in couples, to serious involvement with a boyfriend or girlfriend (Carlson & Rose, 2012). Generally, casual socializing with other-sex peers and experiences in a mixed-sex social network occur before the development of romantic relationships (Connolly & McIsaac, 2009). As a consequence, more adolescents have experience in mixed-sex group activities like parties or dances than in dating, and more have dated than have had a serious boyfriend or girlfriend, or

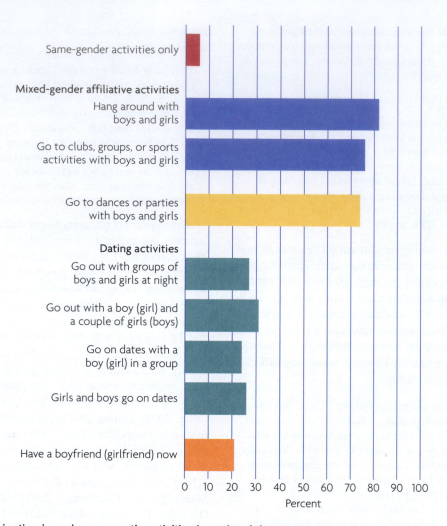

Figure 10 **Participation in various romantic activities in early adolescence.** (Connolly et al., 2004)

a sexual relationship (see Figure 10) (Connolly, Craig, Goldberg, & Pepler, 2004; O'Sullivan, Cheng, Harris, & Brooks-Gunn, 2007). However, involvement in one-on-one romantic relationships does not replace same-sex or mixed-sex group activities—like other aspects of intimacy in adolescence, new forms of relationships are added to the adolescent's repertoire while old ones are retained. The sequence of transitioning into romantic relationships follows similar patterns across ethnic groups, although Asian American youth appear to make this transition at a somewhat later stage than their peers from other backgrounds, consistent with other findings on ethnic differences in beliefs about the appropriate age at which adolescents should begin dating and engaging in other adultlike activities (Connolly et al., 2004).

Even for adolescents with a history of intimate friendships with same- and other-sex peers, the transition into romantic relationships can be difficult. In one study, in which adolescents were asked to discuss social situations they thought were difficult, themes having to do with communicating with the other sex were mentioned frequently. Many adolescents discussed difficulty in initiating or

maintaining conversations, in person ("He will think I am an idiot," "Sometimes you don't know, if you're like sitting with a guy and you're watching a basketball game or something, you don't know if you should start talking or if you should just sit there") and on the phone ("I think it is hard to call. After it's done with, you don't know how to get off the phone"). Others mentioned problems in asking people out ("Asking a girl out on a first date—complete panic!") or in turning people down ("How about if you go on a date and you're really not interested, but he keeps calling?"). Still others noted problems in making or ending romantic commitments ("You don't know if you are going out with someone or if you are just seeing them," "It is hard to say, 'so, are we gonna make a commitment?'" "I avoided [breaking up] for two weeks because I was trying to think of what to say") (Grover & Nangle, 2003, pp. 133–134).

The Development of Dating Relationships

It is not until late adolescence that dating relationships begin to be characterized by a level of emotional depth and maturity that can be described as intimate, and it is not until late adolescence that individuals develop genuinely deep attachments to individuals other than their parents (Furman & Simon, 1999; Montgomery, 2005). One study comparing the way adolescents interacted with their mother, a close friend, and a romantic partner found that interactions with romantic partners were characterized by more conflict and fewer positive interactions than with friends, and more off-task behavior than with mothers (Furman & Shomaker, 2008). Over the course of adolescence, the importance of a romantic partner—relative to other relationships—increases, and by college, individuals typically name their romantic partner first on a list of significant others (up from fourth in grade 7 and third in grade 10) (Buhrmester, 1996; Furman & Wehner, 1994).

The ways in which adolescents interact with romantic partners also changes with development, with increasing willingness to acknowledge, analyze, and work through disagreements. (The major sources of conflict between boyfriends and girlfriends are issues related to how the relationship is going, such as jealousy, neglect, betrayal, and trust [McIsaac, Connolly, McKenney, Pepler, & Craig, 2008].) One study of age differences in couples' conflict resolution found that whereas 70% of the adolescent couples either denied having conflicts or dismissed them as insignificant, only 20% of the young adults did. Interestingly, the adolescents whose conversations looked more like those of the young adults were less likely to break up (Shulman, Tuval-Mashiach, Levran, & Anbar, 2006).

Reasons for Dating   Prior to middle or late adolescence, dating may be less important for the development of intimacy than it is for other purposes, including establishing emotional and behavioral autonomy from parents (Dowdy & Kliewer, 1998; Gray & Steinberg, 1999), furthering the development of gender identity (Feiring, 1999), learning about oneself as a romantic partner (Furman & Simon, 1999), and establishing and maintaining status and popularity in the peer group (B. Brown, 1999). Younger adolescents' choice of dating partners may have more to do with how they will be seen by others (for example, as "grown up," "macho," or "popular") than with the actual quality of the relationship itself. This explains why, between elementary school and middle school, there is an increase in girls' attraction to aggressive boys who stand out in the peer group (Bukowski, Sippola, & Newcomb, 2000).

Phases of Romance   The development of intimacy and more sophisticated social cognitive abilities is paralleled by changes in the ways adolescents think about and behave within romantic relationships. Several stage theories of romantic relationships have been proposed, but they make roughly the same points (Connolly &

One of the fundamental developmental tasks of adolescence is to begin to develop the capacity for intimate, romantic relationships. © Andrey_Popov/Shutterstock.com RF

McIsaac, 2009). The evolution of romance in the adolescent's life proceeds through three distinct phases. During the first phase (roughly between 11 and 13), adolescents first discover an interest in socializing with potential romantic and sexual partners. The focus of activity during this phase is primarily on learning about themselves, as adolescents broaden their self-conceptions to include seeing themselves as a potential romantic partner. Actual romantic relationships tend to be short-lived (the average romantic relationship at this age lasts only a few weeks), though, and are frequently based on superficial infatuations. Success in socializing with the other sex becomes an important determinant of status in the peer group, and high-status adolescents generally start dating before their lower-status peers (Connolly & McIsaac, 2009). The main purpose of romantic activity at this age involves establishing, improving, or maintaining one's social status.

During the second phase (from about 14 to 16), adolescents slowly move toward more meaningful dyadic relationships. Dating is very casual and often occurs in a group context in which peer networks start to include couples who have a special relationship. Although adolescents are still learning about themselves as romantic and sexual partners and are still aware of the way their peers view their romantic relationships, they are now sufficiently involved in the emotional side of romance for this to completely overshadow the personal and status concerns that dominated the earlier phases of romantic involvement. Relationships become a source of passion and preoccupation—recalling the themes expressed in popular love songs that appeal to teenagers. Although relationships are more enduring at this age than they were during early adolescence, the average romance still

LGBTQ youth
Lesbian, gay, bisexual, transgender, and questioning youth,
sometimes referred to as
sexual-minority youth.

sexual-minority youth
Lesbian, gay, bisexual, trans-
gender, and questioning
(LGBTQ) youth.

lasts only about six months (Connolly & McIsaac, 2009). One reason for this is that "dating the 'wrong' person or conducting romantic relationships in the 'wrong' way can seriously damage one's standing in the group. . . . This makes it difficult to sustain relationships that are too heavily focused inward, on the quality of the interaction or needs of the couple" (B. Brown, 1999, p. 297).

Finally, toward the later years of high school (around 17 or 18), concerns about commitment begin to move to the forefront, as adolescents begin to think about the long-term survival and growth of their romantic attachments. Often during this stage, there are tensions between partners' needs for intimacy (which draw them together) and their needs for autonomy (which distance them). As conceptions of romance develop, adolescents come to value commitment and caring as features of relationships that are as important as passion and pleasure, if not more so (B. Brown, 1999; Seiffge-Krenke, 2003). Relationships begin to look more like those seen among young adults, and couples increasingly spend time by themselves, rather than in the larger peer group. The average romantic relationship at age 18 lasts more than a year (Connolly & McIsaac, 2009).

Although the progression through the different phases of dating and romance may characterize the development of most adolescents, a number of writers interested in the experiences of lesbian, gay, bisexual, transgender, and questioning (LGBTQ) adolescents have pointed out that this picture may be less applicable to

LGBTQ youth—adolescents who are not exclusively or conventionally heterosexual (Diamond, 2000; Diamond, Savin-Williams, & Dubé, 1999). Although great strides have been made in increasing the public's tolerance and understanding of **sexual-minority youth,** stigmas and stereotypes still make the development of intimate relationships—whether nonsexual friendships, dating relationships, or sexual relationships—more complicated among LGBTQ youth than among their straight peers. For example, because LGBTQ youth don't always have the freedom to publicly express their romantic and sexual interests, they often find it difficult, if not impossible, to engage in many of the social and interpersonal activities that their heterosexual friends are permitted to enjoy. Thus, many LGBTQ youth end up pursuing sexual activity *outside* the context of a dating relationship, because the prejudices and harassment of others may preclude any public display of romantic intimacy with a same-sex partner. At the same time, for LGBTQ youth who are even somewhat open about their sexual identity, the development of close, nonsexual friendships with same-sex peers may be hampered by the suspicions and homophobia of others. As one group of writers explains the special predicament faced by LGBTQ adolescents, "A sexual-minority adolescent may already be privately plagued by the sense that he or she is profoundly different from other youths. To have this differentness acknowledged and perhaps ridiculed by peers may prove intolerable" (Diamond, Savin-Williams, & Dubé, 1999).

Sex Differences in Partner Preferences   There are both age and sex differences in what adolescents look for in romantic partners, and these differences parallel what is known about age and sex differences in romantic relationships. During middle adolescence, boys are more likely than girls to emphasize physical attractiveness and girls are more likely than boys to place more weight on interpersonal qualities, such as support or intimacy, although controlled studies, in which characteristics of potential dates are experimentally manipulated, find that girls are influenced more by attractiveness than they think they are (Ha, Overbeek, & Engels, 2010). By late adolescence, both sexes emphasize interpersonal qualities, and the ingredients of a satisfying relationship are very similar for males and females (and quite similar to those mentioned by adults): passion, communication, commitment, emotional support, and togetherness (W. A. Collins, 2003).

The Impact of Dating on Adolescent Development

When considering the impact of dating on adolescents' development and mental health, it is important to differentiate between group and couple activities. Participating

The interpersonal challenges of adolescence can be more complicated for LGBTQ youth. © Eddie linssen/Alamy

in mixed-sex activity in group situations—going to parties or dances, for example—has a positive impact on the psychological well-being of adolescents, because at this stage of development, participating in these activities is status enhancing. The impact of more serious dating is complicated and depends on the adolescent's age. Early starters (those who enter into dating relationships well before their peers) and late bloomers (those who do not have a romantic relationship until young adulthood) may both be at risk, although for different reasons and with different consequences. This is not to say that dating is not a valuable interpersonal experience for the adolescent, just that its benefits may only accrue among teenagers who begin dating at a certain age (Neemann et al., 1995).

Early Starters Entering into a serious romantic relationship before it is normative (say, before age 15) is associated with a wide range of negative correlates (Connolly, Nguyen, Craig, & Jiang, 2013; Connolly & McIsaac, 2009; Furman & Collibee, 2014; Orpinas, Horne, Song, Reeves, & Hsieh, 2013). This is probably true for both sexes, but researchers have focused primarily on girls because boys are less likely to begin serious dating quite so early. Even so, the few studies that have looked at early dating among boys do not show consistent effects.

The links between early dating and poorer mental health have been reported consistently for more than 50 years. Girls who begin serious dating early are worse off psychologically than their peers—less mature socially, less imaginative, less oriented toward achievement, less happy with who they are and how they look, more depressed, more likely to engage in disordered eating, less likely to do well in school, and more likely to be involved in delinquency, substance use, and risky behavior (Connolly & McIsaac, 2009). Early dating seems to have particularly negative implications for White girls (Compian et al., 2004), girls whose family relationships are more strained (Doyle et al., 2003), girls who date older boys (Haydon & Halpern, 2010; Loftus, Kelly, & Mustillo, 2011), and girls who are early maturers (Natsuaki, Biehl, & Ge, 2009). Adolescents who are unpopular with same-sex peers are especially harmed by early serious dating, perhaps because having few same-sex friends makes the dating relationships excessively important (Brendgen, Vitaro, Doyle, Markiewicz, & Bukowski, 2002). Research also shows that adolescents who begin dating early and who have multiple dating partners experience a drop in the quality of their relationships over time (W. A. Collins, 2003) and poorer quality relationships in young adulthood (Madsen & Collins, 2011). Adolescents who begin dating early are also more likely to be victims of dating violence (Halpern, Spriggs, Martin, & Kupper, 2009).

A variety of explanations for the link between early dating and psychological problems have been offered, but before we get ahead of ourselves, let's keep in mind the difficulty in distinguishing between cause and effect (Zimmer-Gembeck, Siebenbrunner, & Collins, 2001). There are all sorts of reasons that girls with psychological problems are more likely to get involved in dating relationships at a younger age, and because we cannot randomly assign some teenagers to date and others to remain single, we cannot be sure that early dating actually *causes* problems. Moreover, early dating may be part of a larger profile that includes precocious involvement in many adultlike activities (often because girls' dating partners are older), and there is a good deal of evidence that this sort of "pseudomaturity" is associated with a range of psychological problems (Connolly & McIsaac, 2009). Because this profile is itself associated with many factors known to place adolescents at risk (poor parenting, early puberty, or family instability, for example), it is hard to pinpoint early dating as the culprit. One recent study found, for example, that individuals who had poorer-quality relationships *prior* to adolescence were more likely to be dating at age 15 (Roisman, Booth-LaForce, Cauffman, Spieker, & The NICHD Early Child Care Research Network, 2009).

That said, it has been suggested that the link between early dating and poor mental health may have something to do with pressures on girls to engage in sexual activity before they are willing or psychologically ready (Marin, Kirby, Hudes, Coyle, & Gomez, 2006). Sexual coercion and date rape are common during the high school years (B. Brown, 2004; McMaster, Connolly, & Craig, 1997; W. Patton & Mannison, 1995). Although boys may feel peer pressure to become sexually active, this may be a very different sort of pressure—with very different consequences—from what girls feel. Because boys generally begin dating at a later age

The impact of dating on adolescent development depends on the age of the adolescent and the intensity of the relationship. Early, serious dating may have a negative impact on psychological development. © J. Hardy/PhotoAlto RF

than girls, and date people who are younger, dating may be less anxiety-provoking for boys, who have the advantage of a few additional years of "maturity."

To Date, or Not to Date?   About 10% of late adolescents report having had no serious romantic relationships, and another 15% have not been in a relationship that lasted more than a few months (Connolly & McIsaac, 2009). In looking at the effects of being a "late bloomer," it is important to distinguish between adolescents who delay dating because it is culturally normative to do so (as is the case in many Asian American communities) and those who delay because they are shy, unattractive, or unpopular (Connolly & McIsaac, 2009). Although one would think that it is the latter group whose development is most at risk, not enough research has been done on late bloomers to draw definitive conclusions.

In general, adolescents who do not date at all show signs of retarded social development and feelings of insecurity (Connolly & McIsaac, 2009), while adolescents who date and go to parties regularly are more popular, have a stronger self-image, and report greater acceptance by their friends; they also are more skilled at relational aggression (Houser, Mayeux, & Cross, 2015). Conversely, stopping or cutting back on dating after having dated heavily is associated with a drop in self-image and an increase in symptoms of depression (Davies & Windle, 2000).

It is not clear, of course, whether age-appropriate dating leads to better social development or whether more socially advanced adolescents are simply more likely to date; both are probably true. But it does seem safe to conclude that a moderate degree of dating—and a delay in serious involvement until age 15 or so—appears to be the most potentially valuable pattern.

This conclusion must be tempered by the fact that characteristics of the romantic partner play a role in shaping the impact of dating on psychological development. Adolescents who are not all that popular to begin with, but who date popular peers, gain in popularity over time, and adolescents with problems who date peers whose mental health is good show improvements in their psychological functioning over time (Simon, Aikins, & Prinstein, 2008). It is also the case, just as in the selection of friends, that adolescents tend to select romantic partners with whom they share certain attributes. (Generally speaking, research suggests that "birds of a feather flock together" is more often true than "opposites attract.") And, as is the case with friendships, dating a romantic partner with a history of delinquent behavior leads to more antisocial behavior, especially among females (Herrera, Wiersma, & Cleveland, 2011; Monahan, Dmitrieva, & Cauffman, 2014).

Regardless of the impact that dating does or doesn't have on adolescents' psychosocial development, studies show that romance has a powerful impact on their emotional state. According to several studies, adolescents' real and fantasized relationships trigger more strong emotional feelings during the course of a day (one-third of girls' strong feelings and one-quarter of boys') than do family, school, or friends. Not surprisingly, the proportion of strong emotions attributed to romantic relationships increases dramatically between preadolescence and early adolescence, and between early and middle adolescence as well. And although the majority of adolescents' feelings about their romantic relationships are positive, a substantial minority of their feelings—more than 40%, in fact—are negative, involving anxiety, anger, jealousy, and depression (Larson, Clore, & Wood, 1999).

Adolescents who have entered into a romantic relationship in the past year report more symptoms of depression than do those who have not (Joyner & Udry, 2000). One reason for this is that many adolescents who are involved romantically also experience breakups during the same time period (Z. Chen et al., 2009b; W. A. Collins, 2003), and the breakup of a romantic relationship is the single most common trigger of the first episode of major depression (Monroe, Rohde, Seeley, & Lewinsohn, 1999). Breaking up is also associated with increases in substance use and delinquency (Hou et al., 2013; Larson & Sweeten, 2012). As you would expect, negative emotions associated with being in a relationship are more common among adolescents who are high in rejection sensitivity (G. Downey et al., 1999) or who have an insecure working model, especially those who form preoccupied attachments to romantic partners (because they are unable to fully trust their partner or see themselves as worthy of their partner's affection) (Davila, 2008).

Breaking up does not have severe effects on all adolescents. Those who are most vulnerable to the potential negative consequences of ending a relationship are

Unfortunately, a substantial number of teenagers end up in violent or abusive romantic relationships. © Pixland/PunchStock RF

adolescents high in rejection sensitivity, those who have experienced a series of breakups, those who have other sorts of problems (such as binge drinking or involvement in delinquency), and, not surprisingly, those who identify themselves as the one who was broken up with (rather than the breaker-upper) (Connolly & McIsaac, 2009).

Violence in Dating Relationships   Unfortunately, many romantic relationships in adolescence are characterized by hostility, aggression, and abuse (B. Brown, 2004; Exner-Cortens, 2014). More distressingly, a high proportion of young adolescents believe that physical violence in a relationship is acceptable. In a recent study of more than 5,000 American 6th-graders, over half said that it was acceptable for a girl to hit her boyfriend if he had made her mad or jealous, and a quarter of the students thought it was fine for a boy to hit his girlfriend. Nearly a third of the girls in the sample and more than 25% of the boys who either were in, or had been in, a romantic relationship had been physically aggressive toward their partner (Simon, Miller, Gorman-Smith, Orpinas, & Sullivan, 2010) (see Figure 11). Although more than half of all parents talk to their adolescent about dating violence, parents are less likely to talk about this topic than about drugs, alcohol, family finances, money management, or

even the economy (Rothman, Miller, Terpeluk, Glauber, & Randel, 2011).

Estimates vary from study to study, but recent national surveys find that about 40% of American adolescents have been the victim of violence within the context of a romantic relationship (Halpern et al., 2009). About 25% of dating teenagers report having been the victim of "cyber dating abuse"—abuse via technology and social media—during the past year (Zweig, Dank, Yahner, & Lachman, 2013). As with other forms of cyberbullying, individuals who perpetrate cyber dating abuse are more likely to be abusive toward their partners in other ways, such as sexual coercion (Zweig, Lachman, Yahner, & Dank, 2014).

Dating abuse increases between early adolescence and mid-adolescence, and then becomes somewhat less common (Foshee et al., 2009). Male and female adolescents are equally likely to be the victims of violence in dating relationships (Halpern, Oslak, Young, Martin, & Kupper, 2001; J. Miller & White, 2003; O'Leary, Slep, Avery-Leaf, & Cascardi, 2008), and violence is often associated with drinking and drug use (Reyes, Foshee, Bauer, & Ennett, 2012; Schnurr & Lohman, 2013; Temple, Shorey, Fite, Stuart, & Le, 2013) and exposure to stressful life events (Chen & Foshee, 2015). Because beliefs about the acceptability of violence in romantic relationships

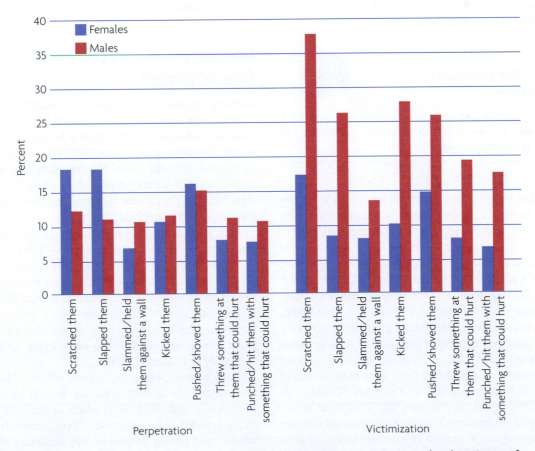

Figure 11   **Proportion of American 6th-graders reporting being victims or perpetrators of various types of dating violence.** (Simon et al., 2010)

influence adolescents' behavior toward their partners (Reyes, Foshee, Niolon, Reidy, & Hall, 2015), adolescents whose friends perpetrate dating violence are themselves more likely to do so (Foshee et al., 2013).

Dating violence is more common in rural areas than in suburban or urban communities (G. A. Spencer & Bryant, 2000), and among ethnic minority adolescents, adolescents from single-parent households, adolescents from lower socioeconomic homes, and LGBTQ youth (Dank, Lachman, Zweig, & Yahner, 2013; Foshee et al., 2009; Freedner, Freed, Yang, & Austin, 2002; Halpern et al., 2009; Luo, Stone, & Tharp, 2014; Martin-Storey, 2014). Individuals who are aggressive in romantic relationships are more likely to have had problems with aggression earlier in life (Foshee et al., 2014; Vagi et al., 2013). Being in a violent relationship also increases the chances of an adolescent girl behaving violently as a young adult (Herrera et al., 2011). Adolescents who have been the victims of violence within the context of a romantic relationship are more likely to be depressed, contemplate suicide, use illegal drugs, become pregnant during adolescence, and drop out of school (Hagan & Foster, 2001; Kim & Capaldi, 2004; Silverman, Raj, Mucci, & Hathaway, 2001), with many of these problems persisting into young adulthood (Adam et al., 2010). They are also more likely to be victimized again in the future (Cui, Ueno, Gordon, & Fincham, 2013; P. H. Smith, White, & Holland, 2003).

making the practical connection

What can be done to reduce the prevalence of violence in adolescents' dating relationships? Is this something that schools should become involved in?

We also know that adolescents behave in a variety of ways within dating relationships that are shaped by "scripts" for how males and females are expected to behave—scripts that are learned at home and from the mass media (Feiring, 1999; Gray & Steinberg, 1999; Larson, Clore, & Wood, 1999). In general, adolescents' ways of dealing with conflict in their romantic relationships are linked to the models they've had at home. Adolescents who have witnessed a great deal of conflict between their parents (either physical or verbal) report higher levels of verbal aggression, physical aggression, and relationship difficulties with their romantic partners, as both perpetrators and victims (Kinsfogel & Grych, 2004; Simon & Furman, 2010; Tschann et al., 2009). Other studies have found that adolescents who are either perpetrators or victims of violence in dating relationships are more likely to have had parents who were abusive, harsh, or behaved inappropriately toward them

(Manchikanti Gómez, 2011; Linder & Collins, 2005; Makin-Byrd, Bierman, & Conduct Problems Prevention Research Group, 2013). These studies, along with those discussed earlier about adolescent attachments, suggest that variations in adolescents' romantic relationships may have their origins—at least in part—in adolescents' family experiences.

The main point to keep in mind is that the qualities of adolescents' relationships with others—whether with parents, siblings, friends, or romantic partners—are correlated across different types of relationships (B. Brown, 2004; Shulman, Zlotnik, Shachar-Shapira, Connolly, & Bohr, 2012). Adolescents who have supportive and satisfying relationships at home are more likely to have high-quality friendships, and adolescents who have high-quality friendships are more likely to have high-quality romantic relationships. Thus, individuals' early experiences in the family, in interaction with their cumulative experiences with peers during childhood and preadolescence, affect the nature and quality of their romantic relationships in adolescence (Dhariwal, Connolly, Paciello, & Caprara, 2009; Rauer, Pettit, Lansford, Bates, & Dodge, 2013), and the quality of adolescents' family relationships affect the quality of the romantic relationships they have in young adulthood (R. Conger, Cui, Bryant, & Elder, 2000; Donnellan, Larsen-Rife, & Conger, 2005).

Intimacy and Psychosocial Development

Intimate relationships during adolescence—whether with peers or adults, inside or outside the family, sexual or nonsexual—play an important role in young people's overall psychological development. Close friends serve as a sounding board for adolescents' fantasies and questions about the future. Adolescents often talk to their friends about the careers they hope to have, the people they hope to get involved with, and the life they expect to lead after they leave home. Friends provide advice on a range of identity-related matters—from how to act in different situations to what sorts of occupational and educational paths to pursue. Having an intimate friendship is more central to adolescents' mental health than it is to children's (Buhrmester, 1990). Intimacy with same-sex friends and intimacy with romantic partners make distinct contributions to adolescents' self-esteem (Connolly & Konarski, 1994).

Keep in mind, however, that the effects of having an intimate friendship with someone depend on who that someone is and what takes place in the relationship. Being popular is less important than genuinely having friends, and having friends is less important than having *good* friendships (Asher, Parker, & Walker, 1996; Berndt, 1996; Fontaine et al., 2009; Hartup & Stevens,

1997; Hussong, 2000). Not all friendships are consistently good. Some provide for positive things like self-disclosure, intimacy, and companionship, but others give rise to insecurity, conflict, jealousy, and mistrust (J. Parker, Low, Walker, & Gamm, 2005). Adolescents who are close to peers or romantic partners who have antisocial values or habits are themselves more likely to develop similar patterns of behavior (Cauffman et al., 2008; Haynie, Giordano, Manning, & Longmore, 2005; Hussong & Hicks, 2003). It is easy to forget, but important to remember, that not all close relationships foster positive developmental outcomes.

Nevertheless, studies consistently show that individuals with satisfying close friendships fare better than those without them, not only in adolescence but in adulthood as well. Adolescence is an especially important time in the development of close relationships because many of the capacities and capabilities that permit intimacy in adult relationships make their debut in adolescence.

11

Sexuality

Sexuality as an Adolescent Issue

Sexual Activity During Adolescence

Stages of Sexual Activity

Sexual Intercourse During Adolescence

Changes in Sexual Activity Over Time

The Sexually Active Adolescent

Psychological and Social Characteristics of Sexually Active Adolescents

Hormonal and Contextual Influences on Sexual Activity

Parental and Peer Influences on Sexual Activity

Sex Differences in the Meaning of Sex

Sexual Orientation

Sexual Harassment, Rape, and Sexual Abuse During Adolescence

Risky Sex and its Prevention

Contraceptive Use

AIDS and Other Sexually Transmitted Diseases

Teen Pregnancy

Adolescent Parenthood

Sex Education

© J. Hardy/PhotoAlto RF

American adults have an ambivalent attitude toward adolescent sexuality. On the one hand, they are fascinated by it—it is nearly impossible to turn on the television and avoid seeing sexual imagery that either depicts or is directed at adolescents (D. Roberts et al., 2009). On the other hand, adults deplore it—most adults (80%, in fact) say that teenage sex is always or almost always wrong (Diamond & Savin-Williams, 2009). Adults look, and then they look the other way, and then they look again. Talk about a love–hate relationship!

This same ambivalence is reflected in the way that social scientists have studied adolescent sexuality. Sex has always been a popular subject among adolescence researchers. But rather than try to understand it, most research focuses simply on enumerating it—counting how many people have done which things how often, at what age, and with whom. Until fairly recently, the problematic aspects of adolescent sexuality—-precocious sex, promiscuous sex, unsafe sex, unwanted sex, and so forth—have received far more attention than its normative aspects (Tolman & McClelland, 2011). This is not to make light of these problems, which for many adolescents are very real. But it is worth pointing out that the study of other aspects of adolescent psychosocial development is not similarly dominated by research on what can go wrong. Imagine if researchers interested in identity, autonomy, intimacy, or achievement studied only negative self-conceptions, angry rebellion, failed friendships, or flunking out. As you will read, and in contrast to adults' concerns, most of the time, sex during adolescence is not associated with problems.

Fortunately, in recent years the last decade, there has been increased interest in positive sexual development (Diamond & Savin-Williams, 2009). There are four distinct aspects to positive sexuality in adolescence that can serve as the basis for how parents and educators discuss sex with teenagers (Brooks-Gunn & Paikoff, 1993; Zimmer-Gembeck, Ducat, & Boislard-Pepin, 2011). First, the adolescent needs to come to feel comfortable with his or her maturing body—its shape, size, and attractiveness. Second, the adolescent should accept having feelings of sexual arousal as normal and appropriate. Third, the adolescent needs to feel comfortable about choosing to engage in—or not to engage in—various sexual activities; that is, healthy sexual development involves understanding that sex is a *voluntary* activity for oneself and for one's partner. Finally, the adolescent (at least, one who is sexually active) must understand and practice safe sex—sex that avoids pregnancy and sexually transmitted infections.

Sexuality as an Adolescent Issue

Like other aspects of psychosocial development, sexuality is not an entirely new issue that surfaces for the first time during adolescence. Young children are curious

Most individuals' first experiences in sexual relationships occur during adolescence. © Patrick Sheandell/PhotoAlto/Fotosearch RF

about their sex organs and at a very early age derive pleasure from them. And, although sexual development may be more dramatic and more obvious prior to adulthood, it by no means ceases at the end of adolescence. Nonetheless, most of us would agree that adolescence is a fundamentally important time—if not the most important time in the life cycle—for the development of sexuality. There are several reasons for this.

Puberty and Adolescent Sexuality   Perhaps most obvious is the link between adolescent sexuality and puberty (Bogin, 2011; Diamond & Savin-Williams, 2011). The substantial increase in the sex drive that takes place in early adolescence is the result of hormonal changes. Moreover, not until puberty do individuals become capable of sexual reproduction. Before puberty, children are capable of kissing, fondling, masturbating, and even having sexual intercourse, and erotic feelings are reported by individuals prior to adolescence. Sexual feelings do not suddenly switch on at puberty (Herdt & McClintock, 2000). But not until puberty can males ejaculate semen or do females ovulate, and the fact that pregnancy is a possible outcome of sexual activity changes the nature and meaning of sexual behavior markedly—for the adolescent and for others. Finally, not until puberty do individuals develop the secondary sex characteristics that serve as a basis for sexual attraction

Although most research on adolescent sexuality has focused on sexual intercourse, adolescents' initial forays into the world of sex typically begin with less intimate sexual activity and gradually build toward intercourse. © Stockbyte/Punchstock RF

and as dramatic indicators that the young person is no longer physically a child.

Cognitive Change and Adolescent Sexuality The increased importance of sexuality at adolescence is not solely a result of puberty. The cognitive changes of adolescence play a part in the changed nature of sexuality as well. One obvious difference between the sex play of children and the sexual activity of adolescents is that children are not introspective or reflective about sexual behavior. In contrast, sex during adolescence is the subject of sometimes painful conjecture ("Will she or won't she?"), decision making ("Should I or shouldn't I?"), hypothetical thinking ("What if he wants to do it tonight?"), and self-conscious concern ("Am I good-looking enough?"). One of the chief tasks of adolescence is to figure out how to deal with sexual desires and

how to incorporate sex successfully and appropriately into social relationships. Much of this task is cognitive in nature, and much of it is made possible by the expansion of intellectual abilities that takes place during the period.

Social Roles and Adolescent Sexuality In addition to the influence of puberty and the growth of sophisticated thinking on sexuality during adolescence, the new social meaning given to sexual and dating behavior at this time in the life cycle makes sexuality an especially important psychosocial concern. Adolescence is a turning point in the development of sexuality because it marks the onset of deliberate sexually motivated behavior that is recognized, both by an adolescent and by others, as primarily and explicitly sexual in nature. Sexual activity in adolescence is motivated by more than hormones. For many adolescents (especially girls, but boys as well), sex is motivated by love and the desire for the sort of serious emotional relationship that begins to take on features of adult romance. For many adolescents (especially boys, but girls as well), sex is motivated by a desire to enhance their status with peers (Diamond & Savin-Williams, 2009).

Sexual Activity During Adolescence

Given the field's historical focus on problematic aspects of adolescent sexuality, such as precocious sex (having sex at too young an age), promiscuous sex (having sex with too many partners), unwanted sex (having sex against one's will), or unsafe sex (having sex that can result in pregnancy or a sexually transmitted disease), most of the research conducted into the sexual behavior of adolescents has focused on sexual intercourse (Tolman & McClelland, 2011). With the possible exception of oral sex, adults have tended not to worry about sexual behavior other than intercourse, and worries about oral sex have surfaced only in recent years, in response to exaggerated media reports about teenagers reporting giving or receiving oral sex promiscuously. Although national surveys show that slightly more teenagers have had oral sex than intercourse, they also indicate that the vast majority of teenagers who have oral sex also engage in sexual intercourse, and that promiscuity is not the norm for either activity (Hensel, Fortenberry, & Orr, 2008; L. Lindberg, Jones, & Santelli, 2008).

Although adolescents' involvement in sexual intercourse is an important topic, it is wise to remember that a good deal of the sexual activity of adolescents—even sexually experienced adolescents—involves activities other than sexual intercourse, such as kissing and touching parts of each other's body (broadly referred to as "noncoital activity," or, to use a more familiar term, "fooling around") (Tolman & McClelland, 2011). Moreover, because most individuals do not begin their sexual experiences with intercourse but progress toward it through stages of gradually increasing intimacy, it is important to view intercourse as one activity in a long progression, rather than as an isolated behavior (Diamond & Savin-Williams, 2009).

Stages of Sexual Activity

Before we turn to statistics on adolescent sexual activity, a word of caution is in order. Reports of sexual behavior vary markedly as a function of the ways in which questions are worded and data are collected. When former president Bill Clinton, referring to his affair with Monica Lewinsky, infamously said, "I did not have sexual relations with that woman," what he meant (we assume) is that he did not have vaginal intercourse with her. Whether the possibility that they engaged in oral sex makes his statement false depends on what one takes the expression "sexual relations" to mean.

Similarly, when adolescents respond to questions asking whether they have "had sex," have been "sexually active," or are "still a virgin," it is not clear how they interpret the question. Is genital touching "sex"? Are you a "virgin" if you have engaged in anal sex but not vaginal intercourse? Adolescents, like adults, don't always agree. And to make things even more complicated, adolescents distinguish between acts that culminate in orgasm (which are more likely to be viewed as leading to a loss of virginity) and those that don't (Bersamin, Fisher, Walker, Hill, & Grube, 2007). Moreover, adolescents who have engaged in a specific behavior are more likely to say that the behavior doesn't "count" in their definition of losing one's virginity, which means that adolescents' responses to surveys about sex are biased by their actual experience. So bear in mind that all figures to follow are necessarily approximate.

Most adolescents' first experience with sex falls into the category of **autoerotic behavior**—sexual behavior that is experienced alone. The most common autoerotic activities reported by adolescents are having erotic fantasies (about three-quarters of all teenagers report having sexual fantasies) and masturbation (different surveys yield different estimates, depending on the age of the respondents and the wording of the questions, but about half of all adolescent boys and about one-fourth of all adolescent girls masturbate prior to age 18) (Diamond & Savin-Williams, 2009).

By the time most adolescents reach high school, they have made the transition from autoerotic behavior to sexual activity that involves another person. By the time

individuals have turned 16, about 80% have engaged in some type of noncoital activity with another person. By about 18, 80% have had either vaginal or oral sex; nearly all of those who hadn't by 18 have done so before the end of their 20s (Halpern & Haydon, 2012; Haydon, Cheng, Herring, McRee, & Halpern, 2014).

The developmental progression of sexual behaviors, from less intimate to more intimate, has not changed very much over the past 50 years, and the sequence in which males and females engage in various sexual activities is remarkably similar. According to recent, large-scale studies of American adolescents, holding hands comes first, followed (in this order) by kissing, making out (kissing for a long time), feeling breasts through clothes, feeling breasts under clothes, feeling a penis through clothes, feeling a penis under clothes or while naked, feeling a vagina through clothes, feeling a vagina under clothes or while naked, and intercourse or oral sex. For about half of all adolescents, intercourse precedes oral sex by about a year and for another third, both types of sex are initiated around the same time; the rest report a range of different patterns (Halpern & Haydon, 2012; Haydon, Herring, Prinstein, & Halpern, 2012). One worrisome finding is that most adolescents report talking about contraception *after* they first have intercourse, rather than before (O'Sullivan, Cheng, Harris, & Brooks-Gunn, 2007). For most adolescents, this sequence of increasingly advanced behaviors unfolds gradually over time, but for a significant minority, it is compressed into a shorter interval (de Graaf, Vanwesenbeeck, Meijer, Woertman, & Meeus, 2009). The expected timetable for progressive sexual activities is faster among adolescents who expect a relatively faster timetable for achieving autonomy from parents and experimenting with drugs and alcohol, suggesting that earlier involvement in more intimate forms of sex may be part of a larger pattern of earlier involvement in "adult" activities (Rosenthal & Smith, 1997).

> **autoerotic behavior**
> Sexual behavior that is experienced alone, such as masturbation or sexual fantasizing.

Sexual Intercourse During Adolescence

Prevalence of Sexual Intercourse Estimates of the prevalence of sexual intercourse among contemporary adolescents vary from study to study, depending on the nature of the sample surveyed, the year and region in which the study was undertaken, the reliability of the data gathered, and the wording of the questions (Santelli, Lindberg, Abma, McNeely, & Resnick, 2000). Adolescents do not always report their sexual activity honestly or accurately. Males tend to overstate their level of activity and females tend to understate it (Kaestle, Halpern, Miller, & Ford, 2005). The following paragraphs summarize what social scientists have concluded from recent surveys with these caveats in mind.

Although regional and ethnic variations make it difficult—if not misleading—to generalize about the average age at which American adolescents initiate sexual intercourse, national surveys indicate that more adolescents are sexually active at an earlier age today than several decades ago, although this number has declined a bit (Centers for Disease Control and Prevention, 2014a). However, there has been a slight decrease in the proportion of sexually experienced teenagers since the mid-1990s—in other words, compared to 25 years ago, fewer adolescents are having sexual intercourse, but those who are do so at a somewhat earlier age (Diamond & Savin-Williams, 2009).

The best estimates we have are that, by the end of their sophomore year in high school, more than 40% of American adolescents have had heterosexual vaginal intercourse (these estimates, which are based on large national surveys, do not include same-sex intercourse or other types of sex, like oral or anal sex). By age 18, this number has risen to about 65% (see Figure 1) (Centers for Disease Control and Prevention, 2014a). Whatever we might think about these figures, one conclusion is inescapable: Sexual intercourse during high school is now a part of the normative experience of adolescence in America.

Ethnic Differences in Age of Sexual Initiation The average age at which American teenagers have intercourse for the first time is around 17 (Guttmacher Institute, 2014). There are substantial ethnic differences in age of sexual initiation, especially among males (Centers for Disease Control and Prevention, 2014a). Nearly one-fourth of Black boys report having had sex

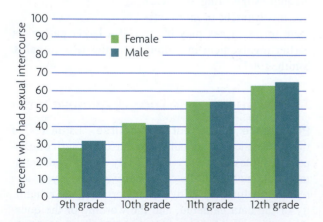

Figure 1 **Nearly one-third of American 9th-graders have had sexual intercourse. By senior year, about two-thirds have.** (Centers for Disease Control and Prevention, 2014a)

for the first time by age 13, compared to 4% among White boys and 9% of Hispanic boys. One recent study of Black children found that about 15% of boys as young as 9 are already thinking about sex and that one-fifth of 12-year-old boys expect to begin having sex within the next year (Miller et al., 2012). In all ethnic groups, the average reported age of first sex is slightly older among females than males (Centers for Disease Control and Prevention, 2014a). Ethnic differences in the age of sexual initiation are far smaller among females, although Hispanic and Asian American females generally have their first sexual intercourse at a later age than is the case among their Black and White counterparts (Grunbaum, Lowry, Kann, & Pateman, 2000).

One reason for the relatively high rate of early sexual activity among Black males is the higher proportion of Black youth who grow up in single-parent homes and in poor neighborhoods, both of which, as you will read later in this chapter, are risk factors for early sexual activity. Although first-generation Mexican American girls are more likely to become sexually active than either immigrant youth or those who are second-generation Americans (Bámaca-Colbert, Greene, Killoren, & Noah, 2014; Killoren & Deutsch, 2014), girls who are more Americanized and who have expectations for earlier autonomy are more likely than their less acculturated peers to have sex at a younger age, to have multiple sex partners, to contract STDs, and to become pregnant (J. Lee & Hahm, 2010; Ma et al., 2014; McDonald, Manlove, & Ikramullah, 2009), and more acculturated Asian American girls are more likely to be sexually active than their less Americanized peers (Hahm, Lahiff, & Barreto, 2006). Studies also indicate that, among all ethnic groups, rates of sexual activity are higher among economically disadvantaged youth, although the gap in rates of sexual activity between rich and poor is substantially narrower now than it was a decade ago, again pointing to the increasingly normative nature of sexual intercourse among American teenagers (Singh & Darroch, 1999). The average age at first intercourse varies considerably across nations; one survey of European adolescents found that the proportion of 15-year-olds who ever had intercourse ranged from 15% in Poland to 75% in Greenland (Madkour, Farhat, Halpern, Godeau, & Gabhainn, 2010a). Adolescents' beliefs about the age at which it is OK to initiate sex vary across Europe as well (see Figure 2) (Madkour et al., 2014).

For many girls, their first sexual experience is forced (Diamond & Savin-Williams, 2009). Involuntary sex is especially frequent among girls who have sex for the first time when they are 12 or younger (Finer & Philbin, 2013); one-fourth of younger adolescents report that their first intercourse was against their will, in contrast to 10% of women whose first intercourse was after age 18. Many other young women who report

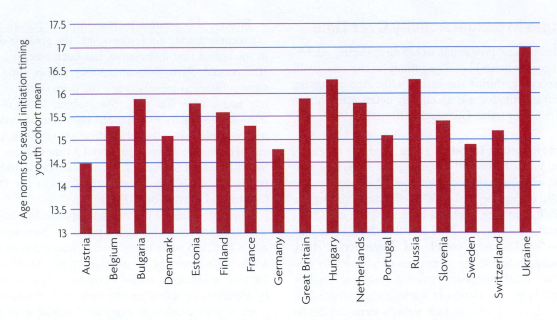

Figure 2   Adolescents' beliefs about the age at which it is acceptable to begin having sex vary across countries. (Madkour et al., 2014).

that they had sex voluntarily the first time nevertheless report that they did not really *want* to have sex; girls in relationships where the balance of power favors the boy are more likely to have sex than those whose relationship is more equal (Giordano et al., 2010). Young girls whose first partner was at least 7 years older are twice as likely as others to report having had voluntary but unwanted intercourse (Abma, Driscoll, & Moore, 1998). Young adolescents, both male and female, with a significantly older romantic partner are far more likely to have sexual intercourse than those whose partner is the same age (Kaestle, Morisky, & Wiley, 2002; Leitenberg & Saltzman, 2000; Loftus & Kelly, 2012).

Timing of Sexual Initiation   Adolescents are more likely to lose their virginity during certain times of the

year than during others. There are two seasonal peaks in the timing of first intercourse: June and December (Levin, Xu, & Bartkowski, 2002) (see Figure 3). June and, to a lesser extent, May and July, are common months for first intercourse regardless of whether the adolescents are romantically involved; December, however, is a peak time only among adolescents who are with a serious boyfriend or girlfriend, and particularly so among girls. Several explanations for these seasonal trends have been offered, including the general tendency for people to be more sexually active when the weather is very hot or very cold and the fact that adolescents have more unsupervised time when they are on summer or winter vacation. As for what has been called "the holiday effect" (the rise in sexual debuts among romantic partners in December)—well, you can probably figure that out for yourself.

Figure 3   Adolescents are most likely to have intercourse for the first time during early summer or in December. (Levin et al., 2002)

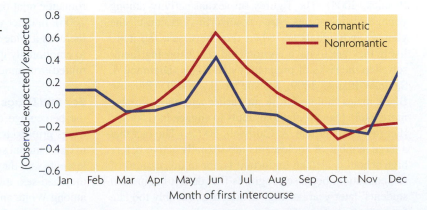

Changes in Sexual Activity Over Time

Attitudes toward premarital intercourse during adolescence became more liberal beginning in the mid-1960s and, especially, during the early 1970s. Accompanying this shift in attitudes was an equally noteworthy shift in sexual behavior (Alan Guttmacher Institute, 1994).

Recent Historical Trends Three trends are of special interest. First, the overall percentage of American adolescents who had engaged in premarital sex accelerated markedly during the early 1970s and again during the late 1980s, and then declined between 1995 and 2001; it has remained flat, at a little less than 50%, since then (Centers for Disease Control and Prevention, 2014a). The recent decline in the proportion of adolescents who have had sexual intercourse has not been paralleled by a decline in the proportion of adolescents who are having other types of sex—in fact, today's teenagers are far more "active" sexually than were previous generations (Diamond & Savin-Williams, 2009). It is likely that the threat of AIDS and other sexually transmitted diseases has led many adolescents to substitute a safer type of sex (such as oral sex, which, although safer than vaginal or anal intercourse, still carries some risk) for intercourse, with what appear to be the desired results: Adolescents who engage in oral sex, but not sexual intercourse, are less likely to feel guilty or used and less likely to contract a sexually transmitted infection (Brady & Halpern-Felsher, 2007).

Second, the proportion of individuals who have sexual intercourse *early* in adolescence is substantial. Although the median age at which adolescents first engage in intercourse has remained somewhere between 16 and 17 for some time, today, nearly one-third of all contemporary American adolescents have had intercourse by the time they are 9th-graders, and more than 5% have had intercourse by age 13 (Centers for Disease Control and Prevention, 2014a). Among adolescents who have not had sex, fears of pregnancy and disease (including HIV/AIDS) are the most common reasons for abstaining (Blinn-Pike, 1999; Loewensen, Ireland, & Resnick, 2004). The figures on sexual activity among younger adolescents are noteworthy, because the younger individuals are when they have sex, the more likely they are to have unprotected sex, exposing themselves to the risks of pregnancy and STDs (Diamond & Savin-Williams, 2009; Kaestle et al., 2005). (Because Black males initiate sex at an earlier age, they are also more likely than other adolescents to engage in risky sex [Fergus, Zimmerman, & Caldwell, 2007].) The fact that a large number of adolescents are sexually active before high school is also an important factor in discussions of sex education, because programs that do not begin until students' later years of high school are probably too late for a substantial number of young people.

Finally, the greatest increase in the prevalence of intercourse among adolescents, and the greatest decline in the age at first intercourse, has been among females (Diamond & Savin-Williams, 2009). Before 1965, there were substantial gaps between the proportions of sexually active boys and girls. Since about 1965, the proportion of sexually experienced high school males has nearly tripled, but the proportion of sexually experienced high school females is about 5 times higher today. Sex differences in rates of sexual intercourse today are negligible, especially by age 15 (Centers for Disease Control and Prevention, 2014a).

The bottom line: Whether adults approve or not, sexual activity has become a normative part of the American teenager's life. And while many parents, educators, and other adults are alarmed by sexual activity among the young, for most adolescents, sexual involvement is accompanied by affection, emotional involvement, and commitment to a relationship. Although many high school students are sexually active on a regular basis, promiscuity is not the norm (Singh & Darroch, 1999). According to recent data, 80% of sexually active high school girls, and 67% of sexually active high school boys, had intercourse with only one partner during the past 3 months, and the proportion of adolescents who have had multiple sex partners has decreased substantially over the past decade, although it is still substantial today—15% of contemporary high school students have had intercourse with four or more persons (Centers for Disease Control and Prevention, 2014a). Rates of promiscuity vary considerably across localities, however, as Figure 4 illustrates.

About one-third of sexually active adolescents have had intercourse with someone they are not in a romantic relationship with (Manning, Longmore, & Giordano, 2005). Although many adults have expressed concern about adolescents having sex with someone outside the context of a dating relationship, or "hooking up," these encounters are usually with someone the adolescent knows well, like a friend or ex-partner (sometimes referred to as "friends with benefits"). And in one-third of these "nonromantic" encounters, one of the persons was hoping that the friendship would turn into (or return to) a romantic relationship (Manning, Giordano, & Longmore, 2006). In other words, the broad category of "casual sex" includes a wide range of behavior, from one-night stands to emotionally close sex with a desired (but not yet committed) romantic partner (Williams & Russell, 2013).

Sex and Drugs One particular cause for concern is that the percentage of adolescents who use alcohol or other drugs prior to having sex has increased in recent years—in one national survey, about one-fourth of American adolescents said they drank or used drugs before the last time they had sex, a behavior that is relatively more common among White and Hispanic male adolescents (Centers for Disease Control and Prevention, 2014a). Not surprisingly,

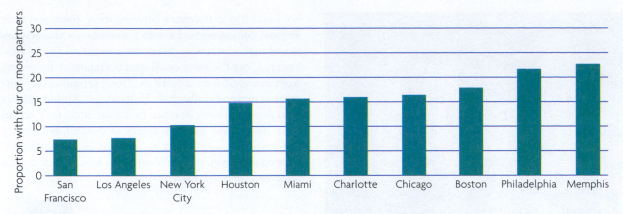

Figure 4   The rate of sexual promiscuity varies considerably across the United States. (Centers for Disease Control and Prevention, 2014a)

sexual risk taking, as well as casual sex, is more likely when alcohol or marijuana is involved, mainly because of impaired judgment and loss of control (Bryan, Schmiege, & Magnan, 2012; Kiene, Barta, Tennen, & Armeli, 2009; Patrick, Maggs, & Lefkowitz, 2014). One study of British adolescents found that one-fourth of those interviewed were so drunk during sex that they did not even remember it (something that by no means is limited to teenagers in England), as these two 16-year-olds (the first male, the second female) describe:

> I've actually woken up next to a girl and I didn't have a clue who she was. And when I woke up I was like, "What's your name? Like, Who were you?" She explained herself, I couldn't remember it, man. I was thinking, "How the hell couldn't I remember that?" . . . I don't remember.

> I've had previous problems with alcohol where I've been so drunk that I can't actually remember things that have happened and the next morning, or the next couple of weeks, I get told about things and then it [having sex with someone] suddenly comes back and I think, oh my God, what have I done? (L. M. Coleman & Cater, 2005, p. 656)

The Sexually Active Adolescent

Psychological and Social Characteristics of Sexually Active Adolescents

For many years, researchers studied the psychological and social characteristics of sexually active adolescents on the assumption that these teenagers were more troubled than their peers (either before or as a consequence of becoming sexually active). This view has been replaced as sexual activity has become more prevalent among "normal" adolescents.

Sexual Activity and Psychological Development
Numerous studies show that sexual activity during adolescence is decidedly *not* associated with psychological

disturbance (Diamond & Savin-Williams, 2011; Tolman & McClelland, 2011). Adolescents who are sexually active earlier than their peers have levels of self-esteem and life satisfaction similar to those of other adolescents (Goodson, Buhi, & Dunsmore, 2006; Vrangalova & Savin-Williams, 2011). Losing one's virginity does not have negative psychological repercussions, either in the short or long term (Bingham & Crockett, 1996; Langer, Zimmerman, & Katz, 1995), even when one's sexual debut is outside the context of a romantic relationship (Monahan & Lee, 2008). Thus, both the belief that only "troubled" adolescents have sex and the belief that sexual activity during adolescence leads to later psychological disturbance are incorrect (Goodson, Buhi, & Dunsmore, 2006; A. M. Meier, 2007; Spriggs & Halpern, 2008).

It is important, however, to distinguish between predictors of being sexually active and predictors of engaging in *risky sex* (unprotected sex, sex with multiple partners, etc.). Risky sex is associated with the same sorts of psychological and behavioral factors correlated with other forms of risk taking (Dogan, Stockdale, Widaman, & Conger, 2010; Kirby, 2011; Lansford et al., 2010; Moilanen, Crockett, Raffaelli, & Jones, 2010a; Price & Hyde, 2011; Van Ryzin, Johnson, Leve, & Kim, 2011). One factor that *isn't* correlated with risky sexual behavior, however, is exposure to pornography (Luder et al., 2011).

Although sexually active adolescents do not differ psychologically from those who are not, *early* sexual activity (having intercourse before age 16) is associated with a more general attitudinal and behavioral profile that includes more permissive attitudes toward sex, experimentation with drugs and alcohol, minor delinquency, low levels of religious involvement, lower interest in academic achievement, and a stronger orientation toward independence (Armour & Haynie, 2007; Cavazos-Rehg et al., 2010; Harden & Mendle, 2011a; Lohman & Billings, 2008). One study that measured adolescents' likelihood of losing their virginity found that individuals who fit the profile in 7th or 8th grade were *25* times more

Many adolescents have sex after drinking or using drugs, which increases the likelihood of sexual risk-taking. © Monkey Business Images/Shutterstock.com RF

not find major differences between these youth and their virginal counterparts. Less is known about characteristics of individuals who do not have sex at all during adolescence, but the most consistent correlate of abstaining from sex until after age 18 is strong religious commitment (Zimmer-Gembeck & Helfand, 2008). Individuals who don't have sex for the first time until they are in their 20s are less likely to marry or cohabit, but among those who do, they report greater satisfaction with their relationship than people who start having sex during their teen years (Harden, 2012).

making the practical connection

Why do you think the psychological correlates of early sexual intercourse are different from the correlates of sexual intercourse when it is delayed until the last years of high school? Would you be in favor of sex education courses whose focus was on persuading adolescents to wait until they were 16 before having intercourse?

likely to lose their virginity within the next 2 years than those who did not (L'Engle & Jackson, 2008; L'Engle, Jackson, & Brown, 2006) (see Figure 5). In the United States, but not in all countries, early sexual intercourse is also associated with higher rates of depression (Madkour et al., 2010b), especially when it takes place outside the context of a romantic relationship (Mendle, Ferrero, Moore, & Harden, 2013). In contrast, studies of adolescents who become sexually active at *age 16 or later* do

Causation or Correlation? Although many studies have found a link between early sexual activity and small-scale deviance, why they are correlated is not entirely clear (Diamond & Savin-Williams, 2009; Zimmer-Gembeck, Siebenbruner, & Collins, 2004). There is little support for the idea that early sex leads to other types of risky or antisocial activity. Just the opposite: Several studies show that involvement in deviance (especially alcohol and drug use, but aggression and

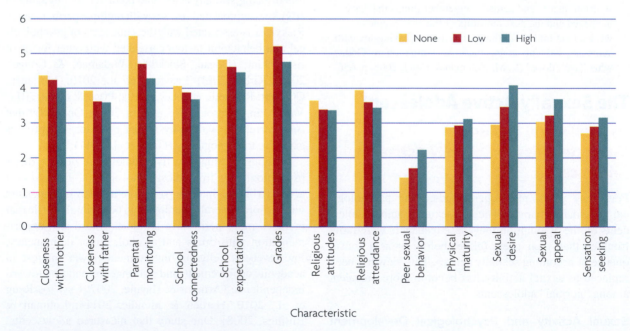

Figure 5 **Characteristics that distinguish adolescents who are low, moderate, or high in their likelihood of becoming sexually active.** (L'Engle, Jackson, & Brown, 2006)

bullying as well) precedes early involvement with sex (Boisard, Dussault, Brendgen, & Vitaro, 2013; Holt, Matjasko, Espelage, Reid, & Koenig, 2013; Lansford, Dodge, Fontaine, Bates, & Pettit, 2014; Parkes et al., 2014). But some studies find that experimentation with deviant activity and early sex are connected because they share some common underlying factor, such as impulsivity or the propensity to take risks (Derefinko et al., 2014; Harden, Mendle, Hill, Turkheimer, & Emery, 2008).

Many experts believe that a general inclination toward problem behavior and lack of impulse control is behind an overarching pattern that includes minor delinquency, precocious or promiscuous sex, disengagement from school, and drug and alcohol use (Crockett et al., 2006; Goldenberg, Telzer, Lieberman, Fuligni, & Galván, 2013; Khurana et al., 2012; Parkes et al., 2014). Engaging in delinquency and in casual sex are influenced by some of the same genes, but that delinquency and sex within a romantic relationship are not, consistent with other research on the genetic bases of traits like sensation-seeking and impulsivity (Harden & Mendle, 2011c). It probably makes sense to view sexual risk taking as a specific instance of risky behavior more generally (Huang, Murphy, & Hser, 2012; Madkour, Farhat, Halpern, Godeau, & Gabhainn, 2010a; Secor-Turner, McMorris, Sieving, & Bearinger, 2013).

Another factor that affects adolescents' sexual activity is the extent to which they are supervised by their parents or other adults. Most sexual activity between teenagers takes place in one of the two individuals' homes—most often, the boy's. (The third most popular setting is at the home of another friend.) And the most common time for adolescents to have sex is not on the weekend, but on weekdays, after school. Adolescents who are unsupervised after school and who do not participate in after-school programs are more likely to be sexually active, more likely to have multiple sexual partners, and more likely to contract an STD (Buhi & Goodson, 2007; D. Cohen, Farley, Taylor, Martin, & Schuster, 2002).

Hormonal and Contextual Influences on Sexual Activity

One factor that is consistently related to the age at which adolescents initiate sex is physical maturation. Adolescents who mature earlier are also likely to have sex earlier, including both risky and non-risky sex (Baams, Dubas, Overbeek, & van Aken, 2015; Diamond & Savin-Williams, 2009; Lam et al., 2002). Increased interest in sex at adolescence is likely to have social as well as biological causes, however. Adolescents are thought to become interested in sex in part because of increases in sex hormones at puberty and in part because sexual activity becomes accepted—even encouraged—in their peer group. A fuller understanding of adolescent sexual behavior necessitates looking at biological and

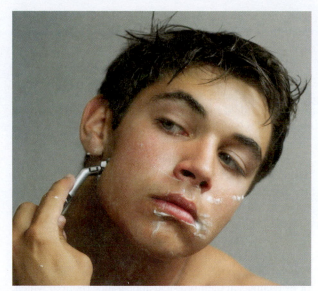

Adolescents who go through puberty earlier than their peers are more likely to start having sex earlier, too. © UpperCut Images/Alamy images RF

social influences in interaction with each other, rather than at either set of influences alone (Halpern, 2003). And the story line is different for males than females.

testosterone
One of the sex hormones secreted by the gonads, found in both sexes but in higher levels among males than females.

Hormonal Influences Boys' and girls' initial interest in sex is influenced primarily by the surge in certain hormones at puberty—**testosterone,** to be specific. Adolescents with higher levels of androgens (testosterone is an androgen) are more likely than their peers to report masturbating, thinking about sex, and planning to have sexual intercourse within the next year. This hormonal change appears to increase adolescents' interest in sex as well as their arousal when exposed to sexual stimuli. This is true for both males and females, although females' interest in sex is also influenced by estrogen.

Motivation to have sex is one thing; becoming sexually active is another. How important is the rise in testosterone at puberty in triggering the onset of sexual intercourse? The answer differs between boys and girls. Among boys, the increased level of androgens is directly related to the likelihood of being sexually active (B. C. Campbell, Prossinger, & Mbzivo, 2005). Younger boys who are more mature biologically are more likely to be sexually active than older boys whose hormone levels are lower. Early-maturing boys also are more likely than their peers to download pornography off the Internet (Skoog, Stattin, & Kerr, 2009).

Whether boys actually have sex is not entirely dependent on their hormone levels, however, because actually having sex depends on how receptive girls are to them. Not surprisingly, boys who are more popular with girls in their school are more likely to initiate sex early than are boys who are less popular with girls. Sex hormones do not just contribute to increases in boys' sex drive—they also affect height, strength, and the development of secondary sex characteristics, like facial hair. In other words, increases in androgens lead to boys' increased sexual activity both because they increase their sex drive (which may make boys with higher testosterone levels want to have sex more) and because they change their physical appearance (which may make them more attractive to girls).

Hormonal influences on sexual desire and physical appearance are easier to separate in girls. Although androgens also are responsible for increases in girls' sex drive, a different set of hormones—estrogens—is primarily responsible for changes in their appearance, including breast development. Because of this, it is possible to study whether increased sexual activity among girls after puberty is more influenced by increases in their sex drive or by changes in their physical appearance (both of which, presumably, influence their sexual attractiveness to boys). It turns out that differences in adolescent girls' sexual activity have little to do with differences in their androgen levels but is correlated with differences in their estrogen levels. Estrogen influences girls' sexual activity mainly through its impact on their physical attractiveness to boys.

Of course, girls' involvement in sex is not solely determined by whether boys want them as sexual partners. Girls' own interest in sex and their receptivity to boys' interest in them are also crucial. But in girls, it turns out, these factors are much more determined by context than by biology.

The Role of Context Social factors are far more important in influencing girls' involvement in sexual intercourse than boys' (Crockett, Bingham, Chopak, & Vicary, 1996; D. B. Henry, Schoeny, Deptula, & Slavick, 2007). Although increases in androgens lead to increased interest in sex among girls, and although increases in estrogens lead to increased attractiveness to boys, whether this interest and attractiveness are translated into behavior depends largely on the social environment (Diamond & Savin-Williams, 2009). Among girls with high levels of androgens, for example, those who have sexually permissive attitudes and whose friends are sexually active are more likely to engage in intercourse. But girls whose social environment is less encouraging of sex—even those with high levels of androgens—are unlikely to be sexually active. In other words, whereas hormones seem to have a direct and powerful effect on the sexual behavior of boys, the impact of hormones on the sexual behavior of girls seems to depend on the social context.

Why might this be? One explanation is that boys develop in an environment that is more uniformly tolerant and encouraging of sexual behavior than do girls. All that boys need to become sexually active is the biological jolt from the increase in androgens at puberty—there is nothing in the environment to hold them back. For girls, however, the environment is more varied. Some girls develop within a context that permits and even encourages sexual activity; others do not. Although the increase in androgens also provides a jolt to the sex drive of the adolescent girl, and although the increase in estrogens makes her more attractive to boys, if she develops within a context that places strong social controls on sexual activity, this hormonal awakening will not be translated into sexual activity. Among the most important forces in this context are parents and peers.

Parental and Peer Influences on Sexual Activity

Many researchers have asked whether adolescents who become sexually active earlier than their peers have different sorts of relationships with their parents or their peers. The answer is clear: Not surprisingly, given the correlation between early sexual activity and other forms of problem behavior, adolescents from authoritative homes—that is, homes where parents are warm, are involved in their adolescent's life, and monitor their adolescent's behavior—are less likely to become sexually active at an early age and less likely to engage in risky sexual activity, such as having unprotected sex (de Graaf, Vanwesenbeeck, Meijer, Woertman, & Meeus, 2009; Ellis, Schlomer, Tilley, & Butler, 2012; Kan, Cheng, Landale, & McHale, 2010; Pingel et al., 2012; Van Campen & Romero, 2012). Parent-adolescent conflict is also associated with early sexual activity, especially among adolescents who are relatively more mature physically (McBride, Paikoff, & Holmbeck, 2003). These strong and consistent links between effective parenting and safer sexual behavior have been found across ethnic groups (Biddlecom, Awusabo-Asare, & Bankole, 2009; Meschke, Bartholomae, & Zentall, 2000; B. Miller, Benson, & Galbraith, 2001). Consistent with the idea that the underpinnings of risky sexual behavior are the underpinnings of risky behavior more generally, one recent study of Black youth found that sexual risk taking was the outcome of a pathway that included suboptimal parenting, academic disengagement, and affiliation with risk-taking peers (Kogan et al., 2011) (see Figure 6).

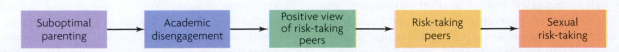

Figure 6 The antecedents of risky sexual behavior are similar to the antecedents of risk taking more generally. (Kogan et al., 2011)

Parent-Adolescent Communication A great deal of attention has been devoted by researchers to the study of parent-adolescent communication about sex, although it is quite clear from this research that any conclusions you might draw about the nature and impact of these conversations depends on whom you ask. Many more parents report communicating with their adolescent about sex than vice versa. In addition, parents often say that they have communicated about a particular topic (such as AIDS) when their teenager says they have not (K. Miller, Kotchick, Dorsey, Forehand, & Ham, 1998). Other discrepancies abound as well. Parents underestimate their adolescents' sexual activity and unrealistically assume that if they disapprove of it, their adolescents are not likely to be sexually active. On the other hand, sexually active adolescents underestimate their parents' disapproval of sexual activity (Jaccard, Dittus, & Gordon, 1998). Generally, teenagers are more likely to talk about sex with mothers than fathers, and they rate their mothers as better sex educators (Raffaelli & Green, 2003). Adolescents also are likely to be more receptive to having multiple conversations over a period of time about sex than to having one "big talk" (Martino, Elliott, Corona, Kanouse, & Schuster, 2008).

Most discussions parents and teenagers have about sex focus on issues of safety (AIDS, condom use) rather than issues of sexual behavior or relationships (DiIorio

Talking to teenagers about sex does not increase their likelihood of becoming sexually active, but may encourage adolescents to practice safe sex.
© SW Productions/Photodisc/Getty Images RF

et al., 1999; K. Miller, Levin, Whitaker, & Xu, 1998). Adolescents are more likely to be well educated about sex when their conversations with their parents are genuinely interactive, rather than dominated by the parents (Lefkowitz, Romo, Corona, Au, & Sigman, 2000). This is important because conversations between mothers and daughters about sex tend to be more interactive than conversations between mothers and sons (Lefkowitz, Boone, Sigman, & Kit-fong Au, 2002). Perhaps because of this, parent-adolescent communication about sex is more predictive of daughters' behavior than of sons' (McNeely et al., 2002). Conversations about sex are very infrequent in Asian American homes (J. L. Kim & Ward, 2007).

It is often assumed that it is beneficial for adolescents to discuss sex with their parents; however, the effect of parent-child communication on adolescents' sexual behavior depends on who is doing the communicating and what is being communicated. Overall, the impact of parent-adolescent communication on the likelihood of an adolescent being sexually active is very small (B. Miller et al., 2001; Paikoff et al., 1997). Parent-child communication specifically about contraception lowers the rate of *risky* sex (Aspy et al., 2007; Donenberg, Emerson, & Mackesy-Amiti, 2011; Hutchinson, Jemmott, Jemmott, Braverman, & Fong, 2003; K. Miller & Whitaker, 2001), however, especially if the discussions take place before the adolescent becomes sexually active (K. Miller, Levin, Whitaker, & Xu, 1998). Communication with older siblings about safe sex is also effective (Kolburn Kowal & Blinn-Pike, 2004).

A growing body of research suggests that what is most important are the attitudes and values communicated by parents during discussions of sex and the ways in which these attitudes and values are interpreted by the adolescent (Bersamin, Walker, Waiters, Fisher, & Grube, 2005; Deutsch & Crockett, 2015; Khurana & Cooksey, 2012; Longmore, Eng, Giordano, & Manning, 2009). Among girls with liberal parents, talking about sex is associated with *more* sexual activity, but this is not true among girls with parents who disapprove of premarital sex (Dittus & Jaccard, 2000; Fingerson, 2005; Usher-Seriki, Bynum, & Callands, 2008). In Hispanic families, in which parental attitudes about sex tend to be relatively more conservative, communication with adolescents about values and beliefs concerning sex is associated with less sexual activity, but the degree to which parents directly caution their teenagers against sex does not seem to make a difference (Romo, Lefkowitz, Sigman, & Au, 2002). In addition, adolescents who speak regularly with their parents about sex are more likely to turn down unwanted sex when they are pressured by others (Sionéan et al., 2002). Studies find that it is important for parents to maintain a close relationship with their teenager after the adolescent has become sexually active and to resist the temptation to pull away in anger over the teenager's behavior (G. Ream & Savin-Williams, 2005).

In summary, parent-adolescent communication about sex is more effective in deterring *risky* sexual activity than in promoting abstinence, and even here, the effect that parents have is small. Thus, despite some parents' beliefs that they can prevent their adolescent's sexual activity by talking about it, and despite other parents' fears that talking about sex will have the unintended effect of encouraging their teenager's sexual behavior, parent-adolescent communication about sex has surprisingly little impact on whether adolescents are sexually active, one way or the other. While it is possible to teach parents how to talk more effectively to their teenagers about sex, it is not clear that doing so leads to dramatic changes in teenagers' knowledge, attitudes, or behavior (Lefkowitz, Sigman, & Au, 2000). Adolescents' opportunity to have sex (for example, whether they are in a steady relationship or date frequently), their having sexually active friends, and their use of alcohol and drugs are far better predictors of early sexual initiation than is parent-adolescent communication (M. Black, Ricardo, & Stanton, 1997; B. Miller et al., 1997; Whitbeck, Yoder, Hoyt, & Conger, 1999).

Sexual Activity and Household Composition   One family factor that does predict adolescent sexual involvement, however—especially among girls—is household composition. Adolescents whose parents are in the process of divorcing as well as those who live in single-parent households—regardless of when (or if) a divorce took place—are more likely to be sexually active earlier than their peers (Ellis et al., 2003; Ryan, 2015). One hypothesis is that parental divorce temporarily disrupts the parent-child relationship, leading the adolescent into early involvement with drugs, alcohol, and minor delinquency, which, according to some studies, increases the likelihood of sex. In other words, it is not family structure per se, but the quality of family relationships in divorced homes, that helps explain why girls from single-parent homes are more sexually active at an earlier age (E. Davis & Friel, 2001). Another possibility is that some of the same personality characteristics that are associated with adults' marital instability, like impulsivity and substance abuse, are transmitted genetically from parents to children, making adolescents with divorced parents more likely to engage in early sex; in other words, it may not only be what divorced parents do, but who they are (Mendle et al., 2009). Adolescents whose mothers had been sexually active at an early age are themselves more likely to begin having sex early (Mott, Fondell, Hu, Kowaleski-Jones, & Menaghan, 1996).

Why should growing up in a single-parent home affect girls' sexual behavior more than boys'? At least four possibilities exist. One, as noted earlier, is that social influences on girls' sexual behavior are stronger and more varied than are the influences on boys' behavior. Parents simply may not attempt to exert much control over sons' sexual activity, regardless of whether the household has one parent or two, and as a result, boys from single- and two-parent homes may be equally likely to be sexually active. Girls' sexual behavior, in contrast, may be more subject to parental controls. Single-parent homes are typically more permissive than two-parent homes (Laursen & Collins, 2009), and this difference in control may be enough to make a difference in girls' sexual activity.

A second possibility is that many single-parent mothers are likely to be dating and, in so doing, may inadvertently be role models of sexual activity to their adolescents (Ivanova, Mills, & Veenstra, 2014). To the extent that this modeling effect is stronger between parents and children of the same sex, we would expect to find a more powerful effect of growing up in a single-parent home on the sexual behavior of daughters than sons.

Yet a third possibility is that girls are more likely than boys to respond to problems at home by going outside the family for alternative sources of warmth and support. If their family environment is not satisfying, girls (whether in divorced homes or not) may be more likely than boys to seek the attention of a romantic partner (Whitbeck, Hoyt, Miller, & Kao, 1992). During or immediately following their parents' divorce, girls may seek the support of individuals with whom they become sexually involved.

Finally, some researchers suggest that the link between growing up in a single-parent household and earlier involvement in sex is genetic in a way that is specific to girls. They have shown that the same gene that makes men more likely to leave their family may, when passed on to daughters, make adolescent girls more likely to go through puberty early and become sexually active at an earlier age (Comings, Muhleman, Johnson, & MacMurray, 2002).

Influences Other Than Parents   Additional studies have examined the influence of forces other than parents on adolescents' sexual behavior. Generally, adolescents are more likely to be sexually active when their peers are (and more likely to engage in risky sex when their peers do) (D. B. Henry et al., 2007); when they *believe* that their friends are sexually active, whether or not their friends actually are (Babalola, 2004; DiIorio et al., 2001; Prinstein, Meade, & Cohen, 2003); and when they have older siblings who model more sexually advanced behavior (East, 2009). Although religious involvement deters adolescents' sexual activity, regular church attendance is associated with delayed sexual activity only among adolescents whose friends attend the same church (Mott et al., 1996). Importantly, adolescents whose parents discuss sex with them in an open and understanding way are less influenced by having sexually active peers (Fasula & Miller, 2006; Whitaker & Miller, 2000).

Peer influences on adolescents' sexual activity appear to operate in two different, but compatible, ways. First, when an adolescent's peers are sexually active, they establish a normative standard that having sex is acceptable (Kogan et al., 2011; White & Warner, 2015). One of the reasons that minor drug use is associated with earlier involvement in sexual activity is that drug use may lead an adolescent to form friendships with a different group of friends, a group that is sexually more permissive (D. French & Dishion, 2003; Whitbeck, Conger, Simons, & Kao, 1993). Adolescents' initiation of sexual activity varies from neighborhood to neighborhood, with earlier sexual activity more likely in relatively more disorganized neighborhoods, where adults have little control over teenagers and where peer groups are relatively more powerful (Carlson, McNulty, Bellair, & Watts, 2014; T. Leventhal, Dupéré, & Brooks-Gunn, 2009); the effect of living in a disadvantaged neighborhood on early sexual initiation is exacerbated by parental hostility (Gardner, Martin, & Brooks-Gunn, 2012). Generally, the more individual **risk factors** there are in an adolescent's life for involvement in early sexual activity (for example, drug and alcohol use, poor parental monitoring, sexually active friends, antisocial peers, disengagement from school, a disadvantaged neighborhood), the more likely the adolescent is to be sexually active (Small & Luster, 1994). The factors that place adolescents at risk for early sexual activity are the same across ethnic groups (D. Perkins, Luster, Villarruel, & Small, 1998). One study of girls in nine European countries found that although the percent of girls who became sexually active by 15 varied across the countries—from 33% in Finland to 10% in Greece—in all locations, adolescents were especially likely to have sex early when their parents had little knowledge of their whereabouts and friends (Madkour, Farhat, Halpern, Gabhainn, & Godeau, 2012).

Peers also influence each other's sexual behavior directly, either through communication among friends ("You haven't done it yet! What's the matter with you?" "You're thinking of doing what?") or, more commonly, between potential sex partners. Several studies show that sexual activity spreads within a community of adolescents much like an epidemic, with sexually experienced adolescents initiating their less experienced partners into increasingly more advanced sex (J. Rodgers & Rowe, 1993). Once they become sexually experienced, previously inexperienced adolescents then "infect" other adolescents. Over time, the percentage of sexually experienced adolescents within a community grows and grows.

Virginity Pledges Studies of "virginity pledges" also shed light on the way in which the social context can influence adolescent sexual activity (Bearman & Brückner, 2001; Rosenbaum, 2009). Over the past 30 years, several million American adolescents have taken a virginity pledge, promising to abstain from sex until they are married. How effective is this? Research finds that virginity pledges work only for younger adolescents—they have no effect on high

Over the past two decades, several million American adolescents have taken a virginity pledge, promising to abstain from sex until they are married. Research has found, however, that high school students who have pledged to remain virgins are just as likely to have sex as those who haven't made such pledges. © Johannes Kroemer/Visum/The Image Works

school students. Among high school students, "pledgers" are just as likely to have sex (including intercourse, oral sex, and anal sex) as "nonpledgers." And longitudinal studies show that

risk factors
Factors that increase the likelihood of some behavior or condition.

after having sex, adolescents who had taken a virginity pledge frequently deny having made one (Hollander, 2006; Rosenbaum, 2006). One study found that 82% of the adolescents who took a virginity pledge denied having done so 5 years later (Rosenbaum, 2009)! Ironically, one way in which those who take a virginity pledge differ from their nonpledging peers is that those who take the pledge are less likely to use contraception, suggesting that encouraging abstinence may actually promote unsafe sex (as you will read later, it does) (Rosenbaum, 2009). The impact of pledging varies as a function of how many other adolescents in the same school have taken the pledge. Pledging has little effect in schools in which few students take virginity pledges (presumably because there is little encouragement of abstinence) or in schools in which nearly everyone pledges (because one of the ways in which pledging works is by allowing those who pledge to make a statement about their values). Making a promise to oneself to delay becoming sexually active is more effective than making a formal, public pledge (Bersamin, Walker, Waiters, Fisher, & Grube, 2005).

Finally, several studies have examined the role of the broader environment in influencing adolescent sexual behavior. Adolescents growing up in poor neighborhoods, for example, are more likely to engage in early sexual activity than adolescents from more affluent communities (Dupéré, Lacourse, Willms, Leventhal, & Tremblay, 2008; T. Leventhal et al., 2009). When adolescents grow up in poverty, they may see little hope for the future, and they therefore may be more likely to risk their occupational and economic future by becoming sexually active (Raiford et al., 2014). To a young person who believes that the chances of getting a good job are slim, an early pregnancy does not seem as costly as it might to someone who hopes to complete high school, attend college, and secure a good job. Adolescents' sexual behavior is more strongly influenced by the values and attitudes of their schoolmates than the characteristics of their neighborhood, however (Teitler & Weiss, 2000).

Sex Differences in the Meaning of Sex

Any discussion of the psychosocial significance of sexual experience during adolescence must be sensitive to the very substantial sex differences in how early sexual activity is experienced. Despite the convergence of males' and females' rates of sexual activity in recent decades, the early sexual experiences of adolescent boys and girls are still very different and, as a consequence, are imbued with very different meanings (Diamond & Savin-Williams, 2009). In other words, the sexual behavior of males and females may be similar, but the **sexual socialization** of males and females is quite different.

sexual socialization
The process through which adolescents are exposed to and educated about sexuality.

The Way Boys Feel   The typical boy's first sexual experience is masturbation in early adolescence (Diamond & Savin-Williams, 2009). At the outset, then, the sexual socialization of males typically places sex outside of an interpersonal context. Before adolescent boys begin dating, they have generally already experienced orgasm and know how to arouse themselves. For males, the development of sexuality during adolescence revolves around efforts to integrate the capacity to form close relationships into an already existing sense of sexual capability.

Perhaps because of this, at the time of first intercourse, boys are likely to keep matters of sex and intimacy separate. Boys often have as their first partner someone they just met or describe as a casual date, and it is generally the male partner of a couple who is likely to initiate sex (Diamond & Savin-Williams, 2009). The early sexual experiences of males are often interpreted not in terms of intimacy and emotional involvement, but in terms of recreation (Hendrick & Hendrick, 1994). Consistent with this, boys are more likely than girls to mention sexual arousal (rather than emotional factors) as a reason for having sex (Eyre & Millstein, 1999). And males typically report that the people to whom they describe their first sexual liaison—most probably, male peers—are overwhelmingly approving. The most

common immediate reactions among adolescent males to having intercourse for the first time are excitement, satisfaction, exhilaration, and happiness (Diamond & Savin-Williams, 2009; Oswald, Bahne, & Feder, 1994). Here's how one 14-year-old boy described his first time, which was outside of a romantic relationship:

> It was really terrific . . . the sex itself felt good, yeah, but when you come, that's really the nicest feeling that I've ever had. . . . The sex itself, I thought that it would have been better, the whole time, but coming, I hadn't expected that it would be that good. (Symons, Vermeersch, & Van Houtte, 2014, pp. 547–548)

Or, consider this unemotional response from a 13-year-old:

> It wasn't the fairly tale story that I had imagined about losing virginity. I can't even say what it was. Yeah, sex, nothing more than that. (Symons, Vermeersch, & Van Houtte, 2014, p. 548)

making the personal connection

If you are sexually experienced, see if you can recall the first time you had sex. What was your immediate reaction?

The Way Girls Feel   The typical girl's first experience and feelings afterward are likely to be very different. Masturbation is far less prevalent among girls than boys, and it is far less regularly practiced (Diamond & Savin-Williams, 2009). As a consequence, the typical adolescent girl, in contrast to the typical boy, is more likely to experience sex for the first time with another person. For girls, unlike boys, the development of sexuality involves the integration of sexual activity into an already existing capacity for intimacy and emotional involvement. As a consequence, the girl's sexual script is one that, from the outset, tinges sex with romance, love, friendship, and intimacy. Girls are more likely than boys to engage in sex in order to enhance an emotional connection (Diamond & Savin-Williams, 2009). Compare these 14-year-old girls' reactions to those of the two boys who were quoted earlier:

> It's a whole new experience and you love that person and you long for him, and yeah, it's a step further in your relationship . . . I think that you trust each other more, you give yourself more to that person and the bond grows. You get closer to each other. (Symons, Vermeersch, & Van Houtte, 2014, p. 547)

> It was fun, and intimate, mainly intimate actually. I mean, he was really sweet. But apart from that, I can't say that I really enjoyed it. I mean, it mainly just hurt. I thought "I just have to go through this." I think that, even if I had waited another year, it would have hurt just as much. (Symons, Vermeersch, & Van Houtte, 2014, pp. 548–549)

Boys and girls also encounter very different social attitudes about sex. Because of the possibility of pregnancy, the potential adverse consequences of sexual activity are far more serious for girls than for boys. For this reason, society monitors the sexual activity of girls more carefully, and girls are more likely to be encouraged to approach sex cautiously (Rosenthal, 1994). Girls have an easier time saying no to unwanted sex than do boys (R. Zimmerman, Sprecher, Langer, & Holloway, 1995).

The adolescent girl's first sexual partner is likely to be someone she says she was in love with at the time (Diamond & Savin-Williams, 2009). After losing her virginity, she is more likely to encounter disapproval or mixed feelings on the part of others in whom she confides (generally, peers) than is the typical boy (Diamond & Savin-Williams, 2009). And although the majority of girls report more positive than negative feelings about their first sexual experience, girls are more likely than boys to report feeling afraid, guilty, and worried as well as happy or excited about the experience (Diamond & Savin-Williams, 2009; Oswald et al., 1994).

Differences between males and females in the meaning of sex are neither inevitable nor consistent across cultures or historical time. Nor is it the case that all adolescent boys follow the male script and all adolescent girls follow the female one. In fact, "girls are more sexually oriented and boys more romantically oriented than previous research might suggest" (Diamond & Savin-Williams, 2009, p. 514). Moreover, as they mature, adolescent boys and girls become more similar in their motives to have sex (males increasingly emphasize the place of sex in an emotional relationship and place less importance on the role of sex in elevating their social status, whereas females become less likely to justify their interest in sex solely in terms of their intimate relationships).

Sexual Orientation

Same-Sex Attraction   It is not uncommon for young adolescents to engage in sex play with members of the same sex, to have sexual fantasies about people of the same sex, or to have questions about the nature of their feelings for same-sex peers (Diamond & Savin-Williams, 2009). According to the national (and confidential) Add Health survey, about 6% of boys and 13% of girls reported having had same-sex attractions, a homosexual or bisexual preference, or engaging in same-sex activity during adolescence. A smaller number of adolescents—between 2% and 5%—identify themselves as gay, lesbian, or bisexual, and this number increases to about 10% among adults (IOM and NRC, 2011b). Between 2% and 3% of adolescents describe themselves as "unsure" of their sexual orientation; when they are a bit older, about two-thirds of these individuals describe themselves as

exclusively heterosexual (Ott, Corliss, Wypij, Rosario, & Austin, 2011; Zhao, Montoro, Igartua, & Thombs, 2010).

Researchers have not found consistent predictors that distinguish individuals who experiment with same-sex relations in adolescence and who later identify themselves as gay, lesbian, or bisexual from those whose experimentation during adolescence is passing and who later identify themselves as exclusively heterosexual. By the same token, the majority of gay, lesbian, and bisexual adults engaged in heterosexual activity during adolescence. As two experts noted, "contrary to the widespread notion that desire, behavior, and identity coalesce neatly in adolescence and young adulthood to signal an unambiguously heterosexual or homosexual orientation, the reality is much more complicated" (Diamond & Savin-Williams, 2009, p. 505).

It is important to distinguish between homosexuality as an exclusive preference and homosexuality as an interest that may exist simultaneously with strong heterosexual interests (Diamond & Savin-Williams, 2009; Russell, Thompson, & Harris, 2011). Many people mistakenly view sexual orientation as an "either-or" attribute, with individuals being either exclusively heterosexual or exclusively homosexual. In fact, however, of the individuals who do not develop an exclusive preference for heterosexual relationships (about 10% of the adult population), only one-third are exclusively homosexual in their orientation. Twice as many describe themselves as bisexual. Between 2% and 3% of adult men and women describe themselves as exclusively homosexual (IOM and NRC, 2011b).

The development of sexual orientation follows different patterns among sexual minority males and females (Saewyc, 2011). Males are more likely to have had same-sex relations before identifying themselves as gay or bisexual, whereas the reverse sequence is more characteristic among females. And whereas more lesbian and bisexual females had heterosexual experiences before their first same-sex sexual activity, the opposite is true for males. In addition, females who have had same-sex contact during adolescence almost always pursue same-sex contact in adulthood (whereas the same is not true for males—only about 60% do) (Diamond & Savin-Williams, 2009).

The Antecedents of Homosexuality   Studies of the antecedents of homosexuality generally have focused on two sets of factors: biological influences, such as hormones, and social influences, such as the parent-child relationship. More is known about the development of homosexuality among men than among women, but the weight of the evidence suggests that an adolescent's sexual orientation is likely to be shaped by a complex interaction of social and biological influences (Saewyc, 2011; Savin-Williams, 2006).

Support for the contention that homosexuality is determined at least partly by biological factors comes from two sources. The hormonal changes of puberty activate sexual behavior, but the particular pattern of sexual behavior that is activated may depend on the way in which hormonal pathways in the brain were organized early in life. There is some evidence that gay and lesbian adults may have been exposed prenatally to certain hormones that, in theory, could affect sexual orientation and gender-atypical behavioral preferences through their effects on early brain organization (Saewyc, 2011). Second, some evidence indicates that homosexuality has a strong genetic component, since sexual orientation is more likely to be similar among close relatives than distant relatives, and between identical twins than fraternal twins (Savin-Williams, 2006). Although environmental explanations for this similarity cannot be ruled out, chances are that at least some of the predisposition to develop a homosexual orientation is inherited (Saewyc, 2011). Same-sex attraction does not spread through adolescent social networks, which would be the case if its determinants were largely environmental (Brakefield et al., 2014).

Several studies suggest as well that a higher proportion of homosexuals than heterosexuals report having had problems in their early family relationships—specifically, in their relationship with their father. The stereotype of the homosexual's father as cold and distant once was rejected as an artifact of popular stereotype and poor research designs. But more carefully designed studies have offered at least partial confirmation of this notion. Both bisexual and homosexual adolescents are more likely than heterosexuals to describe their fathers as distant and rejecting (Bos, Sandfort, de Bruyn, & Hakvoort, 2008; Busseri, Willoughby, Chalmers, & Bogaert, 2008). Whereas gay men are more likely than heterosexuals to report having had close and generally positive relationships with their mothers, lesbians are more likely than heterosexuals to describe their mothers as cold and unpleasant (A. Bell, Weinberg, & Hammersmith, 1981). However, gay and lesbian adolescents are no more likely than heterosexual youth to have had gay or lesbian parents—in fact, studies of adolescents with same-sex parents find few differences between them and their peers with opposite-sex parents (Patterson, 2009).

Although these studies point to certain factors that appear more often than not in the early histories of gay, lesbian, or bisexual individuals, all homosexual individuals do not have identical developmental histories. For example, although, on average, homosexuals are more likely than heterosexuals to describe their parents in negative terms, not all gay and lesbian individuals feel this way. Indeed, only about half do, suggesting that a large number of gay and lesbian individuals had quite positive family relationships growing up. And, of course, many

Sexual orientation is influenced by a complex interplay of biological and contextual factors. © Digital Vision/PunchStock RF

heterosexuals describe their parents in exceedingly negative terms. Similarly, although the majority of boys with persistently feminine behavior preferences may grow up to be gay, a substantial number of feminine boys do not.

making the scientific connection

Should social scientists be interested in the antecedents of homosexuality? Is it important to know whether homosexuality is biologically or contextually determined? Why or why not?

Sexual Harassment, Rape, and Sexual Abuse During Adolescence

Sexual Harassment and Date Rape   Although most research on adolescent sexual activity has focused on voluntary sexual behavior between consenting individuals, there is growing public awareness that a large proportion of teenagers are sexually harassed and that a significant minority are forced to have sex against their will (Chiodo, Wolfe, Crooks, Hughes, & Jaffe, 2009;

V. Lee, Croninger, Linn, & Chen, 1996). This latter group includes adolescents who have been the victims of forcible rape by a stranger, sexual abuse within the family, or **date rape**—when a young person, typically a woman, is forced by a date to have sex when she does not want to. Sexual coercion and sex under the influence of alcohol or drugs are more likely to occur when there is a large age difference (3 years or more) between a girl and her partner (Gowen, Feldman, Diaz, & Yisrael, 2004). Adolescents who are sexually coerced are more likely to report depression, behavior problems, and alcohol and drug use (Bucchianeri, Eisenberg, Wall, Piran, & Neumark-Sztainer, 2014; Young, Furman, & Jones, 2012).

For all the concern that is expressed about the sexual harassment of teenagers over the Internet, adolescents are far more at risk at school than online. Recent studies indicate that sexual harassment—both cross-sex and between members of the same sex—is widespread within American public schools (Leaper & Brown, 2008; V. Lee et al., 1996; McMaster, Connolly, Pepler, & Craig, 2002; Young, Grey, & Boyd, 2009) (see Figure 7). According to one study of a nationally representative sample of middle and secondary school students, more than 80% of girls and 60% of boys reported having received unwanted sexual attention while in school (V. Lee at al., 1996). Sexual harassment is especially distressing to early-maturing girls, whose physical maturity, which makes them the targets of harassment,

already makes them stand apart from their peers (S. M. Lindberg, Grabe, & Hyde, 2007; Skoog & Özdemir, 2015). Girls who are sexually harassed are more likely to focus on their appearance and develop eating disorders as a consequence (Petersen & Hyde, 2013).

Because the majority of those who had been sexually harassed had themselves harassed others, and because many incidents occurred within full view of teachers and other school personnel—indeed, a significant percentage of students report having been sexually harassed by their *teachers*—numerous experts have suggested the need for wholesale changes in the moral and ethical climate of secondary schools (V. Lee et al., 1996; Timmerman, 2002; A. M. Young et al., 2009). This is easier said than done, however; one evaluation of a school-based program called Safe Dates found significant reductions in psychological abuse and sexual violence 1 month after the program was implemented, but these effects had disappeared within 1 year (Foshee et al., 2000). Other research, on the histories of individuals who commit dating violence, indicates that perpetrators themselves were likely to have been exposed to physical punishment and abuse at home (Basile et al., 2006; Capaldi & Clark, 1998; R. Simons, Lin, & Gordon, 1998). Given that sexual harassment is a form of bullying, it is not surprising that studies find considerable overlap between

> **date rape**
> Being forced by a date to have sex against one's will.

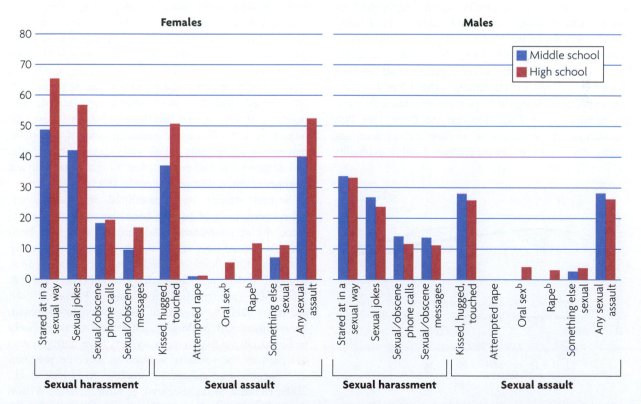

Figure 7   Percentage reporting sexual victimization. Respondents could report multiple forms of victimization. Questions about oral sex and rape were not asked of middle school students. (Young, Grey, & Boyd, 2009)

adolescents who bully others and those who harass others sexually (Espelage, Basile, & Hamburger, 2012; Reyes & Foshbee, 2012).

Harassment of Sexual-Minority Youth A substantial number of sexual-minority youth are harassed, physically abused, or verbally abused by peers or adults while growing up (Berlan, Corliss, Field, Goodman, & Bryn Austin, 2010; Russell, Everett, Rosario, & Birkett, 2014; Saewyc, 2011). Abuse of this sort, as well having more distant family relationships, contribute to the relatively higher rates of truancy, depression, suicide, substance abuse, running away from home, and school difficulties reported by sexual-minority adolescents (Birkett, Russell, & Corliss, 2014; Burton, Marshal, Chisholm, Sucato, & Friedman, 2013; Needham, 2012; Pearson & Wilkinson, 2013; Poteat, Scheer, DiGiovanni, & Mereish, 2014; Seil, Desai, & Smith, 2014; Shilo & Savaya, 2012) as well as mental health problems that persist into adulthood (Dermody et al., 2014; Marshal et al., 2013). Over the course of adolescence, prejudice against both gay and lesbian individuals declines (see Figure 8) (Poteat and Anderson, 2012), and parental acceptance of their adolescents' sexual orientation increases (Samarova, Shilo, & Diamond, 2014).

As with other types of discrimination, hostility toward sexual-minority youth is greater in small schools, rural schools, schools in lower-SES communities, and schools with fewer explicit rules for student behavior, and less racially diverse schools tend to have climates that are more hostile toward sexual-minority youth (Hatzenbuehler, Birkett, Van Wagenen, & Meyer, 2014; Martin-Story, Cheadle, Skalamera, & Crosnoe, 2015; Poteat, Espelage, & Koenig, 2009; Sandfort, Bos, Collier, & Metselaar, 2010). This has prompted many experts to call for more concerted efforts to implement school-based educational programs designed to promote tolerance. In 2012, for example, Lady Gaga founded the Born This Way Foundation, whose mission is "to foster a more accepting society, where differences are embraced and individuality

is celebrated" (Born This Way Foundation, 2012). The attitudes of teachers and other school personnel also are important: Sexual-minority adolescents who feel they have the support of at least one adult at school are less likely to suffer from the adverse consequences of having been verbally abused (e.g., teased, sworn at, shamed, etc.) for their sexual orientation. Studies also find that the establishment of gay–straight alliances within schools have had positive effects on school climate (Poteat, Sinclair, DiGiovanni, Koenig, & Russell, 2013; Walls, Kane, & Wisneski, 2010).

Sexual Abuse Because both perpetrators and victims of sexual assaults are often reluctant to admit their experiences, it is difficult to obtain accurate estimates of the numbers of adolescents who have been sexually victimized. We do know that adolescent victims of sexual abuse are disproportionately female and poor (Cappelleri, Eckenrode, & Powers, 1993). According to several studies, between 7% and 18% of adolescents report having had nonvoluntary sexual intercourse before age 18; reports by females are substantially higher than those by males, but it is not known how much of this is due to different prevalence rates and how much to different willingness on the part of females and males to report having been raped (Diamond & Savin-Williams, 2009). (These figures on sexual abuse do not include adolescents who have been physically forced to engage in sexual activity other than intercourse and, as such, clearly underestimate the proportion of teenagers who have been sexually abused.) Women who were most likely to have been raped during adolescence were those who lived apart from their parents before age 16; who were physically, emotionally, or mentally impaired; who were raised at or below the poverty level; or whose parents abused alcohol or used other drugs. Indeed, two-thirds of all women who had three or more of these risk factors were raped as adolescents. In contrast to popular perception, adolescents are abused (sexually, physically, and emotionally) and neglected at a higher rate than are younger children (Cappelleri et al., 1993).

Several studies have examined the psychological consequences of having been the victim of sexual abuse during adolescence. Adolescents who have been sexually abused have relatively lower self-esteem, more academic difficulties, and higher rates of anxiety, fear, eating disorders, and depression (D. Perkins, Luster, & Jank, 2002; Trickett, McBride-Chang, & Putnam, 1994); are more likely to engage in risky behavior (Tubman, Montgomery, Gil, & Wagner, 2004); and are more likely to be sexually active, have risky sex, have multiple sexual partners, be sexually victimized, become pregnant as teenagers, and engage in prostitution (Black et al., 2009; Homma, Wang, Saewyc, & Kishor, 2012; Wilson & Widom, 2010; Young, Deardorff, Ozer, & Lahiff, 2011). Girls who have been chronically sexually abused

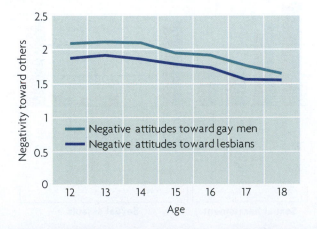

Figure 8 With age, adolescents become less prejudiced against gay and lesbian people. (Poteat & Anderson, 2012).

by their biological father are at greatest risk for problems (Trickett, Noll, Reiffman, & Putnam, 2001). There is also some evidence that sexual abuse prior to adolescence may lead to precocious (that is, very early) puberty (J. Brown, Cohen, Chen, Smailes, & Johnson, 2004).

At the same time, it is worth noting that there are substantial differences among individuals in the extent to which they show problems as a result of having been sexually abused and in the form those problems take (Bauserman & Rind, 1997). Generally, individuals who have been both sexually and physically abused fare worse than those who experience sexual abuse alone. But adolescents who have been sexually abused fare better psychologically when they have parents (presumably not the perpetrators of the abuse) who are authoritative (firm and supportive) and when they are successful in school (Luster & Small, 1997).

Risky Sex and Its Prevention

Contraceptive Use

One reason for the great concern among adults over the sexual activity of adolescents is the failure of many sexually active young people to use contraception regularly. Among sexually active high school students in the United States, 40% report not having used a condom the last time they had sex. Adolescents' condom use increased significantly during the 1990s (from less than half to close to 60%), but dropped between 2003 and 2013 (see Figure 9) (Centers for Disease Control and Prevention, 2014a). Condom use is slightly higher among sexually active 9th-graders (63%) than sexually active 12th-graders (53%), most likely because nearly twice as many 12th-grade girls (28%) than 9th-grade

girls (15%) are on the birth control pill. Of course, using the pill prevents pregnancy but provides no protection against sexually transmitted diseases. Condom use is higher among Black adolescents than White or Hispanic adolescents, whereas proportionately more White adolescents are on the pill (Centers for Disease Control and Prevention, 2014a).

Among adolescents who do use contraception, the most popular method by far is using a condom, the method used by close to 60% of sexually active teenage couples, followed by the birth control pill, which is used by about one-fifth of couples; this is a significant change from previous generations of adolescents, who were far more likely to depend on the pill than on condoms (Everett et al., 2000). (About 10% of girls who are on the pill or some other longer-acting form of birth control report that their partner uses a condom as well [Centers for Disease Control and Prevention, 2014a].) Withdrawal, a highly ineffective method of preventing pregnancy, and a practice that provides no protection against sexually transmitted diseases, unfortunately is still used by a large number of teenagers. Nearly 60% of sexually active teenagers have relied on withdrawal at least once (Horner et al., 2009).

One important recent trend has been a sharp increase in the number of sexually active adolescent girls who use long-acting reversible contraception (LARC), such as intrauterine devices (IUDs) or contraceptive implants (Romero et al., 2015). These methods work because, once installed, they don't require any thinking on the part of teenagers, many of whom find themselves in situations in which they want to have sex but did not plan for it in advance. Many experts believe that the increased use of LARCs has contributed to the largest drop in teen pregnancies seen in many years (Boonstra, 2014). It is

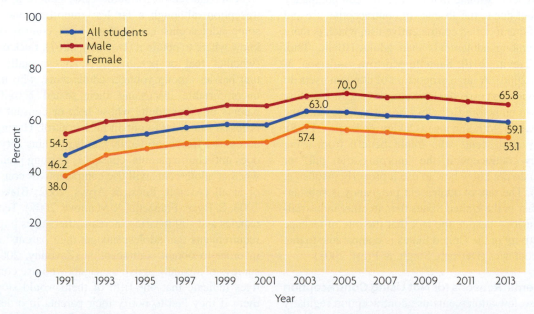

Figure 9 **Adolescent condom use over time.** (Centers for Disease Control and Prevention, 2014).

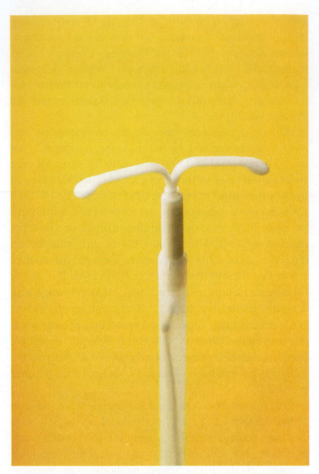

One of the reasons for adults' concern about adolescent sexual activity is the failure of many sexually active teenagers to use contraception regularly. The increasing popularity of long-acting reversible contraceptives is a welcome sign. © BSIP SA/Alamy RF

important to note, however, that LARC does not provide protection against STDs.

Researchers estimate that the risk of teen pregnancy is about half due to the absence of contraceptive use and about half due to failed contraceptive use, which is more frequent among adolescents than adults (Blanc, Tsui, Croft, & Trevitt, 2010; Santelli, Morrow, Anderson, & Lindberg, 2006). A large proportion of condom users do not use condoms correctly, for example (e.g., not putting the condom on before first entry or not holding onto the condom while withdrawing) (Oakley & Bogue, 1995), and many adolescents who might benefit from using emergency contraception (the "morning after pill," or "Plan B") do not know how to use it properly (Mollen et al., 2008). The rate of adolescent pregnancy is substantially higher in the United States than in other industrialized countries—despite the fact that the rate of teenage sexual activity in the United States is comparable to that in other countries (Darroch, Singh, & Frost, 2001).

Adolescents' Reasons for Not Using Contraception

Why do so few adolescents use contraception regularly and effectively? Social scientists point to three broad

factors: lack of planning, lack of access, and lack of knowledge.

By far the most important reason many adolescents fail to use birth control is that their sexual activity is unplanned (D. Kirby, 2007). This absence of planning may reflect adolescents' resistance to admitting that they are choosing to be sexually active, which may explain why adolescents who have taken virginity pledges often do not use contraception when they break their pledge and have sex (Brückner & Bearman, 2005; Rosenbaum, 2009) and why conservatively religious adolescents are less likely to be sexually active but also are less likely to consistently use birth control if they do have sex (Burdette, Haynes, Hill, & Bartkowski, 2014). Adolescents' failure to use contraceptives also may reflect the fact that adolescents are just generally less likely to plan ahead and think about the future consequences of their behavior than adults (Steinberg, Cauffman, Woolard, Graham, & Banich, 2009). In either case, going on the pill or purchasing a condom requires an adolescent to acknowledge that he or she is having or is going to have sexual relations and engage in some advance planning. One reason long-acting reversible contraception is effective is that once the device is in place, no further planning is required.

One of the best predictors of condom use is the individual's intent to use a condom and willingness to communicate about it with his or her partner (Sheeran, Abraham, & Orbell, 1999; Tschann & Adler, 1997; Widman, Welsh, McNulty, & Little, 2006). Interventions designed to strengthen adolescents' intentions and their ability to communicate with their partner about contraception, and not just increase their knowledge, have been shown to be effective in promoting condom use, even within high-risk populations (DiClemente et al., 2004; Jemmott, Jemmott, Fong, & McCaffree, 1999).

A second reason for adolescents' failure to use contraception, although a far less important one, is that some adolescents can't afford birth control or don't know where to obtain it (D. Kirby, 2007). Lack of access (whether real or perceived) is an especially important barrier among younger adolescents, who may feel uncomfortable discussing their sexual activity with parents or other adults whose help or consent may be necessary in order to obtain birth control. Having ready access to a free, confidential family planning service that does not require parents' consent is a strong predictor of whether adolescents will use contraceptives consistently or at all (Averett, Rees, & Argys, 2002; Blake et al., 2003; S. Ryan, Franzetta, & Manlove, 2007). Teen pregnancies and childbearing increase after states implement requirements that adolescents get their parents' consent in order to obtain contraception (Zavodny, 2004), and surveys of sexually active teenagers who use contraceptives indicate that one-fifth of them would stop using them if they had to notify their parents in order to get them (R. K. Jones, Purcell, Singh, & Finer, 2005).

Finally, many young people are insufficiently educated about sex, contraception, and pregnancy, which may leave them misinformed about when and how to use contraception (D. Kirby, 2007; S. Ryan et al., 2007). For example, although it is important for adolescents to understand the need to use contraception every time they have sex, a very large proportion of teenagers who have had sex with contraception have also had sex without contraception (Arnett & Balle-Jensen, 1993; Gillmore, Morrison, Lowery, & Baker, 1994). That said, knowledge alone does not seem to be sufficient to promote contraceptive use; individuals must be motivated to use contraception as well as know why they need to (Sheeran, Abraham, & Orbell, 1999).

Given all these reasons—lack of planning, lack of access, and lack of knowledge—it is not surprising that one of the best predictors of contraceptive use is the adolescent's age: Older teenagers are better at thinking ahead, less guilty about having sex, more likely to be able to discuss contraception with their partner, and better able to grasp the potential negative consequences of an unwanted pregnancy (Sheeran et al., 1999). Relatively younger women are even less likely to use contraception if their partner is older and more likely, as a result, to contract an STD (Bauermeister, Zimmerman, Xue, Gee, & Caldwell, 2009; Pettifor, O'Brien, MacPhail, Miller, & Rees, 2009; S. Ryan, Franzetta, Manlove, & Schelar, 2008).

Improving Contraceptive Behavior   There is a great deal that adults can do to improve the contraceptive behavior of adolescents (R. K. Jones, Biddlecom, Hebert, & Mellor, 2011b). First, adults can see that contraceptives are made accessible to young people who want them. Second, parents and schools can provide sex education at an early enough age to instruct young people in the fundamentals of contraceptive use before, rather than after, they've become sexually active; such education should try to strengthen adolescents' intentions to use contraception and not just increase their contraceptive knowledge. Third, parents can be more open and responsive in the ways in which they communicate with their teenagers about sex, and about safe sex in particular, so that when adolescents become sexually active, they find it easier to plan ahead without feeling guilty. Finally, adolescents can be encouraged to consider the potential future consequences of an unplanned pregnancy or a sexually transmitted disease. One way to do this is to engage adolescents in school, which may improve their aspirations for the future (D. Kirby, 2007; Manlove, Steward-Streng, Peterson, Scott, & Wildsmith, 2013). Adolescents who do not believe that a pregnancy will be an impediment to their future goals are less likely to take steps to avoid getting pregnant (Mireless-Rios & Romo, 2014). However, adolescents with high educational aspirations who have a child as a result of an unwanted pregnancy are often insecure and unaffectionate mothers (East & Barber, 2014).

AIDS and Other Sexually Transmitted Diseases

Helping youngsters understand sex, pregnancy, and contraception is an important goal of sex education programs for adolescents. Helping them avoid the risks of **sexually transmitted diseases (STDs)** (also referred to as sexually transmitted infections, or STIs) is another. STDs are caused by viruses, bacteria, or parasites that are transmitted through sexual contact. About 3 million adolescents are diagnosed with a sexually transmitted infection each year (Ozer & Irwin, 2009). Some of the most common STDs among adolescents are **gonorrhea** and **chlamydia** (both caused by a bacterium), **herpes** and **human papillomavirus (HPV)** (both caused by a virus), and **trichomoniasis** (caused by a parasite) (Forhan et al., 2009). One-fourth of all American young women between the ages of 14 and 19, and nearly 40% of sexually active women of this age, had at least one of these five infections, with HPV by far the most prevalent (Forhan et al., 2009). These infections pose a significant health risk, because they are associated with increased rates of cancer and infertility. Countries vary considerably in rates of STD infection, with the United States having one of the highest rates in the world (Panchaud, Singh, Feivelson, & Darroch, 2000).

HIV/AIDS   Since the 1980s, a new and far more serious STD has commanded the world's attention: **AIDS,** or **acquired immune deficiency syndrome.** The virus that causes AIDS, **human immunodeficiency virus (HIV),** is transmitted through bodily fluids, especially semen, during sex, or blood when drug users share needles. AIDS itself has no symptoms, but HIV attacks the body's immune system, interfering with the body's ability to defend itself against life-threatening diseases like pneumonia or cancer. Because there is a long period of time between HIV infection and the actual manifestation of illness—sometimes as long as 10 years—infected adolescents are likely to be asymptomatic carriers of the HIV virus who may develop AIDS in young adulthood. In recent decades,

---

sexually transmitted disease (STD)
Any of a group of infections—including HPV, gonorrhea, trichomoniasis, herpes, chlamydia, and AIDS—passed on through sexual contact.

gonorrhea
A sexually transmitted infection caused by a bacterium.

chlamydia
A sexually transmitted infection caused by a bacterium.

herpes
A sexually transmitted infection caused by a virus.

human papillomavirus (HPV)
One of several viruses that causes a sexually transmitted disease.

trichomoniasis
A sexually transmitted infection caused by a parasite.

AIDS (acquired immune deficiency syndrome)
A disease, caused by a virus transmitted by means of bodily fluids, that devastates the immune system.

HIV (human immunodeficiency virus)
The virus associated with AIDS.

cases of AIDS increased by 7% among adolescents, but by 47% among 20- to 24-year-olds (Ozer & Irwin, 2009).

Although the incidence of AIDS in the United States was initially concentrated within two groups, gay men and drug users who use needles, surveys indicate that the transmission of AIDS through heterosexual activity is a clear danger to male and female adolescents and is especially prevalent among inner-city ethnic minority youngsters (Prado, Lightfoot, & Brown, 2013). Nor is HIV infection limited to poor, inner-city adolescents (Gayle et al., 1990). Because adolescents' condom use is sporadic, straight, bisexual, and gay youth are *all* at high risk for HIV (Rotheram-Borus, Marelich, & Srinivasan, 1999). HIV infection is particularly high in Sub-Saharan Africa, where it has reached epidemic proportions (Hindin & Fatusi, 2009). The chances of contracting HIV are greatest among individuals who use drugs, have unprotected sex, have many sexual partners, and already have another STD (such as gonorrhea) (Elkington, Bauermeister, & Zimmerman, 2010). Because these risk factors are more common among young people than adults, the risk of HIV infection among adolescents is substantial.

Protecting Against STDs Adults often forget that adolescents' sexual behavior is as much, if not more, influenced by their perceptions of benefits (for example, the fun of having different partners or the physical sensation of unprotected intercourse) as it is by their perceptions of costs (for example, the risks of contracting an STD) (R. Levinson, Jaccard, & Beamer, 1995). Adolescents have sex because they want intimacy with their partner, status with their peers, and, of course, physical pleasure (Ott, Millstein, Offner, & Halpern-Felsher, 2006). Even adolescents who know they are vulnerable to infection are less likely to protect themselves when they feel negatively about using condoms, when they are positively inclined toward risk taking, and when their friends are actively engaged in risky sex (Serovich & Greene, 1997; St. Lawrence, Brasfield, Jefferson, Allyene, & Shirley, 1994). One large-scale evaluation of a media campaign targeted at Black youth (who are four times more likely than other youth to have an STD) and designed to promote the messages that using condoms would make sex more worry-free and therefore more enjoyable, that waiting to have sex was a way of showing respect for one's partner, and that a "steady partner is a safe partner" was shown to be effective in changing adolescents' attitudes and condom use (Romer et al., 2009).

Short of abstinence, the best way for teenagers to protect themselves against contracting HIV and many other STDs is by using condoms during sex; adolescents who consistently use condoms are half as likely as those who do not to contract an STD (Crosby, DiClemente, Wingood, Lang, & Harrington, 2003). Educating young

people about the risk factors associated with AIDS is also important, because studies show that adolescents who believe that they are at risk for HIV infection and who are motivated to avoid the risk are more likely to take precautions during intercourse (Hausser & Michaud, 1994; Jemmott et al., 1999). Increasing adolescents' perceptions of vulnerability to HIV infection is not sufficient to motivate them to use condoms, however (Gerrard, Gibbons, & Bushman, 1996).

Teen Pregnancy

Given the high rate of sexual activity and poor record of contraceptive use among contemporary adolescents, it comes as little surprise to learn that many young women become pregnant before the end of adolescence. Each year, more than 600,000 American adolescents between 15 and 19 become pregnant—giving the United States the highest rate of teen pregnancy in the industrialized world (see Table 1) (Sedgh, Finer, Bankole, Eilers, & Sinh, 2015). The rate of unintended pregnancy is far greater among adolescents than adults once age differences in sexual activity are taken into account (Finer, 2010). Close to 90% of teen pregnancies are unintended (Committee on Adolescence, 2014). This is important, because having an unintended pregnancy increases the odds that an adolescent mother will experience difficulties in parenting (East, Chien, & Barber, 2012).

making the cultural connection

Although rates of sexual activity are no higher in the United States than in many other industrialized countries, rates of STDs, teen pregnancy, and teen childbearing are. What factors do you think contribute to this?

Prevalence of Teen Pregnancy Recent statistics indicate that about one-sixth of American young women become pregnant at least once by age 20. This rate is dramatically lower than it had been a few decades ago (it peaked in the early 1990s, when it was twice as high as it is today). Teen pregnancy has become less common mainly because of increased contraceptive use (and, especially, long-acting reversible contraception) but also because somewhat fewer younger teenagers are sexually active. Rates of teen pregnancy vary considerably by ethnicity: The rate is nearly three times higher among Black youth, and more than twice as high among Hispanic youth, than among White youth; the rate among Asian-American adolescents is lowest of all (National Campaign to Prevent Teen and Unplanned Pregnancy, 2015).

Table 1 Rates of adolescent pregnancies, abortions, and births in Europe and the United States. (Sedgh et al., 2015)

Country	Year	Rate per 1,000 females 15–19 years old			Pregnancies that end in abortion (%)
		Pregnancies	**Abortions**	**Births**	
Belgium	2009	21	8	10	38
Denmark	2011	21	14	5	67
England and Wales	2011	47	20	21	42
Estonia	2011	43	19	19	43
Finland	2011	23	13	8	55
France	2011	25	15	7	61
Hungary	2011	38	16	18	41
Iceland	2011	30	15	11	51
Israel	2011	23	8	13	32
Netherlands	2008	14	7	5	50
New Zealand	2011	51	18	26	36
Norway	2011	23	13	7	56
Portugal	2011	25	8	13	33
Scotland	2011	46	17	23	37
Singapore	2011	14	8	5	54
Slovakia	2011	33	6	22	17
Slovenia	2009	14	7	5	48
Spain	2011	26	13	10	50
Sweden	2010	29	20	6	69
Switzerland	2011	8	5	2	59
United States	2010	57	15	34	26

As rates of teen pregnancy have fallen, so have rates of teen births (Office of Adolescent Health, 2015) (see Figure 10). Keep in mind that not all adolescent pregnancies result in childbirth. The proportion of teen pregnancies that are aborted differs from country to country, from a low of about 20% in Ireland to a high of close to 70% in Sweden (Singh & Darroch, 2000). In the United States, about 25% of all teenage pregnancies are aborted, and slightly more than 15% end in miscarriage (Kost & Henshaw, 2014; Office of Adolescent Health, 2015). Thus, more than half of teenage pregnancies in

the United States result in the birth of an infant who will be raised by his or her mother (with or without the help of a partner or other family members). Among American adolescents who carry their pregnancy full term, very few put the baby up for adoption.

Abortion Researchers have asked whether teenagers who choose to abort an unwanted pregnancy are harmed psychologically by the experience. The consensus among experts is that they are not (Adler, Ozer, & Tschann, 2003). Several studies indicate that

Figure 10 **Trends in teen births.**
(Office of Adolescent Health, 2015)

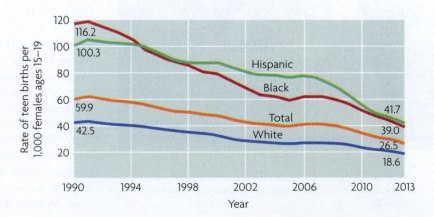

pregnant teenage women who abort their pregnancy are significantly better off, psychologically, socially, and economically, than women who give birth to their child, both in the United States (Zabin, Hirsch, & Emerson, 1989) and abroad (Bailey et al., 2001). Among the most important differences between pregnant adolescents who abort their pregnancy and those who do not is that young women who terminate their pregnancy by abortion are less likely over the next 2 years to experience a subsequent pregnancy and more likely to practice contraception.

Given the psychological and economic benefits of terminating an unwanted adolescent pregnancy, it is easy to understand why many social scientists have questioned the wisdom of court decisions designed to restrict adolescents' access to abortion services (Blum, Resnick, & Stark, 1990). While some studies show that laws requiring parental notification or limiting access to legal abortion do, in fact, result in fewer terminated pregnancies among adolescents (Joyce & Mocan, 1990; J. Rogers, Boruch, Stoms, & DeMoya, 1991), not all studies reach the same conclusion (e.g., Henshaw, 1995). An analysis of the parental notification law in Texas found that it was associated with an overall decrease in abortion, but an increase in late-term abortion (Joyce, Kaestner, & Colman, 2006). Policies limiting access to abortion lead to higher rates of unintended childbearing, especially among Black, Hispanic, and poor youth (Coles, Makino, Stanwood, Dozier, & Klein, 2010).

Causes of Teen Pregnancy Many myths permeate discussions of the causes of adolescent pregnancy and complicate what is actually a fairly simple matter. The most important differences between young women who do and do not become pregnant during adolescence are in their sexual activity and contraceptive use. As you have read, sexual activity among American young people is high, while contraceptive use is sporadic and inadequate. Although some evidence indicates that Black and Hispanic teenagers are more likely than White teenagers to say they intend to have a baby at an early age, the large racial difference in teenage childbearing is due mainly to racial differences in *unintended* pregnancies (Mosher & Bachrach, 1996; Trent & Crowder, 1997).

Deep down inside, do adolescents who become pregnant actually want to have a baby? This has been an extremely difficult question to answer. According to national surveys, 85% of births to women ages 15–19 are unintended, so we know that the vast majority of adolescent mothers did not become pregnant intentionally. Yet, studies that plumb the issue a bit deeper find that many young women who say they do not want to become pregnant are actually ambivalent, and not unequivocally negative, about the prospect of having a child (Jaccard, Dodge, & Dittus, 2003a). For example, consider the following response from a 17-year-old Australian girl, when asked about her pregnancy: "I knew it was going to happen, like I didn't stop it from happening so if it was going to happen it was going to happen and if it didn't, it didn't" (J. L. Smith, Skinner, & Fenwick, 2011, p. 628). She doesn't explicitly say that she wanted to get pregnant, but she doesn't say that she didn't want to, either.

Adolescents who are ambivalent about childbearing or who believe that having a child will be a positive experience are less likely to use contraception effectively (Unger, Molina, & Teran, 2002; Zabin, Astone, & Emerson, 1993). Thus, while the vast majority of sexually active teenagers do not actively wish to become pregnant, a significant minority feel less troubled by the prospect of early parenthood than do their peers, and these youngsters are more likely to risk pregnancy by having unprotected sex. As one team of authors wrote, "Adolescent childbearing is more an unintended result of risky behaviors than a result of rational choice" (Trent & Crowder, 1997, p. 532). The younger sisters of adolescent mothers may be more likely to become adolescent parents themselves, in part because the older sisters may communicate some acceptance of early motherhood (East, 2009).

The Role of the Father A number of studies have focused on the male partners of pregnant adolescents. In general, research indicates that these males share a number of distinguishing characteristics that differentiate them from their peers who have not gotten a teenager pregnant. Most important is the fact that they are relatively more likely to have problems with self-esteem, school, work, aggression, drugs and alcohol, and the law, and to have fathered a child previously (Fagot, Pears, Capaldi, Crosby, & Leve, 1998; Miller-Johnson, Winn, Coie, Malone, & Lochman, 2004; Thornberry, Smith, &

Each year, more than 600,000 American adolescents become pregnant—giving the United States the highest rate of teen pregnancy in the industrialized world. © harpazo_hope/Getty Images RF

Howard, 1997). They are also more likely to have been the child of an adolescent father (Sipsma, Biello, Cole-Lewis, & Kershaw, 2010).

Much has been made in the popular media about the age gap between teenage mothers and the men who have fathered their children, but the proportion of teenage births fathered by adult men (that is, age 20 or older) has declined over the past 40 years, and the age difference between teenage mothers (most of whom are 18 or 19) and their sexual partners is generally about 2 or 3 years—a gap not substantially different from the age gap between adolescent boyfriends and girlfriends in general, or between husbands and wives in the general population (Elo, King, & Furstenberg, 1999). Moreover, girls who choose to get involved with older partners have more psychological problems than girls who do not, well before the relationship begins (Young & D'Arcy, 2005). Nevertheless, adolescent girls who have sex for the first time before 16 with a man who is more than 3 years older are less likely to use contraception and more likely to bear a child (Manlove, Terry-Humen, & Ikramullah, 2006). Regardless of the age difference between mother and father, however, the higher rates of problem behavior among the male partners of pregnant adolescents help to explain why marriage may not be the best response to pregnancy for teenage women, as we'll see shortly.

Although many of their problems precede the pregnancy, young men's educational development and mental health are adversely affected by fathering a child early in life, even if they do not marry the child's mother (Furstenberg, Brooks-Gunn, & Chase-Lansdale, 1989; Nock, 1998; Sigler-Rushton, 2005; Vera Institute of Justice, 1990). Men who impregnate adolescent women are more likely to drop out of school and to report feeling anxious and depressed as young adults than their peers. The adverse effects of teenage fatherhood appear to be greater among White and Hispanic men than among Black men, however, perhaps because teenage fatherhood is more disruptive and is seen as less acceptable within the White and Hispanic communities (M. Buchanan & Robbins, 1990). In general, however, teenage fathers receive little in the way of supportive services or assistance in becoming responsible parents (Kiselica & Sturmer, 1993).

Adolescent Parenthood

It is important to distinguish between pregnancies and actual births—a distinction that often is lost in debates over the consequences of teenage pregnancy. Because of the many pregnant adolescents choosing abortion, the birthrate among teenage women is far lower than it would otherwise be, and it may surprise you to learn that the birthrate among adolescent women today is considerably lower than it was in previous eras. Contrary to the popular idea that teenage childbearing has reached epidemic proportions in this country, relatively more women gave birth to an infant before reaching adulthood in previous decades than do so today—and by a large margin.

Nevertheless, the rate of teenage births in the United States continues to be more than twice as high as in Canada; 3 times greater than in Ireland; 5 times greater than in France; 10 times greater than in Japan; and 17 times greater than in Korea (UNICEF, 2001). All sorts of explanations for the astoundingly high rate of teenage childbearing in the United States have been offered (often, the finger is pointed at the mass media, which are blamed for pretty much everything adolescents do that adults disapprove of). More likely candidates are income inequality and school attendance: The greater the gap between rich and poor, and the lower the rate of school attendance among young people, the higher the rate of teen childbearing. The United States leads the list of industrialized countries in income inequality and comes in 25th (out of 28) in school enrollment (UNICEF, 2001).

Rates of teenage childbearing vary markedly across ethnic and socioeconomic groups. Middle-class women are far more likely to abort their pregnancies than are poor women, and as a consequence, the problem of teenage childbearing is densely concentrated among economically disadvantaged youth (Russell, 1994). Because minority adolescents are more likely to grow up poor, teenage childbearing is especially prevalent in non-White communities.

Part of the controversy surrounding teenage childbearing is linked to the public's concern about the large number of teenage mothers who spend extended periods of time on welfare. Among White adolescents, nearly two-thirds of all births occur outside of marriage, but a large proportion of these births occur within the context of cohabitation; among Black adolescents, virtually all childbirths are out of wedlock, and relatively few of these occur even among cohabiting couples (Manning & Landale, 1996). The rate for Hispanic teenagers falls somewhere in between; interestingly, young Mexican American women are more likely to bear their first child within marriage, whereas young Puerto Rican women are more likely to bear children out of wedlock but within the context of cohabitation. This suggests that cultural attitudes toward marriage and cohabitation influence the context of childbearing in important ways (East & Blaustein, 1995; Manning & Landale, 1996; Milan et al., 2006).

Because minority youth are more likely to experience problems such as school failure or unemployment, early childbearing is likely to take place in the context of limited social and economic resources. Indeed, the main reason for the high rate of out-of-wedlock childbearing among Black teenagers is the higher proportion of adolescents growing up in single-parent homes (Bumpass & McLanahan, 1987), which experience more economic stress. In addition, many poor, young, Black women believe that it is perfectly normal to become a mother while still a teenager and to become a grand-mother before turning 40 (Perez-Febles, Allison, & Burton, 1999), norms that may be handed down from one generation to the next (Hardy, Astone, Brooks-Gunn, Shapiro, & Miller, 1998).

Because teenage childbearing tends to go hand in hand with a variety of other problems—the most criti-cal of which is poverty—it is extremely difficult to know whether any problems of teenage mothers or their children result from the mother's young age or from other, corre-lated factors. Separating the effects of early childbearing from poverty is a matter of more than theoretical impor-tance: If early childbearing is, in fact, a problem in and of itself, it becomes important to direct preventive programs at deterring adolescent pregnancy (either by discouraging sexual activity or by encouraging effective contraceptive use) and childbearing (by encouraging adoption and abor-tion). But if poverty, not the mother's age, is the key, an entirely different set of strategies is called for, aimed not at youngsters' sexual behavior but at all individuals' eco-nomic circumstances. It is extremely important, therefore, to ask whether and in what ways a mother's age at the time she gives birth affects her and her child's well-being.

Children of Teen Mothers Many of the problems that afflict children born to adolescent mothers result primarily from poverty and single parenthood, and from other qualities that often characterize young women who become teen parents (such as poor school achievement), rather than from the mother's youth (e.g., J. A. Levine,

Because adolescent mothers are more likely than adult mothers to be both unmarried and poor, their children are at greater risk of developing a variety of psychological and social problems.
© moodboard/Alamy

Emery, & Pollack, 2007; Pittard, Laditka, & Laditka, 2008). Babies born to middle-class adolescents differ little from their counterparts born to older middle-class mothers, and infants born to poor adolescents are similar to children born to equally poor adults.

One important exception to this general similarity between the children of adolescent and adult mothers is that adolescent mothers—even of similar socioeconomic status—may perceive their babies as being especially difficult and may interact with their infants less often in ways that are known to be beneficial to the child's cogni-tive and social development (Coley & Chase-Lansdale, 1998). Children born to adolescent mothers are more likely to have school problems, to be involved in mis-behavior and delinquent activity, to be sexually active at an early age, and to become an adolescent parent (Campa & Eckenrode, 2006; Coley & Chase-Lansdale, 1998; Hofferth & Reid, 2002; Tang, Davis-Kean, Chen, & Sexton, 2015). In general, and for reasons that are not known, the cognitive and psychosocial problems of children born to adolescent mothers grow increasingly more apparent with age (that is, the differences between children born to teen versus adult mothers are more evi-dent in adolescence than infancy). Again, though, stud-ies show that the adverse outcomes of being born to an adolescent mother—even outcomes not visible until the children have reached young adulthood—are attribut-able both to characteristics of young women who are likely to become teen parents (for example, the adverse effects of being raised by someone who is poorly edu-cated) and to the circumstances that characterize the family environments of young mothers (for example, the adverse effects of growing up in poverty) (Jaffee, Caspi, Moffitt, Belsky, & Silva, 2001; Pogarsky, Lizotte, & Thornberry, 2003). Adolescent mothers who were rela-tively more intelligent and better adjusted *before* the birth of their infant have greater parenting skills later (Mylod, Whitman, & Borkowski, 1997; O'Callaghan, Borkowski, Whitman, Maxwell, & Keogh, 1999), and children whose adolescent mothers are better edu-cated, married, and better off financially do better in school than those whose mothers are less accomplished and single (Luster, Bates, Fitzgerald, Vandenbelt, & Key, 2000).

Because adolescent mothers are more likely than adult mothers to be both unmarried and poor, their children are at greater risk of developing a variety of psychologi-cal and social problems. Many of the problem behaviors seen among children of adolescent mothers are prevalent among poor children growing up in single-parent homes generally. In other words, the greater incidence of prob-lems among offspring of adolescent mothers may reflect the overall environment in which the children grow up, rather than the ways in which they are raised. Although in theory we can separate the effects of poverty on chil-dren from the effects of adolescent childbearing, in reality, the two usually go together, and the end result is that children born to adolescent mothers are more likely than other children to suffer the effects both of malnutrition—in the womb as well as in the world—and of environmental deprivation.

Consequences for Teen Mothers Studies of the long-term consequences of adolescent parenthood indicate that the problems associated with it may actually be greater for the mothers than for their children. In general, women who bear children early suffer disruptions in their educational and occupational careers (Gibb, Fergusson, Horwood, & Boden, 2014; Hofferth, Reid, & Mott, 2001), the consequences of which often continue into midlife (Lounds Taylor, 2009). Not only are adolescent mothers more likely to come from a poor background and to have a history of academic difficulties, but they are also more likely to remain poor than their equally disadvantaged peers who delay childbearing until after their schooling is completed (Mollborn, 2007; K. Moore et al., 1993; R. Richardson, 1996). Remember, however, that many adolescent mothers were low-achieving students *before* becoming pregnant, and the limited educational attainment of teenage mothers is at least partly due to factors that were in play long before the pregnancy, perhaps even during early childhood (Fergusson & Woodward, 2000; Frisco, 2008; Russell, 2002; Shearer et al., 2002). In short, poverty and low achievement are both causes *and* consequences of early childbearing.

Having a child early in life does not inevitably cast in concrete a life of poverty and misery for the mother and her youngster, however. There is considerable diversity among teenage mothers in the routes that their adult lives take (Coley & Chase-Lansdale, 1998; Oxford, Gilchrist, Gillmore, & Lohr, 2006). One study identified three distinct groups: a problem-prone group (15% of the sample), who had chronic problems in many areas of life, including antisocial behavior; a psychologically vulnerable group (42%), who had relatively high rates of mental health problems but who were able to transition into adult roles with some degree of success; and a normative group (43%), who defied common stereotypes of adolescent mothers as doomed to failure and poverty and who were able to make a successful transition to adulthood (Oxford et al., 2005). The long-term consequences of early childbearing may not be as negative among Black adolescents as among Whites or Hispanics, especially among Black youth living in communities in which early childbearing is accepted as normative (K. Moore et al., 1993; E. Smith & Zabin, 1993).

In general, young mothers who remain in, or return to, high school and delay subsequent childbearing fare a great deal better over the long run—as do their children—than those who drop out of school or have more children relatively early (Leadbeater, 1996;

Upchurch & McCarthy, 1990). Remaining in school and living at home with one's parents significantly diminishes the chances of a second unwanted pregnancy (Manlove, Mariner, & Papillo, 2000). Marriage, in contrast, is a high-risk strategy (Furstenberg, Morgan, & Allison, 1987b). In some cases, when a stable relationship is formed and economic resources are available, marriage improves the mother's and the child's chances for life success; this seems to be especially true for women who marry somewhat later. In other cases, however, a hasty decision to marry in the absence of a stable relationship and economic security actually exacerbates many other problems (Teti & Lamb, 1989).

After the Baby Is Born Many of the negative effects of having children as a teenager can be prevented or at least minimized by lessening the disruptive economic impact of teenage parenthood on young women's lives (Sandfort & Hill, 1996). What do we know about the factors that work? First, marrying the father of the child may place the adolescent mother at greater risk if the father is not capable of supporting himself economically, much less his family. If the father is able to find a good job and remain employed, he can be an important source of psychological and economic support and a healthy influence on the mother and child. Given the characteristic problems of male partners of adolescent mothers that we discussed earlier, however, it is all too likely that marriage may diminish, rather than enhance, an adolescent mother's economic circumstances. In addition, marriage places the adolescent mother at greater risk of having another child relatively soon, which further jeopardizes her already precarious economic situation; having another child soon is one of the factors most likely to worsen her other problems (Apfel & Seitz, 1997; Kalmuss & Namerow, 1994). Moreover, teenage marriage is very likely to end in divorce, which itself is an additional stressor on the mother and child.

Adolescent mothers therefore cannot always look to the father of the child to help break the cycle of poverty. However, in many cases they can look to their own parents for support, and this may be an effective strategy (J. Stevens, 1988). Teenage mothers who move in with their own family for a short time—a practice far more common among Black than among Hispanic or White adolescents—are more likely to enjoy educational and occupational success than their counterparts who live on their own, because the family's help allows the young mother to return to school or find employment (Roye & Balk, 1996; Trent & Harlan, 1994). Without this help, many young mothers drop out of school and have to find and pay for child care, which often is more costly than the income their low-paying jobs generate. Without a high school diploma, these women have little chance of improving their economic situation or their child's opportunities.

Although having the support of her own family is important for the adolescent mother's well-being, living with her family of origin for an extended period after having a baby is not uniformly beneficial, as several studies of three-generational Black families show. When the adolescent mother lives with her own mother, the living arrangement may undermine the development of her own parenting skills and increase her risk of getting pregnant again (Chase-Lansdale, Brooks-Gunn, & Zamsky, 1994; Gillmore, Lewis, Lohr, Spencer, & White, 1997), and problems in the relationship between the adolescent and her mother can adversely affect the teen parent's mental health (A. Davis & Rhodes, 1994; East & Felice, 1996; Musick, 1994). However, living with one's mother is associated with continued schooling, which confers long-term economic advantages (Spieker & Bensley, 1994). Several studies have found that support from the adolescent's father, in addition to that of her mother, may be especially beneficial (A. Davis, Rhodes, & Hamilton-Leaks, 1997; Oyserman, Radin, & Benn, 1993).

One fact is certain: Adolescent mothers who receive social support fare better, are better parents, and have healthier children than do adolescent mothers who lack support (Riggs, Holmbeck, Paikoff, & Bryant, 2004; Turner, Sorenson, & Turner, 2000). The best arrangement for a teenage mother may be to live independently from her own parents but rely on them for emotional support and child care (Coley & Chase-Lansdale, 1998).

Because it is so important for young mothers to have an adequate income and a chance for adequate employment, many policy makers have called for changes in the ways that schools and other social institutions treat pregnant students and changes in the provision of day care. Among the most important are adaptations in school schedules and the development of school-based child care centers so that pregnant students can remain in school after the birth of their child; the expansion of subsidized child care for young mothers who are out of school so that the economic benefits of having a job are not outweighed by the costs of child care; and the expansion of family planning services to adolescent mothers so that they can prevent yet another pregnancy. Unfortunately, evaluations of programs aimed at enhancing teen mothers' employability, decreasing their reliance on welfare, or preventing their subsequent pregnancies have been largely disappointing (Coley & Chase-Lansdale, 1998), although occasional successes have been reported (e.g., Solomon & Liefeld, 1998).

Although there are stories of young women whose lives are not devastated by early childbearing, the successes are young women who have avoided poverty, rather than achieving great economic success. Although the picture of adolescent parenthood is less uniformly dire than typically painted in the media, there is still consensus among experts that it is important to try to prevent teenage pregnancy and childbearing.

comprehensive sex education
Programs that not only provide information about contraception, STDs, and pregnancy but also teach adolescents how to refuse unwanted sex and avoid unintended sex, increase their motivation to engage in safe sex, and change perceptions about peer norms and attitudes.

Sex Education

Each year, millions of dollars are spent attempting to prevent teen pregnancy and the spread of sexually transmitted diseases. Many adolescents receive some sort of classroom instruction about sex—whether through high school health classes, biology classes, classes designated exclusively for the purpose of sex education, or educational programs administered through youth or religious organizations. Do these programs do any good?

The answer to this question is complicated and depends on the nature of the program and the outcome it is trying to achieve. A recent comprehensive review of more than 50 curriculum-based programs concluded that carefully constructed educational interventions can delay the initiation of sex and reduce rates of risky sexual activity among adolescents (D. Kirby & Laris, 2009), although the long-term effectiveness of these programs has not been adequately studied (Kågesten, Parekh, Tuncalp, Turke, & Blum, 2014). Generally speaking, programs are more effective in reducing risky sex than in reducing sexual activity more generally. But experts agree that successful interventions must do more than provide information about contraception, STDs, and pregnancy. They must also teach adolescents how to refuse unwanted sex and avoid unintended sex, increase adolescents' motivation to engage in safe sex, and change perceptions about peer norms and attitudes (Anderman et al., 2011). These approaches, collectively, are referred to as **comprehensive sex education.** Although many adults are concerned that teaching adolescents how to engage in safe sex sends a message encouraging more teenagers to become sexually active, evaluations of effective comprehensive sex education programs (even those that distribute condoms to teenagers) show that this is not the case (D. Kirby & Laris, 2009; Minguez, Santelli, Gibson, Orr, & Samant, 2015). Expanding access to family planning services and contraceptives is more effective than sex education in deterring teen childbearing (Beltz, Sacks, Moore, & Terzian, 2015). This is consistent with evaluations of other health education interventions, which find that they are good at changing what teenagers know but not at changing how they behave (Steinberg, 2015).

We also know a fair amount about what *doesn't* work. Programs designed to increase safe sex (which includes both abstinence as well as condom use) are far more effective than those that emphasize abstinence alone.

Careful evaluations of **abstinence-only sex education** programs have shown unequivocally that they are not successful, either in changing adolescents' sexual behavior or in reducing rates of pregnancy or STDs (D. Kirby, 2007; P. K. Kohler, Manhart, & Lafferty, 2008; Lindberg & Maddow-Zimet, 2012). In fact, abstinence-only education programs cause an *increase* in teen pregnancy and childbearing (Stanger-Hall & Hall, 2011; Yang & Gaydos, 2010). Programs that attempt to reduce sexual risk taking by reducing other forms of risky behavior (such as delinquency or substance use) also are not effective, consistent with the notion that sexual risk taking, while correlated with other types of risk taking, may have some unique causes (Santelli, Carter, Orr, & Dittus, 2009). The evidence on other types of programs designed to reduce unsafe sex, such as those designed to encourage safe sex indirectly, by facilitating positive youth development, is inconclusive (D. Kirby, 2007).

abstinence-only sex education
Programs that encourage adolescents to avoid sexual activity but that do not provide information about safe sex.

12 Achievement

Achievement as an Adolescent Issue

The Importance of Noncognitive Factors
Achievement Motivation
Beliefs about Success and Failure

Environmental Influences On Achievement
The Influence of the Home Environment
The Influence of Friends

Educational Achievement
The Importance of Socioeconomic Status
Ethnic Differences in Educational Achievement
Changes in Educational Achievement Over Time
Dropping Out of High School

Occupational Achievement
The Development of Occupational Plans
Influences on Occupational Choices

© focal point/Shutterstock.com RF

Because adolescence is typically a time of preparation for the roles of adulthood, considerable attention has been paid to the development and expression of achievement during these years. Broadly defined, achievement concerns the development of motives, capabilities, interests, and behavior that have to do with performance in evaluative situations. More specifically, the study of achievement during adolescence has focused on young people's performance in educational settings and on their hopes and plans for future scholastic and occupational careers. Since most young people form their first realistic educational and vocational plans during adolescence, researchers have long been interested in the factors that play the greatest role in influencing individuals' futures.

Achievement is a particularly important consideration in the study of adolescence in contemporary society. Industrialized societies place an extraordinary emphasis on achievement, competition, and success. During childhood and adolescence, youngsters are continually tested to determine how they stand in relation to their peers. In most industrialized societies, the amount of education a person has completed and the job he or she holds—two of the most important indicators of achievement—provide a basis for the individual's self-conceptions and image in the eyes of others.

A second reason for the importance of achievement in the study of adolescence concerns the range and rapidly changing nature of the choices faced by today's young people. Adolescents in modern societies are confronted with an array of difficult occupational and educational decisions before they turn 25. Beyond such fundamental questions as what type of career to follow and whether to continue with schooling after high school, adolescents must think about what specific sorts of jobs should be pursued within a particular career path, what kind of educational preparation would be most appropriate, and how to get a decent job.

For the college student contemplating a career as a therapist who works with teenagers, is it better to major in some sort of counseling or to follow a more general, liberal arts course of study? How early do you have to decide which specific profession to specialize in (e.g., counseling, social work, psychology, psychiatry)? Is it necessary to go to graduate school right away, or is it better to get some work experience before applying? These are all difficult questions to answer. And they are made more difficult because the nature of work, and the preparation one needs for specific careers, changes so rapidly. What might have been good advice 10 years ago might be terrible advice today.

Finally, achievement is a particularly important issue in the study of adolescence in contemporary society because individuals vary so widely in levels of educational and occupational success (Byrnes, 2011). By the end of high school, many adolescents demonstrate a high enough level of academic achievement to enter selective colleges and universities; at the other extreme are their peers who enter adulthood unable even to read a newspaper or understand a bus schedule. Although three-quarters of adolescents in the United States today complete high school and go on to college, nearly 10% leave high school before graduating (the figure is even higher in many inner-city school districts).

Similar disparities exist in the world of work: Most youth make the transition from school to work without a great deal of difficulty, but a significant number experience frustrating unemployment. Even within the population of young people who enter the labor force, there is considerable variation in earnings and in occupational status. Many important questions in the study of adolescent achievement concern factors that distinguish between young people who are successful—however success is defined—and those who are not.

Achievement as an Adolescent Issue

Development in the realm of achievement neither begins nor ends during adolescence. Educational institutions— even for young children—stress performance, competition, and success on tests of knowledge and ability, perhaps even more so today than in the past. Concerns over achievement continue throughout adulthood as well. Like their younger counterparts, adults often place a premium on success, and in American society, what one does for a living is an important part of one's identity.

Achievement during the adolescent years, though, merits special attention for several reasons. First, the fact that adolescence is a time of preparation for adult work roles raises questions about the nature of the preparation young people receive and the processes through which they sort themselves (or are sorted) into the jobs that may influence the remainder of their lives. Individuals' options for later school and work are often influenced by decisions they make during high school and college, and it is important to ask how such options are perceived and defined and how decisions are made.

Second, although differences in school performance and achievement are apparent as early as the 1st grade, not until adolescence do individuals begin to fully appreciate the implications of these differences for immediate and future success. Children's occupational plans are often the product of fantasy and passing interests, without any realistic assessment of their practicality or feasibility. Not until adolescence do individuals begin to evaluate their occupational choices in light of their actual talents, abilities, and opportunities, and by comparing their own performance to that of those around them.

Third, the educational and occupational decisions made during adolescence are more numerous, and the consequences of such decisions more serious, than the decisions made during childhood. In most elementary schools, although children may be grouped by ability, they generally are all exposed to fairly similar curricula and have few opportunities to veer from the educational program established by their school system. In high school, however, students can select how much science and math they want to take, whether they wish to study a foreign language, whether they want to pursue an academic or vocational track—even whether they want to remain in school once they have reached the legal age for leaving school. (In most parts of the United States, students can leave school before turning 18, but only if they have their parents' permission to do so.) Moreover, it is during adolescence that most individuals decide whether they want to go to college or enter a full-time job directly from high school. All these decisions have important implications for the sort of choices and plans the adolescent will make in the future, which, in turn, will influence his or her earnings, lifestyle, identity, and subsequent psychosocial development.

How might the biological, cognitive, and social changes of adolescence affect the ways in which individuals respond in achievement-related situations?

Puberty and Achievement Although the biological changes of puberty are less obvious influences on achievement than are the cognitive and social transitions of the period, they may nevertheless affect the development of achievement in important ways. As you will read, the transition into secondary school is usually marked by a temporary drop in individuals' motivation to achieve, and some of this may be related to puberty, because it introduces new issues (like dating and sex) into the adolescent's mix of concerns. To the extent that puberty changes what's important for maintaining status in the peer group, it may lead some adolescents to worry about whether trying too hard to do well will make them less attractive to their classmates. Puberty also increases

Noncognitive factors Influences on achievement that do not have to do with intellectual ability, such as determination, perseverance, and grit.

adolescents' interest in risky behavior (like experimenting with drugs), which may conflict or interfere with what's expected of them in school. In addition, puberty intensifies differences between males and females, and one impact of this is to make individuals think about what is "appropriate" achievement-related behavior for each of the sexes.

Cognitive Change and Achievement The intellectual changes of the period obviously are important influences on achievement. Certain subjects, like algebra, demand the use of the sorts of higher-order cognitive skills that don't fully mature until adolescence. Perhaps more important, not until adolescence are individuals cognitively capable of seeing the long-term consequences of their educational and occupational choices or of realistically considering the range of scholastic and work possibilities open to them. Thus, a second reason for the prominence of achievement-related issues during adolescence is related to the advent of more sophisticated forms of thinking. The ability to think in hypothetical terms, for example, raises new achievement concerns for the individual ("Should I go to college after I graduate, or should I work for a while?"); it also permits the young person to think through such questions in a logical and systematic fashion ("If I decide to go to college, then . . .").

Social Roles and Achievement The main reason that many achievement-related issues take on new significance during adolescence involves the social transition of the period. In virtually all societies, adolescence is the age when important educational and occupational decisions are made, and society has structured its educational and work institutions around this. In most industrialized societies, it is not until adolescence that individuals attain the status necessary to decide whether they will continue or end their formal education (i.e., stop at high school or continue on to college). Similarly, it is not until adolescence that individuals are allowed to enter the labor force in an official capacity, since child labor regulations typically prohibit the formal employment of youngsters under the age of 14 or so. In other words, the transition from school to work—one of the central issues in the study of achievement during adolescence—is a socially defined passage that society has determined will be negotiated during adolescence.

In this chapter, we look at the nature of achievement during the adolescent years. As you'll see, the extent to which an adolescent is successful in school and in preparing for work is influenced by a complex array of personal and environmental factors. We begin with a look at one set of factors that reliably differentiates adolescents who are successful from their peers who are not. It turns out that **noncognitive factors,** such as how motivated someone is to achieve, or what the person believes about the causes of successes and failure, are far more important than had been thought.

The Importance of Noncognitive Factors
Achievement Motivation

There is no question that success is partly determined by sheer ability (Bornstein, Hahn, & Wolke, 2013). But as many writers have pointed out, it takes more than talent to succeed—it also takes desire and determination—what some experts have referred to as "grit" (Duckworth, Peterson, Matthews, & Kelly, 2007). Individuals differ in the extent to which they strive for success, and this differential striving—which can be measured independently of ability—helps to account for different degrees of actual achievement (Casilas et al., 2012; Mega, Ronconi, & De Beni, 2014; Wigfield et al., 2011). Two students may both score equally on an intelligence or aptitude test, but if one student simply tries much harder than the other, their actual grades will probably differ. As someone who has been advising undergraduate and graduate students for more than three decades, I can assure you that the difference between those who are successful and those who are not usually has much more to do with their drive and capacity for self-direction than with their intelligence—an observation that is borne out by scientific study (Andersson & Bergman, 2011; Duckworth & Seligman, 2005; Murayama, Pekrun, Lichtenfeld, & vom Hofe, 2013). As far as success in school or work is concerned, a certain amount of intelligence is necessary, but it's more important to be hard-working than to be brilliant. Adolescents with greater mental toughness even sleep better than their peers, most probably because getting a good night's sleep helps us stay focused (Brand et al., 2014).

In recent years, there has been growing interest in understanding the social and personality factors that predict success in school and work, especially things like self-control and persistence (Padilla-Walker, Day, Dyer, & Black, 2013; Valiente, Swanson, & Eisenberg, 2012; Veronneau, Racer, Fosco, & Dishion, 2014). In a classic study conducted nearly 50 years ago, researchers presented preschoolers with the choice between receiving a single marshmallow immediately or waiting 15 minutes to get two of them. This test measured what psychologists call **delay of gratification,** the ability to wait longer to get a larger, better, or more valuable reward instead of a less attractive one available immediately. In the marshmallow study, children who had a stronger ability to delay gratification *when they were just preschoolers* were far more likely than the others to be successful in school throughout childhood and adolescence, and, as adults, at work (Mischel, 2014). Motivation becomes a more and more important determinant of success during adolescence, as individuals increasingly are expected to take charge of their own educational careers. By the time one enters college, doing well is influenced as much by conscientiousness as it is by intelligence (Poropat, 2009).

Individuals who are intrinsically motivated strive to achieve because of the pleasure they get out of learning and mastering the material. Generally speaking, they perform better in school than students who are extrinsically motivated. © Bananastock/ Age Fotostock RF

Fear of Failure Being motivated to achieve is only part of the story. Even students who are determined to succeed are sometimes so afraid of failing that their strong achievement motivation is undermined. Fear of failure, which often creates feelings of anxiety during tests or in other evaluative situations, can interfere with successful performance. When the achievement situation involves an easy task, and when a little anxiety helps to focus attention (if, for example, the task is boring), a moderate amount of anxiety may improve performance by increasing one's concentration. But the anxiety generated by a strong fear of failure interferes with successful performance. This often happens when the task involves learning something new or solving a complex problem—like many tasks faced by adolescents in school settings. Studies of adolescents from affluent backgrounds who are under strong pressure to do well in school find that it isn't so much parents' pressure to do well that creates mental health problems, but rather, parents' criticism when expectations are not achieved (Luthar, Shoum, & Brown, 2006).

An adolescent's achievement motivation and her or his fear of failure work together to pull the individual toward (or repel the individual from) achievement situations.

> **delay of gratification**
> The capacity to wait longer to get a larger, better, or more valuable reward instead of a smaller, less attractive, or less valuable one that is available immediately.

Individuals with a relatively strong need for achievement and a relatively weak fear of failure are more likely to actively approach challenging achievement situations—by taking more difficult classes, for example—and to look forward to them. In contrast, those whose fear of failure is relatively intense and whose need for achievement is relatively weak will dread challenging situations and do what they can to avoid them. Many students who have trouble persisting at tasks and who fear failure become **underachievers**—students whose grades are far lower than one would expect based on their intellectual ability.

Self-Handicapping Distinguishing between students whose underachievement is due mainly to anxiety and those who underperform for other reasons is important (Klassen et al., 2009; Midgley, Arunkumar, & Urdan, 1996; Midgley & Urdan, 1995). Some students actually want to appear uninterested in school because in some contexts this presentation may garner more respect and admiration from peers than academic success. Others want to make sure that they have an excuse for poor performance other than a lack of ability (Nurmi, Onatsu, & Haavisto, 1995). Still others may downplay the importance of academics as a response to their poor performance (Loose, Regner, Morin, & Dumas, 2012). These students may use various **self-handicapping** strategies—such as joking around in class, procrastination, turning in incomplete homework, or partying excessively the night before a big exam—as a way of self-protection ("I failed the test because I didn't try hard, not because I'm stupid") or as a means of enhancing their self-presentation ("I'm too cool to care about doing well in school").

Although self-handicapping is common among both males and females, there are sex differences in the ways in which adolescent girls and boys undermine their own success in school: Boys who self-handicap tend to attribute their poor performance to a lack of effort, whereas girls are more likely to mention emotional problems (Warner & Moore, 2004). A number of writers have drawn special attention to the use of self-handicapping strategies among ethnic minority youth, who may disengage from school because they perceive their long-term prospects as being limited by discrimination and prejudice (Mickelson, 1990; R. Taylor, Casten, Flickinger, Roberts, & Fulmore, 1994).

underachievers
Individuals whose actual school performance is lower than what would be expected on the basis of objective measures of their aptitude or intelligence.

self-handicapping
Deliberately behaving in ways that will likely interfere with doing well, in order to have an excuse for failing.

mastery motivation
Motivation to succeed based on the pleasure one will experience from mastering a task.

performance motivation
Motivation to succeed based on the rewards one will receive for successful performance.

Achievement Goal Orientation Two individuals can be equally motivated to achieve, but for very different reasons. Psychologists draw a distinction between **mastery motivation** (similar to *intrinsic motivation*) and **performance motivation** (similar to *extrinsic motivation*). Individuals who have a strong mastery orientation strive to achieve because of the pleasure they get out of learning and mastering the material. Individuals who are mainly performance oriented strive to achieve because of the rewards they get for performing well (typically, good grades) and the punishments they receive for performing poorly (like parental disapproval).

Individuals with a strong mastery orientation perform better in school than those whose motivation is mainly driven by performance goals, because intrinsically motivated individuals are more confident about their ability and more likely to persist in the face of failure (Eccles & Roeser, 2011; Yeager et al., 2014). There is a drop in students' mastery motivation as they transition from elementary into secondary school (Bong, 2009; Wang & Pomerantz, 2009), in part because teachers themselves become more performance-oriented and less mastery-oriented during this time (Eccles & Roeser, 2011). Students who believe that their teachers value and encourage autonomy are less likely to show this decline in motivation (Hafen et al., 2012).

Important adults in the adolescent's life affect the extent to which an adolescent's achievement motives are more aimed at mastery or more targeted toward performance (Kim, Schallert, & Kim, 2010; Murayama & Elliot, 2009). It's valuable for students to have perfectionistic tendencies, but it's essential that this drive to do well comes from inside, and not from the demands of others (Bong, Hwang, Noh, & Kim, 2014). When adults attempt to control an adolescent's achievement behavior by rewarding good grades (e.g., giving prizes or money), punishing bad grades (e.g., restricting privileges), or excessively supervising their performance (e.g., constantly checking up on their homework), adolescents are more likely to develop a performance orientation and, as a result, are less likely to do well in school. In contrast, adolescents whose parents and teachers encourage their autonomy, provide a cognitively stimulating home environment, and are supportive of school success (without rewarding it concretely) are more likely to develop a strong mastery orientation and tend to perform better in school as a consequence (Dumont, Trautwein, Nagy, & Nagengast, 2014; Gottfried, Marcoulides, Gottfried, & Oliver, 2009; Kim et al., 2010; Mouratidis, Vansteenkiste, Lens, Michou, & Soenens, 2013).

Beliefs About Success and Failure

How we behave in achievement situations is also influenced by our beliefs about our abilities and our chances for success and failure. You may have a very strong need for achievement, but if you are put into a situation in which you see little likelihood of succeeding, you will behave very differently than if you are in a situation in which you think your odds of doing well are good. For this reason, researchers have studied adolescents' beliefs about achievement, and not simply their motives.

Adolescents make judgments about their likelihood of succeeding or failing and exert different degrees of effort accordingly (Dweck, 2002). For example, choices of what classes to take in school are influenced by students' beliefs about their abilities. Students who believe that they are good at math will take more, and more difficult, math courses than their peers (Wang, 2012). This potentially has ramifications for the future: Because course selection influences achievement (students who take more challenging math classes perform better on math tests), and achievement, in turn, influences students' beliefs about their abilities (students who do well on math tests come to see themselves as better math students). A cycle is set in motion in which students' beliefs, abilities, classroom engagement, and actual achievement have a reciprocal influence on each other (Chow, Eccles, & Salmela-Aro, 2012; Poorthuis et al., 2014). One of the most interesting applications of this idea involves what psychologists call stereotype threat.

Stereotype Threat Students' beliefs about their abilities and, as a consequence, their performance can also be affected by situational factors operating when they are being evaluated. When students are told that members of their ethnic group usually perform poorly on a particular test (for example, before the test is administered, students are told that previous studies have shown that members of their ethnic group do not score as well as other students), their performance actually suffers, whereas the reverse is true when students are told that members of their ethnic group usually perform better than others (Steele, 1997), a phenomenon referred to as **stereotype threat.** To the extent that adolescents believe widely held stereotypes about ethnic or sex differences in ability (for example, that boys are just better at math than girls or that Asians are more intelligent than individuals from other ethnic groups), their achievement may be enhanced or depressed, depending on how they think they are expected to perform (Woodcock, Hernandez, Estrada, & Schultz, 2012). For instance, biracial students who identify themselves as Black or Hispanic (groups often stereotyped as poor achievers) achieve lower grades in school than those with identical backgrounds who identify themselves as White or Asian (groups often stereotyped as high achievers) (Herman, 2009). Certain stereotypes about ethnic differences in intelligence (e.g., that Asians are better at math) are present even before adolescence (Cvencek, Nasir, O'Connor, Wischnia, & Meltzoff, 2014). Interventions designed to counter students' beliefs about their group's

Students who are good at math take more, and more difficult, math courses, which enhances their academic self-conceptions. This leads them to take more challenging math courses in the future. © Pixtal/AGE Fotostock RF

intellectual deficiencies have been successful (Hanselman, Bruch, Gamoran, & Borman, 2014).

Changing views of male and female intellectual ability have affected adolescent girls' test performance. For many years, experts were concerned about the achievement motives and beliefs of adolescent girls, particularly with regard to performance in math and science, but more studies have shown that many previously observed sex differences have gotten much smaller, at least in the United States (Watt et al., 2012). One possible reason for this is that stereotypes about sex differences in cognitive ability have weakened considerably. Many decades ago, raters in experiments judged successful females as less likable, less attractive, and less likely to be happy. Today, similar experiments show the opposite effect, perhaps because we have become that much more accustomed to seeing successful girls and women in a variety of settings and endeavors (Quatman, Sokolik, & Smith, 2000).

It is striking how much things have changed. As a result of improvements in girls' achievement—across all subject areas—the achievement gap between males and females in math and science is very small (Reilly, Neumann, & Andrews, 2014). Today, people tend to be worried about the poor achievement of boys, not girls (Sommers, 2000). On average, boys do not do as well in school, are less invested in doing well, are disciplined more often by their teachers, and are more likely to perceive their schools and teachers as unfair (Kiang, Supple, Stein, & Gonzalez, 2012; Pomerantz, Altermatt, & Saxon, 2002). Sex differences in educational

stereotype threat
The harmful effect that exposure to stereotypes about ethnic or sex differences in ability has on student performance.

attainment have grown in recent years, with females now far outnumbering males on American college campuses (T. Lewin, 2006). Sex differences in educational attainment, favoring females, are especially great among Black adolescents (J. King, 2006; Saunders, Davis, Williams, & Williams, 2004), in part because Black parents are more likely to practice authoritative parenting with daughters than with sons (Dotterer, Loew, & McHale, 2014; Varner & Mabdara, 2014)

The Nature of Intelligence The way adolescents think about intelligence in general (in addition to how they view their own capability) also enters into the achievement equation. What's especially crucial is whether intelligence is thought of as something that is fixed or as something that is changeable (Stipek & Gralinski, 1996). Studies show that three factors interact to predict students' behavior in school: whether they believe that intelligence is fixed or malleable, whether they are oriented more toward performance or mastery, and whether they are confident about their abilities, or, as some theorists have put it, have a strong sense of **self-efficacy** (Bandura, Barbaranelli, Caprara, & Pastorelli, 1996). But it's how these qualities are combined that really matters (De Castella, Byrne, & Covington, 2013; Martin, Nejad, Colmar, & Liem, 2013).

Students who believe that intelligence is fixed tend to be oriented toward their performance and to be greatly affected by their degree of self-efficacy (Stipek & Gralinski, 1996). If they are confident about their abilities, this is fine; they tend to work hard and to seek out challenges. If they are insecure, though, they tend to give up easily and feel helpless. In other words, if you believe that intelligence is fixed, you'd better have confidence in your own abilities.

Students who believe that intelligence is malleable approach achievement situations from a different perspective. They are more likely to be intrinsically than extrinsically motivated; for them, satisfaction comes from mastering the material, not simply from getting a good grade. They are also far less affected by their level of confidence, because they are less concerned about their performance. Whether assured or insecure, these students exert extra effort and seek out challenges, because they are motivated by learning rather than by performing (Purdie, Hattie, & Douglas, 1996). Beliefs in the capacity of people to change are especially helpful during times of stressful transition (Yeager et al., 2014).

These newer models of the noncognitive aspects of achievement during adolescence illustrate how students' beliefs (about the nature of ability in general and the nature of their own ability in particular) influence their motivation, which, in turn, influences their

self-efficacy
The sense that an individual has some control over his or her life.

performance (Bassi, Steca, Delle Fave, & Caprara, 2007; Legault, Green-Demers, & Pelletier, 2006; Simpkins, Davis-Kean, & Eccles, 2006). Their performance, in turn, influences their beliefs about their competence (T. Williams & Williams, 2010) (Figure 1). Understanding how these forces work together has important implications for teachers, because, as you will read, adolescents' motives and beliefs are influenced by the context in which they are educated. In other words, there are specific steps teachers can take that will help bring out the best in their students.

The Importance of Context Although students' orientation toward mastery versus performance is determined in part by psychological factors, the educational context matters as well. When classroom conditions change so that performance becomes more important than learning, students' motives and beliefs change as a result. You've probably experienced this when you enrolled in a course in which the instructor stressed grades rather than mastery of the material. This sort of emphasis brings out the worst in students—literally. Under some circumstances, performance goals make students more extrinsically motivated, more insecure about their abilities, more hesitant to challenge themselves, and less likely to ask for help (R. Newman & Schwager, 1995). This is especially likely when students are motivated mainly by trying to avoid looking stupid (which diminishes their performance) rather than by trying to compete with and outperform their classmates (which enhances their performance) (Pintrich, 2000). In classrooms in which teachers are very performance-oriented (rather than mastery-oriented), students feel more alienated from school, have lower feelings of self-efficacy, and are more likely to engage in self-handicapping behavior (Kalil & Ziol-Guest, 2008; Patall, Cooper, & Wynn, 2010; Urdan, 2004).

Students' feelings of self-efficacy influence, and are influenced by, their experiences, the messages they receive from teachers and parents, and the ways in which they compare themselves to their classmates (Gniewosz, Eccles, & Noack, 2014; Simpkins, 2015; Simpkins & Eccles, 2012). Around the world, adolescents also use peers as a basis of social comparison, and develop beliefs about their academic competence by comparing their grades to the grades their friends

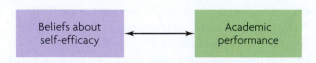

Figure 1 Individuals' sense of self-efficacy influences their academic performance, which further shapes their sense of self-efficacy. (T. Williams & Williams, 2010)

get (Bissell-Havran, 2014; Marsh et al., 2014). Here is how Jamaal, an 8th-grade student who is high in self-efficacy, described his reaction to the performance of a high-achieving classmate:

> I was real mad when Stacey had got a 100. I wasn't really mad, but I was kind of jealous. Like I envied it. Like I wished I was that one that got 100. I mean sometimes, now that, *that's* one of the things that give me the extra drive. That gives me the extra determination to work harder in math to get good grades like everyone else. (Usher, 2009, p. 295)

When he felt challenged by a math problem, Jamaal would give himself pep talks:

> I'll be like, "Come on." I'll be thinking about different ways to solve problems and stuff like that. I'll be saying, "Come on, Jamaal, you can do this," and stuff like that. . . . I don't know what it does, but it's just like extra comfort to me. (p. 295)

Compare this sentiment to that expressed by Tanisha, a classmate of Jamaal's who is low in self-efficacy:

> Some of my friends tell me about [algebra], and, you know, some of their tests that they told me about, they said it was hard. But, you know, that's kind of what makes me feel like I'm not going to do good in it. Because, like, if they can't do it, then I probably can't do it. (p. 297)

Attributions for Success and Failure How students interpret their successes and failures is also important. Researchers who are interested in **achievement attributions** have studied how the explanations that people give for their success or failure influence their performance (Dweck, 2002). According to these theorists, individuals attribute their performance to a combination of four factors: ability, effort, task difficulty, and luck. When people succeed and attribute their success to internal causes, such as their ability or effort, they are more likely to approach future tasks confidently and with self-assurance. If, however, they attribute their success to external factors outside their control, such as luck or an easy task, they are more likely to remain unsure of their abilities. Successful students, who tend to be high in achievement motivation, are likely to attribute their successes to internal causes (Durik, Vida, & Eccles, 2006; Randel, Stevenson, & Witruk, 2000; Swinton, Kurtz-Costes, Rowley, & Okeke-Adeyanju, 2011).

When teachers emphasize performance, rather than mastery, students are more likely to disengage from class. ©Photodisc/PunchStock RF

How adolescents interpret their failures is also important. Some youngsters try harder in the face of failure, whereas others withdraw and exert less effort. When students attribute their failures to a lack of effort, they are more likely to try harder on future tasks (Dweck, 2002). Adolescents who attribute their failure to factors that they feel cannot be changed (such as bad luck, lack of intelligence, or task difficulty) are more likely to feel helpless and to exert less effort in subsequent situations.

Suppose, for instance, a student takes the SAT and receives a mediocre score. He then is told by his guidance counselor that the SAT is a measure of intelligence, that intelligence is fixed, and that his score reflects how smart he is. The counselor tells the student that he can retake the test if he wants to but that he should not expect to score much higher the next time. Now imagine a different student, who has the same score on the test. She is told by her guidance counselor that effort has a great deal to do with scores on the SAT and that she can raise her score by trying harder. In all likelihood, the next time these students take the test, the first student will not try as hard as the second student, because he is more likely to feel helpless.

Students who are led to believe that their efforts do not make a difference—by being told, for example, that they are stupid or that the work is too difficult for them—develop what psychologists call **learned helplessness:** the belief that failure is inevitable (Dweck, 2002). As a result of learned helplessness, some students try less hard than their peers, and they don't do as well as they might. Students

achievement attributions
The beliefs an individual holds about the causes of her or his successes and failures.

learned helplessness
The acquired belief that an individual is not able to influence events through his or her own efforts or actions.

making the personal connection

When you succeed in school, to what do you attribute your success? When you fail, how do you explain your failure? Have you had teachers who influenced your beliefs about your own abilities?

who suffer from learned helplessness and who use a lot of self-handicapping strategies tend not only to perform worse in school but also to have more overall adjustment problems than their peers (Määta, Nurmi, & Stattin, 2007; Määta, Stattin, & Nurmi, 2002). Instead of dismissing low-achieving students as having "low needs for achievement" or "low intelligence," teachers and other school personnel can help students achieve more by helping them learn to attribute their performance to factors that are under their control (Blackwell, Trzesniewski, & Dweck, 2007; Hudley, 1997; Usher, 2009).

The Drop in Motivation during the Transition into Secondary School One of the most interesting applications of research on achievement-related beliefs has been in studies of changes in adolescents' academic motivation during the transition from elementary school to junior high school (Eccles & Roeser, 2011). Studies find that students' motivation and school performance decline when they move into secondary school (see Figure 2) (Eccles & Rosser, 2009; Wang & Eccles, 2012). Why might this be?

Among the other important changes that take place during this school transition is a shift on the part of teachers toward a more performance-oriented style of instruction and evaluation (Fine, 2014). Elementary school teachers tend to stress the importance of mastering the material. During secondary school, however, more of an emphasis is placed on grades. This shift undermines many students' intrinsic motivation and their self-confidence, which, in turn, diminishes their performance. Indeed, during the early years of high school, there is a general decline in adolescents' feelings of self-efficacy and their mastery motivation, and an increase in their use of self-handicapping strategies (Gottfried, Fleming, & Gottfried, 2001; Pintrich, 2000). In addition, beliefs about intelligence change as students move into and through adolescence, with older students more likely to view intelligence as stable (Ablard & Mills, 1996) and to endorse dysfunctional attributions (e.g., attributing failure to a lack of ability, rather than a lack of effort) (Swinton et al., 2011).

Several experiments have demonstrated that this decline does not have to be inevitable. In one, researchers randomly assigned students enrolled in 7th-grade math classes to one of two groups: an experimental group, which received two class sessions on how it is possible to "grow your intelligence" and on how experience can actually affect brain development, and a control group, which was taught strategies to improve memory (Blackwell et al., 2007). While both groups showed a comparable drop in math grades initially, after the intervention, the group that was taught that intelligence is malleable improved, whereas the control group continued to decline. Another study found that having students write essays about the potential benefits of the transition into high school helped maintain positive academic self-conceptions during this time (Facchin, Margola, & Revenson, 2014).

Environmental Influences on Achievement

Ability, beliefs, and motivation play a large role in influencing academic performance, but opportunity and situational factors also have a great deal to do with achievement (Eccles & Roeser, 2011). Many differences in achievement observed among adolescents result not from differences in their abilities, motives, or beliefs but from differences in the schools and classrooms where their abilities and motives are expressed.

School environments differ markedly—in physical facilities, in opportunities for pursuing academically enriched programs, and in classroom atmospheres. Students are more engaged and successful in schools that are more personal, less departmentalized, and less rigidly tracked, and in which team teaching is used more frequently (V. Lee & Smith, 1993). Unfortunately, many school districts, plagued with shrinking tax bases, have decaying school buildings, outdated equipment, and shortages of textbooks and teachers. In some schools, disciplinary problems and crime have become so overwhelming that dealing with them has taken precedence over learning and instruction. Many young people who genuinely want to succeed are impeded not by a lack of talent or motivation but by a school environment that makes their academic success virtually impossible. Students who attend schools with a high concentration of poor, minority students are especially disadvantaged, as are students who attend schools with a high proportion of students from single-parent families (Bankston & Caldas, 1998; Pong, 1998). The decline in school engagement seen during the transition from elementary to secondary school is especially pronounced among students in low-income neighborhoods (Benner & Wang, 2014a) and among disadvantaged students in schools in which they are a small minority (Benner & Wang, 2014b).

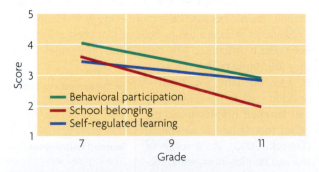

Figure 2 As students move through adolescence, they become increasingly disengaged from school. (Wang & Eccles, 2012)

Schools in the United States vary considerably in the resources their students have access to. © Thomas Trutschel/Getty Images

The Influence of The Home Environment

The school, of course, is not the only environment that makes a difference in adolescents' achievement, and few would argue that schools should accept full responsibility for adolescents who do not succeed at a level consonant with their abilities. If anything, important aspects of the home environment are better predictors of adolescents' academic achievement than are features of the school environment (Azmitia, Cooper, & Brown, 2009; Steinberg, 1996). Researchers have studied three ways in which the adolescent's home may influence his or her level of achievement (see Figure 3).

Parental Values and Expectations   Adolescents' achievement is directly related to their parents' values and expectations (Jodl, Michael, Malanchuk, Eccles, & Sameroff, 2001). Parental encouragement of academic success are manifested in a number of ways, all of which benefit adolescents' school performance. First, parents who encourage school success set higher standards for their child's school performance and homework; they have higher aspirations for their child, which, in turn, contribute to school success (Luthar et al., 2006). Parents' and adolescents' expectations influence each other over time, so that adolescents who grow up with parents who

expect a lot come to expect a lot of themselves (Y. Zhang, Haddad, Torres, & Chen, 2011b), whereas low parental expectations can contribute to a self-fulfilling prophecy,

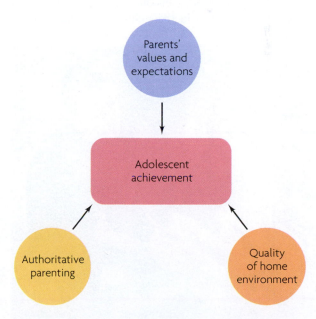

Figure 3   Parents influence adolescent achievement through three processes: their values and expectations, the way they parent, and the quality of the home environment.

leading to poor achievement (Wood, Kurtz-Costes, Rowley, & Okeke-Adeyanju, 2010). The relation between parents' and adolescents' expectations is complicated, though: In the long run, adolescents achieve more when their parents' expectations for them actually exceed their own (perhaps because parents then provide encouragement that bolsters adolescents' school performance), but in the short term they achieve less when they believe that their parents expect more of them than they are capable of (perhaps because this creates stress) (Bowen, Hopson, Rose, & Glennie, 2012; Randall, Bohnert, & Travers, 2015; Wang & Benner, 2014). One arena in which parental expectations play an especially important role is mathematics, where traditional views of gender roles may lead adolescent boys and girls to develop very different sorts of self-conceptions that inspire male students to develop relatively stronger interests in math from an early age (Frenzel, Goetz, Pekrun, & Watt, 2010; Nagy et al., 2010). When parents are told how useful it is for students to take math and science, girls' enrollment in these classes increases (Rozek, Hyde, Svoboda, Hulleman, & Harackiewicz, 2014).

Second, parents who encourage school success also have values that are consistent with doing well in school. They structure the home environment to support academic pursuits, so that the messages children receive from their teachers are echoed at home (Benner, Graham, & Mistry, 2008; Grolnick, Raftery-Helmer, Flamm, Marbell, & Cardemil, 2014; Roche & Ghazarian, 2012). Even high school students profit from having parents who help them learn more effective time management strategies and healthier work habits (Xu, 2004).

Finally, parents who encourage success are likely to be more involved in their child's education—more likely to attend school programs, help in course selection, maintain interest in school activities and assignments, and the like—all of which contribute to students' success (Benner et al., 2008; N. E. Hill et al., 2004; Shumow & Miller, 2001). Parental involvement in schooling may make academic success seem both more important and more attainable to the adolescent, which may enhance the young person's academic self-conceptions (Grolnick & Slowiaczek, 1994; Ibañez, Kuperminc, Jurkovic, & Perilla, 2004); it also sends an important message to teachers (Kuperminc, Darnell, & Alvarez-Jiminez, 2008). In contrast, parental disengagement from school makes students themselves more likely to disengage and do poorly (Roeser, Lord, & Eccles, 1994). Parental involvement seems to be an especially strong influence on the achievement of Mexican American youth, perhaps because of the importance of the family in Mexican culture (Trusty, Plata, & Salazar, 2003; Woolley, Kol, & Bowen, 2009). The way in which parents are involved matters, however: Encouraging and expecting achievement in school and being involved in school-based activities are both effective forms of parental involvement, whereas helping with homework is not (N. E. Hill & Tyson, 2009). Parental involvement in schooling has a more substantial effect when the adolescent attends a school in which a large proportion of other students' parents are involved as well (Darling & Steinberg, 1997; Pong, 1998) and in higher-income communities (Gordon & Cui, 2014).

Authoritative Parenting A second way in which parents influence student achievement is through their general approach to parenting. Authoritative parenting—parenting that is warm, firm, and fair—is linked to school success during adolescence, as indexed by better grades, better attendance, higher expectations, more positive academic self-conceptions, and stronger engagement in the classroom (Cheung, Pomerantz, & Dong, 2013; Hill & Wang, 2015; Lowe & Dotterer, 2013; Wang, Hill, & Hofkens, 2014). In contrast, parenting that is especially punitive, harsh, overcontrolling, or inept is associated with lower school engagement and diminished achievement (Blondal & Adalbjamardottir, 2014; Q. Wang, Pomerantz, & Chen, 2007). Interestingly, extreme parental permissiveness, not authoritarianism, is associated with higher rates of dropping out of school (Rumberger, Ghatak, Poulos, Ritter, & Dornbusch, 1990).

Why do adolescents achieve more in school when they come from authoritative homes? Authoritative parenting promotes the development of a healthy achievement orientation—including an emphasis on mastery and a healthier attributional style—which, in turn, enhances adolescent school performance (Duchesne & Ratelle, 2010; Suizzo et al., 2012). This is in part because authoritative parents are more likely themselves to hold healthier beliefs about their child's

Adolescents whose parents are involved in their schooling perform better than adolescents whose parents are not. One reason that students from higher social classes do better in school is that their parents tend to be more involved. © sturti/Getty Images RF

achievement and less likely to be overly controlling—two factors that strengthen adolescents' work ethic and intrinsic motivation (Arbeton, Eccles, & Harold, 1994; Grolnick & Slowiaczek, 1994). Having a strong work orientation enhances achievement both directly, as we saw earlier, and indirectly, through the positive impression it makes on teachers (Farkas, Grobe, & Shuan, 1990).

In general, these findings are in line with a good deal of research suggesting that consistent, authoritative parenting is associated with a wide array of benefits to the adolescent, including higher achievement motivation, greater self-esteem, and enhanced competence (Steinberg, 2001). Authoritative parents also tend to be more involved in school activities, which is associated with scholastic success, although parents' involvement both affects and is affected by adolescents' achievement (Cheung & Pomerantz, 2012; Juang & Silbereisen, 2002; Wang & Sheikh-Khalil, 2014). Students also perform better when the values and expectations they encounter at home are consistent with those they encounter in school (Arunkumar, Midgley, & Urdan, 1999).

The Quality of the Home Environment A third mechanism of familial influence is through the quality of the home environment, as measured by the presence of such items as a television, dictionary, encyclopedia, newspaper, vacuum cleaner, and other indicators of family income. The quality of the home environment is more strongly correlated with academic achievement than is the quality of the physical facility of the school students attend, the background and training of their teachers, or their teachers' salaries (Armor, 1972). The extent to which parents provide **cultural capital**—by exposing the adolescent to art, music, literature, and so forth—exerts a positive impact on achievement above and beyond the effects of the parents' own level of education (Waithaka, 2014). Access to the Internet at home is important, too (Chen, Hsaio, Chern, & Chen, 2014; Hofferth & Moon, 2012).

Several researchers have asked whether adolescents' school achievement is affected by genetic factors. Whereas intelligence and cognitive achievement both have strong genetic components (and influence grades through this mechanism), school performance is highly influenced by environmental factors, both inside and outside the family (W. Johnson, McGue, & Iacono, 2006; Teachman, 1997). With this in mind, it is important to point out that a disheartening number of young people in this country live in overcrowded, inadequate housing and come from families that are under severe economic and social stress—so much so that parental encouragement and involvement are often undermined by neighborhood conditions (Gonzales, Cauce, Friedman, & Mason, 1996). It is extremely difficult for a parent under severe economic stress to provide a supportive home environment. Stress at home, in turn, spills over into the adolescent's school life, leading to academic problems and lower achievement (Flook & Fuligni, 2008). One recent study found, for example, that adolescents from homes in which there had been a lot of family instability did not do as well as other students when they attended schools that had a large proportion of high-achieving students; in schools with fewer high achievers, coming from an unstable family environment mattered much less (Cavanagh & Fomby, 2012).

Put succinctly, many American youngsters do not grow up in an atmosphere that is conducive to academic achievement. Many communities lack **social capital**—the support, encouragement, and involvement of adults necessary to facilitate youngsters' success (J. Coleman & Hoffer, 1987). Social capital, which is strengthened when families have strong ties to other families in the community, is an important contributor to success in school, above and beyond the contribution of adolescents' family income, their parents' education, or their household composition (Waithaka, 2014). In contrast, students who can draw on resources provided not only by the family, but by friends, mentors, and teachers, stand a far better chance of succeeding in school (Fruiht & Wray-Lake, 2013; Maulana, Opdenakker, Stroet, & Bosker, 2013; Rice et al., 2013; Song, Bong, Lee, & Kim, 2014). One recent study of undocumented immigrant Latino college students described the way that these individuals created "families" of support that extended well beyond their immediate family (Enriquez, 2011).

> **cultural capital**
> The resources provided within a family through the exposure of the adolescent to art, music, literature, and other elements of "high culture."
>
> **social capital**
> The interpersonal resources available to an adolescent or family.

The Influence of Friends

Friends also influence adolescents' achievement. Friends, not parents, are the most salient influences on adolescents' day-to-day school behaviors, such as doing homework and exerting effort in class (Steinberg, 1996; Wang & Eccles, 2012). That is, although parents are stronger influences on long-range educational plans, what adolescents do in school on a daily basis is more affected by their friends. One of the main reasons that adolescents growing up in poor neighborhoods achieve less is that they are often surrounded by peers who are disengaged from school (South, Baumer, & Lutz, 2003).

When most of us think about the influence of adolescents' peers on achievement, we tend to think of the ways in which peers undermine academic success. But the impact of friends on adolescents' school performance depends on the academic orientation of the peer group. Having friends who earn high grades and aspire to further education enhances adolescents' achievement, whereas having friends who earn low grades or disparage school success interferes with it (Steinberg, 1996). Students whose friends are more engaged in school are themselves more engaged and less likely to drop out (R. Ream & Rumberger, 2008). Friends also influence course selection and play an important role in decisions to take math and science classes, which may be an especially powerful influence on girls' choice of classes (Leaper, Farkas, & Brown, 2012; Robnet & Leaper, 2013).

Students' grades change in parallel to the grades their friends get (Shin & Ryan, 2014). Students with best friends who achieve high grades in school are more likely to show improvements in their own grades than are students who begin at similar levels of achievement but whose friends are not high achievers. Peers also exert a small but significant influence on each other's future plans (Kiuru et al., 2012). Among low-achieving adolescents, those with high-achieving friends are more likely to plan to continue their education than are those with low-achieving friends. The causal direction works the other way, too: When adolescents' grades go up, they tend to befriend more high-achieving classmates, but when their grades drop, they tend to become friends with lower-achieving peers (Flashman, 2012; Véronneau, Vitaro, Brendgen, Dishion, & Tremblay, 2010).

Although peers can influence achievement for better or for worse, many observers have noted that in the contemporary United States, the influence of the peer culture on academic achievement is far more negative than positive (Bishop, Bishop, Gelbwasser, Green, & Zuckerman, 2003). Perhaps because of this, adolescents with an extremely high orientation toward peers tend to perform worse in school (Fuligni & Eccles, 1993). Conversely, adolescents who are neglected by their peers often have a stronger academic orientation than relatively more popular students (Luthar & McMahon, 1996; Wentzel & Asher, 1995). As they move into middle school, adolescents become increasingly worried about their friends' reactions to success in school. By 8th grade, students do not want their classmates to know that they worked hard in school, even though they knew that it would be helpful to convey this impression to their teachers (Juvonen & Murdock, 1995). High-achieving, popular students believe that it is important to hide their grades from their friends (Zook & Russotti, 2013), which may make sense in many schools, in which high-achieving students are ostracized (Schwartz, Kelly, & Duong, 2013).

Doing well in school does not have to come at the cost of having a decent social life, however. A study in which adolescents maintained daily diaries of their time use sheds interesting light on the differences between high- and low-achieving students in how they spend their time (Witkow, 2009). Not surprisingly, students who earn higher grades than their peers spend more time studying, both on weekdays and on weekends. But as Figure 4 shows, a key difference between the groups is in how much—and when—they spend time with their friends. As you can see, high-achieving students spend less time with their friends than do low-achieving students on weekdays, but not on weekends. In other words, high-achieving students are able to maintain an active social life by allocating their time more judiciously during the week. In all likelihood, one reason that high-achieving students spend less time with friends on weekdays is that their friends are also busy studying.

A number of researchers have studied how the influences of parents and peers operate together to affect adolescents' achievement. These studies show that the family environment has an effect on adolescents' choice of friends, which in turn influences school achievement (B. Brown, Mounts, Lamborn, & Steinberg, 1993). Having academically oriented peers is especially beneficial to adolescents from single-parent homes, where parental involvement in schooling is typically lower (Garg, Melanson, & Levin, 2007). By the same token, having friends who disparage school success may offset the benefits of authoritative parenting (Steinberg, 1996); having friends who are disengaged from school is especially detrimental to the achievement of students with more distant relationships at home (Espinoza, Gillen-O'Neel, Gonzales, & Fuligni, 2014; Marion, Laursen, Kiuru, Nurmi, & Salmela-Aro, 2014). Rather than asking whether family or friends influence adolescents' school performance, it may make more sense to ask how these two forces—along with the influence of the school itself—work together.

The broader context in which schooling takes place affects the degree to which peers and parents influence adolescents' achievement. Peers and parents more strongly influence student achievement in countries

Peers influence how much effort adolescents devote to school, for better and for worse. © Hero/Corbis/Glow Images RF

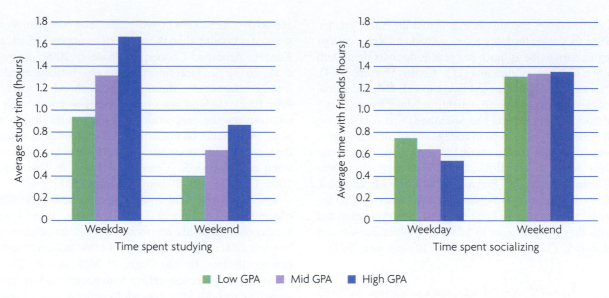

Figure 4   High- and low-achieving students allocate their time spent studying and socializing differently. (Witkow, 2009)

where schools serve more heterogeneous groups of students, as in the United States. In countries where students with different long-term educational aspirations attend different schools (e.g., in countries like Germany, where there are separate schools for adolescents who are planning to go to college and those who are not), peers and parents are less influential (Buchmann & Dalton, 2002).

In summary, although psychological factors play a key role in determining scholastic success, it is important to take into account the broader environment in which individuals pursue their education (Gonzales, Cauce, Friedman, & Mason, 1996; Li, Lerner, & Lerner, 2010; Steinberg, 1996). Distinguishing between psychological and environmental factors is hard, though, because they typically go hand in hand. Living in an environment that offers few opportunities for success induces feelings of learned helplessness, which, in turn, leads individuals to feel that exerting any effort to succeed is futile. Attending school in an environment in which achievement is not encouraged engenders attitudes and beliefs inconsistent with striving to do well. Rather than being determined by one single factor, such as ability or motivation, patterns of achievement are the result of a cumulative process that includes a long history of experience and socialization in school, at home, in the peer group, and in the community.

Educational Achievement

Educational achievement is usually defined in one of three ways: **school performance** (the grades students earn in school), **academic achievement** (their performance on standardized tests), or **educational attainment** (the number of years of schooling they complete).

These different measures of educational achievement are interrelated, but they are less tied to each other than you might expect.

No single factor adequately accounts for differences in educational achievement. Intellectual ability as assessed by IQ tests is highly correlated with performance on achievement tests (hardly a surprise, since IQ tests and achievement tests are designed to tap similar abilities). But grades in school—and to an even greater extent, educational attainment—are influenced by a wider range of factors than intellectual abilities. Grades are influenced by teachers' judgments of students' mastery of the material, and these judgments are influenced by teachers' evaluations of students' efforts and behaviors in the classroom (Farkas, Grobe, & Shuan, 1990). How many years of school an adolescent completes is likely to be influenced by his or her family background and living circumstances, as well as by school performance. Two adolescents may have similar grade point averages, but if one comes from a poor family and cannot afford to go to college, the two will have different levels of educational attainment. Even as early as elementary school many inner-city youth have very limited occupational expectations, and these low expectations affect their educational achievement and attainment (T. Cook et al., 1996).

Regardless of what influences it, educational attainment has important implications for subsequent earnings (Ceci & Williams, 1999). The gap in earnings between high school graduates and college graduates

school performance
A measure of achievement based on an individual's grades in school.

academic achievement
Achievement that is measured by standardized tests of scholastic ability or knowledge.

educational attainment
The number of years of schooling completed by an individual.

is considerable, and this is true across all ethnic groups. When they enter the labor force, individuals with a college degree earn twice as much per year as do individuals with only a high school diploma (U.S. Census Bureau, 2014). This state of affairs has led many to call for educational policies that encourage all students to "shoot for the stars." Although some experts had speculated that encouraging all students to strive to go to college would ultimately have negative effects on the mental health of students whose expectations are unrealistic, this has not proven to be true (Domina, Conley, & Farkas, 2011; Reynolds & Baird, 2010). It is important, however, that adolescents who are encouraged to go to college be given the information and skills they need in order to fulfill their plans and succeed (Roderick, Coca, & Nagaoka, 2011; Rosenbaum, 2011).

The Importance of Socioeconomic Status

One of the most powerful influences on educational achievement is the socioeconomic status of the adolescent's family. Although some of the socioeconomic gaps in school achievement have narrowed, disparities in achievement between the social classes remain strong, and the importance of socioeconomic status in determining educational achievement remains substantial across all ethnic groups and in different countries (Goza & Ryabov, 2009; Parker et al., 2012; Tynkkyen, Tolvanen, & Salmela-Aro, 2012). One recent study found that adolescents from higher income groups had more gray matter in brain regions important to performance on achievement tests (Mackey et al., 2015).

A Head Start for the More Affluent Five decades of studies have shown over and over that middle-class adolescents score higher on basic tests of academic skills

Intervening in early childhood can help close the achievement gap between disadvantaged and affluent children. © Jim West/PhotoEdit

and achievement, earn higher grades, and complete more years of schooling than their less affluent peers (Sackett, Kuncel, Arneson, Cooper, & Waters, 2009; Sackett et al., 2012). Socioeconomic status also influences adolescent achievement through neighborhood processes. Poor Black students who live in neighborhoods with a relatively higher proportion of middle-class neighbors place more value on education and try harder in school than comparably poor students who live in disadvantaged neighborhoods (Ceballo, McLoyd, & Toyokawa, 2004; E. B. Stewart, Stewart, & Simons, 2007).

One big reason that family background is related to educational achievement is that children from lower socioeconomic levels are more likely to enter elementary school scoring low on tests of basic academic competence (Rouse, Brooks-Gunn, & McLanahan, 2005). These initial differences reflect both genetic and environmental factors. Middle-class adults generally have higher IQs than lower-class adults, and this advantage is passed on to their children—both through genetics and through the benefit that middle-class youngsters receive from growing up under more favorable environmental conditions (C. S. Chen, Lee, & Stevenson, 1996; Teachman, 1996). Affluent youngsters receive better health care and better nutrition, for example, both of which contribute to their higher performance on IQ tests. The disadvantages of poorer youngsters in achievement test scores persist—and may even increase—throughout elementary and secondary school (Rouse, Brooks-Gunn, & McLanahan, 2005). Because progress in high school depends so heavily on having a solid foundation of basic academic competence, adolescents who enter secondary school without having mastered basic academic skills quickly fall behind, and some leave high school before graduating.

Early Intervention One bit of encouraging news comes from long-term evaluations of interventions designed to improve the academic achievement of very poor youngsters who, by virtue of their poverty, are at high risk for academic failure (F. Campbell & Ramey, 1995; A. Reynolds & Temple, 1998). In these evaluations, researchers compared groups of adolescents who had participated in an intensive educational program during their preschool and elementary school years with matched samples of adolescents who had had the preschool intervention only, the elementary school intervention only, or no educational intervention at all. The interventions were targeted at improving the children's school skills and at strengthening the links between parents and their child's school.

Children who participated in preschool interventions (with or without participation in elementary school interventions) perform significantly better in school during adolescence than those who did not (F. Campbell & Ramey, 1995). In one study, participating in both the preschool and the elementary school programs provided additional advantages over the preschool program alone (A. Reynolds, Temple, Robertson, & Mann, 2001). Interestingly, however, adolescents who had been in the elementary school program but not the preschool program had no advantages over those who had been in no intervention at all (F. Campbell & Ramey, 1995). These findings suggest that intervening prior to entering first grade is extremely important in preventing long-term academic problems among impoverished adolescents, and that extended participation in educational programs may be better than short-term participation. Consistent with this, school difficulties as early as kindergarten are predictive of poor school performance in adolescence (Hamre & Pianta, 2001).

One reason for the relatively poorer school performance of disadvantaged youth, therefore, is that these youngsters begin school at a distinct academic disadvantage. A second reason for the disparity is stress, both before and during adolescence. Adolescents who come from lower-class backgrounds experience more stressful life events, report more daily hassles, and attend schools with more negative climates (DuBois, Felner, Meares, & Krier, 1994; Felner et al., 1995; Gillock & Reyes, 1999; Pungello, Kupersmidt, Burchinal, & Patterson, 1996). Stress adversely affects adolescents' mental health, well-being, and school performance (DuBois, Felner, Brand, Adan, & Evans, 1992; Felner et al., 1995).

making the scientific connection

In light of the profound impact that socioeconomic status has on student achievement, what would you suggest as policies or practices to raise the achievement of poor youth? Think about people you know who overcame economic disadvantage and were highly successful in school (perhaps *you* are in this category). To what would you attribute this success?

Parental Involvement   Parents from higher social classes are more likely to be involved in their adolescent's education, especially through formal parent-teacher organizations, like the PTA or PTO (Shumow & Miller, 2001). Middle- and upper-middle-class parents are also more likely to have information about their child's school, to be responsive to their child's school problems, and to help select more rigorous courses for their child to take (Crosnoe & Huston, 2007). Because adolescents whose parents are involved in their schooling perform better than those whose parents are not involved, youngsters from higher social classes achieve more in school than their less advantaged peers in part because of their parents' more active involvement (Henry, Cavanagh,

& Oetting, 2011; V. Lee & Croninger, 1994). In addition, parents with greater economic resources are able to provide their children with more cultural capital, which is an important contributor to school success (Waithaka, 2014).

Socioeconomic differences in school achievement obviously reflect the cumulative and combined effects of a variety of influences, and it is simplistic to explain social class differences in achievement without considering these factors simultaneously. What is perhaps more interesting—and more worthy of scientific study—is the question of what it is about the many youngsters from economically disadvantaged backgrounds who are successful that accounts for their overcoming the tremendous odds against them. The successful college student who comes from an environment of severe economic disadvantage has had to overcome incredible barriers. Researchers have been studying various types of interventions designed to encourage such students, many of whom are the first in their family to aspire to college, to make a successful transition into postsecondary education (Stephens, Hamedani, & Destin, 2014).

Although more research on successful students from poor backgrounds is sorely needed, what might be most important is the presence of warm and encouraging parents who raise their children authoritatively, take an interest in their children's academic progress, and hold high aspirations for their children's educational attainment, as well as the availability of peers who support and encourage academic success (Goza & Ryabov, 2009; Melby, Conger, Fang, Wickrama, & Conger, 2008). In other words, positive relations at home and the encouragement of significant others can in some circumstances overcome the negative influence of socioeconomic disadvantage.

Ethnic Differences In Educational Achievement

Among the most controversial and intriguing findings in research on adolescents' achievement concern ethnic differences in school success. On average, the educational achievement of Black and Hispanic students—virtually however indexed—lags behind that of White students, and all three groups achieve less in school than Asian students. Although some of these differences can be attributed to socioeconomic differences among these ethnic groups, the group disparities persist even after socioeconomic factors are taken into account (Fuligni, Hughes, & Way, 2009).

The academic superiority of Asian students tends to emerge during the transition into junior high school—when most other students' grades typically decline—and it persists through high school and into college (Fuligni, 1994; Fuligni & Witkow, 2004). What has been most intriguing to social scientists is that Black and Hispanic students have educational aspirations and attitudes that are similar to those of Asian and White students but significantly poorer academic skills, habits, and behavior (Ainsworth-Darnell & Downey, 1998). If Black and Hispanic students have the same long-term goals as other students, why don't they behave in similar ways?

False Optimism Rather Than Realistic Pessimism
Several theories have been advanced to explain this finding. One set of theories involves the perceptions that adolescents have about the likely payoff of hard work in school. Some writers have argued that even though they have high aspirations in the abstract, many minority youth do not believe that educational success will have a substantial occupational payoff for them, because discrimination and prejudice will limit their actual opportunities (Mickelson, 1990). Although intuitively appealing, this theory has not received convincing empirical support (Fuligni et al., 2009; Herman, 2009). It is true that adolescents who believe they have been victims of discrimination, or who believe that their opportunities for occupational success are unfairly constrained, achieve less in school and report more emotional distress than their peers who do not hold these beliefs (C. Fisher, Wallace, & Fenton, 2000; P. Wood & Clay, 1996). It is also true that students who are more confident about and oriented to the future do better in school (Beal & Crockett, 2010; W. T. Brown & Jones, 2004; Oyserman, Bybee, & Terry, 2006).

But it is not true that Black or Hispanic youngsters are more likely than other adolescents to believe that their opportunities for success are blocked (Ainsworth-Darnell & Downey, 1998; D. Downey & Ainsworth-Darnell, 2002; Kao & Tienda, 1998). Indeed, several studies indicate that Black and Hispanic youth have *more* optimistic beliefs and positive feelings about school than other students (e.g., Ainsworth-Darnell & Downey, 1998; D. Downey, Ainsworth, & Qian, 2009; Shernoff & Schmidt, 2008; Voelkl, 1997). Plus, some research suggests that beliefs about the likelihood of future discrimination may motivate adolescents to perform better in school (perhaps because they feel that they will need to be even better prepared than others to overcome prejudicial treatment), although feeling discriminated against in the present, by classmates or teachers, hinders academic achievement (perhaps by causing psychological distress or hopelessness) (Benner, Crosnoe, & Eccles, 2014; Mattison & Aber, 2007). All in all, however, adolescents' hopes and aspirations for the future are very similar across ethnic groups (Chang, Chen, Greenberger, Dooley, & Heckhausen, 2006).

If anything, it may be adolescents' fear of failure, rather than their desire (or lack of desire) to succeed, that matters most (Steinberg, Dornbusch, & Brown, 1992). Asian youngsters not only believe in the value of school success but also are very anxious about the possible negative repercussions of not doing well in school, in terms of both occupational success and their parents' disappointment (Eaton & Dembo, 1997; Herman, 2009; Steinberg, 1996). Moreover, many Asian youth believe that the only way they can succeed in mainstream American society is through educational achievement (Sue & Okazaki, 1990). Asian students' sense of obligation to their parents—a factor frequently suggested as a reason for their high rates of school success—does not seem to play a very important role in predicting school achievement. If anything, being expected to assist the family by performing household chores and other family work—something that is especially salient in Asian and Hispanic households—has a negative impact on school performance (Fuligni, Tseng, & Lam, 1999; Telzer & Fuligni, 2009).

The Burden of "Acting White"   Another popular explanation for ethnic differences in achievement is that ethnic minority students underperform in school because they are stigmatized for "acting White" if they try to do well and, as a consequence, develop an "oppositional" identity that is hostile to doing well in school (Fordham & Ogbu, 1986). This view has not held up, however, perhaps because the extent of this negative peer pressure varies from school to school and from peer group to peer group (Lynch, Lerner, & Leventhal, 2013). Black peer groups are not all the same, and while some may disparage academic achievement, many admire it. Here's how one academically successful Black student replied when asked if students from different peer groups treated her differently:

> I think, yes. The black people who, say, aren't as smart as me or Renée or whoever else they say, "Oh, you act white" because we're in high classes or whatever, and that really upsets me. They say we talk white. I don't even have like proper English or whatever, but they say we talk white because we use all these big words and everything. To me, that's total ignorance.

When asked to describe her own friends, however, she said:

> They're always, "I'm so proud of you. You have a job, you're still in school, and you're not pregnant." All this other good stuff. But it makes me feel good. (Horvat & Lewis, 2003, pp. 270–272)

Another successful student from the same school noted that even her friends who had dropped out of school in the 8th or 9th grade were supportive of her achievement:

> They just treat me as one of them. School's not a subject that really comes up as far as my neighborhood is concerned. They'll say, "How was your day at school?" "Fine." They accept me for what I am and what I do. If I am smart, I am smart. It seems they really congratulated

me, if anything, especially now. So many of my friends have told me, "I'm so proud of you." Basically pushing me on. (Horvat & Lewis, 2003, p. 272)

Ethnic Differences in Beliefs   A third account of ethnic differences in achievement stresses differences in beliefs about ability. We noted earlier that adolescents who believe that intelligence is malleable are more likely to be intrinsically motivated and, as a consequence, academically successful. It is therefore interesting that Asian cultures tend to place more emphasis on effort than on ability in explaining school success and are more likely to believe that all students have the capacity to succeed (H. Stevenson & Stigler, 1992). By and large, students from Asian backgrounds tend to be more invested in mastering the material than in simply performing well—an orientation that, as we saw earlier, contributes to school success (J. Li, 2006). It is also important to note that Asian students—both in the United States and in Asia— spend significantly more time each week than their peers on homework and other school-related activities, and significantly less time socializing and watching television (Asakawa & Csikszentmihalyi, 2000; Fuligni & Stevenson, 1995; Steinberg, 1996).

Contrary to popular belief, Asian students do not pay a price for their superior achievement in terms of increased anxiety, depression, stress, or social awkwardness; the suicide rate among American teenagers is higher than it is among Asian youth, for example (Wasserman, Cheng, & Jiang, 2005). During regular periods of school in the United States, Asian students' moods while studying are significantly more positive than those of other students (Asakawa & Csikszentmihalyi, 1998), and the links between academic motivation and various indices of happiness and adjustment are stronger among Asian adolescents than other youth (Asakawa & Csikszentmihalyi, 2000). Among Asian students more than their peers from other ethnic groups, then, engagement in academics is linked to positive emotion and well-being.

The Success of Immigrants   There are large and important variations in achievement within as well as between ethnic groups. First, there are differences in educational achievement among youngsters from different countries of origin who may be classified together by researchers into the same larger ethnic group for purposes of statistical comparison. For example, although both groups are classified as Asian, Chinese American adolescents have much higher academic achievement than Filipino Americans; similarly, there are large differences in academic achievement among Puerto Rican, Cuban American, and Mexican American adolescents, all of whom are classified as Hispanic (Fuligni et al., 2009).

Second, studies of ethnic minority youngsters show that foreign-born adolescents, as well as those who are children of immigrants, tend to be more cognitively

One reason Asian students outperform adolescents from other ethnic groups is the belief that success in school is a function of how hard one works. © Gary Conner/PhotoEdit

engaged (although less socially engaged) and achieve more in school than do minority youngsters who are second- or third-generation Americans, a finding that has now emerged in many studies of Asian, Latino, and Caribbean youth (Chiu, Pong, Mori, & Chow, 2012; Fuligni et al., 2009; Lansford, 2011). One explanation for the so-called "immigrant paradox" has been that part of becoming acculturated to American society—at least among teenagers—may be learning to devalue academic success (Santiago, Gudiño, Baweja, & Nadeem, 2014). There is also some evidence that the higher school achievement of immigrant youth—at least among adolescents who have immigrated from Mexico—may be due to the higher quality of the schooling they receive before coming to the United States (Padilla & Gonzalez, 2001). The exceptional achievement of immigrant youth is all the more remarkable in light of the fact that these adolescents typically have much greater family obligations—providing financial support to their parents, for instance—than their American-born peers (Fuligni & Witkow, 2004). A stronger sense of family obligation contributes to, rather than interferes with, school success (Chang, 2013; Roche, Ghazarian, & Fernandez-Esquer, 2012; van Geel & Vedder, 2011).

making the cultural connection

Many immigrant adolescents in the United States achieve more in school than their counterparts from the same ethnic group who were born in America—despite the fact that adolescents who are immigrants often arrive without proficiency in English or familiarity with American culture. How do you account for this?

Third, and most important, within all ethnic groups, students achieve more when they feel a sense of belonging to their school, when they see the connection between academic accomplishment and future success, when their friends and parents value and support educational achievement, and when their parents are effective monitors of their children's behavior and schooling (Chun & Dickson, 2011; Hernández, Robins, Widaman, & Conger, 2014). The especially close and supportive relationships characteristic of immigrant families likely contribute to school success (Suárez-Orozco, Rhodes, & Milburn, 2009).

Changes in Educational Achievement Over Time

Today, three-fourths of high school graduates enroll in college, two-thirds of them immediately after graduation (National Center for Education Statistics, 2015). Although ethnic differences in educational attainment have narrowed over the past 40 years, there remain substantial gaps in attainment between White and non-White individuals, and especially between White and Hispanic individuals. Thus, whereas 35% of all non-Hispanic White adults ages 25 and over, and more than 50% of all Asian adults of this age, are college graduates, slightly more than 20% of Black adults and only 15% of Hispanic adults are (U.S. Census Bureau, 2014). Discrepancies in rates of high school graduation between Hispanic and non-Hispanic Americans are also substantial—90% of non-Hispanic White adults have completed high school, compared with 82% of Blacks and 89% of Asian Americans, but only 64% of Hispanic adults

National Assessment of Educational Progress (NAEP)

A periodic testing of American 4th-, 8th-, and 12th-graders by the federal government, used to track achievement.

have (U.S. Census Bureau, 2014). In light of the rapidly increasing size of the Latino population in the United States, the gap in educational attainment between Latinos and non-Latinos is one of the most important challenges facing American educational institutions.

More Schooling, But Less Learning Trends in academic achievement (what students know) have not paralleled trends in educational attainment (how many years of schooling they have completed). In other words, although more students are staying in school longer, they are not necessarily learning more. For example, as Figure 5 indicates, between 1970 and 1980, average scores on the Scholastic Assessment Test (SAT) declined by about 35 points on the verbal portion and 20 points on the math. Scores remained more or less flat between 1980 and 1990, when math (but not verbal) scores began to rise. Verbal, math, and writing scores all dropped slightly from 2005 on. (The one exception to this general trend is among Asian students, whose scores on both subscales have risen substantially in the last 10 years.) Moreover, the gap in SAT scores between Black and Hispanic students on the one hand, and Asian and White students on the other, remains substantial and virtually unchanged over the past two decades (College Board, 2014).

The relatively poor showing of American adolescents on standardized tests of achievement has been carefully documented in a series of reports based on the **National Assessment of Educational Progress (NAEP).** This national assessment of student achievement is conducted by the federal government in order to track trends in educational achievement over time. Because the NAEP tests have been administered regularly for more than 40 years, it is possible to compare the achievement levels of today's adolescents with their counterparts 4 decades ago.

Figure 5 Changes in SAT scores over time. (College Board, 2014)

High school graduation year of examinee

According to recent NAEP reports, over the past 45 years adolescent achievement in reading, writing, math, and science has improved only slightly among 13-year-olds and not at all among 17-year-olds, despite massive national efforts at education reform. This is consistent with other trends in achievement data, which show that American elementary and middle school students have been making gains, but that high school student achievement has not improved at all (Steinberg, 2014). Contemporary 17-year-olds, for example, score no better than their counterparts did in the early 1970s in reading or math, and *worse* than their counterparts did in science. Perhaps more importantly, most analyses of the NAEP data indicate that the modest gains in achievement that have occurred during recent years have been in relatively simple skills. Only a handful of students, at any age, or in any subject area, score at a level that is designated "advanced" or "superior," whereas large proportions of students score in the lowest category, "below basic." When gains have been made (and they are generally very small), they tend to be in the proportion of students who have moved from the basic into the "proficient" range, rather than from "proficient" to "advanced."

As is the case in rates of high school graduation and SAT scores, the gap in achievement test performance among ethnic groups narrowed during the 1970s, but a wide disparity still exists. The achievement gap did not shrink at all during the 1980s, widened a bit during the 1990s, and has not changed since then (National Center for Education Statistics, 2013). About three times as many White and Asian middle school students score in the proficient range in reading, for example, as do Black students, and more than twice as many White and Asian students score in the proficient range as do Hispanic students. The gaps are even larger in math. Obviously, the achievement gap has important implications for the labor market success of adolescents from different ethnic groups.

International Competitions Although the poor achievement test performance of Black and Latino students is certainly cause for concern, there is no reason to be sanguine about the performance of White high school students. Since the 1970s, their achievement test scores have remained more or less stagnant, and U.S. scores on standardized tests of math and science are mediocre in comparison with scores of other industrialized countries. More interestingly, the gap between American students' performance and that of students from other countries widens as they move from elementary to middle to high school. That is, when elementary school students from around the world are compared, American students fare just about as well as students from other countries. When middle school students are compared, Americans perform more poorly than their counterparts

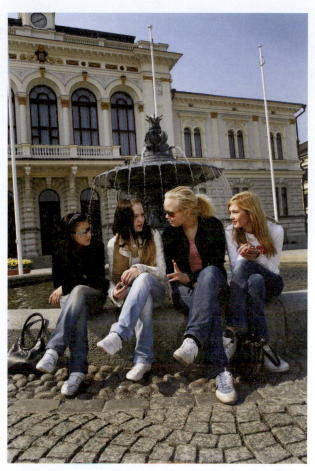

On tests of achievement, American high school students lag behind those from many European countries. © Martin Thomas Photography/Alamy

from most industrialized Asian countries, but at a level comparable to young adolescents from most western European countries, and considerably better than adolescents from less developed nations (National Center for Education Statistics, 2009). But when the comparison focuses on high school students, the gap between the United States and other countries is substantial (J. Schmidt, 2003). According to recent international comparisons, 15-year-olds in the United States ranked slightly above average in reading, well below average in science, and near the bottom of the list in math (OECD, 2014a) (see Table 1).

The relatively poor performance of American high school students in international competitions persists despite the fact that spending on education in the United States is among the world's highest (OECD, 2014b). Despite how much is spent, at 4-year American colleges and universities, 20% of entering college freshmen require some sort of remedial education in order to do college-level work; at community colleges, half of all entering students do. As a result, employers and postsecondary educational institutions alike today devote vast amounts of money to remedial education—colleges and universities spend an estimated $3 billion annually

Table 1 An International Education Test: Results of 2012 PISA (Program for International Student Assessment) of 15-year-old students in selected countries. (OECD, 2014a)

	Mathematics	Reading	Science
	Mean score in PISA 2012	Mean score in PISA 2012	Mean score in PISA 2012
China	613	570	580
Korea	554	536	538
Japan	536	538	547
Netherlands	523	511	522
Finland	519	524	545
Canada	518	523	525
Germany	514	508	524
Australia	504	512	521
Denmark	500	496	498
France	495	505	499
United Kingdom	494	499	514
Norway	489	504	495
Italy	485	490	494
Russian Federation	482	475	486
United States	481	498	497
Sweden	478	483	485
Israel	466	486	470
Turkey	448	475	463
United Arab Emirates	434	442	448
Chile	423	441	445
Mexico	413	424	415
Costa Rica	407	441	429
Brazil	391	410	405
Jordan	386	399	409
Colombia	376	403	399

covering subject matter that students should have mastered before graduating from high school (Complete College, 2012). And, as astounding as it may sound, more than 80% of college students enrolled in remedial education graduated from high school with a GPA of 3.0 or better (Strong American Schools, 2008).

If more American students are remaining in high school, and so many are going on to college, why are their achievement test scores so low according to absolute, historical, and international standards? Experts suggest several reasons: that teachers are not challenging students to work hard; that very little time is spent on writing; that there has been a pervasive decline in the difficulty of textbooks; that parents are not encouraging academic pursuits at home; that students are not spending sufficient time on their studies outside of school; that students are permitted to choose what courses they take;

and that students know that, thanks to "grade inflation," they can earn good grades without working very hard (Steinberg, 2014).

Dropping Out of High School

There was a time when leaving high school before graduating did not have the dire consequences that it does today. With changes in the labor force, however, have come changes in the educational requirements for entry into the world of work. Today, educational attainment is a powerful predictor of adult occupational success and earnings. High school dropouts are far more likely than graduates to live at or near the poverty level, to experience unemployment, to depend on government-subsidized income maintenance programs, to become pregnant while still a teenager, and

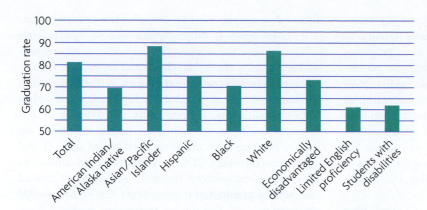

Figure 6 High school graduation rates of American adolescents (based on data from EDfacts). (National Center for Education Statistics, 2015)

to be involved in delinquent and criminal activity (Rumberger, 2012).

Because there are different ways of counting dropouts, different studies often report very different figures. For example, many students drop out of school temporarily but return in their early 20s and obtain a diploma or GED—so while these students would be classified as dropouts at the age of 17, they would be classified as graduates if they were surveyed just a few years later. A few years ago, the U.S. Department of Education began measuring high school graduation rates using a new metric, which is the proportion of students who graduate high school on time (i.e., in 4 years). As you can see from Figure 6, although more than 80% of American adolescents graduate from high school on time, there are wide variations in graduation rates as a function of ethnicity and other background characteristics (National Center for Education Statistics, 2015).

Correlates of Dropping Out Given the findings on educational achievement discussed earlier, the other correlates of dropping out come as no surprise. Adolescents who leave high school before graduating are more likely to come from lower socioeconomic levels, poor communities, large families, single-parent families, permissive or disengaged families, and households where little reading material is available. In short, adolescents who drop out of school are more likely to come from backgrounds with limited **family capital,** which has three components: economic capital, social capital, and cultural capital (see Figure 7) (Waithaka, 2014).

Coupled with this disadvantage in background, adolescents who drop out of high school also are more likely to have a history of poor school performance, low school involvement, multiple changes of schools, poor performance on standardized tests of achievement and intelligence, negative school experiences, and a variety of emotional and behavioral problems, some of which contribute to academic failure and some of which result from it. Many high school dropouts had to repeat one or

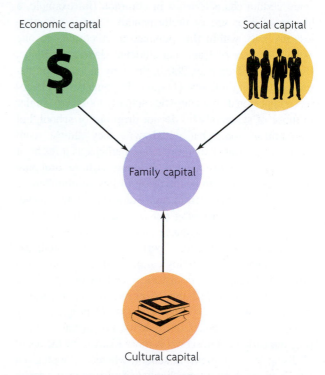

Figure 7 Families provide three kinds of capital: economic, social, and cultural. (adapted from Waithaka, 2014)

more grades in elementary school; indeed, having been held back is one of the strongest predictors of dropping out (Qiroga, Janosz, Bisset, & Morin, 2013; Rumberger, 2012; Wang & Fredricks, 2014).

In other words, dropping out of high school is not so much a discrete decision made during the adolescent years as it is the culmination of a long process (Rumberger, 2012; Sweeten, Bushway, & Paternoster, 2009). Specific factors may instigate a student's final decision to leave school—a suspension for misbehavior, a failed course, an unintended pregnancy, the lure of a job—but by and large, dropping out is a process characterized by a history of repeated academic

family capital
The economic, social, and cultural resources provided by the family.

failure and increasing alienation from school (Henry et al., 2012). While programs designed to enhance adolescents' academic skills have been largely unsuccessful in preventing dropping out, one approach that has met with success has focused on involving at-risk adolescents in service learning and in guided discussions of their life options, which may help them see how important it is to graduate from high school (J. Allen, Philliber, Herrling, & Kuperminc, 1997).

Although adolescents who drop out of school often share certain characteristics in common (for example, a history of poor school performance), there is nevertheless diversity within this population. According to one extensive study of Canadian students (Janosz, LeBlanc, Boulerice, & Tremblay, 2000), there are at least four distinct groups of dropouts: (1) quiet dropouts (whose histories and personal characteristics actually look very similar to those of students who do not drop out of school, but who appear somewhat withdrawn—they almost seem to "fade out" rather than drop out, perhaps as a result of depression), (2) disengaged dropouts (whose dropping out appears mainly to be the result of low commitment to school and poor academic motivation), (3) low-achiever dropouts (whose dropping out is primarily the result of very poor school performance), and (4) maladjusted dropouts (whose dropping out is part of a larger constellation of behavioral and psychological problems). The idea that different developmental histories lead to dropping out is important to the design of preventive interventions, because it suggests that different sorts of programs may work for different sorts of students. For instance, dropping out early in high school is more likely to be the result of disciplinary problems at school, whereas dropping out later in high school is more likely to be driven by the desire to work (Stearns & Glennie, 2006). Other studies indicate that it is important to distinguish between students who temporarily drop out of school but return at some later point and obtain their GED—as do between one-third and one-half of all dropouts—and those who leave and never return (Entwisle, Alexander, & Olson, 2004).

making the practical connection

Based on what we know about the causes and consequences of dropping out, what steps should be taken to reduce the dropout rate?

School Factors Although most research on the causes of dropping out has focused on characteristics of adolescents who leave school prematurely, some studies have focused on the schools that dropouts leave (Rumberger, 2012). In general, dropping out is less likely from schools where the environment is orderly, where academic pursuits are emphasized, and where the faculty is supportive and committed (V. Lee & Burkam, 2003). Students who are at particularly high risk of dropping out (low-achieving, economically disadvantaged, and foreign-born Hispanic youth) are helped especially by having teachers who are sources of social support and guidance (Enriquez, 2011). Although some educators have expressed concern about the recent trend toward toughening graduation requirements and ending **social promotion**—the practice of promoting students from one grade to the next on the basis of age rather than actual achievement—evaluations of policies such as the use of high school exit examinations to determine whether students can graduate show that they do not increase the rate of dropping out or differentially affect minority and White students (Warren, Grodsky, & Lee, 2008; Warren & Jenkins, 2005).

Occupational Achievement

School, rather than work, is the setting in which achievement is most often studied by contemporary scholars interested in adolescence. Although many individuals in previous generations began their occupational careers during adolescence, this is very rare today in most industrialized societies, where the majority of individuals pursue some form of postsecondary education before entering into full-time work. With the exception of apprenticeships, which are popular in only a handful of European countries, the work individuals perform during adolescence is rarely relevant to their future careers; it is mainly a means of earning spending money. Work experiences in adolescence, in general, have little or no impact on adolescents' plans or aspirations for adult work, especially among students from nonpoor families (Entwisle, Alexander, & Olson, 2005; M. Johnson, 2002), although it is possible that the small minority of adolescents who hold "good" jobs may learn something about their career interests from them. Fast food, restaurant, and retail jobs provide the fewest opportunities to build career-related skills, whereas office and clerical jobs are among the best (Staff, Messersmith, & Schulenberg, 2009).

Researchers who are interested in occupational achievement during adolescence have examined several issues, including the ways in which young people make decisions about their careers and the influences on their occupational aspirations and expectations. We begin with a look at the development of adolescents' occupational plans.

The Development of Occupational Plans

In many respects, the development of occupational plans during adolescence parallels the identity development process (Skorikov & Vondracek, 2007; Staff et al., 2009). Occupational development follows a sequence that involves an examination of one's traits, abilities, and interests; a period of experimentation with different work roles; and an integration of influences from one's past (primarily, identification with familial role models) with one's hopes for the future. And as is also the case with identity development, the development of an occupational identity is profoundly influenced by the social environment in which it takes place.

Changes in the broader environment in which adolescents develop—in this case, changes in the need for and accessibility of higher education—have exerted a powerful influence on the developmental course of occupational planning. For many individuals, the development of occupational plans may not take place until the final years of college, and deciding on a specific career may not even begin until well after college graduation.

Influences on Occupational Choices

What makes one individual choose to become an attorney and another decide to be a teacher? Why do some students pursue careers in psychology while others major in engineering? Researchers have long been interested in the reasons that individuals end up in certain careers (Neuenschwander & Kracke, 2011).

Work Values When you think about your future work, what will you look for in a job? **Work values** refer to the sorts of rewards individuals seek from their jobs (e.g., M. Johnson, 2002). For example, are you most interested in making a lot of money, in having a secure job, or in having a job that permits you to have a lot of vacation time? According to most theories of work values, seven basic types of work rewards define individuals' work values: extrinsic rewards (earning a high income), security (enjoying job stability), intrinsic rewards (being able to be creative or to learn things from work), influence (having authority over others or power over decision making), altruistic rewards (helping others), social rewards (working with people you like), and leisure (having an opportunity for free time or vacation). Individuals choose jobs based on the relative importance of these various work rewards to them (see Table 2).

Many contemporary adolescents have unrealistic and overly ambitious ideas about the rewards they will derive from their future work. A very large proportion of adolescents aspire to levels of work rewards that they are highly unlikely to attain (Schneider & Stevenson, 1999). One problem is that adolescents tend to rate almost all work rewards very highly, optimistically believing that they can find jobs that satisfy multiple rewards simultaneously. When they actually enter their first full-time adult jobs, though, they soon discover that it is difficult, if not impossible, to have a career in which one makes a lot of money, is creative, helps other people, enjoys job security, and has a lot of free time.

Over the course of young adulthood, one of the most important changes that occurs in the domain of occupational development is that individuals become both somewhat disillusioned and more focused on what they want from a job, abandoning the unrealistic notion that one can "have it all" (B. Roberts, O'Donnell, & Robins, 2004). As adolescents move into young adulthood, the degrees to which they value the extrinsic, altruistic, and social rewards of jobs, which are all strongly valued when individuals are seniors in high school, decline most dramatically, whereas the values they place on intrinsic rewards and job security, which are also strong at the end of high school, remain strong (M. Johnson, 2002) (see Figure 8).

> **work values**
> The particular sorts of rewards an individual looks for in a job (extrinsic, intrinsic, social, altruistic, security, influence, leisure).

Table 2 People look for different things in a job. Which types of rewards are most important to you?

Type of Reward	Example
Extrinsic	Earning a good income
Security	Enjoying job stability
Intrinsic	Having opportunities for creativity
Influence	Wielding power over others
Altruistic	Helping others
Social	Enjoying one's coworkers
Leisure	Having opportunities for vacation or time off

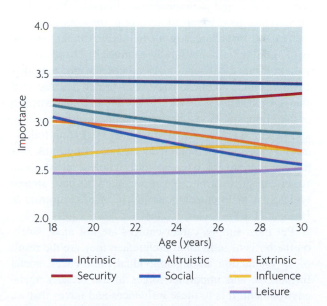

Figure 8 As adolescents move into young adulthood, the value they place on the extrinsic, altruistic, and social rewards of a job declines, whereas the value they place on intrinsic job rewards and job security remains strong. (Johnson, 2002)

occupational attainment
A measure of achievement based on the status or prestige of the job an individual holds.

There are important limitations to theories of career choice that are based solely on reward preferences assessed in adolescence. First, interests and abilities are not fixed during adolescence, but continue to develop and change during the adult years, and one of the most important influences on personality development during adulthood is work itself (M. Johnson, 2002). Through working in a job that emphasizes certain personality characteristics, requires certain abilities, or provides certain types of rewards, individuals begin to change their personality, skills, and values. A job that seems like a bad match during early adulthood may over time become a good match. For example, someone may not be especially interested in a job that involves a lot of social interaction but may, because of a tight job market, end up in a teaching position after graduating from college. Over time, the more he interacts with students, the more appealing the interpersonal aspects of the job may become. Eventually, he may come to feel that having opportunities for social interaction on the job is very important.

A second problem with theories of career choice that emphasize adolescents' work values is that they may underestimate the importance of other factors that influence and shape vocational decisions, most importantly, the social context in which adolescents make career decisions (Staff et al., 2009). Many career decisions are influenced more by individuals' beliefs about what sorts of jobs are accessible or "appropriate" for them than by their interests and preferences (M. Johnson, 2002). It is all well and good for an adolescent to discover that he is well suited for a career in medicine, but the realization is of little value if his family cannot afford the cost of college or medical school. An adolescent girl may discover through taking a vocational preference test that she is well suited for work in the area of construction or building, but find that her parents, peers, teachers, and potential employers all discourage her from following this avenue of employment because they think it is not appropriate for women. Early adolescent Mexican American girls, in particular, are likely to have stereotypically female career goals (N. E. Hill, Ramirez, & Dumka, 2003).

Put most simply, career choices are not made solely on the basis of individual preference; they are the result of an interaction among individual preferences, social influences, and important forces in the broader social environment. It is to these influences and forces that we now turn.

The Influence of Parents and Peers No influence on occupational choice is stronger than socioeconomic status, and as a result, adolescents' occupational ambitions and achievements are highly correlated with the ambitions and achievements of those around them (Ashby & Schoon, 2012). Youngsters from middle-class families are more likely than their less advantaged peers to aspire to and enter middle-class occupations. Socioeconomic status also influences work values, with individuals from higher classes more likely to value intrinsic rewards and influence and less likely to value extrinsic rewards and security. The importance of social class as a determinant of what people look for in their jobs is strong and constant throughout adolescence and young adulthood (M. Johnson, 2002).

A variety of explanations have been offered for the fit between adolescents' ambitions and the socioeconomic status of those around them. First, and perhaps most important, **occupational attainment**—the prestige or status an individual achieves in the world of work—depends strongly on educational attainment (Elmore, 2009). As we saw earlier, educational attainment is greatly influenced by socioeconomic status. Because middle-class adolescents are likely to complete more years of schooling than their lower-class peers, economically advantaged adolescents are more likely to seek and enter higher-status occupations.

Second, middle-class parents, as noted earlier, are more likely to raise their children in ways that foster the development of strong achievement orientation and career exploration (Kracke, 2002). The development of achievement motivation, which has an impact on school performance, also has an impact on youngsters' occupational ambitions—both directly (in that individuals with strong needs for achievement will express these needs by aspiring to occupations that provide opportunities to achieve status or wealth) and indirectly, through the effects of achievement motivation on academic achievement (in that youngsters who are successful in school are likely to be encouraged to seek higher-status occupations and engage in identity exploration). Parents influence their adolescents' career aspirations mainly by influencing their educational achievement (Jodl et al., 2001).

Third, the same opportunities that favor economically advantaged youngsters in the world of education—better facilities, more opportunities for enrichment, greater accessibility of higher education—also favor middle-class youngsters in the world of work. Because their parents are more likely to work in positions of power and leadership, middle-class youngsters often have important family connections and sources of information about the world of work that are less available to youngsters from poorer families. In addition, coming from a family that is economically well off may provide an adolescent with more time to explore career options and to wait for an especially desirable position, rather than having to take the first job that becomes available out of economic necessity. This advantage is particularly

An individual's choice of occupation is influenced by many factors, including the work values he or she has. Contextual factors, such as job opportunities, are important as well.
© Lars A. Niki RF

important during economic downturns, when it is relatively more difficult to find employment.

Fourth, parents, siblings, and other important sources of influence serve as models for adolescents' occupational choices. Although some young people establish career choices through the explicit rejection of their parents' careers, adolescents' and parents' vocations are more similar than different, particularly when the adolescent's family relationships have been warm and close and when strong identifications have formed between the adolescent and his or her parents.

Finally, parents—and, to a lesser extent, peers—influence adolescents' occupational plans by creating a context in which certain occupational choices are encouraged and others are discouraged (Kohn, 1977). Middle-class families and middle-class schools encourage children to value autonomy, self-direction, and independence—three features that are more likely to be found in middle-class than in working-class jobs. Middle-class children are told, implicitly and explicitly, how important it is to have freedom, power, and status. Adolescents who have been raised to value attributes that are characteristic of middle-class jobs will seek those attributes when they plan their careers.

In working-class families, children are more likely to be raised to value obedience and conformity—two characteristics that are highly valued in most working-class jobs. For people from this socioeconomic background, jobs that appeal to these values will be relatively more attractive. They will have been raised to value such things as job security and not having to worry too much about making high-pressured decisions. Indeed, to many working-class youngsters, the high-stress world of the business executive is not at all an attractive career possibility.

The Broader Context of Occupational Choice

Adolescents' occupational choices are made, of course, within a broader social context that profoundly influences the nature of their plans (Staff et al., 2009). Today's young people see work as a less central part of life than their counterparts did in the past. Contemporary young people, for example, are more likely than past generations to say that if they had enough money, they would not work; that they are less willing to work overtime to make sure their job was done well; and that it is important to have a job that allows sufficient time for leisure (Wray-Lake, Syvertsen, Briddell, Osgood, & Flanagan, 2009).

At different times, different employment opportunities arise, and young people—particularly by the time they reach the end of their formal schooling—are often very aware of the prospects for employment in different fields. One study of inner-city youngsters found that many had developed ideas about their future job prospects by the time they were in 2nd grade (T. Cook et al., 1996). Young people often tailor their plans in response to what they perceive as the future needs and demands of the labor market and the acceptability of given occupational choices within their community. In addition, whether an adolescent's occupational expectations are actually realized depends on many factors that are not in his or her control (as anyone graduating during the economic downturn of the last decade could certainly attest).

Unfortunately, adolescents also tailor their plans based on their beliefs regarding which jobs society says are "acceptable" for individuals of particular social class, ethnicity, or sex (M. Johnson, 2002). One manifestation of this is seen in the disproportionate numbers of males in jobs in the sciences. (see Figure 9). Although sex differences in the value adolescents place on extrinsic rewards are small, there are significant sex differences in the extent to which individuals value power (associated with masculine jobs, and more valued by males) and altruism (associated with feminine jobs, and more valued by females) (M. Johnson, 2002; Weisgram, Bigler, & Liben, 2010). Moreover, many more adolescent girls than boys express concern about having to balance family and work demands in adulthood, and this further affects their occupational decision making, since they may be reluctant to pursue careers that they believe will interfere with family life (Cinamon & Rich, 2002). Perhaps because of this, adolescent boys' occupational expectations are predictive of what they actually end up doing as adults, whereas this is not the case for adolescent girls (Mello, 2008).

One problem faced by all young people in making career plans is obtaining accurate information about the labor market needs of the future and the appropriate means of pursuing positions in various fields. The majority of young people do not have educational plans that are consistent with the educational requirements of the jobs they hope to enter, and many adolescents

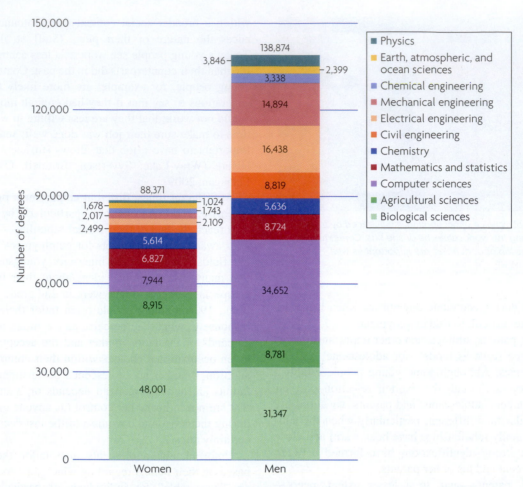

Figure 9 Bachelor's degrees earned in selected science and engineering fields, by gender, 2007. Although gender roles have changed considerably in recent decades, there remain large sex differences in occupational choices.
(Hill, Corbett, & Rose, 2010)

are overly optimistic about their chances for success (Chang et al., 2006; Schneider & Stevenson, 1999). One goal of career educators is to help adolescents make more informed and more realistic choices about their careers and to free them from stereotypes that constrain their choices. Career counselors, especially on college campuses, have come to play an increasingly important role in individuals' career decision making, because the rapid pace at which the labor market changes has made it less likely that adolescents will be able to obtain accurate information from their family (Staff et al., 2009).

Psychosocial Problems in Adolescence

13

Some General Principles about Problems in Adolescence

Psychosocial Problems: Their Nature and Covariation

    Comorbidity of Externalizing Problems

    Comorbidity of Internalizing Problems

Substance Use and Abuse

    Prevalence of Substance Use and Abuse

    Causes and Consequences of Substance Use and Abuse

    Drugs and the Adolescent Brain

    Prevention and Treatment of Substance Use and Abuse

Externalizing Problems

    Categories of Externalizing Problems

    Developmental Progression of Antisocial Behavior

    Changes in Juvenile Offending Over Time

    Causes of Antisocial Behavior

    Prevention and Treatment of Externalizing Problems

Internalizing Problems

    The Nature and Prevalence of Depression

    Sex Differences in Depression

    Suicide and Non-Suicidal Self-Injury

    Causes of Depression and Internalizing Disorders

    Treatment and Prevention of Internalizing Problems

Stress and Coping

© Comstock/PunchStock RF

Although the majority of young people move through the adolescent years without major difficulty, some experience serious psychological and behavioral problems, such as substance abuse, delinquency, and depression, that disrupt not only their lives but also the lives of those around them. These problems indirectly touch the lives of all of us, either directly, through the personal contact we may have with a troubled young person, or indirectly, through increased taxes for community services or heightened anxiety about the safety of our neighborhoods. In this chapter, we look at some of the more serious psychological problems we typically associate with adolescence.

Some General Principles about Problems in Adolescence

The mass media like nothing more than to paint extreme pictures of the world in which we live. This exaggerated view is obvious in the presentation of teenage problem behavior. Rarely are popular portrayals of adolescents' behavioral disorders, psychological distress, or drug use accurate: A breakup with a boyfriend is followed that evening by a suicide attempt. An after-school prank develops into a life of crime. A weekend of heavy drinking fades into a commercial, and when the program returns, the adolescent is on his way to a life of addiction, delinquency, and school failure. Those of you for whom adolescence was not that long ago know that these "facts" about adolescent problem behavior are rarely true. But we are so often bombarded with images of young people in trouble that it is easy to be fooled into believing that "adolescence" equals "problems."

We should not gloss over the fact that many healthy adolescents at one time or another experience self-doubt, family squabbles, academic setbacks, or broken hearts, of course. But it is important to keep in mind as we look at psychosocial problems during adolescence that there is an important distinction between the normative, and usually transitory, difficulties encountered by many young people and the serious psychosocial problems experienced by a minority of youth. One of the purposes of this chapter is to put these problems in perspective. It's helpful, before we look at several specific categories of problems in detail, to lay out some general principles about adolescent psychosocial problems that apply to all of them.

Most Problems Reflect Transitory Experimentation
First, let's distinguish between occasional experimentation and enduring patterns of dangerous or troublesome behavior. Rates of occasional, usually harmless, experimentation far exceed rates of enduring problems. The majority of adolescents experiment with alcohol sometime before high school graduation, and the majority will have been drunk at least once. But, as we'll see, relatively few teenagers develop drinking problems or permit alcohol to adversely affect their schooling or personal relationships, and as they move into adulthood, get married, and change their patterns of socializing, their drinking declines (Staff, Schulenberg et al., 2010).

Similarly, although the vast majority of teenagers do something during adolescence that is against the law, very few of these young people go on to have criminal careers. In a period of development during which it is normal—maybe even expected—that individuals will seek independence and explore themselves and their relationships with others, it is hardly surprising that some of the experimentation in which individuals engage is risky (Hayden et al., 2011; Steinberg, 2008). In fact, adolescents who experiment occasionally with risky behavior report a quality of life that is more similar to that reported by adolescents who abstain from risk taking entirely than it is to the quality of life reported by frequent risk takers (Topolski et al., 2001).

It is important to differentiate between occasional experimentation with risky or unhealthful activities and enduring patterns of troublesome behavior. © BananaStock/PunchStock RF

Not All Problems Begin in Adolescence Second, let's distinguish between problems that have their origins and onset during adolescence, and those that have their roots during earlier periods of development (Drabick & Steinberg, 2011). Some teenagers fall into patterns of criminal or delinquent behavior during adolescence, and we tend to associate delinquency with the adolescent years. But most teenagers who have recurrent problems with the law had problems at home and at school from an early age; in some samples of delinquents, the problems were evident as early as preschool (Farrington, 2009; Hartung, Lefner, & Fedele, 2011). Many individuals who develop depression during adolescence suffered from other types of psychological distress, such as excessive anxiety, as children (Flynn & Rudolph, 2011; Graber & Sontag, 2009; Puelo, Settipani, Crawley, Beidas, & Kendall, 2011). According to a study of more than 10,000 American adolescents, although one-third of all teenagers report having had an anxiety disorder by age 18, almost all of these individuals had developed an anxiety disorder before turning 12. Similarly, of the 20% of adolescents who reported having had a behavioral disorder at some point in time, two-thirds had the first occurrence before entering adolescence (Merikangas et al., 2010) (see Figure 1). In other words, simply because a problem may be displayed *during* adolescence does not mean that it is a problem *of* adolescence.

Most Problems Do Not Persist into Adulthood

Third, it is important to remember that many of the behavioral problems experienced by adolescents are transitory and are resolved by the beginning of adulthood, with few long-term repercussions. Substance abuse, delinquency, and eating disorders are three good examples: Rates of drug and alcohol use, delinquency, and disordered eating are all higher within the adolescent population than in the adult population, but most individuals who abused drugs and alcohol, committed delinquent acts, or were bulimic as teenagers grow up to be sober, law-abiding adults without eating disorders. Nevertheless, we should not lose sight of the fact that adolescence is the most common age for the onset of a serious mental illness, or that 20% of adolescents have a mental illness that will persist into adulthood (Lee et al., 2014). Individuals for whom problem behavior persists into adulthood are likely to have had a problematic childhood as well as a problematic adolescence.

Problems During Adolescence Are Not Caused by Adolescence Finally, problem behavior during adolescence is virtually never a direct consequence of the normative changes of adolescence itself. Popular theories about "raging hormones" causing oppositional or deviant behavior have no scientific support whatsoever, nor do the widely held beliefs that problem behaviors are manifestations of an inherent need to rebel against authority or that bizarre behavior results from an identity crisis. The hormonal changes of puberty have only a modest direct effect on adolescent behavior; rebellion during adolescence is atypical, not normal; and few adolescents experience a tumultuous identity crisis. When a young person exhibits a serious psychosocial problem,

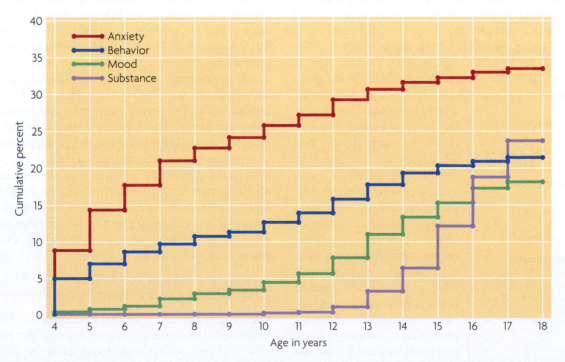

Figure 1 Anxiety disorders and behavioral disorders typically begin during childhood, whereas mood disorders and substance abuse first appear during adolescence. (Merikangas et al., 2010)

such as depression, the worst possible interpretation is that it is a normal part of growing up. It is more likely a sign that something is wrong.

Psychosocial Problems: Their Nature and Covariation

Clinical practitioners (psychologists, psychiatrists, social workers, and counselors) and other experts on the development and treatment of psychosocial problems during adolescence distinguish among three broad categories of problems: substance abuse, externalizing disorders, and internalizing disorders (Achenbach & Edelbrock, 1987). **Substance abuse** refers to the maladaptive use of drugs, including legal drugs like alcohol or nicotine; illegal drugs like marijuana (even in states that have legalized marijuana, it is still illegal for adolescents to use it without a prescription), cocaine, or ecstasy; and prescription drugs such as stimulants or sedatives. **Externalizing disorders** are those in which the young person's problems are turned outward and are manifested in behavioral problems (some writers use the expression "acting out" to refer to this set of problems). Common externalizing problems during adolescence are delinquency, antisocial aggression, and truancy. **Internalizing disorders** are those in which the young person's problems are turned inward and are manifested in emotional and cognitive distress, such as depression or anxiety.

Although we often think of adolescent substance abuse as an externalizing disorder, research indicates that it is just as likely to accompany depression and other internalizing disorders as it is to be a part of "acting out" behavior (Kleinjan, Rozing, Engels, & Verhagen, 2014; Scholes-Balog, Hemphill, Patton, & Toumbourou, 2015; Verona & Javdani, 2011; White, Fite, Pardini, Mun, & Loeber, 2013). We are simply more likely to be aware of substance abuse problems when they are seen among adolescents who are antisocial (such as a rowdy group of drunk delinquent youth) than when they occur along with internalizing problems (such as a depressed teenager who drinks herself to sleep each night). Because substance abuse problems co-occur, or are **comorbid,** with both externalizing and internalizing problems, and because many adolescents who experiment with drugs have neither internalizing nor externalizing problems, we look at substance abuse as a separate category of problem behavior.

substance abuse
The misuse of alcohol or other drugs to a degree that causes problems in the individual's life.

externalizing disorders
Psychosocial problems that are manifested in a turning of the symptoms outward, as in aggression or delinquency.

internalizing disorders
Psychosocial problems that are manifested in a turning of the symptoms inward, as in depression or anxiety.

comorbid
Co-occurring, as when an individual has more than one problem at the same time.

While the distinction between internalizing disorders and externalizing disorders is useful for organizing information about psychosocial problems during adolescence, it is important to bear in mind that some adolescents experience problems in both domains simultaneously (Cosgrove, Rhee, Gelhorn, Boeldt, & Hewitt, 2011). Some adolescents who engage in delinquency or show other behavior problems also suffer from depression (Lee & Stone, 2012; Loeber & Burke, 2011; Reinke, Eddy, Dishion, & Reid, 2012). Many depressed or anxious adolescents, as well as many antisocial adolescents, also abuse drugs and alcohol (Coker, Smith, Westphal, Zonana, & McKee, 2014; Maslowsky, Schulenberg, & Zucker, 2014; Monahan, Rhew, Hawkins, & Brown, 2014).

It is important to distinguish among adolescents who exhibit one specific problem without any others (for example, depressed adolescents who do not have other internalizing or externalizing problems), adolescents who exhibit more than one problem within the same general category (for example, violent delinquent youth or anxious-depressed youth), and adolescents who exhibit both internalizing and externalizing problems (for example, depressed delinquents). Multiproblem adolescents tend not only to have more problems, but more *serious* problems (Kessler et al., 2012). These adolescents may have followed very different developmental pathways and may require very different types of treatment. Multiproblem teenagers typically have had far worse family experiences than those with one problem (R. Chen & Simons-Morton, 2009; Yong, Fleming, McCarty, & Catalano, 2014).

The links between co-occurring internalizing and externalizing problems are different among females than among males (Klostermann, Connell, & Stormshak, 2015; Kofler et al., 2011). In girls, more often than not, internalizing problems, like depression, usually precede conduct problems. Girls who are depressed often experience problems with their peers, which may lead them into antisocial peer groups, where their chances of developing conduct problems increase. Boys, on the other hand, are more likely to have conduct problems that lead to depression, often because their conduct problems lead to academic difficulties, which cause emotional distress. One important implication of research on comorbidity is that successfully treating one sort of problem (e.g., antisocial behavior) may also help reduce other sorts of problems as well (e.g., depression) (Monahan, Oesterle, Rhew, & Hawkins, 2014).

Comorbidity of Externalizing Problems

One of the reasons it is helpful to differentiate between internalizing and externalizing disorders is that the specific problems within each broad category are often highly intercorrelated. Delinquency is often associated with problems such as truancy, defiance, sexual promiscuity, academic difficulties, and violence (Farrington, 2009; Savolainen et al., 2012). All these problems are different sorts of manifestations of a lack of impulse control, and adolescents who engage in these behaviors are often described as "undercontrolled" (Martel et al., 2009; Robins, John, Caspi, Moffitt, & Stouthamer-Loeber, 1996; S. E. Young et al., 2009).

Problem Behavior Syndrome Researchers have devoted a great deal of attention to studying the covaria-tion among externalizing problems, and a number of theories about the origins of what some experts call **prob-lem behavior syndrome** have been proposed (Jessor & Jessor, 1977). According to many writers, the underly-ing cause of externalizing problems during adolescence is unconventionality in both the adolescent's personality and the social environment. Unconventional individuals are tolerant of deviance, not highly connected to educa-tional or religious institutions, and very liberal in their views. Unconventional environments are those in which a large number of individuals share these same attitudes. Unconventional individuals in unconventional environ-ments are more likely to engage in a wide variety of risk-taking behavior, including experimentation with ille-gal drugs, risky sex, delinquent activity, and risky driv-ing (Brack, Brack, & Orr, 1996; M. L. Cooper, Wood, Orcutt, & Albino, 2003; Monshouwer et al., 2012). A comparison of adolescents in the United States and China found that the same factors heighten or diminish adoles-cents' risk for problem behavior in both countries (Jessor et al., 2003).

A number of possibilities have been proposed about the origins of unconventionality. One set of theories emphasizes the biological underpinnings of the trait and argues that a predisposition toward deviance may actually be inherited (McAdams, Rowe, Rijsdijk, Maughan, & Eley, 2012). A second view stresses biologically based differences (either inherited or acquired through experi-ence) among individuals in arousal, sensation seeking, and fearlessness (e.g., Dunlop & Romer, 2010; Ortiz & Raine, 2004). Yet a third view emphasizes the early family context in which deviance-prone children are reared and frames problem behavior as a sort of adaptive response to a hostile environment (Belsky, Steinberg, & Draper, 1991). Indeed, many writers have argued that some types of antisocial behavior, especially those that involve risk taking, actually make a lot of evolutionary sense (Ellis et al., 2012).

Problem Clusters An alter-native to the view that an underlying trait drives all prob-lem behavior is that different types of deviance have different origins, but that involvement in a given problem behavior may lead to involvement in a second one. Thus, problem behaviors cluster together not because of a common underlying trait like unconventionality, but because engaging in some problematic activities (such as drug and alcohol use) leads to others (such as delinquency) (Bingham & Shope, 2004; Glaser, Shelton, & van den Bree, 2010; Hussong, Curran, & Moffitt, 2004; Malone, Taylor, & Marmorstein, 2004). Some writers have talked about "cascading" effects, where one sort of problem causes another, which triggers a third (Bornstein, Hahn, & Haynes, 2010; Burt & Roisman, 2010; Lynne-Landsman, Bradshaw, & Ialongo, 2010; Rogosch, Oshri, & Cicchetti, 2010). One study of individuals followed from preadoles-cence into adulthood found that externalizing problems in childhood led to academic difficulties in adolescence, which, in turn, led to internalizing problems in adult-hood (see Figure 2) (A. Masten et al., 2005). Studies of the relationship between drug use and depression, and between drug use and conduct problems, have found simi-lar sorts of cascades (Felton, Kofler, Lopez, Saunders, & Kilpatrick, 2015; Sitnick, Shaw, & Hyde, 2014).

Social Control Theory According to a third view, **social control theory** (Gottfredson & Hirschi, 1990), individuals who do not have strong bonds to society's institutions—such as the family, school, or workplace—will be likely to behave unconventionally in a variety of ways. Thus, the clustering of different problem behav-iors may stem not from a problem "in" the person (such as a biological predisposition toward risky behavior), but from an underlying weakness in the individual's attach-ment to society. This underlying problem leads to the development of an unconventional attitude, to member-ship in an unconventional peer group, or to involvement in one or several problem behaviors that may set a chain of problem activities in motion. Social control theory helps to explain why behavior problems are not just clus-tered together but are far more prevalent among poor, inner-city, minority youngsters.

> **problem behavior syndrome** The covariation among various types of externalizing disorders believed to result from an underlying trait of unconventionality.
>
> **social control theory** A theory of delinquency that links deviance with the absence of bonds to society's main institutions.

Figure 2 One explanation for comorbidity is that problems in one domain can create problems in another. (Masten et al., 2005)

Overstating the Case? Finally, a number of researchers stress that we should be careful about overstating the case for a single problem behavior "syndrome" (Farrell, Sullivan, Esposito, Meyer, & Valois, 2005; Willoughby, Chalmers, & Busseri, 2004). They note that although engaging in one type of problem behavior increases the likelihood of engaging in another, the overlap among behavior problems is far from perfect. Indeed, the majority of delinquents are *not* serious drug users (D. Elliott, Huizinga, & Menard, 1989). Other studies suggest that it is important to differentiate between problem behavior that adults disapprove of but that many adolescents consider normative (such as smoking, drinking, or having sex) versus problem behavior that both adults and adolescents view as serious (such as violent crime) (Dong & Ding, 2012; Sullivan, Childs, & O'Connell, 2010; Zweig, Lindberg, & McGinley, 2001). Context matters, too: One international comparison found that adolescent alcohol use was predictive of violence in Scandinavia and Eastern Europe, but not in Mediterranean countries, in part because adolescents in Mediterranean countries are less likely to drink to intoxication and more likely to drink in settings where adults are present (Felson, Savolainen, Bjarnason, Anderson, & Zohra, 2011).

Comorbidity of Internalizing Problems

There is also a good deal of comorbidity in internalizing disorders, which tend to have in common the subjective state of distress. For example, depressed adolescents are more likely than their peers to experience anxiety, panic, phobia, obsessional thinking, suicidal ideation, eating disorders, and various psychosomatic disturbances (physical problems that have psychological causes) (Ferreiro, Seoane, & Senra, 2012; Graber & Sontag, 2009; Kouros, Quasem, & Garber, 2013). Some experts question whether it even makes sense to consider some of these problems as separate entities when speaking about children or adolescents (for example, to draw a distinction between anxiety and depression) because rates of comorbidity are so high (Graber & Sontag, 2009).

Just as different externalizing problems are hypothesized to reflect an underlying antisocial syndrome, various indicators of internalizing problems may be thought of as different manifestations of a common underlying factor. This factor is referred to as **negative emotionality** (Barrocas & Hankin, 2011; Wetter & Hankin, 2009). Individuals who are high in negative emotionality—who become distressed easily—are at greater risk for depression, anxiety disorders, and a range of internalizing problems, as

negative emotionality
The presumed underlying cause of internalizing disorders, characterized by high levels of subjective distress.

anhedonic
Having difficulty experiencing positive emotions, a risk factor for depression.

are individuals who are **anhedonic,** or low in positive emotionality, who are especially prone to depression. Like externalizing problems, the underpinnings of internalizing problems are believed to have both biological and environmental origins, including high levels of biological reactivity to stress (Bardone, Moffitt, Caspi, Dickson, & Silva, 1996; Susman, Dorn, Inoff-Germain, Nottelmann, & Chrousos, 1997).

In this chapter, we examine the nature, prevalence, consequences, and amelioration of the three sets of problems often seen during adolescence: substance abuse, antisocial behavior and other externalizing problems, and depression and other internalizing problems. In each case, we ask four central questions: (1) What is the nature of this sort of problem in adolescence? (2) How many, and which, young people have these problems? (3) What do we know about factors that contribute to these problems?, and (4) What approaches to prevention and intervention appear to have the most promise?

Substance Use and Abuse

Society sends young people mixed messages about drugs and alcohol. Television programs aimed at pre-adolescents urge viewers to "Just Say No!" but the football games and sitcoms that many of these same viewers watch tell them, no less subtly, that having a good time with friends is virtually impossible without something alcoholic to drink. Many celebrities who are idolized by teenagers speak out against cocaine and marijuana, but many equally famous stars admit to using these same drugs. Tobacco and alcohol use are common in music videos and often linked to sex, and more often than not, the lead performer is the individual doing the drinking, smoking, and lovemaking (DuRant et al., 1997). Tobacco and alcohol companies label their products as causing health problems, but they spend enormous amounts of money marketing their cigarettes and beverages to teenagers (Arnett, 2001; Biener & Siegel, 2000).

The mixed signals sent to young people about drugs reflect the inconsistent way that we view these substances as a society: Some drugs (like alcohol or Adderall) are fine, as long as they are not abused, but others (like cocaine or meth) are not; some drinking (enough to relax at a party) is socially appropriate, but too much (enough to impair an automobile driver) is not; some people (those over 21) are old enough to handle drugs, but others (those under 21) are not. It is easy to see why teenagers do not follow the dictates of their elders when it comes to alcohol and other drugs. How, then, should we view substance use and abuse among teenagers, when our backdrop is a society that much of the time tolerates, if not actively encourages, adults who use these same substances?

Alcohol and marijuana remain the main drugs of choice among American adolescents. © Janine Wiedel Photolibrary/Alamy

As with most of the problem behaviors that are common during adolescence, discussions of teenage substance use are often filled more with rhetoric than reality. The popular stereotype of contemporary young people is that they use and abuse a wide range of drugs more than their counterparts did previously, that the main reason adolescents use drugs is peer pressure, and that the "epidemic" level of substance use among American teenagers is behind many of the other problems associated with this age group—including academic underachievement, early pregnancy, suicide, and crime. The simplicity of these assertions is undeniably tempting—after all, what could be more reassuring than to identify the "real" culprit (drugs) and the "real" causes (peers and mass media) of all the maladies of young people? And what could be even more comforting than the belief that, if we simply teach young people to "just say no," these problems will disappear?

Unfortunately, what we might like to believe about adolescent substance use is not necessarily correct. As we shall see, there are grains of truth to many of the popular claims about the causes, nature, and consequences of teenage substance use and abuse, but there are many widely held misconceptions about the subject, too.

Prevalence of Substance Use and Abuse

Each year since 1975, a group of researchers from the University of Michigan has surveyed a nationally representative sample of about 15,000 American high school seniors on several aspects of their lifestyle and values, including their use and abuse of a variety of drugs. Beginning in 1991, comparable samples of 8th- and 10th-graders were added to the annual survey. Because of the size and representativeness of the sample of respondents, this survey, called **Monitoring the Future** (L. D. Johnston, O'Malley, Miech, Bachman, & Schulenberg, 2015), is an excellent source of information about patterns of adolescent drug and alcohol use, at least among young people who have not dropped out of school. (The latest survey results can be accessed at www.monitoringthefuture.org.)

Monitoring the Future
An annual survey of a nationwide sample of American 8th-, 10th-, and 12th-graders, mainly known for its data on adolescent substance use.

binge drinking
Consuming five or more drinks in a row on one occasion, an indicator of alcohol abuse.

Drugs of Choice The surveys consistently indicate that alcohol is by far the most commonly used and abused substance, in terms of both prevalence (the percentage of teenagers who have ever used the drug) and recency of use (the percentage of teenagers who have used the drug within the last month), followed by marijuana and tobacco. By the time they are seniors in high school, 66% of teenagers have tried alcohol, 44% have smoked marijuana, and 34% have smoked cigarettes. After marijuana and tobacco, however, the percentage of young people who have tried various other drugs drops precipitously, and only about 8% of teenagers have used an illicit drug other than marijuana within the last month (L. D. Johnston et al., 2015) (see Figure 3). Although alcohol and tobacco use among adolescents in most European countries is substantially higher than it is in the United States, twice as many American than European adolescents regularly use illicit drugs (mainly marijuana) (Wadley, 2012).

Prevalence statistics, especially those that tap whether an individual has ever tried the substance in question, tell us little about the nature and extent of drug use from the standpoint of adolescents' health and well-being. It is one thing to have tried alcohol or marijuana; it is something else to use either of these substances so often that one's life and behavior are markedly affected.

One of the best ways to examine this issue is to look at the percentage of young people who report using various substances daily or nearly daily. Daily use is infrequent, even among older teens. About 10% of high school seniors smoke daily, marijuana is used daily by 7% of teenagers, and daily use of alcohol is rare (only 2% of seniors drink daily). However, about 20% of all seniors, 13% of all 10th-graders, and 4% of all 8th-graders report having abused alcohol (had more than five drinks in a row, sometimes called **binge drinking**) at least once during the previous 2 weeks (L. D. Johnston et al., 2015). Also worrisome is that 13% of high school seniors report having driven a car after drinking at least once in the past month (Centers for Disease Control and Prevention, 2014).

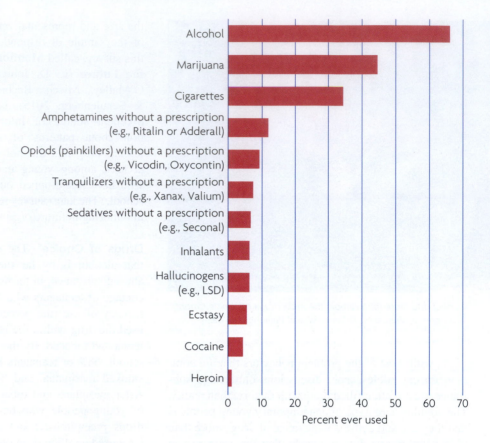

Figure 3 Percentages of American high school seniors who have ever used various drugs. (L. D. Johnston et al., 2015)

making the cultural connection

The use of illicit drugs is more common among American teenagers than their European counterparts, but adolescent smoking and drinking are more common in Europe. Why do you think this is?

Taken together, the findings from these surveys cast doubt on some of the most fervently held stereotypes about adolescent drug use in the United States. Many adolescents who drink do so to excess—a quarter of all seniors and more than 10% of all sophomores have been drunk at least once in the last month (L. D. Johnston et al., 2015). But only a very small proportion of young people have serious drug dependency problems (which would lead to daily use) or use hard drugs at all. Moreover, it is very unlikely that drug and alcohol use lurks behind the wide assortment of adolescent problems for which it is so frequently blamed. Rather, the pattern suggests that most adolescents have experimented with alcohol, marijuana, and tobacco; that many have used one or more of these drugs regularly; that alcohol is clearly the drug of choice among teenagers (a substantial proportion of whom drink to excess); and that most teenagers have not experimented with other drugs. One point worth noting is that a substantial number of high school students

have used painkillers (like Vicodin), amphetamines (like Adderall), tranquilizers (like Xanax), and sedatives (like Seconal) that they have obtained without a prescription, a pattern that also is seen on college campuses (McCabe & West, 2013; Young, Glover, & Havens, 2012).

Changes in Substance Use Over Time The Monitoring the Future study has also been used to chart changes over time in adolescent substance use. Recent administrations of the survey have given experts both cause for relief and cause for concern (L. D. Johnston et al., 2015) (see Figure 4). Things haven't gotten worse, but for the most part, they haven't gotten better, either. Marijuana use, which had been on a steady decline since the late 1970s, rose quite sharply during the mid-1990s, has not declined to its former levels, and has not changed appreciably in recent years. Alcohol use, which declined steadily during the 1980s (from more than 70% of seniors drinking monthly to about 50%), has declined more slowly since then, and not at all in recent years. One bit of very good news is that teen smoking, which increased during the 1990s, has declined dramatically and continues to fall—probably because there has been a gargantuan increase in the price of cigarettes during the past two decades. The high price of cigarettes is a far more powerful deterrent to teen smoking (Gruber & Zinman, 2001; Pampel & Aguilar, 2008). In fact, exposure to some antismoking and antidrug ads may *increase*

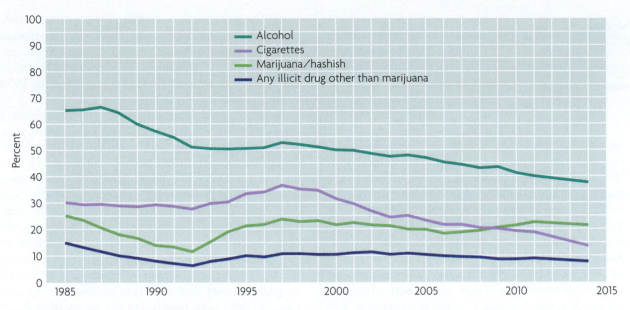

Figure 4 Over-time trends in the proportion of high school seniors who report having used various drugs in the 30 days preceding the survey. (L. D. Johnston et al., 2015)

adolescents' drug use (Hornik, Jacobsohn, Orwin, Piesse, & Kalton, 2008; Wakefield et al., 2006).

Although pundits and political commentators frequently claim to have discovered the "real" reason for changes in rates of adolescent substance use, no one really knows why rates of adolescent substance use fluctuate over time, except, perhaps, because of fluctuations in price and availability. Many historical patterns are puzzling and hard to make sense of. For instance, during the same time period that heavy drinking among high school seniors declined dramatically (between 1976 and 2004), it increased just as significantly among college students who were just a few years older. And during this very same era, rates of marijuana use were far more stable at both ages (Jager, Schulenberg, O'Malley, & Bachman, 2013).

We know that adolescents' drug use fluctuates with changes in their perceptions of how normative, harmful, and disapproved of drug use is (Farhat et al., 2012; Keyes et al., 2012), but scientists have not been able to determine what influences these perceptions, although it is likely that the messages teenagers receive about drugs—from parents, teachers, and mass media—are important. Sex differences in drug use are very small among 8th-graders (for some drugs, use is more prevalent among females than males, for others, the reverse is true) but grow a little bit over the course of high school, so that by senior year, rates are slightly higher among males than females (Johnston, O'Malley, Bachman, Schulenberg, & Miech, 2014). Even among older adolescents, though, sex differences in alcohol, tobacco, and marijuana use are so small that they are unimportant.

Perhaps the most encouraging finding to emerge in recent surveys is that experimentation with drugs is less common among younger teens than it had been in the past (Brooks-Russell, Farhat, Haynie, & Simons-Morton, 2014; L. D. Johnston et al., 2015). In the mid-1990s, about 25% of all 8th-graders reported drinking at least once a month; by 2011, fewer than 10% of young adolescents did. Four times as many 8th-graders were regular smokers in the 1990s than is the case today. Nevertheless, more than one-fourth of all 8th-graders have tried alcohol, one in six has tried marijuana, and one in ten has been drunk at least once. Curiously, while young adolescents' attitudes toward drinking and smoking have gotten progressively more negative over the years, their views of marijuana have not changed. Neither have their rates of marijuana use, at least not in the past decade.

Rates of substance use among 8th-graders are important to watch, because the chances of becoming addicted to alcohol or nicotine are dramatically increased when substance use begins prior to age 15 (G. C. Patton, Coffey, Carlin, Sawyer, & Wakefield, 2006). Because the typical adolescent who smokes cigarettes begins around the 7th or 8th grade, looking at changes in the number of 8th-graders who smoke is a good way of forecasting rates of smoking among adults in the future. Unfortunately, although smoking among 8th-graders has declined markedly since the 1990s, when close to half of all 8th-graders had tried cigarettes, the rate has leveled off, at a little less than 15% (L. D. Johnston et al., 2015).

Ethnic Differences in Substance Use Several national surveys have examined ethnic differences in rates of adolescent substance use and abuse. In general, White adolescents are more likely to use drugs and alcohol than minority youngsters, especially

gateway drugs
Drugs that, when used over time, lead to the use of other, more dangerous substances.

developmental trajectories
Patterns of change over time.

Black and Asian youth, although differences between White and Black adolescents have been getting smaller (L. D. Johnston et al., 2014). Although rates of drug use among Hispanic adolescents had been comparable to those of White youngsters, rates have increased among Hispanic youth in recent years (L.D. Johnston et al., 2014). Use among Native American adolescents is the highest of any ethnic group (Chassin, Hussong, & Beltran, 2009; L. D. Johnston et al., 2012b; Whitbeck, Yu, Johnson, Hoyt, & Walls, 2008). Foreign-born and less Americanized minority youngsters—whether Asian or Hispanic in background—use alcohol, drugs, and tobacco at a lower rate than do American-born and more acculturated immigrant youth; part of becoming an "American" teenager means experimenting with drugs (Delva et al., 2005; Georgiades, Boyle, Duku, & Racine, 2006; Nagoshi, Marsiglia, Parsai, & Castro, 2011). The rate of drug use among immigrant adolescents is *half* the rate of use among adolescents from the same ethnic group who were born in the United States (K. Harris, 1999).

Does Substance Use Follow a Particular Progression?

Young people experiment with beer and wine before trying cigarettes or hard liquor, which precedes marijuana use, which, in turn, precedes the use of other illicit drugs. However, although experimentation may follow this sequence, this does not mean that alcohol use or smoking invariably lead to marijuana use, or that marijuana use necessarily leads to experimentation with harder drugs (van Leeuwen et al., 2011). In fact, there is little evidence to support the idea that marijuana is an inevitable stepping-stone to hard-drug use (it depends on how frequently marijuana is used) (Treaster, 1994).

The fact that there is a fairly standard sequence of drug use suggests that virtually all users of hard drugs have also tried alcohol, cigarettes, and marijuana and, moreover, that one way to prevent adolescents from experimenting with more serious drugs might be to stop them from drinking, smoking, and using marijuana. Adolescents who have not experimented with alcohol or marijuana by the time they are in their 20s are unlikely ever to use these or any other drugs (K. Chen & Kandel, 1996). For this reason, tobacco, alcohol, and marijuana are considered **gateway drugs,** in the sense that they represent a gate through which individuals pass on the way to using harder drugs. (Nicotine exposure, whether through cigarettes or e-cigarettes, may sensitize the adolescent brain to other drugs and make future abuse more likely [Yuan, Cross, Loughlin, & Leslie, 2015]). Whether an individual passes through the gate is influenced by many factors beyond his or her previous patterns of drug use, including the era in which he or she grows up. Progression from tobacco and alcohol to marijuana and other illegal drugs was far more common among people who were born around 1960 than among people born before 1950 or after 1970 (Golub & Johnson, 2001).

On average, smoking and drinking (and problematic drinking in particular) increase during adolescence, peak in the early 20s, and then decline (Brodbeck, Bachmann, Croudace, & Brown, 2013), but not all individuals follow this pattern. Researchers have identified several distinct **developmental trajectories** of alcohol, tobacco, and drug use (Chassin et al., 2009; Jackson & Schulenberg, 2013; Patrick & Schulenberg, 2011). In one study, six distinct groups were identified. Nonusers (one-third of the sample) rarely experimented with substances at any point in adolescence. Alcohol experimenters (25% of the sample) first tried alcohol early in adolescence and continued to drink occasionally, but did not try other drugs and did not increase their drinking over time. Low escalators (5%) began using substances early in adolescence and increased their use slowly but steadily over time. Early starters (6%) showed very high substance use in early adolescence and escalated gradually over time, so that by the end of high school they were smoking and drinking frequently and experimenting with drugs. Late starters (20%) used substances infrequently during early adolescence but increased their use rapidly during high school—so much so that by the end of high school their substance use was similar to that of the early starters. Finally, high escalators (8%) showed moderate use in early adolescence, escalated rapidly between early and middle adolescence, and continued to increase their use throughout high school (Zapert, Snow, & Tebes, 2002).

Exposure to nicotine, whether through tobacco or e-cigarettes, may sensitize the adolescent brain to other substances, increasing the likelihood of future substance abuse. © ppi09/Shutterstock.com RF

Adolescents whose substance use begins early or escalates rapidly, as well as those with a history of solitary use, are most at risk for substance use problems as adults (D. Belsky et al., 2013; Nelson, Van Ryzin, & Dishion. 2014; Tucker et al., 2014).

Causes and Consequences of Substance Use and Abuse

In looking at the causes and consequences of substance use and abuse in adolescence, it is especially important to keep in mind the distinction between occasional experimentation and problematic use.

Users, Abusers, and Abstainers Because the majority of adolescents have experimented with alcohol and marijuana, there are plenty of normal, healthy young people who have used these drugs at least once. Adolescents who experiment with alcohol and marijuana are no worse adjusted than their peers who abstain from them (Alex Mason & Spoth, 2011; Scheier & Botvin, 1998; J. S. Tucker, Ellickson, Collins, & Klein, 2006). In

order to understand the relation between substance use and psychological adjustment, it is important to differentiate among four groups of adolescents: frequent drug users (for example, at least once a week); hard-drug users (that is, drugs other than alcohol, tobacco, or marijuana); those who experiment with marijuana and alcohol but who do not use them frequently (that is, no more than once a month); and those who abstain (Connell, Gilreath, Aklin, & Brex, 2010; Hughes, Power, & Francis, 1992; C. Mitchell et al., 1996; Wills, McNamara, Vaccaro, & Hirky, 1996). Experimenters and abstainers score higher on measures of psychological adjustment than frequent users. Relative to experimenters, though, abstainers tend to be overcontrolled, narrow in their interests, anxious, and inhibited (Shedler & Block, 1990). The age at which adolescents experiment with substances is also important. One study of people in their mid-20s found that those who had experimented with substance use at age 17 (when experimentation is normative, at least in the United States) generally were better adjusted than those who had been abstainers, abusers, or problematic users (see Figure 5) (Englund et al., 2013).

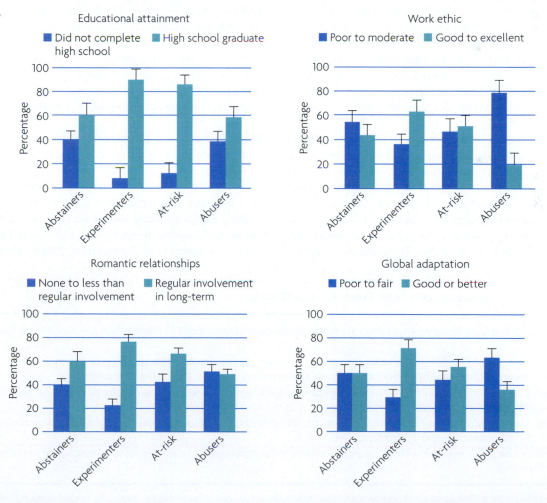

Figure 5 **Experimentation with substances later in adolescence is associated with better adjustment in young adulthood.** (Englund et al., 2013)

Longer-term follow-up studies also show that moderate alcohol use during adolescence does not have negative long-term effects (Haller, Handley, Chassin, & Bountress, 2010; Paschall, Freisthler, & Lipton, 2005). In contrast, cigarette use during adolescence has more harmful long-term health consequences because nicotine is a more addictive drug, and its use is more likely to persist into middle adulthood (K. Chen & Kandel, 1996; Elders, Perry, Eriksen, & Giovino, 1994; Pierce & Gilpin, 1996).

This does not mean that occasional experimentation with drugs during adolescence *leads* to better adjustment, of course. In fact, the psychological advantages observed among adolescents who experiment with alcohol and marijuana were evident well before they began experimenting, even when they were young children (Shedler & Block, 1990). Well-adjusted adolescents are more socially competent and are more likely to be in social situations in which other teenagers are drinking and smoking marijuana (Ludden & Eccles, 2007). In this sense, psychological adjustment increases the likelihood of alcohol and marijuana use, rather than the reverse.

Taken together, research indicates that moderate alcohol and marijuana use has become normative among adolescents in contemporary society (however troublesome some adults may find this), that these substances are typically used in social situations, and that better-adjusted and more interpersonally competent young people are likely to participate in social activities in which alcohol and other drugs are present.

Predictors and Consequences of Substance Abuse

Substance abuse (using drugs in a way that causes significant problems at home, school, work, or with the law) is a different matter (see Table 1). Adolescents who are frequent users of alcohol, tobacco, and other drugs score lower on measures of psychological adjustment as teenagers and were more likely to have been maladjusted as children (Hicks et al., 2014). Drug and alcohol abuse during adolescence is often a symptom of prior psychological disturbance.

Substance abuse during adolescence, whatever its antecedents, is associated with a host of other problems. Young people who abuse alcohol, tobacco, and other drugs are more likely to experience problems at school; suffer from psychological distress and depression; become involved in dangerous or deviant activities, including crime, delinquency, and truancy; and engage in unprotected sexual activity. As adults, they are more likely to have physical health problems, experience unemployment and out-of-wedlock childbearing, and continue to have substance abuse problems (Aseltine, Schilling, James, Glanovsky, & Jacobs, 2009; Chassin et al., 2009; Green & Ensminger, 2006; Holmen, Barrett-Connor, Holmen, & Bjermer, 2000; Stuart & Green, 2008). Alcohol and other drugs are often implicated in adolescent automobile crashes, the leading cause of death and disability among American teenagers (O'Malley & Johnston, 1999), and in other fatal and nonfatal accidents, such as drownings, falls, and burns (Hingson & Zha, 2009). Adolescent substance abusers also expose themselves to the long-term physical health risks of excessive drug use. In the case of cigarettes, alcohol, and marijuana, these risks are substantial and well documented—among them, cancer, heart disease, and kidney and liver damage. It is also now well established that heavy cigarette smoking during adolescence can exacerbate feelings of emotional distress and lead to depression and anxiety disorders (Chassin et al., 2009).

Risk Factors for Substance Abuse

Which adolescents are most likely to become substance abusers? Generally, four sets of risk factors—psychological, familial, social, and contextual—have been identified, and the more risk factors that are present for an individual, the more likely she or he is to use and abuse drugs (O'Loughlin, Karp, Koulis, Paradis, & DiFranza, 2009; Ostaszewski & Zimmerman, 2006). These same

---

Table 1 DSM–5 diagnostic criteria for Substance Use Disorder

The DSM-5 defines a Substance Use Disorder as the presence of at least 2 of 11 criteria, which are clustered in four groups:

1. *Impaired control:* (1) taking more or for longer than intended, (2) unsuccessful efforts to stop or cut down use, (3) spending a great deal of time obtaining, using, or recovering from use, (4) craving for substance.
2. *Social impairment:* (5) failure to fulfill major obligations due to use, (6) continued use despite problems caused or exacerbated by use, (7) important activities given up or reduced because of substance use.
3. *Risky use:* (8) recurrent use in hazardous situations, (9) continued use despite physical or psychological problems that are caused or exacerbated by substance use.
4. *Pharmacologic dependence:* (10) tolerance to effects of the substance, (11) withdrawal symptoms when not using or using less.*

---

* Persons who are prescribed medications such as opioids may exhibit these two criteria, but would not necessarily be considered to have a substance use disorder.

Source: American Psychiatric Association, 2013.

risk factors have been found across a variety of studies and in samples of adolescents from a wide range of ethnic and socioeconomic backgrounds, although there is evidence that family factors may be more influential in early adolescence and peer factors more so in middle adolescence (M. J. Cleveland, Feinberg, Bontempo, & Greenberg, 2008). In other words, the factors that place an adolescent at risk for substance abuse are more or less the same regardless of the adolescent's sex, social class, or ethnicity (Aspy, Tolma, Oman, & Vesely, 2014; Choi, Harachi, Gillmore, & Catalano, 2005). This is good news, because it suggests that preventive interventions do not need to be specifically tailored to different subgroups of adolescents (Hu, Davies, & Kandel, 2006).

The first set of risk factors is psychological. Individuals with certain personality characteristics—which typically are present prior to adolescence—are more likely to develop drug and alcohol problems than their peers. These characteristics include anger, impulsivity, inattentiveness, and sensation seeking (Chassin et al., 2009; Colder et al., 2013; Malone, Van Eck, Flory, & Lamis, 2010; Wilens et al., 2011). The combination of poor impulse control and heightened sensation seeking is especially problematic (Khurana et al., 2014; Willoughby & Fortner, 2014). Many of these traits have a strong genetic component, although the effects of having a genetic propensity toward substance use can be diminished by a context that discourages smoking or drinking (Brody et al. 2009; D. Li et al., 2011; Park, Sher, Todorov, & Heath, 2011). In addition, individuals who have more tolerant attitudes about drug use (and about deviance in general) are at greater risk for drug abuse (Schulenberg, Wadsworth, O'Malley, Bachman, & Johnston, 1996; Petraitis et al., 1995), as are those who expect alcohol or other drugs to improve their social relationships (Griffin, Epstein, Botvin, & Spoth, 2001). Children who expect alcohol to have positive effects on them are more likely to become heavy drinkers in adolescence (M. Dunn & Goldman, 1998).

Second, individuals with distant, hostile, or conflicted family relationships are more likely to develop substance abuse problems than are their peers who grow up in close, nurturing families (J. A. Ford, 2009; King, Molina, & Chassin, 2009; Sale et al., 2005). Drug-abusing youngsters are also more likely than their peers to have parents who are excessively permissive, uninvolved, neglectful, or rejecting (Abar, Jackson, & Wood, 2014; Chassin et al., 2009; Tobler & Komro, 2010). In addition, they are more likely to come from homes where one or more other family members (parents or siblings) smoke, drink, or use drugs (as a result of both genetics and the environment) (Chassin et al., 2009; Gilman et al., 2009; Mays et al., 2014). One explanation for especially high rates of substance use among affluent suburban teenagers is that their parents often are tolerant of this behavior (Botticello, 2009; Luthar & Goldstein, 2008).

Third, individuals with substance abuse problems are more likely to have friends who use and tolerate the use of drugs (Alli, Amialchuk, & Dwyer, 2011; Cruz, Emery, & Turkheimer, 2012; Parsai, Voisine, Marsiglia, Kulis, & Nieri, 2009). Whether and how often adolescents use drugs is an important defining characteristic of peer groups—abstainers tend to have other abstainers as friends, and users tend to be friends with other users. Drug-using adolescents seek drug-using peers, and drug-using peers encourage even more drug use among their friends (Chassin, Presson, Todd, Rose, & Sherman, 1998; Schulenberg et al., 1999). Substance-using adolescents who have many substance-using friends may also overestimate how common substance use is because they are so much more likely to see other people engaged in it (Unger & Rohrbach, 2002).

Finally, adolescents who become substance abusers are more likely to live in a social context that makes drug use easier (Chassin et al., 2009; Stanley, Henry, & Swaim, 2011). Important factors are the availability of drugs, the community's norms regarding drug use, the degree to which drug laws are enforced, and the ways in which drug use is presented via the mass media (Bendtsen, Damsgaard, Tolstrup, Ersbøll, & Holstein, 2013; X. Li, Stanton, & Feigelman, 2000; Thrul, Lipperman-Kreda, Grube, & Friend, 2014). Lowering the minimum purchasing age for alcohol (as was done in New Zealand) significantly increases the rate of alcohol-related car crashes among younger drivers, whereas raising it (as was done in the United States) decreases crashes (Kypri et al., 2006). Binge drinking and drinking while driving are higher among adolescents who live in neighborhoods with relatively more retail outlets for alcohol (M.-J. Chen, Gruenewald, & Remer, 2009a; Resko et al., 2010; Truong & Sturm, 2009), and smoking is more common among adolescents who live in neighborhoods with relatively more stores that sell cigarettes (McCarthy et al., 2009; Novak et al., 2006) or attend schools where a high proportion of other students smoke (Sabiston et al., 2009). Adolescent marijuana use is not higher in states that have legalized the drug for medical use, however (Choo et al., 2014; Lynne-Landsman, Livingston, & Wagenaar, 2013).

Researchers have also identified important **protective factors** that decrease the likelihood of adolescents' engaging in substance abuse (Jessor & Turbin, 2014). Among the most important are positive mental health (including high self-esteem and the absence of depression), high academic achievement, engagement in school, close family relationships, and involvement in religious activities (C. Jordan & Lewis, 2005; Sanchez, Opaleye, Chaves, Noto, & Nappo, 2011). These protective factors appear to operate over and above the effects of the risk factors discussed previously. As with

protective factors
Factors that limit individual vulnerability to harm.

dopamine
A neurotransmitter especially important in the brain circuits that regulate the experience of reward.

the factors that place adolescents at risk for substance abuse, the protective factors identified operate similarly among adolescents from different ethnic groups and explain why some groups of adolescents use drugs more than others do (G. Barnes & Farrell, 1992; Ennett et al., 2008; Flannery, Vazsonyi, & Rowe, 1996). One of the reasons for the lower rate of drinking among Black youth is that their parents are less likely to drink or tolerate adolescent drinking (Peterson, Hawkins, Abbott, & Catalano, 1994).

Drugs and the Adolescent Brain

Scientists have long speculated that, because the brain is still very malleable early in adolescence, experimentation with drugs is more harmful then than later in development. Experimental research in which scientists have compared the brains of animals exposed to drugs, either close to the time of puberty or after reaching full maturity, has illuminated some of the specific neurobiological pathways that explain why the potential for addiction is much greater in adolescence than adulthood (Brenhouse, Sonntag, & Andersen, 2008; Hardin & Ernst, 2009; Lydon, Wilson, Child, & Geier, 2014). In order to understand what these studies say, we need to digress slightly and look at certain aspects of adolescent brain development.

Changes in the limbic system during adolescence, a region of the brain that is important for the experience of reward and punishment, affect receptors for **dopamine,** one of the neurotransmitters that influence our experience of pleasure. We experience things like great sex or fabulous food as enjoyable because they result in higher levels of dopamine in the brain; these higher levels permit more electrical activity through the synapses that connect the circuits in the brain that regulate feelings of pleasure.

Certain drugs make users feel good primarily because they affect the same receptors that are sensitive to the dopamine that is in the brain naturally. The molecules of addictive drugs are so similar to dopamine molecules that dopamine receptors act in the same way in their presence as they do in the presence of natural dopamine. As a result, when drugs enter the brain (which is where they go whether they enter the body through the mouth, nose, or blood vessels), they are "read" by dopamine receptors as the real thing. On the positive side, this makes the user feel good (the same way that natural dopamine does)—which, of course, is why people use drugs. The problem, though, is that frequent drug use during adolescence interferes with the normal maturation of the brain's dopamine system. The animal studies referred to earlier have shown that experiences in early adolescence,

when the limbic system is changing naturally, can *permanently* affect the way the brain functions (Spear & Swartzwelder, 2014). (Various brain systems and regions are malleable, or "plastic," during different periods of development, and it is during periods of heightened plasticity that these brain systems are most easily and irreversibly affected by outside influences.) Repeated exposure to drugs during this period of heightened malleability in the limbic system can affect the brain in ways that make it *necessary* to use drugs in order to experience normal amounts of pleasure.

How many exposures to a drug does it take to permanently alter the adolescent brain's dopamine system? No one knows for sure, and the answer varies from person to person, largely because of genetic factors (this is why some people are more likely to develop addictions than others) (Laucht et al., 2008). This permanent alteration in the dopamine system is more likely to happen in adolescence, when the limbic system is still malleable, than in adulthood, when it is less changeable.

Exposure to drugs during adolescence is more likely to lead to addiction than is the same amount of exposure during adulthood (Swendsen et al., 2012). Compared with people who delay drinking until they are 21, people who begin in early adolescence (before age 14) are *7 times* more likely to binge drink as teenagers and *5 times* more likely to develop a substance abuse or dependence disorder at some point in life (Hingson, Heeren, & Winter, 2006). Similarly, people who begin smoking regularly before age 14 are at much greater risk for nicotine dependence as adults than are those who start in late adolescence (Orlando, Tucker, Ellickson, & Klein, 2004).

Studies of juvenile mice have furthered our understanding of the impact of drinking on adolescent brain development.
© Adam Gault/OJO Images/Getty Images RF

It's not simply that people who start using drugs early are different from those who wait in ways that make them more prone to addiction. Experimental studies with animals, in which some are randomly assigned to drug exposure shortly after puberty and others to exposure in adulthood, have proven that it is easier to become addicted during adolescence than during adulthood (Wong, Ford, Pagels, McCutcheon, & Marinelli, 2013).

The increased vulnerability of the adolescent brain to the addicting effects of alcohol is compounded by the fact that adolescents don't feel the negative consequences of drinking as profoundly as adults do (this can only be studied experimentally in animals, because researchers are not allowed to give teenagers alcohol). Studies comparing juvenile rodents with adult rodents find that juveniles can drink more than adults before they become tired or have their reflexes slow, and the unpleasant consequences of drinking too much (otherwise known as a hangover) are less intense among juveniles than adults. To make matters worse, juveniles feel the positive effects of alcohol more intensely than adults—alcohol makes juvenile rodents want to socialize but it makes adults want to be left alone (Spear, 2013). And whereas the presence of "peers" increases alcohol consumption among juvenile rodents, it has no such effect among adult animals (Logue, Chein, Gould, Holliday, & Steinberg, 2014).

Although the short-term effects of alcohol are less severe in adolescents than adults, the lasting effects of alcohol on brain functioning are worse in adolescence than in adulthood—again, because the brain is more vulnerable to influences during periods of plasticity. One area of the adolescent brain that is especially vulnerable to the harmful effects of alcohol is the hippocampus, which is important for memory and, along with the prefrontal cortex, for "putting the brakes" on impulsive behavior (Squeglia, Jacobus, & Tapert, 2009; Sturmhöfel & Swartzwelder, 2004; E. Walker et al., 2004). Alcohol also has harmful effects on the development of regions of the brain involved in higher-order cognitive abilities, such as planning and decision making, and in self-regulation (Butler, 2006; Nasrallah et al., 2011; Nasrallah, Yang, & Bernstein, 2009). Although some of the harmful neurobiological consequences of drinking in early adolescence can be reversed, the fact that early exposure is more likely to lead to addiction and long-term use indicates that interventions designed to prevent substance abuse should begin prior to adolescence. Less is known about the impact of marijuana use on adolescent brain development (DuPont & Lieberman, 2014), although chronic use may be associated with brain abnormalities in many of the same areas that are also affected by drinking, including the hippocampus and prefrontal cortex (Abush & Akirav, 2012; Batalla et al., 2013). Not all studies have reached this conclusion, though (Weiland et al., 2015).

Prevention and Treatment of Substance Use and Abuse

Efforts to prevent substance use and abuse among teenagers focus on one of three factors: the supply of drugs, the environment in which teenagers may be exposed to drugs, and characteristics of the potential drug user (Newcomb & Bentler, 1988). One huge problem is that two of the three most commonly used and abused drugs—cigarettes and alcohol—are both legal and widely available, and laws prohibiting the sale of these substances to minors are not well enforced (Centers for Disease Control and Prevention, 2006). Research does show, however, that raising the price of alcohol and cigarettes reduces adolescents' use of them (Bishai, Mercer, & Tapales, 2005; Lovato et al., 2013), that raising the minimum legal drinking age leads to a decline in binge drinking among teenagers (but not young adults) (Andersen, Rasmussen, Bendtsen, Due, & Holstein, 2014; Grucza, Norberg, & Bierut, 2009), and that raising the minimum purchase age for tobacco products lowers rates of teen smoking (Institute of Medicine, 2015). Attempts to enforce laws governing the purchase of cigarettes are less effective than those governing alcohol, in part, because many adolescents obtain cigarettes through means other than purchasing them from stores (for example, bumming them from older friends or stealing them from parents) (Fichtenberg & Glantz, 2002; Pokorny, Jason, & Schoeny, 2006).

Many different types of drug abuse prevention interventions have been tried, either alone or in combination. In programs designed to change some characteristic of the adolescent, drug use is targeted indirectly either by attempting to enhance adolescents' psychological development in general or by helping adolescents develop other interests and participate in other activities that will make drug use less likely. The idea behind these sorts of efforts is that adolescents who have high self-esteem, for example, or who are gainfully employed will be less likely to use drugs. In other programs, the intervention is directly focused on preventing drug use. These programs include information-based efforts (in which adolescents are educated about the dangers of drugs), social skills training (in which adolescents are taught how to turn down drugs), and some combination of informational and general psychological intervention (in which adolescents are educated about drug abuse and exposed to a program designed to enhance their self-esteem or social skills) (Newcomb & Bentler, 1988).

The results of research designed to evaluate these sorts of individual-focused approaches have not been encouraging (Dielman, 1994; H. Leventhal & Keeshan, 1993). Careful evaluations of Project DARE—the most widely implemented drug education program in the United States—show that the program is largely ineffective (Ennett, Tobler, Ringwall, & Flewelling, 1994). Experts are now fairly confident that drug education alone, whether based on rational information or scare tactics, does not prevent drug use (Steinberg, 2015). This is reminiscent of research on sex education, which has shown that informational programs are simply not effective on their own. As a rule, educational programs may change individuals' knowledge, but they rarely affect their behavior. Research on the effectiveness of drug testing in schools has yielded inconsistent findings (James-Burdumy, Goesling, Deke, & Einspruch, 2012; Yamaguchi, Johnston, & O'Malley, 2003).

The most encouraging results have been found in programs that do not focus only on the individual adolescent but rather combine some sort of social competence training with a communitywide intervention aimed not only at adolescents but also at their peers, parents, and teachers (Fletcher, Bonell, & Hargreaves, 2008; J. Hawkins et al., 2008; Liddle, Rowe, Dakoff, Henderson, & Greenbaum, 2009; M. Siegel & Biener, 2000). These multifaceted efforts have been shown to be effective in reducing adolescents' use of alcohol, cigarettes, and other drugs, especially if the programs begin when youngsters are preadolescents and continue well into high school (Bruvold, 1993; Dielman, 1994; Ellickson, Bell, & McGuigan, 1993; Flynn et al., 1994; Perry et al., 1996).

Overall, most experts agree that efforts designed simply to change the potential adolescent drug user without transforming the environment in which the adolescent lives are not likely to succeed. Despite their intuitive appeal, efforts to help adolescents "Just Say No" have been remarkably unsuccessful.

One of the problems with all prevention programs is that they often do not distinguish between drug *use* and drug *abuse*. Trying to stop teenagers from *ever* using alcohol, for instance, is both unlikely to succeed and probably not a very wise allocation of resources, whereas preventing binge drinking and drunk driving are far more important—and attainable—goals.

Distinguishing between use and abuse is also important in treatment. Some experts worry that adolescents who are mistakenly enrolled in treatment programs (because their parents have overreacted to the adolescent's normative and probably harmless experimentation with drugs) may end up more alienated and more distressed—and more likely to become drug abusers—as a result of the "treatment." Evaluations of treatment programs for adolescents who are genuine drug abusers suggest that efforts that involve the adolescent's family, and not just the teenager, are more likely to be successful (Liddle et al., 2009). Unfortunately, many adolescents who would benefit from substance abuse treatment, especially those from ethnic minority groups, do not receive it, often because they can't afford it or have inadequate health insurance (Cummings, Wen, & Druss, 2011).

Externalizing Problems

Experts distinguish among three main categories of externalizing problems in adolescence: conduct disorder, aggression, and delinquency. Although these three classes of problems are highly interrelated, their definitions differ.

Categories of Externalizing Problems

Conduct Disorder The first category of externalizing problems is **conduct disorder,** which is a clinical diagnosis that refers to a repetitive and persistent pattern of antisocial behavior in which the rights of others or age-appropriate societal norms are violated and where, as a result of this behavior, the individual has problems in social relationships, school, or the workplace (see Table 2) (Farrington, 2009). (A related, but less serious, diagnosis is **oppositional-defiant disorder,** which refers to behavior that is spiteful, angry, and argumentative, but not necessarily aggressive.) An estimated 6%–16% of adolescent males and 2%–9% of adolescent females have conduct disorder (Farrington, 2009). Conduct disorder is very stable between childhood and adolescence—about half of all individuals who are diagnosed with it as children are also diagnosed with it as teenagers, and many had oppositional-defiant disorder when they were younger. One reason for this is that the risk factors for these two disorders are pretty much the same (Boden, Fergusson, & Horwood, 2010).

Individuals who have been diagnosed with conduct disorder and who persist in their antisocial behavior after age 18 may subsequently be diagnosed with **antisocial personality disorder,** which is characterized by a lack of regard for the moral or legal standards of the community and a marked inability to get along with others or abide by societal rules. Some individuals with antisocial personality disorder are **psychopaths**—individuals who are not only antisocial in their behavior but manipulative, superficially charming, impulsive, and indifferent to the feelings of others, a cluster of characteristics referred to as **callous-unemotional (CU) traits** (Frick & White, 2008;

conduct disorder

A repetitive and persistent pattern of antisocial behavior that results in problems at school or work, or in relationships with others.

oppositional-defiant disorder

A disorder of childhood and adolescence characterized by excessive anger, spite, and stubbornness.

antisocial personality disorder

A disorder of adulthood characterized by antisocial behavior and persistent disregard for the rules of society and the rights of others.

psychopaths

Individuals who are not only antisocial but also manipulative, superficially charming, impulsive, and indifferent to the feelings of others.

callous-unemotional traits (CU)

A cluster of traits characteristic of psychopathic individuals, which includes a lack of empathy and indifference toward the feelings of others.

Table 2 DSM-5 diagnostic criteria for Conduct Disorder

In Conduct Disorder, a repetitive and persistent pattern of behavior occurs in which the basic rights of others or major age-appropriate societal norms or rules are violated. This manifests as the presence of at least 3 of the following 15 criteria in the past 12 months from any of the categories below, with at least one criterion present in the past 6 months:

Aggression to people and animals:	• Often bullies, threatens, or intimidates others
	• Often initiates physical fights
	• Has used a weapon that can cause serious physical harm to others (e.g., a bat, brick, broken bottle, knife, gun)
	• Has been physically cruel to people
	• Has been physically cruel to animals
	• Has stolen while confronting a victim (e.g., mugging, purse snatching, extortion, armed robbery)
	• Has forced someone into sexual activity
Destruction of property:	• Has deliberately engaged in fire setting with the intention of causing serious damage
	• Has deliberately destroyed others' property (other than by fire setting)
Deceitfulness or theft:	• Has broken into someone else's house, building, or car
	• Often lies to obtain goods or favors or to avoid obligations (i.e., "cons" others)
	• Has stolen items of nontrivial value without confronting a victim (e.g., shoplifting, but without breaking and entering; forgery)
Serious violations of rules:	• Often stays out at night despite parental prohibitions, beginning before age 13 years
	• Has run away from home overnight at least twice while living in the parental or parental surrogate home, or once without returning for a lengthy period
	• Is often truant from school, beginning before age 13 years

The disturbance in behavior causes clinically significant impairment in social, academic, or occupational functioning.

Source: American Psychiatric Association, 2013.

Shirtcliff et al., 2009). Because the terms "antisocial personality disorder" and "psychopath" imply a deep-seated personality problem that is unlikely to change, experts advise against applying them to people younger than 18, because, as you will read, most individuals who engage in antisocial behavior as teenagers do not continue to do so after their mid-20s.

Social scientists disagree about whether it is possible to identify "juvenile psychopaths" or "fledgling psychopaths"—individuals who, despite their youth, exhibit many of the same characteristics as adult psychopaths and are likely to grow into them. Some contend that it is possible to do so (e.g., M. A. Campbell, Porter, & Santor, 2004; Frick, Kotov, Loney, & Vasey, 2005; Lynam et al., 2009; Salekin, 2008), while others note that some of the distinguishing features of adult psychopaths that are considered pathological (impulsivity, irresponsibility, instability in romantic relationships) may be transient characteristics that reflect immaturity, not pathology (Hawes, Mulvey, Schubert, & Pardini, 2014; Skeem & Cauffman, 2003; Vincent, Vitacco, Grisso, & Corrado, 2003). Nevertheless, some adolescents have stronger psychopathic tendencies than others (Edens, Marcus, & Vaughn, 2011), and while

not all adolescents who score high on measures of CU traits grow up to be adult psychopaths, they are more likely to commit crimes, as adolescents and as adults (McMahon, Witkiewitz, Kotler, & Conduct Problems Prevention Research Group, 2010; Moran et al., 2009; Stickle, Kirkpatrick, & Brush, 2009). For this reason, when making a diagnosis of conduct disorder, practitioners distinguish between conduct-disordered adolescents with CU traits and those without them.

aggression
Acts done to be intentionally harmful.

Aggression A second category of externalizing problems is **aggression,** which is behavior that is done to intentionally hurt someone. "Aggression" is a very broad term that includes physical fighting, relational aggression, and intimidation, and it can be either instrumental (planned) or reactive (unplanned).

It is very difficult to estimate the prevalence of aggression during adolescence, because the category is so far-reaching. Virtually everyone has done *something* aggressive at one time or another, and about one-fourth of high school students report having been in a fight during the past year (Centers for Disease Control and Prevention, 2014). Most psychologists are concerned with adolescents whose aggression is persistent and causes serious injury to others. Aggressive behavior actually declines over the course of childhood and adolescence—in sheer quantity, the most aggressive period of development is the preschool years, when children frequently hit, kick, or bite each other—although aggression committed by adolescents is usually more serious than that committed by children (Bongers, Koot, van der Ende, & Verhulst, 2004). Like conduct disorder, aggression is also very stable, although much more so in boys than girls (Broidy et al., 2003). One likely reason for this sex difference is that aggressive little girls are more often forced to curtail their bad behavior than aggressive little boys are.

Juvenile Offending The third main category of externalizing problems is **juvenile offending**, which includes **delinquency** (crimes committed by minors that are dealt with in the juvenile justice system) and **criminal behavior** (crimes that are dealt with in the criminal justice system, regardless of the age of the offender), and **status offenses,** a special category of delinquent acts that are not against the law for adults but that nevertheless violate established codes of conduct for juveniles, like truancy or running away from home (Woolard & Scott, 2009). Unlike conduct disorder or aggression, which are defined in terms of behavior, juvenile offending is defined legally. A large proportion of juvenile offenders have conduct disorder, and most are aggressive, but not all adolescents who have conduct disorder or who are aggressive are juvenile offenders, because that depends entirely on whether they have broken the law.

making the scientific connection

The age-crime curve is found all over the world. How do you account for this, in light of the fact that the contexts in which adolescents develop vary so much?

Both violent crimes (such as assault, rape, robbery, and murder) and property crimes (such as burglary, theft, and arson) increase in frequency between the preadolescent and adolescent years, peak during the late high school years, and decline during young adulthood (Sweeten, Piquero, & Steinberg, 2013), a pattern seen for externalizing problems more generally (Petersen, Bates, Dodge, Lansford, & Pettit, 2014). The so-called **age–crime curve** has been remarkably stable over time and is consistently seen around the world (Piquero, Farrington, & Blumstein, 2003). In the United States, almost one-third of arrests for serious crimes involve a suspect under 18, and individuals under 18 account for one-sixth of all violent crimes (Bureau of Justice Statistics, 2010) (see Figure 6). The onset of serious delinquency generally begins between the ages of 13 and 16 (Farrington, 2009).

Developmental Progression of Antisocial Behavior

Antisocial behavior can take different forms: **authority conflicts** (such as truancy or running away from home), **covert antisocial behavior** (such as stealing), and **overt antisocial behavior** (such as attacking someone with a

juvenile offending
An externalizing problem that includes delinquency and criminal behavior.

delinquency
Juvenile offending that is processed within the juvenile justice system.

criminal behavior
Crimes that are dealt with in the criminal justice system, regardless of the age of the offender.

status offenses
Violations of the law that pertain to minors but not adults.

age–crime curve
The relationship between chronological age and offending, showing that the prevalence of offending peaks in late adolescence.

authority conflicts
A type of antisocial behavior characterized by stubbornness and rebelliousness.

covert antisocial behavior
A type of antisocial behavior characterized by misdeeds that are not always detected by others, such as lying or stealing.

overt antisocial behavior
A type of antisocial behavior characterized by aggression toward others.

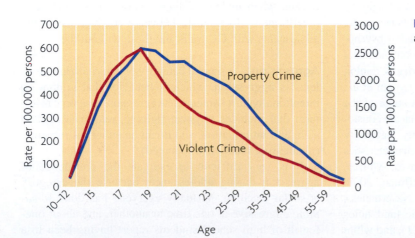

Figure 6 Age differences in criminal activity. (Bureau of Justice Statistics, 2010)

Arrests for both violent and nonviolent crime peak in late adolescence. © AP Images/Carline Jean

weapon). With-in these broad categories, there are some fairly predictable progressions (Farrington, 2009; Loeber & Burke, 2011). Authority conflicts usually first appear as stubborn behavior, which escalates into defiance and disobedience, and then progresses to more serious signs of problems with authority, such as truancy and running away from home. Covert antisocial behavior typically begins with acts like lying and shoplifting; progresses to property damage, such as vandalism; and then to more serious property crimes, such as burglary. Overt antisocial behavior generally first presents itself as fighting or bullying, which escalates to things like gang fighting and, ultimately, to violent criminal activity.

This is not to say that all bullies grow up to be violent criminals or that all stubborn preschoolers run away from home as teenagers. But the reverse is almost always true. Virtually all violent juveniles have a history of escalating aggressive behavior, most adolescents who commit serious property crimes started with less serious forms of overt behavior, and most chronically rebellious teenagers were oppositional children.

Some juveniles commit all three types of acts. Generally, the more serious an adolescent's behavior is in one category, the more likely he or she is to have displayed the others. That is, most adolescents who commit violent crimes have also engaged in covert and authority-related antisocial behavior, but not all adolescents who have conflicts with authority or who engage in covert antisocial behavior are necessarily aggressive (Van Lier, Vitaro, Barker, Koot, & Tremblay, 2009). The authority conflict pathway almost always starts in childhood (contrary to the stereotype, few people suddenly develop serious authority problems for the first time as teenagers). The covert and overt pathways, in contrast, can begin either in childhood or in adolescence—and, as you will read, individuals whose antisocial behavior begins in childhood are very different from those whose antisocial behavior doesn't start until adolescence (Moffitt, 2006).

Changes in Juvenile Offending Over Time

When social scientists track changes in antisocial behavior over time, they generally look at juvenile offending, because statistics are kept on the numbers of juveniles arrested each year and the crimes with which they have been charged. Between 1965 and 1988, and especially after 1984, arrests for the most serious violent crimes—murder, rape, armed robbery, and aggravated assault—increased substantially among young people. After 1993, violent crime among young people declined dramatically; it began to rise very slightly in the middle of the first decade of the new century, but started to decline again in 2006. As of 2013, violent crime among adolescents was at its lowest level since 1980 (Office of Juvenile Justice and Delinquency Prevention, 2011) (see Figure 7). Property crime among adolescents is also less prevalent today than in 1980.

Bad Girls Much attention has been devoted to what appears to be a substantial reduction in the gender gap

Figure 7 Rates of juvenile crime in the United States are lower than they have been at any time in the past 30 years. (Office of Juvenile Justice and Delinquency Prevention, 2013)

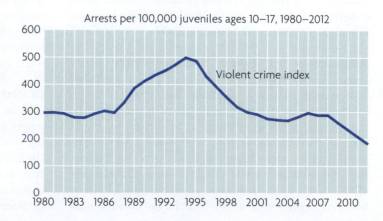

Arrests per 100,000 juveniles ages 10–17, 1980–2012

Violent crime index

in serious offenses over the past several decades (Federal Bureau of Investigation, 2009). Although antisocial behavior is still far more common among males than females, the male-to-female ratio in juvenile arrests today (for violent crime, it is about 4 to 1) is about half of what it was in 1980 (Office of Juvenile Justice and Delinquency Prevention, 2011).

It is not clear whether this change is mainly due to changes in actual offending or to changes in arrest practices. Changes in arrest rates can occur without there being any changes in actual offending (if, for example, the police crack down on crime, more people will be arrested, even if more people are not offending), and studies that rely on official statistics often reach conclusions different from those that rely on police or court records (Farrington, Loeber, & Stouthamer-Loeber, 2003). In fact, an analysis of data on actual offending found that there has *not* been an increase in violent acts committed by adolescent girls; rather, girls are simply being arrested more frequently for the same things they did in the past but were not arrested for (Steffensmeier, Schwartz, Zhong, & Ackerman, 2005). Analyses of underage drinking among girls have reached a similar conclusion: Although the proportion of girls who drink illegally has not increased in recent years, there has been a disproportionate increase in girls who are arrested for underage drinking (Zhong & Schwartz, 2010).

The ratio of males to females who have been arrested has changed not so much because of an increase in female offending, but because the drop in juvenile offending since 1993 was much steeper for males than females (Office of Juvenile Justice and Delinquency Prevention, 2011). If female offending remained relatively flat, but male offending dropped by more than 50%, the ratio of male-to-female offending would be cut in half. Regardless of the size or causes of the gender gap in arrests, violent females have significantly more mental health problems than do violent males, consistent with the notion that gender-inappropriate displays of aggression may be indicative of greater maladjustment (Cauffman, 2008; Grande et al., 2012). Girls' antisocial behavior may be especially influenced by the boys who are their friends and boyfriends (Arndorfer & Stormshak, 2008; Cauffman, Farruggia, & Goldweber, 2008; Lonardo, Giordano, Longmore, & Manning, 2009).

Adolescents as Crime Victims Violent crime among young people is a significant and understandable source of worry to adults. But crime is also a major source of worry to adolescents themselves, who are the age group most likely to be *victims* of crimes such as theft, robbery, rape, and assault. Adolescents are 2.5 times more likely than adults to be the victim of a nonfatal violent crime (Snyder & Sickmund, 2006). Adolescent victims of violent crimes are more likely to report a wide range of problems than are other

adolescents, including posttraumatic stress disorder, depressed mood, sleep deprivation, and academic difficulties, and they are more likely themselves to engage in aggression and antisocial behavior (Boney-McCoy & Finkelhor, 1995; Cooley-Quille & Lorion, 1999; Moses, 1999). Adolescents living in single-parent homes in the inner city are disproportionately likely to be the victims of violent crime; although Black and Hispanic adolescents are more likely to be victimized than White adolescents, this is due to the higher proportion of non-White adolescents living in single-parent homes in poor neighborhoods (Snyder & Sickmund, 2006; Wright & Younts, 2009). For many adolescents growing up in the inner city, gang violence and victimization are chronic problems. Among 15- to 19-year-olds, homicide accounts for 44% of all deaths among Blacks and 25% of all deaths among Hispanic Americans, but about 10% of deaths among Asian Americans, Native Americans, and Whites (National Center for Health Statistics, 2008).

Violence and aggression among youth are strongly linked to poverty for a number of reasons (Stoddard et al., 2013; Stoddard, Zimmerman, & Bauermeister, 2012). First, when families live in impoverished neighborhoods, parents are less effective in nurturing and monitoring their children, and this diminished effectiveness leads to increased aggression and crime (Snyder & Sickmund, 2006). Second, concentrated poverty upsets the social fabric of a neighborhood, making it more difficult for adults and social institutions to provide the guidance and supervision that adolescents need (Sampson, 1992). Third, in many inner-city communities devastated by unemployment, aggression is used by males to demonstrate their standing and power—characteristics that are typically demonstrated in middle-class communities through occupational success (M. Wilson & Daly, 1985). Finally, the widespread prevalence of guns in inner-city neighborhoods changes the sorts of interactions that take place when adolescents fight, transforming what might have been aggressive disputes into lethal exchanges (P. J. Cook & Ludwig, 2004; D. Wilkinson & Fagan, 1996). The significance of neighborhood influences on violence was confirmed in an experiment in which poor families with adolescents were randomly selected to be relocated into better neighborhoods: After their relocation, rates of violent behavior among the juveniles dropped significantly (J. R. Kling, Ludwig, & Katz, 2005).

Official Statistics Versus Adolescents' Reports Official figures about adolescent crime both underreport and selectively report rates of juvenile offending (Farrington, Loeber, & Stouthamer-Loeber, 2003). Underreporting results from the fact that many adolescents commit offenses that are undetected by authorities or that are handled outside official reporting procedures, as when an adolescent who is caught shoplifting is reprimanded by the storekeeper instead of being referred to the police. Selective reporting results from the fact that poor and minority youngsters are more likely to be arrested and, if convicted, to be treated more harshly than other youngsters who commit similar offenses, so that official statistics may artificially inflate the proportion of crimes committed by poor, minority youth (Chauhan, Reppucci, Burnette, & Reiner, 2010; Kakade et al., 2012; Rodriguez, 2010). People hold such strong negative stereotypes about Black males that when provided with information about a crime and asked to evaluate the perpetrator, individuals who were unconsciously led to believe that the offender was Black were significantly more likely than those who were not to rate him as likely to reoffend in the future and as deserving of harsh punishment, an effect that was consistent regardless of the race of the rater (S. Graham & Lowery, 2004). Racial bias is especially strong in the processing of relatively more *minor* crimes, like drug possession. When a very serious crime like armed robbery is committed, juveniles of different ethnic backgrounds are likely to receive similar treatment (Cauffman, Piquero, Kimonis, Steinberg, & Chassin, 2007).

An alternative to relying on official records is to go to adolescents directly and ask them about their involvement in various criminal or status offenses. Several researchers have done this, promising the respondents anonymity and confidentiality. The results of these surveys do not necessarily provide a more accurate picture of juvenile crime, but they certainly paint a different one. Two conclusions are especially interesting.

First, a very large proportion of adolescents—between 60% and 80%, depending on the survey sample—report having engaged in delinquent behavior at one time or another; nearly one-third of American 17-year-old boys have committed a violent crime in the past year, and nearly half of all males report being responsible for an assault sometime during adolescence (Farrington, 2009). Second, ethnic differences in the prevalence of offending derived from surveys of teenagers are smaller than those derived from official records (Farrington et al., 2003). More minority than White youth admit to having committed a serious crime, but ethnic differences in self-reported offending are far smaller than ethnic differences in rates of arrest. There also are social class and neighborhood differences in rates of serious criminal activity, and because minority youth are overrepresented among the poor, they are also overrepresented among those who commit crimes (McNulty & Bellair, 2003). Delinquency is by no means limited to poor adolescents, however. One-third of adolescents in affluent neighborhoods report involvement in violent and serious delinquency (J. M. Beyers, Loeber, Wikström, & Stouthamer-Loeber, 2001).

Although studies indicate that most adolescents—regardless of their social backgrounds—do something that violates the law at one time or another, the vast majority of teenagers who violate the law do so only once, and not violently. In fact, a relatively small number of adolescents—between 5% and 10%, depending on the study—account for most serious criminal activity (Piquero et al., 2003). It is important, therefore, in thinking about the causes of delinquent behavior, to distinguish between delinquent behavior that is serious and chronic and delinquent behavior that is less worrisome. As you will see, these two sets of delinquent behavior have very different antecedents (Moffitt, 2006).

Causes of Antisocial Behavior

The earlier an adolescent's "criminal career" begins—in particular, if it begins before adolescence—the more likely he or she is to become a chronic offender, to commit serious and violent crimes, and to continue committing crimes as an adult (Farrington, 2009). Conversely, the older an adolescent is when the delinquent activity first appears, the less worrisome his or her behavior is likely to become. For purposes of discussion, therefore, it is helpful to distinguish between youngsters who begin misbehaving before adolescence and those whose delinquent activity first appears during adolescence.

Two Types of Offenders   One of the most influential ways of characterizing these two groups of delinquents distinguishes between **life-course-persistent offenders** and **adolescence-limited offenders** (Moffitt, 2006). The first group demonstrates antisocial behavior before adolescence, is involved in delinquency during adolescence, and is at great risk for continuing criminal activity in adulthood. The second group engages in antisocial behavior *only* during adolescence; some adolescence-limited offenders become involved in crime relatively early in adolescence, whereas others begin during mid-adolescence (Fergusson & Horwood, 2002). Some researchers have suggested that there are other groups of offenders as well (for example, individuals who do not start offending until adolescence but who continue on into adulthood, and those who display antisocial behavior as children but desist before adulthood) (Piquero et al., 2003; Veenstra, Lindenberg, Verhulst, & Ormel, 2009), and others have pointed out that virtually everybody desists from crime by midlife, so that there really is no such thing as "life-course-persistent" offending (Sampson & Laub, 2003). Nevertheless, experts agree that the causes and consequences of delinquent behavior that begins during childhood or preadolescence are

life-course-persistent offenders Individuals who begin demonstrating antisocial or aggressive behavior during childhood and continue their antisocial behavior throughout adolescence and into adulthood.

adolescence-limited offenders Antisocial adolescents whose delinquent or violent behavior begins and ends during adolescence.

quite different from those of delinquency that begins—and typically ends—during adolescence or young adulthood (e.g., Dandreaux & Frick, 2009; Moffitt, 2006; van der Geest, Blokland, & Bijleveld, 2009). Although many more males than females are life-course-persistent offenders, the risk factors for early-onset antisocial behavior are similar for the sexes (Fergusson & Horwood, 2002; Storvoll & Wichstrøm, 2002).

What this means is that it is extremely difficult to predict which antisocial adolescents will persist in their bad behavior solely on the basis of their behavior during adolescence. Social scientists who have attempted to assess juvenile offenders' risk for future reoffending based solely on their adolescent characteristics have a remarkably poor track record (Mulvey et al., 2004). It's necessary to have information on the juvenile's behavior and history *before* adolescence in order to predict whether her or his offending is likely to be adolescence-limited or life-course-persistent, because the best predictor of continued offending in adulthood isn't whether someone is antisocial in adolescence. It's the presence of serious antisocial behavior in childhood.

Life-Course-Persistent Offenders Youngsters whose problems with the law begin before adolescence are often psychologically troubled. Most of these delinquents are male, many are poor, and a disproportionate number come from homes in which divorce has occurred (Farrington, 2009). More importantly, chronic delinquents typically come from disorganized families with hostile, inept, or neglectful parents who have mistreated their children and failed to instill in them proper standards of behavior or the psychological foundations of self-control (Compton, Snyder, & Schrepferman, 2003; Dogan, Conger, Kim, & Masyn, 2007). There is some evidence that exposure to harsh parenting may adversely affect the developing child's brain chemistry—in particular, the activity of serotonin receptors—which may increase the risk of antisocial behavior (Pine et al., 1996).

As Figure 8 illustrates, serious adolescent violence is typically the result of a cascade that begins early in life (Dodge, Greenberg, Malone, & Conduct Problems Prevention Research Group, 2008). Early economic disadvantage in the home leads to harsh and inconsistent parenting, which leads to cognitive and social deficits. These deficits, in turn, lead to conduct problems, which contribute

It is important to distinguish between adolescents whose "criminal careers" begin early and those who do not engage in delinquency until they are teenagers. Early-onset offending is a risk factor for chronic criminality. © Chet Gordon/The Image Works

to peer rejection and academic failure in elementary school and, over time, a reduction in parental supervision and monitoring (Ettekal & Ladd, 2015). Once poorly monitored, adolescents tend to drift into antisocial peer groups, which heightens their involvement in violence.

The idea that family factors may underlie chronic delinquency—because of genetic factors, environmental influences, or both—is supported by observations that preadolescent delinquency tends to run in families (Farrington, 2009; Thornberry, Freeman-Gallant, Lizotte, Krohn, & Smith, 2003). Many adolescents who have been in trouble with the law from an early age have siblings and parents who have had similar problems (Farrington, 2009; Tzoumakis, Lussier, & Corrado, 2012). Although studies have identified genetic influences on all types of antisocial behavior (Newsome & Sullivan, 2014), aggression is especially heritable (Deater-Deckard & Plomin, 1999; Eley, Lichtenstein, & Stevenson, 1999).

In addition to family factors, certain characteristics distinguish persistently delinquent youngsters from their peers at a relatively early age. First and most importantly,

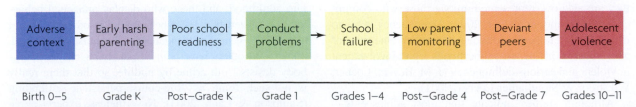

| Adverse context | Early harsh parenting | Poor school readiness | Conduct problems | School failure | Low parent monitoring | Deviant peers | Adolescent violence |

| Birth 0–5 | Grade K | Post–Grade K | Grade 1 | Grades 1–4 | Post–Grade 4 | Post–Grade 7 | Grades 10–11 |

Figure 8 Adolescent violence is often the long-term consequence of a process that begins early in life. (Dodge et al., 2008)

children who become delinquent—especially those who engage in violence—have histories of aggressive and antisocial behavior that are identifiable as early as age 8 (Broidy et al., 2003; Farrington, 2009; Kokko, Pulkkinen, Huesmann, Dubow, & Boxer, 2009; Patterson, Forgatch, Yoerger, & Stoolmiller, 1998). Although this has been confirmed in hundreds of studies, it is important to keep in mind that the majority of children who have histories of aggressive behavior problems do *not* grow up to be delinquent. (If this seems confusing, think about it this way: The majority of delinquents probably have eaten in fast-food restaurants at some point in their childhood, but the majority of children who eat in fast-food restaurants don't grow up to be delinquent.)

Second, studies show that many children who become persistent offenders have problems in self-regulation (Monahan, Steinberg, Cauffman, & Mulvey, 2013). They are more impulsive, less able to control their anger, and more likely than their peers to suffer from attention deficit/hyperactivity disorder (ADHD) (Calkins & Keane, 2009; A. Carroll et al., 2006; Sourander et al., 2006). ADHD is primarily biological in origin, strongly influenced by genes, and characterized by impulsivity, inattentiveness, restlessness, and inappropriately high levels of activity, especially in learning situations (Greven, Rijsdijk, & Plomin, 2011). Although ADHD does not directly cause antisocial behavior, it does elevate the risk for other family and academic problems, which, in turn, increase the likelihood of an adolescent developing externalizing problems (Bussing, Mason, Bell, Porter, & Garvan, 2010; Sibley et al., 2014; von Polier & Herpetz-Dahlmann, 2012).

Current thinking is that chronically conduct-disordered adolescents are born with strong biological predispositions toward antisocial behavior, some of which are genetic in origin, including low levels of serotonin (which diminish their ability to delay gratification), an emotional system that is easily aroused and difficult to regulate, and a temperament that makes them hard to control (Dodge & Pettit, 2003; Guo, Roettger, & Cai, 2008; Vloet, Konrad, Huebner, Herpetz, & Herpetz-Dahlmann, 2008). One recent brain imaging study found that the connections between brain regions that are important for impulse control are less well developed among juvenile offenders (Shannon et al., 2011). Poor self-regulation is an especially potent risk factor for continued problem behavior (P. Chen & Vazsonyi, 2011; T. W. Gardner, Dishion, & Connell, 2008; Monahan, Steinberg, Cauffman, & Mulvey, 2009).

Many researchers have examined the biological underpinnings of chronic antisocial behavior. There is considerable evidence that antisocial adolescents, especially those who are callous and unemotional, have a significantly lower resting heart rate than other youth, which may indicate a biologically inherited tendency toward fearlessness (Syngelaki, Fairchild, Moore, Savage, & van Goozen,

2013). In addition, CU adolescents show a blunted biological response to emotional and painful stimuli, as evidenced both in neuroimaging studies (Blair, Leibenluft, & Pine, 2014), and in studies of stress reactivity (Haltigan, Roisman, Susman, Barnett-Walker, & Monahan, 2011; Susman, 2006). Because individuals high in CU traits don't experience distress as easily or often as others, they are less likely to empathize with others or behave prosocially (Shirtcliff et al., 2009). Some antisocial adolescents, especially those who have CU traits, show abnormal brain development in regions that govern how we process emotionally arousing stimuli (Ermer, Cope, Nyalakanti, Calhoun, & Kiehl, 2013; Herpers, Scheepers, Bons, Buitelaar, & Rommelse, 2014; Hyde, Shaw, & Hariri, 2013; Wallace et al., 2014). All CU adolescents do not become delinquents, however; it also takes a willingness to engage in antisocial activity, sometimes referred to as "moral disengagement" (Hyde, Shaw, & Moilanen, 2010; Shulman, Cauffman, Piquero, & Fagan, 2011). The identification of the biological underpinnings of problematic functioning does not necessarily mean that they are inborn or hard-wired. Child maltreatment, for example, has been shown to affect children's stress reactivity, which may be one reason that abused and neglected children are at greater risk for developing subsequent behavior problems (Trickett, Negriff, Ji, & Peckins, 2011).

Third, and probably as a result of these biological inclinations, children who become chronically delinquent are more likely than their peers to score low on standardized tests of intelligence and neuropsychological functioning and to perform poorly in school (Cauffman, Steinberg, & Piquero, 2005; Pajer et al., 2008; Raine et al., 2005). Some of this is due to genetic factors, but some is also due to conditions surrounding their birth and prenatal care. A disproportionate number of persistently violent adolescents were born to mothers who abused drugs during pregnancy and had medical complications during delivery that likely affected their baby's neuropsychological and intellectual development (J. Liu, Raine, Wuerker, Venables, & Mednick, 2009).

Especially aggressive youngsters are likely to suffer from a tendency toward what has been called a **hostile attributional bias** (Dodge & Pettit, 2003; Fontaine, Yang, Dodge, Bates, & Pettit, 2008; Lansford et al., 2006). Individuals with this predisposition are likely to interpret ambiguous interactions with other children as deliberately hostile and to react aggressively. What might be viewed by the average adolescent as an innocent and accidental bump on the basketball court may be interpreted as an intentional shove by someone with a biased viewpoint, and it may lead to a fight. Adolescents with a hostile attributional bias are more likely to believe that people's personalities are unlikely to change (Yeager,

hostile attributional bias
The tendency to interpret ambiguous interactions with others as deliberately hostile.

Miu, Powers, & Dweck, 2013). In addition, some adolescents have more positive views about using aggression as a means to solve problems, and this inclination, in combination with a hostile attributional bias, leads to aggressive behavior that is almost automatic (Griffith Fontaine, Salzer Burks, & Dodge, 2002). This research has led to the development of interventions designed to change the way aggressive adolescents think about their interactions with others. Evaluations of Fast Track, a program designed to prevent disruptive behavior by improving individuals' social skills, found that reducing individuals' hostile attributional biases, as well as the extent to which they value aggression as a response to problems, led to a modest reduction in antisocial behavior (Dodge, Godwin, & The Conduct Problems Prevention Research Group, 2013).

Because aggressiveness, impulsivity, hyperactivity, and intelligence are relatively stable, there is a great deal of continuity in problem behaviors over time. Studies that have followed individuals from childhood through adolescence and into adulthood find very high correlations between behavior problems at one point in time and antisocial behavior later in life (Farrington, 2009; Lussier, Farrington, & Moffitt, 2009). This does not mean that all individuals who show antisocial behavior early invariably show it later—in fact, the majority do not. Nevertheless, many chronically antisocial adolescents grow up to be adults who persist in their antisocial behavior and who are at increased risk for other problems as well, such as substance abuse and depression (Wiesner, Kim, & Capaldi, 2005; Wiesner & Windle, 2006).

Adolescence-Limited Offenders In contrast to youngsters who begin their delinquent activity prior to adolescence (and who often continue their antisocial behavior into adulthood), those who begin during adolescence do not ordinarily show signs of serious psychological abnormality or severe family pathology (Moffitt, 2006; Van Lier, Wanner, & Vitaro, 2007). However, some individuals are genetically inclined to experience a greater-than-average increase in sensation-seeking during early adolescence, and this contributes to increased delinquency as well (Harden, Quinn, & Tucker-Drob, 2012). Typically, the offenses committed by these youngsters do not develop into serious criminality, and these individuals do not commit serious violations of the law after adolescence, although they may be more likely to have subsequent problems with drugs and alcohol (Nagin, Farrington, & Moffitt, 1995). In general, individuals who are involved in adolescence-limited antisocial activities have learned the norms and standards of society and are far better socialized than life-course-persistent antisocial individuals. Nor do adolescence-limited offenders show the sorts of temperamental difficulties and neuropsychological problems seen among life-course-persistent offenders (Moffitt, Caspi,

Harrington, & Milne, 2002). In contrast to the greatly disproportionate number of males who make up the life-course-persistent population (10 times more of these offenders are males than females), the ratio of males to females whose delinquency begins in adolescence is much smaller (about 1.5 to 1) (Moffitt & Caspi, 2001).

Although adolescence-limited offenders do not show the same degree of pathology as life-course-persistent offenders, they do have more problems during adolescence and early adulthood than youth who are not at all delinquent (Aguilar, Sroufe, Egeland, & Carlson, 2000; X. Chen & Adams, 2010; Roisman et al., 2010); although studies have found that many antisocial adolescents are nevertheless popular with their peers, there is no evidence that abstaining from antisocial behavior leads to peer rejection (Rulison, Kreager, & Osgood, 2014). One long-term follow-up of individuals who had earlier been classified as life-course-persistent offenders, adolescence-limited offenders, or neither found that the adolescence-limited offenders had more mental health, substance abuse, and financial problems as young adults than individuals who had not been delinquent as teenagers (Moffitt et al., 2002). It is incorrect, therefore, to assume that just because an adolescent's antisocial behavior is limited to adolescence that he or she is not troubled. Their serious offending may be limited to adolescence, but other problems may persist into early adulthood.

The main risk factors for adolescence-limited offending are well established: poor parenting (especially poor monitoring) and affiliation with antisocial peers (Burt, McGue, & Iacono, 2009; Goodnight, Bates, Newman, Dodge, & Pettit, 2006; Monahan, Steinberg, & Cauffman, 2009; Wiesner, Capaldi, & Kim, 2012;

Some aggressive adolescents are prone to having a "hostile attributional bias"—they are more likely to interpret ambiguous interactions with others as intentionally hostile. © Ken Karp/ McGraw-Hill Companies

Wissink, Deković, & Meijer, 2009). The first of these (poor parenting) usually leads to the second (hanging around with antisocial peers) (Laird, Criss, Pettit, Dodge, & Bates, 2008), often through the impact of poor parenting on school problems. Adolescents who have problems in school start spending time with antisocial peers, which leads to violence and other types of antisocial behavior (Dishion, Véronneau, & Myers, 2010). Influences on adolescence-limited offending are virtually identical for males and females and among adolescents from different ethnic groups (Fite, Wynn, & Pardini, 2009; Malsonado-Molina, Piquero, Jennings, Bird, & Canino, 2009; S. Miller, Malone, & Dodge, 2010).

One of the strongest predictors of delinquency and other forms of problem behavior is the extent to which the adolescent spends unsupervised time in unstructured activities with peers—activities like hanging out, driving around, and going to parties (Osgood, Wilson, O'Malley, Bachman, & Johnston, 1996). Most delinquent activity occurs in situations in which adolescents are pressured by their friends to go along with the group (Zimring, 1998). It is not coincidental that the peak years of susceptibility to peer pressure overlap with the peak years for this sort of delinquency. Indeed, adolescence-limited offending is largely done in an effort to impress other teenagers with one's bravado and independence from adult authority; nondelinquent youth often mimic antisocial peers to increase their status and popularity (Moffitt, 2006; Rebellon, 2006).

Prevention and Treatment of Externalizing Problems

Given the important differences between the causes of life-course-persistent and adolescence-limited antisocial behavior, it makes sense that these two groups of adolescents would be best served by different sorts of preventive and after-the-fact interventions. In order to lower the rate of chronic antisocial behavior, experts argue that we need mainly to prevent disruption in early family relationships and head off early academic problems through a combination of family support and preschool intervention (Loeber & Farrington, 2000; Tolan & Gorman-Smith, 2002). There is also some evidence that interventions designed to improve the transition into school and work roles in young adulthood may prove helpful (Roisman, Aguilar, & Egeland, 2004; Stouthamer-Loeber, Wei, & Loeber, 2004). These sorts of preventive strategies are easier proposed than done, however. Society is hesitant to intervene to prevent family problems, and we typically wait until we see a sign of trouble in a family before acting.

Unfortunately, research shows that the outlook for delinquents who have begun criminal careers early is not very good, although recent evaluations of a variety of interventions that follow **evidence-based practices**

(programs that have a proven track record) have been encouraging (Lipsey, 2009). This is the case for approaches that employ individual psychotherapy, family-based interventions, and diversion programs designed to remove delinquents from the juvenile justice system and provide them with alternative opportunities for productive behavior. One analysis found that every dollar spent on **multisystemic family therapy,** a proven intervention for antisocial youth (Weiss et al., 2013), saved taxpayers five times that amount (Dopp, Bourdin, Wagner, & Sawyer, 2014). In contrast, interventions that group antisocial youth together tend to be less effective, because they may inadvertently foster friendships among delinquent peers, and more antisocial adolescents may teach less antisocial ones some of the "tricks of the trade" (Mager, Milich, Harris, & Howard, 2005).

evidence-based practices Programs and practices that have a proven scientific basis.

multisystemic family therapy An intervention designed to reduce antisocial behavior that has been proven to be effective.

The prognosis for delinquents whose antisocial behavior is adolescence-limited is considerably better. Many juvenile offenders "age out" of crime; as they settle into adult roles, a criminal lifestyle becomes more difficult and less attractive (Massoglia & Uggen, 2010). Because they have internalized a basic foundation of norms and moral standards, it is easier to help these youngsters control their own behavior and stop misbehaving. Four types of strategies have been proposed. First, we can teach delinquent adolescents how to learn to resist peer pressure and to settle conflicts without resorting to aggression (Conduct Problems Prevention Research Group, 1999). Second, we can train parents to monitor their children more effectively, thereby minimizing opportunities adolescents have to engage in peer-oriented misbehavior (Forgatch, Patterson, Degarmo, & Beldavs, 2009). Third, by intervening within classrooms, schools, and neighborhoods, we may be able to alter the broader climate to discourage antisocial behavior and encourage prosocial behavior (Beets et al., 2009). Finally, by treating delinquency seriously when it occurs—by making sure that an adolescent knows that misbehavior has definite consequences—we can deter her or him from doing the same thing again in the future (E. Scott & Steinberg, 2008). Treating juvenile offending seriously does not require that we incarcerate juveniles for long periods, however; this has been shown to be ineffective in deterring future crime (Loughran et al., 2009).

Internalizing Problems

Most individuals emerge from adolescence confident, with a healthy sense of who they are and where they are headed. But for some, the changes and demands of adolescence create feelings of helplessness, confusion, and pessimism.

depression
A psychological disturbance characterized by low self-esteem, decreased motivation, sadness, and difficulty in finding pleasure in formerly pleasurable activities.

Although minor fluctuations in self-esteem during early adolescence are commonplace, it is not normal for adolescents (or adults, for that matter) to feel a prolonged or intense sense of hopelessness or frustration. Such young people are likely to be psychologically depressed and in need of professional help. Depression is by far the most significant internalizing problem that has its onset in adolescence. Many adolescents have experienced bouts of severe anxiety as well, but these generally make their first appearance in childhood (Merikangas et al., 2010).

The Nature and Prevalence of Depression

In its mild form, **depression** is the most common psychological disturbance among adolescents (Graber & Sontag, 2009). Although we associate depression with feelings of sadness, there are other symptoms that are important signs of the disorder, and sadness alone without any other symptoms may not indicate depression, at least in the clinical sense of the term. Depression has emotional symptoms, including dejection, decreased enjoyment of pleasurable activities, and low self-esteem. It has cognitive symptoms, such as pessimism and hopelessness. It has motivational symptoms, including apathy and boredom. Finally, it often has physical symptoms, such as a loss of appetite, difficulty sleeping, and loss of energy. The symptoms of major depression are the same in adolescence as in adulthood and among males and females, although, as you'll read, there are large sex differences in the prevalence of the illness (Lewinsohn, Pettit, Joiner, & Seeley, 2003).

Mood, Syndromes, and Disorder Psychologists believe that it is important to distinguish among depressed mood (feeling sad), depressive syndromes (having multiple symptoms of depression), and depressive disorder (having enough symptoms to be diagnosed with the illness) (Graber & Sontag, 2009). According to one large-scale survey, 30% of all high school students feel so sad and hopeless so often that they stop engaging in their usual activities, and each year, 17% of this age group seriously contemplate committing suicide (Centers for Disease Control and Prevention, 2014).

Fewer individuals report a pattern of depressive symptoms that includes a wider range of symptoms than sadness alone. About 8% of American teenagers between the ages of 13 and 18 meet the DSM diagnostic criteria for a depressive disorder during the past year (Avenevoli, Swendsen, He, Burstein, & Merikangas, 2015) (see Table 3). As many as 15% of individuals will experience at least one bout of depression by the age of 18 (Merikangas et al., 2010). Some studies also indicate that there have been increases over time in the prevalence of depression and other signs of internalized distress, especially among adolescents, with the rates increasing in each generation (Lewinsohn, Rohde, Seeley, & Fischer, 1993). Visits to psychiatrists by adolescents have increased at a much faster rate in recent decades among adolescents than adults (Olfson, Blanco, Wang, Laje, & Correll, 2014).

Depressed mood, depressive syndrome, and depressive disorder all become more common over adolescence, in part because of the increasing prevalence of stressful events during the adolescent years (Graber & Sontag, 2009) and in part because the cognitive changes of adolescence permit

Table 3   DSM-5 diagnostic criteria for Persistent Depressive Disorder

The essential feature of Persistent Depressive Disorder is a depressed mood that occurs for most of the day, for more days than not, for at least 2 years (at least 1 year for children and adolescents). Individuals with persistent depressive disorder describe their mood as sad or "down in the dumps." During periods of depressed mood (in children and adolescents, the mood can be irritable), at least two of the following six symptoms are present:

- Poor appetite or overeating
- Insomnia or hypersomnia
- Low energy or fatigue
- Low self-esteem
- Poor concentration or difficulty making decisions
- Feelings of hopelessness

Because these symptoms have become a part of the individual's day-to-day experience, particularly in the case of early onset (e.g., "I've always been this way"), they may not be reported unless the individual is directly prompted. During the 2-year period (1 year for children or adolescents), any symptom-free intervals last no longer than 2 months. The symptoms may not be due to the direct physiological effects of the use or abuse of a substance (for instance, alcohol, drugs, or medications) or a general medical condition (e.g., cancer or a stroke). The symptoms must also cause significant distress or impairment in social, occupational, educational or other important areas of functioning.

Source: American Psychiatric Association, 2013.

the introspection and rumination that often accompany depression (Avenevoli & Steinberg, 2001). There is also a significant decline in positive mood over the adolescent years (Weinstein, Mermelstein, Hankin, Hedeker, & Flay, 2007).

There is an especially dramatic increase in the prevalence of depressive feelings around the time of puberty; depression is one-third as common during childhood as it is during adolescence (Graber & Sontag, 2009). Depressive symptoms increase between 14 and 17, and then begin to decline (see Figure 9) (Rawana & Morgan, 2014). One intriguing idea links the increase in depression to the same changes in the brain's dopamine system that increase the vulnerability to alcohol and other drugs (Davey, Yücel, & Allen, 2008). According to this view, the coincidence of increased reward seeking caused by this brain change with changes in the adolescent's social world leads to an intensification in adolescents' desire for the rewards of intimate friendships and romantic relationships. When these rewards don't materialize, adolescents may become frustrated and depressed. Symptoms of depression increase steadily throughout adolescence and then start to decline—making late adolescence the period of the life span with the highest risk for the disorder (Wight, Sepúlveda, & Aneshensel, 2004). One reason that depression declines after late adolescence is that individuals report a significant decline in stress during this period (J. S. Brown, Meadows, & Elder, Jr., 2007; Seiffge-Krenke, Aunola, & Nurmi, 2009).

Sex Differences in Depression

One of the most consistent findings in the study of adolescent depression involves the emergence of a very large sex difference in rates of depression in early adolescence (Avenevoli et al., 2015). Before adolescence, boys are somewhat more likely to exhibit depressive symptoms than girls, but after puberty, the sex difference

in prevalence of depression reverses. From early adolescence until very late in adulthood, twice as many females as males suffer from depressive disorder, and females are somewhat more likely than males to report depressed mood (Avenevoli et al., 2015). The increased risk for depression among girls emerges during puberty, rather than at a particular age or grade in school (Angold, Costello, & Worthman, 1998; G. C. Patton et al., 2008). Although sex differences in major depression persist beyond adolescence, reports of depressive symptoms tend to diminish in early adulthood, but the decline is steeper among females, perhaps because they experience a greater drop in stress as they leave adolescence behind (Galambos, Barker, & Krahn, 2006; Ge, Natsuaki, & Conger, 2006; Meadows, Brown, & Elder, Jr., 2006; Stoolmiller, Kim, & Capaldi, 2005).

Psychologists do not have a definitive explanation for the emergence of sex differences in depressive disorder at adolescence. Some evidence indicates that females are more susceptible than males to genetic influences on depression, such that even when males and females inherit the same genetic predisposition toward depression from their parents, that predisposition is more likely to be manifested among girls (Jacobson & Rowe, 1999), but it is not known why this is the case. More likely, changes in social relationships around the time of puberty may leave girls more vulnerable than boys to some forms of psychological distress (with some individuals inheriting a stronger predisposition than others), and depression may be a stereotypically feminine way of manifesting it.

Gender Roles It is well-known that rates of depression are about twice as high among adult women than men; it is less well-known that this sex difference is entirely due to the higher prevalence of depression among girls than boys, which persists into adulthood. Sex differences in the appearance of depression for the first time after adolescence (which is rare) are very small.

Social scientists speculate that the emergence of sex differences in depression has something to do with the social role that the adolescent girl may find herself in as she enters the world of boy–girl relationships, which may bring heightened self-consciousness over her physical appearance and increased concern over popularity with peers (Wichstrøm, 1999). Because many of these feelings may provoke helplessness, hopelessness, and anxiety, adolescent girls may be more susceptible to depressive feelings. To make matters worse, pressures on young women to behave in sex-stereotyped ways may lead girls to adopt some behaviors and dispositions—passivity, dependency, and fragility, for example—that they have been socialized to believe are part of the feminine role and that may contribute to their depressed mood. Depression in girls is significantly correlated with having a poor body image and being low in masculinity

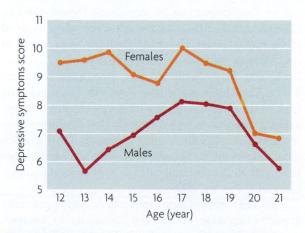

Figure 9 **Depressive symptoms increase during adolescence, peak in middle adolescence, and then decline.** (Rawana & Morgan, 2014)

One reason the incidence of depression is greater among adolescent girls than boys is that girls are more likely to react to stress by ruminating about the problem and feeling helpless. © Jetta Productions/Walter Hodges/Tetra Images/Getty Images RF

(Bearman & Stice, 2008; Eberhart, Shih, Hammen, & Brennan, 2006).

The gender-role hypothesis is only one explanation for sex differences in the prevalence of depression during adolescence. Three other accounts focus on sex differences in the degree to which adolescence is stressful, in how people cope with stress, and in vulnerability to different types of stressors.

Stress, Rumination, and Sensitivity to Others   The link between stress and depression during adolescence is well documented among both males and females; individuals who experience more stress are more vulnerable to depression and other internalizing problems (Ge, Natsuaki, Neiderhiser, & Reiss, 2009). But there is evidence that early adolescence is generally a more stressful time for girls than boys (Charbonneau, Mezulis, & Hyde, 2009; Rudolph & Hammen, 1999). This is because the bodily changes of puberty, especially when they occur early in adolescence, are more likely to be stressful for girls than boys; because girls are more likely than boys to experience multiple stressors at the same time (for example, going through puberty while making the transition into junior high school); and because girls are likely to experience more stressful life events than boys, including sexual abuse and harassment (Graber & Sontag, 2009; Vaughan & Halpern, 2010).

Second, there is evidence that girls are more likely than boys to react to stress by turning their feelings inward—for instance, by ruminating about the problem (sometimes with a friend) and feeling helpless—whereas boys are more likely to respond either by distracting themselves or by turning their feelings outward, in aggressive behavior or in drug and alcohol abuse (Cox, Mezulis, & Hyde, 2010; Daughters, Gorka, Matusiewicz, & Anderson, 2013; Jose & Weir, 2013). Girls' greater tendency to ruminate, especially with their friends, likely contributes to their greater risk for depression (Stone, Hankin, Gibb, & Abela, 2011). As a result, even when exposed to the same degree of stress, girls are more likely to respond to the stressors by becoming depressed (Kiang & Buchanan, 2014; Rood, Roelofs, Bögels, & Meesters, 2012). This difference in the ways that boys and girls react to stress helps explain why the prevalence of externalizing disorders is higher in boys, while the prevalence of internalizing disorders is higher in girls. Girls who are more able to tolerate conflicts in their relationships are less likely to develop internalizing symptoms (Gunlicks-Stoessel & Powers, 2008).

The third explanation emphasizes girls' generally greater orientation toward and sensitivity to interpersonal relations (Cyranowski & Frank, 2000; Guyer, McClure-Tone, Shiffrin, Pine, & Nelson, 2009; Hankin, Stone, & Wright, 2010). Sex differences in levels of the hormone **oxytocin** may both encourage females to invest more in their close relationships and make them more vulnerable to the adverse consequences of relational disruptions and interpersonal difficulties (Bakker, Ormel, Verhulst, & Oldehinkel, 2010). Girls are much more likely than boys to develop emotional problems as a result of family discord or problems with peers (Conley, Rudolph, & Bryant, 2012; St. Clair et al., 2014; Telzer & Fuligni, 2013). Because adolescence is a time of many changes in relationships—in the family, with friends, and with romantic partners—the capacity of females to invest heavily in their relationships with others may be both a strength and a source of vulnerability.

making the practical connection

In light of what we know about the likely causes of sex differences in depression, what preventive interventions should be targeted at young adolescent girls?

Suicide and Non-Suicidal Self-Injury

Prevalence of Suicide   According to recent national surveys, in any given year, more than 10% of American female high school students and about 5% of males attempt suicide; nearly one-third of these attempts are serious enough to require treatment by a physician or nurse. More than twice as many adolescents think about killing themselves than actually attempt suicide—referred to as **suicidal ideation**—but the majority of these have gone so far as to make a plan (Centers for Disease Control and Prevention, 2014). Suicidal ideation increases during early adolescence, peaks around age 15, and then declines (Nock et al., 2013). Adolescents who attempt to kill themselves usually have made appeals for help and have tried but failed to get emotional support from family or friends.

They report feeling trapped, lonely, worthless, and hopeless (Kidd, 2004).

The adolescent suicide rate among 15- to 19-year-olds increased alarmingly between 1950 and 1990, fueled by the increased use of drugs and alcohol and the increased availability of firearms (Judge & Billick, 2004). The rate peaked and declined somewhat during the 1990s. But the adolescent suicide rate began increasing again in 2007 and is higher now than it was 10 years ago (see Figure 10) (Centers for Disease Control and Prevention, 2014).

You may have read that suicide is a leading cause of death among young people, but this is primarily because very few young people die from other causes, such as disease. Although the rate of suicide rises rapidly during the middle adolescent years, it continues to rise throughout adulthood, and suicide is a much more common cause of death among adults than it is among young people, largely because very few suicide attempts by adolescents are successful. The most common method of suicide among adolescents is with a firearm, followed by hanging. Drug overdoses and carbon monoxide poisoning are also common (Judge & Billick, 2004). The suicide rate is highest among American Indian and Alaskan Native adolescents and lowest among Black and White adolescents; rates among Hispanic and Asian adolescents fall in between these extremes (Goldston et al., 2008).

Non-Suicidal Self-Injury   Many adolescents do not contemplate suicide, but commit acts of **non-suicidal self-injury (NSSI),** such as deliberately burning or cutting themselves (Nock, Prinstein, & Sterba, 2009). Some studies estimate that nearly 25% of adolescents

oxytocin
A hormone known to influence emotional bonding to others.

suicidal ideation
Thinking about ending one's life.

non-suicidal self-injury (NSSI)
Deliberate attempts to hurt oneself in nonlethal ways, including cutting or burning one's skin.

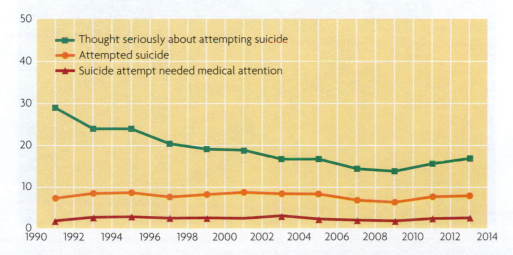

Figure 10   Suicidal thoughts and suicide attempts among U.S. adolescents, which had been declining, are on the rise. (Centers for Disease Control and Prevention, 2014)

suicide contagion
The process through which learning about another's suicide can lead people to try to take their own lives.

have engaged in NSSI at least once, and that the prevalence has been rising in recent years (Jacobson & Gould, 2007). The most common reasons given for NSSI are to reduce feelings of tension, anger, anxiety, or depression or to prompt feelings when none exist. Less is known about this group of adolescents than about those who attempt suicide, but at least one study found that levels of depressive symptomatology among adolescents who attempt to harm themselves, as well as risk factors for depression, fall somewhere between non-suicidal and suicidal adolescents (Brausch & Gutierrez, 2010; Guan, Fox, & Prinstein, 2012). Adolescents who engage in NSSI often have the same cognitive vulnerabilities associated with depression (Tatnell, Kelada, Hasking, & Martin, 2014; Voon, Hasking, & Martin, 2014). They are also more likely than other adolescents to have a friend who has attempted NSSI (Hasking, Andrews, & Martin, 2013)

Risk Factors for Suicide   There are four established sets of risk factors for attempting suicide during adolescence, and they are similar for males and females and among Black, Hispanic, and White adolescents: having a psychiatric problem, especially depression or substance abuse; having a history of suicide in the family; being under stress, especially in the areas of achievement and sexuality; and, especially, experiencing parental rejection, family disruption, or extensive family conflict (Boeninger, Masyn, & Conger, 2013; Karch, Logan, McDaniel, Floyd, & Vagi, 2013; Miller, Esposito-Smythers, & Leichtweis, 2015). Adolescents who have one of these risk factors are significantly more likely to attempt suicide than their peers, and adolescents who have more than one risk factor are dramatically more likely to try to kill themselves. Adolescents who have attempted suicide once are at risk for attempting it again (Lewinsohn, Rohde, & Seely, 1994).

Suicide Contagion   Adolescents are also more likely to attempt suicide if one of their friends or someone else in their community has committed suicide, which is referred to as **suicide contagion** (Abrutyn & Mueller, 2014; Institute of Medicine, 2013). Teenagers are more susceptible to suicide contagion than adults. Studies of media reports show that adolescents are susceptible to both fictionalized (e.g., television dramas) and nonfictionalized reports of suicide, especially those involving celebrities. The way in which a suicide victim is portrayed in the media has a significant impact on the likelihood that adolescents will copy the behavior. When the

Shortly after the actor and comedian Robin Williams committed suicide, the American Academy of Motion Picture Arts and Sciences posted this image on Twitter, with the text, "Genie, you're free." This was sharply criticized by suicide experts, because the message that suicide is a liberating act encourages others who are depressed to try to take their own lives.

victim is portrayed as someone who is suffering from some sort of abnormality or psychopathology, there is far less chance that the suicide will be "contagious." When the victim is portrayed in a positive light, though, it increases the odds that adolescents who learn about it will attempt to take their own lives. This is especially the case when coverage of the death presents a celebrity suicide as having been a means of liberating himself or herself from a painful situation. Suicide experts prefer that media coverage of celebrity suicides (which is inevitable) emphasize the fact that individuals who are under duress or hopeless seek treatment for their mental health.

Causes of Depression and Internalizing Disorders

A variety of theories have been proposed to account for the onset of depression and other types of internalizing problems during adolescence. The current consensus is that internalizing problems are likely to result from interacting environmental conditions and individual predispositions rather than either set of factors alone. Today, most experts endorse a **diathesis–stress model** of depression, which suggests that depression may occur when individuals who are predisposed toward internalizing problems (the term "diathesis" refers to this predisposition) are exposed to chronic or acute stressors that precipitate a depressive reaction (Auerbach, Eberhart, & Abela, 2010; Lewinsohn, Joiner, & Rohde, 2001). Individuals without the diathesis—who are not predisposed toward depression—are able to withstand a great deal of stress, for instance, without developing any psychological problems. In contrast, individuals who have strong predispositions toward the disorder may become depressed in the face of mildly stressful circumstances that most of us would consider to be normal. Research has focused on both the diathesis and the stress—on identifying individual predispositions toward depression and on identifying the environmental circumstances likely to precipitate the disorder.

The Diathesis   Two categories of predispositions have received the most attention. First, because depression has been found to have a strong genetic component, it is believed that at least some of the diathesis is biological in origin and may be related to problematic patterns of neuroendocrine functioning (**neuroendocrine** refers to hormonal activity in the brain and nervous system). In particular, researchers have focused on the predisposition toward intense problems in the regulation of neural activity in the hypothalamus, a brain structure that plays a crucial role in how we respond to stress (Paten, 2013). This biological predisposition may make it difficult for individuals to regulate their emotions, which, in turn, may make them susceptible to depression and other psychological problems (Silk et al., 2007). Individuals

who are prone to intense activation of the hypothalamic-pituitary-adrenocortical (HPA) axis, in particular, are more biologically reactive to stress than others, and they are more prone to depression and other internalizing disorders (Diamond, Fagundes, & Cribbet, 2012). Abnormalities in one of several genes, in particular, may make some individuals more likely to develop depression in the face of stress (Caspi et al., 2003; Cicchetti, Rogosch, & Sturge-Apple, 2007; Petersen et al., 2012). Not surprisingly, given the role that genes play in the development of depression, vulnerability to depression tends to run in families—adolescents with a depressed parent are 3 times as likely to develop depression as are other youth (Graber & Sontag, 2009).

Other researchers have focused more on the cognitive style of depressed individuals, suggesting that people with tendencies toward hopelessness, pessimism, and self-blame are more likely to interpret events in their lives in ways that lead to the development of depression (Alloy et al., 2012; Auerbach, Ho, & Kim, 2014; Calvete, Orue, & Hankin, 2013; Nicolai, Laney, & Mezulis, 2013). These sorts of cognitive sets, which may be linked to the ways in which children think they are viewed first by parents and later by peers, develop during childhood and are thought to play a role in the onset of depression during adolescence (Abela & Hankin, 2011). Individuals who tend to ruminate in the face of stress are especially at risk for the development of depression and anxiety (Michl, McLaughlin, Shepherd, & Nolen-Hoeksema, 2013). As with the case of stress-reactivity, there is some evidence that individuals' cognitive style is stable and moderately heritable (Rudolph & Klein, 2009).

The Stress   Researchers who have been more concerned with the stress component of the diathesis–stress model—that is, with environmental influences on depression—have focused on three broad sets of stressors. First, depression is more common among adolescents from families characterized by high conflict and low cohesion, and rates are higher among adolescents from divorced homes (Graber & Sontag, 2009; Hamza & Willoughby, 2011; Karevold, Røysamb, Ystrom, & Mathiesen, 2009). Second, depression is more prevalent among adolescents who are unpopular, have poor peer relations, or have friends who are depressed (Agoston & Rudolph, 2011; Conley & Rudolph, 2009; Mendle, Harden, Brooks-Gunn, & Graber, 2012; Sontag & Graber, 2010; Van Zalk, Kerr, Branje, Stattin, & Meeus, 2010). Third, depressed adolescents report more chronic and acute adversity than nondepressed adolescents do,

diathesis–stress model
A perspective on psychological disorder that posits that problems are the result of an interaction between a preexisting condition (the diathesis) and exposure to a stressful event or condition.

neuroendocrine
Referring to activity in the brain and nervous system.

such as the loss of a parent, maltreatment, and poverty (Garber & Cole, 2010; Graber & Sontag, 2009; McLaughlin et al., 2012). There is also evidence that academic difficulties are correlated with depression, especially among adolescents from Asian cultures, in which relatively more stress may be placed on achievement (Greenberger, Chen, Tally, & Dong, 2000). Similar findings on the connection between academic pressure and depression have emerged from studies of affluent suburban youth in the United States (Luthar & Becker, 2002). Although all sorts of stressors have been linked to the onset of psychological problems, the single most common trigger of the first episode of major depression in adolescence is the breakup of a romantic relationship (Monroe, Rohde, Seeley, & Lewinsohn, 1999).

You read earlier that the prevalence of depression rises during adolescence. Can diathesis–stress models of depression account for this increase? For the most part, they can. Biological theorists can point to the hormonal changes of puberty, because one of the effects of pubertal hormones is to make individuals more sensitive to stress (Edwards, Rose, Kaprio, & Dick, 2011; E. Walker, Sabuwalla, & Huot, 2004). Depression and negative affect among both boys and girls are correlated with various hormones known to change at puberty (Graber & Sontag, 2009). Many studies show that the increase in depression in adolescence is more closely linked to puberty than age (Conley & Rudolph, 2009), although it is difficult to pinpoint puberty as the *cause* of the problem, since many other changes typically occur around the same time (such as the transition out of elementary school). Cognitive theorists can point to the onset of hypothetical thinking at adolescence, which may result in new (and perhaps potentially more depressing) ways of viewing the world (Kuhn, 2009). And theorists who emphasize environmental factors draw attention to the new environmental demands of adolescence, such as changing schools, beginning to date, or coping with transformations in family relationships—all of which may be stressful (Graber & Sontag, 2009; Morris, Ciesla, & Garber, 2010). Thus, there are many good reasons to expect that the prevalence of depression would increase as individuals pass from childhood into adolescence. Individuals who develop internalizing disorders such as depression and anxiety in adolescence are at elevated risk to suffer from these problems as adults (Lewinsohn, Rohde, Seeley, Klein, & Gotlib, 2003).

Treatment and Prevention of Internalizing Problems

The treatment of depression during adolescence is very similar to its treatment at other points in the life span.

Clinicians use a wide range of approaches, including biological therapies employing antidepressant medication (these address the neuroendocrine problem, if one exists); psychotherapies designed to help depressed adolescents understand the roots of their depression, to increase the degree to which they experience pleasure in their daily activities, or to change the nature of their cognitive set; and family therapy, which focuses on changing patterns of family relationships that may be contributing to the adolescent's symptoms. A comprehensive review found that psychotherapy with depressed and anxious adolescents has a significant, but modest, effect; although most of the treatment studies employed cognitive-behavioral therapy, the review found that other evidence-based practices (e.g., interpersonal therapy) were equally effective (Weisz, McCarty, & Valeri, 2006). Importantly, evidence-based approaches are superior to approaches that do not have a scientific basis, which, unfortunately, are widely used (Beardslee et al., 2013; Weisz et al., 2009). With regard to antidepressants, research has confirmed the effectiveness of a class of drugs called **selective serotonin reuptake inhibitors (SSRIs)** in the treatment of depression in adolescence (Graber & Sontag, 2009). These medications are also effective in treating other types of internalizing problems, such as anxiety disorders and social phobias, especially when used in conjunction with cognitive-behavioral therapy (Brent et al., 2008; Kennard et al., 2009; Walkup et al., 2008). The use of antidepressant medications among adolescents has nearly doubled since the 1990s (Olfson, Druss, & Marcus, 2015).

Stress and Coping

Many adolescents report difficulty in coping with stressful situations at home or at school. These stressors include major life changes (such as a parental divorce, changing schools, or having someone in the family suddenly become seriously ill), chronically stressful conditions (such as poverty, a disabling illness, or constant family conflict), and day-to-day hassles (such as school exams, fights with friends, and arguments with siblings and parents) (Compas & Reeslund, 2009).

Stress can affect individuals in different ways (Steinberg & Avenevoli, 2000). For some teenagers, it can lead to internalized disorders, such as anxiety, depression, headaches, and indigestion—even compromised immune system functioning (Birmaher et al., 1994). For others, the consequences of stress are externalized, in behavior and conduct problems. For still others, the impact of stress is manifested in drug and alcohol abuse. These links between stress and psychosocial problems have been documented in studies of youngsters from all ethnic groups and family backgrounds and among youth exposed to both relatively common stressors (such as breaking up with a romantic partner) and relatively severe ones (such as exposure to war trauma, terrorism, or natural disasters) (Gershoff, Aber, Ware, & Kotler, 2010; La Greca & Silverman, 2009).

Yet, for some adolescents, the very same sources and levels of stress do not seem to be associated with psychological or physical upset at all. Thus, although we tend to think of stress as having negative effects on our well-being, the connection between stress and dysfunction is not clear-cut. Some adolescents show enormous **resilience** in the face of enormous adversity (Compas & Reeslund, 2009). What makes some adolescents more vulnerable to the effects of stress than others? Psychologists point to three sets of factors.

First, the effect of any one stressor is exacerbated if it is accompanied by other stressors. Stress tends to have a multiplicative effect: An adolescent who faces two stressors at the same time (parental divorce and a change of schools, for example) is more than twice as likely to experience psychological problems as someone who has experienced only one of the two stressors (Compas & Reeslund, 2009; Forehand, Biggar, & Kotchick, 1998).

Second, adolescents who have other resources—either internal resources, such as high self-esteem, healthy identity development, high intelligence, or strong feelings of competence, or external resources, such as social support from others—are less likely to be adversely affected by stress than their peers (Compas & Reeslund, 2009; Luthar, 1991; Masten et al., 1999; Monahan, Guyer, Silk, Fitzwater, & Steinberg, L., 2016). Adolescents with close friends and good social skills seem to be better able to handle stressors such as parental divorce or starting junior high school than are teenagers who lack close friendships or have fewer interpersonal resources. Most importantly, teenagers who have warm and close family relationships are less likely to be distressed by a stressful experience than are teenagers without such familial support (Weist, Freedman, Paskewitz, Proescher, & Flaherty, 1995). Indeed, studies consistently show that the presence of a close parent-adolescent relationship is probably the single most important factor in protecting adolescents from psychological harm (Raffaelli et al., 2013). The importance of social support as a buffer against the adverse effects of stress has been documented in studies of adolescents around the world.

Finally, some adolescents use more effective coping strategies than do others. Specialists who study coping strategies distinguish between strategies that involve taking steps to change the source of the stress, called **primary control strategies,** and those that involve efforts to adapt to the problem, called **secondary control strategies** (Compas & Reeslund, 2009). For instance, if you are very worried about an upcoming exam, a primary control strategy might be to form a study group with other students in order to review the material, whereas a secondary control strategy might be to go out to a movie or for a run in order to relax yourself. Individuals who use primary or secondary control strategies are better adjusted, less depressed, and less likely to have behavioral problems than those who react to stress through disengagement or avoidance (Compas & Reeslund, 2009; L. D. Scott & House, 2005; Seiffge-Krenke & Klessinger, 2000; Tolan, Gorman-Smith, Henry, Chung, & Hunt, 2002; Weisz, Francis, & Bearman, 2010).

resilience
The ability of an individual to continue to function competently in the face of adversity or stress.

primary control strategies
Coping strategies in which an individual attempts to change the stressor.

secondary control strategies
Coping strategies that involve attempts by the individual to adapt to the stressor.

making the personal connection

How do you cope with stress? Are you more likely to use primary or secondary control strategies?

In some situations, secondary control strategies are quite effective. These tend to be stressful situations that are clearly uncontrollable, such as being diagnosed with a serious illness or learning that one's parents are getting a divorce (Hall, Chipperfield, Perry, Ruthig, & Goetz, 2006). In these instances, trying to distract and calm oneself may help alleviate some of the stress, and trying to exert control over an uncontrollable situation may only make matters worse (Jaser et al., 2007). But, adolescents who employ primary control strategies when the source of the stress is controllable are less vulnerable to its detrimental health consequences (Clarke, 2006).

Glossary

A

abstinence-only sex education Programs that encourage adolescents to avoid sexual activity but that do not provide information about safe sex.

academic achievement Achievement that is measured by standardized tests of scholastic ability or knowledge.

achievement The psychosocial domain concerning behaviors and feelings in evaluative situations.

achievement attributions The beliefs an individual holds about the causes of her or his successes and failures.

adolescence The second decade of life.

adolescence-limited offenders Antisocial adolescents whose delinquent or violent behavior begins and ends during adolescence.

adolescent growth spurt The dramatic increase in height and weight that occurs during puberty.

adolescent health care A field of study and health care devoted to understanding the health care needs of individuals during the second decade of life.

adrenarche The maturation of the adrenal glands that takes place during adolescence.

Adult Attachment Interview A structured interview used to assess an individual's past attachment history and "internal working model" of relationships.

adult plasticity Relatively minor changes in brain circuits as a result of experiences during adulthood, after the brain has matured.

age grading The process of grouping individuals within social institutions on the basis of age.

age of majority The designated age at which an individual is recognized as an adult.

age–crime curve The relationship between chronological age and offending, showing that the prevalence of offending peaks in late adolescence.

agency The sense that one has an impact on one's world.

aggression Acts done to be intentionally harmful.

AIDS (acquired immune deficiency syndrome) A disease, caused by a virus transmitted by means of bodily fluids, that devastates the immune system.

androgens A class of sex hormones secreted by the gonads, found in both sexes, but in higher levels among males than females following puberty.

anhedonic Having difficulty experiencing positive emotions, a risk factor for depression.

anorexia nervosa An eating disorder found chiefly among young women, characterized by dramatic and severe self-induced weight loss.

anxious-avoidant attachment An insecure attachment between infant and caregiver, characterized by indifference on the part of the infant toward the caregiver.

anxious-resistant attachment An insecure attachment between infant and caregiver, characterized by distress at separation and anger at reunion.

attachment The strong affectional bond that develops between an infant and a caregiver.

attention deficit/hyperactivity disorder (ADHD) A biologically based psychological disorder characterized by impulsivity, inattentiveness, and restlessness, often in school situations.

authoritarian parents Parents who use punitive, absolute, and forceful discipline, and who place a premium on obedience and conformity.

authoritative parents Parents who use warmth, firm control, and rational, issue-oriented discipline, in which emphasis is placed on the development of self-direction.

authority conflicts A type of antisocial behavior characterized by stubbornness and rebelliousness.

autobiographical memory The recall of personally meaningful past events.

autoerotic behavior Sexual behavior that is experienced alone, such as masturbation or sexual fantasizing.

autonomy The psychosocial domain concerning the development and expression of independence.

B

baby boom The period following World War II, during which the number of infants born was extremely large.

Bar (Bas) Mitzvah In Judaism, the religious ceremony marking the young person's transition to adulthood.

basal metabolism rate The minimal amount of energy used by the body during a resting state.

behavioral autonomy The capacity to make independent decisions and to follow through with them.

behavioral decision theory An approach to understanding adolescent risk taking, in which behaviors are seen as the outcome of systematic decision-making processes.

behavioral genetics The scientific study of genetic influences on behavior.

big fish–little pond effect The reason that individuals who attend high school with high-achieving peers feel worse about themselves than comparably successful individuals with lower-achieving peers.

binge drinking Consuming five or more drinks in a row on one occasion, an indicator of alcohol abuse.

binge eating disorder An eating disorder characterized by a pattern of binge eating that is not accompanied by drastic attempts to lose weight.

body mass index (BMI) A measure of an individual's body fat, the ratio of weight to height; used to gauge overweight and obesity.

brain function Patterns of brain activity.

brain structure The physical form and organization of the brain.

bulimia An eating disorder found primarily among young women, characterized by a pattern of binge eating and extreme weight loss measures, including self-induced vomiting.

C

causation The correlation between two things attributable to the effect one thing has on the other.

charter schools Public schools that have been given the autonomy to establish their own curricula and teaching practices.

child protectionists Individuals who argued, early in the 20th century, that adolescents needed to be kept out of the labor force in order to protect them from the hazards of the workplace.

chlamydia A sexually transmitted infection caused by a bacterium.

circumcision A procedure in which some part of the genitals is cut and permanently altered.

civic engagement Involvement in political and community affairs, as reflected in knowledge about politics and current affairs, participation in conventional and alternative political activities, and engaging in community service.

cliques Small, tightly knit groups of between 2 and 12 friends, generally of the same sex and age.

cognitive autonomy The establishment of an independent set of values, opinions, and beliefs.

cognitive-developmental view A perspective on development, based on the work of Piaget, that takes a qualitative, stage-theory approach.

cohort A group of individuals born during the same general historical era.

collective efficacy A community's social capital, derived from its members' common values and goals.

comorbid Co-occurring, as when an individual has more than one problem at the same time.

Common Core A proposed set of standards in language arts and mathematics that all American schools would be expected to use.

comprehensive high school An educational institution that evolved during the first half of the 20th century, offering a varied curriculum and designed to meet the needs of a diverse population of adolescents.

comprehensive sex education Programs that not only provide information about contraception, STDs, and pregnancy but also teach adolescents how to refuse unwanted sex and avoid unintended sex, increase their motivation to engage in safe sex, and change perceptions about peer norms and attitudes.

concrete operations The third stage of cognitive development, according to Piaget, spanning the period roughly between age 6 and early adolescence.

continuous transitions Passages into adulthood in which adult roles and statuses are entered into gradually.

conventional moral reasoning The second level of moral development, which occurs during late childhood and early adolescence and is characterized by reasoning that is based on the rules and conventions of society.

correlation The extent to which two things vary systematically with each other.

cortisol A hormone produced when a person is exposed to stress.

covert antisocial behavior A type of antisocial behavior characterized by misdeeds that are not always detected by others, such as lying or stealing.

criminal behavior Crimes that are dealt with in the criminal justice system, regardless of the age of the offender.

criminal justice system The system of courts and related institutions developed to handle adult crime.

critical thinking Thinking that involves analyzing, evaluating, and interpreting information, rather than simply memorizing it.

cross-sectional study A study that compares two or more groups of individuals at one point in time.

crowds Large, loosely organized groups of young people, composed of several cliques and typically organized around a common shared activity.

cultivation theory A perspective on media use that emphasizes the impact media exposure has on individuals.

cultural capital The resources provided within a family through the exposure of the adolescent to art, music, literature, and other elements of "high culture."

D

date rape Being forced by a date to have sex against one's will.

deductive reasoning A type of logical reasoning in which one draws logically necessary conclusions from a general set of premises, or givens.

delayed phase preference A pattern of sleep characterized by later sleep and wake times, which usually emerges during puberty.

delay of gratification The capacity to wait longer to get a larger, better, or more valuable reward instead of a smaller, less attractive, or less valuable one that is available immediately.

delinquency Juvenile offending that is processed within the juvenile justice system.

depression A psychological disturbance characterized by low self-esteem, decreased motivation, sadness, and difficulty in finding pleasure in formerly pleasurable activities.

detachment In psychoanalytic theory, the process through which adolescents sever emotional attachments to their parents or other authority figures.

developmental plasticity Extensive remodeling of the brain's circuitry in response to experiences during childhood and adolescence, while the brain is still maturing.

developmental trajectories Patterns of change over time.

diathesis–stress model A perspective on disorder that posits that problems are the result of an interaction between a preexisting condition (the diathesis) and exposure to a stressful event or condition.

diffusion tensor imaging (DTI) A technique used to produce images of the brain that shows connections among different regions.

discontinuous transitions Passages into adulthood in which adult roles and statuses are entered into abruptly.

disordered eating Mild, moderate, or severe disturbance in eating habits and attitudes.

divided attention The process of paying attention to two or more stimuli at the same time.

dopamine A neurotransmitter especially important in the brain circuits that regulate the experience of reward.

dyscalculia   Impaired ability in arithmetic.

dysgraphia   Impaired ability in handwriting.

dyslexia   Impaired ability in reading or spelling.

E

early adolescence   The period spanning roughly ages 10–13, corresponding roughly to the junior high or middle school years.

ecological perspective on human development   A perspective on development that emphasizes the broad context in which development occurs.

educational attainment   The number of years of schooling completed by an individual.

electroencephalography (EEG)   A technique for measuring electrical activity at different locations on the scalp.

emotional autonomy   The establishment of more adultlike and less childish close relationships with family members and peers.

endocrine system   The system of the body that produces, circulates, and regulates hormones.

epiphysis   The closing of the ends of the bones, which terminates growth after the adolescent growth spurt has been completed.

estrogens   A class of sex hormones secreted by the gonads, found in both sexes, but in higher levels among females than males following puberty.

ethnic identity   The aspect of individuals' sense of identity concerning ancestry or racial group membership.

ethnic socialization   The process through which individuals develop an understanding of their ethnic or racial background, also referred to as racial socialization.

ethnography   A type of research in which individuals are observed in their natural settings.

event-related potentials (ERP)   Changes in electrical activity in areas of the brain in response to specific stimuli or events.

evidence-based practices   Programs and practices that have a proven scientific basis.

executive function   More advanced thinking abilities, enabled chiefly by the maturation of the prefrontal cortex, especially in early adolescence.

experience sampling method (ESM)   A method of collecting data about adolescents' emotional states, in which individuals are paged and asked to report on their mood and activity.

externalizing disorders   Psychosocial problems that are manifested in a turning of the symptoms outward, as in aggression or delinquency.

F

false-self behavior   Behavior that intentionally presents a false impression to others.

familism   An orientation toward life in which the needs of one's family take precedence over the needs of the individual.

family capital   The economic, social, and cultural resources provided by the family.

family systems theory   A perspective on family functioning that emphasizes interconnections among different family relationships (such as marital, parent–child, sibling).

feedback loop   A cycle through which two or more bodily functions respond to and regulate each other, such as that formed by the hypothalamus, the pituitary gland, and the gonads.

female genital mutilation   The cutting or removal of the clitoris, performed in some cultures as part of the initiation of female adolescents.

five-factor model   The theory that there are five basic dimensions to personality: extraversion, agreeableness, conscientiousness, neuroticism, and openness to experience.

flow experience   The experience of high levels of both concentration and interest at the same time.

formal operations   The fourth stage of cognitive development, according to Piaget, spanning the period from early adolescence through adulthood.

foster care   A placement in a temporary living arrangement when a child's parents are not able to provide care, nurturance, or safety.

functional connectivity   The extent to which multiple brain regions function at the same time, which improves during adolescence.

functional magnetic resonance imaging (fMRI)   A technique used to produce images of the brain, often while the subject is performing some sort of mental task.

future orientation   The extent to which an individual is able and inclined to think about the potential consequences of decisions and choices.

G

gangs   Organized peer groups of antisocial individuals.

gateway drugs   Drugs that, when used over time, lead to the use of other, more dangerous substances.

gender identity   One's sense of oneself as male, female, or transgender.

gender intensification hypothesis   The idea that pressures to behave in sex-appropriate ways intensify during adolescence.

gender-role behavior   The extent to which an individual behaves in traditionally "masculine" or "feminine" ways.

generational dissonance   Divergence of views between adolescents and parents that is common in families of immigrant parents and American-born adolescents.

gifted students   Students who are unusually talented in some aspect of intellectual performance.

glands   Organs that stimulate particular parts of the body to respond in specific ways to particular hormones.

gonadotropin-releasing hormone (GnRH) neurons   Specialized neurons that are activated by certain pubertal hormones.

gonads   The glands that secrete sex hormones: in males, the testes; in females, the ovaries.

gonorrhea   A sexually transmitted infection caused by a bacterium.

graduated driver licensing   A licensing system in which full adult driving privileges are not granted all at once to teen drivers, but phased in over time.

H

herpes   A sexually transmitted infection caused by a virus.

HIV (human immunodeficiency virus)   The virus associated with AIDS.

hormones   Highly specialized substances secreted by one or more endocrine glands.

hostile attributional bias   The tendency to interpret ambiguous interactions with others as deliberately hostile.

HPG (hypothalamic-pituitary-gonadal) axis   The neurophysiological pathway that involves the hypothalamus, the pituitary gland, and the gonads.

human papillomavirus (HPV)   One of several viruses that causes a sexually transmitted disease.

hypothalamus   A part of the brain that controls the functioning of the pituitary gland.

I

iatrogenic effects   Unintended adverse consequences of a treatment or intervention.

identity   The domain of psychosocial development involving self-conceptions, self-esteem, and the sense of who one is.

identity diffusion   The incoherent, disjointed, incomplete sense of self characteristic of not having resolved the crisis of identity.

identity foreclosure   The premature establishment of a sense of identity, before sufficient role experimentation has occurred.

identity versus identity diffusion   According to Erikson, the normative crisis characteristic of the fifth stage of psychosocial development, predominant during adolescence.

imaginary audience   The belief, often brought on by the heightened self-consciousness of early adolescence, that everyone is watching and evaluating one's behavior.

immigrant paradox   The fact that on many measures of psychological functioning and mental health, adolescents who have immigrated more recently to the United States score higher on measures of adjustment than adolescents from the same ethnic group whose family has lived in the United States for several generations.

indifferent parents   Parents who are characterized by low levels of both responsiveness and demandingness.

individuation   The progressive sharpening of an individual's sense of being an autonomous, independent person.

indulgent parents   Parents who are characterized by responsiveness but low demandingness, and who are mainly concerned with the child's happiness.

information-processing perspective   A perspective on cognition that derives from the study of artificial intelligence and attempts to explain cognitive development in terms of the growth of specific components of the thinking process (such as memory).

initiation ceremony   The formal induction of a young person into adulthood.

instrumental aggression   Aggressive behavior that is deliberate and planned.

internal working model   The implicit model of interpersonal relationships that an individual employs throughout life, believed to be shaped by early attachment experiences.

internalizing disorders   Psychosocial problems that are manifested in a turning of the symptoms inward, as in depression or anxiety.

Internet addiction   A disorder in which an individual's use of the Internet is pathological, defined by six symptoms: *salience, mood change, tolerance, withdrawal, conflict*, and *relapse and reinstatement*.

intimacy   The psychosocial domain concerning the formation, maintenance, and termination of close relationships.

inventionists   Theorists who argue that the period of adolescence is mainly a social invention.

J

junior high school   An educational institution designed during the early era of public secondary education, in which young adolescents are schooled separately from older adolescents.

juvenile justice system   A separate system of courts and related institutions developed to handle juvenile crime and delinquency.

juvenile offending   An externalizing problem that includes delinquency and criminal behavior.

K

kisspeptin   A brain chemical believed to trigger the onset of puberty.

L

late adolescence   The period spanning roughly ages 18–21, corresponding approximately to the college years.

learned helplessness   The acquired belief that an individual is not able to influence events through his or her own efforts or actions.

learning disability   A difficulty with academic tasks that cannot be traced to an emotional problem or sensory dysfunction.

leptin   A protein produced by the fat cells that may play a role in the onset of puberty through its impact on kisspeptin.

LGBTQ youth   Lesbian, gay, bisexual, and transgender and questioning youth, sometimes referred to as sexual-minority youth.

life-course-persistent offenders   Individuals who begin demonstrating antisocial or aggressive behavior during childhood and continue their antisocial behavior throughout adolescence and into adulthood.

limbic system   An area of the brain that plays an important role in the processing of emotional experience, social information, and reward and punishment.

long-term memory   The ability to recall something from a long time ago.

longitudinal study   A study that follows the same group of individuals over time.

M

mainstreaming   The integration of adolescents who have educational handicaps into regular classrooms.

mastery motivation   Motivation to succeed based on the pleasure one will experience from mastering a task.

media practice model   A perspective on media use that emphasizes the fact that adolescents not only choose what media they are exposed to but also interpret the media in ways that shape their impact.

melatonin   A hormone secreted by the brain that contributes to sleepiness and that triggers the onset of puberty through its impact on kisspeptin.

menarche   The time of first menstruation, one of the most important changes to occur among females during puberty.

mentalizing   The ability to understand someone else's mental state.

metacognition   The process of thinking about thinking itself.

middle adolescence   The period spanning roughly ages 14–17, corresponding to the high school years.

middle school   An educational institution housing 7th- and 8th-grade students along with adolescents who are 1 or 2 years younger.

midlife crisis   A psychological crisis over identity believed to occur between the ages of 35 and 45, the age range of most adolescents' parents.

Monitoring the Future   An annual survey of a nationwide sample of American 8th-, 10th-, and 12th-graders, mainly known for its data on adolescent substance use.

moral disengagement   Rationalizing immoral behavior as legitimate, as a way of justifying one's own bad acts.

multidimensional model of racial identity   A perspective on ethnic identity, that emphasizes three different phenomena: racial centrality (how important race is in defining individuals' identity), private regard (how individuals feel about being a member of their race), and public regard (how individuals think others feel about their race).

multisystemic family therapy   An intervention designed to reduce antisocial behavior that has been proven to be effective.

multiethnic   Having two parents of different ethnic or racial backgrounds.

myelination   The process through which brain circuits are insulated with myelin, which improves the efficiency of information processing.

N

National Assessment of Educational Progress (NAEP)   A periodic testing of American 4th-, 8th-, and 12th-graders by the federal government, used to track achievement.

negative emotionality   The presumed underlying cause of internalizing disorders, characterized by high levels of subjective distress.

negative identity   The selection of an identity that is obviously undesirable in the eyes of significant others and the broader community.

neuroendocrine   Referring to activity in the brain and nervous system.

neurons   Nerve cells.

neurotransmitters   Specialized chemicals that carry electrical impulses between neurons.

new media   Digital media typically accessed via computers, smartphones, or other Internet-based devices.

Noncognitive factors   Influences on achievement that do not have to do with intellectual ability, such as determination, perseverance, and grit.

nonshared environmental influences   The nongenetic influences in individuals' lives that make them different from people they live with.

non-suicidal self-injury (NSSI)   Deliberate attempts to hurt oneself in nonlethal ways, including cutting or burning one's skin.

O

occupational attainment   A measure of achievement based on the status or prestige of the job an individual holds.

ovaries   The female gonads.

overt antisocial behavior   A type of antisocial behavior characterized by aggression toward others.

oxytocin   A hormone known to influence emotional bonding to others.

P

parental demandingness   One of two important dimensions of parenting; demandingness refers to the degree to which the parent expects and insists on mature, responsible behavior from the child.

parental responsiveness   One of the two important dimensions of parenting; responsiveness refers to the degree to which the parent responds to the child's needs in an accepting, supportive manner.

peak height velocity   The point at which the adolescent is growing most rapidly.

peer groups   Groups of individuals of approximately the same age.

perceived popularity   How much status or prestige an individual has.

performance motivation   Motivation to succeed based on the rewards one will receive for successful performance.

personal fable   An adolescent's belief that he or she is unique and therefore not subject to the rules that govern other people's behavior.

pheromones   A class of chemicals secreted by animals that stimulate certain behaviors in other members of the species.

pituitary gland   One of the chief glands responsible for regulating levels of hormones in the body.

plasticity   The capacity of the brain to change in response to experience.

platonic relationships   Nonsexual relationships with individuals who might otherwise be romantic partners.

positive youth development   The goal of programs designed to facilitate healthy psychosocial development and not simply to deter problematic development.

possible selves   The various identities an adolescent might imagine for him- or herself.

postconventional moral reasoning   The level of moral reasoning during which society's rules and conventions are seen as relative and subjective rather than as authoritative; also called principled moral reasoning.

preconventional moral reasoning   The first level of moral reasoning, which is typical of children and is characterized by reasoning that is based on rewards and punishments associated with different courses of action.

prefrontal cortex   The region of the brain most important for sophisticated thinking abilities, such as planning, thinking ahead, weighing risks and rewards, and controlling impulses.

premature affluence   Having more income than one can manage maturely, especially during adolescence.

preoperational period   The second stage of cognitive development, according to Piaget, spanning roughly ages 2–5.

primary control strategies   Coping strategies in which an individual attempts to change the stressor.

problem behavior syndrome   The covariation among various types of externalizing disorders believed to result from an underlying trait of unconventionality.

prosocial behavior   Behaviors intended to help others.

protective factors   Factors that limit individual vulnerability to harm.

psychological control   Parenting that attempts to control the adolescent's emotions and opinions.

psychosocial   Referring to aspects of development that are both psychological and social in nature, such as developing a sense of identity or sexuality.

psychosocial moratorium   A period during which individuals are free from excessive obligations and responsibilities and can therefore experiment with different roles and personalities.

puberty   The biological changes of adolescence.

Q

quinceañera   An elaborate sort of "coming-out" celebration for adolescent girls that is practiced in many Latino communities.

R

reactive aggression   Aggressive behavior that is unplanned and impulsive.

reference groups   A group against which an individual compares him- or herself.

rejection sensitivity   Heightened vulnerability to being rejected by others.

relational aggression   Acts intended to harm another through the manipulation of his or her relationships with others, as in malicious gossip.

religiosity   The degree to which one engages in religious practices, like attending services.

reminiscence bump   The fact that experiences from adolescence are generally recalled more than experiences from other stages of life.

resilience   The ability of an individual to continue to function competently in the face of adversity or stress.

response inhibition   The suppression of a behavior that is inappropriate or no longer required.

reverse causation   Relationship in which the correlation between two things is due not to the first thing causing the second, but to the second causing the first.

risk factors   Factors that increase the likelihood of some behavior or condition.

rite of passage   A ceremony or ritual marking an individual's transition from one social status to another, especially marking the young person's transition to adulthood.

routine activity theory   A perspective on adolescence that views unstructured, unsupervised time with peers as a main cause of misbehavior.

S

scaffolding   Structuring a learning situation so that it is just within the reach of the student.

scarification   The intentional creation of scars on some part or parts of the body, often done as part of an initiation ceremony.

school performance   A measure of achievement based on an individual's grades in school.

school vouchers   Government-subsidized vouchers that can be used for private school tuition.

schools within schools   Subdivisions of the student body within large schools created to foster feelings of belongingness.

secondary control strategies   Coping strategies that involve attempts by the individual to adapt to the stressor.

secondary educational system   The system of middle schools, junior high schools, and high schools.

secondary sex characteristics   The manifestations of sexual maturity at puberty, including the development of breasts, the growth of facial and body hair, and changes in the voice.

secular trend   The tendency, over the past two centuries, for individuals to be larger in stature and to reach puberty earlier, primarily because of improvements in health and nutrition.

secure attachment   A healthy attachment between infant and caregiver, characterized by trust.

selective attention   The process by which we focus on one stimulus while tuning out another.

selective serotonin reuptake inhibitors (SSRIs)   A class of antidepressant medications that has proven to be effective with adolescents suffering from internalizing problems, such as depression.

self-conceptions   The collection of traits and attributes that individuals use to describe or characterize themselves.

self-consciousness   The degree to which an individual is preoccupied with his or her self-image.

self-efficacy   The sense that an individual has some control over his or her life.

self-esteem   The degree to which individuals feel positively or negatively about themselves.

self-fulfilling prophecy   The idea that individuals' behavior is influenced by others' expectations for them.

self-handicapping   Deliberately behaving in ways that will likely interfere with doing well, in order to have an excuse for failing.

self-image stability   The degree to which an individual feels that his or her self-image changes from day to day.

sensation seeking   The pursuit of experiences that are novel or exciting.

sense of identity   The extent to which individuals feel secure about who they are and who they are becoming.

sensorimotor period   The first stage of cognitive development, according to Piaget, spanning the period roughly between birth and age 2.

serotonin   A neurotransmitter that is especially important for the experience of different moods.

service learning   The process of learning through involvement in community service.

set point   A physiological level or setting (e.g., of a specific hormone) that the body attempts to maintain through a self-regulating system.

sexual orientation   Whether one is sexually attracted to individuals of the same sex, other sex, or both.

sexual socialization   The process through which adolescents are exposed to and educated about sexuality.

sexuality   The psychosocial domain concerning the development and expression of sexual feelings.

sexually transmitted disease (STD)   Any of a group of infections—including HPV, gonorrhea, trichomoniasis, herpes, chlamydia, and AIDS—passed on through sexual contact.

shared environmental influences   Nongenetic influences that make individuals living in the same family similar to each other.

sibling deidentification   The process through which siblings deliberately try to be different from each other.

sibling rivalry   Competition between siblings, often for parental attention.

social capital   The interpersonal resources available to an adolescent or family.

social cognition   The aspect of cognition that concerns thinking about other people, about interpersonal relations, and about social institutions.

social control theory   A theory of delinquency that links deviance with the absence of bonds to society's main institutions.

social conventions   The norms that govern everyday behavior in social situations.

social promotion   The practice of promoting students from one grade to the next automatically, regardless of their school performance.

social redefinition   The process through which an individual's position or status is redefined by society.

social support   The extent to which an individual receives emotional or instrumental assistance from his or her social network.

sociometric popularity   How well-liked an individual is.

spirituality   The degree to which one places importance on the quest for answers to questions about God and the meaning of life.

spurious causation   Relationship in which the correlation between two things is due to the fact that each of them is correlated with some third factor.

standards-based reform   Policies designed to improve achievement by holding schools and students to a predetermined set of standards measured by achievement tests.

status offense   A violation of the law that pertains to minors but not adults.

statutory rape   Sex between two individuals, even when it is consensual, when at least one of the persons is below the legal age of consent; in the United States, the specific age of consent varies from state to state.

stereotype threat   The harmful effect that exposure to stereotypes about ethnic or sex differences in ability has on student performance.

student engagement   The extent to which students are psychologically committed to learning and mastering the material rather than simply completing the assigned work.

substance abuse   The misuse of alcohol or other drugs to a degree that causes problems in the individual's life.

suicide contagion   The process through which learning about another's suicide can lead people to try to take their own lives.

synapse   The gap in space between neurons, across which neurotransmitters carry electrical impulses.

synaptic pruning   The process through which unnecessary connections between neurons are eliminated, improving the efficiency of information processing.

T

Tanner stages   A widely used system that describes the five stages of pubertal development.

teenager   A term popularized about 50 years ago to refer to young people; it connoted a more frivolous and lighthearted image than did "adolescent."

testes   The male gonads.

testosterone   One of the sex hormones secreted by the gonads, found in both sexes but in higher levels among males than females.

theory of mind   The ability to understand that others have beliefs, intentions, and knowledge that may be different from one's own.

tracking   The practice of separating students into ability groups, so that they take classes with peers at the same skill level.

trichomoniasis   A sexually transmitted infection caused caused by a parasite.

U

underachievers   Individuals whose actual school performance is lower than what would be expected on the basis of objective measures of their aptitude or intelligence.

uses and gratification approach   A perspective on media use that emphasizes the active role users play in selecting the media to which they are exposed.

V

viral marketing   A way of promoting products or services by encouraging individuals to pass information on to others.

W

work values The particular sorts of rewards an individual looks for in a job (extrinsic, intrinsic, social, altruistic, security, influence, leisure).

working memory That aspect of memory in which information is held for a short time while a problem is being solved.

Y

youth Today, a term used to refer to individuals ages 18–22; it once referred to individuals ages 12–24.

Z

zero tolerance A get-tough approach to adolescent misbehavior that responds seriously or excessively to the first infraction.

zone of proximal development In Vygotsky's theory, the level of challenge that is still within the individual's reach but that forces an individual to develop more advanced skills.

References

Abar, C. C., Jackson, K. M., & Wood, M. (2014). Reciprocal relations between perceived parental knowledge and adolescent substance use and delinquency: The moderating role of parent-teen relationship quality. *Developmental Psychology, 50,* 2176–2187.

Abecassis, M., Hartup, W. W., Haselager, G. T., Scholte, R. J., & Van Lieshout, C. M. (2002). Mutual antipathies and their significance in middle childhood and adolescence. *Child Development, 73,* 1543–1556.

Abela, J. R. Z., & Hankin, B. L. (2011). Rumination as a vulnerability factor to depression during the transition from early to middle adolescence: A multiwave longitudinal study. *Journal of Abnormal Psychology, 120,* 259–271.

Ablard, K., & Mills, C. (1996). Implicit theories of intelligence and self-perceptions of academically talented adolescents and children. *Journal of Youth and Adolescence, 25,* 137–148.

Abma, J., Driscoll, A., & Moore, K. (1998). Young women's degree of control over first intercourse: An exploratory analysis. *Family Planning Perspectives, 30,* 12–18.

Abrahamson, A., Baker, L. A., & Caspi, A. (2002). Rebellious teens? Genetic and environmental influences on the social attitudes of adolescents. *Journal of Personality and Social Psychology, 83,* 1392–1408.

Abrutyn, S., & Mueller, A. S. (2014). Are Suicidal Behaviors Contagious in Adolescence? Using Longitudinal Data to Examine Suicide Suggestion. *American Sociological Review, 79,* 211–227.

Aceves, M. J., & Cookston, J. T. (2007). Violent victimization, aggression, and parent–adolescent relations: Quality parenting as a buffer for violently victimized youth. *Journal of Youth and Adolescence, 36,* 635–647.

Aceves, M. J., Hinshaw, S. P., Mendoza-Denton, R., & Page-Gould, E. (2010). Seek help from teachers or fight back? Student perceptions of teachers' actions during conflicts and responses to peer victimization. *Journal of Youth and Adolescence, 39,* 658–669.

Achenbach, T., & Edelbrock, C. (1987). *The manual for the Youth Self-Report and Profile.* Burlington: University of Vermont.

Ackerman, R. A., Kashy, D. A., Donnellan, M. B., Neppl, T., Lorenz, F. O., & Conger, R. D. (2013). The interpersonal legacy of a positive family climate in adolescence. *Psychological Science, 24,* 243–250.

Adachi, P. J., & Willoughby, T. (2013a). More than just fun and games: the longitudinal relationships between strategic video games, self-reported problem solving skills, and academic grades. *Journal of Youth & Adolescence, 42,* 1041–1052.

Adachi, P. J., & Willoughby, T. (2013b). Demolishing the competition: the longitudinal link between competitive video games, competitive gambling, and aggression. *Journal of Youth & Adolescence, 42,* 1090–1104.

Adalbjarnardottir, S., & Hafsteinsson, L. G. (2001). Adolescents' perceived parenting styles and their substance use: Concurrent and longitudinal analyses. *Journal of Research on Adolescence, 11,* 401–423.

Adam, E., & Chase-Lansdale, P. (2002). Home sweet home(s): Parental separations, residential moves, and adjustment problems in low-income adolescent girls. *Developmental Psychology, 38,* 792–805.

Adam, E., Chyu, L., Hoyt, L. T., Doane, L. D., Boisjoly, J., Duncan, G., McDade, T. (2011). Adverse adolescent relationship histories and young adult health: Cumulative effects of loneliness, low parental support, relationship instability, intimate partner violence, and loss. *Journal of Adolescent Health, 49,* 278–286.

Adamczyk-Robinette, S. L., Fletcher, A. C., & Wright, K. (2002). Understanding the authoritative parenting–early adolescent tobacco use link: The mediating role of peer tobacco use. *Journal of Youth and Adolescence, 31,* 311–318.

Adams, R. E., Bukowski, W. M., & Bagwell, C. (2005). Stability of aggression during early adolescence as moderated by reciprocated friendship status and friend's aggression. *International Journal of Behavioral Development, 29,* 139.

Adams, R., & Laursen, B. (2001). The organization and dynamics of adolescent conflict with parents and friends. *Journal of Marriage and the Family, 63,* 97–110.

Adegoke, A. (1993). The experience of spermarche (the age of onset of sperm emission) among selected adolescent boys in Nigeria. *Journal of Youth and Adolescence, 22,* 201–209.

Adelson, J. (1972). The political imagination of the young adolescent. In J. Kagan & R. Coles (Eds.), *Twelve to sixteen: Early adolescence.* New York: Norton.

Adiele, I., & Olatokun, W. (2014). Prevalence and determinants of Internet addiction among adolescents. *Computers in Human Behavior, 32,* 100–110.

Adler, N., Boyce, T., Chesney, M., Cohen, S., Folkman, S., Kahn, R., & Syme, S. (1994). Socioeconomic status and health: The challenge of the gradient. *American Psychologist, 49,* 15–24.

Adler, N., Ozer, E. J., & Tschann, J. (2003). Abortion among adolescents. *American Psychologist, 58,* 211–217.

Adolescent Sleep Working Group, Committee on Adolescence, Council on School Health. (2014a). School start times for adolescents. *Pediatrics, 134,* 642–649.

Agans, J. P., Champine, R. B., DeSouza, L. M., Mueller, M. K., Johnson, S. K., Lerner, R. M. (2014). Activity involvement as an ecological asset: profiles of participation and youth outcomes. *Journal of Youth & Adolescence, 43,* 919–932.

Agliata, D., & Tantleff-Dunn. (2004). The impact of media exposure on males' body image. *Journal of Social and Clinical Psychology, 23,* 7–22.

Agoston, A. M., & Rudolph, K. D. (2011). Transactional associations between youths' responses to peer stress and depression: The moderating roles of sex and stress exposure. *Journal of Abnormal Child Psychology, 39,* 159–171.

Aguilar, B., Sroufe, L. A., Egeland, B., & Carlson, E. (2000). Distinguishing the early onset/persistent and adolescence-onset antisocial behavior types: From birth to 16 years. *Development and Psychopathology, 12,* 109–132.

Ahmad, I., Smetana, J. G., & Klimstra, T. (2015). Maternal monitoring, adolescent disclosure, and adolescent adjustment among Palestinian refugee youth in Jordan. *Journal of Research on Adolescence, 25,* 403–411.

Ahn, N. (1994). Teenage childbearing and high school completion: Accounting for individual heterogeneity. *Family Planning Perspectives, 26,* 17–21.

Ainsworth, J. W. (2002). Why does it take a village? The mediation of neighborhood effects on educational achievement. *Social Forces, 81,* 117–152.

Ainsworth-Darnell, J., & Downey, D. (1998). Assessing the oppositional culture explanation for racial/ethnic differences in school performance. *American Sociological Review, 63,* 536–553.

Akom, A. A. (2003). Reexamining resistance as oppositional behavior: The nation of Islam and the creation of a Black achievement ideology. *Sociology of Education, 76,* 305–325.

Aksglaede, L., Sørensen, K., Petersen, J. H., Skakkebæk, N. E., & Juul, A. (2009). Recent decline in age at breast development: The Copenhagen Puberty Study, *Pediatrics, 123,* 932–939.

Alan Guttmacher Institute. (1994). *Sex and America's teenagers.* New York: Author.

Alasker, F., & Flammer, A. (1999). Time use by adolescents in an international perspective. II: The case of necessary activities. In F. Alasker & A. Flammer (Eds.), *The adolescent experience: European and American adolescents in the 1990s* (pp. 61–83). Hillsdale, NJ: Erlbaum.

Albers, A. B., & Biener, L. (2003). Adolescent participation in tobacco promotions: The role of psychosocial factors. *Pediatrics, 111,* 402–406.

Albert, D., & Steinberg, L. (2011a). Age differences in strategic planning as indexed by the Tower of London. *Child Development, 82,* 1501–1517.

Albert, D., & Steinberg, L. (2011b). Judgment and decision making in adolescence. *Journal of Research on Adolescence, 21,* 211–224.

Albert, D., Chein, J., & Steinberg, L. (2013). The teenage brain: Peer influences on adolescent decision making. *Current Directions in Psychological Science, 22,* 114–120.

Alberts, A., Elkind, D., & Ginsberg, S. (2007). The personal fable and risk-taking in early adolescence. *Journal of Youth and Adolescence, 36,* 71–76.

Albrecht, A. K., Galambos, N. L., & Jansson, S. M. (2007). Adolescents' internalizing and aggressive behaviors and perceptions of parents' psychological control: A panel study examining direction of effects. *Journal of Youth and Adolescence, 36,* 673–684.

Albrecht, C., & Teachman, J. D. (2003). Childhood living arrangements and the risk of premarital intercourse. *Journal of Family Influence, 24,* 867–894.

Alex Mason, W., & Spoth, R. L. (2011). Longitudinal associations of alcohol involvement with subjective well-being in adolescence and prediction to alcohol problems in early adulthood. *Journal of Youth and Adolescence, 40,* 1215–1224.

Alexander, K. L., Entwisle, D. R., & Kabbani, N. S. (2001). The dropout process in life course perspective: Early risk factors at home and school. *Teachers College Record, 103,* 760–822.

Alexander, K., Natriello, G., & Pallas, A. (1985). For whom the cognitive bell tolls: The impact of dropping out on cognitive performance. *American Sociological Review, 50,* 409–420.

Ali, M. M., Rizzo, J. A., & Heiland, F. W. (2013). Big and beautiful? Evidence of racial differences in perceived attractiveness of obese females. *Journal of Adolescence, 36,* 539–549.

Allen, J. P., Chango J., Szwedo, D., Schad, M., & Marston, E. (2012). Predictors of susceptibility to peer influence regarding substance use in adolescence. *Child Development, 83,* 337–350.

Allen, J. P., Chango, J., & Szwedo, D. (2014). The Adolescent Relational Dialectic and the Peer Roots of Adult Social Functioning. *Child Development, 85,* 192–204.

Allen, J. P., Schad, M. M., Oudekerk, B., & Chango, J. (2014). What Ever Happened to the "Cool" Kids? Long-Term Sequelae of Early Adolescent Pseudomature Behavior. *Child Development, 85,* 1866–1880.

Allen, J., & McElhaney, K. (March, 2000). *Autonomy in discussions vs. autonomy in decision-making as predictors of developing close friendship competence.* Paper presented at the biennial meetings of the Society for Research on Adolescence, Chicago.

Allen, J., Hauser, S., O'Connor, T., & Bell, K. (2002). Prediction of peer-rated adult hostility from autonomy struggles in adolescent–family interactions. *Development and Psychopathology, 14,* 123–137.

Allen, J., McElhaney, K., Kuperminc, G., & Jodl, K. (2004). Stability and change in attachment security across adolescence. *Child Development, 75,* 1792–1805.

Allen, J., Philliber, S., Herrling, S., & Kuperminc, G. (1997). Preventing teen pregnancy and academic failure: Experimental evaluation of a developmentally based approach. *Child Development, 64,* 729–742.

Allen, J., Pianta, R., Gregory, A., Mikami, A., & Lun, J. (2011). An interaction-based approach to enhancing secondary school instruction and student achievement. *Science, 333,* 1034–1037.

Allen, J., Porter, M. R., & McFarland, F. C. (2006). Leaders and followers in adolescent close friendships: Susceptibility to peer influence as a predictor of risky behavior, friendship instability, and depression. *Development and Psychopathology, 18,* 155–172.

Allen, J., Porter, M., McFarland, C., McElhaney, K. B., & Marsh, P. (2007). The relation of attachment security to adolescents' paternal and peer relationships, depression, and externalizing behavior. *Child Development, 78,* 1222–1239.

Allen, J., Porter, M., McFarland, F., Marsh, P., & McElhaney, K. (2005). The two faces of adolescents' success with peers: Adolescent popularity, social adaptation, and deviant behavior. *Child Development, 76,* 747–760.

Allen, K. L., Byrne, S. M., Oddy, W. H., & Crosby, R. D. (2014). DSM–IV–TR and DSM-5 eating disorders in adolescents: Prevalence, stability, and psychosocial correlates in a population-based sample of male and female adolescents. *Journal of Abnormal Psychology, 122,* 720–732.

Allen, M. L., Elliott, M. N., Morales, L. S., Diamant, A. L., Hambarsoomian, K., & Schuster, M. A. (2007). Adolescent participation in preventive health behaviors, physical activity, and nutrition: Differences across immigrant generations for Asians and Latinos compared with Whites. *American Journal of Public Health, 97,* 337–343.

Allen, R., & Mirabell, J. (1990, May). *Shorter subjective sleep of high school students from early compared to late starting schools.* Paper presented at the second meeting of the Society for Research on Biological Rhythms, Jacksonville, FL.

Alli, M. M., Amialchuk, A., & Dwyer, D. S. (2011). The social contagion effect of marijuana use among adolescents. *PLoS ONE, 6,* e16183.

Allison, K., Crawford, I., Leone, P., Trickett, E., Perez-Febles, A., Burton, L., & Le Blanc, R. (1999). Adolescent substance use: Preliminary examinations of school and neighborhood context. *American Journal of Community Psychology, 27,* 111–141.

Alloy, L., Black, S., Young, M., Goldstein, K., Shapero, B, Stange, J., … Abramson, L. (2012). Cognitive vulnerabilities and depression versus other psychopathology symptoms and diagnoses in early adolescence. *Journal of Clinical Child and Adolescent Psychology, 41,* 539–560.

Allwood, M., & Bell, D. (2008). A preliminary examination of emotional and cognitive mediators in the relations between violence exposure and violent behaviors in youth. *Journal of Community Psychology, 36,* 989–1007.

Almeida, J., Johnson, R. M., Corliss, H. L., Molnar, B. E., & Azrael, D. (2009). Emotional distress among LGBT youth: The influence of perceived discrimination based on sexual orientation. *Journal of Youth and Adolescence, 38,* 1001–1014.

Althaus, F. (1997). Female circumcision: Rite of passage or violation of rights? *International Family Planning Perspectives, 23,* 130–133.

Altschul, I., Oyserman, D., & Bybee, D. (2006). Racial-ethnic identity in mid-adolescence: Content and change as predictors of academic achievement. *Child Development, 77,* 1155–1169.

Alva, S. (1993). Differential patterns of achievement among Asian-American adolescents. *Journal of Youth and Adolescence, 22,* 407–423.

Alvaro, P. K., Roberts, R. M., & Harris, J. K. A. (2013). Systematic review assessing bidirectionality between sleep disturbances, anxiety, and depression. *Sleep, 36,* 1059–1068.

Amato, P. R., & Anthony, C. J. (2014). Estimating the effects of parental divorce and death with fixed effects models. *Journal of Marriage and Family, 76,* 370–386.

Amato, P., & Booth, A. (1996). A prospective study of divorce and parent–child relationships. *Journal of Marriage and the Family, 58,* 356–365.

Amato, P., & Cheadle, J. (2008). Parental divorce, marital conflict, and children's behavior problems: A comparison of adopted and biological children. *Social Forces, 86,* 1139–1161.

Amato, P., & Fowler, F. (2002). Parenting practices, child adjustment, and family diversity. *Journal of Marriage and the Family, 64,* 703–716.

Amato, P., & Keith, B. (1991). Parental divorce and the well-being of children: A meta-analysis. *Psychological Bulletin, 110,* 26–46.

Amato, P., & Sobolewski, J. M. (2001). The effects of divorce and marital discord on adult children's psychological well being. *American Sociological Review, 66,* 900–921.

American Psychiatric Association. (2013). *Diagnostic and statistical manual of the American Psychiatric Association (DSM-V).* Washington: Author.

American Psychological Association Zero Tolerance Task Force. (2008). Are zero tolerance policies effective in the schools?: An evidentiary review and recommendations. *American Psychologist, 63,* 852–862.

Amso, D., Haas, S., McShane, L., & Badre, D. (2014). Working memory updating and the development of rule-guided behavior. *Cognition, 133,* 201–210

Analitis, F., Velderman, M. K., Ravens-Sieberer, U., Detmar, S., Erhart, M., Herdman, M., European Kidscreen Group. (2009). Being bullied: Associated factors in children and adolescents 8 to 18 years old in 11 European countries. *Pediatrics, 123,* 569–577.

Anderman, E. (2002). School effects on psychological outcomes during adolescence. *Journal of Educational Psychology, 94,* 795–809.

Anderman, E., & Midgley, C. (1996, March). *Changes in achievement goal orientations after the transition to middle school.* Paper presented at the biennial meetings of the Society for Research on Adolescence, Boston.

Anderman, E., Cupp, P. K., Lane, D. R., Zimmerman, R., Gray, D. L., & O'Connell, A. (2011). Classroom goal structures and HIV and pregnancy prevention education in rural high school health classrooms. *Journal of Research on Adolescence, 21,* 904–922.

Andersen, A., Rasmussen, M., Bendtsen, P., Due, P., & Holstein, B. E. (2014). Secular trends in alcohol drinking among Danish 15-year-olds: Comparable representative samples from 1988 to 2010. *Journal of Research on Adolescence, 24,* 748–756.

Anderson, A. L., & Hughes, L. A. (2009). Exposure to situations conducive to delinquent behavior: The effects of time use, income, and transportation. *Journal of Research in Crime and Delinquency, 46,* 5–34.

Anderson, C. A., Carnagey, N. L., & Eubanks, J. (2003). Exposure to violent media: The effects of songs with violent lyrics on aggressive thoughts and feelings. *Journal of Personality and Social Psychology, 84,* 960–971.

Anderson, M., Kaufman, J., Simon, T. R., Barrios, L., Paulozzi, L., Ryan, G., School Associated Violent Deaths Study Group. (2001). School-associated violent deaths in the United States, 1994–1999. *Journal of the American Medical Association, 286,* 2695–2702.

Anderson, S. E., Dallal, G. E., & Must, A. (2003). Relative weight and race influence average age at menarche: Results from two nationally representative surveys of U.S. girls studied 25 years apart. *Pediatrics, 111,* 844–891.

Andersson, H., & Bergman, L. R. (2011). The role of task persistence in young adolescence for successful educational and occupational attainment in middle adulthood. *Developmental Psychology, 47,* 950–960.

Ando, M., Asakura, T., & Simons-Morton, B. (2005). Psychosocial influences on physical, verbal, and indirect bullying among Japanese early adolescents. *Journal of Early Adolescence, 25,* 268–297.

Andrews, J., Alpert, A., Hops, H., & Davis, B. (1996, March). *The relation of competence in middle adolescence to depression and antisocial behavior: A multi-method assessment.* Paper presented at the biennial meetings of the Society for Research on Adolescence, Boston.

Andrews-Hanna, J., Seghete, K., Claus, E., Burgess, G., Ruzic, L., & Banich, M. (2011). Cognitive control in adolescence: Neural underpinnings and relation to self-report behaviors. *PLoS ONE, 6,* e21598.

Andrinopoulos, K., Kerrigan, D., & Ellen, J. M. (2006). Understanding sex partner selection from the perspective of inner-city Black adolescents. *Perspectives on Sexual and Reproductive Health, 38,* 132–138.

Angold, A., Costello, E. J., & Worthman, C. (1998). Puberty and depression: The roles of age, pubertal status, and pubertal timing. *Psychological Medicine, 28,* 51–61.

Angold, A., Costello, E. J., Erkanli, A., & Worthman, C. M. (1999). Pubertal changes in hormone levels and depression in girls. *Psychological Medicine, 29,* 1043–1053.

Angold, A., Worthman, C., Costello, E., Stangl, D., Messer, S., & Tweed, D. (1996, March). *Puberty and depression.* Paper presented at the Society for Research on Adolescence, Boston.

Ansary, N. S., & Luthar, S. S. (2009). Distress and academic achievement among adolescents of affluence: A study of externalizing and internalizing problem behaviors and school performance. *Development and Psychopathology, 21,* 319–341.

Antheunis, M. L., Schouten, A. P., & Krahmer, E. (2014). The role of social networking sites in early adolescents' social lives. *The Journal of Early Adolescence.* DOI: 10.1177/0272431614564060.

Antshel, K., & Barkley, R. (2011). Attention Deficit/Hyperactivity Disorder. (2011). In B. Brown & M. Prinstein (Eds.), *Encyclopedia of adolescence* (Vol. 3, pp. 56–61). New York: Academic Press.

Apel, R., & Kaukinen, C. (2008). On the relationship between family structure and antisocial behavior: Parental cohabitation and blended households. *Criminology: An Interdisciplinary Journal, 46,* 35–69.

Apel, R., Bushway, S., Brame, R., Haviland, A. M., Nagin, D. S., & Paternoster, R. (2007). Unpacking the relationship between adolescent employment and antisocial behavior: A matched samples comparison. *Criminology, 45,* 67–97.

Apfel, N., & Seitz, V. (1997). The firstborn sons of African American teen mothers: Perspectives on risk and resilience. In S. Luthar, J. Burack, D. Cicchetti, & J. Weisz (Eds.), *Developmental psychopathology: Perspectives on risk and disorder* (pp. 484–506). New York: Cambridge University Press.

Aquilino, W. (2005). Impact of family structure on parental attitudes toward the economic support of adult children over the transition to adulthood. *Journal of Family Influence, 26,* 143–167.

Aquilino, W., & Supple, A. J. (2001). Long-term effects of parenting practices during adolescence on well-being: Outcomes in young adulthood. *Journal of Family Issues, 22,* 289–308.

Arbeton, A., Eccles, J., & Harold, R. (1994, February). *Parents' perceptions of their children's competence: The role of parent attributions.* Paper presented at the biennial meetings of the Society for Research on Adolescence, San Diego.

Archibald, A., Graber, J., & Brooks-Gunn, J. (1999). Associations among parent–adolescent relationships, pubertal growth, dieting, and body image in young adolescent girls: A short-term longitudinal study. *Journal of Research on Adolescence, 9,* 395–415.

Archibald, A., Linver, M., Graber, J., & Brooks-Gunn, J. (2002). Parent–adolescent relationships and girls' unhealthy eating: Testing reciprocal effects. *Journal of Research on Adolescence, 12,* 451–461.

Ardekani, B. A., Figarsky, K., & Sidtis, J. J. (2013). Sexual dimorphism in the human corpus callosum: An MRI study using the OASIS brain database. *Cerebral Cortex, 23,* 2514–2520.

Ardelt, M., & Day, L. (2002). Parents, siblings, and peers: Close social relationships and adolescent deviance. *Journal of Early Adolescence, 22,* 310–349.

Arens, A., Yeung, A., Craven, R., & Hasselhorn, M. (2011). The twofold multidimensionality of academic self-concept: Domain specificity and separation between competence and affect components. *Journal of Educational Psychology, 103,* 970–981.

Arias, D. F., & Hernández, A. M. (2007). Emerging adulthood in Mexican and Spanish youth: Theories and realities. *Journal of Adolescent Research, 22,* 476–503.

Arim, R. G., Tramonte, L., Shapka, J. D., Susan Dahinten, V., & Douglas Willms, J. (2011). The family antecedents and the subsequent outcomes of early puberty. *Journal of Youth and Adolescence, 40,* 1423–1435.

Armor, D. (1972). School and family effects on Black and White achievement: A reexamination of the USOE data. In F. Mosteller & D. Moynihan (Eds.), *On equality of educational opportunity.* New York: Random House.

Armour, S., & Haynie, D. L. (2007). Adolescent sexual debut and later delinquency. *Journal of Youth and Adolescence, 36,* 141–152.

Armstrong, T. D., & Costello, E. (2002). Community studies on adolescent substance use, abuse, or dependence and psychiatric comorbidity. *Journal of Consulting and Clinical Psychology, 70,* 1224–1239.

Arndorfer, C. L., & Stormshak, E. A. (2008). Same-sex versus other-sex best friendship in early adolescence: Longitudinal predictors of antisocial behavior throughout adolescence. *Journal of Youth and Adolescence, 37,* 1059–1070.

Arnett, J. (1994). Are college students adults? Their conceptions of the transition to adulthood. *Journal of Adult Development, 1,* 213–224.

Arnett, J. (1998). Learning to stand alone: The contemporary American transition to adulthood in cultural and historical context. *Human Development, 41,* 295–315.

Arnett, J. (2000). Emerging adulthood: A theory of development from the late teens through the twenties. *American Psychologist, 55,* 469–480.

Arnett, J. (2001). Adolescents' responses to cigarette advertisements for five "youth brands" and one "adult brand." *Journal of Research on Adolescence, 11,* 425–443.

Arnett, J. (2002). Adolescents in Western countries on the threshold of the 21st century. In B. Brown, R. Larson, & T. Saraswathi (Eds.), *The world's youth: Adolescence in eight regions of the globe.* New York: Cambridge University Press.

Arnett, J. (2004). *Emerging adulthood: The winding road from the late teens through the twenties.* New York: Oxford University Press.

Arnett, J. (2007). Suffering, selfish, slackers? Myths and reality about emerging adults. *Journal of Youth and Adolescence, 36,* 23–29.

Arnett, J. (2009). Emerging adulthood: What is it, and what is it good for? *Child Development Perspectives, 1,* 68–73.

Arnett, J. J., & Padilla-Walker, L. M. (2015). Brief report: Danish emerging adults' conceptions of adulthood. *Journal of Adolescence, 38,* 39–44.

Arnett, J., & Balle-Jensen, L. (1993). Cultural bases of risk behavior: Danish adolescents. *Child Development, 64,* 1842–1855.

Arnett, J. J. (2013). Adolescence and emerging adulthood: a cultural approach (5th ed.). Upper Saddle River, NJ: Pearson.

Aronson, J., Jannone, S., McGlone, M., & Johnson-Campbell, T. (2009). The Obama effect: An experimental test. *Journal of Experimental Social Psychology, 45,* 957–960.

Arseneault, L., Tremblay, R. E., Boulerice, B., & Saucier, J. (2002). Obstetrical complications and violent delinquency: Testing two developmental pathways. *Child Development, 73,* 496–508.

Arum, R., & Hout, M. (1998). The early returns: The transition from school to work in the United States. In Y. Shavit & W. Mueller (Eds.), *From school to work: A comparative study of educational qualifications and occupational destinations* (pp. 471–510). Oxford: Clarendon Press.

Arunkumar, R., Midgley, C., & Urdan, T. (1999). Perceiving high or low home–school dissonance: Longitudinal effects on adolescent emotional and academic well-being. *Journal of Research on Adolescence, 9,* 441–466.

Asakawa, K., & Csikszentmihalyi, M. (1998). The quality of experience of Asian American adolescents in academic activities: An exploration of educational achievement. *Journal of Research on Adolescence, 8,* 241–262.

Asakawa, K., & Csikszentmihalyi, M. (2000). Feelings of connectedness and internalization of values in Asian American adolescents. *Journal of Youth and Adolescence, 29,* 121–145.

Asato, M., Terwilliger, R., Woo, J., & Luna, B. (2010). White matter development in adolescence: a DTI study. *Cerebral Cortex, 20,* 2122–2131.

Aseltine, R. H., Schilling, E. A., James, A., Glanovsky, J. L., & Jacobs, D. (2009). Age variability in the association between heavy episodic drinking and adolescent suicide attempts: Findings from a large-scale, school-based screening program. *Journal of the American Academy of Child and Adolescent Psychiatry, 48,* 262–270.

Aseltine, R., & Gore, S. (2005). Work, post-secondary education, and psychosocial functioning following the transition from high school. *Journal of Adolescent Research, 20,* 615–639.

Aseltine, R., Gore, S., & Colten, M. (1994). Depression and the social developmental context of adolescence. *Journal of Personality and Social Psychology, 67,* 252–263.

Aseltine, R., Jr., Gore, S., & Colten, M. (1998). The co-occurrence of depression and substance abuse in late adolescence. *Development & Psychopathology, 10,* 549–570.

Ashby, J. S., & Schoon, I. (2012). Living the dream? A qualitative retrospective study exploring the role of adolescent aspirations across the life span. *Developmental Psychology, 48,* 1694–1706.

Asher, S., Parker, J., & Walker, D. (1996). Distinguishing friendship from acceptance: Implications for intervention and assessment. In W. Bukowski, A. Newcomb, & W. Hartup (Eds.), *The company they keep: Friendship in childhood and adolescence* (pp. 366–405). New York: Cambridge University Press.

Ashikali, E. M., Dittmar, H., & Ayers, S. (2014). The effect of cosmetic surgery reality tv shows on adolescent girls' body image. *Psychology of Popular Media Culture, 3,* 141–153.

Asmussen, L., & Larson, R. (1991). The quality of family time among young adolescents in single-parent and married-parent families. *Journal of Marriage and the Family, 53,* 1021–1030.

Aspy, C. B., Tolma, E. L., Oman, R. F., & Vesely, S. K. (2014). The influence of assets and environmental factors on gender differences in adolescent drug use. *Journal of Adolescence, 37,* 827–837.

Aspy, C. B., Vesely, S. K., Oman, R. F., Rodine, S., Marshall, L., & McLeroy, K. (2007). Parental communication and youth sexual behaviour. *Journal of Adolescence, 30,* 449–466.

Astor, R. (1994). Children's moral reasoning about family and peer violence: The role of provocation and retribution. *Child Development, 65,* 1054–1067.

Atkins, R., Hart, D., & Donnelly, T. M. (2005). The association of childhood personality type with volunteering during adolescence. *Merrill-Palmer Quarterly, 2,* 145–162.

Attie, I., & Brooks-Gunn, J. (1989). The development of eating problems in adolescent girls: A longitudinal study. *Developmental Psychology, 25,* 70–79.

Auerbach, R. P., Eberhart, N. K., & Abela, J. R. Z. (2010). Cognitive vulnerability to depression in Canadian and Chinese adolescents. *Journal of Abnormal Child Psychology, 38,* 57–68.

Auerbach, R. P., Ho, M. H., & Kim, J. C. (2014). Identifying cognitive and interpersonal predictors of adolescent depression. *Journal of Abnormal Child Psychology, 42,* 913–924.

Augustyn, M. B., Thornberry, T. P., & Krohn, M. D. (2014). Gang membership and pathways to maladaptive parenting. *Journal of Research on Adolescence, 24,* 252–267.

Aunola, K., Stattin, H., & Nurmi, J.-E. (2000). Parenting styles and adolescents' achievement strategies. *Journal of Adolescence, 23,* 205–222.

Austin, S. B., & Gortmaker, S. L. (2001). Dieting and smoking initiation in early adolescent girls and boys: A prospective study. *American Journal of Public Health, 91,* 446–450.

Avenevoli, S., & Steinberg, L. (2001). The continuity of depression across the adolescent transition. In H. Reese & R. Kail (Eds.), *Advances in child development and behavior* (Vol. 28, pp. 139–173). New York: Academic Press.

Avenevoli, S., Swendsen, J., He, J., Burstein, M.,& Merikangas, K. (2015). Major depression in the National Comorbidity Survey–Adolescent Supplement: Prevalence, correlates, and treatment. *Journal of the American Academy of Child & Adolescent Psychiatry , 54 ,* 37–44.

Averett, S. L., Rees, D. I., & Argys, L. M. (2002). The impact of government policies and neighborhood characteristics on teenage sexual activity and contraceptive use. *American Journal of Public Health, 92,* 1773–1778.

Azmitia, M., Cooper, C. R., & Brown, J. R. (2009). Support and guidance from families, friends, and teachers in Latino early adolescents' math pathways. *Journal of Early Adolescence, 29,* 142–169.

Baams, L., Dubas, J. S., Overbeek, G., & van Aken, M. A. G. (2015). Transitions in body and behavior: A meta-analytic study on the relationship between pubertal development and adolescent sexual behavior. *Journal of Adolescent Health, 56,* 586–598.

Baams, L., Grossman, A. H., & Russell, S. T. (2015). Minority stress and mechanisms of risk for depression and suicidal ideation among lesbian, gay, and bisexual youth. *Developmental Psychology, 51,* 688–696.

Babalola, S. (2004). Perceived peer behavior and the timing of sexual debut in Rwanda: A survival analysis of youth data. *Journal of Youth and Adolescence, 33,* 353–363.

Bachman, J. (1983, Summer). Premature affluence: Do high school students earn too much? *Economic Outlook USA,* 64–67.

Bachman, J. G., Staff, J., O'Malley, P. M., & Freedman-Doan, P. (2013). Adolescent work intensity, school performance, and substance use: Links vary by race/ethnicity and socioeconomic status. *Developmental Psychology, 49,* 2125–2134.

Bachman, J. G., Staff, J., O'Malley, P. M., Schulenberg, J. E., & Freedman-Doan, P. (2011). Twelfth-grade student work intensity linked to later educational attainment and substance use: New longitudinal evidence. *Developmental Psychology, 47,* 344–363.

Bachman, J., & Schulenberg, J. (1993). How part-time work intensity relates to drug use, problem behavior, time use, and satisfaction among high school seniors: Are these consequences or merely correlates? *Developmental Psychology, 29,* 220–235.

Badaly, D., Kelly, B. M., Schwartz, D., Dabnet-Lieras, K. (2013). Longitudinal associations of electronic aggression and victimization with social standing during adolescence. *Journal of Youth & Adolescence, 42,* 891–904.

Bae, D., Wickrama, K. A. S., & O'Neal, C. W. (2014). Social consequences of early socioeconomic adversity and youth BMI trajectories: Gender and race/ethnicity differences. *Journal of Adolescence, 37,* 883–892.

Baer, J. (2002). Is family cohesion a risk or protective factor during adolescent development? *Journal of Marriage and the Family, 64,* 668–675.

Baer, J., & Schmitz, M. F. (2007). Ethnic differences in trajectories of family cohesion for Mexican American and non-Hispanic White adolescents. *Journal of Youth and Adolescence, 36,* 583–592.

Bagwell, C., Newcomb, A., & Bukowski, W. (1998). Preadolescent friendship and peer rejection as predictors of adult adjustment. *Child Development, 69,* 140–153.

Bailey, P. E., Bruno, Z. V., Bezerra, M. F., Queiroz, I., Oliveira, C. M., & Chen-Mok, M. (2001). Adolescent pregnancy 1 year later: The effects of abortion vs. motherhood in Northeast Brazil. *Journal of Adolescent Health, 29,* 223–232.

Baird, A., Fugelsang, J., & Bennett, C. (2005, April). "What were you thinking?": An fMRI study of adolescent decision making. Poster presented at the 12th Annual Cognitive Neuroscience Society (CNS) Meeting, New York.

Bakan, D. (1972). Adolescence in America: From idea to social fact. In J. Kagan & R. Coles (Eds.), *Twelve to sixteen: Early adolescence.* New York: Norton.

Baker, L., Tuvblad, C., Reynolds, C., Zheng, M., Lozano, D. I., & Raine, A. (2009). Resting heart rate and the development of antisocial behavior from age 9 to 14: Genetic and environmental influences. *Development and Psychopathology, 21,* 939–960.

Baker, T., & Velez, W. (1996). Access to and opportunity in postsecondary education in the United States: A review. *Sociology of Education, Extra Issue, 69,* 82–101.

Bakken, J., & Brown, B. (2010). Adolescent secretive behavior: African American and Hmong Adolescents "strategies and justifications for

managing parents" knowledge about peers. *Journal of Research on Adolescence, 20,* 359–388.

Bakker, M. P., Ormel, J., Verhulst, F. C., & Oldehinkel, A. J. (2010). Peer stressors and gender differences in adolescents' mental health: The TRAILS study. *Journal of Adolescent Health, 46,* 444–450.

Balfanz, R., Legters, N., West, T. C., & Weber, L. M. (2007). Are NCLB's measures, incentives, and improvement strategies the right ones for the nation's low-performing high schools? *American Education Research Journal, 44,* 559–593.

Balsa, A., Homer, J., French, M., & Norton, E. (2011). Alcohol use and popularity: Social payoffs from conforming to peers' behavior. *Journal of Research on Adolescence, 21,* 559–568.

Balsano, A., Theokas, C., & Bobek, D. (2009). A shared commitment to youth: The integration of theory, research, practice, and policy. In R. Lerner & L. Steinberg (Eds.), *Handbook of adolescent psychology* (3rd ed., Vol. 2, pp. 623–650). New York: Wiley.

Bámaca, M. Y., & Umaña-Taylor, A. J. (2006). Testing a model of resistance to peer pressure among Mexican-origin adolescents. *Journal of Youth and Adolescence, 35,* 631–645.

Bámaca-Colbert, M. Y., Greene, K. M., Killoren, S. E., & Noah, A. J. (2014). Contextual and developmental predictors of sexual initiation timing among Mexican-origin girls. *Developmental Psychology, 50,* 2353–2359.

Bámaca-Colbert, M. Y., Umaña-Taylor, A. J., Espinosa-Hernández, G., & Brown, A. M. (2012). Behavioral autonomy age expectations among Mexican-origin mother-daughter dyads: An examination of within-group variability. *Journal of Adolescence, 35,* 691–700.

Bandura, A., & Walters, R. (1959). *Adolescent aggression.* New York: Ronald Press.

Bandura, A., Barbaranelli, C., Caprara, G., & Pastorelli, C. (1996). Multifaceted impact of self-efficacy beliefs on academic functioning. *Child Development, 67,* 1206–1222.

Banister, E. (1999). Women's midlife experience of their changing bodies. *Qualitative Health Research, 9,* 520–537.

Bank, L., Burraston, B., & Snyder, J. (2004). Sibling conflict and ineffective parenting as predictors of adolescent boys' antisocial behavior and peer difficulties: Additive and interactional effects. *Journal of Research on Adolescence, 14,* 99–125.

Bankston, C. L., III, & Caldas, S. (1998). Family structure, schoolmates, and racial inequalities in school achievement. *Journal of Marriage & the Family, 60,* 715–723.

Banny, A. M., Heilbron, N., Ames, A., & Prinstein, M. J. (2011). Relational benefits of relational aggression: Adaptive and maladaptive associations with adolescent friendship quality. *Developmental Psychology, 47,* 1153–1166.

Barber, B. (1996). Parental psychological control: Revisiting a neglected construct. *Child Development, 67,* 3296–3319.

Barber, B., & Eccles, J. (1992). Long-term influence of divorce and single parenting on adolescent family- and work-related values, behaviors, and aspirations. *Psychological Bulletin, 111,* 108–126.

Barber, B., & Olsen, J. (1997). Socialization in context: Connection, regulation, and autonomy in the family, school, neighborhood, and with peers. *Journal of Adolescent Research, 12,* 287–315.

Barber, B., & Olsen, J. (2004). Assessing the transitions to middle and high school. *Journal of Adolescent Research, 19,* 3–30.

Barber, B., Eccles, J., & Stone, M. (2001). Whatever happened to the jock, the brain, and the princess? Young adult pathways linked to adolescent activity involvement and social identity. *Journal of Adolescent Research, 16,* 429–455.

Barber, B., Stone, M., Hunt, J., & Eccles, J. (2005). Benefits of activity participation: The roles of identity affirmation and peer norm sharing. In J. Mahoney, R. Larson, & J. Eccles (Eds.), *Organized activities as contexts of development* (pp. 185–210). Hillsdale, NJ: Erlbaum.

Barboza, G. E., Schiamberg, L. B., Oehmke, J., Korzeniewski, S. J., Post, L. A., & Heraux, C. G. (2009). Individual characteristics and the multiple contexts of adolescent bullying: An ecological perspective. *Journal of Youth and Adolescence, 38,* 101–121.

Bardone, A., Moffitt, T., Caspi, A., Dickson, N., & Silva, P. (1996). Adult mental health and social outcomes of adolescent girls with depression and conduct disorder. *Development and Psychopathology, 8,* 811–829.

Barnes, G. M., Hoffman, J. H., Welte, J. W., Farrell, M. P., & Dintcheff, B. A. (2006). Effects of parental monitoring and peer deviance on substance use and delinquency. *Journal of Marriage and Family, 68,* 1084–1104.

Barnes, G., & Farrell, M. (1992). Parental support and control as predictors of adolescent drinking, delinquency, and related problem behaviors. *Journal of Marriage and the Family, 54,* 763–776.

Barnes, R. (2007, June 29). Divided court limits use of race by school districts. *Washington Post,* p. A01.

Barnett, T. A., O'Loughlin, J., Sabiston, C. M., Karp, I., Belanger, M., Van Hulst, A., & Lambert, M. (2010). Teens and screens: The influence of screen time on adiposity in adolescents. *American Journal of Epidemiology, 172,* 255–262.

Barnett, T., Rowley, S., Zimmerman, M., Vansadia, P., & Howard Caldwell, C. (2011). A longitudinal study of household change on African American adolescents. *Journal of Community Psychology, 39,* 303–315.

Barratt, M., Roach, M., Morgan, K., & Colbert, K. (1996). Adjustment to motherhood by single adolescents. *Family Relations, 45,* 209–215.

Barrett-Singer, A. T., & Weinstein, R. S. (2000). Differential parent treatment predicts achievement and self-perceptions in two cultural contexts. *Journal of Family Psychology, 14,* 491–509.

Barrocas, A. L., & Hankin, B. L. (2011). Developmental pathways to depressive symptoms in adolescence: A multi-wave prospective study of negative emotionality, stressors, and anxiety. *Journal of Abnormal Child Psychology, 39,* 489–500.

Barry, C. M., & Nelson, L. J. (2005). The role of religion in the transition to adulthood for young emerging adults. *Journal of Youth and Adolescence 34,* 245–255.

Barry, C. M., & Wentzel, K. R. (2006). Friend influence on prosocial behavior: The role of motivational factors and friendship characteristics. *Developmental Psychology, 42,* 153–163.

Bartko, W. T., & Eccles, J. (2003). Adolescent participation in structured and unstructured activities: A person-oriented analysis. *Journal of Youth and Adolescence, 32,* 233–241.

Barton, P., & Coley, R. (2010). *The Black-White achievement gap: When progress stopped.* Princeton: Educational Testing Service.

Bascoe, S. M., Davies, P. T., & Cummings, E. M. (2012). Beyond warmth and conflict: The developmental utility of a boundary conceptualization of sibling relationship processes. *Child Development, 83,* 2121–2138.

Basile, K. C., Black, M. C., Simon, T. R., Arias, I., Brener, N. D., & Saltzman, L. E. (2006). The association between self-reported lifetime history of forced sexual intercourse and recent health-risk behaviors: Findings from the 2003 national youth risk behavior survey. *Journal of Adolescent Health, 39,* e1–e7.

Bassi, M., Steca, P., Delle Fave, A., & Caprara, G. V. (2007). Academic self-efficacy beliefs and quality of experience in learning. *Journal of Youth and Adolescence, 36,* 301–312.

Bastaits, K., Ponnet, K., Mortelmans, D. (2012). Parenting of divorced fathers and the association with children's self-esteem. *Journal of Youth & Adolescence, 41,* 1643–1656.

Batalla, A., Bhattacharyya, S., Yücel, M., Fusar-Poli, P., Crippa, J. A., Nogué, S., Torrens, M., Pujol, J., Farré, M., & Martin-Santos, R. (2013). Structural and functional imaging studies in chronic cannabis users: A systematic review of adolescent and adult findings. *PLoS One, 8,* 55821.

Batterink, L., Yokum, S., & Stice, E. (2010). Body mass correlates inversely with inhibitory control in response to food among adolescent girls: An fMRI study. *Neuroimage, 52,* 1696–1703.

Battin-Pearson, S., Newcomb, M. D., Abbott, R. D., Hill, K. G., Catalano, R. F., & Hawkins, J. (2000). Predictors of early high school dropout: A test of five theories. *Journal of Educational Psychology, 92,* 568–582.

Bauermeister, J. A., Zimmerman, M. A., Barnett, T. E., & Caldwell, C. H. (2007). Working in high school and adaptation in the transition to young adulthood among African American youth. *Journal of Youth and Adolescence, 36,* 877–890.

Bauermeister, J. A., Zimmerman, M., Xue, Y., Gee, G. C., & Caldwell, C. H. (2009). Working, sex partner age differences, and sexual behavior among African American youth. *Archives of Sexual Behavior, 38,* 802–813.

Baumer, E. P., & South, S. J. (2001). Community effects on youth sexual activity. *Journal of Marriage and the Family, 63,* 540–554.

Baumrind, D. (1978). Parental disciplinary patterns and social competence in children. *Youth and Society, 9,* 239–276.

Bauserman, R., & Rind, B. (1997). Psychological correlates of male child and adolescent sexual experiences with adults: A review of the nonclinical literature. *Archives of Sexual Behavior, 26,* 105–141.

Bayer, P., Hjalmarsson, R., & Pozen, D. (2009). Building criminal capital behind bars: Peer effects in juvenile corrections. *Quarterly Journal of Economics, 124,* 105–147.

Bayley, N. (1949). Consistency and variability in the growth of intelligence from birth to eighteen years. *Journal of General Psychology, 75,* 165–196.

Bayram Özdemir, S., & Stattin, H. (2014). Why and when is ethnic harassment a risk for immigrant adolescents' school adjustment? Understanding the processes and conditions. *Journal of Youth & Adolescence, 43,* 1252–1265.

Beal, S. J., & Crockett, L. J. (2010). Adolescents' occupational and educational aspirations and expectations: Links to high school activities and adult educational attainment. *Developmental Psychology, 46,* 258–265.

Beam, M. R., Chen, C., & Greenberger, E. (2002). The nature of adolescents' relationship with their "very important" nonparental adults. *American Journal of Community Psychology, 30,* 305–325.

Bean, R. A., Barber, B. K., & Crane, D. R. (2006). Parental support, behavioral control, and psychological control among African American youth: The relationships to academic grades, delinquency, and depression. *Journal of Family Issues, 27,* 1335–1355.

Bean, R. A., Bush, K. R., McKenry, P. C., & Wilson, S. M. (2003). The impact of parental support, behavioral control, and psychological control on the academic achievement and self-esteem of African American and European American adolescents. *Journal of Adolescent Research, 18,* 523–541.

Beardslee, W. R., Brent, D. A., Weersing, V. R., Clarke, G. N., Porta, G., Hollon, S. D., Gladstone, T. R., Gallop, R., Lynch, F. L., Iyengar, S., DeBar, L., & Garber, J. (2013). Prevention of depression in at-risk adolescents: Longer-term effects. *JAMA Psychiatry, 70,* 1161–1170.

Bearman, P. S., & Brückner, H. (2001). Promising the future: Virginity pledges and first intercourse. *American Journal of Sociology, 106,* 859–912.

Bearman, P., & Moody, J. (2004). Suicide and friendships among American adolescents. *American Journal of Public Health, 94,* 89–96.

Bearman, S. K., & Stice, E. (2008). Testing a gender additive model: The role of body image in adolescent depression. *Journal of Abnormal Child Psychology, 36,* 1251–1263.

Beaumont, S. (1996). Adolescent girls' perceptions of conversations with mothers and friends. *Journal of Adolescent Research, 11,* 325–346.

Beaver, K. M., & Wright, J. P. (2007). A child effects explanation for the association between family risk and involvement in an antisocial lifestyle. *Journal of Adolescent Research, 22,* 640–664.

Beaver, K. M., DeLisi, M., Wright, J. P., & Vaughn, M. G. (2009). Gene–environmental interplay and delinquent involvement: Evidence of direct, indirect, and interactive effects. *Journal of Adolescent Research, 24,* 147–168.

Bechara, A. (2005). Decision making, impulse control and loss of willpower to resist drugs: A neurocognitive perspective. *Nature Neuroscience, 8,* 1458–1463.

Beck, S. R., & Riggs, K. J. (2014). Developing thoughts about what might have been. *Child Development Perspectives, 8,* 175–179.

Becker, B. E., & Luthar, S. S. (2007). Peer-perceived admiration and social preference: Contextual correlates of positive peer regard among suburban and urban adolescents. *Journal of Research on Adolescence, 17,* 117–144.

Becker, M., Neumann, M., Tetzner, J., Böse, S., Knoppick, H., Maaz, K., Baumert, J., & Lehmann, R. (2014). Is early ability grouping good for high-achieving students' psychosocial development? Effects of the transition into academically selective schools. *Journal of Educational Psychology, 106,* 555–568.

Beckwith, L., Cohen, S., & Hamilton, C. (1999). Maternal sensitivity during infancy and subsequent life events relate to attachment representation at early adulthood. *Developmental Psychology, 35,* 693–700.

Beets, M. W., Flay, B. R., Vuchinich, S., Snyder, F. J., Acock, A., Li, K. K., . . . Durlack, J. (2009). Use of a social and character development program to prevent substance use, violent behaviors, and sexual activity among elementary-school students in Hawaii. *American Journal of Public Health, 99,* 1438–1445.

Bell, A., Weinberg, M., & Hammersmith, S. (1981). *Sexual preference: Its development in men and women.* Bloomington: Indiana University Press.

Bell, J., & Bromnick, R. (2000, March). *A grounded approach to understanding modern dilemmas of individuality.* Paper presented at the eighth biennial meeting of the Society for Research on Adolescence, Chicago.

Bellmore, A. (2011). Peer rejection and unpopularity: Associations with GPAs across the transition to middle school. *Journal of Educational Psychology, 103,* 282–295.

Bellmore, A., Villarreal, V. M., & Ho, A. Y. (2011). Staying cool across the first year of middle school. *Journal of Youth and Adolescence, 40,* 776–785.

Belsky, D. W., Moffitt, T. E., Baker, T. B., Biddle, A. K., Evans, J. P., Harrington, H., . . . Caspi, A. (2013). Polygenic risk and the developmental progression to heavy, persistent smoking and nicotine dependence evidence from a 4-decade longitudinal study. *JAMA Psychiatry, 70,* 534–542.

Belsky, J., Steinberg, L., & Draper, P. (1991). Childhood experience, interpersonal development, and reproductive strategy: An evolutionary theory of socialization. *Child Development, 62,* 647–670.

Belsky, J., Steinberg, L., Houts, R. M., Halpern-Felsher, B. L., & NICHD Early Child Care Research Network. (2010). The development of reproductive strategy in females: Early maternal harshness → earlier menarche → increased sexual risk taking. *Developmental Psychology, 46,* 120–128.

Belsky, J., Steinberg, L., Houts, R., Friedman, S., DeHart, G., . . . Cauffman, E. (2007). Family rearing antecedents of pubertal timing. *Child Development, 78,* 1302–1321.

Beltz, M. A., Sacks, V. H., Moore, K. A., & Terzian, M. (2015). State policy and teen childbearing: A review of research studies. *Journal of Adolescent Health, 56,* 130–138.

BeLue, R., Francis, L. A., & Colaco, B. (2009). Mental health problems and overweight in a nationally representative sample of adolescents: Effects of race and ethnicity. *Pediatrics, 123,* 697–702.

Benda, B., & Corwyn, R. (1998). Race and gender differences in theories of sexual behavior among rural adolescents residing in AFDC families. *Youth and Society, 30,* 59–88.

Bender, H., Allen, J., McElhaney, K., Antonishak, J., Moore, C., O'Beirne Kelly, H., & Davis, S. (2007). Use of harsh physical discipline and developmental outcomes in adolescence. *Development and Psychopathology, 19,* 227–242.

Bendtsen, P., Damsgaard, M. T., Tolstrup, J. S., Ersbøll, A. K., & Holstein, B. E. (2013). Adolescent alcohol use reflects community-level alcohol consumption irrespective of parental drinking. *Journal of Adolescent Health, 53,* 368–373.

Benedict, R. (1934). *Patterns of culture.* New York: Houghton Mifflin.

Benenson, J. F., & Christakos, A. (2003). The greater fragility of females' versus males' closest same-sex friendships. *Child Development, 74,* 1123–1129.

Benhorin, S., & McMahon, S. (2008). Exposure to violence and aggression: Protective roles of social support among urban African American youth. *Journal of Community Psychology, 36,* 723–743.

Benish-Weisman, M., Levy, S., & Knafo, A. (2013). Parents differentiate between their personal values and their socialization values: The role of adolescents' values. *Journal of Research on Adolescence, 23,* 614–620.

Benjet, C., & Hernandez-Guzman, L. (2002). A short-term longitudinal study of pubertal change, gender, and psychological well-being of Mexican early adolescents. *Journal of Youth and Adolescence, 31,* 429–442.

Benner, A. D. (2011). Latino adolescents' loneliness, academic performance, and the buffering nature of friendships. *Journal of Youth and Adolescence, 40,* 556–567.

Benner, A. D., & Graham, S. (2009). The transition to high school as a developmental process among multiethnic urban youth. *Child Development, 80,* 356–376.

Benner, A. D., & Graham, S. (2011). Latino adolescents' experiences of discrimination across the first 2 years of high school: Correlates and influences on educational outcomes. *Child Development, 82,* 508–519.

Benner, A. D., & Graham, S. (2013). The antecedents and consequences of racial/ethnic discrimination during adolescence: Does the source of discrimination matter? *Developmental Psychology, 49,* 1602–1613.

Benner, A. D., & Kim, S. Y. (2009). Experiences of discrimination among Chinese American adolescents and the consequences for socioemotional and academic development. *Developmental Psychology, 45,* 1682–1694.

Benner, A. D., & Kim, S. Y. (2010). Understanding Chinese American adolescents' developmental outcomes: Insights from the family stress model. *Journal of Research on Adolescence, 20,* 1–12.

Benner, A. D., & Mistry, R. S. (2007). Congruence of mother and teacher educational expectations and low-income youth's academic competence. *Journal of Educational Psychology, 99,* 140–153.

Benner, A. D., & Wang, Y. (2014). Shifting attendance trajectories from middle to high school: Influences of school transitions and changing school contexts. *Developmental Psychology, 50,* 1288–1301.

Benner, A. D., Crosnoe, R., & Eccles, J. S. (2014). Schools, peers, and prejudice in adolescence. *Journal of Research on Adolescence, 25,* 173–188.

Benner, A. D., Graham, S., & Mistry, R. S. (2008). Discerning direct and mediated effects of ecological structures and processes on adolescents' educational outcomes. *Developmental Psychology, 44,* 840–854.

Benner, A. D., & Wang, Y. (2014). Demographic marginalization, social integration, and adolescents' educational success. *Journal of Youth & Adolescence, 43,* 1611–1627.

Bennett, P. R., Lutz, A. C., & Jayaram, L. (2012). Beyond the schoolyard: The role of parenting logics, financial resources, and social institutions in the social class gap in a structured activity participation. *Sociology of Education, 85,* 131–157.

Benoit, A., Lacourse, E., & Claes, M. (2013). Pubertal timing and depressive symptoms in late adolescence: The moderating role of individual, peer, and parental factors. *Development and Psychopathology, 25,* 455–471.

Benson, M. J., & Buehler, C. (2012). Family process and peer deviance influences on adolescent aggression: Longitudinal effects across early and middle adolescence. *Child Development, 83,* 1213–1228.

Ben-Zur, H., & Reshef-Kfir, Y. (2003). Risk taking and coping strategies among Israeli adolescents. *Journal of Adolescence, 26,* 255–265.

Berge, J., Wall, M., Loth, K., & Neumark-Sztainer, D. (2010). Parenting style as a predictor of adolescent weight and weight-related behaviors. *Journal of Adolescent Health, 46,* 331–338.

Berger, C., & Dijkstra, J. K. (2013). Competition, envy, or snobbism? How popularity and friendships shape antipathy networks of adolescents. *Journal of Research on Adolescence, 23,* 586–595.

Berkel, C., Knight, G., Zeiders, K., Tein, J., Roosa, M., Gonzales, N., & Saenz, D. (2010). Discrimination and adjustment for Mexican American adolescents: A prospective examination of the benefits of culturally related values. *Journal of Research on Adolescence, 20,* 893–915.

Berkel, C., Murry, V. M., Hurt, T. R., Chen, Y., Brody, G. H., Simons, R. L., . . . Gibbons, F. (2009). It takes a village: Protecting rural African American youth in the context of racism. *Journal of Youth and Adolescence, 38,* 175–188.

Berkowitz, R. I., Wadden, T. A., Tershakovec, A. M., & Cronquist, J. L. (2003). Behavior therapy and sibutramine for the treatment of adolescent obesity. *Journal of the American Medical Association, 289,* 1805–1812.

Berlan, E. D., Corliss, H. L., Field, A. E., Goodman, E., & Bryn Austin, S. (2010). Sexual orientation and bullying among adolescents in the growing up today study. *Journal of Adolescent Health, 46,* 366–371.

Berliner, D., & Biddle, B. (1995). *The manufactured crisis: Myths, fraud, and attack on America's public schools.* Reading, MA: Addison-Wesley.

Berndt, T. (1996). Exploring the effects of friendship quality on social development. In W. Bukowski, A. Newcomb, & W. Hartup (Eds.), *The company they keep: Friendship in childhood and adolescence* (pp. 346–365). New York: Cambridge University Press.

Berndt, T., & Keefe, K. (1995). Friends' influence on adolescents' adjustment to school. *Child Development, 66,* 1312–1329.

Berndt, T., & Perry, T. (1990). Distinctive features and effects of early adolescent friendships. In R. Montemayor, G. Adams, & T. Gullota (Eds.), *Advances in adolescence research* (Vol. 2, pp. 269–287). Beverly Hills, CA: Sage.

Berninger, V., & Miller, B. (2011). Adolescent specific learning disabilities. In B. Brown & M. Prinstein (Eds.), *Encyclopedia of adolescence* (Vol. 3, pp. 21–29). New York: Academic Press.

Berns, G., Capra, C., Moore, S., & Noussair, C. (2010). Neural mechanisms of the influence of popularity on adolescent ratings of music. *Neuroimage, 49,* 2687–2696.

Bersamin, M., Fisher, D., Walker, S., Hill, D., & Grube, J. (2007). Defining virginity and abstinence: Adolescents' interpretations of sexual behaviors. *Journal of Adolescent Health, 41,* 182–188.

Bersamin, M., Walker, S., Waiters, E., Fisher, D., & Grube, J. (2005). Promising to wait: Virginity pledges and adolescent sexual behavior. *Journal of Adolescent Health, 36,* 428–436.

Berzonsky, M. (2004). Identity style, parental authority, and identity commitment. *Journal of Youth and Adolescence, 33,* 213–220.

Best, A. L. (2006). Freedom, constraint, and family responsibility: Teens and parents collaboratively negotiate around the car, class, gender, and culture. *Journal of Family Issues, 27,* 55–84.

Beyers, J. M., Bates, J. E., Pettit, G. S., & Dodge, K. A. (2003). Neighborhood structure, parenting processes, and the development of youths' externalizing behaviors: A multilevel analysis. *American Journal of Community Psychology, 31,* 35–53.

Beyers, J. M., Loeber, R., Wikström, P. H., & Stouthamer-Loeber, M. (2001). What predicts adolescent violence in better-off neighborhoods? *Journal of Abnormal Psychology, 29,* 369–381.

Beyers, W., & Goossens, L. (2008). Dynamics of perceived parenting and identity formation in late adolescence. *Journal of Adolescence, 31,* 165–184.

Beyers, W., Goossens, L., Vasant, I., & Moors, E. (2003). A structural model of autonomy in middle and late adolescence: Connectedness, separation, detachment, and agency. *Journal of Youth and Adolescence, 32,* 351–365.

Beyth-Marom, R., Austin, L., Fischoff, B., Palmgren, C., & Jacobs-Quadrel, M. (1993). Perceived consequences of risky behaviors: Adults and adolescents. *Developmental Psychology, 29,* 549–563.

Bezold, C. P., Konty, K. J., Day, S. E., Berger, M., Harr, L., Larkin, M., Napier, M. D., Nonas, C., Saha, S., Harris, T. G., & Stark, J. H. (2014). The effects of changes in physical fitness on academic performance among New York City youth. *Journal of Adolescent Health, 55,* 774–781.

Biddlecom, A. E., Awusabo-Asare, K., & Bankole, A. (2009). Role of parents in adolescent sexual activity and contraceptive use in four African countries. *International Perspectives on Sexual and Reproductive Health, 35,* 72–81.

Biehl, M. C., Natsuaki, M. N., & Ge, X. (2007). The influence of pubertal timing on alcohol use and heavy drinking trajectories. *Journal of Youth and Adolescence, 36,* 153–167.

Biehl, M., & Halpern-Felsher, B. L. (2001). Adolescents' and adults' understanding of probability expressions. *Journal of Adolescent Health, 28,* 30–35.

Biener, L., & Siegel, M. (2000). Tobacco marketing and adolescent smoking: More support for a causal inference. *American Journal of Public Health, 90,* 407–411.

Bierman, K., & Furman, W. (1984). The effects of social skills training and peer involvement on the social adjustment of preadolescents. *Child Development, 55,* 151–162.

Bierman, K., & Wargo, J. (1995). Predicting the longitudinal course associated with aggressive-rejected, aggressive-nonrejected, and rejected non-aggressive status. *Development and Psychopathology, 7,* 669–682.

Bijvank, M., Konijn, E., Bushman, B., & Roelofsma, P. (2009). Age and violent-content labels make video games forbidden fruits for youth. *Pediatrics, 123,* 870–876.

Bills, D., Helms, L., & Ozcan, M. (1995). The impact of student employment on teachers' attitudes and behaviors toward working students. *Youth and Society, 27,* 169–193.

Bimmel, N., van IJzendoorn, M. H., Bakermans-Kranenburg, M., Juffer, F., & De Geus, E. (2008). Problem behavior and heart rate reactivity in adopted adolescents: Longitudinal and concurrent relations. *Journal of Research on Adolescence, 18,* 201–214.

Bingenheimer, J. B. (2005). Firearm violence exposure and serious violent behavior. *Science, 308,* 1323–1326.

Bingham, C., & Crockett, L. (1996). Longitudinal adjustment patterns of boys and girls experiencing early, middle, and late sexual intercourse. *Developmental Psychology, 32,* 647–658.

Bingham, C., & Shope, J. T. (2004). Adolescent problem behavior and problem driving in young adulthood. *Journal of Adolescent Research, 19,* 205–223.

Birkeland, M. S., Melkevik, O., Holsen, I., & Wold, B. (2012). Trajectories of global self-esteem development during adolescence. *Journal of Adolescence, 35,* 43–54.

Birkeland, M. S., Breivik, K., & Wold, B. (2014). Peer acceptance protects global self-esteem from negative effect of low closeness to parents during adolescence and early adulthood. *Journal of Youth & Adolescence, 43,* 70–80.

Birkett, M., Espelage, D. L., & Koenig, B. (2009). LGB and questioning students in schools: The moderating effects of homophobic bullying and school climate on negative outcomes. *Journal of Youth and Adolescence, 38,* 989–1000.

Birkett, M., Russell, S. T., Corliss, H. L. (2014). Sexual-orientation disparities in school: the mediational role of indicators of victimization in achievement and truancy because of feeling unsafe. *American Journal of Public Health, 104,* 1124–1128.

Birmaher, B., Rabin, B., Garcia, M., Jain, U., Whiteside, T., Williamson, D., . . . Ryan, N. (1994). Cellular immunity in depressed, conduct disorder, and normal adolescents: Role of adverse life events. *Journal of the American Academy of Child and Adolescent Psychiatry, 33,* 671–678.

Biro F., Huang, B., Crawford, P., Lucky, A., Striegel-Moore, R., . . . Barton, B. (2006). Pubertal correlates in Black and White girls. *Journal of Pediatrics, 148,* 234–240.

Biro, F., Galvez, M. P., Greenspan, L. C., Succop, P. A., Vangeepuram, N., . . . Pinney, S. M., (2010). Pubertal assessment method and baseline characteristics in a mixed longitudinal study of girls, *Pediatrics, 126,* 583–590.

Biro, F., Striegel-Moore, R., Franko, D. L., Padgett, J., & Bean, J. A. (2006). Self-esteem in adolescent females. *Journal of Adolescent Health, 39,* 501–507.

Bishai, D., Mercer, D., & Tapales, A. (2005). Can government policies help adolescents avoid risky behavior? *Preventive Medicine, 40,* 197–202.

Bishop, D., Hardiman, M., Uwer, R., & von Suchodoletz, W. (2007). Maturation of the long-latency auditory ERP: Step function changes at start and end of adolescence. *Developmental Science, 10,* 565–575.

Bishop, J. (1999). Nerd harrassment, incentives, school priorities and learning. In S. Mayer & P. Peterson (Eds.), *Earning and learning.* Washington, DC: Brookings Institution.

Bishop, J. (2001). The role of end-of-course exams and minimum competency exams in standards-based reforms. In D. Ravitch (Ed.), *Brookings papers on educational policy.* Washington, DC: Brookings Institution.

Bishop, J., Bishop, M., Gelbwasser, L., Green, S., & Zuckerman, A. (2003). Why do we harass nerds and freaks?: Towards a theory of student culture and norms. In D. Ravitch (Ed.), *Brookings papers on education policy.* Washington, DC: Brookings Institution.

Bissell-Havran, J. M. (2014). Dispositional hope as a moderator of the link between social comparison with friends and eighth-grade students' perceptions of academic competence. *The Journal of Adolescence.* DOI: 10.1177/0272431614554705

Bjork, J. M., Lynne-Landsman, S. D., Sirocco, K., Boyce, C. A. (2012). Brain Maturation and Risky Behavior: The Promise and the Challenges of Neuroimaging-Based Accounts. *Child Development Perspectives, 6,* 385–391.

Black, M., Oberlander, S. E., Lewis, T., Knight, E. D., Zolotor, A. J., & Litrownik, A. J., English, D. (2009). Sexual intercourse among adolescents maltreated before age 12: A prospective investigation. *Pediatrics, 124,* 941–949.

Black, M., Ricardo, I., & Stanton, B. (1997). Social and psychological factors associated with AIDS risk behaviors among low-income, urban, African American adolescents. *Journal of Research on Adolescence, 7*, 173–195.

Blackwell, L. S., Trzesniewski, K. H., & Dweck, C. S. (2007). Implicit theories of intelligence predict achievement across an adolescent transition: A longitudinal study and an intervention. *Child Development, 78*, 246–263.

Blair, J. (2007). The amygdala and ventromedial prefrontal cortex in morality and psychopathy. *Trends in Cognitive Science, 11*, 387–392.

Blair, R. J. R., Leibenluft, E., & Pine, D. S. (2014). Conduct disorder and callous-unemotional traits in youth. *New England Journal of Medicine, 371*, 2207–2216.

Blais, J. J., Craig, W. M., Pepler, D., & Connolly, J. (2008). Adolescents online: The importance of Internet activity choices to salient relationships. *Journal of Youth and Adolescence, 37*, 522–536.

Blake, S. M., Ledsky, R., Goodenow, C., Sawyer, R., Lohrmann, D., & Windsor, R. (2003). Condom availability programs in Massachusetts high schools: Relationships with condom use and sexual behavior. *American Journal of Public Health, 93*, 955–962.

Blakemore, S.-J., & Robbins, T. W. (2012). Decision-making in the adolescent brain. *Nature Neuroscience, 15*, 1184–1191.

Blakemore, S-J. (2012). Imaging brain development: The adolescent brain. *Neuroimage, 61*, 397–406.

Blanc, A. K., Tsui, A. O., Croft, T. N., & Trevitt, J. L. (2010). Patterns and trends in adolescents' contraceptive use and discontinuation in developing countries and comparisons with adult women. *International Perspectives on Sexual and Reproductive Health, 35*, 63–71.

Bleakley, A., Hennessy, M., Fishbein, M., & Jordan, A. (2008). It works both ways: The relationship between sexual content in the media and adolescent sexual behavior. *Media Psychology, 11*, 443–461.

Bleakley, A., Jamieson, P. E., & Romer, D. (2012). Trends of sexual and violent content by gender in top-grossing U.S. films, 1950–2006. *Journal of Adolescent Health, 51*, 73–79.

Blinn-Pike, L. (1999). Why abstinent adolescents report they have not had sex: Understanding sexually resilient youth. *Family Relations, 48*, 295–301.

Blodgett Salafia, E., Gondoli, D., & Grundy, A. (2009). The longitudinal interplay of maternal warmth and adolescents' self-disclosure in predicting maternal knowledge. *Journal of Research on Adolescence, 19*, 654–668.

Blomfield, C. J., & Barber, B. L. (2011). Developmental experiences during extracurricular activities and Australian adolescents' self-concept: Particularly important for youth from disadvantaged schools. *Journal of Youth and Adolescence, 40*, 582–594.

Blondal, K. S., & Adalbjarnardottir, S. (2014). Parenting in relation to school dropout through student engagement: A longitudinal study. *Journal of Marriage and Family, 76*, 778–795.

Blos, P. (1967). The second individuation process of adolescence. In R. S. Eissler et al. (Eds.), *Psychoanalytic study of the child* (Vol. 15). New York: International Universities Press.

Blos, P. (1979). *The adolescent passage.* New York: International Universities Press.

Blum, R., & Nelson-Mmari, K. (2004). The health of young people in a global context. *Journal of Adolescent Health, 35*, 402–418.

Blum, R., & Rinehart, P. (2000). *Reducing the risk: Connections that make a difference in the lives of youth.* Minneapolis: Division of General Pediatrics and Adolescent Health, University of Minnesota.

Blum, R., Beuhring, T., Wunderlich, M., & Resnick, M. (1996). Don't ask, they won't tell: The quality of adolescent health screening in five practice settings. *American Journal of Public Health, 86*, 1767–1772.

Blum, R., Resnick, M., & Stark, T. (1990). Factors associated with the use of court bypass by minors to obtain abortions. *Family Planning Perspectives, 22*, 158–160.

Blumenthal, H., Leen-Feldner, E. W., Babson, K. A., Gahr, J. L., Trainor, C. D., & Frala, J. L. (2011). Elevated social anxiety among early maturing girls. *Developmental Psychology, 47*, 1133–1140.

Blyth, D., Simmons, R., & Zakin, D. (1985). Satisfaction with body image for early adolescent females: The impact of pubertal timing within different school environments. *Journal of Youth and Adolescence, 14*, 227–236.

Boden, J. M., Fergusson, D. M., & Horwood, L. J. (2010). Risk factors for conduct disorder and oppositional/defiant disorder: Evidence from a New Zealand birth cohort. *Journal of the American Academy of Child & Adolescent Psychiatry, 49*, 1125–1133.

Boden, J., Fergusson, D., & Horwood, J. (2011). Age of menarche and psychosocial outcomes in a New Zealand birth cohort. *Journal of the American Academy of Child & Adolescent Psychiatry, 50*, 132–140.

Boeninger, D. K., Masyn, K. E., & Conger, R. D. (2013). Testing alternative explanations for the associations between parenting and adolescent suicidal problems. *Journal of Research on Adolescence, 23*, 331–344.

Bogart, L. M., Elliott, M. N., Kanouse, D. E., Klein, D. J., Davies, S. L., Cuccaro, P. M., . . . Schuster, M. (2013). Association between perceived discrimination and racial/ethnic disparities in problem behaviors among preadolescent youths. *American Journal of Public Health, 103*, 1074–1081

Bogdan, R., & Hariri, A. R. (2012). Neural embedding of stress reactivity. *Nature Neuroscience, 15*, 1605–1607.

Bogenschneider, K. (1997). Parental involvement in adolescent schooling: A proximal process with transcontextual validity. *Journal of Marriage and the Family, 59*, 1–16.

Bogin, B. (2011). Puberty and adolescence: An evolutionary perspective. In B. Brown & M. Prinstein (Eds.), *Encyclopedia of adolescence* (Vol. 1, pp. 275–286). New York: Academic Press.

Bohnert, A. M., Kane, P., & Garber, J. (2008). Organized activity participation and internalizing and externalizing symptoms: Reciprocal relations during adolescence. *Journal of Youth and Adolescence, 37*, 239–250.

Boislard, M. A., Dussault, F., Brendgen, M., & Vitaro, F. (2013). Internalizing and externalizing behaviors as predictors of sexual onset in early adolescence. *The Journal of Early Adolescence, 33*, 920–945.

Boldero, J., & Fallon, B. (1995). Adolescent help-seeking: What do they get help for and from whom? *Journal of Adolescence, 18*, 193–209.

Bolland, J. M., Lian, B. E., & Formichella, C. M. (2005). The origins of hopelessness among inner-city African American adolescents. *American Journal of Community Psychology, 36*, 293–305.

Bolling, D., Pitskel, N., Deen, B., Crowley, M., Mayes, L., & Pelphrey, K. (2011). Development of neural systems for processing social exclusion from childhood to adolescence. *Developmental Psychology, 14*, 1431–1444.

Bomar, J., & Sabatelli, R. (1996). Family system dynamics, gender, and psychosocial maturity in late adolescence. *Journal of Adolescent Research, 11*, 421–439.

Bonanno, R.A., & Hymel, S. (2013). Cyber bullying and internalizing difficulties: above and beyond the impact of traditional forms of bullying. *Journal of Youth & Adolescence, 42*, 685–697.

Boney-McCoy, S., & Finkelhor, D. (1995). The psychosocial impact of violent victimization in a national youth sample. *Journal of Consulting and Clinical Psychology, 63*, 726–736.

Bong, M. (2009). Age-related differences in achievement goal differentiation. *Journal of Educational Psychology, 101*, 879–896.

Bong, M., Hwang, A., Noh, A., & Kim, S-i. (2014). Perfectionism and motivation of adolescents in academic contexts. *Journal of Educational Psychology, 106*, 711–729.

Bongers, I. L., Koot, H. M., van der Ende, J., & Verhulst, F. C. (2004). Developmental trajectories of externalizing behaviors in childhood and adolescence. *Child Development, 75*, 1523–1537.

Bontempo, D. E., & D'Augelli, A. R. (2002). Effects of at-school victimization and sexual orientation on lesbian, gay, or bisexual youths' health risk behavior. *Journal of Adolescent Health, 30*, 364–374.

Boone, E., & Leadbeater, B. (2006). Game on: Diminishing risks for depressive symptoms in early adolescence through positive involvement in team sports. *Journal of Research on Adolescence, 16*, 79–90.

Boone, L., Soenens, B., & Luyten, P. (2014). When or why does perfectionism translate into eating disorder pathology? A longitudinal examination of the moderating and mediating role of body dissatisfaction. *Journal of Abnormal Psychology, 123,* 412–418.

Boonstra, H. (2014). What is behind the decline in teen pregnancy rates? *Guttmacher Policy Review, 17,* 15–21.

Booth, A., Johnson, D., Granger, D., Crouter, A., & McHale, S. (2003). Testosterone and child and adolescent adjustment: The moderating role of parent–child relationships. *Developmental Psychology, 39,* 85–98.

Booth, A., Scott, M., & King, V. (2010). Father residence and adolescent problem behavior: Are youth always better off in two-parent families? *Journal of Family Issues, 31,* 585–605.

Booth, M. Z., & Gerard, J. M. (2014). Adolescents' stage-environment fit in middle and high school: The relationship between students' perceptions of their schools and themselves. *Youth & Society, 46,* 735–755.

Booth, M. Z., & Sheehan, H. C. (2008). Perceptions of people and place: Young adolescents' interpretation of their schools in the United States and the United Kingdom. *Journal of Adolescent Research, 23,* 722–744.

Borelli, J. L., & Prinstein, M. J. (2006). Reciprocal, longitudinal associations among adolescents' negative feedback-seeking, depressive symptoms, and peer relations. *Journal of Abnormal Child Psychology, 34,* 159–169.

Borkowski, J., & Sneed, M. (2006). Will NCLB improve or harm public education? *Harvard Educational Review, 76,* 503–525.

Born this Way Foundation. (2012). Website accessed at http://bornthiswayfoundation.org/pages/our-mission/ on July 2, 2012.

Bornstein, M. H., Hahn, C. S., & Wolke, D. (2013). Systems and cascades in cognitive development and academic achievement. *Child Development, 84,* 154–162.

Bornstein, M. H., Hahn, C.-S., & Haynes, O. M. (2010). Social competence, externalizing, and internalizing behavioral adjustment from early childhood through early adolescence: Developmental cascades. *Development and Psychopathology, 22,* 717–735.

Borzekowski, D., Fobil, J., & Asante, K. (2006). Online access by adolescents in Accra: Ghanaian teens' use of the Internet for health information. *Developmental Psychology, 42,* 450–458.

Bos, H., Sandfort, T., de Bruyn, E., & Hakvoort, E. (2008). Same-sex attraction, social relationships, psychosocial functioning, and school performance in early adolescence. *Developmental Psychology, 44,* 59–68.

Botticello, A. L. (2009). School contextual influences and the risk for adolescent alcohol misuse. *American Journal of Community Psychology, 43,* 85–97.

Botvin, M., & Vitaro, F. (1995). The impact of peer relationships on aggression in childhood: Inhibition through coercion or promotion through peer support. In J. McCord (Ed.), *Coercion and punishment in long-term perspectives* (pp. 183–197). New York: Cambridge University Press.

Bouchey, H. A., Shoulberg, E. K., Jodl, K. M., & Eccles, J. S. (2010). Longitudinal links between older sibling features and younger siblings' academic adjustment during early adolescence. *Journal of Educational Psychology, 102,* 197–211.

Bowen, G. L., Hopson, L. M., Rose, R. A., & Glennie, E. J. (2012). Students' perceived parental school behavior expectations and their academic performance: A longitudinal analysis. *Family Relations, 61,* 175–191.

Bowen, N. K., & Bowen, G. L. (2002). Neighborhood social disorganization, families, and the educational behavior of adolescents. *Journal of Adolescent Research, 17,* 468–490.

Bowers, E. P., Geldhof, G. J., Johnson, S. K., Lerner, J. V., Lerner, R. M. (2014). Special issue introduction: thriving across the adolescent years: a view of the issues. *Journal of Youth & Adolescence, 43,* 859–868.

Bowers, E. P., Johnson, S. K., Buckingham, M. H., Gasca, S., Warren, D. J., Lerner, J. V., & Lerner, R. M. (2014). Important non-parental adults and positive youth development across mid-to-late adolescence: the moderating effect of parenting profiles. *Journal of Youth & Adolescence, 43,* 897–918.

Bowker, A. (2004). Predicting friendship stability during early adolescence. *Journal of Early Adolescence, 24,* 85–112.

Bowker, J. C. (2011). Examining two types of best friendship dissolution during early adolescence. *Journal of Early Adolescence, 31,* 656–670.

Bowker, J. C., & Etkin, R. G. (2013). Does humor explain why relationally aggressive adolescents are popular? *Journal of Youth & Adolescence, 43,* 1322–1332.

Bowker, J. C., & Spencer, S. V. (2010). Friendship and adjustment: A focus on mixed-grade friendships. *Journal of Youth and Adolescence, 39,* 1318–1329.

Bowlby, J. (1969). *Attachment and loss:* Vol. 1. *Attachment.* New York: Basic Books.

Boyd, D. (2014). *It's complicated: The social life of networked teens.* New Haven: Yale University Press.

Boyer, B. P., & Nelson, J. A. (2015). Longitudinal associations of childhood parenting and adolescent health: the mediating influence of social competence. *Child Development, 86,* 828–843.

Boyer, T. W. (2006). The development of risk-taking: A multi-perspective review. *Developmental Review, 26,* 291–345.

Boyle, M. H., Georgiades, K., Racine, Y., & Mustard, C. (2007). Neighborhood and family influences on educational attainment: Results from the Ontario Child Health Study follow-up 2001. *Child Development, 78,* 168–189.

Boynton-Jarrett, R., Wright, R. J., Putnam, F. W., Lividoti Hibert, E., Michels, K. B., Forman, M. R., Rich-Edwards, J. (2013). Childhood abuse and age of menarche. *Journal of Adolescent Health, 52,* 241–247.

Braams, B. R., van Duijvenvoorde, A. C. K., Pepper, J. S., & Crone, E. A. (2015). Longitudinal changes in adolescent risk-taking: A comprehensive study of neural responses to rewards, pubertal development, and risk-taking behavior. *Journal of Neuroscience, 35,* 7226–7238.

Brack, C., Brack, G., & Orr, D. (1996). Adolescent health promotion: Testing a model using multidimensional scaling. *Journal of Research on Adolescence, 6,* 139–149.

Bradford, K., Vaughn, L. B., & Barber, B. K. (2008). When there is conflict: Interparental conflict, parent–child conflict, and youth problem behaviors. *Journal of Family Issues, 29,* 780–805.

Bradley, R. H., Corwyn, R. F., Pipes McAdoo, H., & Garcia-Coll, C. (2001). The home environments of children in the United States, part 1: Variations by age, ethnicity, and poverty status. *Child Development, 72,* 1844–1867.

Bradshaw, C. P., Sawyer, A. L., & O'Brennan, L. M. (2009). A social disorganization perspective on bullying-related attitudes and behaviors: The influences of school context. *American Journal of Community Psychology, 43,* 204–220.

Bradshaw, C. P., Waasdorp, T. E., Goldweber, A., Johnson, S. L. (2013). Bullies, gangs, drugs, and school: understanding the overlap and the role of ethnicity and urbanicity. *Journal of Youth & Adolescence, 42,* 220–234.

Brady, S., & Halpern-Felsher, B. (2007). Adolescents' reported consequences of having oral sex versus vaginal sex. *Pediatrics, 119,* 229–236.

Brahmbhatt, S. B., McAuley, T., & Barch, D. M. (2008). Functional developmental similarities and differences in the neural correlates of verbal and nonverbal working memory tasks. *Neuropsychologia, 46,* 1020–1031.

Brain Development Cooperative Group. (2012). Total and Regional Brain Volumes in a Population-Based Normative Sample from 4 to 18 Years: The NIH MRI Study of Normal Brain Development. *Cerebral Cortex, 22,* 1–12.

Braithwaite, I., Stewart, A. W., Hancox, R. J., Beasley, R., Murphy, R., Mitchell, E. A., & ISAAC Phase Three Study Group. (2013). The worldwide association between television viewing and obesity in children and adolescents: Cross sectional study. *PLoS One, 8,* 74263.

Brakefield, T. A., Mednick, S. C., Wilson, H. W., De Neve, J. E., Christakis, N.A., Fowler, J. H. (2014). Same-sex sexual attraction does not spread in adolescent social networks. *Archives of Sexual Behavior, 43,* 335–344.

Bramen, J. E., Hranilovich, J. A., Dahl, R. E., Chen, J., Rosso, C., Forbes, E. E., Dinov, I. D., Worthman, C. M., & Sowell, E. R. (2012). Sex matters during adolescence: testosterone-related cortical thickness maturation differs between boys and girls. *PLoS One, 7,* 33850.

Branch, C. (1995, August). *Gang bangers: Ethnic variations.* Paper presented at the American Psychological Association, New York.

Brand, S., Gerber, M., Beck, J., Hatzinger, M., Puhse, U., & Holsboer-Trachsler, E. (2010). High exercise levels are related to favorable sleep patterns and psychological functioning in adolescents: A comparison of athletes and controls. *Journal of Adolescent Health, 46,* 133–141.

Brand, S., Gerber, M., Kalak, N., Kirov, R., Lemola, S., Clough, P. J., Pühse, U., & Holsboer-Trachsler, E. Adolescents with greater mental toughness show higher sleep efficiency, more deep sleep and fewer awakenings after sleep onset. *Journal of Adolescent Health, 54,* 109–113.

Branstetter, S. A., Furman, W., & Cottrell, L. (2009). The influence of representations of attachment, maternal–adolescent relationship quality, and maternal monitoring on adolescent substance use: A 2-year longitudinal examination. *Child Development, 80,* 1448–1462.

Bratt, C. (2008). Guardians to counter adolescent drug use? Limitations of a routine activities approach. *Youth and Society, 39,* 385–405.

Braun, H., Jenkins, F., & Grigg, W. (2006). *Comparing private schools and public schools using hierarchical linear modeling.* U.S. Department of Education, National Center for Education Statistics. Washington, DC: U.S. Government Printing Office.

Brausch, A. M., & Gutierrez, P. M. (2010). Differences in non-suicidal self-injury and suicide attempts in adolescents. *Journal of Youth and Adolescence, 39,* 233–242.

Bray, J., Adams, G., Getz, J., & McQueen, A. (2003). Individuation, peers, and adolescent alcohol use: A latent growth analysis. *Journal of Consulting and Clinical Psychology, 71,* 553–564.

Bray, J., Adams, J., Getz, J., & Baer, P. E. (2001). Developmental, family, and ethnic influences on adolescent alcohol usage: A growth curve approach. *Journal of Family Psychology, 15,* 301–314.

Brechwald, W., & Prinstein, M. (2011). Beyond homophily: A decade of advances in understanding peer influence processes. *Journal of Research on Adolescence, 21,* 166–179.

Brendgen, M., Lamarche, V., Wanner, B., & Vitaro, F. (2010). Links between friendship relations and early adolescents' trajectories of depressed mood. *Developmental Psychology, 46,* 491–501.

Brendgen, M., Vitaro, F., & Bukowski, W. (2000). Deviant friends and early adolescents' emotional and behavioral adjustment. *Journal of Research on Adolescence, 10,* 173–189.

Brendgen, M., Vitaro, F., Barker, E. D., Girard, A., Dionne, G., Tremblay, R. E., & Boivin, M. (2013). Do other people's plights matter? A genetically informed twin study of the role of social context in the link between peer victimization and children's aggression and depression symptoms. *Developmental Psychology, 49,* 327–340.

Brendgen, M., Vitaro, F., Doyle, A., Markiewicz, D., & Bukowski, W. (2002). Same-sex peer relations and romantic relationships during early adolescence: Interactive links to emotional, behavioral, and academic adjustment. *Merrill-Palmer Quarterly, 48,* 77–103.

Brenhouse, H. C., Sonntag, K. C., & Andersen, S. L. (2008). Transient D-sub-1 dopamine receptor expression on prefrontal cortex projection neurons: Relationship to enhanced motivational salience of drug cues in adolescence. *Journal of Neuroscience, 28,* 2375–2382.

Brenick, A., & Killen, M. (2014). Moral judgements about Jewish-Arab intergroup exclusion: The role of cultural identity and contact. *Developmental Psychology, 50,* 86–99.

Brennan, P. A., Hall, J., Bor, W., Najman, J. M., & Williams, G. (2003). Integrating biological and social processes in relation to early-onset persistent aggression in boys and girls. *Developmental Psychology, 39,* 309–323.

Brenner, A. B., Zimmerman, M. A., Bauermeister, J. A., & Caldwell, C. H. (2013). Neighborhood context and perceptions of stress over time: an ecological model of neighborhood stressors and intrapersonal and interpersonal resources. *American Journal of Community Psychology, 51,* 544–556

Brenner, A. B., Zimmerman, M. A., Bauermeister, J. A., Caldwell, C. H. (2013). The physiological expression of living in disadvantaged neighborhoods for youth. *Journal of Youth & Adolescence, 42,* 792–806.

Brent, D., Emslie, G., Clarke, G., Wagner, K. D., Asarnow, J. R., Keller, M. . . . Zelazny, J. (2008). Switching to another SSRI or to venlafaxine with or without cognitive behavioral therapy for adolescents with SSRI-resistant depression: The TORDIA randomized controlled trial. *JAMA: Journal of the American Medical Association, 299,* 901–913.

Bridges, G., & Steen, S. (1998). Racial disparities in official assessments of juvenile offenders: Attributional stereotypes as mediating mechanisms. *American Sociological Review, 63,* 554–570.

Briley, D. A., & Tucker-Drob, E. M. (2013). Explaining the increasing heritability of cognitive ability across development: A meta-analysis of longitudinal twin and adoption studies. *Psychological Science, 24,* 1704–1713.

Brinch, C., & Galloway, T. (2012). Schooling in adolescence raises IQ scores. *Proceedings of the National Academy of Sciences, 109,* 425–430.

Brodbeck, J., Bachmann, M. S., Croudace, T. J., & Brown, A. (2013). Comparing growth trajectories of risk behaviors from late adolescence through young adulthood: An accelerated design. *Developmental Psychology, 49,* 1732–1738.

Brody, G. H., Chen, Y. F., Yu, T., Beach, S. R., Kogan, S. M., Simons, R. L., et al. (2012). Life stress, the dopamine receptor gene, and emerging adult drug use trajectories: A longitudinal, multilevel, mediated moderation analysis. *Development and Psychopathology, 24,* 941–951.

Brody, G., Beach, S., Philibert, R., Chen, Y., & Murry, V. (2009). Prevention effects moderate the association of 5-httlpr and youth risk behavior initiation: G3E hypotheses tested via a randomized prevention design. *Child Development, 80,* 645–661.

Brody, G., Beach, S., Philibert, R., Chen, Y.-F., Lei, M.-K., Murry, V., & Brown, A. (2009). Parenting moderates a genetic vulnerability factor in longitudinal increases in youths' substance use. *Journal of Consulting and Clinical Psychology, 77,* 1–11.

Brody, G., Chen, Y., Murry, V., Ge, X., Simons, R., Gibbons, F., . . . Cutrona, C. (2006). Perceived discrimination and the adjustment of African American youths: A five-year longitudinal analysis with contextual moderation effects. *Child Development, 77,* 1170–1189.

Brody, G., Ge, X., Kim, S., Murry, V., Simons, R., Gibbons, F., . . . Conger, R. (2003). Neighborhood disadvantage moderates associations of parenting and older sibling problem attitudes and behavior with conduct disorders in African American children. *Journal of Consulting and Clinical Psychology, 71,* 211–222.

Brody, G., Murry, V., Kogan, S., Gerrard, M., Gibbons, F., Molgaard, V., . . . Wills, T. (2006). The Strong African American Families Program: A cluster-randomized prevention trial of long-term effects and a mediational model. *Journal of Consulting and Clinical Psychology, 74,* 356–366.

Brody, G., Stoneman, Z., & Flor, D. (1995). Linking family processes and academic competence among rural African American youths. *Journal of Marriage and the Family, 57,* 567–579.

Brody, G., Stoneman, Z., & Flor, D. (1996). Parental religiosity, family processes, and youth competence in rural, two-parent African-American families. *Developmental Psychology, 32,* 696–706.

Brody, G., Stoneman, Z., & McCoy, J. (1994). Forecasting sibling relationships in early adolescence from child temperaments and family processes in middle childhood. *Child Development, 65,* 771–784.

Brody, G. H., Kogan, S. M., & Chen, Y. F. (2012). Perceived discrimination and longitudinal increases in adolescent substance use: gender differences and mediational pathways. *American Journal of Public Health, 102,* 1006–1011.

Broh, B. A. (2002). Linking extracurricular programming to academic achievement: Who benefits and why? *Sociology of Education, 75,* 69–95.

Broidy, L., Nagin, D., Tremblay, R., Bates, J., Brame, B., Dodge, K., . . . Vitaro, F. (2003). Developmental trajectories of childhood disruptive behaviors and adolescent delinquency: A six-site, cross-national study. *Developmental Psychology, 39,* 222–245.

Bronfenbrenner, U. (1979). *The ecology of human development.* Cambridge, MA: Harvard University Press.

Bronstein, P., Duncan, P., Clauson, J., Abrams, C. L., Yannett, N., Ginsburg, G., & Milne, M. (1998). Preventing middle school adjustment problems for children from lower-income families: A program for aware parenting. *Journal of Applied Developmental Psychology, 19,* 129–152.

Bronstein, P., Ginsburg, G., & Herrera-Leavitt, I. (2000). *Parental predictors of motivational orientation and academic performance in early adolescence: A longitudinal study.* Unpublished manuscript. Burlington, VT: Department of Psychology, University of Vermont.

Brooker, R. J., Berenbaum, S. A., Bricker, J., Corley, R. P., & Wadsworth, S. A. (2012). Pubertal timing as a potential mediator of adoption effects on problem behaviors. *Journal of Research on Adolescence, 22,* 739–745.

Brookmeyer, K. A., Henrich, C. C., & Schwab-Stone, M. (2005). Adolescents who witness community violence: Can parent support and prosocial cognitions protect them from committing violence? *Child Development, 76,* 917–929.

Brooks-Gunn, J., & Donahue, E. (Eds.) (2008). Children and electronic media. *The Future of Children, 18.*

Brooks-Gunn, J., & Paikoff, R. (1993). "Sex is a gamble, kissing is a game": Adolescent sexuality and health promotion. In S. Millstein, A. Petersen, & E. Nightingale (Eds.), *Promoting the health of adolescents: New directions for the twenty-first century* (pp. 180–208). New York: Oxford University Press.

Brooks-Gunn, J., & Reiter, E. (1990). The role of pubertal processes. In S. Feldman & G. Elliott (Eds.), *At the threshold: The developing adolescent* (pp. 16–23). Cambridge, MA: Harvard University Press.

Brooks-Gunn, J., & Warren, M. (1985). The effects of delayed menarche in different contexts: Dance and nondance students. *Journal of Youth and Adolescence, 14,* 285–300.

Brooks-Gunn, J., Graber, J., & Paikoff, R. (1994). Studying links between hormones and negative affect: Models and measures. *Journal of Research on Adolescence, 4,* 469–486.

Brooks-Gunn, J., Newman, D., Holderness, C., & Warren, M. (1994). The experience of breast development and girls' stories about the purchase of a bra. *Journal of Youth and Adolescence, 23,* 539–565.

Brooks-Russell, A., Farhat, T., Haynie, D., & Simons-Morton, B. (2014). Trends in substance use among 6th- to 10th-grade students from 1998 to 2010: Findings from a national probability study. *The Journal of Early Adolescence, 34,* 667–680.

Brown, B. (1990). Peer groups. In S. Feldman & G. Elliott (Eds.), *At the threshold: The developing adolescent* (pp. 171–196). Cambridge, MA: Harvard University Press.

Brown, B. (1996). Visibility, vulnerability, development, and context: Ingredients for a fuller understanding of peer rejection in adolescence. *Journal of Early Adolescence, 16,* 27–36.

Brown, B. (1999). "You're going out with who?" Peer group influences on adolescent romantic relationships. In W. Furman, B. Brown, & C. Feiring (Eds.), *Contemporary perspectives on adolescent romantic relationships* (pp. 291–329). New York: Cambridge University Press.

Brown, B. (2004). Adolescents' relationships with peers. In R. Lerner & L. Steinberg (Eds.), *Handbook of adolescent psychology.* New York: Wiley.

Brown, B., & Bakken, J. (2011). Parenting and peer relationships: Reinvigorating research on family–peer linkages in adolescence. *Journal of Research on Adolescence, 21,* 153–165.

Brown, B., & Larson, J. (2009). Peer relationships in adolescence. In R. Lerner & L. Steinberg (Eds.), *Handbook of adolescent psychology* (3rd ed., Vol. 2, pp. 74–103). New York: Wiley.

Brown, B., & Mounts, N. (1989, April). *Peer group structures in single versus multiethnic high schools.* Paper presented at the biennial meetings of the Society for Research in Child Development, Kansas City.

Brown, B., Herman, M., Hamm, J. V., & Heck, D. (2008). Ethnicity and image: Correlates of minority adolescents' affiliation with individual-based versus ethnically defined peer crowds. *Child Development, 79,* 529–546.

Brown, B., Mory, M., & Kinney, D. (1994). Casting crowds in a relational perspective: Caricature, channel, and context. In R. Montemayor, G. Adams, & T. Gullotta (Eds.), *Advances in adolescent development: Vol. 5. Personal relationships during adolescence.* Newbury Park, CA: Sage.

Brown, B., Mounts, N., Lamborn, S., & Steinberg, L. (1993). Parenting practices and peer group affiliation in adolescence. *Child Development, 64,* 467–482.

Brown, B., Von Bank, H., & Steinberg, L. (2008). Smoke in the looking glass: Effects of discordance between self- and peer-rated crowd affiliation on adolescent anxiety, depression, and self-feelings. *Journal of Youth and Adolescence, 37,* 1163–1177.

Brown, C. S., Alabi, B. O., Huynh, V. W., & Masten, C. L. (2011). Ethnicity and gender in late childhood and early adolescence: Group identity and awareness of bias. *Developmental Psychology, 47,* 463–471.

Brown, J. D., L'Engle, K. L., Pardun, C. J., Guo, G., Kenneavy, K., & Jackson, C. (2006). Sexy media matter: Exposure to sexual content in music, movies, television, and magazines predicts Black and White adolescents' sexual behavior. *Pediatrics, 117,* 1018–1027.

Brown, J. S., Meadows, S. O., & Elder, G. H., Jr. (2007). Race-ethnic inequality and psychological distress: Depressive symptoms from adolescence to young adulthood. *Developmental Psychology, 43,* 1295–1311.

Brown, J., & Bobkowski, P. (2011a). Media, influence of. In B. Brown & M. Prinstein (Eds.), *Encyclopedia of adolescence* (Vol. 2, pp. 189–195). New York: Academic Press.

Brown, J., & Bobkowski, P. (2011b). Older and newer media: Patterns of use and effects on adolescents' health and well-being. *Journal of Research on Adolescence, 21,* 95–113.

Brown, J., & L'Engle, K. (2009). X-Rated: Sexual attitudes and behaviors associated with U.S. early adolescents' exposure to sexually explicit media. *Communication Research, 36,* 129–151.

Brown, J., Cohen, P., Chen, H., Smailes, E., & Johnson, J. (2004). Sexual trajectories of abused and neglected youths. *Journal of Developmental & Behavioral Pediatrics, 25,* 77–82.

Brown, K., McMahon, R., Biro, F., Crawford, P., Schreiber, G., Similo, S., . . . Striegel-Moore, S. (1998). Changes in self-esteem in Black and White girls between the ages of 9 and 14 years: The NHLBI Growth and Health Study. *Journal of Adolescent Health, 23,* 7–19.

Brown, L. K., Tolou-Shams, M., Lescano, C., Houck, C., Zeidman, J., Pugatch, D., . . . Project SHIELD Study Group. (2006). Depressive symptoms as a predictor of sexual risk among African American adolescents and young adults. *Journal of Adolescent Health, 39,* e1–e8.

Brown, S., & Rinelli, L. (2010). Family structure, family processes, and adolescent smoking and drinking. *Journal of Research on Adolescence, 20,* 259–273.

Brown, W. T., & Jones, J. M. (2004). The substance of things hoped for: A study of the future orientation, minority status perceptions, academic engagement, and academic performance of Black high school students. *Journal of Black Psychology, 30,* 248–273.

Browning, C. R., Gardner, M., Maimon, D., & Brooks-Gunn, J. (2014). Collective efficacy and the contingent consequences of exposure to life-threatening violence. *Developmental Psychology, 50,* 1878–1890.

Browning, C. R., Leventhal, T., & Brooks-Gunn, J. (2005). Sexual initiation in early adolescence: The nexus of parental and community control. *American Sociological Review, 70,* 758–778.

Brubacher, J., & Rudy, W. (1976). *Higher education in transition* (3rd ed.). New York: Harper & Row.

Brückner, H., & Bearman, P. (2005). After the promise: The STD consequences of adolescent virginity pledges. *Journal of Adolescent Health, 36,* 271–278.

Brumberg, J. (1997). *The body project: An intimate history of American girls.* New York: Random House.

Bruvold, W. (1993). A meta-analysis of adolescent smoking prevention programs. *American Journal of Public Health, 83,* 872–880.

Bryan, A. D., Schmiege, S. J., & Magnan, R. E. (2012). Marijuana use and risky sexual behavior among high-risk adolescents: Trajectories, risk factors, and event-level relationships. *Developmental Psychology, 48,* 1429–1442.

Bryant, A., & Zimmerman, M. (2003). Role models and psychosocial outcomes among African American adolescents. *Journal of Adolescent Research, 18,* 36–67.

Bryant, A., & Zimmerman, M. A. (2002). Examining the effects of academic beliefs and behaviors on changes in substance use among urban adolescents. *Journal of Educational Psychology, 94,* 621–637.

Bryant, A., Schulenberg, J., O'Malley, P., Bachman, J., & Johnston, L. (2003). How academic achievement, attitudes, and behaviors relate to the course of substance use during adolescence: A 60-year, multiwave national longitudinal study. *Journal of Research on Adolescence, 13,* 361–397.

Bucchianeri, M. M., Eisenberg, M. E., Wall, M. M., Piran, N., & Neumark-Sztainer, D. (2014). Multiple types of harassment: Associations with emotional well-being and unhealthy behaviors in adolescents. *Journal of Adolescent Health, 54,* 724–729.

Buchanan, C., & Maccoby, E. (1993, March). *Relationships between adolescents and their nonresidential parents: A comparison of nonresidential mothers and fathers.* Paper presented at the biennial meetings of the Society for Research in Child Development, New Orleans.

Buchanan, C., Eccles, J., & Becker, J. (1992). Are adolescents the victims of raging hormones? Evidence for activational effects of hormones on moods and behavior at adolescence. *Psychological Bulletin, 111,* 62–107.

Buchanan, C., Maccoby, E., & Dornbusch, S. (1996). *Adolescents after divorce.* Cambridge, MA: Harvard University Press.

Buchanan, M., & Robbins, C. (1990). Early adult psychological consequences for males of adolescent pregnancy and its resolution. *Journal of Youth and Adolescence, 19,* 413–424.

Buchmann, C., & Dalton, B. (2002). Interpersonal influences and educational aspirations in 12 countries: The importance of institutional context. *Sociology of Education, 75,* 99–122.

Buck, K. A., Kretsch, N., & Harden, K. P. (2013). Positive attentional bias, attachment style, and susceptibility to peer influence. *Journal of Research on Adolescence, 23,* 605–613.

Buechel, F., & Duncan, G. (1998). Do parents' social activities promote children's school attainments? Evidence from the German Socioeconomic Panel. *Journal of Marriage and the Family, 60,* 95–108.

Buehler, C. (2006). Parents and peers in relation to early adolescent problem behavior. *Journal of Marriage and Family, 68,* 109–124.

Buehler, C., & Welsh, D. P. (2009). A process model of adolescents' triangulation into parents' marital conflict: The role of emotional reactivity. *Journal of Family Psychology, 23,* 167–180.

Buehler, C., Benson, M., & Gerard, J. (2006). Interpersonal hostility and early adolescent problem behavior: The mediating role of specific aspects of parenting. *Journal of Research on Adolescence, 16,* 265–292.

Buehler, C., Franck, K., & Cook, E. (2009). Adolescents' triangulation in marital conflict and peer relations. *Journal of Research on Adolescence, 19,* 669–689.

Buehler, C., Krishnakumar, A., Stone, G., Anthony, C., Pemberton, S., Gerard, J., & Barber, B. (1998). Interparental conflict styles and youth problem behaviors: A two-sample replication study. *Journal of Marriage and the Family, 60,* 119–132.

Buelow, M. T., Okdie, B. M., & Cooper, A. B. (2015). The influence of video games on executive functions in college students. *Computers in Human Behavior, 45,* 228–234.

Buhi, E. R., & Goodson, P. (2007). Predictors of adolescent sexual behavior and intention: A theory-guided systematic review. *Journal of Adolescent Health, 40,* 4–21.

Buhrmester, D. (1990). Intimacy of friendship, interpersonal competence, and adjustment during preadolescence and adolescence. *Child Development, 61,* 1101–1111.

Buhrmester, D. (1996). Need fulfillment, interpersonal competence, and the developmental contexts of early adolescent friendship. In W. Bukowski, A. Newcomb, & W. Hartup, (Eds.), *The company they keep: Friendship in childhood and adolescence* (pp. 158–185). New York: Cambridge University Press.

Buhrmester, D., & Furman, W. (1987). The development of companionship and intimacy. *Child Development, 58,* 1101–1113.

Buhrmester, D., & Furman, W. (1990). Perceptions of sibling relationships during middle childhood and adolescence. *Child Development, 61,* 1387–1396.

Buhrmester, D., & Yin, J. (1997, April). *A longitudinal study of friends' influence on adolescents' adjustment.* Paper presented at the biennial meetings of the Society for Research in Child Development, Washington, DC.

Bukowski, W., Gauze, C., Hoza, B., & Newcomb, A. (1993). Differences and consistency between same-sex and other-sex peer relationships during early adolescence. *Developmental Psychology, 29,* 255–263.

Bukowski, W., Sippola, L., & Hoza, B. (1999). Same and other: Interdependency between participation in same- and other-sex friendships. *Journal of Youth and Adolescence, 28,* 439–459.

Bukowski, W., Sippola, L., & Newcomb, A. F. (2000). Variations in patterns of attraction of same- and other-sex peers during early adolescence. *Developmental Psychology, 36,* 147–154.

Bulcroft, R., Carmody, D., & Bulcroft, K. (1996). Patterns of parental independence giving to adolescents: Variations by race, age, and gender of child. *Journal of Marriage and the Family, 58,* 866–883.

Bullock, B., & Dishion, T. J. (2002). Sibling collusion and problem behavior in early adolescence: Toward a process model for family mutuality. *Journal of Abnormal Child Psychology, 30,* 143–153.

Bumpass, L., & McLanahan, S. (1987, April). *Unmarried motherhood: A note on recent trends, composition and Black-White differences.* Paper presented at the annual meeting of the Population Association of America, Chicago.

Bumpus, M. F., Crouter, A., & McHale, S. (2001). Parental autonomy granting during adolescence: Exploring gender differences in context. *Developmental Psychology, 37,* 163–173.

Burdette, A. M., Haynes, S. H., Hill, T. D., & Bartkowski, J. P. (2014). Religious variations in perceived infertility and inconsistent contraceptive use among unmarried young adults in the United States. *Journal of Adolescent Health, 54,* 704–709.

Burdette, A., & Needham, B. (2012). Neighborhood environment and body mass index trajectories from adolescence to adulthood. *Journal of Adolescent Health, 50,* 30–37.

Bureau of Labor Statistics. (2012). *Current population survey.* Washington: Author.

Bureau of Labor Statistics. (2015) *Earnings and unemployment rates by educational attainment.* Washington: Author.

Bureau of Labor Statistics. (2015b). *Employment status of the civilian noninstitutional population 16 to 24 years of age by school enrollment, age, sex, race, Hispanic or Latino ethnicity, and educational attainment.* Washington: Author.

Bureau of Labor Statistics. (2015c). *Labor force status of 2014 high school graduates and 2013–14 high school dropouts 16 to 24 years old by school enrollment, educational attainment, sex, race, and Hispanic or Latino ethnicity, October 2014.* Washington: Author.

Bureau of Labor Statistics. (2015d). *Employment characteristics of families summary.* Washington: Author.

Burg, S., Mayers, R., & Miller, L. (2011). Spirituality, religion, and healthy development in adolescents. In B. Brown & M. Prinstein (Eds.), *Encyclopedia of adolescence* (Vol. 1, pp. 353–359). New York: Academic Press.

Burke, J. D., Pardini, D. A., & Loeber, R. (2008). Reciprocal relationships between parenting behavior and disruptive psychopathology from childhood through adolescence. *Journal of Abnormal Child Psychology, 36,* 679–692.

Burnett, S., Bault, N., Coricelli, G., & Blakemore, S.-J. (2010). Adolescents' heightened risk-seeking in a probabilistic gambling task. *Cognitive Development, 25,* 183–196.

Burnett, S., Sebastian, C., Kadosh, K., & Blakemore, S-J. (2011). The social brain in adolescence: Evidence from functional magnetic resonance imaging and behavioural studies. *Neuroscience and Biobehavioral Reviews, 35,* 1654–1664.

Burrell, G., & Roosa, M. (2009). Mothers' economic hardship and behavior problems in their early adolescents. *Journal of Family Issues, 30,* 511–531.

Burt, K. B., & Paysnick, A. A. (2012). Resilience in the transition to adulthood. *Development and Psychopathology, 24,* 493–505.

Burt, K. B., & Roisman, G. I. (2010). Competence and psychopathology: Cascade effects in the NICHD Study of Early Child Care and Youth Development. *Development and Psychopathology, 22,* 557–567.

Burt, K., Obradović, J., Long, J., & Masten, A. (2008). The interplay of social competence and psychopathology over 20 years: Testing transactional and cascade models. *Child Development, 79,* 359–374.

Burt, S. A., Barnes, A. R., McGue, M., & Iacono, W. G. (2008). Parental divorce and adolescent delinquency: Ruling out the impact of common genes. *Developmental Psychology, 44,* 1668–1677.

Burt, S. A., McGue, M., & Iacono, W. G. (2009). Nonshared environmental mediation of the association between deviant peer affiliation and adolescent externalizing behaviors over time: Results from a cross-lagged monozygotic twin differences design. *Developmental Psychology, 45,* 1752–1760.

Burt, S. A., McGue, M., Krueger, R. F., & Iacono, W. G. (2007). Environmental contributions to adolescent delinquency: A fresh look at the shared environment. *Journal of Abnormal Child Psychology, 35,* 787–800.

Burton, C. M., Marshal, M. P., Chisolm, D. J., Sucato, G. S., & Friedman, M. S. (2013). Sexual minority-related victimization as a mediator of mental health disparities in sexual minority youth: a longitudinal analaysis. *Journal of Youth & Adolescence, 42,* 394–402.

Burton, L. (2007). Childhood adultification in economically disadvantaged families: A conceptual model. *Family Relations, 56,* 329–345.

Busseri, M. A., Willoughby, T., Chalmers, H., & Bogaert, A. F. (2008). On the association between sexual attraction and adolescent risk behavior involvement: Examining mediation and moderation. *Developmental Psychology, 44,* 69–80.

Bussing, R., Mason, D. M., Bell, L., Porter, P., & Garvan, C. (2010). Adolescent outcomes of childhood attention-deficit/hyperactivity disorder in a diverse community sample. *Journal of the American Academy of Child and Adolescent Psychiatry, 49,* 595–605.

Butler, K. (2006, July 4). The grim neurology of teenage drinking. *The New York Times.*

Buzy, W. M., McDonald, R., Jouriles, E. N., Swank, P. R., Rosenfield, D., Shimek, J. S., & Corbitt-Shindler, D. (2004). Adolescent girls' alcohol use as a risk factor for relationship violence. *Journal of Research on Adolescence, 14,* 449–470.

Byrd, C., & Chavous, T. (2011). Racial identity, school racial climate, and school intrinsic motivation among African American youth: The importance of person–context congruence. *Journal of Research on Adolescence, 21,* 849–860.

Byrne, B., & Shavelson, R. (1996). On the structure of social self-concept for pre-, early, and late adolescents: A test of the Shavelson, Hubner, and Stanton (1976) model. *Journal of Personality and Social Psychology, 70,* 599–613.

Byrnes, J. (2011). Academic achievement. In B. Brown & M. Prinstein (Eds.), *Encyclopedia of adolescence* (Vol. 1, pp. 1–9). New York: Academic Press.

Cairns, R., Leung, M., Buchanan, L., & Cairns, B. (1995). Friendships and social networks in childhood and adolescence: Fluidity, reliability, and interrelations. *Child Development, 66,* 1330–1345.

Caldwell, C. H., Kohn-Wood, L. P., Schmeelk-Cone, K. H., Chavous, T. M., & Zimmerman, M. A. (2004). Racial discrimination and racial identity as risk or protective factors for violent behaviors in African American young adults. *American Journal of Community Psychology, 33,* 91–105.

Caldwell, C. H., Sellers, R. M., Bernat, D. H., & Zimmerman, M. A. (2004). Racial identity, parental support, and alcohol use in a sample of academically at-risk African American high school students. *American Journal of Community Psychology, 34,* 71–82.

Caldwell, L., & Darling, N. (1999). Leisure context, parental control, and resistance to peer pressure as predictors of adolescent partying and substance use: An ecological perspective. *Journal of Leisure Research, 31,* 57–77.

Caldwell, M. S., Rudolph, K. D., Troop-Gordon, W., & Kim, D. Y. (2004). Reciprocal influence among relational self-views, social disengagement, and peer stress during early adolescence. *Child Development, 75,* 1140–1154.

Calkins, S. D., & Keane, S. P. (2009). Developmental origins of early antisocial behavior. *Development and Psychopathology, 21,* 1095–1109.

Call, K. T., Riedel, A. A., Hein, K., McLoyd, V., Petersen, A., & Kipke, M. (2002). Adolescent health and well-being in the twenty-first century: A global perspective. *Journal of Research on Adolescence, 12,* 69–98.

Callahan, R. (2005). Tracking and English learners: Limiting opportunity to learn. *American Educational Research Journal, 42,* 305–328.

Calvert, S. (2008). Children as consumers: Advertising and marketing. *The Future of Children, 18,* 205–234.

Calvete, E., & Cardeñoso, O. (2005). Gender differences in cognitive vulnerability to depression and behavior problems in adolescents. *Journal of Abnormal Child Psychology, 33,* 179–192.

Calvete, E., Orue, I., & Hankin, B. L. (2013). Transactional relationships among cognitive vulnerabilities, stressors, and depressive symptoms in adolescence. *Journal of Abnormal Child Psychology, 41,* 399–410.

Calzo, J. P., Sonneville, K. R., Haines, J., Blood, E. A., Field, A. E., & Austin, S. B. (2012). The development of associations among body mass index, body dissatisfaction, and weight and shape concern in adolescent boys and girls. *Journal of Adolescent Health, 51,* 517–523.

Campa, M. I., & Eckenrode, J. J. (2006). Pathways to intergenerational adolescent childbearing in a high-risk sample. *Journal of Marriage and Family, 68,* 558–572.

Campbell, B. (2011). Adrenarche and middle childhood. *Human Nature, 22,* 327–349.

Campbell, B. C., Prossinger, H., & Mbzivo, M. (2005). Timing of pubertal maturation and the onset of sexual behavior among Zimbabwe school boys. *Archives of Sexual Behavior, 34,* 505–516.

Campbell, F., & Ramey, C. (1995). Cognitive and school outcomes for high-risk African-American students at middle adolescence: Positive effects of early intervention. *American Educational Research Journal, 32,* 743–772.

Campbell, F., Pungello, E., Miller-Johnson, S., Burchinal, M., & Ramey, C. (2001). The development of cognitive and academic abilities: Growth curves from an early childhood educational experiment. *Developmental Psychology, 37,* 231–242.

Campbell, M. A., Porter, S., & Santor, D. (2004). Psychopathic traits in adolescent offenders: An evaluation of criminal history, clinical, and psychosocial correlates. *Behavioral Sciences and the Law, 22,* 23–47.

Campione-Barr, N., & Smetana, J. G. (2004). In the eye of the beholder: Subjective and observer ratings of middle-class African American mother–adolescent interactions. *Developmental Psychology, 40,* 927–934.

Campione-Barr, N., & Smetana, J. G. (2010). "Who said you could wear my sweater?" Adolescent siblings' conflicts and associations with relationship quality. *Child Development, 81,* 464–471.

Campione-Barr, N., Bassett Greer, K., & Kruse, A. (2013). Differential associations between domains of sibling conflict and adolescent emotional adjustment. *Child Development, 84,* 938–954.

Cantillon, D. (2006). Community social organization, parents, and peers as mediators of perceived neighborhood block characteristics on delinquent and prosocial activities. *American Journal of Community Psychology, 37,* 111–127.

Capaldi, D., & Clark, S. (1998). Prospective family predictors of aggression toward female partners for at-risk young men. *Developmental Psychology, 34,* 1175–1188.

Capaldi, D., Dishion, T., Stoolmiller, M., & Yoerger, K. (2001). Aggression toward female partners by at-risk young men: The contribution of male adolescent friendships. *Developmental Psychology, 37,* 61–73.

Capaldi, D., Stoolmiller, M., Clark, S., & Owen, L. (2002). Heterosexual risk behaviors in at-risk young men from early adolescence to young adulthood: Prevalence, prediction, and association with STD contraction. *Developmental Psychology, 38,* 394–406.

Caplan, N., Choy, M., & Whitmore, J. (1992, February). Indochinese refugee families and academic achievement. *Scientific American,* pp. 36–42.

Cappelleri, J., Eckenrode, J., & Powers, J. (1993). The epidemiology of child abuse: Findings from the Second National Incidence and Prevalence Study of Child Abuse and Neglect. *American Journal of Public Health, 83,* 1622–1624.

Carbonaro, W. (2005). Tracking, students' effort, and academic achievement. *Sociology of Education, 78,* 27–49.

Carbonaro, W., & Covay, E. (2010). School sector and student achievement in the era of standards-based reforms. *Sociology of Education, 83,* 160–182.

Card, N. A., & Hodges, E. V. E. (2008). Peer victimization among schoolchildren: Correlations, causes, consequences, and consideration in assessment and intervention. *School Psychology Quarterly, 23,* 451–461.

Card, N. A., Stucky, B. D., Sawalani, G. M., & Little, T. D. (2008). Direct and indirect aggression during childhood and adolescence: A meta-analytic review of gender differences, intercorrelations, and relations to maladjustment. *Child Development, 79,* 1185–1229.

Carlo, G., Crockett, L. J., Randall, B. A., & Roesch, S. C. (2007). A latent growth curve analysis of prosocial behavior among rural adolescents. *Journal of Research on Adolescence, 17,* 301–324.

Carlo, G., Knight, G., McGinley, M., & Hayes, R. (2011a). The roles of parental inductions, moral emotions, and moral cognitions in prosocial tendencies among Mexican American and European American early adolescents. *Journal of Early Adolescence, 31,* 757–781.

Carlo, G., Koller, S., Eisenberg, N., Da Silva, M., & Frohlich, C. (1996). A cross-national study of the relations among prosocial moral reasoning, gender role orientations, and prosocial behaviors. *Developmental Psychology, 32,* 231–240.

Carlo, G., Padilla-Walker, L. P., & Day, R. (2011b). A test of the economic strain model on adolescents' prosocial behaviors. *Journal of Research on Adolescence, 21,* 842–848.

Carlson Jones, D. (2004). Body image among adolescent girls and boys: A longitudinal study. *Developmental Psychology, 40,* 823–835.

Carlson, D. L., McNulty, T. L., Bellair, P. E., & Watts, S. (2014). Neighborhoods and racial/ethnic disparities in adolescent sexual risk behavior. *Journal of Youth & Adolescence, 43,* 1536–1549.

Carlson, E., Sroufe, L. A., Collins, W. A., Jimerson, S., Weinfield, N., Henninghausen, K., … Meyer, S. (1999). Early environmental support and elementary school adjustment as predictors of school adjustment in middle adolescence. *Journal of Adolescent Research, 14,* 72–94.

Carlson, W., & Rose, A. (2012). Activities in heterosexual romantic relationships: Grade differences and associations with relationship satisfaction. *Journal of Adolescence, 35,* 219–224.

Carrion, V. G., & Wong, S. S. (2012). Can traumatic stress alter the brain? Understanding the implications of early trauma on brain development and learning. *Journal of Adolescent Health, 51,* S23–S28.

Carroll, A., Hemingway, F., Bower, J., Ashman, A., Houghton, S., & Durkin, K. (2006). Impulsivity in juvenile delinquency: Differences among early-onset, late-onset, and non-offenders. *Journal of Youth and Adolescence, 35,* 519–529.

Carroll, J. S., Badger, S., Willoughby, B. J., Nelson, L. J., Madsen, S. D., & McNamara Barry, C. (2009). Ready or not?: Criteria for marriage readiness among emerging adults. *Journal of Adolescent Research, 24,* 349–375.

Carroll, J. S., Willoughby, B., Badger, S., Nelson, L. J., Barry, C. M., & Madsen, S. D. (2007). So close, yet so far away: The impact of varying marital horizons on emerging adulthood. *Journal of Adolescent Research, 22,* 219–247.

Carskadon, M. (2011). Sleep in adolescents: The perfect storm. *Pediatric Clinics of North America, 58,* 637–647.

Carskadon, M., & Acebo, C. (2002). Regulation of sleepiness in adolescence: Update, insights, and speculation. *Sleep, 25,* 606–616.

Carson, D., Chowdhury, A., Perry, C., & Pati, C. (1999). Family characteristics and adolescent competence in India: Investigation of youth in southern Orissa. *Journal of Youth and Adolescence, 28,* 211–233.

Carter, P. M., Bingham, C. R., Zakrajsek, J. S., Shope, J. T., & Sayer, T. B. (2014). Social norms and risk perception: Predictors of distracted driving behavior among novice adolescent drivers. *Journal of Adolescent Health, 54,* S32–S41.

Carter, R., Caldwell, C. H., Matusko, N., Antonucci, T., & Jackson, J. S. (2011). Ethnicity, perceived pubertal timing, externalizing behaviors, and depressive symptoms among Black adolescent girls. *Journal of Youth and Adolescence, 40,* 1394–1406.

Casella, R. (2003). Zero tolerance policy in schools: Rationale, consequences, and alternatives. *Teachers College Review, 105,* 872–892.

Casey, B. J., & Caudle, K. (2013). The teenage brain: Self control. *Current Directions in Psychological Science 22,* 82–87.

Casey, B. J., Duhoux, S., & Cohen, M. (2010). Adolescence: what do transmission, transition, and translation have to do with it? *Neuron, 67,* 749–760.

Casey, B. J., Jones, R., & Somerville, L. (2011). Braking and accelerating of the adolescent brain. *Journal of Research on Adolescence, 21,* 21–33.

Casey, B. J., Tottenham, N., Liston, C., & Durston, S. (2005). Imaging the developing brain: What have we learned about cognitive development? *Trends in Cognitive Science, 9,* 104–110.

Cash, T. F., Morrow, J., Hrabosky, J. I., & Perry, A. A. (2004). How has body image changed? A cross-sectional investigation of college women and men from 1983 to 2001. *Journal of Consulting and Clinical Psychology, 72,* 1081–1089.

Casillas, A., Robbins, S., Allen, J., Kuo, Y-L., Hanson, M. A., & Schmeiser, C. (2012). Predicting early academic failure in high school from prior academic achievement, psychosocial characteristics, and behavior. *Journal of Educational Psychology, 104,* 407–420.

Casper, D., & Card, N. (2010). "We were best friends, but . . .": Two studies of antipathetic relationships emerging from broken friendships. *Journal of Adolescent Research, 25,* 499–526.

Caspi, A. (2000). The child is father of the man: Personality continuities from childhood to adulthood. *Journal of Personality and Social Psychology, 78,* 158–172.

Caspi, A., Henry, B., McGee, R. O., Moffitt, T. E., & Silva, P. A. (1995). Temperamental origins of child and adolescent behavior problems: From age 3 to age 15. *Child Development, 66,* 55–68.

Caspi, A., Lynam, D., Moffitt, T., & Silva, P. (1993). Unraveling girls' delinquency: Biological, dispositional, and contextual contributions to adolescent misbehavior. *Developmental Psychology, 29,* 19–30.

Caspi, A., Sugden, K., Moffitt, T., Taylor, A., Craig, I., Harrington, H., et al. (2003). Influence of life stress on depression: Moderation by a polymorphism in the 5-HTT gene. *Science, 301,* 386–389.

Cassidy, J., Ziv, Y., Mehta, T. G., & Feeney, B. C. (2003). Feedback seeking in children and adolescents: Associations with self-perceptions, attachment representations, and depression. *Child Development, 74,* 612–628.

Casteel, M. (1993). Effects of inference necessity and reading goal on children's inferential generation. *Developmental Psychology, 29,* 346–357.

Castellanos-Ryan, N., Parent, S., Vitaro, F., Tremblay, R. E., & Séguin, R. (2013). Pubertal development, personality, and substance use: A 10-year longitudinal study from childhood to adolescence. *Journal of Abnormal Psychology, 122,* 782–796.

Catsambis, S. (1992, March). *The many faces of tracking in middle school grades: Between- and within-school differentiation of students and resources.* Paper presented at the biennial meetings of the Society for Research on Adolescence, Washington, DC.

Catterall, J. (1998). Risk and resilience in student transitions to high school. *American Journal of Education, 106,* 302–333.

Cauffman, E. (2008). Understanding the female offender. *Future of Children, 18,* 119–142.

Cauffman, E., & Steinberg, L. (1996). Effects of menarche, dating, and heterosocial involvement on dieting behavior in early adolescence. *Developmental Psychology, 32,* 631–635.

Cauffman, E., Farruggia, S. P., & Goldweber, A. (2008). Bad boys or poor parents: Relations to female juvenile delinquency. *Journal of Research on Adolescence, 18,* 699–712.

Cauffman, E., Piquero, A., Kimonis, E., Steinberg, L., & Chassin, L. (2007). Legal, individual, and contextual predictors of court disposition. *Law and Human Behavior, 31,* 519–535.

Cauffman, E., Shulman, E., Bechtold, J., & Steinberg, L. (2015). Children and the law. In R. M. Lerner (Series Ed.) & M. Bornstein & T. Leventhal (Vol. Eds.), *Handbook of child psychology and developmental science* (7th ed.). *Volume 4: Ecological settings and processes in developmental systems* (pp. 616–653). New York: Wiley.

Cauffman, E., Shulman, E., Steinberg, L., Claus, E., Banich, M., Graham, S., & Woolard, J. (2010). Age differences in affective decision making as indexed by performance on the Iowa Gambling Task. *Developmental Psychology, 46,* 193–207.

Cauffman, E., Steinberg, L., & Piquero, A. R. (2005). Psychological, neuropsychological and physiological correlates of serious antisocial behavior in adolescence: The role of self-control. *Criminology, 43,* 133–175.

Caughy, M. O., Franzini, L., Windle, M., Dittus, P., Cuccaro, P., Elliot, M. N., Schuster, M. A. (2012). Social competence in late elementary school: relationships to parenting and neighborhood context. *Journal of Youth & Adolescence, 41,* 1613–1627.

Cavanagh, S. E., & Fomby, P. (2012). Family instability, school context, and the academic careers of adolescents. *Sociology of Education, 85,* 81–97.

Cavanagh, S. E., Crissey, S. R., & Raley, R. K. (2008). Family structure history and adolescent romance. *Journal of Marriage and Family, 70,* 698–714.

Cavanagh, S., & Fomby, P. (2012) School context, family instability, and the academic careers of adolescents. *Sociology of Education, 85,* 81–97.

Cavazos-Rehg, P. A., Spitznagel, E. L., Bucholz, K. K., Nurnberger, J., Edenberg, H. J., Kramer, J. R., . . . Beirut, L. (2010). Predictors of sexual debut at age 16 or younger. *Archives of Sexual Behavior, 39,* 664–673.

Ceballo, R., McLoyd, V. C., & Toyokawa, T. (2004). The influence of neighborhood quality on adolescents' educational values and school effort. *Journal of Adolescent Research, 19,* 716–739.

Ceci, S., & Williams, W. (1999). Schooling, intelligence, and income. *American Psychologist, 52,* 1051–1058.

Centers for Disease Control and Prevention (2014a). *Youth risk behavior surveillance, 2013.* Washington: Author.

Centers for Disease Control and Prevention (2014b). *School-associated violent death study.* Washington: Author.

Centers for Disease Control and Prevention. (2006). Youth behavior surveillance—United States, 2005. *Morbidity and Mortality Weekly Report, 55,* SS–5.

Centers for Disease Control and Prevention. (2012). Youth risk behavior surveillance—United States, 2011. *Morbidity and Mortality Weekly Report, 61(4).*

Cepeda, A., & Valdez, A. (2003). Risk behaviors among young Mexican American gang-associated females: Sexual relations, partying, substance abuse, and crime. *Journal of Adolescent Research, 18,* 90–106.

Cervantes, R., & Cordova, D. (2011). Life experiences of Hispanic adolescents: developmental and language considerations in acculturation stress. *Journal of Community Psychology, 39,* 336–352.

Chaloupka, F. (2004). The effects of price on alcohol use, abuse, and their consequences. In R. Bonnie & M. O'Connell (Eds.,) *Reducing underage drinking: a collective responsibility.* Washington: The National Academies Press.

Chan, D. (1997). Depressive symptoms and perceived competence among Chinese secondary school students in Hong Kong. *Journal of Youth and Adolescence, 26,* 303–319.

Chan, S. M., & Chan, K.W. (2013). Adolescents' susceptibility to peer pressure: Relations to parent–adolescent relationship and adolescents' emotional autonomy from parents. *Youth & Society, 45,* 286–302.

Chan, W. Y., Ou, S. R., Reynolds, A. J. (2014). Adolescent civic engagement and adult outcomes: an examination among urban racial minorities. *Journal of Youth & Adolescence, 43,* 1829–1843.

Chandler, M. (1987). The Othello effect: Essay on the emergence and eclipse of skeptical doubt. *Human Development, 30,* 137–159.

Chandra, A., Martino, S., Collins, R., Elliott, M., Berry, S., Kanouse, D., & Miu, A. (2008). Does watching sex on television predict teen pregnancy? Findings from a national longitudinal survey of youth. *Pediatrics, 122,* 1047–1054.

Chang, E. S. (2013). Negotiating family obligations and educational goals among college-enrolled youth on Jeju Island, Korea. *Journal of Research on Adolescence, 23,* 25–34.

Chang, E. S., Chen, C., Greenberger, E., Dooley, D., & Heckhausen, J. (2006). What do they want in life?: The life goals of a multi-ethnic, multi-generational sample of high school seniors. *Journal of Youth and Adolescence, 35,* 321–332.

Chang, E. S., Greenberger, E., Chen, C., Heckhausen, J., & Farruggia, S. P. (2010). Nonparental adults as social resources in the transition to adulthood. *Journal of Research on Adolescence, 20,* 1065–1082.

Chang, Z., Lichtenstein, P., & Larsson, H. (2012). The effects of childhood ADHD symptoms on early-onset substance use: A Swedish twin study. *Journal of Abnormal Child Psychology, 40,* 425–35.

Chang, Z., Lichtenstein, P., Asherson, P. J., & Larsson, H. (2013). Developmental twin study of attention problems high heritabilities throughout development. *JAMA Psychiatry, 70,* 311–318.

Chango, J. M., Allen, J. P., Szwedo, D., & Schad, M. M. (2014). Early adolescent peer foundations of late adolescent and young adult psychological adjustment. *Journal of Research*

on Adolescence, Early view. DOI: 10.1111/jora.12162

Chango, J. M., McElhaney, K. B., Allen, J. P., Schad, M. M., & Marston, E. (2012). Relational stressors and depressive symptoms in late adolescence: Rejection sensitivity as a vulnerability. *Journal of Abnormal Child Psychology, 40,* 369–379.

Chao, R., & Otsuki-Clutter, M. (2011). Racial and ethnic differences: Sociocultural and contextual explanations. *Journal of Research on Adolescence, 21,* 47–60.

Charbonneau, A. M., Mezulis, A. H., & Hyde, J. S. (2009). Stress and emotional reactivity as explanations for gender differences in adolescents' depressive symptoms. *Journal of Youth and Adolescence, 38,* 1050–1058.

Chase-Landsdale, P. L., Brooks-Gunn, J., & Zamsky, E. (1994). Young African-American multigenerational families in poverty: Quality of mothering and grandmothering. *Child Development, 65,* 373–393.

Chase-Landsdale, P. L., Moffit, R. A., Lohman, B. J., Cherlin, A. J., Coley, R. L., Pittman, L. D., Roff, J., & Votruba-Drazl, E. (2003). Mothers' transitions from welfare to work and the well-being of preschooler and adolescents. *Science, 299,* 15–28.

Chassin, L., Hussong, A., & Beltran, I. (2009). Adolescent substance use. In R. Lerner & L. Steinberg (Eds.), *Handbook of adolescent psychology* (3rd ed., Vol. 1, pp. 723–764). New York: Wiley.

Chassin, L., Presson, C., Todd, M., Rose, J., & Sherman, S. (1998). Maternal socialization of adolescent smoking: The intergenerational transmission of parenting and smoking. *Developmental Psychology, 34,* 1189–1201.

Chauhan, P., Reppucci, N. D., Burnette, M., & Reiner, S. (2010). Race, neighborhood disadvantage, and antisocial behavior among female juvenile offenders. *Journal of Community Psychology, 38,* 532–540.

Chauhan, P., Reppucci, N., & Turkheimer, E. (2009). Racial differences in the associations of neighborhood disadvantage, exposure to violence, and criminal recidivism among female juvenile offenders. *Behavioral Sciences & the Law, 27,* 531–552.

Chavez, R. S., & Heatherton, T. F. (2015). Multimodal frontostriatal connectivity underlies individual differences in self-esteem. *Social Cognitive Affective Neuroscience, 10,* 364–370.

Chavous, T., Bernat, D., Schmeelk-Cone, K., Caldwell, C., Kohn-Wood, L., & Zimmerman, M. (2003). Racial identity and academic attainment among African American adolescents. *Child Development, 74,* 1076–1090.

Chavous, T., Rivas-Drake, D., Smalls, C., Griffin, T., & Cogburn, C. (2008). Gender matters, too: The influences of school racial discrimination and racial identity on academic engagement outcomes among African American adolescents. *Developmental Psychology, 44,* 637–654.

Chein, J., Albert, D., O'Brien, L., Uckert, K., & Steinberg, L. (2011). Peers increase adolescent risk taking by enhancing activity in the brain's reward circuitry. *Developmental Psychology, 14,* F1–F10.

Chen, C. S., Greenberger, E., Lester, J., Dong, Q., & Guo, M. (1998). A cross-cultural study of family and peer correlates of adolescent misconduct. *Developmental Psychology, 34,* 770–781.

Chen, C. S., Lee, S. Y., & Stevenson, H. W. (1996). Academic achievement and motivation of Chinese students: A cross-national perspective. In S. Lau (Ed.), *Growing up the Chinese way: Chinese child and adolescent development.* Hong Kong: Chinese University Press.

Chen, C. Y., Dormitzer, C. M., Bejarno, J., & Anthony, J. C. (2004). Religiosity and the earliest stages of adolescent drug involvement in seven countries of Latin America. *American Journal of Epidemiology, 159,* 1180–1188.

Chen, E., Langer, D. A., Raphaelson, Y. E., & Matthews, K. (2004). Socioeconomic status and health in adolescents: The role of stress interpretations. *Child Development, 75,* 1039–1052.

Chen, K., & Kandel, D. (1996). The natural history of drug use from adolescence to the mid-thirties in a general population sample. *American Journal of Public Health, 85,* 41–47.

Chen, M.-J., Gruenewald, P. J., & Remer, L. G. (2009a). Does alcohol outlet density affect youth access to alcohol? *Journal of Adolescent Health, 44,* 582–589.

Chen, M. S., & Foshee, V. A. (2015). Stressful life events and the perpetration of adolescent dating abuse. *Journal of Youth & Adolescence, 44,* 696–707.

Chen, P., & Jacobson, K. C. (2012). Developmental trajectories of substance use from early adolescence to young adulthood: Gender and racial/ethnic differences. *Journal of Adolescent Health, 50,* 154–163.

Chen, P., & Vazsonyi, A. T. (2011). Future orientation, impulsivity, and problem behaviors: A longitudinal moderation model. *Developmental Psychology, 47,* 1633–1645.

Chen, R., & Simons-Morton, B. (2009). Concurrent changes in conduct problems and depressive symptoms in early adolescents: A developmental person-centered approach. *Development and Psychopathology, 21,* 285–307.

Chen, W-I. (2010). Exposure to community violence and adolescents' internalizing behaviors among African American and Asian American adolescents. *Journal of Youth and Adolescence, 39,* 403–413.

Chen, X. (2012). Culture, peer interaction, and socioemotional development. *Child Development Perspectives, 6,* 27–34.

Chen, X., & Adams, M. (2010). Are teen delinquency abstainers social introverts?: A test of Moffitt's theory. *Journal of Research in Crime and Delinquency, 47,* 439–468.

Chen, X., & Graham, S. (2012). Close relationships and attributions for peer victimization among late adolescents. *Journal of Adolescence, 35,* 1547–1556.

Chen, X., & Graham, S. (2015). Cross-ethnic friendships and intergroup attitudes among Asian American adolescents. *Child Development, 86,* 749–764.

Chen, X., Rubin, K., & Li, D. (1997). Relation between academic achievement and social adjustment: Evidence from Chinese children. *Developmental Psychology, 33,* 518–525.

Chen, Z., Guo, F., Yang, X., Li, X., Duan, Q., Zhang, J., & Ge, X. (2009b). Emotional and behavioral effects of romantic relationships in Chinese adolescents. *Journal of Youth and Adolescence, 38,* 1282–1293.

Chen-Gaddini, M. (2012). Chinese mothers and adolescents' views of authority and autonomy: A study of parent–adolescent conflict in urban and rural china. *Child Development, 83,* 1846–1852.

Cherlin, A., Chase-Lansdale, P., & McRae, C. (1998). Effects of parental divorce on mental health throughout the life course. *American Sociological Review, 63,* 239–249.

Cherney, I. D., & Shing, Y. L. (2008). Children's nurturance and self-determination rights: A cross-cultural perspective. *Journal of Social Issues, 64,* 835–856.

Cheung, C. S., Pomerantz, E. M., & Dong, W. (2013). Does adolescents' disclosure to their parents matter for their academic adjustment? *Child Development, 84,* 693–710.

Cheung, C. S. S., & Pomerantz, E. M. (2012). Why does parents' involvement enhance children's achievement? The role of parent-oriented motivation. *Journal of Educational Psychology, 104,* 820–832.

Child Trends. (2010). *High school students carrying weapons.* Washington: Author.

Child Trends. Databank. (2014). *Attendance at religious services.* Available at: http://www.childtrends.org/?indicators5religious-service-attendance. Accessed on July 9, 2015.

Chiodo, D., Wolfe, D. A., Crooks, C., Hughes, R., & Jaffe, P. (2009). Impact of sexual harassment victimization by peers on subsequent adolescent victimization and adjustment: A longitudinal study. *Journal of Adolescent Health, 45,* 246–252.

Chisholm, L., & Hurrelmann, K. (1995). Adolescence in modern Europe: Pluralized transition patterns and their implications for personal and social risks. *Journal of Adolescence, 18,* 129–158.

Chiu, M. M., Pong, S. L., Mori, I., Chow, B. W. (2012). Immigrant students' emotional and cognitive engagement at school: a multilevel analysis of students in 41 countries. *Journal of Youth & Adolescence, 41,* 1409–1425.

Choe, D. E., & Zimmerman, M. A. (2014). Transactional process of African American adolescents' family conflict and violent behavior. *Journal of Research on Adolescence, 24,* 591–597.

Choi, Y., Harachi, T. W., Gillmore, M. R., & Catalano, R. F. (2005). Applicability of the social development model to urban ethnic minority youth: Examining the relationship between external constraints, family socialization, and problem behaviors. *Journal of Research on Adolescence, 15,* 505–534.

Choi, Y., He, M., & Harachi, T. W. (2008). Intergenerational cultural dissonance, parent–child conflict and bonding, and youth problem behaviors among Vietnamese and Cambodian immigrant families. *Journal of Youth and Adolescence, 37,* 85–96.

Choo, E. K., Benz, M., Zaller, N., Warren, O., Rising, K. L., & McConnell, K. J. (2014). The impact of state medical marijuana legislation on adolescent marijuana use. *Journal of Adolescent Health, 55,* 160–166.

Choudhury, S., Blakemore, S., & Charman, T. (2006). Social cognitive development during adolescence. *Social Cognitive and Affective Neuroscience, 3,* 165–174.

Choukas-Bradley, S., Giletta, M., Neblett, E. W., & Prinstein, M. J. (2015). Ethnic differences in associations among popularity, likability, and trajectories of adolescents' alcohol use and frequency. *Child Development, 86,* 519–535.

Choukas-Bradley, S., Giletta, M., Widman, L., Cohen, G. L., & Prinstein, M. J. (2014). Experimentally measured susceptibility to peer influence and adolescent sexual behavior trajectories: A preliminary study. *Developmental Psychology, 50,* 2221–2227.

Chow, A., Eccles, J. S., & Salmela-Aro, K. (2012). Task value profiles across subjects and aspirations to physical and IT-related sciences in the United States and Finland. *Developmental Psychology, 48,* 1612–1628.

Christakou, A. (2014). Present simple and continuous: Emergence of self-regulation and contextual sophistication in adolescent decision-making. *Neuropsychologia, 65,* 302–312.

Christakou, A., Brammer, M., & Rubia, K. (2011). Maturation of limbic corticostriatal activation and connectivity associated with developmental changes in temporal discounting. *Neuroimage, 54,* 1344–1354.

Chua, A. (2011). Battle hymn of the Tiger Mother. New York: Penguin.

Chumlea, W., Schubert, C., Roche, A., Kulin, H., Lee, P., . . . Himes, J. (2003). Age at menarche and racial comparisons in U.S. girls. *Pediatrics, 111,* 110–113.

Chun, H., & Dickson, G. (2011). A psychoecological model of academic performance among Hispanic adolescents. *Journal of Youth and Adolescence, 40,* 1581–1594.

Chun, Y.-J., & MacDermid, S. M. (1997). Perceptions of family differentiation, individuation, and self-esteem among Korean adolescents. *Journal of Marriage and the Family, 59,* 451–462.

Chung, G. H., Flook, L., & Fuligni, A. (2011). Reciprocal associations between family and peer conflict in adolescents' daily lives. *Child Development, 82,* 1390–1396.

Chung, G. H., Flook, L., & Fuligni, A. J. (2009). Daily family conflict and emotional distress among adolescents from Latin American, Asian, and European backgrounds. *Developmental Psychology, 45,* 1406–1415.

Chung, H. L., & Steinberg, L. (2006). Relations between neighborhood factors, parenting behaviors, peer deviance, and delinquency among serious juvenile offenders. *Developmental Psychology, 42,* 319–331.

Chung, J. M., Robins, R. W., Trzesniewski, K. H., Noftle, E. E., Roberts, B. W., & Widaman, K. F. (2014). Continuity and change in self-esteem during emerging adulthood. *Journal of Personality and Social Psychology, 106,* 469–483.

Church, R. (1976). *Education in the United States.* New York: Free Press.

Churchwell, J. C., & Yurgelun-Todd, D. A. (2013). Age-related changes in insula cortical thickness and impulsivity: Significance for emotional development and decision-making. *Developmental Cognitive Neuroscience, 6,* 80–86.

Cicchetti, D., Rogosch, F. A., & Sturge-Apple, M. (2007). Interactions of child maltreatment and serotonin transporter and monoamine oxidase A polymorphisms: Depressive symptomatology among adolescents from low socioeconomic status backgrounds. *Development and Psychopathology, 19,* 1161–1180.

Cillessen, A. H. N., & Rose, A. J. (2005). Understanding popularity in the peer system. *Current Directions in Psychological Science, 14,* 102–105.

Cinamon, R. G., & Rich, Y. (2002). Gender difference in the importance of work and family roles: Implications for work–family conflict. *Sex Roles, 47,* 531–541.

Claes, M. (1998). Adolescents' closeness with parents, siblings, and friends in three countries: Canada, Belgium, and Italy. *Journal of Youth and Adolescence, 27,* 165–184.

Clampet-Lundquist, S., Edin, K., Kling, J., & Duncan, G. (2011). Moving teenagers out of high-risk neighborhoods: How girls fare better than boys. *American Journal of Sociology, 116,* 1154–1189.

Clancy, S., & Dollinger, S. (1993). Identity, self, and personality, I: Identity status and the five-factor model of personality. *Journal of Research on Adolescence, 3,* 227–246.

Clardy, C., & King, P. (2011). Religious involvement. In B. Brown & M. Prinstein (Eds.), *Encyclopedia of adolescence* (Vol. 2, pp. 279–288.). New York: Academic Press.

Clark, J., & Barber, B. (1994). Adolescents in postdivorce and always-married families: Self-esteem and perceptions of fathers' interest. *Journal of Marriage and the Family, 56,* 608–614.

Clark, R., Dogan, R. R., & Akbar, N. J. (2003). Youth and parental correlates of externalizing symptoms, adaptive functioning, and academic performance: An exploratory study in preadolescent Blacks. *Journal of Black Psychology, 29,* 210–229.

Clark, R., Novak, J. D., & Dupree, D. (2002). Relationship of perceived parenting practices to anger regulation and coping strategies in African American adolescents. *Journal of Adolescence, 25,* 373–384.

Clarke, A. T. (2006). Coping with interpersonal stress and psychosocial health among children and adolescents: A meta-analysis. *Journal of Youth and Adolescence, 35,* 11–24.

Clasen, D., & Brown, B. (1985). The multidimensionality of peer pressure in adolescence. *Journal of Youth and Adolescence, 14,* 451–468.

Clements, M., Aber, J. L., & Seidman, E. (2008). The dynamics of life stressors and depressive symptoms in early adolescence: A test of six theoretical models. *Child Development, 79,* 1168–1182.

Clentifanti, L. C. M., Modecki, K. L., MacLellan, S., & Gowling, H. (2014). Driving under the influence of risky peers: An experimental study of adolescent risk taking. *Journal of Research on Adolescence,* Early view. DOI: 10.1111/jora.12187

Cleveland, H. (2003). The influence of female and male risk on the occurrence of sexual intercourse within adolescent relationships. *Journal of Research on Adolescence, 13,* 81–112.

Cleveland, H., & Wiebe, R. P. (2003). The moderation of adolescent-to-peer similarity in tobacco and alcohol use by school levels of substance use. *Child Development, 74,* 279–291.

Cleveland, M. J., Feinberg, M. E., & Greenberg, M. T. (2010). Protective families in high- and low-risk environments: Implications for adolescent substance use. *Journal of Youth and Adolescence, 39,* 114–126.

Cleveland, M. J., Feinberg, M. E., Bontempo, D. E., & Greenberg, M. T. (2008). The role of risk and protective factors in substance use across adolescence. *Journal of Adolescent Health, 43,* 157–164.

Cleveland, M. J., Gibbons, F., Gerrard, M., Pomery, E., & Brody, G. (2005). The impact of parenting on risk cognitions and risk behavior: A study of mediation and moderation in a panel of African American adolescents. *Child Development, 76,* 900–916.

Clinkinbeard, S. S., Simi, P., Evans, M. K., & Anderson, A. L. (2011). Sleep and delinquency: Does the amount of sleep matter? *Journal of Youth and Adolescence, 40,* 916–930.

Clotfelter, C. T., Ladd, H. F., & Vigdor, J. L. (2012). New destinations, new trajectories? The educational progress of Hispanic youth in North Carolina. *Child Development, 83,* 1608–1622.

Coatsworth, J. D., & Conroy, D. E. (2009). The effects of autonomy-supportive coaching, need satisfaction, and self-perceptions on initiative and identity in youth swimmers. *Developmental Psychology, 45,* 320–328.

Coatsworth, J. D., Sharp, E. H., Palen, L., Darling, N., Cumsille, P., & Marta, E. (2005). Exploring adolescent self-defining leisure activities and identity experiences across three countries. *International Journal of Behavioral Development, 29,* 361–370.

Cochran, B. N., Stewart, A. J., Ginzler, J. A., & Cauce, A. (2002). Challenges faced by homeless sexual minorities: Comparison of gay, lesbian, bisexual, and transgender homeless adolescents with their heterosexual counterparts. *American Journal of Public Health, 92,* 773–777.

Cohen, D., Farley, T., Taylor, S., Martin, D., & Schuster, M. (2002). When and where do youths have sex? The potential role of adult supervision. *Pediatrics, 110,* E66.

Cohen, G. L., & Prinstein, M. J. (2006). Peer contagion of aggression and health risk behavior among adolescent males: An experimental investigation of effects on public conduct and private attitudes. *Child Development, 77,* 967–983.

Cohen, P. K., Chen, H., Hartmark, C., & Gordon, K. (2003). Variations in patterns of developmental transmissions in the emerging adulthood period. *Developmental Psychology, 39,* 657–669.

Cohen-Gilbert, J. E., & Thomas, K. M. (2013). Inhibitory Control During Emotional Distraction Across Adolescence and Early Adulthood. *Child Development, 84,* 1954–1966.

Coie, J., Terry, R., Lenox, K., Lochman, J., & Hyman, C. (1995). Childhood peer rejection and aggression as predictors of stable patterns of adolescent disorder. *Development and Psychopathology, 7,* 697–713.

Coiro, M., & Emery, R. (1996, March). *Adolescents' adjustment as a function of their involvement in post-divorce conflict.* Paper presented at the biennial meetings of the Society for Research on Adolescence, Boston.

Coker, K. L., Smith, P. H., Westphal, A., Zonana, H. V., & McKee, S. A. (2014). Crime and psychiatric disorders among youth in the US population: An analysis of the national comorbidity survey–adolescent supplement. *Journal of the American Academy of Child & Adolescent Psychiatry, 53,* 888–898.

Coker, T., Elliott, M., Kanouse, D., & Grunbaum, J. (2009). Perceived racial/ethnic discrimination among fifth-grade students and its association with mental health. *American Journal of Public Health, 99,* 878–884.

Colder, C. R., Hawk, L. W. Jr., Lengua, L. J., Wiezcorek, W., Das Eiden, R., & Read, J. P. (2013). Trajectories of reinforcement sensitivity during adolescence and risk for substance use. *Journal of Research on Adolescence, 23,* 345–356.

Cole, A., & Kerns, K. A. (2001). Perceptions of sibling qualities and activities of early adolescents. *Journal of Early Adolescence, 21,* 204–226.

Cole, D. A., Jacquez, F. M., LaGrange, B., Pineda, A. Q., Truss, A. E., Weitlauf, A. S., . . . Dufton, L. (2011). A longitudinal study of cognitive risks for depressive symptoms in children and young adolescents. *Journal of Early Adolescence, 31,* 782–816.

Cole, D. A., Martin, N. C., Sterba, S. K., Sinclair-McBride, K., Roeder, K. M., Zelkowitz, R., Bilsky, A. (2014). Peer victimization (and harsh parenting) as developmental correlates of cognitive reactivity, a diathesis for depression. *Journal of Abnormal Psychology, 123,* 336–349.

Cole, D., & Jordan, A. (1995). Competence and memory: Integrating psychosocial and cognitive correlates of child depression. *Child Development, 66,* 459–473.

Cole, D., Martin, J., & Powers, B. (1997). A competency-based model of child depression: A longitudinal study of peer, parent, teacher, and self-evaluations. *Journal of Child Psychology and Psychiatry and Allied Disciplines, 38,* 505–514.

Cole, D., Maxwell, S., Martin, J., Peeke, L., Seroczynski, A., Tram, J., ... Maschman, T. (2001). The development of multiple domains of child and adolescent self-concept: A cohort sequential longitudinal design. *Child Development, 72,* 1723–1746.

Cole, D., Peeke, L., Dolezal, S., Murray, N., & Canzoniero, A. (1999). A longitudinal study of negative affect and self-perceived competence in young adolescents. *Journal of Personality and Social Psychology, 77,* 851–862.

Cole, M. W., Yarkoni, T., Repovš, G., Anticevic, A., & Braver, T. S. (2012). Global connectivity of prefrontal cortex predicts cognitive control and intelligence. *Journal of Neuroscience, 32,* 8988–8999.

Coleman, J. (1961). *The adolescent society.* Glencoe, IL: Free Press.

Coleman, J., & Hoffer, T. (1987). *Public and private high schools: The impact of communities.* New York: Basic Books.

Coleman, J., Hoffer, T., & Kilgore, S. (1982). *High school achievement: Public, Catholic and other private schools compared.* New York: Basic Books.

Coleman, L. M., & Cater, S. M. (2005). A qualitative study of the relationship between alcohol consumption and risky sex in adolescents. *Archives of Sexual Behavior, 34,* 649–661.

Coleman, P. K. (2006). Resolution of unwanted pregnancy during adolescence through abortion versus childbirth: Individual and family predictors and psychological consequences. *Journal of Youth and Adolescence, 35,* 903–911.

Coles, M. S., Makino, K. K., Stanwood, N. L., Dozier, A., & Klein, J. D. (2010). How are restrictive abortion statutes associated with unintended teen birth? *Journal of Adolescent Health, 47,* 160–167.

Coley, R. L., & Chase-Lansdale, P. L. (1998). Adolescent pregnancy and parenthood: Recent evidence and future directions. *American Psychologist, 53,* 152–166.

Coley, R. L., & Medeiros, B. L. (2007). Reciprocal longitudinal relations between nonresident father involvement and adolescent delinquency. *Child Development, 78,* 132–147.

Coley, R. L., Leventhal, T., Lynch, A. D., & Kull, M. (2013). Relations between housing characteristics and the well-being of low-income children and adolescents. *Developmental Psychology, 49,* 1775–1789.

Coley, R. L., Medeiros, B. L., & Schindler, H. S. (2008). Using sibling differences to estimate effects of parenting on adolescent sexual risk behaviors. *Journal of Adolescent Health, 43,* 133–140.

Coley, R. L., Morris, J. E., & Hernandez, D. (2004). Out-of-school care and problem behavior trajectories among low-income adolescents: Individual, family, and neighborhood characteristics as added risks. *Child Development, 75,* 948–965.

Coley, R. L., Votruba-Drzal, E., & Schindler, H. S. (2008). Trajectories of parenting processes and adolescent substance use: Reciprocal effects. *Journal of Abnormal Child Psychology, 36,* 613–625.

Coley, R., Votruba-Drzal, E., & Schindler, H. S. (2009). Fathers' and mothers' parenting predicting and responding to adolescent sexual risk behaviors. *Child Development, 80,* 808–827.

Collaer, M., & Hines, M. (1995). Human behavioral sex differences: A role for gonadal hormones during early development? *Psychological Bulletin, 118,* 55–107.

College Board (2014). SAT data tables. http://research.collegeboard.org/content/sat-data-tables. Accessed on July 16, 2015.

College Board. (2012). *College-bound seniors, 2011.* New York: Author.

Collins, N. L., & Feeney, B. C. (2004). Working models of attachment shape perceptions of social support: Evidence from experimental and observational studies. *Journal of Personality and Social Psychology, 87,* 363–383.

Collins, R. L., Martino, S. C., Elliott, M. N., & Miu, A. (2011). Relationships between adolescent sexual outcomes and exposure to sex in media: Robustness to propensity-based analysis. *Developmental Psychology, 47,* 585–591.

Collins, W. A. (1990). Parent–child relationships in the transition to adolescence: Continuity and change in interaction, affect, and cognition. In R. Montemayor, G. Adams, & T. Gullotta (Eds.), *Advances in adolescent development:* Vol. 2. *The transition from childhood to adolescence* (pp. 85–106). Beverly Hills, CA: Sage.

Collins, W. A. (2003). More than a myth: The developmental significance of romantic relationships during adolescence. *Journal of Research on Adolescents, 13,* 1–24.

Collins, W. A., & Steinberg, L. (2006). Adolescent development in interpersonal context. In W. Damon & R. Lerner (Ser. Eds.) & N. Eisenberg (Vol. Ed.), *Handbook of child psychology:* Vol. 3. *Social, emotional, and personality development* (6th ed., pp. 1003–1067). New York: Wiley.

Collins, W. A., Maccoby, E., Steinberg, L., Hetherington, E. M., & Bornstein, M. (2000). Contemporary research on parenting: The case for nature and nurture. *American Psychologist, 55,* 218–232.

Comings, D. E., Muhleman, D., Johnson, J. P., & MacMurray, J. P. (2002). Parent–daughter transmission of the androgen receptor gene as an explanation of the effect of father absence on age of menarche. *Child Development, 73,* 1046–1051.

Committee on Adolescence. (2014). Addendum—Adolescent pregnancy: Current trends and issues. *Pediatrics, 133,* 954–957.

Common Sense Media. (2014). *Advertising to children and teens.* New York: Author.

Compas, B., & Reeslund, K. (2009). Processes of risk and resilience during adolescence. In R. Lerner & L. Steinberg (Eds.), *Handbook of adolescent psychology* (3rd ed., Vol. 1, pp. 561–588). New York: Wiley.

Compian, L., Gowen, L., & Hayward, C. (2004). Peripubertal girls' romantic and platonic involvement with boys: Associations with body image and depression symptoms. *Journal of Research on Adolescence, 14,* 23–47.

Complete College. (2012). *Remediation: Higher education's bridge to nowhere.* Washington: Author.

Compton, K., Snyder, J., & Schrepferman, L. (2003). The contribution of parents and siblings to antisocial and depressive behavior in adolescents: A double jeopardy coercion model. *Development and Psychopathology, 15,* 163–182.

Conant, J. (1959). *The American high school today.* New York: McGraw-Hill.

Conchas, G. Q. (2001). Structuring failure and success: Understanding the variability in Latino school engagement. *Harvard Educational Review, 71,* 475–504.

Conduct Problems Prevention Research Group (1999). Initial impact of the Fast Track Prevention Trial for Conduct Problems, II: Classroom effects. *Journal of Consulting and Clinical Psychology, 67,* 648–657.

Conger, K., Conger, R., & Elder, G., Jr. (1994). Sibling relationships during hard times. In R. Conger & G. Elder, Jr. (Eds.), *Families in troubled times: Adapting to change in rural America* (pp. 235–252). New York: Aldine.

Conger, K., Conger, R., & Scaramella, L. (1997). Parents, siblings, psychological control, and adolescent adjustment. *Journal of Adolescent Research, 12,* 113–138.

Conger, R., Cui, M., Bryant, C. M., & Elder, G. H., Jr. (2000). Competence in early adult romantic relationships: A developmental perspective on family influences. *Journal of Personality and Social Psychology, 79,* 224–237.

Conger, R., Ge, X., Elder, G., Jr., Lorenz, F., & Simons, R. (1994). Economic stress, coercive family process, and developmental problems of adolescents. *Child Development, 65,* 541–561.

Conklin, H. M., Luciana, M., Hooper, C. J., & Yarger, R. S. (2007). Working memory performance in typically developing children and adolescents: Behavioral evidence of protracted frontal lobe development. *Developmental Neuropsychology, 31,* 103–128.

Conley, C. S., & Rudolph, K. D. (2009). The emerging sex difference in adolescent depression: Interacting contributions of puberty and peer stress. *Development and Psychopathology, 21,* 593–620.

Conley, C. S., Rudolph, K. D., & Bryant, F. B. (2012). Explaining the longitudinal association between puberty and depression: Sex differences in the mediating effects of peer stress. *Development and Psychopathology, 24,* 691–701.

Connell, A. M., & Dishion, T. J. (2008). Reducing depression among at-risk early adolescents: Three-year effects of a family-centered intervention embedded within schools. *Journal of Family Psychology, 22,* 574–585.

Connell, C. M., Gilreath, T. D., Aklin, W. M., & Brex, R. A. (2010). Social-ecological influences on patterns of substance use among non-metropolitan high school students. *American Journal of Community Psychology, 45(1–2),* 36–48.

Connell, J., Spencer, M., & Aber, J. (1994). Educational risk and resilience in African-American youth: Context, self, action, and outcomes in school. *Child Development, 65,* 493–506.

Conner, J. O., & Poper, D. C. (2013). Not just robo-students: why full engagement matters and how school can promote it. *Journal of Youth & Adolescence, 42,* 1426–1442.

Connolly, J., & Goldberg, A. (1999). Romantic relationships in adolescence: The role of friends and peers in their emergence and development. In W. Furman, B. Brown, & C. Feiring (Eds.), *Contemporary perspectives on adolescent romantic relationships* (pp. 266–290). New York: Cambridge University Press.

Connolly, J., & Johnson, A. (1993, March). *The psychosocial context of romantic relationships in adolescence.* Paper presented at the biennial meetings of the Society for Research in Child Development, New Orleans.

Connolly, J., & Konarski, R. (1994). Peer self-concept in adolescence: Analysis of factor structure and of associations with peer experience. *Journal of Research on Adolescence, 4,* 385–403.

Connolly, J., & McIsaac, C. (2009). Romantic relationships in adolescence. In R. Lerner & L. Steinberg (Eds.), *Handbook of adolescent psychology* (3rd ed., Vol. 2, pp. 104–151). New York: Wiley.

Connolly, J., Craig, W., Goldberg, A., & Pepler, D. (1999). Conceptions of cross-sex friendships and romantic relationships in early adolescence. *Journal of Youth and Adolescence, 28,* 481–494.

Connolly, J., Craig, W., Goldberg, A., & Pepler, D. (2004). Mixed-gender groups, dating, and romantic relationships in early adolescence. *Journal of Research on Adolescence, 14,* 185–207.

Connolly, J., Furman, W., & Konarski, R. (2000). The role of peers in the emergence of heterosexual romantic relationships in adolescence. *Child Development, 71,* 1395–1408.

Connolly, J., Nguyen, H. N. T., Pepler, D., Craig, W., & Jiang, D. (2013). Developmental trajectories of romantic stages and associations with problem behaviours during adolescence. *Journal of Adolescence, 36,* 1013–1024.

Conseur, A., Rivara, F., Barnoski, R., & Emanuel, I. (1997). Maternal and perinatal risk factors for later delinquency. *Pediatrics, 99,* 785–790.

Cooc, N., & Gee, K. A. (2014). National trends in school victimization among Asian American adolescents. *Journal of Adolescence, 37,* 839–849.

Cook, E. C., Buehler, C., & Blair, B. L. (2013). Adolescents' emotional reactivity across relationship contexts. *Developmental Psychology, 49,* 341–352.

Cook, P. J., & Ludwig, J. (2004). Does gun prevalence affect teen gun carrying after all? *Criminology, 42,* 27–54.

Cook, T., Church, M., Ajanaku, S., Shadish, W., Jr., Kim, J., & Cohen, R. (1996). The development of occupational aspirations and expectations among inner-city boys. *Child Development, 67,* 3368–3385.

Cook, T., Deng, Y., & Morgano, E. (2007). Friendship influences during early adolescence: The special role of friends' grade point average. *Journal of Research on Adolescence, 17,* 325–356.

Cook, T., Herman, M., Phillips, M., & Settersten, R., Jr. (2002). Some ways in which neighborhoods, nuclear families, friendship groups, and schools jointly affect changes in early adolescent development. *Child Development, 73,* 1283–1309.

Cook, W. L. (2001). Interpersonal influence in family systems: A social relations model analysis. *Child Development, 72,* 1179–1197.

Cooksey, E. C., Mott, F. L., & Neubauer, S. A. (2002). Friendships and early relationships: Links to sexual initiation among American adolescents born to young mothers. *Perspectives on Sexual and Reproductive Health, 34,* 118–126.

Cooley-Quille, M., & Lorion, R. (1999). Adolescents' exposure to community violence: Sleep and psychophysiological functioning. *Journal of Community Psychology, 27,* 367–375.

Cooper, C. (1994). Cultural perspectives on continuity and change in adolescents' relationships. In R. Montemayor, G. Adams, & T. Gullotta (Eds.), *Personal relationships during adolescence.* Thousand Oaks, CA: Sage.

Cooper, H., Charlton, K., Valentine, J., & Muhlenbruck, L. (2000). Making the most of summer school: A meta-analytic and narrative review. *Monographs of the Society for Research in Child Development, 65,* Serial No. 260.

Cooper, M. L., Shaver, P. R., & Collins, N. L. (1998). Attachment styles, emotion regulation, and adjustment in adolescence. *Journal of Personality and Social Psychology, 74,* 1380–1397.

Cooper, M. L., Wood, P. K., Orcutt, H. K., & Albino, A. (2003). Personality and the predisposition to engage in risky or problem behaviors during adolescence. *Journal of Personality and Social Psychology, 84,* 390–410.

Copeland, W. E., Wolke, D., Angold, A., Costello, E. J. (2013). Adult psychiatric outcomes of bullying and being bullied by peers in childhood and adolescence. *JAMA Psychiatry, 70,* 419–426.

Copeland-Linder, N., Lambert, S. F., Chen, Y.-F., & Ialongo, N. S. (2010). Contextual stress and health risk behaviors among African American adolescents. *Journal of Youth and Adolescence, 40,* 158–173.

Coplan, R. J., Rose-Krasnor, L., Weeks, M., Kingsbury, A., Kingsbury, M., & Bullock, A. (2013). Alone is a crowd: Social motivations, social withdrawal, and socioemotional functioning in later childhood. *Developmental Psychology, 49,* 861–875.

Cordova, D., Ciofu, A., & Cervantes, R. (2014). Exploring culturally based intrafamilial stressors among Latino adolescents. *Family Relations, 63,* 693–706.

Corenblum, B. (2014). Relationships between racial-ethnic identity, self-esteem and in-group attitudes among first nation children. *Journal of Youth & Adolescence, 43,* 387–404.

Cornell, D., Gregory, A., Huang, F., & Fan, X. (2013). Perceived prevalence of teasing and bullying predicts high school dropout rates. *Journal of Educational Psychology, 105,* 138–149.

Cortina, K., & Arel, S. (2011). Schools and schooling. In B. Brown & M. Prinstein (Eds.), *Encyclopedia of adolescence* (Vol. 2, pp. 299–305). New York: Academic Press.

Cosgrove, V. E., Rhee, S. H., Gelhorn, H. L., Boeldt, D., Corley, R. C., Ehringer, M. A., . . . Hewitt, J. K. (2011). Structure and etiology of co-occurring internalizing and externalizing disorders in adolescents. *Journal of Abnormal Child Psychology, 39,* 109–123.

Côté, J. (2000). *Arrested adulthood: The changing nature of maturity and identity.* New York: New York University Press.

Côté, J. (2009). Identity formation and self development in adolescence. In R. Lerner & L. Steinberg (Eds.), *Handbook of adolescent psychology* (3rd ed., Vol. 1, pp. 266–304). New York: Wiley.

Côté, J. (2014). The dangerous myth of emerging adulthood: An evidence-based critique of a flawed developmental theory. *Applied Developmental Science, 18,* 177–188.

Côté, J., & Bynner, J. (2008). Changes in the transition to adulthood in the UK and Canada: The role of structure and agency in emerging adulthood. *Journal of Youth Studies, 11,* 251–268.

Couperus, J. W., & Nelson, C. A. (2006). Early brain development and plasticity. In K. McCartney & D. Phillips (Eds.), *Blackwell handbook of early childhood development* (pp. 85–105). Malden, MA: Blackwell Publishing.

Courtney, M., & Cohen, R. (1996). Behavior segmentation by boys as a function of aggressiveness and prior information. *Child Development, 67,* 1034–1047.

Cox, M., Wang, F., & Gustafsson, H. (2011). Family organization and adolescent development. In B. Brown & M. Prinstein (Eds.), *Encyclopedia of adolescence* (Vol. 2, pp. 75–83). New York: Academic Press.

Cox, S. J., Mezulis, A. H., & Hyde, J. S. (2010). The influence of child gender role and maternal feedback to child stress on the emergence of the gender difference in depressive rumination in adolescence. *Developmental Psychology, 46,* 842–852.

Coyne, S. M., & Padilla-Walker, L. M. (2015). Sex, violence, & rock n' roll: Longitudinal effects of music on aggression, sex, and prosocial behavior during adolescence. *Journal of Adolescence, 41,* 96–104.

Coyne, S. M., Padilla-Walker, L. M., Fraser, A. M., Fellows, K., & Day, R. D. (2014). "Media time = family time": Positive media use in families with adolescents. *Journal of Adolescent Research, 29,* 663–688.

Coyne, S., Padilla-Walker, L., Stockdale, L., & Day, R. (2011). Game on . . . girls: Associations between co-playing video games and adolescent behavioral and family outcomes. *Journal of Adolescent Health, 49,* 160–165.

Crane, D. R., So Wa, N., Larson, J. H., & Hafen, M., Jr. (2005). The influence of family functioning and parent–adolescent acculturation on North American Chinese adolescent outcomes. *Family Relations, 54,* 400–410.

Crapanzano, A., Frick, P., Childs, K., & Terranova, A. (2011). Gender differences in the assessment, stability, and correlates to bullying roles in middle school children. *Behavioral Sciences & the Law, 29,* 677–694.

Crawford, T. N., Cohen, P., Midlarsky, E., & Brook, J. S. (2001). Internalizing symptoms in adolescents: Gender differences in vulnerability to parental distress and discord. *Journal of Research on Adolescence, 11,* 95–118.

Crean, H. F. (2012). Youth activity involvement, neighborhood adult support, individual decision making skills, and early adolescent delinquent behaviors: Testing a conceptual model. *Journal of Applied Developmental Psychology, 33,* 175–188.

Creasey, G., & Kaliher, G. (1994). Age differences in grandchildren's perceptions of relations with grandparents. *Journal of Adolescence, 17,* 411–426.

Crespo, C., Jose, P. E., Kielpikowski, M., & Pryor, J. (2013). "On solid ground": Family and school connectedness promotes adolescents'

future orientation. *Journal of Adolescence, 36,* 993–1002.

Crick, N. (1996). The role of overt aggression, relational aggression, and prosocial behavior in the prediction of children's future social adjustment. *Child Development, 67,* 2317–2327.

Crick, N. (1997). Engagement in gender normative versus nonnormative forms of aggression: Links to social-psychological adjustment. *Developmental Psychology, 33,* 610–617.

Crick, N., & Dodge, K. (1994). A review and reformulation of social information-processing mechanisms in children's social adjustment. *Psychological Bulletin, 115,* 74–101.

Criss, M. M., & Shaw, D. (2005). Sibling relationships as contexts for delinquency training in low-income families. *Journal of Family Psychology, 19,* 592–600.

Crocetti, E., Klimstra, T., Keijsers, L., Hale, W. W., & Meeus, W. (2009). Anxiety trajectories and identity development in adolescence: A five-wave longitudinal study. *Journal of Youth and Adolescence, 38,* 839–849.

Crocetti, E., Klimstra, T. A., Hale, W. W. 3rd., Koot, H. M., Meeus, W. (2013). Impact of early adolescent externalizing problem behaviors on identity development in middle to late adolescence: a prospective 7-year longitudinal study. *Journal of Youth & Adolescence, 42,* 1745–1758.

Crockett, L. J., Carlo, G., Wolff, J. M., & Hope, M. O. (2013). The role of pubertal timing and temperamental vulnerability in adolescents' internalizing symptoms. *Development and Psychopathology, 25,* 377–389.

Crockett, L., & Hayes, R. (2011). Parenting practices and styles. In B. Brown & M. Prinstein (Eds.), *Encyclopedia of adolescence* (Vol. 2, pp. 241–248). New York: Academic Press.

Crockett, L., Bingham, C., Chopak, J., & Vicary, J. (1996). Timing of first sexual intercourse: The role of social control, social learning and problem behavior. *Journal of Youth and Adolescence, 25,* 89–111.

Crockett, L., Brown, J., Russell, S. T., & Shen, Y. (2007). The meaning of good parent–child relationships for Mexican American adolescents. *Journal of Research on Adolescence, 17,* 639–668.

Crockett, L., Raffaelli, M., & Shen, Y. (2006). Linking self-regulation and risk proneness to risky sexual behavior: Pathways through peer pressure and early substance use. *Journal of Research on Adolescence, 16,* 503–525.

Croll, J., Neumark-Sztainer, D., Story, M., & Ireland, M. (2002). Prevalence and risk and protective factors related to disordered eating behaviors among adolescents: Relationship to gender and ethnicity. *Journal of Adolescent Health, 31,* 166–175.

Crone, E. (2009). Executive functions in adolescence: Inferences from brain and behavior. *Developmental Science, 12,* 825–830.

Crone, E. A., & van der Molen, M. W. (2007). Development of decision making in school-aged

children and adolescents: Evidence from heart rate and skin conductance analysis. *Child Development, 78,* 1288–1301.

Crone, E., Somsen, R., Zanolie, K., & Van der Molen, M. (2006). A heart rate analysis of developmental change in feedback processing and rule shifting from childhood to early adulthood. *Journal of Experimental Child Psychology, 95,* 99–116.

Crone, E.A. (2013). Considerations of fairness in the adolescent brain. *Child Development Perspectives, 7,* 97–103.

Croninger, R. G., & Lee, V. E. (2001). Social capital and dropping out of school: Benefits to at-risk students of teachers' support and guidance. *Teachers College Record, 103,* 548–581.

Crosby, R. A., DiClemente, R. J., Wingood, G. M., Lang, D., & Harrington, K. F. (2003). Value of consistent condom use: A study of sexually transmitted disease prevention among African American adolescent females. *American Journal of Public Health, 93,* 901–902.

Crosnoe, R. (2001). Academic orientation and parental involvement in education during high school. *Sociology of Education, 74,* 210–230.

Crosnoe, R. (2002). High school curriculum track and adolescent association with delinquent friends. *Journal of Adolescent Research, 17,* 143–167.

Crosnoe, R. (2006). The connection between academic failure and adolescent drinking in secondary school. *Sociology of Education, 79,* 44–60.

Crosnoe, R. (2007). Gender, obesity, and education. *Sociology of Education, 80,* 241–260.

Crosnoe, R. (2009). Low-income students and the socioeconomic composition of public high schools. *American Sociological Review, 74,* 709–730.

Crosnoe, R., & Cavanagh, S. (2010). Families with children and adolescents: A review, critique, and future agenda. *Journal of Marriage and Family, 72,* 594–611.

Crosnoe, R., & Huston, A. C. (2007). Socioeconomic status, schooling, and the developmental trajectories of adolescents. *Developmental Psychology, 43,* 1097–1110.

Crosnoe, R., & Needham, B. (2004). Holism, contextual variability, and the study of friendships in adolescent development. *Child Development, 75,* 264–279.

Crosnoe, R., Erickson, K., & Dornbusch, S. M. (2002). Protective functions of family relationships and school factors on the deviant behavior of adolescent boys and girls: Reducing the impact of risky friendships. *Youth and Society, 33,* 515–544.

Crosnoe, R., Mistry, R. S., & Elder, G. H., Jr. (2002). Economic disadvantage, family dynamics, and adolescent enrollment in higher education. *Journal of Marriage and the Family, 64,* 690–702.

Crouter, A., Bumpus, M., Davis, K., & McHale, S. (2005). How do parents learn about adolescents' experiences? Implications for parental knowledge and adolescent risky behavior. *Child Development, 76,* 869–882.

Crouter, A., Whiteman, S., McHale, S., & Osgood, D. W. (2007). Development of gender attitude traditionality across middle childhood and adolescence. *Child Development, 78,* 911–926.

Crow, S., Eisenberg, M. E., Story, M., & Neumark-Sztainer, D. (2006). Psychosocial and behavioral correlates of dieting among overweight and non-overweight adolescents. *Journal of Adolescent Health, 38,* 569–574.

Cruz, J. E., Emery, R. E., & Turkheimer, E. (2012). Peer network drinking predicts increased alcohol use from adolescence to early adulthood after controlling for genetic and shared environmental selection. *Developmental Psychology, 48,* 1390–1402.

Crystal, D., Chen, C., Fuligni, A., Stevenson, H., Hsu, C., Ko, H., … Kimura, S. (1994). Psychological maladjustment and academic achievement: A cross-cultural study of Japanese, Chinese, and American high school students. *Child Development, 65,* 738–753.

Csikszentmihalyi, M. (1990). *Flow: The psychology of optimal experience.* New York: Harper and Row.

Csikszentmihalyi, M., & Larson, R. (1984). *Being adolescent.* New York: Basic Books.

Cubbin, C., Santelli, J., Brindis, C. D., & Braveman, P. (2005). Neighborhood context and sexual behaviors among adolescents: Findings from the National Longitudinal Study of Adolescent Health. *Perspectives on Sexual and Reproductive Health, 37,* 125–134.

Çuhadaroğlu Çetin, F., Tüzün, Z., Pehlivantürk, B., Ünal, F., & Gökler, B. (2010). Attachment styles and self-image in Turkish adolescents. *Journal of Research on Adolescence, 20,* 840–848.

Cui, M., & Conger, R. (2008). Parenting behavior as mediator and moderator of the association between marital problems and adolescent maladjustment. *Journal of Research on Adolescence, 18,* 261–284.

Cui, M., Conger, R., & Lorenz, F. O. (2005). Predicting change in adolescent adjustment from change in marital problems. *Developmental Psychology, 41,* 812–823.

Cui, M., Donnellan, M. B., & Conger, R. (2007). Reciprocal influences between parents' marital problems and adolescent internalizing and externalizing behavior. *Developmental Psychology, 43,* 1544–1552.

Cui, M., Ueno, K., Gordon, M., & Fincham, F. D. (2013). The continuation of intimate partner violence from adolescence to young adulthood. *Journal of Marriage and Family, 75,* 300–313.

Cummings, E. M., Cheung, R. Y., Koss, K., & Davies, P. T. (2014). Parental depressive symptoms and adolescent adjustment: A prospective test of an explanatory model for the role of marital conflict. *Journal of Abnormal Child Psychology, 42,* 1153–1166.

Cummings, E. M., George, M. R. W., McCoy, K. P., & Davies, P. T. (2012). Interparental conflict in kindergarten and adolescent adjustment: Prospective investigation of emotional security as an explanatory mechanism. *Child Development, 83,* 1703–1715.

Cummings, E., Ballard, M., El-Sheikh, M., & Lake, M. (1991). Resolution and children's responses to interadult anger. *Developmental Psychology, 27,* 462–470.

Cummings, J. R., Wen, H., & Druss, B. G. (2011). Racial/ethnic differences in treatment for substance use disorders among U.S. adolescents. *Journal of the American Academy of Child & Adolescent Psychiatry, 50,* 1265–1274.

Cumsille, P., Darling, N., Flaherty, B., & Martinez, M. (2009). Heterogeneity and change in the patterning of adolescents' perceptions of the legitimacy of parental authority: A latent transition model. *Child Development, 80,* 418–432.

Cunningham, M. (1999). African-American adolescent males' perceptions of their community resources and constraints: A longitudinal analysis. *Journal of Community Psychology, 27,* 569–588.

Curran, P., Stice, E., & Chassin, L. (1997). The relation between adolescent alcohol use and peer alcohol use: A longitudinal random coefficients model. *Journal of Consulting and Clinical Psychology, 65,* 130–140.

Currie, C., Ahluwalia, N., Godeau, E., Nic Gabhainn, S., Due, P., & Currie, D. B. (2012). Is obesity at individual and national level associated with lower age at menarche? Evidence from 34 countries in the health behaviour in school-aged children study. *Journal of Adolescent Health, 50,* 621–626.

Curry, A. E., Mirman, J. H., Kallan, M. J., Winston, F. K., & Durbin, D. R. (2012). Peer passengers: How do they affect teen crashes? *Journal of Adolescent Health, 50,* 588–594.

Curtner-Smith, M., & MacKinnon-Lewis, C. (1994). Family process effects on adolescent males' susceptibility to antisocial peer pressure. *Family Relations, 43,* 462–468.

Cusick, P. A. (1973). *Inside high school.* New York: Holt, Rinehart & Winston.

Cvencek, D., Nasir, N. S., O'Connor, K., Wischnia, S., & Meltzoff, A. (2014). The development of math-race stereotypes: "They say Chinese people are the best at math." *Journal of Research on Adolescence, Early view.* DOI: 10.1111/jora.12151

Cvijanovich, N. Z., Cook, L. J., Mann, N. C., & Dean, J. M. (2001). A population-based study of crashes involving 16- and 17-year-old drivers: The potential benefit of graduated driver licensing restrictions. *Pediatrics, 107,* 632–637.

Cyranowski, J., & Frank, E. (2000). Adolescent onset of the gender difference in lifetime rates of major depression. *Archives of General Psychiatry, 57,* 21–27.

D'Onofrio, B. M., Turkheimer, E., Emery, R. E., Slutske, W. S., Heath, A. C., … Madden, P. A.,

(2006). A genetically informed study of the processes underlying the association between parental marital instability and offspring adjustment. *Developmental Psychology, 42,* 486–499.

Daddis, C. (2011). Desire for increased autonomy and adolescents' perceptions of peer autonomy: "Everyone else can; Why can't I?" *Child Development, 82,* 1310–1326.

Daddis, C., & Smetana, J. (2005). Middle-class African American families' expectations for adolescents' behavioral autonomy. *International Journal of Behavioral Development, 29,* 371–381.

Daha, M. (2011). Contextual factors contributing to ethnic identity development of second-generation Iranian American adolescents. *Journal of Adolescent Research, 26,* 543–569.

Dahl, R. (2008). Biological, developmental, and neurobehavioral factors relevant to adolescent driving risks. *American Journal of Preventive Medicine, 35,* S278–S284.

Dahl, R. (2011). Understanding the risky business of adolescence. *Neuron, 69,* 837–839.

Dahl, R., & Hariri, A. (2005). Lessons from G. Stanley Hall: Connecting new research in biological science to the study of adolescent development. *Journal of Research on Adolescence 15,* 367–382.

Dallago, L., Perkins, D., Santinello, M., Boyce, W., Molcho, M., & Morgan, A. (2009). Adolescent place attachment, social capital, and perceived safety: A comparison of 13 countries. *American Journal of Community Psychology, 44,* 148–160.

Dandreaux, D. M., & Frick, P. J. (2009). Developmental pathways to conduct problems: A further test of the childhood and adolescent-onset distinction. *Journal of Abnormal Child Psychology, 37,* 375–385.

Daniel, D. B., & Klaczynski, P. A. (2006). Developmental and individual differences in conditional reasoning: Effects of logic instructions and alternative antecedents. *Child Development, 77,* 339–354.

Daniels, D., Dunn, J., Furstenberg, F., Jr., & Plomin, R. (1985). Environmental differences within the family and adjustment differences within pairs of adolescent siblings. *Child Development, 56,* 764–774.

Daniels, E., & Leaper, C. (2011). Gender issues. In B. Brown & M. Prinstein (Eds.), *Encyclopedia of adolescence* (Vol. 1, pp. 151–159). New York: Academic Press.

Dank, M., Lachman, P., Zweig, J. M., & Yahner, J. (2014). Dating violence experiences of lesbian, gay, bisexual, and transgender youth. *Journal of Youth & Adolescence, 43,* 846–857.

Darling, N., & Steinberg, L. (1993). Parenting style as context: An integrative model. *Psychological Bulletin, 113,* 487–496.

Darling, N., & Steinberg, L. (1997). Community influences on adolescent achievement and deviance. In J. Brooks-Gunn, G., Duncan, & L. Aber (Eds.), *Neighborhood poverty: Context and consequences for children:* Vol. 2. *Conceptual, methodological, and policy approaches to studying neighborhoods* (pp. 120–131). New York: Russell Sage Foundation.

Darling, N., Cumsille, P., & Martínez, M. (2008). Individual differences in adolescents' beliefs about the legitimacy of parental authority and obligation to obey: A longitudinal investigation. *Child Development, 79,* 1103–1118.

Darling, N., Cumsille, P., & Martínez, M. L. (2007). Adolescents as active agents in the socialization process: Legitimacy of parental authority and obligation to obey as predictors of obedience. *Journal of Adolescence, 30,* 297–311.

Darling, N., Cumsille, P., Peña-Alampay, L., & Coatsworth, D. (2009). Individual and issue-specific differences in parental knowledge and adolescent disclosure in Chile, the Philippines, and the United States. *Journal of Research on Adolescence, 19,* 715–740.

Darling, N., Dowdy, B. B., Van Horn, M. L., & Caldwell, L. L. (1999). Mixed-sex settings and the perception of competence. *Journal of Youth and Adolescence, 28,* 461–480.

Darling, N., Hamilton, S., & Matsuda, S. (1990, March). *Functional roles and social roles: Adolescents' significant others in the United States and Japan.* Paper presented at the biennial meetings of the Society for Research on Adolescence, Atlanta.

Darling-Hammond, L. (1997). *The right to learn.* San Francisco: Jossey-Bass.

Darling-Hammond, L. (2006). No child left behind and high school reform. *Harvard Educational Review, 76,* 642–667.

Darroch, J. E., Singh, S., & Frost, J. J. (2001). Differences in teenage pregnancy rates among five developed countries: The roles of sexual activity and contraceptive use. *Family Planning Perspectives, 33,* 244–250.

Darwich, L., Hymel, S., & Waterhouse, T. (2012). School avoidance and substance use among lesbian, gay, bisexual, and questioning youths: The impact of peer victimization and adult support. *Journal of Educational Psychology, 104,* 381–392.

Dauber, S., Alexander, K., & Entwisle, D. (1996). Tracking and transitions through the middle grades: Channeling educational trajectories. *Sociology of Education, 69,* 290–307.

Daughters, S. B., Gorka, S. M., Matusiewicz, A., & Anderson, K. (2013). Gender specific effect of psychological stress and cortisol reactivity on adolescent risk taking. *Journal of Abnormal Child Psychology, 41,* 749–758.

Davey, C. G., Yücel, M., & Allen, N. B. (2008). The emergence of depression in adolescence: Development of the prefrontal cortex and the representation of reward. *Neuroscience & Biobehavioral Reviews, 32,* 1–19.

Davies, P. T., Martin, M. J., & Cicchetti, D. (2012). Delineating the sequelae of destructive and constructive interparental conflict for children within an evolutionary framework. *Developmental Psychology, 48,* 939–955.

Davies, P. T., Sturge-Apple, M. L., Bascoe, S. M., & Cummings, E. M. (2014). The legacy of early insecurity histories in shaping adolescent adaptation to interparental conflict. *Child Development, 85,* 338–354.

Davies, P., & Lindsay, L. (2004). Interparental conflict and adolescent adjustment: Why does gender moderate early adolescent vulnerability? *Journal of Family Psychology, 18,* 160–170.

Davies, P., & Windle, M. (2000). Middle adolescents' dating pathways and psychosocial adjustment. *Merrill-Palmer Quarterly, 46,* 90–118.

Davies, P., & Windle, M. (2001). Interparental discord and adolescent adjustment trajectories: The potentiating and protective role of intrapersonal attributes. *Child Development, 72,* 1163–1178.

Davila, J. (2008). Depressive symptoms and adolescent romance: Theory, research, and implications. *Child Development Perspectives, 2,* 26–31.

Davis, A., & Rhodes, J. (1994). African-American teenage mothers and their mothers: An analysis of supportive and problematic interactions. *Journal of Community Psychology, 22,* 12–19.

Davis, A., Rhodes, J., & Hamilton-Leaks, J. (1997). When both parents may be a source of support and problems: An analysis of pregnant and parenting female African American adolescents' relationships with their mothers and fathers. *Journal of Research on Adolescence, 7,* 331–348.

Davis, B., & Carpenter, C. (2009). Proximity of fast-food restaurants to schools and adolescent obesity. *American Journal of Public Health, 99,* 505–510.

Davis, E., & Friel, L. V. (2001). Adolescent sexuality: Disentangling the effects of family structure and family context. *Journal of Marriage and the Family, 63,* 669–681.

Davis, K. (2013). Young people's digital lives: the impact of interpersonal relationships and digital media use on adolescents' sense of identity. *Computers in Human Behavior, 29,* 2281–2293.

Davis, K. A., & Epkins, C. (2009). Do private religious practices moderate the relation between family conflict and preadolescents' depression and anxiety symptoms? *Journal of Early Adolescence, 29,* 693–717.

Davis, K., & Kirkpatrick, L. (1994). Attachment style, gender, and relationship stability: A longitudinal analysis. *Journal of Personality and Social Psychology, 66,* 502–512.

Davis, L. E., Ajzen, I., Saunders, J., & Williams, T. (2002). The decision of African American students to complete high school: An application of the theory of planned behavior. *Journal of Educational Psychology, 94,* 810–819.

Davis-Kean, P., Huesmann, L. R., Jager, J., Collins, W. A., Bates, J. E., & Lansford, J.

E. (2008). Changes in the relation of self-efficacy beliefs and behaviors across development. *Child Development, 79,* 1257–1269.

Davison, T., & McCabe, M. (2011). Physical attractiveness. In B. Brown & M. Prinstein (Eds.), *Encyclopedia of adolescence* (Vol. 1, pp. 269–274). New York: Academic Press.

Dawes, M., & Xie, H. (2014). The role of popularity goal in early adolescents' behaviors and popularity status. *Developmental Psychology, 50,* 489–497.

Dawes, N. P., & Larson, R. (2011). How youth get engaged: Grounded-theory research on motivational development in organized youth programs. *Developmental Psychology, 47,* 259–269.

de Boer, H., Bosker, R., & van der Werf, M. (2010). Sustainability of teacher expectation bias effects on long-term student performance. *Journal of Educational Psychology, 102,* 168–179.

De Bolle, M., De Fruyt, F., McCrae, R. R., Löckenhoff, C. E., Costa Jr., P. T., Aguilar-Vafaie, M. E., et al. (2015). The emergence of sex differences in personality traits in early adolescence: A cross-sectional, cross-cultural study. *Journal of Personality and Social Psychology, 108,* 171–185.

de Bruyn, E., & Cillessen, A. (2006). Heterogeneity of girls' consensual popularity: Academic and interpersonal behavioral profiles. *Journal of Youth and Adolescence, 35,* 435–445.

de Bruyn, E., Cillessen, A., & Wissink, I. (2010). Associations of peer acceptance and perceived popularity with bullying and victimization in early adolescence. *Journal of Early Adolescence, 30,* 543–566.

De Castella, K., Byrne, D., & Covington, M. (2013). Unmotivated or motivated to fail? A cross-cultural study of achievement motivation, fear of failure, and student disengagement. *Journal of Educational Psychology, 105,* 861–880.

De Goede, I. H. A., Branje, S. J. T., Delsing, M. J. M. H., & Meeus, W. H. J. (2009). Linkages over time between adolescents' relationships with parents and friends. *Journal of Youth and Adolescence, 38,* 1304–1315.

De Goede, I., Branje, S., & Meeus, W. (2009). Developmental changes in adolescents' perceptions of relationships with their parents. *Journal of Youth and Adolescence, 38,* 75–88.

de Graaf, H., van de Schoot, R., Woertman, L., Hawk, S.T., & Meeus, W. (2012). Family cohesion and romantic and sexual initiation: a three wave longitudinal study. *Journal of Youth & Adolescence, 41,* 583–592.

de Graaf, H., Vanwesenbeeck, I., Meijer, S., Woertman, L., & Meeus, W. (2009). Sexual trajectories during adolescence: Relation to demographic characteristics and sexual risk. *Archives of Sexual Behavior, 38,* 276–282.

de Haan A. D., Prinzie, P., & Deković, M. (2012). Change and reciprocity in adolescent aggressive and rule-breaking behaviors and parental support and dysfunctional discipline. *Development and Psychopathology, 24,* 301–315.

de la Haye, K., Green, H. D. Jr., Kennedy, D. P., Pollard, M. S., & Tucker, J. S. (2013). Selection and influence mechanisms associated with marijuana initiation and use in adolescent friendship networks. *Journal of Research on Adolescence, 23,* 474–486.

de la Haye, K., Robins, G., Mohr, P., & Wilson, C. (2013). Adolescents' intake of junk food: Processes and mechanisms driving consumption similarities among friends. *Journal of Research on Adolescence, 23,* 524–536.

De Lorme, K., Bell, M. R., & Sisk, C. L. (2013). The teenage brain: Social reorientation and the adolescent brain—The role of gonadal hormones in the male Syrian hamster. *Current Directions in Psychological Science, 22,* 128–133.

de Water, E., Cillessen, A. H. N., & Scheres, A. (2014). Distinct age-related differences in temporal discounting and risk taking in adolescents and young adults. *Child Development, 85,* 1881–1897.

Deardorff, J., Cham, H., Gonzales, N. A., White, R. M. B., Tein, J. Y., Wong, J. J., & Roosa, M. W. (2013). Pubertal timing and Mexican-origin girls' internalizing and externalizing symptoms: The influence of harsh parenting. *Developmental Psychology, 49,* 1790–1804.

Deardorff, J., Gonzales, N. A., Christopher, F. S., Roosa, M. W., & Millsap, R. E. (2005). Early puberty and adolescent pregnancy: The influence of alcohol use. *Pediatrics 116,* 1451–1456.

Deary, I. J. (2014). The stability of intelligence from childhood to old age. *Current Directions in Psychological Science, 23,* 239–245.

Deater-Deckard, K. (2014). Family matters: Intergenerational and interpersonal processes of executive function and attentive behavior. *Current Directions in Psychological Science, 23,* 230–236.

Deater-Deckard, K., & Plomin, R. (1999). An adoption study of etiology of teacher and parent reports of externalizing behavior problems in middle childhood. *Child Development, 70,* 144–154.

DeBerry, K., Scarr, S., & Weinberg, R. (1996). Family racial socialization and ecological competence: Longitudinal assessments of African-American transracial adoptees. *Child Development, 67,* 2375–2399.

Debnam, K. J., Johnson, S. L., Waasdorp, T. E., & Bradshaw, C. P. (2014). Equity, connection, and engagement in the school context to promote positive youth development. *Journal of Research on Adolescence, 24,* 447–459.

Decety, J., & Michalska, K. (2010). Neurodevelopmental changes in the circuits underlying empathy and sympathy from childhood to adulthood. *Developmental Science, 13,* 886–899.

Dee, T., & Evans, W. (2001). Teens and traffic safety. In J. Gruber (Ed.), *Risky behavior among youths: An economic analysis* (pp. 121–165). Chicago: University of Chicago Press.

Defoe, I. N., Dubas, J. S., Figner, B., & van Aken, M. A. (2015). A meta-analysis on age differences in risky decision making: Adolescents versus children and adults. *Psychological Bulletin, 141,* 48–84.

Değirmencioğlu, S., & Urberg, K. (1994, February). *Cross-gender friendships in adolescence: Who chooses the "other"?* Paper presented at the biennial meetings of the Society for Research on Adolescence, San Diego.

Değirmencioğlu, S., Tolson, J., & Urberg, K. (1993, March). *Stability of adolescent social networks over the school year.* Paper presented at the biennial meetings of the Society for Research in Child Development, New Orleans.

Değirmencioğlu, S., Urberg, K., Tolson, J., & Richard, P. (1998). Adolescent friendship networks: Continuity and change over the school year. *Merrill-Palmer Quarterly, 44,* 313–337.

DeGarmo, D. S., & Martinez, C. R. J. (2006). A culturally informed model of academic well-being for Latino youth: The importance of discriminatory experiences and social support. *Family Relations, 55,* 267–278.

Del Giudice, M., Angeleri, R., & Manera, V. (2009). The juvenile transition: A developmental switch point in human life history. *Developmental Review, 29,* 1–31.

DeLay, D., Laursen, B., Kiuru, N., Salmela-Aro, K., & Nurmi, J. E. (2013). Selecting and retaining friends on the basis of cigarette smoking similarity. *Journal of Research on Adolescence, 23,* 464–473.

Delevi, R., & Weisskirch, R. (2013). Personality factors as predictors of sexting. *Computers in Human Behavior, 29,* 2589–2594.

Delgado, M. Y., Updegraff, K. A., Roosa, M. W., & Umaña-Taylor, A. J. (2011). Discrimination and Mexican-Origin adolescents' adjuroles of adolescents', mothers', and fathers' cultural orientations and values. *Journal of Youth and Adolescence, 40,* 125–139.

Delsing, M. J. M. H., ter Bogt, T. F. M., Engels, R. C. M. E., & Meeus, W. H. J. (2007). Adolescents' peer crowd identification in the Netherlands: Structure and associations with problem behaviors. *Journal of Research on Adolescence, 17,* 467–480.

Delva, J., Wallace, J. M., Jr., O'Malley, P. M., Bachman, J. G., Johnston, L. D., & Schulenberg, J. E. (2005). The epidemiology of alcohol, marijuana, and cocaine use among Mexican American, Puerto Rican, Cuban American, and other Latin American eighth-grade students in the United States: 1991–2002. *American Journal of Public Health, 95,* 696–702.

Demetriou, A., Christou, C., Spanoudis, G., & Platsidou, M. (2002). The development of mental processing: Efficiency, working memory, and thinking. *Monographs of the Society for Research in Child Development, 67,* Serial No. 268.

Demo, D., & Acock, A. (1996). Family structure, family process, and adolescent well-being. *Journal of Research on Adolescence, 6,* 457–488.

Demurie, E., Roeyers, H., Baeyens, D., & Sonuga-Barke, E. (2012). Temporal discounting of monetary rewards in children and adolescents with ADHD and autism spectrum disorders. *Developmental Science, 15,* 791–800.

Deng, S., Kim, S. Y., Vaughan, P. W., & Li, J. (2010). Cultural orientation as a moderator of the relationship between Chinese American adolescents' discrimination experiences and delinquent behaviors. *Journal of Youth and Adolescence, 39,* 1027–1040.

Denissen, J. J. A., van Aken, M. A. G., & Dubas, J. S. (2009). It takes two to tango: How parents' and adolescents' personalities link to the quality of their mutual relationship. *Developmental Psychology, 45,* 928–941.

Denissen, J. J. A., van Aken, M. A. G., Lars, P., & Wood, D. (2013). Self-Regulation Underlies Temperament and Personality: An Integrative Developmental Framework. *Child Development Perspectives, 7,* 255–260.

Dennison, M., Whittle, S., Yücel, M., Vijayakumar, N., Kline, A., Simmons, J., & Allen, N. B. (2013). Mapping subcortical brain maturation during adolescence: Evidence of hemisphere and sex-specific longitudinal changes. *Developmental Science, 16,* 772–791.

Denton, K., & Zarbatany, L. (1996). Age differences in support processes in conversations between friends. *Child Development, 67,* 1360–1373.

Derefinko, K. J., Peters, J. R., Eisenlohr-Moul, T. A., Walsh, E. C., Adams, Z. W., Lynam, D. R. (2014). Relations between trait impulsivity, behavioral impulsivity, physiological arousal, and risky sexual behavior among young men. *Archives of Sexual Behavior, 43,* 1149–1158.

Derlan, C. L., Umaña-Taylor, A. J., Toomey, R. B., Updegraff, K. A., Jahromi, L. B., & Flores, L. I. (2014). Perceived discrimination and ethnic affirmation: anglo culture orientation as a moderator among mexican-origin adolescent mothers. *Child Development, 85,* 1357–1365.

Dermody, S. S., Marshal, M. P., Cheong, J., Burton, C., Hughes, T., Aranda, F., Friedman, M. S. (2014). Longitudinal disparities of hazardous drinking between sexual minority and heterosexual individuals from adolescence to young adulthood. *Journal of Youth & Adolescence, 43,* 30–39.

DeRose, L. M., Shiyko, M. P., Foster, H., & Brooks-Gunn, J. (2011). Associations between menarcheal timing and behavioral developmental trajectories for girls from age 6 to age 15. *Journal of Youth and Adolescence, 40,* 1329–1342.

Desjardins, T. L., & Leadbeater, B. J. (2011). Relational victimization and depressive symptoms in adolescence: Moderating effects of mother, father, and peer emotional support. *Journal of Youth and Adolescence, 40,* 531–544.

DesRoches, A., & Willoughby, T. (2014). Bidirectional associations between valued activities and adolescent positive adjustment in a longitudinal study: positive mood as a mediator. *Journal of Youth & Adolescence, 43,* 208–220.

Deutsch, A. R., & Crockett, L. J. (2015). Gender, generational status, and parent-adolescent sexual communication: Implications for Latino/a adolescent sexual behavior. *Journal of Research on Adolescence,* DOI: 10.1111/jora.12192

Deutsch, A. R., Crockett, L. J., Wolff, J. M., Russell, S. T. (2012). Parent and peer pathways to adolescence delinquency: variations by ethnicity and neighborhood context. *Journal of Youth and Adolescence, 41,* 1078–1094.

Dhariwal, A., & Connolly, J. (2013). Romantic experiences of homeland and diaspora South Asian Youth: Westernizing processes of media and friends. *Journal of Research on Adolescence, 23,* 45–56.

Dhariwal, A., Connolly, J., Paciello, M., & Caprara, G. V. (2009). Adolescent peer relationships and emerging adult romantic styles: A longitudinal study of youth in an Italian community. *Journal of Adolescent Research, 24,* 579–600.

Diamond, L. (1998). Development of sexual orientation among adolescent and young adult women. *Developmental Psychology, 34,* 1085–1095.

Diamond, L. (2000). Passionate friendships among adolescent sexual-minority women. *Journal of Research on Adolescence, 10,* 191–209.

Diamond, L. (2008). Female bisexuality from adolescence to adulthood: Results from a 10-year longitudinal study. *Developmental Psychology, 44,* 5–14.

Diamond, L. M., Fagundes, C. P., & Cribbet, M. R. (2012). Individual differences in adolescents' sympathetic and parasympathetic functioning moderate associations between family environment and psychosocial adjustment. *Developmental Psychology, 48,* 918–931.

Diamond, L., & Dubé, E. M. (2002). Friendship and attachment among heterosexual and sexual-minority youths: Does the gender of your friend matter? *Journal of Youth and Adolescence, 31,* 155–166.

Diamond, L., & Lucas, S. (2004). Sexual-minority and heterosexual youths' peer relationships: Experiences, expectations, and implications for well-being. *Journal of Research of Adolescence, 14,* 313–340.

Diamond, L., & Savin-Williams, R. (2009). Adolescent sexuality. In R. Lerner & L. Steinberg (Eds.), *Handbook of adolescent psychology* (3rd ed., Vol. 1, pp. 479–523). New York: Wiley.

Diamond, L., & Savin-Williams, R. (2011). Sexuality. In B. Brown & M. Prinstein (Eds.), *Encyclopedia of adolescence* (Vol. 2, pp. 314–321). New York: Academic Press.

Diamond, L., Savin-Williams, R., & Dubé, E. (1999). Sex, dating, passionate friendships, and romance: Intimate peer relations among lesbian, gay, and bisexual adolescents. In W. Furman, B. Brown, & C. Feiring (Eds.), *Contemporary perspectives on adolescent romantic relationships* (pp. 175–210). New York: Cambridge University Press.

Diazgranados, S., & Selman, R. L. (2014). How students' perceptions of the school climate influence their choice to upstand, bystand, or join perpetrators of bullying. *Harvard Educational Review, 84,* 162–187.

Diazgranados, S., Selman, R., & Feigenberg, L. (2012). Rules of the culture and personal needs: Witnesses' decision-making processes to deal with situations of bullying in middle school. *Harvard Educational Review, 82,* 445–470.

Dick, D. (2011). Developmental changes in genetic influences on alcohol use and dependence. *Child Development Perspectives, 5,* 223–230.

Dick, D., Rose, R. J., Viken, R. J., & Kaprio, J. (2000). Pubertal timing and substance use: Associations between and within families across late adolescence. *Developmental Psychology, 36,* 180–189.

Dick, D., Rose, R., Pulkkinen, L., & Kaprio, J. (2001). Measuring puberty and understanding its impact: A longitudinal study of adolescent twins. *Journal of Youth and Adolescence, 30,* 385–400.

Dick, D., Viken, R., Purcell, S., Kaprio, J., Pulkkinen, L., & Rose, R. J. (2007). Parental monitoring moderates the importance of genetic and environmental influences on adolescent smoking. *Journal of Abnormal Psychology, 116,* 213–218.

DiClemente, R., Durbin, M., Siegel, D., Krasnovsky, F., Lazarus, N., & Comacho, T. (1992). Determinants of condom use among junior high school students in a minority, inner-city school district. *Pediatrics, 89,* 197–202.

DiClemente, R., Wingood, G., Harrington, K., Lang, D., Davies, S., . . . Hook, E., (2004). Efficacy of an HIV prevention intervention for African American adolescent girls: A randomized controlled trial. *Journal of the American Medical Association, 292,* 171–179.

Diehl, L., Vicary, J., & Deike, R. (1997). Longitudinal trajectories of self-esteem from early to middle adolescence and related psychosocial variables among rural adolescents. *Journal of Research on Adolescence, 7,* 393–411.

Dielman, T. (1994). School-based research on the prevention of adolescent alcohol use and misuse: Methodological issues and advances. *Journal of Research on Adolescence, 4,* 271–293.

DiIorio, C., Dudley, W. N., Kelly, M., Soet, J. E., Mbwara, J., & Sharpe Potter, J. (2001). Social cognitive correlates of sexual experience and condom use among 13- through 15-year-old adolescents. *Journal of Adolescent Health, 29,* 208–216.

DiIorio, C., Kelley, M., & Hockenberry-Eaton, M. (1999). Communication about sexual issues: Mothers, fathers, and friends. *Journal of Adolescent Health, 24,* 181–189.

Dijkstra, J. K., Cillessen, A. H., & Borch, C. (2013). Popularity and adolescent friendship networks: Selection and influence dynamics. *Developmental Psychology, 49,* 1242–1252.

Dijkstra, J. K., Lindenberg, S., & Veenstra, R. (2008). Beyond the class norm: Bullying behavior of popular adolescents and its relation to peer acceptance and rejection. *Journal of Abnormal Child Psychology, 36,* 1289–1299.

Dijkstra, J., & Veenstra, R. (2011). Peer relations. In B. Brown & M. Prinstein (Eds.), *Encyclopedia of adolescence* (Vol. 2, pp. 255–259). New York: Academic Press.

Dijkstra, J., Cillessen, A., Lindenberg, S., & Veenstra, R. (2010a). Same-gender and cross-gender likeability: Associations with popularity and status enhancement: The TRAILS study. *Journal of Early Adolescence, 30,* 773–802.

Dijkstra, J., Cillessen, A., Lindenberg, S., & Veenstra, R. (2010b). Basking in reflected glory and its limits: Why adolescents hang out with popular peers. *Journal of Research on Adolescence, 20,* 942–958.

Dijkstra, J., Lindenberg, S., Veenstra, R., Steglich, C., Isaacs, J., Card, N., & Hodges, E. (2010). Influence and selection processes in weapon carrying during adolescence: The roles of status, aggression, and vulnerability. *Criminology, 48,* 187–220.

Dijkstra, J., Lindenberg, S., Verhulst, F., Ormel, J., & Veenstra, R. (2009). The relation between popularity and aggressive, destructive, and norm-breaking behaviors: Moderating effects of athletic abilities, physical attractiveness, and prosociality. *Journal of Research on Adolescence, 19,* 401–413.

Dir, A. L., Cyders, M. A., & Coskunpinar, A. (2013). From the bar to the bed via mobile phone: A first test of the role of problematic alcohol use, sexting, and impulsivity-related traits in sexual hookups. *Computers in Human Behavior, 29,* 1664–1670.

Dirghangi, S., Kahn, G., Laursen, B., Brendgen, M., Vitaro, F., Dionne, G., & Boivin, M. (2015). Co-rumination cultivates anxiety: A genetically informed study of friend influence during early adolescence. *Developmental Psychology, 51,* 564–571.

Dishion, T. J., Véronneau, M.-H., & Myers, M. W. (2010). Cascading peer dynamics underlying the progression from problem behavior to violence in early to late adolescence. *Development and Psychopathology, 22,* 603–619.

Dishion, T., & Owen, L. (2002). A longitudinal analysis of friendships and substance use: Bidirectional influence from adolescence to adulthood. *Developmental Psychology, 38,* 480–491.

Dishion, T., Andrews, D., & Crosby, L. (1995). Antisocial boys and their friends in early adolescence: Relationship characteristics, quality, and interactional process. *Child Development, 66,* 139–151.

Dishion, T., Capaldi, D., & Yoerger, K. (1999). Middle childhood antecedents to progressions in male adolescent substance use: An ecological analysis of risk and protection. *Journal of Adolescent Research, 14,* 175–205.

Dishion, T., McCord, J., & Poulin, F. (1999). When interventions harm: Peer groups and problem behavior. *American Psychologist, 54,* 755–764.

Dishion, T., Nelson, S., & Bullock, B. (2004). Premature adolescent autonomy: Parent disengagement and deviant peer process in the amplification of problem behavior. *Journal of Adolescence, 27,* 515–530.

Dishion, T., Nelson, S., Winter, C., & Bullock, B. (2004). Adolescent friendship as a dynamic system: Entropy and deviance in the etiology and course of male antisocial behavior. *Journal of Abnormal Child Psychology, 32,* 651–663.

Dishion, T., Patterson, G., Stoolmiller, M., & Skinner, M. (1991). Family, school, and behavioral antecedents to early adolescent involvement with antisocial peers. *Developmental Psychology, 27,* 172–180.

Dittus, P. J., & Jaccard, J. (2000). Adolescents' perceptions of maternal disapproval of sex: Relationship to sexual outcomes. *Journal of Adolescent Health, 26,* 268–278.

Dmitrieva, J., Chen, C., Greenberger, E., & Gil-Rivas, V. (2004). Family relationships and adolescent psychosocial outcomes: Converging findings from Eastern and Western cultures. *Journal of Research on Adolescence, 14,* 425–447.

Dmitrieva, J., Gibson, L., Steinberg, L., Piquero, A., & Fagan, J. (2014). Predictors and consequences of gang membership: Comparing gang members, gang leaders, and non-gang-affiliated adjudicated youth. *Journal of Research on Adolescence, 24,* 220–234.

Dobkin, P., Tremblay, R., & Sacchitelle, C. (1997). Predicting boys' early-onset substance abuse from father's alcoholism, son's disruptiveness, and mother's parenting behavior. *Journal of Consulting and Clinical Psychology, 65,* 86–92.

Dobkin, P., Tremblay, R., Mâsse, L., & Vitaro, F. (1995). Individual and peer characteristics in predicting boys' early onset of substance abuse: A seven-year longitudinal study. *Child Development, 66,* 1198–1214.

Dodge, K. (1986). A social information-processing model of social competence in children. In M. Perlmutter (Ed.), *Minnesota Symposium on Child Psychology* (Vol. 18, pp. 77–125). Hillsdale, NJ: Erlbaum.

Dodge, K. A., Godwin, J., & Conduct Problems Prevention Research Group. (2013). Social-information-processing patterns mediate the impact of preventive intervention on adolescent antisocial behavior. *Psychological Science, 24,* 456–465.

Dodge, K., & Coie, J. (1987). Social information-processing factors in reactive and proactive

aggression in children's peer groups. *Journal of Personality and Social Psychology, 53,* 1146–1158.

Dodge, K., & Pettit, G. (2003). A biopsychosocial model of the development of chronic conduct problems in adolescence. *Developmental Psychology, 39,* 349–371.

Dodge, K., Coie, J., & Lynam, D. (2006). Aggression and antisocial behavior in youth. In W. Damon & R. Lerner (Ser. Eds.) & N. Eisenberg (Vol. Ed.), *Handbook of child psychology: Vol. 3. Social, emotional, and personality development* (6th ed., pp. 719–788). New York: Wiley.

Dodge, K., Greenberg, M., Malone, P., & Conduct Problems Prevention Research Group. (2008). Testing an idealized dynamic cascade model of the development of serious violence in adolescence. *Child Development, 79,* 1907–1927.

Dogan, S. J., Stockdale, G. D., Widaman, K. F., & Conger, R. D. (2010). Developmental relations and patterns of change between alcohol use and number of sexual partners from adolescence through adulthood. *Developmental Psychology, 46,* 1747–1759.

Dogan, S., Conger, R., Kim, K., & Masyn, K. (2007). Cognitive and parenting pathways in the transmission of antisocial behavior from parents to adolescents. *Child Development, 78,* 335–349.

Dolev-Cohen, M., & Barak, A. (2013). Adolescents' use of Instant Messaging as a means of emotional relief. *Computers in Human Behavior, 29,* 58–63.

Dollahite, D., Layton, E., Bahr, H., Walker, A., & Thatcher, J. (2009). Giving up something good for something better: Sacred sacrifices made by religious youth. *Journal of Adolescent Research, 24,* 691–725.

Dolliver, M. (2010, November 15). Teen girls as avid shoppers. *Adweek* (accessed online at http://www.adweek.com/news/advertising-branding/teen-girls-avid-shoppers-103813).

Domina, T., Conley, A., & Farkas, G. (2011). The link between educational expectations and effort in the college-for-all era. *Sociology of Education, 84,* 93–112.

Donahue, K. L., D'Onofrio, B. M., Bates, J. E., Lansford, J. E., Dodge, K. A., & Pettit, G. S. (2010). Early exposure to parents' relationship instability: Implications for sexual behavior and depression in adolescence. *Journal of Adolescent Health, 47,* 547–554.

Donenberg, G. R., Emerson, E., & Mackesy-Amiti, M. E. (2011). Sexual risk among African American girls: Psychopathology and mother–daughter relationships. *Journal of Consulting and Clinical Psychology, 79,* 153–158.

Dong, Y., & Ding, C. (2012). Adolescent risk behaviors: Studying typical and atypical individuals via multidimensional scaling profile analysis. *Journal of Adolescence, 35,* 197–205.

Donnellan, M., Larsen-Rife, D., & Conger, R. (2005). Personality, family history, and competence in early adult romantic relationships.

Journal of Personality and Social Psychology, 88, 562–576.

Doornwaard, S. M., Branje, S., Meeus, W. H., & ter Bogt, T. F. (2012). Development of adolescents' peer crowd identification in relation to changes in problem behaviors. *Developmental Psychology, 48,* 1366–1380.

Dopp, A. R., Borduin, C. M., Wagner, D. V., & Sawyer, A. M. (2014). The economic impact of multisystemic therapy through midlife: A cost-benefit analysis with serious juvenile offenders and their siblings. *Journal of Consulting and Clinical Psychology, 82,* 694–705.

Dorn, L., & Biro, F. (2011). Puberty and its measurement: A decade in review. *Journal of Research on Adolescence, 21,* 180–195.

Dorn, L., Dahl, R., Woodward, H., & Biro, F. (2006). Defining the boundaries of early adolescence: A user's guide to assessing pubertal status and pubertal timing in research with adolescents. *Applied Developmental Science, 1,* 30–56.

Dorn, L., Nottelmann, E. D., Susman, E. J., Inoff-Germain, G., Cutler, G. B., Jr., & Chrousos, G. P. (1999). Variability in hormone concentrations and self-reported menstrual histories in young adolescents: Menarche as an integral part of a developmental process. *Journal of Youth and Adolescence, 28,* 283–304.

Dornbusch, S., Carlsmith, J., Bushwall, S., Ritter, P., Leiderman, P., Hastorf, A., & Gross, T. (1985). Single parents, extended households, and the control of adolescents. *Child Development, 56,* 326–341.

Dornbusch, S., Erickson, K., Laird, J., & Wong, C. (2001). The relation of family and school attachment to adolescent deviance in diverse groups and communities. *Journal of Adolescent Research, 16,* 396–422.

Dosenbach, N. U. F., Petersen, S. E., & Schlaggar, B. (2013). The teenage brain: Functional connectivity. *Current Directions in Psychological Science, 22,* 101–107.

Dosenbach, N., Nardos, B., Cohen, A., Fair, D., Power, J., Church, J. A., . . . Schlaggar, B. (2010). Prediction of individual brain maturity using fMRI. *Science, 329,* 1358–1361.

Dotterer, A. M., & Lowe, K. (2011). Classroom context, school engagement, and academic achievement in early adolescence. *Journal of Youth and Adolescence, 40,* 1649–1660.

Dotterer, A. M., Lowe, K., & McHale, S. M. (2014). Academic growth trajectories and family relationships among African American youth. *Journal of Research on Adolescence, 24,* 734–747.

Dotterer, A., McHale, S., & Crouter, A. (2007). Implications of out-of-school activities for school engagement in African American adolescents. *Journal of Youth and Adolescence, 36,* 391–401.

Dotterer, A., McHale, S., & Crouter, A. C. (2009). The development and correlates of academic interests from childhood through adolescence. *Journal of Educational Psychology, 101,* 509–519.

Douglass, S., Yip, T., & Shelton, J. N. (2014). Intragroup contact and anxiety among ethnic minority adolescents: considering ethnic identity and school diversity transitions. *Journal of Youth & Adolescence, 43,* 1628–1641.

Dowdy, B. B., & Kliewer, W. (1998). Dating, parent–adolescent conflict, and behavioral autonomy. *Journal of Youth and Adolescence, 27,* 473–492.

Downey, D., & Ainsworth-Darnell, J. W. (2002). The search for oppositional culture among Black students. *American Sociological Review, 67,* 156–164.

Downey, D., & Pribesh, S. (2004). When race matters: Teachers' evaluations of students' classroom behavior. *Sociology of Education, 77,* 267–282.

Downey, D., Ainsworth, J. W., & Qian, Z. (2009). Rethinking the attitude-achievement paradox among Blacks. *Sociology of Education, 82,* 1–19.

Downey, D., Ainsworth-Darnell, J., & Dufur, M. (1998). Sex of parent and children's well-being in single-parent households. *Journal of Marriage and the Family, 60,* 878–893.

Downey, G., Bonica, C., & Rincón, C. (1999). Rejection sensitivity and adolescent romantic relationships. In W. Furman, B. Brown, & C. Feiring (Eds.), *Contemporary perspectives on adolescent romantic relationships* (pp. 148–174). New York: Cambridge University Press.

Downey, G., Lebolt, A., Rincón, C., & Freitas, A. (1998). Rejection sensitivity and children's interpersonal difficulties. *Child Development, 69,* 1074–1091.

Doyle, A., & Markiewicz, D. (2005). Parenting, marital conflict, and adjustment from early to mid-adolescence: Mediated by adolescent attachment style? *Journal of Youth and Adolescence, 34,* 97–110.

Doyle, A., Lawford, H., & Markiewicz, D. (2009). Attachment style with mother, father, best-friend, and romantic partner during adolescence. *Journal of Research on Adolescence, 19,* 690–714.

Drabick, D., & Steinberg, L. (2011). Developmental psychopathology. In B. Brown & M. Prinstein (Eds.), *Encyclopedia of adolescence* (Vol. 3, pp. 135–142). New York: Academic Press.

Drapela, L. A., Gebelt, J. L., & McRee, N. (2006). Pubertal development, choice of friends, and smoking initiation among adolescent males. *Journal of Youth and Adolescence, 35,* 717–727.

Dregan, A., & Armstrong, D. (2010). Adolescence sleep disturbances as predictors of adulthood sleep disturbances—A cohort study. *Journal of Adolescent Health, 46,* 482–487.

Dreyfuss, M., Caudle, K., Drysdale, A. T., Johnston, N. E., Cohen, A. O., Somerville, L. H., Galván, A., Tottenham, N., Hare, T. A., & Casey, B. J. (2014). Teens impulsively react rather than retreat from threat. *Developmental Neuroscience, 36,* 220–227.

Drumm, P., & Jackson, D. (1996). Developmental changes in questioning strategies during adolescence. *Journal of Adolescent Research, 11,* 285–305.

Drummond, A., & Sauer, J. D. (2014). Videogames do not negatively impact adolescent academic performance in science, mathematics or reading. *PLoS One, 9,* 87943.

Dryfoos, J. (1993). Schools as places for health, mental health, and social services. *Teachers College Record, 94,* 540–567.

Dubas, J., Graber, J., & Petersen, A. (1991). A longitudinal investigation of adolescents' changing perceptions of pubertal timing. *Developmental Psychology, 27,* 580–586.

Dubé, E., & Savin-Williams, R. (1999). Sexual identity development among ethnic sexual-minority male youths. *Developmental Psychology, 35,* 1389–1398.

Dube, S. R., Felitti, V. J., Dong, M., Chapman, D. P., Giles, W. H., & Anda, R. F. (2003). Childhood abuse, neglect, and household dysfunction and the risk of illicit drug use: The adverse childhood experiences study. *Pediatrics, 111,* 564–572.

DuBois, D., & Hirsch, B. (1990). School and neighborhood friendship patterns of Blacks and Whites in early adolescence. *Child Development, 61,* 524–536.

DuBois, D., & Silverthorn, N. (2005). Natural mentoring relationships and adolescent health: Evidence from a national study. *American Journal of Public Health, 95,* 518–524.

DuBois, D., & Tevendale, H. (1999). Self-esteem in childhood and adolescence: Vaccine or epiphenomenon. *Applied and Preventive Psychology, 8,* 103–117.

DuBois, D., Bull, C., Sherman, M., & Roberts, M. (1998). Self-esteem and adjustment in early adolescence: A social-contextual perspective. *Journal of Youth and Adolescence, 27,* 557–583.

DuBois, D., Burk-Braxton, C., Swenson, L. P., Tevendale, H. D., & Hardesty, J. L. (2002). Race and gender influences on adjustment in early adolescence: Investigation of an integrative model. *Child Development, 73,* 1573–1592.

DuBois, D., Felner, R., Brand, S., & George, G. (1999). Profiles of self-esteem in early adolescence: Identification and investigation of adaptive correlates. *American Journal of Community Psychology, 27,* 899–932.

DuBois, D., Felner, R., Brand, S., Adan, A., & Evans, E. (1992). A prospective study of life stress, social support, and adaptation in early adolescence. *Child Development, 63,* 542–557.

DuBois, D., Felner, R., Meares, H., & Krier, M. (1994). Prospective investigation of the effects of socioeconomic disadvantage, life stress, and social support on early adolescent adjustment. *Journal of Abnormal Psychology, 103,* 511–522.

DuBois, D., Holloway, B., Valentine, J., & Cooper, H. (2002). Effectiveness of mentoring programs for youth: A meta-analytic review. *American Journal of Community Psychology, 30,* 157–197.

DuBois, D., Tevendale, H., Burk-Braxton, C., Swenson, L., & Hardesty, J. (2000). Self-system influences during early adolescence: Investigation of an integrative model. *Journal of Early Adolescence, 20,* 12–43.

Dubow, E. F., Huesmann, L. R., Boxer, P., Pulkkinen, L., & Kokko, K. (2006). Middle childhood and adolescent contextual and personal predictors of adult educational and occupational outcomes: A mediational model in two countries. *Developmental Psychology, 42,* 937–949.

Duchesne, S., & Ratelle, C. (2010). Parental behaviors and adolescents' achievement goals at the beginning of middle school: Emotional problems as potential mediators. *Journal of Educational Psychology, 102,* 497–507.

Duckworth, A. L., & Seligman, M. E. P. (2005). Self-discipline outdoes IQ in predicting academic performance of adolescents. *Psychological Science, 16,* 939–944.

Duckworth, A. L., Quinn, P. D., & Tsukayama E. (2012). What no child left behind leaves behind: The roles of IQ and selfcontrol in predicting standardized achievement test scores and report card grades. *Journal of Educational Psychology, 104,* 439–451.

Duckworth, A., Peterson, C., Matthews, M., & Kelly, D. (2007). Grit: Perseverance and passion for long-term goals. *Journal of Personality and Social Psychology, 92,* 1087–1101.

Due, P., Merlo, J., Harel-Fisch, Y., Damsgaard, M., Holstein, B., Hetland, J., Currie, C., et al. (2009). Socioeconomic inequality in exposure to bullying during adolescence: a comparative, cross-sectional, multilevel study in 35 countries. *American Journal of Public Health, 99,* 907–915.

Duke, S. A., Balzer, B. W. R., & Steinbeck, K. S. (2014). Testosterone and its effects on human male adolescent mood and behavior: A systematic review. *Journal of Adolescent Health, 55,* 315–322.

Dukes, R., Martinez, R., & Stein, J. (1997). Precursors and consequences of membership in youth gangs. *Youth and Society, 29,* 139–165.

Dumas, T. M., Lawford, H., Tieu, T.-T., & Pratt, M. W. (2009). Positive parenting in adolescence and its relation to low-point narration and identity status in emerging adulthood: A longitudinal analysis. *Developmental Psychology, 45,* 1531–1544.

Dumont, H., Trautwein, U., Nagy, G., & Nagengast, B. (2014). Quality of parental homework involvement: Predictors and reciprocal relations with academic functioning in the reading domain. *Journal of Educational Psychology, 106,* 144–161.

Dumont, M., & Provost, M. (1999). Resilience in adolescents: Protective role of social support, coping strategies, self-esteem, and social activities on experience of stress and depression. *Journal of Youth and Adolescence, 28,* 343–363.

Dumontheil, I., Apperly, I., & Blakemore, S.-J. (2010). Online usage of theory of mind continues to develop in late adolescence. *Developmental Science, 13,* 331–338.

Duncan, G. (1994). Families and neighbors as sources of disadvantage in the schooling decisions of White and Black adolescents. *American Journal of Education, 103,* 20–53.

Dunifon, R. (2013). The influence of grandparents on the lives of children and adolescents. *Child Development Perspectives, 7,* 55–60.

Dunlop, S. M., & Romer, D. (2010). Adolescent and young adult crash risk: Sensation seeking, substance use propensity, and substance use behaviors. *Journal of Adolescent Health, 46,* 90–92.

Dunn, J., Slomkowski, C., & Beardsall, L. (1994). Sibling relationships from the preschool period through middle childhood and early adolescence. *Developmental Psychology, 30,* 315–324.

Dunn, M., & Goldman, M. (1998). Age and drinking-related differences in the memory organization of alcohol expectances in 3rd-, 6th-, 9th-, and 12th-grade children. *Journal of Consulting & Clinical Psychology, 66,* 579–585.

Dunn, S., Putallaz, M., Sheppard, B., & Lindstrom, R. (1987). Social support and adjustment in gifted adolescents. *Journal of Educational Psychology, 79,* 467–473.

Dupéré, V., Lacourse, E., Willms, D., Leventhal, T., & Tremblay, R. (2008). Neighborhood poverty and early transition to sexual activity in young adolescents: A developmental ecological approach. *Child Development, 79,* 1463–1476.

Dupéré, V., Lacourse, É., Willms, J. D., Vitaro, F., & Tremblay, R. E. (2007). Affiliation to youth gangs during adolescence: The interaction between childhood psychopathic tendencies and neighborhood disadvantage. *Journal of Abnormal Child Psychology, 35,* 1035–1045.

DuPont, R. L., & Lieberman, J. A. (2014). Young brains on drugs. *Science, 344,* 557.

DuRant, R., Rome, E., Rich, M., Allred, E., Emans, S., & Woods, E. (1997). Tobacco and alcohol use behaviors portrayed in music videos: A content analysis. *American Journal of Public Health, 87,* 1131–1135.

Durik, A. M., Vida, M., & Eccles, J. (2006). Task values and ability beliefs as predictors of high school literacy choices: A developmental analysis. *Journal of Educational Psychology, 98,* 382–393.

Dweck, C. S. (2002). The development of ability conceptions. In A. Wigfield & J. Eccles (Eds.), *The development of achievement motivation* (pp. 57–88). New York: Academic Press.

Dwyer, D. B., Harrison, B. J., Yücel, M., Whittle, S., Zalesky, A., Pantelis, C., et al. (2014). Large-scale brain network dynamics supporting adolescent cognitive control. *Journal of Neuroscience, 34,* 14096–14107.

Dykas, M. J., Woodhouse, S. S., Ehrlich, K. B., & Cassidy, J. (2012). Attachment-related differences in perceptions of an initial peer interaction emerge over time: Evidence of reconstructive memory processes in adolescents. *Developmental Psychology, 48,* 1381–1389.

Dykas, M. J., Woodhouse, S. S., Jones, J. D., & Cassidy, J. (2014). Attachment-related biases in adolescents' memory. *Child Development, 85,* 2185–2201.

Eamon, M. K. (2005). Social-demographic, school, neighborhood, and parenting influences on the academic achievement of Latino young adolescents. *Journal of Youth and Adolescence, 34,* 163–174.

Earls, F., Cairns, R., & Mercy, J. (1993). The control of violence and the promotion of nonviolence in adolescents. In S. Millstein, A. Petersen, & E. Nightingale (Eds.), *Promoting the health of adolescents: New directions for the twenty-first century* (pp. 285–304). New York: Oxford University Press.

East, P. (2009). Adolescents' relationships with siblings. In R. Lerner & L. Steinberg (Eds.), *Handbook of adolescent psychology* (3rd ed., Vol. 2, pp. 43–73). New York: Wiley.

East, P. L., & Barber, J. S. (2014). High educational aspirations among pregnant adolescents are related to pregnancy unwantedness and subsequent parenting stress and inadequacy. *Journal of Marriage and Family, 76,* 652–664.

East, P. L., Chien, N. C., & Barber, J. S. (2012). Adolescents' pregnancy intention, wantedness, and regret: Cross-lagged relations with mental health and harsh parenting. *Journal of Marriage and Family, 74,* 167–185.

East, P., & Blaustein, E. (1995, March). *Perceived timing of life-course transitions: Race differences in early adolescent girls' sexual, marriage, and childbearing expectations.* Paper presented at the biennial meetings of the Society for Research in Child Development, Indianapolis.

East, P., & Felice, M. (1996). *Adolescent pregnancy and parenting: Findings from a racially diverse sample.* Mahwah, NJ: Erlbaum.

East, P., & Jacobson, L. (2003). Mothers' differential treatment of their adolescent childbearing and nonchildbearing children: Contrasts between and within families. *Journal of Family Psychology, 19,* 384–396.

East, P., & Khoo, S. (2005). Longitudinal pathways linking family factors and sibling relationship qualities to adolescent substance use and sexual risk behaviors. *Journal of Family Psychology, 19,* 571–580.

East, P., & Rook, K. (1992). Compensatory patterns of support among children's peer relationships: A test using school friends, nonschool friends, and siblings. *Developmental Psychology, 28,* 163–172.

East, P., Felice, M., & Morgan, M. (1993). Sisters' and girlfriends' sexual and childbearing behavior: Effects on early adolescent girls' sexual outcomes. *Journal of Marriage and the Family, 55,* 953–963.

East, P., Reyes, B. T., & Horn, E. J. (2007). Association between adolescent pregnancy and a family history of teenage births. *Perspectives on Sexual and Reproductive Health, 39,* 108–115.

Eaton, D., McKnight-Eily, L., Lowry, R., Perry, G., Presley-Cantrell, L., & Croft, J. (2010). Prevalence of insufficient, borderline, and optimal hours of sleep among high school students–United States, 2007. *Journal of Adolescent Health, 46,* 399–401.

Eaton, M. J., & Dembo, M. H. (1997). Differences in the motivational beliefs of Asian American and non-Asian students. *Journal of Educational Psychology, 89,* 433–440.

Eberhart, N. K., Shih, J. H., Hammen, C. L., & Brennan, P. A. (2006). Understanding the sex difference in vulnerability to adolescent depression: An examination of child and parent characteristics. *Journal of Abnormal Child Psychology, 34,* 495–508.

Ebin, V. J., Sneed, C. D., Morisky, D. E., Rotherman-Borus, M., Magnusson, A. M., & Malotte, C. (2001). Acculturation and interrelationships between problem and health-promoting behaviors among Latino adolescents. *Journal of Adolescent Health, 28,* 62–72.

Eccles, J. (2004). Schools, academic motivation, and stage-environment fit. In R. Lerner & L. Steinberg (Eds.), *Handbook of adolescent psychology.* New York: Wiley.

Eccles, J., & Roeser, R. (2009). Schools, academic motivation, and stage-environment fit. In R. Lerner & L. Steinberg (Eds.), *Handbook of adolescent psychology* (3rd ed., Vol. 1, pp. 404–434). New York: Wiley.

Eccles, J., & Roeser, R. (2011). Schools as developmental contexts during adolescence. *Journal of Research on Adolescence, 21,* 225–241.

Eccles, J., Early, D., Frasier, K., Belansky, E., & McCarthy, K. (1997). The relation of connection, regulation, and support for autonomy to adolescents' functioning. *Journal of Adolescent Research, 12,* 263–286.

Eccles, J., Lord, S. E., Roeser, R. (1996). Round holes, square pegs, rocky roads, and sore feet: The impact of stage/environment fit on young adolescents' experiences in schools and families. In S. L. Toth & D. Cicchetti (Eds.), *Adolescence: Opportunities and challenges* (Vol. 7, pp. 49–93). Rochester, NY: University of Rochester Press.

Eccles, J., Midgley, C., Wigfield, A., Buchanan, C., Reuman, D., Flanagan, C., & Mac Iver, D. (1993). Development during adolescence: The impact of stage-environment fit on young adolescents' experiences in schools and families. *American Psychologist, 48,* 90–101.

Echeverria, S. E., Vélez-Valle, E., Janevic, T., & Prystowsky, A. (2014). The role of poverty status and obesity on school attendance in the United States. *Journal of Adolescent Health, 55,* 402–407.

Edens, J. F., Marcus, D. K., & Vaughn, M. G. (2011). Exploring the taxometric status of psychopathy among youthful offenders: Is there a juvenile psychopath taxon? *Law and Human Behavior, 35,* 13–24.

Edens, J., Skeem, J., Cruise, K., & Cauffman, E. (2000). The assessment of juvenile psychopathy and its association with violence: A critical review. *Behavioral Sciences and the Law, 18,* 53–80.

Eder, D. (1985). The cycle of popularity: Interpersonal relations among female adolescence. *Sociology of Education, 58,* 154–165.

Edwards, A. C., Rose, R. J., Kaprio, J., & Dick, D. M. (2011). Pubertal development moderates the importance of environmental influences on depressive symptoms in adolescent girls and boys. *Journal of Youth and Adolescence, 40,* 1383–1393.

Egan, S., & Perry, D. (1998). Does low self-regard invite victimization? *Developmental Psychology, 34,* 299–309.

Egan, S., & Perry, D. (2001). Gender identity: A multidimensional analysis with implications for psychosocial adjustment. *Developmental Psychology, 37,* 451–463.

Ehrlich, K. B., Richards, J. M., Lejuez, C. W., & Cassidy, J. (2015). When parents and adolescents disagree about disagreeing: Observed parent-adolescent communication predicts informant discrepancies about conflict. *Journal of Research on Adolescence, Early view.* DOI: 10.1111/jora.12201

Eichen, D. M., Conner, B. T., Daly, B. P., & Fauber, R. L. (2012). Weight perception, substance use, and disordered eating behaviors: Comparing normal weight and overweight high-school students. *Journal of Youth and Adolescence, 41,* 1–13.

Eisenberg, M., & Neumark-Sztainer, D. (2010). Friends' dieting and disordered eating behaviors among adolescents five years later: Findings from Project EAT. *Journal of Adolescent Health, 47,* 67–73.

Eisenberg, M., Neumark-Sztainer, D., Haines, J., & Wall, M. (2006). Weight-teasing and emotional well-being in adolescents: Longitudinal findings from project EAT. *Journal of Adolescent Health, 38,* 675–683.

Eisenberg, N., Carlo, G., Murphy, B., & Van Court, P. (1995). Prosocial development in late adolescence: A longitudinal study. *Child Development, 66,* 1179–1197.

Eisenberg, N., Cumberland, A., Guthrie, I. K., Murphy, B. C., & Shepard, S. A. (2005). Age changes in prosocial responding and moral reasoning in adolescence and early adulthood. *Journal of Research on Adolescence, 15,* 235–260.

Eisenberg, N., Morris, A., McDaniel, B., & Spinrad, T. (2009). Moral cognitions and prosocial responding in adolescence. In R. Lerner & L. Steinberg (Eds.), *Handbook of adolescent psychology* (3rd ed., Vol. 1, pp. 229–265). New York: Wiley.

Eisenberg, N., VanSchyndel, S. K., & Hofer, C. (2015). The association of maternal socialization in childhood and adolescence with adult offsprings' sympathy/caring. *Developmental Psychology, 51,* 7–16.

Eisenberg, N., Zhou, Q., & Koller, S. (2001). Brazilian adolescents' prosocial moral judgment and behavior: Relations to sympathy, perspective taking, gender-role orientation, and demographic characteristics. *Child Development, 72,* 518–534.

Elder, G. H., Jr. (1980). Adolescence in historical perspective. In J. Adelson (Ed.), *Handbook of adolescent psychology.* New York: Wiley.

Elders, M., Perry, C., Eriksen, M., & Giovino, G. (1994). The report of the Surgeon General: Preventing tobacco use among young people. *American Journal of Public Health, 84,* 543–547.

Eley, T., Lichenstein, P., & Stevenson, J. (1999). Sex differences in the etiology of aggressive and nonaggressive antisocial behavior: Results from two twin studies. *Child Development, 70,* 155–168.

Elkind, D. (1967). Egocentrism in adolescence. *Child Development, 38,* 1025–1034.

Elkington, K. S., Bauermeister, J. A., & Zimmerman, M. A. (2010). Psychological distress, substance use, and HIV/STI risk behaviors among youth. *Journal of Youth and Adolescence, 39,* 514–527.

Ellickson, P., Bell, R., & McGuigan, K. (1993). Preventing adolescent drug use: Long-term results of a junior high program. *American Journal of Public Health, 83,* 856–861.

Elliott, D., Huizinga, D., & Menard, S. (1989). *Multiple problem youth: Delinquency, substance abuse, and mental health problems.* New York: Springer-Verlag.

Ellis, B. (2004). Timing of pubertal maturation in girls: An integrated life history approach. *Psychological Bulletin, 130,* 920–958.

Ellis, B. J., Schlomer, G. L., Tilley, E. H., & Butler, E. A. (2012). Impact of fathers on risky sexual behavior in daughters: A genetically and environmentally controlled sibling study. *Development and Psychopathology, 24,* 317–332.

Ellis, B., Bates, J., Dodge, K., Fergusson, D., Horwood, L., . . . Pettit, G. (2003). Does father absence place daughters at special risk for early sexual activity and teenage pregnancy? *Child Development, 74,* 801–821.

Ellis, B., Del Guidice, M., Dishion, T., Figueredo, A., Gray, G., Griskevicius, G., . . . Wilson, D. (2012). The evolutionary basis of risky adolescent behavior: Implications for science, policy, and practice. *Developmental Psychology, 48,* 598–623.

Ellis, B., Shirtcliff, E., Boyce, W., Deardoff, J., & Essex, M. (2011). Quality of early family relationships and the timing and tempo of puberty: Effects depend on biological sensitivity to context. *Development and Psychopathology, 23,* 85–99.

Elmen, J. (1991). Achievement orientation in early adolescence: Developmental patterns and social correlates. *Journal of Early Adolescence, 11,* 125–151.

Elmore, R. (2009). Schooling adolescents. In R. Lerner & L. Steinberg (Eds.), *Handbook of adolescent psychology* (3rd ed., Vol. 2, pp. 193–227). New York: Wiley.

Elo, I., King, R., & Furstenberg, F., Jr. (1999). Adolescent females: Their sexual partners and the fathers of their children. *Journal of Marriage and the Family, 61,* 74–84.

Emery, R., Beam, C., & Rowen, J. (2011). Adolescents' experience of parental divorce. In B. Brown & M. Prinstein (Eds.), *Encyclopedia of adolescence* (Vol. 2, pp. 10–17). New York: Academic Press.

Engle, R. (2013). The teen brain. *Current Directions in Psychological Science, 22* (whole issue).

English, D., Lambert, S. F., & Ialongo, N. S. (2014). Longitudinal associations between experienced racial discrimination and depressive symptoms in African American adolescents. *Developmental Psychology, 50,* 1190–1196.

Englund, M. M., Siebenbruner, J., Oliva, E. M., Egeland, B., Chung, C. T., & Long, J. D. (2013). The developmental significance of late adolescent substance use for early adult functioning. *Developmental Psychology, 49,* 1554–1564.

Ennett, S., & Bauman, K. (1994). The contribution of influence and selection to adolescent peer group homogeneity: The case of adolescent cigarette smoking. *Journal of Personality and Social Psychology, 67,* 653–663.

Ennett, S., & Bauman, K. (1996). Adolescent social networks: School, demographic, and longitudinal considerations. *Journal of Adolescent Research, 11,* 194–215.

Ennett, S., Bauman, K., Hussong, A., Faris, R., Foshee, V., Cai, L., & DuRant, R. (2006). The peer context of adolescent substance use: Findings from social network analysis. *Journal of Research on Adolescence, 16,* 159–186.

Ennett, S., Foshee, V. A., Bauman, K. E., Hussong, A., Faris, R., . . . Durant, R. (2008). The social ecology of adolescent alcohol misuse. *Child Development, 79,* 1777–1791.

Ennett, S., Tobler, N., Ringwalt, C., & Flewelling, R. (1994). How effective is drug abuse resistance education? A meta-analysis of Project DARE outcome evaluations. *American Journal of Public Health, 84,* 1394–1401.

Enright, R., Levy, V., Harris, D., & Lapsley, D. (1987). Do economic conditions influence how theorists view adolescents? *Journal of Youth and Adolescence, 16,* 541–560.

Enriquez, L. E. (2011). "Because we feel the pressure and we also feel the support": Examining the educational success of undocumented immigrant Latina/o students. *Harvard Educational Review, 81,* 476–499.

Ensminger, M., Lamkin, R., & Jacobson, N. (1996). School leaving: A longitudinal perspective including neighborhood effects. *Child Development, 67,* 2400–2416.

Entwisle, D. (1990). Schools and the adolescent. In S. Feldman & G. Elliott (Eds.), *At the threshold: The developing adolescent* (pp. 197–224). Cambridge, MA: Harvard University Press.

Entwisle, D., Alexander, K., & Olson, L. (2004). Temporary as compared to permanent high school dropout. *Social Forces, 82,* 1181–1205.

Entwisle, D., Alexander, K., & Olson, L. (2005). Urban teenagers work and dropout. *Youth and Society, 37,* 3–32.

Epstein, R. (2007). *The case against adolescence: Rediscovering the adult in every teen.* Sanger, CA: Quill Driver Books.

Erath, S. A., Flanagan, K. S., & Bierman, K. L. (2007). Social anxiety and peer relations in early adolescence: Behavioral and cognitive factors. *Journal of Abnormal Child Psychology, 35,* 405–416.

Erel, O., & Burman, B. (1995). Interrelatedness of marital relations and parent–child relations: A meta-analytic review. *Psychological Bulletin, 118,* 108–132.

Erickson, K., Crosnoe, R., & Dornbusch, S. M. (2000). A social process model of adolescent deviance: Combining social control and differential association perspectives. *Journal of Youth and Adolescence, 29,* 395–425.

Erikson, E. (1959). Identity and the life cycle. *Psychological Issues, 1,* 1–171.

Erikson, E. (1963). *Childhood and society.* New York: Norton.

Erikson, E. (1968). *Identity: Youth and crisis.* New York: Norton.

Erkut, S., Szalacha, L. A., Garcia Coll, C., & Alarcon, O. (2000). Puerto Rican early adolescents' self-esteem patterns. *Journal of Research on Adolescence, 10,* 339–364.

Ermer, E., Cope, L. M., Nyalakanti, P. K., Calhoun, V. D., & Kiehl, K. A. (2013). Aberrant paralimbic gray matter in incarcerated male adolescents with psychopathic traits. *Journal of the American Academy of Child & Adolescent Psychiatry, 52,* 94–103.

Ernst, M., Nelson, E., Jazbec, S., McClure, E., Monk, C., Leibenluft, E., . . . Pine, D. (2005). Amygdala and nucleus accumbens in response to receipt and omission of gains in adults and adolescents. *Neuroimage, 25,* 1279–1291.

Erol, R. Y., & Orth, U. (2011). Self-esteem development from age 14 to 30 years: A longitudinal study. *Journal of Personality and Social Psychology, 101,* 607–619.

Esbensen, F., Deschenes, E., & Winfree, L., Jr. (1999). Differences between gang girls and gang boys: Results from a multisite survey. *Youth and Society, 31,* 27–53.

Espelage, D. L., Basile, K. C., & Hamburger, M. E. (2012). Bullying perpetration and subsequent sexual violence perpetration among middle school students. *Journal of Adolescent Health, 50,* 60–65.

Espelage, D. L., Holt, M. K., & Henkel, R. R. (2003). Examination of peer-group contextual effects on aggression during early adolescence. *Child Development, 74,* 205–220.

Espelage, D., Anderman, E. M., Brown, V. E., Jones, A., Lane, K. L., McMahon, S. D., . . . Reynolds, C. R. (2013). Understanding and preventing violence directed against teachers: Recommendations for a national research, practice, and policy agenda. *American Psychologist, 68,* 75–87.

Espenshade, T. J., Hale, L. E., & Chung, C. Y. (2005). The frog pond revisited: High school academic context, class rank, and elite college admission. *Sociology of Education, 78,* 269–293.

Espinoza, G., Gillen-O'Neel, C., Gonzales, N. A., & Fuligni, A. J. (2014). Friend affiliations and school adjustment among Mexican-American adolescents: the moderating role of peer and parent support. *Journal of Youth & Adolescence, 43,* 1969–1981.

Espinoza, G., Gonzales, N. A., Fuligni, A. J. (2013). Daily school peer victimization experiences among Mexican-American adolescents: associations with psychosocial, physical and school adjustment. *Journal of Youth & Adolescence, 42,* 1775–1788.

Ettekal, I. & Ladd, G. W. (2015). Development pathways from childhood aggression-disruptiveness, chronic peer rejection, and deviant friendships to early-adolescent rule breaking. *Child Development, 86,* 614–631.

Eurostat. (2010). *Young adults in the EU27 in 2008.* Luxembourg: Author.

Evans, A. D., & Lee, K. (2011). Verbal deception from late childhood to middle adolescence and its relation to executive functioning skills. *Developmental Psychology, 47,* 1108–1116.

Evans, A. B., Banerjee, M., Meyer, R., Aldana, A., Foust, M., & Rowley, S. (2012). Racial Socialization as a Mechanism for Positive Development Among African American Youth. *Child Development Perspectives, 6,* 251–257.

Evans, E., Schweingruber, H., & Stevenson, H. W. (2002). Gender differences in interest and knowledge acquisition: The United States, Taiwan, and Japan. *Sex Roles, 47,* 153–167.

Evans, G. W. & Fuller-Rowell, T. E. (2013). Childhood poverty, chronic stress, and young adult working memory: the protective role of self-regulatory capacity. *Developmental Science, 16,* 688–696.

Evans, G. W., & Kim, P. (2012). Childhood poverty and young adults' allostatic load: The mediating role of childhood cumulative risk exposure. *Psychological Science, 23,* 979–983.

Eveleth, P., & Tanner, J. (1990). *Worldwide variation in human growth* (2nd ed.). New York: Cambridge University Press.

Everett, S. A., Warren, C. W., Santelli, J. S., Kann, L., Collins, J. L., & Kolbe, L. J. (2000). Use of birth control pills, condoms, and withdrawal among U.S. high school students. *Journal of Adolescent Health, 27,* 112–118.

Exner-Cortens, D. (2014). Theory and teen dating violence victimization: Considering adolescent development. *Developmental Review, 34,* 168–188.

Eyre, S., & Millstein, S. (1999). What leads to sex? Adolescent preferred partners and reasons for sex. *Journal of Research on Adolescence, 9,* 277–307.

Facchin, F., Margola, D., Molgora, S., & Revenson, T. A. (2014). Effects of benefit-focused versus standard expressive writing on adolescents' self-concept during the high school transition. *Journal of Research on Adolescence, 24,* 131–144.

Fagot, B., Pears, K., Capaldi, D., Crosby, L., & Leve, C. (1998). Becoming an adolescent father: Precursors and parenting. *Developmental Psychology, 34,* 1209–1219.

Faircloth, B. (2009). Making the most of adolescence: Harnessing the search for identity to understand classroom belonging. *Journal of Adolescent Research, 24,* 321–348.

Falk, E. B., Cascio, C. N., O'Donnell, M. B., Carp, J., Tinney, F. J. Jr., Bingham, C. R., Shope, J. T., Ouimet, M. C., Paradhan, A. K., & Simons-Morton, B. G. (2014). Neural responses to exclusion predict susceptibility to social influence. *Journal of Adolescent Health, 54,* S22–S31.

Falk, R., & Wilkening, F. (1998). Children's construction of fair chances: Adjusting probabilities. *Developmental Psychology, 34,* 1340–1357.

Fallon, B. J., & Bowles, T. V. (1997). The effect of family structure and family functioning on adolescents' perceptions of intimate time spent with parents, siblings, and peers. *Journal of Youth and Adolescence, 26,* 25–43.

Fang, X., Stanton, B., Li, X., Feigelman, S., & Baldwin, R. (1998). Similarities in sexual activity and condom use among friends within groups before and after a risk-reduction intervention. *Youth and Society, 29,* 431–450.

Fanti, K., & Kimonis, E. R. (2012). Bullying and victimization: The role of conduct problems and psychopathic traits. *Journal of Research on Adolescence, 22,* 617–631.

Fanti, K., Brookmeyer, K., Henrich, C., & Kuperminc, G. (2009). Aggressive behavior and quality of friendships. *Journal of Early Adolescence, 29,* 826–838.

Farb, A., & Matjasko, J. (2012). Recent advances in research on school-based extracurricular activities and adolescent development. *Developmental Review, 32,* 1–48.

Farhat, T., Simons-Morton, B. G., Kokkevi, A., Van der Sluijs, W., Fotiou, A., & Kuntsche, E. (2012). Early adolescent and peer drinking homogeneity: Similarities and differences among European and North American countries. *The Journal of Early Adolescence, 32,* 81–103.

Farkas, G., Grobe, R., & Shuan, Y. (1990). Cultural resources and school success: Gender, ethnicity, and poverty groups within an urban school district. *American Sociological Review, 55,* 127–142.

Farkas, G., Lleras, C., & Maczuga, S. (2002). Does oppositional culture exist in minority and poverty peer groups? *American Sociological Review, 67,* 148–155.

Farley, J. P., & Kim-Spoon, J. (2014). The development of adolescent self-regulation: Reviewing the role of parent, peer, friend, and romantic relationships. *Journal of Adolescence, 37,* 433–440.

Farmer, T. W., Estell, D. B., Bishop, J. L., O'Neal, K. K., & Cairns, B. D. (2003). Rejected bullies or popular leaders? The social relations of aggressive subtypes of rural African American early adolescents. *Developmental Psychology, 39,* 992–1004.

Farmer, T. W., Hamm, J. V., Leung, M.-C., Lambert, K., & Gravelle, M. (2011). Early adolescent peer ecologies in rural communities: Bullying in schools that do and do not have a transition during the middle grades. *Journal of Youth and Adolescence, 40,* 1106–1117.

Farrell, A. D., & Sullivan, T. (2004). Impact of witnessing violence on growth curves for problem behaviors among early adolescents in urban and rural settings. *Journal of Community Psychology, 32,* 505–525.

Farrell, A. D., & White, K. S. (1998). Peer influences and drug use among urban adolescents: Family structure and parent–adolescent relationship as protective factors. *Journal of Consulting and Clinical Psychology, 66,* 248–258.

Farrell, A. D., Erwin, E. H., Allison, K. W., Meyer, A., Sullivan, T., Camou, S., ... Esposito, L. (2007). Problematic situations in the lives of urban African American middle school students: A qualitative study. *Journal of Research on Adolescence, 17,* 413–454.

Farrell, A. D., Mehari, K. R., Kramer-Kuhn., A., & Goncy, E. A. (2014). The impact of victimization and witnessing violence on physical aggression among high-risk adolescents. *Child Development, 85,* 1694–1710.

Farrell, A. D., Sullivan, T. N., Esposito, L. E., Meyer, A. L., & Valois, R. F. (2005). A latent growth curve analysis of the structure of aggression, drug use, and delinquent behaviors and their interrelations over time in urban and rural adolescents. *Journal of Research on Adolescence, 15,* 179–203.

Farrell, A. D., Mays, S., Bettencourt, A., Erwin, E., Vullin-Reynolds, M., & Allision, K. (2010). Environmental influences on fighting versus nonviolent behavior in peer situations: A qualitative study with urban African American adolescents. *American Journal of Community Psychology, 46,* 19–35.

Farrelly, M. C., Davis, K. C., Haviland, M. L., Healton, C. G., & Messeri, P. (2005). Evidence of a dose-response relationship between "truth" antismoking ads and youth smoking prevalence. *American Journal of Public Health, 95,* 425–431.

Farrington, D. (2009). Conduct disorder, aggression, and delinquency. In R. Lerner & L. Steinberg (Eds.), *Handbook of adolescent psychology* (3rd ed., Vol. 1, pp. 683–722). New York: Wiley.

Farrington, D., Loeber, R., & Stouthamer-Loeber, M. (2003). How can the relationship between race and violence be explained? In D. Hawkins (Ed.), *Violent crimes: Assessing race and ethnic differences* (pp. 213–237). New York: Cambridge University Press.

Farruggia S. P., Bullen, P., & Davidson, J. (2013). Important nonparental adults as an academic resource for youth. *The Journal of Early Adolescence, 33,* 498–522.

Fasick, F. (1994). On the "invention" of adolescence. *Journal of Early Adolescence, 14,* 6–23.

Fasula, A. M., & Miller, K. S. (2006). African-American and Hispanic adolescents' intentions to delay first intercourse: Parental communication as a buffer for sexually active peers. *Journal of Adolescent Health, 38,* 193–200.

Fauth, R. C., Leventhal, T., & Brooks-Gunn, J. (2007). Welcome to the neighborhood? Long-term impacts of moving to low-poverty neighborhoods on poor children's and adolescents' outcomes. *Journal of Research on Adolescence, 17,* 249–284.

Fauth, R. C., Roth, J. L., & Brooks-Gunn, J. (2007). Does the neighborhood context alter the link between youth's after-school time activities and developmental outcomes? A multilevel analysis. *Developmental Psychology, 43,* 760–777.

Federal Bureau of Investigation. (2009). *Crime in the United States, 2008.* Washington, DC: Author.

Federal Interagency Forum on Child and Family Statistics. (2005). *America's children.* Washington: Author.

Feinberg, I., & Campbell, I. (2010). Sleep EEG changes during adolescence: An index of a fundamental brain reorganization. *Brain and Cognition, 72,* 56–65.

Feinberg, M. E., & Hetherington, E. (2000). Sibling differentiation in adolescence: Implications for behavioral genetic theory. *Child Development, 71,* 1512–1524.

Feinberg, M. E., Howe, G. W., Reiss, D., & Hetherington, E. (2000). Relationship between perceptual differences of parenting and adolescent antisocial behavior and depressive symptoms. *Journal of Family Psychology, 14,* 531–555.

Feinberg, M., McHale, S., Crouter, A., & Cumsille, P. (2003). Sibling differentation: Sibling and parent relationship trajectories in adolescence. *Child Development, 74,* 1261–1274.

Feinberg, M., Neiderhiser, J., Simmens, S., Reiss, D., & Hetherington, E. (2000). Sibling comparison of differential parental treatment in adolescence: Gender, self-esteem, and emotionality as mediators of the parenting-adjustment association. *Child Development, 71,* 1611–1628.

Feiring, C. (1993, March). *Developing concepts of romance from 15 to 18 years.* Paper presented at the biennial meetings of the Society for Research in Child Development, New Orleans.

Feiring, C. (1999). Gender identity and the development of romantic relationships in adolescence. In W. Furman, B. Brown, & C. Feiring (Eds.), *Contemporary perspectives on adolescent romantic relationships* (pp. 211–232). New York: Cambridge University Press.

Feiring, C., & Lewis, M. (1991). The transition from middle childhood to early adolescence: Sex differences in the social network and perceived self-competence. *Sex Roles, 24,* 489–510.

Feiring, C., & Lewis, M. (1993). Do mothers know their teenagers' friends? Implications for individuation in early adolescence. *Journal of Youth and Adolescence, 22,* 337–354.

Feldman, A. F., & Matjasko, J. L. (2007). Profiles and portfolios of adolescent school-based extracurricular activity participation. *Journal of Adolescence, 30,* 313–332.

Feldman, S., & Fisher, L. (1997). The effect of parents' marital satisfaction on young adults' adaptation: A longitudinal study. *Journal of Research on Adolescence, 7,* 55–80.

Feldman, S., & Gehring, T. (1988). Changing perceptions of family cohesion and power across adolescence. *Child Development, 59,* 1034–1045.

Feldman, S., & Quatman, T. (1988). Factors influencing age expectations for adolescent autonomy: A study of early adolescents and parents. *Journal of Early Adolescence, 8,* 325–343.

Feldman, S., & Rosenthal, D. (2000). The effect of communication characteristics on family members' perceptions of parents as sex educators. *Journal of Research on Adolescence, 10,* 119–150.

Felix, E., & You, S. (2011). Peer victimization within the ethnic context of high school. *Journal of Community Psychology, 39,* 860–875.

Felner, R., Brand, S., DuBois, D., Adan, A., Mulhall, P., & Evans, E. (1995). Socioeconomic disadvantage, proximal environmental experiences, and socioemotional and academic adjustment in early adolescence: Investigation of a mediated effects model. *Child Development, 66,* 774–792.

Felson, R. B., Savolainen, J., Bjarnason, T., Anderson, A. L., & Zohra, I. T. (2011). The cultural context of adolescent drinking and violence in 30 European countries. *Criminology, 49,* 699–728.

Felton, J. W., Kofler, M. J., Lopez, C. M., Saunders, B. E., & Kilpatrick, D. G. (2015). The emergence of co-occurring adolescent polysubstance use and depressive symptoms: A latent growth modeling approach. *Development and Psychopathology, FirstView Articles.* DOI: 10.1017/S0954579414001473

Fenzel, L. (2001). Prospective study of changes in global self-worth and strain during the transition to middle school. *Journal of Early Adolescence, 20,* 93–116.

Fergus, S., Zimmerman, M. A., & Caldwell, C. H. (2007). Growth trajectories of sexual risk behavior in adolescence and young adulthood. *American Journal of Public Health, 97,* 1096–1101.

Ferguson, C. (2011). Video games and youth violence: A prospective analysis in adolescents. *Journal of Youth and Adolescence, 40,* 377–391.

Ferguson, C., & Kilburn, J. (2009). The public health risks of media violence: A meta-analytic review. *Journal of Pediatrics, 154,* 759–763.

Ferguson, C.J. (2013). Violent video games and the Supreme Court: Lessons for the scientific community in the wake of Brown v. Entertainment Merchants Association. *American Psychologist, 68,* 57–74.

Ferguson, C. J., & Olson, C. K. (2014). Video game violence use among "vulnerable" populations: the impact of violent games on delinquency and bullying among children with clinically elevated depression or attention deficit symptoms. *Journal of Youth & Adolescence, 43,* 127–136.

Ferguson, C. J., Garza, A., Jerabeck, J., Ramos, R., Galindo, M. (2013). Not woth the fuss after all? Cross-sectional and prospective data on violent video game influences on aggression, visuospatial cognition and mathematics ability in a sample of youth. *Journal of Youth & Adolescence, 42,* 109–122.

Ferguson, Y., Kasser, T., & Jahng, S. (2011). Differences in life satisfaction and school satisfaction among adolescents from three nations: The role of perceived autonomy support. *Journal of Research on Adolescence, 21,* 649–661.

Fergusson, D., & Horwood, L. (2002). Male and female offending trajectories. *Development and Psychopathology, 14,* 159–177.

Fergusson, D., & Lynskey, M. (1996). Alcohol misuse and adolescent sexual behaviors and risk taking. *Pediatrics, 98,* 91–96.

Fergusson, D., & Woodward, L. (2000). Teenage pregnancy and female educational under-achievement: A prospective study of a New Zealand birth cohort. *Journal of Marriage and the Family, 62,* 147–161.

Fergusson, D., Lynskey, M., & Horwood, L. (1996). Factors associated with continuity and changes in disruptive behavior patterns between childhood and adolescence. *Journal of Abnormal Child Psychology, 24,* 533–553.

Ferrar, K., Chang, C., Li, M., & Olds, T. S. (2013). Adolescent time use clusters: A systematic review. *Journal of Adolescent Health, 52,* 259–270.

Ferreira, P. D., Azevedo, C. N., & Menezes, I. (2012). The developmental quality of participation experiences: Beyond the rhetoric that "participation is always good!" *Journal of Adolescence, 35,* 599–610.

Ferreiro, F., Seoane, G., & Senra, C. (2014). Toward understanding the role of body dissatisfaction in the gender differences in depressive symptoms and disordered eating: A longitudinal study during adolescence. *Journal of Adolescence, 37,* 73–84.

Ferreiro, F., Seoane, G., Senra, C. (2012). Gender-related risk and protective factors for depressive symptoms and disordered eating in adolescence: a 4-year longitudinal study. *Journal of Youth & Adolescence, 41,* 607–622.

Ferreiro, F., Wichstrøm, L., Seoane, G., & Senra, C. (2014). Reciprocal associations between depressive symptoms and disordered eating among adolescent girls and boys: A multiwave, prospective study. *Journal of Abnormal Child Psychology, 42,* 803–812.

Ferrer, E., Whitaker, K. J., Steele, J. S., Green, C. T., Wendelken, C., & Bunge, S. A. (2013). White matter maturation supports the development of reasoning ability through its influence on processing speed. *Developmental Science, 16,* 941–951.

Fichtenberg, C. M., & Glantz, S. A. (2002). Youth access interventions do not affect youth smoking. *Pediatrics, 109,* 1088–1092.

Field, T., Greenwald, P., Morrow, C., Healy, B., Foster, T., . . . Guthertz, M. (1992). Behavior state matching during interactions of preadolescent friends versus acquaintances. *Developmental Psychology, 28,* 242–250.

Fields, J. (2003). *Children's living arrangements and characteristics: March 2002.* Current Population Reports P20–547. Washington, DC: U.S. Census Bureau.

Figner, B., & Weber, E. (2011). Who takes risks when and why?: Determinants of risk taking. *Current Directions in Psychological Science, 20,* 211–216.

Filardo, E. (1996). Gender patterns in African American and White adolescents' social interactions in same-race, mixed-gender groups. *Journal of Personality and Social Psychology, 71,* 71–82.

Fincham, F. (1994). Understanding the association between marital conflict and child adjustment: Overview. *Journal of Family Psychology, 8,* 123–127.

Fine, S. M. (2014). "A slow revolution": Toward a theory of intellectual playfulness in high school classrooms. *Harvard Educational Review, 84,* 1–23, 134–135.

Finer, L. B. (2010). Unintended pregnancy among U.S. adolescents: Accounting for sexual activity. *Journal of Adolescent Health, 47,* 312–314.

Finer, L. B., & Philbin, J. M. (2013). Sexual initiation, contraceptive use, and pregnancy among young adolescents. *Pediatrics, 131,* 886–891.

Fingerson, L. (2005). Do mother's opinions matter in teens' sexual activity? *Journal of Family Influence, 26,* 947–974.

Finken, L., & Jacobs, J. (1996). Consultant choice across decision contexts: Are abortion decisions different? *Journal of Adolescent Research, 11,* 235–260.

Finkenauer, C., Engles, R., & Meeus, W. (2002). Keeping secrets from parents: Advantages and disadvantages of secrecy in adolescence. *Journal of Youth and Adolescence, 31,* 123–136.

Finn, A. S., Kraft, M. A., West, M. R., Leonard, J. A., Bish, C. E., Martin, R. E., Sheridan, M. A., Gabrieli, C. F., & Gabrieli, J. D. (2014). Cognitive skills, student achievement test, and schools. *Psychological Science, 25,* 736–744.

Finn, A., Sheridan, M., Kam, C., Hinshaw, S., & D'Esposito, M. (2010). Longitudinal evidence for functional specialization of the neural circuit supporting working memory in the human brain. *Journal of Neuroscience, 30(33),* 11062–11067.

Finn, J., Gerber, S. B., & Boyd-Zaharias, J. (2005). Small classes in the early grades, academic achievement, and graduating from high school. *Journal of Educational Psychology, 97,* 214–223.

Fischhoff, B., & Quadrel, M. (1995). Adolescent alcohol decisions. In G. Boyd, J. Howard, & R. Zucker (Eds.), *Alcohol problems among adolescents: Current directions in prevention research* (pp. 59–84). Hillsdale, NJ: Erlbaum.

Fischhoff, B., de Bruin, W. B., Parker, A., Millstein, S., & Halpern-Felsher, B. (2010). Adolescents' perceived risk of dying. *Journal of Adolescent Health, 46,* 265–269.

Fisher, C., Wallace, S. A., & Fenton, R. E. (2000). Discrimination distress during adolescence. *Journal of Youth and Adolescence, 29,* 679–695.

Fisher, M., Golden, N., Katzman, D., Kriepe, R., Rees, J., Schebendach, J., . . . Hoberman, H. (1995). Eating disorders in adolescents: A background paper. *Journal of Adolescent Health, 16,* 420–437.

Fisher, P., Stoolmiller, M., Mannering, A., Takahashi, A., & Chamberlain, P. (2011). Foster placement disruptions associated with problem behavior: Mitigating a threshold effect. *Journal of Consulting and Clinical Psychology, 79,* 481–487.

Fisher, S., Reynolds, J. L., Hsu, W. W., Barnes, J., & Tyler, K. (2014). Examining multiracial youth in context: ethnic identity development and mental health outcomes. *Journal of Youth & Adolescence, 43,* 1688–1699.

Fite, P. J., Wynn, P., & Pardini, D. A. (2009). Explaining discrepancies in arrest rates between Black and White male juveniles. *Journal of Consulting and Clinical Psychology, 77,* 916–927.

Fitzpatrick, K. M., Dulin, A., & Piko, B. (2010). Bullying and depressive symptomatology among low-income, African–American youth. *Journal of Youth and Adolescence, 39,* 634–645.

Flamm, E. S., & Grolnick, W. S. (2013). Adolescent adjustment in the context of life change: The supportive role of parental structure provision. *Journal of Adolescence, 36,* 899–912.

Flammer, A., Alasker, F., & Noack, P. (1999). Time use by adolescents in an international perspective, I: The case of leisure activities. In F. Alasker & A. Flammer (Eds.), *The adolescent experience: European and American adolescents in the 1990s* (pp. 33–60). Hillsdale, NJ: Erlbaum.

Flanagan, C. (2004). Volunteerism, leadership, political socialization, and civic engagement. In R. Lerner & L. Steinberg (Eds.), *Handbook of adolescent psychology.* New York: Wiley.

Flanagan, C. A., Kim, T., Collura, J., & Kopish, M. A. (2015). Community service and adolescents' social capital. *Journal of Research on Adolescence, 25,* 295–309.

Flanagan, C. A., Kim, T., Pykett, A., Finlay, A., Gallay, E. E., & Pancer, M. (2014). Adolescents' theories about economic inequality: Why are some people poor while others are rich? *Developmental Psychology, 50,* 2512–2525.

Flanagan, C., & Galay, L. (1995). Reframing the meaning of "political" in research with adolescents. *Perspectives on Political Science, 24,* 34–41.

Flanagan, C., & Stout, M. (2010). Developmental patterns of social trust between early and late adolescence: Age and school climate effects. *Journal of Research on Adolescence, 20,* 748–773.

Flanagan, C., & Tucker, C. (1999). Adolescents' explanations for political issues: Concordance with their views of self and society. *Developmental Psychology, 35,* 1198–1209.

Flanagan, C., & Wray-Lake, L. (2011). Civic and political engagement. In B. Brown & M. Prinstein (Eds.), *Encyclopedia of adolescence* (Vol. 2, pp. 35–43). New York: Academic Press.

Flannery, D., Torquati, J., & Lindemeier, L. (1994). The method and meaning of emotional expression and experience during adolescence. *Journal of Adolescent Research, 9,* 8–27.

Flannery, D., Vazsonyi, A., & Rowe, D. (1996). Caucasian and Hispanic early adolescent substance use: Parenting, personality, and school adjustment. *Journal of Early Adolescence, 16,* 71–89.

Flannery, D., Weseter, K., & Singer, M. (2004). Impact of exposure to violence in school on child and adolescent mental health and behavior. *Journal of Community Psychology, 32,* 559–573.

Flashman, J. (2012). Academic achievement and its impact on friend dynamics. *Sociology of Education, 85,* 61–80.

Flavell, J., Green, F., & Flavell, E. (1998). The mind has a mind of its own: Developing knowledge about mental uncontrollability. *Cognitive Development, 13,* 127–138.

Fletcher, A., Bonell, C., & Hargreaves, J. (2008). School effects on young people's drug use: A systematic review of intervention and observational studies. *Journal of Adolescent Health, 42,* 209–220.

Fletcher, A., Darling, N., Steinberg, L., & Dornbusch, S. (1995). The company they keep: Relation of adolescents' adjustment and behavior to their friends' perceptions of authoritative parenting in the social network. *Developmental Psychology, 31,* 300–310.

Fletcher, A., Elder, G., Jr., & Mekos, D. (2000). Parental influences on adolescent involvement in community activities. *Journal of Research on Adolescence, 10,* 29–48.

Fletcher, A., Fitzgerald-Yau, N., Jones, R., Allen, E., Viner, R. M., & Bonell, C. (2014). Brief report: Cyberbullying perpetration and its associations with socio-demographics, aggressive behaviour at school, and mental health outcomes. *Journal of Adolescence, 37,* 1393–1398.

Fletcher, A., Steinberg, L., & Williams-Wheeler, M. (2004). Parental influences on adolescent problem-behavior: Revisiting Stattin and Kerr. *Child Development, 75,* 781–796.

Flieller, A. (1999). Comparison of the development of formal thought in adolescent cohorts aged 10 to 15 years (1967–1996 and 1972–1993). *Developmental Psychology, 35,* 1048–1058.

Flisher, A. J., Kramer, R. A., Hoven, C. W., King, R. A., Bird, H. R., Davies, M., . . . Shaffer, D. (2000). Risk behavior in a community sample of children and adolescents. *Journal of the American Academy of Child and Adolescent Psychiatry, 39,* 881–887.

Flook, L. (2011). Gender differences in adolescents' daily interpersonal events and well-being. *Child Development, 82,* 454–461

Flook, L., & Fuligni, A. J. (2008). Family and school spillover in adolescents' daily lives. *Child Development, 79,* 776–787.

Flory, K., Lynam, D., & Milich, R. (2004). Early adolescent through young adult alcohol and marijuana use trajectories: Early predictors, young adult outcomes, and predictive utility. *Development and Psychopathology, 16,* 193–213.

Flynn, B., Worden, J., Secker-Walker, R., Pirie, P., Badger, G., Carpenter, J., & Geller, B. (1994). Mass media and school interventions for cigarette smoking prevention: Effects 2 years after completion. *American Journal of Public Health, 84,* 1148–1150.

Flynn, M., & Rudolph, K. (2011). Depression and depressive disorders. In B. Brown & M. Prinstein (Eds.), *Encyclopedia of adolescence* (Vol. 3, pp. 127–135). New York: Academic Press.

Fomby, P., & Bosick, S. J. (2013). Family instability and the transition to adulthood. *Journal of Marriage and Family, 75,* 1266–1287.

Fontaine, R. G., Yang, C., Burks, V. S., Dodge, K. A., Price, J. M., Pettit, G. S., & Bates, J. E. (2009). Loneliness as a partial mediator of the relation between low social preference in childhood and anxious/depressed symptoms in adolescence. *Development and Psychopathology, 21,* 479.

Fontaine, R., Yang, C., Dodge, K., Bates, J., & Pettit, G. (2008). Testing an individual systems model of response evaluation and decision (RED) and antisocial behavior across adolescence. *Child Development, 79,* 462–475.

Forbes, E. E., Phillips, M. L., Silk, J. S., Ryan, N. D., & Dahl, R. E. (2011). Neural systems of threat processing in adolescents: Role of pubertal maturation and relation to measures of negative affect. *Developmental Neuropsychology, 36,* 429–452.

Forbes, E., & Dahl, R. (2010). Pubertal development and behavior: Hormonal activation of social and motivational tendencies. *Brain and Cognition, 72,* 66–72.

Forbes, E., Ryan, N., Phillips, M., Manuck, S., Worthman, C. M., Moyles, D. L., . . . Dahl, R. (2010). Healthy adolescents' neural response to reward: Associations with puberty, positive affect, and depressive symptoms. *Journal of the American Academy of Child and Adolescent Psychiatry, 49,* 162–172.

Ford, D., & Harris, J. I. (1996). Perceptions and attitudes of Black students toward school, achievement, and other educational variables. *Child Development, 67,* 1141–1152.

Ford, J. A. (2009). Nonmedical prescription drug use among adolescents: The influence of bonds to family and school. *Youth and Society, 40,* 336–352.

Ford, K. R., Hurd, N. M., Jagers, R. J., & Sellers, R. M. (2013). Caregiver experiences of discrimination and African American adolescents' psychological health over time. *Child Development, 84,* 485–499.

Fordham, C., & Ogbu, J. (1986). Black students' school success: Coping with the burden of "acting White." *Urban Review, 18,* 176–206.

Forehand, R., Biggar, H., & Kotchick, B. (1998). Cumulative risk across family stressors: Short- and long-term effects for adolescents. *Journal of Abnormal Child Psychology, 26,* 119–128.

Forehand, R., Neighbors, B., Devine, D., & Armistead, L. (1994). Interparental conflict and parental divorce: The individual, relative, and interactive effects on adolescents across four years. *Family Relations, 43,* 387–393.

Forest, A. L., & Wood, J. V. (2012). When social networking is not working: Individuals with low self-esteem recognize but do not reap the benefits of self-disclosure on Facebook. *Psychological Science, 23,* 295–302.

Forgatch, M., DeGarmo, D., & Knutson, N. (1994, February). *Transitions within transitions: The impact of adolescence and family structure on boys' antisocial behavior.* Paper presented at the biennial meetings of the Society for Research on Adolescence, San Diego.

Forgatch, M., Patterson, G. R., Degarmo, D. S., & Beldavs, Z. G. (2009). Testing the Oregon delinquency model with 9-year follow-up of the Oregon Divorce Study. *Development and Psychopathology, 21,* 637–660.

Forhan, S., Gottlieb, S., Sternberg, M., Xu, F., Datta, S., McQuillan, G., . . . Markowitz, L. (2009). Prevalence of sexually transmitted infections among female adolescents aged 14 to 19 in the United States. *Pediatrics, 124,* 1505–1512.

Fortner, M., Crouter, A., & McHale, S. (2004). Is parents' work involvement responsive to the quality of relationships with adolescent offspring? *Journal of Family Psychology, 19,* 530–538.

Fortuin, J., van Geel, M., Vedder, P. (2015). Peer influences on internalizing and externalizing problems among adolescents: a longitudinal social network analysis. *Journal of Youth & Adolescence, 44,* 887–897.

Fosco, G. M., & Feinberg, M. E. (2015). Cascading effects of interparental conflict in adolescence: Linking threat appraisals, self-efficacy, and adjustment. *Development and Psychopathology, 27,* 239–252.

Fosco, G., & Grych, J. (2010). Adolescent triangulation into parental conflicts: Longitudinal implications for appraisals and adolescent-parent relations. *Journal of Marriage and Family, 72,* 254–266.

Foshee, V. A., McNaughton Reyes, H. L., Vivolo-Kantor, A. M., Basile, K. C., Chang, L. Y., Faris, R., & Ennett, S. T. (2014). Bullying as a longitudinal predictor of adolescent dating violence. *Journal of Adolescent Health, 55,* 439–444.

Foshee, V., Bauman, K., Greene, W., Koch, G., Linder, G., & MacDougall, J. (2000). The safe dates program: 1-year follow-up results. *American Journal of Public Health, 90,* 1619–1622.

Foshee, V., Benefield, T., Suchindran, C., Ennett, S. T., Bauman, K. E., Karriker-Jaffe, K., … Mathias, J. (2009). The development of four types of adolescent dating abuse and selected demographic correlates. *Journal of Research on Adolescence, 19,* 380–400.

Foshee, V. A., Benefield, T. S., Reyes, H. L., Ennett, S. T., Faris, R., Chang, L. Y., Hussong, A., & Suchindran, C. M. (2013). The peer context and the development of the perpetration of adolescent dating violence. *Journal of Youth & Adolescence, 42,* 471–486.

Foss, R. D., & Goodwin, A. H. (2014). Distracted driver behaviors and distracting conditions among adolescent drivers: findings from a naturalistic driving study. *Journal of Adolescent Health, 54,* S50–S60.

Fowler, P., Ahmed, S., Tompsett, C., Jozefowicz-Simbeni, D., & Toro, P. (2008). Community violence and externalizing problems: Moderating effects of race and religiosity in emerging adulthood. *Journal of Community Psychology, 36,* 835–850.

Fowler, P., Tompsett, C., Braciszewski, J., Jacques-Tiura, A., & Baltes, B. (2010). Community violence: a meta-analysis on the effect of exposure and mental health outcomes of children and adolescents. *Development and Psychopathology, 21,* 227–259.

Fowler, P., Toro, P., & Miles, B. (2009). Pathways to and from homelessness and associated psychosocial outcomes among adolescents leaving the foster care system. *American Journal of Public Health, 99,* 1453–1458.

Frabutt, J. M., Walker, A. M., & MacKinnon-Lewis, C. (2002). Racial socialization messages and the quality of mother/child interactions in African American families. *Journal of Early Adolescence, 22,* 200–217.

Fraley, R. C., Roisman, G. I., Booth-LaForce, C., Owen, M. T., & Holland, A. S. (2013). Interpersonal and genetic origins of adult attachment styles: A longitudinal study from infancy to early adulthood. *Journal of Personality and Social Psychology, 104,* 817–838.

Francisco, R., Espinoza, P., González, M. L., Penelo, E., Mora, M., Rosés, R., & Raich, R. M. (2015). Body dissatisfaction and disordered eating among Portuguese and Spanish adolescents: The role of individual characteristics and internalization of sociocultural ideals. *Journal of Adolescence, 41,* 7–16.

Francois, S., Overstreet, S., & Cunningham, M. (2012). Where we live: The unexpected influence of urban neighborhoods on the academic performance of African American adolescents. *Youth & Society, 44,* 307–328.

Frank, K. A., Muller, C., Schiller, K. S., Riegle-Crumb, C., Mueller, A. S., Crosnoe, R., & Pearson, J. (2008). The social dynamics of mathematics coursetaking in high school. *American Journal of Sociology, 113,* 1645–1696.

Frank, S., & Jackson, S. (1996). Family experiences as moderators of the relationship between eating symptoms and personality disturbance. *Journal of Youth and Adolescence, 25,* 55–72.

Frank, S., Pirsch, L., & Wright, V. (1990). Late adolescents' perceptions of their relationships with their parents: Relationships among de-idealization, autonomy, relatedness, and insecurity and implications for adolescent adjustment and ego identity status. *Journal of Youth and Adolescence, 19,* 571–588.

Frankenberger, K. D. (2000). Adolescent egocentrism: A comparison among adolescents and adults. *Journal of Adolescence, 23,* 343–354.

Franzoi, S., Davis, M., & Vasquez-Suson, K. (1994). Two social worlds: Social correlates and stability of adolescent status groups. *Journal of Personality and Social Psychology, 67,* 462–473.

Fredricks, J. A., & Eccles, J. (2002). Children's competence and value beliefs from childhood through adolescence: Growth trajectories in two male-sex-typed domains. *Developmental Psychology, 38,* 519–533.

Fredricks, J. A., & Eccles, J. (2008). Participation in extracurricular activities in the middle school years: Are there developmental benefits for African American and European American youth? *Journal of Youth and Adolescence, 37,* 1029–1043.

Fredricks, J., & Eccles, J. S. (2010). Breadth of extracurricular participation and adolescent adjustment among African American and European American youth. *Journal of Research on Adolescence, 20,* 307–333.

Fredricks, J. A., & Simpkins, S. D. (2012). promoting positive youth development through organized after-school activities: Taking a closer look at participation of ethnic minority youth. *Child Development Perspectives, 6,* 280–287.

Fredriksen, K., Rhodes, J., Reddy, R., & Way, N. (2004). Sleepless in Chicago: Tracking the effects of adolescent sleep loss during the middle school years. *Child Development, 75,* 84–95.

Fredstrom, B. K., Adams, R. E., & Gilman, R. (2011). Electronic and school-based victimization: Unique contexts for adjustment difficulties during adolescence. *Journal of Youth and Adolescence, 40,* 405–415.

Freedner, N., Freed, L. H., Yang, Y., & Austin, S. (2002). Dating violence among gay, lesbian, and bisexual adolescents: Results from a community survey. *Journal of Adolescent Health, 31,* 469–474.

Freeman, H., & Brown, B. (2001). Primary attachment to parents and peers during adolescence: Differences by attachment style. *Journal of Youth and Adolescence, 30,* 653–674.

French, D. C., Christ, S., Lu, T., & Purwono, U. (2014). Trajectories of Indonesian adolescents' religiosity, problem behavior, and friends' religiosity: Covariation and sequences. *Child Development, 85,* 1634–1646.

French, D. C., Eisenberg, N., Vaughan, J., Purwono, U., & Suryanti, T. A. (2008). Religious involvement and the social competence and adjustment of Indonesian Muslim adolescents. *Developmental Psychology, 44,* 597–611.

French, D. C., Jansen, E., & Pidada, S. (2002). United States and Indonesian children's and adolescents' reports of relational aggression by disliked peers. *Child Development, 73,* 1143–1150.

French, D. C., Purwono, U., & Rodkin, P. C. (2012). Religiosity of adolescents and their friends and network associates: Homophily and associations with antisocial behavior. *Journal of Research on Adolescence, 22,* 326–332.

French, D. C., Purwono, U., & Triwahyuni, A. (2011). Friendship and the religiosity of Indonesian Muslim adolescents. *Journal of Youth and Adolescence, 40,* 1623–1633.

French, D. C., Rianasari, M., Pidada, S., Nelwan, P., & Buhrmester, D. (2001). Social support of Indonesian and U.S. children and adolescents by family members and friends. *Merrill-Palmer Quarterly, 47,* 377–394.

French, D., & Conrad, J. (2001). School dropout as predicted by peer rejection and antisocial behavior. *Journal of Research on Adolescence, 11,* 225–244.

French, D., & Dishion, T. (2003). Predictors of early initiation of sexual intercourse among high-risk adolescents. *Journal of Early Adolescence, 23,* 295–315.

French, D., Conrad, J., & Turner, T. (1995). Adjustment of antisocial and nonantisocial rejected adolescents. *Development and Psychopathology, 7,* 857–874.

French, S. E., Seidman, E., Allen, L., & Aber, J. L. (2006). The development of ethnic identity during adolescence. *Developmental Psychology, 42,* 1–10.

French, S., Story, M., Downes, B., Resnick, M., & Blum, R. (1995). Frequent dieting among adolescents: Psychosocial and health behavior correlates. *American Journal of Public Health, 85,* 695–701.

Frenzel, A. C., Goetz, T., Pekrun, R., & Watt, H. M. G. (2010). Development of mathematics interest in adolescence: Influences of gender, family, and school context. *Journal of Research on Adolescence, 20,* 507–537.

Freud, A. (1958). Adolescence. *Psychoanalytic Study of the Child, 13,* 255–278.

Freud, S. (1938). *An outline of psychoanalysis.* London: Hogarth Press.

Frey, S., Balu, S., Greusing, S., Rothen, N., & Cajochen, C. (2009). Consequences of the timing of menarche on female adolescent sleep phase preference. *PLoS ONE, 4,* e5217.

Frey, W. (2012, April 25). Analysis of U.S. Census data. *The Washington Post*. Accessed on June 8, 2012 at http://www.washingtonpost.com/local/an-increasing-number-of-interracial-babies-nationwide/2012/04/25/gIQAzKFohT_graphic.html

Frick, P., & White, S. F. (2008). The importance of callous-unemotional traits for the development of aggressive and antisocial behavior. *Journal of Child Psychology and Psychiatry, 49*, 359–375.

Frick, P., Kotov, R., Loney, B., & Vasey, M. (2005). The latent structure of psychopathy in youth: A taxometric investigation. *Journal of Abnormal Child Psychology, 33*.

Fried, M., & Fried, M. (1980). *Transitions: Four rituals in eight cultures*. New York: Norton.

Friedenberg, E. (1959). *The vanishing adolescent*. Boston: Beacon Press.

Friedenberg, E. (1967). *Coming of age in America*. New York: Vintage Books.

Friedlander, L. J., Connolly, J. A., Pepler, D. J., & Craig, W. M. (2007). Biological, familial, and peer influences on dating in early adolescence. *Archives of Sexual Behavior, 36*, 821–830.

Frijns, T., Finkenauer, C., Vermulst, A. A., & Engels, R. (2005). Keeping secrets from parents: Longitudinal associations of secrecy in adolescence. *Journal of Youth and Adolescence, 34*, 137–148.

Frisch, R. (1983). Fatness, puberty, and fertility: The effects of nutrition and physical training on menarche and ovulation. In J. Brooks-Gunn & A. Petersen (Eds.), *Girls at puberty*. New York: Plenum.

Frisco, M. L. (2005). Parental involvement and young women's contraceptive use. *Journal of Marriage and the Family, 67*, 110.

Frisco, M. L. (2008). Adolescents' sexual behavior and academic attainment. *Sociology of Education, 81*, 284–311.

Frisco, M. L., Muller, C., & Frank, K. (2007). Parents' union dissolution and adolescents' school performance: Comparing methodological approaches. *Journal of Marriage and Family, 69*, 721–741.

Frison, E., & Eggermont, S. (2015). The impact of daily stress on adolescents' depressed mood: The role of social support seeking through Facebook. *Computers in Human Behavior, 44*, 315–325.

Fromme, K., Corbin, W. R., & Kruse, M. I. (2008). Behavioral risks during the transition from high school to college. *Developmental Psychology, 44*, 1497–1504.

Fruiht, V. M., & Wray-Lake, L. (2013). The role of mentor type and timing in predicting educational attainment. *Journal of Youth & Adolescence, 42*, 1459–1472.

Fuhrman, T., & Holmbeck, G. (1995). A contextual-moderator analysis of emotional autonomy and adjustment in adolescence. *Child Development, 66*, 793–811.

Fujimoto, K., Unger, J. B., & Valente, T. W. (2012). A network method of measuring affiliation-based peer influence: Assessing the influences of teammates' smoking on adolescent smoking. *Child Development, 83*, 442–451.

Fuligni, A. (1994, February). *Academic achievement and motivation among Asian-American and European-American early adolescents*. Paper presented at the biennial meetings of the Society for Research on Adolescence, San Diego.

Fuligni, A. (1998). Authority, autonomy, and parent–adolescent conflict and cohesion: A study of adolescents from Mexican, Chinese, Filipino, and European backgrounds. *Developmental Psychology, 34*, 782–792.

Fuligni, A., & Eccles, J. (1993). Perceived parent–child relationships and early adolescents' orientation toward peers. *Developmental Psychology, 29*, 622–632.

Fuligni, A., & Hardway, C. (2006). Daily variation in adolescents' sleep, activities, and psychological well-being. *Journal of Research on Adolescence, 16*, 353–378.

Fuligni, A., & Pedersen, S. (2002). Family obligation and the transition to young adulthood. *Developmental Psychology, 38*, 856–868.

Fuligni, A., & Stevenson, H. (1995). Time-use and mathematics achievement among American, Chinese, and Japanese high school students. *Child Development, 66*, 830–842.

Fuligni, A., & Witkow, M. (2004). The postsecondary educational progress of youth from immigrant families. *Journal of Research on Adolescence, 14*, 159–183.

Fuligni, A., Eccles, J., &, Barber, B. (1995). The long-term effects of seventh grade ability grouping in mathematics. *Journal of Early Adolescence, 15*, 58–89.

Fuligni, A., Eccles, J., Barber, B., & Clements, P. (2001). Early adolescent peer orientation and adjustment during high school. *Developmental Psychology, 37*, 28–36.

Fuligni, A., Hughes, D., & Way, N. (2009). Ethnicity and immigration. In R. Lerner & L. Steinberg (Eds.), *Handbook of adolescent psychology* (3rd ed., Vol. 2, pp. 527–569). New York: Wiley.

Fuligni, A., Kiang, L., Witkow, M., & Baldelomar, O. (2008). Stability and change in ethnic labeling among adolescents from Asian and Latin American immigrant families. *Child Development, 79*, 944–956.

Fuligni, A., Tseng, V., & Lam, M. (1999). Attitudes toward family obligations among American adolescents from Asian, Latin American, and European backgrounds. *Child Development, 70*, 1030–1044.

Fuligni, A., Witkow, M., & Garcia, C. (2005). Ethnic identity and the academic adjustment of adolescents from Mexican, Chinese, and European backgrounds. *Developmental Psychology, 41*, 799–811.

Fuligni, A., Yip, T., & Tseng, V. (2002). The impact of family obligation on the daily activities and psychological well-being of Chinese American adolescents. *Child Development, 73*, 302–314.

Fulkerson, J. A., & French, S. A. (2003). Cigarette smoking for weight loss or control among adolescents: Gender and racial/ethnic differences. *Journal of Adolescent Health, 32*, 306–313.

Furbey, M., & Beyth-Marom, R. (1992). Risk-taking in adolescence: A decision-making perspective. *Developmental Review, 12*, 1–44.

Furman, W., & Buhrmester, D. (1985). Children's perceptions of the personal relationships in their social networks. *Developmental Psychology, 21*, 1016–1024.

Furman, W., & Collibee, C. (2014). A matter of timing: Developmental theories of romantic involvement and psychosocial adjustment. *Development and Psychopathology, 26*, 1149–1160.

Furman, W., & Shomaker, L. B. (2008). Patterns of interaction in adolescent romantic relationships: Distinct features and links to other close relationships. *Journal of Adolescence, 31*, 771–788.

Furman, W., & Simon, V. (1999). Cognitive representations of adolescent romantic relationships. In W. Furman, B. Brown, & C. Feiring (Eds.), *Contemporary perspectives on adolescent romantic relationships* (pp. 75–98). New York: Cambridge University Press.

Furman, W., & Simon, V. (2006). Actor and partner effects of adolescents' romantic working models and styles on interactions with romantic partners. *Child Development, 77*, 588–604.

Furman, W., & Wehner, E. (1994). Romantic views: Toward a theory of adolescent romantic relationships. In R. Montemayor (Ed.), *Advances in adolescent development:* Vol. 3. *Relationships in adolescence* (pp. 168–195). Newbury Park, CA: Sage.

Furman, W., Brown, B., & Feiring, C. (Eds.). (1999). *Contemporary perspectives on adolescent romantic relationships*. New York: Cambridge University Press.

Furman, W., Simon, V., Shaffer, L., & Bouchey, H. A. (2002). Adolescents' working models and styles for relationships with parents, friends, and romantic partners. *Child Development, 73*, 241–255.

Furr-Holden, C., Milam, A., Reynolds, E., MacPherson, L., & Lejuez, C. (2012). Disordered neighborhood environments and risk-taking propensity in late childhood through adolescence. *Journal of Adolescent Health, 50*, 100–102.

Furstenberg, F., Jr. (1990). Coming of age in a changing family system. In S. Feldman & G. Elliott (Eds.), *At the threshold: The developing adolescent* (pp. 147–170). Cambridge, MA: Harvard University Press.

Furstenberg, F., Jr. (1996). *Family management of adolescent success in inner-city Philadelphia*. Paper presented at the biennial meetings of the Society for Research on Adolescence, Boston.

Furstenberg, F., Jr. (2000). The sociology of adolescence and youth in the 1990s: A critical commentary. *Journal of Marriage and Family, 62*, 896–910.

Furstenberg, F., Jr. (2006, March). *Diverging development: The not-so-invisible hand of social class in the United States.* Invited address, Society for Research on Adolescence, San Francisco.

Furstenberg, F., Jr., Brooks-Gunn, J., & Chase-Lansdale, P. L. (1989). Teenaged pregnancy and childbearing. *American Psychologist, 44,* 313–320.

Furstenberg, F., Jr., Cook, T., Eccles, J., Elder, G., Jr., & Sameroff, A. (1999). *Managing to make it: Urban families and adolescent success.* Chicago: University of Chicago Press.

Furstenberg, F., Jr., Morgan, S. P., & Allison, P. (1987b). Paternal participation and children's well-being after marital dissolution. *American Sociological Review, 52,* 695–701.

Furstenberg, F., Jr., Morgan, S. P., Moore, K. A., & Peterson, J. L. (1987a). Race differences in the timing of adolescent intercourse. *American Sociological Review, 52,* 511–518.

Fussell, M., & Greene, M. (2002). Demographic trends affecting youth around the world. In B. Brown, R. Larson, & T. Saraswathi (Eds.), *The world's youth: Adolescence in eight regions of the globe.* New York: Cambridge University Press.

Gage, J. C., Overpeck, M. D., Nansel, T. R., & Kogan, M. D. (2005). Peer activity in the evenings and participation in aggressive and problem behaviors. *Journal of Adolescent Health, 37,* 517.e7–517.e14.

Galambos, N., & Maggs, J. (1991). Out-of-school care of young adolescents and self-reported behavior. *Developmental Psychology, 27,* 644–655.

Galambos, N., Barker, E., & Almeida, D. (2003). Parents do matter: Trajectories of change in externalizing and internalizing problems in adolescence. *Child Development, 74,* 578–594.

Galambos, N., Barker, E., & Krahn, H. (2006). Depression, self-esteem, and anger in emerging adulthood: Seven-year trajectories. *Developmental Psychology, 42,* 350–365.

Galambos, N., Barker, E., & Tilton-Weaver, L. (2003). Who gets caught at maturity gap? A study of pseudomature, immature, and mature adolescents. *International Journal of Behavioral Development, 27,* 253–263.

Galambos, N., Berenbaum, S., & McHale, S. (2009). Gender development in adolescence. In R. Lerner & L. Steinberg (Eds.), *Handbook of adolescent psychology* (3rd ed., Vol. 1, pp. 305–357). New York: Wiley.

Galambos, N., Dalton, A., & Maggs, J. (2009). Losing sleep over it: Daily variation in sleep quantity and quality in Canadian students' first semester of university. *Journal of Research on Adolescence, 19,* 741–761.

Galambos, N., Kolaric, G., Sears, H., & Maggs, J. (1999). Adolescents' subjective age: An indicator of perceived maturity. *Journal of Research on Adolescence, 9,* 309–337.

Galambos, N., Turner, P., & Tilton-Weaver, L. (2005). Chronological and subjective age in emerging adulthood: The crossover effect. *Journal of Adolescent Research, 20,* 538–556.

Galliher, R. V., Jones, M. D., & Dahl, A. (2011). Concurrent and longitudinal effects of ethnic identity and experiences of discrimination on psychosocial adjustment of Navajo adolescents. *Developmental Psychology, 47,* 509–526.

Galliher, R. V., Rostosky, S. S., & Hughes, H. K. (2004). School belonging, self-esteem, and depressive symptoms in adolescents: An examination of sex, sexual attraction status, and urbanicity. *Journal of Youth and Adolescence, 33,* 235–245.

Gallup, G., & Bezilla, R. (1992). *The religious life of young Americans.* Princeton, NJ: Gallup Institute.

Galvan, A. (2010). Adolescent development of the reward system. *Frontiers in Neuroscience, 4,* 1–9.

Galván, A. (2013). The teenage brain: Sensitivity to rewards. *Current Directions in Psychological Science, 22,* 88–93.

Galvan, A., Hare, T. A., Parra, C. E., Penn, J., Voss, K., Glover, G., & Casey, B. J. (2006). Earlier development of the accumbens relative to orbitofrontal cortex might underlie risk-taking behavior in adolescents. *Journal of Neuroscience, 26,* 6885–6892.

Galvan, A., Hare, T., Voss, H., Glover, G., & Casey, B. J. (2007). Risk-taking and the adolescent brain: Who is at risk? *Developmental Science, 10,* f8–f14.

Gamoran, A. (1993). Alternative uses of ability grouping in secondary schools: Can we bring high-quality instruction to low-ability classes? *American Journal of Education, 102,* 1–22.

Gamoran, A. (1996). Curriculum standardization and equality of opportunity in Scottish secondary education: 1984–90. *Sociology of Education, 69,* 1–21.

Gano-Overway, L., Newton, M., Magyar, T. M., Fry, M. D., Kim, M., & Guivernau, M. R. (2009). Influence of caring youth sport contexts on efficacy-related beliefs and social behaviors. *Developmental Psychology, 45,* 329–340.

Gans, J. (1990). *America's adolescents: How healthy are they?* Chicago: American Medical Association.

Garber, J., & Cole, D. A. (2010). Intergenerational transmission of depression: A launch and grow model of change across adolescence. *Development and Psychopathology, 22,* 819–830.

Garber, J., Robinson, N., & Valentiner, D. (1997). The relation between parenting and adolescent depression: Self-worth as a mediator. *Journal of Adolescent Research, 12,* 12–33.

Garcia Coll, C., Lamberty, G., Jenkins, R., McAdoo, H., Crnic, K., Wasik, B., . . . Vasquez Garcia, H. (1996). An integrative model for the study of developmental competencies in minority children. *Child Development, 67,* 1891–1914.

Garcia, N. V. & Scherf, K. S. (2015). Emerging sensitivity to socially complex expressions: A unique role for adolescence? *Child Development Perspectives, 9,* 84–90.

Garcia-Reid, P. (2007). Examining social capital as a mechanism for improving school engagement among low income Hispanic girls. *Youth and Society, 39,* 164–181.

Gardner, H. (1983). *Frames of mind.* New York: Basic Books.

Gardner, M., & Brooks-Gunn, J. (2009). Adolescents' exposure to community violence: Are neighborhood youth organizations protective? *Journal of Community Psychology, 37,* 505–525.

Gardner, M., & Steinberg, L. (2005). Peer influence on risk taking, risk preference, and risky decision making in adolescence and adulthood: An experimental study. *Developmental Psychology, 41,* 625–635.

Gardner, M., Browning, C., & Brooks-Gunn, J. (2012). Can organized youth activities protect against internalizing problems among adolescents living in violent homes? *Journal of Research on Adolescence, 22,* 662–667.

Gardner, M., Martin, A., & Brooks-Gunn, J. (2012). Exploring the link between caregiver affect and adolescent sexual behavior: Does neighborhood disadvantage matter? *Journal of Research on Adolescence, 22,* 135–149.

Gardner, M., Roth, J., & Brooks-Gunn, J. (2008). Adolescents' participation in organized activities and developmental success 2 and 8 years after high school: Do sponsorship, duration, and intensity matter? *Developmental Psychology, 44,* 814–830.

Gardner, T. W., Dishion, T. J., & Connell, A. M. (2008). Adolescent self-regulation as resilience: Resistance to antisocial behavior within the deviant peer context. *Journal of Abnormal Child Psychology, 36,* 273–284.

Garg, R., Melanson, S., & Levin, E. (2007). Educational aspirations of male and female adolescents from single-parent and two biological parent families: A comparison of influential factors. *Journal of Youth and Adolescence, 36,* 1010–1023.

Gargiulo, J., Attie, I., Brooks-Gunn, J., & Warren, M. (1987). Girls' dating behavior as a function of social context and maturation. *Developmental Psychology, 23,* 730–737.

Garnefski, N. (2000). Age differences in depressive symptoms, antisocial behavior, and negative perceptions of family, school, and peers among adolescents. *Journal of the American Academy of Child and Adolescent Psychiatry, 39,* 1175–1181.

Garner, R., Bootcheck, J., Lorr, M., & Rauch, K. (2006). The adolescent society revisited: Cultures, crowds, climates, and status structures in seven secondary schools. *Journal of Youth and Adolescence, 35,* 1023–1035.

Garnier, H., & Stein, J. (2002). An 18-year model of family and peer effects on adolescent drug use and delinquency. *Journal of Youth and Adolescence, 31,* 45–56.

Garthe, R.C., Sullivan, T. Kliewer, W. (2015). Longitudinal relations between adolescent and parental behaviors, parental knowledge, and internalizing behaviors among urban adolescents. *Journal of Youth & Adolescence, 44,* 819–832.

Gartner, M., Kiang, L., & Supple, A. (2014). Prospective links between ethnic socialization, ethnic and American identity, and well-being among Asian-American adolescents. *Journal of Youth & Adolescence, 43,* 1715–1727.

Gartrell, N., Bos, H., Peyser, H., Deck, A., & Rodas, C. (2011). Family characteristics, custody arrangements, and adolescent psychological well-being after lesbian mothers break up. *Family Relations, 60,* 572–585.

Gartstein, M., Seamon, E., & Dishion, T. J. (2014). Geospatial ecology of adolescent problem behavior: Contributions of community factors and parental monitoring. *Journal of Community Psychology, 42,* 299–315.

Gathercole, S. E., Pickering, S. J., Ambridge, B., & Wearing, H. (2004). The structure of working memory from 4 to 15 years of age. *Developmental Psychology, 40,* 177–190.

Gau, S. S., Soong, W., & Merikangas, K. R. (2004). Correlates of sleep-wake patterns among children and young adolescents in Taiwan. *Sleep, 27,* 512–519.

Gaudreau, P., Amiot, C. E., & Vallerand, R. J. (2009). Trajectories of affective states in adolescent hockey players: Turning point and motivational antecedents. *Developmental Psychology, 45,* 307–319.

Gault-Sherman, M. (2012). It's a two-way street: The bidirectional relationship between parenting and delinquency. *Journal of Youth and Adolescence, 41,* 121–145.

Gauze, C., Bukowski, W., Aquan-Assee, J., & Sippola, L. (1996). Interactions between family environment and friendship and associations with self-perceived well-being during early adolescence. *Child Development, 67,* 2201–2216.

Gavin, L., & Furman, W. (1996). Adolescent girls' relationships with mothers and best friends. *Child Development, 67,* 375–386.

Gayle, H., Keeling, R., Garcia-Tunon, M., Kilbourne, B., Narkunas, J., Ingram, F., & Curran, J. (1990). Prevalence of the human immunodeficiency virus among university students. *New England Journal of Medicine, 323,* 1538–1541.

Gaylord-Harden, N., Ragsdale, B. L., Mandara, J., Richards, M. H., & Petersen, A. C. (2007). Perceived support and internalizing symptoms in African American adolescents: Self-esteem and ethnic identity as mediators. *Journal of Youth and Adolescence, 36,* 77–88.

Gaysina, D., Richards, M., Kuh, D., & Hardy, R. (2015). Pubertal maturation and affective symptoms in adolescence and adulthood: Evidence from a prospective birth cohort. *Development and Psychopathology, FirstView Articles.*

Ge, X., Best, K., Conger, R., & Simons, R. (1996). Parenting behaviors and the occurrence and co-occurrence of adolescent depressive symptoms and conduct problems. *Developmental Psychology, 32,* 717–731.

Ge, X., Brody, G., Conger, R., Simons, R., & Murry, V. (2002). Contextual amplification of pubertal transition effects on deviant peer affiliation and externalizing behavior among African American children. *Developmental Psychology, 38,* 42–54.

Ge, X., Conger, R., & Elder, G. H., Jr. (2001). The relation between puberty and psychological distress in adolescent boys. *Journal of Research on Adolescence, 11,* 49–70.

Ge, X., Kim, I. J., Brody, G., Conger, R., Simons, R., Gibbons, F., & Cutrona, C. (2003). It's about timing and change: Pubertal transition effects on symptoms of major depression among African American youths. *Developmental Psychology, 39,* 430–439.

Ge, X., Natsuaki, M. N., Neiderhiser, J. M., & Reiss, D. (2009). The longitudinal effects of stressful life events on adolescent depression are buffered by parent–child closeness. *Development and Psychopathology, 21,* 621–635.

Ge, X., Natsuaki, M., & Conger, R. (2006). Trajectories of depressive symptoms and stressful life events among male and female adolescents in divorced and nondivorced families. *Development and Psychopathology, 18,* 253–273.

Ge, X., Natsuaki, M., Neiderhiser, J., & Reiss, D. (2007). Genetic and environmental influences on pubertal timing: Results from two national sibling studies. *Journal of Research on Adolescence, 17,* 767–788.

Gecas, V., & Seff, M. (1990). Families and adolescents: A review of the 1980s. *Journal of Marriage and the Family, 52,* 941–958.

Geier, C. F., & Luna, B. (2012). Developmental effects of incentives on response inhibition. *Child Development, 83,* 1262–1274.

Geier, C., Terwilliger, R., Teslovich, T., & Luna, B. (2010). Immaturities in reward processing and its influence on inhibitory control in adolescence. *Cerebral Cortex, 20,* 1613–1629.

Gennetian, L. A., Duncan, G., Knox, V., Vargas, W., Clark-Kauffman, E., & London, A. S. (2004). How welfare policies affect adolescents' school outcomes: A synthesis of evidence from experimental studies. *Journal of Research on Adolescence, 14,* 399–423.

Gentile, D. (2009). Pathological video game use among youth 8 to 18: A national study. *Psychological Science, 20,* 594–602.

Gentile, D. A., Swing, E. L., Lim, C. G., & Khoo, A. (2012). Video game playing, attention problems, and impulsiveness: Evidence of bidirectional causality. *Psychology of Popular Media Culture, 1,* 62–70.

Gentile, D., Choo, H., Liau, A., Sim, T., Li, D., Fung, D., & Khoo, A. (2011). Pathological video game use among youths: a two-year longitudinal study. *Pediatrics, 127,* e319–e329.

Gentile, D., Lynch, P. J., Linder, J. R., & Walsh, D. A. (2004). The effects of violent video game habits on adolescent hostility, aggressive behaviors, and school performance. *Journal of Adolescence, 27,* 5–22.

Gentry, M., Gable, R. K., & Rizza, M. G. (2002). Students' perceptions of classroom activities: Are there grade-level and gender differences? *Journal of Educational Psychology, 94,* 539–544.

Georgiades, K., Boyle, M. H., Duku, E., & Racine, Y. (2006). Tobacco use among immigrant and nonimmigrant adolescents: Individual and family level influences. *Journal of Adolescent Health, 38,* 443.e1–443.e7.

Georgiades, K., Boyle, M. H., & Fife, K. A. (2013). Emotional and behavioral problems among adolescent students: the role of immigrant, racial/ethnic congruence and belongingness in school. *Journal of Youth & Adolescence, 42,* 1473–1492.

Gerard, J. M., & Buehler, C. (2004). Cumulative environmental risk and youth maladjustment: The role of youth attributes. *Child Development, 75,* 1832–1849.

Gerbner, G., Gross, L., Morgan, M., & Signorelli, N. (1994). Growing up with television: The cultivation perspective. In J. Bryant & D. Zillman (Eds.), *Media effects: Advances in theory and research* (pp. 17–41). Hillsdale, NJ: Erlbaum.

Germán, M., Gonzales, N., & Dumka, L. (2009). Familism values as a protective factor for Mexican-origin adolescents exposed to deviant peers. *Journal of Early Adolescence, 29,* 16–42.

Gerrard, M., Gibbons, F., & Bushman, B. (1996). Relation between perceived vulnerability to HIV and precautionary sexual behavior. *Psychological Bulletin, 119,* 390–409.

Gershoff, E. T., Aber, J. L., Ware, A., & Kotler, J. A. (2010). Exposure to 9/11 among youth and their mothers in New York City: Enduring associations with mental health and sociopolitical attitudes. *Child Development, 81,* 1142–1160.

Gest, S. (1997). Behavioral inhibition: Stability and associations with adaptation from childhood to early adulthood. *Journal of Personality and Social Psychology, 72,* 467–475.

Gestsdóttir, S., & Lerner, R. M. (2007). Intentional self-regulation and positive youth development in early adolescence: Findings from the 4-H study of positive youth development. *Developmental Psychology, 43,* 508–521.

Gfroerer, J. C., & Tan, L. L. (2003). Substance use among foreign-born youths in the United States: Does the length of residence matter? *American Journal of Public Health, 93,* 1892–1895.

Ghetti, S., DeMaster, D., Yonelinas, A., & Bunge, S. (2010). Developmental differences in medial temporal lobe function during memory encoding. *Journal of Neuroscience, 30(28),* 9548–9556.

Gibb, S. J., Fergusson, D. M., Horwood, L. J., & Boden, J. M. (2014). Early motherhood and long-term economic outcomes: findings from a 30-year longitudinal study. *Journal of Research on Adolescence, 25,* 163–172.

Gibbons, F., Benbow, C., & Gerrard, M. (1994). From top dog to bottom half: Social comparison strategies in response to poor performance. *Journal of Personality and Social Psychology, 67,* 638–652.

Gibbs, J., Basinger, K. S., Grime, R., & Snarney, J. (2007). Moral judgment development across cultures: Revisiting Kohlberg's universality claims. *Developmental Review, 27,* 443–500.

Giedd, J. N. (2008). The teen brain: Insights from neuroimaging. *Journal of Adolescent Health, 42,* 335–343.

Giletta, M., Scholte, R. H. J., Burk, W. J., Engels, R. C. M. E., Larsen, J. K., Prinstein, M. J., & Ciairano, S. (2011). Similarity in depressive symptoms in adolescents' friendship dyads: Selection or socialization? *Developmental Psychology, 47,* 1804–1814.

Gillen-O'Neel, C., & Fuligni, A. (2013). A longitudinal study of school belonging and academic motivation across high school. *Child Development, 84,* 678–692.

Gilliam, F., & Bales, S. (2001). Strategic frame analysis: Reframing America's youth. *SRCD Social Policy Report, 15.*

Gillmore, M., Archibald, M. E., Morrison, D. M., Wilsdon, A., Wells, E. A., Hoppe, M. J., . . . Murowchick, E. (2002). Teen sexual behavior: Applicability of the theory of reasoned action. *Journal of Marriage and the Family, 64,* 885–897.

Gillmore, M., Lewis, S., Lohr, M., Spencer, M., & White, R. (1997). Repeat pregnancies among adolescent mothers. *Journal of Marriage and the Family, 59,* 536–550.

Gillmore, M., Morrison, D., Lowery, C., & Baker, S. (1994). Beliefs about condoms and their association with intentions to use condoms among youths in detention. *Journal of Adolescent Health, 15,* 228–237.

Gillock, K., & Reyes, O. (1996). High school transition-related changes in urban minority students' academic performance and perceptions of self and school environment. *Journal of Community Psychology, 24,* 245–261.

Gillock, K., & Reyes, O. (1999). Stress, support, and academic performance of urban, low-income, Mexican-American adolescents. *Journal of Youth and Adolescence, 28,* 259–282.

Gilman, A. B., Hill, K. G., Hawkins, J. D., Howell, J. C., & Kosterman, R. (2014). The development dynamics of joining a gang in adolescence: Patterns and predictors of gang membership. *Journal of Research on Adolescence, 24,* 204–219.

Gilman, A. B., Hill, K. G., & Hawkins, J. D. (2014). Long-term consequences of adolescent gang membership for adult functioning. *American Journal of Public Health, 104,* 938–994.

Gilman, S. E., Rende, R., Boergers, J., Abrams, D. B., Buka, S. L., Clark, M. A., . . . Niaura, R. (2009). Parental smoking and adolescent smoking initiation: An intergeneration perspective on tobacco control. *Pediatrics, 123,* 274–281.

Giordano, P. C., Longmore, M. A., & Manning, W. D. (2006). Gender and the meanings of adolescent romantic relationships: A focus on boys. *American Sociological Review, 71,* 260–287.

Giordano, P. C., Manning, W. D., & Longmore, M. A. (2010). Affairs of the heart: Qualities of adolescent romantic relationships and sexual behavior. *Journal of Research on Adolescence, 20,* 983–1013.

Giorgio, A., Watkins, K., Chadwick, M., James, S., Winmill, L., Douaud, G., . . . James, A. (2010). Longitudinal changes in grey and white matter during adolescence. *Neuroimage, 49,* 94–103.

Glaberson, W. (2007, June 7). A legal debate in Guantánamo on boy fighters. *The New York Times,* p. A1.

Glaser, B., Shelton, K. H., & van den Bree, M. B. M. (2010). The moderating role of close friends in the relationship between conduct problems and adolescent substance use. *Journal of Adolescent Health, 47,* 35–42.

Glasgow, K., Dornbusch, S., Ritter, P., Troyer, L., & Steinberg, L. (1997). Parenting styles, dysfunctional attributions, and adolescent outcomes in diverse groups. *Child Development, 67,* 507–529.

Glenwright, M., & Pexman, P. (2010). Development of children's ability to distinguish sarcasm and verbal irony. *Journal of Child Language, 37,* 429–451.

Glick, G. C., & Rose, A. J. (2011). Prospective associations between friendship adjustment and social strategies: Friendship as a context for building social skills. *Developmental Psychology, 47,* 1117–1132.

Gniewosz, B., Eccles, J. S., & Noack, P. (2015). Early adolescents' development of academic self-concept and intrinsic task value: The role of contextual feedback. *Journal of Research on Adolescence, 25,* 459–473.

Goddings, A., Heyes, S. B., Bird, G., Viner, R. M., & Blakemore, S. (2012). The relationship between puberty and social emotion processing. *Developmental Science, 15,* 801–811.

Goeke-Morey, M. C., Papp, L. M., & Cummings, E. M. (2013). Changes in marital conflict and youths' responses across childhood and adolescence: A test of sensitization. *Development and Psychopathology, 25,* 241–251.

Goldenberg, D., Telzer, E. H., Lieberman, M. D., Fuligini, A., & Galván, A. (2013). Neural mechanisms of impulse control in sexually risky adolescents. *Developmental Cognitive Neuroscience, 6,* 23–29.

Goldfield, G., Kenny, G., Hadjiyannakis, S., Phillips, P., Alberga, A., Saunders, T., . . . Sigal, R. (2011). Video game playing is independently associated with blood pressure and lipids in overweight and obese adolescents. *PLoS ONE, 6.*

Goldsmith, P. A. (2004). Schools' racial mix, students' optimism, and the Black–White and Latino–White achievement gaps. *Sociology of Education, 77,* 121–147.

Goldstein, B. (1976). *Introduction to human sexuality.* Belmont, CA: Star.

Goldstein, S., Davis-Kean, P., & Eccles, J. (2005). Parents, peers, and problem behavior: A longitudinal investigation of the impact of relationship perceptions and characteristics on the development of adolescent problem behavior. *Developmental Psychology, 41,* 401–413.

Goldston, D., Molock, S., Whitbeck, L., Murakami, J., Zayas, L., & Hall, G. (2008). Cultural considerations in adolescent suicide prevention and psychosocial treatment. *American Psychologist, 63,* 14–31.

Goleman, D. (1995). *Emotional intelligence.* New York: Bantam Books.

Golombok, S., Rust, J., Zervoulis, K., Golding, J., & Hines, M. (2012). Continuity in sex-typed behavior from preschool to adolescence: A longitudinal population study of boys and girls aged 3–13 years. *Archives of Sexual Behavior, 41,* 591–597.

Golub, A., & Johnson, B. D. (2001). Variation in youthful risks of progression from alcohol and tobacco to marijuana and to hard drugs across generations. *American Journal of Public Health, 91,* 225–232.

Gonzales, N. A., Deardorff, J., Formoso, D., Barr, A., & Barrera, M. Jr. (2006). Family mediators of the relation between acculturation and adolescent mental health. *Family Relations, 55,* 318–330.

Gonzales, N., Cauce, A., Friedman, R., & Mason, C. (1996). Family, peer, and neighborhood influences on academic achievement among African-American adolescents: One-year prospective effects. *American Journal of Community Psychology, 24,* 365–387.

Gonzales, R. (2011). Learning to be illegal undocumented youth and shifting legal contexts in the transition to adulthood. *American Sociological Review, 76,* 602–619.

Good, M., & Willoughby, T. (2006). The role of spirituality versus religiosity in adolescent psychosocial adjustment. *Journal of Youth and Adolescence, 35,* 41–55.

Good, M., & Willoughby, T. (2007). The identity formation experiences of church-attending rural adolescents. *Journal of Adolescent Research, 22,* 387–412.

Good, M., & Willoughby, T. (2011). Evaluating the direction of effects in the relationship between religious versus non-religious activities, academic success, and substance use. *Journal of Youth and Adolescence, 40,* 680–693.

Good, M., & Willoughby, T. (2014). Institutional and personal spirituality/religiosity and psychosocial adjustment in adolescence: concurrent and longitudinal associations. *Journal of Youth & Adolescence, 43,* 757–774.

Good, M., Willoughby, T., & Busseri, M. A. (2011). Stability and change in adolescent spirituality/religiosity: A person-centered approach. *Developmental Psychology, 47,* 538–550.

Good, M., Willoughby, T., & Fritjers, J. (2009). Just another club? The distinctiveness of the relation between religious service attendance and adolescent psychosocial adjustment. *Journal of Youth and Adolescence, 38,* 1153–1171.

Goodnight, J. A., Bates, J. E., Newman, J. P., Dodge, K. A., & Pettit, G. S. (2006). The interactive influences of friend deviance and reward dominance on the development of externalizing behavior during middle adolescence. *Journal of Abnormal Child Psychology, 34,* 573–583.

Goodson, P., Buhi, E. R., & Dunsmore, S. C. (2006). Self-esteem and adolescent sexual behaviors, attitudes, and intentions: A systematic review. *Journal of Adolescent Health, 38,* 310–319.

Goodwin, N. P., Mrug, S., Borch, C., Cillessen, A.H. (2012). Peer selection and socialization in adolescent depression: the role of school transitions. *Journal of Youth & Adolescence, 41,* 320–332.

Goosby, B. J. (2007). Poverty duration, maternal psychological resources, and adolescent socioemotional outcomes. *Journal of Family Issues, 28,* 1113–1134.

Goossens, L., Seiffge-Krenke, I., & Marcoen, A. (1992, March). *The many faces of adolescent egocentrism: Two European replications.* Paper presented at the biennial meetings of the Society for Research on Adolescence, Washington, DC.

Goran, M., et al. (1998). Developmental changes in energy expenditure and physical activity in children: Evidence for a decline in physical activity in girls before puberty. *Pediatrics, 101,* 887–891.

Gordis, E., Margolin, G., & St. John, R. (1997). Marital aggression, observed parental hostility, and child behavior during triadic family interaction. *Journal of Family Psychology, 11,* 76–89.

Gordon, K. (1995). Self-concept and motivational patterns of resilient African American high school students. *Journal of Black Psychology, 21,* 239–255.

Gordon, M., & Cui, M. (2014). School-related parental involvement and adolescent academic achievement: The role of community poverty. *Family Relations, 63,* 616–626.

Gordon, R. A., Lahey, B. B., Kawai, E., Loeber, R., Stouthamer-Loeber, M., & Farrington, D. P. (2004). Antisocial behavior and youth gang membership. *Criminology, 42,* 55–87.

Gordon, R. A., Rowe, H. L., Pardini, D., Loeber, R., White, H. R., & Farrington, D. P. (2014). Serious delinquency and gang participation: Combining and specializing in drug selling, theft, and violence. *Journal of Research on Adolescence, 24,* 235–251.

Gore, S., & Aseltine, R., Jr. (1995). Protective processes in adolescence: Matching stressors with social resources. *American Journal of Community Psychology, 23,* 301–327.

Gorrese, A., & Ruggieri, R. (2012). Peer attachment: a meta-analytic review of gender and age differences and associations with parent attachment. *Journal of Youth & Adolescence, 41,* 650–672.

Gottfredson, D., & DiPietro, S. (2011). School size, social capital, and student victimization. *Sociology of Education, 84,* 69–89.

Gottfredson, M., & Hirschi, T. (1990). *A general theory of crime.* Stanford, CA: Stanford University Press.

Gottfried, A. E., Marcoulides, G. A., Gottfried, A. W., & Oliver, P. H. (2009). A latent curve model of parental motivational practices and developmental decline in math and science academic intrinsic motivation. *Journal of Educational Psychology, 101,* 729–739.

Gottfried, A., Fleming, J. S., & Gottfried, A. W. (2001). Continuity of academic intrinsic motivation from childhood through late adolescence: A longitudinal study. *Journal of Educational Psychology, 93,* 3–13.

Gottlieb, B. H., Still, E., & Newby-Clark, I. (2007). Types and precipitants of growth and decline in emerging adulthood. *Journal of Adolescent Research, 22,* 132–155.

Gould, M., Munfakh, J., Lubell, K., Kleinman, M., & Parker, S. (2002). Seeking help from the Internet during adolescence. *Journal of the American Academy of Child and Adolescent Psychiatry, 41,* 1182–1189.

Gowen, L. K., Feldman, S. S., Diaz, R., & Yisrael, D. S. (2004). A comparison of the sexual behaviors and attitudes of adolescent girls with older vs. similar-aged boyfriends. *Journal of Youth and Adolescence, 33,* 167–175.

Gowen, L., Hayward, C., Killen, J., Robinson, T., & Taylor, C. (1999). Acculturation and eating disorder symptoms in adolescent girls. *Journal of Research on Adolescence, 9,* 67–83.

Goyette, K., & Xie, Y. (1999). Educational expectations of Asian American youths: Determinants and ethnic differences. *Sociology of Education, 72,* 22–36.

Goza, F., & Ryabov, I. (2009). Adolescents' educational outcomes: Racial and ethnic variations in peer network importance. *Journal of Youth and Adolescence, 38,* 1264–1279.

Graber, J., & Sontag, L. (2009). Internalizing problems during adolescence. In R. Lerner & L. Steinberg (Eds.), *Handbook of adolescent psychology* (3rd ed., Vol. 1, pp. 642–682). New York: Wiley.

Graber, J., Brooks-Gunn, J., & Warren, M. P. (2006). Pubertal effects on adjustment in girls: Moving from demonstrating effects to identifying pathways. *Journal of Youth and Adolescence, 35,* 391–401.

Graber, J., Brooks-Gunn, J., Paikoff, R., & Warren, M. (1994). Prediction of eating problems: An 8-year study of adolescent girls. *Developmental Psychology, 30,* 823–834.

Graber, J., Lewinsohn, P., Seeley, J., & Brooks-Gunn, J. (1997). Is psychopathology associated with the timing of pubertal development? *Journal of the American Academy of Child and Adolescent Psychiatry, 36,* 1768–1776.

Graber, J., Seeley, J., Brooks-Gunn, J., & Lewinsohn, P. (2004). Is pubertal timing associated with psychopathology in young adulthood? *Journal of the American Academy of Child and Adolescent Psychiatry, 43,* 718–726.

Graham, C. (1991). Menstrual synchrony: An update and review. *Human Nature, 2,* 293–311.

Graham, S. (1993, March). *Peer-directed aggression in African-American youth from an attributional perspective.* Paper presented at the biennial meetings of the Society for Research in Child Development, New Orleans.

Graham, S., & Hudley, C. (1994). Attributions of aggressive and nonaggressive African-American male early adolescents: A study of construct accessibility. *Developmental Psychology, 30,* 365–373.

Graham, S., & Juvonen, J. (1998). Self-blame and peer victimization in middle school: An attributional analysis. *Developmental Psychology, 34,* 587–599.

Graham, S., & Lowery, B. (2004). Priming unconscious racial stereotypes about adolescent offenders. *Law and Human Behavior, 28,* 483–504.

Graham, S., Bellmore, A., Nishina, A., & Juvonen, J. (2009). "It must be 'me'": Ethnic diversity and attributions for peer victimization in middle school. *Journal of Youth and Adolescence, 38,* 487–499.

Graham, S., Munniksma, A., & Juvonen, J. (2014). Psychosocial benefits of cross-ethnic friendships in urban middle schools. *Child Development, 85,* 469–483.

Granberg, E., Simons, L., & Simons, R. (2009). Body size and social self-image among adolescent african american girls the moderating influence of family racial socialization. *Youth & Society, 41,* 256–277.

Grande, T. L., Hallman, J., Rutledge, B., Caldwell, K., Upton, B., Underwood, L. A., Warren, K. M., Rehfuss, M. (2012). Examining mental health symptoms in male and female incarcerated juveniles. *Behavioral Sciences & the Law, 30,* 365–369.

Granic, I., Hollenstein, T., Dishion, T. K., & Patterson, G. R. (2003). Longitudinal analysis of flexibility and reorganization in early adolescence: A dynamic systems study of family interactions. *Developmental Psychology, 39,* 606–617.

Granillo, M., Grogan-Kaylor, A., Delva, J., & Castillo, M. (2011). Eating disorders among a community-based sample of Chilean female adolescents. *Journal of Research on Adolescence, 21,* 762–768.

Granot, D., & Mayseless, O. (2012). Representations of mother-child attachment relationships and social-information processing of peer relationships in early adolescence. *The Journal of Early Adolescence, 32,* 537–564.

Grant, K., Lyons, A., Finkelstein, J., Conway, K., Reynolds, L., O'Koon, J., . . . Hicks, K. (2004). Gender differences in rates of depressive symptoms among low-income, urban, African American youth: A test of two mediational hypotheses. *Journal of Youth and Adolescence, 33,* 523–533.

Gray, M., & Steinberg, L. (1999). Adolescent romance and the parent–child relationship: A contextual perspective. In W. Furman, B. Brown, & C. Feiring (Eds.), *Contemporary perspectives on adolescent romantic relationships* (pp. 235–265). New York: Cambridge University Press.

Gray-Little, B., & Carels, R. (1997). The effect of racial dissonance on academic achievement in elementary, junior high, and high school students. *Journal of Research on Adolescence, 7*, 109–131.

Gray-Little, B., & Hafdahl, A. (2000). Factors influencing racial comparisons of self-esteem: A quantitative review. *Psychological Bulletin, 126*, 26–54.

Green, K. M., & Ensminger, M. E. (2006). Adult social behavioral effects of heavy adolescent marijuana use among African Americans. *Developmental Psychology, 42*, 1168–1178.

Greenberg, M., & Kusche, C. (1998). *Promoting alternative thinking strategies.* Boulder: Institute of Behavioral Sciences, University of Colorado.

Greenberg, M., Siegel, J., & Leitch, C. (1983). The nature and importance of attachment relationships to parents and peers during adolescence. *Journal of Youth and Adolescence, 12*, 373–386.

Greenberger, E., & Chen, C. (1996). Perceived family relationships and depressed mood in early and late adolescence: A comparison of European and Asian Americans. *Developmental Psychology, 32*, 707–716.

Greenberger, E., & Steinberg, L. (1986). *When teenagers work: The psychological and social costs of adolescent employment.* New York: Basic Books.

Greenberger, E., Chen, C., & Beam, M. R. (1998). The role of "very important" nonparental adults in adolescent development. *Journal of Youth and Adolescence, 27*, 321–343.

Greenberger, E., Chen, C., Beam, M., Whang, S., & Dong, Q. (2000a). The perceived social contexts of adolescents' misconduct: A comparative study of youths in three cultures. *Journal of Research on Adolescence, 10*, 365–388.

Greenberger, E., Chen, C., Tally, S., & Dong, Q. (2000b). Family, peer, and individual correlates of depressive symptomatology among U.S. and Chinese adolescents. *Journal of Consulting and Clinical Psychology, 68*, 209–219.

Greene, M. L., & Way, N. (2005). Self-esteem trajectories among ethnic minority adolescents: A growth curve analysis of the patterns and predictors of change. *Journal of Research on Adolescence, 15*, 151–177.

Greene, M. L., Way, N., & Pahl, K. (2006). Trajectories of perceived adult and peer discrimination among Black, Latino, and Asian American adolescents: Patterns and psychological correlates. *Developmental Psychology, 42*, 218–236.

Green-Hennessy, S. (2014). Homeschooled adolescents in the United States: Developmental outcomes. *Journal of Adolescence, 37*, 441–449.

Greenspan, L., & Deardorff, J. (2014). *The new puberty.* New York: Rodale.

Gregory, A., & Weinstein, R. S. (2004). Connection and regulation at home and in school: Predicting growth in achievement for adolescents. *Journal of Adolescent Research, 19*, 405–427.

Gregory, A., Cornell, D., & Fan, X. (2011). The relationship of school structure and support to suspension rates for Black and White high school students. *American Educational Research Journal, 48*, 904–934.

Gregory, A., Cornell, D., Fan, X., Sheras, P., Shih, T., & Huang, F. (2010). Authoritative school discipline: High school practices associated with lower bullying and victimization. *Journal of Educational Psychology, 102*, 483–496.

Gregory, E. (2007). *Ready: Why women are embracing the new later motherhood.* New York: Basic Books.

Grenard, J. L., Dent, C. W., & Stacy, A. W. (2013). Exposure to alcohol advertisements and teenage alcohol-related problems. *Pediatrics, 131*, e369–e379.

Greven, C. U., Rijsdijk, F. V., & Plomin, R. (2011). A twin study of ADHD symptoms in early adolescence: Hyperactivity-impulsivity and inattentiveness show substantial genetic overlap but also genetic specificity. *Journal of Abnormal Child Psychology, 39*, 265–275.

Griffin, K. W., Epstein, J. A., Botvin, G. J., & Spoth, R. L. (2001). Social competence and substance use among rural youth: Mediating role of social benefit expectancies of use. *Journal of Youth and Adolescence, 30*, 485–498.

Griffith Fontaine, R., Salzer Burks, V., & Dodge, K. (2002). Response decision processes and externalizing behavior problems in adolescents. *Development and Psychopathology, 14*, 107–122.

Grisso, T., Steinberg, L., Woolard, J., Cauffman, E., Scott, E., Graham, S., et al. (2003). Juveniles' competence to stand trial: A comparison of adolescents' and adults' capacities as trial defendants. *Law and Human Behavior, 27*, 333–363.

Grolnick, W. S., Raftery-Helmer, J. N., Flamm, E. S., Marbell, K. N., & Cardemil, E. V. (2014). Parental provision of academic structure and the transition to middle school. *Journal of Research on Adolescence*, DOI: 10.1111/jora.12161

Grolnick, W., & Slowiaczek, M. (1994). Parents' involvement in children's schooling: A multidimensional conceptualization and motivational model. *Child Development, 65*, 237–252.

Grolnick, W., Kurowski, C. O., Dunlap, K. G., & Hevey, C. (2000). Parental resources and the transition to junior high. *Journal of Research on Adolescence, 10*, 465–488.

Grosbras, M., Jansen, M., Leonard, G., McIntosh, A., Osswald, K., Poulsen, C., ... Paus, T. (2007). Neural mechanisms of resistance to peer influence in early adolescence. *Journal of Neuroscience, 27*, 8040–8045.

Grossman, J. M., & Charmaraman, L. (2009). Race, context, and privilege: White adolescents' explanations of racial-ethnic centrality. *Journal of Youth and Adolescence, 38*, 139–152.

Grossman, M., Chaloupka, F., Saffer, H., & Laixuthai, A. (1994). Effects of alcohol price policy on youth: A summary of economic research. *Journal of Research on Adolescence, 4*, 347–364.

Grotevant, H. (1997). Adolescent development in family contexts. In N. Eisenberg (Ed.), *Handbook of child psychology: Vol. 3. Social, emotional, and personality development* (5th ed., pp. 1097–1149). New York: Wiley.

Grotpeter, J., & Crick, N. (1996). Relational aggression, overt aggression, and friendship. *Child Development, 67*, 2328–2338.

Grover, R. L., & Nangle, D. W. (2003). Adolescent perceptions of problematic heterosocial situations: A focus group study. *Journal of Youth and Adolescence, 32*, 129–139.

Gruber, J. (Ed.). (2001). *Risky behavior among youths: An economic analysis.* Chicago: University of Chicago Press.

Gruber, J., & Zinman, J. (2001). Youth smoking in the United States. In J. Gruber (Ed.), *Risky behavior among youths: An economic analysis* (pp. 69–120). Chicago: University of Chicago Press.

Grucza, R. A., Norberg, K. E., & Bierut, L. J. (2009). Binge drinking among youths and young adults in the United States: 1979–2006. *Journal of the American Academy of Child and Adolescent Psychiatry, 48*, 692–702.

Grumbach, M., Roth, J., Kaplan, S., & Kelch, R. (1974). Hypothalamic-pituitary regulation of puberty in man: Evidence and concepts derived from clinical research. In M. Grumbach, G. Grave, & F. Mayer (Eds.), *Control of the onset of puberty.* Philadelphia: Lippincott Williams & Wilkins.

Grunbaum, J., Lowry, R., Kann, L., & Pateman, B. (2000). Prevalence of health risk behaviors among Asian American/Pacific Islander high school students. *Journal of Adolescent Health, 27*, 322–330.

Grundy, A., Gondoli, D., & Salafia, E. B. (2010). Hierarchical linear modeling analysis of change in maternal knowledge over the transition to adolescence. *Journal of Early Adolescence, 30*, 707–732.

Grych, J. H., Raynor, S. R., & Fosco, G. M. (2004). Family processes that shape the impact of interparental conflict on adolescents. *Development and Psychopathology, 16*, 649–665.

Guan, K., Fox, K. R., & Prinstein, M. J. (2012). Nonsuicidal self-injury as a time-invariant predictor of adolescent suicide ideation and attempts in a diverse community sample. *Journal of Consulting and Clinical Psychology, 80*, 842–849.

Guarini, T. E., Marks, A. K., Patton, F., Coll, C. G. (2013). The immigrant paradox in pregnancy: Explaining the first-generation advantage for Latina adolescent. *Journal of Research on Adolescence, 25*, 14–19.

Guberman, S. (1996). The development of everyday mathematics in Brazilian children with limited formal education. *Child Development, 67*, 1609–1623.

Gudiño, O., Nadeem, E., Kataoka, S., & Lau, A. (2011). Relative impact of violence exposure and immigrant stressors on Latino youth psychopathology. *Journal of Community Psychology, 39,* 316–335.

Guerra, N. G., Williams, K. R., & Sadek, S. (2011). Understanding bullying and victimization during childhood and adolescence: A mixed methods study. *Child Development, 82,* 295–310.

Guest, A., & Schneider, B. (2003). Adolescents' extracurricular participation in context: The mediating effects of schools, communities, and identity. *Sociology of Education, 76,* 89–109.

Guillen, E., & Barr, S. (1994). Nutrition, dieting, and fitness messages in a magazine for adolescent women, 1970–1990. *Journal of Adolescent Health, 15,* 464–472.

Guion, K., Mrug, S., & Windle, M. (2009). Predictive value of informant discrepancies in reports of parenting: Relations to early adolescents' adjustment. *Journal of Abnormal Child Psychology, 37,* 17–30.

Guldi, M., Page, M., & Stevens, A. (2007). Family background and children's transition to adulthood over time. In S. Danziger & C. Rouse (Eds.), *The price of independence: The economics of early adulthood.* New York: Russell Sage Foundation.

Gummerum, M., Keller, M., Takezawa, M., & Mata, J. (2008). To give or not to give: Children's and adolescents' sharing and moral negotiations in economic decision situations. *Child Development, 79,* 562–576.

Gunlicks-Stoessel, M., & Powers, S. I. (2008). Adolescents' emotional experiences of mother–adolescent conflict predict internalizing and externalizing symptoms. *Journal of Research on Adolescence, 18,* 621–642.

Gunnar, M., Wewerka, S., Frenn, K., Long, J., & Griggs, C. (2009). Developmental changes in hypothalamus–pituitary–adrenal activity over the transition to adolescence: Normative changes and associations with puberty. *Development and Psychopathology, 21,* 69–85.

Gunnoe, M. (1994, February). *Noncustodial mothers' and fathers' contributions to the adjustment of adolescents in stepfamilies.* Paper presented at the biennial meetings of the Society for Research on Adolescence, San Diego.

Gunnoe, M., Hetherington, E. M., & Reiss, D. (1999). Parental religiosity, parenting style, and adolescent social responsibility. *Journal of Early Adolescence, 19,* 199–225.

Gunter, W., & Bakken, N. (2010). Transitioning to middle school in the sixth grade: A hierarchical linear modeling (HLM) analysis of substance use, violence, and suicidal thoughts. *Journal of Early Adolescence, 30,* 895–915.

Gunther Moor, B., Bos, M. G., Crone, E. A., & van der Molen, M. W. (2014). Peer rejection cues induce cardiac slowing after transition into adolescence. *Developmental Psychology, 50,* 947–955.

Guo, G., Roettger, M. E., & Cai, T. (2008). The integration of genetic propensities into social-control models of delinquency and violence among male youths. *American Sociological Review, 73,* 543–568.

Guo, G., Tong, Y., & Cai, T. (2008). Gene by social context interactions for number of sexual partners among White male youths: Genetics informed sociology. *American Journal of Sociology, 114,* 36–66.

Gupta, T., Way, N., McGill, R. K., Hughes, D., Santos, C., Jia, Y., Yoshikawa, H., Chen, X., & Deng, H. (2013). Gender-typed behaviors in friendships and well-being: A cross-cultural study of Chinese and American boys. *Journal of Research on Adolescence, 23,* 57–68.

Güroğlu, B., Haselager, G. J. T., van Lieshout, C., & Scholte, R. H. J. (2009). Antagonists in mutual antipathies: A person-oriented approach. *Journal of Research on Adolescence, 19,* 35–46.

Gutierrez, R. (2000). Advancing African American, urban youth in mathematics: Unpacking the success of one math department. *American Journal of Education, 109,* 63–111.

Gutman, L., & Eccles, J. (2007). Stage-environment fit during adolescence: Trajectories of family relations and adolescent outcomes. *Developmental Psychology, 43,* 522–537.

Gutman, L., & Midgley, C. (2000). The role of protective factors in supporting the academic achievement of poor African American students during the middle school transition. *Journal of Youth and Adolescence, 29,* 223–248.

Gutman, L., McLoyd, V., & Tokoyawa, T. (2005). Financial strain, neighborhood stress, parenting behaviors, and adolescent adjustment in urban African American families. *Journal of Research on Adolescence, 15,* 425–449.

Guttmacher Institute. (2014). American teens' sexual and reproductive health. www.guttmacher.org/pubs/FB-ATSRH.html. Accessed on July 13, 2015.

Guyer, A. E., Benson, B., Choate, V. R., Bar-Haim, Y., Perez-Edgar, K., Jarcho, J. M., Pine, D. S., Ernst, M., Fox, N. A., & Nelson, E. E. (2014). Lasting associations between early-childhood temperament and late-adolescent rewardcircuitry response to peer feedback. *Development and Psychopathology, 26,* 229–243.

Guyer, A. E., Choate, V. R., Pine, D. S., & Nelson, E. E. (2012). Neural circuitry underlying affective response to peer feedback in adolescence. *Social Cognitive Affective Neuroscience, 7,* 81–92.

Guyer, A., McClure-Tone, E., Shiffrin, N., Pine, D., & Nelson, E. (2009). Probing the neural correlates of anticipated peer evaluation in adolescence. *Child Development, 80,* 1000–1015.

Ha, T., Overbeek, G., & Engels, R. C. M. E. (2010). Effects of attractiveness and social status on dating desire in heterosexual adolescents: An experimental study. *Archives of Sexual Behavior, 39,* 1063–1071.

Habermas, T., & de Silveira, C. (2008). The development of global coherence in life narratives across adolescence: Temporal, causal, and thematic aspects. *Developmental Psychology, 44,* 707–721.

Habib, M., Borst, G., Poirel, N., Houdé, O., Moutier, S., & Cassotti, M. (2013). Socioemotional context and adolescents' decision making: The experience of regret and relief after social comparison. *Journal of Research on Adolescence, 25,* 81–91.

Haddad, A. D. M., Harrison, F., Norman, T., & Lau, J. Y. F. (2014). Adolescent and adult risk-taking in virtual social contexts. *Developmental Psychology, 5,* 1–7.

Haddad, E., Chen, C., & Greenberger, E. (2011). The pole of important nonparental adults (VIPs) in the lives of older adolescents: A comparison of three ethnic groups. *Journal of Youth and Adolescence, 40,* 310–319.

Hafen, C. A., Spilker, A., Chango, J., Marston, E. S., & Allen, J. P. (2014). To accept or reject? The impact of adolescent rejection sensitivity on early adult romantic relationships. *Journal of Research on Adolescence, 24,* 55–64.

Hafen, C. A., Allen, J. P., Mikami, A. Y., Gregory, A., Hamre, B., & Pianta, R. C. (2012). The pivotal role of adolescent automony in secondary school classrooms. *Journal of Youth & Adolescence, 41,* 245–255.

Hagan, J., & Foster, H. (2001). Youth violence and the end of adolescence. *American Sociological Review, 66,* 874–899.

Hahm, H., Lahiff, M., & Barreto, R. M. (2006). Asian American adolescents' first sexual intercourse: Gender and acculturation differences. *Perspectives on Sexual and Reproductive Health, 38,* 28–36.

Hahm, H., Lahiff, M., & Guterman, N. (2003). Acculturation and parental attachment in Asian-American adolescents' alcohol use. *Journal of Adolescent Health, 33,* 119–129.

Hahm, H., Lahiff, M., & Guterman, N. (2004). Asian American adolescents' acculturation, binge drinking, and alcohol- and tobacco-using peers. *Journal of Community Psychology, 32,* 295–308.

Haines, J., Neumark-Sztainer, D., Eisenberg, M., & Hannan, P. (2006). Weight teasing and disordered eating behaviors in adolescents: Longitudinal findings from Project EAT (Eating Among Teens). *Pediatrics, 117,* e209–15.

Hair, E. C., Moore, K. A., Garrett, S. B., Ling, T., & Cleveland, K. (2008). The continued importance of quality parent–adolescent relationships during late adolescence. *Journal of Research on Adolescence, 18,* 187–200.

Haj-Yahia, M. M., Musleh, K., & Haj-Yahia, Y. (2002). The incidence of adolescent maltreatment in Arab society and some of its psychological effects. *Journal of Family Issues, 23,* 1032–1064.

Hale, D. R., Fitzgerald-Yau, N., & Mark Viner, R. (2014). A systematic review of effective interventions for reducing multiple health risk behaviors in adolescence. *American Journal of Public Health. 104,* e19-41.

Hale, S., Bronik, M., & Fry, A. (1997). Verbal and spatial working memory in school-age children: Developmental differences in susceptibility to interference. *Developmental Psychology, 33,* 364–371.

Halgunseth, L., Ispa, J., & Rudy, D. (2006). Parental control in Latino families: An integrated review of the literature. *Child Development, 77,* 1282–1297.

Hall, G. S. (1904). *Adolescence.* New York: Appleton.

Hall, N. C., Chipperfield, J. G., Perry, R. P., Ruthig, J. C., & Goetz, T. (2006). Primary and secondary control in academic development: Gender-specific implications for stress and health in college students. *Anxiety, Stress & Coping: An International Journal, 19,* 189–210.

Haller, M., Handley, E., Chassin, L., & Bountress, K. (2010). Developmental cascades: Linking adolescent substance use, affiliation with substance use promoting peers, and academic achievement to adult substance use disorders. *Development and Psychopathology, 22,* 899–916.

Halligan, S. L., & Philips, K. J. (2010). Are you thinking what I'm thinking? Peer group similarities in adolescent hostile attribution tendencies. *Developmental Psychology, 46,* 1385–1388.

Hallinan, M. (1996). Track mobility in secondary school. *Social Forces, 74,* 983–1002.

Hallinan, M. (2008). Teacher influences on students' attachment to school. *Sociology of Education, 81,* 271–283.

Hallinan, M., & Kubitschek, W. (2012). A comparison of academic achievement and adherence to the common school ideal in public and Catholic schools. *Sociology of Education, 85,* 1–22.

Hallinan, M., & Williams, R. (1989). Interracial friendship choices in secondary schools. *American Sociological Review, 54,* 67–78.

Hallquist, S., Cuthbertson, C., Killeya-Jones, L., Halpern, C., & Harris, K. (November, 2011). *Living arrangements in young adulthood: Results from wave iv of the national longitudinal study of adolescent health.* Add Health Research Brief, Carolina Population Center, The University of North Carolina at Chapel Hill.

Halpem, C. T., & Haydon, A. A. (2012). Sexual Timetables for oral-genital, vaginal, and anal intercourse: Sociodemographic comparisons in a nationally representative sample of adolescents. *American Journal of Public Health, 102,* 1221–1228.

Halpern, C. T. (2003). Biological influences on adolescent romantic and sexual behavior. In P. Florsheim (Ed.), *Adolescent romantic relations and sexual behavior: Theory, research, and practical implications* (pp. 57–84). Mahwah, NJ: Lawrence Erlbaum.

Halpern, C. T., Spriggs, A. L., Martin, S. L., & Kupper, L. L. (2009). Patterns of intimate partner violence victimization from adolescence to young adulthood in a nationally representative sample. *Journal of Adolescent Health, 45,* 508–516.

Halpern, C., King, R., Oslak, S., & Udry, J. (2005). Body mass index, dieting, romance, and sexual activity in adolescent girls: Relationships over time. *Journal of Research on Adolescence, 15,* 535–559.

Halpern, C., Oslak, S., Young, M., Martin, S., & Kupper, L. (2001). Partner violence among adolescents in opposite-sex romantic relationships: Findings from the National Longitudinal Study of Adolescent Health. *American Journal of Public Health, 91,* 1679–1685.

Halpern, C., Udry, J., & Suchindran, C. (1996, March). *Monthly measures of salivary testosterone predict sexual activity in adolescent males.* Paper presented at the biennial meetings of the Society for Research on Adolescence, Boston.

Halpern, C., Udry, J., Campbell, B., & Suchindran, C. (1999). Effects of body fat on weight concerns, dating, and sexual activity: A longitudinal analysis of Black and White adolescent girls. *Developmental Psychology, 35,* 721–736.

Halpern-Felsher, B. (2011). Adolescent decision-making. In B. Brown & M. Prinstein (Eds.), *Encyclopedia of adolescence* (Vol. 1, pp. 30–37). New York: Academic Press.

Halpern-Felsher, B., & Cauffman, E. (2001). Costs and benefits of a decision: Decision-making competence in adolescents and adults. *Journal of Applied Developmental Psychology, 22,* 257–273.

Halpern-Meekin, S., & Tach, L. (2008). Heterogeneity in two-parent families and adolescent well-being. *Journal of Marriage and Family, 70,* 435–451.

Haltigan, J. D., & Vaillancourt, T. (2014). Joint trajectories of bullying and peer victimization across elementary and middle school and associations with symptoms of psychopathology. *Developmental Psychology, 50,* 2426–2436.

Haltigan, J. D., Roisman, G. I., Susman, E. J., Barnett-Walker, K., & Monahan, K. C. (2011). Elevated trajectories of externalizing problems are associated with lower awakening cortisol levels in midadolescence. *Developmental Psychology, 47,* 472–478.

Hamill, S. (1994). Parent–adolescent communication in sandwich generation families. *Journal of Adolescent Research, 9,* 458–482.

Hamilton, B., Martin, J., & Ventura, S. (2007). Births: Preliminary data for 2006. *National Vital Statistics Reports, 56,* Number 7.

Hamilton, C. (2000). Continuity and discontinuity of attachment from infancy through adolescence. *Child Development, 71,* 690–694.

Hamilton, J. L., Hamlat, E. J., Strange, J. P., Abramson, L. Y., & Alloy, L. B. (2014). Pubertal timing and vulnerabilities to depression in early adolescence: Differential pathways to depressive symptoms by sex. *Journal of Adolescence, 37,* 165–174.

Hamilton, S., & Hamilton, M. (2009). The transition to adulthood: Challenges of poverty and structural lag. In R. Lerner & L. Steinberg (Eds.), *Handbook of adolescent psychology* (3rd ed., Vol. 2, pp. 492–526). New York: Wiley.

Hamm, J. (2000). Do birds of a feather flock together? The variable bases for African American, Asian American, and European American adolescents' selection of similar friends. *Developmental Psychology, 36,* 209–219.

Hamm, J., Brown, B., & Heck, D. (2005). Bridging the ethnic divide: Student and school characteristics in African American, Asian-descent, Latino, and White adolescents' cross-ethnic friend nominations. *Journal of Research on Adolescence, 15,* 21–46.

Hammons, A., & Fiese, B. (2011). Is frequency of shared family meals related to the nutritional health of children and adolescents? *Pediatrics, 127,* 1565–1574.

Hampson, S. E., & Goldberg, L. R. (2006). A first large cohort study of personality trait stability over the 40 years between elementary school and midlife. *Journal of Personality and Social Psychology, 91,* 763–779.

Hamre, B. K., & Pianta, R. C. (2001). Early teacher–child relationships and the trajectory of children's school outcomes through eighth grade. *Child Development, 72,* 625–638.

Hamza, C. A., & Willoughby, T. (2011). Perceived parental monitoring, adolescent disclosure, and adolescent depressive symptoms: A longitudinal examination. *Journal of Youth and Adolescence, 40,* 902–915.

Han, W., Miller, D., & Waldfogel, J. (2010). Parental work schedules and adolescent risky behaviors. *Developmental Psychology, 46,* 1245–1267.

Hankin, B. L., Mermelstein, R., & Roesch, L. (2007). Sex differences in adolescent depression: Stress exposure and reactivity models. *Child Development, 78,* 279–295.

Hankin, B. L., Stone, L., & Wright, P. A. (2010). Corumination, interpersonal stress generation, and internalizing symptoms: Accumulating effects and transactional influences in a multiwave study of adolescents. *Development and Psychopathology, 22,* 217–235.

Hanselman, P., Bruch, S. K., Gamoran, A., & Borman, G. D. (2014). Threat in context: School moderation of the impact of social identity threat on racial/ethnic achievement gaps. *Sociology of Education, 87,* 106–124.

Hansen, D. M., Janssen, I., Schiff, A., Zee, P. C., & Dubocovich, M. L. (2005). The impact of school daily schedule on adolescent sleep. *Pediatrics, 115,* 1555–1561.

Hanson, J. L., Adluru, N., Chung, M. K., Alexander, A. L., Davidson, R. J., & Pollak, S. D. (2013). Early neglect is associated with alterations in white matter integrity and cognitive functioning. *Child Development, 84,* 1566–1578.

Hanson, J. L., Chung, M. K., Avants, B. B., Rudolph, K. D., Shirtcliff, E. A., Gee, J. C., ... Pollak, S. (2012). Structural variations in prefrontal cortex mediate the relationship between early childhood stress and spatial working memory. *Journal of Neuroscience, 32,* 7917–7925.

Hanson, S. (1994). Lost talent: Unrealized educational aspirations and expectations among U.S. youths. *Sociology of Education, 67,* 159–183.

Hanson, T., McLanahan, S., & Thomson, E. (1996). Double jeopardy: Parental conflict and stepfamily outcomes for children. *Journal of Marriage and the Family, 58,* 141–154.

Hao, L., & Woo, H. S. (2012). Distinct trajectories in the transition to adulthood: Are children of immigrants advantaged? *Child Development, 83,* 1623–1639.

Harber, K. D., Gorman, J. L., Gengaro, F. P., Butisingh, S., Tsang W., & Ouellette, R. (2012). Students' race and teachers' social support affect the positive feedback bias in public schools. *Journal of Educational Psychology, 104,* 1149–1161.

Harcourt, T. H., Adler-Baeder, F., Erath, S., & Pettit, G. S. (2015). Examining family structure and half-sibling influence on adolescent well-being. *Journal of Family Issues, 36,* 250–272.

Hardaway, C. R., & Cornelius, M. D. (2014). Economic hardship and adolescent problem drinking: family processes as mediating influences. *Journal of Youth & Adolescence, 43,* 1191–1202.

Hardaway, C. R., McLoyd, V. C., & Wood, D. (2012). Exposure to violence and socioemotional adjustment in low-income youth: An examination of protective factors. *American Journal of Community Psychology, 49,* 112–126.

Harden, K. P. (2012). True love waits? A sibling-comparison study of age at first sexual intercourse and romantic relationships in young adulthood. *Psychological Science, 23,* 1324–1336.

Harden, K. P., & Mendle, J. (2011a). Adolescent sexual activity and the development of delinquent behavior: The role of relationship context. *Journal of Youth and Adolescence, 40,* 825–838.

Harden, K. P., & Mendle, J. (2011b). Gene-environment interplay in the association between pubertal timing and delinquency in adolescent girls. *Journal of Abnormal Psychology, 120,* 73–87.

Harden, K. P., & Mendle, J. (2012). Gene-environment interplay in the association between pubertal timing and delinquency in adolescent girls. *Journal of Abnormal Psychology, 121,* 73–87.

Harden, K. P., & Tucker-Drob, E. M. (2011). Individual differences in the development of sensation seeking and impulsivity during adolescence: Further evidence for a dual systems model. *Developmental Psychology, 47,* 739–746.

Harden, K. P., Mendle, J., Hill, J. E., Turkheimer, E., & Emery, R. E. (2008). Rethinking timing of first sex and delinquency. *Journal of Youth and Adolescence, 37,* 373–385.

Harden, K. P., Quinn, T., & Tucker-Drob, E. (2012). Genetically influenced change in sensation seeking drives the rise of delinquent behavior during adolescence. *Developmental Science, 15,* 150–163.

Hardie, J. H., & Tyson, K. (2013). Other people's racism: Race, rednecks, and riots in a southern high school. *Sociology of Education, 86,* 83–102.

Hardin, M., & Ernst, M. (2009). Functional brain imaging of development-related risk and vulnerability for substance use in adolescents. *Journal of Addiction Medicine, 3,* 47–54.

Harding, D. J. (2003). Counterfactual models of neighborhood effects: The effect of neighborhood poverty on dropping out and teenage pregnancy. *American Journal of Sociology, 109,* 676–719.

Hardway, C., & Fuligni, A. (2006). Dimensions of family connectedness among adolescents with Mexican, Chinese, and European backgrounds. *Developmental Psychology, 42,* 1246–1258.

Hardy, D., Astone, N., Brooks-Gunn, J., Shapiro, X., & Miller, X. (1998). Like mother, like child: Intergenerational patterns of age at first birth and associations with childhood and adolescent characteristics and adult outcomes in the second generation. *Developmental Psychology, 34,* 1220–1232.

Hardy, S. A., & Raffaelli, M. (2003). Adolescent religiosity and sexuality: An investigation of reciprocal influences. *Journal of Adolescence, 26,* 731–739.

Hardy, S. A., Carlo, G., & Roesch, S. C. (2010). Links between adolescents' expected parental reactions and prosocial behavioral tendencies: The mediating role of prosocial values. *Journal of Youth and Adolescence, 39,* 84–95.

Hare, A. L., Marston, E. G., & Allen, J. P. (2011). Maternal acceptance and adolescents' emotional communication: A longitudinal study. *Journal of Youth and Adolescence, 40,* 744–751.

Hare, A. L., Szwedo, D. E., Schad, M. M., & Allen, J. P. (2014). Undermining adolescent autonomy with parents and peers: The enduring implications of psychologically controlling parenting. *Journal of Research on Adolescence,* DOI: 10.1111/jora.12167.

Harenski, C. L., Harenski, K. A., Shane, M. S., & Kiehl, K. A. (2012). Neural development of mentalizing in moral judgment from adolescence to adulthood. *Development Cognitive Neuroscience, 2,* 162–173.

Hargreaves, D., & Tiggemann, M. (2003). The effect of thin ideal television commercials on body dissatisfaction and schema activation during early adolescence. *Journal of Youth and Adolescence, 32,* 367–373.

Harker, K. (2001). Immigrant generation, assimilation, and adolescent psychological well-being. *Social Forces, 79,* 969–1004.

Harold, G., & Conger, R. (1997). Marital conflict and adolescent distress: The role of adolescent awareness. *Child Development, 68,* 333–350.

Harper, B. D. (2012). Parents' and children's beliefs about peer victimization: Attributions, coping responses, and child adjustment. *The Journal of Early Adolescence, 32,* 387–413.

Harper, G., & Robinson, W. L. (1999). Pathways to risk among inner-city African-American adolescent females: The influence of gang membership. *American Journal of Community Psychology, 27,* 383–404.

Harper, J. M., Padilla-Walker, L. M., & Jensen, A. C. (2014). Do siblings matter independent of both parents and friends? Sympathy as a mediator between sibling relationship quality and adolescent outcomes. *Journal of Research on Adolescence,* DOI: 10.1111/jora.12174

Harré, N. (2000). Risk evaluation, driving, and adolescents: A typology. *Developmental Review, 20,* 206–226.

Harris, J. (1995). Where is the child's environment? A group socialization theory of development. *Psychological Bulletin, 102,* 458–489.

Harris, J. (1998). *The nurture assumption: Why children turn out the way they do.* New York: Free Press.

Harris, K. (1999). The health status and risk behavior of adolescents in immigrant families. In D. Hernandez (Ed.), *Children of immigrants: Health, adjustment, and public assistance* (pp. 286–347). Washington, DC: National Academy Press.

Harris, M. (1994). Cholas, Mexican-American girls, and gangs. *Sex Roles, 30,* 289–301.

Harris, M. A., Gruenfelder-Steiger, A. E., Ferrer, E., Donnellan, M. B., Allemand, M., Fend, H., . . . Trzesniewski, K. H. (2015). Do parents foster self-esteem? Testing the prospective impact of parent closeness on adolescent self-esteem. *Child Development,* DOI: 10.1111/cdev.12356.

Harris-Britt, A., Valrie, C. R., Kurtz-Costes, B., & Rowley, S. J. (2007). Perceived racial discrimination and self-esteem in African American youth: Racial socialization as a protective factor. *Journal of Research on Adolescence, 17,* 669–682.

Harrison, K., & Heffner, V. (2008). Media, body image, and eating disorders. In S. L. Calvert & B. J. Wilson (Eds.), *The handbook of children, media, and development* (pp. 381–406). Oxford: Wiley-Blackwell.

Hart, D., & Fegley, S. (1995). Prosocial behavior and caring in adolescence: Relations to self-understanding and social judgment. *Child Development, 66,* 1346–1359.

Hart, D., Donnelly, T. M., Youniss, J., & Atkins, R. (2007). High school community service as a predictor of adult voting and volunteering. *American Educational Research Journal, 44,* 197–219.

Hart, D., Hofmann, V., Edelstein, W., & Keller, M. (1997). The relation of childhood personality types to adolescent behavior and development: A longitudinal study of Icelandic children. *Developmental Psychology, 33,* 195–205.

Harter, S. (1990). Identity and self development. In S. Feldman & G. Elliott (Eds.), *At the threshold: The developing adolescent* (pp. 352–387). Cambridge, MA: Harvard University Press.

Harter, S. (1999). *The construction of the self.* New York: Guilford Press.

Harter, S. (2011). Self-development during adolescence. In B. Brown & M. Prinstein (Eds.), *Encyclopedia of adolescence* (Vol. 1, pp. 307–315). New York: Academic Press.

Harter, S., & Monsour, A. (1992). Developmental analysis of conflict caused by opposing attributes in the adolescent self-portrait. *Developmental Psychology, 28,* 251–260.

Harter, S., Marold, D., Whitesell, N., & Cobbs, G. (1996). A model of the effects of parent and peer support on adolescent false-self behavior. *Child Development, 67,* 360–374.

Harter, S., Stocker, C., & Robinson, N. (1996). The perceived directionality of the link between approval and self-worth: The liabilities of a looking glass self orientation among young adolescents. *Journal of Research on Adolescence, 6,* 285–308.

Harter, S., Waters, P., & Whitesell, N. (1998). Relational self-worth: Differences in perceived worth as a person across interpersonal contexts among adolescents. *Child Development, 69,* 756–766.

Hartman, S., Widaman, K. F., & Belsky, J. (2015). Genetic moderation of effects of maternal sensitivity on girl's age of menarche: Replication of the Manuck et al. study. *Development and Psychopathology, 27,* 747–756.

Hartney, C. (2006). *Youth under 18 in the criminal justice system.* Oakland: National Council on Crime and Delinquency.

Hartung, C., Lefner, E., & Fedele, D. (2011). Disruptive behaviors and aggression. In B. Brown & M. Prinstein (Eds.), *Encyclopedia of adolescence* (Vol. 3, pp. 143–150). New York: Academic Press.

Hartup, W. (1977). Adolescent peer relations: A look to the future. In J. Hill & F. Monks (Eds.), *Adolescence and youth in prospect.* Guildford, England: IPC Press.

Hartup, W., & Stevens, N. (1997). Friendships and adaptation in the life course. *Psychological Bulletin, 121,* 335–370.

Hasebe, Y., Nucci, L., & Nucci, M. S. (2004). Parental control of the personal domain and adolescent symptoms of psychopathology: A cross-national study in the United States and Japan. *Child Development, 75,* 815–828.

Hasking, P., Andrews, T., Martin, G. (2013). The role of exposure to self-injury among peers in predicting later self-injury. *Journal of Youth & Adolescence, 42,* 1543–1556.

Hastings, J. S., & Weinstein, J. M. (2008). Information, school choices, and academic achievement: Evidence from two experiments. *Quarterly Journal of Economics, 123,* 1373–1414.

Hatzenbuehler, M. L., Birkett, M., Van Wagenen, A., & Meyer, I. H. (2014). Protective school climates and reduced risk for suicide ideation in sexual minority youths. *American Journal of Public Health, 104,* 279–286.

Hatzichristou, C., & Hopf, D. (1996). A multi-perspective comparison of peer sociometric status groups in childhood and adolescence. *Child Development, 67,* 1085–1102.

Hauser, S., & Bowlds, M. (1990). Stress, coping, and adaptation. In S. Feldman & G. Elliott (Eds.), *At the threshold: The developing adolescent* (pp. 388–413). Cambridge, MA: Harvard University Press.

Hausser, D., & Michaud, P. (1994). Does a condom-promoting strategy (the Swiss STOP-AIDS campaign) modify sexual behavior among adolescents? *Pediatrics, 93,* 580–585.

Havighurst, R. (1952). *Developmental tasks and education.* New York: McKay.

Hawes, S. W., Mulvey, E. P., Schubert, C. A., Pardini, D. A. (2014). Structural coherence and temporal stability of psychopathic personality features during emerging adulthood. *Journal of Abnormal Psychology, 123,* 623–633.

Hawk, S. T., Becht, A., & Branje, S. (2015). "Snooping" as a distinct parental monitoring strategy: Comparisons with overt solicitation and control. *Journal of Research on Adolescence, Early view.* DOI: 10.1111/jora.12204

Hawkins, D. N., Amato, P. R., & King, V. (2006). Parent–adolescent involvement: The relative influence of parent gender and residence. *Journal of Marriage and Family, 68,* 125–136.

Hawkins, D. N., Amato, P. R., & King, V. (2007). Nonresident father involvement and adolescent well-being: Father effects or child effects? *American Sociological Review, 72,* 990–1010.

Hawkins, J., Brown, E. C., Oesterle, S., Arthur, M. W., Abbott, R. D., & Catalano, R. F. (2008). Early effects of communities that care on targeted risks and initiation of delinquent behavior and substance use. *Journal of Adolescent Health, 43,* 15–22.

Hay, C., & Meldrum, R. (2010). Bullying victimization and adolescent self-harm: Testing hypotheses from general strain theory. *Journal of Youth and Adolescence, 39,* 446–459.

Hay, C., Fortson, E. N., Hollist, D. R., Altheimer, I., & Schaible, L. M. (2007). Compounded risk: The implications for delinquency of coming from a poor family that lives in a poor community. *Journal of Youth and Adolescence, 36,* 593–605.

Haydon, A. A., & Halpern, C. T. (2010). Older romantic partners and depressive symptoms during adolescence. *Journal of Youth and Adolescence, 39,* 1240–1251.

Haydon, A. A., Herring, A. H., Prinstein, M. J., & Halpern, C. T. (2012). Beyond age at first sex: Patterns of emerging sexual behavior in adolescence and young adulthood. *Journal of Adolescent Health, 50,* 456–463.

Haydon, A., McRee, A-L., & Halpern, C. (2011). Risk-taking behavior. In B. Brown & M. Prinstein (Eds.), *Encyclopedia of adolescence* (Vol. 3, pp. 255–263). New York: Academic Press.

Haydon, A. A., Cheng, M. M., Herring, A. H., McRee, A. L., Halpern, C. T. (2014). Prevalence and Predictors of Sexual Inexperience in Adulthood. *Archives of Sexual Behavior, 43,* 221–230.

Hayes, D., Wolfer, L., & Wolfe, M. (1996). Schoolbook simplification and its relation to the decline in SAT-Verbal scores. *American Educational Research Journal, 33,* 489–508.

Hayford, S. R., & Furstenberg, F. F. J. (2008). Delayed adulthood, delayed desistance? Trends in the age distribution of problem behaviors. *Journal of Research on Adolescence, 18,* 285–304.

Haynie, D. L. (2003). Contexts of risk? Explaining the link between girls' pubertal development and their delinquency involvement. *Social Forces, 82,* 355–397.

Haynie, D. L., & McHugh, S. (2003). Sibling deviance in the shadows of mutual and unique friendship effects? *Criminology, 41,* 355–391.

Haynie, D. L., & Osgood, D. W. (2005). Reconsidering peers and delinquency: How do peers matter? *Social Forces, 84,* 1109–1130.

Haynie, D. L., Doogan, N. J., & Soller, B. (2014). Gender, friendship networks, and delinquency: A dynamic network approach. *Criminology, 52,* 688–722.

Haynie, D. L., Giordano, P. C., Manning, W. D., & Longmore, M. A. (2005). Adolescent romantic relationships and delinquency involvement. *Criminology, 43,* 177–210.

Haynie, D. L., Nansel, T., Eitel, P., Crump, A., Saylor, K., Yu, K., & Simons-Morton, B. (2001). Bullies, victims, and bully/victims: Distinct groups of at-risk youth. *Journal of Early Adolescence, 21,* 29–49.

Hayward, C., Gotlib, I., Schraedley, P., & Litt, I. (1999). Ethnic differences in the association between pubertal status and symptoms of depression in adolescent girls. *Journal of Adolescent Health, 25,* 143–149.

Hazan, C. (1994, February). *The role of sexuality in peer attachment formation.* Paper presented at the biennial meetings of the Society for Research on Adolescence, San Diego.

Hazel, N. A., Oppenheimer, C. W., Technow, J. R., Young, J. F., & Hankin, B. L. (2014). Parent relationship quality buffers against the effect of peer stressors on depressive symptoms from middle childhood to adolescence. *Developmental Psychology, 50,* 2115–2123.

Heard, H. E. (2007). The family structure trajectory and adolescent school performance: Differential effects by race and ethnicity. *Journal of Family Issues, 28,* 319–354.

Heatherton, T. F., & Sargent, J. D. (2009). Does watching smoking in movies promote teenage smoking? *Current Directions in Psychological Science, 18,* 63–67.

Hebert, K. R., Faes, J., Nangle, D. W., Papadakis, A. A., Grover, R. L. (2013). Linking social anxiety and adolescent romantic relationship functioning: Indirect effects and the importance of peers. *Journal of Youth & Adolescence, 42,* 1708–1720.

Hechinger, F. (1993). Schools for teenagers: A historic dilemma. *Teachers College Record, 94,* 522–539.

Heck, R. H., Price, C. L., & Thomas, S. L. (2004). Tracks as emergent structures: A network analysis of student differentiation in a high school. *American Journal of Education, 110,* 321–353.

Hein, K., Dell, R., Futterman, D., Rotheram-Borus, M., & Shaffer, N. (1995). Comparison of HIV1 and HIV2 adolescents: Risk factors and psychosocial determinants. *Pediatrics, 95,* 96–104.

Hektner, J. M., & Swenson, C. A. (2012). Links from teacher beliefs to peer victimization and bystander intervention: Tests of mediating processes. *The Journal of Early Adolescence, 32,* 516–536.

Heller, S. B. (2014). Summer jobs reduce violence among disadvantaged youth. *Science, 346,* 1219–1223.

Hellström, C., Nilsson, K.W., Leppert, J., & Åslund, C. (2012). Influences of motives to play and time spent gaming on the negative consequences of adolescent online computer gaming. *Computers in Human Behavior, 28,* 1379–1387.

Helms, S. W., Choukas-Bradley, S., Widman, L., Giletta, M., Cohen, G. L., & Prinstein, M. J. (2014). Adolescents misperceive and are influenced by high-status peers' health risk, deviant, and adaptive behavior. *Developmental Psychology, 50,* 2697–2714.

Helsen, M., Vollebergh, W., & Meeus, W. (2000). Social support from parents and friends and emotional problems in adolescence. *Journal of Youth and Adolescence, 29,* 319–335.

Helwig, C. (1995). Adolescents' and young adults' conceptions of civil liberties: Freedom of speech and religion. *Child Development, 66,* 152–166.

Helwig, C. (1997). The role of agent and social context in judgments of freedom of speech and religion. *Child Development, 68,* 484–495.

Helwig, C. C., To, S., Wang, Q., Liu, C., & Yang, S. (2014). Judgments and reasoning about parental discipline involving induction and psychological control in China and Canada. *Child Development, 85,* 1150–1167.

Helwig, C., Arnold, M. L., Tan, D., & Boyd, D. (2007). Mainland Chinese and Canadian adolescents' judgments and reasoning about the fairness of democratic and other forms of government. *Cognitive Development, 22,* 96–109.

Helwig, C., Yang, S., Tan, D., Liu, C., & Shao, T. (2011). Urban and rural Chinese adolescents' judgments and reasoning about personal and group jurisdiction. *Child Development, 82,* 701–716.

Henderson, A., Brown, S. D., Pancer, S. M., & Ellis-Hale, K. (2007). Mandated community service in high school and subsequent civic engagement: The case of the "double cohort" in Ontario, Canada. *Journal of Youth and Adolescence, 36,* 849–860.

Henderson, A., Pancer, S. M., & Brown, S. D. (2014). Creating effective civic engagement policy for adolescents: Quantitative and qualitative evaluations of compulsory community service. *Journal of Adolescent Research, 29,* 120–154.

Henderson, C., Hayslip, B., Sanders, L., & Louden, L. (2009). Grandmother–grandchild relationship quality predicts psychological adjustment among youth from divorced families. *Journal of Family Issues, 30,* 1245–1264.

Hendrick, S., & Hendrick, C. (1994, February). *Gender, sexuality, and close relationships.* Paper presented at the biennial meetings of the Society for Research on Adolescence, San Diego.

Henry, B., Caspi, A., Moffitt, T., & Silva, P. (1996). Temperamental and familial predictors of violent and nonviolent criminal convictions: Age 3 to age 18. *Developmental Psychology, 32,* 614–623.

Henry, B., Caspi, A., Moffitt, T., Harrington, H., & Silva, P. (1999). Staying in school protects boys with poor self-regulation in childhood from later crime: A longitudinal study. *International Journal of Behavioral Development, 23,* 1049–1073.

Henry, D. B., Schoeny, M. E., Deptula, D. P., & Slavick, J. T. (2007). Peer selection and socialization effects on adolescent intercourse without a condom and attitudes about the costs of sex. *Child Development, 78,* 825–838.

Henry, K. L., Cavanagh, T. M., & Oetting, E. R. (2011). Perceived parental investment in school as a mediator of the relationship between socio-economic indicators and educational outcomes in rural America. *Journal of Youth and Adolescence, 40,* 1164–1177.

Henry, K. L., Knight, K. E., & Thornberry, T. P. (2012). School disengagement as a predictor of dropout, delinquency, and problem substance use during adolescence and early adulthood. *Journal of Youth and Adolescence, 41,* 156–166.

Hensel, D., Fortenberry, J., & Orr, D. (2008). Variations in coital and noncoital sexual repertoire among adolescent women. *Journal of Adolescent Health, 42,* 170–176.

Henshaw, S. (1995). The impact of requirements for parental consent on minors' abortions in Mississippi. *Family Planning Perspectives, 27,* 120–122.

Herbers, J. E., Reynolds, A. J., & Chen, C. C. (2013). School mobility and developmental outcomes in young adulthood. *Development and Psychopathology, 25,* 501–515.

Herdt, G., & McClintock, M. (2000). The magical age of 10. *Archives of Sexual Behavior, 29,* 587–606.

Herman, M. (2004). Forced to choose: Some determinants of racial identification in multiracial adolescents. *Child Development, 75,* 730–748.

Herman, M. (2009). The Black-White-other achievement gap: Testing theories of academic performance among multiracial and monoracial adolescents. *Sociology of Education, 82,* 20–46.

Herman-Giddens, M., Slora, E., Wasserman, R., Bourdony, C., Bhapkar, M., Koch, G., . . . Hasemeier, C. (1997). Secondary sexual characteristics and menses in young girls seen in office practice: A study from the Pediatric Research in Office Settings Network. *Pediatrics, 88,* 505–512.

Herman-Giddens, M., Steffes, J., Harris, D., Slora, E., Hussey, M., Dowshen, S., . . . Reiter, E. (2012, October 20). Secondary sexual characteristics in boys: Data from the Pediatric Research in Office Settings Network. Pediatrics, published online (DOI: 10.1542/peds.2011-3291).

Herman-Stahl, M., Stemmler, M., & Petersen, A. (1995). Approach and avoidant coping: Implications for adolescent mental health. *Journal of Youth and Adolescence, 24,* 649–665.

Hernandez, D. C., Pressler, E., Dorius, C., & Mitchell, K. S. (2014). Does family instability make girls fat? Gender differences between instability and weight. *Journal of Marriage and Family, 76,* 175–190.

Hernández, M. M., Conger, R. D., Robins, R. W., Beaumont Bacher, K., & Widaman, K. F. (2014). Cultural socialization and ethnic pride among Mexican-origin adolescents during the transition to middle school. *Child Development, 85,* 695–708.

Hernández, M. M., Robins, R. W., Widaman, K. F., & Conger, R. D. (2014). School belonging, generational status, and socioeconomic effects on Mexican-origin children's later academic competence and expectations. *Journal of Research on Adolescence, Early view.* DOI: 10.1111/jora.12188

Herpers, P. C., Scheepers, F. E., Bons, D. M., Buitelaar, J. K., & Rommelse, N. N. (2014). The cognitive and neural correlates of psychopathy and especially callous–unemotional traits in youths: A systematic review of the evidence. *Development and Psychopathology, 26,* 245–273.

Herrenkohl, T. I., Hill, K. G., Hawkins, J. D., Chung, I., & Nagin, D. (2006). Developmental trajectories of family management and risk for violent behavior in adolescence. *Journal of Adolescent Health, 39,* 206–213.

Herrenkohl, T. I., Kosterman, R., Hawkins, J. D., & Mason, W. A. (2009). Effects of growth in family conflict in adolescence on adult depressive symptoms: Mediating and moderation effects of stress and school bonding. *Journal of Adolescent Health, 44,* 146–152.

Herrenkohl, T. I., Maguin, E., Hill, K. G., Hawkins, J., Abbott, R. D., & Catalano, R. F. (2000).

Developmental risk factors for youth violence. *Journal of Adolescent Health, 26,* 176–186.

Herrera, V. M., Wiersma, J. D., & Cleveland, H. H. (2011). Romantic partners' contribution to the continuity of male and female delinquent and violent behavior. *Journal of Research on Adolescence, 21,* 608–618.

Herting, M. M., Colby, J. B., Sowell, E. R., & Nagel, B. J. (2014). White matter connectivity and aerobic fitness in male adolescents. *Developmental Cognitive Neuroscience, 7,* 65–75.

Herting, M. M., Maxwell, E. C., Irvine, C., & Nagel, B.J. (2012) .The impact of sex, puberty, and hormones on white matter microstructure in adolescents. *Cerebral Cortex, 22,* 1979–1992.

Herts, K. L., McLaughlin, K. A., Hatzenbuehler, M. L. (2012). Emotion dysregulation as a mechanism linking stress exposure to adolescent aggressive behavior. *Journal of Abnormal Child Psychology, 40,* 1111–1122.

Hetherington, E. M. (1991). The role of individual differences and family relationships in children's coping with divorce and remarriage. In P. Cowan & E. M. Hetherington (Eds.), *Advances in family research:* Vol. 2. *Family transitions.* Hillsdale, NJ: Erlbaum.

Hetherington, E. M. (1993). An overview of the Virginia longitudinal study of divorce and remarriage with a focus on early adolescence. *Journal of Family Psychology, 7,* 39–56.

Hetherington, E. M., Bridges, M., & Insabella, G. (1998). What matters? What does not? Five perspectives on the association between marital transitions and children's adjustment. *American Psychologist, 53,* 167–184.

Hetherington, E. M., Henderson, S., & Reiss, D. (1999). Adolescent siblings in stepfamilies: Family functioning and adolescent adjustment. *Monographs of the Society for Research in Child Development, 64,* Serial No. 259.

Hicks, B. M., Johnson, W., Durbin, C. E., Blonigen, D. M., Iacono, W. G., & McGue, M. (2014). Delineating selection and mediation effects among childhood personality and environmental risk factors in the development of adolescent substance abuse. *Journal of Abnormal Child Psychology, 42,* 845–859.

Hightower, E. (1990). Adolescent interpersonal and familial predictors of positive mental health at midlife. *Journal of Youth and Adolescence, 19,* 257–276.

Hill, C., Corbett, C., & Rose, A. (2010). *Why so few?* Washington: AAUW.

Hill, J. P. (1983). Early adolescence: A framework. *Journal of Early Adolescence, 3,* 1–21.

Hill, J., Emery, R. E., Harden, K. P., Mendle, J., & Turkheimer, E. (2008). Alcohol use in adolescent twins and affiliation with substance using peers. *Journal of Abnormal Child Psychology, 36,* 81–94.

Hill, K. G., Hawkins, J. D., Catalano, R. F., Abbott, R. D., & Guo, J. (2005). Family influences on the risk of daily smoking initiation. *Journal of Adolescent Health, 37,* 202–210.

Hill, N. E., & Tyson, D. (2009). Parental involvement in middle school: A meta-analytic assessment of the strategies that promote achievement. *Developmental Psychology, 45,* 740–763.

Hill, N. E., & Wang, M. T. (2015). From middle school to college: Developing aspirations, promoting engagement, and indirect pathways from parenting to post high school enrollment. *Developmental Psychology, 51,* 224–235.

Hill, N. E., Castellino, D. R., Lansford, J. E., Nowlin, P., Dodge, K. A., Bates, J. E., & Pettit, G. S. (2004). Parent academic involvement as related to school behavior, achievement, and aspirations: Demographic variations across adolescence. *Child Development, 75,* 1491–1509.

Hill, N. E., Ramirez, C., & Dumka, L. E. (2003). Early adolescents' career aspirations: A qualitative study of perceived barriers and family support among low-income, ethnically diverse adolescents. *Journal of Family Issues, 24,* 934–959.

Hill, P. L., Burrow, A. L., Sumner, R. (2013). Addressing important questions in the field of adolescent purpose. *Child Development Perspectives, 7,* 232–236.

Hilsman, R., & Garber, J. (1995). A test of the cognitive diathesis–stress model of depression in children: Academic stressors, attributional style, perceived competence, and control. *Journal of Personality and Social Psychology, 69,* 370–380.

Hilt, L. M., McLaughlin, K. A., & Nolen-Hoeksema, S. (2010). Examination of the Response Styles Theory in a community sample of young adolescents. *Journal of Abnormal Child Psychology, 38,* 545–556.

Hindin, M. J., & Fatusi, A. O. (2009). Adolescent sexual and reproductive health in developing countries: An overview of trends and interventions. *International Perspectives on Sexual and Reproductive Health, 35,* 58–62.

Hinduja, S., Patchin, J. W. (2013). Social influences on cyberbullying behaviors among middle and high school students. *Journal of Youth & Adolescence, 42,* 711–722.

Hine, T. (1999). *The rise and fall of the American teenager.* New York: Bard Books.

Hingson, R., & Zha, W. (2009). Age of drinking onset, alcohol use disorders, frequent heavy drinking, and unintentionally injuring oneself and others after drinking. *Pediatrics, 123,* 1477–1484.

Hingson, R., Heeren, T., & Winter, M. (2006). Age at drinking onset and alcohol dependence: Age at onset, duration, and severity. *Archives of Pediatric and Adolescent Medicine, 160,* 739–746.

Hirsch, B., & DuBois, D. (1991). Self-esteem in early adolescence: The identification and prediction of contrasting longitudinal trajectories. *Journal of Youth and Adolescence, 20,* 53–72.

Hirsch, B., Mickus, M., & Boerger, R. (2002). Ties to influential adults among Black and White adolescents: Culture, social class, and family networks. *American Journal of Community Psychology, 30,* 289–303.

Hirschfield, P. (2009). Another way out: The impact of juvenile arrests on high school dropout. *Sociology of Education, 82,* 368–393.

Hitlin, S., Brown, J. S., & Elder, G. H. J. (2006). Racial self-categorization in adolescence: Multiracial development and social pathways. *Child Development, 77,* 1298–1308.

Hochberg, Z., Gawlik, A., & Walker, R. S. (2011). Evolutionary fitness as a function of pubertal age in 22 subsistence-based traditional societies. *International Journal of Pediatric Endocrinology, 2,* 1–7.

Hock, E., Eberly, M., Bartle-Haring, S., Ellwanger, P., & Widaman, K. F. (2001). Separation anxiety in parents of adolescents: Theoretical significance and scale development. *Child Development, 72,* 284–298.

Hodges, E., & Perry, D. (1999). Personal and interpersonal antecedents and consequences of victimization by peers. *Journal of Personality and Social Psychology, 76,* 677–685.

Hodges, E., Boivin, M., Vitaro, F., & Bukowski, W. (1999). The power of friendship: Protection against an escalating cycle of peer victimization. *Developmental Psychology, 35,* 94–101.

Hoeve, M., Blokland, A., Dubas, J. S., Loeber, R., Gerris, J., & van der Laan, P. (2008). Trajectories of delinquency and parenting styles. *Journal of Abnormal Child Psychology, 36,* 223–235.

Hofferth, S. L., & Moon, U. J. (2012). Electronic play, study, communication, and adolescent achievement, 2003–2008. *Journal of Research on Adolescence, 22,* 215–224.

Hofferth, S. L., & Reid, L. (2002). Early childbearing and children's achievement and behavior over time. *Perspectives on Sexual and Reproductive Health, 34,* 41–49.

Hofferth, S. L., Reid, L., & Mott, F. L. (2001). The effects of early childbearing on schooling over time. *Family Planning Perspective, 33,* 259–267.

Hoffman, J. P. (2002). The community context of family structure and adolescent drug use. *Journal of Marriage and the Family, 64,* 314–330.

Hoffman, J. P. (2003). A contextual analysis of differential association, social control, and strain theories of delinquency. *Social Forces, 81,* 753–785.

Hoffman, K. L., Kiecolt, J., & Edwards, J. N. (2005). Physical violence between siblings: A theoretical and empirical analysis. *Journal of Family Issues, 26,* 1103–1130.

Hogan, D., Sun, R., & Cornwell, G. (2000). Sexual and fertility behaviors of American females aged 15–19 years: 1985, 1990, and 1995. *American Journal of Public Health, 90,* 1421–1425.

Hogue, A., & Steinberg, L. (1995). Homophily of internalized distress in adolescent peer groups. *Developmental Psychology, 31,* 897–906.

Holas, I., & Huston, A. C. (2012). Are middle school harmful? The role of transition timing, classroom quality and school characteristics. *Journal of Youth & Adolescence, 41,* 333–345.

Holder, D. W., DuRant, R. H., Harris, T. L., Daniel, J. H., Obeidallah, D., & Goodman, E. (2000). The association between adolescent spirituality and voluntary sexual activity. *Journal of Adolescent Health, 26,* 295–302.

Holland, M. M. (2012). Only here for the day: The social integration of minority students at a majority white high school. *Sociology of Education, 85,* 101–120.

Hollander, D. (2006). Many teenagers who say they have taken a virginity pledge retract that statement after having intercourse. *Perspectives on Sexual and Reproductive Health, 38,* 168.

Hollenstein, T., & Lougheed, J. P. Beyond storm and stress: Typicality, transactions, timing, and temperament to account for adolescent change. (2013). *American Psychologist, 68,* 444–454.

Hollingshead, A. (1975). *Elmtown's youth and Elmtown revisited.* New York: Wiley. (Original work published 1949).

Holmbeck, G. (1996). A model of family relational transformations during the transition to adolescence: Parent–adolescent conflict and adaptation. In J. Graber, J. Brooks-Gunn, & A. Petersen (Eds.), *Transitions through adolescence: Interpersonal domains and context* (pp. 167–199). Mahwah, NJ: Erlbaum.

Holmbeck, G., & Hill, J. P. (1991). Conflictive engagement, positive affect, and menarche in families with seventh-grade girls. *Child Development, 62,* 1030–1048.

Holmbeck, G., Durbin, D., & Kung, E. (1995, March). *Attachment, autonomy, and adjustment before and after leaving home: Sullivan and Sullivan revisited.* Paper presented at the Society for Research in Child Development, Indianapolis.

Holmbeck, G., Shapera, W., Westhoven, V., Johnson, S., Millstein, R., & Hommeyer, J. (2000, March). *A longitudinal study of observed and perceived parenting behaviors and autonomy development in families of young adolescents with spina bifida.* Paper presented at the biennial meetings of the Society for Research on Adolescence, Chicago.

Holmen, T., Barrett-Connor, E., Holmen, J., & Bjermer, L. (2000). Health problems in teenage daily smokers versus nonsmokers, Norway, 1995–1997. *American Journal of Epidemiology, 151,* 148–155.

Holsen, I., Kraft, P., & Vitterso, J. (2000). Stability in depressed mood in adolescence: Results from a 6-year longitudinal panel study. *Journal of Youth and Adolescence, 29,* 61–78.

Holt, M. K., Matjasko, J. L., Espelage, D., Reid, G., & Koenig, B. (2013). Sexual risk taking and bullying among adolescents. *Pediatrics, 132,* e1481–e1487.

Homma, Y., Wang, N., Saewyc, E., & Kishor, N. (2012). The relationship between sexual abuse

and risky sexual behavior among adolescent boys: A meta-analysis. *Journal of Adolescent Health, 51,* 18–24.

Hooper, C. J., Luciana, M., Conklin, H. M., & Yarger, R. S. (2004). Adolescents' performance on the Iowa gambling task: Implications for the development of decision making and ventromedial prefrontal cortex. *Developmental Psychology, 40,* 1148–1158.

Hope, E. C., Skoog, A. B., & Jagers, R. J. (2015). "It'll never be the white kids, it'll always be us": Black high school students' evolving critical analysis of racial discrimination and inequity in schools. *Journal of Adolescent Research, 30,* 83–112.

Horan, P., & Hargis, P. (1991). Children's work and schooling in the late nineteenth-century family economy. *American Sociological Review, 56,* 583–596.

Horn, A. S. (2012). The cultivation of a prosocial value orientation through community service: an examination of organizational context, social facilitation, and duration. *Journal of Youth & Adolescence, 41,* 948–968.

Horn, S. S. (2003). Adolescents' reasoning about exclusion from social groups. *Developmental Psychology, 39,* 71–84.

Horn, S. S. (2007). Adolescents' acceptance of same-sex peers based on sexual orientation and gender expression. *Journal of Youth and Adolescence, 36,* 363–371.

Horner, J., Jamieson, P., & Romer, D. (2008). The changing portrayal of alcohol use in television. In P. Jamieson & D. Romer (Eds.), *The changing portrayal of adolescents in the media since 1950* (pp. 284–312). New York: Oxford University Press.

Horner, J., Salazar, L. F., Romer, D., Vanable, P. A., DiClemente, R., Carey, M. P., . . . Brown, L. (2009). Withdrawal (coitus interruptus) as a sexual risk reduction strategy: perspectives from African-American adolescents. *Archives of Sexual Behavior, 38,* 779–787.

Hornik, R., Jacobsohn, L., Orwin, R., Piesse, A., & Kalton, G. (2008). Effects of the national youth anti-drug media campaign on youths. *American Journal of Public Health, 98,* 2229–2236.

Horvat, E. M., & Lewis, K. S. (2003). Reassessing the "burden of 'acting White'": The importance of peer group in managing academic success. *Sociology of Education, 76,* 265–280.

Hou, J., Natsuaki, M. N., Zhang, J., Guo, F., Huang, Z., Wang, M., & Chen, Z. (2013). Romantic relationships and adjustment problems in China: The moderating effect of classroom romantic context. *Journal of Adolescence, 36,* 171–180.

Houser, J. J., Mayeux, L., & Cross, C. (2015). Peer status and aggression as predictors of dating popularity in adolescence. *Journal of Youth & Adolescence, 44,* 683–695.

Howard, A. L., Kimonis, E. R., Muñoz, L. C., Frick, P. J. (2012). Violence exposure mediates the relation between callous-unemotional traits and offending patterns in adolescents.

Journal of Abnormal Child Psychology, 40, 1237–1247.

Howard, A., & Galambos, N. (2011). Transitions to adulthood. In B. Brown & M. Prinstein (Eds.), *Encyclopedia of adolescence* (Vol. 1, pp. 376–383). New York: Academic Press.

Howard, K., Budge, S., & McKay, K. (2010). Youth exposed to violence: the role of protective factors. *Journal of Community Psychology, 38,* 63–79.

Howell, W., & Peterson, P. (2002). *The education gap: Vouchers and urban schools.* Washington, DC: Brookings Institution.

Hoyt, L. T., Kushi, L. H., Leung, C. W., Nickleach, D. C., Adler, N., Laraia, B. A., Hiatt, R. A., & Yen, I. H. (2014). Neighborhood influences on girls' obesity risk across the transition to adolescence. *Pediatrics, 134,* 942–949.

Hoyt, L., Chase-Lansdale, P., McDade, T., & Adam, E. K. (2011). Positive youth, healthy adults: Does positive well-being in adolescence predict better perceived health and fewer risky health behaviors in young adulthood? *Journal of Adolescent Health, 50,* 66–73.

Hu, M., Davies, M., & Kandel, D. (2006). Epidemiology and correlates of daily smoking and nicotine dependence among young adults in the United States. *American Journal of Public Health, 96,* 299–308.

Huang, D., Murphy, D. A., & Hser, Y-H. (2012). Developmental trajectory of sexual risk behaviors from adolescence to young adulthood. *Youth & Society, 44,* 479–499.

Hudley, C. (1995). Assessing the impact of separate schooling for African American male adolescents. *Journal of Early Adolescence, 15,* 38–57.

Hudley, C. (1997). Supporting achievement beliefs among ethnic minority adolescents: Two case examples. *Journal of Research on Adolescence, 7,* 133–152.

Huebner, A. J., & Howell, L. W. (2003). Examining the relationship between adolescent sexual risk-taking and perceptions of monitoring, communication, and parenting styles. *Journal of Adolescent Health, 33,* 71–78.

Huebner, A. J., & Mancini, J. A. (2003). Shaping structured out-of-school time use among youth: The effects of self, family, and friend systems. *Journal of Youth and Adolescence, 32,* 453–463.

Huesmann, L. R. (2007). The impact of electronic media violence: Scientific theory and research. *Journal of Adolescent Health, 41,* S6–S13.

Hughes, D., Way, N., & Rivas-Drake, D. (2011). Stability and change in private and public ethnic regard among African American, Puerto Rican, Dominican, and Chinese American early adolescents. *Journal of Research on Adolescence, 21,* 861–870.

Hughes, J. N., Im, M., Kwok, O., Cham, H., & West, S. G. (2015). Latino students' transition to middle school: Role of bilingual education and school ethnic context. *Journal of Research on Adolescence, 25,* 443–458.

Hughes, S., Power, T., & Francis, D. (1992). Defining patterns of drinking in adolescence: A cluster analytic approach. *Journal of Studies on Alcohol, 53,* 40–47.

Huh, D., Stice, E., Shaw, H., & Boutelle, K. (2012). Female overweight and obesity in adolescence: Developmental trends and ethnic differences in prevalence, incidence, and remission. *Journal of Youth and Adolescence, 41,* 76–85.

Huh, D., Tristan, J., Wade, E., & Stice, E. (2006). Does problem behavior elicit poor parenting?: A prospective study of adolescent girls. *Journal of Adolescent Research, 21,* 185–204.

Huizenga, H., Crone, E., & Jansen, B. (2007). Decision-making in healthy children, adolescents, and adults explained by the use of increasingly complex proportional reasoning rules. *Developmental Science, 10,* 814–825.

Hulleman, C. S., & Harackiewicz, J. M. (2009). Promoting interest and performance in high school science classes. *Science, 326(5958),* 1410–1412.

Hulme, S., Jones, O., & Abraham, W. (2013). Emerging roles of metaplasticity in behaviour and disease, *Trends in Neurosciences 36,* 353–362.

Hunter, S., Barber, B., Olsen, J., McNeely, C., & Bose, K. (2011). Adolescents' self-disclosure to parents across cultures: Who discloses and why. *Journal of Adolescent Research, 26,* 447–478.

Huntsinger, C. S., & Jose, P. E. (2006). A longitudinal investigation of personality and social adjustment among Chinese American and European American adolescents. *Child Development, 77,* 1309–1324.

Hurd, N. M., Sánchez, B., Zimmerman, M. A., & Caldwell, C. H. (2012). Natural mentors, racial identity, and educational attainment among African American adolescents: Exploring pathways to success. *Child Development, 83,* 1196–1212.

Hurd, N. M., Stoddard, S. A., & Zimmerman, M. A. (2013). Neighborhoods, social support, and African American adolescents' mental health outcomes: A multilevel path analysis. *Child Development, 84,* 858–874.

Hurd, N. M., Varner, F. A., Caldwell, C. H., & Zimmerman, M. A. (2014). Does perceived racial discrimination predict changes in psychological distress and substance use over time? An examination among Black emerging adults. *Developmental Psychology, 50,* 1910–1918.

Hurd, N. M., Varner, F. A., Rowley, S. J. (2013). Involved-vigilant parenting and socio-emotional well-being among black youth: the moderating influence of natural mentoring relationships. *Journal of Youth & Adolescence, 42,* 1583–1595.

Hurley, D. (2005, April 19). Divorce rate: It's not as high as you think. *The New York Times.*

Hussong, A. M. (2000). Perceived peer context and adolescent adjustment. *Journal of Research on Adolescence, 10,* 391–415.

Hussong, A. M., & Hicks, R. E. (2003). Affect and peer context interactively impact adolescent substance use. *Journal of Abnormal Child Psychology, 31,* 413–426.

Hussong, A. M., Curran, P. J., & Moffitt, T. E. (2004). Substance abuse hinders desistance in young adults' antisocial behavior. *Development and Psychopathology, 16,* 1029–1046.

Hutchinson, D., Rapee, R., & Taylor, A. (2010). Body dissatisfaction and eating disturbances in early adolescence: A structural modeling investigation examining negative affect and peer factors. *Journal of Early Adolescence, 30,* 489–517.

Hutchinson, M. K., Jemmott, J. B., III, Jemmott, L. S., Braverman, P., & Fong, G. T. (2003). The role of mother–daughter sexual risk communication in reducing sexual risk behaviors among urban adolescent females: A prospective study. *Journal of Adolescent Health, 33,* 98–107.

Huynh, V., & Fuligni, A. (2008). Ethnic socialization and the academic adjustment of adolescents from Mexican, Chinese, and European backgrounds. *Developmental Psychology, 44,* 1202–1208.

Huynh, V., & Fuligni, A. (2010). Discrimination hurts: The academic, psychological, and physical well-being of adolescents. *Journal of Research on Adolescence, 20,* 916–941.

Huynh, V. W. (2012). Ethnic microaggressions and the depressive and somatic symptoms of Latino and Asian American adolescents. *Journal of Youth & Adolescence, 41,* 831–846.

Hwang, K., Hallquist, M. N., and Luna, B. (2013). The development of hub architecture in the human functional brain network. *Cerebral Cortex, 23,* 2380–2393.

Hwang, K., Velanova, K., & Luna, B. (2010). Strengthening of top-down frontal cognitive control networks underlying the development of inhibitory control: a functional magnetic resonance imaging effective connectivity study. *Journal of Neuroscience, 30(46),* 15535–15545.

Hyde, L. W., Shaw, D. S., & Hariri, A. R. (2013). Understanding youth antisocial behavior using neuroscience through a developmental psychopathology lens: Review, integration, and directions for research. *Developmental Review, 33,* 168–223.

Hyde, L. W., Shaw, D. S., & Moilanen, K. L. (2010). Developmental precursors of moral disengagement and the role of moral disengagement in the development of antisocial behavior. *Journal of Abnormal Child Psychology, 38,* 197–209.

Iannotti, R. J., & Wang, J. (2013). Patterns of physical activity, sedentary behavior, and diet in U.S. adolescents. *Journal of Adolescent Health, 53,* 280–286.

Iannotti, R. J., & Wang, J. (2013). Trends in physical activity, sedentary behavior, diet, and BMI among US adolescents, 2001–2009. *Pediatrics, 132,* 606–614.

Ibañez, G. E., Kuperminc, G. P., Jurkovic, G., & Perilla, J. (2004). Cultural attributes and adaptations linked to achievement motivation among Latino adolescents. *Journal of Youth and Adolescence, 33,* 559–568.

Iglowstein, I., Jenni, O., Molinari, L., & Largo, R. (2003). Sleep duration from infancy to adolescence: Reference values and generational trends. *Pediatrics, 111,* 302–307.

Impett, E. A., Sorsoli, L., Schooler, D., Henson, J. M., & Tolman, D. L. (2008). Girls' relationship authenticity and self-esteem across adolescence. *Developmental Psychology, 44,* 722–733.

Ingoldsby, E. M., Kohl, G. O., McMahon, R. J., & Lengua, L. (2006). Conduct problems, depressive symptomatology, and their co-occurring presentation in childhood as predictors of adjustment in early adolescence. *Journal of Abnormal Child Psychology, 34,* 603–621.

Inhelder, B., & Piaget, J. (1958). *The growth of logical thinking from childhood to adolescence.* New York: Basic Books.

Institute of Medicine (2013). *Contagion of violence: Workshop summary.* Washington: National Academies Press.

Institute of Medicine. (2015). *Investing in the health and well-being of young adults.* Washington: National Academies Press.

IOM (Institute of Medicine) and NRC (National Research Council) (2006). *Food marketing to children and youth: Threat or opportunity?* Washington, DC: National Academies Press.

IOM (Institute of Medicine) and NRC (National Research Council). (2011a). *The science of adolescent risk-taking: Workshop report.* Committee on the Science of Adolescence. Washington, DC: The National Academies Press.

IOM (Institute of Medicine) and NRC (National Research Council). (2011b). *The health of lesbian, gay, bisexual, and transgender people: Building a foundation for better understanding.* Washington, DC: The National Academies Press.

Irwin, K. (2004). The violence of adolescent life experiencing and managing everyday threats. *Youth and Society, 35,* 452–479.

Isakson, K., & Jarvis, P. (1999). The adjustment of adolescents during the transition into high school: A short-term longitudinal study. *Journal of Youth and Adolescence, 28,* 1–26.

Iselin, A. M., Mulvey, E. P., Loughran, T. A., Chung, H. L., & Schubert, C. A. (2012). A longitudinal examination of serious adolescent offenders' perceptions of chances for success and engagement in behaviors accomplishing goals. *Journal of Abnormal Child Psychology, 40,* 237–249.

Ispa-Landa, S. (2013). Gender, race, and justifications for group exclusion: Urban black students bussed to affluent suburban schools. *Sociology of Education, 86,* 218–233.

Israelashvili, M., Kim, T., & Bukobza, G. (2012). Adolescents' over-use of the cyber-world:

Internet addiction or identity exploration? *Journal of Adolescence, 35,* 417–424.

Ivanova, K., Mills, M., & Veenstra, R. (2011). The initiation of dating in adolescence: The effect of parental divorce. The TRAILS study. *Journal of Research on Adolescence, 21,* 769–775.

Ivanova, K., Mills, M., & Veenstra, R. (2014). Parental residential and partnering transitions and the initiation of adolescent romantic relationships. *Journal of Marriage and Family, 76,* 465–475.

Ivers, R., Senserrick, T., Boufous, S., Stevenson, M., Chen, H., Woodward, M., & Norton, R. (2009). Novice drivers' risky driving behavior, risk perception, and crash risk: Findings from the DRIVE study. *American Journal of Public Health, 99,* 1638–1644.

Ivory, J. (2008). The games, they are a-changin': Technological advancements in video games and implications for effects on youth. In P. Jamieson & D. Romer (Eds.), *The changing portrayal of adolescents in the media since 1950* (pp. 347–376). New York: Oxford University Press.

Jaccard, J., Blanton, H., & Dodge, T. (2005). Peer influences on risk behavior: An analysis of the effects of a close friend. *Developmental Psychology, 41,* 135–147.

Jaccard, J., Dittus, P., & Gordon, V. (1998). Parent–adolescent congruency in reports of adolescent sexual behavior and in communications about sexual behavior. *Child Development, 69,* 247–261.

Jaccard, J., Dodge, T., & Dittus, P. (2003a). Do adolescents want to avoid pregnancy? Atttitudes toward pregnancy as predictors of pregnancy. *Journal of Adolescent Health, 33,* 79–83.

Jaccard, J., Dodge, T., & Dittus, P. (2003b). Maternal discussion about pregnancy and adolescents' attitudes towards pregnancy. *Journal of Adolescent Health, 33,* 84–87.

Jackson, C. (2002). Perceived legitimacy of parental authority and tobacco and alcohol use during early adolescence. *Journal of Adolescent Health, 31,* 425–432.

Jackson, K. M., & Schulenberg, J. E. (2013). Alcohol use during the transition from middle school to high school: National panel data on prevalence and moderators. *Developmental Psychology, 49,* 2147–2158.

Jackson, L. (2008). Adolescents and the Internet. In P. Jamieson & D. Romer (Eds.), *The changing portrayal of adolescents in the media since 1950* (pp. 377–411). New York: Oxford University Press.

Jackson, T., & Chen, H. (2011). Risk factors for disordered eating during early and middle adolescence: Prospective evidence from mainland Chinese boys and girls. *Journal of Abnormal Psychology, 120,* 454–464.

Jackson, T., & Chen, H. (2014). Risk factors for disordered eating during early and middle adolescence: A two year longitudinal study of mainland chinese boys and girls. *Journal of Abnormal Child Psychology, 42,* 791–802.

Jackson-Newsom, J., Buchanan, C. M., & McDonald, R. M. (2008). Parenting and perceived maternal warmth in European American and African American adolescents. *Journal of Marriage and Family, 70,* 62–75.

Jacobi, C., Hayward, C., de Zwaan, M., Kraemer, H. C., & Agras, W. S. (2004). Coming to terms with risk factors for eating disorders: Application of risk terminology and suggestions for a general taxonomy. *Psychological Bulletin, 130,* 19–65.

Jacobs, J. E., Chin, C. S., & Shaver, K. (2005). Longitudinal links between perceptions of adolescence and the social beliefs of adolescents: Are parents' stereotypes related to beliefs held about and by their children? *Journal of Youth and Adolescence, 34,* 61–72.

Jacobs, J. E., Lanza, S., Osgood, D. W., Eccles, J., & Wigfield, A. (2002). Changes in children's self-competence and values: Gender and domain differences across grades one through twelve. *Child Development, 73,* 509–527.

Jacobson, C., & Gould, M. (2007). The epidemiology and phenomenology of non-suicidal self-injurious behavior among adolescents: A critical review of the literature. *Archives of Suicide Research, 11,* 129–147.

Jacobson, K., & Rowe, D. (1999). Genetic and environmental influences on the relationships between family connectedness, school connectedness, and adolescent depressed mood: Sex differences. *Developmental Psychology, 35,* 926–939.

Jaeger, A., Selmeczy, D., O'Connor, A. R., Diaz, M., & Dobbins, I. G. (2012). Prefrontal cortex contributions to controlled memory judgment: fMRI evidence from adolescents and young adults. *Neuropsychologia, 50,* 3745–3756.

Jaffari-Bimmel, N., Juffer, F., van IJzendoorn, M. H., Bakermans-Kranenburg, M., & Mooijaart, A. (2006). Social development from infancy to adolescence: Longitudinal and concurrent factors in an adoption sample. *Developmental Psychology, 42,* 1143–1153.

Jaffee, S., Caspi, A., Moffitt, T. E., Belsky, J., & Silva, P. (2001). Why are children born to teen mothers at risk for adverse outcomes in young adulthood? Results from a 20-year longitudinal study. *Development and Psychopathology, 13,* 377–397.

Jager, J., Schulenberg, J. E., O'Malley, P. M., & Bachman, J. G. (2013). Historical variation in drug use trajectories across the transition to adulthood: The trend toward lower intercepts and steeper, ascending slopes. *Development and Psychopathology, 25,* 527–543.

Jager, J., Yuen, C. X., Putnick, D. L., Hendricks, C., & Bornstein, M. H. (2015). Adolescent-peer relationships, separation and detachment from parents, and internalizing and externalizing behaviors: Linkages and interactions. *The Journal of Early Adolescence, 35,* 511–537.

James-Burdumy, S., Goesling, B., Deke, J., & Einspruch, E. (2012). The effectiveness of mandatory-random student drug testing: A cluster randomized trial. *Journal of Adolescent Health, 50,* 172–178.

Jang, S. J., & Franzen, A. B. (2013). Is being "spiritual" enough without being religious? A study of violent and property crimes among emerging adults. *Criminology, 51,* 595–627.

Jang, S., & Thornberry, T. (1998). Self-esteem, delinquent peers, and delinquency: A test of the self-enhancement thesis. *American Sociological Review, 63,* 586–598.

Janosz, M., Archambault, I., Pagani, L. S., Pascal, S., Morin, A. J. S., & Bowen, F. (2008). Are there detrimental effects of witnessing school violence in early adolescence? *Journal of Adolescent Health, 43,* 600–608.

Janosz, M., LeBlanc, M., Boulerice, B., & Tremblay, R. E. (2000). Predicting different types of school dropouts: A typological approach with two longitudinal samples. *Journal of Educational Psychology, 92,* 171–190.

Janssen, S., Chessa, A., & Jaap M. (2007). Temporal distribution of favourite books, movies, and records: Differential encoding and re-sampling. *Memory, 15,* 755–67.

Jarrett, R. (1995). Growing up poor: The family experiences of socially mobile youth in low-income African American neighborhoods. *Journal of Adolescent Research, 10,* 111–135.

Jarvinen, M., & Østergaard, J. (2009). Governing adolescent drinking. *Youth & Society, 40,* 377–402.

Jaser, S. S., Champion, J. E., Reeslund, K. L., Keller, G., Merchant, M. J., Benson, M., & Compas, B. (2007). Cross-situational coping with peer and family stressors in adolescent offspring of depressed parents. *Journal of Adolescence, 30,* 917–932.

Jemmott, J., III, Jemmott, L., Fong, G., & McCaffree, K. (1999). Reducing HIV risk-associated sexual behavior among African American adolescents: Testing the generality of intervention effects. *American Journal of Community Psychology, 27,* 161–187.

Jensen, L. A., Arnett, J. J., Feldman, S. S., & Cauffman, E. (2004). The right to do wrong: Lying to parents among adolescents and emerging adults. *Journal of Youth and Adolescence, 33,* 101–112.

Jenssen, B., Klein, J., Salazar, L., Daluga, N., & DiClemente, R. (2009). Exposure to tobacco on the internet: Content analysis of adolescents' internet use. *Pediatrics, 124,* e180–e186.

Jeong, Y.-J., & Chun, Y.-J. (2010). The pathways from parents' marital quality to adolescents' school adjustment in South Korea. *Journal of Family Issues, 31,* 1604–1621.

Jessor, R., & Jessor, S. (1977). Problem behavior and psychosocial development: A longitudinal study of youth. New York: Academic Press.

Jessor, R., & Turbin, M.S. (2014). Parsing protection and risk for problem behavior versus pro-social behavior among U.S. and Chinese adolescents. *Journal of Youth & Adolescence, 43,* 1037–1051.

Jessor, R., Turbin, M. S., Costa, F. M., Dong, Q., Zhang, H., & Wang, C. (2003). Adolescent problem behavior in China and the United States: A cross-national study of psychosocial protective factors. *Journal of Research on Adolescence, 13,* 329–360.

Jessor, R., Turbin, M., & Costa, F. (2010). Predicting developmental change in healthy eating and regular exercise among adolescents in China and the United States: The role of psychosocial and behavioral protection and risk. *Journal of Research on Adolescence, 20,* 707–725.

Jessor, R., Van Den Bos, J., Vanderryn, J., Costa, F., & Turbin, M. (1995). Protective factors in adolescent problem behavior: Moderator effects and developmental change. *Developmental Psychology, 31,* 923–933.

Jewell, J., Brown, C. S., & Perry, B. (2014). All my friends are doing it: Potentially offensive sexual behavior perpetration within adolescent social networks. *Journal of Research on Adolescence, Early view.* DOI: 10.1111/jora.12150

Jewett, R., Sabiston, C. M., Brunet, J., O'Loughlin, E. K., Scarapicchia, T., & O'Loughlin, J. (2014). School sport participation during adolescence and mental health in early adulthood. *Journal of Adolescent Health, 55,* 640–644.

Jeynes, W. (1999). Effects of remarriage following divorce on the academic achievement of children. *Journal of Youth and Adolescence, 28,* 385–393.

Jeynes, W. (2001). The effects of recent parental divorce on their children's consumption of alcohol. *Journal of Youth and Adolescence, 30,* 305–319.

Jeynes, W. (2002). A meta-analysis of the effects of attending religious schools and religiosity on Black and Hispanic academic achievement. *Education and Urban Society, 35,* 27–49.

Jia, Y., Way, N., Ling, G., Yoskikawa, H., Chen, X., Hughes, D., ... Lu, Z. (2009). The influence of student perceptions of school climate on socioemotional and academic adjustment: A comparison of Chinese and American adolescents. *Child Development, 80,* 1514–1530.

Jodl, K. M., Michael, A., Malanchuk, O., Eccles, J., & Sameroff, A. (2001). Parents' roles in shaping early adolescents' occupational aspirations. *Child Development, 72,* 1247–1265.

John, O., Caspi, A., Robins, R., Moffitt, T., & Stouthamer-Loeber, M. (1994). The "Little Five": Exploring the nomological network of the five-factor model of personality in adolescent boys. *Child Development, 65,* 160–178.

Johnson, C. A., Xiao, L., Palmer, P., Sun, P., Wang, Q., Wei, Y., ... Bechara, A. (2008). Affective decision-making deficits, linked to a dysfunctional ventromedial prefrontal cortex, revealed in 10th grade Chinese adolescent binge drinkers. *Neuropsychologia, 46,* 714–726.

Johnson, E., Roth, T., Schultz, L., & Breslau, N. (2006). Epidemiology of DSM-IV insomnia in adolescence: Lifetime prevalence, chronicity, and emergent gender difference. *Pediatrics, 117,* 247–256.

Johnson, J. G., Cohen, P., Kotler, L., Kasen, S., & Brook, J. S. (2002). Psychiatric disorders associated with risk for the development of eating disorders during adolescence and early adulthood. *Journal of Consulting and Clinical Psychology, 70,* 1119–1128.

Johnson, M. (2002). Social origins, adolescent experiences, and work value trajectories during the transition to adulthood. *Social Forces, 80,* 1307–1341.

Johnson, M. D., & Galambos, N. L. (2014). Paths to intimate relationship quality from parent-adolescent relations and mental health. *Journal of Marriage and Family, 76,* 145–160.

Johnson, R., & Gerstein, D. (1998). Initiation of use of alcohol, cigarettes, marijuana, cocaine, and other substances in U.S. birth cohorts since 1919. *American Journal of Public Health, 88,* 27–33.

Johnson, R., Johnson, D., Wang, M., Smiciklas-Wright, H., & Guthrie, H. (1994). Characterizing nutrient intakes of adolescents by sociodemographic factors. *Journal of Adolescent Health, 15,* 149–154.

Johnson, W., McGue, M., & Iacono, W. G. (2006). Genetic and environmental influences on academic achievement trajectories during adolescence. *Developmental Psychology, 42,* 514–532.

Johnson, W., McGue, M., & Iacono, W. G. (2009). School performance and genetic and environmental variance in antisocial behavior at the transition from adolescence to adulthood. *Developmental Psychology, 45,* 973–987.

Johnston, L. D., O'Malley, P., Bachman, J., & Schulenberg, J. (2012a). *Monitoring the Future national results on adolescent drug use: Overview of key findings, 2011.* Ann Arbor: Institute for Social Research, The University of Michigan.

Johnston, L. D., O'Malley, P., Bachman, J., & Schulenberg, J. (2012b). *Demographic subgroup trends for various licit and illicit drugs, 1975–2011* (Monitoring the Future Occasional Paper No. 77). Ann Arbor, MI: Institute for Social Research.

Johnston, L., O'Malley, P., Bachman, J., Schulenberg, J., & Miech, R. (2014). Demographic subgroup trends among adolescents in the use of various licit and illicit drugs, 1975–2013. Ann Arbor: Institute for Social Research, The University of Michigan.

Johnston, L., O'Malley, P., Miech, R., Bachman, J., & Schulenberg, J. (2015). *Monitoring the Future national survey results on drug use: 1975–2014: Overview, key findings on adolescent drug use.* Ann Arbor: Institute for Social Research, The University of Michigan.

Johnston, M., Crosnoe, R., & Elder, G. H., Jr. (2001). Students' attachment and academic engagement: The role of race and ethnicity. *Sociology of Education, 74,* 318–340.

Jolles, D., Kleibeuker, S., Rombouts, S. A. R. B., & Crone, E. A. (2011). Developmental differences in prefrontal activation during working memory maintenance and manipulation for different memory loads. *Developmental Science, 14,* 713–724.

Jones, D. C., Vigfusdottir, T. H., & Lee, Y. (2004). Body image and the appearance culture among adolescent girls and boys: An examination of friend conversations, peer criticism, appearance magazines, and the internalization of appearance ideals. *Journal of Adolescent Research, 19,* 323–339.

Jones, D. J., Forehand, R., Brody, G., & Armistead, L. (2002). Psychosocial adjustment of African American children in single-mother families: A test of three risk models. *Journal of Marriage and the Family, 64,* 105–115.

Jones, D., & Smolak, L. (2011). Body image during adolescence: A developmental perspective. In B. Brown & M. Prinstein (Eds.), *Encyclopedia of adolescence* (Vol. 1, pp. 77–86). New York: Academic Press.

Jones, D., Costin, S., & Ricard, R. (1994, February). *Ethnic and sex differences in best friendship characteristics among African-American, Mexican-American, and European-American adolescents.* Paper presented at the biennial meetings of the Society for Research on Adolescence, San Diego.

Jones, J., Vanfossen, B., & Ensminger, M. (1995). Individual and organizational predictors of track placement. *Sociology of Education, 68,* 287–300.

Jones, L., Mitchell, K., & Finkelhor, D. (2011). Trends in youth internet victimization: Findings from three youth internet safety surveys 2000–2010. *Journal of Adolescent Health, 50,* 179–186.

Jones, M. C., & Bayley, N. (1950). Physical maturing among boys as related to behavior. *Journal of Educational Psychology, 41,* 129–148.

Jones, M. D., & Galliher, R. V. (2007). Ethnic identity and psychosocial functioning in Navajo adolescents. *Journal of Research on Adolescence, 17,* 683–696.

Jones, M., Luce, K. H., Osborne, M. I., Taylor, K., Cunning, D., Doyle, A. C., & Taylor, C. (2008). Randomized, controlled trial of an Internet-facilitated intervention for reducing binge eating and overweight in adolescents. *Pediatrics, 121,* 453–462.

Jones, N., Pieper, C., & Robertson, L. (1992). The effect of legal drinking age on fatal injuries of adolescents and young adults. *American Journal of Public Health, 82,* 112–115.

Jones, R. K., Biddlecom, A. E., Hebert, L., & Mellor, R. (2011b). Teens reflect on their sources of contraceptive information. *Journal of Adolescent Research, 26,* 423–446.

Jones, R. K., Darroch, J. E., & Singh, S. (2005). Religious differentials in the sexual and reproductive behaviors of young women in the United States. *Journal of Adolescent Health, 36,* 279–288.

Jones, R. K., Purcell, A., Singh, S., & Finer, L. B. (2005). Adolescents' reports of parental knowledge of adolescents' use of sexual health services and their reactions to mandated parental notification for prescription contraception. *Journal of the American Medical Association, 293,* 340–348.

Jonkman, K., Trautwein, U., & Lüdtke, O. (2009). Social dominance in adolescence: The moderating role of the classroom context and behavioral heterogeneity. *Child Development, 80,* 338–355.

Jordan, A., & Cole, D. (1996). Relation of depressive symptoms to the structure of self-knowledge in childhood. *Journal of Abnormal Psychology, 105,* 530–540.

Jordan, L. C., & Lewis, M. L. (2005). Paternal relationship quality as a protective factor: Preventing alcohol use among African American adolescents. *Journal of Black Psychology, 31,* 152–171.

Jordan-Conde, Z., Mennecke, B., & Townsend, A. (2014). Late adolescent identity definition and intimate disclosure on Facebook. *Computers in Human Behavior, 33,* 356–366.

Jose, P. E., & Brown, I. (2008). When does the gender difference in rumination begin? Gender and age differences in the use of rumination by adolescents. *Journal of Youth and Adolescence, 37,* 180–192.

Jose, P. E., Kljakovic, M., Scheib, E., & Notter, O. (2012). The joint development of traditional bullying and victimization with cyber bullying and victimization in adolescence. *Journal of Research on Adolescence, 22,* 301–309.

Jose, P. E., Ryan, N., & Pryor, J. (2012). Does social connectedness promote a greater sense of well-being in adolescence over time? *Journal of Research on Adolescence, 22,* 235–251.

Jose, P. E., & Weir, K. F. (2013). How is anxiety involved in the longitudinal relationship between brooding rumination and depressive symptpms in adolescents? *Journal of Youth & Adolescence, 42,* 1210–1222.

Joshi, S. P., Peter, J., & Valkenburg, P. M. (2014). Virginity loss and pregnancy in U.S. and Dutch teen girl magazines: A content-analytic comparison. *Youth & Society, 46,* 70–88.

Joyce T., Kaestner, R., & Colman, S. (2006). Changes in abortions and births and the Texas parental notification law. *New England Journal of Medicine, 354,* 1031–1038.

Joyce, T., & Mocan, N. (1990). The impact of legalized abortion on adolescent childbearing in New York City. *American Journal of Public Health, 80,* 273–278.

Joyner, K., & Udry, J. R. (2000). You don't bring me anything but down: Adolescent romance and depression. *Journal of Health and Social Behavior, 41,* 369–391.

Juang, L., & Alvarez, A. (2010). Discrimination and adjustment among Chinese American adolescents: Family conflict and family cohesion as vulnerability and protective factors. *American Journal of Public Health, 100,* 2403–2409.

Juang, L., & Silbereisen, R. K. (2002). The relationship between adolescent academic capability beliefs, parenting and school grades. *Journal of Adolescence, 25,* 3–18.

Juang, L., Lerner, J., McKinney, J., & von Eye, A. (1999). The goodness of fit in autonomy time-table expectations between Asian-American late adolescents and their parents. *International Journal of Behavioral Development, 23,* 1023–1048.

Juang, L., Nguyen, H. H., & Lin, Y. (2006). The ethnic identity, other-group attitudes, and psychosocial functioning of Asian American emerging adults from two contexts. *Journal of Adolescent Research, 21,* 542–568.

Judge, B., & Billick, S. B. (2004). Suicidality in adolescence: Review and legal considerations. *Behavioral Sciences and the Law, 22,* 681–695.

Jumping-Eagle, S., Sheeder, J., Kelly, L. S., & Stevens-Simon, C. (2008). Association of conventional goals and perceptions of pregnancy with female teenagers' pregnancy avoidance behavior and attitudes. *Perspectives on Sexual and Reproductive Health, 40,* 74–80.

Jung, J., & Forbes, G. B. (2013). Body dissatisfaction and characteristics of disordered eating among black and white early adolescent girls and boys. *The Journal of Early Adolescence, 33,* 737–764.

Juonala, M., Magnussen, C., & Berenson, G. (2011). Childhood adiposity, adult adiposity, and cardiovascular risk factors. *New England Journal of Medicine, 365,* 1876–1885.

Jussim, L., Eccles, J., & Madon, S. (1996). Social perception, social stereotypes, and teacher expectations: Accuracy and the quest for the powerful self-fulfilling prophecy. *Advances in Experimental Social Psychology, 28,* 281–388.

Juvonen, J., & Gross, E. F. (2008). Extending the school grounds? Bullying experiences in cyberspace. *Journal of School Health, 78,* 496–505.

Juvonen, J., & Murdock, T. (1995). Grade-level differences in the social value of effort: Implications for self-presentation tactics of early adolescents. *Child Development, 66,* 1694–1705.

Juvonen, J., Graham, S., & Schuster, M. A. (2003). Bullying among young adolescents: The strong, the weak, and the troubled. *Pediatrics, 112,* 1231–1237.

Juvonen, J., Nishina, A., & Graham, S. (2006). Ethnic diversity and perceptions of safety in urban middle schools. *Psychological Science, 17,* 393–400.

Juvonen, J., Wang, Y., & Espinoza, G. (2011). Bullying experiences and compromised academic performance across middle school grades. *Journal of Early Adolescence, 31,* 152–173.

Juvonen, J., Wang, Y., Espinoza, G. (2013). Physical aggression, spreading of rumors, and social

prominence in early adolescence: reciprocal effects supporting gender similarities. *Journal of Youth & Adolescence, 42,* 1801–1810.

Kaestle, C. E., Halpern, C. T., Miller, W. C., & Ford, C. A. (2005). Young age at first sexual intercourse and sexually transmitted infections in adolescents and young adults. *American Journal of Epidemiology, 161,* 774–780.

Kaestle, C. E., Morisky, D. E., & Wiley, D. J. (2002). Sexual intercourse and the age difference between adolescent females and their romantic partners. *Perspectives on Sexual and Reproductive Health, 34,* 304–305.

Kågesten, A., Parekh, J., Tunçalp, Ö., Turke, S., Blum, R.W. (2014). Comprehensive adolescent health programs that include sexual and reproductive health services: A systematic review. *American Journal of Public Health, 104,* 23–36.

Kahneman, D. (2011). *Thinking, fast and slow.* New York: Farrar, Strauss, and Giroux.

Kail, R. V., & Ferrer, E. (2007). Processing speed in childhood and adolescence: Longitudinal models for examining developmental change. *Child Development, 78,* 1760–1770.

Kakade, M., Duarte, C. S., Liu, X., Fuller, C. J., Drucker, E., Hoven, C. W., Fan, B., & Wu, P. (2012). Adolescent substance use and other illegal behaviors and racial disparities in criminal justice system involvement: Findings from a US national survey. *American Journal of Public Health, 102,* 1307–1310.

Kakihara, F., Tilton-Weaver, L., Kerr, M., & Stattin, H. (2010). The relationship of parental control to youth adjustment: Do youths' feelings about their parents play a role? *Journal of Youth and Adolescence, 39,* 1442–1456.

Kalakoski, V., & Nurmi, J.-E. (1998). Identity and educational transitions: Age differences in adolescent exploration and commitment related to education, occupation, and family. *Journal of Research on Adolescence, 8,* 29–47.

Kalil, A., & Eccles, J. (1998). Does welfare affect family processes and adolescent adjustment? *Child Development, 69,* 1597–1613.

Kalil, A., & Kunz, J. (2002). Teenage childbearing, marital status, and depressive symptoms in later life. *Child Development, 73,* 1748–1760.

Kalil, A., & Ziol-Guest, K. (2008). Teacher support, school goal structures, and teenage mothers' school engagement. *Youth and Society, 39,* 524–548.

Kalmuss, D., & Namerow, P. (1994). Subsequent childbearing among teenage mothers: The determinants of a closely spaced second birth. *Family Planning Perspectives, 26,* 149–153, 159.

Kaltiala-Heino, R., Koivisto, A.-M., Marttunen, M., & Fröjd, S. (2011). Pubertal timing and substance use in middle adolescence: A 2-year follow-up study. *Journal of Youth and Adolescence, 40,* 1288–1301.

Kam, J. A., & Wang, N. (2014). Longitudinal effects of best-friend communication against substance use for Latino and non-Latino white early adolescents. *Journal of Research on Adolescence, 25,* 534–550.

Kambam, P., & Thompson, C. (2009). The development of decision-making capacities in children and adolescents: Psychological and neurological perspectives and their implications for juvenile defendants. *Behavioral Sciences & the Law, 27,* 173–190.

Kamenetz, A. (2006, May 30). Take this internship and shove it. *The New York Times,* p. A19.

Kaminski, J. W., Puddy, R. W., Hall, D. M., Cashman, S. Y., Crosby, A. E., & Ortega, L. A. G. (2010). The relative influence of different domains of social connectedness on self-directed violence in adolescence. *Journal of Youth and Adolescence, 39,* 460–473.

Kan, M. L., Cheng, Y.-H. A., Landale, N. S., & McHale, S. M. (2010). Longitudinal predictors of change in number of sexual partners across adolescence and early adulthood. *Journal of Adolescent Health, 46,* 25–31.

Kandel, D., Johnson, J., Bird, H., & Canino, G. (1997). Psychiatric disorders associated with substance use among children and adolescents: Findings from the Methods for the Epidemiology of Child and Adolescent Mental Disorders (MECA) Study. *Journal of Abnormal Child Psychology, 25,* 121–132.

Kandler, C. (2012). Nature and nurture in personality development: The case of neuroticism and extraversion. *Current Directions in Psychological Science, 21,* 290–296.

Kang, H., Okazaki, S., Abelmann, N., Kim-Prieto, C., & Lan, S. (2010). Redeeming immigrant parents: How Korean American emerging adults reinterpret their childhood. *Journal of Adolescent Research, 25,* 441–464.

Kantor, H., & Brenzel, B. (1992). Urban education and the "truly disadvantaged": The historical roots of the contemporary crisis, 1945–1990. *Teachers College Record, 94,* 278–314.

Kao, G. (1999). Psychological well-being and educational achievement among immigrant youth. In D. Hernandez (Ed.), *Children of immigrants: Health, adjustment, and public assistance* (pp. 410–477). Washington, DC: National Academy Press.

Kao, G., & Tienda, M. (1998). Educational aspirations of minority youth. *American Journal of Education, 106,* 349–384.

Kaplan, C., Erickson, P., & Juarez-Reyes, M. (2002). Acculturation, gender role orientation, and reproductive risk-taking behavior among Latina adolescent family planning. *Journal of Adolescent Research, 17,* 103–121.

Karch, D. L., Logan, J., McDaniel, D. D., Floyd, C. F., & Vagi, K. J. (2013). Precipitating circumstances of suicide among youth aged 10–17 years by sex: Data from the national violent death reporting system, 16 states, 2000–2008. *Journal of Adolescent Health, 53,* S51–S53.

Karevold, E., Røysamb, E., Ystrom, E., & Mathiesen, K. S. (2009). Predictors and pathways from infancy to symptoms of anxiety and depression in early adolescence. *Developmental Psychology, 45,* 1051–1060.

Karre, J. K., & Mounts, N. S. (2012). Nonresident fathers' parenting style and the adjustment of late-adolescent boys. *Journal of Family Issues, 33,* 1642–1657.

Karriker-Jaffe, K., Foshee, V. A., Ennett, S. T., & Suchindran, C. (2008). The development of aggression during adolescence: Sex differences in trajectories of physical and social aggression among youth in rural areas. *Journal of Abnormal Child Psychology, 36,* 1227–1236.

Karriker-Jaffe, K., Foshee, V. A., Ennett, S. T., & Suchindran, C. (2009). Sex differences in the effects of neighborhood socioeconomic disadvantage and social organization on rural adolescents' aggression trajectories. *American Journal of Community Psychology, 43,* 189–203.

Kaslow, N. J., Adamson, L. B., & Collins, M. H. (2000). A developmental psychopathology perspective on the cognitive components of child and adolescent depression. In A. J. Sameroff, M. Lewis, & S. M. Miller (Eds.), *Handbook of developmental psychopathology* (2nd ed., pp. 491–510). New York: Plenum.

Kassin, S. (2008). The psychology of confessions. *Annual Review of Law and Social Science, 4,* 193–217.

Katainen, S., Raeikkoenen, K., & Keltikangas-Jaervinen, L. (1998). Development of temperament: Childhood temperament and the mother's childrearing attitudes as predictors of adolescent temperament in a 9-year follow-up study. *Journal of Research on Adolescence, 8,* 485–509.

Katz, E., Blumler, J., & Gurevitch, M. (1974). Uses and gratifications research. *Public Opinion Quarterly, 37,* 509–523.

Katz, M. (1975). *The people of Hamilton, Canada West: Family and class in a mid-nineteenth-century city.* Cambridge, MA: Harvard University Press.

Kaufman, K., Gregory, W., & Stephan, W. (1990). Maladjustment in statistical minorities within ethnically unbalanced classrooms. *American Journal of Community Psychology, 18,* 757–762.

Kawabata, Y., Alink, L., Tseng, W., van IJzendoorn, M., & Crick, N. (2011). Maternal and paternal parenting styles associated with relational aggression in children and adolescents: A conceptual analysis and meta-analytic review. *Developmental Review, 31,* 240–278.

Kaye, K. (2009). *Changes in the teen birth rate from 1991 to 2005 and 2005 to 2006: Assessing the role of changes in the teen population.* Washington, DC: National Campaign to Prevent Teen and Unplanned Pregnancy.

Kazis, R. (1993). *Improving the transition from school to work in the United States.* Washington, DC: American Youth Policy Forum, Competitiveness Policy Council, and Jobs for the Future.

Keating, D. (2004). Cognitive and brain development. In R. Lerner & L. Steinberg (Eds.), *Handbook of adolescent psychology* (2nd ed.). New York: Wiley.

Keating, D. (2011). Cognitive development. In B. Brown & M. Prinstein (Eds.), *Encyclopedia of adolescence* (Vol. 1, pp. 106–114). New York: Academic Press.

Keating, D., & Hertzman, C. (Eds.). (2000). *Developmental health and the wealth of nations: Social, biological, and educational dynamics.* New York: Guilford Press.

Keel, P. K., & Klump, K. L. (2003). Are eating disorders culture-bound syndromes? Implications for conceptualizing their etiology. *Psychological Bulletin, 129,* 747–769.

Keijsers, L., & Laird, R. D. (2014). Mother-adolescent monitoring dynamics and the legitimacy of parental authority. *Journal of Adolescence, 37,* 515–524.

Keijsers, L., & Poulin, F. (2013). Developmental changes in parent-child communication throughout adolescence. *Developmental Psychology, 49,* 2301–2308.

Keijsers, L., Branje, S., Frijns, T., Finkenauer, C., & Meeus, W. (2010a). Gender differences in keeping secrets from parents in adolescence. *Developmental Psychology, 46,* 293–298.

Keijsers, L., Branje, S., Hawk, S., Schwartz, S., Frijns, T., Koot, H., . . . Meuss, W. (2012). Forbidden friends as forbidden fruit: Parental supervision of friendships, contact with deviant peers, and adolescent delinquency. *Child Development, 83,* 651–656.

Keijsers, L., Branje, S., VanderValk, I., & Meeus, W. (2010b). Reciprocal effects between parental solicitation, parental control, adolescent disclosure, and adolescent delinquency. *Journal of Research on Adolescence, 20,* 88–113.

Keijsers, L., Frijns, T., Branje, S. J. T., & Meeus, W. (2009). Developmental links of adolescent disclosure, parental solicitation, and control with delinquency: Moderation by parental support. *Developmental Psychology, 45,* 1314–1327.

Kellam, S., Ling, X., Merisca, R., Brown, C., & Ialongo, N. (1998). The effect of the level of aggression in the first grade classroom on the course and malleability of aggressive behavior into middle school. *Development and Psychopathology, 10,* 165–185.

Keller, J. (2002). Blatant stereotype threat and women's math performances: Self-handicapping as a strategic means to cope with obtrusive negative performance expectations. *Sex Roles, 47,* 193–198.

Keller, M., Edelstein, W., Schmid, C., Fang, F., & Fang, G. (1998). Reasoning about responsibilities and obligations in close relationships: A comparison across two cultures. *Developmental Psychology, 34,* 731–741.

Kelly, A., Wall, M., Eisenberg, M., Story, M., & Neumark-Sztainer, D. (2005). Adolescent girls with high body satisfaction: Who are they and what can they teach us? *Journal of Adolescent Health, 37,* 391–396.

Kelly, S. (2009). The Black–White gap in mathematics course taking. *Sociology of Education, 82,* 47–69.

Kendig, S. M., Mattingly, M. J., & Bianchi, S. M. (2014). Childhood poverty and the transition to adulthood. *Family Relations, 63,* 271–286.

Kendrick, K., Jutengren, G., & Stattin, H. (2012). The protective role of supportive friends against bullying perpetration and victimization. *Journal of Adolescence, 35,* 1069–1080.

Keniston, K. (1970). Youth: A "new" stage of life. *American Scholar, 39,* 631–641.

Kennard, B. D., Silva, S. G., Tonev, S., Rohde, P., Hughes, J. L., Vitiello, B., . . . March, J. (2009). Remission and recovery in the treatment for adolescents with depression study (TADS): Acute and long-term outcomes. *Journal of the American Academy of Child and Adolescent Psychiatry, 48,* 186–195.

Kenyon, D. B., Rankin, L. A., Koerner, S. S., & Dennison, R. P. (2007). What makes an adult? Examining descriptions from adolescents of divorce. *Journal of Youth and Adolescence, 36,* 813–823.

Kercher, A., & Rapee, R. M. (2009). A test of a cognitive diathesis–stress generation pathway in early adolescent depression. *Journal of Abnormal Child Psychology, 37,* 845–855.

Kern, M., Benson, L., Steinberg, E., & Steinberg, L. (in press). The EPOCH measure of adolescent well-being. *Psychological Assessment.*

Kerns, K. (1996). Individual differences in friendship quality: Links to child–mother attachment. In W. Bukowski, A. Newcomb, & W. Hartup, (Eds.), *The company they keep: Friendship in childhood and adolescence* (pp. 137–157). New York: Cambridge University Press.

Kerns, K. A., & Brumariu, L. E. (2014). Is insecure parent–child attachment a risk factor for the development of anxiety in childhood or adolescence? *Child Development Perspectives, 8,* 12–17.

Kerr, D., Capaldi, D., Pears, K., & Owen, L. (2009). A prospective three-generational study of fathers' constructive parenting: Influences from family of origin, adolescent adjustment, and offspring temperament. *Developmental Psychology, 45,* 1257–1275.

Kerr, M., Stattin, H., & Burk, W. (2010). A reinterpretation of parental monitoring in longitudinal perspective. *Journal of Research on Adolescence, 20,* 39–64.

Kerr, M., Stattin, H., & Özdemir, M. (2012). Perceived parenting style and adolescent adjustment: Revisiting directions of effects and the role of parental knowledge. *Developmental Psychology, 48,* 1540–1553.

Kessler, R. C., Avenevoli, S., Costello, J., Green, J. G., Gruber, M. J., McLaughlin, K. A., Petukhova, M., Sampson, N. A., Zaslavsky, A. M., & Merikangas, K. R. (2012). Severity of 12-month DSM-IV disorders in the national comorbidity survey replication adolescent supplement. *Arch Gen Psychiatry, 69,* 381–389.

Kessler, R., Avenevoli, S., Costello, E., Georgiades, K., Green, J., . . . Gruber, M. (2012). Prevalence, persistence, and sociodemographic correlates of DSM-IV disorders in the National Comorbidity Survey Replication Adolescent Supplement. *Archives of General Psychiatry, 69,* 372–380.

Kessler, R., Berglun, P., Demler, O., Jin, R., Merikangas, K., & Walters, E. (2005). Lifetime prevalence and age-of-onset distributions of DSM-IV disorders in the National Comorbidity Survey Replication, *Archives of General Psychiatry* 62, no. 6 (2005), 593–602.

Kett, J. (1977). *Rites of passage: Adolescence in America, 1790 to the present.* New York: Basic Books.

Keyes, K. M., Maslowsky, J., Hamilton, A., & Schulenberg, J. (2015). The great sleep recession: Changes in sleep duration among US adolescents, 1991–2012. *Pediatrics, 135,* 460–468.

Keyes, K. M., Schulenberg, J. E., O'Malley, P. M., Johnston, L. D., Bachman, J. D., Li, G., & Hasin, D. (2012). Birth cohort effects on adolescent alcohol use: The influence of social norms from 1976 to 2007. *Arch Gen Psychiatry, 69,* 1304–1313.

Khalife, N., Kantomaa, M., Glover, V., Tammelin, T., Laitinen, J., Ebeling, H., et al. (2014). Childhood attention-deficit/hyperactivity disorder symptoms are risk factors for obesity and physical inactivity in adolescence. *Journal of the American Academy of Child & Adolescent Psychiatry, 53,* 425–436.

Khoury-Kassibri, M., Benbensihty, R., Astor, R. A., & Zeira, A. (2004). The contributions of community, family, and school variables to student victimization. *American Journal of Community Psychology, 34,* 187–204.

Khundrakpam, B. S., Reid, A., Brauer, J., Carbonell, F., Lewis, J., Ameis, S., Karama, S., Lee, J., Chen, Z., Das, S., Evans, A. C, & Brain Development Cooperative Group. (2013). Developmental changes in organization of structural brain networks. *Cerebral Cortex, 23,* 2072–2085.

Khurana, A., & Cooksey, E. C. (2012). Examining the effect of maternal sexual communication and adolescents' perceptions of maternal disapproval on adolescent risky sexual involvement. *Journal of Adolescent Health, 51,* 557–565.

Khurana, A., Romer, D., Betancourt, L. M., Brodsky, N. L., Giannetta, J. M., & Hurt, H. (2012). Early adolescent sexual debut: The mediating role of working memory ability, sensation seeking, and impulsivity. *Developmental Psychology, 48,* 1416–1428.

Khurana, A., Romer, D., Betancourt, L. M., Brodsky, N. L., Giannetta, J. M., & Hurt, H. (2015). Experimentation versus progression in adolescent drug use: A test of an emerging neurobehavioral imbalance model. *Development and Psychopathology, 27,* 901–913.

Kiang, L. (2012). Deriving daily purpose through daily events and role fulfillment among Asian American youth. *Journal of Research on Adolescence, 22,* 185–198.

Kiang, L., & Buchanan, C. M. (2014). Daily stress and emotional well-being among Asian American adolescents: Same-day, lagged, and chronic associations. *Developmental Psychology, 50,* 611–621.

Kiang, L., & Fuligni, A. (2009). Ethnic identity and family processes among adolescents from Latin American, Asian, and European backgrounds. *Journal of Youth and Adolescence, 38,* 228–241.

Kiang, L., & Fuligni, A. (2010). Meaning in life as a mediator of ethnic identity and adjustment among adolescents from Latin, Asian, and European American backgrounds. *Journal of Youth and Adolescence, 39,* 1253–1264.

Kiang, L., Andrews, K., Stein, G. L., Supple, A. J., Gonzales, L. M. (2013). Socioeconomic stress and academic adjustment among Asian American adolescents: the protective role of family obligation. *Journal of Youth & Adolescence, 42,* 837–847.

Kiang, L., Peterson, J. L., & Thompson, T. L. (2011). Ethnic peer preferences among Asian American adolescents in emerging immigrant communities. *Journal of Research on Adolescence, 21,* 754–761.

Kiang, L., Supple, A. J., Stein, G. L., & Gonzales, L. M. (2012). Gendered academic adjustment among Asian American adolescents in an emerging immigrant community. *Journal of Youth & Adolescence, 41,* 283–294.

Kiang, L., Witkow, M., Baldelomar, O., & Fuligni, A. (2010). Change in ethnic identity across the high school years among adolescents with Latin American, Asian, and European backgrounds. *Journal of Youth and Adolescence, 39,* 683–693.

Kiang, L., Yip, T., Gonzales-Backen, M., Witkow, M., & Fuligni, A. (2006). Ethnic identity and the daily psychological well-being of adolescents from Mexican and Chinese backgrounds. *Child Development, 77,* 1338–1350.

Kidd, S. A. (2004). "The walls were closing in, and we were trapped": A qualitative analysis of street youth suicide. *Youth and Society, 36,* 30–55.

Kiene, S. M., Barta, W. D., Tennen, H., & Armeli, S. (2009). Alcohol, helping young adults to have unprotected sex with casual partners: Findings from a daily diary study of alcohol use and sexual behavior. *Journal of Adolescent Health, 44,* 73–80.

Kiesner, J. (2002). Depressive symptoms in early adolescence: Their relations with classroom problem behavior and peer status. *Journal of Research on Adolescence, 12,* 463–478.

Kiesner, J., & Pastore, M. (2005). Differences in the relations between antisocial behavior and peer acceptance across contexts and across adolescence. *Child Development, 76,* 1278–1293.

Kiesner, J., Cadinu, M., Poulin, F., & Bucci, M. (2002). Group identification in early adolescence: Its relation with peer adjustment and its moderator effect on peer influence. *Child Development, 73,* 196–208.

Kiesner, J., Poulin, F., & Nicotra, E. (2003). Peer relations across contexts: Individual–network homophily and network inclusion in and after school. *Child Development, 74,* 1328–1343.

Killen, M., Henning, A., Kelly, M. C., Crystal, D., & Ruck, M. (2007). Evaluations of interracial peer encounters by majority and minority U.S. children and adolescents. *International Journal of Behavioral Development, 31,* 491–500.

Killen, M., Rutland, A., Abrams, D., Mulvey, K. L., & Hitti, A. (2013). Development of intra- and intergroup judgments in the context of moral and social-conventional norms. *Child Development, 84,* 1063–1080.

Killoren, S. E., & Deutsch, A. R. (2014). A longitudinal examination of parenting processes and Latino youth's risky sexual behaviors. *Journal of Youth & Adolescence, 43,* 1982–1993.

Kilpatrick, D., Acierno, R., Saunders, B., Resnick, H., Best, C., & Schnurr, P. (2000). Risk factors for adolescent substance abuse and dependence: Data from a national sample. *Journal of Consulting and Clinical Psychology, 68,* 19–30.

Kim, H., & Capaldi, D. (2004). The association of antisocial behavior and depressive symptoms between partners and risk for aggression in romantic relationships. *Journal of Family Psychology 18,* 82–96.

Kim, H., Capaldi, D., & Stoolmiller, M. (2003). Depressive symptoms across adolescence and young adulthood in men: Predictions from parental and contextual risk factors. *Development and Psychopathology, 15,* 469–495.

Kim, I. J., Zane, N., & Hong, S. (2002). Protective factors against substance use among Asian American youth: A test of the peer cluster theory. *Journal of Community Psychology, 30,* 565–584.

Kim, J. L., & Ward, L. M. (2007). Silence speaks volumes: Parental sexual communication among Asian American emerging adults. *Journal of Adolescent Research, 22,* 3–31.

Kim, J., McHale, S. M., Crouter, A. C., & Osgood, D. W. (2007). Longitudinal linkages between sibling relationships and adjustment from middle childhood through adolescence. *Developmental Psychology, 43,* 960–973.

Kim, J., McHale, S. M., Osgood, D. W., & Crouter, A. C. (2006). Longitudinal course and family correlates of sibling relationships from childhood through adolescence. *Child Development, 77,* 1746–1761.

Kim, J.-I., Schallert, D. L., & Kim, M. (2010). An integrative cultural view of achievement motivation: Parental and classroom predictors of children's goal orientations when learning mathematics in Korea. *Journal of Educational Psychology, 102,* 418–437.

Kim, K., Conger, R. D., Elder, G. H., Jr., & Lorenz, F. O. (2003). Reciprocal influences between stressful life events and adolescent internalizing and externalizing problems. *Child Development, 74,* 127–143.

Kim, K., Conger, R. D., Lorenz, F. O., & Elder, G. H., Jr. (2001). Parent–adolescent reciprocity in negative affect and its relation to early adult social development. *Developmental Psychology, 37,* 775–790.

Kim, S., & Brody, G. H. (2005). Longitudinal pathways to psychological adjustment among Black youth living in single-parent households. *Journal of Family Psychology, 19,* 305–313.

Kim, S., & Ge, X. (2000). Parenting practices and adolescent depressive symptoms in Chinese American families. *Journal of Family Psychology, 14,* 420–435.

Kim, S., Wang, Y., Deng, S., Alvarez, R., & Li, J. (2011). Accent, perpetual foreigner stereotype, and perceived discrimination as indirect links between English proficiency and depressive symptoms in Chinese American adolescents. *Developmental Psychology, 47,* 289–301.

Kim-Spoon, J., Farley, J. P., Holmes, C., Longo, G. S., McCullough, M. E. (2014). Processes linking parents' and adolescents' religiousness and adolescent substance use: Monitoring and self-control. *Journal of Youth & Adolescence, 43,* 745–756.

Kim-Spoon, J., McCullough, M. E., Bickel, W. K., Farley, J. P., & Longo, G. S. (2014). Longitudinal associations among religiousness, delay discounting, and substance use initiation in early adolescence. *Journal of Research on Adolescence, 25,* 36–43.

King, C., Akiyama, M., & Elling, K. (1996). Self-perceived competencies and depression among middle school students in Japan and the United States. *Journal of Early Adolescence, 16,* 192–210.

King, J. (2006). *Gender equity in higher education, 2006.* Washington: American Council on Education.

King, K. M., Molina, B. S. G., & Chassin, L. (2009). Prospective relations between growth in drinking and familial stressors across adolescence. *Journal of Abnormal Psychology, 118,* 610–622.

King, M. D, Jennings, J., & Fletcher, J. M. (2014). Medical adaptation to academic pressure schooling, stimulant use, and socioeconomic status. *American Sociological Review, 79,* 1039–1066.

King, P., & Furrow, J. (2004). Religion as a resource for positive youth development: Religion, social capital, and moral outcomes. *Developmental Psychology, 40,* 703–713.

King, P., & Roeser, R. (2009). Religion and spirituality in adolescent development. In R. Lerner & L. Steinberg (Eds.), *Handbook of adolescent psychology* (3rd ed., Vol. 1, pp. 435–478). New York: Wiley.

King, P., Carr, A., & Boiter, C. (2011). Spirituality, religiosity, and youth thriving. In R. M. Lerner, J. V. Lerner, and J. B. Benson (Eds.). *Advances in Child Development and Behavior, Vol (41). Positive Youth Development: Research and Applications for Promoting Thriving in Adolescence.* Amsterdam: Elsevier Press.

King, P., Ramos, J., & Clardy, C. (2013). Searching for the sacred: Religious and spiritual development among adolescents. In K. I. Pargament, J. Exline, & J. Jones (Eds.), *APA Handbook of Psychology, Religion and Spirituality,* Washington D.C.: American Psychological Association.

King, V. (2006). The antecedents and consequences of adolescents' relationships with stepfathers and nonresident fathers. *Journal of Marriage and Family, 68,* 910–928.

King, V., Elder, G. H., Jr., & Whitbeck, L. B. (1997). Religious involvement among rural youth: An ecological and life-course perspective. *Journal of Research on Adolescence, 7,* 431–456.

Kingston, B., Huizinga, D., & Elliot, D. (2009). A test of social disorganization theory in high-risk urban neighborhoods. *Youth & Society, 41,* 53–79.

Kinney, D. (1993). From nerds to normals: The recovery of identity among adolescents from middle school to high school. *Sociology of Education, 66,* 21–40.

Kinsfogel, K. M., & Grych, J. H. (2004). Interparental conflict and adolescent dating relationships: Integrating cognitive, emotional, and peer influences. *Journal of Family Psychology, 18,* 505–515.

Kirby, D. (2007). *Emerging answers 2007: Research findings on programs to reduce teen pregnancy and sexually transmitted diseases.* Washington, DC: National Campaign to Prevent Teen and Unplanned Pregnancy.

Kirby, D. (2011). Risky sexual behavior. In B. Brown & M. Prinstein (Eds.), *Encyclopedia of adolescence* (Vol. 3, pp. 264–275). New York: Academic Press.

Kirby, D., & Laris, B. A. (2009). Effective curriculum-based sex and STD/HIV education programs for adolescents. *Child Development Perspectives, 3,* 21–29.

Kirby, D., Coyle, K., & Gould, J. B. (2001). Manifestations of poverty and birthrates among young teenagers in California zip code areas. *Family Planning Perspectives, 33,* 63–69.

Kirby, J. B. (2006). From single-parent families to stepfamilies: Is the transition associated with adolescent alcohol initiation? *Journal of Family Issues, 27,* 685–711.

Kirk, D. (2009). Unraveling the contextual effects on student suspension and juvenile arrest: The independent and interdependent influences of school, neighborhood, and family social controls. *Criminology, 47,* 479–520.

Kirschenbaum, D. S., & Gierut, K. (2013). Treatment of childhood and adolescent obesity: An integrative review of recent recommendations from five expert groups. *Journal of Consulting and Clinical Psychology, 81,* 347–360.

Kirshner, B., & Ginwright, S. (2012). Youth organizing as a developmental context for African American and Latino Adolescents. *Child Development Perspectives, 6,* 288–294.

Kiselica, M., & Sturmer, P. (1993). Is society giving teenage fathers a mixed message? *Youth and Society, 24,* 487–501.

Kistler, M., Rodgers, K., Power, T., Austin, E., & Hill, L. (2010). Adolescents and music media: Toward an involvement-mediational model of consumption and self-concept. *Journal of Research on Adolescence, 20,* 616–630.

Kiuhara, S. A., Graham, S., & Hawken, L. S. (2009). Teaching writing to high school students: A national survey. *Journal of Educational Psychology, 101,* 136–160.

Kiuru, N., Burk, W. J., Laursen, B., Nurmi, J. E., & Salmela-Aro, K. (2012). Is depression contagious? A test of alternative peer socialization mechanisms of depressive symptoms in adolescent peer networks. *Journal of Adolescent Health, 50,* 250–255.

Kiuru, N., Salmela-Aro, K., Nurmi, J. E., Zettergren, P., Andersson, H., & Bergman, L. (2012). Best friends in adolescence show similar educational careers in early adulthood. *Journal of Applied Developmental Psychology, 33,* 102–111.

Klaczynski, P. (2000). Motivated scientific reasoning biases, epistemological beliefs, and theory polarization: A two-process approach to adolescent cognition. *Child Development, 71,* 1347–1366.

Klaczynski, P. (2001). Analytic and heuristic processing influences on adolescent reasoning and decision making. *Child Development, 72,* 844–861.

Klaczynski, P., & Narasimham, G. (1998). Development of scientific reasoning biases: Cognitive versus ego-protective explanations. *Developmental Psychology, 34,* 175–187.

Klahr, A., McGue, M., Iacono, W., & Burt, S. (2011a). The association between parent–child conflict and adolescent conduct problems over time: Results from a longitudinal adoption study. *Journal of Abnormal Psychology, 120,* 46–56.

Klahr, A., Rueter, M., McGue, M., Iacono, W., & Burt, S. (2011b). The relationship between parent–child conflict and adolescent antisocial behavior: Confirming shared environmental mediation. *Journal of Abnormal Child Psychology, 39,* 683–694.

Klassen, R. M., Ang, R. P., Chong, W. H., Krawchuk, L. L., Huan, V. S., Wong, I., & Yeo, L. S. (2009). A cross-cultural study of adolescent procrastination. *Journal of Research on Adolescence, 19,* 799–811.

Kleibeuker, S. W., Koolschijn, P. C., Jolles, D. D., De Dreu, C. K., & Crone, E. A. (2013). The neural coding of creative idea generation across adolescence and early adulthood. *Frontiers in Human Neuroscience, 7,* 905.

Klein, J., & Cornell, D. (2010). Is the link between large high schools and student victimization an illusion? *Journal of Educational Psychology, 102,* 933–946.

Kleinjan, M., Rozing, M., Engels, R., & Verhagen, M. (2015). Co-development of early adolescent alcohol use and depressive feelings: The role of the mu-opioid receptor A118G polymorphism. *Development and Psychopathology, 27,* 915–925.

Klepinger, D., Lundberg, S., & Plotnick, R. (1995). Adolescent fertility and the educational attainment of young women. *Family Planning Perspectives, 27,* 23–28.

Klerman, L. (1993). The influence of economic factors on health-related behaviors in adolescents. In S. Millstein, A. Petersen, & E. Nightingale (Eds.), *Promoting the health of adolescents: New directions for the twenty-first century* (pp. 38–57). New York: Oxford University Press.

Kliewer, W., Murrelle, L., Prom, E., Ramirez, M., Obando, P., . . . Sandi, L. (2006). Violence exposure and drug use in Central American youth: Family cohesion and parental monitoring as protective factors. *Journal of Research on Adolescence, 16,* 455–478.

Klimstra, T. (2013). Adolescent personality development and identity formation. *Child Development Perspectives, 7,* 80–84.

Klimstra, T., Hale, W., Raaijmakers, Q., Branje, S., & Meeus, W. (2009). Maturation of personality in adolescence. *Journal of Personality and Social Psychology, 96,* 898–912.

Klimstra, T., Hale, W., Raaijmakers, Q., Branje, S., & Meeus, W. (2010). Identity formation in adolescence: Change or stability? *Journal of Youth and Adolescence, 39,* 150–162.

Kling, J. R., Ludwig, J., & Katz, L. F. (2005). Neighborhood effects on crime for female and male youth: Evidence from a randomized housing voucher experiment. *Quarterly Journal of Economics, 120,* 87–130.

Klingberg, T. (2006). Development of a superior frontal-intraparietal network for visuospatial working memory. *Neuropsychologia, 44,* 2171–2177.

Klodnick, V. V., Guterman, N., Haj-Yahia, M. M., & Leshem, B. (2014). Exploring adolescent community violence exposure and posttraumatic stress cross-culturally in Israel. *Journal of Community Psychology, 42,* 47–60.

Kloep, M., & Hendry, L. B. (2014). Some ideas on the emerging future of developmental research. *Journal of Adolescence, 37,* 1541–1545.

Klomek, A. B., Marrocco, F., Kleinman, M., Schonfeld, I. S., & Gould, M. S. (2007). Bullying, depression, and suicidality in adolescents. *Journal of the American Academy of Child & Adolescent Psychiatry, 46,* 40–49.

Klostermann, S., Connell, A., & Stormshak, E. A. (2014). Gender differences in the developmental links between conduct problems and depression across early adolescence. *Journal of Research on Adolescence, Early view.* DOI: 10.1111/jora.12170

Knack, J. M., Tsar, V., Vaillancourt, T., Hymel, S., & McDougall, P. (2012). What protects rejected adolescents from also being bullied by their peers? The moderating role of peer-valued characteristics. *Journal of Research on Adolescence, 22,* 467–479.

Knafo, A., & Schwartz, S. H. (2003). Parenting and adolescents' accuracy in perceiving parental values. *Child Development, 74,* 595–611.

Knecht, A., Burk, W., Weesie, J., & Steglich, C. (2011). Friendship and alcohol use in early adolescence: A multilevel social network approach. *Journal of Research on Adolescence, 21,* 475–487.

Kniefsend, C.A., & Graham, S. (2012). Too much of a good thing? How breadth of extracurricular participation relates to school-related affect and academic outcomes during adolescence. *Journal of Youth & Adolescence, 41,* 379–389.

Knifsend, C. A., & Juvonen, J. (2014). Social identity complexity, cross-ethnic friendships, and intergroup attitudes in urban middle schools. *Child Development, 85,* 709–721.

Knight, G. P., Carlo, G., Basilio, C. D., & Jacobson, R. P. (2014). Familism values, perspective taking, and prosocial moral reasoning: Predicting prosocial tendencies among Mexican American adolescents. *Journal of Research on Adolescence, Early view.* DOI: 10.1111/jora.12164

Knoester, C., & Haynie, D. L. (2005). Community context, social integration into family, and youth violence. *Journal of Marriage and the Family, 67,* 767.

Knoester, C., Haynie, D. L., & Stephens, C. M. (2006). Parenting practices and adolescents' friendship networks. *Journal of Marriage and Family, 68,* 1247–1260.

Knutson, B., & Adcock, R. (2005). Remembrance of rewards past. *Neuron, 45,* 331–32.

Ko, L., & Perreira, K. (2010). "It turned my world upside down": Latino youths' perspectives on immigration. *Journal of Adolescent Research, 25,* 465–493.

Kobak, R., & Madsen, S. (2011). Attachment. In B. Brown & M. Prinstein (Eds.), *Encyclopedia of adolescence* (Vol. 2, pp. 18–24). New York: Academic Press.

Kobak, R., Cole, H., Ferenz-Gillies, R., Fleming, W., & Gamble, W. (1993). Attachment and emotion regulation during mother–teen problem-solving: A control theory analysis. *Child Development, 64,* 231–245.

Kobak, R., Zajac, K., & Smith, C. (2009). Adolescent attachment and trajectories of hostile–impulsive behavior: Implications for the development of personality disorders. *Development and Psychopathology, 21,* 839.

Kochel, K., Ladd, G., & Rudolph, K. (2012). Longitudinal associations among youth depressive symptoms, peer victimization, and low peer acceptance: An interpersonal process perspective. *Child Development, 83,* 637–650.

Kochel, K. P., Miller, C. F., Updegraff, K. A., Ladd, G. W., & Kochenderfer-Ladd, B. (2012). Associations between fifth graders' gender atypical problem behavior and peer relationships: a short-term longitudinal study. *Journal of Youth & Adolescence, 41,* 1022–1034.

Koenig, L., McGue, M., & Iacono, W. G. (2008). Stability and change in religiousness during emerging adulthood. *Developmental Psychology, 44,* 532–543.

Koerner, S., Jacobs, S., & Raymond, M. (2000). When mothers turn to their adolescent daughters: Predicting daughters' vulnerability to negative adjustment outcomes. *Family Relations, 49,* 301–309.

Koerner, S., Korn, M., Dennison, R., & Witthoft, S. (2011). Future money-related worries among adolescents after divorce. *Journal of Adolescent Research, 26,* 299–317.

Koerner, S., Wallace, S. R., Lehman, S. J., Lee, S., & Escalante, K. A. (2004). Sensitive mother-to-adolescent disclosures after divorce: Is the experience of sons different from that of daughters? *Journal of Family Psychology, 18,* 46–57.

Koff, E., & Rierdan, J. (1996). Premenarcheal expectations and postmenarcheal experiences of positive and negative menstrual related changes. *Journal of Adolescent Health, 18,* 286–291.

Kofler, M. J., McCart, M. R., Zajac, K., Ruggiero, K. J., Saunders, B. E., & Kilpatrick, D. G. (2011). Depression and delinquency covariation in an accelerated longitudinal sample of adolescents. *Journal of Consulting and Clinical Psychology, 79,* 458–469.

Kogan, S. M., Brody, G. H., Gibbons, F. X., Chen, Y.-F., Grange, C. M., Simons, R. L., . . . Cutrona, C. (2011). Mechanisms of family impact on African American adolescents' HIV-related behavior. *Journal of Research on Adolescence, 21,* 361–375.

Kohler, J. K., Grotevant, H. D., & McRoy, R. G. (2002). Adopted adolescents' preoccupation with adoption: The impact on adoptive family relationships. *Journal of Marriage and Family, 64,* 93–104.

Kohler, P. K., Manhart, L. E., & Lafferty, W. E. (2008). Abstinence-only and comprehensive sex education and the initiation of sexual activity and teen pregnancy. *Journal of Adolescent Health, 42,* 344–351.

Kohls, G., Peltzer, J., Herpertz-Dahlman, B., & Konrad, K. (2009). Differential effects of social and non-social reward on response inhibition in children and adolescents. *Developmental Science, 12,* 614–625.

Kohn, M. (1977). *Class and conformity* (2nd ed.). Chicago: University of Chicago Press.

Kokko, K., Pulkkinen, L., Huesmann, L. R., Dubow, E. F., & Boxer, P. (2009). Intensity of aggression in childhood as a predictor of different forms of adult aggression: A two-country (Finland and the United States) analysis. *Journal of Research on Adolescence, 19,* 9–34.

Kolburn Kowal, A., & Blinn-Pike, L. (2004). Sibling influences on adolescents' attitudes toward safe sex practices. *Family Relations, 53,* 377–384.

Kolloren, S. E., & Deutsch, A. R. (2014). A longitudinal examination of parenting processes and Latino youth's risky sexual behaviors. *Journal of Youth & Adolescence, 43,* 1982–1993.

Konijn, E. A., Nije Bijvank, M., & Bushman, B. J. (2007). I wish I were a warrior: The role of wishful identification in the effects of violent video games on aggression in adolescent boys. *Developmental Psychology, 43,* 1038–1044.

Koolschijn, P. C., & Crone, E. A. (2013). Sex differences and structural brain maturation from childhood to early adulthood. *Developmental Cognitive Neuroscience, 5,* 106–118.

Koolschijn, P. C., Peper, J. S., & Crone, E. A. (2014). The influence of sex steroids on structural brain maturation in adolescence. *PLoS One, 9,* 83929.

Kort-Butler, L. A., & Hagewen, K. J. (2011). School-based extracurricular activity involvement and adolescent self-esteem: A growth-curve analysis. *Journal of Youth and Adolescence, 40,* 568–581.

Kosciw, J. G., Greytak, E. A., & Diaz, E. M. (2009). Who, what, where, when, and why: Demographic and ecological factors contributing to hostile school climate for lesbian, gay, bisexual, and transgender youth. *Journal of Youth and Adolescence, 38,* 976–988.

Kost K., & Henshaw S. (2014). US teen pregnancies, births, and abortions. New York: Guttmacher Institute. Avalableonline at http://www.childtrends.org/wp-content/uploads/2012/07/27_fig1.jpg. Accessed on July 14, 2015.

Kouros, C. D., & Garber, J. (2014). Trajectories of individual depressive symptoms in adolescents: Gender and family relationships as predictors. *Developmental Psychology, 50,* 2633–2643.

Kouros, C. D., Quasem, S., & Garber, J. (2013). Dynamic temporal relations between anxious and depressive symptoms across adolescence. *Development and Psychopathology, 25,* 683–697.

Kowal, A., & Kramer, L. (1997). Children's understanding of parental differential treatment. *Child Development, 68,* 113–126.

Kowaleski-Jones, L. (2000). Staying out of trouble: Community resources and problem behavior among high-risk adolescents. *Journal of Marriage and the Family, 62,* 449–464.

Kowaleski-Jones, L., & Dunifon, R. (2006). Family structure and community context: Evaluating influences on adolescent outcomes. *Youth and Society, 38,* 110–130.

Kracke, B. (2002). The role of personality, parents, and peers in adolescents career exploration. *Journal of Adolescence, 25,* 19–30.

Kragel, P. A., Zucker, N. L., Covington, V. E., & LaBar, K. S. (2015). Developmental trajectories of cortical-subcortical interactions underlying the evaluation of trust in adolescence. *Social Cognitive Affective Neuroscience, 10,* 240–247.

Krahé, B., Busching, R., & Möller, I. (2012). Media violence use and aggression among German adolescents: Associations and trajectories of change in a three-wave longitudinal study. *Psychology of Popular Media Culture, 1,* 152–166.

Kramer, L., & Conger, K. (2011). Adolescent sibling relations. In B. Brown & M. Prinstein (Eds.), *Encyclopedia of adolescence* (Vol. 2. pp. 1–9). New York: Academic Press.

Kramer, L., & Kowal, A. K. (2005). Sibling relationship quality from birth to adolescence: The enduring contributions of friends. *Journal of Family Psychology, 19,* 503–511.

Kreager, D. A. (2004). Strangers in the halls: Isolation and delinquency in social networks. *Social Forces, 83,* 351–390.

Kreager, D. A. (2007a). Unnecessary roughness? School sports, peer networks, and male adolescent violence. *American Sociological Review, 72,* 705–724.

Kreager, D. A. (2007b). When it's good to be "bad": Violence and adolescent peer acceptance. *Criminology: An Interdisciplinary Journal, 45,* 893–923.

Kreager, D. A., Molloy, L. E., Moody, J., & Feinberg, M. E. (2015). Friends first? The peer network origins of adolescent dating. *Journal of Research on Adolescence, Early view.* DOI: 10.1111/jora.12189

Kreager, D., & Haynie, D. (2011). Dangerous liaisons? Dating and drinking diffusion in adolescent peer networks. *American Sociological Review, 76,* 737–763.

Krei, M., & Rosenbaum, J. E. (2001). Career and college advice to the forgotten half: What do counselors and vocational teachers advise? *Teachers College Record, 103,* 823–842.

Kretsch, N., & Harden, K. P. (2014). Pubertal development and peer influence on risky decision making. *The Journal of Early Adolescence, 34,* 339–359.

Kretsch, N., Mendle, J., & Harden, P. (2014). A twin study of objective and subjective pubertal timing and peer influence on risk-taking. *Journal of Research on Adolescence, Early view.* DOI: 10.1111/jora.12160

Kretschmer, T., Oliver, B. R., & Maughan, B. (2014). Pubertal development, spare time activities, and adolescent delinquency: Testing the contextual amplification hypothesis. *Journal of Youth and Adolescence, 43,* 1346–1360.

Kroger, J. (1993). The role of historical context in the identity formation process of late adolescence. *Youth and Society, 24,* 363–376.

Kroger, J. (2003). Identity development during adolescence. In G. R. Adams, & M. D. Berzonsky (Eds.), *Blackwell Handbook of Adolescence* (pp. 205–226). Malden, MA: Blackwell.

Kroger, J., & Green, K. (1996). Events associated with identity status change. *Journal of Adolescence, 19,* 477–490.

Kuhn, D. (2009). Adolescent thinking. In R. Lerner & L. Steinberg (Eds.), *Handbook of adolescent psychology* (3rd ed., Vol. 1, pp. 152–186). New York: Wiley.

Kuhn, E. S., & Laird, R. (2011). Individual differences in early adolescents' beliefs in the legitimacy of parental authority. *Developmental Psychology, 47,* 1353–1365.

Kuhn, E. S., Phan, J. M., Laird, R. D. (2014). Compliance with parents' rules: between-person and within-person predictions. *Journal of Youth & Adolescence, 43,* 245–256.

Kulis, S., Marsiglia, F., & Hurdle, D. (2003). Gender identity, ethnicity, acculturation, and drug use: Exploring differences among adolescents in the Southwest. *Journal of Community Psychology, 31,* 167–188.

Kumpfer, K. L., & Alvarado, R. (2003). Family-strengthening approaches for the prevention of youth problem behaviors. *American Psychologist, 58,* 457–465.

Kunkel, D., Eyal, E., Finnerty, K., Biely, E., & Donnerstein, E. (2005). *Sex on TV.* Menlo Park, CA: Kaiser Family Foundation.

Kupchik, A., & Ellis, N. (2008). School discipline and security: Fair for all students? *Youth and Society, 39,* 549–574.

Kuperminc, G., Blatt, S., Shahar, B., Henrich, C., & Leadbeater, B. (2004). Cultural equivalence and cultural variance in longitudinal associations of young adolescents' self-definition and interpersonal relatedness to psychological and school adjustment. *Journal of Youth and Adolescence, 33,* 13–30.

Kuperminc, G., Darnell, A., & Alvarez-Jimenez, A. (2008). Parent involvement in the academic adjustment of Latino middle and high school youth: Teacher expectations and school belonging as mediators. *Journal of Adolescence, 31,* 469–483.

Kupersmidt, J., Burchinal, M., & Patterson, C. (1995). Developmental patterns of childhood peer relations as predictors of externalizing behavior problems. *Development and Psychopathology, 7,* 825–843.

Kuppens, S., Laurent, L., Heyvaert, M., & Onghena, P. (2013). Associations between parental psychological control and relational aggression in children and adolescents: A multilevel and sequential meta-analysis. *Developmental Psychology, 49,* 1697–1712.

Kurdek, L., & Fine, M. (1993). The relation between family structure and young adolescents' appraisals of family climate and parenting behavior. *Journal of Family Issues, 14,* 279–290.

Kurdek, L., Fine, M., & Sinclair, R. (1995). School adjustment in sixth graders: Parenting transitions, family climate, and peer norm effects. *Child Development, 66,* 430–445.

Kurlychek, M., & Johnson, B. (2010). Juvenility and punishment: Sentencing juveniles in adult criminal court. *Criminology, 48,* 725–758.

Kuss, D., van Rooij, A., Shorter, G. W., Griffiths, M. D., & Mheen, D. (2013). Internet addiction in adolescents: Prevalence and risk factors. *Computers in Human Behavior, 29,* 1987–1996.

Kuttler, A. F., & La Greca, A. M. (2004). Linkages among adolescent girls' romantic relationships, best friendships, and peer networks. *Journal of Adolescence, 27,* 395–414.

Kuttler, A. F., La Greca, A. M., & Prinstein, M. J. (1999). Friendship qualities and social-emotional functioning of adolescents with

close, cross-sex friendships. *Journal of Research on Adolescence, 9,* 339–366.

Kwak, K. (2003). Adolescents and their parents: A review of intergenerational family relations for immigrant and non-immigrant families. *Human Development, 46,* 115–136.

Kypri, K., Voas, R. B., Langley, J. D., Stephenson, S. C. R., Begg, D. J., Tippetts, A. S., & Davie, G. (2006). Minimum purchasing age for alcohol and traffic crash injuries among 15- to 19-year-olds in New Zealand. *American Journal of Public Health, 96,* 126–131.

L'Engle, K. L., & Jackson, C. (2008). Socialization influences on early adolescents' cognitive susceptibility and transition to sexual intercourse. *Journal of Research on Adolescence, 18,* 353–378.

L'Engle, K. L., Brown, J. D., & Kenneavy, K. (2006). The mass media are an important context for adolescents' sexual behavior. *Journal of Adolescent Health, 38,* 186–192.

L'Engle, K. L., Jackson, C., & Brown, J. D. (2006). Early adolescents' cognitive susceptibility to initiating sexual intercourse. *Perspectives on Sexual and Reproductive Health, 38,* 97–105.

La Greca, A., & Silverman, W. K. (2009). Treatment and prevention of posttraumatic stress reactions in children and adolescents exposed to disasters and terrorism: What is the evidence? *Child Development Perspectives, 3,* 4–10.

la Haye, de, K., Robins, G., Mohr, P., & Wilson, C. (2011). Homophily and contagion as explanations for weight similarities among adolescent friends. *Journal of Adolescent Health, 49,* 421–427.

Lachman, M. (2004). Development in midlife. *Annual Review of Psychology, 55,* 305–331.

Lacourse, R., Nagin, D., & Tremblay, R. E. (2003). Developmental trajectories of boys' delinquent group membership and facilitation of violent behaviors during adolescence. *Development and Psychopathology, 15,* 183–197.

Ladd, G. W., Ettekal, I., Kochenderfer-Ladd, B., Rudolph, K. D., & Andrews, R. K. (2014). Relations among chronic peer group rejection, maladaptive behavioral dispositions, and early adolescents' peer perceptions. *Child Development, 85,* 971–988.

Ladouceur, C. D., Dahl, R. E., & Carter, C. S. (2007). Development of action monitoring through adolescence into adulthood: ERP and source localization. *Developmental Science, 10,* 874–891.

Ladouceur, C. D., Peper, J. S., Crone, E. A., & Dahl, R. E. (2012). White matter development in adolescence: The influence of puberty and implications for affective disorders. *Developmental Cognitive Neuroscience, 2,* 36–54.

Lahat, A., Helwig, C. C., & Zelazo, P. D. (2013). An event-related potential study of adolescents' and young adults' judgments of moral and social conventional violations. *Child Development, 84,* 938–954.

Lahey, B., Van Hulle, C. A., D'Onofrio, B. M., Rodgers, J. L., & Waldman, I. D. (2008).

Is parental knowledge of their adolescent offspring's whereabouts and peer associations spuriously associated with offspring delinquency? *Journal of Abnormal Child Psychology, 36,* 807–823.

Laible, D., Carlo, G., & Raffaelli, M. (2000). The differential relations of parent and peer attachment to adolescent adjustment. *Journal of Youth and Adolescence, 29,* 45–59.

Laird, R. D., Bridges, B. J., & Marsee, M. A. (2013). Secrets from friends and parents: Longitudinal links with depression and antisocial behavior. *Journal of Adolescence, 36,* 685–693.

Laird, R. D., Marrero, M. D., Melching, J. A., & Kuhn, E. S. (2013). Information management strategies in early adolescence: Developmental change in use and transactional associations with psychological adjustment. *Developmental Psychology, 49,* 928–937.

Laird, R., & Marrero, M. (2011). Mothers' knowledge of early adolescents' activities following the middle school transition and pubertal maturation. *Journal of Early Adolescence, 31,* 209–233.

Laird, R., Criss, M., Pettit, G., Dodge, K., & Bates, J. (2008). Parents' monitoring knowledge attenuates the link between antisocial friends and adolescent delinquent behavior. *Journal of Abnormal Child Psychology, 36,* 299–310.

Laird, R., Marrero, M., & Sentse, M. (2010). Revisiting parental monitoring: Evidence that parental solicitation can be effective when needed most. *Journal of Youth and Adolescence, 39,* 1431–1441.

Laird, R., Pettit, G., Bates, J., & Dodge, K. (2003). Parents' monitoring relevant knowledge and adolescents' delinquent behavior: Evidence of correlated developmental changes and reciprocal influences. *Child Development, 74,* 752–768.

Laird, R., Pettit, G., Dodge, K., & Bates, J. (2005). Peer relationship antecedents of delinquent behavior in late adolescence: Is there evidence of demographic group differences in developmental processes? *Development and Psychopathology, 17,* 127–144.

Lam, C. B., McHale, S. M., & Crouter, A. C. (2014). Time with peers from middle childhood to late adolescence: Developmental course and adjustment correlates. *Child Development, 85,* 1677–1693.

Lam, L. T., & Yang, L. (2007). Overweight/obesity and attention deficit and hyperactivity disorder tendency among adolescents in China. *International Journal of Obesity, 31,* 584–590.

Lam, T., Shi, H., Ho, L., Stewart, S. M., & Fan, S. (2002). Timing of pubertal maturation and heterosexual behavior among Hong Kong Chinese adolescents. *Archives of Sexual Behavior, 31,* 359–366.

Lambert, S. F., Herman, K. C., Bynum, M. S., & Ialongo, N. S. (2009). Perceptions of racism and depressive symptoms in African American adolescents: The role of perceived academic and social control. *Journal of Youth and Adolescence, 38,* 519–531.

Lamborn, S., & Nguyen, D. T. (2004). African American adolescents' perceptions of family interactions: Kinship support, parent–child relationships, and teen adjustment. *Journal of Youth and Adolescence, 33,* 547–558.

Lamborn, S., & Steinberg, L. (1993). Emotional autonomy redux: Revisiting Ryan and Lynch. *Child Development, 64,* 483–499.

Lammers, C., Ireland, M., Resnick, M., & Blum, R. (2000). Influences on adolescents' decision to postpone onset of sexual intercourse: A survival analysis of virginity among youths aged 13 to 18 years. *Journal of Adolescent Health, 26,* 42–48.

Lampard, A. M., MacLehose, R. F., Eisenberg, M. E., Neumark-Sztainer, D., Davison, K. K. (2014). Weight-related teasing in the school environment: associations with psychosocial health and weight control practices among adolescent boys and girls. *Journal of Youth and Adolescence, 43,* 1770–1780.

Lang, F., & Carstensen, L. (2002). Time counts: Future time perspective, goals, and social relationships. *Psychology and Aging, 17,* 125–139.

Lang, S., Waller, P., & Shope, J. (1996). Adolescent driving: Characteristics associated with single-vehicle and injury crashes. *Journal of Safety Research, 27,* 241–257.

Langer, J. A. (2001). Beating the odds: Teaching middle and high school students to read and write well. *American Educational Research Journal, 38,* 837–880.

Langer, L., Zimmerman, R., & Katz, J. (1995). Virgins' expectations and nonvirgins' reports: How adolescents feel about themselves. *Journal of Adolescent Research, 10,* 291–306.

Langhout, R. D., Rhodes, J. E., & Osborne, L. N. (2004). An exploratory study of youth mentoring in an urban context: Adolescents' perceptions of relational styles. *Journal of Youth and Adolescence, 33,* 293–306.

Lansford, J. (2011). Immigrant issues. In B. Brown & M. Prinstein (Eds.), *Encyclopedia of adolescence* (Vol. 2, pp. 143–151). New York: Academic Press.

Lansford, J. E., Yu, T., Pettit, G. S., Bates, J. E., & Dodge, K. A. (2014). Pathways of peer relationships from childhood to young adulthood. *Journal of Applied Developmental Psychology, 35,* 111–117.

Lansford, J., Criss, M., Laird, R., Shaw, D., Pettit, G., Bates, J., & Dodge, K. (2011). Reciprocal relations between parents' physical discipline and children's externalizing behavior during middle childhood and adolescence. *Development and Psychopathology, 23,* 225–238.

Lansford, J., Killeya-Jones, L. A., Miller, S., & Costanzo, P. R. (2009). Early adolescents' social standing in peer groups: Behavioral correlates of stability and change. *Journal of Youth and Adolescence, 38,* 1084–1095.

Lansford, J., Malone, P., Dodge, K., Crozier, J., Pettit, G., & Bates, J. (2006). A 12-year

prospective study of patterns of social information processing problems and externalizing behaviors. *Journal of Abnormal Child Psychology, 34,* 715–724.

Lansford, J., Yu, T., Erath, S., Pettit, G., Bates, J., & Dodge, K. (2010). Developmental precursors of number of sexual partners from ages 16 to 22. *Journal of Research on Adolescence, 20,* 651–677.

Lansford, J. E., Dodge, K. A., Fontaine, R. G., Bates, J. E., & Pettit, G. S. (2014). Peer rejection, affiliation with deviant peers, delinquency, and risky sexual behavior. *Journal of Youth & Adolescence, 43,* 1742–1751.

Lansford, J. E., Laird, R. D., Pettit, G. S., Bates, J. E., Dodge, K. A. (2014). Mothers' and fathers' autonomy-relevant parenting: longitudinal links with adolescents' externalizing and internalizing behavior. *Journal of Youth & Adolescence, 43,* 1877–1889.

Lansu, T. A. M., & Cillessen, A. H. N. (2011). Peer status in emerging adulthood: Associations of popularity and preference with social roles and behavior. *Journal of Adolescent Research, 27,* 132–150.

Lansu, T. A. M., Cillessen, A. H. N., & Karremans, J. C. (2012). Implicit associations with popularity in early adolescence: An approach-avoidance analysis. *Developmental Psychology, 48,* 65–75.

Lansu, T. A. M., Cillessen, A. H. N., & Karremans, J. C. (2014). Adolescents' selective visual attention for high-status peers: the role of perceiver status and gender. *Child Development, 85,* 421–428.

Lanz, M., Scabini, E., Vermulst, A. A., & Gerris, J. M. (2001). Congruence on child rearing in families with early adolescent and middle adolescent children. *International Journal of Behavioral Development, 25,* 133–139.

Lapsley, D., Enright, R., & Serlin, R. (1985). Toward a theoretical perspective on the legislation of adolescence. *Journal of Early Adolescence, 5,* 441–466.

Larson, M., & Sweeten, G. (2012). Breaking up is hard to do: Romantic dissolution, offending, and substance use during the transition to adulthood. *Criminology, 50,* 605–636.

Larson, R. (1983). Adolescents' daily experience with family and friends: Contrasting opportunity systems. *Journal of Marriage and the Family, 11,* 739–750.

Larson, R. (1995). Secrets in the bedroom: Adolescents' private use of media. *Journal of Youth and Adolescence, 24,* 535–550.

Larson, R. (1997). The emergence of solitude as a constructive domain of experience in early adolescence. *Child Development, 68,* 80–93.

Larson, R. (2000). Toward a psychology of positive youth development. *American Psychologist, 55,* 170–183.

Larson, R., & Angus, R. (2011). Adolescents' development of skills for agency in youth programs: Learning to think strategically. *Child Development, 82,* 277–294.

Larson, R., & Brown, J. (2007). Emotional development in adolescence: What can be learned from a high school theater program? *Child Development, 78,* 1083–1099.

Larson, R., & Gillman, S. (1996, March). *Daily processes in single parent families.* Paper presented at the biennial meetings of the Society for Research on Adolescence, Boston.

Larson, R., & Richards, M. (1991). Daily companionship in late childhood and early adolescence: Changing developmental contexts. *Child Development, 62,* 284–300.

Larson, R., & Richards, M. (1994). Family emotions: Do young adolescents and their parents experience the same states? *Journal of Research on Adolescence, 4,* 567–583.

Larson, R., & Richards, M. (1998). Waiting for the weekend: Friday and Saturday night as the emotional climax of the week. *New Directions for Child and Adolescent Development, Winter,* 37–51.

Larson, R., & Seepersad, S. (2003). Adolescents' leisure time in the United States: Partying, sports, and the American experiment. *New Directions for Child and Adolescent Development, 99,* 53–64.

Larson, R., & Verma, S. (1999). How children and adolescents spend time across the world: Work, play, and developmental opportunities. *Psychological Bulletin, 125,* 701–736.

Larson, R., Clore, G., & Wood, G. (1999). The emotions of romantic relationships: Do they wreak havoc on adolescents? In W. Furman, B. Brown, & C. Feiring (Eds.), *Contemporary perspectives on adolescent romantic relationships* (pp. 19–49). New York: Cambridge University Press.

Larson, R., Hansen, D. M., & Moneta, G. (2006). Differing profiles of developmental experiences across types of organized youth activities. *Developmental Psychology, 42,* 849–863.

Larson, R., Moneta, G., Richards, M. H., & Wilson, S. (2002). Continuity, stability, and change in daily emotional experience across adolescence. *Child Development, 73,* 1151–1165.

Larson, R., Pearce, N., Sullivan, P., & Jarrett, R. (2007). Participation in youth programs as a catalyst for negotiation of family autonomy with connection. *Journal of Youth and Adolescence, 36,* 31–45.

Larson, R., Richards, M., Moneta, G., Holmbeck, G., & Duckett, E. (1996). Changes in adolescents' daily interactions with their families from ages 10 to 18: Disengagement and transformation. *Developmental Psychology, 32,* 744–754.

Larson, R., Richards, M., Sims, B., & Dworkin, J. (2001). How urban African American young adolescents spend their time: Time budgets for locations, activities, and companionship. *American Journal of Community Psychology, 29,* 565–597.

Larson, R., Wilson, S., & Rickman, A. (2009). Globalization, societal change, and adolescence across the world. In R. Lerner & L. Steinberg (Eds.), *Handbook of adolescent psychology* (3rd ed., Vol. 2, pp. 590–622). New York: Wiley.

Latendresse, S. J., Bates, J. E., Goodnight, J. A., Lansford, J. E., Budde, J. P., Goate, A., Dick, D. (2011). Differential susceptibility to adolescent externalizing trajectories: Examining the interplay between CHRM2 and peer group antisocial behavior. *Child Development, 82,* 1797–1814.

Lau, J., & Eley, T. (2008). Attributional style as a risk marker of genetic effects for adolescent depressive symptoms. *Journal of Abnormal Psychology, 117,* 849–859.

Lau, M., Markham, C., Lin, H., Flores, G., & Chacko, M. R. (2009). Dating and sexual attitudes in Asian-American adolescents. *Journal of Adolescent Research, 24,* 91–113.

Laucht, M., Becker, K., Frank, J., Schmidt, M. H., Esser, G., Treutlein, J., . . . Schumann, G. (2008). Genetic variation in dopamine pathways differentially associated with smoking progression in adolescence. *Journal of the American Academy of Child & Adolescent Psychiatry, 47,* 673–681.

Laursen, B. (1993). The perceived impact of conflict on adolescent relationships. *Merrill-Palmer Quarterly, 39,* 535–550.

Laursen, B. (1995). Conflict and social interaction in adolescent relationships. *Journal of Research on Adolescence, 5,* 55–70.

Laursen, B. (1996). Closeness and conflict in adolescent peer relationships: Interdependence with friends and romantic partners. In W. Bukowski, A. Newcomb, & W. Hartup (Eds.), *The company they keep: Friendship in childhood and adolescence* (pp. 186–210). New York: Cambridge University Press.

Laursen, B., & Collins, W. A. (1994). Interpersonal conflict during adolescence. *Psychological Bulletin, 115,* 197–209.

Laursen, B., & Collins, W. A. (2009). Parent–child relationships during adolescence. In R. Lerner & L. Steinberg (Eds.), *Handbook of adolescent psychology* (3rd ed., Vol. 2, pp. 3–42). New York: Wiley.

Laursen, B., & DeLay, D. (2011). Parent-child relationship. In B. Brown & M. Prinstein (Eds.), *Encyclopedia of adolescence* (Vol. 2, pp. 233–240). New York: Academic Press.

Laursen, B., & Hartl, A. C. (2013). Understanding loneliness during adolescence: Developmental changes that increase the risk of perceived social isolation. *Journal of Adolescence, 36,* 1261–1268.

Laursen, B., & Jensen-Campbell, L. (1999). The nature and functions of social exchange in adolescent romantic relationships. In W. Furman, B. Brown, & C. Feiring (Eds.), *Contemporary perspectives on adolescent romantic relationships* (pp. 50–74). New York: Cambridge University Press.

Laursen, B., Coy, K., & Collins, W. A. (1998). Reconsidering changes in parent–child conflict across adolescence: A meta-analysis. *Child Development, 69,* 817–832.

Laursen, B., DeLay, D., & Adams, R. E. (2010). Trajectories of perceived support in mother–adolescent relationships: The poor (quality) get poorer. *Developmental Psychology, 46,* 1792–1798.

Laursen, B., Finkelstein, B. D., & Townsend Betts, N. (2001). A developmental meta-analysis of peer conflict resolution. *Developmental Review, 21,* 423–449.

Laursen, B., Hafen, C. A., Kerr, M., & Stattin, H. (2012). Friend influence over adolescent problem behaviors as a function of relative peer acceptance: To be liked is to be emulated. *Journal of Abnormal Psychology, 121,* 88–94.

Laursen, B., Hafen, C., Kerr, M., & Stattin, H. (2012). Friend influence over adolescent problem behaviors as a function of relative peer acceptance: To be liked is to be emulated. *Journal of Abnormal Psychology, 121,* 88–94.

Lavoie, F., Hebert, M., Tremblay, R., Vitaro, F., Vezina, L., & McDuff, P. (2002). History of family dysfunction and perpetration of dating violence by adolescent boys: A longitudinal study. *Journal of Adolescent Health, 30,* 375–383.

LaVoie, J. (1994). Identity in adolescence: Issues of theory, structure, and transition. *Journal of Adolescence, 17,* 17–28.

Lawford, H., Pratt, M. W., Hunsberger, B., & Pancer, S. M. (2005). Adolescent generativity: A longitudinal study of two possible contexts for learning concern for future generations. *Journal of Research on Adolescence, 15,* 261–273.

Lawler, M., & Nixon, E. (2011). Body dissatisfaction among adolescent boys and girls: The effects of body mass, peer appearance culture and internalization of appearance ideals. *Journal of Youth and Adolescence, 40,* 59–71.

Leadbeater, B. (1996). School outcomes for minority-group adolescent mothers at 28 to 36 months postpartum: A longitudinal follow-up. *Journal of Research on Adolescence, 6,* 629–648.

Leadbeater, B., Kuperminc, G., Blatt, S., & Hertzog, C. (1999). A multivariate model of gender differences in adolescents' internalizing and externalizing problems. *Developmental Psychology, 35,* 1268–1282.

Leahy, E. (2001). Gender differences in mathematical trajectories. *Social Forces, 80,* 713–732.

Leaper, C., & Brown, C. S. (2008). Perceived experiences with sexism among adolescent girls. *Child Development, 79,* 685–704.

Leaper, C., Farkas, T., & Brown, C. P. (2012). Adolescent girls' experiences and gender-related beliefs in relation to their motivation in math/science and English. *Journal of Youth & Adolescence, 41,* 268–282.

Leatherdale, S. T., & Papadakis, S. (2011). A multilevel examination of the association between older social models in the school environment and overweight and obesity among younger students. *Journal of Youth and Adolescence, 40,* 361–372.

Lebel, C., & Beaulieu, C. (2011). Longitudinal development of human brain wiring continues from childhood into adulthood. *Journal of Neuroscience, 31(30),* 10937–10947.

LeBlanc, A. (2003). *Random family: Love, drugs, trouble, and coming of age in the Bronx.* New York: Scribner.

LeBlanc, L., Swisher, R., Vitaro, F., & Tremblay, R. E. (2008). High school social climate and antisocial behavior: A 10 year longitudinal and multilevel study. *Journal of Research on Adolescence, 18,* 395–419.

LeBlanc, M., Self-Brown, S., Shepard, D., & Kelley, M. (2011). Buffering the effects of violence: communication and problem-solving skills as protective factors for adolescents exposed to violence. *Journal of Community Psychology, 39,* 353–367.

Lee, B., & Thompson, R. (2009). Examining externalizing behavior trajectories of youth in group homes: Is there evidence for peer contagion? *Journal of Abnormal Child Psychology, 37,* 31–44.

Lee, E. J., & Stone, S. I. (2012). Co-occurring internalizing and externalizing behavioral problems: the mediating effect of negative self-concept. *Journal of Youth & Adolescence, 41,* 717–731.

Lee, H. J., Park, S., Kim, C. I., Choi, D. W., Lee, J. S., Oh, S. M. . . . & Oh, S. W. (2013). The association between disturbed eating behavior and socioeconomic status: The online Korean adolescent panel survey (OnKAPS). *PLoS One, 8,* 57880.

Lee, H., Lee, D., Guo, G., & Harris, K. (2011). Trends in body mass index in adolescence and young adulthood in the United States: 1959–2002. *Journal of Adolescent Health, 49,* 601–608.

Lee, J. (2008). "A Kotex and a Smile": Mothers and daughters at menarche. *Journal of Family Issues, 29,* 1325–1347.

Lee, J. (2010). Tripartite growth trajectories of reading and math achievement: Tracking national academic progress at primary, middle, and high school levels. *American Educational Research Journal, 47,* 800–832.

Lee, J. C., & Staff, J. (2007). When work matters: The varying impact of work intensity on high school dropout. *Sociology of Education, 80,* 158–178.

Lee, J., & Hahm, H. C. (2010). Acculturation and sexual risk behaviors among Latina adolescents transitioning to young adulthood. *Journal of Youth and Adolescence, 39,* 414–427.

Lee, J., Edwards, K., Menson, R., & Rawls, A. (2011). *The college completion agenda: 2011 progress report.* New York: The College Board.

Lee, K. H., Siegle, G. J., Dahl, R. E., Hooley, J. M., & Silk, J. S. (2014). Neural responses to maternal criticism in healthy youth. *Social Cognitive Affective Neuroscience, 10,* 902–912.

Lee, M., & Larson, R. (2000). The Korean "examination hell": Long hours of studying, distress, and depression. *Journal of Youth and Adolescence, 29,* 249–271.

Lee, S. (2001). More than "model minorities" or "delinquents": A look at Hmong American high school students. *Harvard Educational Review, 71,* 505–528.

Lee, S. (2011). Deviant peer affiliation and antisocial behavior: Interaction with Monoamine Oxidase A (MAOA) genotype. *Journal of Abnormal Child Psychology, 39,* 321–332.

Lee, T. K., Wickrama, K. A. S., Simons, L. G. (2013). Chronic family economic hardship, family processes and progression of mental and physical health symptoms in adolescence. *Journal of Youth & Adolescence, 42,* 821–836.

Lee, V., & Burkam, D. (1992). Transferring high schools: An alternative to dropping out? *American Journal of Education, 100,* 420–453.

Lee, V., & Burkam, D. (2003). Dropping out of high school: The role of school organization and structure. *American Educational Research Journal, 40,* 353–393.

Lee, V., & Croninger, R. (1994). The relative importance of home and school in the development of literacy skills for middle-grade students. *American Journal of Education, 102,* 286–329.

Lee, V., & Smith, J. (1993). Effects of school restructuring on the achievement and engagement of middle-grade students. *Sociology of Education, 66,* 164–187.

Lee, V., & Smith, J. (1995). Effects of high school restructuring and size in early gains in achievement and engagement. *Sociology of Education, 68,* 241–270.

Lee, V., & Smith, J. (1996). Collective responsibility for learning and its effects on gains in achievement for early secondary school students. *American Journal of Education, 104,* 103–147.

Lee, V., & Smith, J. (1997). High school size: Which works best, and for whom? *Educational Evaluation and Policy Analysis, 19,* 205–227.

Lee, V., Burkam, D., Zimiles, H., & Ladewski, B. (1994). Family structure and its effect on behavioral and emotional problems in young adolescents. *Journal of Research on Adolescence, 4,* 405–437.

Lee, V., Croninger, R., Linn, E., & Chen, X. (1996). The culture of sexual harassment in secondary schools. *American Educational Research Journal, 33,* 383–417.

Lee, V., Smith, J., & Croninger, R. (1997). How high school organization influences the equitable distribution of learning in mathematics and science. *Sociology of Education, 70,* 128–150.

Leech, T. G. J., & Dias, J. J. (2012). Risky sexual behavior: A race-specific social consequence of obesity. *Journal of Youth and Adolescence, 41,* 41–52.

Leel, F. S., Heimer, H., Giedd, J. N., Lein, E. S., Šestan, N., Weinberger, D. R., & Casey, B. J. (2014). Adolescent mental health–Opportunity and obligation. *Science, 346,* 547–549.

Leets, L., & Sunwolf. (2005). Adolescent rules for social exclusion: When is it fair to exclude someone else? *Journal of Moral Education, 34,* 343–362.

Lefkowitz, E. (2005). "Things have gotten better": Developmental changes among emerging adults after the transition to university. *Journal of Adolescent Research, 20,* 40–63.

Lefkowitz, E., Boone, T. L., Sigman, M., & Kitfong Au, T. (2002). He said, she said: Gender differences in mother–adolescent conversations about sexuality. *Journal of Research on Adolescence, 12*(2), 217–242.

Lefkowitz, E., Romo, L., Corona, R., Au, T., & Sigman, M. (2000). How Latino American and European American adolescents discuss conflicts, sexuality, and AIDS with their mothers. *Developmental Psychology, 36,* 315–325.

Lefkowitz, E., Sigman, M., & Au, T. (2000). Helping mothers discuss sexuality and AIDS with adolescents. *Child Development, 71,* 1383–1394.

Legault, L., Green-Demers, I., & Pelletier, L. (2006). Why do high school students lack motivation in the classroom? Toward an understanding of academic amotivation and the role of social support. *Journal of Educational Psychology, 98,* 567–582.

Leitenberg, H., & Saltzman, H. (2000). A statewide survey of age at first intercourse for adolescent females and age of their male partners: Relation to other risk behaviors and statutory rape implications. *Archives of Sexual Behavior, 29,* 203–215.

Lekes, N., Gingras, I., Philippe, F. L., Koestner, R., & Fang, J. (2010). Parental autonomy-support, intrinsic life goals, and well-being among adolescents in China and North America. *Journal of Youth and Adolescence, 39,* 858–869.

Lemola, S., Perkinson-Gloor, N., Brand, S., Dewalk-Kaufmann, J. F., Grob, A. (2015). Adolescents' electronic media use at night, sleep disturbance, and depressive symptoms in the smartphone age. *Journal of Youth & Adolescence, 44,* 405–418.

LeMoult, J., Colich, N. L. Sherdell, L., Hamilton, J. P., & Gotlib, I. H. (2015). Influence of menarche on the relation between diurnal cortisol production and ventral striatum activity during reward anticipation. *Social Cognitive Affective Neuroscience, Epub ahead of print.* DOI: 10.1093/scan/nsv016

Lengua, L. J. (2006). Growth in temperament and parenting as predictors of adjustment during children's transition to adolescence. *Developmental Psychology, 42,* 819–832.

Lenhart, A. (2012). *Teens, smartphones, and texting.* Washington: Pew Research Center.

Lenhart, A. (2015). *Teens, social media, and technology.* Washington: Pew Research Center.

Lenhart, A., Madden, M., Smith, A., Purcell, K., Zickuhr, K., & Rainie, L. (2011). *Teens, kindness and cruelty on social network sites.* Washington: Pew Research Center.

Lenhart, L., & Rabiner, D. (1995). An integrative approach to the study of social competence in adolescence. *Development and Psychopathology, 7,* 543–561.

Lenroot, R. K., & Giedd, J. N. (2008). The changing impact of genes and environment on brain development during childhood and adolescence: Initial findings from a neuroimaging study of pediatric twins. *Development and Psychopathology, 20,* 1161–1175.

Lenzi, M., Vieno, A., Perkins, D. D., Pastore, M., Santinello, M., & Mazzardis, S. (2012). Perceived neighborhood social resources as determinants of prosocial behavior in early adolescence. *American Journal of Community Psychology, 50,* 37–49.

Lenzi, M., Vieno, A., Perkins, D. D., Santinello, M., Elgar, F. J., Morgan, A., & Mazzardis, S. (2012). Family affluence, school and neighborhood contexts and adolescents' civic engagement: A cross-national study. *American Journal of Community Psychology, 50,* 197–210.

Lenzi, M., Vieno, A., Santinello, M., & Perkins, D. D. (2013) How neighborhood structural and institutional features can shape neighborhood social connectedness: A multilevel study of adolescent perceptions. *American Journal of Community Psychology, 51,* 451–467.

Lenzi, M., Vieno, A., Santinello, M., Nation, M. & Voight, A. (2014). The role played by the family in shaping early and middle adolescent civic responsibility. *The Journal of Early Adolescence, 34,* 251–278.

Leon, G., Fulkerson, J. A., Perry, C. L., Keel, P. K., & Klump, K. L. (1999). Three to four year prospective evaluation of personality and behavioral risk factors for later disordered eating in adolescent girls and boys. *Journal of Youth and Adolescence, 28,* 181–196.

Leopold, T. (2012). The legacy of leaving home: Long-term effects of coresidence on parent-child relationships. *Journal of Marriage and Family, 74,* 399–412.

Lerner, J., Phelps, E., Forman, Y., & Bowers, E. (2009). Positive youth development. In R. Lerner & L. Steinberg (Eds.), *Handbook of adolescent psychology* (3rd ed., Vol. 1, pp. 524–558). New York: Wiley.

Lerner, R., & Steinberg, L. (Eds.) (2009). *Handbook of adolescent psychology* (3rd ed.). New York: Wiley.

Lerner, R., Lerner, J. V., Almerigi, J. B., Theokas, C., Phelps, E., Gestsdottir, S., . . . von Eye, A. (2005). Positive youth development, participation in community youth development programs, and community contributions of fifth-grade adolescents findings from the first wave of the 4-H study of positive youth development. *Journal of Early Adolescence, 25,* 17–71.

Lerner, R., von Eye, A., Lerner, J. V., Lewin-Bizan, S., & Bowers, E. P. (2010). Special issue introduction: The meaning and measurement of thriving: A view of the issues. *Journal of Youth and Adolescence, 39,* 707–719.

Lesane-Brown, C. (2006). A review of race socialization within Black families. *Developmental Review, 26,* 400–426.

Lesko, N. (1996). Denaturalizing adolescence: The politics of contemporary representations. *Youth and Society, 28,* 139–161.

Lesthaeghe, R., & Neidert, L. (2006). *The "Second Demographic Transition" in the U.S.: Spatial patterns and correlates.* PSC Research Report No. 06–592. Ann Arbor: Institute for Social Research, University of Michigan.

Leventhal, H., & Keeshan, P. (1993). Promoting healthy alternatives to substance abuse. In S. Millstein, A. Petersen, & E. Nightingale (Eds.), *Promoting the health of adolescents: New directions for the twenty-first century* (pp. 260–284). New York: Oxford University Press.

Leventhal, T., & Brooks-Gunn, J. (2004). Diversity in developmental trajectories across adolescence: Neighborhood influences. In R. Lerner & L. Steinberg (Eds.), *Handbook of adolescent psychology.* New York: Wiley.

Leventhal, T., & Brooks-Gunn, J. (2011). Changes in neighborhood poverty from 1990 to 2000 and youth's problem behaviors. *Developmental Psychology, 47,* 1680–1698.

Leventhal, T., Dupéré, V., & Brooks-Gunn, J. (2009). Neighborhood influences on adolescent development. In R. Lerner & L. Steinberg (Eds.), *Handbook of adolescent psychology* (3rd ed., Vol. 2, pp. 411–443). New York: Wiley.

Leventhal, T., Fauth, R. C., & Brooks-Gunn, J. (2005). Neighborhood poverty and public policy: A 5-year follow-up of children's educational outcomes in the New York City Moving to Opportunity demonstration. *Developmental Psychology, 41,* 933–952.

Leversen, I., Danielsen, A. G., Birkeland, M. S., Samdal, O. (2012). Basic psychological need satisfaction in leisure activities and adolescents' life satisfaction. *Journal of Youth & Adolescence, 41,* 1588–1599.

Levesque, R. (1993). The romantic experience of adolescents in satisfying love relationships. *Journal of Youth and Adolescence, 22,* 219–251.

Levin, M., Xu, X., & Bartkowski, J. (2002). Seasonality of sexual debut. *Journal of Marriage and the Family, 64,* 871–884.

Levine, J. A., Emery, C. R., & Pollack, H. (2007). The well-being of children born to teen mothers. *Journal of Marriage and Family, 69,* 105–122.

Levine, M., & Harrison, K. (2004). Media's role in the perpetuation and prevention of negative body image and disordered eating. In J. K. Thompson (Ed.), *Handbook of eating disorders and obesity* (pp. 695–717). New York: John Wiley.

Levine, M., Smolak, L., & Hayden, H. (1994). The relation of sociocultural factors to eating attitudes and behaviors among middle school girls. *Journal of Early Adolescence, 14,* 471–490.

Levine, P. (2001). The sexual activity and birth control use of American teenagers. In J. Gruber (Ed.), *Risky behavior among youths: An economic analysis* (pp. 167–218). Chicago: University of Chicago Press.

Levinson, R., Jaccard, J., & Beamer, L. (1995). Older adolescents' engagement in casual sex: Impact of risk perception and psychosocial motivations. *Journal of Youth and Adolescence, 24,* 349–364.

Levitt, M., Guacci-Franci, N., & Levitt, J. (1993). Convoys of social support in childhood and early adolescence: Structure and function. *Developmental Psychology, 29,* 811–818.

Levitt, S., & Dubner, S. (2005). *Freakonomics.* New York: William Morrow.

Lewin, K. (1951). *Field theory and social science.* New York: Harper & Row.

Lewin, T. (July 9, 2006). At colleges, women are leaving men in the dust. *The New York Times,* pp. 1ff.

Lewin-Bizan, S., Bowers, E., & Lerner, R. (2010). One good thing leads to another: Cascades of positive youth development among American adolescents. *Development and Psychopathology, 22,* 759–770.

Lewinsohn, P., Gotlib, I., & Seeley, J. (1997). Depression-related psychosocial variables: Are they specific to depression in adolescents? *Journal of Abnormal Psychology, 106,* 365–375.

Lewinsohn, P., Joiner, T. E., Jr., & Rohde, P. (2001). Evaluation of cognitive diathesis–stress models in predicting major depressive disorder in adolescents. *Journal of Abnormal Psychology, 110,* 203–215.

Lewinsohn, P., Pettit, J., Joiner, T., Jr., & Seeley, J. (2003). The symptomatic expression of major depressive disorder in adolescents and young adults. *Journal of Abnormal Psychology, 112,* 244–252.

Lewinsohn, P., Roberts, R., Seeley, J., Rohde, P., Gotlib, I., & Hops, H. (1994). Adolescent psychopathology, II: Psychosocial risk factors for depression. *Journal of Abnormal Psychology, 103,* 302–325.

Lewinsohn, P., Rohde, P., & Seeley, J. (1994). Psychosocial risk factors for future adolescent suicide attempts. *Journal of Consulting and Clinical Psychology, 62,* 297–305.

Lewinsohn, P., Rohde, P., Seeley, J., & Fischer, S. (1993). Age-cohort changes in the lifetime occurrence of depression and other mental disorders. *Journal of Abnormal Psychology, 102,* 110–120.

Lewinsohn, P., Rohde, P., Seeley, J., Klein, D., & Gotlib, I. (2003). Psychosocial functioning of young adults who have experienced and recovered from major depressive disorder during adolescence. *Journal of Abnormal Psychology, 112,* 353–363.

Lewis, M., Feiring, C., & Rosenthal, S. (2000). Attachment over time. *Child Development, 71,* 707–720.

Li, D., London, S. J., Liu, J., Lee, W., Jiang, X., Van Den Berg, D., . . . Conti, D. (2011). Association of the calcyon neuron-specific vesicular protein gene (CALY) with adolescent smoking initiation in China and California. *American Journal of Epidemiology, 173,* 1039–1048.

Li, J. (2006). Self in learning: Chinese adolescents' goals and sense of agency. *Child Development, 77,* 482–501.

Li, J. (2009). Forging the future between two different worlds: Recent Chinese immigrant adolescents tell their cross-cultural experiences. *Journal of Adolescent Research, 24,* 477–504.

Li, J. L., Berk, M. S., & Lee, S. S. (2013). Differential susceptibility in longitudinal models of gene–environment interaction for adolescent depression. *Development and Psychopathology, 25,* 991–1003.

Li, S. T., Nussbaum, K. M., & Richards, M. H. (2007). Risk and protective factors for urban African American youth. *American Journal of Community Psychology, 39,* 21–35.

Li, X., Stanton, B., & Feigelman, S. (2000). Impact of perceived parental monitoring on adolescent risk behavior over 4 years. *Journal of Adolescent Health, 27,* 49–56.

Li, X., Stanton, B., Pack, R., Harris, C., Cottrell, L., & Burns, J. (2002). Risk and protective factors associated with gang involvement among urban African American adolescents. *Youth and Society, 34,* 172–194.

Li, Y., & Lerner, R. M. (2011). Trajectories of school engagement during adolescence: Implications for grades, depression, delinquency, and substance use. *Developmental Psychology, 47,* 233–247.

Li, Y., Lerner, J. V., & Lerner, R. M. (2010). Personal and ecological assets and academic competence in early adolescence: The mediating role of school engagement. *Journal of Youth and Adolescence, 39,* 801–815.

Lichtwarck-Aschoff, A., Kunnen, S. E., & van Geert, P. L. C. (2009). Here we go again: A dynamic systems perspective on emotional rigidity across parent–adolescent conflicts. *Developmental Psychology, 45,* 1364–1375.

Liddle, H. A., Rowe, C. L., Dakof, G. A., Henderson, C. E., & Greenbaum, P. E. (2009). Multidimensional family therapy for young adolescent substance abuse: Twelve-month outcomes of a randomized controlled trial. *Journal of Consulting and Clinical Psychology, 77,* 12–25.

Lieberman, M., Doyle, A., & Markiewicz, D. (1999). Developmental patterns in security of attachment to mother and father in late childhood and early adolescence: Associations with peer relations. *Child Development, 70,* 202–213.

Lien, L., Sagatun, A., Heyerdahl, S., Søgaard, A. J., & Bjertness, E. (2009). Is the relationship between smoking and mental health influenced by other unhealthy lifestyle factors? Results from a 3-year follow-up study among adolescents in Oslo, Norway. *Journal of Adolescent Health, 45,* 609–617.

Light, J. M., Greenan, C. C., Rusby, J. C., Nies, K. M., & Snijders, T. A. B (2013). Onset to first alcohol use in early adolescence: A network diffusion model. *Journal of Research on Adolescence, 23,* 487–499.

Lightwood, J., Bibbins-Domingo, K., Coxson, P., & Wang, Y. (2009). Forecasting the future economic burden of current adolescent overweight: An estimate of the coronary heart disease policy model. *American Journal of Public Health, 99,* 2230–2237.

Lillard, A., & Erisir, A. (2011). Old dogs learning new tricks: Neuroplasticity beyond the juvenile period. *Developmental Review, 31,* 207–39.

Lin, W., Cheong, P., Kim, Y., & Jung, J. (2010). Becoming citizens: Youths' civic uses of new media in five digital cities in East Asia. *Journal of Adolescent Research, 25,* 839–857.

Lin, W. H., & Yi, C. C. (2015). Unhealthy sleep practices, conduct problems, and daytime functioning during adolescence. *Journal of Youth and Adolescence, 44,* 431–446.

Lindberg, L. D., & Maddow-Zimet, I. (2012). Consequences of sex education on teen and young adult sexual behaviors and outcomes. *Journal of Adolescent Health, 51,* 332–338.

Lindberg, L., Jones, R., Santelli, J. (2008). Noncoital sexual activities among adolescents. *Journal of Adolescent Health, 43,* 231–238.

Lindberg, S. M., Grabe, S., & Hyde, J. S. (2007). Gender, pubertal development, and peer sexual harassment predict objectified body consciousness in early adolescence. *Journal of Research on Adolescence, 17,* 723–742.

Linder, J. R., & Collins, W. A. (2005). Parent and peer predictors of physical aggression and conflict management in romantic relationships in early adulthood. *Journal of Family Psychology, 19,* 252–262.

Linver, M. R., Brooks-Gunn, J., & Kohen, D. E. (2002). Family processes as pathways from income to young children's development. *Developmental Psychology, 38,* 719–734.

Linver, M. R., Roth, J. L., & Brooks-Gunn, J. (2009). Patterns of adolescents' participation in organized activities: Are sports best when combined with other activities? *Developmental Psychology, 45,* 354–367.

Lippold, M. A., Greenberg, M. T., Graham, J. W., & Feinberg, M. E. (2014). Unpacking the effect of parental monitoring on early adolescent problem behavior: Mediation by parental knowledge and moderation by parent–youth warmth. *Journal of Family Issues, 35,* 1800–1823.

Lipsey, M. (2009). The primary factors that characterize effective interventions with juvenile offenders: A meta-analytic overview. *Victims and Offenders, 4,* 124–147.

Little, S. A., & Garber, J. (2004). Interpersonal and achievement orientations and specific stressors predict depressive and aggressive symptoms. *Journal of Adolescent Research, 19,* 63–84.

Little, T. D., Brauner, J., Jones, S. M., Nock, M. K., & Hawley, P. H. (2003). Rethinking aggression: A typological examination of the functions of aggression. *Merrill-Palmer Quarterly, 49,* 343–369.

Litwack, S. D., Aikins, J. W., & Cillessen, A. H. N. (2012). The distinct roles of sociometric and perceived popularity in friendship: Implications for adolescent depressive affect and self-esteem. *The Journal of Early Adolescence, 32,* 226–251.

Liu, D., & Xin, Z. (2014). Birth cohort and age changes in the self-esteem of Chinese adolescents: A cross-temporal meta-analysis, 1996–2009. *Journal of Research on Adolescence, 25,* 366–376.

Liu, J., Raine, A., Wuerker, A., Venables, P. H., & Mednick, S. (2009). The association of birth complications and externalizing behavior in early adolescents: Direct and mediating effects. *Journal of Research on Adolescence, 19,* 93–111.

Liu, R. X. (2006). Vulnerability to friends' suicide influence: The moderating effects of gender and adolescent depression. *Journal of Youth and Adolescence, 35,* 479–489.

Liu, X., Kaplan, H., & Risser, W. (1992). Decomposing the reciprocal relationships between academic achievement and general self-esteem. *Youth and Society, 24,* 123–148.

Lobel, T. E., Nov-Krispin, N., Schiller, D., Lobel, O., & Feldman, A. (2004). Gender discriminatory behavior during adolescence and young adulthood: A developmental analysis. *Journal of Youth and Adolescence, 33,* 535–546.

Lochman, J., Bierman, K. L., Coie, J. D., Dodge, K. A., Greenberg, M. T., McMahon, R. J., & Pinderhughes, E. E. (2010). The difficulty of maintaining positive intervention effects: A look at disruptive behavior, deviant peer relations, and social skills during the middle school years. *Journal of Early Adolescence, 30,* 593–624.

Loeber, R., & Burke, J. D. (2011). Developmental pathways in juvenile externalizing and internalizing problems. *Journal of Research on Adolescence, 21,* 34–46.

Loeber, R., & Farrington, D. P. (2000). Young children who commit crime: Epidemiology, developmental origins, risk factors, early interventions, and policy implications. *Development and Psychopathology, 12,* 737–762.

Loehlin, J. C., Neiderhiser, J. M., & Reiss, D. (2005). Genetic and environmental components of adolescent adjustment and parental behavior: A multivariate analysis. *Child Development, 76,* 1104–1115.

Loewenson, P. R., Ireland, M., & Resnick, M. D. (2004). Primary and secondary sexual abstinence in high school students. *Journal of Adolescent Health, 34,* 209–215.

Loftus, J., & Kelly, B. C. (2012). Short-term sexual health effects of relationships with significantly older females on adolescent boys. *Journal of Adolescent Health, 50,* 195–197.

Loftus, J., Kelly, B. C., & Mustillo, S. A. (2011). Depressive symptoms among adolescent girls in relationships with older partners: Causes and lasting effects? *Journal of Youth and Adolescence, 40,* 800–813.

Logis, H. A., Rodkin, P. C., Gest, S. D., & Ahn, H. J. (2013). Popularity as an organizing factor of preadolescent friendship networks: Beyond prosocial and aggressive behavior. *Journal of Research on Adolescence, 23,* 413–423.

Logue, S., Chein, J., Gould, T., Holliday, E., & Steinberg, L. (2014). Adolescent mice, unlike adults, consume more alcohol in the presence of peers than alone. *Developmental Science, 17,* 79–85.

Lohman, B. J., & Billings, A. (2008). Protective and risk factors associated with adolescent boys' early sexual debut and risky sexual behaviors. *Journal of Youth and Adolescence, 37,* 723–735.

Lomniczi, A., Loche, A., Castellano, J. M., Ronnekleiv, O. K., Bosch, M., Kaidar, G., . . . Ojeda, S. (2013). Epigenetic control of female puberty. *Nature Neuroscience, 16,* 281–289.

Lonardo, R. A., Giordano, P. C., Longmore, M. A., & Manning, W. D. (2009). Parents, friends, and romantic partners: Enmeshment in deviant networks and adolescent delinquency involvement. *Journal of Youth and Adolescence, 38,* 367–383.

Longest, K. C., & Shanahan, M. J. (2007). Adolescent work intensity and substance use: The mediational and moderational roles of parenting. *Journal of Marriage and Family, 69,* 703–720.

Longmore, M. A., Eng, A. L., Giordano, P. C., & Manning, W. D. (2009). Parenting and adolescents' sexual initiation. *Journal of Marriage and Family, 71,* 969–982.

Longmore, M. A., Manning, W. D., & Giordano, P. C. (2001). Preadolescent parenting strategies and teens' dating and sexual initiation: A longitudinal analysis. *Journal of Marriage and the Family, 63,* 322–335.

Loose, F., Régner, I., Morin, A. J. S., & Florence, D. (2012). Are academic discounting and devaluing double-edged swords? Their relations to global self-esteem, achievement goals, and performance among stigmatized students. *Journal of Educational Psychology, 104,* 713–725.

Lopez, A. B., Huynh, V. W., & Fuligni, A. J. (2011). A longitudinal study of religious identity and participation during adolescence. *Child Development, 82,* 1297–1309.

Lopez, E. M., Wishard, A., Gallimore, R., & Rivera, W. (2006). Latino high school students? Perceptions of gangs and crews. *Journal of Adolescent Research, 21,* 299–318.

Lopez, S. (2009). The rigors of life unplugged. *Los Angeles Times,* May 6.

Lopez-Larson, M., Anderson, J., Ferguson, M., & Yurkelun-Todd, D. A. (2011). Local brain connectivity and associations with gender and age. *Developmental Cognitive Neuroscience, 1,* 187–197.

Lord, S., Eccles, J., & McCarthy, K. (1994). Surviving the junior high transition: Family processes and self-perceptions as protective and risk factors. *Journal of Early Adolescence, 14,* 162–199.

Loughran, T. A., Mulvey, E. P., Schubert, C. A., Fagan, J., Piquero, A. R., & Losoya, S. H. (2009). Estimating a dose-response relationship between length of stay and future recidivism in serious juvenile offenders. *Criminology, 47,* 699–740.

Louis, K., & Smith, B. (1992). Breaking the iron law of social class: The renewal of teachers' professional status and engagement. In F. Newmann (Ed.), *Student engagement and achievement in American high schools.* New York: Teachers College Press.

Loukas, A. (2009). Examining temporal associations between perceived maternal psychological control and early adolescent internalizing problems. *Journal of Abnormal Child Psychology, 37,* 1113–1122.

Loukas, A., & Pasch, K. E. (2013). Does school connectedness buffer the impact of peer victimization on early adolescents' subsequent adjustment problems? *The Journal of Early Adolescence, 33,* 245–266.

Loukas, A., Ripperger-Suhler, K. G., & Horton, K. D. (2009). Examining temporal associations between school connectedness and early adolescent adjustment. *Journal of Youth and Adolescence, 38,* 804–812.

Loukas, A., Roalson, L., & Herrera, D. (2010). School connectedness buffers the effects of negative family relations and poor effortful control on early adolescent conduct problems. *Journal of Research on Adolescence, 20,* 13–22.

Lounds Taylor, J. (2009). Midlife impacts of adolescent parenthood. *Journal of Family Issues, 30,* 484–510.

Lovato, C., Watts, A., Brown, K. S., Lee, D., Sabiston, C., Nykiforuk, C. . . . & Thompson, M. (2013). School and community predictors of smoking: A longitudinal study of Canadian high schools. *American Journal of Public Health, 103,* 362–368.

Loveless, T. (2002). *How well are American students learning? The 2002 Brown Center Report on American Education.* Washington, DC: Brookings Institution.

Low, S., Polanin, J. R., Espelage, D. L. (2013). The role of social networks in physical and relational aggression among young adolescents. *Journal of Youth & Adolescence, 42,* 1078–1089.

Low, S., Shortt, J. W., & Snyder, J. (2012). Sibling influences on adolescent substance use: The role of modeling, collusion, and conflict. *Development and Psychopathology, 24,* 287–300.

Lowe, K., & Dotterer, A. M. (2013). Parental monitoring, parental warmth, and minority youths'

academic outcomes: Exploring the integrative model of parenting. *Journal of Youth & Adolescence, 42,* 1413–1425.

Lowry, R., Holtzman, D., Truman, B., Kann, L., Collins, J., & Kolbe, L. (1994). Substance use and HIV-related sexual behaviors among US high school students: Are they related? *American Journal of Public Health, 84,* 1116–1120.

Lubienski, S. T., & Lubienski, C. (2006). School sector and academic achievement: A multilevel analysis of NAEP mathematics data. *American Education Research Journal, 43,* 651–698.

Lucas, S. (1996). Selective attrition in a newly hostile regime: The case of 1980 sophomores. *Social Forces, 75,* 511–533.

Lucas, S., & Berends, M. (2002). Sociodemographic diversity, correlated achievement, and de facto tracking. *Sociology of Education, 75,* 328–348.

Luciana, M. (2013). Adolescent brain development in normality and psychopathology. *Development and Psychopathology, 25,* 1325–1345.

Luciana, M., & Collins, P. F. (2012). Incentive motivation, cognitive control, and the adolescent brain: Is it time for a paradigm shift? *Child Development Perspectives, 6,* 392–399.

Luciana, M., Conklin, H. M., Hooper, C. J., & Yarger, R. S. (2005). The development of nonverbal working memory and executive control processes in adolescents. *Child Development, 76,* 697.

Ludden, A. B. (2011). Engagement in school and community civic activities among rural adolescents. *Journal of Youth and Adolescence, 40,* 1254–1270.

Ludden, A. B., & Eccles, J. (2007). Psychosocial, motivational, and contextual profiles of youth reporting different patterns of substance use during adolescence. *Journal of Research on Adolescence, 17,* 51–88.

Luder, M. T., Pittet, I., Berchtold, A., Akré, C., Michaud, P. A., & Suris, J. C. (2011). Associations between online pornography and sexual behavior among adolescents: Myth or reality? *Archives of Sexual Behavior, 40,* 1027–1035.

Ludwig, J., Duncan, G., & Hirschfield, P. (2001). Urban poverty and juvenile crime: Evidence from a randomized housing-mobility experiment. *Quarterly Journal of Economics, 116,* 665–679.

Lumeng, J. C., Wendorf, K., Pesch, M. H., Appugliese, D. P., Kaciroti, N., Corwyn, R. F., & Bradley, R. H. (2013). Overweight adolescents and life events in childhood. *Pediatrics, 132,* e1506–e1512.

Luna, B., Garver, K., Urban, T., Lazar, N., & Sweeney, J. (2004). Maturation of cognitive processes from late childhood to adulthood. *Child Development, 75,* 1357–1372.

Luna, B., Paulsen, D. J., Padmanabhan, A., & Geier, C. (2013). The teenage brain: Cognitive

control and motivation. *Current Directions in Psychological Science, 22,* 94–100.

Lund, T. J., & Dearing, E. (2013). Is growing up affluent risky for adolescents or is the problem growing up in an affluent neighborhood? *Journal of Research on Adolescence, 23,* 274–282.

Luo, F., Stone, D. M., & Tharp, A. T. (2014). Physical dating violence victimization among sexual minority youth. *American Journal of Public Health, 104,* 66–73.

Luo, Q., Urberg, K., & Rao, P. (1995, March). *Selection of best friends among Chinese adolescents.* Paper presented at the biennial meetings of the Society for Research in Child Development, Indianapolis.

Lussier, P., Farrington, D. P., & Moffitt, T. E. (2009). Is the antisocial child father of the abusive man? A 40-year prospective longitudinal study on the developmental antecedents of intimate partner violence. *Criminology, 47,* 741–779.

Luster, T., & McAdoo, H. (1995). Factors related to self-esteem among African American youths: A secondary analysis of the High/Scope Perry Preschool data. *Journal of Research on Adolescence, 5,* 451–467.

Luster, T., & Small, S. (1997). Sexual abuse history and problems in adolescence: Exploring the effects of moderating variables. *Journal of Marriage and the Family, 59,* 131–142.

Luster, T., Bates, L., Fitzgerald, H., Vandenbelt, M., & Key, J. (2000). Factors related to successful outcomes among preschool children born to low-income adolescent mothers. *Journal of Marriage and the Family, 62,* 133–146.

Luthar, S. (1991). Vulnerability and resilience: A study of high-risk adolescents. *Child Development, 62,* 600–616.

Luthar, S. (1994, February). *Social competence of inner-city adolescents: A six-month prospective study.* Paper presented at the biennial meetings of the Society for Research on Adolescence, San Diego.

Luthar, S. S., & Barkin, S. H. (2012). Are affluent youth truly "at risk"? Vulnerability and resilience across three diverse samples. *Development and Psychopathology, 24,* 429–449.

Luthar, S. S., Barkin, S. H., & Crossman, E. J. (2013). "I can, therefore I must": Fragility in the upper-middle clases. *Development and Psychopathology, 25,* 1529–1549.

Luthar, S., & Becker, B. (2002). Privileged but pressured? A study of affluent youth. *Child Development, 73,* 1593–1610.

Luthar, S., & Goldstein, A. S. (2008). Substance use and related behaviors among suburban late adolescents: The importance of perceived parent containment. *Development and Psychopathology, 20,* 591–614.

Luthar, S., & Latendresse, S. (2005). Comparable "risks" at the socioeconomic status extremes: Preadolescents' perceptions of parenting. *Development and Psychopathology, 17,* 207–230.

Luthar, S., & McMahon, T. (1996). Peer reputation among inner-city adolescents: Structure and correlates. *Journal of Research on Adolescence, 6,* 581–603.

Luthar, S., Cicchetti, D., & Becker, B. (2000). The construct of resilience: A critical evaluation and guidelines for future work. *Child Development, 71,* 543–562.

Luthar, S., Shoum, K. A., & Brown, P. J. (2006). Extracurricular involvement among affluent youth: A scapegoat for "ubiquitous achievement pressures"? *Developmental Psychology, 42,* 583–597.

Luyckx, K., Goossens, L., & Soenens, B. (2006). A developmental contextual perspective on identity construction in emerging adulthood: Change dynamics in commitment formation and commitment evaluation. *Developmental Psychology, 42,* 366–380.

Luyckx, K., Teppers, E., Kilmstra, T. A., & Rassart, J. (2014). Identity processes and personality traits and types in adolescence: Directionality of effects and developmental trajectories. *Developmental Psychology, 50,* 2144–2153.

Lydon, D. M., Wilson, S. J., Child, A., & Geier, C. F. (2014). Adolescent brain maturation and smoking: What we know and where we're headed. *Neuroscience and Biobehavioral Reviews, 45,* 323–342.

Lynam, D. R., Caspi, A., Moffitt, T. E., Wikstroem, P. O., Loeber, R., & Novak, S. (2000). The interaction between impulsivity and neighborhood context on offending: The effects of impulsivity are stronger in poorer neighborhoods. *Journal of Abnormal Psychology, 109,* 563–574.

Lynam, D. R., Charnigo, R., Moffitt, T. E., Raine, A., Loeber, R., & Stouthamer-Loeber, M. (2009). The stability of psychopathy across adolescence. *Development and Psychopathology, 21,* 1133–1153.

Lynch, A. D., Lerner, R. M, & Leventhal, T. (2013). Adolescent academic achievement and school engagement: an examination of the role of school-wide peer culture. *Journal of Youth & Adolescence, 42,* 6–19.

Lynne-Landsman, S. D., Bradshaw, C. P., & Ialongo, N. S. (2010a). Testing a developmental cascade model of adolescent substance use trajectories and young adult adjustment. *Development and Psychopathology, 22,* 933–948.

Lynne-Landsman, S. D., Graber, J. A., & Andrews, J. A. (2010b). Do trajectories of household risk in childhood moderate pubertal timing effects on substance initiation in middle school? *Developmental Psychology, 46,* 853–868.

Lynne-Landsman, S. D., Livingston, M. D., & Wagenaar, A. C. (2013). Effects of state medical marijuana laws on adolescent marijuana use. *American Journal of Public Health, 103,* 1500–1506.

Ma, H.-M., Du, M.-L., Luo, X.-P., Chen, S.-K., Liu, L., Chen, R.-M., ... Chinese Medical Association (2009). Onset of breast and pubic hair development and menses in urban Chinese girls. *Pediatrics, 124,* 269–277.

Ma, J., Flanders, W., Ward, E., & Jemal, A. (2011). Body mass index in young adulthood and premature death: analyses of the US National Health Interview Survey linked mortality files. *American Journal of Epidemiology, 174,* 934–944.

Ma, M., Malcolm, L. R., Diaz-Albertini, K., Klinoff, V. A., Leeder, E., Barrientos, S., & Kibler, J. L. (2014). Latino cultural values as protective factors against sexual risks among adolescents. *Journal of Adolescence, 37,* 1215–1225.

Ma, T. L., & Bellmore, A. (2012). Peer victimization and parental psychological control in adolescence. *Journal of Abnormal Child Psychology, 40,* 413–424.

Määttä, S., Nurmi, J., & Stattin, H. (2007). Achievement orientations, school adjustment, and well-being: A longitudinal study. *Journal of Research on Adolescence, 17,* 789–812.

Määttä, S., Stattin, H., & Nurmi, J. E. (2002). Achievement strategies at school: Types and correlates. *Journal of Adolescence, 25,* 31–46.

Maccoby, E. (1990). Gender and relationships: A developmental account. *American Psychologist, 45,* 513–520.

Maccoby, E., & Martin, J. (1983). Socialization in the context of the family: Parent–child interaction. In E. M. Hetherington (Ed.), *Handbook of child psychology:* Vol. 4. *Socialization, personality, and social development* (pp. 1–101). New York: Wiley.

MacDonald, W., & DeMaris, A. (1995). Remarriage, stepchildren, and marital conflict: Challenges to the incomplete institutionalization hypothesis. *Journal of Marriage and the Family, 57,* 387–398.

Maciejewski, D. F., van Lier, P. A., Neumann, A., Van der Giessen, D., Branje, S. J., Meeus, W. H., & Koot, H. M. (2014). The development of adolescent generalized anxiety and depressive symptoms in the context of adolescent mood variability and parent-adolescent negative interactions. *Journal of Abnormal Child Psychology, 42,* 515–526.

Mackey, A. P., Finn, A. S., Leonard, J. A., Jacoby-Senghor, D. S., West, M. R., Gabrieli, C. F. O., & Gabrieli, J. D. E. (2015). Neuroanatomical correlates of the income-achievement gap. *Psychological Science,* 1–9.

Mackey, E. R., & La Greca, A. M. (2008). Does this make me look fat? Peer crowd and peer contributions to adolescent girls' weight control behaviors. *Journal of Youth and Adolescence, 37,* 1097–1110.

Mackey, K., Arnold, M. L., & Pratt, M. W. (2001). Adolescents' stories of decision making in more and less authoritative families: Representing the voices of parents in narrative. *Journal of Adolescent Research, 16,* 243–268.

Macmillan, R., & Hagan, J. (2004). Violence in the transition to adulthood: Adolescent victimization, education, and socioeconomic attainment in later life. *Journal of Research on Adolescence, 14,* 127–158.

Madkour, A. S., de Looze, M., Ma, P., Halpem, C. T., Farhat, T., Ter Bogt, T. F. M., Ehlinger, V., Nic Gabhainn, S., Currie, C., & Godeau, E. (2014). Macro-level age norms for the timing of sexual initiation and adolescents' early sexual initiation in 17 European countries. *Journal of Adolescent Health, 55,* 114–121.

Madkour, A. S., Farhat, T., Halpern, C. T., Godeau, E., & Gabhainn, S. (2010a). Early adolescent sexual initiation as a problem behavior: A comparative study of five nations. *Journal of Adolescent Health, 47,* 389–398.

Madkour, A. S., Farhat, T., Halpern, C. T., Godeau, E., & Gabhainn, S. (2010b). Early adolescent sexual initiation and physical/psychological symptoms: A comparative analysis of five nations. *Journal of Youth and Adolescence, 39,* 1211–1225.

Madkour, A. S., Farhat, T., Halpern. C. T., Gabhainn, N. S., & Godeau, E. (2012). Parents' support and knowledge of their daughters' lives, and females' early sexual initiation in nine European countries. *Perspectives on Sexual & Reproductive Health, 44,* 167–175.

Madon, S., Willard, J., Guyll, M., Trudeau, L., & Spoth, R. (2006). Self-fulfilling prophecy effects of mothers' beliefs on children's alcohol use: Accumulation, dissipation, and stability over time. *Journal of Personality and Social Psychology, 90,* 911–926.

Madsen, S. D., & Collins, W. A. (2011). The salience of adolescent romantic experiences for romantic relationship qualities in young adulthood. *Journal of Research on Adolescence, 21,* 789–801.

Mager, W., Milich, R., Harris, M. J., & Howard, A. (2005). Intervention groups for adolescents with conduct problems: Is aggregation harmful or helpful? *Journal of Abnormal Child Psychology, 33,* 349–362.

Magnusson, D., Stattin, H., & Allen, V. (1986). Differential maturation among girls and its relation to social adjustment in a longitudinal perspective. In P. Baltes, D. Featherman, & R. Lerner (Eds.), *Life span development and behavior* (Vol. 7). Hillsdale, NJ: Erlbaum.

Maharaj, S., & Connolly, J. (1994). Peer network composition of acculturated and ethnoculturally affiliated adolescents in a multicultural setting. *Journal of Adolescent Research, 9,* 218–240.

Mahoney, A., Donelly, W. O., Boxer, P., & Lewis, T. (2003). Marital and severe parent-to-adolescent physical aggression in clinic-referred families: Mother and adolescent reports on co-occurrence and links to child behavior problems. *Journal of Family Psychology, 17,* 3–19.

Mahoney, J. (2000). School extracurricular activity participation as a moderator in the development of antisocial patterns. *Child Development, 71,* 502–516.

Mahoney, J. L., & Vest, A. E. (2012). The over-scheduling hypothesis revisited: Intensity of organized activity participation during adolescence and young adult outcomes. *Journal of Research on Adolescence, 22,* 409–418.

Mahoney, J., & Cairns, R. (1997). Do extracurricular activities protect against early school dropout? *Developmental Psychology, 33,* 241–253.

Mahoney, J., & Parente, M. (2009). Should we care about adolescents who care for themselves? What we have learned and what we need to know about youth in self-care. *Child Development Perspectives, 3,* 189–195.

Mahoney, J., & Stattin, H. (2000). Leisure activities and adolescent antisocial behavior: The role of structure and social context. *Journal of Adolescence, 23,* 113–127.

Mahoney, J., Larson, R., Eccles, J., & Lord, H. (2005). Organized activities as developmental contexts for children and adolescents. In J. Mahoney, R. Larson, & J. Eccles (Eds.), *Organized activities as contexts of development* (pp. 3–22). Hillsdale, NJ: Erlbaum.

Mahoney, J., Schweder, A. E., & Stattin, H. (2002). Structured after-school activities as a moderator of depressed mood for adolescents with detached relations to their parents. *Journal of Community Psychology, 30,* 69–86.

Mahoney, J., Stattin, H., & Lord, H. (2004). Unstructured youth recreation centre participation and antisocial behaviour development: Selective influences and the moderating role of antisocial peers. *International Journal of Behavioral Development, 28,* 553–560.

Mahoney, J., Vandell, D., Simpkins, S., & Zarrett, N. (2009). Adolescent out-of-school activities. In R. Lerner & L. Steinberg (Eds.), *Handbook of adolescent psychology* (3rd ed., Vol. 2, pp. 228–269). New York: Wiley.

Maimon, D., & Browning, C. (2010). Unstructured socializing, collective efficacy, and violent behavior among urban youth. *Criminology, 48,* 443–474.

Main, M., Kaplan, N., & Cassidy, J. (1985). Security in infancy, childhood, and adulthood: A move to the level of representation. In I. Bretherton and E. Waters (Eds.), *Growing points of attachment theory and research, Monographs of the Society for Research on Child Development, 50*(1–2), Serial No. 209, pp. 66–106.

Makel, M. C., Lee, S.-Y., Olszewki-Kubilius, P., & Putallaz, M. (2012). Changing the pond, not the fish: Following high-ability students across different educational environments. *Journal of Educational Psychology, 104,* 778–792.

Makin-Byrd, K., Bierman, K. L., & Conduct Problems Prevention Research Group. (2013). Individual and family predictors of the perpetration of dating violence and victimization in late adolescence. *Journal of Youth & Adolescence, 42,* 536–550.

Malanchuk, O., & Eccles, J. (April, 1999). *Determinants of self-esteem in African-American and White adolescent girls.* Paper presented at the biennial meetings of the Society for Research on Child Development, Albuquerque.

Maldonado-Molina, M. M., Piquero, A. R., Jennings, W. G., Bird, H., & Canino, G.

(2009). Trajectories of delinquency among Puerto Rican children and adolescents at two sites. *Journal of Research in Crime and Delinquency, 46,* 144–181.

Males, M., & Chew, K. (1996). The ages of fathers in California adolescent births. *American Journal of Public Health, 86,* 565–568.

Malone, P. S., Van Eck, K., Flory, K., & Lamis, D. A. (2010). A mixture-model approach to linking ADHD to adolescent onset of illicit drug use. *Developmental Psychology, 46,* 1543–1555.

Malone, S. M., Taylor, J., & Marmorstein, N. R. (2004). Genetic and environmental influences on antisocial behavior and alcohol dependence from adolescence to early adulthood. *Development and Psychopathology, 16,* 943–966.

Malti, T., Killen, M., & Gasser, L. (2012). Social judgments and emotion attributions about exclusion in Switzerland. *Child Development, 83,* 697–711.

Manchikanti Gomez, A. (2011). Testing the cycle of violence hypothesis: Child abuse and adolescent dating violence as predictors of intimate partner violence in young adulthood. *Youth & Society, 43,* 171–192.

Mandara, J., & Murray, C. B. (2000). Effects of parental marital status, income, and family functioning on African American adolescent self-esteem. *Journal of Family Psychology, 14,* 475–490.

Mandara, J., Gaylord-Harden, N., Richards, M. H., & Ragsdale, B. L. (2009a). The effects of changes in racial identity and self-esteem on changes in African American adolescents' mental health. *Child Development, 80,* 1660–1675.

Mandara, J., Varner, F., Greene, N., & Richman, S. (2009b). Intergenerational family predictors of the Black–White achievement gap. *Journal of Educational Psychology, 101,* 867–878.

Manlove, J. (1998). The influence of high school dropout and school disengagement on the risk of school-age pregnancy. *Journal of Research on Adolescence, 8,* 187–220.

Manlove, J., Logan, C., Moore, K. A., & Ikramullah, E. (2008). Pathways from family religiosity to adolescent sexual activity and contraceptive use. *Perspectives on Sexual and Reproductive Health, 40,* 105–117.

Manlove, J., Mariner, C., & Papillo, A. (2000). Subsequent fertility among teen mothers: Longitudinal analyses of recent national data. *Journal of Marriage and the Family, 62,* 430–448.

Manlove, J., Steward-Streng, N., Peterson, K., Scott, M., & Wildsmith, E. (2013). Racial and ethnic differences in the transition to a teenage birth in the United States. *Perspectives on Sexual & Reproductive Health, 45,* 89–100.

Manlove, J., Terry-Humen, E., & Ikramullah, E. (2006). Young teenagers and older sexual partners: Correlates and consequences for

males and females. *Perspectives on Sexual and Reproductive Health, 38,* 197–207.

Mannheim, K. (1952). The problem of generations. In K. Mannheim (Ed.), *Essays on the sociology of knowledge.* London: Routledge & Kegan Paul.

Manning, W. D., Brown, S. L., & Payne, K. K. (2014). Two decades of stability and change in age at first union formation. *Journal of Marriage and Family, 76,* 247–260.

Manning, W. D., Giordano, P. C., & Longmore, M. A. (2006). Hooking up: The relationship contexts of 'nonrelationship' sex. *Journal of Adolescent Research, 21,* 459–483.

Manning, W. D., Longmore, M. A., & Giordano, P. (2007). The changing institution of marriage: Adolescents' expectations to cohabit and to marry. *Journal of Marriage and Family, 69,* 559–575.

Manning, W. D., Longmore, M., & Giordano, P. (2005). Adolescents' involvement in non-romantic sexual activity. *Social Science Research, 34,* 384–407.

Manning, W., & Lamb, K. (2003). Adolescent well-being in cohabiting, married, and single-parent families. *Journal of Marriage and Family, 65,* 876–893.

Manning, W., & Landale, N. (1996). Racial and ethnic differences in the role of cohabitation in premarital childbearing. *Journal of Marriage and the Family, 58,* 63–77.

Manuck, S., Craig, A., Flory, J., Halder, I., & Ferrell, R. (2011). Reported early family environment covaries with menarcheal age as a function of polymorphic variation in estrogen receptor-a. *Development and Psychopathology, 23,* 69–83.

Marceau, K., Ram, N., & Susman, E. J. (2014). Development and lability in the parent-child relationship during adolescence: Associations with pubertal timing and tempo. *Journal of Research on Adolescence, Early view.* DOI: 10.1111/jora.12139.

Marcia, J. (1966). Development and validation of ego identity status. *Journal of Personality and Social Psychology, 3,* 551–558.

Marin, B. V., Kirby, D. B., Hudes, E. S., Coyle, K. K., & Gomez, C. A. (2006). Boyfriends, girlfriends, and teenagers' risk of sexual involvement. *Perspectives on Sexual and Reproductive Health, 38,* 76–83.

Marion, D., Laursen, B., Kiuru, N., Nurmi, J. E., & Salmela-Aro, K. (2014). Maternal affection moderates friend influence on schoolwork engagement. *Developmental Psychology, 50,* 766–771.

Marion, D., Laursen, B., Zettergren, P., Bergman, L. R. (2013). Predicting life satisfaction during middle adulthood from peer relationships during mid-adolescence. *Journal of Youth & Adolescence, 42,* 1299–1307.

Markey, C. N., & Markey, P. M. (2012). Emerging adults' responses to a media presentation of idealized female beauty: An examination of cosmetic surgery in reality television. *Psychology of Popular Media Culture, 1,* 209–219.

Markey, P., Markey, C., & French, J. (2014). Violent video games and real-world violence: Rhetoric versus data. *Psychology of Popular Media Culture.* Advance online publication.

Markiewicz, D., Lawford, H., Doyle, A. B., & Haggart, N. (2006). Developmental differences in adolescents' and young adults' use of mothers, fathers, best friends, and romantic partners to fulfill attachment needs. *Journal of Youth and Adolescence, 35,* 127–140.

Marks, A. K., Patton, F., & Coll, C. G. (2011). Being bicultural: A mixed-methods study of adolescents' implicitly and explicitly measured multiethnic identities. *Developmental Psychology, 47,* 270–288.

Marks, A. K., Ejesi, K., García Coll, C. (2014). Understanding the U.S. immigrant paradox in childhood and adolescence. *Child Development Perspectives, 8,* 59–64.

Marks, H. M. (2000). Student engagement in instructional activity: Patterns in the elementary, middle, and high school years. *American Educational Research Journal, 37,* 153–184.

Markstrom, C. (2011a). Identity formation of American Indian adolescents: Local, national, and global considerations. *Journal of Research on Adolescence, 21,* 519–535.

Markstrom, C. (2011b). Initiation ceremonies and rites of passage. In B. Brown & M. Prinstein (Eds.), *Encyclopedia of adolescence* (Vol. 2, pp. 152–159). New York: Academic Press.

Markstrom-Adams, C., & Adams, G. (1995). Gender, ethnic group, and grade differences in psychosocial functioning during middle adolescence? *Journal of Youth and Adolescence, 24,* 397–417.

Markus, H., & Nurius, P. (1986). Possible selves. *American Psychologist, 41,* 954–969.

Marsh, H. W., Abduljabbar, A., Morin, A. J. S., Parker, P. D., Abdelfattah F., Nagengast, B., & Abu-Hilal, M. M. (2014). The big-fish-little-pond effect: Generalizability of social comparison processes over two age cohorts from Western, Asian, and Middle Eastern Islamic countries. *Journal of Educational Psychology, 107,* 258–271.

Marsh, H., & Hau, K. (2003). Big-fish–little-pond effect on academic self-concept: A cross-cultural (26-country) test of the negative effects of academically selective schools. *American Psychologist, 58,* 364–376.

Marsh, H., & Hau, K. (2004). Explaining paradoxical relationship between academic self-concepts and achievements: Cross-cultural generalizability of the internal/external frame of reference predictions across 26 countries. *Journal of Educational Psychology, 96,* 56–67.

Marsh, H., & Kleitman, S. (2002). Extracurricular school activities: The good, the bad, and the nonlinear. *Harvard Educational Review, 72,* 464–514.

Marsh, H., & Kleitman, S. (2005). Consequences of employment during high school: Character building, subversion of academic goals, or a threshold? *American Educational Research Journal, 42,* 331–369.

Marsh, H., & Yeung, A. (1997). Coursework selection: Relations to academic self-concept and achievement. *American Educational Research Journal, 34,* 691–720.

Marsh, H., Chessor, D., Craven, R., & Roche, L. (1995). The effects of gifted and talented programs on academic self-concept: The big fish strikes again. *American Educational Research Journal, 32,* 285–319.

Marsh, H., Kong, C., & Hau, K. (2000). Longitudinal multilevel models of the big-fish–little-pond effect on academic self-concept: Counterbalancing contrast and reflected-glory effects in Hong Kong schools. *Journal of Personality and Social Psychology, 78,* 337–349.

Marsh, H., Trautwein, U., Ludtke, O., Baumert, J., & Koller, O. (2007). The big-fish–little-pond effect: Persistent negative effects of selective high schools on self-concept after graduation. *American Education Research Journal, 44,* 631–669.

Marsh, P., McFarland, F. C., & Allen, J. P. (2003). Attachment, autonomy, and multifinality in adolescent internalizing and risky behavioral symptoms. *Development and Psychopathology, 15,* 451–467.

Marshal, M. P., Dermody, S. S., Cheong, J., Burton, C. M., Friedman, M. S., Aranda, F., & Hughes, T. L. (2013). Trajectories of depressive symptoms and suicidality among heterosexual and sexual minority youth. *Journal of Youth & Adolescence, 42,* 1243–1256.

Marshall, S. (1995). Ethnic socialization of African American children: Implications for parenting, identity development, and academic achievement. *Journal of Youth and Adolescence, 24,* 377–396.

Marshall, S. L., Parker, P. D., Ciarrochi, J., & Heaven, P. C. L. (2014). Is self-esteem a cause or consequence of social support? A 4-year longitudinal study. *Child Development, 85,* 1275–1291.

Marshall, W. (1978). Puberty. In F. Faulkner & J. Tanner (Eds.), *Human growth* (Vol. 2, pp. 141–181). New York: Plenum.

Marshall, W., & Tanner, J. (1969). Variations in the pattern of pubertal change in girls. *Archive of Diseases of Childhood, 44,* 130.

Marsiglia, F. F., Nagoshi, J. L., Parsai, M., Booth, J. M., & Castro, G. F. (2014). The parent-child acculturation gap, parental monitoring, and substance use in Mexican heritage adolescents in Mexican neighborhoods of the Southwest U.S. *Journal of Community Psychology, 42,* 530–543.

Marsiglia, F., Kulis, S., & Hecht, M. L. (2001). Ethnic labels and ethnic identity as predictors of drug use among middle school students in the Southwest. *Journal of Research on Adolescence, 11,* 21–48.

Marston, E. G., Hare, A., & Allen, J. P. (2010). Rejection sensitivity in late adolescence: Social and emotional sequelae. *Journal of Research on Adolescence, 20,* 959–982.

Martel, M. M., Pierce, L., Nigg, J. T., Jester, J. M., Adams, K., Puttler, L. I., . . . Zucker, R. (2009). Temperament pathways to childhood disruptive behavior and adolescent substance abuse: Testing a cascade model. *Journal of Abnormal Child Psychology, 37,* 363–373.

Martin, A. J., Nejad, H. G., Colmar, S., Liem, G. A. D. (2013). Adaptability: How students' responses to uncertainty and novelty predict their academic and non-academic outcomes. *Journal of Educational Psychology, 105,* 728–746.

Martin, M., Bascoe, S., & Davies, P. (2011). Family relationships. In B. Brown & M. Prinstein (Eds.), *Encyclopedia of adolescence* (Vol. 2, pp. 84–94). New York: Academic Press.

Martin, M., McCarthy, B., Conger, R., Gibbons, F., Simons, R., Cutrona, C., & Brody, G. (2011). The enduring significance of racism: Discrimination and delinquency among Black American youth. *Journal of Research on Adolescence, 21,* 662–676.

Martinez, C. R., Jr. (2006). Effects of differential family acculturation on Latino adolescent substance use. *Family Relations, 55,* 306–317.

Martinez, R., & Dukes, R. (1997). The effects of ethnic identity, ethnicity, and gender on adolescent well-being. *Journal of Youth and Adolescence, 26,* 503–516.

Martino, S. C., Elliott, M. N., Corona, R., Kanouse, D. E., & Schuster, M. A. (2008). Beyond the "big talk": The roles of breadth and repetition in parent–adolescent communication about sexual topics. *Pediatrics, 121,* 612–618.

Martin-Storey, A. (2015). Prevalence of dating violence among sexual minority youth: variation across gender, sexual minority identity and gender of sexual partners. *Journal of Youth & Adolescence, 44,* 211–224.

Martin-Storey, A., Cheadle, J. E., Skalamera, J., & Crosnoe, R. (2015). Exploring the social integration of sexual minority youth across high school contexts. *Child Development, 86,* 965–975.

Marx, D., Ko, S., & Friedman, R. (2009). The "Obama Effect": How a salient role model reduces race-based performance differences. *Journal of Experimental Social Psychology, 45,* 953–956.

Masi, G., Millepiedi, S., Mucci, M., Poll, P., Bertini, N., & Milantoni, L. (2004). Generalized anxiety disorder in referred children and adolescents. *Journal of the American Academy of Child and Adolescent Psychiatry, 43,* 752–760.

Maslowsky, J. & Ozer, E. J. (2014). Developmental trends in sleep duration in adolescence and young adulthood: Evidence from a national United States sample. *Journal of Adolescent Health, 54,* 691–697.

Maslowsky, J., Schulenberg, J. E., & Zucker, R. A. (2014). Influence of conduct problems and depressive symptomatology on adolescent substance use: Developmentally proximal versus distal effects. *Developmental Psychology, 50,* 1179–1189.

Mason, C., Cauce, A., Gonzales, N., & Hiraga, Y. (1996). Neither too sweet nor too sour: Problem peers, maternal control, and problem behavior in African American adolescents. *Child Development, 67,* 2115–2130.

Mason, W. (2001). Self-esteem and delinquency revisited (again): A test of Kaplan's self-derogation theory of delinquency using latent growth curve modeling. *Journal of Youth and Adolescence, 30,* 83–102.

Mason, W., & Windle, M. (2002). Reciprocal relations between adolescent substance use and delinquency: A longitudinal latent variable analysis. *Journal of Abnormal Psychology, 111,* 63–76.

Massoglia, M., & Uggen, C. (2010). Settling down and aging out: Toward an interactionist theory of desistance and the transition to adulthood. *The American Journal of Sociology, 116,* 543–582.

Masten, A. (2001). Ordinary magic: Resilience processes in development. *American Psychologist, 56,* 227–238.

Masten, A., Burt, K. B., & Roisman, G. I. (2004). Resources and resilience in the transition to adulthood: Continuity and change. *Development and Psychopathology, 16,* 1071–1094.

Masten, A., Hubbard, J., Gest, S., Tellegen, A., Garmezy, N., & Ramirez, M. (1999). Competence in the context of adversity: Pathways to resilience and maladaptation from childhood to late adolescence. *Development and Psychopathology, 11,* 143–169.

Masten, A., Miliotis, D., Graham-Bermann, S., Ramirez, M., & Neemann, J. (1993). Children in homeless families: Risks to mental health and development. *Journal of Consulting and Clinical Psychology, 61,* 335–343.

Masten, A., Roisman, G. I., Long, J. D., Burt, K. B., Obradovic, J., Riley, J. R., Boelcke-Stennes, K., et al. (2005). Developmental cascades: Linking academic achievement and externalizing and internalizing symptoms over 20 years. *Developmental Psychology, 41,* 733–746.

Masten, C. L., Eisenberger, N. I., Borofsky, L. A., McNealy, K., Pfeifer, J. H., & Dapretto, M. (2011). Subgenual anterior cingulate responses to peer rejection: A marker of adolescents' risk for depression. *Development and Psychopathology, 23,* 283–292.

Masten, C. L., Eisenberger, N. I., Pfeifer, J. H., & Dapretto, M. (2013). Neural responses to witnessing peer rejection after being socially excluded: fMRI as a window into adolescents' emotional processing. *Developmental Science, 16,* 743–759.

Masten, C. L., Eisenberger, N. I., Pfeifer, J. H., Colich, N. L., & Dapretto, M. (2013). Associations among pubertal development, empathic ability, and neural responses while witnessing peer rejection in adolescence. *Child Development, 84,* 1338–1354.

Masten, C. L., Telzer, E. H., Fuligni, A. J., Lieberman, M. D., & Eisenberger, N. I. (2012). Time spent with friends in adolescence relates to less neural sensitivity to later peer rejection. *Social Cognitive Affective Neuroscience, 7,* 106–114.

Masten, C., Eisenberger, N., Pfeifer, J., & Dapretto, M. (2010). Witnessing peer rejection during early adolescence: Neural correlates of empathy for experiences of social exclusion. *Social Neuroscience, 5,* 496–507.

Masten, S. V., Foss, R. D., & Marshall, S. W. (2011). Graduated driver licensing and fatal crashes involving 16- to 19-year-old drivers. *JAMA, 306,* 1098–1103.

Matas, L., Arend, R., & Sroufe, L. (1978). Continuity in adaptation in the second year: The relationship between quality of attachment and later competence. *Child Development, 49,* 547–556.

Mathieson, L. C., Klimes-Dougan, B., & Crick, N. C. (2014). Dwelling on it may make it worse: The links between relational victimization, relational aggression, rumination, and depressive symptoms in adolescents. *Development and Psychopathology, 26,* 735–747.

Matricciani, L., Olds, T., Blunden, S., Rigney, G., & Williams, M. (2012). Never enough sleep: A brief history of sleep recommendations for children. *Pediatrics, 129,* 548–556.

Matsuba, M. K., & Walker, L. J. (2005). Young adult moral exemplars: The making of self through stories. *Journal of Research on Adolescence, 15,* 275–297.

Matsueda, R. L., Kreager, D. A., & Huizinga, D. (2006). Deterring delinquents: A rational choice model of theft and violence. *American Sociological Review, 71,* 95–122.

Matthews, D., & Keating, D. (1995). Domain specificity and habits of mind: An investigation of patterns of high-level development. *Journal of Early Adolescence, 15,* 319–343.

Matthews, L. S., & Conger, R. D. (2004). "He did it on purpose!" Family correlates of negative attributions about an adolescent sibling. *Journal of Research on Adolescence, 14,* 257–284.

Mattison, E., & Aber, M. S. (2007). Closing the achievement gap: The association of racial climate with achievement and behavioral outcomes. *American Journal of Community Psychology, 40,* 1–12.

Matza, L. S., Kupersmidt, J. B., & Glenn, D. (2001). Adolescents' perceptions and standards of their parents as a function of sociometric status. *Journal of Research on Adolescence, 11,* 245–272.

Maulana, R., Opdenakker, M. C., Stroet, K., & Bosker, R. (2013). Changes in teachers' involvement versus rejection and links with academic motivation during the first year of secondary education: a multilevel growth curve analysis. *Journal of Youth & Adolescence, 42,* 1348–1371.

Mauras, C. P., Grolnick, W. S., & Friendly, R. W. (2013). Time for "the talk" . . . Now what? Autonomy support and structure in mother-daughter conversations about sex. *The Journal of Early Adolescence, 33,* 458–481.

Mayberry, M. L., Espelage, D. L., & Koenig, B. (2009). Multilevel modeling of direct effects and interactions of peers, parents, school, and community influences on adolescent substance use. *Journal of Youth and Adolescence, 38,* 1038–1049.

Mayeux, L., Sandstrom, M. J., & Cillessen, A. H. N. (2008). Is being popular a risky proposition? *Journal of Research on Adolescence, 18,* 49–74.

Mays, D., & Thompson, N. (2009). Alcohol-related risk behaviors and sports participation among adolescents: An analysis of 2005 youth risk behavior survey data. *Journal of Adolescent Health, 44,* 87–89.

Mays, D., Gilman, S. E., Rende, R., Luta, G., Tercyak, K. P., & Niaura, R. S. (2014). Parental smoking exposure and adolescent smoking trajectories. *Pediatrics, 133,* 983–991.

Mayseless, O., & Scharf, M. (2007). Adolescents' attachment representations and their capacity for intimacy in close relationships. *Journal of Research on Adolescence, 17,* 23–50.

Mayseless, O., Scharf, M., & Sholt, M. (2003). From authoritative parenting practices to an authoritarian context: Exploring the person–environment fit. *Journal of Research on Adolescence, 13,* 427–457.

McAdams, T., Rowe, R., Rijsdijk, F., Maughan, B., & Eley, T. C. (2012). The covariation of antisocial behavior and substance use in adolescence: A behavioral genetic perspective. *Journal of Research on Adolescence, 22,* 100–112.

McAloney, K., McCrystal, P., Percy, A., & McCartan, C. (2009). Damaged youth: prevalence of community violence exposure and implications for adolescent well-being in post-conflict Northern Ireland. *Journal of Community Psychology, 37,* 635–648.

McBride, C. K., Paikoff, R. L., & Holmbeck, G. N. (2003). Individual and familial influences on the onset of sexual intercourse among urban African American adolescents. *Journal of Consulting and Clinical Psychology, 71,* 159–167.

McCabe, K., Hough, R., Wood, P. A., & Yeh, M. (2001). Childhood and adolescent onset conduct disorder: A test of the developmental taxonomy. *Journal of Abnormal Child Psychology, 29,* 305–316.

McCabe, S. E., & West, B. T. (2013). Medical and nonmedical use of prescription stimulants: Results from a national multicohort study. *Journal of the American Academy of Child & Adolescent Psychiatry, 52,* 1272–1280.

McCarthy, K., Lord, S., Eccles, J., Kalil, A., & Furstenberg, F., Jr. (1992, March). *The impact of family management strategies on adolescents in high risk environments.* Paper presented at the biennial meetings of the Society for Research on Adolescence, Washington.

McCarthy, W. J., Mistry, R., Lu, Y., Patel, M., Zheng, H., & Dietsch, B. (2009). Density of tobacco retailers near schools: Effects of tobacco use among students. *American Journal of Public Health, 99,* 2006–2013.

McClintock, M. (1980). Major gaps in menstrual cycle research: Behavioral and physiological controls in a biological context. In P. Komenich, M. McSweeney, J. Noack, & N. Elder (Eds.), *The menstrual cycle* (Vol. 2, pp. 7–23). New York: Springer.

McClintock, M., & Herdt, G. (1996). Rethinking puberty: The development of sexual attraction. *Psychological Sciences, 5,* 178–183.

McCoy, J. (1996, March). *Parents' involvement in youths' peer relationships as a predictor of youths' later psychological well-being.* Paper presented at the biennial meetings of the Society for Research on Adolescence, Boston.

McCrae, R., & John, O. (1992). An introduction to the five-factor model and its applications. *Journal of Personality, 60,* 175–215.

McCrae, R., Costa, P. T., Jr., Terracciano, A., Parker, W. D., Mills, C. J., De Fruyt, F., & Mervielde, I. (2002). Personality trait development from age 12 to age 18: Longitudinal, cross-sectional, and cross-cultural analyses. *Journal of Personality and Social Psychology, 83,* 1456–1468.

McCree, D. J., Wingood, G. M., DiClemente, R., Davies, S., & Harrington, K. F. (2003). Religiosity and risky sexual behavior in African-American adolescent females. *Journal of Adolescent Health, 33,* 2–8.

McDonald, J. A., Manlove, J., & Ikramullah, E. N. (2009). Immigration measures and reproductive health among Hispanic youth: Findings from the National Longitudinal Survey of Youth, 1997–2003. *Journal of Adolescent Health, 44,* 14–24.

McElhaney, K., Allen, J., Stephenson, J., & Hare, A. (2009). Attachment and autonomy during adolescence. In R. Lerner & L. Steinberg (Eds.), *Handbook of adolescent psychology* (3rd ed., Vol. 1, pp. 358–403). New York: Wiley.

McElhaney, K., Antonishak, J., & Allen, J. P. (2008). "They like me, they like me not": Popularity and adolescents' perceptions of acceptance predicting social functioning over time. *Child Development, 79,* 720–731.

McGill, R. K., Hughes, D., Alicea, S., & Way, N. (2012). Academic adjustment across middle school: The role of public regard and parenting. *Development Psychology, 48,* 1003–1018.

McGlinchey, E. L., & Harvey, A. G. (2015). Risk behaviors and negative health outcomes fo adolescents with late bedtimes. *Journal of Youth and Adolescence, 44,* 478–488.

McGloin, J. (2009). Delinquency balance: Revisiting peer influence. *Criminology, 47,* 439–477.

McGloin, J. M., Sullivan, C. J., Thomas, K. J. (2014). Peer influence and context: the interdependence of friendship groups, schoolmates and network density in predicting substance use. *Journal of Youth & Adolescence, 43,* 1436–1452.

McGrady, P. B., & Reynolds, J. R. (2013). Racial mismatch in the classroom: Beyond black-white difference. *Sociology of Education, 86,* 3–17.

McGue, M., Elkins, I., Walden, B., & Iacono, W. G. (2005). Perceptions of the parent–adolescent relationship: A longitudinal investigation. *Developmental Psychology, 41,* 971–984.

McGue, M., Sharma, A., & Benson, P. (1996). The effects of common rearing on adolescent adjustment: Evidence from a U.S. adoption cohort. *Developmental Psychology, 32,* 604–613.

McGuire, S., Manke, B., Saudino, K., Reiss, D., Hetherington, E. M., & Plomin R. (1999). Perceived competence and self-worth during adolescence: A longitudinal behavioral genetic study. *Child Development, 70,* 1283–1296.

McHale, S. M., Corneal, D., Crouter, A., & Birch, L. (2001). Gender and weight concerns in early and middle adolescence: Links with well-being and family characteristics. *Journal of Clinical Child Psychology, 30,* 338–348.

McHale, S. M., Crouter, A., & Tucker, C. (2001). Free time activities in middle childhood: Links with adjustment in early adolescence. *Child Development, 72,* 1764–1778.

McHale, S. M., Crouter, A., Kim, J., Burton, L., Davis, K., . . . Dotterer, A. (2006). Mothers' and fathers' racial socialization in African American families: Implications for youth. *Child Development, 77,* 1387–1402.

McHale, S. M., Kim, J., Dotterer, A., Crouter, A., & Booth, A. (2009). The development of gendered interests and personality qualities from middle childhood through adolescence: A biosocial analysis. *Child Development, 80,* 482–495.

McHale, S. M., Kim, J., Whiteman, S., & Crouter, A. C. (2004). Links between sex-typed time use in middle childhood and gender development in early adolescence. *Developmental Psychology, 40,* 868–881.

McHale, S. M., Updegraff, K. A., & Whiteman, S. D. (2012). Sibling relationships and influences in childhood and adolescence. *Journal of Marriage and Family, 74,* 913–930.

McHale, S. M., Updegraff, K. A., Kim, J.-Y., & Cansler, E. (2009). Cultural orientations, daily activities, and adjustment in Mexican American youth. *Journal of Youth and Adolescence, 38,* 627–641.

McHale, S., Shanahan, L., Updegraff, K. A., Crouter, A., & Booth, A. (2004). Developmental and individual differences in girls' sex-typed activities in middle childhood and adolescence. *Child Development, 75,* 1575–1593.

McIsaac, C., Connolly, J., McKenney, K., Pepler, D., & Craig, W. (2008). Conflict negotiation and autonomy processes in adolescent romantic relationships: An observational study of interdependence in boyfriend and girlfriend effects. *Journal of Adolescence, 31,* 691–707.

McKenney, S. J., & Bigler, R. S. (2014). High heels, low grades: Internalized sexualization and academic orientation among adolescent girls. *Journal of Research on Adolescence, Early view.* DOI: 10.1111/jora.12179

McKinney, C., & Renk, K. (2008). Differential parenting between mothers and fathers: Implications for late adolescents. *Journal of Family Issues, 29,* 806–827.

McLaughlin, K. A., Green, J. G., Gruber, M. J., Sampson, N. A., Zaslavsky, A. M., & Kessler, R. C. (2012). Childhood adversities and first onset of psychiatric disorders in a national sample of US adolescents. *Arch Gen Psychiatry, 69,* 1151–1160.

McLaughlin, K., Fairbank, J., Gruber, M., Jones, R., Osofsky, J., Pfefferbaum, B., & Kessler, R. (2010). Trends in serious emotional disturbance among youths exposed to Hurricane Katrina. *Journal of the American Academy of Child & Adolescent Psychiatry, 49,* 990–1000.

McLaughlin, K., Hatzenbuehler, M., & Hilt, L. (2009). Emotion dysregulation as a mechanism linking peer victimization to internalizing symptoms in adolescents. *Journal of Consulting and Clinical Psychology, 77,* 894–904.

McLean, K. (2005). Late adolescent identity development: Narrative meaning making and memory telling. *Developmental Psychology, 41,* 683–691.

McLean, K. C., Syed M., Yoder, A., & Greenhoot, A. F. (2014). The role of domain content in understanding identity development processes. *Journal of Research on Adolescence, Early view.* DOI: 10.1111/jora.12169

McLean, K., & Breen, A. V. (2009). Processes and content of narrative identity development in adolescence: Gender and well-being. *Developmental Psychology, 45,* 702–710.

McLean, K., & Pratt, M. (2006). Life's little (and big) lessons: Identity statuses and meaning-making in the turning point narratives of emerging adults. *Developmental Psychology, 42,* 714–722.

McLean, K., & Thorne, A. (2003). Late adolescents' self-defining memories about relationships. *Developmental Psychology, 39,* 635–645.

McLean, K., Breen, A., & Fournier, M. (2010). Constructing the self in early, middle, and late adolescent boys: Narrative identity, individuation, and well-being. *Journal of Research on Adolescence, 20,* 166–187.

McLellan, J. A., & Youniss, J. (2003). Two systems of youth service: Determinants of voluntary and required youth community service. *Journal of Youth and Adolescence, 32,* 47–58.

McLoyd, V., Kaplan, R., Purtell, K. M., & Huston, A. C. (2011). Assessing the effects of a work-based antipoverty program for parents on youth's future orientation and employ-ment experiences. *Child Development, 82,* 113–132.

McLoyd, V., Kaplan, R., Purtell, K., Bagley, E., Hardaway, C., & Smalls, C. (2009). Poverty and socioeconomic disadvantage in adoles-cence. In R. Lerner & L. Steinberg (Eds.), *Handbook of adolescent psychology* (3rd ed., Vol. 2, pp. 444–491). New York: Wiley.

McMahon, R. J., Witkiewitz, K., Kotler, J. S., & Conduct Problems Prevention Research Group. (2010). Predictive validity of callous-unemotional traits measured in early ado-lescence with respect to multiple antisocial outcomes. *Journal of Abnormal Psychology, 119,* 752–763.

McMahon, S., & Watts, R. (2002). Ethnic identity in urban African American youth: Exploring links with self-worth, aggression, and other psychosocial variables. *Journal of Community Psychology, 30,* 411–431.

McMahon, S., Felix, E., Halpert, J., & Petropoulos, L. (2009). Community violence exposure and aggression among urban adolescents: Testing a cognitive mediator model. *Journal of Community Psychology, 37,* 895–910.

McMahon, S. D., Todd, N. R., Martinez, A., Coker, C., Sheu, C. F., Washburn, J., & Shah, S. (2013). Aggressive and prosocial behav-ior: community violence, cognitive, and behavioral predictors among urban African American youth. *American Journal of Community Psychology, 51,* 407–421.

McMaster, L., Connolly, J., & Craig, W. (1997, March). *Sexual harassment and dating violence among early adolescents.* Paper presented at the biennial meetings of the Society for Research in Child Development, Washington, DC.

McMaster, L., Connolly, J., Pepler, D., & Craig, W. (2002). Peer to peer sexual harassment in early adolescence: A developmental perspec-tive. *Development and Psychopathology, 14,* 91–105.

McNaughton Reyes, H. L., Foshee, V. A., Bauer, D. J., & Ennett, S. T. (2011). The role of heavy alcohol use in the developmental pro-cess of desistance in dating aggression dur-ing adolescence. *Journal of Abnormal Child Psychology, 39,* 239–250.

McNeely, C., & Barber, B. (2010). How do par-ents make adolescents feel loved? Perspectives on supportive parenting from adolescents in 12 cultures. *Journal of Adolescent Research, 25,* 601–631.

McNeely, C., Shew, M. L., Beuhring, T., Sieving, R., Miller, B. C., & Blum, R. (2002). Mothers' influence on the timing of first sex among 14- and 15-year olds. *Journal of Adolescent Health, 31,* 256–265.

McNelles, L., & Connolly, J. (1999). Intimacy between adolescent friends: Age and gen-der differences in intimate affect and inti-mate behaviors. *Journal of Research on Adolescence, 9,* 143–159.

McNulty, T., & Bellair, P. (2003). Explaining racial and ethnic differences in serious adolescent violent behavior. *Criminology, 41,* 709–748.

McPhie, M. L. & Rawana, J. S. (2015). The effect of physical activity on depression in adoles-cence and emerging adulthood: A growth-curve analysis. *Journal of Adolescence, 40,* 83–92.

McQueen, A., Getz, J., & Bray, J. (2003). Acculturation, substance use, and deviant behavior: Examining separation and family conflict as mediators. *Child Development, 74,* 1737–1750.

Mead, M. (1978). *Coming of age in Samoa.* New York: Morrow. (Original work published 1928.)

Meadows, S. O., Brown, J. S., & Elder, G. H. J. (2006). Depressive symptoms, stress, and sup-port: Gendered trajectories from adolescence to young adulthood. *Journal of Youth and Adolescence, 35,* 93–103.

Measelle, J. R., Stice, E., & Hogansen, J. M. (2006). Developmental trajectories of co-occurring depressive, eating, antisocial, and substance abuse problems in female adoles-cents. *Journal of Abnormal Psychology, 115,* 524–538.

Mednick, S., Gabrielli, W., & Hitchings, B. (1987). Genetic factors in the etiology of crim-inal behavior. In S. Mednick, T. Moffitt, & S. Stack (Eds.), *The causes of crime: New bio-logical approaches* (pp. 74–91). Cambridge: Cambridge University Press.

Meeus, W. (2011). The study of adolescent iden-tity formation 2000–2010: A review of lon-gitudinal research. *Journal of Research on Adolescence, 21,* 75–94.

Meeus, W., Iedema, J., & Vollebergh, W. (1999). Rejoinder: Identity formation re-revisited: A rejoinder to Waterman in developmental and cross-cultural issues. *Developmental Review, 19,* 480–496.

Meeus, W., van de Schoot, R., Keijsers, L., Branje, S. (2012). Identity statuses as develop-mental trajectories: A five-wave longitudinal study in early-to-middle and middle-to-late adolescents. *Journal of Youth & Adolescence, 41,* 1008–1021.

Meeus, W., Van de Schoot, R., Keijsers, L., Schwartz, S., & Branje, S. (2010). On the pro-gression and stability of adolescent identity formation: A five-wave longitudinal study in early-to-middle and middle-to-late adoles-cence. *Child Development, 81,* 1565–1581.

Meeus, W., Van de Schoot, R., Klimstra, T., & Branje, S. (2011). Personality types in ado-lescence: Change and stability and links with adjustment and relationships: A five-wave longitudinal study. *Developmental Psychology, 47,* 1181–1195.

Mega, C., Ronconi, L., & De Beni, R. (2014). What makes a good student? How emotions, self-regulated learning, and motivation con-tribute to academic achievement. *Journal of Educational Psychology, 106,* 121–131.

Mehari, K. R., & Farrell, A. D. (2013). The rela-tion between peer victimization and adoles-cents' well-being: The moderating role of ethnicity within context. *Journal of Research on Adolescence, 25,* 118–134.

Mehta, C., & Strough, J. (2009). Sex segregation in friendships and normative contexts across the life span. *Developmental Review, 29,* 201–220.

Meier, A. M. (2003). Adolescents' transition to first intercourse, religiosity, and attitudes about sex. *Social Forces, 81,* 1031–1052.

Meier, A. M. (2007). Adolescent first sex and sub-sequent mental health. *American Journal of Sociology, 112,* 1811–1847.

Meier, A., & Musick, K. (2014). Variation in associations between family dinners and ado-lescent well-being. *Journal of Marriage and Family, 76,* 13–23.

Meier, M., Slutske, W., Arndt, S., & Cadoret, R. (2008). Impulsive and callous traits are more strongly associated with delinquent behavior in higher risk neighborhoods among boys and girls. *Journal of Abnormal Psychology, 117,* 377–385.

Mekos, D., Hetherington, E. M., & Reiss, D. (1996). Sibling differences in problem behav-ior and parental treatment in nondivorced and remarried families. *Child Development, 67,* 2148–2165.

Melby, J. (1995, March). *Early family and peer predictors of later adolescent tobacco use.* Paper presented at the biennial meetings of the Society for Research in Child Development, Indianapolis.

Melby, J., & Conger, R. (1996). Parental behav-iors and adolescent academic performance: A longitudinal analysis. *Journal of Research on Adolescence, 6,* 113–137.

Melby, J., Conger, R., Fang, S., Wickrama, K. A. S., & Conger, K. J. (2008). Adolescent family experiences and educational attain-ment during early adulthood. *Developmental Psychology, 44,* 1519–1536.

Melde, C., & Esbensen, F. (2011). Gang mem-bership as the turning point in the life course. *Criminology, 49,* 513–552.

Melde, C., Taylor, T., & Esbensen, F. (2009). "I got your back": An examination of the protec-tive function of gang membership in adoles-cence. *Criminology, 47,* 565–594.

Meldrum, R. C., Barnes, J. C., & Hay, C. (2015). Sleep deprivation, low self-control, and delin-quency: a test of the strength model of self-control. *Journal of Youth and Adolescence, 44,* 465–477.

Mello, Z. R. (2008). Gender variation in develop-mental trajectories of educational and occu-pational expectations and attainment from adolescence to adulthood. *Developmental Psychology, 44,* 1069–1080.

Memmert, D. (2014). Inattentional blindness to unexpected events in 8–15-year-olds. *Cognitive Development, 32,* 103–109.

Mendle, J. (2014). Beyond pubertal timing: New directions for studying individual differences in development. *Current Directions in Psychological Science, 23,* 215–219.

Mendle, J., & Ferrero, J. (2012). Detrimental psychological outcomes associated with pubertal timing in adolescent boys. *Developmental Review, 32,* 49–66.

Mendle, J., Ferrero, J., Moore, S. R., & Harden, K. P. (2013). Depression and adolescent sexual activity in romantic and nonromantic relational contexts: A genetically-informative sibling comparison. *Journal of Abnormal Psychology, 122,* 51–63.

Mendle, J., Harden, K. P., Brooks-Gunn, J., & Graber, J. A. (2010). Development's tortoise and hare: Pubertal timing, pubertal tempo, and depressive symptoms in boys and girls. *Developmental Psychology, 46,* 1341–1353.

Mendle, J., Harden, K. P., Turkheimer, E., Van Hulle, C. A., D'Onofrio, B. M., Brooks-Gunn, J., . . . Lahey, B. (2009). Associations between father absence and age of first sexual intercourse. *Child Development, 80,* 1463–1480.

Mendle, J., Harden, K., Brooks-Gunn, J., & Graber, J. (2012). Peer relationships and depressive symptomatology in boys at puberty. *Developmental Psychology, 48,* 429–435.

Mendle, J., Leve, L. D., Van Ryzin, M., & Natsuaki, M. N. (2014). Linking childhood maltreatment with girls' internalizing symptoms: Early puberty as a tipping point. *Journal of Research on Adolescence, 24,* 689–702.

Mendle, J., Leve, L., Van Ryzin, M., Natsuaki, M., & Ge, X. (2011). Associations between early life stress, child maltreatment, and pubertal development among girls in foster care. *Journal of Research on Adolescence, 21,* 871–880.

Mendle, J., Ryan, R. M., & McKone, K. M. (2015). Early childhood maltreatment and pubertal development: Replication in a population-based sample. *Journal of Research on Adolescence, Early view.* DOI: 10.1111/jora.12201

Mendle, J., Turkheimer, E., & Emery, R. E. (2007). Detrimental psychological outcomes associated with early pubertal timing in adolescent girls. *Developmental Review, 27,* 151–171.

Menning, C. L. (2002). Absent parents are more than money: The joint effect of activities and financial support on youths' educational attainment. *Journal of Family Issues, 23,* 648–671.

Menon, M. (2011). Does felt gender compatibility mediate influences of self-perceived gender nonconformity on early adolescents' psychosocial adjustment? *Child Development, 82,* 1152–1162.

Menzer, M. M., & Torney-Purta, J. (2012). Individualism and socioeconomic diversity at school as related to perceptions of the frequency of peer aggression in fifteen countries. *Journal of Adolescence, 35,* 1285–1294.

Menzies, L., Goddings, A. L., Whitaker, K. J., Blakemore, S. J., & Viner, R. M. (2015). The effects of puberty on white matter development in boys. *Developmental Cognitive Neuroscience, 11,* 116–128.

Merikangas, K. R., He, J., Burstein, M., Swanson, S. A., Avenevoli, S., Cui, L., . . . Swendsen, J. (2010). Lifetime prevalence of mental disorders in U.S. adolescents: Results from the National Comorbidity Survey Replication–Adolescent Supplement (NCS-A). *Journal of the American Academy of Child & Adolescent Psychiatry, 49,* 980–989.

Merskin, D. (1999). Adolescence, advertising, and the ideology of menstruation. *Sex Roles, 40,* 941–957.

Merten, D. (1997). The meaning of meanness: Popularity, competition and conflict among junior high school girls. *Sociology of Education, 70,* 175–191.

Merten, M., Wickrama, K., & Williams, A. (2008). Adolescent obesity and young adult psychosocial outcomes: Gender and racial differences. *Journal of Youth and Adolescence, 37,* 1111–1122.

Mesch, G. S., & Talmud, I. (2007). Similarity and the quality of online and offline social relationships among adolescents in Israel. *Journal of Research on Adolescence, 17,* 455–466.

Meschke, L. L., Bartholomae, S., & Zentall, S. R. (2000). Adolescent sexuality and parent–adolescent processes: Promoting healthy teen choices. *Family Relations: Interdisciplinary Journal of Applied Family Studies, 49,* 143–154.

Meuwese, R., Crone, E. A., de Rooij, M., & Güroğlu, B. (2015). Development of equity preferences in boys and girls across adolescence. *Child Development, 86,* 145–158.

Michl, L. C., McLaughlin, K. A., Shepherd, K., & Nolen-Hoeksema, S. (2013). Rumination as a mechanism linking stressful life events to symptoms of depression and anxiety: Longitudinal evidence in early adolescents and adults. *Journal of Abnormal Psychology, 122,* 339–352.

Mickelson, R. (1990). The attitude–achievement paradox among Black adolescents. *Sociology of Education, 63,* 44–61.

Midgley, C., & Urdan, T. (1995). Predictors of middle school students' use of self-handicapping strategies. *Journal of Early Adolescence, 15,* 389–411.

Midgley, C., Arunkumar, R., & Urdan T. (1996). If I don't do well tomorrow, there's a reason: Predictors of adolescents' use of academic self-handicapping strategies. *Journal of Educational Psychology, 88,* 423–434.

Midgley, C., Berman, E., & Hicks, L. (1995). Differences between elementary and middle school teachers and students: A goal theory approach. *Journal of Early Adolescence, 15,* 90–113.

Midgley, C., Feldlaufer, H., & Eccles, J. (1988). The transition to junior high school: Beliefs of pre- and posttransition teachers. *Journal of Youth and Adolescence, 17,* 543–562.

Miech, R. A., Kumanyika, S. K., Stettler, N., Link, B. G., Phelan, J. C., & Chang, V. W. (2006). Trends in the association of poverty with overweight among US adolescents, 1971–2004. *JAMA: Journal of the American Medical Association, 295,* 2385–2393.

Mihalic, S., & Elliot, D. (1997). Short- and long-term consequences of adolescent work. *Youth and Society, 28,* 464–498.

Mikami, A. Y., Szwedo, D. E., Allen, J. P., Evans, M. A., & Hare, A. L. (2010). Adolescent peer relationships and behavior problems predict young adults' communication on social networking websites. *Developmental Psychology, 46,* 46–56.

Miklikowska, M., Duriez, B., & Soenens, B. (2011). Family roots of empathy-related characteristics: The role of perceived maternal and paternal need support in adolescence. *Developmental Psychology, 47,* 1342–1352.

Milan, S., Ethier, K., Lewis, J., Kershaw, T., Niccolai, L., & Ickovics, J. (2006). Reproductive health of urban adolescents: Differences in the behaviors, cognitions, and social context of African-American and Puerto Rican females. *Journal of Youth and Adolescence, 35,* 959–967.

Milbrath, C., Ohlson, B., & Eyre, S. L. (2009). Analyzing cultural models in adolescent accounts of romantic relationships. *Journal of Research on Adolescence, 19,* 313–351.

Miller, A. B., Esposito-Smythers, C., & Leichtweis, R. N. (2015). Role of social support in adolescent suicidal ideation and suicide attempts. *Journal of Adolescent Health, 56,* 286–292.

Miller, B., & Moore, K. (1990). Adolescent sexual behavior, pregnancy, and parenting: Research through the 1980s. *Journal of Marriage and the Family, 52,* 1025–1044.

Miller, B., Benson, B., & Galbraith, K. A. (2001). Family relationships and adolescent pregnancy risk: A research synthesis. *Developmental Review, 21,* 1–38.

Miller, B., Fan, X., Christensen, M., Grotevant, H. D., & van Dulmen, M. (2000). Comparisons of adopted and nonadopted adolescents in a large, nationally represented sample. *Child Development, 71,* 1458–1473.

Miller, B., Norton, M., Curtis, T., Hill, E., Schvaneveldt, P., & Young, M. (1997). The timing of sexual intercourse among adolescents: Family, peer, and other antecedents. *Youth and Society, 29,* 54–83.

Miller, B., Norton, M., Fan, X., & Christopherson, C. (1998). Pubertal development, parental communication, and sexual values in relation to adolescent sexual behaviors. *Journal of Early Adolescence, 18,* 27–52.

Miller, D. I., & Halpern, D. F. (2014). The new science of cognitive sex differences. *Trends in Cognitive Sciences, 18,* 37–45.

Miller, D. P., Waldfogel, J., & Han, W. J. (2012). Family meals and child academic and behavioral outcomes. *Child Development, 83,* 2104–2120.

Miller, D., & Byrnes, J. (1997). The role of contextual and personal factors in children's risk taking. *Developmental Psychology, 33,* 814–823.

Miller, J. (2013). Individual offending, routine activities, and activity settings: Revisiting the routine activity theory of general deviance. *Journal of Research in Crime and Delinquency, 50,* 390–416.

Miller, J., & White, N. (2003). Gender and adolescent relationship violence: A contextual examination. *Criminology, 41,* 1207–1248.

Miller, K. E., Melnick, M. J., Barnes, G. M., Sabo, D., & Farrell, M. P. (2007). Athletic involvement and adolescent delinquency. *Journal of Youth and Adolescence, 36,* 711–723.

Miller, K. S., Fasula, A. M., Lin, C. Y., Levin, M. L., Wyckoff, S. C., & Forehand, R. (2012). Ready, set go: African American preadolescents' sexual thoughts, intentions, and behaviors. *The Journal of Early Adolescence, 32,* 293–307.

Miller, K., & Whitaker, D. (2001). Predictors of mother–adolescent discussions about condoms: Implications for providers who serve youth. *Pediatrics, 108,* E28.

Miller, K., Kotchick, B., Dorsey, S., Forehand, R., & Ham, A. (1998). Family communication about sex: What are parents saying and are their adolescents listening? *Family Planning Perspectives, 30,* 218–222, 235.

Miller, K., Levin, M., Whitaker, D., & Xu, X. (1998). Patterns of condom use among adolescents: The impact of mother–adolescent communication. *American Journal of Public Health, 88,* 1542–1544.

Miller, L., & Gur, M. (2002). Religiousness and sexual responsibility in adolescent girls. *Journal of Adolescent Health, 31,* 401–406.

Miller, L., Davies, M., & Greenwald, S. (2000). Religiosity and substance use and abuse among adolescents in the National Comorbidity Survey. *Journal of the American Academy of Child and Adolescent Psychiatry, 39,* 1190–1197.

Miller, N. (1928). *The child in primitive society.* New York: Brentano's.

Miller, S. R., Tserakhava, V., & Miller, C. J. (2011). "My child is shy and has no friends: What does parenting have to do with it?" *Journal of Youth and Adolescence, 40,* 442–452.

Miller, S., Malone, P. S., & Dodge, K. A. (2010). Developmental trajectories of boys' and girls' delinquency: Sex differences and links to later adolescent outcomes. *Journal of Abnormal Child Psychology, 38,* 1021–1032.

Miller-Johnson, S., Winn, D. C., Coie, J. D., Malone, P. S., & Lochman, J. (2004). Risk factors for adolescent pregnancy reports among African American males. *Journal of Research on Adolescence 14,* 471–495.

Miller-Johnson, S., Winn, D., Coie, J., Maumary-Gremaud, A., Hyman, C., Retty, R., et al. (1999). Motherhood during the teen years: A developmental perspective on risk factors for childbearing. *Development and Psychopathology, 11,* 85–100.

Mills, B., Reyna, V., & Estrada, S. (2008). Explaining contradictory relations between risk perception and risk taking. *Psychological Science, 19,* 429–433.

Mills, K. L. (2014). Effects of internet use on the adolescent brain: Despite popular claims, experimental evidence remains scarce. *Trends in Cognitive Sciences, 18,* 385–387.

Mills, K. L., Goddings, A. L., Clasen, L. S., Giedd, J. N., & Blakemore, S. J. (2014). The developmental mismatch in structural brain maturation during adolescence. *Developmental Neuroscience, 36,* 147–160.

Mills, K. L., Lalonde, F., Clasen, L. S., Giedd, J. N., & Blakemore, S. J. (2014). Developmental changes in the structure of the social brain in late childhood and adolescence, *Social Cognitive Affective Neuroscience, 9,* 123–131.

Millstein, S. G., & Halpern-Felsher, B. L. (2002). Judgments about risk and perceived invulnerability in adolescents and young adults. *Journal of Research on Adolescence, 12,* 399–422.

Milnitsky-Sapiro, C., Turiel, E., & Nucci, L. (2006). Brazilian adolescents' conceptions of autonomy and parental authority. *Cognitive Development, 21,* 317–331.

Milot, A., & Ludden, A. B. (2009). The effects of religion and gender on well-being, substance use, and academic engagement among rural adolescents. *Youth & Society, 40,* 403–425.

Minguez, M., Santelli, J. S., Gibson, E., Orr, M., & Samant, S. (2015). Reproductive health impact of a school health center. *Journal of Adolescent Health, 56,* 338–344.

Mireles-Rios, R., & Romo, L. F. (2014). Latina daughters' childbearing attitudes: The role of maternal expectations and education communication. *Developmental Psychology, 50,* 1553–1563.

Mischel, W. (in press). *The marshmallow effect.* New York: Little, Brown.

Mitchell, C. M., Whitesell, N. R., Spicer, P., Beals, J., & Kaufman, C. E. (2007). Cumulative risk for early sexual initiation among American Indian youth: A discrete-time survival analysis. *Journal of Research on Adolescence, 17,* 387–412.

Mitchell, C., O'Nell, T., Beals, J., Dick, R., Keane, E., & Manson, S. (1996). Dimensionality of alcohol use among American Indian adolescents: Latent structure, construct validity, and implications for developmental research. *Journal of Research on Adolescence, 6,* 151–180.

Mitchell, E. (Ed.). (1985). *Anorexia nervosa and bulimia: Diagnosis and treatment.* Minneapolis: University of Minnesota Press.

Mitchell, J. A., Rodriguez, D., Schmitz, K. H., Audrain-McGovern, J. (2013). Sleep duration and adolescent obesity. *Pediatrics, 131,* e1428–e1434.

Mitchell, J., Pate, R., Beets, M., & Nader, P. (2013). Time spent in sedentary behavior and changes in childhood BMI: A longitudinal study from ages 9 to 15 years. *International Journal of Obesity, 37,* 54–60.

Mitchell, K. J., Finkelhor, D., Jones, L. M., & Wolak, J. (2012). Prevalence and characteristics of youth sexting: A national study. *Pediatrics, 129,* 13–20.

Mitchell, K. J., Wells, M., Priebe, G., & Ybarra, M. L. (2014). Exposure to websites that encourage self-harm and suicide: Prevalence rates and association with actual thoughts of self-harm and thoughts of suicide in the United States. *Journal of Adolescence, 37,* 1335–1344.

Mitchell, K., Booth, A., & King, V. (2009). Adolescents with nonresident fathers: Are daughters more disadvantaged than sons? *Journal of Marriage and Family, 71,* 650–662.

Mitchell, K., Finkelhor, D., Jones, L., & Wolak, J. (2012). Prevalence and characteristics of youth sexting: A national study. *Pediatrics, 129,* 13–20.

Mitchell, K., Finkelhor, D., Wolak, J., Ybarra, M., & Turner, H. (2011). Youth internet victimization in a broader victimization context. *Journal of Adolescent Health, 48,* 128–134.

Mitru, G., Millrood, D. L., & Mateika, J. H. (2002). The impact of sleep on learning and behavior in adolescents. *Teachers College Record, 104,* 704–726.

Mizuno, K., Tanaka, M., Fukuda, S., Sasabe, T., Imai-Matsumura, K., & Watanabe, Y. (2011). Changes in cognitive functions of students in the transitional period from elementary school to junior high school. *Brain Development, 33,* 412–420.

Modecki, K. L. (2008). Addressing gaps in the maturity of judgment literature: Age differences and delinquency. *Law and Human Behavior, 32,* 78–91.

Modecki, K. L., Minchin, J., Harbaugh, A. G., Guerra, N. G., & Runions, K. C. (2014). Bullying prevalence across contexts: A meta-analysis measuring cyber and traditional bullying. *Journal of Adolescent Health, 55,* 602–611.

Modell, J., & Goodman, M. (1990). Historical perspectives. In S. Feldman & G. Elliott (Eds.), *At the threshold: The developing adolescent* (pp. 93–122). Cambridge, MA: Harvard University Press.

Modell, J., Furstenberg, F., Jr., & Hershberg, T. (1976). Social change and transitions to adulthood in historical perspective. *Journal of Family History, 1,* 7–32.

Moffitt, T. (2006). Life-course persistent versus adolescence-limited antisocial behavior. In D. Cicchetti & D. Cohen (Eds.), *Developmental psychopathology* (2nd ed.). New York: Wiley.

Moffitt, T., & Caspi, A. (2001). Childhood predictors differentiate life-course-persistent and adolescence-limited antisocial pathways among males and females. *Development and Psychopathology, 13,* 355–375.

Moffitt, T., Caspi, A., Harkness, A., & Silva, P. (1993). The natural history of change in intellectual performance: Who changes? How much? Is it meaningful? *Journal of Child Psychology and Psychiatry, 34,* 455–506.

Moffitt, T., Caspi, A., Harrington, H., & Milne, B. J. (2002). Males on the life-course-persistent and adolescence-limited antisocial pathways: Follow-up at age 26 years. *Development and Psychopathology, 14,* 179–207.

Moilanen, K., Crockett, L. J., Raffaelli, M., & Jones, B. L. (2010a). Trajectories of sexual risk from middle adolescence to early adulthood. *Journal of Research on Adolescence, 20,* 114–139.

Moilanen, K., Shaw, D., & Maxwell K. (2010b). Developmental cascades: Externalizing, internalizing, and academic competence from middle childhood to early adolescence. *Development and Psychopathology, 22,* 635–653.

Moilanen, K. L., Rasmussen, K. E., & Padilla-Walker, L. M. (2015). Bidirectional associations between self-regulation and parenting styles in early adolescence. *Journal of Research on Adolescence, 25,* 246–262.

Molano, A., Jones, S. M., Brown, J. L., & Aber, L. (2013). Selection and socialization of aggressive and prosocial behavior: The moderating role of social-cognitive processes. *Journal of Research on Adolescence, 23,* 424–436.

Molina, B., & Chassin, L. (1996). The parent–adolescent relationship at puberty: Hispanic ethnicity and parent alcoholism as moderators. *Developmental Psychology, 32,* 675–686.

Mollen, C. J., Barg, F. K., Hayes, K. L., Gotcsik, M., Blades, N. M., & Schwarz, D. F. (2008). Assessing attitudes about emergency contraception among urban, minority adolescent girls: An in-depth interview study. *Pediatrics, 122,* 395–401.

Molloy, L. E., Gest, S. D., Feinberg, M. E., & Osgood, D. W. (2014). Emergence of mixed-sex friendship groups during adolescence: Developmental associations with substance use and delinquency. *Developmental Psychology, 50,* 2449–2461.

Molloy, L. E., Ram, N., & Gest, S. D. (2011). The storm and stress (or calm) of early adolescent self-concepts: Within- and between-subjects variability. *Developmental Psychology, 47,* 1589–1607.

Molnar, B. E., Cerda, M., Roberts, A. L., & Buka, S. L. (2008). Effects of neighborhood resources on aggressive and delinquent behaviors among urban youths. *American Journal of Public Health, 98,* 1086–1093.

Monahan, K. C., & Booth-LaForce, C. (2015). Deflected pathways: becoming aggressive, socially withdrawn, or prosocial with peers during the transition to adolescence. *Journal of Research on Adolescence, Early view.* DOI: 10.1111/jora.12190

Monahan, K. C., Dmitrieva, J., & Cauffman, E. (2014). Bad romance: Sex differences in the longitudinal association between romantic relationships and deviant behavior. *Journal of Research on Adolescence, 24,* 12–26.

Monahan, K. C., King, K. M., Shulman, E. P., Cauffman, E., & Chassin, L. (2015). The effects of violence exposure on the development of impulse control and future orientation across adolescence and early adulthood: Time-specific and generalized effects in a sample of juvenile offenders. *Development and Psychopathology, FirstView Articles.* DOI: 10.1017/S0954579414001394

Monahan, K. C., Oesterle, S., Rhew, I., & Hawkins, J. D. (2014). The relation between risk and protective factors for problem behaviors and depressive symptoms, antisocial behavior, and alcohol use in adolescence. *Journal of Community Psychology, 42,* 621–638.

Monahan, K. C., Rhew, I. C., Hawkins, J. D., & Brown, E. C. (2014). Adolescent pathway to co-occurring problem behavior: The effects of peer delinquency and peer substance use. *Journal of Research on Adolescence, 24,* 630–645.

Monahan, K. C., Steinberg, L., Cauffman, E., & Mulvey, E. P. (2013). Psychosocial (im)maturity from adolescence to early adulthood: Distinguishing between adolescence-limited and persisting antisocial behavior. *Development and Psychopathology, 25,* 1093–1105.

Monahan, K., & Lee, J. (2008). Adolescent sexual activity: Links between relational context and depressive symptoms. *Journal of Youth and Adolescence, 37,* 917–927.

Monahan, K., & Steinberg, L. (2011). Accentuation of individual differences in social competence during the transition to adolescence. *Journal of Research on Adolescence, 21,* 576–585.

Monahan, K., Egan, E., Van Horn, M., Arthur, M., & Hawkins, D. (2011). Community-level effects of individual and peer risk and protective factors on adolescent substance use. *Journal of Community Psychology, 39,* 478–498.

Monahan, K., Guyer, A., Silk, J., Fitzwater, T., & Steinberg, L. (in press). Integration of developmental neuroscience and contextual approaches to the study of adolescent psychopathology. In D. Cicchetti (Ed.), *Developmental psychopathology* (3rd ed.). New York: Wiley.

Monahan, K., Lee, J., & Steinberg, L. (2011). Revisiting the negative impact of part-time work on adolescent adjustment: Distinguishing between selection and socialization using propensity score matching. *Child Development, 82,* 96–112.

Monahan, K., Steinberg, L., & Cauffman, E. (2009). Affiliation with antisocial peers, susceptibility to peer influence, and desistance from antisocial behavior during the transition to adulthood. *Developmental Psychology, 45,* 1520–1530.

Monahan, K., Steinberg, L., & Cauffman, E. (2013). Age differences in the impact of employment on antisocial behavior. *Child Development.*

Monahan, K., Steinberg, L., Cauffman, E., & Mulvey, E. (2009). Trajectories of antisocial behavior and psychosocial maturity from adolescence to young adulthood. *Developmental Psychology, 45,* 1654–1668.

Monahan, K. C., Vanderhei, S., Bechtold, J., Cauffman, E. (2014). From the school yard to the squad car: school discipline, truancy, and arrest. *Journal of Youth & Adolescence, 43,* 1110–1122.

Monck, E. (1991). Patterns of confiding relationships among adolescent girls. *Journal of Child Psychology and Psychiatry, 32,* 333–345.

Monk, C., McClure, E., Nelson, E., Zarahn, E., Bilder, R., Leibenluft, E., . . . Pine, D. (2003). Adolescent immaturity in attention-related brain engagement to emotional facial expressions. *Neuroimage, 20,* 420–428.

Monroe, S. M., Rohde, P., Seeley, J. R., & Lewinsohn, P. M. (1999). Life events and depression in adolescence: Relationship loss as a prospective risk factor for first onset of major depressive disorder. *Journal of Abnormal Psychology, 108,* 606–614.

Monshouwer, K., Harakeh, Z., Lugtig, P., Huizink, A., Creemers, H. E., Reijneveld, S., . . . & Vollebergh, W. A. (2012). Predicting transitions in low and high levels of risk behavior from early to middle adolescence: The TRAILS study. *Journal of Abnormal Child Psychology, 40,* 923–931.

Montgomery, K., Chester, J., Grier, S., & Dorfman, L. (2012). The new threat of digital marketing. *Pediatric Clinics of North America, 59,* 659–675.

Montgomery, M. (1996). "The fruit that hangs highest": Courtship and chaperonage in New York high society, 1880–1920. *Journal of Family History, 21,* 172–191.

Montgomery, M. J. (2005). Psychosocial intimacy and identity: From early adolescence to emerging adulthood. *Journal of Adolescent Research, 20,* 346–374.

Montgomery, M. J., & Sorell, G. T. (1998). Love and dating experience in early and middle adolescence: Grade and gender comparisons. *Journal of Adolescence, 21,* 677–689.

Moody, J. (2001). Race, school integration, and friendship segregation in America. *American Journal of Sociology, 107,* 679–716.

Moore, K., Myers, D., Morrison, D., Nord, C., Brown, B., & Edmonston, B. (1993). Age at first childbirth and later poverty. *Journal of Research on Adolescence, 3,* 393–422.

Moore, M. J., & Werch, C. E. (2005). Sport and physical activity participation and substance use among adolescents. *Journal of Adolescent Health, 36,* 486–493.

Moore, M. R., & Chase-Lansdale, P. L. (2001). Sexual intercourse and pregnancy among African American girls in high-poverty neighborhoods: The role of family and perceived community environment. *Journal of Marriage and the Family, 63,* 1146–1157.

Moore, M., Petrie, C., Braga, A., & McLaughlin, B. (2003). *Deadly lessons: Understanding lethal school violence.* Washington, DC: National Academies Press.

Moore, S. (1995). Girls' understanding and social construction of menarche. *Journal of Adolescence, 18,* 87–104.

Moore, S. R., Harden, K. P., & Mendle, J. (2014). Pubertal timing and adolescent sexual behavior in girls. *Developmental Psychology, 50,* 1734–1745.

Moore, S., & Gullone, E. (1996). Predicting adolescent risk behavior using a personalized cost-benefit analysis. *Journal of Youth and Adolescence, 25,* 343–359.

Moore, W., Pfeifer, J., Masten, C., Iacoboni, M., Mazziotta, J. & Dapretto, M. (2012). Facing puberty: Associations between pubertal development and neural responses to affective facial displays. *Social Cognitive and Affective Neuroscience, 7,* 35–43.

Moos, R. (1978). A typology of junior high and high school classrooms. *American Educational Research Journal, 15,* 53–66.

Moran, P., Rowe, R., Flach, C., Briskman, J., Ford, T., Maughan, B., ... Goodman, R. (2009). Predictive value of callous-unemotional traits in a large community sample. *Journal of the American Academy of Child and Adolescent Psychiatry, 48,* 1079–1084.

Morin, A. J. S., Maïano, C., Marsh, H. W., Nagengast, B., & Janosz, M. (2013). School life and adolescents' self-esteem trajectories. *Child Development, 84,* 1967–1988.

Morisi, T. (2008). Youth enrollment and employment during the school year. *Monthly Labor Review, 131,* 51–63.

Morris, A. K., & Sloutsky, V. (1998). Understanding of logical necessity: Developmental antecedents and cognitive consequences. *Child Development, 69,* 721–741.

Morris, A. K., & Sloutsky, V. (2001). Children's solutions of logical versus empirical problems: What's missing and what develops? *Cognitive Development, 16,* 907–928.

Morris, A., Eisenberg, N., & Houltberg, B. (2011). Adolescent moral development. In B. Brown & M. Prinstein (Eds.), *Encyclopedia of adolescence* (Vol. 1, pp. 48–55). New York: Academic Press.

Morris, M. C., Ciesla, J. A., & Garber, J. (2010). A prospective study of stress autonomy versus stress sensitization in adolescents at varied risk for depression. *Journal of Abnormal Psychology, 119,* 341–354.

Morris, N., & Udry, J. (1980). Validation of a self-administered instrument to assess stage of adolescent development. *Journal of Youth and Adolescence, 9,* 271–280.

Morrison Gutman, L., Sameroff, A. J., & Eccles, J. (2002). The academic achievement of African American students during early adolescence: An examination of multiple risk, promotive, and protective factors. *American Journal of Community Psychology, 30,* 367–399.

Morrison, G. M., Laughlin, J., Miguel, S. S., Smith, D. C., & Widaman, K. (1997). Sources of support for school-related issues: Choices of Hispanic adolescents varying in migrant status. *Journal of Youth and Adolescence, 26,* 233–252.

Mortimer, J. (2003). *Working and growing up in America.* Cambridge, MA: Harvard University Press.

Mortimer, J., & Johnson, M. (1998). New perspectives on adolescent work and the transition to adulthood. In R. Jessor & M. Chase (Eds.), *New perspectives on adolescent risk behavior.* New York: Cambridge University Press.

Mortimer, J., & Larson, R. (2002). Adolescence in the 21st century: A worldwide perspective. Introduction: Macro societal trends and the changing experiences of adolescence. In J. Mortimer & R. Larson (Eds.), *The future of adolescent experience: Societal trends and the transition to adulthood.* New York: Cambridge University Press.

Mortimer, J., Pimentel, E., Ryu, S., Nash, K., & Lee, C. (1996). Part-time work and occupational value formation in adolescence. *Social Forces, 74,* 1405–1418.

Moses, A. (1999). Exposure to violence, depression, and hostility in a sample of inner city high school youth. *Journal of Adolescence, 22,* 21–32.

Mosher, W., & Bachrach, C. (1996). Understanding U.S. fertility: Continuity and change in the National Survey of Family Growth, 1988–1995. *Family Planning Perspectives, 28,* 4–12.

Moshman, D. (1993). Adolescent reasoning and adolescent rights. *Human Development, 36,* 27–40.

Mosteller, F., Light, R., & Sachs, J. (1996). Sustained inquiry in education: Lessons from skill grouping and class size. *Harvard Educational Review, 66,* 797–842.

Motl, R. W., McAuley, E., Birnbaum, A. S., & Lytle, L. A. (2006). Naturally occurring changes in time spent watching television are inversely related to frequency of physical activity during early adolescence. *Journal of Adolescence, 29,* 19–32.

Mott, F., Fondell, M., Hu, P., Kowaleski-Jones, P., & Menaghan, E. (1996). The determinants of first sex by age 14 in a high-risk adolescent population. *Family Planning Perspectives, 28,* 13–18.

Moua, M., & Lamborn, S. (2010). Hmong American adolescents' perceptions of ethnic socialization practices. *Journal of Adolescent Research, 25,* 416–440.

Mounts, N. (2002). Parental management of adolescent peer relationships in context: The role of parenting style. *Journal of Family Psychology, 16,* 58–69.

Mounts, N. (2004). Adolescents' perceptions of parental management of peer relationships in an ethnically diverse sample. *Journal of Adolescent Research, 19,* 446–467.

Mounts, N. (2007). Adolescents' and their mothers' perceptions of parental management of peer relationships. *Journal of Research on Adolescence, 17,* 169–178.

Mounts, N. (2011). Parental management of peer relationships and early adolescents' social skills. *Journal of Youth and Adolescence, 40,* 416–427.

Mounts, N. S., Karre, J., & Kim, H. S. (2013). Mothers' attitudes about and goals for early adolescents' cross-ethnic peer relationships: A qualitative analysis. *Family Relations, 62,* 312–325.

Mounts, N., & Kim, H. S. (2009). Expectations for parental management of dating in an ethnically diverse sample of early adolescents. *Journal of Adolescent Research, 24,* 531–560.

Mounts, N., & Steinberg, L. (1995). An ecological analysis of peer influence on adolescent grade point average and drug use. *Developmental Psychology, 31,* 915–922.

Mouratidis, A., Vansteenkiste, M., Lens, W., Michou, A., & Soenens, B. (2013). Within-person configurations and temporal relations of personal and perceived parent-promoted aspirations to school correlates among adolescents. *Journal of Educational Psychology, 105,* 895–910.

Mouw, T., & Entwisle, B. (2006). Residential segregation and interracial friendship in schools. *American Journal of Sociology, 112,* 394–441.

Mrug, S., & Windle, M. (2009). Bidirectional influences of violence exposure and adjustment in early adolescence: Externalizing behaviors and school connectedness. *Journal of Abnormal Child Psychology, 37,* 611–623.

Mrug, S., Borch, C., & Cillessen, A. H. N. (2011). Other-sex friendships in late adolescence: Risky associations for substance use and sexual debut? *Journal of Youth and Adolescence, 40,* 875–888.

Mrug, S., Madan, A., & Windle, M. (2012). Temperament alters susceptibility to negative peer influence in early adolescence. *Journal of Abnormal Child Psychology, 40,* 201–209.

Muise, A. M., Stein, D. G., & Arbess, G. (2003). Eating disorders in adolescent boys: A review of the adolescent and young adult literature. *Journal of Adolescent Health, 33,* 427–435.

Mulgrew, K. E., Volcevski-Kostas, D., & Rendell, P. G. (2014). The effect of music video clips on adolescent boys' body image, mood, and schema activation. *Journal of Youth & Adolescence, 43,* 92–103.

Müller, C. M., Hofmann, V., Fleischli, J., & Studer, F. (2015). Effects of classroom composition on the development of antisocial behavior in lower secondary school. *Journal of Research on Adolescence, Early view.* DOI: 10.1111/jora.12195

Muller, P. A., Stage, F. K., & Kinzie, J. (2001). Science achievement growth trajectories: Understanding factors related to gender and racial-ethnic differences in precollege science achievement. *American Educational Research, 3,* 981–1012.

Mulvey, E., & Cauffman, E. (2001). The inherent limits of predicting school violence. *American Psychologist, 56,* 797–802.

Mulvey, E., Steinberg, L., Fagan, J., Cauffman, E., Piquero, A., Chassin, L., . . . Losoya, S. (2004). Theory and research on desistance from antisocial activity among serious adolescent offenders. *Youth Violence and Juvenile Justice, 2,* 213–236.

Mulvey, K. L., & Killen, M. (2015). Challenging gender stereotypes: Resistance and exclusion. *Child Development, 86,* 681–694.

Mun, E. Y., Windle, M., & Schainker, L. M. (2008). A model-based cluster analysis approach to adolescent problem behaviors and young adult outcomes. *Development and Psychopathology, 20,* 291–318.

Munakata, Y., Snyder, H. R., & Chatham, C. H. (2012). Developing cognitive control: Three key transitions. *Current Directions in Psychological Science 21,* 71–77.

Munsch, J., Liang, S., & DeSecottier, L. (1996, March). *Natural mentors: Who they are and the roles they fill. A gender and ethnic comparison.* Paper presented at the biennial meetings of the Society for Research on Adolescence, Boston.

Murayama, K., & Elliot, A. J. (2009). The joint influence of personal achievement goals and classroom goal structures on achievement-relevant outcomes. *Journal of Educational Psychology, 101,* 432–447.

Murayama, K., Pekrun, R., Lichtenfeld, S., & vom Hofe, R. (2013). Predicting long-term growth in students' mathematics achievement: The unique contributions of motivation and cognitive strategies. *Child Development, 84,* 1475–1490.

Murdock, K. K., Gorman, S., & Robbins, M. (2015). Co-rumination via cellphone moderates the association of perceived interpersonal stress and psychosocial well-being in emerging adults. *Journal of Adolescence, 38,* 27–37.

Murdock, T. (1994, February). *Who are you and how do you treat me? Student withdrawal as motivated alienation.* Paper presented at the biennial meetings of the Society for Research on Adolescence, San Diego.

Murdock, T., Anderman, L. H., & Hodge, S. A. (2000). Middle-grade predictors of students' motivation and behavior in high school. *Journal of Adolescent Research, 15,* 327–351.

Murray, C. (2009). Parent and teacher relationships as predictors of school engagement and functioning among low-income urban youth. *Journal of Early Adolescence, 29,* 376–404.

Murray, K. W., Haynie, D. L., Howard, D. E., Cheng, T. L., Simons-Morton, B. (2013). Adolescent reports of aggression as predictors of perceived parenting behaviors and expectations. *Family Relations 62,* 637–648.

Murray, K. W., Dwyer, K. M., Rubin, K. H., Knighton-Wisor, S., Booth-LaForce, C. (2014). Parent-child relationships, parental psychological control, and aggression: maternal and paternal relationships. *Journal of Youth & Adolescence, 43,* 1362–1373.

Musick, J. (1994). Grandmothers and grandmothers-to-be: Effects on adolescent mothers and adolescent mothering. *Infancy and Young Children, 6,* 1–9.

Musick, K., & Meier, A. (2012). Assessing causality and persistence in associations between family dinners and adolescent well-being. *Journal of Marriage and Family, 74,* 476–493.

Mustanski, B. S., Viken, R. J., Kaprio, J., Pulkkinen, L., & Rose, R. J. (2004). Genetic and environmental influences on pubertal development: Longitudinal data from Finnish twins at ages 11 and 14. *Developmental Psychology, 40,* 1188–1198.

Myers, J., Lindentthal, J., & Pepper, M. (1975). Life events, social integration, and psychiatric symptomatology. *Journal of Health and Social Behavior, 16,* 421–429.

Mylod, D., Whitman, T., & Borkowski, J. (1997). Predicting adolescent mothers' transition to adulthood. *Journal of Research on Adolescence, 7,* 457–478.

Nadeem, E., & Graham, S. (2005). Early puberty, peer victimization, and internalizing symptoms in ethnic minority adolescents. *Journal of Early Adolescence, 25,* 197–222.

Nader, P. R., Bradley, R. H., Houts, R. M., McRitchie, S. L., & O'Brien, M. (2008). Moderate-to-vigorous physical activity from ages 9 to 15 years. *Journal of the American Medical Association, 300,* 295–305.

Nagengast, B., & Marsh, H. W. (2012). Big fish in little ponds aspire more: Mediation and cross-cultural generalizability of school-average ability effects on self-concept and career aspirations in science. *Journal of Educational Psychology, 104,* 1033–1053.

Nagengast, B., Marsh, H. W., Chiorri, C., Hau, K.-T. (2014). Character building or subversive consequences of employment during high school: Causal effects based on propensity score models for categorical treatments. *Journal of Educational Psychology, 106,* 584–603.

Nagin, D., & Tremblay, R. (1999). Trajectories of boys' physical aggression, opposition, and hyperactivity on the path to physically violent and nonviolent juvenile delinquency. *Child Development, 70,* 1181–1196.

Nagin, D., Farrington, D., & Moffitt, T. (1995). Life-course trajectories of different types of offenders. *Criminology, 33,* 111–139.

Nagoshi, J. L., Marsiglia, F. F., Parsai, M., & Castro, F. G. (2011). The moderating effects of ethnic identification on the relationship between parental monitoring and substance use in Mexican heritage adolescents in the Southwest United States. *Journal of Community Psychology, 39,* 520–533.

Nagy, G., Watt, H. M. G., Eccles, J. S., Trautwein, U., Lüdtke, O., & Baumert, J. (2010). The development of students' mathematics self-concept in relation to gender: Different countries, different trajectories? *Journal of Research on Adolescence, 20,* 482–506.

Nagy, S., DiClimente, R., & Adcock, A. (1995). Adverse factors associated with forced sex among Southern adolescent girls. *Pediatrics, 96,* 944–946.

Nansel, T. R., Overpeck, M., Pilla, R. S., Ruan, W., Simons-Morton, B., & Scheidt, P. (2001). Bullying behaviors among U.S. youth. *Journal of the American Medical Association, 285,* 2094–2100.

Nasrallah, N. A., Clark, J. J., Collins, A. L., Akers, C. A., Phillips, P. E., & Bernstein, I. L. (2011). Risk preference following adolescent alcohol use is associated with corrupted encoding of costs but not rewards by mesolimbic dopamine. *Proceedings from the National Academy of Sciences, 108,* 5466–5471.

Nasrallah, N. A., Yang, T. W. H., & Bernstein, I. L. (2009). Long-term risk preference and suboptimal decision making following adolescent alcohol use. *Proceedings from the National Academy of Sciences, 106(41),* 17600–17604.

Nation, M., Crusto, C., Wandersman, A., Kumpfer, K. L., Seybolt, D., Morrissey-Kane, E., & Davino, K. (2003). What works in prevention: Principles of effective prevention programs. *American Psychologist, 58,* 449–456.

National Campaign to Prevent Teen and Unplanned Pregnancy. (2015). Fact sheet available at www.thenationalcampaign.org. Accessed on July 14, 2015.

National Center for Children in Poverty. (2010). *Basic facts about low-income children, 2009.* New York: Author.

National Center for Children in Poverty. (2015). *Basic facts about low-income children: Children 12 through 17 years, 2013.* Retrieved from http://www.nccp.org/publications/pub_1099 .html on June 9, 2015.

National Center for Education Statistics. (2006). *The nation's report card: Science 2005 Trial Urban District Assessment.* Washington: Author.

National Center for Education Statistics. (2011a). NAEP Assessment. Washington: Author.

National Center for Education Statistics. (2002). *Digest of education statistics, 2001.* Washington, DC: Author.

National Center for Education Statistics. (2005). *Youth indicators, 2005.* Washington, DC: Author.

National Center for Education Statistics. (2009). *The condition of education 2009.* Washington: Author.

National Center for Education Statistics. (2011b). *The condition of education 2011.* Washington: Author.

National Center for Education Statistics. (2012). *The condition of education 2012.* Washington: Author.

National Center for Education Statistics. (2013). *Digest of education statistics.* Washington: Author.

National Center for Education Statistics. (2014). *Condition of education.* Washington: Author.

National Center for Education Statistics. (2015). *Condition of education*. Washington: Author.

National Center for Education Statistics. (2015). *EDfacts*. Washington: Author.

National Center for Education Statistics. (2015). *The condition of education, 2014*. Washington: Author.

National Center for Education Statistics. (2015). *The nation's report card, 2013*. Washington: Author.

National Center for Health Statistics. (2008). *Leading causes of death, 2005*. Retrieved from http://www.cdc.gov/nchs/data/dvs/LCWK4_2005.pdf

National Coalition for the Homeless. (2007). *NCH fact sheet #13*. Washington: Author.

National Heart, Lung, and Blood Institute Growth and Health Study Research Group. (1992). Obesity and cardiovascular disease risk factors in Black and White girls: The NHLBI Growth and Health Study. *American Journal of Public Health, 82*, 1613–1620.

National Research Council and Institute of Medicine. (2009). *Adolescent health services: Missing opportunities*. Washington: The National Academies Press.

National Research Council. (1998). *Protecting youth at work*. Washington, DC: National Academy Press.

National Research Council. (2004). *Reducing underage drinking: A collective responsibility*. Washington, DC: National Academies Press.

National Research Council. (2005). *Growing up global*. Washington, DC: National Academies Press.

Natsuaki, M. N., Biehl, M. C., & Ge, X. (2009). Trajectories of depressed mood from early adolescence to young adulthood: The effects of pubertal timing and adolescent dating. *Journal of Research on Adolescence, 19*, 47–74.

Neal, J. (2010). Social aggression and social position in middle childhood and early adolescence: Burning bridges or building them? *Journal of Early Adolescence, 30*, 122–137.

Neblett, E., Jr., Gaskin, A., Lee, D., & Carter, S. (2011). Discrimination, racial and ethnic. In B. Brown & M. Prinstein (Eds.), *Encyclopedia of adolescence* (Vol. 2, pp. 53–58). New York: Academic Press.

Neblett, E., Jr., Smalls, C., Ford, K., Nguyên, H., & Sellers, R. (2009). Racial socialization and racial identity: African American parents' messages about race as precursors to identity. *Journal of Youth and Adolescence, 38*, 189–203.

Neblett, E., Jr., White, R., Ford, K., Philip, C., Nguyên, H., & Sellers, R. M. (2008). Patterns of racial socialization and psychological adjustment: Can parental communications about race reduce the impact of racial discrimination? *Journal of Research on Adolescence, 18*, 477–515.

Neckerman, H., Cairns, B., & Cairns, R. (1993, March). *Peers and families: Developmental changes, constraints, and continuities*. Paper presented at the biennial meetings of the Society for Research on Child Development, New Orleans.

Needham, B. L. (2012). Sexual attraction and trajectories of mental health and substance use during the transition from adolescence to adulthood. *Journal of Youth and Adolescence, 41*, 179–190.

Neemann, J., Hubbard, J., & Masten, A. (1995). The changing importance of romantic relationship involvement to competence from late childhood to late adolescence. *Development and Psychopathology, 7*, 727–750.

Negriff, S., & Susman, E. J. (2011). Pubertal timing, depression, and externalizing problems: A framework, review, and examination of gender differences. *Journal of Research on Adolescence, 21*, 717–746.

Negriff, S., Blankson, A. N., & Trickett, P. K. (2015). Pubertal timing and tempo: Associations with childhood maltreatment. *Journal of Research on Adolescence, 25*, 201–213.

Negriff, S., Ji, J., & Trickett, P. (2011b). Exposure to peer delinquency as a mediator between self-report pubertal timing and delinquency: A longitudinal study of mediation. *Development and Psychopathology, 23*, 293–304.

Negriff, S., Susman, E. J., & Trickett, P. K. (2011b). The developmental pathway from pubertal timing to delinquency and sexual activity from early to late adolescence. *Journal of Youth and Adolescence, 40*, 1343–1356.

Neiderhiser, J. M., Reiss, D., Pedersen, N. L., Lictenstein, P., Spotts, E. L., Hansson, K., . . . Ellhammer, O. (2004). Genetic and environmental influences on mothering of adolescents: A comparison of two samples. *Developmental Psychology, 40*, 335–351.

Nelson, C., Bloom, F., Cameron, J., Amaral, D., Dahl, R., & Pine, D. (2002). An integrative, multidisciplinary approach to the study of brain–behavior relations in the context of typical and atypical development. *Development and Psychopathology, 14*, 499–520.

Nelson, E. E., Lau, J. Y. F., & Jarcho, J. M. (2014). Growing pains and pleasures: How emotional learning guides development. *Trends in Cognitive Sciences, 18*, 99–108.

Nelson, E., Leibenluft, E., McClure, E., & Pine, D. (2005). The social re-orientation of adolescence: A neuroscience perspective on the process and its relation to psychopathology. *Psychological Medicine, 35*, 163–174.

Nelson, E., McClure, E., Parrish, J., Leibenluft, E., Ernst, M., Fox, N., . . . Pine, D. (2007). *Brain systems underlying peer social acceptance in adolescents*. Unpublished paper, Development and Anxiety Neuroscience Section, Mood and Activity Disorders Program, National Institute of Mental Health, Washington, DC.

Nelson, I. A., & Gastic, B. (2009). Street ball, swim team and the sour cream machine: A cluster analysis of out of school time participation portfolios. *Journal of Youth and Adolescence, 38*, 1172–1186.

Nelson, L. J., & Barry, C. M. (2005). Distinguishing features of emerging adulthood. *Journal of Adolescent Research, 20*, 242–262.

Nelson, L. J., Badger, S., & Bo, W. (2004). The influence of culture in emerging adulthood: Perspectives of Chinese college students. *International Journal of Behavioral Development, 28*, 26–36.

Nelson, S. E., Van Ryzin, M. J., & Dishion, T. J. (2015). Alcohol, marijuana, and tobacco use trajectories from age 12 to 24 years: Demographic correlates and young adult substance use problems. *Development and Psychopathology, 27*, 253–277.

Neppl, T. K., Jeon, S., Schofield, T. J., & Donnellan, M. B. (2015). The impact of economic pressure on parent positivity, parenting, and adolescent positivity into emerging adulthood. *Family Relations, 64*, 80–92.

Nesbit, K. C., Kolobe, T. H., Sisson, S. B., & Ghement, I. R. (2014). A model of environmental correlates of adolescent obesity in the United States. *Journal of Adolescent Health, 55*, 394–401.

Neuenschwander, M., & Kracke, B. (2011). Career development. In B. Brown & M. Prinstein (Eds.), *Encyclopedia of adolescence* (Vol. 1, pp. 97–105). New York: Academic Press.

Neumark-Sztainer, D., Bauer, K., Friend, S., Hannan, P. J., Story, M., & Berge, J. (2010). Family weight talk and dieting: How much do they matter for body dissatisfaction and disordered eating behaviors in adolescent girls? *Journal of Adolescent Health, 47*, 270–276.

Neumark-Sztainer, D., Paxton, S. J., Hannan, P. J., Haines, J., & Story, M. (2006). Does body satisfaction matter? Five-year longitudinal associations between body satisfaction and health behaviors in adolescent females and males. *Journal of Adolescent Health, 39*, 244–251.

Neumark-Sztainer, D., Story, M., Dixon, L., & Murray, D. (1998). Adolescents engaging in unhealthy weight control behaviors: Are they at risk for other health-compromising behaviors? *American Journal of Public Health, 88*, 952–955.

Neumark-Sztainer, D., Wall, M., Story, M., & Standish, A. R. (2012). Dieting and unhealthy weight control behaviors during adolescence: Associations with 10-year changes in body mass index. *Journal of Adolescent Health, 50*, 80–86.

Newcomb, M., & Bentler, P. (1988). Impact of adolescent drug use and social support on problems of young adults: A longitudinal study. *Journal of Abnormal Psychology, 97*, 64–75.

Newman, B., & Newman, P. (2001a). Group identity and alienation: Giving the we its due. *Journal of Youth and Adolescence, 30*, 515–538.

Newman, B., & Newman, P. (2011b). Adolescence, theories of. In B. Brown & M. Prinstein (Eds.), *Encyclopedia of adolescence* (Vol. 1, pp. 20–29). New York: Academic Press.

Newman, D. L. (2005). Ego development and ethnic identity formation in rural American

Indian adolescents. *Child Development, 76,* 734–746.

Newman, K. (1999). *No shame in my game.* New York: Knopf.

Newman, R., & Schwager, M. (1995). Students' help seeking during problem solving: Effects of grade, goal, and prior achievement. *American Educational Research Journal, 32,* 352–376.

Newmann, F. (1992). Higher order thinking and prospects for classroom thoughtfulness. In F. Newmann (Ed.), *Student engagement and achievement in American high schools.* New York: Teachers College Press.

Newmann, F., Marks, H., & Gamoran, A. (1996). Authentic pedagogy and student performance. *American Journal of Education, 104,* 280–312.

Newsome, J., & Sullivan, C. J. (2014). Resilience and vulnerability in adolescents: genetic influences on differential response to risk for delinquency. *Journal of Youth & Adolescence, 43,* 1080–1095.

Nguyen, J., & Brown, B. (2010). Making meanings, meaning identity: Hmong adolescent perceptions and use of language and style as identity symbols. *Journal of Research on Adolescence, 20,* 849–868.

Nichols, S., & Good, T. (1998). Students' perceptions of fairness in school settings: A gender analysis. *Teachers College Record, 100,* 369–401.

Nicolai, K. A., Laney, T., & Mezulis, A. H. (2013). Different stressors, different strategies, different outcomes: how domain-specific stress responses differentially predict depressive symptoms among adolescents. *Journal of Youth & Adolescence, 42,* 1183–1193.

Nieto, M., Lambert, S., Briggs, E., McCoy, J., Brunson, L., & Aber, M. (1996, March). *Untangling the relationship between ethnic composition of neighborhood and school adjustment.* Paper presented at the biennial meetings of the Society for Research on Adolescence, Boston.

Nishina, A. (2012). Microcontextual characteristics of peer victimization experiences and adolescents' daily well-being. *Journal of Youth and Adolescence, 41,* 191–201.

Nishina, A., & Juvonen, J. (2005). Daily reports of witnessing and experiencing peer harassment in middle school. *Child Development, 76,* 435–450.

Nishina, A., Ammon, N. Y., Bellmore, A. D., & Graham, S. (2006). Body dissatisfaction and physical development among ethnic minority adolescents. *Journal of Youth and Adolescence, 35,* 189–201.

Nishina, A., Bellmore, A., Witkow, M. R., & Nylund-Gibson, K. (2010). Longitudinal consistency of adolescent ethnic identification across varying school ethnic contexts. *Developmental Psychology, 46,* 1389–1401.

Niwa, E. Y., Way, N., & Hughes, D. L. (2014). Trajectories of ethnic-racial discrimination among ethnically diverse early adolescents: Associations with psychological and social adjustment. *Child Development, 85,* 2339–2354.

Noack, P., Kracke, B., & Hofer, M. (1994, February). *The family context of rightist attitudes among adolescents in East and West Germany.* Paper presented at the biennial meetings of the Society for Research on Adolescence, San Diego.

Noakes, M. A., & Rinaldi, C. M. (2006). Age and gender differences in peer conflict. *Journal of Youth and Adolescence, 35,* 881–891.

Noble, K. G., Korgaonkar, M. S., Grieve, S. M., & Brickman, A. M. (2013). Higher education is an age-independent predictor of white matter integrity and cognitive control in late adolescence. *Developmental Science, 16,* 653–664.

Nock, M. K., Green, J. G., Hwang, I., McLaughlin, K. A., Sampson, N. A., Zaslavsky, A. M., & Kessler, R. C. (2013). Prevalence, correlates, and treatment of lifetime suicidal behavior among adolescents: Results from the national comorbidity survey replication adolescent supplement. *JAMA Psychiatry, 70,* 300–310.

Nock, M. K., Prinstein, M. J., & Sterba, S. K. (2009). Revealing the form and function of self-injurious thoughts and behaviors: A real-time ecological assessment study among adolescents and young adults. *Journal of Abnormal Psychology, 118,* 816–827.

Nock, S. (1998). The consequences of premarital fatherhood. *American Sociological Review, 63,* 250–263.

Nofziger, S., & Lee, H. (2006). Differential associations and daily smoking of adolescents: The importance of same-sex models. *Youth and Society, 37,* 453–478.

Noguera, P. (1995). Preventing and producing violence: A critical analysis of responses to school violence. *Harvard Educational Review, 65,* 189–212.

Nolen-Hoeksema, S., & Girgus, J. (1994). The emergence of gender differences in depression during adolescence. *Psychological Bulletin, 115,* 424–443.

Nolle, K., Guerino, P., & Dinkes, R. (2007). *Crime, violence, discipline, and safety in U.S. public schools: Findings from the School Survey on Crime and Safety: 2005–06.* National Center for Education Statistics, Institute of Education Sciences, U.S. Department of Education. Washington, DC.

Noller, P., & Callan, V. (1990). Adolescents' perceptions of the nature of their communication with parents. *Journal of Youth and Adolescence, 19,* 349–362.

Norona, J. C., Salvatore, J. F., Welsh, D. P., & Darling, N. (2014). Rejection sensitivity and adolescents' perceptions of romantic interactions. *Journal of Adolescence, 37,* 1257–1267.

Nosko, A., Tieu, T.-T., Lawford, H., & Pratt, M. W. (2011). How do I love thee? Let me count the ways: Parenting during adolescence, attachment styles, and romantic narratives in emerging adulthood. *Developmental Psychology, 47,* 645–657.

Novaira, H., Yates, M., Diaczok, D., Kim, H., Wolfe, A., & Radovick, S. (2011). The gonadotropin-releasing hormone cell-specific element is required for normal puberty and estrous cyclicity. *Journal of Neuroscience, 31,* 3336–3343.

Novak, S. P., Reardon, S. F., Raudenbush, S. W., & Buka, S. L. (2006). Retail tobacco outlet density and youth cigarette smoking: A propensity-modeling approach. *American Journal of Public Health, 96,* 670–676.

Ntoumanis, N., Taylor, I. M., & Thøgersen-Ntoumanis, C. (2012). A longitudinal examination of coach and peer motivational climates in youth sport: Implications for moral attitudes, well-being, and behavioral investment. *Developmental Psychology, 48,* 213–223.

Nucci, L., Smetana, J., Araki, N., Nakaue, M., & Comer, J. (2014). Japanese adolescents' disclosure and information management with parents. *Child Development, 85,* 901–907.

Nuñez, A. (2009). Latino students' transitions to college: A social and intercultural capital perspective. *Harvard Educational Review, 79,* 22–49.

Nurmi, J. (1993). Adolescent development in an age-graded context: The role of personal beliefs, goals, and strategies in the tackling of developmental tasks and standards. *International Journal of Behavioural Development, 16,* 169–189.

Nurmi, J. (2004). Socialization and self-development: Channeling, selection, adjustment, and reflection. In R. Lerner & L. Steinberg (Eds.), *Handbook of adolescent psychology.* New York: Wiley.

Nurmi, J., Onatsu, T., & Haavisto, T. (1995). Underachievers' cognitive and behavioral strategies: Self-handicapping at school. *Contemporary Educational Psychology, 20,* 188–200.

Nylund, K., Bellmore, A., Nishina, A., & Graham, S. (2007). Subtypes, severity, and structural stability of peer victimization: What does latent class analysis say? *Child Development, 78,* 1706–1722.

O'Brien, L., Albert, D., Chein, J., & Steinberg, L. (2011). Adolescents prefer more immediate rewards when in the presence of their peers. *Journal of Research on Adolescence, 21,* 747–753.

O'Callaghan, M., Borkowski, J., Whitman, T., Maxwell, S., & Keogh, D. (1999). A model of adolescent parenting: The role of cognitive readiness to parent. *Journal of Research on Adolescence, 9,* 203–225.

O'Connor, T., Caspi, A., DeFries, J., & Plomin, R. (2000). Are associations between parental divorce and children's adjustment genetically mediated? An adoption study. *Developmental Psychology, 36,* 429–437.

O'Connor, T., Deater-Deckard, K., Fulker, D., Rutter, M., & Plomin, R. (1998). Genotype-environment correlations in late childhood and early adolescence: Antisocial behavioral problems and coercive parenting. *Developmental Psychology, 34,* 970–981.

O'Donnell, D., Schwab-Stone, M., & Ruchkin, V. (2006). The mediating role of alienation in the development of maladjustment in youth exposed to community violence. *Development and Psychopathology, 18,* 215–232.

O'Donnell, L., Stueve, A., Myint-U. A., Duran, R., Agronick, G., & Wilson-Simmons, R. (2006). Middle school aggression and subsequent intimate partner physical violence. *Journal of Youth and Adolescence, 35,* 693–703.

O'Hara, R. E., Gibbons, F. X., Gerrard, M., Li, Z., & Sarent, J. D. (2012). Greater exposure to sexual content in popular movies predicts earlier sexual debut and increased sexual risk taking. *Psychological Science, 23,* 984–993.

O'Hare, E. D., Lu, L. H., Houston, S. M., Bookheimer, S. Y., & Sowell, E. R. (2008). Neurodevelopmental changes in verbal working memory load-dependency: An fMRI investigation. *Neuroimage, 42,* 1678–1685.

O'Keefe, G., Clarke-Pearson, K., & Council on Communications and Media. (2011). The impact of social media on children, adolescents, and families. *Pediatrics, 127,* 800–804.

O'Leary, K. D., Slep, A. M. S., Avery-Leaf, S., & Cascardi, M. (2008). Gender differences in dating aggression among multiethnic high school students. *Journal of Adolescent Health, 42,* 473–479.

O'Loughlin, J., Karp, I., Koulis, T., Paradis, G., & DiFranza, J. (2009). Determinants of first puff and daily cigarette smoking in adolescents. *American Journal of Epidemiology, 170,* 585–597.

O'Malley, P., & Johnston, L. (1999). Drinking and driving among U.S. high school seniors, 1984–1997. *American Journal of Public Health, 89,* 678–684.

O'Sullivan, L. F., Cheng, M. M., Harris, K. M., & Brooks-Gunn, J. (2007). I wanna hold your hand: The progression of social, romantic, and sexual events in adolescent relationships. *Perspectives on Sexual and Reproductive Health, 39,* 100–107.

Oakes, J. (1995). Two cities' tracking and within-school segregation. *Teachers College Record, 96,* 681–690.

Oakes, J. (2005) *Keeping track: How schools structure inequality.* New Haven: Yale University Press.

Oakley, D., & Bogue, E. (1995). Quality of condom use as reported by female clients of a family planning clinic. *American Journal of Public Health, 85,* 1526–1530.

Obeidallah, D., Brennan, R. T., Brooks-Gunn, J., & Earls, F. (2004). Links between pubertal timing and neighborhood contexts: Implications for girls' violent behavior. *Journal of the American Academy of Child and Adolescent Psychiatry, 43,* 1460–1468.

Obsuth, I., Hennighausen, K., Brumariu, L. E., & Lyons-Ruth, K. (2014). Disorganized behavior in adolescent–parent interaction: Relations to attachment state of mind, partner abuse, and psychopathology. *Child Development, 85,* 370–387.

Odgers, C. L., Caspi, A., Russell, M. A., Sampson, R. J., Arseneault, L., & Moffitt, T. E. (2012). Supportive parenting mediates neighborhood socioeconomic disparities in children's antisocial behavior from ages 5 to 12. *Development and Psychopathology, 24,* 705–721.

OECD. (2014a). *PISA 2012 results in focus: What students know and can do.* Paris: Author.

OECD. (2014b). *Education at a glance.* Paris: Author.

Oelsner, J., Lippold, M., & Greenberg, M. (2011). Factors influencing the development of school bonding among middle school students. *Journal of Early Adolescence, 31,* 463–487.

Oesterle, S., David Hawkins, J., Hill, K. G., & Bailey, J. A. (2010). Men's and women's pathways to adulthood and their adolescent precursors. *Journal of Marriage and Family, 72,* 1436–1453.

Oettinger, G. (1999). Does high school employment affect high school academic performance? *Industrial and Labor Relations Review, 53,* 136–151.

Offer, S. (2013). Family time activities and adolescents' emotional well-being. *Journal of Marriage and Family, 75,* 26–41.

Office of Adolescent Health. (2015). Trends in teen pregnancy and child bearing. Available at http://www.hhs.gov/ash/oah/adolescent-health-topics/reproductive-health/teen-pregnancy/trends.html. Accessed on July 14, 2015.

Office of Juvenile Justice and Delinquency Prevention. (2011, December). *Juvenile arrests, 2009.* Washington: Author.

Ogden, C., Carroll, M. D., & Flegal, K. M. (2008). High body mass index for age among US children and adolescents, 2003–2006. *JAMA: Journal of the American Medical Association, 299,* 2401–2405.

Ogden, C., Carroll, M., Curtin, L., Lamb, M., & Flegal, K. (2010). Prevalence of high body mass index in US children and adolescents, 2007–2008. *JAMA, 303,* 242–249.

Ogle, J. P., & Damhorst, M. L. (2003). Mothers' and daughters' interpersonal approaches to body and dieting. *Journal of Family Influence, 24,* 448–487.

Ogletree, M. D., Jones, R. M., & Coyl, D. D. (2002). Fathers and their adolescent sons: Pubertal development and paternal involvement. *Journal of Adolescent Research, 17,* 418–424.

Ohannessian, C., Lerner, R., Lerner, J., & von Eye, A. (1994). A longitudinal study of perceived family adjustment and emotional adjustment in early adolescence. *Journal of Early Adolescence, 14,* 371–390.

Ohida, T., Osaki, Y., Doi, Y., Tanihata, T., Minowa, M., Suzuki, K., . . . Kaneita, Y. (2004). An epidemiologic study of self-reported sleep problems among Japanese adolescents. *Sleep, 27,* 978–985.

Ojanen, T., & Perry, D. G. (2007). Relational schemas and the developing self: Perceptions of mother and of self as joint predictors of early adolescents' self-esteem. *Developmental Psychology, 43,* 1474–1483.

Olatunji, A. N. (2005). Dropping out of high school among Mexican-origin youths: Is early work experience a factor? *Harvard Educational Review, 75,* 286–305.

Olds, T., Ferrar, K., Schranz, N., & Maher, C. A. (2011). Obese adolescents are less active than their normal-weight peers, but wherein lies the difference? *Journal of Adolescent Health, 48,* 189–195.

Olfson M., Druss, B., & Marcus, S. (2015). Trends in mental health care among children and adolescents. *New England Journal of Medicine, 372,* 2029–2038.

Olfson, M., Blanco, C., Wang, S., Laje, G., & Correll, C. U. (2014). National trends in the mental health care of children, adolescents, and adults by office-based physicians. *JAMA Psychiatry, 71,* 81–90.

Olfson, M., Druss, B. G., Marcus, S. C. (2015). Trends in mental health care among children and adolescents. *New England Journal of Medicine, 372,* 2029–2038.

Olsen, E. O., Shults, R. A., & Eaton, D. K. (2013). Texting while driving and other risky motor vehicle behaviors among US high school students. *Pediatrics, 131,* e1708–e1715.

Olvera, N., McCarley, K., Rodriguez, A. X., Noor, N., & Hernández-Valero, M. A. (2014). Body image disturbances and predictors of body dissatisfaction among Hispanic and white preadolescents. *Journal of Research of Adolescence, Early view.* DOI: 10.1111/jora.12165

Olweus, D. (1993). Victimization by peers: Antecedents and long-term outcomes. In K. Rubin & J. Asendorf (Eds.), *Social withdrawal, inhibition, and shyness in childhood.* Hillsdale, NJ: Erlbaum.

Op de Macks, Z., Moor, B., Overgaauw, S., Guroglu, B., Dahl, R. E., & Crone, E. A. (2011). Testosterone levels correspond with increased ventral striatum activation in response to monetary rewards in adolescents. *Developmental Cognitive Neuroscience, 1,* 506–516.

Oppedal, B., Røysamb, E., & Sam, D. L. (2004). The effect of acculturation and social support on change in mental health among young immigrants. *International Journal of Behavioral Development, 28,* 481–494.

Oransky, M., & Marecek, J. (2009). "I'm not going to be a girl": Masculinity and emotions in boys' friendships and peer groups. *Journal of Adolescent Research, 24,* 218–241.

Ordaz, S. J., Foran, W., Velanova, K., & Luna, B. (2013). Longitudinal growth curves of brain function underlying inhibitory control through adolescence. *Journal of Neuroscience, 33,* 18109–18124.

Organization for Economic Cooperation and Development (OECD). (2010). *PISA 2009 results.* Paris: Author.

Orlando, M., Tucker, J. S., Ellickson, P., & Klein, D. (2004). Developmental trajectories of cigarette smoking and their correlates from early adolescence to young adulthood. *Journal of Consulting and Clinical Psychology, 72,* 400–410.

Orpinas, P., Horne, A. M., Song, X., Reeves, P. M., & Hsieh, H. L. (2013). Dating trajectories from middle to high school: Association with academic performance and drug use. *Journal of Research on Adolescence, 23,* 772–784.

Orr, D., & Langefeld, C. (1993). Factors associated with condom use by sexually active male adolescents at risk for sexually transmitted disease. *Pediatrics, 91,* 873–879.

Ortega, F. B., Konstabel, K., Pasquali, E., Ruiz, J. R., Hurtig-Wennlöf, A., Mäestu, J. . . & Sjöström, M. (2013). Objectively measured physical activity and sedentary time during childhood, adolescence and young adulthood: A cohort study. *PLoS One, 8,* 60871.

Orth, U., & Robins, R. W. (2013). Understanding the link between low self-esteem and depression. *Current Directions in Psychological Science, 22,* 455–460.

Orth, U., & Robins, R. W. (2014). The development of self-esteem. *Current Directions in Psychological Science, 23,* 381–387.

Orth, U., Maes, J., & Schmitt, M. (2015). Self-esteem development across the life span: A longitudinal study with a large sample from Germany. *Developmental Psychology, 51,* 248–259.

Orth, U., Robins, R. W., Widaman, K. F., & Conger, R. D. (2014). Is low self-esteem a risk factor for depression? Findings from a longitudinal study of Mexican-origin youth. *Developmental Psychology, 50,* 622–633.

Ortiz, J., & Raine, A. (2004). Heart rate level and antisocial behavior in children and adolescents. *Journal of the American Academy of Child and Adolescent Psychiatry, 43,* 154–162.

Osgerby, B. (2008). Understanding the "Jackpot Market": Media, marketing, and the rise of the American teenager. In P. Jamieson & D. Romer (Eds.), *The changing portrayal of adolescents in the media since 1950* (pp. 27–58). New York: Oxford University Press.

Osgood, D. W., & Anderson, A. (2004). Unstructured socializing and rates of delinquency. *Criminology, 42,* 519–549.

Osgood, D. W., Anderson, A., & Shaffer, J. (2005). Unstructured leisure in the after-school hours. In J. Mahoney, R. Larson, & J. Eccles (Eds.), *Organized activities as contexts of development* (pp. 45–64). Hillsdale, NJ: Erlbaum.

Osgood, D. W., Ragan, D. T., Wallace, L., Gest, S. D., Feinberg, M. E., & Moody, J. (2013). Peers and the emergence of alcohol use: Influence and selection processes in adolescent friendship networks. *Journal of Research on Adolescence, 23,* 500–512.

Osgood, D. W., Ruth, G., Eccles, J., Jacobs, J., & Barber, B. (2005). Six paths to adulthood. In R. Settersten, R., Furstenberg, F., Jr., & R.

Rumbaut (Eds.), *On the frontier of adulthood* (pp. 340–355). Chicago: University of Chicago Press.

Osgood, D. W., Wilson, J., O'Malley, P., Bachman, J., & Johnston, L. (1996). Routine activities and individual deviant behavior. *American Sociological Review, 61,* 635–655.

Ostaszewski, K., & Zimmerman, M. A. (2006). The effects of cumulative risks and promotive factors on urban adolescent alcohol and other drug use: A longitudinal study of resiliency. *American Journal of Community Psychology, 38,* 237–249.

Oswald, H., Bahne, J., & Feder, M. (1994, February). *Love and sexuality in adolescence: Gender-specific differences in East and West Berlin.* Paper presented at the biennial meetings of the Society for Research on Adolescence, San Diego.

Osypuk, T. L., Tchetgen, E. J., Acevedo-Garcia, D., Earls, F. J., Lincoln, A., Schmidt, N. M., & Glymour, M. (2012). Differential mental health effects of neighborhood relocation among youth in vulnerable families: Results from a randomized trial. *Archives of General Psychiatry, 69,* 1284–1294.

Ott, M. A., Millstein, S. G., Ofner, S., & Halpern-Felsher, B. L. (2006). Greater expectations: Adolescents' positive motivations for sex. *Perspectives on Sexual and Reproductive Health, 38,* 84–89.

Ott, M. Q., Corliss, H. L., Wypij, D., Rosario, M., & Austin, S. B. (2011). Stability and change in self-reported sexual orientation identity in young people: Application of mobility metrics. *Archives of Sexual Behavior, 40,* 519–532.

Otterblad Olausson, P., Haglund, B., Ringback Weitoft, G., & Cnattingius, S. (2001). Teenage childbearing and long-term socioeconomic consequences: A case study in Sweden. *Family Planning Perspectives, 33,* 70–74.

Oudekerk, B. A., Allen, J. P., Hessel, E. T., & Molloy, L. E. (2015). The cascading development of autonomy and relatedness from adolescence to adulthood. *Child Development, 86,* 472–485.

Overbaugh, K., & Allen, J. (1994). The adolescent athlete, II: Injury patterns and prevention. *Journal of Pediatric Health Care, 8,* 203–211.

Overbeek, G., Stattin, H., Vermulst, A., Ha, T., & Engels, R. (2007). Parent–child relationships, partner relationships, and emotional adjustment: A birth-to-maturity prospective study. *Developmental Psychology, 43,* 429–437.

Overton, W. (1990). Competence and procedures: Constraints on the development of logical reasoning. In W. Overton (Ed.), *Reasoning, necessity, and logic: Developmental perspectives* (pp. 1–32). Hillsdale, NJ: Erlbaum.

Owen, J. (1995). *Why our kids don't study.* Baltimore: Johns Hopkins University Press.

Owen-Kostelnik, J., Reppucci, N. D., & Meyer, J. R. (2006). Testimony and interrogation of minors: Assumptions about maturity and morality. *American Psychologist, 61,* 286–304.

Owens, A. (2010). Neighborhoods and schools as competing and reinforcing contexts for educational attainment. *Sociology of Education, 83,* 287–311.

Owens, J., & Adolescent Sleep Working Group, Committee on Adolescence. (2014b). Insufficient sleep in adolescents and young adults: An update on causes and consequences. *Pediatrics, 134,* e921–e932.

Owens, T., Mortimer, J., & Finch, M. (1996). Self-determination as a source of self-esteem in adolescence. *Social Forces, 74,* 1377–1404.

Oxford, M. L., Gilchrist, L. D., Gillmore, M. R., & Lohr, M. J. (2006). Predicting variation in the life course of adolescent mothers as they enter adulthood. *Journal of Adolescent Health, 39,* 20–26.

Oxford, M. L., Gilchrist, L. D., Lohr, M. J., Gillmore, M. R., Morrison, D. M., & Spieker, S. J. (2005). Life course heterogeneity in the transition from adolescence to adulthood among adolescent mothers. *Journal of Research on Adolescence, 15,* 479–504.

Oyserman, D., & Markus, H. (1990). Possible selves and delinquency. *Journal of Personality and Social Psychology, 59,* 112–125.

Oyserman, D., Bybee, D., & Terry, K. (2006). Possible selves and academic outcomes: How and when possible selves impel action. *Journal of Personality and Social Psychology, 91,* 188–204.

Oyserman, D., Radin, N., & Benn, R. (1993). Dynamics in a three-generational family: Teens, grandparents, and babies. *Developmental Psychology, 29,* 564–572.

Ozer, E., & Irwin, C. (2009). Adolescent and young adult health: From basic health status to clinical interventions. In R. Lerner & L. Steinberg (Eds.), *Handbook of adolescent psychology* (3rd ed., Vol. 1, pp. 618–641). New York: Wiley.

Pabon, E., Rodriguez, O., & Gurin, G. (1992). Clarifying peer relations and delinquency. *Youth and Society, 24,* 149–165.

Paciello, M., Fida, R., Tramontano, C., Lupinetti, C., & Caprara, G. V. (2008). Stability and change of moral disengagement and its impact on aggression and violence in late adolescence. *Child Development, 79,* 1288–1309.

Packaged Facts. (2007). *The teens market in the U.S.* New York: Market Research Group.

Padilla, A. M., & Gonzalez, R. (2001). Academic performance of immigrant and U.S.-born Mexican heritage students: Effects of schooling in Mexico and bilingual/English language instruction. *American Educational Research Journal, 38,* 727–742.

Padilla-Walker, L. (2008). Domain-appropriateness of maternal discipline as a predictor of adolescents' positive and negative outcomes. *Journal of Family Psychology, 22,* 456–464.

Padilla-Walker, L. M., & Christensen, K. J. (2011). Empathy and self-regulation as mediators between parenting and adolescents' prosocial behaviors toward strangers, friends, and family. *Journal of Research on Adolescence, 21,* 545–551.

Padilla-Walker, L. M., Carlo, G., Christensen, K. J., & Yorgason, J. B. (2012). Bidirectional relations between authoritative parenting and adolescents' prosocial behaviors. *Journal of Research on Adolescence, 22,* 400–408.

Padilla-Walker, L. M., Day, R. D., Dyer, W. J., & Black, B. C. (2013). "Keep on keeping on, even when it's hard!": Predictors and outcomes of adolescent persistence. *The Journal of Early Adolescence, 33,* 433–457.

Padilla-Walker, L. M., Dyer, W. J., Yorgason, J. B., Fraser, A. M., Coyne, S. M. (2013). Adolescents' prosocial behavior toward family, friends, and strangers: A person-centered approach. *Journal of Research on Adolescence, 25,* 135–150.

Padilla-Walker, L. M., Fraser, A. M., & Harper, J. M. (2012). Walking the walk: The moderating role of proactive parenting on adolescents' value-congruent behaviors. *Journal of Adolescence, 35,* 1141–1152.

Padmanabhan, A., Geier, C., Ordaz, S., Teslovich, T., & Luna, B. (2011). Developmental changes in brain function underlying the influence of reward processing on inhibitory control. *Developmental Cognitive Neuroscience, 1,* 517–529.

Pahl, K., & Way, N. (2006). Longitudinal trajectories of ethnic identity among urban Black and Latino adolescents. *Child Development, 77,* 1403–1415.

Paikoff, R., & Brooks-Gunn, J. (1991). Do parent–child relationships change during puberty? *Psychological Bulletin, 110,* 47–66.

Paikoff, R., Parfenoff, S., Williams, S., McCormick, A., Greenwood, G., & Holmbeck, G. (1997). Parenting, parent–child relationships, and sexual possibility situations among urban African American preadolescents: Preliminary findings and implications for HIV prevention. *Journal of Family Psychology, 11,* 11–22.

Pajer, K., Chung, J., Leininger, L., Wang, W., Gardner, W., & Yeates, K. (2008). Neuropsychological function in adolescent girls with conduct disorder. *Journal of the American Academy of Child & Adolescent Psychiatry, 47,* 416–425.

Paley, B., Conger, R., & Harold, G. (2000). Parents' affect, adolescent cognitive representations, and adolescent social development. *Journal of Marriage and the Family, 62,* 761–776.

Palladino, G. (1996). *Teenagers: An American history.* New York: Basic Books.

Pallock, L., & Lamborn, S. (2006). Beyond parenting practices: Extended kinship support and the academic adjustment of African-American and European-American teens. *Journal of Adolescence, 29,* 813–828.

Pampel, F. C., & Aguilar, J. (2008). Changes in youth smoking, 1976–2002: A time-series analysis. *Youth and Society, 39,* 453–479.

Panchaud, C., Singh, S., Feivelson, D., & Darroch, J. E. (2000). Sexually transmitted diseases among adolescents in developed countries. *Family Planning Perspectives, 32,* 24–32, 45.

Papadakis, A. A., Prince, R. P., Jones, N. P., & Strauman, T. J. (2006). Self-regulation, rumination, and vulnerability to depression in adolescent girls. *Development and Psychopathology, 18,* 815–829.

Pardini, D. A., Loeber, R., & Stouthamer-Loeber, M. (2005). Developmental shifts in parent and peer influences on boys' beliefs about delinquent behavior. *Journal of Research on Adolescence, 15,* 299–323.

Park, A., Sher, K. J., Todorov, A. A., & Heath, A. C. (2011). Interaction between the DRD4 VNTR polymorphism and proximal and distal environments in alcohol dependence during emerging and young adulthood. *Journal of Abnormal Psychology, 120,* 585–595.

Park, M. J., Scott, J. T., Adams, S. H., Brindis, C. D., & Irwin, C. E. Jr. (2014). Adolescent and young adult health in the United States in the past decade: Little improvement and young adults remain worse off than adolescents. *Journal of Adolescent Health, 55,* 3–16.

Parker, J., & Seal, J. (1996). Forming, losing, renewing, and replacing friendships: Applying temporal parameters to the assessment of children's friendship experiences. *Child Development, 67,* 2248–2268.

Parker, J., Low, C., Walker, A. R., & Gamm, B. K. (2005). Friendship jealousy in young adolescents: Individual differences and links to sex, self-esteem, aggression, and social adjustment. *Developmental Psychology, 41,* 235–250.

Parker, K. (2012). *The boomerang generation.* Washington: Pew Research Center.

Parker, K. F., & Reckdenwald, A. (2008). Concentrated disadvantage, traditional male role models, and African-American juvenile violence. *Criminology, 46,* 711–735.

Parker, P. D., Ciarrochi, J., Heaven, P., Marshall, S., Sahdra, B., & Kiuru, N. (2015). Hope, friends, and subjective well-being: A social network approach to peer group contextual effects. *Child Development, 86,* 642–650.

Parker, P. D., Schoon, I., Tsai, Y. M., Nagy, G., Trautwein, U., & Eccles, J. S. (2012). Achievement, agency, gender, and socioeconomic background as predictors of postschool choices: A multicontext study. *Developmental Psychology, 48,* 1629–1642.

Parkes, A., Waylen, A., Saval, K., Heron, J., Henderson, M., Wight, D., Mcleoud, J. (2014). Which behavioral, emotional and school problems in middle-childhood predict early sexual behavior? *Journal of Youth & Adolescence, 43,* 507–527.

Parkin, C. M., & Kuczynski, L. (2012). Adolescent perspectives on rules and resistance within the parent-child relationship. *Journal of Adolescent Research, 27,* 632–658.

Parra, A., Oliva, A., & Sánchez-Queija, I. (2015). Development of emotional autonomy from adolescence to young adulthood in Spain. *Journal of Adolescence, 38,* 57–67.

Parsai, M., Voisine, S., Marsiglia, F. F., Kulis, S., & Nieri, T. (2009). The protective and risk effects of parents and peers on substance use, attitudes, and behaviors of Mexican and Mexican American female and male adolescents. *Youth and Society, 40,* 353–376.

Parvanta, S., Brown, J., Du, S., Zimmer, C., Zhao, X., & Zhai, F. (2010). Television use and snacking behaviors among children and adolescents in China. *Journal of Adolescent Health, 46,* 339–345.

Pascarella, E., & Terenzini, P. (2005). *How college affects students: Vol. 2. A third decade of research.* San Francisco: Jossey-Bass.

Pasch, K. E., Latimer, L. A., Duncan Cance, J., Moe, S. G., Lytle, L. A. (2012). Longitudinal bi-directional relationships between sleep and youth sustance use. *Journal of Youth and Adolescence, 41,* 1184–1196.

Paschall, M. J., Flewelling, R. L., & Russell, T. (2004). Why is work intensity associated with heavy alcohol use among adolescents? *Journal of Adolescent Health, 34,* 79–87.

Paschall, M. J., Freisthler, B., & Lipton, R. I. (2005). Moderate alcohol use and depression in young adults: Findings from a national longitudinal study. *American Journal of Public Health, 95,* 453–457.

Pasley, K., & Gecas, V. (1984). Stresses and satisfactions of the parental role. *Personnel and Guidance Journal, 2,* 400–404.

Patall, E. A., Cooper, H., & Wynn, S. R. (2010). The effectiveness and relative importance of choice in the classroom. *Journal of Educational Psychology, 102,* 896–915.

Paten, S. (2013). Major depression epidemiology from a diathesis-stress conceptualization. *BMC Psychiatry, 13,* 19.

Paternoster, R., McGloin, J. M., Nguyen, H., & Thomas, K. J. (2013). The causal impact of exposure to deviant peers: An experimental investigation. *Journal of Research in Crime and Delinquency, 50,* 476–503.

Patrick, M. E., & Schulenberg, J. E. (2011). How trajectories of reasons for alcohol use relate to trajectories of binge drinking: National panel data spanning late adolescence to early adulthood. *Developmental Psychology, 47,* 311–317.

Patrick, M. E., Maggs, J. L., & Lefkowitz, E. S. (2015). Daily associations between drinking and sex among college students: A longitudinal measurement burst design. *Journal of Research on Adolescence, 25,* 377–386.

Patrikakou, E. (1996). Investigating the academic achievement of adolescents with learning disabilities: A structural modeling approach. *Journal of Education Psychology, 88,* 435–450.

Patten, C. A., Choi, W. S., Gillin, C. J., & Pierce, J. P. (2000). Depressive symptoms and cigarette smoking predict development and persistence of sleep problems in U.S. adolescents. *Pediatrics, 106,* Article e23.

Patterson, C. J. (2009). Children of lesbian and gay parents: Psychology, law, and policy. *American Psychologist, 64*, 727–736.

Patterson, G., DeGarmo, D., & Knutson, M. (2000). Hyperactive and antisocial behaviors: Comorbid or two points in the same process? *Development and Psychopathology, 12*, 91–106.

Patterson, G., Forgatch, M., Yoerger, K., & Stoolmiller, M. (1998). Variables that initiate and maintain an early-onset trajectory for juvenile offending. *Development and Psychopathology, 10*, 531–547.

Patton, D. U., Hong, J. S., Ranney, M., Patel, S., Kelley, C., Eschmann, R., Washington, T. (2014). Social media as a vector for youth violence: A review of the literature. *Computers in Human Behavior, 35*, 548–553.

Patton, G. C., Bond, L., Carlin, J. B., Thomas, L., Butler, H., Glover, S., ... Bowes, G. (2006). Promoting social inclusion in schools: A group-randomized trial of effects on student health risk behavior and well-being. *American Journal of Public Health, 96*, 1582–1587.

Patton, G. C., Olsson, C., Bond, L., Toumbourou, J. W., Carlin, J. B., ... Hemphill, S. A. (2008). Predicting female depression across puberty: A two-nation longitudinal study. *Journal of the American Academy of Child & Adolescent Psychiatry, 47*, 1424–1432.

Patton, W., & Mannison, M. (1995). Sexual coercion in high school dating. *Sex Roles, 33*, 447–457.

Paus, T. (2009). Brain development. In R. Lerner & L. Steinberg (Eds.), *Handbook of adolescent psychology* (3rd ed., Vol. 1, pp. 95–115). New York: Wiley.

Paus, T., Keshavan, B., & Giedd, J. (2008). Why do so many psychiatric disorders emerge during adolescence? *Nature Reviews Neuroscience, 9*, 947–957.

Paus, T., Toro, R., Leonard, G., Lerner, J., Lerner, R., Perron, M., ... Pausova, Z. (2008). Morphological properties of the action-observation cortical network in adolescents with low and high resistance to peer influence. *Social Neuroscience, 3*, 303–316.

Paxton, S., Wertheim, E., Gibbons, K., Szmukler, G., Hillier, L., & Petrovich, J. (1991). Body image satisfaction, dieting beliefs, and weight loss behaviors in adolescent girls and boys. *Journal of Youth and Adolescence, 20*, 361–380.

Payne, A. (2009). Girls, boys, and schools: Gender differences in the relationships between school-related factors and student deviance. *Criminology, 47*, 1167–1200.

Pea, R., Nass, C., Meheula, L., Rance, M., Kumar, A., Bamford, H., ... Zhou, M. (2012). Media use, face-to-face communication, media multitasking, and social well-being among 8- to 12-year-old girls. *Developmental Psychology, 48*, 327–336.

Pearce, M. J., Jones, S. M., Schwab-Stone, M. E., & Ruchkin, V. (2003). The protective effects of religiousness and parent involvement on the development of conduct problems among youth exposed to violence. *Child Development, 74*, 1682–1696.

Pearson, J., & Wilkinson, L. (2013). Family relationships and adolescent well-being: are families equally protective for same-sex attracted youth? *Journal of Youth & Adolescence, 42*, 376–393.

Pechmann, C., Levine, L., Loughlin, S., & Leslie, F. (2005). Impulsive and self-conscious: Adolescents' vulnerability to advertising and promotion. *Journal of Public Policy and Marketing, 24*, 202–221.

Pedersen, S., Seidman, E., Yoshikawa, H., Rivera, A. C., Allen, L., & Aber, J. L. (2005). Contextual competence: Multiple manifestations among urban adolescents. *American Journal of Community Psychology, 35*, 65–82.

Pedersen, S., Vitaro, F., Barker, E. D., & Borge, A. I. H. (2007). The timing of middle-childhood peer rejection and friendship: Linking early behavior to early-adolescent adjustment. *Child Development, 78*, 1037–1051.

Peeters, M., Cillessen, A. H. N., & Scholte, R. H. J. (2010). Clueless or powerful? Identifying subtypes of bullies in adolescence. *Journal of Youth and Adolescence, 39*, 1041–1052.

Pellegrini, A. D. (2003). Perceptions and functions of play and real fighting in early adolescence. *Child Development, 74*, 1522–1533.

Pellegrini, A. D., & Long, J. D. (2007). An observational study of early heterosexual interaction at middle-school dances. *Journal of Research on Adolescence, 17*, 613–638.

Pellerin, L. A. (2005). Student disengagement and the socialization styles of high schools. *Social Forces, 84*, 1159–1179.

Peper, J. S., Mandl, R. C., Braams, B. R., de Water, E., Heijboer, A. C., Koolschijn, P. C., & Crone, E. A. (2013). Delay discounting and frontostriatal fiber tracts: A combined DTI and MTR study on impulsive choices in healthy young adults. *Cerebral Cortex, 23*, 1695–1702.

Pepler, D., Jiang, D., Craig, W., & Connolly, J. (2008). Developmental trajectories of bullying and associated factors. *Child Development, 79*, 325–338.

Perez-Febles, A., Allison, K., & Burton, L. (April, 1999). *Sociocultural context and the construction of research questions: The case of adolescent childbearing.* Paper presented at the biennial meetings of the Society for Research on Child Development, Albuquerque.

Perius, J. G., Brooks-Russell, A., Jing, W., & Iannotti, R. J. (2014). Trends in bullying, physical fighting, and weapon carrying among 6th- through 10th-grade students from 1998 to 2010: Findings from a national study. *American Journal of Public Health, 104*, 1100–1106.

Perkins, D., Jacobs, J. E., Barber, B. L., & Eccles, J. (2003). Childhood and adolescent sports participation as predictors of participation in sports and physical fitness activities during young adulthood. *Youth and Society, 35*, 295–520.

Perkins, D., Luster, T., & Jank, W. (2002). Protective factors, physical abuse, and purging from community-wide surveys of female adolescents. *Journal of Adolescent Research, 17*, 377–400.

Perkins, D., Luster, T., Villarruel, F., & Small, S. (1998). An ecological, risk-factor examination of adolescents' sexual activity in three ethnic groups. *Journal of Marriage and the Family, 60*, 660–673.

Perkins, S. A., & Turiel, E. (2007). To lie or not to lie: To whom and under what circumstances. *Child Development, 78*, 609–621.

Perry, C., Williams, C., Veblen-Mortenson, S., Toomey, T., Komro, K., Anstine, P., McGovern, P., ... Wolfson, M. (1996). Project Northland: Outcomes of a communitywide alcohol use prevention program during early adolescence. *American Journal of Public Health, 86*, 956–965.

Perry, D., & Pauletti, R. (2011). Gender and adolescent development. *Journal of Research on Adolescence, 21*, 61–74.

Persike, M., & Seiffge-Krenke, I. (2014). Is stress perceived differently in relationships with parents and peers? Inter- and intra-regional comparisons on adolescents from 21 nations. *Journal of Adolescence, 37*, 493–504.

Persson, A., Kerr, M., & Stattin, H. (2007). Staying in or moving away from structured activities: Explanations involving parents and peers. *Developmental Psychology, 43*, 197–207.

Peskin, H. (1967). Pubertal onset and ego functioning: A psychoanalytic approach. *Journal of Abnormal Psychology, 72*, 1–15.

Petersen, A. (1988). Adolescent development. *Annual Review of Psychology, 39*, 583–607.

Petersen, I. T., Bates, J. E., Dodge, K. A., Lansford, J. E., & Pettit, G. S. (2015). Describing and predicting developmental profiles of externalizing problems from childhood to adulthood. *Development and Psychopathology, 27*, 791–818.

Petersen, I. T., Bates, J. E., Goodnight, J. A., Dodge, K. A., Lansford, J. E., Pettit, G. S., ... & Dick, D. M. (2012). Interaction between serotonin transporter polymorphism (5-HTTLPR) and stressful life events in adolescents' trajectories of anxious/depressed symptoms. *Developmental Psychology, 48*, 1463–1475.

Petersen, J. L., & Hyde, J. S. (2013). Peer sexual harassment and disordered eating in early adolescence. *Developmental Psychology, 49*, 184–195.

Peterson, P., Hawkins, J., Abbott, R., & Catalano, R. (1994). Disentangling the effects of parental drinking, family management, and parental alcohol norms on current drinking by Black and White adolescents. *Journal of Research on Adolescence, 4*, 203–227.

Petraitis, J., Flay, B., & Miller, T. (1995). Reviewing theories of adolescent substance use: Organizing pieces in the puzzle. *Psychological Bulletin, 117*, 67–86.

Pettifor, A., O'Brien, K., MacPhail, C., Miller, W. C., & Rees, H. (2010). Early coital debut and associated HIV risk factors among young women and men in South Africa. *International Perspectives on Sexual and Reproductive Health, 35,* 74–82.

Pettit, G., Bates, J., Dodge, K., & Meece, D. (1999). The impact of after-school peer contact on early adolescent externalizing problems is moderated by parental monitoring, perceived neighborhood safety, and prior adjustment. *Child Development, 70,* 768–778.

Pfeifer, J. H., & Peake, S. J. (2012). Self-development: Integrating cognitive, socioemotional, and neuroimaging perspectives. *Developmental Cognitive Neuroscience, 2,* 55–69.

Pfeifer, J., & Blakemore, S-J. (2012). Adolescent social cognitive and affective neuroscience: past, present, and future. *Social Cognitive and Affective Neuroscience, 7,* 1–10.

Pfeifer, J., Masten, C. L., Borofsky, L. A., Dapretto, M., Fuligni, A. J., & Lieberman, M. D. (2009). Neural correlates of direct and reflected self-appraisals in adolescents and adults: When social perspective-taking informs self-perception. *Child Development, 80,* 1016–1038.

Pfeifer, J., Masten, C., Moore, W., III, & Oswald, T. (2011). Entering adolescence: Resistance to peer influence, risky behavior, and neural changes in emotion reactivity. *Neuron, 69,* 1029–1036.

Pfeifer, J., Masten, C., Moore, W., Oswald, T., Mazziotta, J., Iacoboni, M., & Dapretto, M. (2012). Entering adolescence: Resistance to peer influence, risky behavior, and neural changes in emotion reactivity *Neuron, 69,* 1029–1036.

Phares, V., Steinberg, A. R., & Thompson, J. K. (2004). Gender differences in peer and parental influences: Body image disturbance, self-worth, and psychological functioning in preadolescent children. *Journal of Youth and Adolescence, 33,* 421–429.

Phelan, P., Yu, H., & Davidson, A. (1994). Navigating the psychosocial pressures of adolescence: The voices and experiences of high school youth. *American Educational Research Journal, 31,* 415–447.

Phillipsen, L. C. (1999). Associations between age, gender, and group acceptance and three components of friendship quality. *Journal of Early Adolescence, 19,* 438–464.

Phinney, J., & Chavira, V. (1995). Parental ethnic socialization and adolescent coping with problems related to ethnicity. *Journal of Research on Adolescence, 5,* 31–53.

Phinney, J., & Ong, A. D. (2002). Adolescent–parent disagreements and life satisfaction in families from Vietnamese- and European-American backgrounds. *Journal of Behavioral Development, 26,* 556–561.

Phinney, J., Ferguson, D., & Tate, J. (1997). Intergroup attitudes among ethnic minority adolescents: A causal model. *Child Development, 68,* 955–969.

Phinney, J., Romero, I., Nava, M., & Huang, D. (2001). The role of language, parents, and peers in ethnic identity among adolescents in immigrant families. *Journal of Youth and Adolescence, 30,* 135–153.

Piehler, T. (2011). Peer influence. In B. Brown & M. Prinstein (Eds.), *Encyclopedia of adolescence* (Vol. 2, pp. 249–254). New York: Academic Press.

Piehler, T. F., & Dishion, T. J. (2014). Dyadic coregulation and deviant talk in adolescent friendships: Interaction patterns associated with problematic substance use in early adulthood. *Developmental Psychology, 50,* 1160–1169.

Piehler, T., & Dishion, T. (2007). Interpersonal dynamics within adolescent friendships: Dyadic mutuality, deviant talk, and patterns of antisocial behavior. *Child Development, 78,* 1611–1624.

Pierce, J., & Gilpin, E. (1996). How long will today's new adolescent smoker be addicted to cigarettes? *American Journal of Public Health, 86,* 253–256.

Pieters, S., Burk, W. J., Van der Vorst, H., Dahl, R. E., Wiers, R. W., Engels, R. C. M. E. (2015). Prospective relationship between sleep problems and substance use, internalizing and externalizing beahviors. *Journal of Youth and Adolescence, 44,* 379–388.

Pietiläinen, K. H., Kaprio, J., Rasanen, M., Winter, T., Rissanen, A., & Rose, R. (2001). Tracking of body size from birth to late adolescence: Contributions of birth length, birth weight, duration of gestation, parents' body size, and twinship. *American Journal of Epidemiology, 154,* 21–29.

Pike, A., McGuire, S., Hetherington, E. M., Reiss, D., et al. (1996). Family environment and adolescent depressive symptoms and antisocial behavior: A multivariate genetic analysis. *Developmental Psychology, 32,* 590–604.

Pilgrim, C., Luo, Q., Urberg, K. A., & Fang, X. (1999). Influence of peers, parents, and individual characteristics on adolescent drug use in two cultures. *Merrill-Palmer Quarterly, 45,* 85–107.

Pillay, Y. (2005). Racial identity as a predictor of the psychological health of African American students at a predominantly White university. *Journal of Black Psychology, 31,* 46–66.

Pinderhughes, E., Jones Harden, B., & Guyer, A. (2007). Children in foster care. In D. Phillips, L. Aber, L. Allen, & S. Jones (Eds.), *Child development and social policy: Knowledge for action.* Washington: American Psychological Association.

Pine, D., Wasserman, G., Coplan, J., Fried, J., Huang, Y., Kassir, S., . . . Parsons, B. (1996). Platelet serotonin 2A ($5HT_{2A}$) receptor characteristics and parenting factors for boys at risk for delinquency: A preliminary report. *American Journal of Psychiatry, 153,* 538–544.

Pingel, E. S., Bauermeister, J. A., Elkington, K. S., Fergus, S., Caldwell, C. H., & Zimmerman, M. A. (2012). Condom use trajectories in adolescence and the transition to adulthood: The role of mother and father support. *Journal of Research on Adolescence, 22,* 350–366.

Pinquart, M., & Silbereisen, R. (2002). Changes in adolescents' and mothers' autonomy and connectedness in conflict discussions: An observation study. *Journal of Adolescence, 25,* 509–522.

Pintrich, P. (2000). Multiple goals, multiple pathways: The role of goal orientation in learning and achievement. *Journal of Educational Psychology, 92,* 544–555.

Piquero, A., & Chung, H. L. (2001). On the relationship between gender, early onset, and the seriousness of offending. *Journal of Criminal Justice, 29,* 189–206.

Piquero, A., Farrington, D., & Blumstein, A. (2003). The criminal career paradigm: Background and recent developments. *Crime and Justice: A Review of Research, 30,* 359–506.

Pitner, R. O., Astor, R. A., Benbenishty, R., Haj-Yahia, M. M., & Zeira, A. (2003). The effects of group stereotypes on adolescents' reasoning about peer retribution. *Child Development, 74,* 413–425.

Pittard, W., Laditka, J., & Laditka S. (2008). Associations between maternal age and infant health outcomes among Medicaid-insured infants in South Carolina: Mediating effects of socioeconomic factors, *Pediatrics, 122,* e100–e106.

Pittman, L. D., & Chase-Lansdale, P. L. (2001). African American adolescent girls in impoverished communities: Parenting style and adolescent outcomes. *Journal of Research on Adolescence, 11,* 199–224.

Plaisier, X. S., & Konijn, E. A. (2013). Rejected by peers-attracted to antisocial media content: Rejection-based anger impairs moral judgment among adolescents. *Developmental Psychology, 49,* 1165–1173.

Planty, M., Bozick, R., & Regnier, M. (2006). Helping because you have to or helping because you want to?: Sustaining participation in service work from adolescence through young adulthood. *Youth and Society, 38,* 177–202.

Plomin, R., & Daniels, D. (1987). Why are children in the same family so different from one another? *Behavioral and Brain Sciences, 10,* 1–60.

Plumert, J. (1994). Flexibility in children's use of spatial and categorical organizational strategies in recall. *Developmental Psychology, 30,* 738–747.

Pogarsky, G., Lizotte, A. J., & Thornberry, T. P. (2003). The delinquency of children born to young mothers: Results from the Rochester Youth Development Study. *Criminology, 41,* 1249–1286.

Pollack, C., & Bright, D. (2003). Caffeine consumption and weekly sleep patterns in U.S. seventh-, eighth-, and ninth-graders. *Pediatrics, 111,* 42–46.

Pomerantz, E. (2001). Parent–child socialization: Implications for the development of depressive symptoms. *Journal of Family Psychology, 15,* 510–525.

Pomerantz, E., Altermatt, E., & Saxon, J. L. (2002). Making the grade but feeling distressed: Gender differences in academic performance and internal distress. *Journal of Educational Psychology, 94,* 396–404.

Pomerantz, E., Qin, L., Wang, Q., & Chen, H. (2009). American and Chinese early adolescents' inclusion of their relationships with their parents in their self-construals. *Child Development, 80,* 792–807.

Pong, S. (1997). Family structure, school context, and eighth-grade math and reading achievement. *Journal of Marriage and the Family, 59,* 734–746.

Pong, S. (1998). The school compositional effect of single parenthood on 10th-grade achievement. *Sociology of Education, 71,* 23–42.

Pong, S., & Ju, D. (2000). The effects of change in family structure and income on dropping out in middle and high school. *Journal of Family Issues, 21,* 147–169.

Ponnet, K., Van Leeuwen, K., Wouters, E., & Mortelmans, D. (2014). A family system approach to investigate family-based pathways between financial stress and adolescent problem behavior. *Journal of Research on Adolescence, Early view.* DOI: 10.1111/jora.12171

Poorthuis, A. M. G., Juvonen, J., Thomaes, S., Denissen, J. J. A., Orobio de Castro, B., & van Aken, M. A. G. (2014). Do grades shape students' school engagement? The psychological consequences of report card grades at the beginning of secondary school. *Journal of Educational Psychology,* http://dx.doi.org/10.1037/edu0000002.

Poropat, A. E. (2009). A meta-analysis of the five-factor model of personality and academic performance. *Psychological Bulletin, 135,* 322–338.

Porter, J. N., Roy, A. K., Benson, B., Carlisi, C., Collins, P. F., Leibenluft, E., . . . & Ernst, M. (2015). Age-related changes in the intrinsic functional connectivity of the human ventral vs. dorsal striatum from childhood to middle age. *Developmental Cognitive Neuroscience, 11,* 83–95.

Pössel, P., Rudasill, K. M., Sawyer, M. G., Spence, S. H., & Bjerg, A. C. (2013). Associations between teacher emotional support and depressive symptoms in Australian adolescents: A 5-year longitudinal study. *Developmental Psychology, 49,* 2135–2146.

Poteat, P. V., Espelage, D. L., & Koenig, B. W. (2009). Willingness to remain friends and attend school with lesbian and gay peers: relational expressions of prejudice among heterosexual youth. *Journal of Youth and Adolescence, 38,* 952–962.

Poteat, V. P., & Anderson, C. J. (2012). Developmental changes in sexual prejudice

from early to late adolescence: The effects of gender, race, and ideology on different patterns of change. *Developmental Psychology, 48,* 1403–1415.

Poteat, V. P., Sinclair, K. O., DiGiovanni, C. D., Koenig, B. W., & Russell, S. T. (2013). Gay-straight alliances are associated with student health: A multischool comparison of LGBTQ and heterosexual youth. *Journal of Research on Adolescence, 23,* 319–330.

Poteat, V. P., Scheer, J. R., DiGiovanni, C. D., & Mereish, E. H. (2014). Short-term prospective effects of homophobic victimization on the mental health of heterosexual adolescents. *Journal of Youth & Adolescence, 43,* 1240–1251.

Potkin, K. T., & Bunney, W. E. (2012). Sleep improves memory: The effect of sleep on long term memory in early adolescence. *PLoS One, 7,* 42191.

Poulin, F., & Chan, A. (2010). Friendship stability and change in childhood and adolescence. *Developmental Review, 30,* 257–272.

Poulin, F., & Denault, A. S. (2012). Other-sex friendships as a mediator between parental monitoring and substance use in girls and boys. *Journal of Youth & Adolescence, 41,* 1488–1501.

Poulin, F., & Pedersen, S. (2007). Developmental changes in gender composition of friendship networks in adolescent girls and boys. *Developmental Psychology, 43,* 1484–1496.

Poulin, F., Denault, A.-S., & Pedersen, S. (2011). Longitudinal associations between other-sex friendships and substance use in adolescence. *Journal of Research on Adolescence, 21,* 776–788.

Poulin, F., Dishion, T., & Haas, E. (1999). The peer influence paradox: Friendship quality and deviancy training within male adolescent friendships. *Merrill-Palmer Quarterly, 45,* 42–61.

Power, J., Fair, D., Schlaggar, B., & Petersen, S. (2010). The development of human functional brain networks. *Neuron, 67,* 735–748.

Pozzoli, T., Gini, G., & Viene, A. (2012). The role of individual correlates and class norms in defending and passive bystanding behavior in bullying: A multilevel analysis. *Child Development, 83,* 1917–1931.

Pradhan, A. K., Li, K., Bingham, C. R., Simons-Morton, B. G., Ouimet, M. C., & Shope, J. T. (2014). Peer passenger influences on male adolescent drivers' visual scanning behavior during simulated driving. *Journal of Adolescent Health, 54,* S42–S49.

Prado, G., Huang, S., Schwartz, S., Maldonado-Molina, M., Bandiera, F., la Rosa, de, M., & Pantin, H. (2009). What accounts for differences in substance use among US-born and immigrant Hispanic adolescents?: Results from a longitudinal prospective cohort study. *Journal of Adolescent Health, 45,* 118–125.

Prado, G., Lightfoot, M., & Brown, C. H. (2013). Macro-level approaches to HIV prevention among ethnic minority youth: State of

the science, opportunities, and challenges. *American Psychologist, 68,* 286–299.

Prelow, H., Danoff-Burg, S., Swenson, R., & Pulgiano, D. (2004). The impact of ecological risk and perceived discrimination on the psychological adjustment of African American and European American youth. *Journal of Community Psychology, 32,* 375–389.

President's Science Advisory Committee. (1974). *Youth: Transition to adulthood.* Chicago: University of Chicago Press.

Price, M. N., & Hyde, J. S. (2011). Perceived and observed maternal relationship quality predict sexual debut by age 15. *Journal of Youth and Adolescence, 40,* 1595–1606.

Priess, H., & Hyde, J. (2011). Gender roles. In B. Brown & M. Prinstein (Eds.), *Encyclopedia of adolescence* (Vol. 2, pp. 99–108). New York: Academic Press.

Priess, H., Lindberg, S., & Hyde, J. (2009). Adolescent gender-role identity and mental health: Gender intensification revisited. *Child Development, 80,* 1531–1544.

Prinstein, M. J., & Aikins, J. W. (2004). Cognitive moderators of the longitudinal association between peer rejection and adolescent depressive symptoms. *Journal of Abnormal Child Psychology, 32,* 147–158.

Prinstein, M. J., & Cillessen, A. H. (2003). Forms and functions of adolescent peer aggression associated with high levels of peer status. *Merrill-Palmer Quarterly, 49,* 310–342.

Prinstein, M. J., & La Greca, A. M. (2002). Peer crowd affiliation and internalizing distress in childhood and adolescence: A longitudinal follow-back study. *Journal of Research on Adolescence, 12,* 325–351.

Prinstein, M. J., Brechwald, W. A., & Cohen, G. L. (2011). Susceptibility to peer influence: Using a performance-based measure to identify adolescent males at heightened risk for deviant peer socialization. *Developmental Psychology, 47,* 1167–1172.

Prinstein, M. J., Meade, C., & Cohen, G. (2003). Adolescent oral sex, peer popularity, and perceptions of best friends' sexual behavior. *Journal of Pediatric Psychology, 28,* 243–249.

Prinstein, M., Heilbron, N., Guerry, J., Franklin, J., Rancourt, D., Simon, V., & Spirito, A. (2010). Peer influence and nonsuicidal self injury: longitudinal results in community and clinically referred adolescent samples. *Journal of Abnormal Child Psychology, 38,* 669–682.

Proctor, L., Skriner, L., Roesch, S., & Litrownik, A. (2010). Trajectories of behavioral adjustment following early placement in foster care: Predicting stability and change over 8 years. *Journal of the American Academy of Child and Adolescent Psychiatry, 49,* 464–473.

Pronk, R., & Zimmer-Gembeck, M. (2010). It's 'mean,' but what does it mean to adolescents? Relational aggression described by victims, aggressors, and their peers. *Journal of Adolescent Research, 25,* 175–204.

Prosser, E., & Carlson, C. (April, 1999). *Ethnic differences in fluctuations in female self-esteem during early adolescence.* Paper presented at the biennial meetings of the Society for Research on Child Development, Albuquerque.

Prot, S., Gentile, D. A., Suzuki, K., Lim, K. M., Horiuchi, Y., Jelic, M. . . . & Lam, B. (2013). Long-term relationships among prosocial-media use, empathy, and prosocial behavior. *Psychological Science, 25,* 358–368.

Public Agenda. (1997). *Getting by: What American teenagers really think about their schools.* New York: Author.

Puelo, C., Settipani, C., Crawley, S., Beidas, R., & Kendall, P. (2011). Anxiety disorders. In B. Brown & M. Prinstein (Eds.), *Encyclopedia of adolescence* (Vol. 3, pp. 48–55). New York: Academic Press.

Punamäki, R., Qouta, S., & Sarraj, E. (1997). Models of traumatic experiences and children's psychological adjustment: The roles of perceived parenting and the children's own resources and activity. *Child Development, 68,* 718–728.

Punamäki, R., Wallenius, M., Nygård, C., Saarni, L., & Rimpelä, A. (2007). Use of information and communication technology (ICT) and perceived health in adolescence: The role of sleeping habits and waking-time tiredness. *Journal of Adolescence, 30,* 569–585.

Pungello, E., Kupersmidt, J., Burchinal, M., & Patterson, C. (1996). Environmental risk factors and children's achievement from middle childhood to early adolescence. *Developmental Psychology, 32,* 755–767.

Purdie, N., Hattie, J., & Douglas, G. (1996). Student conceptions of learning and their use of self-regulated learning strategies: A cross-cultural comparison. *Journal of Educational Psychology, 88,* 87–100.

Purtell, K. M., & McLoyd, V. C. (2013). A longitudinal investigation of employment among low-income youth: Patterns, predictors, and correlates. *Youth & Society, 45,* 243–264.

Pyrooz, D. C. (2014). From colors and guns to caps and gowns? The effects of gang membership on educational attainment. *Journal of Research in Crime and Delinquency, 51,* 56–87.

Qin, D. (2008). Doing well vs. feeling well: Understanding family dynamics and the psychological adjustment of Chinese immigrant adolescents. *Journal of Youth and Adolescence, 37,* 22–35.

Qin, D. (2009). Being "good" or being "popular": Gender and ethnic identity negotiations of Chinese immigrant adolescents. *Journal of Adolescent Research, 24,* 37–66.

Qin, D., Way, N., & Mukherjee, P. (2008). The other side of the model minority story: The familial and peer challenges faced by Chinese American adolescents. *Youth and Society, 39,* 480–506.

Qin, L., & Pomerantz, E. M. (2013). Reciprocal pathways between American and Chinese early adolescents' sense of responsibility and disclosure to parents. *Child Development, 84,* 1887–1895.

Qin, L., Pomerantz, E. M., & Wang, Q. (2009). Are gains in decision-making autonomy during early adolescence beneficial for emotional functioning? The case of the United States and China. *Child Development, 80,* 1705–1721.

Qu, Y., Pomerantz, E. M., & Deng, C. (2014). Mothers' goals for adolescents in the United States and China: Content and transmission. *Journal of Research on Adolescence, Early view.* DOI: 10.1111/jora.12176

Quadrel, M., Fischhoff, B., & Davis, W. (1993). Adolescent (in)vulnerability. *American Psychologist, 48,* 102–116.

Quatman, T., Sokolik, E., & Smith, K. (2000). Adolescent perception of peer success: A gendered perspective over time. *Sex Roles, 43,* 61–84.

Quillian, L., & Campbell, M. E. (2003). Beyond Black and White: The present and future of multiracial friendship segregation. *American Sociological Review, 68,* 540–566.

Quinn, P. D., & Harden, K. P. (2013). Differential changes in impulsivity and sensation seeking and the escalation of substance use from adolescence to early adulthood. *Development and Psychopathology, 25,* 223–239.

Quintana, S., Castaneda-English, P., & Ybarra, V. C. (1999). Role of perspective-taking abilities and ethnic socialization in development of adolescent ethnic identity. *Journal of Research on Adolescence, 9,* 161–184.

Quiroga, C. V., Janosz, M., Bisset, S., & Morin, A. J. S. (2013). Early adolescent depression symptoms and school dropout: Mediating processes involving self-reported academic competence and achievement. *Journal of Educational Psychology, 105,* 552–560.

Quittner, A., Romero, S., Kimberg, C., Blackwell, L., & Cruz, I. (2011). Chronic illness. In B. Brown & M. Prinstein (Eds.), *Encyclopedia of adolescence* (Vol. 3, pp. 91–99). New York: Academic Press.

Raabe, T., & Beelman, A. (2011). Development of ethnic, racial, and national prejudice in childhood and adolescence: A multinational meta-analysis of age differences. *Child Development, 82,* 1715–1737.

Raby, K. L., Roisman, G. I., Fraley, R. C., & Simpson, J. A. (2015). The enduring predictive significance of early maternal sensitivity: Social and academic competence through age 32 years. *Child Development, 86,* 695–708.

Radmacher, K., & Azmitia, M. (2006). Are there gendered pathways to intimacy in early adolescents' and emerging adults' friendships? *Journal of Adolescent Research, 21,* 415–448.

Raffaelli, M. (1997). Young adolescents' conflicts with siblings and friends. *Journal of Youth and Adolescence, 26,* 539–558.

Raffaelli, M., & Green, S. (2003). Parent–adolescent communication about sex: Retrospective reports by Latino college students. *Journal of Marriage and the Family, 65,* 474.

Raffaelli, M., Andrade, F. C. D., Wiley, A. R., Sanchez-Armass, O., Edwards, L. L., & Aradillas-Garcia, C. (2013). Stress, Social support, and depression: A test of the stress-buffering hypothesis in a Mexican sample. *Journal of Research on Adolescence, 23,* 283–289.

Raiford, J. L., Herbst, J. H., Carry, M., Browne, F. A., Doherty, I., & Wechsberg, W. M. (2014). Low prospects and high risk: Structural determinants of health associated with sexual risk among young African American women residing in resource-poor communities in the South. *American Journal of Community Psychology, 54,* 243–250.

Raine, A., Loeber, R., Stouthamer-Loeber, M., Moffitt, T. E., Caspi, A., & Lynam, D. (2005). Neurocognitive impairments in boys on the life-course-persistent antisocial path. *Journal of Abnormal Psychology, 114,* 38–49.

Ramchand, R., Ialongo, N. S., & Chilcoat, H. D. (2007). The effect of working for pay on adolescent tobacco use. *American Journal of Public Health, 97,* 2056–2062.

Ramey, H. L., & Rose-Krasnor, L. (2012). Contexts of structured youth activities and positive youth development. *Child Development Perspectives, 6,* 85–91.

Ramirez-Valles, J., Zimmerman, M. A., & Juarez, L. (2002). Gender differences of neighborhood and social control processes: A study of the timing of first intercourse among low-achieving, urban, African American youth. *Youth and Society, 33,* 418–441.

Ramos, D., Victor, T., Seidl-de-Moura, M. L., Daly, M. (2013). Future discounting by slum-dwelling youth versus university students in Rio de Janeiro. *Journal of Research on Adolescence, 23,* 95–102.

Rampey, B. D., Dion, G. S., & Donahue, P. L. (2009). *NAEP 2008 Trends in Academic Progress.* Washington, DC: National Center for Education Statistics.

Ramsden, S., Richardson, F., Josse, G., Thomas, M., & Ellis, C. (2011). Verbal and non-verbal intelligence changes in the teenage brain. *Nature, 479,* 113–116.

Randall, E. T., & Bohnert, A. M. (2009). Organized activity involvement, depressive symptoms, and social adjustment in adolescents: Ethnicity and socioeconomic status as moderators. *Journal of Youth and Adolescence, 38,* 1187–1198.

Randall, E. T., Bohnert, A. M., & Travers, L. V. (2015). Understanding affluent adolescent adjustment: The interplay of parental perfectionism, perceived parental pressure, and organized activity involvement. *Journal of Adolescence, 41,* 56–66.

Randel, B., Stevenson, H. W., & Witruk, E. (2000). Attitudes, beliefs, and mathematics achievement of German and Japanese high school students. *International Journal of Behavioral Development, 24,* 190–198.

Rangel, M. C., Gavin, L., Reed, C., Fowler, M. G., & Lee, L. M. (2006). Epidemiology of HIV and AIDS among adolescents and young adults in the United States. *Journal of Adolescent Health, 39,* 156–163.

Rankin, J., Lane, D., Gibbons, F., & Gerrard, M. (2004). Adolescent self-consciousness: Longitudinal age changes and gender differences in two cohorts. *Journal of Research on Adolescence, 14,* 1–21.

Ranney, J. D., & Troop-Gordon, W. (2012). Computer-mediated communication with distant friends: Relations with adjustment during students' first semester in college. *Journal of Educational Psychology, 104,* 848–861.

Rao, M. A., Berry, R., Gonsalves, A., Hastak, Y., Shah, M., & Roeser, R. W. (2013). Globalization and the identity remix among urban adolescents in India. *Journal of Research on Adolescence, 23,* 9–24.

Raskauskas, J., & Stoltz, A. D. (2007). Involvement in traditional and electronic bullying among adolescents. *Developmental Psychology, 43,* 564–575.

Raudino, A., Fergusson, D. M., & Horwood, L. J. (2013). The quality of parent/child relationships in adolescence is associated with poor adult psychosocial adjustment. *Journal of Adolescence, 36,* 331–340.

Rauer, A. J., Pettit, G. S., Lansford, J. E., Bates, J. E., & Dodge, K. A. (2013). Romantic relationship patterns in young adulthood and their developmental antecedents. *Developmental Psychology, 49,* 2159–2171.

Rauscher, K. J., Wegman, D. H., Wooding, J., Davis, L., & Junkin, R. (2013). Adolescent work quality: A view from today's youth. *Journal of Adolescent Research, 28,* 557–590.

Ravitch, D. (2000). *Left back: A century of failed school reforms.* New York: Simon & Schuster.

Ravitch, D. (Ed.). (2001). *Brookings papers on education policy.* Washington, DC: Brookings Institution.

Rawana, J. S., & Morgan, A. S. (2014). Trajectories of depressive symptoms from adolescence to young adulthood: the role of self-esteem and body-related predictors. *Journal of Youth & Adolescence, 43,* 597–611.

Rayner, K. E., Schniering, C. A., Rapee, R. M., Taylor, A., & Hutchinson, D. M. (2013). Adolescent girls' friendship networks, body dissatisfaction, and disordered eating: Examining selection and socialization processes. *Journal of Abnormal Psychology, 122,* 93–104.

Raznahan, A., Lerch, J., Lee, N., Greenstein, D., Wallace, G. L., Stockman, M., . . . Giedd, J. (2011). Patterns of coordinated anatomical change in human cortical development: A longitudinal neuroimaging study of maturational coupling. *Neuron, 72,* 873–884.

Ready, D. D., Lee, V., & Welner, K. G. (2004). Educational equity and school structure: School size, overcrowding, and schools-within-schools. *Teachers College Review, 106,* 1989–2014.

Ream, G., & Savin-Williams, R. (2005). Reciprocal associations between adolescent sexual activity and quality of youth–parent interactions. *Journal of Family Psychology, 19,* 171–179.

Ream, R., & Rumberger, R. (2008). Student engagement, peer social capital, and school dropout among Mexican American and non-Latino White students. *Sociology of Education, 81,* 109–139.

Rebellon, C. J. (2006). Do adolescents engage in delinquency to attract the social attention of peers?: An extension and longitudinal test of the social reinforcement hypothesis. *Journal of Research in Crime and Delinquency, 43,* 387–411.

Recchia, H. E., Wainryb, C., Bourne, S., & Pasupathi, M. (2014). The construction of moral agency in mother-child conversations about helping and hurting across childhood and adolescence. *Developmental Psychology, 50,* 34–44.

Recchia, H., Wainryb, C., & Pasupathi, M. (2013). "Two for flinching": Children's and adolescents' narrative accounts of harming their friends and siblings. *Child Development, 84,* 1459–1474.

Recchia, H. E., Brehl, B. A., & Wainryb, C. (2012). Children's and adolescents' reasons for socially excluding others. *Cognitive Development, 27,* 195–203.

Reddy, R., Rhodes, J. E., & Mulhall, P. (2003). The influence of teacher support on student adjustment in the middle school years: A latent growth curve study. *Development and Psychopathology, 15,* 119–138.

Redlich, A., & Goodman, G. (2003). Taking responsibility for an act not committed: The influence of age and suggestibility. *Law and Human Behavior, 27,* 141–156.

Redlich, A., Silverman, A., & Steiner, H. (2003). Pre-adjudicative competence in juveniles and young adults. *Behavioral Sciences and the Law, 21,* 393–410.

Reese, E., Jack, F., & White, N. (2010). Origins of adolescents' autobiographical memories. *Cognitive Development, 25,* 352–367.

Reese-Weber, M. (2000). Middle and late adolescents' conflict resolution skills and siblings: Associations with interparental and parent–adolescent conflict resolution. *Journal of Youth and Adolescence, 29,* 697–711.

Reich, K., Oser, F., & Valentin, P. (1994). Knowing why I now know better: Children's and youth's explanations of their worldview changes. *Journal of Research on Adolescence, 4,* 151–173.

Reich, S. (2010). Adolescents' sense of community on Myspace and Facebook: A mixed-methods approach. *Journal of Community Psychology, 38,* 688–705.

Reich, S., Subrahmanyam, K., & Espinosa, G. (2012). Friending, IMing, and hanging out face-to-face: Overlap in adolescents' online and offline social networks. *Developmental Psychology, 48,* 356–368.

Reichhardt, T. (2003). Playing with fire. *Nature, 424,* 367–368.

Reijneveld, S., Veenstra, R., de Winter, A., Verhulst, F., Ormel, J., & de Meer, G. (2010). Area deprivation affects behavioral problems of young adolescents in mixed urban and rural areas: The TRAILS study. *Journal of Adolescent Health, 46,* 189–196.

Reilly, D., Neumann, D. L., & Andrews, G. (2014). Sex differences in mathematics and science achievement: A meta-analysis of national assessment of educational progress assessments. *Journal of Educational Psychology, First posting,* http://dx.doi.org/10.1037/edu0000012

Reinders, H., & Youniss, J. (2006). School-based required community service and civic development in adolescents. *Applied Developmental Science, 10,* 2–12.

Reinke, W. M., Eddy, J. M., Dishion, T. J., Reid, J. B. (2012). Joint trajectories of symptoms of disruptive behavior problems and depressive symptoms during early adolescence and adjustment problems during emerging adulthood. *Journal of Abnormal Child Psychology, 40,* 1123–1136.

Reiss, D., Hetherington, E. M., Plomin, R., Howe, G., Simmens, S., Henderson S., . . . Law, T. (1995). Genetic questions for environmental studies. *Archives of General Psychiatry, 52,* 925–936.

Reitz, A. K., Motti-Stefanidi, F., & Asendorpf, J. B. (2014). Mastering developmental transitions in immigrant adolescents: The longitudinal interplay of family functioning, developmental and acculturative tasks. *Developmental Psychology, 50,* 754–765.

Repetti, R. (1996). The effects of perceived daily social and academic failure experiences on school-age children's subsequent interactions with parents. *Child Development, 67,* 1467–1482.

Repetto, P. B., Zimmerman, M. A., & Caldwell, C. H. (2008). A longitudinal study of depressive symptoms and marijuana use in a sample of inner-city African Americans. *Journal of Research on Adolescence, 18,* 421–447.

Repinski, D., & Leffert, N. (1994, February). *Adolescents' relations with friends: The effects of a psychoeducational intervention.* Paper presented at the biennial meetings of the Society for Research on Adolescence, San Diego.

Reppucci, N., Scott, E., & Antonishak, J. (2009). Political orientation and perceptions of adolescent autonomy and judicial culpability. *Behavioral Sciences & the Law, 27,* 29–34.

Resko, S. M., Walton, M. A., Bingham, C. R., Shope, J. T., Zimmerman, M., Chermack, S. T., . . . Cunningham, R. (2010). Alcohol availability and violence among inner-city adolescents: A multi-level analysis of the role of alcohol outlet density. *American Journal of Community Psychology, 46(3–4),* 253–262.

Resnick, M., Bearman, P., Blum, R., Bauman, K., Harris, K., Jones, J., . . . Udry, J. (1997). Protecting adolescents from harm: Findings from the National Longitudinal Study of Adolescent Health. *Journal of the American Medical Association, 278,* 823–832.

Rest, J., Narvaez, D., Bebeau, M., & Thoma, S. (1999). *Postconventional moral thinking: A neo-Kohlbergian approach.* Mahwah, NJ: Erlbaum.

Reuman, D. (1989). How social comparison mediates the relation between ability-grouping practices and students' achievement expectancies in mathematics. *Journal of Educational Psychology, 81,* 178–189.

Reyes, H. L., Foshee, V. A., Bauer, D. J., & Ennett, S. T. (2012). Developmental associations between adolescent alcohol use and dating aggression. *Journal of Research on Adolescence, 22,* 526–541.

Reyes, H. L., & Foshee, V. A. (2013). Sexual dating aggression across grades 8 through 12: Timing and predictors of onset. *Journal of Youth & Adolescence, 42,* 581–595.

Reyes, H. L., Foshee, V. A., Niolon, P. H., Reidy, D. E., & Hall, J. E. (2015). Gender role attitudes and male adolescent dating violence perpetration: normative beliefs as moderators. *Journal of Youth & Adolescence.* DOI: 10.1007/s10964-015-0278-0

Reyes, M. R., Brackett, M. A., Rivers, S. E., White, M., & Salovey, P. (2012). Classroom emotional climate, student engagement, and academic achievement. *Journal of Educational Psychology, 104,* 700–712.

Reyes, O., & Jason, L. (1993). Pilot study examining factors associated with academic success for Hispanic high school students. *Journal of Youth and Adolescence, 22,* 57–71.

Reyna, V., & Brainerd, C. (2011). Dual processes in decision making and developmental neuroscience: A fuzzy-trace model. *Developmental Review, 31,* 180–206.

Reyna, V., & Farley, F. (2006). Risk and rationality in adolescent decision making: Implications for theory, practice, and public policy. *Psychological Science in the Public Interest, 7,* 1–44.

Reynolds, A., & Temple, J. (1998). Extended early childhood intervention and school achievement: Age thirteen findings from the Chicago Longitudinal Study. *Child Development, 69,* 231–246.

Reynolds, A., Temple, J., Robertson, D. L., & Mann, E. A. (2001). Long-term effects of an early childhood intervention on educational achievement and juvenile arrest: A 15-year follow-up of low-income children in public schools. *Journal of the American Medical Association, 285,* 2339–2346.

Reynolds, B. M., & Juvonen, J. (2011). The role of early maturation, perceived popularity, and rumors in the emergence of internalizing symptoms among adolescent girls. *Journal of Youth and Adolescence, 40,* 1407–1422.

Reynolds, B. M., & Juvonen, J. (2012). Pubertal timing fluctuations across middle school: implications for girls' psychological health. *Journal of Youth and Adolescence, 41,* 677–690.

Reynolds, J. R., & Baird, C. L. (2010). Is there a downside to shooting for the stars?: Unrealized educational expectations and symptoms of depression. *American Sociological Review, 75,* 151–172.

Rhodes, J. (2004). *Stand by me.* Cambridge, MA: Harvard University Press.

Rhodes, J., & Lowe, S. (2009). Mentoring in adolescence. In R. Lerner & L. Steinberg (Eds.), *Handbook of adolescent psychology* (3rd ed., Vol. 2, pp. 152–190). New York: Wiley.

Rhodes, J., Haight, W., & Briggs, E. (1999). The influence of mentoring on the peer relationships of foster youth in relative and nonrelative care. *Journal of Research on Adolescence, 9,* 185–201.

Ricciardelli, L. A., & McCabe, M. P. (2001). Self-esteem and negative affect as moderators of sociocultural influences on body dissatisfaction, strategies to decrease weight, and strategies to increase muscles among adolescent boys and girls. *Sex Roles, 44*(3–4), 189–207.

Ricciardelli, L. A., & McCabe, M. P. (2004). A biopsychosocial model of disorder eating and the pursuit of muscularity in adolescent boys. *Psychological Bulletin, 130,* 179–205.

Rice, F., Harold, G., Shelton, K., & Thapar, A. (2006). Family conflict interacts with genetic liability in predicting childhood and adolescent depression. *Journal of the American Academy of Child & Adolescent Psychiatry, 45,* 841–848.

Rice, K., & Mulkeen, P. (1995). Relationships with parents and peers: A longitudinal study of adolescent intimacy. *Journal of Adolescent Research, 10,* 338–357.

Rice, L., Barth, J. M., Guadagno, R. E., Smith, G. P., McCallum, D. M., & ASERT. (2013). The role of social support in students' perceived abilities and attitudes toward math and science. *Journal of Youth & Adolescence, 42,* 1028–1040.

Rich, L. M., & Kim, S.-B. (2002). Employment and the sexual and reproductive behavior of female adolescents. *Perspectives on Sexual and Reproductive Health, 34,* 127–134.

Richards, M., & Larson, R. (1993). Pubertal development and the daily subjective states of young adolescents. *Journal of Research on Adolescence, 3,* 145–169.

Richards, M., Boxer, A., Petersen, A., & Albrecht, R. (1990). Relation of weight to body image in pubertal girls and boys from two communities. *Developmental Psychology, 26,* 313–321.

Richards, M., Crowe, P., Larson, R., & Swarr, A. (1998). Developmental patterns and gender differences in the experience of peer companionship during adolescence. *Child Development, 69,* 154–163.

Richardson, J. (2009). Men do matter: Ethnographic insights on the socially supportive role of the African American uncle in the lives of inner-city African American youth. *Journal of Family Issues, 30,* 1041–1069.

Richardson, R. (1996, March). *Competence in the transition to adulthood: Exploring the influence of adolescent motherhood for low-income, urban, African-American women.* Paper presented at the biennial meetings of the Society for Research on Adolescence, Boston.

Richman, S. B., & Mandara, J. (2013). Do socialization goals explain differences in parental control between black and white parents? *Family Relations 62,* 625–636.

Ridenour, T., Cottier, L., Robins, L., Campton, W., Spitznagel, E., & Cunningham-Williams, R. (2002). Test of the plausibility of adolescent substance use playing a causal role in developing adulthood antisocial behavior. *Journal of Abnormal Psychology, 111,* 144–155.

Rideout, V., Foeher, U., & Roberts, D. (2010). *Generation M²: Media in the lives of 8- to 18-year-olds.* Palo Alto: Kaiser Family Foundation.

Riegle-Crumb, C., Farkas, G., & Muller, C. (2006). The role of gender and friendship in advanced course taking. *Sociology of Education, 79,* 206–228.

Riggs, L., Holmbeck, G., Paikoff, R., & Bryant, F. (2004). Teen mothers parenting their own teen offspring: The moderating role of parenting support. *Journal of Early Adolescence, 24,* 200–230.

Rigon, F., Bianchin, L., Bernasconi, S., Bona, G., Bozzola, M., Buzi, F., . . .Perissinotto, E. (2010). Update on age at menarche in Italy: toward the leveling off of the secular trend. *Journal of Adolescent Health, 46,* 238–244.

Rigsby, L., & McDill, E. (1975). Value orientations of high school students. In H. R. Stub (Ed.), *The sociology of education: A sourcebook* (3rd ed., pp. 53–74). Homewood, IL: Dorsey.

Riina, E. M., & McHale, S. M. (2012). Adolescents' experiences of discrimination and parent–adolescent relationship quality: The moderating roles of sociocultural processes. *Journal of Family Issues, 33,* 851–873.

Risch, S., Jodl, K., & Eccles, J. (2004). Role of the father–adolescent relationship in shaping adolescents' attitudes toward divorce. *Journal of Marriage and the Family, 66,* 46.

Ritakallio, M., Koivisto, A., von der Pahlen, B., Pelkonen, M., Marttunen, M., & Kaltiala-Heino, R. (2008). Continuity, comorbidity, and longitudinal associations between depression and antisocial behaviour in middle adolescence: A 2-year prospective follow-up study. *Journal of Adolescence, 31,* 355–370.

Rivas-Drake, D., & Witherspoon, D. (2013). Racial identity from adolescence to young adulthood: Does prior neighborhood experience matter? *Child Development, 84,* 1918–1932.

Rivas-Drake, D., Hughes, D., & Way, N. (2009). A preliminary analysis of associations among ethnic racial socialization, ethnic discrimination, and ethnic identity among urban sixth graders. *Journal of Research on Adolescence, 19,* 558–584.

Rivas-Drake, D., Seaton, E. K., Markstrom, C., Quintana, S., Syed, M., Lee, R. M., . . . & Ethnic and Racial Identity in the 21st Century Study Group. (2014). Ethnic and racial identity in adolescence: Implications for psychosocial, academic, and health outcomes. *Child Development, 85,* 40–57.

Rivas-Drake, D., Syed, M., Umaña-Taylor, A., Markstrom, C., French, S., Schwartz, S., . . . & Ethnic and Racial Identity in the 21st Century Study Group. (2014). Feeling good, happy, and proud: A meta-analysis of positive ethnic–racial affect and adjustment. *Child Development, 85,* 77–102.

Rivers, S., Reyna, V., & Mills, B. (2008). Risk taking under the influence: A fuzzy-trace theory of emotion in adolescence. *Developmental Review, 28,* 107–144.

Roberts, A. L., Rosario, M., Slopen, N., Calzo, J. P., & Austin, S. B. (2013). Childhood gender nonconformity, bullying victimization, and depressive symptoms across adolescence and early adulthood: An 11-year longitudinal study. *Journal of the American Academy of Child & Adolescent Psychiatry, 52,* 143–152.

Roberts, A., Seidman, E., Pederson, S., Chesir-Teran, D., Allen, L., Aber, J., . . . Hseuh, J. (2000). Perceived family and peer transactions and self-esteem among urban early adolescents. *Journal of Early Adolescence, 20,* 68–92.

Roberts, B., & DelVecchio, W. F. (2000). The rank-order consistency of personality traits from childhood to old age: A quantitative review of longitudinal studies. *Psychological Bulletin, 126,* 3–25.

Roberts, B., Caspi, A., & Moffitt, T. E. (2001). The kids are alright: Growth and stability in personality development from adolescence to adulthood. *Journal of Personality and Social Psychology, 81,* 670–683.

Roberts, B., O'Donnell, M., & Robins, R. (2004). Goal and personality trait development in emerging adulthood. *Journal of Personality and Social Psychology, 87,* 541–550.

Roberts, B., Walton, K., & Viechtbauer, W. (2006). Patterns of mean-level change in personality traits across the life course: A meta-analysis of longitudinal studies. *Psychological Bulletin, 132,* 1–25.

Roberts, D. (1993). Adolescents and the mass media: From "Leave It to Beaver" to "Beverly Hills 90210." *Teachers College Record, 94,* 629–644.

Roberts, D., Henriksen, L., & Foehr, U. (2009). Adolescence, adolescents, and media. In R. Lerner & L. Steinberg (Eds.), *Handbook of adolescent psychology* (3rd ed., Vol. 2, pp. 314–344). New York: Wiley.

Roberts, D., Foehr, U., & Rideout, V. (2005). *Generation M: Media in the lives of 8–18-year-olds.* Menlo Park, CA: Kaiser Family Foundation.

Roberts, M., Gibbons, F., Gerard, M., Weng, C., Murry, V., Simons, L., . . .Lorenz, F. (2012). From racial discrimination to risky sex: Prospective relations involving peers and parents. *Developmental Psychology, 48,* 89–102.

Roberts, R. E., Roberts, C. R., & Duong, H. T. (2008). Chronic insomnia and its negative consequences for health and functioning of adolescents: A 12-month prospective study. *Journal of Adolescent Health, 42,* 294–302.

Roberts, R. E., Roberts, C., & Chen, Y. (1997). Ethno cultural differences in prevalence of adolescent depression. *American Journal of Community Psychology, 25,* 95–110.

Roberts, R., Phinney, J., Mâsse, L., Chen, Y., Roberts, C., & Romero, A. (1999). The structure of ethnic identity of young adolescents from diverse ethnocultural groups. *Journal of Early Adolescence, 19,* 301–322.

Robertson, A., Stein, J., & Schaefer-Rohleder, L. (2010). Effects of Hurricane Katrina and other adverse life events on adolescent female offenders: A test of General Strain Theory. *Journal of Research in Crime & Delinquency, 47,* 469–495.

Robertson, L. A., McAnally, H. M., & Hancox, R. J. (2013). Childhood and adolescent television viewing and antisocial behavior in early adulthood. *Pediatrics, 131,* 439–446.

Robins, R., John, O., Caspi, A., Moffitt, T., & Stouthamer-Loeber, M. (1996). Resilient, overcontrolled, and undercontrolled boys: Three replicable personality types. *Journal of Personality and Social Psychology, 70,* 157–171.

Robinson, N. (1995). Evaluating the nature of perceived support and its relation to perceived self-worth in adolescents. *Journal of Research on Adolescence, 5,* 253–280.

Robnett, R. D., & Leaper, C. (2013). Friendship groups, personal motivation, and gender in relation to high school students' STEM career interest. *Journal of Research on Adolescence, 23,* 652–664.

Roche, K. M., & Ghazarian, S. R. (2012). The value of family routines for the academic success of vulnerable adolescents. *Journal of Family Issues, 33,* 874–897.

Roche, K. M., Ensminger, M. E., & Cherlin, A. J. (2007). Variations in parenting and adolescent outcomes among African American and Latino families living in low-income, urban areas. *Journal of Family Issues, 28,* 882–909.

Roche, K. M., Ensminger, M. E., Chilcoat, H., & Storr, C. (2003). Establishing independence in low-income urban areas: The relationship to adolescent aggressive behavior. *Journal of Marriage and the Family, 65,* 668.

Roche, K., Ghazarian, S., Little, T., & Leventhal, T. (2011). Understanding links between punitive parenting and adolescent adjustment: The relevance of context and reciprocal associations. *Journal of Research on Adolescence, 21,* 448–460.

Roche, K. M., Caughy, M. O., Schuster, M. A., Bogart, L. M., Dittus, P.J., & Franzini, L. (2014). Cultural orientations, parental beliefs and practices, and Latino adolescents' autonomy and independence. *Journal of Youth & Adolescence, 43,* 1389–1403.

Roche, K. M., Ghazarian, S. R., Fernandez-Esquer, M. E. (2012). Unpacking acculturation: cultural orientation and educational attainment among Mexican-Origin youth. *Journal of Youth & Adolescence, 41,* 920–931.

Rocheleau, G. C., & Swisher, R. R. (2012). Adolescent work and alcohol use revisited: Variations by family structure. *Journal of Research on Adolescence, 22,* 694–703.

Roderick, M., & Camburn, E. (1999). Risk and recovery from course failure in the early years of high school. *American Educational Research Journal, 36,* 303–343.

Roderick, M., Coca, V., & Nagaoka, J. (2011). Potholes on the road to college: High school effects in shaping urban students' participation in college application, four-year college enrollment, and college match. *Sociology of Education, 84,* 178–211.

Rodgers, J., & Rowe, D. (1993). Social contagion and adolescent sexual behavior: A developmental EMOSA model. *Psychological Review, 100,* 479–510.

Rodgers, K., & Rose, H. A. (2002). Risk and resiliency factors among adolescents who experience marital transitions. *Journal of Marriage and the Family, 64,* 1024–1037.

Rodgers, R. F., McLean, S. A., & Paxton, S. J. (2015). Longitudinal relationships among internalization of the media ideal, peer social comparison, and body dissatisfaction: Implications for the tripartite influence model. *Developmental Psychology, 51,* 706–713.

Rodgers, R. F., Paxton, S.J., McLean, S. A. (2014). A biopsychosocial model of body image concerns and disordered eating in early adolescent girls. *Journal of Youth and Adolescence, 43,* 814–823.

Rodkin, P., Farmer, T., Pearl, R., & Van Acker, R. (2000). Heterogeneity of popular boys: Antisocial and prosocial configurations. *Developmental Psychology, 36,* 14–24.

Rodriguez, N. (2010). The cumulative effect of race and ethnicity in juvenile court outcomes and why preadjudication detention matters. *Journal of Research in Crime & Delinquency, 47,* 391–413.

Rodriguez, S. A., Perez-Brena, N. J., Updegraff, K. A., & Umaña-Taylor, A. J. (2014). Emotional closeness in Mexican-origin adolescents' relationships with mothers, fathers, and same-sex friends. *Journal of Youth & Adolescence, 43,* 1953–1968.

Roe, K. (1995). Adolescents' use of socially disvalued media: Towards a theory of media delinquency. *Journal of Youth and Adolescence, 24,* 617–631.

Roenkae, A., & Pulkkinen, L. (1998). Work involvement and timing of motherhood in the accumulation of problems in social functioning in young women. *Journal of Research on Adolescence, 8,* 221–239.

Roenneberg, T., Kuehnle, T., Pramstaller, P., Ricken, J., Havel, M., Guth, A., & Merrow, M.

(2004). A marker for the end of adolescence. *Current Biology, 14,* 1038–1039.

Roeser, R., Eccles, J., & Freedman-Doan, C. (1999). Academic functioning and mental health in adolescence: Patterns, progressions, and routes from childhood. *Journal of Adolescent Research, 14,* 135–174.

Roeser, R., Lord, S., & Eccles, J. (1994, February). *A portrait of academic alienation in adolescence: Motivation, mental health, and family experience.* Paper presented at the biennial meetings of the Society for Research on Adolescence, San Diego.

Roeser, R., Midgley, C., & Urdan, T. (1996). Perceptions of the school psychological environment and early adolescents' psychological and behavioral functioning in school: The mediating role of goals and belonging. *Journal of Educational Psychology, 88,* 408–422.

Rogers, I., Northstone, K., Dunger, D., Cooper, A., Ness, A., & Emmett, P. (2010). Diet throughout childhood and age at menarche in a contemporary cohort of British girls. *Public Health Nutrition, 13,* 2052–2063.

Rogers, J., Boruch, R., Stoms, G., & DeMoya, D. (1991). Impact of the Minnesota parental notification law on abortion and birth. *American Journal of Public Health, 81,* 294–298.

Rogers, L. O., Scott, M. A., & Way, N. (2015). Racial and gender identity among black adolescent males: An intersectionality perspective. *Child Development, 86,* 407–424.

Rogers, M., & Holmbeck, G. (1997). Effects of brief interparental aggression on children's adjustment: The moderating role of cognitive appraisal and coping. *Journal of Family Psychology, 11,* 125–130.

Rogers, R., Steadham, J. A., Fiduccia, C. E., Drogin, E. Y., & Robinson, E. V. (2014). Mired in Miranda misconceptions: A study of legally involved juveniles at different levels of psychosocial maturity. *Behavioral Sciences & the Law, 32,* 104–120.

Rogosch, F. A., Oshri, A., & Cicchetti, D. (2010). From child maltreatment to adolescent cannabis abuse and dependence: A developmental cascade model. *Development and Psychopathology, 22,* 883–897.

Rohde, P., Lewinsohn, P. M., Kahler, C. W., Seeley, J. R., & Brown, R. A. (2001). Natural course of alcohol use disorders from adolescence to young adulthood. *Journal of the American Academy of Child and Adolescent Psychiatry, 40,* 83–90.

Roisman, G. I. (2002). Beyond main effect models of adolescent work intensity, family closeness and school disengagement: Mediational and conditional hypotheses. *Journal of Adolescent Research, 17,* 331–345.

Roisman, G. I., Aguilar, B., & Egeland, B. (2004). Antisocial behavior in the transition to adulthood: The independent and interactive roles of developmental history and emerging developmental tasks. *Development and Psychopathology, 16,* 857–871.

Roisman, G. I., Booth-LaForce, C., Cauffman, E., Spieker, S., & The NICHD Early Child Care Research Network. (2009). The developmental significance of adolescent romantic relationships: parent and peer predictors of engagement and quality at age 15. *Journal of Youth and Adolescence, 38,* 1294–1303.

Roisman, G. I., Masten, A. S., Coatsworth, J. D., & Tellegen, A. (2004). Salient and emerging developmental tasks in the transition to adulthood. *Child Development, 75,* 123–133.

Roisman, G., Monahan, K., Campbell, S., Steinberg, L., Cauffman, E., & The National Institute of Child Health and Human Development Early Child Care Research Network. (2010). Is adolescence-onset antisocial behavior developmentally normative? *Development and Psychopathology, 22,* 295–311.

Romeo, R. S. (2013). The teenage brain: The stress response and the adolescent brain. *Current Directions in Psychological Science, 22,* 140–145.

Romer, D., Betancourt, L., Brodsky, N., Giannetta, J., Yang, W., & Hurt, H. (2011). Does adolescent risk taking imply weak executive function? A prospective study of relations between working memory performance, impulsivity, and risk taking in early adolescence. *Developmental Science, 14,* 1119–1133.

Romer, D., Betancourt, L., Giannetta, J., Brodsky, N., Farah, M., & Hurt, H. (2009a). Executive cognitive functions and impulsivity as correlates of risk taking and problem behavior in preadolescents. *Neuropsychologia, 47,* 2916–2926.

Romer, D., Black, M., Ricardo, I., Feigelman, S., Kaljee, L., Galbraith, J., . . . Stanton, B. (1994). Social influences on the sexual behavior of youth at risk for HIV exposure. *American Journal of Public Health, 84,* 977–985.

Romer, D., Sznitman, S., DiClemente, R., Salazar, L. F., Vanable, P. A., Carey, M. P., . . . Juzang, I. (2009b). Mass media as an HIV-prevention strategy: Using culturally sensitive messages to reduce HIV-associated sexual behavior of at-risk African American youth. *American Journal of Public Health, 99,* 2150–2159.

Romero, A. J., Carvajal, S. C., Valle, F., & Orduña, M. (2007). Adolescent bicultural stress and its impact on mental well-being among Latinos, Asian Americans, and European Americans. *Journal of Community Psychology, 35,* 519–534.

Romero, L., Pazol, K., Warner, L., Gavin, L., Moskosky, S., Besera, M., . . . Barfield, W. (2015). Trends in Use of Long-Acting Reversible Contraception Among Teens Aged 15–19 Years Seeking Contraceptive Services— United States, 2005–2013. *MMWR, 64,* 363–369.

Romich, J., Lundberg, S., & Tsang, K. (2009). Independence giving or autonomy taking? Childhood predictors of decision-sharing patterns between young adolescents and parents. *Journal of Research on Adolescence, 19,* 587–600.

Romo, L. F., Lefkowitz, E. S., Sigman, M., & Au, T. K. (2002). A longitudinal study of maternal messages about dating and sexuality and their influence on Latino adolescents. *Journal of Adolescent Health, 31,* 59–69.

Romo, L. F., Mireles-Rios, R., & Lopez-Tello, G. (2014). Latina mothers' and daughters' expectations for autonomy at age 15 (La Quinceañera). *Journal of Adolescent Research, 29,* 271–294.

Rong, X., & Brown, F. (2001). The effects of immigrant generation and ethnicity on educational attainment among young African and Caribbean Blacks in the United States. *Harvard Educational Review, 71,* 536–565.

Rood, L., Roelofs, J., Bögels, S. M., & Meesters, C. (2012). Stress-reactive rumination, negative cognitive style, and stressors in relationship to depressive symptoms in non-clinical youth. *Journal of Youth & Adolescence, 41,* 414–425.

Roosa, M. W., Zeiders, K. H., Knight, G. P., Gonzales, N. A., Tein, J.-Y., Saenz, D., . . . Berkel, C. (2011). A test of the social development model during the transition to junior high with Mexican American adolescents. *Developmental Psychology, 47,* 527–537.

Roper, Z. J., Vecera, S. P., & Vaidya, J. G. (2014). Value-driven attentional capture in adolescence. *Psychological Science, 25,* 1987–1993.

Rosario, M., Salzinger, S., Feldman R., & Ng-Mak, D. (2008). Intervening processes between youths' exposure to community violence and internalizing symptoms over time: The roles of social support and coping. *American Journal of Community Psychology, 41,* 43–62.

Roscigno, V., & Ainsworth-Darnell, J. (1999). Race, cultural capital, and educational resources: Persistent inequalities and achievement returns. *Sociology of Education, 72,* 158–178.

Rose, A. J. (2002). Co-rumination in the friendships of girls and boys. *Child Development, 73,* 1830–1843.

Rose, A. J., & Swenson, L. P. (2009). Do perceived popular adolescents who aggress against others experience emotional adjustment problems themselves? *Developmental Psychology, 45,* 868–872.

Rose, A. J., Carlson, W., & Waller, E. M. (2007). Prospective associations of co-rumination with friendship and emotional adjustment: Considering the socioemotional trade-offs of co-rumination. *Developmental Psychology, 43,* 1019–1031.

Rose, A. J., Schwartz-Mette, R. A., Glick, G. C., Smith, R. L., & Luebbe, A. M. (2014). An observational study of co-rumination in adolescent friendships. *Developmental Psychology, 50,* 2199–2209.

Rose, A. J., Schwartz-Mette, R., Smith, R., Asher, S., Swenson, L., Carlson, W., & Waller, E. (2012). How girls and boys expect that talking about problems will make them feel: Associations with disclosure to friends in childhood and adolescence. *Child Development, 83,* 844–863.

Rose, A. J., Swenson, L. P., & Waller, E. M. (2004). Overt and relational aggression and perceived popularity: Developmental differences in concurrent and prospective relations. *Developmental Psychology, 40,* 378–387.

Rose, S., & Feldman, J. (1995). Prediction of IQ and specific cognitive abilities at 11 years from infancy measures. *Developmental Psychology, 31,* 685–696.

Rose, T., Joe, S., Shields, J., & Caldwell, C. H. (2014). Social integration and the mental health of Black adolescents. *Child Development, 85,* 1003–1018.

Rosen, L., Underwood, M., Beron, K., Gentsch, J., Wharton, M., & Rahdar, A. (2009). Persistent versus periodic experiences of social victimization: Predictors of adjustment. *Journal of Abnormal Child Psychology, 37,* 693–704.

Rosen, L. D., Lim, A.F., Felt, J., Carrier, L. M., Cheever, N. A., Lara-Ruiz, J. M. . . . & Rokkum, J. (2014). Media and technology use predicts ill-being among children, preteens and teenagers independent of the negative health impacts of exercise and eating habits. *Computers in Human Behavior, 35,* 364–375.

Rosenbaum, J. E. (2009). Patient teenagers? A comparison of the sexual behavior of virginity pledgers and matched nonpledgers. *Pediatrics, 123,* e110–120.

Rosenbaum, J. E. (2011). The complexities of college for all: Beyond fairy-tale dreams. *Sociology of Education, 84,* 113–117.

Rosenberg, M. (1975). The dissonant context and the adolescent self-concept. In S. Dragastin & G. Elder, Jr. (Eds.), *Adolescence in the life cycle.* Washington, DC: Hemisphere.

Rosenberg, M. (1986). Self-concept from middle childhood through adolescence. In J. Suls & A. Greenwald (Eds.), *Psychological perspectives on the self* (Vol. 3). Hillsdale, NJ: Erlbaum.

Rosenbloom, S. R., & Way, N. (2004). Experiences of discrimination among African American, Asian American, and Latino adolescents in an urban high school. *Youth and Society, 35,* 420–451.

Rosenblum, G., & Lewis, M. (1999). The relations among body image, physical attractiveness, and body mass in adolescence. *Child Development, 70,* 50–64.

Rosenthal, D. (1994, February). *Gendered constructions of adolescent sexuality.* Paper presented at the biennial meetings of the Society for Research on Adolescence, San Diego.

Rosenthal, D., & Feldman, S. (1990). The acculturation of Chinese immigrants: The effects on family functioning of length of residence in two cultural contexts. *Journal of Genetic Psychology, 151,* 493–514.

Rosenthal, D., & Smith, A. (1997). Adolescent sexual timetable. *Journal of Youth and Adolescence, 26,* 619–636.

Rosenthal, D., Smith, A., & de Visser, R. (1999). Personal and social factors influencing age at first sexual intercourse. *Archives of Sexual Behavior, 28,* 319–333.

Rosenthal, N. L., & Kobak, R. (2010). Assessing adolescents' attachment hierarchies: Differences across developmental periods and associations with individual adaptation. *Journal of Research on Adolescence, 20,* 678–706.

Roseth, C. J., Johnson, D. W., & Johnson, R. T. (2008). Promoting early adolescents' achievement and peer relationships: The effects of cooperative, competitive, and individualistic goal structures. *Psychological Bulletin, 134,* 223–246.

Roseweir, A., & Millar, R. (2009). The Role of Kisspeptin in the Control of Gonadotrophin Secretion, *Human Reproduction Update* 15, no. 2 (2009), 203–212.

Rossa, K. R., Smith, S. S., Allan, A. C., & Sullivan, K. A. (2014). The effects of sleep restriction on executive inhibitory control and affect in young adults. *Journal of Adolescent Health, 55,* 287–292.

Rote, W. M., & Smetana, J. G. (2015). Acceptability of information management strategies: Adolescents' and parents' judgement and links with adjustment and relationships. *Journal of Research on Adolescence, 25,* 490–505.

Rote, W. M., & Smetana, J. G. (2015). Beliefs about parents' right to know: Domain differences and associations with change in concealment. *Journal of Research on Adolescence, Early view.* DOI: 10.1111/jora.12194

Rote, W., & Smetana, J. (2011). Social cognition. In B. Brown & M. Prinstein (Eds.), *Encyclopedia of adolescence* (Vol. 1, pp. 333–341). New York: Academic Press.

Roth, J., Brooks-Gunn, J., Murray, L., & Foster, W. (1998). Promoting healthy adolescents: Synthesis of youth development program evaluations. *Journal of Research on Adolescence, 8,* 423–459.

Rotheram-Borus, M., & Koopman, C. (1991). Sexual risk behaviors, AIDS knowledge, and beliefs about AIDS among runaways. *American Journal of Public Health, 81,* 206–208.

Rotheram-Borus, M., Marelich, W., & Srinivasan, S. (1999). HIV risk among homosexual, bisexual, and heterosexual male and female youths. *Archives of Sexual Behavior, 28,* 159–177.

Rothman, E. F., Miller, E., Terpeluk, A., Glauber, A., & Randel, J. (2011). The proportion of U.S. parents who talk with their adolescent children about dating abuse. *Journal of Adolescent Health, 49,* 216–218.

Rouse, C. E., Brooks-Gunn, J., & McLanahan, S. (Eds.) (2005). *The future of children: School Readiness: Closing racial and ethnic gaps.* Brooking Institution and Woodrow Wilson School of Public and International Affairs, Princeton University.

Rousseau, J. (1911). *Emile* (B. Foxley, trans.). London: Dent. (Original work published 1762.)

Rovner, A., Nansel, T., Wang, J., & Iannotti, R. (2011). Food sold in school vending machines is associated with overall dietary intake. *Journal of Adolescent Health, 48,* 13–19.

Rowe, C., La Greca, A., & Alexandersson, A. (2010). Family and individual factors associated with substance involvement and PTS symptoms among adolescents in greater New Orleans after Hurricane Katrina. *Journal of Consulting and Clinical Psychology, 78,* 806–817.

Rowe, D., Rodgers, J., Meseck-Bushey, S., & St. John, C. (1989). Sexual behavior and nonsexual deviance: A sibling study of their relationship. *Developmental Psychology, 25,* 61–69.

Rowe, D., Vazsonyi, A., & Flannery, D. (1994). No more than skin deep: Ethnic and racial similarity in developmental processes. *Psychological Review, 101,* 396–413.

Rowland, B., Toumbourou, J. W., & Livingston, M. (2015). The association of alcohol outlet density with illegal underage adolescent purchasing of alcohol. *Journal of Adolescent Health, 56,* 146–152.

Roye, C., & Balk, S. (1996). The relationship of partner support to outcomes for teenage mothers and their children: A review. *Journal of Adolescent Health, 19,* 86–93.

Rozek, C. S., Hyde, J. S., Svoboda, R. C., Hulleman, C. S., & Harackiewicz, J. M. (2014). Gender differences in the effects of a utility-value intervention to help parents motivate adolescents in mathematics and science. *Journal of Educational Psychology, 107,* 195–206.

Rozin, P., Bauer, R., & Catanese, D. (2003). Food and life, pleasure and worry, among American college students: Gender differences and regional similarities. *Journal of Personality and Social Psychology, 85,* 132–141.

Rubin, D., et al. (1986). Autobiographical memory across the adult life span. In D. Rubin (Ed.), *Autobiographical Memory* (pp. 202–221). Cambridge, UK: Cambridge University Press.

Rubin, K., Bukowski, W., & Parker, J. (2006). Peer interactions, relationships, and groups. In W. Damon & R. Lerner (Series Eds.), & N. Eisenberg (Vol. Ed.), *Handbook of child psychology: Vol 3. Social, emotional, and personality development* (6th ed., pp 571–645). Hoboken, NJ: Wiley.

Rubin, K., LeMare, L., & Lollis, S. (1990). Social withdrawal in childhood: Developmental pathways to peer rejection. In S. Asher & J. Coie (Eds.), *Peer rejection in childhood* (pp. 217–249). New York: Cambridge University Press.

Ruchkin, V., Henrich, C. C., Jones, S. M., Vermeiren, R., & Schwab-Stone, M. (2007). Violence exposure and psychopathology in urban youth: The mediating role of post-traumatic stress. *Journal of Abnormal Child Psychology, 35,* 578–593.

Ruck, M., Abramovitch, R., & Keating, D. (1998). Children and adolescents' understanding of rights: Balancing nurturance and self-determination. *Child Development, 64,* 404–417.

Ruck, M., Peterson-Badali, M., & Day, D. M. (2002). Adolescents' and mothers' understanding of children's rights in the home. *Journal of Research on Adolescence, 12,* 373–398.

Rudolph, K. D., Lansford, J. E., Agoston, A. M., Sugimura, N., Schwartz, D., Dodge, K. A., et al. (2014). Peer victimization and social alienation: Predicting deviant peer affiliation in middle school. *Child Development, 85,* 124–139.

Rudolph, K. D., Troop-Gordon, W., Lambert, S. F., & Natsuaki, M. N. (2014). Long-term consequences of pubertal timing for youth depression: Identifying personal and contextual pathways of risk. *Development and Psychopathology, 26,* 1423–1444.

Rudolph, K., & Hammen, C. (1999). Age and gender as determinants of stress exposure, generation, and reactions in youngsters: A transactional perspective. *Child Development, 70,* 660–677.

Rudolph, K., & Klein, D. (2009). Exploring depressive personality traits in youth: Origins, correlates, and developmental consequences. *Development and Psychopathology, 21,* 1155–1180.

Rueger, S. Y., Chen, P., Jenkins, L. N., & Choe, H. J. (2014). Effects of perceived support from mothers, fathers, and teachers on depressive symptoms during the transition to middle school. *Journal of Youth & Adolescence, 43,* 655–670.

Rueter, M., & Kwon, H. (2005). Developmental trends in adolescent suicidal ideation. *Journal of Research on Adolescence, 15,* 205–222.

Ruggles, S. (1994). The origins of African-American family structure. *American Sociological Review, 59,* 136–151.

Ruhl, H., Dolan, E. A., & Buhrmester, D. (2014). Adolescent attachment trajectories with mothers and fathers: The importance of parent-child relationship experiences and gender. *Journal of Research on Adolescence, 25,* 427–442.

Ruiz, S., Roosa, M., & Gonzales, N. (2002). Predictors of self-esteem for Mexican American and European American youths: A reexamination of the influence of parenting. *Journal of Family Psychology, 16,* 70–80.

Rulison, K. L., Gest, S. D., & Loken, E. (2013). Dynamic social networks and physical aggression: The moderating role of gender and social status among peers. *Journal of Research on Adolescence, 23,* 437–449.

Rulison, K. L., Kreager, D. A., & Osgood, D. W. (2014). Delinquency and peer acceptance in adolescence: A within-person test of Moffitt's hypotheses. *Developmental Psychology, 50,* 2437–2448.

Rumbaut, R. (1997). Assimilation and its discontents: Between rhetoric and reality. *International Migration Review, 31,* 923–960.

Rumberger, R. (2012). *Dropping out.* Cambridge, MA: Harvard University Press.

Rumberger, R., & Palardy, G. (2005). Test scores, dropout rates, and transfer rates as alternative indicators of high school performance. *American Education Research Journal, 42,* 3–42.

Rumberger, R., Ghatak, R., Poulos, G., Ritter, P., & Dornbusch, S. (1990). Family influences on dropout behavior in one California high school. *Sociology of Education, 63,* 283–299.

Rusby, J. C., Forrester, K. K., Biglan A., & Metzler, C. W. (2005). Relationships between peer harassment and adolescent problem behaviors. *Journal of Early Adolescence, 25,* 453–477.

Russell, S. (1994). Life course antecedents of premarital conception in Great Britain. *Journal of Marriage and the Family, 56,* 480–492.

Russell, S. (2002). Childhood development risk for teen childbearing in Britain. *Journal of Research on Adolescence, 12,* 305–324.

Russell, S., Elder, G. H., Jr., & Conger, R. (1997, April). *School transitions and academic achievement.* Paper presented at the biennial meetings of the Society for Research in Child Development, Washington, DC.

Russell, S., Thompson, E., & Harris, R. (2011). Sexual orientation. In B. Brown & M. Prinstein (Eds.), *Encyclopedia of adolescence* (Vol. 1, pp. 325–332). New York: Academic Press.

Russell, S. T., Everett, B. G., Rosario, M., & Birkett, M. (2014). Indicators of victimization and sexual orientation among adolescents: Analyses from youth risk behavior surveys. *American Journal of Public Health, 104,* 255–261.

Ryan, A. M. (2001). The peer group as a context for the development of young adolescent motivation and achievement. *Child Development, 72,* 1135–1150.

Ryan, A. M., & Patrick, H. (2001). The classroom social environment and changes in adolescents' motivation and engagement during middle school. *American Educational Research Journal, 38,* 437–460.

Ryan, J., Marshall, J., Herz, D., & Hernandez, P. (2008). Juvenile delinquency in child welfare: Investigating group home effects. *Children and Youth Services Review, 30,* 1088–1099.

Ryan, R. M. (2015). Nonresident fatherhood and adolescent sexual behavior: A comparison of siblings approach. *Developmental Psychology, 51,* 211–223.

Ryan, R., & Lynch, J. (1989). Emotional autonomy versus detachment: Revisiting the vicissitudes of adolescence and young adulthood. *Child Development, 60,* 340–356.

Ryan, S., Franzetta, K., & Manlove, J. (2007). Knowledge, perceptions, and motivations for contraception: Influence on teens' contraceptive consistency. *Youth and Society, 39,* 182–208.

Ryan, S., Franzetta, K., Manlove, J., & Schelar, E. (2008). Older sexual partners during

adolescence: Links to reproductive health outcomes in young adulthood. *Perspectives on Sexual and Reproductive Health, 40,* 17–26.

Sabiston, C. M., Lovato, C. Y., Ahmed, R., Pullman, A. W., Hadd, V., Campbell, H. S., . . .Brown, K. (2009). School smoking policy characteristics and individual perceptions of the school tobacco context: Are they linked to students' smoking status? *Journal of Youth and Adolescence, 38,* 1374–1387.

Sackett, P. R., Kuncel, N. R., Arneson, J. J., Cooper, S. R., & Waters, S. D. (2009). Does socioeconomic status explain the relationship between admissions tests and post-secondary academic performance? *Psychological Bulletin, 135,* 1–22.

Sackett, P. R., Kuncel, N. R., Beatty, A. S., Rigdon, J. L., Shen, W., & Kiger, T. B. (2012). The role of socioeconomic status in SAT-grade relationships and in college admissions decision. *Psychological Science, 23,* 1000–1007.

Saewyc, E. M. (2011). Research on adolescent sexual orientation: Development, health disparities, stigma, and resilience. *Journal of Research on Adolescence, 21,* 256–272.

Safron, J., Sy, S., & Schulenberg, J. (2003). Wishing to work: New perspectives on how adolescents' part-time work intensity is linked to educational disengagement, substance use, and other problem behaviours. *International Journal of Behavioral Development, 27,* 301–315.

Sagar, H., Schofield, J., & Snyder, H. (1983). Race and gender barriers: Preadolescent peer behavior in academic classrooms. *Child Development, 54,* 1032–1040.

Sagrestano, L., McCormick, S., Paikoff, R., & Holmbeck, G. (1999). Pubertal development and parent–child conflict in low-income, urban, African American adolescents. *Journal of Research on Adolescence, 9,* 85–107.

Salafia, E., & Gondoli, D. (2011). A 4-year longitudinal investigation of the processes by which parents and peers influence the development of early adolescent girls' bulimic symptoms. *Journal of Early Adolescence, 31,* 390–414.

Salas-Wright, C. P., Vaughn, M. G., Hodge, D. R., Perron, B. E. (2012). Religiosity profiles of American youth in relation to substance use, violence, and delinquency. *Journal of Youth & Adolescence, 41,* 1560–1575.

Sale, E., Sambrano, S., Springer, J. F., Pena, C., Pan, W., & Kasim, R. (2005). Family protection and prevention of alcohol use among Hispanic youth at high risk. *American Journal of Community Psychology, 36,* 195–205.

Salekin, R. T. (2008). Psychopathy and recidivism from mid-adolescence to young adulthood: Cumulating legal problems and limiting life opportunities. *Journal of Abnormal Psychology, 117,* 386–395.

Salem, D., Zimmerman, M., & Notaro, P. (1998). Effects of family structure, family process, and father involvement on psychosocial outcomes among African American adolescents. *Family Relations, 47,* 331–341.

Salinger, J. D. (1964). *The catcher in the rye.* New York: Bantam Books. (Original work published 1951)

Sallquist, J., Eisenberg, N., French, D. C., Purwono, U., & Suryanti, T. A. (2010). Indonesian adolescents' spiritual and religious experiences and their longitudinal relations with socioemotional functioning. *Developmental Psychology, 46,* 699–716.

Salmivalli, C. (1998). Intelligent, attractive, well-behaving, unhappy: The structure of adolescents' self-concept and its relations to their social behavior. *Journal of Research on Adolescence, 8,* 333–354.

Salsberry, P., Reagan, P., & Pajer, K. (2009). Growth differences by age of menarche in African American and White girls. *Nursing Research, 58,* 382–390.

Salusky, I., Larson, R. W., Griffith, A., Wu, J., Raffaelli, M., Sugimura, N., & Guzman, M. (2014). How adolescents develop responsibility: What can be learned from youth programs. *Journal of Research on Adolescence, 24,* 417–430.

Salzinger, S., Feldman, R., Rosario, M., & Ng-Mak, D. (2011). Role of parent and peer relationships and individual characteristics in middle school children's behavioral outcomes in the face of community violence. *Journal of Research on Adolescence, 21,* 395–407.

Samarova, V., Shilo, G., & Diamond, G. M. (2014). Changes in youths' perceived parental acceptance of their sexual minority status over time. *Journal of Research on Adolescence, 24,* 681–688.

Samek, D. R., McGue, M., Keyes, M., & Iacono, W. G. (2014). Sibling facilitation mediates the association between older and younger sibling alcohol use in late adolescence. *Journal of Research on Adolescence, Early view.* DOI: 10.1111/jora.12154

Samela-Aro, K. (2011). Stages of adolescence. In B. Brown & M. Prinstein (Eds.), *Encyclopedia of adolescence* (Vol. 1, pp. 360–368). New York: Academic Press.

Sampson, R. (1992). Family management and child development: Insights from social disorganization theory. In J. McCord (Ed.), *Advances in criminological theory* (Vol. 3, pp. 63–93). New Brunswick, NJ: Transaction.

Sampson, R. (1997). Collective regulation of adolescent misbehavior: Validation results from eighty Chicago neighborhoods. *Journal of Adolescent Research, 12,* 227–244.

Sampson, R., & Laub, J. (2003). Life-course desistors? Trajectories of crime among delinquent boys followed to age 70. *Criminology, 41,* 555–592.

Sampson, R., Raudenbusch, S., & Earls, F. (1997). Neighborhoods and violent crime: A multilevel study of collective efficacy for children. *Science, 277,* 918–924.

Sánchez, B., Esparza, P., & Colón, Y. (2008). Natural mentoring under the microscope: An investigation of mentoring relationships and Latino adolescents' academic performance. *Journal of Community Psychology, 36,* 468–482.

Sanchez, Z. M., Opaleye, E. S., Chaves, T. V., Noto, A. R., & Nappo, S. A. (2011). God forbids or mom disapproves? Religious beliefs that prevent drug use among youth. *Journal of Adolescent Research, 26,* 591–616.

Sandfort, J., & Hill, M. (1996). Assisting young, unmarried mothers to become self-sufficient: The effects of different types of early economic support. *Journal of Marriage and the Family, 58,* 311–326.

Sandfort, T. G., Bos, H., Collier, K. L., & Metselaar, M. (2010). School environment and the mental health of sexual minority youths: A study among Dutch young adolescents. *American Journal of Public Health, 100,* 1696–1700.

Santelli, J., Abma, J., Ventura, S., Lindberg, L., Morrow, B., Anderson, J. E., . . .Hamilton, B. (2004). Can changes in sexual behaviors among high school students explain the decline in teen pregnancy rates in the 1990s? *Journal of Adolescent Health, 35,* 80–90.

Santelli, J., Carter, M., Orr, M., & Dittus, P. (2009). Trends in sexual risk behaviors, by nonsexual risk behavior involvement, U.S. high school students, 1991–2007. *Journal of Adolescent Health, 44,* 372–379.

Santelli, J., Lindberg, L., Abma, J., McNeely, C., & Resnick, M. (2000). Adolescent sexual behavior: Estimates and trends from four nationally representative surveys. *Family Planning Perspectives, 32,* 156–165.

Santelli, J., Morrow, B., Anderson, J., & Lindberg, L. (2006). Contraceptive use and pregnancy risk among U.S. high school students, 1991–2003. *Perspectives on Sexual and Reproductive Health, 38,* 106–111.

Santelli, J., Orr, M., Lindberg, L., & Diaz, D. (2009). Changing behavioral risk for pregnancy among high school students in the United States, 1991–2007. *Journal of Adolescent Health, 45,* 25–32.

Santelli, J., Warren, C., Lowry, R., Sogolow, E., Collins, J., Kann, L., . . .Celentano, D. (1997). The use of condoms with other contraceptive methods among young men and women. *Family Planning Perspectives, 29,* 261–267.

Santesso, D. L., & Segalowitz, S. J. (2008). Developmental differences in error-related ERPs in middle- to late-adolescent males. *Developmental Psychology, 44,* 205–217.

Santiago, D. C., Gudiño, O. G., Baweja, S., & Nadeem, E. (2014). Academic achievement among immigrant and U.S.-Born Latino adolescents: Associations with cultural, family, and acculturation factors. *Journal of Community Psychology, 42,* 735–747.

Santo, J. B., Bukowski, W. M., Stella-Lopez, L., Carmago, G., Mayman, S. B., & Adams, R. E.

(2013). Factors underlying contextual variations in the structure of the self: Differences related to SES, gender, culture, and "majority/nonmajority" status during early adolescence. *Journal of Research on Adolescence, 23,* 69–80.

Santrock, J. W. (2014). Adolescence (15th ed.). New York, NY: McGraw-Hill.

Saporito, S., & Sohoni, D. (2006). Coloring outside the lines: Racial segregation in public schools and their attendance boundaries. *Sociology of Education, 79,* 81–105.

Sargent, J., & Dalton, M. (2001). Does parental disapproval of smoking prevent adolescents from becoming established smokers? *Pediatrics, 108,* 1256–1262.

Sarwer, D. B., & Dilks, R. J. (2012). Invited commentary: Childhood and adolescent obesity: Psychological and behavioral issues in weight loss treatment. *Journal of Youth and Adolescence, 41,* 98–104.

Saunders, J., Davis, L., Williams, T., & Williams, J. H. (2004). Gender differences in self-perceptions and academic outcomes: A study of African American high school students. *Journal of Youth and Adolescence, 33,* 81–90.

Savage, M., & Scott, L. (1998). Physical activity and rural middle school adolescents. *Journal of Youth and Adolescence, 27,* 245–253.

Savin-Williams, R. (2006). Who's gay? Does it matter? *Current Directions in Psychological Science, 15,* 40–44.

Savin-Williams, R. C., & Vrangalova, Z. (2013). Mostly heterosexual as a distinct sexual orientation group: A systematic review of the empirical evidence. *Developmental Review, 33,* 58–88.

Savin-Williams, R., & Berndt, T. (1990). Friendship and peer relations. In S. Feldman & G. Elliott (Eds.), *At the threshold: The developing adolescent* (pp. 277–307). Cambridge, MA: Harvard University Press.

Savin-Williams, R., & Demo, D. (1983). Situational and transituational determinants of adolescent self-feelings. *Journal of Personality and Social Psychology, 44,* 824–833.

Savin-Williams, R., & Ream, G. (2007). Prevalence and stability of sexual orientation components during adolescence and young adulthood. *Archives of Sexual Behavior, 36,* 385–394.

Savin-Williams, R. C., Joyner, K., & Rieger, G. (2012). Prevalence and stability of self-reported sexual orientation identity during young adulthood. *Archives of Sexual Behavior, 41,* 103–110.

Savolainen, J., Hughes, L. A., Mason, W. A., Hurtig, T. M., Ebeling, H., Moilanen, I. K., . . . & Taanila, A. M. (2012). Antisocial propensity, adolescent school outcomes, and the risk of criminal conviction. *Journal of Research on Adolescence, 22,* 54–64.

Saxbe, D. E., Margolin, G., Spies Shapiro, L. A., & Baucom, B. R. (2012). Does dampened physiological reactivity protect youth in aggressive family environments? *Child Development, 83*, 821–830.

Scales, P., Benson, P., & Mannes, M. (2006). The contribution to adolescent well-being made by nonfamily adults: An examination of developmental assets as contexts and processes. *Journal of Community Psychology, 34*, 401–413.

Scales, P., Benson, P., Roehlkepartain, E., Sesma, Jr., A., & van Dulmen, M. (2006). The role of developmental assets in predicting academic achievement: A longitudinal study. *Journal of Adolescence, 29*, 691–708.

Scanlan, T., Bakes, M., & Scanlan, L. (2005). Participation in sport: A developmental glimpse at emotion. In J. Mahoney, R. Larson, & J. Eccles (Eds.), *Organized activities as contexts of development* (pp. 275–309). Hillsdale, NJ: Erlbaum.

Scaramella, L., Conger, R. D., Spoth, R., & Simons, R. L. (2002). Evaluation of a social contextual model of delinquency: A cross-study replication. *Child Development, 73*, 175–195.

Schaefer, D. R., Simpkins, S. D., Vest, A. E., & Price, C. D. (2011). The contribution of extra-curricular activities to adolescent friendships: New insights through social network analysis. *Developmental Psychology, 47*, 1141–1152.

Schaefer, D. R., & Simpkins, S. D. (2014). Using social network analysis to clarify the role of obesity in selection of adolescent friends. *American Journal of Public Health, 104*, 1223–1229.

Schaefer, D. R., Haas, S. A., & Bishop, N. J. (2012). A dynamic model of US adolescents' smoking and friendship networks. *American Journal of Public Health, 102*, 12–18.

Scharf, M., Shulman, S., & Avigad-Spitz, L. (2005). Sibling relationships in emerging adulthood and in adolescence. *Journal of Adolescent Research, 20*, 64–90.

Scheier, L., & Botvin, G. (1998). Relations of social skills, personal competence, and adolescent alcohol use: A developmental exploratory study. *Journal of Early Adolescence, 18*, 77–114.

Scheier, L., Botvin, G. J., Griffin, K. W., & Diaz, T. (2000). Dynamic growth models of self-esteem and adolescent alcohol use. *Journal of Early Adolescence, 20*, 178–209.

Schelleman-Offermans, K., Knibbe, R. A., & Kuntsche, E. (2013). Are the effects of early pubertal timing on the initiation of weekly alcohol use mediated by peers and/or parents? A longitudinal study. *Developmental Psychology, 49*, 1277–1285.

Schellenbach, C., Whitman, T., & Borkowski, J. (1992). Toward an integrative model of adolescent parenting. *Human Development, 35*, 81–99.

Schepis, T. S., & Krishnan-Sarin, S. (2009). Sources of prescriptions for misuse by adolescents: Differences in sex, ethnicity, and severity of misuse in a population-based study.

Journal of the American Academy of Child and Adolescent Psychiatry, 48, 828–836.

Scherf, K., Behrmann, M., & Dahl, R. (2012). Facing changes and changing faces in adolescence: A new model for investigating adolescent-specific interactions between pubertal, brain and behavioral development. *Developmental Cognitive Neuroscience, 2*, 199–219.

Schiller, K. (1999). Effects of feeder patterns on students' transition to high school. *Sociology of Education, 72*, 216–233.

Schilling, E. A., Aseltine, R. H. J., Glanovsky, J. L., James, A., & Jacobs, D. (2009). Adolescent alcohol use, suicidal ideation, and suicide attempts. *Journal of Adolescent Health, 44*, 335–341.

Schleepen, T., & Jonkman, L. (2009). The development of non-spatial working memory capacity during childhood and adolescence and the role of interference control: An n-back task study. *Developmental Neuropsychology, 35*, 37–56.

Schlegel, A. (2009). Cross-cultural issues in the study of adolescent development. In R. Lerner & L. Steinberg (Eds.), *Handbook of adolescent psychology* (3rd ed., Vol. 2, pp. 570–589). New York: Wiley.

Schlegel, A., & Barry, H. (1991). *Adolescence: An anthropological inquiry.* New York: Free Press.

Schmidt, J. (2003). Correlates of reduced misconduct among adolescents facing adversity. *Journal of Youth and Adolescence, 32*, 439–452.

Schmidt, J., & Padilla, B. (2003). Self-esteem and family challenge: An investigation of their effects on achievement. *Journal of Youth and Adolescence, 32*, 37–46.

Schmidt, J., Shumow, L., & Kackar, H. (2007). Adolescents' participation in service activities and its impact on academic, behavioral, and civic outcomes. *Journal of Youth and Adolescence, 36*, 127–140.

Schmidt, J. A., Shumow, L., Kackar, H. Z (2012). Associations of participation in service activities with academic, behavioral, and civic outcomes of adolescents at varying risk levels. *Journal of Youth & Adolescence, 41*, 932–947.

Schmidt, M. G., Reppucci, N. D., & Woolard, J. (2003). Effectiveness of participation as a defendant: The attorney–juvenile client relationships. *Behavioral Sciences and the Law, 21*, 175–198.

Schmiedek, F., Lövdén, M., & Lindenberger, U. (2014). Younger adults show long-term effects of cognitive training on broad cognitive abilities over 2 years. *Developmental Psychology, 50*, 2304–2310.

Schneider, B., & Stevenson, D. (1999). *The ambitious generations: America's teenagers, motivated but directionless.* New Haven, CT: Yale University Press.

Schneiders, J., Nicolson, N. A., Berkhof, J., Feron, F. J., van Os, J., & deVries, M. W. (2006).

Mood reactivity to daily negative events in early adolescence: Relationship to risk for psychopathology. *Developmental Psychology, 42*, 543–554.

Schnurr, M. P., & Lohman, B. J. (2013). The impact of collective efficacy on risks for adolescents perpetration of dating violence. *Journal of Youth & Adolescence, 42*, 518–535.

Schochet, T., Kelley, A., & Landry, C. (2004). Differential behavioral effects of nicotine exposure in adolescent and adult rats. *Psychopharmacology, 175*, 265–273.

Schochet, T., Kelley, A., & Landry, C. (2005). Differential expression of arc mRNA and other plasticity-related genes induced by nicotine in adolescent rat forebrain. *Neuroscience, 135*, 285–297.

Schofield, H. T., Bierman, K. L., Heinrichs, B., & Nix, R. L. (2008). Predicting early sexual activity with behavior problems exhibited at school entry and in early adolescence. *Journal of Abnormal Child Psychology, 36*, 1175–1188.

Schofield, T. J., Conger, R. D., Martin, M. J., Stockdale, G. D., Conger, K. J., & Widaman, K. F. (2009). Reciprocity in parenting of adolescents within the context of marital negativity. *Developmental Psychology, 45*, 1708–1722.

Scholes-Balog, K. E., Hemphill, S. A., Patton, G. C., & Toumbourou, J. W. (2015). Relationships between substance use and depressive symptoms: A longitudinal study of Australian adolescents. *The Journal of Early Adolescence, 35*, 538–561.

Scholte, R., van Lieshout, C., & van Aken, C. (2001). Perceived relational support in adolescence: Dimensions, configurations, and adolescent adjustment. *Journal of Research on Adolescence, 11*, 71–94.

Schommer, M., Calvert, C., Gariglietti, G., & Bajaj, A. (1997). The development of epistemological beliefs among secondary school students: A longitudinal study. *Journal of Educational Psychology, 89*, 37–40.

Schooler, D., Sorsoli, C., Kim, J., & Tolman, D. (2009). Beyond exposure: A person-oriented approach to adolescent media diets. *Journal of Research on Adolescence, 19*, 484–508.

Schoon, I., Bynner, J., Joshi, H., Parsons, S., Wiggins, R. D., & Sacker, A. (2002). The influence of context, timing, and duration of risk experiences for the passage from childhood to midadulthood. *Child Development, 73*, 1486–1504.

Schoon, I., Parsons, S., & Sacker, A. (2004). Socioeconomic adversity, educational resilience, and subsequent levels of adult adaptation. *Journal of Adolescent Research, 19*, 383–404.

Schroeder, R. D., & Mowen, T. J. (2014). Parenting style transitions and delinquency. *Youth & Society, 46*, 228–254.

Schulenberg, J., Bryant, A. L., & O'Malley, P. (2004). Taking hold of some kind of life: How developmental tasks relate to trajectories of well-being during the transition to adulthood.

Development and Psychopathology, 16, 1119–1140.

Schulenberg, J., Maggs, J., Dielman, T., Leech, S., Kloska, D., Shope, J., & Laetz, V. (1999). On peer influences to get drunk: A panel study of young adolescents. *Merrill-Palmer Quarterly, 45,* 108–142.

Schulenberg, J., Wadsworth, K., O'Malley, P., Bachman, J., & Johnston, L. (1996). Adolescent risk factors for binge drinking during the transition to young adulthood: Variable- and pattern-centered approaches to change. *Developmental Psychology, 32,* 659–674.

Schwartz, D., Kelly, B. M., & Duong, M. T. (2013). Do academicaly-engaged adolescents experience social sanctions from the peer group? *Journal of Youth & Adolescence, 42,* 1319–1330.

Schwartz, S. E. O., Rhodes, J. E., Chan, C. S., & Herrera, C. (2011). The impact of school-based mentoring on youths with different relational profiles. *Developmental Psychology, 47,* 450–462.

Schwartz, S. J., Côté, J. E., & Arnett, J. J. (2005). Identity and agency in emerging adulthood: Two developmental routes in the individualization process. *Youth and Society, 37,* 201–229.

Schwartz, S. J., Pantin, H., Prado, G., Sullivan, S., & Szapocznik, J. (2005). Family functioning, identity and problem behavior in Hispanic immigrant early adolescents. *Journal of Early Adolescence, 25,* 392–420.

Schwartz, S., Rhodes, J. E., Spencer, R., & Grossman, J. B. (2013). Youth initiated mentoring: Investigating a new approach to working with vulnerable adolescents. *American Journal of Community Psychology, 52,* 155–169.

Schwartz, S. J., Des Rosiers, S., Huang, S., Zamboanga, B. L., Unger, J. B., Knight, G. P., & Szapocznik, P. (2013). Developmental trajectories of acculturation in Hispanic adolescents: associations with family functioning and adolescent risk behavior. *Child Development, 84,* 1355–1372.

Schwartz, S. J., Unger, J. B., Zamboanga, B. L., Córdova D., Mason, C.A., Huang, S., . . . *Szapocznik, J.* (2015). Developmental trajectories of acculturation: Links with family functioning and mental health in recent-immigrant Hispanic adolescents. *Child Development, 86,* 726–748.

Schwartz-Mette, R., & Rose, A. (2012). Co-rumination mediates contagion of internalizing symptoms within youths' friendships. *Developmental Psychology, 48,* 1355–1365.

Schwartz-Mette, R. A., & Rose, A. J. (2012). Co-rumination mediates contagion of internalizing symptoms within youths' friendships. *Developmental Psychology, 48,* 1355–1365.

Schwarz, B., Mayer, B., Trommsdorff, G., Ben-Arieh, A., Friedlmeier, M., Lubiewska, K., . . . & Peltzer, K. (2012). Does the importance of parent and peer relationships for adolescents' life satisfaction vary across cultures? *The Journal of Early Adolescence, 32,* 55–80.

Schwarz, B., Stutz, M., & Ledermann, T. (2012). Perceived interparental conflict and early adolescents friendships: the role of attachment security and emotion regulation. *Journal of Youth & Adolescence, 41,* 1240–1252.

Schweder, R. (Ed.). (1998). *Welcome to middle age! And other cultural fictions.* Chicago: University of Chicago Press.

Schweingruber, H. A., & Kalil, A. (2000). Decision making and depressive symptoms in Black and White multigenerational teen-parent families. *Journal of Family Psychology, 14,* 556–569.

Scott, E., & Steinberg, L. (2008). *Rethinking juvenile justice.* Cambridge, MA: Harvard University Press.

Scott, L. D., & House, L. E. (2005). Relationship of distress and perceived control to coping with perceived racial discrimination among Black youth. *Journal of Black Psychology, 31,* 254–272.

Scull, T. M., Kupersmidt, J. B., Erausquin, J. T. (2014). The impact of media-related cognitions on children's substance use outcomes in the context of parental and peer substance use. *Journal of Youth & Adolescence, 43,* 717–728.

Seaton, E. K., Upton, R., Gilbert, A., & Volpe, V. (2014). A moderated mediation model: racial discrimination, coping strategies, and racial identity among black adolescents. *child development, 85,* 882–890.

Seaton, E., & Gilbert, A. (2011). Ethnic/racial identity among minority youth. In B. Brown & M. Prinstein (Eds.), *Encyclopedia of adolescence* (Vol. 2, pp. 68–74). New York: Academic Press.

Seaton, E., & Yip, T. (2009). School and neighborhood contexts, perceptions of racial discrimination, and psychological well-being among African American adolescents. *Journal of Youth and Adolescence, 38,* 153–163.

Seaton, E., Caldwell, C., Sellers, R., & Jackson, J. (2008). The prevalence of perceived discrimination among African American and Caribbean Black youth. *Developmental Psychology, 44,* 1288–1297.

Seaton, E., Caldwell, C., Sellers, R., & Jackson, J. (2010a). An intersectional approach for understanding perceived discrimination and psychological well-being among African American and Caribbean Black youth. *Developmental Psychology, 46,* 1372–1379.

Seaton, E., Neblett, E., Upton, R., Hammond, W., & Sellers, R. (2011). The moderating capacity of racial identity between perceived discrimination and psychological well-being over time among African American youth. *Child Development, 82,* 1850–1867.

Seaton, E., Scottham, K., & Sellers, R. (2006). The status model of racial identity development in African American adolescents: Evidence of structure, trajectories, and well-being. *Child Development, 77,* 1416–1426.

Seaton, E., Yip, T., & Sellers, R. (2009). A longitudinal examination of racial identity and racial discrimination among African American adolescents. *Child Development, 80,* 406–417.

Sebastian, C., Burnett, S., & Blakemore, S. (2008). Development of the self-concept during adolescence. *Trends in Cognitive Science, 12,* 441–446.

Sebastian, C., Tan, G., Roiser, J., Viding, E., Dumontheil, I., & Blakemore, S.-J. (2011). Developmental influences on the neural bases of responses to social rejection: Implications of social neuroscience for education. *Neuroimage, 57,* 686–694.

Secor-Turner, M., McMorris, B., Sieving, R., & Bearinger, L. H. (2013). Life experiences of instability and sexual risk behaviors among high-risk adolescent females. *Perspectives on Sexual & Reproductive Health, 45,* 101–107.

Sedgh, G., Finer, L. B., Bankole, A., Eilers, M. A., & Singh, S. (2015). Adolescent pregnancy, birth, and abortion rates across countries: Levels and recent trends. *Journal of Adolescent Health, 56,* 223–230.

Seegers, V., Petit, D., Falissard, B., Vitaro, F., Tremblay, R., Montplaisir, J., & Touchette, E. (2011). Short sleep duration and body mass index: A prospective longitudinal study in preadolescence. *American Journal of Epidemiology, 173,* 621–629.

Segalowitz, S. J., & Davies, P. L. (2004). Charting the maturation of the frontal lobe: An electrophysiological strategy. *Brain and Cognition, 55,* 116–133.

Segalowitz, S. J., Santesso, D. L., Willoughby, T., Reker, D. L., Campbell, K., Chalmers, H., & Rose-Krasnor, L. (2012). Adolescent peer interaction and trait surgency weaken medial prefrontal cortex responses to failure. *Social Cognitive Affective Neuroscience, 7,* 115–124.

Seguin, J., Arseneault, L., & Tremblay, R. (2007). The contribution of "cool" and "hot" components of decision-making in adolescence: Implications for developmental psychopathology. *Cognitive Development, 22,* 530–543.

Seidman, E., & French, S. E. (2004). Developmental trajectories and ecological transitions: A two-step procedure to aid in the choice of prevention and promotion interventions. *Development and Psychopathology, 16,* 1141–1159.

Seidman, E., Aber, J., Allen, L., & French, S. (1996). The impact of the transition to high school on the self-system and perceived social context of poor urban youth. *American Journal of Community Psychology, 24,* 489–515.

Seidman, E., Lambert, L. E., Allen, L., & Aber, J. L. (2003). Urban adolescents' transition to junior high school and protective family transactions. *Journal of Early Adolescence, 23,* 166–193.

Seiffge-Krenke, I. (2003). Testing theories of romantic development from adolescence to young adulthood: Evidence of a developmental sequence. *International Journal of Behavioral Development, 27,* 519–531.

Seiffge-Krenke, I. (2006). Leaving home or still in the nest? Parent–child relationships and psychological health as predictors of different leaving home patterns. *Developmental Psychology, 42,* 864–876.

Seiffge-Krenke, I., & Beyers, W. (2005). Coping trajectories from adolescence to young adulthood: Links to attachment state of mind. *Journal of Research on Adolescence, 15,* 561–582.

Seiffge-Krenke, I., & Klessinger, N. (2000). Long-term effects of avoidant coping on adolescents' depressive symptoms. *Journal of Youth and Adolescence, 29,* 617–630.

Seiffge-Krenke, I., & Stemmler, M. (2002). Factors contributing to gender differences in depressive symptoms: A test of three developmental models. *Journal of Youth and Adolescence, 31,* 405–417.

Seiffge-Krenke, I., Persike, M., Karaman, N. G., Cok, F., Herrera, D., Rohail, I., . . . & Hyeyoun, H. (2013). Stress with parents and peers: How adolescents from six nations cope with relationship stress. *Journal of Research on Adolescence, 23,* 103–117.

Seil, K. S., Desai, M. M., & Smith, M. V. (2014). Sexual orientation, adult connectedness, substance use, and mental health outcomes among adolescents: Findings from the 2009 New York City Youth Risk Behavior Survey. *American Journal of Public Health, 104,* 1950–1956.

Selemon, L. (2013). A role for synaptic plasticity in the adolescent development of executive function, *Translational Psychiatry, 3,* e238 and ff.

Selfhout, M., Branje, S., & Meeus, W. (2008). The development of delinquency and perceived friendship quality in adolescent best friendship dyads. *Journal of Abnormal Child Psychology, 36,* 471–485.

Sellers, R., Copeland-Linder, N., Martin, P., & Lewis, R. (2006). Racial identity matters: The relationship between racial discrimination and psychological functioning in African American adolescents. *Journal of Research on Adolescence, 16,* 187–216.

Sells, C., & Blum, R. (1996). Morbidity and mortality among U.S. adolescents: An overview of data and trends. *American Journal of Public Health, 86,* 513–519.

Sentse, M., Kiuru, N., Veenstra, R., Salmivalli, C. (2014). A social network approach to the interplay between adolescents' bullying and likeability over time. *Journal of Youth & Adolescence, 43,* 1409–1420.

Serovich, J., & Greene, K. (1997). Predictors of adolescent sexual risk taking behaviors which put them at risk for contracting HIV. *Journal of Youth and Adolescence, 26,* 429–444.

Settersten, R., Furstenberg, F., Jr., & Rumbaut, R. (Eds.). (2005). *On the frontier of adulthood.* Chicago: University of Chicago Press.

Seymour, K. E., Chronis-Tuscano, A., Iwamoto, D. K., Kurdziel, G., & MacPherson, L. (2014). Emotion regulation mediates the association between ADHD and depressive symptoms in a community sample of youth. *Journal of Abnormal Child Psychology, 42,* 611–621.

Shahinfar, A., Kupersmidt, J. B., & Matza, L. S. (2001). The relation between exposure to violence and social information processing among incarcerated adolescents. *Journal of Abnormal Psychology, 110,* 136–141.

Shanahan, L., McHale, S., Crouter, A., & Osgood, D. W. (2008). Linkages between parents' differential treatment, youth depressive symptoms, and sibling relationships. *Journal of Marriage and Family, 70,* 480–494.

Shanahan, L., McHale, S., Osgood, D. W., & Crouter, A. (2007). Conflict frequency with mothers and fathers from middle childhood to late adolescence: Within- and between-families comparisons. *Developmental Psychology, 43,* 539–550.

Shanahan, M. J., & Bauer, D. J. (2004). Developmental properties of transactional models: The case of life events and mastery from adolescence to young adulthood. *Development and Psychopathology, 16,* 1095–1117.

Shanahan, M. J., & Flaherty, B. P. (2001). Dynamic patterns of time use in adolescence. *Child Development, 72,* 385–401.

Shanahan, M. J., Porfeli, E., Mortimer, J. T., & Erickson, L. (2005). Subjective age identity and the transition to adulthood: When do adolescents become adults? In R. Settersten, F. Furstenberg, Jr., & R. Rumbaut (Eds.), *On the frontier of adulthood* (pp. 225–255). Chicago: University of Chicago Press.

Shannon, B. J., Raichle, M. E., Snyder, A. Z., Fair, D. A., Mills, K. L., Zhang, D., . . . Kiehl, K. (2011). Premotor functional connectivity predicts impulsivity in juvenile offenders. *Proceedings of the National Academy of Sciences, 108(27),* 11241–11245.

Sharabany, R., Gershoni, R., & Hofman, J. (1981). Girlfriend, boyfriend: Age and sex differences in intimate friendship. *Developmental Psychology, 17,* 800–808.

Sharkey, P., & Sampson, R. (2010). Destination effects: Residential mobility and trajectories of adolescent violence in a stratified metropolis. *Criminology, 48,* 639–681.

Sharp, C., Ha, C., & Fonagy, P. (2011). Get them before they get you: Trust, trustworthiness, and social cognition in boys with and without externalizing behavior problems. *Development and Psychopathology, 23,* 647–658.

Shaw, P., Gilliam, M., Liverpool, M., Weddle, C., Malek, M., Sharp, W., . . . Giedd, J. (2011). Cortical development in typically developing children with symptoms of hyperactivity and impulsivity: Support for a dimensional view of Attention Deficit Hyperactivity Disorder. *American Journal of Psychiatry, 168,* 143–151.

Shaw, P., Greenstein, D., Lerch, J., Klasen, L., Lenroot, R., Gogtay, N., . . . Giedd, J. (2006). Intellectual ability and cortical development in children and adolescents. *Nature, 440,* 676–679.

Shaywitz, S., Gruen, J., & Shaywitz, B. (2007). Management of dyslexia, its rationale and underlying neurobiology. *Pediatric Clinics of North America, 54,* 609–623.

Shearer, D. L., Mulvihill, B. A., Klerman, L. V., Wallander, J. L., Hovinga, M. E., & Redden, D. T. (2002). Association of early childbearing and low cognitive ability. *Perspectives on Sexual and Reproductive Health, 34,* 236.

Shedler, J., & Block, J. (1990). Adolescent drug use and psychological health: A longitudinal inquiry. *American Psychologist, 45,* 612–630.

Sheeran, P., Abraham, C., & Orbell, S. (1999). Psychosocial correlates of heterosexual condom use: A meta-analysis. *Psychological Bulletin, 125,* 90–132.

Sheidow, A. J., Gorman-Smith, D., Tolan, P. H., & Henry, D. B. (2001). Family and community characteristics: Risk factors for violence exposure in inner-city youth. *Journal of Community Psychology, 29,* 345–360.

Sheidow, A. J., Strachan, M. K., Minden, J. A., Henry, D. B., Tolan, P. H., & Gorman-Smith, D. (2008). The relation of antisocial behavior patterns and changes in internalizing symptoms for a sample of inner-city youth: Comorbidity within a developmental framework. *Journal of Youth and Adolescence, 37,* 821–829.

Shek, D. (2007). A longitudinal study of perceived differences in parental control and parent–child relational qualities in Chinese adolescents in Hong Kong. *Journal of Adolescent Research, 22,* 156–188.

Shen, Y. L., Carlo, G., & Knight, G. P. (2013). Relations between parental discipline, empathy-related traits, and prosocial moral reasoning: A multicultural examination. *The Journal of Early Adolescence, 33,* 994–1021.

Sher, K. J., Gotham, H. J., & Watson, A. L. (2004). Trajectories of dynamic predictors of disorder: Their meanings and implications. *Development and Psychopathology, 16,* 825–856.

Sher-Censor, E., Parke, R. D., & Coltrane, S. (2011). Parents' promotion of psychological autonomy, psychological control, and Mexican–American adolescents' adjustment. *Journal of Youth and Adolescence, 40,* 620–632.

Sherman, L. E., Rudie, J. D., Pfeifer, J. H., Masten, C. L., McNealy, K., & Dapretto, M. (2014). Development of the default mode and central executive networks across early adolescence: A longitudinal study. *Developmental Cognitive Neuroscience, 10,* 148–159.

Shernoff, D. J., & Schmidt, J. A. (2008). Further evidence of an engagement–achievement paradox among U.S. high school students. *Journal of Youth and Adolescence, 37,* 564–580.

Shernoff, D. J., & Vandell, D. L. (2007). Engagement in after-school program activities: Quality of experience from the perspective of participants. *Journal of Youth and Adolescence, 36,* 891–903.

Sherrod, L., & Lauckhardt, J. (2009). The development of citizenship. In R. Lerner & L.

Steinberg (Eds.), *Handbook of adolescent psychology* (3rd ed., Vol. 2, pp. 372–408). New York: Wiley.

Shih, T. (1998). Finding the niche: Friendship formation of immigrant adolescents. *Youth and Society, 30,* 209–240.

Shilo, G., & Savaya, R. (2012). Mental health of lesbian, gay, and bisexual youth and young adults: Differential effects of age, gender, religiosity, and sexual orientation. *Journal of Research on Adolescence, 22,* 310–325.

Shin, H., & Ryan, A. M. (2014). Early adolescent friendships and academic adjustment: Examining selection and influence processes with longitudinal social network analysis. *Developmental Psychology, 50,* 2462–2472.

Shiner, R. L., Masten, A. S., & Tellegen, A. (2002). A developmental perspective on personality in emerging adulthood: Childhood antecedents and concurrent adaptation. *Journal of Personality and Social Psychology, 83,* 1165–1177.

Shirtcliff, E. A., Vitacco, M. J., Graf, A. R., Gostisha, A. J., Merz, J. L., & Zahn-Waxler, C. (2009). Neurobiology of empathy and callousness: Implications for the development of antisocial behavior. *Behavioral Sciences & the Law, 27,* 137–171.

Shoop, D., & Davidson, P. (1994). AIDS and adolescents: The relation of parent and partner communication to adolescent condom use. *Journal of Adolescence, 17,* 137–148.

Shtarkshall, R. A., Carmel, S., Jaffe-Hirschfield, D., & Woloski-Wruble, A. (2009). Sexual milestones and factors associated with coitus initiation among Israeli high school students. *Archives of Sexual Behavior, 38,* 591–604.

Shulman, E. P., & Cauffman, E. (2013). Reward-biased risk appraisal and its relation to juvenile versus adult crime. *Law and Human Behavior, 37,* 412–423.

Shulman, E. P., & Cauffman, E. (2014). Deciding in the dark: Age differences in intuitive risk judgment. *Developmental Psychology, 50,* 167–177.

Shulman, E. P., Cauffman, E., Piquero, A. R., & Fagan, J. (2011). Moral disengagement among serious juvenile offenders: A longitudinal study of the relations between morally disengaged attitudes and offending. *Developmental Psychology, 47,* 1619–1632.

Shulman, E. P., Harden, K. P., Chein, J. M., & Steinberg, L. (2014). The development of impulse control and sensation-seeking in adolescence: independent or interdependent processes? *Journal of Research on Adolescence.* DOI: 10.1111/jora.12181

Shulman, E. P., Harden, K. P., Chein, J. M., Steinberg, L. (2015). Sex differences in the developmental trajectories of impulse control and sensation-seeking from early adolescence to early adulthood. *Journal of Youth & Adolescence, 44,* 1–17.

Shulman, S., & Laursen, B. (2002). Adolescent perceptions of conflict in interdependent and disengaged friendships. *Journal of Research on Adolescence, 12,* 353–372.

Shulman, S., & Scharf, M. (2000). Adolescent romantic behaviors and perceptions: Age- and gender-related differences, and links with family and peer relationships. *Journal of Research on Adolescence, 10,* 99–118.

Shulman, S., Connolly, J., & McIssac, C. (2011). Romantic relationships. In B. Brown & M. Prinstein (Eds.), *Encyclopedia of adolescence* (Vol. 2, pp. 289–298). New York: Academic Press.

Shulman, S., Laursen, B., Kalman, Z., & Karpovsky, S. (1997). Adolescent intimacy revisited. *Journal of Youth and Adolescence, 26,* 597–617.

Shulman, S., Tuval-Mashiach, R., Levran, E., & Anbar, S. (2006). Conflict resolution patterns and longevity of adolescent romantic couples: A 2-year follow-up study. *Journal of Adolescence, 29,* 575–588.

Shulman, S., Zlotnik, A., Shachar-Shapira, L., Connolly, J., & Bohr, Y. (2012). Adolescent daughters' romantic competence, quality of parenting, and maternal romantic history. *Journal of Youth & Adolescence, 41,* 593–606.

Shumow, L., & Miller, J. D. (2001). Parents' at-home and at-school academic involvement with youth adolescents. *Journal of Early Adolescence, 21,* 68–91.

Shumow, L., Smith, T., & Smith, M. (2009). Academic and behavioral characteristics of young adolescents in self-care. *Journal of Early Adolescence, 29,* 233–257.

Sibley, M. H., Pelham, W. E., Jr., Molina, B. S. G., Gnagy, E. M., Waschbusch, D. A., Garefino, A. C. . . . & Karch, K. M. (2012). Diagnosing ADHD in adolescence. *Journal of Consulting and Clinical Psychology, 80,* 139–150.

Sibley, M. H., Pelham, W. E., Molina, B. S. G., Gnagy, E. M., Waschbusch, D. A., Biswas, A., . . . Karch, K. (2011). The delinquency outcomes of boys with ADHD with and without comorbidity. *Journal of Abnormal Child Psychology, 39,* 21–32.

Sibley, M. H., Pelham, W. E., Molina, B. S., Coxe, S., Kipp, H., Gnagy, E. M. . . . & Lahey, B. B. (2014). The role of early childhood ADHD and subsequent CD in the initiation and escalation of adolescent cigarette, alcohol, and marijuana use. *Journal of Abnormal Psychology, 123,* 362–374.

Siebenbruner, J., Englund, M. M., Egeland, B., & Hudson, K. (2006). Developmental antecedents of late adolescence substance use patterns. *Development and Psychopathology, 18,* 551–571.

Siegel, A., & Scovill, L. C. (2000). Problem behavior: The double symptom of adolescence. *Development and Psychopathology, 12,* 763–793.

Siegel, J., Aneshensel, C., Taub, B., Cantwell, D., & Driscoll, A. (1998). Adolescent depressed mood in a multiethnic sample. *Journal of Youth and Adolescence, 27,* 413–427.

Siegel, J., Yancey, A., Aneshensel, C., & Schuler, R. (1999). Body image, perceived pubertal timing, and adolescent mental health. *Journal of Adolescent Health, 25,* 155–165.

Siegel, M., & Biener, L. (2000). The impact of an antismoking media campaign on progression to established smoking: Results of a longitudinal study. *American Journal of Public Health, 90,* 380–386.

Siegel, R. S., La Greca, A. M., & Harrison, H. M. (2009). Peer victimization and social anxiety in adolescents: Prospective and reciprocal relationships. *Journal of Youth and Adolescence, 38,* 1096–1109.

Siegler, R. (2006). Microgenetic analyses of learning. In W. Damon & R. Lerner (Series Eds.) & D. Kuhn & R. Siegler (Eds.), *Handbook of child psychology: Vol. 2. Cognition, perception, and language* (6th ed., pp. 464–510). Hoboken, NJ: Wiley.

Siennick, S. E., & Osgood, D. W. (2012). Hanging out with which friends? Friendship-level predictors of unstructured and unsupervised socializing in adolescence. *Journal of Research on Adolescence, 22,* 646–661.

Sieving, R. E., Eisenberg, M. E., Pettingell, S., & Skay, C. (2006). Friends' influence on adolescents' first sexual intercourse. *Perspectives on Sexual and Reproductive Health, 38,* 13–19.

Siffert, A., Schwartz, B., Stutz, M. (2012). Marital conflict and early adolescents' self-evaluation: the role of parenting quality and early adolescents' appraisals. *Journal of Youth & Adolescence, 41,* 749–763.

Sigler-Rushton, W. (2005). Young fatherhood and subsequent disadvantage in the United Kingdom. *Journal of Marriage and the Family, 67,* 735.

Sijtsema, J. J., Rambaran, J. A., Caravita, S. C., & Gini, G. (2014). Friendship selection and influence in bullying and defending: Effects of moral disengagement. *Developmental Psychology, 50,* 2093–2104.

Silbereisen, R., Petersen, A., Albrecht, H., & Kracke, B. (1989). Maturational timing and the development of problem behavior: Longitudinal studies in adolescence. *Journal of Early Adolescence, 9,* 247–268.

Silk, J. S., Stroud, L. R., Siegle, G. J., Dahl, R. E., Lee, K. H., & Nelson, E. E. (2012). Peer acceptance and rejection through the eyes of youth: Pupillary, eyetracking and ecological data from the Chatroom Interact task. *Social Cognitive Affective Neuroscience, 7,* 93–105.

Silk, J., Morris, A., Kanaya, T., & Steinberg, L. (2003). Psychological control and autonomy granting: Opposite ends of a continuum or distinct constructs? *Journal of Research on Adolescence, 13,* 113–128.

Silk, J., Siegle, G., Whalen, D., Ostapenko, L., Ladouceur, D., & Dahl, R. (2009). Pubertal changes in emotional information processing: Pupillary, behavioral, and subjective evidence during emotional word identification. *Development and Psychopathology, 21,* 7–26.

Silk, J., Vanderbilt-Adriance, E., Shaw, D. S., Forbes, E. E., Whalen, D. J., Ryan, N. D., . . .Dahl, R. (2007). Resilience among children and adolescents at risk for depression: Mediation and moderation across social and neurobiological context. *Development and Psychopathology, 19,* 841–865.

Silverberg, S., & Steinberg, L. (1990). Psychological well-being of parents at midlife: The impact of early adolescent children. *Developmental Psychology, 26,* 658–666.

Silverberg, S., Marczak, M., & Gondoli, D. (1996). Maternal depressive symptoms and achievement-related outcomes among adolescent daughters: Variations by family structure. *Journal of Early Adolescence, 16,* 90–109.

Silverman, J., Raj, A., Mucci, L. A., & Hathaway, J. E. (2001). Dating violence against adolescent girls and associated substance abuse, unhealthy weight control, sexual risk behavior, pregnancy, and suicidality. *Journal of the American Medical Association, 286,* 572–579.

Silvers, J. A., Insel, C., Powers, A., Franz, P., Weber, J., Mischel, W. . . . & Ochsner, K. N. (2014). Curbing craving: Behavioral and brain evidence that children regulate craving when instructed to do so but have higher baseline craving than adults. *Psychological Science, 25,* 1932–1942.

Sim, T. (2000). Adolescent psychosocial competence: The importance and role of regard for parents. *Journal of Research on Adolescence, 10,* 49–64.

Sim, T. N., & Yeo, G. H. (2012). Peer crowds in singapore. *Youth & Society, 44,* 201–216.

Sim, T., & Koh, S. (2003). A domain conceptualization of adolescent susceptibility to peer pressure. *Journal of Research on Adolescence, 13,* 57–80.

Simmons, R. (2003). *Odd girl out.* New York: Harvest Books.

Simmons, R., Blyth, D., & McKinney, K. (1983). The social and psychological effects of puberty on White females. In J. Brooks-Gunn & A. Petersen (Eds.), *Girls at puberty* (pp. 229–272). New York: Plenum.

Simmons, R., Rosenberg, F., & Rosenberg, M. (1973). Disturbance in the self-image at adolescence. *American Sociological Review, 38,* 553–568.

Simon, T. R., Miller, S., Gorman-Smith, D., Orpinas, P., & Sullivan, T. (2010). Physical dating violence norms and behavior among sixth-grade students from four U.S. sites. *Journal of Early Adolescence, 30,* 395–409.

Simon, V. A., & Furman, W. (2010). Interparental conflict and adolescents' romantic relationship conflict. *Journal of Research on Adolescence, 20,* 188–209.

Simon, V. A., Aikins, J. W., & Prinstein, M. J. (2008). Romantic partner selection and socialization during early adolescence. *Child Development, 79,* 1676–1692.

Simons, L., & Conger, R. (2007). Linking mother–father differences in parenting to a typology of family parenting styles and adolescent outcomes. *Journal of Family Issues, 28,* 212–241.

Simons, L. G., Simons, R. L., Su, X. (2013). Consequences of corporal punishment among African Americans: the importance of context and outcome. *Journal of Youth & Adolescence, 42,* 1273–1285.

Simons, R., & Burt, C. (2011). Learning to be bad: Adverse social conditions, social schemas, and crime. *Criminology, 49,* 553–598.

Simons, R., Chao, W., Conger, R., & Elder, G. H., Jr. (2001). Quality of parenting as mediator of the effect of childhood defiance on adolescent friendship choice and delinquency: A growth curve analysis. *Journal of Marriage and the Family, 63,* 63–79.

Simons, R., Johnson, C., Beaman, J., Conger, R., & Whitbeck, L. (1996). Parents and peer group as mediators of the effect of community structure on adolescent problem behavior. *American Journal of Community Psychology, 24,* 145–171.

Simons, R., Lin, K., & Gordon, L. (1998). Socialization in the family of origin and male dating violence: A prospective study. *Journal of Marriage and the Family, 60,* 467–478.

Simons, R., Simons, L., Burt, C., Brody, G., & Cutrona, C. (2005). Collective efficacy, authoritative parenting and delinquency: A longitudinal test of a model integrating community- and family-level processes. *Criminology, 43,* 989–1029.

Simons, R., Whitbeck, L., Conger, R., & Chyi-In, W. (1991). Intergenerational transmission of harsh parenting. *Developmental Psychology, 27,* 159–171.

Simons-Morton, B. (2011). Adolescent driving behavior: A developmental challenge. In B. Brown & M. Prinstein (Eds.), *Encyclopedia of adolescence* (Vol. 1, pp. 38–47). New York: Academic Press.

Simons-Morton, B., & Chen, R. (2009). Peer and parent influences on school engagement among early adolescents. *Youth & Society, 41,* 3–25.

Simons-Morton, B., Hartos, J., Leaf, W., & Preusser, D. (2005). Persistence of effects of the Checkpoints Program on parental restrictions on teen driving privileges. *American Journal of Public Health, 95,* 447–452.

Simons-Morton, B., Ouimet, M., Zhang, Z., Klauer, S., Lee, S., Wang, J., . . . Dingus, T. (2011). The effect of passengers and risk-taking friends on risky driving and crashes/near crashes among novice teenagers. *Journal of Adolescent Health, 49,* 587–593.

Simpkins, S. D. (2015). The role of parents in the ontogeny of achievement-related motivation and behavioral choices. *Monographs of the Society for Research in Child Development, 80,* 1–169.

Simpkins, S. D., Fredricks, J. A., & Eccles, J. S. (2012). Charting the Eccles' expectancy-value model from mothers' beliefs in childhood to youths' activities in adolescence. *Developmental Psychology, 48,* 1019–1032.

Simpkins, S. D., Schaefer, D. R., Price, C. D., & Vest, A. E. (2013). Adolescent friendships, BMI, and physical activity: Untangling selection and influence through longitudinal social network analysis. *Journal of Research on Adolescence, 23,* 537–549.

Simpkins, S., Bouffard, S., Dearing, E., Kreider, H., Wilmer, C., Caronongan, P., & Weiss, H. (2009). Adolescent adjustment and patterns of parents' behaviors in early and middle adolescence. *Journal of Research on Adolescence, 19,* 530–557.

Simpkins, S., Davis-Kean, P., & Eccles, J. (2006). Math and science motivation: A longitudinal examination of the links between choices and beliefs. *Developmental Psychology, 42,* 70–83.

Simpkins, S., Eccles, J., & Becnel, J. N. (2008). The mediational role of adolescents' friends in relations between activity breadth and adjustment. *Developmental Psychology, 44,* 1081–1094.

Simpson, J. A., Collins, W. A., Tran, S., & Haydon, K. C. (2007). Attachment and the experience and expression of emotions in romantic relationships: A developmental perspective. *Journal of Personality and Social Psychology, 92,* 355–367.

Singh, P., & Bussey, K. (2011). Peer victimization and psychological maladjustment: The mediating role of coping self-efficacy. *Journal of Research on Adolescence, 21,* 420–433.

Singh, S., & Darroch, J. (1999). Trends in sexual activity among adolescent American women: 1982–1995. *Family Planning Perspectives, 31,* 212–219.

Singh, S., & Darroch, J. E. (2000). Adolescent pregnancy and childbearing: Levels and trends in developed countries. *Family Planning Perspectives, 32*(1), 14–23.

Sinha, J. W., Cnaan, R. A., & Gelles, R. J. (2007). Adolescent risk behaviors and religion: Findings from a national study. *Journal of Adolescence, 30,* 231–249.

Sinopoli, K. J., Schachar, R., & Dennis, M. (2011). Reward improves cancellation and restraint inhibition across childhood and adolescence. *Developmental Psychology, 47,* 1479–1489.

Sionéan, C., DiClemente, R. J., Wingood, G. M., Crosby, R., Cobb, B. K., Harrington, K., . . . Oh, M. (2002). Psychosocial and behavioral correlates of refusing unwanted sex among African-American adolescent females. *Journal of Adolescent Health, 30,* 55–63.

Sipsma, H., Biello, K. B., Cole-Lewis, H., & Kershaw, T. (2010). Like father, like son: The intergenerational cycle of adolescent fatherhood. *American Journal of Public Health, 100,* 517–524.

Sirin, S. R., & Rogers-Sirin, L. (2004). Exploring school engagement of middle-class African American adolescents. *Youth and Society, 35,* 323–340.

Sirin, S. R., Rogers-Sirin, L., Cressen, J., Gupta, T., Ahmed, S. F., & Novoa, A. D. (2015). Discrimination-related stress effects on the development of internalizing symptoms among Latino adolescents. *Child Development, 86,* 709–725.

Sisk, C. L., & Foster, D. L. (2004). The neural basis of puberty and adolescence. *Nature Neuroscience, 7,* 1040–1047.

Sitnick, S. L., Shaw, D. S., & Hyde, L. W. (2014). Precursors of adolescent substance use from early childhood and early adolescence: Testing a developmental cascade model. *Development and Psychopathology, 26,* 125–140.

Skeem, J., & Cauffman. E. (2003). Views of the downward extension: Comparing the youth version of the Psychopathy Checklist with the Youth Psychopathic Traits Inventory. *Behavioral Sciences and the Law, 21,* 737–770.

Skeer, M. R., Ballard, E. L. (2013). Are family meals as food for youth as we think they are? A review of the literature on family meals as they pertain to adolescent risk prevention. *Journal of Youth & Adolescence, 42,* 943–963.

Skinner, B. F. (1953). *Science and human behavior.* New York: Free Press.

Skitch, S. A., & Abela, J. R. Z. (2008). Rumination in response to stress as a common vulnerability factor to depression and substance misuse in adolescence. *Journal of Abnormal Child Psychology, 36,* 1029–1045.

Skoog, T., & Özdemir, S. B. (2015). Explaining why early-maturing girls are more exposed to sexual harassment in early adolescence. *The Journal of Early Adolescence.* DOI: 10.1177/0272431614568198

Skoog, T., & Stattin, H. (2014). Why and under what contextual conditions do early-maturing girls develop problem behaviors. *Child Development Perspectives, 8,* 158–162.

Skoog, T., Stattin, H., & Kerr, M. (2009). The role of pubertal timing in what adolescent boys do online. *Journal of Research on Adolescence, 19,* 1–7.

Skorikov, V. B., & Vondracek, F. W. (2007). Vocational identity. In V. B. Skorikov & W. Patton (Eds.), *Career development in childhood and adolescence* (pp. 143–168). Rotterdam, The Netherlands: Sense.

Slap, G., Goodman, E., & Huang, B. (2001). Adoption as a risk factor for attempted suicide during adolescence. *Pediatrics, 108,* Article E30.

Slater, A., Tiggemann, M., Hawkins, K., & Werchon, D. (2012). Just one click: A content analysis of advertisements on teen web sites. *Journal of Adolescent Health, 50,* 339–345.

Smahel, D., Brown, B., & Blinka, L. (2012). Associations between online friendship and internet addiction among adolescents and emerging adults. *Developmental Psychology, 48,* 381–388.

Small, S., & Luster, T. (1994). Adolescent sexual activity: An ecological, risk-factor approach. *Journal of Marriage and the Family, 56,* 181–192.

Small, S., & Memmo, M. (2004). Contemporary models of youth development and problem prevention: Toward an integration of terms, concepts and models. *Family Relations, 53,* 3–11.

Smetana, J. (1989). Adolescents' and parents' reasoning about actual family conflict. *Child Development, 59,* 1052–1067.

Smetana, J. (1995a). Conflict and coordination in adolescent–parent relationships. In S. Shulman (Ed.), *Close relationships and socioemotional development* (pp. 155–184). Norwood, NJ: Ablex.

Smetana, J. (1995b). Parenting styles and conceptions of parental authority during adolescence. *Child Development, 66,* 299–316.

Smetana, J. (2005). Adolescent–parent conflict: Resistance and subversion as developmental process. In L. Nucci (Ed.), *Conflict, contradiction, and contrarian elements in moral development and education* (pp. 69–91). Mahwah, NJ: Erlbaum.

Smetana, J., & Asquith, P. (1994). Adolescents' and parents' conceptions of parental authority and personal autonomy. *Child Development, 65,* 1147–1162.

Smetana, J., & Bitz, B. (1996). Adolescents' conceptions of teachers' authority and their relations to rule violations in school. *Child Development, 67,* 1153–1172.

Smetana, J., & Chuang, S. (2001). Middle-class African American parents' conceptions of parenting in the transition to adolescence. *Journal of Research on Adolescence, 11,* 177–198.

Smetana, J., & Daddis, C. (2002). Domain-specific antecedents of parental psychological control and monitoring: The role of parenting beliefs and practices. *Child Development, 73,* 563–580.

Smetana, J., & Gaines, C. (2000). Adolescent–parent conflict in middle-class African American families. *Child Development, 70,* 1447–1463.

Smetana, J., & Gettman, D. C. (2006). Autonomy and relatedness with parents and romantic development in African American adolescents. *Developmental Psychology, 42,* 1347–1351.

Smetana, J., & Villalobos, M. (2009). Social cognitive development in adolescence. In R. Lerner & L. Steinberg (Eds.), *Handbook of adolescent psychology* (3rd ed., Vol. 1, pp. 187–228). New York: Wiley.

Smetana, J., Campione-Barr, N., & Daddis, C. (2004). Longitudinal development of family decision making: Defining healthy behavioral autonomy for middle-class African American adolescents. *Child Development, 75,* 1418–1434.

Smetana, J., Crean, H. F., & Daddis, C. (2002). Family processes and problem behaviors in middle-class African American adolescents. *Journal of Research on Adolescence, 12,* 275–304.

Smetana, J., Daddis, C., & Chuang, S. (2003). "Clean your room!" *Journal of Adolescent Research, 18,* 631–650.

Smetana, J., Metzger, A., Gettman, D., & Campione-Barr, N. (2006). Disclosure and secrecy in adolescent–parent relationships. *Child Development, 77,* 201–217.

Smetana, J., Yau, J., Restrepo, A., & Braeges, J. (1991). Adolescent–parent conflict in married and divorced families. *Developmental Psychology, 27,* 1000–1010.

Smith, A. R., Chein, J., & Steinberg, L. (2014). Peers increase adolescent risk taking even when the probabilities of negative outcomes are known. *Developmental Psychology, 50,* 1564–1568.

Smith, A. R., Steinberg, L., & Chein, J. (2014). The role of the anterior insula in adolescent decision making. *Developmental Neuroscience, 36,* 196–209.

Smith, A. R., Steinberg, L., Strang, N., & Chein, J. (2015). Age differences in the impact of peers on adolescents' and adults' neural response to reward. *Development Cognitive Neuroscience, 11,* 75–82.

Smith, A., & Lalonde, R. N. (2003). "Racelessness" in a Canadian context? Exploring the link between Black students' identity, achievement, and mental health. *Journal of Black Psychology, 29,* 142–164.

Smith, A., Steinberg, L., Strang, N., & Chein, J. (2015). Age differences in the impact of peers on adolescents' and adults' neural response to reward. *Developmental Cognitive Neuroscience, 11,* 75–82.

Smith, C., & Denton, M. (2005). *Soul searching: The religious and spiritual lives of American teenagers.* New York: Oxford University Press.

Smith, D. G., Xiao, L., & Bechara, A. (2012). Decision making in children and adolescents: Impaired Iowa gambling task performance in early adolescence. *Developmental Psychology, 48,* 1180–1187.

Smith, D. T., Kelly, A. B., Chan, G. C. K., Toumbourou, J. W., Patton, G. C., & Williams, J. W. (2014). Beyond the primary influences of parents and peers on very young adolescent alcohol use: Evidence of independent community associations. *The Journal of Early Adolescence, 34,* 569–584.

Smith, E., & Zabin, L. (1993). Marital and birth expectations of urban adolescents. *Youth and Society, 25,* 62–74.

Smith, G., Goldman, M., Greenbaum, P., & Christiansen, B. (1995). Expectancy for social facilitation from drinking: The divergent paths of high-expectancy and low-expectancy adolescents. *Journal of Abnormal Psychology, 104,* 32–40.

Smith, J. L., Skinner, S. R., & Fenwick, J. (2011). How Australian female adolescents prioritize pregnancy protection: A grounded theory study of contraceptive histories. *Journal of Adolescent Research, 26,* 617–644.

Smith, P. H., White, J. W., & Holland, L. J. (2003). A longitudinal perspective on dating violence among adolescent and college-age women. *American Journal of Public Health, 93,* 1104–1109.

Smith, R., & Rose, A. (2011). The "cost of caring" in youths' friendships: Considering associations among social perspective-taking, co-rumination, and empathetic distress. *Developmental Psychology, 47,* 1792–1803.

Smith, T. E., & Leaper, C. (2006). Self-perceived gender typicality and the peer context during adolescence. *Journal of Research on Adolescence, 16,* 91–103.

Smith-Bynum, M. A., Lambert, S. F., English, D., & Ialongo, N. S. (2014). Associations between trajectories of perceived racial discrimination and psychological symptoms among African American adolescents. *Development and Psychopathology, 26,* 1049–1065.

Smokowski, P., Bacallao, M., & Buchanan, R. (2009). Interpersonal mediators linking acculturation stressors to subsequent internalizing symptoms and self-esteem in Latino adolescents. *Journal of Community Psychology, 37,* 1024–1045.

Smokowski, P. R., Evans, C. B., Cotter, K. L., Webber, K. C. (2014). Ethnic identity and mental health in American Indian youth: examining mediation pathways through self-esteem, and future optimism. *Journal of Youth & Adolescence, 43,* 343–355.

Smolak, L., Levine, M., & Gralen, S. (1993). The impact of puberty and dating on eating problems among middle school girls. *Journal of Youth and Adolescence, 22,* 355–368.

Smoll, F., & Schutz, R. (1990). Quantifying gender differences in physical performance: A developmental perspective. *Developmental Psychology, 26,* 360–369.

Smollar, J., & Youniss, J. (1985). *Transformation in adolescents' perceptions of parents.* Paper presented at the biennial meetings of the Society for Research in Child Development, Baltimore.

Snell, E. K., Adam, E. K., & Duncan, G. J. (2007). Sleep and the body mass index and over-weight status of children and adolescents. *Child Development, 78,* 309–323.

Snell, E. K., Castells, N., Duncan, G., Gennetian, L., Magnuson, K., & Morris, P. (2013). Promoting the positive development of boys in high-poverty neighborhoods: Evidence from four anti-poverty experiments. *Journal of Research on Adolescence, 23,* 357–374.

Snyder, H., & Sickmund, M. (2006). *Juvenile offenders and victims: 2006 national report.* Washington, DC: Office of Juvenile Justice and Delinquency Prevention.

Snyder, J., Bank, L., & Burraston, B. (2005). The consequences of antisocial behavior in older male siblings for younger brothers and sisters. *Journal of Family Psychology, 19,* 643–653.

Sobesky, W. (1983). The effects of situational factors on moral judgments. *Child Development, 54,* 575–584.

Soenens, B., Vansteenkiste, M., Luyckx, K., & Goossens, L. (2006). Parenting and adolescent problem behavior: An integrated model with adolescent self-disclosure and perceived parental knowledge as intervening variables. *Developmental Psychology, 42,* 305–318.

Soli, A. R., McHale, S. M., & Feinberg, M. E. (2009). Risk and protective effects of sibling relationships among African American adolescents. *Family Relations, 58,* 578–592.

Solmeyer, A. R., McHale, S. M., & Crouter, A. C. (2014). Longitudinal associations between sibling relationship qualities and risky behavior across adolescence. *Developmental Psychology, 50,* 600–610.

Solomon, R., & Liefeld, C. (1998). Effectiveness of a family support center approach to adolescent mothers: Repeat pregnancy and school drop-out rates. *Family Relations, 47,* 139–144.

Somerville, L. H. (2013). The teenage brain: Sensitivity to social evaluation. *Current Directions in Psychological Science, 22,* 121–127.

Somerville, L. H., Ruberry, E. J., Dyke, J. P., Glover, G., & Casey, B. J. (2013). The medial prefrontal cortex and the emergence of self-conscious emotion in adolescence. *Psychological Science, 24,* 1554–1562.

Sommer, K., Whitman, T., Borkowski, J., Schellenbach, C., Maxwell, S., & Keogh, D. (1993). Cognitive readiness and adolescent parenting. *Developmental Psychology, 29,* 389–398.

Sommers, C. (2000). *The war against boys.* New York: Simon & Schuster.

Song, J., Bong, M., Lee, K., Kim, S-il. (2014). Longitudinal investigation into the role of perceived social support in adolescents' academic motivation and achievement. *Journal of Educational Psychology.* http://dx.doi.org/10.1037/edu0000016

Sonneville, K. R., Grilo, C. M., Richmond, T. K., Thurston, I. B., Jernigan, M., Gianini, L., & Field, A. E. (2015). Prospective association between overvaluation of weight and binge eating among overweight adolescent girls. *Journal of Adolescent Health, 56,* 25–29.

Sontag, L. M., & Graber, J. A. (2010). Coping with perceived peer stress: Gender-specific and common pathways to symptoms of psychopathology. *Developmental Psychology, 46,* 1605–1620.

Sontag, L. M., Clemans, K. H., Graber, J. A., & Lyndon, S. T. (2011). Traditional and cyber aggressors and victims: A comparison of psychosocial characteristics. *Journal of Youth and Adolescence, 40,* 392–404.

Sontag, L. M., Graber, J. A., & Clemans, K. H. (2011). The role of peer stress and pubertal timing on symptoms of psychopathology during early adolescence. *Journal of Youth and Adolescence, 40,* 1371–1382.

Sontag, L. M., Graber, J. A., Brooks-Gunn, J., & Warren, M. P. (2008). Coping with social stress: Implications for psychopathology in young adolescent girls. *Journal of Abnormal Child Psychology, 36,* 1159–1174.

Sorensen, S., Richardson, B., & Peterson, J. (1993). Race/ethnicity patterns in the homicide of children in Los Angeles, 1980 through 1989. *American Journal of Public Health, 83,* 725–727.

Sorhagen, N. S. (2013). Early teacher expectations disproportionately affect poor children's high school performance. *Journal of Educational Psychology, 105,* 465–477.

Sourander, A., Elonheimo, H., Niemelä, S., Nuutila, A., Helenius, H., Sillanmäki, L., ...Almqvist, F. (2006). Childhood predictors of male criminality: A prospective population-based follow-up study from age 8 to late adolescence. *Journal of the American Academy of Child & Adolescent Psychiatry, 45,* 578–586.

South, S. J., & Baumer, E. P. (2000). Deciphering community and race effects on adolescent premarital childbearing. *Social Forces, 78,* 1379–1407.

South, S. J., & Baumer, E. P. (2001). Community effects on the resolution of adolescent premarital pregnancy. *Journal of Family Issues, 22,* 1025–1043.

South, S. J., & Haynie, D. L. (2004). Friendship networks of mobile adolescents. *Social Forces, 83,* 315–350.

South, S. J., Baumer, E. P., & Lutz, A. (2003). Interpreting community effects on youth educational attainment. *Youth and Society, 35,* 3–36.

Sparks, S. (2015, May 24). Study points to fewer "dropout factory" schools. *Education Week.*

Spear, L. (2010). *The behavioral neuroscience of adolescence.* New York: Norton.

Spear, L. (2011a). Brain development. In B. Brown & M. Prinstein (Eds.), *Encyclopedia of adolescence* (Vol. 1, pp. 87–95). New York: Academic Press.

Spear, L. (2013). Adolescent neurodevelopment. *Journal of Adolescent Health, 52,* S7–S13.

Spear, L. (2013). The teenage brain: Adolescents and alcohol. *Current Directions in Psychological Science, 22,* 152–157.

Spear, L. P. (2011b). Adolescent neurobehavioral characteristics, alcohol sensitivities, and intake: Setting the stage for alcohol use disorders? *Child Development Perspectives, 5,* 231–238.

Spear, L. P., & Swartzwelder, H. S. (2014). Adolescent alcohol exposure and persistence of adolescent-typical phenotypes into adulthood: A mini-review. *Neuroscience and Biobehavioral Reviews, 45,* 1–8.

Specht, J., Luhmann, M., & Geiser, C. (2014). On the consistency of personality types across adulthood: Latent profile analyses in two large-scale panel studies. *Journal of Personality and Social Psychology, 107,* 540–556.

Spencer, G. A., & Bryant, S. A. (2000). Dating violence: A comparison of rural, suburban, and urban teens. *Journal of Adolescent Health, 27,* 302–305.

Spencer, M. B. (2005). Crafting identities and accessing opportunities post-Brown. *American Psychologist, 60,* 821–830.

Spieker, S., & Bensley, L. (1994). Roles of living arrangements and grandmother social support in adolescent mothering and infant attachment. *Developmental Psychology, 30,* 102–111.

Spielberg, J. M., Forbes, E. E., Ladouceur, C. D., Worthman, C., M., Olino, T., M., Ryan, N. D., & Dahl, R. E. (2015). Pubertal testosterone influences threat-related amygdala-orbitofrontal cortex coupling. *Social Cognitive Affective Neuroscience, 10,* 408–415.

Spielberg, J. M., Olino, T. M., Forbes, E. E., & Dahl, R. E. (2014). Exciting fear in adolescence: Does pubertal development alter threat processing? *Development Cognitive Neuroscience, 8,* 86–95.

Spies, L. A., Margolin, G., Susman, E. J., & Gordis, E. B. (2011). Adolescents' cortisol reactivity and subjective distress in response to family conflict: The moderating role of internalizing symptoms. *Journal of Adolescent Health, 49,* 386–392.

Spilman, S. K., Neppl, T. K., Donnellan, M. B., Schofield, T. J., & Conger, R. D. (2013). Incorporating religiosity into a developmental model of positive family functioning across generations. *Developmental Psychology, 49,* 762–774.

Spotts, E. L., Neiderheiser, J. M., Hetherington, E., & Reiss, D. (2001). The relation between observational measures of social problem solving and familial antisocial behavior: Genetic and environmental influences. *Journal of Research on Adolescence, 11,* 351–374.

Spriggs, A. L., & Halpern, C. T. (2008). Sexual debut timing and depressive symptoms in emerging adulthood. *Journal of Youth and Adolescence, 37,* 1085–1096.

Sprondel, V., Kipp, K. H., & Mecklinger, A. (2011). Developmental changes in item and source memory: Evidence from an ERP recognition memory study with children, adolescents, and adults. *Child Development, 82,* 1638–1953.

Spruijt-Metz, D. S. (2011). Etiology, treatment, and prevention of obesity in childhood and adolescence: A decade in review. *Journal of Research on Adolescence, 129,* 129–152.

Squeglia, L. M., Jacobus, J., & Tapert, S. F. (2009). The influence of substance use on adolescent brain development. *Clinical EEG and Neuroscience, 40,* 32–39.

Srikanth, S., Petrie, T. A., Greenleaf, C., & Martin, S. B. (2015). The relationship of physical fitness, self-beliefs, and social support to the academic performance of middle school boys and girls. *The Journal of Early Adolescence, 35,* 353–377.

St Clair, M. C., Croudace, T., Dunn, V. J., Jones, P. B., Herbert, J., & Goodyer, L. M. (2015). Childhood adversity subtypes and depressive symptoms in early and late adolescence. *Development and Psychopathology, 27,* 885–899.

St. George, I., Williams, S., & Silva, P. (1994). Body size and menarche: The Dunedin study. *Journal of Adolescent Health, 15,* 573–576.

St. Lawrence, J., Brasfield, T., Jefferson, K., Allyene, E., & Shirley, A. (1994). Social support as a factor in African-American adolescents' sexual risk behavior. *Journal of Adolescent Research, 9,* 292–310.

Staff, J., & Mortimer, J. T. (2007). Educational and work strategies from adolescence to early adulthood: Consequences for educational attainment. *Social Forces, 85,* 1169–1194.

Staff, J., Messersmith, E., & Schulenberg, J. (2009). Adolescents and the world of work. In R. Lerner & L. Steinberg (Eds.), *Handbook of adolescent psychology* (3rd ed., Vol. 2, pp. 270–313). New York: Wiley.

Staff, J., Osgood, D. W., Schulenberg, J., Bachman, J., & Messersmith, E. (2010). Explaining the relationship between employment and juvenile delinquency. *Criminology, 48,* 1101–1131.

Staff, J., Schulenberg, J. E., Maslowsky, J., Bachman, J. G., O'Malley, P. M., Maggs, J. L., & Johnston, L. D. (2010). Substance use changes and social role transitions: Proximal developmental effects on ongoing trajectories from late adolescence through early adulthood. *Development and Psychopathology, 22,* 917–932.

Staff, J., VanEseltine, M., Woolnough, A., Silver, E., & Burrington, L. (2012). Adolescent work experiences and family formation behaviors. *Journal of Research on Adolescence, 22,* 150–164.

Stams, G. J., Brugman, D., Dekovic, M., van Rosmalen, L., van der Laan, P., & Gibbs, J. C. (2006). The moral judgment of juvenile delinquents: A meta-analysis. *Journal of Abnormal Child Psychology, 34,* 697–713.

Stanger-Hall, K. F., & Hall, D. W. (2011). Abstinence-only education and teen pregnancy rates: Why we need comprehensive sex education in the U.S. *PLoS ONE, 6,* e24658.

Stanley, L. R., Henry, K. L., & Swaim, R. C. (2011). Physical, social, and perceived availabilities of alcohol and last month alcohol use in rural and small urban communities. *Journal of Youth and Adolescence, 40,* 1203–1214.

Stanton-Salazar, R., & Spina, S. (2005). Adolescent peer networks as a context for social and emotional support. *Youth and Society, 36,* 379–417.

Starr, L. R., & Davila, J. (2009). Clarifying co-rumination: Associations with internalizing symptoms and romantic involvement among adolescent girls. *Journal of Adolescence, 32,* 19–37.

Stattin, H., Kerr, M., & Skoog, T. (2011). Early pubertal timing and girls' problem behavior: Integrating two hypotheses. *Journal of Youth and Adolescence, 40,* 1271–1287.

Stearns, E. (2004). Interracial friendliness and the social organization of schools. *Youth and Society 35,* 395–419.

Stearns, E., & Glennie, E. J. (2006). When and why dropouts leave high school. *Youth and Society, 38,* 29–57.

Stearns, E., Buchmann, C., & Bonneau, K. (2009). Interracial friendships in the transition to college: Do birds of a feather flock together once they leave the nest? *Sociology of Education, 82,* 173–195.

Stedman, L. (1998). An assessment of the contemporary debate over U.S. achievement. In D. Ravitch (Ed.). *Brookings papers on education policy: 1998,* pp. 53–121. Washington: Brookings Institution.

Steeger, C. M., & Gondoli, D. M. (2013). Mother-adolescent conflict as a mediator between adolescent problem behaviors and maternal psychological control. *Developmental Psychology, 49,* 804–814.

Steele, C. M. (1997). A threat in the air: How stereotypes shape intellectual identity and performance. *American Psychologist, 52,* 613–619.

Steele, J., & Brown, J. (1995). Adolescent room culture: Studying media in the context of everyday life. *Journal of Youth and Adolescence, 24,* 551–576.

Steffensmeier, D., Schwartz, J., Zhong, H., & Ackerman, J. (2005). An assessment of recent trends in girls' violence using diverse longitudinal sources: Is the gender gap closing? *Criminology, 43,* 355–406.

Stein, J., & Reiser, L. (1994). A study of White middle-class adolescent boys' responses to "semenarche" (the first ejaculation). *Journal of Youth and Adolescence, 23,* 373–384.

Steinberg, L. (1987). Single parents, stepparents, and the susceptibility of adolescents to antisocial peer pressure. *Child Development, 58,* 269–275.

Steinberg, L. (1990). Autonomy, conflict, and harmony in the family relationship. In S. Feldman & G. Elliott (Eds.), *At the threshold: The developing adolescent* (pp. 255–276). Cambridge, MA: Harvard University Press.

Steinberg, L. (1996). *Beyond the classroom: Why school reform has failed and what parents need to do.* New York: Simon & Schuster.

Steinberg, L. (2000). Youth violence: Do parents and families make a difference? *National Institute of Justice Journal,* April, 30–38.

Steinberg, L. (2001). We know some things: Adolescent–parent relationships in retrospect and prospect. *Journal of Research on Adolescence, 11,* 1–19.

Steinberg, L. (2003). The state of adolescence. In D. Ravitch (Ed.), *Brookings papers on education policy.* Washington, DC: Brookings Institution.

Steinberg, L. (2005). *The 10 basic principles of good parenting.* New York: Simon & Schuster.

Steinberg, L. (2007). Risk-taking in adolescence: New perspectives from brain and behavioral science. *Current Directions in Psychological Science, 16,* 55–59.

Steinberg, L. (2008). A social neuroscience perspective on adolescent risk-taking. *Developmental Review, 28,* 78–106.

Steinberg, L. (2010). A dual systems model of adolescent risk-taking. *Developmental Psychobiology, 52,* 216–224.

Steinberg, L. (2011). *You and your adolescent: The essential guide for ages 10–25.* New York: Simon & Schuster.

Steinberg, L. (2012). Should the science of adolescent brain development inform public policy? *Issues in Science and Technology, Spring,* 67–78.

Steinberg, L. (2014). *Age of opportunity: Lessons from the new science of adolescence.* New York, NY: Houghton Mifflin Harcourt.

Steinberg, L. (2014). *Age of Opportunity: Lessons From the New Science of Adolescence.* New York: Houghton Mifflin Harcourt.

Steinberg, L. (2014, October 31). Injuries. Stress. Divided attention. Are coaches damaging our kids? *TIME.*

Steinberg, L. (in press). How to improve the health of American adolescents. *Perspectives on Psychological Science.*

Steinberg, L., & Avenevoli, S. (2000). The role of context in the development of psychopathology: A conceptual framework and some speculative propositions. *Child Development, 71,* 66–74.

Steinberg, L., & Belsky, J. (1996). A sociobiological perspective on psychopathology in adolescence. In D. Cicchetti and S. Toth (Eds.), *Rochester Symposium on Developmental Psychopathology* (Vol. 7, pp. 93–124). Rochester, NY: University of Rochester Press.

Steinberg, L., & Cauffman, E. (1996). Maturity of judgment in adolescence: Psychosocial factors in adolescent decisionmaking. *Law and Human Behavior, 20,* 249–272.

Steinberg, L., & Dornbusch, S. (1991). Negative correlates of part-time work in adolescence: Replication and elaboration. *Developmental Psychology, 17,* 304–313.

Steinberg, L., & Monahan, K. (2007). Age differences in resistance to peer influence. *Developmental Psychology, 43,* 1531–1543.

Steinberg, L., & Monahan, K. (2011). Adolescents' exposure to sexy media does not hasten the initiation of sexual intercourse. *Developmental Psychology, 47,* 562–576.

Steinberg, L., & Morris, A. (2001). Adolescent development. *Annual Review of Psychology, 52,* 83–110.

Steinberg, L., & Silk, J. (2002). Parenting adolescents. In M. Bornstein (Ed.), *Handbook of parenting:* Vol. 1. *Children and parenting* (2nd ed., pp. 103–133). Mahwah, NJ: Erlbaum.

Steinberg, L., & Silverberg, S. (1986). The vicissitudes of autonomy in early adolescence. *Child Development, 57,* 841–851.

Steinberg, L., & Steinberg, W. (1994). *Crossing paths: How your child's adolescence triggers your own crisis.* New York: Simon & Schuster.

Steinberg, L., Albert, D., Cauffman, E., Banich, M., Graham, S., & Woolard, J. (2008). Age differences in sensation seeking and impulsivity as indexed by behavior and self-report: Evidence for a dual systems model. *Developmental Psychology, 44,* 1764–1778.

Steinberg, L., Blatt-Eisengart, I., & Cauffman, E. (2006). Patterns of competence and adjustment among adolescents from authoritative, authoritarian, indulgent, and neglectful homes: Replication in a sample of serious juvenile offenders. *Journal of Research on Adolescence, 16,* 47–58.

Steinberg, L., Cauffman, E., Woolard, J., Graham, S., & Banich, M. (2009). Are adolescents less mature than adults? Minors' access to abortion, the juvenile death penalty, and the alleged APA "flip-flop." *American Psychologist, 64,* 583–594.

Steinberg, L., Dahl, R., Keating, D., Kupfer, D., Masten, A., & Pine, D. (2006). Psychopathology in adolescence: Integrating affective neuroscience with the study of context. In D. Cicchetti & D. Cohen (Eds.), *Developmental psychopathology:* Vol. 2. *Developmental neuroscience* (pp. 710–741). New York: Wiley.

Steinberg, L., Dornbusch, S., & Brown, B. (1992). Ethnic differences in adolescent achievement: An ecological perspective. *American Psychologist, 47,* 723–729.

Steinberg, L., Graham, S., O'Brien, L., Woolard, J., Cauffman, E., & Banich, M. (2009). Age differences in future orientation and delay discounting. *Child Development, 80,* 28–44.

Steinberg, L., Lamborn, S., Darling, N., Mounts, N., & Dornbusch, S. (1994). Over-time changes in adjustment and competence among adolescents from authoritative, authoritarian, indulgent, and neglectful families. *Child Development, 65,* 754–770.

Steinberg, L., Lamborn, S., Dornbusch, S., & Darling, N. (1992). Impact of parenting practices on adolescent achievement: Authoritative parenting, school involvement, and encouragement to succeed. *Child Development, 63,* 1266–1281.

Steinberg, S. J., Davila, J., & Fincham, F. (2006). Adolescent marital expectations and romantic experiences: Associations with perceptions about parental conflict and adolescent attachment security. *Journal of Youth and Adolescence, 35,* 333–348.

Steinman, K. J., & Zimmerman, M. A. (2004). Religious activity and risk behavior among African American adolescents: Concurrent and developmental effects. *American Journal of Community Psychology, 33,* 151–161.

Stephens, L. (1996). Will Johnny see Daddy this week? An empirical test of three theoretical perspectives of postdivorce contact. *Journal of Family Issues, 17,* 466–494.

Stephens, N. M., Hamedani, M. G., & Destin, M. (2014). Closing the social-class achievement gap: A difference-education intervention improves first-generation students' academic performance and all students' college transition. *Psychological Science, 25,* 943–953.

Sternberg, R. (1988). *The triarchic mind.* New York: Viking Penguin.

Stevens, E. A., & Prinstein, M. J. (2005). Peer contagion of depressogenic attributional styles among adolescents: A longitudinal study. *Journal of Abnormal Child Psychology, 33,* 25–38.

Stevens, J. (1988). Social support, locus of control, and parenting in three low-income groups of mothers: Black teenagers, Black adults, and White adults. *Child Development, 59,* 635–642.

Stevenson, C. E., Kleibeuker, S. W., de Dreu, C. K. & Crone, E. A. (2014) Training creative cognition: Adolescence as a flexible period for improving creativity. *Frontiers in Human Neuroscience, 8,* 827.

Stevenson, D., Schiller, K., & Schneider, B. (1994). Sequences of opportunities for learning. *Sociology of Education, 67,* 184–198.

Stevenson, H., & Stigler, J. (1992). *The learning gap: Why our schools are failing and what we can learn from Japanese and Chinese education.* New York: Simon & Schuster.

Stevenson, H., Jr., Reed, J., Bodison, P., & Bishop, A. (1997). Racism stress management: Racial social beliefs and the experience of depression and anger in African American youth. *Youth and Society, 29,* 197–222.

Stewart, E. B., Stewart, E. A., & Simons, R. L. (2007). The effect of neighborhood context on the college aspirations of African American adolescents. *American Education Research Journal, 44,* 896–919.

Stewart, S. D. (2003). Nonresident parenting and adolescent adjustment: The quality of nonresident father–child interaction. *Journal of Family Issues, 24,* 217–244.

Stice, E., & Bearman, S. (2001). Body-image and eating disturbances prospectively predict increases in depressive symptoms in adolescent girls: A growth curve analysis. *Developmental Psychology, 37,* 597–607.

Stice, E., & Gonzales, N. (1998). Adolescent temperament moderates the relation of parenting to antisocial behavior and substance use. *Journal of Adolescent Research, 13,* 5–31.

Stice, E., & Shaw, H. (2003). Prospective relations of body image, eating, and affective disturbances to smoking onset in adolescent girls: How Virginia Slims. *Journal of Consulting and Clinical Psychology, 71,* 129–135.

Stice, E., & Whitenton, K. (2002). Risk factors for body dissatisfaction in adolescent girls: A longitudinal investigation. *Developmental Psychology, 38,* 669–678.

Stice, E., Burton, E., & Shaw, H. (2004). Prospective relations between bulimic pathology, depression, and substance abuse: Unpacking comorbidity in adolescent girls. *Journal of Consulting and Clinical Psychology, 72,* 62–71.

Stice, E., Hayward, C., Cameron, R. P., Killen, J., & Taylor, C. (2000). Body-image and eating disturbances predict onset of depression among female adolescents: A longitudinal study. *Journal of Abnormal Psychology, 109,* 438–444.

Stice, E., Marti, C. N., & Rohde, P. (2013). Prevalence, incidence, impairment, and course of the proposed DSM-5N eating disorder diagnoses in an 8-year prospective community study of young women. *Journal of Abnormal Psychology, 122,* 445–457.

Stice, E., Presnell, K., Shaw, H., & Rohde, P. (2005). Psychological and behavioral risk factors for obesity onset in adolescent girls: A prospective study. *Journal of Consulting and Clinical Psychology, 73,* 195–202.

Stice, E., Shaw, H., & Marti, C. N. (2006). A meta-analytic review of obesity prevention programs for children and adolescents: The skinny on interventions that work. *Psychological Bulletin, 132,* 667–691.

Stice, E., Shaw, H., & Ochner, C. (2011). Eating disorders. In B. Brown & M. Prinstein (Eds.), *Encyclopedia of adolescence* (Vol. 3, pp. 151–159). New York: Academic Press.

Stice, E., Yokum, S., Burger, K., Epstein, L., & Small, D. (2011). Youth at risk for obesity show greater activation of striatal and somatosensory regions to food. *Journal of Neuroscience, 31,* 4360–4366.

Stickle, T. R., Kirkpatrick, N. M., & Brush, L. N. (2009). Callous-unemotional traits and social information processing: Multiple risk-factor models for understanding aggressive behavior in antisocial youth. *Law and Human Behavior, 33,* 515–529.

Stipek, D., & Gralinski, J. (1996). Children's beliefs about intelligence and school performance. *Journal of Educational Psychology, 88,* 397–407.

Stocker, C. M., Burwell, R. A., & Briggs, M. L. (2002). Sibling conflict in middle childhood predicts children's adjustment in early adolescence. *Journal of Family Psychology, 16,* 50–57.

Stocker, C. M., Lanthier, R. P., & Furman, W. (1997). Sibling relationships in early adulthood. *Journal of Family Psychology, 11,* 210–221.

Stoddard, S. A., Zimmerman, M. A., & Bauermeister, J. A. (2012). A longitudinal analysis of cumulative risks, cumulative promotive factors, and adolescent violent behavior. *Journal of Research on Adolescence, 22,* 542–555.

Stoddard, S. A., Whiteside, L., Zimmerman, M. A., Cunningham, R. M., Chermack, S. T., & Walton, M. A. (2013). The relationship between cumulative risk and promotive factors and violent behavior among urban adolescents. *American Journal of Community Psychology, 51,* 57–65.

Stone, J. (2011). Employment. In B. Brown & M. Prinstein (Eds.), *Encyclopedia of adolescence* (Vol. 2, pp. 59–67). New York: Academic Press.

Stone, L. B., & Gibb, B. E. (2015). Brief report: Preliminary evidence that co-rumination fosters adolescents' depression risk by increasing rumination. *Journal of Adolescence, 38,* 1–4.

Stone, L. B., Hankin, B. L., Gibb, B. E., & Abela, J. R. Z. (2011). Co-rumination predicts the onset of depressive disorders during adolescence. *Journal of Abnormal Psychology, 120,* 752–757.

Stoolmiller, M., Kim, H. K., & Capaldi, D. M. (2005). The course of depressive symptoms in men from early adolescence to young adulthood: Identifying latent trajectories and early predictors. *Journal of Abnormal Psychology, 114,* 331–345.

Storvoll, E. E., & Wichstrøm, L. (2002). Do the risk factors associated with conduct problems vary according to gender? *Journal of Adolescence, 25,* 183–202.

Stouthamer-Loeber, M., Wei, E., & Loeber, R. (2004). Desistance from persistent serious delinquency in the transition to adulthood. *Development and Psychopathology, 16,* 897–918.

Strachman, A., Impett, E. A., Henson, J. M., & Pentz, M. A. (2009). Early adolescent alcohol use and sexual experience by emerging adulthood: A 10-year longitudinal investigation. *Journal of Adolescent Health, 45,* 478–482.

Strang, N. M., & Pollak, S. D. (2014). Development continuity in reward-related enhancement of cognitive control. *Development Cognitive Neuroscience, 10,* 34–43.

Strang, N., Pruessner, J., & Pollack, S. (2011). Developmental changes in adolescents' neural response to challenge. *Developmental Cognitive Neuroscience, 1,* 560–569.

Strasburger, V., & Donnerstein, E. (1999). Children, adolescents, and the media: Issues and solutions. *Pediatrics, 103,* 129–139.

Strasburger, V., Jordan, A., & Donnerstein, E. (2010). Health effects of media on children and adolescents. *Pediatrics, 125,* 756–767.

Straub, D. M., Hills, N. K., Thompson, P. J., & Moscicki, A. (2003). Effects of pro- and anti-tobacco advertising on nonsmoking adolescents' intentions to smoke. *Journal of Adolescent Health, 32,* 36–43.

Straus, M., & Yodanis, C. (1996). Corporal punishment in adolescence and physical assaults on spouses in later life: What accounts for the link? *Journal of Marriage and the Family, 58,* 825–841.

Strenziok, M., Krueger, F., Pulaski, S., Openshaw, A., Zamboni, G., van de Meer, E., & Grafman, J. (2010). Lower lateral orbitofrontal cortex density associated with more frequent exposure to television and movie violence in male adolescents. *Journal of Adolescent Health, 46,* 607–609.

Strong American Schools. (2008). *Diploma to nowhere.* Washington, DC: Author.

Stroud, L., Foster, E., Papandonatos, G., Handwerger, K., Granger, D., Kivlighan, K., . . . Niaura, R. (2009). Stress response and the adolescent transition: Performance versus peer rejection stressors. *Development and Psychopathology, 21,* 47–68.

Strough, J., & Berg, C. (2000). Goals as a mediator of gender differences in high-affiliation dyadic conversations. *Developmental Psychology, 36,* 117–125.

Stuart, E. A., & Green, K. M. (2008). Using full matching to estimate causal effects in nonexperimental studies: Examining the relationship between adolescent marijuana use and adult outcomes. *Developmental Psychology, 44,* 395–406.

Sturman, D., & Moghaddam, B. (2012). Striatum processes reward differently in adolescents versus adults. *Proceedings of the National Academy of Sciences, 109,* 1719–1724.

Sturmhöfel, S., & Swartzwelder, H. (2004). Alcohol's effects on the adolescent brain: What can be learned from animal models? *Alcohol Research and Health, 28,* 213–221.

Su, X., Simons, R. L., & Simons, L. G. (2011). Interparental aggression and antisocial behavior among African American youth: A simultaneous test of competing explanations. *Journal of Youth and Adolescence, 40,* 1489–1502.

Suárez-Orozco, C., Rhodes, J., & Milburn, M. (2009). Unraveling the immigrant paradox: Academic engagement and disengagement among recently arrived immigrant youth. *Youth & Society, 41,* 151–185.

Sue, S., & Okazaki, S. (1990). Asian-American educational achievements: A phenomenon in search of an explanation. *American Psychologist, 45,* 913–920.

Sui-Chu, E., & Willms, J. (1996). Effects of parental involvement on eighth-grade achievement. *Sociology of Education, 69,* 126–141.

Suizzo, M. A., Jackson, K. M., Pahlke, E., Marroquin, Y., Blondeau, L., & Martinez, A. (2012). Pathways to achievement: How low-income Mexican-origin parents promote their adolescents through school. *Family Relations, 61,* 533–547.

Sullivan, C. J., Childs, K. K., & O'Connell, D. (2010). Adolescent risk behavior subgroups: An empirical assessment. *Journal of Youth and Adolescence, 39,* 541–562.

Sullivan, H. S. (1953a). *The interpersonal theory of psychiatry.* New York: Norton.

Sullivan, H. S. (1953b). *Conceptions of modern psychiatry.* New York: Norton.

Sullivan, T. N., Farrell, A. D., & Kliewer, W. (2006). Peer victimization in early adolescence: Association between physical and relational victimization and drug use, aggression, and delinquent behaviors among urban middle school students. *Development and Psychopathology, 18,* 119–137.

Sun, Y. (2001). Family environment and adolescents' well-being before and after parents' marital disruption: A longitudinal analysis. *Journal of Marriage and the Family, 63,* 697–713.

Sun, Y. (2003). The well-being of adolescents in households with no biological parents. *Journal of Marriage and Family, 65,* 894.

Sun, Y., & Li, Y. (2002). Children's well-being during the parents' marital disruption process: A pooled time-series analysis. *Journal of Marriage and the Family, 64,* 472–488.

Sun, Y., & Li, Y. (2009). Postdivorce family stability and changes in adolescents' academic performance: A growth-curve model. *Journal of Family Issues, 30,* 1527–1555.

Supple, A. J., Ghazarian, S. R., Frabutt, J. M., Plunkett, S. W., & Sands, T. (2006). Contextual influences on Latino adolescent ethnic identity and academic outcomes. *Child Development, 77,* 1427–1433.

Supple, A. J., Peterson, G. W., & Bush, K. R. (2004). Assessing the validity of parenting measures in a sample of Chinese adolescents. *Journal of Family Psychology, 18,* 539–544.

Susman, E. (1997). Modeling developmental complexity in adolescence: Hormones and behavior in context. *Journal of Research on Adolescence, 7,* 283–306.

Susman, E. (2006). Psychobiology of persistent antisocial behavior: Stress, early vulnerabilities, and the attenuation hypothesis. *Neuroscience Biobehavioral Reviews, 30,* 376–389.

Susman, E. J., Dockray, S., Schiefelbein, V. L., Herwehe, S., Heaton, J. A., & Dorn, L. D. (2007). Morningness/eveningness, morning-to-afternoon cortisol ratio, and antisocial behavior problems during puberty. *Developmental Psychology, 43,* 811–822.

Susman, E., & Dorn, L. (2009). Puberty: Its role in development. In R. Lerner & L. Steinberg (Eds.), *Handbook of adolescent psychology* (3rd ed., Vol. 1, pp. 116–151). New York: Wiley.

Susman, E., Dorn, L., Inoff-Germain, G., Nottelmann, E., & Chrousos, G. (1997). Cortisol reactivity, distress behavior, and behavioral and psychological problems in young adolescents: A longitudinal perspective. *Journal of Research on Adolescence, 7,* 81–105.

Swahn, M. H., Bossarte, R. M., & Sullivent, E. E. I., II. (2008). Age of alcohol use initiation, suicidal behavior, and peer and dating violence victimization and perpetration among high-risk, seventh-grade adolescents. *Pediatrics, 121,* 297–305.

Swanson, C. (2009). *Cities in crisis 2009.* Bethesda, MD: EPE Research Center.

Swarr, A., & Richards, M. (1996). Longitudinal effects of adolescent girls' pubertal development, perceptions of pubertal timing, and parental relations on eating problems. *Developmental Psychology, 32,* 636–646.

Sweeten, G., Bushway, S. D., & Paternoster, R. (2009). Does dropping out of school mean dropping into delinquency? *Criminology: An Interdisciplinary Journal, 47,* 47–91.

Sweeten, G., Piquero, A. P., & Steinberg, L. (2013). Age and the explanation of crime, revisited. *Journal of Youth & Adolescence, 42,* 921–938.

Swendsen, J., Burstein, M., Case, B., Conway, K. P., Dierker, L., He, J., & Merikangas, K. R. (2012). Use and abuse of alcohol and illicit drugs in US adolescents: Results of the national comorbidity survey–adolescent supplement. *Archives of General Psychiatry, 69,* 390–398.

Swenson, L. P., & Rose, A. J. (2003). Friends as reporters of children's and adolescents' depressive symptoms. *Journal of Abnormal Child Psychology, 31,* 619–631.

Swinton, A. D., Kurtz-Costes, B., Rowley, S. J., & Okeke-Adeyanju, N. (2011). A longitudinal examination of African American adolescents' attributions about achievement outcomes. *Child Development, 82,* 1486–1500.

Swisher, R. R., & Warner, T. D. (2013). If they grow up: Exploring the neighborhood context of adolescent and young adult survival expectations. *Journal of Research on Adolescence, 23,* 678–694.

Syed, M., & Azmitia, M. (2008). A narrative approach to ethnic identity in emerging adulthood: Bringing life to the identity status model. *Developmental Psychology, 44,* 1012–1027.

Syed, M., & Seiffge-Krenke, I. (2013). Personality development from adolescence to emerging adulthood: Linking trajectories of ego development to the family context and identity formation. *Journal of Personality and Social Psychology, 104,* 371–384.

Symons, K., Vermeersch, H., & Van Houtte, M. (2014). The emotional experiences of early first intercourse: A multi-method study. *Journal of Adolescent Research, 29,* 533–560.

Syngelaki, E. M., Fairchild, G., Moore, S. C., Savage, J. C., & Van Goozen, S. H. M. (2013). Fearlessness in juvenile offenders is associated with offending rate. *Developmental Science, 16,* 84–90.

Syvertsen, A., Flanagan, C., & Stout, M. (2009). Code of silence: Students' perceptions of school climate and willingness to intervene in a peer's dangerous plan. *Journal of Educational Psychology, 101,* 219–232.

Syvertsen, A., Wray-Lake, L., Flanagan, C., Osgood, D. W., & Briddell, L. (2011). Thirty-year trends in U.S. adolescents' civic engagement: A story of changing participation and educational differences. *Journal of Research on Adolescence, 21,* 586–594.

Szeszulski, P., Martinez, A., & Reyes, B. (1994, February). *Patterns and predictors of self-satisfaction among culturally diverse high school students.* Paper presented at the biennial meetings of the Society for Research on Adolescence, San Diego.

Szwedo, D. E., Mikami, A. Y., & Allen, J. P. (2012). Social networking site use predicts changes in young adults' psychological adjustment.

Journal of Research on Adolescence, 22, 453–466.

Szwedo, D., Mikami, A., & Allen, J. (2011). Qualities of peer relations on social networking websites: Predictions from negative mother–teen interactions. *Journal of Research on Adolescence, 21,* 595–607.

Tabak, I., Mazur, J., del Carmen Granado Alcón, M., rkenyi, A., Zaborskis, A., Aasvee, K., & Moreno, C. (2012). Examining trends in parent-child communication in Europe over 12 years. *Journal of Early Adolescence, 32,* 26–54.

Talwar, V., Gomez-Garibello, C., & Shariff S. (2014). Adolescents' moral evaluations and ratings of cyberbullying: The effect of veracity and intentionality behind the event. *Computers in Human Behavior, 36,* 122–128.

Tamnes, C., Østby, Y., Fjell, A., Westlye, L., Due-Tonnessen, P., & Walhovd, K. (2010). Brain maturation in adolescence and young adulthood: regional age-related changes in cortical thickness and white matter volume and microstructure. *Cerebral Cortex, 20,* 534–548.

Tanaka, C., Matsui, M., Uematsu, A., Noguchi, K., & Miyawaki, T. (2012) Developmental trajectories of the fronto-temporal lobes from infancy to early adulthood in healthy individuals. *Developmental Neuroscience, 34,* 477–487.

Tang, C. S., Yeung, D. Y., & Lee, A. M. (2003). Psychosocial correlates of emotional responses to menarche among Chinese adolescent girls. *Journal of Adolescent Health, 33,* 193–201.

Tang, C. S., Yeung, D. Y., & Lee, A. M. (2004). A comparison of premenarcheal expectations and postmenarcheal experiences in Chinese early adolescents. *Journal of Early Adolescence, 24,* 180–195.

Tang, S., Davis-Kean, P. E., Chen, M., & Sexton, H. R. (2015). Adolescent pregnancy's intergenerational effects: Does an adolescent mother's education have consequences for her children's achievement. *Journal of Research on Adolescence.* DOI: 10.1111/jora.12182.

Tanner, D. (1972). *Secondary education.* New York: Macmillan.

Tanner, J. (1972). Sequence, tempo, and individual variation in growth and development of boys and girls aged twelve to sixteen. In J. Kagan & R. Coles (Eds.), *Twelve to sixteen: Early adolescence.* New York: Norton.

Tanner-Smith, E. E. (2010). Negotiating the early developing body: Pubertal timing, body weight, and adolescent girls' substance use. *Journal of Youth and Adolescence, 39,* 1402–1416.

Tapert, S. F., Baratta, M. V., Abrantes, A. M., & Brown, S. A. (2002). Attention dysfunction predicts involvement in community youths. *Journal of the American Academy of Child and Adolescent Psychiatry, 41,* 680–686.

Taradash, A., Connolly, J., Pepler, D., Craig, W., & Costa, M. (2001). The interpersonal context of romantic autonomy in adolescence. *Journal of Adolescence, 24,* 365–377.

Tartakovsky, E. (2009). Cultural identities of adolescent immigrants: A three-year longitudinal study including the pre-migration period. *Journal of Youth and Adolescence, 38,* 654–671.

Tatnell, R., Kelada, L., Hasking, P., & Martin, G. (2014). Longitudinal analysis of adolescent NSSI: The role of intrapersonal and interpersonal factors. *Journal of Abnormal Child Psychology, 42,* 885–896.

Tavernier, R., & Willoughby, T. (2012). Adolescent turning points: The association between meaning-making and psychological well-being. *Developmental Psychology, 48,* 1058–1068.

Tavernise, S. (2015, April 8). *More teens using long-term contraception. The New York Times,* p. A18.

Taylor, D., Jenni, O., Acebo, C., & Carskadon, M. (2005). Sleep tendency during extended wakefulness: Insights into adolescent sleep regulation and behavior. *Journal of Sleep Research, 14,* 239–244.

Taylor, N. (2011). "Guys, she's humongous!": Gender and weight-based teasing in adolescence. *Journal of Adolescent Research, 26,* 178–199.

Taylor, R., & Roberts, D. (1995). Kinship support and maternal and adolescent well-being in economically disadvantaged African-American families. *Child Development, 66,* 1585–1597.

Taylor, R., Casten, R., Flickinger, S., Roberts, D., & Fulmore, C. (1994). Explaining the school performance of African-American adolescents. *Journal of Research on Adolescence, 4,* 21–44.

Taylor, R., Rodriguez, A. U., Seaton, E. K., & Dominguez, A. (2004). Association of financial resources with parenting and adolescent adjustment in African American families. *Journal of Adolescent Research, 19,* 267–283.

Taylor, T. J., Peterson, D., Esbensen, F., & Freng, A. (2007). Gang membership as a risk factor for adolescent violent victimization. *Journal of Research in Crime and Delinquency, 44,* 351–380.

Teachman, J. (1996). Intellectual skill and academic performance: Do families bias the relationship? *Sociology of Education, 69,* 35–48.

Teachman, J. (1997). Gender of siblings, cognitive achievement, and academic performance: Familial and nonfamilial influences on children. *Journal of Marriage and the Family, 59,* 363–374.

Teachman, J., & Paasch, K. (1998). The family and educational aspirations. *Journal of Marriage and the Family, 60,* 704–714.

Teachman, J., Paasch, K., & Carver, K. (1996). Social capital and dropping out of school early. *Journal of Marriage and the Family, 58,* 773–783.

Teachman, J., Paasch, K., & Carver, K. (1997). Social capital and the generation of human capital. *Social Forces, 75,* 1343–1359.

Teitler, J. O., & Weiss, C. C. (2000). Effects of neighborhood and school environments on transitions to first sexual intercourse. *Sociology of Education, 73,* 112–132.

Telzer, E. H., & Fuligni, A. (2009). A longitudinal daily diary study of family assistance and academic achievement among adolescents from Mexican, Chinese, and European backgrounds. *Journal of Youth and Adolescence, 38,* 560–571.

Telzer, E. H., & Fuligni, A. J. (2013). Positive daily family interactions eliminate gender differences in internalizing symptoms among adolescents. *Journal of Youth & Adolescence, 42,* 1498–1511.

Telzer, E. H., Fuligni, A. J., Lieberman, M. D., Miernicki, M. E., & Galván, A. (2015). The quality of adolescents' peer relationships modulates neural sensitivity to risk taking. *Social Cognitive Affective Neuroscience, 10,* 389–398.

Telzer, E. H., Gonzales, N., Fuligni, A. J. (2014). Family obligation values and family assistance behaviors: protective and risk factors for Mexican-American adolescents' substance use. *Journal of Youth & Adolescence, 43,* 270–283.

Telzer, E. H., Ichien, N. T., & Qu, Y. (2015). Mothers know best: Redirecting adolescent reward sensitivity towards safe behavior during risk taking. *Social Cognitive Affective Neuroscience, Epub ahead of print.* DOI: 10.1093/scan/nsv026.

Telzer, E. H., Tsai, K. M., Gonzales, N., & Fuligni, A. J. (2015). Mexican American adolescents' family obligation values and behaviors: Links to internalizing symptoms across time and context. *Developmental Psychology, 51,* 75–86.

Temple, J. R., Le, V. D., van den Berg, P., Ling, Y., Paul, J. A, & Temple, B. W. (2014). Brief report: Teen sexting and psychosocial health. *Journal of Adolescence, 37,* 33–26.

Temple, J. R., Shorey, R. C., Fite, P., Stuart, G. L., & Le, V. D. (2013). Substance use as a longitudinal predictor of the perpetration of teen dating violence. *Journal of Youth & Adolescence, 42,* 596–606.

Tenenbaum, H. R., & Ruck, M. D. (2012). British adolescents' and young adults' understanding and reasoning about the religious and nonreligious rights of asylum-seeker youth. *Child Development, 83,* 1102–1115.

Terry, M., Ferris, J., Tehranifar, P., Wei, Y., & Flom, J. (2009). Birth weight, postnatal growth, and age at menarche. *American Journal of Epidemiology, 170,* 72–79.

Terry, R., & Winston, C. (2010). Personality characteristic adaptations: Multiracial adolescents' patterns of racial self-identification change. *Journal of Research on Adolescence, 20,* 432–455.

Teslovich, T., Mulder, M., Franklin, N. T., Ruberry, E. J., Millner, A., Somerville, L. J. . . . . & Casey, B. J. (2014). Adolescents let sufficient evidence accumulate before making a

decision when large incentives are at stake. *Developmental Science, 17,* 59–70.

Teti, D., & Lamb, M. (1989). Socioeconomic and marital outcomes of adolescent marriage, adolescent childbirth, and their co-occurrence. *Journal of Marriage and the Family, 51,* 203–212.

Tevendale, H., DuBois, D., Lopez, C., & Prindiville, S. (1997). Self-esteem stability and early adolescent adjustment: An exploratory study. *Journal of Early Adolescence, 17,* 216–237.

Theokas, C. (2009). Youth sport participation—A view of the issues: Introduction to the special section. *Developmental Psychology, 45,* 303–306.

Theokas, C., & Lerner, R. (2006). Promoting positive development in adolescence: The role of ecological assets in families, schools, and neighborhoods. *Applied Developmental Science, 10,* 61–74.

Thijs, J., Verkuyten, M., & Helmond, P. (2010). A further examination of the big-fish–little-pond effect: Perceived position in class, class size, and gender comparisons. *Sociology of Education, 83,* 333–345.

Thomaes, S., Bushman, B. J., de Castro, B. O., & Reijntjes, A. (2012). Arousing "gentle passions" in young adolescents: Sustained experimental effects of value affirmations on prosocial feelings and behaviors. *Developmental Psychology, 48,* 103–110.

Thomaes, S., Poorthuis, A., & Nelemans, S. (2011). Self-esteem. In B. Brown & M. Prinstein (Eds.), *Encyclopedia of adolescence* (Vol. 1, pp. 316–324). New York: Academic Press.

Thomas, A. G, Monahan, K. C., Lukowski, A. F., Cauffman, E. (2015). Sleep problems across development: a pathway to adolescent risk taking through working memory. *Journal of Youth and Adolescence, 44,* 447–464.

Thomas, J., & Daubman, K. A. (2001). The relationship between friendship quality and self-esteem in adolescent girls and boys. *Sex Roles, 45,* 53–65.

Thomas, K. J., & McGloin, J. M. (2013). A dual-systems approach for undersanding differential susceptibility to processes of peer influence. *Criminology 51,* 435–474.

Thomas, L. A., De Bellis, M. D., Graham, R., & LaBar, K. S. (2007). Development of emotional facial recognition in late childhood and adolescence. *Developmental Science, 10,* 547–558.

Thomas, L., Hall, J., Skup, M., Jenkins, S., Pine, D. S., & Leibenluft, E. (2011). A developmental neuroimaging investigation of the change paradigm. *Developmental Science, 14,* 148–161.

Thomas, M., & Johnson, M. (2008). New advances in understanding sensitive periods in brain development. *Current Directions in Psychological Science, 17,* 1–5.

Thomas, O., Caldwell, C., Faison, N., & Jackson, J. (2009). Promoting academic achievement:

The role of racial identity in buffering perceptions of teacher discrimination on academic achievement among African American and Caribbean Black adolescents. *Journal of Educational Psychology, 101,* 420–431.

Thomason, M. E., Marusak, H. A., Tocco, M. A., Vila, A. M., McGarragle, O., & Rosenberg, D. R. (2015). Altered amygdala connectivity in urban youth exposed to trauma. *Social Cognitive Affective Neuroscience, Epub ahead of print.* DOI: 10.1093/scan/nsv030

Thompson, R., & Zuroff, D. C. (1999). Dependency, self-criticism, and mothers' responses to adolescent sons' autonomy and competence. *Journal of Youth and Adolescence, 28,* 365–384.

Thornberry, T., Freeman-Gallant, A., Lizotte, A. J., Krohn, M. D., & Smith, C. (2003). Linked lives: The intergenerational transmission of antisocial behavior. *Journal of Abnormal Child Psychology, 31,* 171–184.

Thornberry, T., Smith, C., & Howard, G. (1997). Risk factors for teenage fatherhood. *Journal of Marriage and the Family, 59,* 505–522.

Thorne, A. (2000). Personal memory telling and personality development. *Personality and Social Psychology Review, 4,* 45–56.

Thornton, A., Orbuch, T. L., & Axinn, W. G. (1995). Parent–child relationships during the transition to adulthood. *Journal of Family Issues, 16,* 538–564.

Thrul, J., Lipperman-Kreda, S., Grube, J. W., & Friend, K. B. (2014). Community-level adult daily smoking prevalence moderates the association between adolescents' cigarette smoking and perceived smoking by friends. *Journal of Youth & Adolescence, 43,* 1527–1535.

Thurber, C. (1995). The experience and expression of homesickness in preadolescent and adolescent boys. *Child Development, 66,* 1162–1178.

Tiggemann, M., & Slater, A. (2014). NetTweens: The internet and body image concerns in preteenage girls. *Journal of Early Adolescence, 34,* 606–620.

Tilton-Weaver, L. (2014). Adolescents' information management: comparing ideas about why adolescents discloe to or keep secrets from their parents. *Journal of Youth & Adolescence, 43,* 803–813.

Tilton-Weaver, L. C., & Galambos, N. L. (2003). Adolescents' characteristics and parents' beliefs as predictors of parents' peer management behaviors. *Journal of Research on Adolescence, 13,* 269–300.

Tilton-Weaver, L. C., Burk, W. J., Kerr, M., & Stattin, H. (2013). Can parental monitoring and peer management reduce the selection or influence of delinquent peers? Testing the question using a dynamic social network approach. *Developmental Psychology, 49,* 2057–2070.

Timmerman, G. (2002). A comparison between unwanted sexual behavior by teachers and by peers in secondary schools. *Journal of Youth and Adolescence, 31,* 397–404.

Timmons, A. C., & Margolin, G. (2015). Family conflict, mood, and adolescents' daily school problems: Moderating roles of internalizing and externalizing symptoms. *Child Development, 86,* 241–258.

Titzmann, P. F. (2014). Immigrant adolescents' adaptation to a new context: ethnic friendship homophily and its predictors. *Child Development Perspectives, 8,* 107–112.

Tobian, A., Serwadda, D., Quinn, T., Kigozi, G., Gravitt, P., Laeyendecker, O., . . .Gray, R. (2009). Male circumcision for the prevention of HSV-2 and HPV infections and syphilis. *New England Journal of Medicine, 360,* 1298–1309.

Tobler, A. L., & Komro, K. A. (2010). Trajectories or parental monitoring and communication and effects on drug use among urban young adolescents. *Journal of Adolescent Health, 46,* 560–568.

Tolan, P. H., & Larsen, R. (2014). Trajectories of life satisfaction during middle school: Relations to developmental-ecological microsystems and student functioning. *Journal of Research on Adolescence, 24,* 497–511.

Tolan, P., & Gorman-Smith, D. (2002). What violence prevention research can tell us about developmental psychopathology. *Development and Psychopathology, 14,* 713–729.

Tolan, P., Gorman-Smith, D., & Henry, D. (2003). The developmental ecology of urban males' youth violence. *Developmental Psychology, 39,* 274–291.

Tolan, P., Gorman-Smith, D., Henry, D., Chung, K., & Hunt, M. (2002). The relation of patterns of coping inner-city youth to psychopathology symptoms. *Journal of Research on Adolescence, 12,* 423–449.

Tolman, D. (1993, March). *"When my body says yes": Adolescent girls' experiences of sexual desire.* Paper presented at the biennial meetings of the Society for Research in Child Development, New Orleans.

Tolman, D. L., & McClelland, S. I. (2011). Normative sexuality development in adolescence: A decade in review, 2000–2009. *Journal of Research on Adolescence, 21,* 242–255.

Tomal, A. (2001). The effect of religious membership on teen abortion rates. *Journal of Youth and Adolescence, 30,* 103–116.

Tomasi, D., & Volkow, N. D. (2012). Laterality patterns of brain functional connectivity: Gender effects. *Cerebral Cortex, 22,* 1455–1462.

Tomasik, M., & Silbereisen, R. (2011). Globalization and adolescence. In B. Brown & M. Prinstein (Eds.), *Encyclopedia of adolescence* (Vol. 2, pp. 109–117). New York: Academic Press.

Tomasik, M. J., & Silbereisen, R. K. (2012). Social change and adolescent developmental tasks: The case of postcommunist Europe. *Child Development Perspectives, 6,* 326–334.

Toomey, R. B., Ryan, C., Diaz, R. M., Card, N. A., & Russell, S. T. (2010). Gender-nonconforming lesbian, gay, bisexual, and transgender youth: School victimization and young adult psychosocial adjustment. *Developmental Psychology, 46,* 1580–1589.

Topolski, T. D., Patrick, D. L., Edwards, T. C., Huebner, C. E., Connell, F. A., & Mount, K. K. (2001). Quality of life and health-risk behaviors among adolescents. *Journal of Adolescent Health, 29,* 426–435.

Torney-Purta, J. (1990). Youth in relation to social institutions. In S. Feldman & G. Elliott (Eds.), *At the threshold: The developing adolescent,* (pp. 457–478). Cambridge, MA: Harvard University Press.

Totura, C. M., Karver, M. S., Gesten, E. L. (2014). Psychological distress and student engagement as mediators of the relationship between peer victimization and achievement in middle school youth. *Journal of Youth & Adolescence, 43,* 40–52.

Tough, P. (2008). *Whatever it takes: Geoffrey Canada's quest to change Harlem and America.* New York: Houghton Mifflin Harcourt.

Tram, J. M., & Cole, D. A. (2000). Self-perceived competence and the relation between life events and depressive symptoms in adolescence: Mediator or moderator? *Journal of Abnormal Psychology, 109,* 753–760.

Treaster, J. (1994, February 1). Survey finds marijuana use is up in high schools. *The New York Times,* pp. A1ff.

Trejos-Castillo, E. & Vazsonyi, A. (2011). Transitions into adolescence. In B. Brown & M. Prinstein (Eds.), *Encyclopedia of adolescence* (Vol. 1, pp. 369–375). New York: Academic Press.

Tremblay, R., Pagani-Kurtz, L., Mâsse, L., Vitaro, F., & Pihl, R. (1995). A bimodal preventive intervention for disruptive kindergarten boys: Its impact through mid-adolescence. *Journal of Consulting and Clinical Psychology, 63,* 560–568.

Trent, K., & Crowder, K. (1997). Adolescent birth intentions, social disadvantage, and behavioral outcomes. *Journal of Marriage and the Family, 59,* 523–535.

Trent, K., & Harlan, S. (1994). Teenage mothers in nuclear and extended households: Differences by marital status and race/ethnicity. *Journal of Family Issues, 15,* 309–337.

Trentacosta, C. J., Criss, M. M., Shaw, D. S., Lacourse, E., Hyde, L. W., & Dishion, T. J. (2011). Antecedents and outcomes of joint trajectories of mother-son conflict and warmth during middle childhood and adolescence. *Child Development, 82,* 1676–1690.

Trepanier, L., Juster, R. P., Marin, M. F., Plusquellec, P., Francois, N., Sindi, S. . . . . & Lupien, S. (2013). Early menarche predicts increased depressive symptoms and cortisol levels in Quebec girls ages 11 to 13. *Development and Psychopathology, 25,* 1017–1027.

Trickett, P., McBride-Chang, C., & Putnam, F. (1994). The classroom performance and behavior of sexually abused females.

Development and Psychopathology, 6, 183–194.

Trickett, P., Negriff, S., Ji, J., & Peckins, M. (2011). Child maltreatment and adolescent development. *Journal of Research on Adolescence, 21,* 3–20.

Trickett, P., Noll, J., & Putnam, F. (2011). The impact of sexual abuse on female development: Lessons from a multigenerational, longitudinal research study. *Development and Psychopathology, 23,* 453–476.

Trifan, T. A., & Stattin, H. (2015). Are adolescents' mutually hostile interactions at home reproduced in other everyday life contexts? *Journal of Youth & Adolescence, 44,* 598–615.

Trinkner, R., Cohn, E. S., Rebellon, C. J., & Van Gundy, K. (2012). Don't trust anyone over 30: Parental legitimacy as a mediator between parenting style and changes in delinquent behavior over time. *Journal of Adolescence, 35,* 119–132.

Trommsdorff, G. (2012). Development of "agentic" regulation in cultural context: The role of self and world views .*Child Development Perspectives, 6,* 19–26.

Trucco, E. M., Colder, C. R., Wieczorek, W. F., Lengua, L. J., & Hawk, L. W. (2014). Early adolescent alcohol use in context: How neighborhoods, parents, and peers impact youth. *Development and Psychopathology, 26,* 425–436.

Trudeau, L., Mason, W. A., Randall, G. K., Spoth, R., & Ralston, E. (2012). Effects of parenting and deviant peers on early to mid-adolescent conduct problems. *Journal of Abnormal Child Psychology, 40,* 1249–1264.

Truong, K. D., & Sturm, R. (2009). Alcohol environments and disparities in exposure associated with adolescent drinking in California. *American Journal of Public Health, 99,* 264–270.

Trusty, J., Plata, M., & Salazar, C. F. (2003). Modeling Mexican Americans' educational expectations: Longitudinal effects of variables across adolescence. *Journal of Adolescent Research, 18,* 131–153.

Trzesniewski, K., & Donnellan, M. (2009). Reevaluating the evidence for increasingly positive self-views among high school students: More evidence for consistency across generations (1976–2006). *Psychological Science, 20,* 920–922.

Trzesniewski, K., Donnellan, M., & Robins, R. (2003). Stability of self-esteem across the life span. *Journal of Personality and Social Psychology, 84,* 205–220.

Trzesniewski, K., Donnellan, M., Moffitt, T., Robins, R., Poulton, R., & Caspi, A. (2006). Low self-esteem during adolescence predicts poor health, criminal behavior, and limited economic prospects during adulthood. *Developmental Psychology, 42,* 381–390.

Tsai, K. M., & Fuligni, A. J. (2012). Change in ethnic identity across the college transition. *Developmental Psychology, 48,* 56–64.

Tsai, K. M., Telzer, E. H., & Fuligni, A. J. (2013). Continuity and discontinuity in perceptions of family relationships from adolescence to young adulthood. *Child Development, 84,* 471–484.

Tsai, K. M., Telzer, E. H., Gonzales, N. A., & Fuligni, A. J. (2015). Parental cultural socialization of Mexican-American adolescents' family obligation values and behaviors. *Child Development.* DOI: 10.1111/cdev.12358

Tschann, J., & Adler, N. (1997). Sexual self-acceptance, communication with partner, and contraceptive use among adolescent females: A longitudinal study. *Journal of Research on Adolescence, 7,* 413–430.

Tschann, J., Flores, E., VanOss Marin, B., Pasch, L. A., Baisch, E., & Wibbelsman, C. J. (2002). Interparental conflict and risk behaviors among Mexican American adolescents: A cognitive-emotional model. *Journal of Abnormal Psychology, 30,* 373–385.

Tschann, J., Pasch, L., Flores, E., Marin, B., Baisch, E., & Wibbelsman, C. (2009). Nonviolent aspects of interparental conflict and dating violence among adolescents. *Journal of Family Issues, 30,* 295–319.

Tseng, V., & Fuligni, A. (2000). Parent–adolescent language use and relationship among immigrant families with East Asian, Filipino and Latin American backgrounds. *Journal of Marriage and the Family, 62,* 465–476.

Tseng, W. L., Kawabata, Y., Gau, S. S., & Crick, N. R. (2014). Symptoms of attention-deficit/hyperactivity disorder and peer functioning: A transactional model of development. *Journal of Abnormal Child Psychology, 42,* 1353–1365.

Tu, K. M., Erath, S. A., & Flanagan, K. S. (2012). Can socially adept friends protect peer victimized early adolescents against lower academic competence? *Journal of Applied Developmental Psychology, 33,* 24–30.

Tubman, J. G., Montgomery, M. J., Gil, A. G., & Wagner, E. F. (2004). Abuse experiences in a community sample of young adults: Relations with psychiatric disorders, sexual risk behaviors, and sexually transmitted diseases. *American Journal of Community Psychology, 34,* 147–162.

Tucker, C., McHale, S., & Crouter, A. (2001). Conditions of sibling support in adolescence. *Journal of Family Psychology, 15,* 254–271.

Tucker, C., McHale, S., & Crouter, A. (2003a). Dimensions of mothers' and fathers' differential treatment of siblings: Links with adolescents' sex-typed personal qualities. *Family Relations: Interdisciplinary Journal of Applied Family Studies, 52,* 82–89.

Tucker, C., McHale, S., & Crouter, A. (2003b). Conflict resolution links with adolescents' family relationships and individual well-being. *Journal of Family Influence, 24,* 715–736.

Tucker, C., Updegraff, K. A., & Baril, M. E. (2010). Who's the boss? Patterns of control in adolescents' sibling relationships. *Family Relations, 59,* 520–532.

Tucker, J. S., Ellickson, P. L., Collins, R. L., & Klein, D. J. (2006). Are drug experimenters better adjusted than abstainers and users?: A longitudinal study of adolescent marijuana use. *Journal of Adolescent Health, 39,* 488–494.

Tucker, J. S., Miles, J. N. V., & D'Amico, E. J. (2013). Cross-lagged associations between substance use-related media exposure and alcohol use during middle school. *Journal of Adolescent Health, 53,* 460-464.

Tucker, J. S., Pedersen, E. R., Miles, J. N. V., Ewing, B. A., Shih, R. A., & D'Amico, E. J. (2014). Alcohol and marijuana use in middle school: Comparing solitary and social-only users. *Journal of Adolescent Health, 55,* 744–749.

Tucker-Drob, E. M., Briley, D. A., & Harden, K. P. (2013). Genetic and environmental influences on cognition across development and context. *Current Directions in Psychological Science, 22,* 349–355.

Tucker-Drob, E., & Harden, K. (2012). Intellectual interest mediates gene–socioeconomic status interaction on adolescent academic achievement. *Child Development, 83,* 743–757.

Turkheimer, E., & Waldron, M. (2000). Nonshared environment: A theoretical, methodological, and quantitative review. *Psychological Bulletin, 126,* 78–108.

Turner, H. A., Finkelhor, D., Hamby, S. L., Shattuck, A., & Ormrod, R. K. (2011). Specifying type and location of peer victimization in a national sample of children and youth. *Journal of Youth and Adolescence, 40,* 1052–1067.

Turner, R., Sorenson, A. M., & Turner, J. (2000). Social contingencies in mental health: A seven-year follow-up study of teenage mothers. *Journal of Marriage and the Family, 62,* 777–791.

Twenge, J. (2000). The age of anxiety? The birth cohort change in anxiety and neuroticism, 1952–1993. *Journal of Personality and Social Psychology, 79,* 1007–1021.

Twenge, J. M., Campbell, W. K., Freeman, & E. C. (2012). Generational differences in young adults' life goals, concern for others, and civic orientation, 1966–2009. *Journal of Personality and Social Psychology, 102,* 1045–1062.

Twenge, J., & Crocker, J. (2002). Race and self-esteem: Meta-analyses comparing Whites, Blacks, Hispanics, Asians, and American Indians and comment on Gray-Little and Hafdahl. *Psychological Bulletin, 128,* 371–408.

Twenge, J., & Nolen-Hoeksema, S. (2002). Age, gender, race, socioeconomic status, and birth cohort difference on the children's depression inventory: A meta-analysis. *Journal of Abnormal Psychology, 111,* 578–588.

Tynes, B. (2007). Role taking in online "classrooms": What adolescents are learning about race and ethnicity. *Developmental Psychology, 43,* 1312–1320.

Tynes, B., Umaña-Taylor, A., Rose, C., Lin, J., & Anderson, C. (2012). Online racial discrimination and the protective function of ethnic identity and self-esteem for African American adolescents. *Developmental Psychology, 48,* 343–355.

Tynkkynen, L., Tolvanen, A., & Salmela-Aro, K. (2012). Trajectories of educational expectations from adolescence to young adulthood in Finland. *Developmental Psychology, 48,* 1674–1685.

Tyrell, F. A., Wheeler, L. A., Gonzales, N. A., Dumka, L., & Millsap, R. (2014). Family influences on Mexican American adolescents' romantic relationships: Moderation by gender and culture. *Journal of Research on Adolescence.* DOI: 10.1111/jora.12177.

Tyrka, A. R., Graber, J. A., & Brooks-Gunn, J. (2000). The development of disordered eating: Correlate and predictors of eating problems in the context of adolescence. In A. J. Sameroff, M. Lewis, & S. M. Miller (Eds.), *Handbook of developmental psychopathology* (2nd ed., pp. 607–624). New York: Kluwer Academic/Plenum.

Tyson, K., Darity, W., & Castellino, D. R. (2005). It's not "a Black thing." Understanding the burden of acting White and other dilemmas of high achievement. *American Sociological Review, 70,* 582–605.

Tzoumakis, S., Lussier, P., & Corrado, R. (2012). Female juvenile delinquency, motherhood, and the intergenerational transmission of aggression and antisocial behavior. *Behavioral Sciences & the Law, 30,* 211–237.

U.S. Census Bureau. (2000). *Projections of the total resident population by 5-year age groups and sex with special age categories: Middle series, 1999 to 2100.* Washington, DC: Author.

U.S. Census Bureau. (2009a). *Educational attainment in the United States: 2007.* Washington, DC: Author.

U.S. Census Bureau. (2009b). *Statistical abstract of the United States.* Washington, DC: Author.

U.S. Census Bureau. (2011). *Current population survey.* Washington, DC: Author.

U.S. Census Bureau. (2012). *Current population survey.* Washington, DC: Author.

U.S. Census Bureau. (2014). *Current Population Survey.* Washington: Author.

U.S. Department of Commerce, Bureau of the Census. (1940). *Characteristics of the population.* Washington, DC: U.S. Government Printing Office.

U.S. Department of Education. (2006). *No Child Left Behind.* Available at www.ed.gov.

U.S. Department of Education. (2009). Creating common standards, turning around schools. Retrieved from http://www.ed.gov/index.jhtml

U.S. Senate Committee on the Judiciary. (1955, March). *Comic books and juvenile delinquency, Interim report.* Washington: Author.

Uçanok, Z., & Güre, A. (2014). Perceived economic strain and psychological well-being: The mediational role of parental relations in Turkish early adolescents. *The Journal of Early Adolescence, 34,* 685–711.

Udry, J., Billy, J., Morris, N., Gruff, T., & Raj, M. (1985). Serum androgenic hormones motivate sexual behavior in boys. *Fertility and Sterility, 43,* 90–94.

Uhls, Y. (2015). *Media mons and digital dads.* Brookline, MA: Bibliomotion.

Uhls, Y., Espinoza, G., Greenfield, P., Subrahmanyam, K., & Šmahel, D. (2011). Internet and other interactive media. In B. Brown & M. Prinstein (Eds.), *Encyclopedia of adolescence* (Vol. 2, pp. 160–168). New York: Academic Press.

Umaña-Taylor, A. J. (2004). Ethnic identity and self-esteem: Examining the role of social context. *Journal of Adolescence, 27,* 139–146.

Umaña-Taylor, A. J., & Bámaca-Gómez, M. Y. (2003). Generational differences in resistance to peer pressure among Mexican-origin adolescents. *Youth and Society, 35,* 183–203.

Umaña-Taylor, A. J., & Guimond, A. B. (2010). A longitudinal examination of parenting behaviors and perceived discrimination predicting Latino adolescents' ethnic identity. *Developmental Psychology, 46,* 636–650.

Umaña-Taylor, A. J., & Updegraff, K. A. (2007). Latino adolescents' mental health: Exploring the interrelations among discrimination, ethnic identity, cultural orientation, self-esteem, and depressive symptoms. *Journal of Adolescence, 30,* 549–567.

Umaña-Taylor, A. J., Alfaro, E. C., Bámaca, M. Y., & Guimond, A. B. (2009). The central role of familial ethnic socialization in Latino adolescents' cultural orientation. *Journal of Marriage and the Family, 71,* 46–90.

Umaña-Taylor, A. J., Bhanot, R., & Shin, N. (2006). Ethnic identity formation during adolescence: The critical role of families. *Journal of Family Issues, 27,* 390–414.

Umaña-Taylor, A. J., Gonzales-Backen, M. A., & Guimond, A. B. (2009). Latino adolescents' ethnic identity: Is there a developmental progression and does growth in ethnic identity predict growth in self-esteem? *Child Development, 80,* 391–405.

Umaña-Taylor, A. J., Quintana, S. M., Lee, R. M., Cross Jr., W. E., Rivas-Drake, D., Schwartz, S. J. . . . & the Ethnic and Racial Identity in the 21st Century Study Group. (2014). Ethnic and racial identity during adolescence and into young adulthood: An integrated conceptualization. *Child Development, 85,* 21–39.

Umaña-Taylor, A. J., Tynes, B. M., Toomey, R. B., Williams, D. R., & Mitchell, K. J. (2015). Latino adolescents' perceived discrimination in online and offline settings: An examination of cultural risk and protective factors. *Developmental Psychology, 51,* 87–100.

Umaña-Taylor, A. J., Wong, J. J., Gonzales, N. A., & Dumka, L. E. (2012). Ethnic identity and gender as moderators of the association between discrimination and academic adjustment among Mexican-origin adolescents. *Journal of Adolescence, 35,* 773–786.

Umlauf, M. G., Bolland, A. C., Bolland, K. A., Tomek, S., Bolland, J. M. (2015). The effects of age, gender, hopelessness, and exposure to violence on sleep disorder symptoms and daytime sleepiness among adolescents in impoverished neighborhoods. *Journal of Youth & Adolescence, 44,* 518–542.

Underwood, M. K., Ehrenreich, S. E., More, D., Solis, J. S., & Brinkley, D. Y. (2013). The BlackBerry project: The hidden world of adolescents' text messaging and relations with internalizing symptoms. *Journal of Research on Adolescence, 25,* 101–117.

Underwood, M., Rosen, L., More, D. Ehrenreich, S., & Gentsch, J. (2012). The BlackBerry project: Capturing the content of adolescents' text messaging. *Developmental Psychology, 48,* 295–302.

Unger, J., Molina G., & Teran, L. (2002). Perceived consequences of teenage childbearing among adolescent girls in an urban sample. *Journal of Adolescent Health, 26,* 205–212.

Unger, J., & Rohrbach, L. (2002). Why do adolescents overestimate their peers' smoking prevalence? Correlates of prevalence estimates among California 8th-grade students. *Journal of Youth and Adolescence, 31,* 147–153.

Unger, J., Kipke, M., Simon, T., Montgomery, S., & Johnson, C. (1997). Homeless youths and young adults in Los Angeles: Prevalence of mental health problems and the relationship between mental health and substance abuse disorders. *American Journal of Community Psychology, 25,* 371–394.

Unger, J. B. (2014). Cultural influences on substance use among hispanic adolescents and young adults: Findings from Project RED. *Child Development Perspectives, 8,* 48–53.

UNICEF. (2001, July). *A league table of teenage births in rich nations.* Innocenti Report Card No. 3. UNICEF Innocenti Research Centre, Florence.

United Nations. (2010). Population by age, sex and urban/rural residence: Latest available year, 2000–2009. *Demographic yearbook.* New York: Author.

United Nations. (2012). Table 4c: Secondary education. *Social indicators.* New York: Author.

Upchurch, D., & McCarthy, J. (1990). The timing of a first birth and high school completion. *American Sociological Review, 55,* 224–234.

Upchurch, D., Aneshensel, C. S., Mudgal, J., & McNeely, C. (2001). Sociocultural contexts of time to first sex among Hispanic adolescents. *Journal of Marriage and the Family, 63,* 1158–1169.

Upchurch, D., Aneshensel, C., Sucoff, C., & Levy-Storms, L. (1999). Neighborhood and family contexts of adolescent sexual activity. *Journal of Marriage and the Family, 61,* 920–933.

Upchurch, D., Levy-Storms, L., Sucoff, C., & Aneshensel, C. (1998). Gender and ethnic differences in the timing of first sexual intercourse. *Family Planning Perspectives, 30,* 121–127.

Updegraff, K. A., Umaña-Taylor, A. J., McHale, S. M., Wheeler, L. A., & Perez-Brena, N. J. (2012). Mexican-origin youth's cultural orientations and adjustment: Changes from early to late adolescence. *Child Development, 83,* 1655–1671.

Updegraff, K., Helms, H., McHale, S., Crouter, A., Thayer, S., & Sales, L. (2004). Who's the boss? Patterns of perceived control in adolescents' friendships. *Journal of Youth and Adolescence, 33,* 403–420.

Updegraff, K., Kim, J., Killoren, S., & Thayer, S. (2010). Mexican American parents' involvement in adolescents' peer relationships: Exploring the role of culture and adolescents' peer experiences. *Journal of Research on Adolescence, 20,* 65–87.

Updegraff, K., Madden-Derdich, D., Estrada, A., Sales, L., & Leonard, S. (2002). Young adolescents' experiences with parents and friends: Exploring the connections. *Family Relations, 51,* 72–80.

Updegraff, K., McHale, S., & Crouter, A. (2000). Adolescents' sex-typed friendship experiences: Does having a sister versus a brother matter? *Child Development, 71,* 1597–1610.

Updegraff, K., McHale, S., Crouter, A., & Kupanoff, K. (2001). Parents' involvement in adolescents' peer relationships: A comparison of mothers' and fathers' roles. *Journal of Marriage and the Family, 63,* 655–668.

Updegraff, K., McHale, S., Whiteman, S., Thayer, S., & Crouter, A. (2006). The nature and correlates of Mexican-American adolescents' time with parents and peers. *Child Development, 77,* 1470–1486.

Urberg, K., Değirmencioğlu, S., Tolson, J., & Halliday-Scher, K. (1995). The structure of adolescent peer networks. *Developmental Psychology, 31,* 540–547.

Urberg, K., Değirmencioğlu, S., & Pilgrim, C. (1997). Close friend and group influence on adolescent cigarette smoking and alcohol use. *Developmental Psychology, 33,* 834–844.

Urdan, T. (2004). Predictors of academic self-handicapping and achievement: Examining achievement goals, classroom goal structures, and culture. *Journal of Educational Psychology, 96,* 251–264.

Urošević, S., Collins, P., Muetzel, R., Lim, K., & Luciana, M. (2012). Longitudinal changes in behavioral approach system sensitivity and brain structures involved in reward processing during adolescence. *Developmental Psychology, 48,* 1488–1500.

Usher, E. L. (2009). Sources of middle school students' self-efficacy in mathematics: A qualitative investigation. *American Educational Research Journal, 46,* 275–314.

Usher-Seriki, K., Bynum, M. S., & Callands, T. A. (2008). Mother-daughter communication about sex and sexual intercourse among middle- to upper-class African American girls. *Journal of Family Issues, 29,* 901–917.

Vagi, K. J., Rothman, E. F., Latzman, N. E., Tharp, A. T., Hall, D. M., & Breiding, M. J. (2013). Beyond correlates: A review of risk and protective factors for adolescent dating violence perpetration. *Journal of Youth & Adolescence, 42,* 633–649.

Valente, T., Fujimoto, K., Chou, C., & Spruijt-Metz, D. (2009). Adolescent affiliations and adiposity: a social network analysis of friendships and obesity. *Journal of Adolescent Health, 45,* 202–204.

Valiente, C., Swanson, J., & Eisenberg, N. (2012). Linking students' emotions and academic achievement: When and why emotions matter. *Child Development Perspectives, 6,* 129–135.

Valkenburg, P. M., & Peter, J. (2007). Preadolescents' and adolescents' online communication and their closeness to friends. *Developmental Psychology, 43,* 267–277.

Valkenburg, P. M., & Peter, J. (2009). Social consequences of the Internet for adolescents: A decade of research. *Current Directions in Psychological Science, 18,* 1–5.

Valkenburg, P., & Peter, J. (2011). Online communication among adolescents: An integrated model of its attraction, opportunities, and risks. *Journal of Adolescent Health, 48,* 121–127.

Valle, G., & Tillman, K. H. (2014). Childhood family structure and romantic relationships during the transition to adulthood. *Journal of Family Issues, 35,* 97–124.

Valois, R., Oeltmann, J., Waller, J., & Hussey, J. (1999). Relationship between number of sexual intercourse partners and selected health risk behaviors among public high school adolescents. *Journal of Adolescent Health, 25,* 328–335.

van Aken, M., Hutteman, R., & Denissen, J. (2011). Personality traits in adolescence. In B. Brown & M. Prinstein (Eds.), *Encyclopedia of adolescence* (Vol. 1, pp. 261–268). New York: Academic Press.

Van Campen, K. S., & Romero, A. J, (2012). How are self-efficacy and family involvement associated with less sexual risk taking among ethnic minority adolescents? *Family Relations, 61,* 548–558.

Van den Akker, A. L., Deković, M., Asscher, J., & Prinzie, P. (2014). Mean-level personality development across childhood and adolescence: A temporary defiance of the maturity principle and bidirectional associations with parenting. *Journal of Personality and Social Psychology, 107,* 736–750.

van den Akker, A., Deković, M., & Prinzie, P. (2010). Transitioning to adolescence: How changes in child personality and overreactive parenting predict adolescent adjustment

problems. *Development and Psychopathology, 22,* 151–163.

van den Berg, P., Mond, J., Eisenberg, M., Ackard, D., & Neumark-Sztainer, D. (2010). The link between body dissatisfaction and self-esteem in adolescents: similarities across gender, age, weight status, race/ethnicity, and socioeconomic status. *Journal of Adolescent Health, 47,* 290–296.

van den Berg, P., Neumark-Sztainer, D., Hannan, P. J., & Haines, J. (2007). Is dieting advice from magazines helpful or harmful? Five-year associations with weight-control behaviors and psychological outcomes in adolescents. *Pediatrics, 119,* 30–37.

van den Berg, Y. H. M., Burk, W. J., & Cillessen, A. H. N. (2014). Identifying subtypes of peer status by combining popularity and preference: A cohort-sequential approach. *The Journal of Early Adolescence.* DOI: 10.1177/0272431614554704

van den Bos, W., Crone, E., & Güroğlu, B. (2012). Brain function during probabilistic learning in relation to IQ and level of education. *Developmental Cognitive Neuroscience, 15,* S78–89.

van den Bos, E., de Rooij, M., Miers, A. C., Bokhorst, C. L., & Westenberg, P. M. (2014). Adolescents' increasing stress response to social evaluation: Pubertal effects on cortisol and alpha-amylase during public speaking. *Child Development, 85,* 220–236.

van den Bos, W., Crone, E. A., & Güroğlu, B. (2012). Brain function during probabilistic learning in relation to IQ and level of education. *Developmental Cognitive Neuroscience, 2,* S78–89.

van den Bos, W., Rodriguez, C., Schweitzer, J., & McClure, S. (2015) Adolescent impatience decreases with frontostriatal connectivity. PNAS 10.1073/pnas.1423095112

van den Bos, W., Westenberg, M., van Dijk, E., & Crone, E. A. (2010). Development of trust and reciprocity in adolescence. *Cognitive Development, 25,* 90–102.

Van den Bulck, J. (2004). Television viewing, computer game playing, and Internet use and self-reported time to bed and time out of bed in secondary-school children. *Sleep, 27,* 101–104.

van den Eijnden, R., Meerkerk, G., Vermulst, A. A., Spijkerman, R., & Engels, R. (2008). Online communication, compulsive Internet use, and psychosocial well-being among adolescents: A longitudinal study. *Developmental Psychology, 44,* 655–665.

van den Eijnden, R., Spijkerman, R., Vermulst, A., Van Rooij, T., & Engels, R. (2010). Compulsive Internet use among adolescents: Bidirectional parent–child relationships. *Journal of Abnormal Child Psychology, 38,* 77–89.

van der Aa, N., Overbeek, G., Engels, R. C. M. E., Scholte, R. H. J., Meerkerk, G.-J., & Eijnden, R. J. J. M. (2009). Daily and compulsive internet use and well-being in adolescence: A diathesis-stress model based on big five personality traits. *Journal of Youth and Adolescence, 38,* 765–776.

van der Geest, V., Blokland, A., & Bijleveld, C. (2009). Delinquent development in a sample of high-risk youth: Shape, content, and predictors of delinquent trajectories from age 12 to 32. *Journal of Research on Crime and Delinquency, 46,* 111–143.

Van der Graaff, J., Branje, S., De Wied, M., Hawk, S., Van Lier, P., & Meeus, W. (2014). Perspective taking and empathic concern in adolescence: Gender differences in developmental changes. *Developmental Psychology, 50,* 881–888.

van der Lely, S., Frey, S., Garbazza, C., Wirz-Justice, A., Jenni, O. G., Steiner, R. . . . & Schmidt, C. (2015). Blue blocker glasses as a countermeasure for alerting effects of evening light-emitting diode screen exposure in male teenagers. *Journal of Adolescent Health, 56,* 113–119.

Van Dijk, M. P., Branje, S., Keijsers, L., Hawk, S. T., Hale, W. W. 3rd, & Meeus, W. (2014). Self-concept clarity across adolescence: longitudinal associations with open communication with parents and internalizing symptoms. *Journal of Youth & Adolescence, 43,* 1861–1876.

Van Doorn, M. D., Branje, S. J. T., & Meeus, W. H. J. (2011). Developmental changes in conflict resolution styles in parent–adolescent relationships: A four-wave longitudinal study. *Journal of Youth and Adolescence, 40,* 97–107.

van Duijvenvoorde, A., Jansen, B. R. J., Bredman, J. C., & Huizenga, H. M. (2012). Age-related changes in decision making: Comparing informed and noninformed situations. *Developmental Psychology, 48,* 192–203.

van Duijvenvoorde, A., Jansen, B., Visser, I., & Huizenga, H. M. (2010). Affective and cognitive decision-making in adolescents. *Developmental Neuropsychology, 35,* 539–554.

van Geel, M., & Vedder, P. (2011). The role of family obligations and school adjustment in explaining the immigrant paradox. *Journal of Youth and Adolescence, 40,* 187–196.

Van Goethem, A. A., van Hoof, A., van Aken, M., de Castro, B. O., & Raaijmakers, Q. (2014). Socialising adolescent volunteering: How important are parents and friends? Age dependent effects of parents and friends on adolescents' volunteering behaviours. *Journal of Applied Developmental Psychology, 35,* 94–101.

van Goethem, A., van Hoof, A., Orobio de Castro, B., Van Aken, M., & Hart, D. (2014). The role of reflection in the effects of community service on adolescent development: A meta-Analysis. *Child Development, 85,* 2114–2130.

van Holst, R., Lemmens, J., Valkenburg, Peter, J., Veltman, D., & Goudriaan, A. (2012). Attentional bias and disinhibition toward gaming cues are related to problem gaming in male adolescents. *Journal of Adolescent Health, 50,* 541–546.

van Hoorn, J., van Dijk, E., Meuwese, R., Rieffe, C., & Crone, E. A. (2014). Peer influence on prosocial behavior in adolescence. *Journal of Research on Adolescence.* DOI: 10.1111/jora.12173

van Leeuwen, A. P., Verhulst, F. C., Reijneveld, S. A., Vollebergh, W. A. M., Ormel, J., & Huizink, A. C. (2011). Can the gateway hypothesis, the common liability model and/or the route of administration model predict initiation of cannabis use during adolescence? A survival analysis—The TRAILS study. *Journal of Adolescent Health, 48,* 73–78.

Van Leeuwen, K. G., Mervielda, I., Braet, C., & Bosmans, G. (2004). Child personality and parental behavior as moderators of problem behavior: Variable- and person-centered approaches. *Developmental Psychology, 40,* 1028–1046.

Van Leijenhorst, L., Westenberg, P. M., & Crone, E. A. (2008). A developmental study of risky decisions on the cake gambling task: Age and gender analyses of probability estimation and reward evaluation. *Developmental Neuropsychology, 33,* 179–196.

Van Leijenhorst, L., Zanolie, K., Van Meel, C., Westenberg, P. M., Rombouts, S. A. R. B., & Crone, E. A. (2010). What motivates the adolescent? Brain regions mediating reward sensitivity across adolescence. *Cerebral Cortex, 20,* 61–69.

Van Lieijenhorst, L., Moor, B., Op de Macks, Z. O., Rombouts, S. A. R. B., Westenberg, P. M., & Crone, E. A. (2010). Adolescent risky decision-making: Neurocognitive development of reward and control regions. *Neuroimage, 51,* 345–355.

Van Lier, P. A. C., Vitaro, F., Barker, E. D., Koot, H. M., & Tremblay, R. E. (2009). Developmental links between trajectories of physical violence, vandalism, theft, and alcohol-drug use from childhood to adolescence. *Journal of Abnormal Child Psychology, 37,* 481–492.

Van Lier, P., Wanner, B., & Vitaro, F. (2007). Onset of antisocial behavior, affiliation with deviant friends, and childhood maladjustment: A test of the childhood- and adolescent-onset models. *Development and Psychopathology, 19,* 167–185.

Van Noorden, T. H., Haselager, G. J., Cillessen, A. H., Bukowski, W. M. (2015). Empathy and involvement in bullying in children and adolescents: a systematic review. *Journal of Youth & Adolescence, 44,* 637–657.

Van Petegem, S., Beyers, W., Vansteenkiste, M., & Soenens, B. (2012). On the association between adolescent autonomy and psychosocial functioning: Examining decisional independence from a self-determination theory perspective. *Developmental Psychology, 48,* 76–88.

van Petegem, S., Soenens, B., Vansteenkiste, M., & Beyers, W. (2015). Rebels with a cause? Adolescent defiance from the perspective of reactance theory and self-determination theory. *Child Development, 86,* 903–918.

Van Petegem, S., Vansteenkiste, M., & Beyers, W. (2013). The jingle-jangle fallacy in adolescent autonomy in the family: In search of an underlying structure. *Journal of Youth & Adolescence, 42,* 994–1014.

van Rijn-van Gelderen, L., Bos, H. M., & Gartrell, N. K. (2015). Dutch adolescents from lesbian-parent families: How do they compare to peers with heterosexual parents and what is the impact of homophobic stigmatization? *Journal of Adolescence, 40,* 65–73.

van Rooij, A., Schoenmakers, T., van de Eijnden, R., & van de Mheen, D. (2010). Compulsive Internet use: the role of online gaming and other internet applications. *Journal of Adolescent Health, 47,* 51–57.

Van Ryzin, M., Johnson, A. B., Leve, L., & Kim, H. K. (2011). The number of sexual partners and health-risking sexual behavior: Prediction from high school entry to high school exit. *Archives of Sexual Behavior, 40,* 939–949.

van Wel, F. (1994). "I count my parents among my best friends": Youths' bonds with parents and friends in the Netherlands. *Journal of Marriage and the Family, 56,* 835–843.

van Workum, N., Scholte, R. H. J., Cillessen, A. H. N., Lodder, G. M. A., & Giletta, M. (2013). Selection, deselection, and socialization processes of happiness in adolescent friendship networks. *Journal of Research on Adolescence, 23,* 563–573.

Van Zalk, M. H. W., Kerr, M., Branje, S. J. T., Stattin, H., & Meeus, W. H. J. (2010). It takes three: Selection, influence, and de-selection processes of depression in adolescent friendship networks. *Developmental Psychology, 46,* 927–938.

Vandell, D., & Ramanan, J. (1991). Children of the National Longitudinal Survey of Youth: Choices in after-school care and child development. *Developmental Psychology, 27,* 637–643.

Vandenbosch, L., & Eggermont, S. (2013). Sexually explicit websites and sexual initiation: Reciprocal relationships and the moderating role of pubertal status. *Journal of Research on Adolescence, 23,* 621–634.

Vandevivere, E., Braet, C., & Bosmans, G. (2015). Under which conditions do early adolescents need maternal support? *Journal of Early Adolescence, 35,* 162–169.

Vanhalst, J., Luyckx, K., Scholte, R. H., Engels, R. C., & Goossens, L. (2013). Low self-esteem as a risk factor for loneliness in adolescence: Perceived—but not actual—social acceptance as an underlying mechanism. *Journal of Abnormal Child Psychology, 41,* 1067–1081.

Vaquera, E., & Kao, G. (2012). Educational achievement of immigrant adolescents in Spain: Do gender and region of origin matter? *Child Development, 83,* 1560–1576.

Vara, A. S., Pang, E. W., Vidal, J., Anagnostou, E., & Taylor, M. J. (2014). Neural mechanisms of inhibitory control continue to mature in adolescence. *Developmental Cognitive Neuroscience, 10,* 129–139.

Varner, F., & Mandara, J. (2014). Differential parenting of African American adolescents as an explanation for gender disparities in achievement. *Journal of Research on Adolescence, 24,* 667–680.

Varner, F., & Mandara, J. (2013). Discrimination concerns and expectations as explanations for gendered socialization in African American families. *Child Development, 84,* 875–890.

Vaughan, C. A., & Halpern, C. T. (2010). Gender differences in depressive symptoms during adolescence: The contributions of weight-related concerns and behaviors. *Journal of Research on Adolescence, 20,* 389–419.

Vaughan, C. A., Foshee, V. A., & Ennett, S. T. (2010). Protective effects of maternal and peer support on depressive symptoms during adolescence. *Journal of Abnormal Child Psychology, 38,* 261–272.

Vaughan, R., McCarthy, J., Armstrong, B., Walter, H., Waterman, P., & Tiezzi, L. (1996). Carrying and using weapons: A survey of minority junior high school students in New York City. *American Journal of Public Health, 86,* 568–572.

Vazsonyi, A. T., & Belliston, L. M. (2006). The cultural and developmental significance of parenting processes in adolescent anxiety and depression symptoms. *Journal of Youth and Adolescence, 35,* 491–505.

Vazsonyi, A. T., Hibbert, J. R., & Black, S. J. (2003). Exotic enterprise no more? Adolescent reports of family and parenting processes from youth in four countries. *Journal of Research on Adolescence, 13,* 129–160.

Vazsonyi, A. T., Trejos-Castillo, E., & Huang, L. (2006). Are developmental processes affected by immigration? Family processes, internalizing behaviors, and externalizing behaviors. *Journal of Youth and Adolescence, 35,* 799–813.

Veenstra, R., Lindenberg, S., Huitsing, G., Sainio, M., & Salmivalli, C. (2014). The role of teachers in bullying: The relation between antibullying attitudes, efficacy, and efforts to reduce bullying. *Journal of Educational Psychology, 106,* 1135–1143.

Veenstra, R., Lindenberg, S., Verhulst, F. C., & Ormel, J. (2009). Childhood-limited versus persistent antisocial behavior: Why do some recover and others do not? The TRAILS study. *Journal of Early Adolescence, 29,* 718–742.

Ventura, S., Abma, J., Mosher, W., & Henshaw, S. (2008). Estimated pregnancy rates by outcome for the United States, 1990–2004. *National Vital Statistics Reports, 56,* Number 15.

Vera Institute of Justice. (1990). *The male role in teenage pregnancy and parenting.* New York: Vera Institute of Justice.

Verhoef, M., van den Eijnden, R. J. J. M., Koning, I. M., Volleberg, W. A. M. (2014). Age of menarche and adolescent alcohol use. *Journal of Youth and Adolescence, 43,* 1333–1345.

Verkuyten, M., & Slooter, L. (2008). Muslim and non-Muslim adolescents' reasoning about freedom of speech and minority rights. *Child Development, 79,* 514–528.

Verma, S., & Larson, R. (Eds.). (2003). Examining adolescent leisure time across cultures. *New Directions for Child and Adolescent Development, 99.*

Vermeer, H. J., Boekaerts, M., & Seegers, G. (2000). Motivational and gender differences: Sixth-grade students' mathematical problem-solving behavior. *Journal of Educational Psychology, 92,* 308–315.

Verona, E., & Javdani, S. (2011). Dimensions of adolescent psychopathology and relationships to suicide risk indicators. *Journal of Youth and Adolescence, 40,* 958–971.

Véronneau, M. H., Racer, K. H., Fosco, G. M., Dishion, T. J. (2014). The contribution of adolescent effortful control to early adult educational attainment. *Journal of Educational Psychology, 106,* 730–743.

Véronneau, M., & Dishion, T. (2011). Middle school friendships and academic achievement in early adolescence: A longitudinal analysis. *Journal of Early Adolescence, 31,* 99–124.

Véronneau, M.-H., Vitaro, F., Brendgen, M., Dishion, T. J., & Tremblay, R. E. (2010). Transactional analysis of the reciprocal links between peer experiences and academic achievement from middle childhood to early adolescence. *Developmental Psychology, 46,* 773–790.

Veroude, K., Jolles, J., Croiset, G., & Krabbendam, L. (2013). Changes in neural mechanisms of cognitive control during the transition from late adolescence to young adulthood. *Developmental Cognitive Neuroscience, 5,* 63–70.

Viau, A. & Poulin, F. (2014). Youths' organized activities and adjustment in emerging adulthood: A multidimensional conception of participation. *Journal of Research on Adolescence.* DOI: 10.1111/jora.12159

Videon, T. M. (2002). The effects of parent-relationships and parental separation on adolescent well-being. *Journal of Marriage and the Family, 64,* 489–503.

Vieno, A., Nation, M., Pastore, M., & Santinello, M. (2009). Parenting and antisocial behavior: A model of the relationship between adolescent self-disclosure, parental closeness, parental control, and adolescent antisocial behavior. *Developmental Psychology, 45,* 1509–1519.

Vieno, A., Nation, M., Perkins, D., Pastore, M., & Santinello, M. (2010). Social capital, safety concerns, parenting, and early adolescents' antisocial behavior. *Journal of Community Psychology, 38,* 314–328.

Vieno, A., Perkins, D. D., Smith, T. M., & Santinello, M. (2005). Democratic school climate and sense of community in the school: A multilevel analysis. *American Journal of Community Psychology, 36,* 327–341.

Viljoen, J. L., Klaver, J., & Roesch, R. (2005). Legal decisions of preadolescent and adolescent defendants: Predictors of confessions, pleas, communication with attorneys, and appeals. *Law and Human Behavior, 29,* 253–277.

Viljoen, J., McLachlan, K., Wingrove, T., & Penner, E. (2010). Defense attorneys' concerns about the competence of adolescent defendants. *Behavioral Sciences & the Law, 28,* 630–646.

Vincent, G. M., Vitacco, M. J., Grisso, T., & Corrado, R. R. (2003). Subtypes of adolescent offenders: Affective traits and antisocial behavior patterns. *Behavioral Sciences and the Law, 21,* 695–712.

Vitaro, F., Brendgen, M., & Tremblay, R. E. (2000). Influence of deviant friends on delinquency: Searching for moderator variables. *Journal of Abnormal Child Psychology, 28,* 313–325.

Vitaro, F., Tremblay, R., Kerr, M., Pagani, L., & Bukowski, W. (1997). Disruptiveness, friends' characteristics, and delinquency in early adolescence: A test of two competing models. *Child Development, 68,* 676–689.

Vloet, T. D., Konrad, K., Huebner, T., Herpertz, S., & Herpertz-Dahlmann, B. (2008). Structural and functional MRI-findings in children and adolescents with antisocial behavior. *Behavioral Sciences & the Law, 26,* 99–111.

Voelkl, K. (1997). Identification with school. *American Journal of Education, 105,* 294–318.

Vogel, M., & Barton, M. S. (2013). Impulsivity, school context, and school misconduct. *Youth & Society, 45,* 455–479.

Vogt Yuan, A. S. (2010). Body perceptions, weight control behavior, and changes in adolescents' psychological well-being over time: A Longitudinal examination of gender. *Journal of Youth and Adolescence, 39,* 927–939.

Voisin, D. R., Hotton, A. L., Neilands, T. B. (2014). Testing pathways linking exposure to community violence and sexual behaviors among African American youth. *Journal of Youth & Adolescence, 43,* 1513–1526.

Vo-Jutabha, E. D., Dinh, K. T., McHale, J. P., & Valsiner, J. (2009). A qualitative analysis of Vietnamese adolescent identity exploration within and outside an ethnic enclave. *Journal of Youth and Adolescence, 38,* 672–690.

Volkow, N., & Ting-Kai, L. (2005). The neuroscience of addiction. *Nature Neuroscience, 8,* 1429–1430.

von Polier, G. G., Vloet, T. D., & Herpertz-Dahlmann, B. (2012). ADHD and delinquency: A developmental perspective. *Behavioral Sciences & the Law, 30,* 121–139.

Voon, D., Hasking P., & Martin G. (2014). Change in emotion regulation strategy use and its impact on adolescent nonsuicidal self-injury: A three-year longitudinal analysis using latent growth modeling. *Journal of Abnormal Psychology, 123,* 487–498.

Vrangalova, Z., & Savin-Williams, R. C. (2011). Adolescent sexuality and positive well-being: A group-norms approach. *Journal of Youth and Adolescence, 40,* 931–944.

Vuchinich, S., Angeletti, J., & Gatherum, A. (1996). Context and development in family problem solving with preadolescent children. *Child Development, 67,* 1276–1288.

Vuchinich, S., Hetherington, E. M., Vuchinich, R., & Clingempeel, W. (1991). Parent–child interaction and gender differences in early adolescents' adaptation to stepfamilies. *Developmental Psychology, 27,* 618–626.

Vygotsky, L. (1978). *Mind in society.* Cambridge, MA: Harvard University Press. (Original work published 1930)

Waasdorp, T. E., & Bradshaw, C. P. (2015). The overlap between cyberbullying and traditional bullying. *Journal of Adolescent Health, 56,* 483–488.

Waasdorp, T., & Bradshaw, C. (2011). Examining student responses to frequent bullying: A latent class approach. *Journal of Educational Psychology, 103,* 336–352.

Waasdorp, T. E., Baker, C. N., Paskwich, B. S., Leff, S. S. (2013). The association between forms of aggression, leadership, and social status among urban youth. *Journal of Youth & Adolescence, 42,* 263–274.

Wade, T. J., Cairney, J., & Pevalin, D. J. (2002). Emergence of gender differences in depression during adolescence: National panel results from three countries. *Journal of the American Academy of Child and Adolescent Psychiatry, 41,* 190–198.

Wadley, J. (2012, June 1). American teens are less likely than European teens to use cigarettes and alcohol, but more likely to use illicit drugs. University of Michigan News Service, Ann Arbor, MI.

Wadsworth, M. E., & Compas, B. E. (2002). Coping with family conflict and economic strain: The adolescent perspective. *Journal of Research on Adolescence, 12,* 243–274.

Waite, E. B., Shanahan, L., Calkins, S. D., Keane, S. P., & O'Brien, M. (2011). Life events, sibling warmth, and youths' adjustment. *Journal of Marriage and Family, 73,* 902–912.

Waite, L., Goldscheider, F., & Witsberger, C. (1986). Nonfamily living and the erosion of traditional family orientations among young adults. *American Sociological Review, 51,* 541–554.

Waithaka, E. N. (2014). Family capital: Conceptual model to unpack the intergenerational transfer of advantage in transitions to adulthood. *Journal of Research on Adolescence, 24,* 471–484.

Waizenhofer, R., Buchanan, C. M., & Jackson-Newsom, J. (2004). Mothers' and fathers' knowledge of adolescents' daily activities: Its

sources and its links with adolescent adjustment. *Journal of Family Psychology, 18,* 348–360.

Wakefield, M., Terry-McElrath, Y., Emery, S., Saffer, H., Chaloupka, F. J., Szczypka, G., . . . Johnston, L. (2006). Effect of televised, tobacco company–funded smoking prevention advertising on youth smoking-related beliefs, intentions, and behavior. *American Journal of Public Health, 96,* 2154–2160.

Wakschlag, L. S., Gordon, R. A., Lahey, B. B., Loeber, R., Green, S. M., & Leventhal, B. L. (2000). Maternal age at first birth and boys' risk for conduct disorder. *Journal of Research on Adolescence, 10,* 417–441.

Walberg, H. (1998). *Spending more while learning less.* New York: Thomas B. Fordham Foundation.

Wald, M. (2005). Foreword. In D. W. Osgood, M. Foster, C. Flanagan, & G. Ruth (Eds.), *On your own without a net: The transition to adulthood for vulnerable populations* (pp. vii–xi). Chicago: University of Chicago Press.

Waldman, I. (1996). Aggressive boys' hostile perceptual and response biases: The role of attention and impulsivity. *Child Development, 67,* 1015–1033.

Walker, E., Sabuwalla, Z., & Huot, R. (2004). Pubertal neuromaturation, stress sensitivity, and psychopathology. *Development and Psychopathology, 16,* 807–824.

Walker, L., Gustafson, P., & Hennig, K. H. (2001). The consolidation/transition model in moral reasoning development. *Developmental Psychology, 37,* 187–197.

Walker, M. (2009). The role of sleep in cognition and emotion. *Annals of the New York Academy of Sciences, 1156,* 168–197.

Walker-Barnes, C. J., & Mason, C. A. (2001). Ethnic difference in the effect of parenting on gang involvement and gang delinquency: A longitudinal, hierarchical linear modeling perspective. *Child Development, 72,* 1814–1831.

Walker-Barnes, C. J., & Mason, C. A. (2004). Delinquency and substance use among gang-involved youth: The moderating role of parenting practices. *American Journal of Community Psychology, 34,* 235–250.

Walkup, J. T., Albano, A. M., Piacentini, J., Birmaher, B., Compton, S. N., . . . Sherrill, J. T. (2008). Cognitive behavioral therapy, sertraline, or a combination in childhood anxiety. *New England Journal of Medicine, 359,* 2753–2766.

Wall, J., Power, T., & Arbona, C. (1993). Susceptibility to antisocial peer pressure and its relation to acculturation in Mexican-American adolescents. *Journal of Adolescent Research, 8,* 403–418.

Wallace, G. K., White, S. F., Robustelli, B., Sinclair, S., Hwang, S., Martin, A., & Blair, R. J. (2014). Cortical and subcortical abnormalities in youths with conduct disorder and elevated callous-unemotional traits. *Journal of*

the American Academy of Child & Adolescent Psychiatry, 53, 456–465.

Wallace, J. M., Forman, T. A., Caldwell, C. H., & Willis, D. S. (2003). Religion and U.S. secondary school students: Current patterns, recent trends, and sociodemographic correlates. *Youth and Society, 35,* 98–125.

Waller, J. M., Silk, J. S., Stone, L. B., & Dahl, R. E. (2014). Co-rumination and Co-problem solving in the daily lives of adolescents with major depressive disorder. *Journal of the American Academy of Child & Adolescent Psychiatry, 53,* 869–878.

Walls, N. E., Kane, S. B., & Wisneski, H. (2010). Gay–straight alliances and school experiences of sexual minority youth. *Youth & Society, 41,* 307–332.

Walsh, B., Kaplan, A., Attia, E., Olmsted, M., Parides, M., . . . Carter, J. (2006). Fluoxetine after weight restoration in anorexia nervosa: A randomized controlled trial. *Journal of the American Medical Association,* i2605–2612.

Walsh, S., Shulman, S., Bar-On, Z. & Tsur, A. (2006). The role of parentification and family climate in adaptation among immigrant adolescents in Israel. *Journal of Research on Adolescence, 16,* 321–350.

Wang, L., Huettel, S., & De Bellis, M. D. (2008). Neural substrates for processing task-irrelevant sad images in adolescents. *Developmental Science, 11,* 23–32.

Wang, L., McCarthy, G., Song, A., & LaBar, K. (2005). Amygdala activation to sad pictures during high-field (4 Tesla) functional magnetic resonance imaging. *Emotion, 5,* 12–22.

Wang, M., & Holcombe, R. (2010). Adolescents' perceptions of school environment, engagement, and academic achievement in middle school. *American Educational Research Journal, 47,* 633–662.

Wang, M., Dishion, T. J., Stormshak, E., & Willett, J. B. (2011). Trajectories of family management practices and early adolescent behavioral outcomes. *Developmental Psychology, 47,* 1324–1341.

Wang, M., Selman, R., Dishion, T., & Stormshak, E. (2010). A tobit regression analysis of the covariation between middle school students' perceived school climate and behavioral problems. *Journal of Research on Adolescence, 20,* 274–286.

Wang, M. T. (2012). Educational and career interests in math: A longitudinal examination of the links between classroom environment, motivational beliefs, and interests. *Developmental Psychology, 48,* 1643–1657.

Wang, M. T., & Eccles, J. S. (2012). Adolescent behavioral, emotional, and cognitive engagement trajectories in school and their differential relations to educational success. *Journal of Research on Adolescence, 22,* 31–39.

Wang, M. T., & Eccles, J. S. (2012). Social support matters: Longitudinal effects of social support on three dimensions of school engagement from middle to high school. *Child Development, 83,* 877–895.

Wang, M. T., & Fredricks, J. A. (2014). The reciprocal links between school engagement, youth problem behaviors, and school dropout during adolescence. *Child Development, 85,* 722–737.

Wang, M. T., & Huguley, J. P. (2012). Parental racial socialization as a moderator of the effects of racial discrimination on educational success among African American adolescents. *Child Development, 83,* 1716–1731.

Wang, M. T., & Kenny, S. (2014). Longitudinal links between fathers' and mothers' harsh verbal discipline and adolescents' conduct problems and depressive symptoms. *Child Development, 85,* 908–923.

Wang, M. T., & Peck, S. C. (2013). Adolescent educational success and mental health vary across school engagement profiles. *Developmental Psychology, 49,* 1266–1276.

Wang, M. T., & Sheikh-Khalil, S. (2014). Does parental involvement matter for student achievement and mental health in high school? *Child Development, 85,* 610–625.

Wang, M. T., Brinkworth, M., & Eccles, J. (2013). Moderating effects of teacher-student relationship in adolescent trajectories of emotional and behavioral adjustment. *Developmental Psychology, 49,* 690–705.

Wang, M. T., Hill, N. E., Hofkens, T. (2014). Parental involvement and african american and european american adolescents' academic, behavioral, and emotional development in secondary school. *Child Development, 85,* 2151–2168.

Wang, Q., & Pomerantz, E. (2009). The motivational landscape of early adolescence in the United States and China: A longitudinal investigation. *Child Development, 80,* 1272–1287.

Wang, Q., Pomerantz, E., & Chen, H. (2007). The role of parents' control in early adolescents' psychological functioning: A longitudinal investigation in the United States and China. *Child Development, 78,* 1592–1610.

Wang, Y., & Benner, A. D. (2014). Parent–child discrepancies in educational expectations: Differential effects of actual versus perceived discrepancies. *Child Development, 85,* 891–900.

Wang, Y., Kim, S. Y., Anderson, E. R., Chen, A. C., Yan, N. (2012). Parent-child acculturation discrepency, perceived parental knowledge, peer deviance, and adolescent delinquency in Chinese immigrant families. *Journal of Youth & Adolescence, 41,* 907–919.

Ward, L. M. (1995). Talking about sex: Common themes about sexuality in the prime-time television programs children and adolescents view most. *Journal of Youth and Adolescence, 24,* 595–615.

Ward, L. M. (2003). Understanding the role of entertainment media in the sexual socialization of American youth: A review of empirical research. *Developmental Review, 23,* 347–388.

Ward, L. M., & Friedman, K. (2006). Using TV as a guide: Associations between television viewing and adolescents' sexual attitudes and behavior. *Journal of Research on Adolescence, 16,* 133–156.

Ward, L. M., Hansbrough, E., & Walker, E. (2005). Contributions of music video exposure to Black adolescents' gender and sexual schemas. *Journal of Adolescent Research, 20,* 143–166.

Ward, L. M., Vandenbosch, L., & Eggermont, S. (2015). The impact of men's magazines on adolescent boys' objectification and courtship beliefs. *Journal of Adolescence, 39,* 49–58.

Warneke, C., & Cooper, S. (1994). Child and adolescent drownings in Harris County, Texas, 1983 through 1990. *American Journal of Public Health, 84,* 593–598.

Warner, S., & Moore, S. (2004). Excuses, excuses: Self-handicapping in an Australian adolescent sample. *Journal of Youth and Adolescence, 33,* 271–281.

Warr, M. (2007). The tangled web: Delinquency, deception, and parental attachment. *Journal of Youth and Adolescence, 36,* 607–622.

Warren, J. R. (2002). Reconsidering the relationship between student employment and academic outcomes: A new theory and better data. *Youth and Society, 33,* 366–393.

Warren, J. R., & Jenkins, K. N. (2005). High school exit examinations and high school dropout in Texas and Florida, 1971–2000. *Sociology of Education, 78,* 122–143.

Warren, J. R., Grodsky, E., & Lee, J. C. (2008). State high school exit examinations and post-secondary labor market outcomes. *Sociology of Education, 81,* 77–107.

Washburn-Ormachea, J. M., Hillman, S. B., & Sawilowsky, S. S. (2004). Gender and gender-role orientation differences on adolescents' coping with peer stressors. *Journal of Youth and Adolescent, 33,* 31–40.

Wasserman, D., Cheng, Q., & Jiang, G. (2005). Global suicide rates among young people aged 15–19. *World Psychiatry, 4,* 114–120.

Wasserman, G., Rauh, V., Brunelli, S., Garcia-Castro, M., & Necos, B. (1990). Psychosocial attributes and life experiences of disadvantaged minority mothers: Age and ethnic variations. *Child Development, 61,* 566–580.

Waters, E., Merrick, S., Treboux, D., Crowell, J., & Albersheim, L. (2000). Attachment security in infancy and early adulthood: A twenty-year longitudinal study. *Child Development, 71,* 684–689.

Waters, S., Lester, L., & Cross, D. (2014). How does support from peers compare with support from adults as students transition to secondary school? *Journal of Adolescent Health, 54,* 543–549.

Watt, H. M. (2004). Development of adolescents' self-perceptions, values, and task perceptions according to gender and domain in 7th-through 11th-grade Australian students. *Child Development, 75,* 1556–1574.

Watt, H. M., Shapka, J. D., Morris, Z. A., Durik, A. M., Keating, D. P., & Eccles, J. S. (2012). Gendered motivational processes affecting high school mathematics participation, educational aspirations, and career plans: A comparison of samples from Australia, Canada, and the United States. *Developmental Psychology, 48,* 1594–1611.

Watt, T. T. (2003). Are small schools and private schools better for adolescents' emotional adjustment? *Sociology of Education, 76,* 344–367.

Way, N. (2013). Boys' friendships during adolescence: Intimacy, desire, and loss. *Journal of Research on Adolescence, 23,* 201–213.

Way, N., & Chen, L. (2000). Close and general friendships among African American, Latino, and Asian American adolescents from low-income families. *Journal of Adolescent Research, 15,* 274–301.

Way, N., & Greene, M. L. (2006). Trajectories of perceived friendship quality during adolescence: The patterns and contextual predictors. *Journal of Research on Adolescence, 16,* 293–320.

Way, N., & Pahl, K. (2001). Individual and contextual predictors of perceived friendship quality among ethnic minority, low-income adolescents. *Journal of Research on Adolescence, 11,* 325–349.

Way, N., & Robinson, M. G. (2003). A longitudinal study of the effects of family, friends, and school experiences on the psychological adjustment of ethnic minority, low-SES adolescents. *Journal of Adolescent Research, 18,* 324–346.

Way, N., Reddy, R., & Rhodes, J. (2007). Students' perceptions of school climate during the middle school years: Associations with trajectories of psychological and behavioral adjustment. *American Journal of Community Psychology, 40,* 194–213.

Weaver, S. R., & Kim, S. Y. (2008). A person-centered approach to studying the linkages among parent–child differences in cultural orientation, supportive parenting, and adolescent depressive symptoms in Chinese American families. *Journal of Youth and Adolescence, 37,* 36–49.

Webb, H. J., & Zimmer-Gembeck, M. J. (2013). The role of friends and peers in adolescent body dissatisfaction: A review and critique of 15 years of research. *Journal of Research on Adolescence, 24,* 564–590.

Weems, C., Taylor, L., Cannon, M., Marino, R., Scott, B., . . . Triplett, V. (2010). Post traumatic stress, context, and the lingering effects of the Hurricane Katrina disaster among ethnic minority youth. *Journal of Abnormal Child Psychology, 38,* 49–56.

Weerman, F. (2011). Delinquent peers in context: a longitudinal network analysis of selection and influence effects. *Criminology, 49,* 253–286.

Wegge, D., Vandebosch, H., Eggermont, S., & Pabian, S. (2014). Popularity through online harm: The longitudinal associations between cyberbullying and sociometric status in early adolescence. *The Journal of Early Adolescence.*

Weigard, A., Chein, J., Albert, D., Smith, A., & Steinberg, L. (2014). Effects of anonymous peer observation on adolescents' preference for immediate rewards. *Developmental Science, 17,* 71–78.

Weiland, B. J., Thayer, R. E., Depue, B. E., Sabbineni, A., Bryan, A. D., & Hutchison, K. E. (2015). Daily marijuana use is not associated with brain morphometric measures in adolescents or adults. *Journal of Neuroscience, 35,* 1505–1512.

Weinfield, N., Ogawa, J. R., & Sroufe, L. A. (1997). Early attachment as a pathway to adolescent peer competence. *Journal of Research on Adolescence, 7*(3), 241–265.

Weinfield, N., Sroufe, A., & Egeland, B. (2000). Attachment from infancy to early adulthood in a high-risk sample: Continuity, discontinuity, and their correlates. *Child Development, 71,* 695–702.

Weinstein, S. M., Mermelstein, R. J., Hankin, B. L., Hedeker, D., & Flay, B. R. (2007). Longitudinal patterns of daily affect and global mood during adolescence. *Journal of Research on Adolescence, 17,* 587–600.

Weiser, J., & Reynolds, B. (2011). Impulsivity and adolescence. In B. Brown & M. Prinstein (Eds.), *Encyclopedia of adolescence* (Vol. 1, pp. 187–192). New York: Academic Press.

Weisgram, E. S., Bigler, R. S., & Liben, L. S. (2010). Gender, values, and occupational interests among children, adolescents, and adults. *Child Development, 81,* 778–796.

Weiss, B., Han, S., Harris, V., Catron, T., Ngo, V. K., Caron, A.... & Guth, C. (2013). An independent randomized clinical trial of multisystemic therapy with non-court-referred adolescents with serious conduct problems. *Journal of Consulting and Clinical Psychology, 81,* 1027–1039.

Weiss, C., & Baker-Smith, E. (2010). Eighth-grade school form and resilience in the transition to high school: A comparison of middle schools and K–8 schools. *Journal of Research on Adolescence, 20,* 825–839.

Weiss, C., Carolan, B. V., & Baker-Smith, E. C. (2010). Big school, small school: (Re) Testing assumptions about high school size, school engagement and mathematics achievement. *Journal of Youth and Adolescence, 39,* 163–176.

Weissberg, R., Caplan, M., & Harwood, R. (1991). Promoting competent young people in competence-enhancing environments: A systems-based perspective on primary prevention. *Journal of Consulting and Clinical Psychology, 59,* 830–841.

Weisskirch, R. S. (2009). Parenting by cell phone: Parental monitoring of adolescents and family relations. *Journal of Youth and Adolescence, 38,* 1123–1139.

Weist, M., Freedman, A., Paskewitz, D., Proescher, E., & Flaherty, L. (1995). Urban youth under stress: Empirical identification of protective factors. *Journal of Youth and Adolescence, 24,* 705–729.

Weisz, J. R., Francis, S. E., & Bearman, S. K. (2010). Assessing secondary control and its association with youth depression symptoms. *Journal of Abnormal Child Psychology, 38,* 883–893.

Weisz, J. R., McCarty, C. A., & Valeri, S. M. (2006). Effects of psychotherapy for depression in children and adolescents: A meta-analysis. *Psychological Bulletin, 132,* 132–149.

Weisz, J. R., Southam-Gerow, M. A., Gordis, E. B., Connor-Smith, J. K., Chu, B. C., Langer, D. A., ... Weiss, B. (2009). Cognitive-behavioral therapy versus usual clinical care for youth depression: An initial test of transportability to community clinics and clinicians. *Journal of Consulting and Clinical Psychology, 77,* 383–396.

Wells, A., & Serna, I. (1996). The politics of culture: Understanding local political resistance to detracking in racially mixed schools. *Harvard Educational Review, 66,* 93–118.

Wentzel, K. (1998). Social relationships and motivation in middle school: The role of parents, teachers, and peers. *Journal of Educational Psychology, 90,* 202–209.

Wentzel, K. (2002). Are effective teachers like good parents? Teaching styles and student adjustment in early adolescence. *Child Development, 73,* 287–301.

Wentzel, K. (2003). Sociometric status and adjustment in middle school: A longitudinal study. *Journal of Early Adolescence, 23,* 5–28.

Wentzel, K., & Asher, S. (1995). The academic lives of neglected, rejected, popular, and controversial children. *Child Development, 66,* 754–763.

Wentzel, K., Barry, C., & Caldwell, K. (2004). Friendships in middle school: Influences on motivation and school adjustment. *Journal of Educational Psychology, 96,* 195–203.

Werner, N., & Nixon, C. L. (2005). Normative beliefs about relational aggression: An investigation of the cognitive bases of adolescent aggressive behavior. *Journal of Youth and Adolescence, 34,* 229–243.

Werner, N., & Silbereisen, R. (2003). Family relationship quality and contact with deviant peers as predictors of adolescent problem behaviors: The moderating role of gender. *Journal of Adolescent Research, 18,* 454–480.

Wetter, E. K., & Hankin, B. L. (2009). Mediational pathways through which positive and negative emotionality contribute to anhedonic symptoms of depression: A prospective study of adolescents. *Journal of Abnormal Child Psychology, 37,* 507–520.

Whitaker, D., & Miller, K. (2000). Parent–adolescent discussions about sex and condoms: Impact on peer influences of sexual risk behavior. *Journal of Adolescent Research, 15,* 251–273.

Whitbeck, L., Conger, R., Simons, R., & Kao, M. (1993). Minor deviant behaviors and adolescent sexuality. *Youth and Society, 25,* 24–37.

Whitbeck, L., Hoyt, D., & Ackley, K. (1997). Abusive family backgrounds and later victimization among runaway and homeless adolescents. *Journal of Research on Adolescence, 7,* 375–392.

Whitbeck, L., Hoyt, D., & Bao, W. (2000). Depressive symptoms and co-occurring depressive symptoms, substance abuse, and conduct problems among runaway and homeless adolescents. *Child Development, 71,* 721–732.

Whitbeck, L., Hoyt, D., Miller, M., & Kao, M. (1992). Parental support, depressed affect, and sexual experience among adolescents. *Youth and Society, 24,* 166–177.

Whitbeck, L., Simons, R., & Kao, M. (1994). The effects of divorced mothers' dating behaviors and sexual attitudes on the sexual attitudes and behaviors of their adolescent children. *Journal of Marriage and the Family, 56,* 615–621.

Whitbeck, L., Yoder, K., Hoyt, D., & Conger, R. (1999). Early adolescent sexual activity: A developmental study. *Journal of Marriage and the Family, 61,* 934–946.

Whitbeck, L., Yu, M., Johnson, K., Hoyt, D., & Walls, M. (2008). Diagnostic prevalence rates from early to mid-adolescence among indigenous adolescents: First results from a longitudinal study. *Journal of the American Academy of Child & Adolescent Psychiatry, 47,* 890–900.

White, A. M., & Gager, C. T. (2007). Idle hands and empty pockets? Youth involvement in extracurricular activities, social capital, and economic status. *Youth and Society, 39,* 75–111.

White, C. N., & Warner, L. A. (2015). Influence of family and school-level factors on age of sexual initiation. *Journal of Adolescent Health, 56,* 231–237.

White, G. (2014, December 18). Inequality between America's rich and poor is at a 30-year high. *The Atlantic.* Retrieved from http://www.theatlantic.com/business/archive/2014/12/inequality-between-americas-rich-and-americas-poor-at-30-year-high/383866/ on June 9, 2015.

White, H. R., Fite, P., Pardini, D., Mun, E. Y., & Loeber, R. (2013). Moderators of the dynamic link between alcohol use and aggressive behavior among adolescent males. *Journal of Abnormal Child Psychology, 41,* 211–222.

White, H. R., Fleming, C. B., Kim, M. J., Catalano, R. F., & McMorris, B. J. (2008). Identifying two potential mechanisms for changes in alcohol use among college-attending and non-college-attending emerging adults. *Developmental Psychology, 44,* 1625–1639.

White, L. O., Wu, J., Borelli, J. L., Mayes, L. C., & Crowley, M. J. (2013). Play it again: Neural responses to reunion with excluders predicted by attachment patterns. *Developmental Science, 16,* 850–863.

White, R. M. B., & Roosa, M. W. (2012). Neighborhood contexts, fathers, and Mexican American young adolescents' internalizing symptoms. *Journal of Marriage and Family, 74,* 152–166.

White, R. M., Liu, Y., Nair, R.L., & Tein, J.Y. (2015). Longitudinal and integrative tests of family stress model effects on Mexican origin adolescents. *Developmental Psychology, 51,* 649–662.

Whitehead, K. A., Ainsworth, A. T., Wittig, M. A., & Gadino, B. (2009). Implications of ethnic identity exploration and ethnic identity affirmation and belonging for intergroup attitudes among adolescents. *Journal of Research on Adolescence, 19,* 123–135.

Whiteman, S., McHale, S. M., & Crouter, A. C. (2011). Family relationships from adolescence to early adulthood: Changes in the family system following firstborns' leaving home. *Journal of Research on Adolescence, 21,* 461–474.

Whiteman, S. D., Jensen, A. C., & Maggs, J. L. (2014). Similarities and differences in adolescent siblings' alcohol-related attitudes, use, and delinquency: Evidence for convergent and divergent influence processes. *Journal of Youth & Adolescence, 43,* 687–697.

Whitesell, N., Mitchell, C., Kaufman, C., & Spicer, P. (2006). Developmental trajectories of personal and collective self-concept among American Indian adolescents. *Child Development, 77,* 1487–1503.

Whitlock, J. L., Powers, J. L., & Eckenrode, J. (2006). The virtual cutting edge: The Internet and adolescent self-injury. *Developmental Psychology, 42,* 407–417.

Wichstrøm, L. (1999). The emergence of gender difference in depressed mood during adolescence: The role of intensified gender socialization. *Developmental Psychology, 35,* 232–245.

Wichstrøm, L. (2001). The impact of pubertal timing on adolescents' alcohol use. *Journal of Research on Adolescence, 11,* 131–150.

Wickrama, K. A. T., Wickrama, K. A. S., & Bryant, C. M. (2006). Community influence on adolescent obesity: Race/ethnic differences. *Journal of Youth and Adolescence, 35,* 647–657.

Widman, L., Welsh, D. P., McNulty, J. K., & Little, K. C. (2006). Sexual communication and contraceptive use in adolescent dating couples. *Journal of Adolescent Health, 39,* 893–899.

Wiesner, M., & Kim, H. K. (2006). Co-occurring delinquency and depressive symptoms of adolescent boys and girls: A dual trajectory modeling approach. *Developmental Psychology, 42,* 1220–1235.

Wiesner, M., & Windle, M. (2006). Young adult substance use and depression as a consequence of delinquency trajectories during middle adolescence. *Journal of Research on Adolescence, 16,* 239–264.

Wiesner, M., Capaldi, D. M., & Kim, H. K. (2012). General versus specific predictors of male arrest trajectories: A test of the Moffitt and Patterson theories. *Journal of Youth and Adolescence, 41,* 217–228.

Wiesner, M., Kim, H. K., & Capaldi, D. M. (2005). Developmental trajectories of offending: Validation and prediction to young adult alcohol use, drug use, and depressive symptoms. *Development and Psychopathology, 17,* 251–270.

Wigfield, A., Ho, A., & Mason-Singh, A. (2011). Achievement motivation. In B. Brown & M. Prinstein (Eds.), *Encyclopedia of adolescence* (Vol. 1, pp. 10–19). New York: Academic Press.

Wight, R. G., Sepúlveda, J. E., & Aneshensel, C. S. (2004). Depressive symptoms: How do adolescents compare with adults? *Journal of Adolescent Health, 34,* 314–323.

Wilcox, W. (1998). Conservative Protestant child rearing: Authoritarian or authoritative? *American Sociological Review, 63,* 796–809.

Wilens, T. E., Martelon, M. K., Joshi, G., Bateman, C., Fried, R., Petty, C., & Biederman, J. (2011). Does ADHD predict substance-use disorders? A 10-year follow-up study of young adults with ADHD. *Journal of the American Academy of Child & Adolescent Psychiatry, 50,* 543–553.

Wilkinson, D., & Carr, P. J. (2008). Violent youths' responses to high levels of exposure to community violence: What violent events reveal about youth violence. *Journal of Community Psychology, 36,* 1026–1051.

Wilkinson, D., & Fagan, J. (1996). The role of firearms in violence "scripts": The dynamics of gun events among adolescent males. *Law and Contemporary Problems, 59,* 55–89.

Wilkinson, R. B. (2004). The role of parental and peer attachment in the psychological health and self-esteem of adolescents. *Journal of Youth and Adolescence, 33,* 479–493.

Wilkinson-Lee, A. M., Zhang, Q., Nuno, V. L., & Wilhelm, M. S. (2011). Adolescent emotional distress: The role of family obligations and school connectedness. *Journal of Youth and Adolescence, 40,* 221–230.

Will, G. J., Crone, E. A., van den Bos, W., & Güroğlu, B. (2013). Acting on observed social exclusion: Developmental perspectives on punishment of excluders and compensation of victims. *Developmental Psychology, 49,* 2236–2244.

William T. Grant Foundation Commission on Work, Family, and Citizenship. (1988). *The forgotten half: Non-college youth in America.* Washington, DC: Author.

Williams, A., & Merten, M. (2009). Adolescents' online social networking following the death of a peer. *Journal of Adolescent Research, 24,* 67–90.

Williams, J. L. Tolan, P. H., Durkee, M. I., Francois, A. G., & Anderson R. E. (2012). Integrating racial and ethnic identity research into developmental understanding of adolescents. *Child Development Perspectives, 6,* 304–311.

Williams, J. L., Aiyer, S. M., Durkee, M. I., Tolan, P. H. (2014). The protective role of ethnic identity for urban adolescent males facing multiple stressors. *Journal of Youth & Adolescence, 43,* 1728–1741.

Williams, K., & Guerra, N. (2007). Prevalence and predictors of Internet bullying. *Journal of Adolescent Health, 31,* S14–S21.

Williams, K., Yeager, D., Cheung, C., & Choi, W. (2012). Cyberball (version 4.0) [Software]. Available from https://cyberball.wikispaces.com.

Williams, L. R., & Steinberg, L. (2011). Reciprocal relations between parenting and adjustment in a sample of juvenile offenders. *Child Development, 82,* 633–645.

Williams, L. R., Degnan, K., Perez-Edgar, K., Henderson, H., Rubin, K., Pine, D. S., . . .Fox, N. (2009). Impact of behavioral inhibition and parenting style on internalizing and externalizing problems from early childhood through adolescence. *Journal of Abnormal Child Psychology, 37,* 1063–1075.

Williams, L. R., & Russell, S. T. (2013). Shared social and emotional activities within adolescent romantic and non-romantic sexual relationships. *Archives of Sexual Behavior, 42,* 649–658.

Williams, P., Holmbeck, G. N., & Greenley, R. N. (2002). Adolescent health psychology. *Journal of Consulting and Clinical Psychology, 70,* 828–842.

Williams, S. K., & Kelly, F. D. (2005). Relationships among involvement, attachment, and behavioral problems in adolescence: Examining fathers' influence. *Journal of Early Adolescence, 25,* 168–196.

Williams, S. T., Conger, K. J., & Blozis, S. A. (2007). The development of interpersonal aggression during adolescence: The importance of parents, siblings, and family economics. *Child Development, 78,* 1526–1542.

Williams, T., & Williams, K. (2010). Self-efficacy and performance in mathematics: Reciprocal determinism in 33 nations. *Journal of Educational Psychology, 102,* 453–466.

Williams, T., Connolly, J., & Cribbie, R. (2008). Light and heavy heterosexual activities of young Canadian adolescents: Normative patterns and differential predictors. *Journal of Research on Adolescence, 18,* 145–172.

Williams, W., Blythe, T., White, N., Li, J., Gardner, H., & Sternberg, R. J. (2002). Practical intelligence for school: Developing metacognitive sources of achievement in adolescence. *Developmental Review, 22,* 162–210.

Williford, A. P., Brisson, D., Bender, K. A., Jenson, J. M., & Forrest-Bank, S. (2011). Patterns of aggressive behavior and peer victimization from childhood to early adolescence: A latent class analysis. *Journal of Youth and Adolescence, 40,* 644–655.

Willoughby, T., & Fortner, A. (2015). At-risk depressive symptoms and alcohol use trajectories in adolescence: a person-centred analysis of co-occurrence. *Journal of Youth & Adolescence, 44,* 793–805.

Willoughby, T., & Hamza, C. A. (2011). A longitudinal examination of the bidirectional associations among perceived parenting behaviors, adolescent disclosure and problem behavior across the high school years. *Journal of Youth and Adolescence, 40,* 463–478.

Willoughby, T., Adachi, P. J. C., & Good, M. (2012). A longitudinal study of the associations between violent video game play and aggression among adolescents. *Developmental Psychology, 48,* 1044–1057.

Willoughby, T., Chalmers, H., & Busseri, M. A. (2004). Where is the syndrome? Examining co-occurrence among multiple problem behaviors in adolescence. *Journal of Consulting and Clinical Psychology, 72,* 1022–1037.

Wills, T., McNamara, G., Vaccaro, D., & Hirky, A. (1996). Escalated substance use: A longitudinal grouping analysis from early to middle adolescence. *Journal of Abnormal Psychology, 105,* 166–180.

Wills, T., Sandy, J. M., Yaeger, A., & Shinar, O. (2001). Family risk factors and adolescent substance use: Moderation effects for temperament dimensions. *Developmental Psychology, 37,* 283–297.

Wilson, H. W., & Widom, C. S. (2010). The role of youth problem behaviors in the path from child abuse and neglect to prostitution: A prospective examination. *Journal of Research on Adolescence, 20,* 210–236.

Wilson, J. L., Peebles, R., Hardy, K. K., & Litt, I. F. (2006). Surfing for thinness: A pilot study of pro-eating disorder web site usage in adolescents with eating disorders. *Pediatrics, 118,* 1635–1643.

Wilson, M., & Daly, M. (1985). Competitiveness, risk taking, and violence: The young male syndrome. *Ethology and Sociobiology, 6,* 59–73.

Wilson, R. (February 1, 2005). The six simple principles of viral marketing. *Web Marketing Today.* Retrieved from www.wilsonweb.com/wmt5/viral-principles.htm

Windle, M., & Wiesner, M. (2004). Trajectories of marijuana use from adolescence to young adulthood: Predictors and outcomes. *Development and Psychopathology, 16,* 1007–1027.

Windle, M., Miller-Tutzauer, C., & Barnes, G. (1991). Adolescent perceptions of help-seeking resources for substance abuse. *Child Development, 62,* 179–189.

Winfree, J. L., Bäckström, T., & Mays, G. (1994). Social learning theory, self-reported delinquency, and youth gangs: A new twist on a general theory of crime and delinquency. *Youth and Society, 26,* 147–177.

Wingo, P. A., Smith, R. A., Tevendale, H. D., & Ferré, C. (2011). Recent changes in the trends of teen birth rates, 1981–2006. *Journal of Adolescent Health, 48,* 281–288.

Winsler, A., Deutsch, A., Vorona, R. D., Payne, P. A, Szklo-Coxe, M. (2015). Sleepless in Fairfax: The difference one more hour of sleep can make for teen hopelessness, suicideal ideation, and substance use. *Journal of Youth and Adolescence, 44,* 362–378.

Winsper, C., Lereya, T., Zanarini, M., & Wolke, D. (2012). Involvement in bullying and suicide-related behavior at 11 years: Prospective birth cohort study. *Journal of the American Academy of Child & Adolescent Psychiatry, 51,* 271–282.

Wiseman, R. (2003). *Queen bees and wannabes.* New York: Three Rivers Press.

Wissink, I. B., Deković, M., & Meijer, A. M. (2009). Adolescent friendship relations and developmental outcomes: Ethnic and gender differences. *Journal of Early Adolescence, 29,* 405–425.

Witkow, M. (2009). Academic achievement and adolescents' daily time use in the social and academic domains. *Journal of Research on Adolescence, 19,* 151–172.

Witkow, M., & Fuligni, A. (2010). In-school versus out-of-school friendships and academic achievement among an ethnically diverse sample of adolescents. *Journal of Research on Adolescence, 20,* 631–650.

Witvliet, M., Brendgen, M., van Lier, P., Koot, H., & Vitaro, F. (2010). Early adolescent depressive symptoms: Prediction from clique isolation, loneliness, and perceived social acceptance. *Journal of Abnormal Child Psychology, 38,* 1045–1056.

Wodtke, G., Harding, D., & Elwert, F. (2011). Neighborhood effects in temporal perspective: The impact of long-term exposure to concentrated disadvantage on High School graduation. *American Sociological Review, 76,* 713–736.

Wolak, J., Finkelhor, D., & Mitchell, K. J. (2012). How often are teens arrested for sexting? Data from a national sample of police cases. *Pediatrics, 129,* 4–12.

Wolak, J., Mitchell, K. J., & Finkelhor, D. (2003). Escaping or connecting? Characteristics of youth who form close online relationships. *Journal of Adolescence, 26,* 105–119.

Wolf, A., Gortmaker, S., Cheung, L., Gray, H., Herzog, D., & Colditz, G. (1993). Activity, inactivity, and obesity: Racial, ethnic, and age differences among schoolgirls. *American Journal of Public Health, 83,* 1625–1627.

Wolfe, S., & Truxillo, C. (1996, March). *The relationship between decisional control, responsibility, and positive and negative outcomes during early adolescence.* Paper presented at the biennial meetings of the Society for Research on Adolescence, Boston.

Wolff, J. M., & Crockett, L. J. (2011). The role of deliberative decision making, parenting, and friends in adolescent risk behaviors. *Journal of Youth and Adolescence, 40,* 1607–1622.

Wolfson, A., & Carskadon, M. (1998). Sleep schedules and daytime functioning in adolescents. *Child Development, 69,* 875–887.

Wolke, D., Copeland, W. E., Angold, A., & Costello, E. J. (2013). Impact of bullying in childhood on adult health, wealth, crime, and social outcomes. *Psychological Science, 24,* 1958–1970.

Wolters, N., Knoors, H., Cillessen, A. H., & Verhoeven, L. (2014). Behavioral, personality, and communicative predictors of acceptance and popularity in early adolescence. *Journal of Early Adolescence, 34,* 585–605.

Wong, C., Crosnoe, R., Laird, J., & Dornbusch, S. (2003). *Relations with parents and teachers, susceptibility to friends' negative influences, and adolescent deviance.* Unpublished manuscript, Department of Sociology, University of Texas at Austin.

Wong, M., Nigg, J., Zucker, R., Puttler, L., Fitzgerald, H., Jester, J., . . .Adams, K. (2006). Behavioral control and resiliency in the onset of alcohol and illicit drug use: A prospective study from preschool to adolescence. *Child Development, 77,* 1016–1033.

Wong, W. C., Ford, K. A., Pagels, N. E., McCutcheon, J. E., & Marinelli, M. (2013). Adolescents are more vulnerable to cocaine addiction: Behavioral and electrophysiological evidence. *Journal of Neuroscience, 33,* 4913–4922.

Wood, D., Kurtz-Costes, B., Rowley, S., & Okeke-Adeyanju, N. (2010). Mothers' academic gender stereotypes and education-related beliefs about sons and daughters in African American families. *Journal of Educational Psychology, 102,* 521–530.

Wood, D., Larson, R. W., & Brown, J. R. (2009). How adolescents come to see themselves as more responsible through participation in youth programs. *Child Development, 80,* 295–309.

Wood, J. J., Lynne-Landsman, S. D., Langer, D. A., Wood, P. A., Clark, S. L., Eddy, J. M., & Lalongo, N. (2012). School attendance problems and youth psychopathology: Structural cross-lagged regression models in three longitudinal data sets. *Child Development, 83,* 351–366.

Wood, P., & Clay, W. (1996). Perceived structural barriers and academic performance among American Indian high school students. *Youth and Society, 28,* 40–61.

Woodcock, A., Hernandez, P. R., Estrada, M., & Schultz, P. W. (2012). The consequences of chronic stereotype threat: Domain disidentification and abandonment. *Journal of Personality and Social Psychology, 103,* 635–646.

Woods, L. N., & Jagers, R. J. (2003). Are cultural values predictors of moral reasoning in African American adolescents? *Journal of Black Psychology, 29,* 102–118.

Woodward, L., & Fergusson, D. (1999). Childhood peer relationship problems and psychosocial adjustment in late adolescence. *Journal of Abnormal Child Psychology, 27,* 87–104.

Woodward, L., Fergusson, D., & Belsky, J. (2000). Timing of parental separation and attachment to parents in adolescence: Results of a prospective study from birth to age 16. *Journal of Marriage and the Family, 62,* 162–174.

Woolard, J., & Scott, E. (2009). The legal regulation of adolescence. In R. Lerner & L. Steinberg (Eds.), *Handbook of adolescent psychology* (3rd ed., Vol. 2, pp. 345–371). New York: Wiley.

Woolley, M. E., Kol, K. L., & Bowen, G. L. (2009). The social context of school success for Latino middle school students: Direct and indirect influences of teachers, family, and friends. *Journal of Early Adolescence, 29,* 43–70.

Worthman, C. (2011). Hormones and behavior. In B. Brown & M. Prinstein (Eds.), *Encyclopedia of adolescence* (Vol. 1, pp. 117–186). New York: Academic Press.

Wouters, S., De Fraine, B., Colpin, H., Van Damme, J., & Verschueren, K. (2012). The effect of track changes on the development of academic selfconcept in high school: A dynamic test of the big-fish–little-pond effect. *Journal of Educational Psychology, 104,* 793–805.

Wray-Lake, L., & Flanagan, C. A. (2012). Parenting practices and the development of adolescents' social trust. *Journal of Adolescence, 35,* 549–560.

Wray-Lake, L., Crouter, A. C., & McHale, S. M. (2010). Developmental patterns in decision-making autonomy across middle childhood and adolescence: European American parents' perspectives. *Child Development, 81,* 636–651.

Wray-Lake, L., Syvertsen, A., Briddell, L, Osgood, D. W., & Flanagan, C. (2011). Exploring the changing meaning of work for American high school seniors from 1976 to 2005. *Youth & Society, 43,* 1110–1135.

Wray-Lake, L., Syvertsen, A., Briddell, L., Osgood, D. W., & Flanagan, C. (2009). *Exploring the changing meaning of work for American high school seniors from 1976 to 2005.* Unpublished paper, Pennsylvania State University, University Park, PA.

Wright, B. R. E., & Younts, C. W. (2009). Reconsidering the relationship between race and crime: Positive and negative predictors of crime among African American youth. *Journal of Research in Crime and Delinquency, 46,* 327–352.

Wright, J., Cullen, F., & Williams, N. (1997). Working while in school and delinquent involvement: Implications for social policy. *Crime and Delinquency, 43,* 203–221.

Wright, K. A., Kim, B., Chassin, L., Losoya, S. H., Piquero, A. R. (2014). Ecological context, concentrated disadvantage, and youth reoffending: identifying the social mechanisms in a sample of serious adolescent offenders. *Journal of Youth & Adolescence, 43,* 1781–1799.

Wu, C., & Chao, R. K. (2011). Intergenerational cultural dissonance in parent–adolescent relationships among Chinese and European Americans. *Developmental Psychology, 47,* 493–508.

Wu, L., & Anthony, J. (1999). Tobacco smoking and depressed mood in late childhood and early adolescence. *American Journal of Public Health, 89,* 1837–1840.

Wu, L., & Thomson, E. (2001). Race differences in family experience and early sexual initiation: Dynamic models of family structure and family change. *Journal of Marriage and the Family, 63,* 682–696.

Wu, L., Pilowsky, D. J., & Schlenger, W. E. (2004). Inhalant abuse and dependence among adolescents in the United States. *Journal of the American Academy of Child and Adolescent Psychiatry, 43,* 1206–1214.

Wu, L., Ringwalt, C. L., Mannelli, P., & Patkar, A. A. (2008). Prescription pain reliever abuse and dependence among adolescents: A nationally representative study. *Journal of the American Academy of Child & Adolescent Psychiatry, 47,* 1020–1029.

Wu, L., Schlenger, W. E., & Galvin, D. M. (2003). The relationship between employment and substance use among students aged 12 to 17. *Journal of Adolescent Health, 32,* 5–15.

Xia, G., & Qian, M. (2001). The relationship of parenting style to self-reported mental health among two subcultures of Chinese. *Journal of Adolescence, 24,* 251–260.

Xing, X. Y., Tao, F. B., Wan, Y. H., Xing, C., Qi, X. Y., Hao, J. H., . . .Huang, L. (2010). Family factors associated with suicide attempts among Chinese adolescent students: A national cross-sectional survey. *Journal of Adolescent Health, 46,* 592–599.

Xu, J. (2004). Family help and homework management in urban and rural secondary schools. *Teachers College Review, 106,* 1786–1803.

Xue, Y., Zimmerman, M., & Cunningham, R. M. (2009). Relationship between alcohol use and violent behavior among urban African American youths from adolescence to emerging adulthood: A longitudinal study. *American Journal of Public Health, 99,* 2041–2048.

Yamaguchi, R., Johnston, L., & O'Malley, P. (2003). Relationship between student illicit drug use and school drug-testing policies. *Journal of School Health, 73,* 159–164.

Yang, Z., & Gaydos, L. M. (2010). Reasons for and challenges of recent increases in teen birth rates: A study of family planning service policies and demographic changes at the state level. *Journal of Adolescent Health, 46,* 517–524.

Yap, M., Schwartz, O., Byrne, M., Simmons, J., & Allen, N. (2010). Maternal positive and negative interaction behaviors and early adolescents' depressive symptoms: Adolescent emotion regulation as a mediator. *Journal of Research on Adolescence, 20,* 1014–1043.

Yasui, M., Dorham, C. L., & Dishion, T. (2004). Ethnic identity and psychological adjustment: A validity analysis for European American and African American adolescents. *Journal of Adolescent Research, 19,* 807–825.

Yates, A., Edman, J., & Aruguete, M. (2004). Ethnic differences in BMI and body/self-dissatisfaction among Whites, Asian subgroups, Pacific Islanders, and African Americans. *Journal of Adolescent Health, 34,* 300–307.

Yates, M., & Youniss, J. (1996). Community service and political–moral identity in adolescents. *Journal of Research on Adolescence, 6,* 271–284.

Yau, J., & Smetana, J. (1996). Adolescent–parent conflict among Chinese adolescents in Hong Kong. *Child Development, 67,* 1262–1275.

Yau, J., & Smetana, J. (2003). Adolescent–parent conflict in Hong Kong and Shenzhen: A comparison of youth in two cultural contexts. *International Journal of Behavioral Development, 27,* 201–211.

Yau, J., Tasopoulos-Chan, M., & Smetana, J. G. (2009). Disclosure to parents about everyday activities among American adolescents from Mexican, Chinese, and European backgrounds. *Child Development, 80,* 1481–1498.

Ybarra, M. L., Alexander, C., & Mitchell, K. J. (2005). Depressive symptomatology, youth Internet use, and online interactions: A national survey. *Journal of Adolescent Health, 36,* 9–18.

Ybarra, M. L., & Mitchell, K. J. (2014). "Sexting" and its relation to sexual activity and sexual risk behavior in a national survey of adolescents. *Journal of Adolescent Health, 55,* 757–764.

Yeager, D. S., Henderson, M. D., Paunesku, D., Walton, G. M., D'Mello, S., Spitzer, B. J., et al. (2014). Boring but important: A self-transcendent purpose for learning fosters academic self-regulation. *Journal of Personality and Social Psychology, 107,* 559–580.

Yeager, D. S., Johnson, R., Spitzer, B. J., Trzesniewski, K. H., Powers, J., & Dweck, C. S. (2014). The far-reaching effects of believing people can change: Implicit theories of personality shape stress, health, and achievement during adolescence. *Journal of Personality and Social Psychology, 106,* 867–884.

Yeager, D. S., Miu, A. S., Powers, J., & Dweck, C. S. (2013). Implicit theories of personality and attributions of hostile intent: A meta-analysis, an experiment, and a longitudinal intervention. *Child Development, 84,* 1651–1667.

Yeager, D. S., Trzesniewski, K. H., & Dweck, C. S. (2013). An implicit theories of personality intervention reduces adolescent aggression in response to victimization and exclusion. *Child Development, 84,* 970–988.

Yeh, H., & Lempers, J. D. (2004). Perceived sibling relationships and adolescent development. *Journal of Youth and Adolescence, 33,* 133–147.

Yeung Thompson, R. S., & Leadbeater, B. J. (2013). Peer victimization and internalizing symptoms from adolescence into young adulthood: Building strength through emotional support. *Journal of Research on Adolescence, 23,* 290–303.

Yeung, R., & Leadbeater, B. (2010). Adults make a difference: The protective effects of parent and teacher emotional support on emotional and behavioral problems of peer-victimized adolescents. *Journal of Community Psychology, 38*, 80–98.

Yip, T. (2014). Ethnic identity in everyday life: The influence of identity development status. *Child Development, 85*, 205–219.

Yip, T., Douglass, S., & Shelton, J. N. (2013). Daily intragroup contact in diverse settings: Implications for Asian adolescents' ethnic identity. *Child Development, 84*, 1425–1441.

Yip, T., Seaton, E., & Sellers, R. (2006). African American racial identity across the lifespan: Identity status, identity content, and depressive symptoms. *Child Development, 77*, 1504–1517.

Yip, T., Seaton, E., & Sellers, R. (2010). Interracial and intraracial contact, school-level diversity, and change in racial identity status among African American adolescents. *Child Development, 81*, 1431–1444.

YMCA. (2000). *Telephone survey conducted for the White House Conference on Teenagers.* Chicago: Author.

YMCA. (2006). Information on the history of the organization is available at www.ymca.net.

Yohalem, N., & Wilson-Ahlstrom, A. (2010). Inside the black box: Assessing and improving quality in youth programs. *American Journal of Community Psychology, 45*, 350–357.

Yong, M., Fleming, C. B., McCarty, C. A., & Catalano, R. F. (2014). Mediators of the associations between externalizing behaviors and internalizing symptoms in late childhood and early adolescence. *The Journal of Early Adolescence, 34*, 967–1000.

Yonker, J. E., Schnabelrauch, C. A., & DeHaan, L. G. (2012). The relationship between spirituality and religiosity on psychological outcomes in adolescents and emerging adults: A meta-analytic review. *Journal of Adolescence, 35*, 299–314.

Yoon, J. S., Barton, E., & Taiarol, J. (2004). Relational aggression in middle school: Educational implications of developmental research. *Journal of Early Adolescence, 24*, 303–318.

Yoon, K., Eccles, J., Wigfield, A., & Barber, B. (1996, March). *Developmental trajectories of early to middle adolescents' academic achievement and motivation.* Paper presented at the biennial meetings of the Society for Research on Adolescence, Boston.

Yorgason, J. B., Padilla-Walker, L., & Jackson, J. (2011). Nonresidential grandparents' emotional and financial involvement in relation to early adolescent grandchild outcomes. *Journal of Research on Adolescence, 21*, 552–558.

Yoshikawa, H. (1994). Prevention as cumulative protection: Effects of early family support and education on chronic delinquency and its risks. *Psychological Bulletin, 115*, 28–54.

Yoshikawa, H., Aber, J. L., & Beardslee, W. R. (2012). The effects of poverty on the mental, emotional, and behavioral health of children and youth: Implications for prevention. *American Psychologist, 67*, 272–284.

Young, A. M., & D'Arcy, H. (2005). Older boyfriends of adolescent girls: The cause or a sign of the problem? *Journal of Adolescent Health, 36*, 410–419.

Young, A. M., Grey, M., & Boyd, C. J. (2009). Adolescents' experiences of sexual assault by peers: Prevalence and nature of victimization occurring within and outside of school. *Journal of Youth and Adolescence, 38*, 1072–1083.

Young, A. M., Glover, N., & Havens, J. R. (2012). Nonmedical use of prescription medications among adolescents in the United States: A systematic review. *Journal of Adolescent Health, 51*, 6–17.

Young, B. J., Furman, W., & Jones, M. C. (2012). Changes in adolescents' risk factors following peer sexual coercion: Evidence for a feedback loop. *Development and Psychopathology, 24*, 559–571.

Young, J. F., Berenson, K., Cohen, P., & Garcia, J. (2005). The role of parent and peer support in predicting adolescent depression: A longitudinal community study. *Journal of Research on Adolescence 15*, 407–423.

Young, J. T. (2014). "Role magnets"? An empirical investigation of popularity trajectories for life-course persistent individuals during adolescence. *Journal of Youth & Adolescence, 43*, 104–115.

Young, M. E. D., Deardorff, J., Ozer, E., & Lahiff, M. (2011). Sexual abuse in childhood and adolescence and the risk of early pregnancy among women ages 18–22. *Journal of Adolescent Health, 49*, 287–293.

Young, S. E., Friedman, N. P., Miyake, A., Willcutt, E. G., Corley, R. P., Haberstick, B. C., & Hewitt, J. (2009). Behavioral disinhibition: Liability for externalizing spectrum disorders and its genetic and environmental relation to response inhibition across adolescence. *Journal of Abnormal Psychology, 118*, 117–130.

Youngstrom, E., Weist, M. D., & Albus, K. E. (2003). Exploring violence exposure, stress, protective factors and behavioral problems among inner-city youth. *American Journal of Community Psychology, 32*, 115–129.

Youniss, J., & Smollar, J. (1985). *Adolescent relations with mothers, fathers, and friends.* Chicago: University of Chicago Press.

Yu, J. J. (2011). Reciprocal associations between connectedness and autonomy among Korean adolescents: Compatible or antithetical? *Journal of Marriage and Family, 73*, 692–703.

Yuan, A. S. V., & Hamilton, H. A. (2006). Stepfather involvement and adolescent well-being: Do mothers and nonresidential fathers matter? *Journal of Family Issues, 27*, 1191–1213.

Yuan, M., Cross, S., Loughlin, S., & Leslie, F. (in press). Nicotine and the adolescent brain. *Journal of Physiology.*

Zabin, L., Astone, N., & Emerson, M. (1993). Do adolescents want babies? The relationship between attitudes and behavior. *Journal of Research on Adolescence, 3*, 67–86.

Zabin, L., Hirsch, M., & Emerson, M. (1989). When urban adolescents choose abortion: Effects on education, psychological status, and subsequent pregnancy. *Family Planning Perspectives, 21*, 248–255.

Zaff, J. F., Moore, K. A., Papillo, A. R., & Williams, S. (2003). Implications of extracurricular activity participation during adolescence on positive outcomes. *Journal of Adolescent Research, 18*, 599–630.

Zaider, T., Johnson, J. G., & Cockell, S. J. (2002). Psychiatric disorders associated with the onset and persistence of bulimia nervosa and binge eating disorder during adolescence. *Journal of Youth and Adolescence, 31*, 319–329.

Zametkin, A. J., Alter, M. R., & Yemini, T. (2001). Suicide in teenagers. *Journal of the American Medical Association, 286*, 3120–3125.

Zametkin, A. J., Zoon, C. K., Klein, H. W., & Munson, S. (2004). Psychiatric aspects of child and adolescent obesity: A review of the past 10 years. *Journal of the American Academy of Child and Adolescent Psychiatry, 43*, 134–150.

Zapert, K., Snow, D. L., & Tebes, J. K. (2002). Patterns of substance use in early through late adolescence. *American Journal of Community Psychology, 30*, 835–852.

Zarrett, N., & Mahoney, J. (2011). Out-of-school activities. In B. Brown & M. Prinstein (Eds.), *Encyclopedia of adolescence* (Vol. 2, pp. 221–231). New York: Academic Press.

Zarrett, N., Fay, K., Li, Y., Carrano, J., Phelps, E., & Lerner, R. (2009). More than child's play: Variable- and pattern-centered approaches for examining effects of sports participation on youth development. *Developmental Psychology, 45*, 368–382.

Zavodny, M. (2004). Fertility and parental consent for minors to receive contraceptives. *American Journal of Public Health, 94*, 1347–1351.

Zelazo, P. D., & Carlson, S. M. (2012). Hot and cool executive function in childhood and adolescence: Development and plasticity. *Child Development Perspectives, 6*, 354–360.

Zeldin, S., & Topitzes, D. (2002). Neighborhood experiences, community connection, and positive beliefs about adolescents among urban adults and youth. *Journal of Community Psychology, 30*, 647–669.

Zeldin, S., Christens, B. D., & Powers, J. L. (2013). The psychology and practice of youth-adult partnership: Bridging generations for youth development and community change. *American Journal of Community Psychology, 51*, 385–397.

Zeman, J., & Shipman, K. (1997). Social-contextual influences on expectancies for managing anger and sadness: The transition from middle childhood to adolescence. *Developmental Psychology, 33*, 917–924.

Zentner, M., & Renaud, O. (2007). Origins of adolescents' ideal self: An intergenerational perspective. *Journal of Personality and Social Psychology, 92,* 557–574.

Zhang, J., Seo, D., Kolbe, L., Lee, A., Middlestadt, S., Zhao, W., & Huang, S. (2011a). Comparison of overweight, weight perception, and weight-related practices among high school students in three large Chinese cities and two large US cities. *Journal of Adolescent Health, 48,* 366–372.

Zhang, W., & Fuligni, A. (2006). Authority, autonomy, and family relationships among adolescents in urban and rural China. *Journal of Research on Adolescence, 16,* 527–537.

Zhang, Y., Haddad, E., Torres, B., & Chen, C. (2011b). The reciprocal relationships among parents' expectations, adolescents' expectations, and adolescents' achievement: A two-wave longitudinal analysis of the NELS data. *Journal of Youth and Adolescence, 40,* 479–489.

Zhao, X., & Gao, M. (2014). "No time for friendship": Shanghai mothers' views of adult and adolescent friendships. *Journal of Adolescent Research, 29,* 587–615.

Zhao, Y., Montoro, R., Igartua, K., & Thombs, B. D. (2010). Suicidal ideation and attempt among adolescents reporting "unsure" sexual identity or heterosexual identity plus same-sex attraction or behavior: Forgotten groups? *Journal of the American Academy of Child & Adolescent Psychiatry, 49,* 104–113.

Zhong, H., & Schwartz, J. (2010). Exploring gender-specific trends in underage drinking across adolescent age groups and measures of drinking: Is girls' drinking catching up with boys'? *Journal of Youth and Adolescence, 39,* 911–926.

Zick, C. (2010). The shifting balance of adolescent time use. *Youth & Society, 41,* 569–596.

Zickler, P. (2004). Early nicotine initiation increases severity of addiction, vulnerability to some effects of cocaine. *NIDA Notes, 19,* 2.

Zillman, D. (2000). Influence of unrestrained access to erotica on adolescents' and young adults' dispositions toward sexuality. *Journal of Adolescent Health, 27,* 41–44.

Zima, B., Wells, K., & Freeman, H. (1994). Emotional and behavioral problems and severe academic delays among sheltered homeless children in Los Angeles County. *American Journal of Public Health, 84,* 260–264.

Zimmer-Gembeck, M. (1999). Stability, change and individual differences in involvement with friends and romantic partners among adolescent females. *Journal of Youth and Adolescence, 28,* 419–438.

Zimmer-Gembeck, M. J., Nesdale, D., McGregor, L., Mastro, S., Goodwin, B., & Downey, G. (2013). Comparing reports of peer rejection: Associations with rejection sensitivity, victimization, aggression, and friendship. *Journal of Adolescence, 36,* 1237–1246.

Zimmer-Gembeck, M., & Helfand, M. (2008). Ten years of longitudinal research on U.S. adolescent sexual behavior: Developmental correlates of sexual intercourse, and the importance of age, gender, and ethnic background. *Developmental Review, 28,* 153–224.

Zimmer-Gembeck, M., Ducat, W., & Boislard-Pepin, M.-A. (2011). A prospective study of young females' sexual subjectivity: Associations with age, sexual behavior, and dating. *Archives of Sexual Behavior, 40,* 927–938.

Zimmer-Gembeck, M., Ducat, W., & Collins, W. A. (2011). Autonomy, development of. In B. Brown & M. Prinstein (Eds.), *Encyclopedia of adolescence* (Vol. 1, pp. 66–76). New York: Academic Press.

Zimmer-Gembeck, M., Siebenbruner, J., & Collins, W. A. (2001). Diverse aspects of dating: Associations with psychosocial functioning from early to middle adolescence. *Journal of Adolescence, 24,* 313–336.

Zimmer-Gembeck, M., Siebenbruner, J., & Collins, W. A. (2004). A prospective study of intraindividual and peer influences on adolescents' heterosexual romantic and sexual behavior. *Archives of Sexual Behavior, 33,* 381–394.

Zimmer-Gembeck, M. J., Trevaskis, S., Nesdale, D., Downey, G. A. (2014). Relational victimization, loneliness and depressive symptoms: Indirect associations between self and peer reports of rejection sensitivity. *Journal of Youth & Adolescence, 43,* 568–582.

Zimmerman, G., & Messner, S. (2010). Neighborhood context and the gender gap in adolescent violent crime. *American Sociological Review, 75,* 958–980.

Zimmerman, M., Bingenheimer, J. B., & Notaro, P. C. (2002). Natural mentors and adolescent resiliency: A study with urban youth. *American Journal of Community Psychology, 30,* 221–243.

Zimmerman, M., Copeland, L., Shope, J., & Dielman, T. (1997). A longitudinal study of self-esteem: Implications for adolescent development. *Journal of Youth and Adolescence, 26,* 117–141.

Zimmerman, R., Sprecher, S., Langer, L., & Holloway, C. (1995). Adolescents' perceived ability to say "No" to unwanted sex. *Journal of Adolescent Research, 10,* 383–399.

Zimmermann, F., Schütte, K., Taskinen, P., & Köller, O. (2013). Reciprocal effects between adolescent externalizing problems and measures of achievement. *Journal of Educational Psychology, 105,* 747–761.

Zimmermann, P., & Becker-Stoll, F. (2002). Stability of attachment representations during adolescence: The influence of ego-identity status. *Journal of Adolescence, 25,* 107–124.

Zimring, F. (1982). *The changing legal world of adolescence.* New York: Free Press.

Zimring, F. (1998). *American youth violence.* New York: Oxford University Press.

Zito, J. M., Safer, D. J., DosReis, S., Gardner, J. F., Soeken, K., Boles, M., & Lynch, F. (2002). Rising prevalence of antidepressants among U.S. youths. *Pediatrics, 109,* 721–727.

Zollo, P. (2004). *Getting wiser to teens: More insights into marketing to teenagers.* Ithaca, NY: New Strategist Publications.

Zook, J. M., & Russotti, J. M. (2013). Academic self-presentation strategies and popularity in middle school. *The Journal of Early Adolescence, 33,* 765–785.

Zweig, J. M., Lindberg, L., & McGinley, K. (2001). Adolescent health risk profiles: The co-occurrence of health risks among females and males. *Journal of Youth and Adolescence, 30,* 707–728.

Zweig, J. M., Dank, M., Yahner, J., & Lachman, P. (2013). The rate of cyber dating abuse among teens and how it relates to other forms of teen dating violence. *Journal of Youth & Adolescence, 42,* 1063–1077.

Zweig, J. M., Lachman, P., Yahner, J., & Dank, M. (2014). Correlates of cyber dating abuse among teens. *Journal of Youth & Adolescence, 43,* 1306–1321.

Zwierzynska, K., Wolke, D., & Lereya, T. S. (2013). Peer victimization in childhood and internalizing problems in adolescence: A prospective longitudinal study. *Journal of Abnormal Child Psychology, 41,* 309–323.

Name Index

A

Abar, C. C., 359
Abbott, R., 360
Abecassis, M., 148
Abela, J.R.Z., 374, 377
Abelmann, N., 225
Aber, J. L., 41, 89, 119, 161, 227, 378–379
Aber, L., 138
Aber, M. S., 336
Ablard, K., 328
Abma, J., 293, 295
Abraham, C., 310, 311
Abrahamson, A., 110
Abramovitch, R., 64, 255
Abrams, D., 64
Abrutyn, S., 376
Acebo, C., 28
Aceves, M. J., 150
Achenbach, T., 350
Ackard, D., 215
Ackerman, J., 366
Ackerman, R. A., 274
Acock, A., 114
Adachi, P. J., 198, 201, 205
Adalbjarnardottir, S., 106–107, 330
Adams, G., 212
Adams, M., 370
Adams, R., 102, 274, 275
Adams, R. E., 96, 141, 149
Adams, S. H., 38
Adan, A., 335
Adcock, R., 49
Adelson, J., 255
Adiele, I., 204
Adler, N., 310, 313
Adler-Baeder, F., 118
Agans, J. P., 191
Agliata, D., 206
Agoston, A. M., 377
Aguilar, B., 370, 371
Aguilar, J., 354
Ahmad, I., 240
Ahn, H. J., 143
Aikins, J. W., 141, 142, 146, 286
Ainsworth, A. T., 227
Ainsworth, J. W., 336
Ainsworth-Darnell, J., 336
Aiyer, S. M., 230
Aklin, W. M., 357
Alabi, B. O., 230
Alarcon, O., 216
Albersheim, L., 266–267
Albert, D., 50, 51, 56, 67, 244, 246, 247
Albino, A., 351
Albrecht, A. K., 108
Alexander, C., 205
Alexander, K., 164, 179, 189, 342
Alexandersson, A., 87
Alex Mason, W., 357
Alfaro, E. C., 227
Ali, M. M., 19
Alicea, S., 227
Alink, L., 146

Allan, A. C., 29
Allen, J., 7, 109, 143, 169, 170, 198, 205, 236, 240, 246, 262–263, 267, 268, 342
Allen, J. P., 108, 138, 143, 144, 204, 239, 242, 247, 265, 267, 268
Allen, L., 161, 227
Allen, M. L., 35
Allen, N., 100
Allen, N. B., 373
Allen, R., 29
Alli, M. M., 359
Allison, K., 316
Allison, P., 317
Alloy, L., 377
Allyene, E., 312
Altermatt, E., 325
Althaus, F., 83
Altheimer, I., 93
Alvarado, R., 121
Alvarez, A., 230
Alvarez, R., 228
Alvarez-Jimenez, A., 171, 330
Alvaro, P. K., 29
Amato, P., 115, 116
Amato, P. R., 114, 117
Ambridge, B., 51
Ames, A., 146
Amialchuk, A., 359
Amiot, C. E., 192
Ammon, N. Y., 19
Amso, D., 49
Analitis, F., 148
Anbar, S., 283
Anderman, E., 158, 159, 167, 318
Andersen, A., 361
Andersen, S. L., 360
Anderson, A. L., 193, 352
Anderson, C., 230
Anderson, C. A., 201
Anderson, C. J., 308
Anderson, J., 52, 310
Anderson, K., 374
Anderson, M., 176
Anderson, S. E., 23
Anderson R. E., 227
Andersson, H., 323
Andrews, D., 218–219
Andrews, G., 325
Andrews, J. A., 32
Andrews, K., 100
Andrews, R. K., 145
Andrews, T., 376
Andrews-Hanna, J., 56
Aneshensel, C., 26–27
Aneshensel, C. S., 373
Angeleri, R., 16
Angeletti, J., 242
Angold, A., 149, 373
Angus, R., 196
Antheunis, M. L., 204
Anthony, C. J., 114
Anticevic, A., 60
Antonishak, J., 144
Antonucci, T., 33–34
Antshel, K., 166

Apel, R., 114
Apfel, N., 317
Apperly, I., 62
Aquan-Assee, J., 276
Aquilino, W., 118
Araki, N., 240
Arbess, G., 37
Arbeton, A., 330–331
Arbona, C., 246
Archibald, A., 37
Ardekani, B. A., 52
Arel, S., 6
Arend, R., 265
Arens, A., 215
Argys, L. M., 310
Arım, R. G., 24
Armeli, S., 297
Armistead, L., 115
Armor, D., 331
Armour, S., 297
Armstrong, D., 29
Arndorfer, C. L., 278, 366
Arndt, S., 92
Arneson, J. J., 334
Arnett, J., 4, 74, 75, 82, 129, 311, 352
Arnett, J. J., 81, 223, 240
Arnold, M. L., 255
Arthur, M., 92
Arunkumar, R., 324, 331
Asakawa, K., 337
Asante, K., 203
Aseltine, R., 179, 276, 358
Asendorpf, J. B., 227
Ashby, J. S., 344
Asher, S., 144, 288–289, 332
Ashikali, E. M., 206
Åslund, C., 198
Asmussen, L., 114
Aspy, C. B., 301, 359
Asquith, P., 242
Asscher, J., 212
Astone, N., 314, 316
Astor, R. A., 174
Atkins, R., 254
Attie, I., 30
Au, T., 301, 302
Audrain-McGovern, J., 29
Auerbach, R. P., 377
Augustyn, M. B., 139
Austin, E., 215
Austin, L., 64–65
Austin, S., 288
Austin, S. B., 38, 234, 305
Avenevoli, S., 372–373, 378
Averett, S. L., 310
Avery-Leaf, S., 287
Avigad-Spitz, L., 110
Awusabo-Asare, K., 300
Ayers, S., 206
Azevedo, C. N., 254
Azmitia, M., 271, 272, 329

B

Baams, L., 31, 33, 231, 299
Babalola, S., 302

Apel, R., 114
Bachman, J., 187, 188, 193, 353, 355, 359, 371
Bachman, J. G., 188–189, 355
Bachmann, M. S., 356
Bachrach, C., 314
Badre, D., 49
Bae, D., 36
Baer, J., 103
Baeyens, D., 166
Bagwell, C., 141
Bahne, J., 304
Bahr, H., 258
Bailey, P. E., 313–314
Baird, A., 68
Baird, C. L., 334
Bakan, D., 11, 154
Baker, C. N., 143
Baker, L. A., 110
Baker, S., 311
Baker, T., 176
Bakermans-Kranenburg, M., 266
Baker-Smith, E., 159, 160
Bakes, M., 193
Bakken, J., 98, 139
Bakken, N., 160–161
Bakker, M. P., 272, 374–375
Baldelomar, O., 226, 227
Balk, S., 317
Ballard, E. L., 107–108
Balle-Jensen, L., 311
Balsa, A., 143
Balsano, A., 90
Baltes, B., 93–94
Balu, S., 28
Balzer, B.W.R., 27
Bámaca, M. Y., 227, 246
Bámaca-Colbert, M. Y., 249, 294
Bámaca-Gómez, M. Y., 246
Bandura, A., 8, 10, 326
Banich, M., 56, 60, 310
Banister, E., 99
Bank, L., 110
Bankole, A., 300, 312
Bankston, C. L., III, 328
Banny, A. M., 146
Bao, W., 120
Barak, A., 204
Barbaranelli, C., 326
Barber, B., 4, 108, 114, 121, 134, 248
Barber, B. K., 106–107, 116
Barber, B. L., 192
Barber, J. S., 311, 312
Barch, D. M., 50
Bardone, A., 352
Baril, M. E., 110
Barker, E., 30, 373
Barker, E. D., 145, 365
Barkin, S. H., 91, 191
Barkley, R., 166
Barnes, A. R., 115
Barnes, G., 359–360
Barnes, J., 230
Barnes, J. C., 29
Barnes, R., 167
Barnett, T., 118

Barnett-Walker, K., 369
Bar-On, Z., 104, 109
Barr, A., 101
Barr, S., 36
Barrera, M. Jr., 101
Barreto, R. M., 294
Barrett-Connor, E., 358
Barrett-Singer, A. T., 112
Barrocas, A. L., 352
Barry, C., 162
Barry, C. M., 224, 253, 258
Barry, H., 80
Barta, W. D., 297
Bartholomae, S., 300
Bartkowski, J., 295
Bartkowski, J. P., 310
Bartle-Haring, S., 241
Barton, E., 146
Barton, M. S., 175, 176
Barton, P., 158
Bascoe, S., 6, 97, 98, 105–107
Bascoe, S. M., 110, 265
Basile, K. C., 307–308
Basilio, C. D., 252
Basinger, K. S., 249
Bassett Greer, K., 241
Bassi, M., 326
Bastaits, K., 117
Batalla, A., 361
Bates, J., 62, 108, 146, 194, 242,
    266, 288, 298–299, 369–371
Bates, L., 316
Batterink, L., 34
Baucom, B. R., 115
Bauer, D. J., 75, 287
Bauer, K., 39
Bauer, R., 36
Bauermeister, J. A., 93, 311,
    312, 366
Bault, N., 64
Bauman, K., 128–129, 135
Baumer, E. P., 92, 331
Baumert, J., 165
Baumrind, D., 105
Bauserman, R., 309
Baweja, S., 337
Bayer, P., 138
Bayram Özdemir, S., 228, 229
Beal, S. J., 336
Beam, C., 112
Beam, M. R., 276–277
Beamer, L., 312
Bean, J. A., 216
Bean, R. A., 106–107
Beardsall, L., 110
Beardslee, w. r., 378
Beardslee, W. R., 41, 89, 119
Bearinger, L. H., 299
Bearman, P., 310
Bearman, P. S., 303
Bearman, S., 38
Bearman, S. K., 373–374, 379
Beaumont Bacher, K., 227
Beaver, K. M., 108, 111
Bechara, A., 66
Becht, A., 98
Bechtold, J., 77, 175
Beck, S. R., 43
Becker, B., 378
Becker, B. E., 143

Becker, J., 27
Becker, M., 165
Beckwith, L., 267
Becnel, J. N., 192
Beelman, A., 135, 137
Beets, M., 203
Beets, M. W., 371
Behrmann, M., 59
Beidas, R., 349
Beldavs, Z. G., 371
Bell, A., 306
Bell, K., 268
Bell, L., 369
Bell, M. R., 58
Bell, R., 362
Bellair, P., 367
Bellair, P. E., 91, 303
Belliston, L. M., 108
Bellmore, A., 143, 145–147,
    227, 242
Bellmore, A. D., 19
Belsky, D. W., 357
Belsky, J., 24, 29, 316, 351
Beltran, I., 8, 356
Beltz, M. A., 318
BeLue, R., 35
Benbensihty, R., 174
Bender, H., 109
Bender, K. A., 148
Bendtsen, P., 359, 361
Benedict, R., 8, 11, 77
Benedit, R., 8
Benenson, J. F., 269
Benhorin, S., 259
Benish-Weisman, M., 242
Benjet, C., 30
Benn, R., 318
Benner, A. D., 119, 162, 171, 229,
    230, 276, 330, 336
Bennett, C., 68
Bennett, P. R., 191
Benoit, A., 33
Bensley, L., 318
Benson, B., 300
Benson, L., 195
Benson, M., 116
Benson, M. J., 140
Benson, P., 111, 192
Bentler, P., 361
Ben-Zur, H., 66
Berenbaum, S., 120, 135, 232, 233,
    253, 277
Berends, M., 164
Berenson, G., 35
Berg, C., 271
Berge, J., 36, 39
Berger, C., 143
Bergman, L. R., 151, 323
Berk, M. S., 111
Berkel, C., 230
Berlan, E. D., 308
Berliner, D., 158
Berman, E., 161
Berndt, T., 262, 268–269, 288–289
Berninger, V., 165, 166
Berns, G., 145
Bernstein, I. L., 361
Bersamin, M., 293, 301, 303
Berzonsky, M., 223, 224
Best, A. L., 236

Best, K., 32
Beyers, J. M., 367
Beyers, W., 98, 224, 239, 242, 267
Beyth-Marom, R., 64–65
Bezilla, R., 256
Bezold, C. P., 35
Bianchi, S. M., 89
Bibbins-Domingo, K., 34
Bickel, W. K., 259
Biddle, S., 158
Biddlecom, A. E., 300, 311
Biehl, M. C., 31, 285
Biello, K. B., 315
Biely, E., 200
Biener, L., 352, 362
Bierman, K., 145, 150
Bierman, K. L., 145, 288
Bierut, L. J., 361
Biggar, H., 379
Biglan A., 149
Bigler, R. S., 234, 346
Bijleveld, C., 367–368
Bijvank, M., 202
Billick, S. B., 375
Billings, A., 297
Bills, D., 188
Bingenheimer, J. B., 93
Bingham, C., 297, 300, 351
Birch, L., 234
Bird, G., 59
Bird, H., 371
Birkeland, M. S., 133, 207, 213,
    215, 218
Birkett, M., 308
Birmaher, B., 378
Birnbaum, A. S., 203
Biro, F., 14, 216
Bishai, D., 361
Bishop, A., 228
Bishop, D., 52
Bishop, J., 332
Bishop, M., 332
Bishop, N. J., 141
Bissell-Havran, J. M., 326–327
Bisset, S., 341
Bitz, B., 63
Bjarnason, T., 352
Bjermer, L., 358
Bjork, J. M., 57
Black, B. C., 323
Black, M., 302, 308
Black, S. J., 106–107
Blackwell, L., 40
Blackwell, L. S., 328
Blair, B. L., 274
Blair, R.J.R., 369
Blake, S. M., 310
Blakemore, S., 59, 62, 210
Blakemore, S-J., 45, 52, 55, 57–59,
    62, 64, 101, 210
Blanc, A. K., 310
Blanco, C., 372, 373
Blankson, A. N., 24
Blanton, H., 141
Blaustein, E., 315
Bleakley, A., 200, 201
Blinka, L., 204
Blinn-Pike, L., 110, 296, 301
Block, J., 357, 358
Blokland, A., 367–368

Blomfield, C. J., 192
Blondal, K. S., 330
Blos, P., 9, 239
Blozis, S. A., 119
Blum, R., 40, 41, 121, 314
Blum, R. W., 318
Blumenthal, H., 32
Blumler, J., 198
Blumstein, A., 364
Blunden, S., 28
Blyth, D., 32
Bobek, D., 90
Bobkowski, P., 6, 197, 198, 200,
    201, 206
Boden, J., 33
Boden, J. M., 317, 362
Bodison, P., 228
Boeninger, D. K., 376
Boerger, R., 276
Bogaert, A. F., 306
Bogart, L. M., 229
Bogdan, R., 93
Bögels, S. M., 374
Bogin, B., 4, 14, 19–21, 23, 24, 291
Bogue, E., 310
Bohnert, A. M., 191, 330
Bohr, Y., 116, 288
Boislard, M. A., 298–299
Boislard-Pepin, M.-A., 291
Boiter, C., 259
Bokhorst, C. L., 58
Bolling, D., 145
Bomar, J., 241
Bonanno, R. A., 149
Bonell, C., 362
Boney-McCoy, S., 366
Bong, M., 324, 331
Bongers, I. L., 364
Bonneau, K., 137
Bons, D. M., 369
Bontempo, D. E., 359
Bookheimer, S. Y., 51–52
Boone, L., 38
Boone, T. L., 301, 301
Boonstra, H., 309
Bootcheck, J., 125
Booth, A., 27, 115, 116, 233, 234
Booth, J. M., 228
Booth, M. Z., 161, 180
Booth-LaForce, C., 145, 242, 253,
    266, 285
Borch, C., 141, 143, 278
Borduin, C. M., 371
Borelli, J. L., 265, 272
Borge, A. I. H., 145
Borkowski, J., 156, 316
Borman, G. D., 325
Bornstein, M, 104, 110–111
Bornstein, M. H., 240, 323, 351
Borofsky, L. A., 45
Boruch, R., 314
Borzekowski, D., 203
Bos, H., 116, 306, 308
Bos, H. M., 120
Bose, K., 108
Bosick, S. J., 118
Bosker, R., 170, 331
Bosmans, G., 267
Botticello, A. L., 359
Botvin, G., 357

Botvin, G. J., 219, 359
Botvin, M., 141
Bouchey, H. A., 112, 265
Boulerice, B., 342
Bountress, K., 358
Bourne, S., 252
Boutelle, K., 34–35
Bowen, G. L., 330
Bowers, E., 195
Bowers, E. P., 195
Bowker, A., 141
Bowker, J. C., 135
Bowker, J. C., 269
Bowlby, J., 265
Bowlds, M., 275
Bowles, T. V., 274, 276
Boxer, P., 368–369
Boyce, C. A., 57
Boyce, W., 24
Boyd, C. J., 307
Boyd, D., 203, 255
Boyd-Zaharias, J., 159–160
Boyer, B. P., 266
Boyer, T. W., 66
Boyle, M. H., 90, 167, 356
Boynton-Jarrett, R., 24
Bozick, R., 254–255
Braams, B. R., 57
Braciszewski, J., 93–94
Brack, C., 351
Brack, G., 351
Brackett, M. A., 169
Bradford, K., 116
Bradley, R. H., 35, 203
Bradshaw, C., 150
Bradshaw, C. P., 149, 171
Brady, S., 296
Braeges, J., 114
Braet, C., 267
Braga, A., 176
Brahmbhatt, S. B., 50
Brainerd, C., 67
Braithwaite, I., 34, 35, 203
Brakefield, T. A., 306
Bramen, J. E., 52
Brammer, M., 56
Brand, S., 191, 218, 335
Branje, S., 98, 133, 213, 220, 224
Branje, S.J.T., 102, 103, 273–274, 377
Branstetter, S. A., 267
Brasfield, T., 312
Braun, H., 168
Brausch, A. M., 376
Braveman, P., 92
Braver, T. S., 60
Braverman, P., 301
Brechwald, W., 133, 134, 140, 247
Brechwald, W. A., 247
Bredman, J. C., 244
Breen, A., 225
Brehl, B. A., 63
Breivik, K., 133, 218
Brendgen, M., 138, 141, 147, 151, 285, 298–299, 332
Brenhouse, H. C., 360
Brenick, A., 63
Brennan, P. A., 373–374
Brennan, R. T., 33
Brenner, A. B., 93

Brent, D., 378
Brenzel, B., 158
Breslau, N., 29
Brex, R. A., 357
Bricker, J., 120, 253
Brickman, A. M., 55
Briddell, L., 185, 256, 346
Bridges, B. J., 268
Bridges, M., 114
Briggs, E., 277
Bright, D., 29
Briley, D. A., 111
Brinch, C., 179
Brindis, C. D., 38, 92
Brinkley, D. Y., 204
Brinkworth, M., 161
Brisson, D., 148
Brodbeck, J., 356
Brody, G., 31, 106–107, 109, 120, 359
Brody, G. H., 111, 229
Broidy, L., 364, 368–369
Bronfenbrenner, U., 6
Bronstein, P, 163
Brooker, R. J., 120, 253
Brookmeyer, K., 143
Brookmeyer, K. A., 253
Brooks-Gunn, J., 27, 30–34, 36, 37, 90–94, 115, 191, 192–193, 281–282, 291, 293, 303, 315, 316, 318, 334, 377
Brooks-Russell, A., 149, 355
Brown, A., 356
Brown, A. M., 249
Brown, B., 7, 98, 123–125, 127–134, 136–139, 141, 142, 204, 226, 227, 262, 275, 276, 283–287, 288, 332, 336
Brown, C. H., 312
Brown, C. P., 332
Brown, C. S., 141, 230, 307
Brown, E. C., 350
Brown, J., 6, 104, 192, 197–201, 206, 309
Brown, J. D., 200, 297–298
Brown, J. L., 138
Brown, J. R., 238, 329
Brown, J. S., 231, 373
Brown, K., 216
Brown, P. J., 323
Brown, S., 118
Brown, S. D., 254
Brown, S. L., 279
Brown, W. T., 336
Browning, C., 92, 191, 193
Browning, C. R., 92, 93
Brubacher, J., 176, 177
Bruch, S. K., 325
Brückner, H., 303, 310
Brumariu, L. E., 265, 267
Brush, L. N., 363
Bruvold, W., 362
Bryan, A. D., 297
Bryant, A., 90
Bryant, A. L., 75
Bryant, C. M., 34–35, 288
Bryant, F., 318
Bryant, F. B., 31, 375
Bryant, S. A., 288
Bryn Austin, S., 308

Bucchianeri, M. M., 307
Buchanan, C., 27, 116, 118–119
Buchanan, C. M., 104, 108–109, 374
Buchanan, M., 315
Buchmann, C., 137, 333
Buck, K. A., 247
Buehler, C., 116, 140, 218, 274
Buelow, M. T., 205
Buhi, E. R., 297, 299
Buhrmester, D., 109, 263, 268, 271, 273, 274, 276–279, 280, 283, 288
Buitelaar, J. K., 369
Buka, S. L., 41, 94
Bukobza, G., 205
Bukowski, W., 138, 262, 271, 276–278, 283, 285
Bukowski, W. M., 141, 148
Bullen, P., 90
Bullock, B., 108, 140
Bumpass, L., 315–316
Bumpus, M., 104
Bumpus, M. F., 248
Bunge, S., 50
Bunney, W. E., 29
Burchinal, M., 335
Burdette, A., 34–35
Burdette, A. M., 310
Burg, S., 256
Burger, K., 34
Burgess, G., 56
Burk, W., 141
Burk, W. J., 107, 139, 141, 142
Burkam, D., 118, 342
Burk-Braxton, C., 215–218
Burke, J. D., 108, 350, 364
Burnett, S., 45, 59, 62, 64, 210
Burnette, M., 367
Burraston, B., 110
Burrell, G., 119
Burrington, L., 188
Burrow, A. L., 219
Burstein, M., 372
Burt, C., 92
Burt, K., 75
Burt, K. B., 90, 351
Burt, S., 102
Burt, S. A., 111, 115, 370–371
Burton, C. M., 308
Burton, L., 236, 316
Busching, R., 201
Bush, G. W., 155
Bushman, B., 202, 312
Bushman, B. J., 253
Bushway, S. D., 341
Busseri, M. A., 258, 306, 352
Bussey, K., 150
Bussing, R., 369
Butler, E. A., 111, 300
Butler, K., 361
Bybee, D., 336
Bynner, J., 4
Bynum, M. S., 301
Byrd, C., 228
Byrne, B., 210
Byrne, D., 326
Byrne, M., 100
Byrnes, J., 66, 321

C

Cadoret, R., 92
Cai, T., 369
Cairns, R., 41, 192
Cajochen, C., 28
Caldas, S., 328
Caldwell, C., 229, 230
Caldwell, C. H., 33–34, 90, 93, 229, 257, 259, 296, 311
Caldwell, K., 162
Caldwell, L., 194
Caldwell, M. S., 266
Calhoun, V. D., 369
Calkins, S. D., 110, 369
Callahan, R., 164
Callan, V., 274
Callands, T. A., 301
Calvete, E., 377
Calzo, J. P., 19, 38, 234
Cameron, R. P., 38
Campa, M. I., 316
Campbell, B., 15, 38
Campbell, B. C., 299
Campbell, F., 334, 335
Campbell, I., 52
Campbell, M. A., 363
Campbell, M. E., 136, 137
Campbell, W. K., 255
Campione-Barr, N., 98, 101, 103, 109, 241
Canino, G., 371
Cannon, M., 87
Cansler, E., 193
Capaldi, D., 104, 287, 307, 314–315
Capaldi, D. M., 370–371, 373
Cappelleri, J., 308
Capra, C., 145
Caprara, G., 326
Caprara, G. V., 252, 288, 326
Caravita, S. C., 141
Carbonaro, W., 164, 168
Card, N., 142
Card, N. A., 145, 146, 232
Cardemil, E. V., 330
Carlo, G., 32, 119, 252, 253, 275
Carlson, D. L., 91, 303
Carlson, E., 370
Carlson, S. M., 54, 56
Carlson, W., 272, 281
Carnagey, N. L., 201
Carolan, B. V., 159
Carr, A., 259
Carrion, V. G., 16
Carroll, A., 369
Carroll, J. S., 75, 261
Carroll, M. D., 34
Carskadon, M., 27–29
Carson, D., 106–107
Carstensen, L., 99
Carter, C. S., 50
Carter, M., 319
Carter, R., 33–34
Carter, S., 88
Cascardi, M., 287
Casella, R., 175
Casey, B. J., 9, 44, 48, 55, 58, 236, 237
Cash, T. F., 38–39

Cashman, S. Y., 121
Casilas, A., 323
Casper, D., 142
Caspi, A., 33, 110, 115, 212, 213, 316, 351, 352, 370, 377
Cassidy, J., 102, 218, 265, 267
Castellanos-Ryan, N., 17
Castellino, D. R., 134
Casten, R., 324
Castillo, M., 39
Castro, F. G., 103, 356
Castro, G. F., 228
Catalano, R., 360
Catalano, R. F., 87, 350, 359
Catanese, D., 36
Cater, S. M., 297
Catsambis, S., 164
Cauce, A., 139, 331, 333
Caudle, K., 44, 48
Cauffman, E., 29, 39, 60, 64, 66, 77, 78, 93, 141, 176, 188, 240, 244–247, 278, 285, 286, 289, 310, 363, 366, 367, 369, 370–371
Caughy, M. O., 92
Cavanagh, S., 115, 118
Cavanagh, S. E., 281, 331
Cavanagh, T. M., 335
Cavazos-Rehg, P. A., 297
Ceballo, R., 334
Ceci, S., 61, 333
Cerda, M., 94
Cervantes, R., 101, 228
Chacko, M. R., 281
Chalmers, H., 306, 352
Chaloupka, F., 68
Chamberlain, P., 121
Chan, A., 141, 142
Chan, C. S., 90
Chan, K. W., 247
Chan, S. M., 247
Chan, W. Y., 254
Chandra, A., 200
Chang, C., 183
Chang, E. S., 276–277, 336, 337, 346–347
Chang, Z., 166
Chango, J., 143, 247
Chango, J. M., 265, 267
Chango J., 138
Chao, R., 108, 225, 227, 228, 230
Chao, R. K., 101
Chao, W., 139
Charbonneau, A. M., 374
Charlton, K., 180
Charman, T., 62
Charmaraman, L., 225
Chase-Lansdale, P., 116, 315–318
Chassin, L., 8, 29, 92, 93, 356, 358, 359, 367
Chatham, C. H., 244
Chauhan, P., 90, 367
Chaves, T. V., 359
Chavez, R. S., 214
Chavous, T., 228, 230
Chavous, T. M., 229
Cheadle, J., 115
Cheadle, J. E., 308
Chein, J., 51, 52, 55, 67, 246–247, 361
Chein, J. M., 66, 243

Chen, C., 102, 106–107, 276–277, 329, 336
Chen, C. C., 161
Chen, C. S., 334
Chen, E., 93
Chen, H., 39, 84, 248, 309, 330
Chen, K., 356, 358
Chen, L., 136, 273
Chen, M., 316
Chen, M. S., 286
Chen, M.-J., 359
Chen, P., 276, 369
Chen, R., 174, 350
Chen, W-I., 94
Chen, X., 128, 137, 147, 306–307, 370
Chen, Y. F., 229
Chen, Z., 286
Cheng, M. M., 281–282, 293
Cheng, Q., 337
Cheng, T. L., 104
Cheng, Y.-H. A., 300
Chen-Gaddini, M., 97, 248
Cheong, P., 198
Cherlin, A., 116
Cherlin, A. J., 93
Cherney, I. D., 64
Chessor, D., 164
Chester, J., 207
Cheung, C., 265
Cheung, C. S., 241, 330
Cheung, C.S.S., 331
Cheung, R. Y., 116
Chien, N. C., 312
Chilcoat, H. D., 188
Child, A., 360
Childs, K., 148
Childs, K. K., 352
Chin, C. S., 96
Chiodo, D., 306–307
Chiorri, C., 188
Chipperfield, J. G., 379
Chisholm, L., 86
Chisolm, D. J., 308
Chiu, M. M., 337
Choate, V. R., 58
Choe, D. E., 116
Choe, H. J., 276
Choi, W., 265
Choi, W. S., 29
Choi, Y., 359
Choo, E. K., 359
Chopak, J., 300
Choudhury, S., 62
Choukas-Bradley, S., 142–143, 247
Chow, A., 325
Chow, B.W., 337
Chowdhury, A., 106–107
Christ, S., 259
Christakopu, A., 243
Christakos, A., 269
Christakou, A., 56
Christensen, K. J., 252
Christopher, F. S., 33
Chrousos, G., 352
Chua, A., 108
Chuang, S., 97, 108
Chumlea, W., 23
Chun, H., 338
Chun, Y.-J., 115
Chung, C. Y., 165

Chung, G. H., 102
Chung, H. L., 88, 93
Chung, I., 107
Chung, J. M., 214, 218
Chung, K., 379
Church, R., 154, 155, 176
Chyi-In, W., 119
Ciarrochi, J., 218
Cicchetti, D., 116, 351, 377
Ciesla, J. A., 378
Cillessen, A., 143, 144
Cillessen, A. H., 141, 143, 144, 148
Cillessen, A.H.N., 66, 134, 141, 142–144, 243, 278
Cinamon, R. G., 346
Ciofu, A., 101
Claes, M., 33
Clampet-Lundquist, S., 91
Clancy, S., 223
Clardy, C., 256–257
Clark, J., 114
Clark, S., 307
Clarke, A. T., 379
Clarke-Pearson, K., 204
Clasen, D., 133
Clasen, L. S., 45, 57, 58
Claus, E., 56
Clay, W., 336
Clemans, K. H., 32, 149
Clements, P., 248
Clentifanti, L.C.M., 67
Cleveland, H. H., 286
Cleveland, M. J., 93, 106–107, 359
Clinton, B., 293
Clore, G., 286, 287
Clotfelter, C. T., 228
Coatsworth, J. D., 59, 196, 207, 237
Cobbs, G., 212
Coca, V., 334
Cogburn, C., 230
Cohen, D., 194, 299
Cohen, G., 302
Cohen, G. L., 143, 247
Cohen, M., 236
Cohen, P., 309
Cohen, P. K., 84
Cohen, S., 267
Cohen-Gilbert, J. E., 59
Cohn, E. S., 98
Coie, J., 62, 145
Coie, J. D., 314–315
Coiro, M., 117
Coker, K. L., 350
Colaco, B., 35
Colby, J. B., 55
Colder, C. R., 92, 359
Cole, D. A., 149, 218, 377–378
Cole, H., 267
Cole, M. W., 60
Cole-Lewis, H., 315
Coleman, J., 11, 125, 169, 331
Coleman, L. M., 297
Coles, M. S., 314
Coley, R., 104, 158
Coley, R. L., 93, 107, 108, 117, 194, 316–318
Colich, N. L., 17
Coll, C. G., 228, 230
Collaer, M., 17
Collibee, C., 285
Collier, K. L., 308

Collins, N. L., 265
Collins, P. F., 57
Collins, R. L., 200, 357
Collins, W. A., 7, 29, 96, 102, 104, 106, 109, 110–111, 190, 236–241, 245, 247, 249, 267, 284–286, 288, 298, 302
Collura, J., 254
Colman, S., 314
Colmar, S., 326
Colpin, H., 165
Comer, J., 240
Comings, D. E., 302
Compas, B., 378, 379
Compian, L., 30, 278, 285
Compton, K., 368
Conant, J., 155
Conger, K., 109, 119
Conger, K. J., 119, 335
Conger, R., 31, 32, 106, 115, 116, 119, 139, 161, 288, 302, 303, 335, 368, 373
Conger, R. D., 218, 227, 259, 297, 338, 376
Conklin, H. M., 49–51, 55
Conley, A., 334
Conley, C. S., 31, 375, 377, 378
Connell, A., 350
Connell, A. M., 107, 369
Connell, C. M., 357
Conner, B. T., 36
Conner, J. O., 173
Connolly, J., 7, 116, 130, 137, 215, 239, 268, 271, 272, 274, 277, 279, 280–287, 288, 307
Connolly, J. A., 281
Conrad, J., 145
Conroy, D. E., 59, 196, 237
Cooc, N., 136
Cook, E., 116
Cook, E. C., 274
Cook, L. J., 40
Cook, P. J., 366
Cook, T., 138, 333, 346
Cooksey, E. C., 131, 301
Cooley-Quille, M., 366
Cooper, A. B., 205
Cooper, C. R., 329
Cooper, H., 180, 326
Cooper, M. L., 351
Cooper, S., 41
Cooper, S. R., 334
Cope, L. M., 369
Copeland, W. E., 149
Copeland-Linder, N., 229, 230
Coplan, R. J., 145
Corbett, C., 347
Corbin, W. R., 86
Cordova, D., 101, 228
Corenblum, B., 227
Coricelli, G., 64
Corley, R. P., 120, 253
Corliss, H. L., 305, 308
Corneal, D., 234
Cornelius, M. D., 119
Cornell, D., 147, 159, 170
Corona, R., 301
Corrado, R., 368
Corrado, R. R., 363
Correll, C. U., 372, 373
Cortina, K., 6

Coskunpinar, A., 205
Costa, M., 239
Costanzo, P. R., 143
Costello, E. J., 149, 373
Costin, S., 273
Côté, J., 4, 75, 77, 210, 214, 215, 221, 223, 225
Côté, J. E., 223
Cotter, K. L., 227
Cottrell, L., 267
Couperus, J. W., 53
Covay, E., 168
Covington, M., 326
Covington, V. E., 59
Cox, M., 6
Cox, S. J., 374
Coxson, P., 34
Coy, K., 29
Coyl, D. D., 29
Coyle, K. K., 285
Coyne, S., 201
Coyne, S. M., 201, 204
Craig, A., 24
Craig, W., 239, 278, 281–285, 307
Craig, W. M., 281
Crane, D. R., 106–107
Crapanzano, A., 148
Craven, R., 164, 165, 215
Crawley, S., 349
Crean, H. F., 107, 192
Creasey, G., 276
Crespo, C., 171
Cribbet, M. R., 377
Crick, M., 145
Crick, N., 146, 147, 269
Crick, N. C., 147
Crick, N. R., 166
Criss, M., 371
Criss, M. M., 110
Crissey, S. R., 281
Crocetti, E., 223, 225
Crocker, J., 216, 217
Crockett, L., 104, 105, 297, 299, 300
Crockett, L. J., 32, 68, 93, 253, 297, 301, 336
Croft, T. N., 310
Croll, J., 38
Crone, E., 50, 60
Crone, E. A., 49–52, 55, 57, 65, 243, 244, 251–253, 270
Croninger, R., 159, 306–307, 335
Crooks, C., 306–307
Crosby, A. E., 121
Crosby, L., 218–219, 314–315
Crosby, R. A., 312
Crosnoe, R., 35, 115, 118, 120, 137, 140, 141, 164, 167, 246, 247, 308, 335, 336
Cross, C., 286
Cross, D., 276
Crossman, E. J., 91
Croudace, T. J., 356
Crouter, A., 100, 103, 104, 109, 111, 136, 174, 191, 192, 233, 234, 248
Crouter, A. C., 110, 123, 127, 161, 193, 232, 248
Crow, S., 39
Crowder, K., 314
Crowe, P., 277

Crowell, J., 266–267
Crowley, M. J., 265
Cruz, I., 40
Cruz, J. E., 359
Csikszentmihalyi, M., 27, 151, 191, 337
Cubbin, C., 92
Çuhadaroğlu Çetin F., 267
Cui, M., 115, 116, 287, 288, 330
Cumberland, A., 252
Cummings, E. M., 110, 116, 265
Cummings, J. R., 362
Cumsille, P., 63, 97, 98, 112, 240
Cunningham, M., 94, 234
Curran, P. J., 351
Currie, C., 25
Cuthbertson, C., 83
Cvencek, D., 325
Cvijanovich, N. Z., 40
Cyders, M. A., 205
Cyranowski, J., 374

D

Daddis, C., 97, 98, 107, 249
Daha, M., 228
Dahl, A., 230
Dahl, R., 3, 9, 17, 59, 66
Dahl, R. E., 27, 50, 55, 57, 59, 271
Dakof, G. A., 362
Dallago, L., 92
Dallal, G. E., 23
Dalton, B., 333
Dalton, M., 247
Daluga, N., 202
Daly, B. P., 36
Daly, M., 92, 366
Damhorst, M. L., 37
Damsgaard, M. T., 359
Dandreaux, D. M., 367–368
Daniel, D. B., 44
Daniels, E., 233
Danielsen, A. G., 207
Dank, M., 287
Dapretto, M., 45, 59
D'Arcy, H., 315
Darity, W., 134
Darling, N., 63, 97, 107, 194, 240, 265, 330
Darling-Hammond, L., 156, 157, 163, 164
Darnell, A., 171, 330
Darroch, J., 294, 296
Darroch, J. E., 259, 310, 311, 313
Darwin, C., 8
Da Silva, M., 253
Dauber, S., 164
Daubman, K. A., 279
Daughters, S. B., 374
Davey, C. G., 373
Davidson, A., 167
Davidson, J., 90
Davies, M., 359
Davies, P., 6, 97, 98, 105–107, 286
Davies, P. L., 52
Davies, P. T., 110, 116, 265
Davila, J., 116, 271, 286
Davis, A., 318
Davis, E., 302

Davis, K., 104, 219–220, 226–227, 267
Davis, K. A., 259
Davis, L., 187, 326
Davis, M., 144
Davis, W., 46
Davis-Kean, P., 210, 248, 326
Davis-Kean, P. E., 316
Davison, K.K., 35
Davison, T., 36
Dawes, M., 146
Dawes, N. P., 195
Day, D. M., 241
Day, R., 119, 201
Day, R. D., 204, 323
Dean, J. M., 40
Deardoff, J., 24
Deardorff, J., 16, 25, 31, 33, 101, 308
Dearing, E., 91
Deater-Deckard, K., 104, 105, 368
De Bellis, M. D., 51–52
De Beni, R., 323
Debnam, K. J., 171
de Boer, H., 170
De Bolle, M., 213
de Bruin, W. B., 65
de Bruyn, E., 143, 306
De Castella, K., 326
de Castro, B. O., 253, 254
Deck, A., 116
De Dreu, C. K., 51
Dee, T., 40
Defoe, I. N., 64
De Fraine, B., 165
DeFries, J., 115
DeGarmo, D., 100, 118
Degarmo, D. S., 371
Değirmencioğlu, S., 130, 141, 278
De Goede, I.H.A., 102, 273–274
de Graaf, H., 281, 293, 300
DeHaan, L. G., 259
de Haan A. D., 108
Deke, J., 362
Deković, M., 108, 212, 370–371
Deković', M., 242
de la Haye, K., 36, 141
DeLay, D., 96–98, 100–103, 141
Delevi, R., 205
Delgado, M. Y., 230
Del Giudice, M., 16
DeLisi, M., 111
Delle Fave, A., 326
De Lorme, K., 58
Delsing, M.J.M.H., 129, 273–274
Delva, J., 39, 356
DelVecchio, W. F., 212
DeMaris, A., 118
DeMaster, D., 50
Dembo, M. H., 336
Demo, D., 114, 214
DeMoya, D., 314
Demurie, E., 166
Denault, A. S., 278
Denault, A.S., 108
Denault, A.-S., 130–131, 278
Deng, C., 46, 108
Deng, S., 228, 230
Deng, Y., 138
Denissen, J., 213
Denissen, J.J.A., 108

Dennison, M., 52
Dennison, R., 117
Dennison, R. P., 82
Dent, C. W., 202
Denton, K., 270–271
Denton, M., 259
Deptula, D. P., 300
Derefinko, K. J., 299
Derlan, C. L., 228
Dermody, S. S., 308
de Rooij, M., 58, 253
DeRose, L. M., 33–34
Desai, M. M., 308
Deschenes, E., 139
DeSecottier, L., 276
de Silveira, C., 224
Desjardins, T. L., 146
D'Esposito, M., 50
Destin, M., 335
Deutsch, A., 29
Deutsch, A. R., 93, 294, 301
Devine, D., 115
de Water, E., 66, 243
Dhariwal, A., 281, 288
Diamond, G. M., 308
Diamond, L., 7, 135, 231, 278, 284, 291–294, 296–300, 304, 305, 308
Diamond, L. M., 377
Dias, J. J., 35
Diaz, M., 57
Diaz, R., 307
Diaz, R. M., 232
Diaz, T., 219
Dick, D., 33, 111
Dick, D. M., 378
Dickson, G., 338
Dickson, N., 352
DiClemente, R., 202, 310
DiClemente, R. J., 312
Diehl, L., 215
Dielman, T., 361, 362
DiFranza, J., 358
DiGiovanni, C. D., 308
DiIorio, C., 301, 302
Dijkstra, J., 6, 123, 127–128, 131, 133, 143, 144, 262
Dijkstra, J. K., 143
Dilks, R. J., 36
Ding, C., 352
Dinh, K. T., 228
Dinkes, R., 174
DiPietro, S., 159
Dir, A .L., 205
Dirghangi, S., 271
Dishion, T., 108, 140, 169–170, 218–219, 303
Dishion, T. J., 92, 104, 107, 108, 140, 323, 332, 350, 369, 371
Dishion, T. K., 98
Dittmar, H., 206
Dittus, P., 301, 314, 319
Dittus, P. J., 301
Dixon, L., 36
Dmitrieva, J., 106–107, 139, 286
Dobbins, I. G., 57
Dobkin, P., 105
Dodge, K., 62, 108, 146, 147, 194, 368–371
Dodge, K. A., 147, 242, 266, 288, 298–299, 370–371

Dodge, T., 141, 314
Dogan, S., 368
Dogan, S. J., 297
Dolan, E. A., 268
Dolev-Cohen, M., 204
Dollahite, D., 258
Dollinger, S., 223
Dolliver, M., 206
Domina, T., 334
Donahue, K. L., 116
Donenberg, G. R., 301
Dong, W., 241, 330
Dong, Y., 352
Donnellan, M., 213, 288
Donnellan, M. B., 115, 259
Donnelly, T. M., 254
Donnerstein, E., 198, 200, 202
D'Onofrio, B. M., 115
Doogan, N. J., 141
Dooley, D., 336
Doornwaard, S. M., 133–134
Dopp, A. R., 371
Dorfman, L., 207
Dorius, C., 118
Dorn, L., 14, 15, 17, 18, 23, 26, 352
Dornbusch, S., 121, 188, 247, 330, 336
Dornbusch, S. M., 140, 246
Dorsey, S., 301
Dosenbach, N., 51–52, 57
Dosenbach, N.U.F., 57
Dotterer, A., 161, 174, 192, 234
Dotterer, A. M., 169, 326
Dotterer, A.M., 330
Douglas, G., 326
Douglass, S., 227
Douglas Willms, J., 24
Dowdy, B. B., 283
Downey, D., 170, 336
Downey, G., 286
Doyle, A., 267–268, 285
Doyle, A. B., 267–268
Dozier, A., 314
Drabick, D., 349
Drapela, L. A., 31
Draper, P., 351
Dregan, A., 29
Dreyfuss, M., 57
Driscoll, A., 295
Drumm, P., 50
Drummond, A., 205
Druss, B., 8, 378
Druss, B. G., 362
Dryfoos, J., 155
Dubas, J. S., 31, 64, 108, 299
Dubé, E., 231, 284
Dubé, E. M., 135, 278
Dube, S. R., 107
Dubner, S., 156
Dubocovich, M. L., 29
DuBois, D., 90, 215–218, 273, 335
Dubow, E. F., 368–369
Ducat, W., 7, 236–239, 291
Duchesne, S., 330
Duckett, E., 98
Duckworth, A., 323
Duckworth, A. L., 156, 323
Due, P., 148, 361
Duhoux, S., 236
Duke, S. A., 27

Duku, E., 356
Dumas, T. M., 224
Dumka, L., 100–101, 281
Dumka, L. E., 230, 344
Dumont, H., 324
Dumontheil, I., 62
Duncan, G., 91
Duncan Cance, J., 29
Dunifon, R., 115, 276
Dunlap, K. G., 109
Dunlop, S. M., 351
Dunn, J., 110
Dunn, M., 359
Dunn, S., 275
Dunsmore, S. C., 297
Duong, H. T., 29
Duong, M. T., 134
Duong, M.T., 332
Dupéré, V., 90–92, 303–304
DuPont, R. L., 361
DuRant, R., 352
Durbin, D., 241
Duriez, B., 107
Durik, A. M., 327
Durkee, M. I., 227, 230
Durston, S., 55
Dussault, F., 298–299
Dweck, C., 147
Dweck, C. S., 147, 325, 327, 328, 369–370
Dwyer, D. B., 55
Dwyer, D. S., 359
Dwyer, K. M., 242
Dyer, W. J., 323
Dykas, M. J., 265, 267

E

Earls, F., 33, 41, 92
East, P., 109, 110, 111, 276, 302, 314, 315, 318
East, P. L., 311, 312
Eaton, D. K., 197
Eaton, M. J., 336
Eberhart, N. K., 373–374, 377
Eberly, M., 241
Eccles, J., 4, 27, 102, 103, 108, 119, 120, 134, 153, 161–163, 169, 170, 179, 190, 192, 213–214, 216, 216, 248, 262, 324, 326–332, 358
Eccles, J. S., 112, 174, 191, 325, 326, 328, 331, 336
Echeverria, S. E., 35
Eckenrode, J., 308
Eckenrode, J. J., 316
Eddy, J. M., 350
Edelbrock, C., 350
Edelstein, W., 213, 269
Edens, J. F., 363
Eder, D., 144
Edin, K., 91
Edwards, A. C., 378
Egan, E., 92
Egan, S., 234
Egeland, B., 266–267, 370, 371
Eggermont, S., 149, 200, 204
Ehrenreich, S. E., 204
Ehrlich, K. B., 102, 267
Eichen, D. M., 36

Eilers, M. A., 312
Einspruch, E., 362
Eisenberg, M., 36, 39, 215
Eisenberg, M. E., 35, 39, 307
Eisenberg, N., 7, 64, 107, 237, 249, 252–254, 258, 272, 323
Eisenberger, N. I., 59, 266
Ejesi, K., 228
Elder, G. H., Jr., 11, 81, 120, 139, 161, 167, 288, 373
Elder, G., Jr., 119
Elder, G.H.J., 231, 373
Elders, M., 358
Eley, T., 368
Eley, T. C., 351
Elkind, D., 45
Elkington, K. S., 312
Elkins, I., 110
Ellickson, P., 360, 362
Ellickson, P. L., 357
Elliot, A. J., 324
Elliot, D., 92, 189
Elliott, D., 352
Elliott, M. N., 200, 301
Ellis, B., 24, 302
Ellis, B. J., 111, 300, 351
Ellis, C., 60
Ellis, N., 175
Ellis-Hale, K., 254
Ellwanger, P., 241
Elmore, R., 153, 154, 156, 160, 344
Elo, I., 315
Elwert, F., 91
Emerson, E., 301
Emerson, M., 313–314
Emery, C. R., 316
Emery, R., 112, 113, 117
Emery, R. E., 299, 359
Eng, A. L., 301
Engels, R., 198, 204, 266
Engels, R. C., 218
Engels, R.C.M.E., 129, 284
Engle, R., 5, 51
English, D., 229
Englund, M. M., 357
Ennett, S., 128–129, 135, 140–141, 359–362
Ennett, S. T., 92, 145, 276, 287
Enright, R., 12
Enriquez, L. E., 331, 342
Ensminger, M., 163
Ensminger, M. E., 93, 358
Entwisle, B., 136
Entwisle, D., 164, 167, 189, 342
Epkins, C., 259
Epstein, J. A., 359
Epstein, L., 34
Epstein, R., 11
Erath, S., 118
Erath, S. A., 145, 150
Erickson, K., 121, 140, 246
Eriksen, M., 358
Erikson, E., 8, 9, 219–221, 223
Erisir, A., 54
Erkut, S., 216
Ermer, E., 369
Ernst, M., 360
Erol, R. Y., 213, 217
Ersbøll, A. K., 359
Esbensen, F., 138, 139
Escalante, K. A., 117

Espelage, D., 174, 298–299
Espelage, D. L., 138, 141, 180, 307–308
Espenshade, T. J., 165
Espinosa, G., 269
Espinosa-Hernández, G., 249
Espinoza, G., 6, 147, 149, 332
Esposito, L. E., 352
Esposito-Smythers, C., 376
Essex, M., 24
Estrada, A., 274
Estrada, M., 325
Estrada, S., 65
Ettekal, I., 145, 368
Eubanks, J., 201
Evans, A. B., 227
Evans, A. D., 62
Evans, C. B., 227
Evans, E., 335
Evans, G. W., 243
Evans, W., 40
Eveleth, P., 24, 25
Everett, B. G., 308
Everett, S. A., 309
Exner-Cortens, D., 287
Eyal, E., 200
Eyre, S., 304
Eyre, S. L., 281

F

Facchin, F., 328
Faes, J., 264
Fagan, J., 139, 366, 369
Fagot, B., 314–315
Fagundes, C. P., 377
Fair, D., 57
Fairchild, G., 369
Falk, E. B., 138, 147, 247
Falk, R., 46
Fallon, B. J., 274, 276
Fan, S., 281
Fan, X., 147, 170
Fang, F., 269
Fang, G., 269
Fang, J., 241
Fang, S., 335
Fang, X., 106–107
Fanti, K., 143, 148
Farb, A., 191
Farhat, T., 294, 299, 303, 355
Farkas, G., 331, 333, 334
Farkas, T., 332
Farley, F., 65
Farley, J. P., 259, 266
Farley, T., 194, 299
Farmer, T., 143
Farmer, T. W., 92, 160–161
Farrell, A. D., 140, 146, 147, 158, 352
Farrell, M., 359–360
Farrington, D., 8, 246, 349, 350–351, 362, 364, 366–371
Farruggia, S. P., 90, 276–278, 366
Fasick, F., 72–74
Fasula, A. M., 302
Fatusi, A. O., 312
Fauber, R. L., 36
Fauth, R. C., 91
Fedele, D., 349

Feder, M., 304
Feeney, B. C., 218, 265
Fegley, S., 253
Feigelman, S., 359
Feinberg, I., 52
Feinberg, M., 112
Feinberg, M. E., 93, 98, 131, 278, 359
Feiring, C., 240, 262, 266–267, 271, 276, 278–280, 283, 287
Feivelson, D., 311
Feldlaufer, H., 162
Feldman, A., 232
Feldman, A. F., 183, 184
Feldman, R., 93
Feldman, S., 248
Feldman, S. S., 240, 307
Felice, M., 318
Felix, E., 174
Fellows, K., 204
Felner, R., 218, 335
Felson, R. B., 352
Felton, J. W., 351
Fenton, R. E., 336
Fenwick, J., 314
Fenzel, L., 162
Ferenz-Gillies, R., 267
Fergus, S., 296
Ferguson, C., 202
Ferguson, C. J., 201, 202
Ferguson, D., 227
Ferguson, M., 52
Ferguson, Y., 241, 242
Fergusson, D., 33, 151, 317, 367, 368
Fergusson, D. M., 266, 317, 362
Fernandez-Esquer, M. E., 227, 337
Ferrar, K., 183
Ferreira, P. D., 254
Ferreiro, F., 39, 352
Ferrell, R., 24
Ferrer, E., 50, 55
Ferrero, J., 25, 31, 298
Ferris, J., 23
Fichtenberg, C. M., 361
Fida, R., 252
Field, A. E., 308
Field, T., 270
Fields, J., 113
Fiese, B., 36
Fife, K. A., 167
Figarsky, K., 52
Figner, B., 64, 66
Filardo, E., 135
Fincham, F., 116
Fincham, F. D., 287
Fine, M., 118
Fine, S. M., 173, 328
Finer, L. B., 294, 310, 312
Fingerson, L., 301
Finkelhor, D., 150, 205, 366
Finkelstein, B. D., 271
Finken, L., 245
Finn, A., 50
Finn, A. S., 179
Finn, J., 159–160
Finnerty, K., 200
Fischer, S., 372
Fischhoff, B., 46, 64–65
Fischoff, B., 65
Fishbein, M., 200

Fisher, C., 336
Fisher, D., 293, 301, 303
Fisher, M., 36
Fisher, P., 121
Fisher, S., 230
Fite, P., 287, 350
Fite, P. J., 371
Fitzgerald, H., 316
Fitzgerald-Yau, N., 40
Fitzwater, T., 16, 379
Flaherty, B., 63
Flaherty, B. P., 182–183, 188
Flaherty, L., 379
Flamm, E. S., 107, 330
Flanagan, C., 176, 185, 253, 255, 256, 346
Flanagan, C. A., 252, 254, 256
Flanagan, K. S., 145, 150
Flanders, W., 35
Flannery, D., 29, 174, 212, 359–360
Flashman, J., 137, 332
Flavell, E., 45
Flavell, J., 45
Flay, B. R., 373
Flegal, K. M., 34
Fleischli, J., 138
Fleming, C. B., 87, 350
Fleming, J. S., 328
Fleming, W., 267
Fletcher, A., 149, 362
Fletcher, J. M., 166
Flewelling, R., 361–362
Flickinger, S., 324
Flom, J., 23
Flook, L., 102, 271, 331
Flor, D., 120
Flores, G., 281
Flory, J., 24
Flory, K., 359
Floyd, C. F., 376
Flynn, B., 362
Flynn, M., 349
Fobil, J., 203
Foeher, U., 197
Foehr, U., 198
Fomby, P., 118, 331
Fondell, M., 302
Fong, G., 310
Fong, G. T., 301
Fontaine, R., 62, 369
Fontaine, R. G., 288–289, 298–299
Foran, W., 55
Forbes, E., 17, 57
Forbes, E. E., 27, 57
Forbes, G. B., 19
Ford, C. A., 293
Ford, J. A., 359
Ford, K., 227
Ford, K. A., 361
Ford, K. R., 227
Fordham, C., 134, 336
Forehand, R., 115, 301, 379
Forest, A. L., 204
Forgatch, M., 100, 118, 368–369, 371
Forhan, S., 311
Forman, T. A., 257
Formoso, D., 101
Forrest-Bank, S., 148
Forrester, K. K., 149

Fortenberry, J., 292
Fortner, M., 100
Fortson, E. N., 93
Fortuin, J., 141
Fosco, G. M., 116, 323
Foshee, V., 287, 307–308
Foshee, V. A., 92, 145, 276, 286–287
Foss, R. D., 67
Foster, D. L., 15, 17
Foster, H., 33–34, 287
Fournier, M., 225
Fowler, P., 93–94, 121, 259
Fox, K. R., 376
Frabutt, J. M., 227
Fraley, R. C., 266
Francis, D., 357
Francis, L. A., 35
Francis, S. E., 379
Francisco, R., 38, 39
Franck, K., 116
Francois, A. G., 227
Francois, S., 94
Frank, E., 374
Frank, K., 115
Frank, K. A., 138
Frank, S., 39
Frankenberger, K. D., 46
Franko, D. L., 216
Franzen, A. B., 259
Franzetta, K., 310, 311
Franzoi, S., 144
Fraser, A. M., 107, 204
Fredricks, J., 191
Fredricks, J. A., 172, 191, 216, 341
Fredstrom, B. K., 149
Freed, L. H., 288
Freedman, A., 379
Freedman-Doan, C., 162
Freedman-Doan, P., 188
Freedner, N., 288
Freeman, & E. C.?, 255
Freeman, H., 275
Freeman-Gallant, A., 368
Freisthler, B., 358
French, D., 145, 303
French, D. C., 258, 259
French, J., 202
French, M., 143
French, S. A., 38
French, S. E., 227
Frenn, K., 16
Frenzel, A. C., 330
Freud, A., 9, 238–239
Freud, S., 9
Frey, S., 28
Frey, W., 230
Frick, P., 148, 362–363
Frick, P. J., 93, 367–368
Fried, M., 80
Friedenberg, E., 10, 180
Friedlander, L. J., 281
Friedman, M. S., 308
Friedman, R., 331, 333
Friel, L. V., 302
Friend, K. B., 359
Friend, S., 39
Friendly, R. W., 242
Frisco, M. L., 115, 317
Frison, E., 204

Frohlich, C., 253
Fröjd, S., 31
Fromme, K., 86
Frost, J. J., 310
Fruiht, V. M., 90, 331
Fugelsang, J., 68
Fujimoto, K., 140–141
Fuligini, A., 299
Fuligni, A., 45, 87, 89, 100–103, 138, 147, 171, 176, 225–229, 240, 248, 257, 266, 269, 274, 275, 331–332, 335–337, 375
Fulker, D., 105
Fulkerson, J. A., 36, 38
Fuller-Rowell, T. E., 243
Fulmore, C., 324
Furbey, M., 65
Furman, W., 109, 130, 150, 262, 265, 267, 268, 274, 276–279, 280, 282–285, 288, 307
Furr-Holden, C., 93
Furstenberg, F., Jr., 72, 86, 88, 114, 120, 315, 317
Furstenberg, F.F.J., 77
Fussell, M., 41

G

Gabhainn, N. S., 303
Gabhainn, S., 294, 299
Gadino, B., 227
Gage, J. C., 193
Galambos, N., 3, 30, 75, 76, 82, 135, 194, 232, 233, 277, 373
Galambos, N. L., 108, 266
Galay, L., 255
Galbraith, K. A., 300
Galliher, R. V., 225, 230
Gallimore, R., 139
Galloway, T., 179
Gallup, G., 256
Galvan, A., 58
Galván, A., 57, 244, 269, 299
Gamble, W., 267
Gamm, B. K., 269, 271, 289
Gamoran, A., 164, 325
Gao, M., 137
Garber, J., 162, 241, 352, 377–378
Garcia, C., 226
Garcia, N. V., 59
Garcia Coll, C., 216
García Coll, C., 228
Gardner, H., 61
Gardner, M., 67, 92, 94, 191–193, 303
Gardner, T. W., 369
Garg, R., 332
Gargiulo, J., 30
Garner, R., 125
Gartner, M., 227
Gartrell, N., 116
Gartrell, N. K., 120
Gartstein, M., 92, 108
Garvan, C., 369
Gaskin, A., 88
Gasser, L., 63
Gastic, B., 183
Gathercole, S. E., 51
Gatherum, A., 242

Gau, S. S., 166
Gaudreau, P., 192
Gauze, C., 271, 276
Gavin, L., 276
Gawlik, A., 21
Gaydos, L. M., 319
Gayle, H., 312
Gaylord-Harden, N., 217
Ge, X., 23, 31, 32, 119, 285, 373, 374
Gebelt, J. L., 31
Gecas, V., 100
Gee, G. C., 311
Gee, K. A., 136
Geier, C., 44, 58, 244
Geier, C. F., 56, 360
Geiser, C., 213
Gelbwasser, L., 332
Geldhof, G. J., 195
Gentile, D., 198
Gentile, D. A., 201
George, G., 218
George, M.R.W., 63, 116
Georgiades, K., 90, 167, 356
Gerard, J., 116
Gerard, J. M., 161, 218
Gerber, S. B., 159–160
Gerbner, G., 198
Germán, M., 100–101
Gerrard, M., 106–107, 200, 312
Gerris, J. M., 103
Gershoff, E. T., 378–379
Gershoni, R., 269
Gest, S., 212, 213
Gest, S. D., 131, 143, 214
Gestsdóttir, S., 247
Gettman, D., 103
Gettman, D. C., 274
Ghatak, R., 330
Ghazarian, S., 104
Ghazarian, S. R., 227, 330, 337
Ghement, I. R., 36
Ghetti, S., 50
Gibb, B. E., 271, 374
Gibb, S. J., 317
Gibbons, F., 106–107, 312
Gibbons, F. X., 200
Gibbs, J., 249
Gibson, E., 318
Gibson, L., 139
Giedd, J., 58
Giedd, J. N., 2, 45, 57, 58, 111
Gierut, K., 36
Gil, A. G., 308
Gilbert, A., 225, 230
Gilchrist, L. D., 317
Giletta, M., 141, 142–143, 247
Gillen-O'Neel, C., 171, 332
Gillin, C. J., 29
Gillman, S., 114
Gillmore, M., 311, 318
Gillmore, M. R., 317, 359
Gillock, K., 335
Gilman, A. B., 138, 139
Gilman, R., 149
Gilman, S. E., 359
Gilpin, E., 358
Gilreath, T. D., 357
Gil-Rivas, V., 106–107
Gingras, I., 241
Gini, G., 141, 150

Ginwright, S., 256
Giordano, P., 280, 296
Giordano, P. C., 280, 281, 289, 295, 296, 301, 366
Giovino, G., 358
Glanovsky, J. L., 358
Glantz, S. A., 361
Glaser, B., 351
Glauber, A., 287
Glennie, E. J., 330, 343
Glenwright, M., 46
Glick, G. C., 262, 269, 271
Glover, N., 354
Gniewosz, B., 326
Goddings, A., 59
Goddings, A. L., 55, 57
Godeau, E., 294, 299, 303
Godwin, J., 147, 370
Goeke-Morey, M. C., 116
Goesling, B., 362
Goetz, T., 330, 379
Gökler, B., 267
Goldberg, A., 278, 281–282
Goldenberg, D., 299
Goldfield, G., 203
Golding, J., 233
Goldman, M., 359
Goldsmith, P. A., 167
Goldstein, A. S., 359
Goldstein, B., 20
Goldstein, S., 248
Goldston, D., 375
Goldweber, A., 278, 366
Goleman, D., 61
Golombok, S., 233
Golub, A., 356
Gomez, C. A., 285
Gomez-Garibello, C., 149
Gondoli, D., 39, 100
Gondoli, D. M., 242
Gonzales, L.M., 100, 325
Gonzales, N., 100–101, 108, 139, 331, 333
Gonzales, N. A., 33, 101, 147, 227, 230, 281, 332
Gonzales, R., 228
Gonzales-Backen, M. A., 227
Gonzalez, R., 337
Good, M., 198, 258
Goodman, E., 308
Goodman, M., 73, 74, 86
Goodnight, J. A., 370–371
Goodson, P., 297, 299
Goodwin, A. H., 67
Goodwin, N. P., 141
Goossens, L., 45, 218, 223, 224
Gordon, K., 84
Gordon, L., 307
Gordon, M., 287, 330
Gordon, R. A., 139
Gordon, V., 301
Gore, S., 179, 276
Gorka, S. M., 374
Gorman, S., 205
Gorman-Smith, D., 139, 287, 371, 379
Gorrese, A., 267
Gortmaker, S. L., 38
Gotlib, I., 378
Gotlib, I. H., 17
Gottfredson, D., 159

Gottfredson, M., 351
Gottfried, A., 328
Gottfried, A. E., 324
Gottfried, A. W., 324, 328
Gould, M., 205, 375–376
Gould, T., 246–247, 361
Gowen, L., 30, 37, 278
Gowen, L. K., 307
Gowling, H., 67
Goza, F., 334, 335
Grabe, S., 307
Graber, J., 8, 27, 31, 34, 37, 349, 352, 372–374, 377–378
Graber, J. A., 31, 32, 36, 149, 377
Graham, C., 24
Graham, J. W., 98
Graham, S., 19, 31, 60, 136, 145, 147, 162, 167, 229, 243, 244, 310, 330, 367
Gralen, S., 39
Gralinski, J., 326
Granberg, E., 19
Grande, T. L., 366
Granic, I., 98
Granillo, M., 39
Granot, D., 267
Gravelle, M., 160–161
Gray, M., 283, 287
Gray-Little, B., 216, 217, 228
Green, F., 45
Green, H. D. Jr., 141
Green, K., 225
Green, K. M., 358
Green, S., 301, 332
Greenan, C. C., 141
Greenbaum, P. E., 362
Greenberg, M., 150, 161, 276, 368
Greenberg, M. T., 93, 98, 359
Greenberger, E., 102, 106–107, 186, 276–277, 336
Green-Demers, I., 326
Greene, K., 312
Greene, K. M., 294
Greene, M., 41
Greene, M. L., 136, 217, 269, 272
Greenfield, P., 6
Green-Hennessy, S., 168
Greenhoot, A. F., 219
Greenley, R. N., 40
Greenspan, L., 16, 25, 31
Greenstein, D., 60
Gregory, A., 147, 169–170, 174
Gregory, E., 100
Gregory, W., 218
Grenard, J. L., 202
Greusing, S., 28
Greven, C. U., 369
Grey, M., 307
Grier, S., 207
Grieve, S. M., 55
Griffin, K. W., 219, 359
Griffin, T., 230
Griffith Fontaine, R., 370
Griffiths, M. D., 204
Grigg, W., 168
Griggs, C., 16
Grime, R., 249
Grisso, T., 78, 244, 363
Grobe, R., 331, 333
Grodsky, E., 342

Grogan-Kaylor, A., 39
Grolnick, W., 109, 330–331
Grolnick, W. S., 107, 242, 330
Grosbras, M., 247
Gross, E. F., 149
Gross, L., 198
Grossman, A. H., 231
Grossman, J. B., 90
Grossman, J. M., 225
Grotevant, H., 101
Grotevant, H. D., 120
Grotpeter, J., 269
Grover, R. L., 264, 282
Grube, J., 293, 301, 303
Grube, J. W., 359
Gruber, J., 41, 354
Grucza, R. A., 361
Gruen, J., 165
Gruenewald, P. J., 359
Grumbach, M., 15
Grunbaum, J., 294
Grych, J. H., 116, 288
Guacci-Franci, N., 274
Guan, K., 376
Guarini, T. E., 228
Gudiño, O., 90
Gudiño, O. G., 337
Guerino, P., 174
Guerra, N. G., 149, 150
Guest, A., 192
Guillen, E., 36
Guimond, A. B., 227
Guion, K., 109
Guldi, M., 89
Gummerum, M., 251
Gunlicks-Stoessel, M., 374
Gunnar, M., 16
Gunnoe, M., 118
Gunter, W., 160–161
Guo, G., 34, 369
Gupta, T., 234
Güre, A., 119
Gurevitch, M., 198
Gurin, G., 139
Güroğlu, B., 60, 148, 253
Gustafson, P., 251
Gustafsson, H., 6
Guterman, N., 93
Guthrie, H., 19
Guthrie, I. K., 252
Gutierrez, P. M., 376
Gutierrez, R., 169
Gutman, L., 102, 103, 163
Guyer, A., 16, 58, 120, 247, 374, 379
Guyer, A. E., 58
Guyll, M., 12

H

Ha, T., 266, 284
Haas, S., 49
Haas, S. A., 141
Haavisto, T., 324
Habermas, T., 224
Haddad, A.D.M., 39, 247
Haddad, E., 276–277, 329
Hafdahl, A., 216, 217, 228
Hafen, C. A., 138, 324
Hafsteinsson, L. G., 106–107

Hagan, J., 287
Hagewen, K. J., 183
Haggart, N., 267–268
Hahm, H., 294
Hahm, H. C., 294
Hahn, C. S., 323
Hahn, C.-S., 351
Haight, W., 277
Haines, J., 39, 206
Haj-Yahia, M. M., 93
Hakvoort, E., 306
Halder, I., 24
Hale, D. R., 40
Hale, L. E., 165
Hale, W., 213, 224
Hale, W. W., 225
Hale, W. W. 3rd., 223
Halgunseth, L., 108–109
Hall, D. M., 121
Hall, D. W., 319
Hall, G. S., 8, 9, 11, 72
Hall, J. E., 288
Hall, N. C., 379
Haller, M., 358
Halliday-Scher, K., 130
Halligan, S. L., 147
Hallinan, M., 136, 164, 168, 169
Hallquist, M. N., 57
Hallquist, S., 83
Halpem, C.T., 293
Halpern, C., 26, 38, 83, 287
Halpern, C. T., 285, 286, 293, 294,
    297, 299, 303, 374
Halpern, D. F., 52
Halpern-Felsher, B., 24, 65, 237,
    245, 296, 312
Halpern-Meekin, S., 114
Haltigan, J. D., 150, 369
Ham, A., 301
Hamburger, M. E., 307–308
Hamby, S. L., 150
Hamedani, M. G., 335
Hamilton, A., 29
Hamilton, C., 266–267
Hamilton, H. A., 118–119
Hamilton, J. L., 32
Hamilton, J. P., 17
Hamilton-Leaks, J., 318
Hamlat, E. J, 32
Hamm, J., 136, 137
Hamm, J. V., 136, 160–161, 227
Hamm, M., 61
Hammen, C., 374
Hammen, C. L., 373–374
Hammersmith, S., 306
Hammond, W., 230
Hammons, A., 36
Hamre, B. K., 335
Hamza, C. A., 104, 377
Han, W., 66
Han, W. J., 107–108
Hancox, R. J., 202
Handley, E., 358
Hankin, B. L., 107, 352, 373,
    374, 377
Hannan, P. J., 39, 206
Hansbrough, E., 200
Hanselman, P., 325
Hansen, D. M., 29, 193
Hanson, J. L., 36, 49–50
Hanson, T., 118

Hao, L., 228
Hara, R. E., 51–52
Harachi, T. W., 359
Harackiewicz, J. M., 174, 330
Harbaugh, A. G., 149
Harber, K. D., 170
Harcourt, T. H., 118
Hardaway, C. R., 94, 119
Harden, K., 111
Harden, K. P., 30, 33, 66, 111, 243,
    247, 297–299, 370, 377
Harden, P., 31
Hardesty, J., 215
Hardesty, J. L., 217
Hardie, J. H., 100, 134, 175
Hardiman, M., 52
Hardin, M., 360
Harding, D., 91
Hardway, C., 100
Hardy, D., 316
Hardy, K. K., 203
Hardy, S. A., 253
Hare, A., 7, 109, 236, 262–263
Hare, A. L., 108, 242
Harenski, C. L., 62
Harenski, K. A., 62
Hargis, P., 184
Hargreaves, J., 362
Hariri, A., 3, 9
Hariri, A. R., 93, 369
Harlan, S., 317
Harold, G., 116
Harold, R., 330–331
Harper, B. D., 147
Harper, G., 139
Harper, J. M., 107, 110
Harré, N., 40
Harrington, H., 370
Harrington, K. F., 312
Harris, D., 12
Harris, J., 125
Harris, J. R., 139–140
Harris, J.K.A., 29
Harris, K., 34, 83, 356
Harris, K. M., 281–282, 293
Harris, M., 139
Harris, M. A., 218
Harris, M. J., 371
Harris, R., 305
Harrison, F., 39, 247
Harrison, H. M., 146
Harrison, K., 206
Hart, D., 213, 253, 254
Harter, S., 7, 209–212, 215,
    218, 241
Hartl, A. C., 262
Hartmark, C., 84
Hartney, C., 81
Hartos, J., 40
Hartung, C., 349
Hartup, W., 288–289
Hartup, W. W., 148
Hasebe, Y., 98
Haselager, G. J., 148
Haselager, G. T., 148
Haselager, G.J.T., 148
Hasking, P., 376
Hasselhorn, M., 215
Hastings, J. S., 98, 168
Hathaway, J. E., 287
Hattie, J., 326

Hatzenbuehler, M. L., 149, 308
Hau, K., 165, 215
Hau, K.-T., 188
Hauser, S., 268, 275
Hausser, D., 312
Havens, J. R., 354
Hawes, S. W., 363
Hawk, L. W., 92
Hawk, S. T., 98, 281
Hawkins, D., 92
Hawkins, D. N., 114, 117
Hawkins, J., 360, 362
Hawkins, J. D., 102, 107, 138,
    139, 350
Hawkins, K., 206
Hay, C., 29, 93
Hayden, A., 348
Hayden, H., 39
Haydon, A. A., 285, 293
Haydon, K. C., 267
Hayes, R., 105
Hayford, S. R., 77
Haynes, O. M., 351
Haynes, S. H., 310
Haynie, D., 141, 355
Haynie, D. L., 33, 93, 104, 108,
    129, 141, 148, 289, 297
Hayslip, B., 115
Hayward, C., 30, 37, 38, 278
Hazel, N. A., 107
He, J., 372
Heard, H. E., 115
Heath, A. C., 359
Heatherton, T. F., 202, 214
Heaven, P.C.L., 218
Hebert, K. R., 264
Hebert, L., 311
Hechinger, F., 160
Heck, D., 136, 227
Heck, R. H., 164
Heckhausen, J., 276–277, 336
Hedeker, D., 373
Heeren, T., 360
Heffner, V., 206
Heiland, F. W., 19
Heilbron, N., 146
Hektner, J. M., 150
Helfand, M., 298
Hellström, C., 198
Helmond, P., 165
Helms, L., 188
Helms, S. W., 143
Helsen, M., 275
Helwig, C., 63, 255
Helwig, C. C., 63
Hemphill, S. A., 350
Henderson, A., 254
Henderson, C., 115
Henderson, C. E., 362
Hendrick, C., 304
Hendrick, S., 304
Hendricks, C., 240
Hendry, L. B., 4
Henkel, R. R., 138
Hennessy, M., 200
Hennig, K. H., 251
Hennighausen, K., 267
Henrich, C., 143
Henry, B., 213
Henry, D., 139, 379
Henry, D. B., 300, 302

Henry, K. L., 335, 342, 359
Hensel, D., 292
Henshaw, S., 314
Henshaw S., 313
Henson, J. M., 212
Herbers, J. E., 161
Herdt, G., 15, 291
Herman, M., 136, 216, 227,
    325, 336
Herman-Giddens, M., 23, 25
Hernandez, D., 194
Hernandez, D. C., 118
Hernández, M. M., 227, 338
Hernandez, P., 121
Hernandez, P. R., 325
Hernandez-Guzman, L., 30
Herpers, P. C., 369
Herpertz, S., 369
Herpertz-Dahlmann, B., 369
Herrenkohl, T. I., 102, 107
Herrera, C., 90
Herrera, D., 161
Herrera, V. M., 286, 287
Herring, A. H., 293
Herrling, S., 342
Hershberg, T., 86
Herting, M. M., 52, 55
Herts, K. L., 149
Hertzman, C., 41
Herz, D., 121
Hessel, E. T., 239
Hetherington, E., 112
Hetherington, E. M., 104, 110–112,
    114–116, 118
Hevey, C., 109
Heyes, S. B., 59
Heyvaert, M., 241
Hibbert, J. R., 106–107
Hicks, B. M., 358
Hicks, L., 161
Hicks, R. E., 289
Hill, C., 347
Hill, D., 293
Hill, J. E., 299
Hill, J. P., 4
Hill, K. G., 107, 138, 139
Hill, L., 215
Hill, M., 317
Hill, N. E., 174, 330, 344
Hill, P. L., 219
Hill, T. D., 310
Hindin, M. J., 312
Hinduja, S., 149
Hine, T., 11, 74, 182
Hines, M., 17, 233
Hingson, R., 358, 360
Hinshaw, S., 50
Hinshaw, S. P., 150
Hiraga, Y., 139
Hirky, A., 357
Hirsch, B., 273, 276
Hirsch, M., 313–314
Hirschi, T., 351
Hitlin, S., 231
Hitti, A., 64
Hjalmarsson, R., 138
Ho, A., 8
Ho, A. Y., 143
Ho, L., 281
Ho, M. H., 377
Hochberg, Z., 21, 25

Hock, E., 241
Hodge, D. R., 259
Hodges, E.V.E., 146
Hoeve, M., 107
Hofer, C., 252
Hoffer, T., 169, 331
Hofferth, S. L., 205, 316, 317, 331
Hoffman, J. P., 114
Hofkens, T., 330
Hofman, J., 269
Hofmann, V., 138, 213
Hogue, A., 141
Holas, I., 160
Holcombe, R., 161
Holder, D. W., 256
Holderness, C., 30
Holland, A. S., 266
Holland, L. J., 287
Holland, M. M., 167
Hollander, D., 303
Hollenstein, T., 9, 26, 98
Holliday, E., 246–247, 361
Hollist, D. R., 93
Holloway, C., 305
Holmbeck, G., 29, 98, 240, 241, 318
Holmbeck, G. N., 40, 300
Holmen, J., 358
Holmen, T., 358
Holmes, C., 259
Holsen, I., 213
Holstein, B. E., 359, 361
Holt, M. K., 138, 298–299
Homer, J., 143
Homma, Y., 308
Hooley, J. M., 59
Hooper, C. J., 49–51, 55
Hope, M. O., 32
Hopson, L. M., 330
Horan, P., 184
Horn, A. S., 254
Horn, E. J., 110
Horn, S. S., 131, 132, 146, 232, 254
Horne, A. M., 285
Horner, J., 206, 309
Hornik, R., 354–355
Horton, K. D., 169
Horvat, E. M., 134, 336
Horwood, J., 33
Horwood, L., 367, 368
Horwood, L. J., 266, 317, 362
Hotton, A. L., 93
Hou, J., 286
Houltberg, B., 7
House, L. E., 379
Houser, J.J., 286
Houston, S. M., 51–52
Houts, R. M., 24, 35, 203
Howard, A., 3, 371
Howard, A. L., 93
Howard, D. E., 104
Howard, G., 314–315
Howard Caldwell, C., 118
Howell, J. C., 138
Hoyt, D., 120, 302, 356
Hoyt, L. T., 36
Hoza, B., 271, 277, 278
Hrabosky, J. I., 38–39
Hser, Y-H., 299
Hsieh, H. L., 285
Hsu, W. W., 230

Hu, M., 359
Hu, P., 302
Huang, D., 299
Huang, F., 147
Hubbard, J., 280
Hudes, E. S., 285
Hudley, C., 328
Huebner, T., 369
Huesmann, L. R., 202, 368–369
Huettel, S., 51–52
Hughes, D., 89, 225, 227, 228, 230, 274, 335
Hughes, D. L., 216
Hughes, L. A., 193
Hughes, R., 306–307
Hughes, S., 357
Huguley, J. P., 230
Huh, D., 34–35
Huizenga, H. M., 66, 244
Huizinga, D., 66, 92, 352
Hulleman, C. S., 174, 330
Hunt, M., 379
Hunter, S., 108
Huot, R., 378
Hurd, N. M., 90, 92, 227, 229
Hurdle, D., 234
Hurley, D., 112
Hurrelmann, K., 86
Hussong, A., 8, 356
Hussong, A. M., 288–289, 351
Huston, A. C., 92, 164, 335
Huston, A.C., 160
Hutchinson, D., 39
Hutchinson, D. M., 141
Hutchinson, M. K., 301
Hutteman, R., 213
Huynh, V., 227, 229
Huynh, V. W., 229, 230, 257
Hwang, A., 324
Hwang, K., 57
Hyde, J., 232–233
Hyde, J. S., 297, 307, 330, 374
Hyde, L. W., 351, 369
Hyman, C., 145
Hymel, S., 147, 149

I
Iacono, W., 102
Iacono, W. G., 110, 111, 115, 258, 331, 370–371
Ialongo, N. S., 188, 229
Iannotti, R. J., 34, 35–36, 149
Ibañez, G. E., 330
Ichien, N. T., 66–67, 246
Iedema, J., 224
Igartua, K., 305
Iglowstein, I., 29
Ikramullah, E., 315
Ikramullah, E. N., 294
Impett, E. A., 212
Inhelder, B., 9
Inoff-Germain, G., 352
Insabella, G., 114
Ireland, M., 38, 296
Irvine, C., 52
Irwin, C., 40, 41, 311–312
Irwin, C. E., Jr., 38
Irwin, K., 174
Isakson, K., 163

Iselin, A. M., 88
Ispa, J., 108–109
Israelashvili, M., 205
Ivanova, K., 115, 302
Ivers, R., 65
Ivory, J., 201, 205

J
Jaccard, J., 141, 301, 312, 314
Jack, F., 49
Jackson, C., 97, 297–298
Jackson, D., 50
Jackson, J., 229, 230, 276
Jackson, J. S., 33–34
Jackson, K. M., 162, 356, 359
Jackson, L., 203, 205
Jackson, S., 39
Jackson, T., 39
Jackson-Newsom, J., 104, 108–109
Jacobi, C., 37
Jacobs, D., 358
Jacobs, J., 4, 245
Jacobs, J. E., 96, 192, 213–214, 232
Jacobs, S., 117
Jacobsohn, L., 354–355
Jacobson, C., 375–376
Jacobson, K., 111, 373
Jacobson, L., 111
Jacobson, R. P., 252
Jacobs-Quadrel, M., 64–65
Jacobus, J., 361
Jacques-Tiura, A., 93–94
Jaeger, A., 57
Jaffari-Bimmel, N., 266
Jaffe, P., 306–307
Jaffee, S., 316
Jager, J., 240, 355
Jagers, R. J., 227
Jahng, S., 241, 242
James, A., 358
James, L., 61
James-Burdumy, S., 362
Jamieson, P., 206
Jamieson, P. E., 201
Janevic, T., 35
Jang, S. J., 259
Jank, W., 308
Janosz, M., 147, 215, 341, 342
Jansen, B., 66
Jansen, B.R.J., 244
Janssen, I., 29
Jansson, S. M., 108
Jarcho, J. M., 246
Jarrett, R., 196
Jarvis, P., 163
Jaser, S. S., 379
Javdani, S., 350
Jayaram, L., 191
Jefferson, K., 312
Jemal, A., 35
Jemmott, J. B., III, 301
Jemmott, J., III, 310, 312
Jemmott, L., 310
Jemmott, L. S., 301
Jenkins, F., 168
Jenkins, K. N., 342
Jenkins, L. N., 276
Jenni, O., 28, 29
Jennings, J., 166

Jennings, W. G., 371
Jensen, A. C., 110
Jensen, L. A., 240
Jensen-Campbell, L., 280
Jenson, J. M., 148
Jenssen, B., 202
Jeong, Y.-J., 115
Jessor, R., 351, 359
Jessor, S., 351
Jewell, J., 141
Jewett, R., 191
Jeynes, W., 114–115, 168
Ji, J., 369
Jia, Y., 169
Jiang, D., 285
Jiang, G., 337
Jing, W., 149
Jodl, K., 119, 268
Jodl, K. M., 112, 329, 344
Joe, S., 259
John, O., 212, 351
Johnson, A., 277
Johnson, A. B., 297
Johnson, B., 77
Johnson, B. D., 356
Johnson, C., 120
Johnson, C. A., 66
Johnson, D., 19
Johnson, D. W., 169
Johnson, E., 29
Johnson, J., 309
Johnson, J. P., 302
Johnson, K., 356
Johnson, M., 187, 342–346
Johnson, M. D., 266
Johnson, R., 19
Johnson, R. T., 169
Johnson, S. K., 195
Johnson, S. L., 171
Johnson, W., 111, 331
Johnston, L., 193, 355, 358, 359, 362, 371
Johnston, L. D., 353–356
Johnston, M., 167
Joiner, T. E., Jr., 377
Joiner, T., Jr., 372
Jolles, D., 49–50
Jolles, D. D., 51
Jones, B. L., 297
Jones, D., 19, 273
Jones, D. C., 39
Jones, J., 163
Jones, J. D., 265
Jones, J. M., 336
Jones, L., 205
Jones, L. M., 205
Jones, M., 203
Jones, M. C., 307
Jones, M. D., 225, 230
Jones, R., 292
Jones, R. K., 259, 310, 311
Jones, R. M., 29
Jones, S. M., 107, 138
Jones Harden, B., 120
Jonkman, K., 142, 143
Jordan, A., 198, 200
Jordan-Conde, Z., 219–220
Jose, P. E., 149, 171, 276, 374
Joshi, S. P., 200
Josse, G., 60
Joyce T., 314

Joyner, K., 231, 286
Ju, D., 115
Juang, L., 230, 248, 331
Judge, B., 375
Juffer, F., 266
Jung, J., 19, 198
Junkin, R., 187
Juonala, M., 35
Jurkovic, G., 330
Jussim, L., 170
Jutengren, G., 147
Juvonen, J., 30, 32, 134, 136, 147, 149, 167, 174, 332

K

Kackar, H., 254
Kackar, H. Z., 254
Kadosh, K., 45
Kaestle, C. E., 293, 295, 296
Kaestner, R., 314
Kågesten, A., 318
Kahneman, D., 48, 64, 67
Kail, R. V., 50
Kakade, M., 367
Kakihara, F., 242
Kalakoski, V., 225
Kaliher, G., 276
Kalil, A., 120, 169, 326
Kalman, Z., 269
Kalmuss, D., 317
Kaltiala-Heino, R., 31
Kalton, G., 354–355
Kam, C., 50
Kam, J. A., 246
Kambam, P., 244
Kamenetz, A., 86
Kaminski, J. W., 121
Kan, M. L., 300
Kandel, D., 356, 358, 359
Kandler, C., 212
Kane, S. B., 308
Kang, H., 225
Kann, L., 294
Kanouse, D. E., 301
Kantor, H., 158
Kao, G., 228, 336
Kao, M., 302, 303
Kaplan, N., 267
Kaplan, R., 92
Kaplan, S., 15
Kaprio, J., 23, 378
Karch, D. L., 376
Karevold, E., 377
Karp, I., 358
Karpovsky, S., 269
Karre, J., 137
Karre, J. K., 117
Karremans, J. C., 134, 144
Karriker-Jaffe, K., 92, 145
Kasser, T., 241, 242
Kataoka, S., 90, 150
Katz, E., 198
Katz, J., 297
Katz, L. F., 91, 366
Katz, M., 84, 86
Kaufman, C., 217
Kaufman, K., 218
Kaukinen, C., 114
Kawabata, Y., 146, 166

Keane, S. P., 110, 369
Keating, D., 4–5, 41, 43, 47–48, 64, 255
Keel, P. K., 36, 38, 39
Keeshan, P., 41, 361
Keijsers, L., 98, 139, 220, 224, 225, 273
Kelada, L., 376
Kelch, R., 15
Keller, M., 213, 251, 269
Kelley, M., 94
Kelly, A., 36
Kelly, B. C., 285, 295
Kelly, B. M., 134, 332
Kelly, D., 323
Kelly, F. D., 104
Kelly, S., 163–164
Kendall, P., 349
Kendig, S. M., 89
Kendrick, K., 147
Keniston, K., 74
Kennard, B. D., 378
Kenneavy, K., 200
Kennedy, D. P., 141
Kenny, S., 104
Kenyon, D. B., 82
Keogh, D., 316
Kern, M., 195
Kerns, K., 266
Kerns, K. A., 265
Kerr, D., 104
Kerr, M., 33, 107, 138, 139, 191, 242, 299, 377
Kershaw, T., 315
Keshavan, B., 58
Kessler, R., 8
Kessler, R. C., 350
Kett, J., 11, 79, 84, 86, 184
Key, J., 316
Keyes, K. M., 29, 355
Keyes, M., 110
Keys, K. M., 29
Khalife, N., 166
Khoo, A., 201
Khoo, S., 110
Khoury-Kassibri, M., 174
Khurana, A., 299, 301
Kiang, L., 100, 136, 218, 226, 227, 230, 325, 374
Kidd, S. A., 375
Kiehl, K. A., 62, 369
Kielpikowski, M., 171
Kiene, S. M., 297
Kiesner, J., 138, 145
Kilburn, J., 202
Kilgore, S., 169
Killen, J., 37, 38
Killen, M., 63, 64, 234
Killeya-Jones, L., 83
Killeya-Jones, L. A., 143
Killoren, S., 139
Killoren, S. E., 294
Kilmstra, T. A., 224
Kilpatrick, D. G., 351
Kim, B., 92
Kim, D. Y., 266
Kim, H., 287
Kim, H. K., 297, 370–371, 373
Kim, H. S., 137
Kim, J., 110, 139, 200, 232, 234
Kim, J. C., 377

Kim, J. L., 301
Kim, J.-I., 324
Kim, J.-Y., 193
Kim, K., 368
Kim, M., 324
Kim, M. J., 87
Kim, S., 228
Kim, S. Y., 119, 230
Kim, S.-B., 188
Kim, S-i., 324
Kim, S-il, 331
Kim, T., 205, 254
Kim, Y., 198
Kimberg, C., 40
Kimonis, E., 367
Kimonis, E. R., 93, 148
Kim-Prieto, C., 225
Kim-Spoon, J., 259, 266
King, J., 326
King, K. M., 93, 359
King, M. D., 166
King, P., 256–259
King, R., 38, 315
King, V., 114, 116, 119
Kingston, B., 92
Kinney, D., 128
Kinsfogel, K. M., 288
Kipke, M., 120
Kipp, K. H., 49
Kirby, D., 297, 310, 311, 318, 319
Kirby, D. B., 285
Kirk, D., 92
Kirkpatrick, L., 267
Kirkpatrick, N. M., 363
Kirschenbaum, D. S., 36
Kirshner, B., 256
Kiselica, M., 315
Kishor, N., 308
Kistler, M., 215
Kit-fong Au, T., 301, 301
Kiuru, N., 137, 141, 332
Klaczynski, P. A., 44
Klahr, A., 102
Klasen, L., 60
Klassen, R. M., 324
Klaver, J., 78
Kleibeuker, S., 49–50
Kleibeuker, S. W., 51
Klein, D., 360, 377, 378
Klein, D. J., 357
Klein, H. W., 34
Klein, J., 159, 202
Klein, J. D., 314
Kleinman, M., 205
Kleitman, S., 188
Klessinger, N., 379
Kliewer, W., 146, 283
Klimes-Dougan, B., 147
Klimstra, T., 213, 223, 225, 240
Klimstra, T. A., 223
Kling, J., 91
Kling, J. R., 91, 366
Klingberg, T., 52
Kljakovic, M., 149
Klodnick, V. V., 93
Kloep, M., 4
Klostermann, S., 350
Klump, K. L., 36, 38, 39
Knack, J. M., 147
Knafo, A., 96, 242
Knecht, A., 141

Knibbe, R. A., 31
Knifsend, C. A., 134
Knight, G. P., 252
Knighton-Wisor, S., 242
Knoester, C., 93, 108
Knoors, H., 144
Knutson, B., 49
Knutson, N., 100, 118
Ko, L., 226
Kobak, R., 262–265, 267, 268
Kochel, K., 147
Kochel, K. P., 147, 233–234
Kochenderfer-Ladd, B., 145, 233–234
Koenig, B., 180, 298–299
Koenig, B. W., 308
Koenig, L., 258
Koerner, S., 117–118
Koerner, S. S., 82
Koestner, R., 241
Koff, E., 30
Kofler, M. J., 350, 351
Kogan, M. D., 193
Kogan, S. M., 229, 300, 302–303
Koh, S., 246
Kohen, D. E., 115
Kohler, J. K., 120
Kohler, P. K., 319
Kohn, M., 346
Kohn-Wood, L. P., 229
Koivisto, A.-M., 31
Kokko, K., 368–369
Kol, K. L., 330
Kolaric, G., 30, 82
Kolburn Kowal, A., 110, 301
Köller, O., 165, 171
Koller, S., 253
Kolobe, T. H., 36
Komro, K. A., 359
Konarski, R., 130, 215, 278, 288
Konijn, E., 202
Konijn, E. A., 149
Konrad, K., 369
Koolschijn, P. C., 51, 52
Koot, H., 151
Koot, H. M., 223, 364, 365
Kopish, M. A., 254
Korgaonkar, M. S., 55
Korn, M., 117
Kort-Butler, L. A., 183
Koss, K., 116
Kosterman, R., 102, 138
Kost K., 313
Kotchick, B., 301, 379
Kotler, J. A., 378–379
Kotler, J. S., 363
Kotov, R., 363
Koulis, T., 358
Kouros, C. D., 241, 352
Kowal, A., 112
Kowal, A. K., 110
Kowaleski-Jones, L., 115
Kowaleski-Jones, P., 302
Kracke, B., 344
Kragel, P. A., 59
Krahé, B., 201
Krahmer, E., 204
Krahn, H., 373
Kramer, L., 109, 110, 112
Kreager, D., 141

Kreager, D. A., 66, 142, 144, 192, 278, 370
Krei, M., 178
Kretsch, N., 30, 66, 247
Kretschmer, T., 31, 33
Krier, M., 335
Kroger, J., 220, 225
Krohn, M. D., 139, 368
Krueger, R. F., 111
Kruse, A., 241
Kruse, M. I., 86
Kubitschek, W., 168
Kuczynski, L., 63
Kuhn, D., 43, 46–50, 60, 378
Kuhn, E. S., 98, 240
Kulis, S., 234, 359
Kull, M., 93
Kumpfer, K. L., 121
Kuncel, N. R., 334
Kung, E., 241
Kunkel, D., 200
Kunnen, S. E., 98
Kuntsche, E., 31
Kupanoff, K., 104
Kupchik, A., 175
Kuperminc, G., 143, 171, 268, 330, 342
Kuperminc, G. P., 330
Kupersmidt, J., 335
Kuppens, S., 242
Kupper, L., 287
Kupper, L. L., 285
Kurdek, L., 118
Kurlychek, M., 77
Kurowski, C. O., 109
Kurtz-Costes, B., 327, 329–330
Kusche, C., 150
Kuss, D., 204
Kuttler, A. F., 130, 131, 279
Kypri, K., 359

L

LaBar, K. S., 59
Lachman, M., 99
Lachman, P., 287
Lacono, W. G., 110
Lacourse, E., 33, 91, 303–304
Lacourse, É., 92
Ladd, G., 147
Ladd, G. W., 145, 233–234, 368
Ladd, H. F., 228
Ladewski, B., 118
Laditka, J., 316
Laditka, S., 316
Ladouceur, C. D., 50, 55
Lafferty, W. E., 319
La Greca, A., 87, 378–379
La Greca, A. M., 39, 130, 131, 133–134, 146, 278
Lahat, A., 63
Lahiff, M., 294, 308
Laible, D., 275
Laird, J., 121, 247
Laird, R., 98, 108, 146, 240, 371
Laird, R. D., 98, 240, 242, 268
Laje, G., 372, 373
Lalonde, F., 45, 58
Lam, C. B., 123, 127, 128
Lam, C. B., 193

Lam, M., 274, 336
Lam, T., 281, 299
Lamar, K., 199
Lamarche, V., 141
Lamb, M., 317
Lambert, K., 160–161
Lambert, L. E., 161
Lambert, S. F., 32, 229
Lamborn, S., 115, 139, 227, 332
Lamis, D. A., 359
Lampard, A. M., 35
Lan, S., 225
Landale, N., 315
Landale, N. S., 300
Laney, T., 377
Lang, D., 312
Lang, F., 99
Langer, D. A., 93
Langer, L., 297, 305
Lansford, J., 89, 108, 143, 297, 337, 369
Lansford, J. E., 242, 266, 288, 298–299
Lansu, T.A.M., 134, 143, 144
Lanthier, R. P., 276
Lanz, M., 103
Lanza, S., 213–214
Lapsley, D., 12
Largo, R., 29
Laris, B. A., 318
Larsen, R., 215
Larsen-Rife, D., 288
Larson, J., 7, 123, 125, 127, 128, 130, 132, 133, 138, 142, 276
Larson, M., 286
Larson, R., 3, 6, 27, 73, 74, 80, 85, 88, 98, 114, 123, 124, 151, 153, 173, 184, 185, 190, 192, 193, 195, 196, 207, 213, 214, 274, 277, 286, 287
Larson, R. W., 238
Larsson, H., 166
Latendresse, S., 106–107
Latendresse, S. J., 111
Latimer, L. A., 29
Lau, A., 90
Lau, J.Y.F., 39, 246, 247
Lau, M., 281
Laub, J. 2003, 367
Laucht, M., 360
Lauckhardt, J., 90, 253–254
Laughlin, J., 246
Laurent, L., 242
Laursen, B., 29, 96–98, 100–103, 138, 141, 151, 190, 236, 237, 239, 240, 262, 269–271, 274, 275, 279, 302, 332
LaVoie, J., 225
Lawford, H., 224, 267–268
Lawler, M., 38
Layton, E., 258
Le, V. D., 287
Leadbeater, B., 317
Leadbeater, B. J., 146
Leaf, W., 40
Leaper, C., 231–234, 307, 332
Leatherdale, S. T., 36
LeBlanc, L., 175
LeBlanc, M., 94, 342
Ledermann, T., 116, 266
Lee, A. M., 30

Lee, B., 138
Lee, C., 186
Lee, D., 34, 88
Lee, E. J., 350
Lee, H., 34
Lee, H. J., 37
Lee, J., 30, 187, 294, 297
Lee, J. C., 342
Lee, K., 62, 331
Lee, K. H., 59, 349
Lee, S., 117
Lee, S. S., 111
Lee, S. Y., 334
Lee, S.-Y., 165
Lee, V., 118, 159, 161, 179, 306–307, 328, 335, 343
Lee, Y., 39
Leech, T.G.J., 35
Leets, L., 63
Leff, S. S., 143
Leffert, N., 150
Lefkowitz, E., 239, 258, 301, 301, 302
Lefkowitz, E. S., 301
Lefner, E., 349
Legault, L., 326
Lehman, S. J., 117
Leibenluft, E., 101, 369
Leichtweis, R. N., 376
Leitch, C., 276
Leitenberg, H., 295
Lejuez, C., 93
Lejuez, C. W., 102
Lekes, N., 241
LeMare, L., 146
LeMoult, J., 17
L'Engle, K., 200
L'Engle, K. L., 200, 297–298
Lengua, L. J., 92
Lenhart, A., 197, 204
Lenox, K., 145
Lenroot, R., 60
Lenroot, R. K., 111
Lens, W., 324
Lenzi, M., 92, 94, 191, 254
Leon, G., 36
Leonard, S., 274
Leopold, T., 87
Leppert, J., 198
Lerch, J., 60
Lereya, T., 150
Lereya, T. S., 149
Lerner, J., 195, 248, 276
Lerner, J. V., 195, 333
Lerner, R., 3, 195, 276, 277
Lerner, R. M., 162, 169, 195, 247, 333, 336
Leshem, B., 93
Lesko, N., 12
Leslie, F., 206
Lester, L., 276
Leung, M.-C., 160–161
Leve, C., 314–315
Leve, L., 297
Leve, L. D., 24
Leventhal, H., 41, 361
Leventhal, T., 90–94, 104, 303–304, 336
Leversen, I., 207
Levin, E., 332
Levin, M., 295, 301

Levine, J. A., 316
Levine, L., 206
Levine, M., 39
Levine, P., 66
Levinson, R., 312
Levitt, J., 274
Levitt, M., 274, 276
Levitt, S., 156
Levran, E., 283
Levy, S., 242
Levy, V., 12
Lewin, K., 10
Lewin, T., 325–326
Lewin-Bizan, S., 195
Lewinsky, M., 293
Lewinsohn, P., 34, 372, 376–378
Lewinsohn, P. M., 286, 378
Lewis, K. S., 134, 336
Lewis, M., 8, 27, 38, 240, 266–267, 276
Lewis, R., 229, 230
Lewis, S., 318
Li, D., 359
Li, J., 226, 228, 230, 337
Li, J. L., 111
Li, M., 183
Li, X., 359
Li, Y., 115, 162, 169, 333
Li, Z., 200
Liang, S., 276
Liben, L. S., 346
Lichenstein, P., 368
Lichtenfeld, S., 323
Lichtenstein, P., 166
Lichtwarck-Aschoff, A., 98
Liddle, H. A., 362
Lieberman, J. A., 361
Lieberman, M. D., 266, 269, 299
Liefeld, C., 318
Liem, G.A.D., 326
Light, J. M., 141
Light, R., 159–160
Lightfoot, M., 312
Lightwood, J., 34
Lillard, A., 54
Lim, C. G., 201
Lin, H., 281
Lin, J., 230
Lin, K., 307
Lin, W., 198
Lindberg, L., 292, 293, 310, 352
Lindberg, L. D., 319
Lindberg, S., 232–233
Lindberg, S. M., 307
Lindenberg, S., 143, 144, 367
Lindenberger, U., 50
Lindentthal, J., 262
Linder, J. R., 288
Lindstrom, R., 275
Linn, E., 306–307
Linver, M. R., 115, 192
Lipperman-Kreda, S., 359
Lippold, M., 161
Lippold, M. A., 98
Lipsey, M., 371
Lipton, R. I., 358
Liston, C., 55
Litrownik, A., 121
Litt, I. F., 203
Little, K. C., 310
Little, S. A., 162

Little, T., 104
Little, T. D., 145
Litwack, S. D., 142
Liu, C., 63
Liu, D., 214
Liu, J., 369
Liu, Y., 93, 119
Livingston, M., 68
Livingston, M. D., 359
Lizotte, A. J., 316, 368
Lobel, O., 232
Lobel, T. E., 232
Lochman, J., 145, 314–315
Lodder, G.M.A., 141
Loeber, R., 108, 139, 350, 364, 366, 367, 371
Loehlin, J. C., 111
Loewenson, P. R., 296
Loftus, J., 285, 295
Logan, J., 376
Logis, H. A., 143
Logue, S., 246–247, 361
Lohman, B. J., 287, 297
Lohr, M., 318
Lohr, M. J., 317
Loken, E., 143
Lollis, S., 146
Lomniczi, A., 16
Lonardo, R. A., 366
Loney, B., 363
Long, J., 16, 75
Long, J. D., 131
Longest, K. C., 189
Longmore, M. A., 280–281, 289, 296, 301, 366
Longo, G. S., 259
Lopez, A. B., 257
Lopez, C., 214
Lopez, C. M., 351
Lopez, E. M., 139
Lopez, S., 196
Lopez-Larson, M., 52
Lopez-Tello, G., 248
Lord, H., 140, 190, 193
Lord, S., 120, 330
Lord, S. E., 161
Lorenz, F., 119
Lorenz, F. O., 116
Lorion, R., 366
Lorr, M., 125
Losoya, S. H., 92
Loth, K., 36
Louden, L., 115
Lougheed, J.P., 9, 26
Loughlin, S., 206
Loughran, T. A., 88, 371
Louis, K., 162
Loukas, A., 98, 161, 169, 171
Lounds Taylor, J., 317
Lovato, C., 361
Lövdén, M., 50
Loveless, T., 168
Low, C., 269, 271, 289
Low, S., 110, 141
Lowe, K., 169, 326, 330
Lowe, S., 90, 276–277
Lowery, B., 367
Lowery, C., 311
Lowry, R., 294
Lu, L. H., 51–52
Lu, T., 259

Lubell, K., 205
Lubienski, C., 168
Lubienski, S. T., 168
Lucas, S., 164, 231
Luciana, M., 49–51, 55, 57
Ludden, A. B., 259, 358
Luder, M. T., 297
Lüdtke, O., 142, 165
Ludwig, J., 91, 366
Luebbe, A. M., 271
Luhmann, M., 213
Lukowski, A. F., 29
Lumeng, J. C., 36
Lun, J., 169
Luna, B., 44, 55–58, 244
Lund, T. J., 91
Lundberg, S., 247
Luo, F., 288
Luo, Q., 106–107, 141
Lupinetti, C., 252
Lussier, P., 368, 370
Luster, T., 303, 308, 309, 316
Luthar, S., 106–107, 323, 329, 332, 359, 378, 379
Luthar, S. S., 91, 143, 191
Lutz, A., 331
Lutz, A. C., 191
Luyckx, K., 218, 223
Luyten, P., 38
Lydon, D. M., 360
Lynam, D., 33, 62
Lynam, D. R., 363
Lynch, A. D., 93, 336
Lyndon, S. T., 149
Lynne-Landsman, S. D., 32, 57, 359
Lyons-Ruth, K., 267
Lytle, L. A., 29, 203

M

Ma, H.-M., 25
Ma, J., 35
Ma, M., 294
Ma, T. L., 242
Määttä, S., 327–328
Maccoby, E., 104, 105, 110–111, 118–119, 135, 273
MacDonald, W., 118
Maciejewski, D. F., 214
Mackesy-Amiti, M. E., 301
Mackey, A. P., 334
Mackey, E. R., 39
MacKinnon-Lewis, C., 227
MacLehose, R. F., 35
MacLellan, S., 67
MacMurray, J. P., 302
MacPherson, L., 93
Madan, A., 138
Madden-Derdich, D., 274
Maddow-Zimet, I., 319
Madkour, A. S., 294, 295, 298, 299, 303
Madon, S., 12, 170
Madsen, S., 262–265
Madsen, S. D., 285
Mager, W., 371
Maggs, J., 30, 82, 194
Magnan, R. E., 297
Magnussen, C., 35

Magnusson, D., 34
Maharaj, S., 137
Mahoney, J., 6, 140, 174, 190–195
Mahoney, J. L., 191
Maïano, C., 215
Maimon, D., 92, 193
Main, M., 267
Makel, M. C., 165
Makin-Byrd, K., 288
Makino, K. K., 314
Malanchuk, O., 216, 329
Maldonado-Molina, M. M., 371
Malone, P., 368
Malone, P. S., 314–315, 359, 371
Malone, S. M., 351
Malti, T., 63
Manchikanti Gómez, A., 288
Mandara, J., 108, 114, 217, 227, 326
Manera, V., 16
Manhart, L. E., 319
Manlove, J., 294, 310, 311, 315, 317
Mann, E. A., 334–335
Mann, N. C., 40
Mannering, A., 121
Mannes, M., 192
Mannheim, K., 8, 11
Manning, W., 315
Manning, W. D., 279–281, 289, 296, 301, 366
Mannison, M., 285
Manuck, S., 24
Marbell, K. N., 330
Marceau, K., 102
Marcia, J., 223
Marcoen, A., 45
Marcoulides, G. A., 324
Marcus, D. K., 363
Marcus, S., 8, 378
Marczak, M., 100
Marecek, J., 135
Marelich, W., 312
Margola, D., 328
Margolin, G., 102, 115
Marin, B. V., 285
Marinelli, M., 361
Mariner, C., 317
Marino, R., 87
Marion, D., 151, 332
Markey, C., 202
Markey, C. N., 206
Markey, P., 202
Markey, P. M., 206
Markham, C., 281
Markiewicz, D., 267–268, 285
Marks, A. K., 228, 230
Marks, H. M., 174
Markstrom, C., 5, 77, 79, 80, 82, 225, 228–229
Markstrom-Adams, C., 212
Markus, H., 210, 211
Mark Viner, R., 40
Marmorstein, N. R., 351
Marold, D., 212
Marrero, M., 108, 240
Marrero, M. D., 240
Marsee, M. A., 268
Marsh, H., 164, 165, 188, 215
Marsh, H. W., 165, 188, 215, 326–327

Marsh, P., 143, 240, 267, 268
Marshal, M. P., 308
Marshall, J., 121
Marshall, S. L., 218
Marshall, W., 18, 22
Marsiglia, F., 234
Marsiglia, F. F., 103, 228, 356, 359
Marston, E., 138, 265
Marston, E. G., 108
Martel, M. M., 351
Marti, C. N., 36
Martin, A., 303
Martin, A. J., 326
Martin, D., 194, 299
Martin, G., 376
Martin, J., 105
Martin, M., 6, 97, 98, 105–107, 229
Martin, M. J., 116
Martin, P., 229, 230
Martin, S., 287
Martin, S. L., 285
Martinez, A., 218
Martinez, C. R., Jr., 101
Martinez, M., 63
Martínez, M., 240
Martínez, M. L., 97
Martino, S. C., 200, 301
Martin-Storey, A., 288, 308
Marttunen, M., 31
Maslowsky, J., 28, 29, 350
Mason, C., 139, 331, 333
Mason, C. A., 140
Mason, D. M., 369
Mason, W., 218–219
Mason, W. A., 102, 140
Mason-Singh, A., 8
Massoglia, M., 371
Masten, A., 75, 280, 351, 379
Masten, A. S., 213
Masten, C., 247
Masten, C. L., 27, 45, 59, 230, 266
Masyn, K., 368
Masyn, K. E., 376
Mata, J., 251
Matas, L., 265
Mathiesen, K. S., 377
Mathieson, L. C., 147
Matjasko, J., 191
Matjasko, J. L., 183, 184, 298–299
Matricciani, L., 28
Matsuba, M. K., 253
Matsueda, R. L., 66
Matsui, M., 54
Matthews, K., 93
Matthews, M., 323
Mattingly, M. J., 89
Mattison, E., 336
Matusiewicz, A., 374
Matusko, N., 33–34
Maughan, B., 31, 351
Maulana, R., 331
Mauras, C. P., 242
Maxwell, E. C., 52
Maxwell, S., 316
Maxwell K., 162
Mayberry, M. L., 180
Mayers, R., 256
Mayes, L. C., 265
Mayeux, L., 143, 144, 286
Mays, D., 192, 359
Mayseless, O., 106–107, 267

Mbzivo, M., 299
McAdams, T., 351
McAloney, K., 93
McAnally, H. M., 202
McAuley, E., 203
McAuley, T., 50
McBride, C. K., 300
McBride-Chang, C., 308
McCabe, M., 36
McCabe, M. P., 37, 39
McCabe, S. E., 354
McCaffree, K., 310
McCartan, C., 93
McCarthy, J., 317
McCarthy, K., 120
McCarthy, W. J., 359
McCarty, C. A., 350, 378
McClelland, S. I., 291, 292–293, 297
McClintock, M., 15, 24, 291
McClure, E., 101
McClure, S., 244
McClure-Tone, E., 58, 374
McCord, J., 140
McCormick, S., 29
McCoy, J., 109
McCoy, K. P., 116
McCrae, R., 212, 213
McCrystal, P., 93
McCullough, M. E., 259
McCutcheon, J. E., 361
McDaniel, B., 64, 107
McDaniel, D. D., 376
McDonald, J. A., 294
McDonald, R. M., 108–109
McDougall, P., 147
McElhaney, K., 7, 109, 143, 144, 236–241, 262–263, 265, 267, 268
McElhaney, K. B., 240, 265, 267
McFarland, C., 240, 267
McFarland, F., 143
McFarland, F. C., 246, 268
McGee, R. O., 213
McGill, R. K., 227
McGinley, K., 352
McGloin, J., 141
McGloin, J. M., 138, 141, 246
McGrady, P. B., 170
McGue, M., 102, 110, 111, 115, 258, 331, 370–371
McGuigan, K., 362
McGuire, S., 111
McHale, J. P., 228
McHale, S., 100, 103, 104, 109, 111, 135, 161, 174, 192, 232, 233, 248, 277
McHale, S. M., 110, 123, 127, 191, 193, 227–230, 232, 234, 248, 300, 326
McIsaac, C., 274, 279, 280, 281, 283–287
McIssac, C., 7
McKee, S. A., 350
McKenney, K., 283
McKenney, S. J., 234
McKinney, C., 106
McKinney, J., 248
McKinney, K., 32
McKone, K. M., 24
McLachlan, K., 78
McLanahan, S., 118, 315–316, 334
McLaughlin, B., 176

McLaughlin, K., 87
McLaughlin, K. A., 149, 377–378
McLean, K., 219, 225, 261, 274
McLean, K. C., 219
McLean, S. A., 37
McLellan, J. A., 90
McLoyd, V., 88, 89, 92, 93, 119
McLoyd, V. C., 94, 189, 334
McMahon, R. J., 363
McMahon, S., 259
McMahon, S. D., 94
McMahon, T., 332
McMaster, L., 285, 307
McMorris, B., 299
McMorris, B. J., 87
McNamara, G., 357
McNeely, C., 108, 121, 293, 301
McNelles, L., 268, 271, 272
McNulty, J. K., 310
McNulty, T., 367
McNulty, T. L., 91, 303
McPhie, M. L., 35
McRae, C., 116
McRee, A. L., 293
McRee, N., 31
McRitchie, S. L., 35, 203
McRoy, R. G., 120
McShane, L., 49
Mead, M., 11, 85
Meade, C., 302
Meadows, S. O., 373
Meares, H., 335
Mecklinger, A., 49
Medeiros, B. L., 107, 117
Mednick, S., 369
Meece, D., 194
Meerkerk, G., 204
Meesters, C., 374
Meeus, W., 213, 220, 223, 224–225, 275, 281, 293, 300
Meeus, W. H., 133
Meeus, W.H.J., 102, 103, 129, 273–274, 377
Mega, C., 323
Mehari, K. R., 147
Mehta, C., 127–128, 135
Mehta, T. G., 218
Meier, A., 107–108
Meier, A. M., 297
Meier, M., 92
Meijer, A. M., 370–371
Meijer, S., 293, 300
Mekos, D., 112
Melanson, S., 332
Melby, J., 335
Melching, J. A., 240
Melde, C., 138, 139
Meldrum, R. C., 29
Melkevik, O., 213
Mello, Z. R., 346
Mellor, R., 311
Meltzoff, A., 325
Memmert, D., 48
Menaghan, E., 302
Menard, S., 352
Mendle, J., 22, 24, 25, 30, 33, 297–299, 302, 377
Mendoza-Denton, R., 150
Menezes, I., 254
Mennecke, B., 219–220
Menning, C. L., 117

Menon, M., 233–234
Menzer, M. M., 148
Menzies, L., 55
Mercer, D., 361
Mercy, J., 41
Mereish, E. H., 308
Merikangas, K., 372
Merikangas, K. R., 349, 372
Mermelstein, R. J., 373
Merrick, S., 266–267
Merskin, D., 30
Merten, D., 144
Mesch, G. S., 135
Meschke, L. L., 300
Messersmith, E., 174, 188, 342
Metselaar, M., 308
Metzger, A., 103
Metzler, C. W., 149
Meuwese, R., 253
Meyer, A. L., 352
Meyer, I.H., 308
Meyer, J. R., 245
Mezulis, A. H., 374, 377
Mheen, D., 204
Michael, A., 329
Michaud, P., 312
Michl, L. C., 377
Michou, A., 324
Mickelson, R., 324, 336
Mickus, M., 276
Midgley, C., 161–163, 324, 331
Miech, R., 353, 355
Miech, R. A., 34–35
Miernicki, M. E., 269
Miers, A. C., 58
Miguel, S. S., 246
Mihalic, S., 189
Mikami, A., 169, 198, 205
Mikami, A. Y., 204
Miklikowska, M., 107
Milam, A., 93
Milan, S., 315
Milbrath, C., 281
Milburn, M., 338
Miles, B., 121
Milich, R., 371
Millar, R., 16
Miller, A. B., 376
Miller, B., 165, 166, 300–302
Miller, C. F., 233–234
Miller, D., 66
Miller, D. I., 52
Miller, D. P., 52, 107–108, 294
Miller, E., 287
Miller, J., 193, 287
Miller, J. D., 330, 335
Miller, K., 120, 247, 301, 302
Miller, K. S., 302
Miller, L., 256
Miller, M., 302
Miller, N., 80, 85
Miller, S., 143, 287, 371
Miller, W. C., 293
Miller, X., 316
Miller-Johnson, S., 314–315
Mills, B., 65, 66
Mills, C., 328
Mills, K. L., 45, 57, 58, 205
Mills, M., 115, 302
Millsap, R., 281
Millsap, R. E., 33

Millstein, S., 65, 304
Millstein, S. G., 312
Milne, B. J., 370
Milnitsky-Sapiro, C., 98
Minchin, J., 149
Minguez, M., 318
Mirabell, J., 29
Mireles-Rios, R., 248, 311
Mistry, R. S., 120, 171, 330
Mitchell, C., 217, 357
Mitchell, J., 203
Mitchell, J. A., 29
Mitchell, K., 117, 205
Mitchell, K. J., 203–205, 229–230
Mitchell, K. S., 118
Miu, A., 200
Miu, A. S., 147, 369–370
Miyawaki, T., 54
Mizuno, K., 48
Mocan, N., 314
Modecki, K. L., 67, 149, 245
Modell, J., 73, 74, 86
Moe, S. G., 29
Moffitt, T., 33, 212, 351, 352, 365, 367–368, 370, 371
Moffitt, T. E., 213, 316, 351, 370
Mohr, P., 36
Moilanen, K., 162, 297
Moilanen, K. L., 369
Molano, A., 138
Molgora, S., 328
Molina, B., 29
Molina, B.S.G., 359
Molina G., 314
Molinari, L., 29
Mollen, C. J., 310
Möller, I., 201
Molloy, L. E., 131, 214, 239, 278
Molnar, B. E., 94
Monahan, K., 16, 66, 92, 132, 141, 162, 187, 188–189, 198, 200, 246, 247, 297, 369, 370–371, 379
Monahan, K. C., 29, 93, 145, 175, 189, 253, 286, 350, 369
Monck, E., 274
Mond, J., 215
Moneta, G., 98, 193, 213
Monroe, S. M., 286, 378
Monshouwer, K., 351, 376
Monsour, A., 211
Montgomery, K., 207
Montgomery, M., 279
Montgomery, M. J., 279, 280, 282–283, 308
Montgomery, S., 120
Montoro, R., 305
Moody, J., 136, 278
Mooijaart, A., 266
Moon, U. J., 205, 331
Moore, K., 295, 317
Moore, K. A., 191, 318
Moore, M., 176
Moore, M. R., 116
Moore, S., 30, 145, 324
Moore, S. C., 369
Moore, S. R., 30, 298
Moore, W., 59
Moore, W., III, 247
Moos, R., 169
Moran, P., 363

More, D., 204
Morgan, A. S., 373
Morgan, M., 198
Morgan, S. P., 317
Morgano, E., 138
Mori, I., 337
Morin, A.J.S., 215, 341
Morisi, T., 184
Morisky, D. E., 295
Morris, A., 7, 64, 107, 237, 249, 252, 253
Morris, A. K., 44, 48
Morris, J. E., 194
Morris, M. C., 378
Morris, N., 21
Morrison, D., 311
Morrison, G. M., 246
Morrison Gutman, L., 108
Morrow, B., 310
Morrow, J., 38–39
Mortelmans, D., 117, 119
Mortimer, J., 88, 186, 187
Mory, M., 128
Moses, A., 366
Mosher, W., 314
Mosteller, F., 159–160
Motl, R. W., 203
Mott, F., 302
Mott, F. L., 131, 317
Motti-Stefanidi, F., 227
Moua, M., 227
Mounts, N., 134, 139, 248, 332
Mounts, N. S., 117, 137
Mouratidis, A., 324
Mouw, T., 136
Mowen, T. J., 139
Mrug, S., 109, 138, 141, 278
Mucci, L. A., 287
Mueller, A.S., 376
Muhleman, D., 302
Muhlenbruck, L, 180
Muise, A. M., 37
Mukherjee, P., 136
Mulgrew, K. E., 206
Mulhall, P., 169
Mulkeen, P., 274
Muller, C., 115
Müller, C. M., 138
Mulvey, E., 176, 246, 247, 368, 369
Mulvey, E. P., 88, 363, 369
Mulvey, K. L., 64, 234
Mun, E. Y., 350
Munakata, Y., 244
Munfakh, J., 205
Munniksma, A., 136
Muñoz, L. C., 93
Munsch, J., 276
Munson, S., 34
Murayama, K., 323, 324
Murdock, K. K., 205
Murdock, T., 162, 332
Murphy, B., 253
Murphy, B. C., 252
Murphy, D. A., 299
Murray, C. B., 114
Murray, D., 36
Murray, K. W., 104, 242
Murry, V., 31
Musick, J., 318
Musick, K., 107–108
Must, A., 23

Mustanski, B. S., 23
Mustard, C., 90
Mustillo, S. A., 285
Myers, J., 262
Myers, M. W., 371
Mylod, D., 316

N

Nadeem, E., 31, 90, 337
Nader, P., 203
Nader, P. R., 35, 203
Nagaoka, J., 334
Nagel, B. J., 52, 55
Nagengast, B., 165, 188, 215, 324
Nagin, D., 107, 370
Nagoshi, J. L., 103, 228, 356
Nagy, G., 324, 330
Nair, R. L., 93, 119
Nakaue, M., 240
Namerow, P., 317
Nangle, D. W., 264, 282
Nansel, T. R., 148, 193
Nappo, S. A., 359
Nash, K., 186
Nasir, N. S., 325
Nasrallah, N. A., 361
Nation, M., 41, 254
Natriello, G., 179
Natsuaki, M., 373, 374
Natsuaki, M. N., 23, 24, 31, 32, 285
Neal, J., 143
Neblett, E., 230
Neblett, E. W., 142–143
Neblett, E., Jr., 88, 227
Needham, B., 34–35, 137, 141
Needham, B. L., 308
Neemann, J., 280, 281, 285
Negriff, S., 24, 31–34, 369
Neiderhiser, J., 112, 374
Neiderhiser, J. M., 23, 110, 111
Neighbors, B., 115
Neilands, T.B., 93
Nejad, H. G., 326
Nelemans, S., 7, 214
Nelson, C., 58
Nelson, C. A., 53
Nelson, E., 58, 82, 101, 374
Nelson, E. E., 58, 246
Nelson, I. A., 183
Nelson, J. A., 266
Nelson, L. J., 224, 258
Nelson, S., 108, 140
Nelson-Mmari, K., 40
Neppl, T. K., 259
Nesbit, K. C., 36
Neubauer, S. A., 131
Neuenschwander, M., 344
Neumann, D. L., 325
Neumark-Sztainer, D., 35, 36, 38, 39, 206, 215, 307
Newcomb, A., 271
Newcomb, A. F., 283
Newcomb, M., 361
Newman, B., 8, 132
Newman, D., 30
Newman, D. L., 225
Newman, J. P., 370–371
Newman, P., 8, 132
Newman, R., 326

Newmann, F., 174
Newsome, J., 368
Ng-Mak, D., 93
Nguyen, D. T., 115
Nguyen, H., 246
Nguyên, H., 227
Nguyen, H.N.T., 285
Nguyen, J., 226
Nicolai, K. A., 377
Nicotra, E., 145
Nieri, T., 359
Nies, K. M., 141
Nilsson, K. W., 198
Niolon, P. H., 288
Nishina, A., 19, 145, 147, 149, 167, 174, 227
Niwa, E. Y., 216, 229
Nixon, C. L., 146
Nixon, E., 38
Noack, P., 326
Noah, A. J., 294
Noakes, M. A., 272
Noble, K. G., 55
Nock, M. K., 375
Nock, S., 315
Noguchi, K., 54
Noguera, P., 174
Noh, A., 324
Nolen-Hoeksema, S., 377
Nolle, K., 174
Noller, P., 274
Norberg, K. E., 361
Norman, T., 247
Norona, J. C., 265
Norton, E., 143
Nosko, A., 267
Noto, A. R., 359
Nottelmann, E., 352
Notter, O., 149
Noussair, C., 145
Novaira, H., 14
Novak, S. P., 41, 359
Nov-Krispin, N., 232
Ntoumanis, N., 192
Nucci, L., 98, 240
Nucci, M. S., 98
Nuñez, A., 177
Nurius, P., 210
Nurmi, J., 210, 224, 324, 327–328
Nurmi, J. E., 141, 327–328, 332
Nurmi, J.-E., 225
Nyalakanti, P. K., 369
Nygård, C., 28
Nylund, K., 145
Nylund-Gibson, K., 227

O

Oakes, J., 163, 164
Oakley, D., 310
Obama, B., 156–157
Obeidallah, D., 33
Obradović, J., 75
O'Brien, L., 67, 246
O'Brien, M., 35, 110, 203
Obsuth, I., 267
O'Callaghan, M., 316
Ochner, C., 37
O'Connell, D., 352
O'Connor, A. R., 57

O'Connor, K., 325
O'Connor, T., 105, 115, 268
Odgers, C. L., 93
O'Donnell, M., 344
Oelsner, J., 161
Oesterle, S., 350
Oetting, E. R., 335
Oettinger, G., 188
Offer, S., 108
Ofner, S., 312
Ogawa, J. R., 266
Ogbu, J., 134, 336
Ogden, C., 34
Ogle, J. P., 37
Ogletree, M. D., 29
Ohannessian, C., 276
O'Hara, R. E., 200
O'Hare, E. D., 51–52
Ohlson, B., 281
Ojanen, T., 218
Okazaki, S., 225, 336
Okdie, B. M., 205
O'Keefe, G., 204
Okeke-Adeyanju, N., 327, 329–330
Olatokun, W., 204
Olatunji, A. N., 189
Oldehinkel, A. J., 272, 374–375
Olds, T., 28
Olds, T. S., 183
O'Leary, K. D., 287
Olfson, M., 372, 373
Olfson M., 8, 378
Olino, T. M., 57
Oliva, A., 240
Oliver, B. R., 31
Oliver, P. H., 324
O'Loughlin, J., 358
Olsen, E.O., 197
Olsen, J., 108
Olson, C. K., 201
Olson, L., 189, 342
Olszewski-Kubilius, P., 165
Olvera, N., 37
Olweus, D., 147
O'Malley, P. M., 355
O'Malley, P., 75, 193, 353, 355, 358, 359, 362, 371
O'Malley, P. M., 188
Oman, R. F., 359
Onatsu, T., 324
O'Neal, C. W., 36
Onghena, P., 242
Opaleye, E. S., 359
Op de Macks, Z., 17
Opdenakker, M. C., 331
Oppenheimer, C. W., 107
Oransky, M., 135
Orbell, S., 310, 311
Orcutt, H. K., 351, 376
Ordaz, S., 58
Ordaz, S. J., 55
Orlando, M., 360
Ormel, J., 144, 272, 367, 374–375
Ormrod, R. K., 150
Orobio de Castro, B., 254
Orpinas, P., 285, 287
Orr, D., 292, 351
Orr, M., 318, 319
Ortega, F. B., 35
Orth, U., 213–214, 217, 218
Ortiz, J., 351

Orue, I., 377
Orwin, R., 354–355
Oser, F., 45
Osgerby, B., 74, 182, 206
Osgood, D. W., 4, 103, 112, 131, 141, 144, 185, 188, 194, 213–214, 233, 256, 346, 370, 371
Oshri, A., 351
Oslak, S., 38, 287
Ostaszewski, K., 358
O'Sullivan, L. F., 281–282, 293
Oswald, H., 304, 305
Oswald, T., 36, 247
Osypuk, T. L., 91
Otsuki-Clutter, M., 108, 225, 227, 228, 230
Ott, M. A., 312
Ott, M. Q., 305
Ou, S. R., 254
Oudekerk, B., 143
Oudekerk, B. A., 239
Overbeek, G., 266, 284, 299
Overpeck, M. D., 31, 193
Overstreet, S., 94
Owen, L., 104
Owen, M. T., 266
Owen-Kostelnik, J., 245
Owens, A., 167
Oxford, M. L., 317
Oyserman, D., 211, 318, 336
Ozcan, M., 188
Özdemir, S. B., 307
Ozer, E., 40, 41, 308, 311–312
Ozer, E. J., 28, 313

P

Pabian, S., 149
Pabon, E., 139
Paciello, M., 252, 288
Padgett, J., 216
Padilla, A. M., 337
Padilla, B., 218
Padilla-Walker, L., 98, 201, 276
Padilla-Walker, L. M., 81, 107, 110, 201, 204, 252, 323
Padilla-Walker, L. P., 119
Padmanabhan, A., 44, 58, 244
Page, M., 89
Page-Gould, E., 150
Pagels, N. E., 360
Pahl, K., 136, 227
Paikoff, R., 27, 29, 291, 301, 318
Paikoff, R. L., 300
Pajer, K., 369
Palardy, G., 179
Palladino, G., 74
Pallas, A., 179
Pallock, L., 115
Palmgren, C., 64–65
Pampel, F. C., 354
Pancer, S. M., 254
Panchaud, C., 311
Papadakis, A. A., 264
Papadakis, S., 36
Papillo, A., 317
Papillo, A. R., 191
Papp, L. M., 116
Paradis, G., 358
Pardini, D., 350

Pardini, D. A., 108, 139, 363, 371
Parekh, J., 318
Parent, S., 17
Parente, M., 194
Park, A., 359
Park, M. J., 38, 40
Parker, A., 65
Parker, J., 144, 262, 269, 271, 288–289
Parker, K., 84, 87
Parker, K. F., 90
Parker, P. D., 141, 218, 334
Parker, S., 205
Parkes, A., 298–299
Parkin, C. M., 63
Parra, A., 240
Parsai, M., 103, 228, 356, 359
Pascarella, E., 225
Pasch, K. E., 29, 171
Paschall, M. J., 358
Paskewitz, D., 379
Paskwich, B. S., 143
Pasley, K., 100
Pastore, M., 138
Pastorelli, C., 326
Pasupathi, M., 110, 252
Patall, E. A., 326
Patchin, J. W., 149
Pate, R., 203
Pateman, B., 294
Paten, S., 377
Paternoster, R., 246, 341
Pati, C., 106–107
Patrick, M. E., 356
Patten, C. A., 29
Patterson, C., 335
Patterson, C. J., 120, 306
Patterson, G., 368–369
Patterson, G. R., 98, 371
Patton, D. U., 149
Patton, F., 228, 230
Patton, G. C., 171, 350, 373
Patton, W., 285
Pauletti, R., 232
Paulsen, D. J., 44, 244
Paus, T., 51, 52, 54, 55, 58, 60
Paus T., 247
Paxton, S., 38
Paxton, S. J., 37
Payne, A., 171
Payne, K. K., 279
Payne, P. A., 29
Paysnick, A. A., 90
Pea, R., 198
Peake, S. J., 62, 214
Pearce, M. J., 107
Pearce, N., 196
Pearl, R., 143
Pears, K., 104, 314–315
Pearson, J., 308
Pechmann, C., 206
Peck, S. C., 172
Peckins, M., 369
Pedersen, S., 87, 130–131, 135, 145, 146, 183, 278
Peebles, R., 203
Pehlivantürk, B., 267
Pekrun, R., 323, 330
Pellegrini, A. D., 131, 277
Pellerin, L. A., 169
Pelletier, L., 326

Penner, E., 78
Peper, J. S., 55, 244
Pepler, D., 239, 278, 281–283, 307
Pepler, D. J., 281
Pepper, J. S., 57
Pepper, M., 262
Percy, A., 93
Perez-Brena, N. J., 228, 274
Perez-Febles, A., 316
Perilla, J., 330
Perius, J. G., 149
Perkins, D., 192, 303, 308
Perkins, D. D., 92, 169
Perkins, S. A., 98, 240, 249
Perreira, K., 226
Perron, B.E., 259
Perry, A. A., 38–39
Perry, B., 141
Perry, C., 106–107, 358, 362
Perry, C. L., 36
Perry, D., 232, 234
Perry, D. G., 218
Perry, R. P., 379
Perry, T., 268, 269
Persike, M., 273
Persson, A., 191
Peter, J., 200, 204, 272
Petersen, A., 32
Petersen, A. C., 217
Petersen, I. T., 377
Petersen, J. L., 307
Petersen, S., 57
Peterson, C., 323
Peterson, J., 41
Peterson, J. L., 136, 230
Peterson, K., 311
Peterson, P., 360
Peterson-Badali, M., 241
Petraitis, J., 359
Petrie, C., 176
Pettit, G., 62, 108, 146, 194, 369, 371
Pettit, G. S., 118, 242, 266, 288, 298–299, 370–371
Pettit, J., 372
Pexman, P., 46
Peyser, H., 116
Pfeifer, J., 45, 59, 101, 210, 211, 247
Pfeifer, J. H., 59, 62, 214
Phares, V., 36
Phelan, P., 167
Philbin, J. M., 294
Philippe, F. L., 241
Philips, K. J., 147
Philliber, S., 342
Phillips, M. L., 27
Phillipsen, L. C., 268
Phinney, J., 227
Piaget, J., 8, 9, 47–48, 249
Pianta, R., 169
Pianta, R. C., 335
Pickering, S. J., 51
Piehler, T., 127
Piehler, T. F., 140
Pierce, J., 358
Pierce, J. P., 29
Piesse, A., 354–355
Pieters, S., 29
Pietiläinen, K. H., 23
Pike, A., 111
Pilgrim, C., 106–107

Pimentel, E., 186
Pinderhughes, E., 120
Pine, D., 58, 101, 368, 374
Pine, D. S., 58, 369
Pingel, E. S., 300
Pinquart, M., 240–241
Pintrich, P., 326, 328
Piquero, A., 139, 364, 367
Piquero, A. P., 364
Piquero, A. R., 92, 369, 371
Piran, N., 307
Pittard, W., 316
Plaisier, X. S., 149
Planty, M., 254–255
Plata, M., 330
Plomin, R., 105, 115, 368, 369
Pogarsky, G., 316
Polanin, J. R., 141
Pollack, C., 29
Pollack, H., 316
Pollack, S., 56
Pollak, S. D., 56
Pollard, M. S., 141
Pomerantz, E., 241, 248, 324, 325, 330
Pomerantz, E. M., 46, 108, 241, 248, 330
Pomerantz, E.M., 331
Pomery, E., 106–107
Pong, S., 115, 328, 330
Pong, S. L., 337
Ponnet, K., 117, 119
Poorthuis, A., 7, 214
Poorthuis, A.M.G., 325
Poper, D. C., 173
Poropat, A. E., 323
Porter, M., 143, 240, 267
Porter, M. R., 246
Porter, R., 369
Porter, S., 363
Poteat, P. V., 308
Poteat, V. P., 308
Potkin, K. T., 29
Poulin, F., 108, 130–131, 135, 140–142, 145, 183, 192, 273, 278
Poulos, G., 330
Power, J., 57
Power, T., 215, 246, 357
Powers, J., 147, 308, 369–370
Powers, S. I., 374
Pozen, D., 138
Pozzoli, T., 150
Pradhan, A. K., 67
Prado, G., 228, 312
Pratt, M. W., 224, 267
Presnell, K., 36
Pressler, E., 118
Presson, C., 359
Preusser, D., 40
Pribesh, S., 170
Price, C. D., 36, 192
Price, C. L., 164
Price, M. N., 297
Priebe, G., 203–2004
Priess, H., 232–233
Prindiville, S., 214
Prinstein, M., 133, 134, 141, 247
Prinstein, M. J., 133–134, 141, 142–144, 146, 247, 272, 278, 286, 293, 302, 375, 376

Prinzie, P., 108, 212, 242
Proctor, L., 121
Proescher, E., 379
Pronk, R., 146
Prossinger, H., 299
Prot, S., 198
Pruessner, J., 56
Pryor, J., 171, 276
Prystowsky, A., 35
Puddy, R. W., 121
Puelo, C., 349
Pulkkinen, L., 23, 368–369
Punamäki, R., 28, 106–107
Pungello, E., 335
Purcell, A., 310
Purdie, N., 326
Purtell, K. M., 92, 189
Purwono, U., 258, 259
Putallaz, M., 165, 275
Putnam, F., 308
Putnick, D. L., 240
Pyrooz, D. C., 139

Q

Qian, Z., 336
Qin, D., 101, 136, 226
Qin, L., 241, 248
Qouta, S., 106–107
Qu, Y., 46, 66–67, 108, 246
Quadrel, M., 46
Quasem, S., 352
Quatman, T., 325
Quillian, L., 136, 137
Quinn, P. D., 66, 156
Quinn, T., 370
Quiroga, C. V., 341
Quittner, A., 40

R

Raabe, T., 135, 137
Raaijmakers, Q., 213, 224, 254
Raby, K. L., 266
Racer, K. H., 323
Racine, Y., 90, 356
Radin, N., 318
Radmacher, K., 271, 272
Raffaelli, M., 269, 271, 272, 275,
    276, 297, 301, 379
Raftery-Helmer, J. N., 330
Ragsdale, B. L., 217
Raiford, J. L., 304
Raine, A., 351, 369
Raj, A., 287
Raley, R. K., 281
Ralston, E., 140
Ram, N., 102, 214
Ramanan, J., 194
Rambaran, J. A., 141
Ramchand, R., 188
Ramey, C., 334, 335
Ramey, H. L., 195
Ramirez, C., 344
Ramos, D., 92
Ramos, J., 257
Ramsden, S., 60
Randall, B. A., 253
Randall, E. T., 191, 330

Randall, G. K., 140
Randel, B., 327
Randel, J., 287
Rankin, L. A., 82
Ranney, J. D., 204–205
Rao, P., 141
Rapee, R., 39
Rapee, R. M., 141
Raphaelson, Y. E., 93
Rasmussen, M., 361
Rassart, J., 223
Ratelle, C., 330
Rauch, K., 125
Raudenbusch, S., 92
Raudenbush, S. W., 41
Raudino, A., 266
Rauer, A. J., 288
Rauscher, K. J., 187
Ravitch, D., 155, 179
Rawana, J. S., 35, 373
Raymond, M., 117
Rayner, K. E., 141
Raynor, S. R., 116
Raznahan, A., 52
Ready, D. D., 159, 160
Ream, G., 231, 301
Ream, R., 332
Reardon, S. F., 41
Rebellon, C. J., 98, 371
Recchia, H., 110
Recchia, H. E., 63, 252
Reckdenwald, A., 90
Reddy, R., 161, 169
Redlich, A., 78
Reed, J., 228
Rees, D. I., 310
Reese, E., 49
Reeslund, K., 378, 379
Reeves, P. M., 285
Regnier, M., 254–255
Reich, K., 45
Reich, S., 204, 269
Reichhardt, T., 202
Reid, G., 298–299
Reid, J. B., 350
Reid, L., 316, 317
Reidy, D. E., 288
Reijneveld, S., 92
Reijntjes, A., 253
Reilly, D., 325
Reinders, H., 254
Reiner, S., 367
Reinke, W. M., 350
Reiser, L., 30
Reiss, D., 23, 111, 374
Reiter, E., 30
Reitz, A. K., 227
Remer, L. G., 359
Renaud, O., 210
Rendell, P. G., 206
Renk, K., 106
Repetti, R., 108
Repinski, D., 150
Repovš, G., 60
Reppucci, N., 90
Reppucci, N. D., 244, 245, 367
Reshef-Kfir, Y., 66
Resko, S. M., 359
Resnick, M., 293, 314
Resnick, M. D., 296
Rest, J., 251

Restrepo, A., 114
Reuman, D., 164
Revenson, T. A., 328
Revenson, T. A., 328
Reyes, B., 218
Reyes, B. T., 110
Reyes, H. L., 288, 307–308
Reyes, M. R., 169
Reyes, O., 335
Reyna, V., 65–67
Reynolds, A., 334–335
Reynolds, A. J., 161, 254
Reynolds, B., 244
Reynolds, B. M., 30, 32
Reynolds, E., 93
Reynolds, J. L., 230
Reynolds, J. R., 170, 334
Rhew, I., 350
Rhew, I. C., 350
Rhodes, J., 90, 161, 276–277,
    318, 338
Rhodes, J. E., 90, 169
Ricard, R., 273
Ricardo, I., 302
Ricciardelli, L. A., 37, 39
Rice, K., 274
Rice, L., 331
Rich, L. M., 188
Rich, Y., 346
Richard, P., 141
Richards, J. M., 102
Richards, M., 39, 98, 123, 173, 190,
    274, 277, 278
Richards, M. H., 213, 217
Richardson, B., 41
Richardson, F., 60
Richardson, J., 115
Richardson, R., 317
Richman, S. B., 108
Rickman, A., 3
Rideout, V., 197, 198, 203
Rieffe, C., 253
Rieger, G., 231
Rierdan, J., 30
Riggs, K. J., 43
Riggs, L., 318
Rigney, G., 28
Riina, E. M., 229–230
Rijsdijk, F., 351
Rijsdijk, F. V., 369
Rimpelä, A., 28
Rinaldi, C. M., 272
Rind, B., 309
Rinehart, P., 121
Rinelli, L., 118
Ringwalt, C., 361–362
Ripperger-Suhler, K. G., 169
Risch, S., 119
Ritter, P., 330
Rivas-Drake, D., 227, 228, 230
Rivera, W., 139
Rivers, S., 66
Rivers, S. E., 169
Rizzo, J. A., 19
Roalson, L., 161
Robbins, C., 315
Robbins, M., 205
Robbins, T. W, 57
Roberts, A. L., 94, 234
Roberts, B., 212, 344
Roberts, C. R., 29

Roberts, D., 120, 182, 196–198,
    200–202, 206, 291, 324
Roberts, M., 229
Roberts, R., 225
Roberts, R. E., 29
Roberts, R. M., 29
Robertson, A., 87
Robertson, D. L., 334–335
Robertson, L. A., 202
Robins, G., 36
Robins, R., 212, 213, 344, 351
Robins, R. W., 213–214, 218, 227,
    338
Robinson, M. G., 169
Robinson, N., 218
Robinson, T., 37
Robinson, W. L., 139
Robnett, R.D., 332
Roche, K., 104, 108
Roche, K. M., 93, 227, 248, 330,
    337
Roche, L., 164
Rocheleau, G. C., 189
Rodas, C., 116
Roderick, M., 334
Rodgers, J., 303
Rodgers, K., 215
Rodgers, R. F., 37
Rodkin, P., 143
Rodkin, P. C., 143, 259
Rodriguez, C., 244
Rodriguez, D., 29
Rodriguez, N., 367
Rodriguez, O., 139
Rodriguez, S. A., 274
Roe, K., 198
Roelofs, J., 374
Roelofsma, P., 202
Roenneberg, T., 28
Roesch, R., 78
Roesch, S., 121
Roesch, S. C., 253
Roeser, R., 153, 161–163, 169,
    170, 179, 257, 259, 262, 324,
    328, 330
Roettger, M. E., 369
Roeyers, H., 166
Rogers, J., 314
Rogers, L. O., 230
Rogers, R., 78
Rogosch, F. A., 351, 377
Rohde, P., 36, 286, 372, 376–378
Rohrbach, L., 359
Roisman, G., 370
Roisman, G. I., 189, 266, 285, 351,
    369, 371
Rombouts, S.A.R.B., 49–50
Romeo, R. S., 16, 55
Romer, D., 60, 201, 206, 351
Romero, A. J., 300
Romero, L., 309
Romero, S., 40
Romich, J., 247
Rommelse, N. N., 369
Romo, L., 301
Romo, L. F., 248, 301, 311
Ronconi, L., 323
Rood, L., 374
Rook, K., 276
Roosa, M., 108, 119
Roosa, M. W., 33, 93, 101, 230

Roper, Z. J., 243
Rosario, M., 93, 234, 305, 308
Rose, A., 271–272, 281, 347
Rose, A. J., 146, 262, 269, 271, 272
Rose, C., 230
Rose, J., 359
Rose, R. A., 330
Rose, R. J., 23, 378
Rose, T., 259
Rose-Krasnor, L., 195
Rosen, L. D., 203
Rosenbaum, J. E., 178, 303, 310
Rosenberg, F., 214
Rosenberg, M., 214, 217–218
Rosenbloom, S. R., 171, 175
Rosenblum, G., 27, 38
Rosenthal, D., 248, 293, 305
Rosenthal, N. L., 268
Rosenthal, S., 266–267
Roseth, C. J., 169
Roseweir, A., 16
Rossa, K. R., 29
Rote, W., 62, 262
Rote, W. M., 98
Roth, J., 15, 94, 192
Roth, J. L., 192
Roth, T., 29
Rothen, N., 28
Rotheram-Borus, M., 312
Rothman, E. F., 287
Rouse, C. E., 334
Rowe, C., 87
Rowe, C. L., 362
Rowe, D., 111, 212, 218, 303,
    359–360, 373
Rowe, R., 351
Rowen, J., 112
Rowland, B., 68
Rowley, S., 118, 329–330
Rowley, S. J., 327
Roye, C., 317
Røysamb, E., 377
Rozek, C. S., 330
Rozin, P., 36
Rubia, K., 56
Rubin, D., 49
Rubin, K., 146, 147, 262
Rubin, K. H., 242
Ruchkin, V., 107
Ruck, M., 64, 241, 255
Ruck, M. D., 255
Rudolph, K., 147, 349, 374, 377
Rudolph, K. D., 31, 32, 145, 149,
    150, 266, 375, 377, 378
Rudy, D., 108–109
Rudy, W., 176, 177
Rueger, S. Y., 276
Rueter, M., 102
Ruggieri, R., 267
Ruhl, H., 268
Ruiz, S., 108
Rulison, K. L., 143, 144, 370
Rumbaut, R., 72
Rumberger, R., 179, 330, 332,
    341–342
Runions, K. C., 149
Rusby, J. C., 141, 149
Russell, S., 161, 305, 315, 317
Russell, S. T., 93, 104, 231, 232,
    296, 308
Russotti, J. M., 332

Rust, J., 233
Ruth, G., 4
Ruthig, J. C., 379
Rutland, A., 64
Rutter, M., 105
Ruzic, L., 56
Ryabov, I., 334, 335
Ryan, A. M., 129, 138, 332
Ryan, C., 232
Ryan, J., 121
Ryan, N., 276
Ryan, N. D., 27
Ryan, R. M., 24, 302
Ryan, S., 310, 311
Ryu, S., 186

S

Saarni, L., 28
Sabatelli, R., 241
Sabiston, C. M., 359
Sabuwalla, Z., 378
Sacchitelle, C., 105
Sachs, J., 159–160
Sackett, P. R., 334
Sacks, V. H., 318
Sadek, S., 150
Saewyc, E., 308
Saewyc, E. M., 231, 305, 306, 308
Safron, J., 188
Sagrestano, L., 29
Salafia, E., 39
Salas-Wright, C. P., 259
Salazar, C. F., 330
Salazar, L., 202
Sale, E., 359
Salekin, R. T., 363
Sales, L., 274
Salinger, J. D., 222
Salmela-Aro, K., 141, 325, 332,
    334
Salmivalli, C., 141, 147
Salovey, P., 169
Saltzman, H., 295
Salusky, I., 195, 196
Salvatore, J. F., 265
Salzer Burks, V., 370
Salzinger, S., 93
Samant, S., 318
Samarova, V., 308
Samdal, O., 207
Samek, D. R., 110
Samela-Aro, K., 4
Sameroff, A., 329
Sameroff, A. J., 108
Sampson, R., 91, 92, 366, 367
Sánchez, B., 90
Sanchez, Z. M., 359
Sánchez-Queija, I., 240
Sanders, L., 115
Sandfort, J., 317
Sandfort, T., 306
Sandfort, T. G., 308
Sandstrom, M. J., 143
Santelli, J., 92, 292, 293, 310, 319
Santelli, J. S., 318
Santiago, D. C., 337
Santinello, M., 92, 169, 254
Santo, J. B., 217
Santor, D., 363

Saporito, S., 168
Sarent, J. D., 200
Sargent, J., 247
Sargent, J. D., 202
Sarraj, E., 106–107
Sarwer, D. B., 36
Sauer, J. D., 205
Saunders, B. E., 351
Saunders, J., 326
Savage, J. C., 369
Savaya, R., 308
Savin-Williams, R., 7, 214, 231,
    262, 269, 284, 291–294,
    296–301, 304–306, 308
Savin-Williams, R. C., 231, 232,
    297
Savolainen, J., 350–352
Sawalani, G. M., 145
Sawyer, A. M., 371
Saxbe, D. E., 115
Saxon, J. L., 325
Scabini, E., 103
Scales, P., 192
Scanlan, L., 193
Scanlan, T., 193
Schad, M., 138
Schad, M. M., 143, 242, 265, 267
Schaefer, D. R., 36, 141, 192
Schaefer-Rohleder, L., 87
Schaible, L. M., 93
Schallert, D. L., 324
Scharf, M., 106–107, 110, 280
Scheepers, F. E., 369
Scheer, J. R., 308
Scheib, E., 149
Scheier, L., 219, 357
Schelar, E., 311
Schelleman-Offermans, K., 31
Scheres, A., 66, 243
Scherf, K., 59
Scherf, K. S., 59
Schiff, A., 29
Schiller, D., 232
Schiller, K., 162, 164
Schilling, E. A., 358
Schindler, H. S., 104, 107, 108
Schlaggar, B., 57
Schlegel, A., 3, 71, 80
Schlomer, G. L., 111, 300
Schmeelk-Cone, K. H., 229
Schmid, C., 269
Schmidt, J., 218, 254
Schmidt, J. A., 254, 336
Schmidt, M. G., 244
Schmiedek, F., 50
Schmiege, S. J., 297
Schmitz, K. H., 29
Schmitz, M. F., 103
Schnabelrauch, C. A., 259
Schneider, B., 164, 192, 344,
    346–347
Schneiders, J., 27
Schniering, C. A., 141
Schnurr, M. P., 287
Schoenmakers, T., 198
Schoeny, M. E., 300
Schofield, T. J., 116, 259
Scholes-Balog, K. E., 350
Scholte, R., 274
Scholte, R. H., 218
Scholte, R. J., 148

Scholte, R.H.J., 141, 148
Schooler, D., 200, 212
Schoon, I., 344
Schouten, A. P., 204
Schrepferman, L., 368
Schroeder, R. D., 139
Schubert, C. A., 88, 363
Schulenberg, J., 29, 75, 76, 174,
    188, 342, 353, 355, 359
Schulenberg, J. E., 162, 348, 350,
    355, 356
Schuler, R., 26–27
Schultz, L., 29
Schultz, P. W., 325
Schuster, M., 194, 299
Schuster, M. A., 301
Schütte, K., 171
Schwab-Stone, M., 253
Schwab-Stone, M. E., 107
Schwager, M., 326
Schwartz, D., 134, 228, 332
Schwartz, J., 366
Schwartz, O., 100
Schwartz, S., 90, 223
Schwartz, S. H., 96
Schwartz, S. J., 223
Schwartz, S.E.O., 90
Schwartz-Mette, R., 271–272
Schwartz-Mette, R. A., 271
Schwarz, B., 116, 121, 266
Schweder, R., 76–77
Schweitzer, J., 244
Scott, E., 70, 71, 78, 79, 245, 364,
    371
Scott, J. T., 38
Scott, L. D., 379
Scott, M., 116, 311
Scott, M. A., 230
Scottham, K., 227
Scovill, L. C., 12
Seamon, E., 92, 108
Sears, H., 30, 82
Seaton, E., 167, 225, 227, 229, 230
Seaton, E. K., 230
Sebastian, C., 45, 210, 247
Secor-Turner, M., 299
Sedgh, G., 312
Seeley, J., 34, 372, 376, 378
Seeley, J. R., 286, 378
Seepersad, S., 184
Seff, M., 100
Segalowitz, S. J., 52, 247
Seghete, K., 56
Séguin, R., 17
Seidl-de-Moura, M. L., 92
Seidman, E., 161, 227
Seiffge-Krenke, I., 45, 212–213,
    267, 268, 271, 273, 284, 379
Seil, K. S., 308
Seitz, V., 317
Selemon, L., 54
Self-Brown, S., 94
Seligman, M.E.P., 323
Sellers, R., 227, 229, 230
Sellers, R. M., 227
Sells, C., 41
Selman, R., 169–170
Selmeczy, D., 57
Senra, C., 39, 352
Sentse, M., 108, 141

Seoane, G., 39, 352
Sepúlveda, J. E., 373
Serna, I., 1634
Serovich, J., 312
Settersten, R., 3, 72
Settipani, C., 349
Sexton, H. R., 316
Shachar-Shapira, L., 116, 288
Shaffer, L., 265
Shanahan, L., 103, 110, 112, 233
Shanahan, M. J., 75, 182–183, 188, 189
Shane, M. S., 62
Shannon, B. J., 369
Shao, T., 63
Shapiro, X., 316
Shapka, J. D., 24
Sharabany, R., 269
Shariff, S., 149
Sharkey, P., 91
Sharma, A., 111
Shattuck, A., 150
Shavelson, R., 210
Shaver, K., 96
Shaw, D., 110, 162
Shaw, D. S., 351, 369
Shaw, H., 34–38
Shaw, P., 60, 166
Shaywitz, B., 165
Shaywitz, S., 165
Shearer, D. L., 317
Shedler, J., 357, 358
Sheehan, H. C., 180
Sheeran, P., 310, 311
Sheikh-Khalil, S., 331
Shek, D., 104
Shelton, J. N., 227
Shelton, K. H., 351
Shen, Y., 104
Shen, Y. L., 252
Shepard, D., 94
Shepard, S. A., 252
Shepherd, K., 377
Sheppard, B., 275
Sher, K. J., 359
Sherdell, L., 17
Sheridan, M., 50
Sherman, L. E., 57
Sherman, S., 359
Shernoff, D. J., 191, 336
Sherrod, L., 90, 253–254
Shi, H., 281
Shields, J., 259
Shiffrin, N., 58, 374
Shih, J. H., 373–374
Shilo, G., 308
Shin, H., 138, 332
Shiner, R. L., 213
Shing, Y. L., 64
Shipman, K., 240
Shirley, A., 312
Shirtcliff, E., 24
Shirtcliff, E. A., 362–363, 369
Shiyko, M. P., 33–34
Sholt, M., 106–107
Shomaker, L. B., 283
Shope, J. T., 351
Shorey, R. C., 287
Shorter, G. W., 204
Shortt, J. W., 110
Shoulberg, E. K., 112

Shoum, K. A., 323
Shuan, Y., 331, 333
Shulman, E., 77
Shulman, E. P., 64, 66, 67, 93, 243, 369
Shulman, S., 7, 109, 110, 116, 269, 270–272, 280, 283, 288
Shults, R. A., 197
Shumow, L., 194, 254, 330, 335
Sibley, M. H., 166, 369
Sickmund, M., 366
Sidtis, J. J., 52
Siebenbruner, J., 285, 298
Siegel, A., 12
Siegel, J., 26–27, 276
Siegel, M., 352, 362
Siegel, R. S., 146, 147
Siegle, G. J., 59
Siegler, R., 50
Siennick, S. E., 193
Sieving, R., 299
Sigler-Rushton, W., 315
Sigman, M., 301, 302
Signorelli, N., 198
Sijtsema, J. J., 141
Silbereisen, R., 31, 33, 85, 87, 88, 240–241, 331
Silk, J., 16, 103, 377, 379
Silk, J. S., 27, 58, 59, 271
Silva, P., 23, 33, 316, 352
Silva, P. A., 213
Silver, E., 188
Silverberg, S., 100, 239–240
Silverman, A., 78
Silverman, J., 287
Silverman, W. K., 378–379
Silvers, J. A., 36
Silverthorn, N., 90
Sim, T., 246
Sim, T. N., 129
Simmens, S., 112
Simmons, J., 100
Simmons, R., 32, 146, 214
Simon, T., 120
Simon, T. R., 287
Simon, V., 265, 280, 282–283
Simon, V. A., 141, 286, 288
Simons, L., 19, 106
Simons, L. G., 116
Simons, R., 19, 31, 32, 92, 119, 139, 303, 307
Simons, R. L., 116, 334
Simons-Morton, B., 40, 66–67, 104, 174, 350, 355
Simpkins, S., 106–107, 174, 192, 326
Simpkins, S. D., 36, 141, 191, 192, 326
Simpson, J. A., 266, 267
Sinclair, K. O., 308
Singer, M., 174
Singh, P., 150
Singh, S., 259, 294, 296, 310–313
Sionéan, C., 301
Sippola, L., 271, 276–278, 283
Sipsma, H., 315
Sirin, S. R., 228
Sirocco, K., 57
Sisk, C. L., 15, 17, 58
Sisson, S. B., 36
Sitnick, S. L., 351

Skalamera, J., 308
Skeem, J., 363
Skeer, M. R., 107–108
Skinner, B. F., 10
Skinner, S. R., 314
Skoog, T., 14, 33, 299, 307
Skorikov, V. B., 343
Skriner, L., 121
Slater, A., 206
Slavick, J. T., 300
Slep, A.M.S., 287
Slomkowski, C., 110
Slopen, N., 234
Sloutsky, V., 44, 48
Slowiaczek, M., 330–331
Slutske, W., 92
Smahel, D., 204, 269
Šmahel, D., 6
Smailes, E., 309
Small, D., 34
Small, S., 303, 309
Smalls, C., 227, 230
Smetana, J., 44, 62–64, 97–98, 103, 107, 108, 114, 237, 240–242, 248, 249, 251, 255, 262, 274
Smetana, J. G., 98, 101, 109, 240
Smiciklas-Wright, H., 19
Smith, A., 247, 293
Smith, A. R., 52, 55, 67, 68, 246, 247
Smith, B., 162
Smith, C., 259, 267, 314–315, 368
Smith, D. C., 246
Smith, D. G., 66
Smith, E., 317
Smith, J., 159, 161, 179, 328
Smith, J. L., 314
Smith, K., 325
Smith, M., 194
Smith, M. V., 308
Smith, P. H., 287, 350
Smith, R., 271–272
Smith, R. L., 271
Smith, S. S., 29
Smith, T., 194
Smith, T. E., 231–234
Smith, T. M., 169
Smith-Bynum, M. A., 229
Smokowski, P., 230
Smokowski, P. R., 227
Smolak, L., 19, 39
Smollar, J., 240, 262
Smoll, F., 19
Snarney, J., 249
Sneed, M., 156
Snell, E. K., 27, 91
Snijders, T.A.B., 141
Snow, D. L., 356
Snyder, H., 366
Snyder, H. R., 244
Snyder, J., 110, 368
Sobesky, W., 252
Sobolewski, J. M., 115, 116
Soenens, B., 38, 98, 107, 223, 239, 242, 324
Sohoni, D., 168
Sokolik, E., 325
Solis, J. S., 204
Soller, B., 141
Solmeyer, A. R., 110
Solomon, R., 318

Somerville, L. H., 45, 50, 58, 246
Sommers, C., 325
Somsen, R., 50
Song, J., 331
Song, X., 285
Sonneville, K. R., 39
Sonntag, K. C., 360
Sontag, L., 8, 349, 352, 372–374, 377–378
Sontag, L. M., 32, 149, 377
Sonuga-Barke, E., 166
Sorell, G. T., 278
Sorensen, S., 41
Sorenson, A. M., 318
Sorhagen, N. S., 170
Sorsoli, C., 200
Sorsoli, L., 212
Sourander, A., 369
South, S. J., 92, 129, 331
Sowell, E. R., 51–52, 55
Sparks, S, 158
Spear, L., 51, 52, 54–55, 361
Spear, L. P., 360
Specht, J., 213
Spencer, G. A., 288
Spencer, M., 318
Spencer, M. B., 170
Spencer, R., 90
Spencer, S. V., 135
Spicer, P., 217
Spieker, S., 285, 318
Spielberg, J. M., 17, 57
Spies Shapiro, L. A., 115
Spijkerman, R., 198, 204
Spilman, S. K., 259
Spina, S., 272, 276, 278
Spinrad, T., 64, 107
Spoth, R., 12, 140
Spoth, R. L., 357, 359
Sprecher, S., 305
Spriggs, A. L., 285, 297
Sprondel, V., 49
Spruijt-Metz, D. S., 34, 36
Squeglia, L. M., 361
Srinivasan, S., 312
Sroufe, A., 266–267
Sroufe, L., 265
Sroufe, L. A., 266, 370
St. George, I., 23
St. Lawrence, J., 312
Stacy, A. W., 202
Staff, J., 174, 182, 184, 186–189, 342, 344–347, 348
Stams, G. J., 251
Standish, A. R., 36
Stanger-Hall, K. F., 319
Stanley, L. R., 359
Stanton, B., 302, 359
Stanton-Salazar, R., 272, 276, 278
Stanwood, N. L., 314
Stark, T., 314
Starr, L. R., 271
Stattin, H., 14, 33, 107, 138–140, 147, 191, 193, 228, 229, 242, 266, 299, 327–328, 377
Stearns, E., 136, 343
Steca, P., 326
Stedman, L., 158
Steeger, C. M., 242
Steele, C. M., 325
Steele, J., 199

Steffensmeier, D., 366
Steglich, C., 141
Stein, D. G., 37
Stein, G. L., 100, 325
Steinbeck, K. S., 27
Steinberg, E., 195
Steinberg, L., 2–4, 7, 9, 12, 16, 24, 25, 29, 39, 40, 44, 50–52, 55, 56, 58, 60, 64–68, 72, 74, 77–79, 81, 86, 88, 93, 96, 99–103, 106, 107, 109, 110–111, 121, 130, 132–134, 139, 141, 150, 156–158, 162, 171–173, 176, 177, 186–188, 195, 198, 200, 210, 236, 237, 239–249, 283, 287, 310, 318, 329–333, 336, 337, 339, 340, 348, 349, 351, 361, 362, 364, 367, 369–373, 378, 379
Steinberg, S. J., 116
Steinberg, W., 99, 100
Steiner, 78
Steinman, K. J., 259
Stephan, W., 218
Stephens, C. M., 108
Stephens, L., 117
Stephens, N. M., 335
Stephenson, J., 7, 109, 236, 262–263
Sterba, S. K., 375
Sternberg, R., 61
Stevens, A., 89
Stevens, J., 317
Stevens, N., 288–289
Stevenson, D., 164, 344, 346–347
Stevenson, H., 337
Stevenson, H. W., 327, 334
Stevenson, H., Jr., 228
Stevenson, J., 368
Steward-Streng, N., 311
Stewart, E. A., 334
Stewart, E. B., 334
Stewart, S. M., 281
Stice, E., 34–39, 373–374
Stickle, T. R., 363
Stigler, J., 337
Stipek, D., 326
Stockdale, G. D., 297
Stockdale, L., 201
Stocker, C., 218
Stocker, C. M., 276
Stoddard, S. A., 92, 366
Stoms, G., 314
Stone, D. M., 288
Stone, J., 6, 184, 185, 188
Stone, L., 374
Stone, L. B., 271, 374
Stone, M., 134
Stone, S. I., 350
Stoneman, Z., 109, 120
Stoolmiller, M., 121, 368–369, 373
Stormshak, E., 104, 169–170
Stormshak, E. A., 278, 350, 366
Storvoll, E. E., 368
Story, M., 36, 38, 39
Stout, M., 176
Stouthamer-Loeber, M., 139, 212, 351, 366, 367, 371
Strang, N., 52, 56, 67, 246

Strang, N. M., 56
Strasburger, V., 198, 201, 202
Straus, M., 119
Strenziok, M., 202
Striegel-Moore, R., 216
Stroet, K., 331
Stroud, L., 16, 145
Strough, J., 127–128, 135, 271
Stuart, E. A., 358
Stuart, G. L., 287
Stucky, B. D., 145
Studer, F., 138
Sturge-Apple, M., 265, 377
Sturm, R., 359
Sturmer, P., 315
Sturmhöfel, S., 361
Stutz, M., 116, 266
Su, X., 116
Suárez-Orozco, C., 338
Subrahmanyam, K., 6, 269
Sucato, G. S., 308
Suchindran, C., 26, 38, 92, 145
Sue, S., 336
Suizzo, M. A., 330
Sullivan, C. J., 141, 352, 368
Sullivan, H. S., 262–264, 266, 268, 271, 280
Sullivan, K. A., 29
Sullivan, P., 196
Sullivan, T., 287
Sullivan, T. N., 146, 352
Sumner, R., 219
Sun, Y., 115
Sunwolf., 63
Supple, A., 227
Supple, A. J., 100, 325
Suryanti, T. A., 258
Susan Dahinten, V., 24
Susman, E., 14, 15, 18, 23, 26, 352, 369
Susman, E. J., 31–34, 102, 369
Svoboda, R. C., 330
Swaim, R. C., 359
Swanson, J., 323
Swarr, A., 39, 277
Swartzwelder, H., 361
Swartzwelder, H. S., 360
Sweeten, G., 341, 364
Sweeten., G., 286
Swendsen, J., 360, 372
Swenson, C. A., 150
Swenson, L., 215
Swenson, L. P., 146, 217, 271
Swing, E. L., 201
Swinton, A. D., 327, 328
Swisher, R., 175
Swisher, R. R., 93, 189
Sy, S., 188
Syed, M., 212–213
Syed M., 219
Symons, K., 304
Syngelaki, E. M., 369
Syvertsen, A., 176, 185, 256, 257, 346
Szalacha, L. A., 216
Szeszulski, P., 218
Szklo-Coxe, M., 29
Szwedo, D., 138, 198, 205, 247, 267
Szwedo, D. E., 204, 242

T

Tabak, I., 96–97
Tach, L., 114
Taiarol, J., 146
Takahashi, A., 121
Takezawa, M., 251
Talmud, I., 135
Talwar, V., 149
Tamnes, C., 56
Tan, D., 63, 255
Tanaka, C., 54
Tang, C. S., 30
Tang, S., 316
Tanner, D., 154, 155
Tanner, J., 17, 20, 22–25
Tanner-Smith, E. E., 31
Tantleff-Dunn, 206
Tapales, A., 361
Tapert, S. F., 361
Taradash, A., 239
Tartakovsky, E., 228
Taskinen, P., 171
Tate, J., 227
Tatnell, R., 376
Tavernier, R., 225
Taylor, A., 39, 141
Taylor, C., 37, 38
Taylor, D., 28
Taylor, I. M., 192
Taylor, J., 351
Taylor, L., 87
Taylor, R., 120, 324
Taylor, S., 194, 299
Taylor, T., 139
Teachman, J., 169, 331, 334
Tebes, J. K., 356
Technow, J. R., 107
Tehranifar, P., 23
Tein, J. Y., 93, 119
Teitler, J. O., 304
Tellegen, A., 213
Telzer, E. H., 66–67, 101, 102, 227, 246, 266, 269, 299, 336, 375
Temple, J., 334–335
Temple, J. R., 205, 287
Tenenbaum, H. R., 255
Tennen, H., 297
Teppers, E., 223
Teran, L., 314
ter Bogt, T. F., 129, 133
Terenzini, P., 225
Terpeluk, A., 287
Terranova, A., 148
Terry, K, 336
Terry, M., 23
Terry, R., 145, 231
Terry-Humen, E., 315
Terzian, M., 318
Teslovich, T., 56, 58
Teti, D., 317
Tevendale, H., 214, 215
Tevendale, H. D., 217
Tharp, A. T., 288
Thatcher, J., 258
Thayer, S., 136, 139
Theokas, C., 90, 191, 277
Thijs, J., 165
Thøgersen-Ntoumanis, C., 192
Thomaes, S., 7, 214, 215, 253
Thomas, A. G., 29

Thomas, J., 279
Thomas, K. J., 138, 141, 246
Thomas, K. M., 59
Thomas, L., 56
Thomas, M., 60
Thomas, O., 230
Thomas, S. L., 164
Thomason, M. E., 93
Thombs, B. D., 305
Thompson, C., 244
Thompson, E., 305
Thompson, J. K., 36
Thompson, N., 192
Thompson, R., 138
Thompson, T. L., 136, 230
Thomson, E., 118
Thornberry, T., 314–315, 368
Thornberry, T. P., 139, 316
Thorne, A., 225, 261, 274
Thrul, J., 359
Tienda, M., 336
Tieu, T.-T., 224, 267
Tiggemann, M., 206
Tilley, E. H., 111, 300
Tillman, K. H., 281
Tilton-Weaver, L., 30, 82, 242
Tilton-Weaver, L. C., 107, 139
Timmerman, G., 307
Timmons, A. C., 102
Titzmann, P. F., 136
Tobian, A., 83
Tobler, A. L., 359
Tobler, N., 361–362
Todd, M., 359
Todorov, A. A., 359
Tolan, P., 139, 371, 379
Tolan, P. H., 215, 227
Tolan, P.H, 230
Tolma, E. L., 359
Tolman, D., 200
Tolman, D. L., 212, 291, 292–293, 297
Tolson, J., 130, 141
Tolstrup, J. S., 359
Tolvanen, A., 334
Tomasi, D., 52
Tomasik, M., 85, 88
Tomasik, M. J., 87
Tompsett, C., 93–94
Toomey, R. B., 229–230, 232
Topitzes, D., 94
Topolski, T. D., 348
Torney-Purta, J., 148
Toro, P., 121
Torres, B., 329
Tottenham, N., 55
Tough, P., 158
Toumbourou, J. W., 68, 350
Townsedn, A., 219–220
Townsend Betts, N., 271
Toyokawa, T., 334
Tram, J. M., 218
Tramontano, C., 252
Tramonte, L., 24
Tran, S., 267
Trautwein, U., 142, 165, 324
Travers, L. V., 191, 330
Treaster, J., 356
Treboux, D., 266–267
Trejos-Castillo, E., 3
Tremblay, R., 91, 105, 303–304

Tremblay, R. E., 17, 92, 175, 332, 342, 365
Trent, K., 314, 317
Trentacosta, C. J., 98
Trépanier, L., 16
Trevitt, J. L., 310
Trickett, P., 308, 369
Trickett, P. K., 24, 33
Trinkner, R., 98
Triwahyuni, A., 259
Trommsdorff, G., 243
Troop-Gordon, W., 32, 204–205, 266
Trucco, E. M., 92
Trudeau, L., 12, 140
Truong, K. D., 359
Trusty, J., 330
Trzesniewski, K., 213, 218
Trzesniewski, K. H., 147, 328
Tsai, K. M., 101, 102, 227
Tsang, K., 247
Tsar, V., 147
Tsarnaev, D., 2
Tschann, J., 288, 310, 313
Tseng, V., 103, 274, 336
Tseng, W., 146
Tseng, W. L., 166
Tsui, A. O., 310
Tsukayama E., 156
Tsur, A., 109
Tu, K. M., 150
Tubman, J. G., 308
Tucker, C., 103, 109, 110, 111, 191
Tucker, J. S., 141, 357, 360
Tucker-Drob, E., 111, 370
Tucker-Drob, E. M., 66, 111
Tunçalp, Ö., 318
Turbin, M. S., 359
Turiel, E., 98, 240, 249
Turke, S., 318
Turkheimer, E., 90, 111, 299, 359
Turner, H. A., 150
Turner, J., 318
Turner, P., 82
Turner, R., 318
Turner, T., 145
Tuval-Mashiach, R., 283
Tüzün, Z., 267
Twenge, J., 216, 217
Twenge, J. M., 255
Tyler, K., 230
Tynes, B., 204, 226–227, 230
Tynes, B. M., 229–230
Tynkkynen, L., 334
Tyrell, F. A., 281
Tyrka, A. R., 36
Tyson, D., 174, 330
Tyson, K., 100, 134, 175
Tzoumakis, S., 368

U

Uçanok, Z., 119
Uckert, K., 246
Udry, J., 21, 26, 38
Udry, J. R., 286
Uematsu, A., 54
Ueno, K., 287
Uggen, C., 371
Uhls, Y., 6, 196

Umaña-Taylor, A., 230
Umaña-Taylor, A. J., 227–230, 246, 249, 274
Ünal, F., 267
Underwood, M. K., 204
Unger, J., 120, 359
Unger, J. B., 140–141, 227
Unger J., 314
Upchurch, D., 317
Updegraff, K., 104, 136, 139, 274
Updegraff, K. A., 110, 193, 228, 230, 233–234, 274
Upton, R., 230
Urberg, K., 130, 141, 278
Urberg, K. A., 106–107
Urdan, T., 324, 326, 331
Usher, E. L., 327, 328
Usher-Seriki, K., 301
Uwer, R., 52

V

Vaccaro, D., 357
Vagi, K. J., 286–288, 376
Vaidya, J. G., 243
Vaillancourt, T., 147, 150
Valente, T. W., 140–141
Valentin, P., 45
Valentine, J., 180
Valeri, S. M., 378
Valiente, C., 323
Valkenburg, P., 204
Valkenburg, P. M., 200, 272
Valle, G., 281
Vallerand, R. J., 192
Valois, R. F., 352
Valsiner, J., 228
Van Acker, R., 143
van Aken, C., 274
van Aken, M., 213, 254
Van Aken, M., 254
van Aken, M. A., 64
van Aken, M.A.G., 31, 108, 299
Van Campen, K. S., 300
Van Court, P., 253
Van Damme, J., 165
Vandebosch, H., 149
van de Eijnden, R., 198
Vandell, D., 174, 194
Vandell, D. L., 191
van de Mheen, D., 198
van den Akker, A., 242
Van den Akker, A. L., 212, 213
Vandenbelt, M., 316
van den Berg, P., 206, 215
van den Berg, Y.H.M., 142, 215
van den Bos, E., 58
van den Bos, M., 244, 253, 270
Vandenbosch, L., 200
van den Bos W., 60
van den Bree, M.B.M., 351
van den Eijnden, R., 198, 204
van der Aa, N., 204
van der Ende, J., 364
van der Geest, V., 367–368
Vanderhei, S., 175
van der Lely, S., 29
Van der Molen, M., 50
van der Molen, M. W., 243
van der Werf, M., 170

van de Schoot, R., 220, 281
Van de Schoot, R., 213, 224
Vandevivere, E., 267
van Dijk, E., 253, 270
Van Dijk, M. P., 211
Van Doorn, M. D., 103
van Duijvenvoorde, A., 66, 244
van Duijvenvoorde, A.C.K., 57
Van Eck, K., 359
VanEseltine, M., 188
Vanfossen, B., 163
van Geel, M., 141, 337
van Geert, P.L.C., 98
van Goethem, A., 254
Van Goethem, A. A., 254
Van Goozen, S.H.M., 369
Van Gundy, K., 98
Vanhalst, J., 218
van Holst, R., 198
van Hoof, A., 254
van Hoorn, J., 253
Van Horn, M., 92
Van Houtte, M., 304
van IJzendoorn, M., 146
van IJzendoorn, M. H., 266
van Leeuwen, A. P., 356
Van Leeuwen, K., 119
Van Leijenhorst, L., 58, 65, 244
Van Lier, P., 151, 370
Van Lier, P.A.C., 365
van Lieshout, C., 148, 274
Van Noorden, T. H., 148
Van Petegem, S., 98, 239, 242
van Rijn-van Gelderen, L., 120
van Rooij, A., 198, 204
Van Rooij, T., 198
Van Ryzin, M., 24, 297
Vansadia, P., 118
VanSchyndel, S. K., 252
Vansteenkiste, M., 98, 239, 242, 324
Van Wagenen, A., 308
Vanwesenbeeck, I., 293, 300
van Workum, N., 141
Van Zalk, M.H.W., 377
Vaquera, E., 228
Varner, F., 227, 229, 326
Vasey, M., 363
Vasquez-Suson, K., 144
Vaughan, C. A., 276, 374
Vaughan, J., 258
Vaughan, P. W., 230
Vaughan, R., 174
Vaughn, L. B., 116
Vaughn, M. G., 111, 259, 363
Vazsonyi, A., 3, 106–108, 212, 359–360, 369
Vecera, S. P., 243
Vedder, P., 141, 337
Veenstra, R., 6, 115, 123, 127–128, 131, 133, 141, 143, 144, 262, 302, 367
Velanova, K., 55
Velez, W., 176
Vélez-Valle, E., 35
Venables, P. H., 369
Verhoeven, L., 144
Verhulst, F., 144
Verhulst, F. C., 272, 364, 367, 374–375

Verkuyten, M., 165
Verma, S., 123, 124, 153, 184, 185
Vermeersch, H., 304
Vermulst, A., 198, 266
Vermulst, A. A., 103, 204
Verona, E., 350
Véronneau, M., 138
Véronneau, M. H., 323, 332, 371
Verschueren, K., 165
Vesely, S. K., 359
Vest, A. E., 36, 191, 192
Viau, A., 183, 192
Vicary, J., 300
Victor, T., 92
Vida, M., 327
Viene, A., 150
Vieno, A., 92, 169, 254
Vigdor, J. L., 228
Vigfusdottir, T. H., 39
Viken, R. J., 23
Viljoen, J., 78
Viljoen, J. L., 78
Villalobos, M., 62–64, 97–98, 237, 249, 251, 255
Villarreal, V. M., 143
Villarruel, F., 303
Vincent, G. M., 363
Viner, R. M., 55, 59
Visser, I., 66
Vitacco, M. J., 363
Vitaro, F., 17, 92, 138, 141, 145, 151, 175, 285, 298–299, 332, 364, 370
Vloet, T. D., 369
Voelkl, K., 336
Vogel, M., 175, 176
Voight, A., 254
Voisin, D. R., 93
Voisine, S., 359
Vo-Jutabha, E. D., 228
Volcevski-Kostas, D., 206
Volkow, N. D., 52
Vollebergh, W., 224, 275
Volpe, V., 230
vom Hofe, R., 323
Von Bank, H., 130, 133, 134
Vondracek, F. W., 343
von Eye, A., 195, 248, 276
von Suchodoletz, W., 52
Voon, D., 376
Vorona, R. D., 29
Votruba-Drzal, E., 104, 108
Vrangalova, Z., 232, 297
Vuchinich, S., 242
Vygotsky, L., 61

W

Waasdorp, T., 150
Waasdorp, T. E., 143, 149, 171
Wadley, J., 353
Wadsworth, K., 359
Wadsworth, S. A., 120, 253
Wagenaar, A. C., 359
Wagner, D. V., 371
Wagner, E. F., 308
Wainryb, C., 63, 110, 252
Waite, E. B., 110
Waiters, E., 301, 303
Waithaka, E. N., 331, 335, 341

Waizenhofer, R., 104
Wakefield, M., 354–355
Wald, M., 178
Walden, B., 110
Waldfogel, J., 66, 107–108
Waldron, M., 111
Walker, A., 258
Walker, A. M., 227
Walker, A. R., 269, 271, 288
Walker, D., 144, 288–289
Walker, E., 200, 361, 378
Walker, L., 251
Walker, L. J., 253
Walker, R. S., 21
Walker, S., 293, 301, 303
Walker-Barnes, C. J., 140
Walkup, J. T., 378
Wall, J., 246
Wall, M., 36, 39
Wall, M. M., 307
Wallace, G. K., 369
Wallace, J. M., 256–259
Wallace, S. A., 336
Wallace, S. R., 117
Wallenius, M., 28
Waller, E. M., 146, 272
Waller, J. M., 271
Walls, M., 356
Walls, N. E., 308
Walsh, B., 39
Walsh, S., 109
Walters, R., 10
Wang, F., 6
Wang, J., 34, 35–36
Wang, L., 51–52
Wang, M., 19, 104, 161, 169–170
Wang, M. T., 104, 172, 174, 230,
    325, 328, 330, 331, 341
Wang, N., 246, 308
Wang, Q., 248, 324, 330
Wang, S., 372, 373
Wang, Y., 34, 149, 228, 330
Wanner, B., 141, 370
Ward, E., 35
Ward, L. M., 200, 301
Ware, A., 378–379
Wargo, J., 145
Warneke, C., 41
Warner, L. A., 302–303
Warner, S., 324
Warner, T. D., 93
Warren, J. R., 342
Warren, M., 30–32
Wasserman, D., 337
Waters, E., 266–267
Waters, P., 215
Waters, S., 276
Waters, S. D., 334
Watt, H. M., 325
Watt, H.M.G., 330
Watt, T. T., 159
Watts, S., 91, 303
Way, N., 89, 136, 161, 169, 171,
    175, 216, 217, 225, 227, 228,
    230, 269, 272–274, 335
Wearing, H., 51
Webb, H. J., 19
Webber, K. C., 227
Weber, E., 66
Weems, C., 87
Weerman, F., 141

Weesie, J., 141
Wegge, D., 149
Wegman, D. H., 187
Wehner, E., 283
Wei, E., 371
Wei, Y., 23
Weigard, A., 247
Weiland, B. J., 361
Weinberg, M., 306
Weinfield, N., 266–267
Weinstein, J. M., 98, 168
Weinstein, R. S., 112, 174
Weinstein, S. M., 373
Weir, K. F., 374
Weiser, J., 244
Weisgram, E. S., 346
Weiss, C., 159, 160
Weiss, C. C., 304
Weiss B., 371
Weisskirch, R., 205
Weisskirch, R. S., 242
Weist, M., 379
Weisz, J. R., 378, 379
Wells, A., 1634
Wells, M., 203–2004
Welner, K. G., 159
Welsh, D. P., 265, 310
Wen, H., 362
Wentzel, K., 162, 169, 332
Wentzel, K. R., 253
Werchon, D., 206
Werner, N., 146
Weseter, K., 174
West, B. T., 354
Westenberg, M., 270
Westenberg, P. M., 58, 65, 244
Westphal, A., 350
Wetter, E. K., 352
Wewerka, S., 16
Wheeler, L. A., 228, 281
Whitaker, D., 247, 301, 302
Whitaker, K. J., 55
Whitbeck, L., 119, 120, 302, 303,
    356
White, C. N., 302–303
White, G., 113
White, H. R., 87, 93, 119, 350
White, J. W., 287
White, L. O., 265
White, M., 169
White, N., 49, 287
White, R., 318
White, R. M., 93, 119
White, R.M.B., 93
White, S. F., 362–363
Whitehead, K. A., 227
Whiteman, S., 110, 136, 232, 233
Whiteman, S. D., 110
Whitesell, N., 212, 215, 217
Whitman, T., 316
Wichstrøm, L., 39, 368, 373
Wickrama, K.A.S., 34–36, 335
Wickrama, K.A.T., 34–35
Widaman, K., 246
Widaman, K. F., 218, 227, 241,
    297, 338
Widman, L., 247, 310
Widom, C. S., 308
Wieczorek, W. F., 92
Wiersma, J. D., 286
Wiesner, M., 370–371

Wigfield, A., 8, 213–214, 323
Wight, R. G., 373
Wikström, P. H., 367
Wildsmith, E., 311
Wilens, T. E., 359
Wiley, D. J., 295
Wilkening, F., 46
Wilkinson, D., 366
Wilkinson, L., 308
Will, G. J., 253
Willard, J., 12
Willett, J. B., 104
Williams, D. R., 229–230
Williams, J. H., 326
Williams, J. L., 227, 230
Williams, K., 265, 266, 326
Williams, K. R., 150
Williams, L. R., 105, 296
Williams, M., 28
Williams, P., 40, 41
Williams, R., 136
Williams, S., 23, 191
Williams, S. K., 104
Williams, S. T., 119
Williams, T., 326
Williams, W., 45, 61, 333
Williford, A. P., 148
Willis, D. S., 257
Willms, D., 91, 303–304
Willms, J. D., 92
Willoughby, T., 104, 198, 201, 205,
    225, 258, 306, 352, 377
Wills, T., 357
Wilson, C., 36
Wilson, H. W., 308
Wilson, J., 193, 371
Wilson, J. L., 203
Wilson, M., 366
Wilson, S., 3, 213
Wilson, S. J., 360
Wilson-Ahlstrom, A., 195
Windle, M., 109, 138, 286, 370
Winfree, L., Jr., 139
Wingood, G. M., 312
Wingrove, T., 78
Winn, D. C., 314–315
Winsler, A., 29
Winsper, C., 150
Winston, C., 231
Winter, C., 140
Winter, M., 360
Wischnia, S., 325
Wiseman, R., 146
Wishard, A., 139
Wisneski, H., 308
Wissink, I., 143
Wissink, I. B., 370–371
Witherspoon, D., 230
Witkiewitz, K., 363
Witkow, M., 138, 176, 183, 226,
    227, 332, 333, 335, 337
Witkow, M. R., 227
Witruk, E., 327
Witthoft, S., 117
Wittig, M. A., 227
Witvliet, M., 151
Wodtke, G., 91
Woertman, L., 281, 293, 300
Wolak, J., 205
Wold, B., 133, 213, 218
Wolf, A., 41

Wolfe, D. A., 306–307
Wolff, J. M., 32, 68, 93
Wolfson, A., 29
Wolke, D., 149, 323
Wolters, N., 144
Wong, C., 121, 247
Wong, J. J., 230
Wong, S. S., 16
Wong, W. C., 361
Woo, H. S., 228
Wood, D., 94, 238, 329–330
Wood, G., 286, 287
Wood, J. J., 171
Wood, J. V., 204
Wood, M., 359
Wood, P., 336
Wood, P. K., 351
Woodcock, A., 325
Woodhouse, S. S., 265, 267
Wooding, J., 187
Woodward, L., 151, 317
Woolard, J., 60, 70, 71, 244, 310,
    365
Woolley, M. E., 330
Woolnough, A., 188
Worthman, C., 16, 373
Wouters, E., 119
Wouters, S., 165
Wray-Lake, L., 90, 185, 248, 252,
    253, 256, 331, 346
Wright, B.R.E., 366
Wright, J. P., 108, 111
Wright, K. A., 92
Wright, P. A., 374
Wu, C., 101
Wu, J., 265
Wuerker, A., 369
Wynn, P., 371
Wynn, S. R., 326
Wypij, D., 305

X
Xiao, L., 66
Xie, H., 146
Xin, Z., 214
Xu, J., 330
Xu, X., 295, 301
Xue, Y., 311

Y
Yahner, J., 287
Yamaguchi, R., 362
Yancey, A., 26–27
Yang, C., 62, 369
Yang, S., 63
Yang, T.W.H., 361
Yang, Y., 288
Yang, Z., 319
Yap, M., 100
Yarger, R. S., 49–51, 55
Yarkoni, T., 60
Yates, M., 253
Yau, J., 97, 114
Ybarra, M. L., 203–2004
Yeager, D., 265
Yeager, D. S., 147, 324, 326,
    369–370

Yeo, G. H., 129
Yeung, A., 215
Yeung, D. Y., 30
Yip, T., 167, 226, 227
Yisrael, D. S., 307
Yodanis, C., 119
Yoder, A., 219
Yoder, K., 302
Yoerger, K., 368–369
Yohalem, N., 195
Yokum, S., 34
Yonelinas, A., 50
Yong, M., 350
Yonker, J. E., 259
Yoon, J. S., 146
Yorgason, J. B., 252, 276
Yoshikawa, H., 41, 89, 119
You, S., 174
Young, A. M., 307, 315, 354
Young, B. J., 307
Young, J. F., 107
Young, J. T., 143
Young, M., 287
Young, M.E.D., 308

Young, S. E., 351
Youniss, J., 90, 240, 253, 254, 262
Younts, C. W., 366
Ystrom, E., 377
Yu, H., 167
Yu, J. J., 239
Yu, M., 356
Yu, T., 266
Yuan, A.S.V., 118–119
Yücel, M., 373
Yuen, C. X., 240
Yurkelun-Todd, D. A., 52

Z

Zabin, L., 313–314, 317
Zaff, J. F., 191
Zajac, K., 267
Zakin, D., 32
Zametkin, A. J., 34, 35
Zamsky, E., 318
Zanarini, M., 150

Zanolie, K., 50, 244
Zapert, K., 356
Zarbatany, L., 270–271
Zarrett, N., 6, 174, 192
Zavodny, M., 310
Zee, P. C., 29
Zeira, A., 174
Zelazo, P. D., 54, 56, 63
Zeldin, S., 94
Zeman, J., 240
Zentall, S. R., 300
Zentner, M., 210
Zervoulis, K., 233
Zettergren, P., 151
Zha, W., 358
Zhang, J., 36
Zhang, W., 240
Zhang, Y., 329
Zhao, X., 137
Zhao, Y., 305
Zhong, H., 366
Zhou, Q., 253
Zick C., 183, 185
Zimiles, H., 118

Zimmer-Gembeck, M., 7, 19, 146, 147, 236–239, 277, 285, 291, 298
Zimmerman, M., 90, 118, 311
Zimmerman, M. A., 90, 92, 93, 116, 229, 259, 296, 312, 358, 366
Zimmerman, R., 297, 305
Zimmermann, F., 171
Zimring, F., 79, 371
Zinman, J., 41, 354
Ziol-Guest, K., 169, 326
Ziv, Y., 218
Zlotnik, A., 116, 288
Zohra, I. T., 352
Zollo, P., 207
Zonana, H. V., 350
Zook, J. M., 332
Zoon, C. K., 34
Zucker, N. L., 59
Zucker, R. A., 350
Zuckerman, A., 332
Zweig, J. M., 287, 352
Zwierzynska, K., 149

Subject Index

A

ability grouping. *See* tracking
abortion, 313–315
abstinence, 312, 318
abstinence-only sex education, **319**
abstract thinking, 45–46
academic achievement. *See also* achievement; education; schools
  changes over time in, 338–341
  cross-cultural variations in, 339–341
  dropping out and, 341–343
  early interventions to improve, 334–335
  employment and, 188
  ethnic differences in, 335–339
  explanation of, **333**–334
  extracurricular activities and, 174
  friendship and, 138
  genetic factors and, 111
  home environment and, 329–331
  importance of context in, 326–327
  parenting and, 171, 329–331, 335
  peer groups and, 331–333
  pubertal maturation and, 34
  socioeconomic status and, 334–335
  teacher expectations and, 170–171
  tracking and, 164
  in urban schools, 158
  victimization and, 147
achievement. *See also* academic achievement
  as adolescent issue, 321–322
  cognitive change and, 322
  environmental influences on, 328–333
  expectations and, 170–171
  explanation of, **7**–8
  motivation for, 323–324
  occupational, 343–347
  overview of, 321
  parenting and, 171, 329–331, 335
  puberty and, 322
  social roles and, 322
  socioeconomic status and, 334–335
  stereotype threat and, 325–326
achievement attributions, **327**
adolescence/adolescents
  achievement in, 321–322
  attachment in, 264, 267–268
  autonomy expectations of, 103
  biological transitions in, 4, 13–41 (*See also* biological transitions)
  birth rate among, 313
  boundaries of, 3–4
  cognitive transitions in, 4–5, 42–68 (*See also* cognitive transitions)

as consumers, 206–207
contexts of, 5–6
as crime victims, 366
as criminal defendants, 78
egocentrism in, 45–46
elongation of, 71–72
emerging adulthood and, 74–77
explanation of, **3**
health care for, 36, 40, 41
health of, 40–41
historical perspective on, 72–74
identity in, 209–232
interpersonal development during, 263–264
legal status and, 77–79
multiethnic, 230
non-college-bound, 178–179, 190
obesity and eating disorders in, 34–39
as parents, 315–318
personality development in, 212–213
phases of, 4
physical health and health care in, 40–41
psychological and social impact of puberty in, 26–34
psychosocial development in, 7–8
puberty and, 14–18
self-care and, 193–194
sexually active, 297–303
social cognition in, 62–64
as social invention, 72–74
social redefinition in, 70–71, 79–80
social transitions in, 5, 69–94 (*See also* social transitions)
somatic development in, 18–21
status changes in, 77–79
stereotypes of, 11–12, 162
theoretical perspectives on, 8–11
timing and tempo of puberty and, 21–25
transitory experimentation in, 348–350
view of self, 81–82
adolescence-limited offenders, **367**, 368, 370–371
adolescent development. *See also* psychosocial development
  biological transitions in, 4, 14–39
  dating and, 284–288
  employment and, 186–190
  extracurricular activities and, 191–193
  family relationships and, 104–105, 121
  genetic and environmental influences on, 111
  hormonal influences in, 17
  leisure activities and, 195–196
  media use and, 198–199, 203–205
  poverty and, 91–92
  religious beliefs and, 256–259
  schools and, 179–180

adolescent growth spurt, **18**–19
adolescent marginality, 10–11
adolescent parents
  consequences for, 317
  girls and, 316–317
  negative effects of, 317–318
  overview of, 315–316
adolescent population, 124–126
adolescent pregnancy
  abortion and, 313–314
  causes of, 314
  poverty and, 92
  prevalence of, 312–313
  role of father and, 314–315
  statistics related to, 312
adoption, 120
adrenarche, **15**–16
Adult Attachment Interview, **267**
adulthood. *See* emerging adulthood
adult plasticity, **54**
Advanced Placement (AP) programs, 185
affluent neighborhoods, 91
African American youth. *See* Black youth
age-crime curve, **364**
age grading, **124**
agency, **223**
age of majority, **71**
age segregation, in cliques, 135
aggression. *See also* violence
  in dating relationships, 286–287
  explanation of, **363**–364
  genetic factors and, 111
  instrumental, 144
  media use and, 199
  popularity and, 143–145
  reactive, 144
  relational, 145–146
AIDS/HIV, **311**–312
Alaska Native youth. *See* American Indian/Alaska Native youth
alcohol use. *See also* substance use/abuse
  binge drinking and, 353
  brain development and, 360–361
  employment and, 189
  media exposure and, 202
  prevalence of, 353
American Indian/Alaska Native youth. *See also* ethnicity; minority youth
  dating relationships and, 281
  initiation ceremonies for, 77
  self-esteem in, 216
  transition to adulthood, 88–89
androgens, **15**, 299, 300
anhedonic, **352**
anorexia nervosa, **37**–39
anthropological theories, 11
antidepressants, 166
antisocial behavior. *See also* delinquency
  adolescence-limited offenders and, 367, 368, 370–371
  causes of, 367–372

developmental progression of, 364–365
early maturation and, 31
friendship and, 138–139
life-course-persistent offenders and, 367–370
parents and, 139–140
prevention and treatment of, 371
rejection and, 143–144
antisocial personality disorder, **362**
anxiety
  affluent backgrounds and, 91
  victimization and, 147–148
anxious-avoidant attachment, **265**
anxious-resistant attachment, **265**
Asian youth. *See also* cultural differences; ethnicity; minority youth
  academic achievement and, 158, 335–337, 339
  adolescent pregnancy and, 312
  clique membership and, 136, 137
  crowd membership and, 134
  dating relationships and, 281
  enrolled in higher education, 176, 177
  ethnic identity and, 229, 230
  expectations for autonomy in, 248
  exposure to violence and, 94
  home leaving and, 87
  identity development in, 228
  individuation and, 241
  self-esteem in, 216, 217
  sexual initiation and, 294
  susceptibility to peer influence, 248
  transition to adulthood, 88, 89
  as victims of violence, 175
attachment
  in adolescence, 264, 267–268
  adolescent intimacy and infant, 265–267
  explanation of, **264**
  in family relationships, 109
  in infancy, 264–265
  to parents, 267–268
  types of, 265
attention, in information-processing perspective, 48
attention deficit/hyperactivity disorder (ADHD), **166**, 369
authoritarian parents
  behavioral autonomy and, 247
  emotional autonomy and, 242
  ethnicity in, 108–109
  explanation of, **105**, 106
authoritative parents
  achievement and, 330–331
  behavioral autonomy and, 247–248
  benefits of, 107–108
  emotional autonomy and, 242
  ethnicity in, 108
  explanation of, **105**
  moral reasoning and, 252
  power of, 106–107

authority, beliefs about, 63
authority conflicts, **364**
autobiographical memory, **49**
autoerotic behavior, **293**
autonomy
 adolescent expectations for, 103
 behavioral autonomy, 243–248
 cognitive, 237–238, 248–259
 emotional, 238–243
 explanation of, **7**
 in family relationships, 109
 overview of, 236, 237
 puberty and, 237
 social roles and, 238
 types of, 238

B

baby boom, **83, 124**
bad girls, 365–366
Bar (Bas) Mitzvah, **80,** 81
basal metabolism rate, **34**
behavioral autonomy
 decision-making abilities and,
  243–245
 ethnic and cultural differences in
  expectations for, 248
 explanation of, **238**
 susceptibility to influence and,
  245–248
behavioral decision theory, **64**–65
behavioral genetics
 adolescent development and, 111
 explanation of, **110**–111
 sibling differences and, 111–112
behaviorism, 10
behavior problems
 in children of adolescent mothers, 316–317
 self-esteem and, 218–219
beliefs
 about ability, 337
 about intelligence, 326
 about occupations, 346
 about success, 324–328
 religious, 259
Big Brothers/Big Sisters, 277
big fish-little pond effect, **165**
binge drinking, **353**
binge eating disorder, **37**
biological transitions. *See also*
  puberty
 adolescent health and health care
  and, 40–41
 body stature and dimensions and,
  18–19
 eating disorders and, 36–39
 endocrine system and, 14–16
 explanation of, **4**
 hormonal influences and, 17
 obesity in, 34–36
 psychological impact of puberty
  and, 26–34
 puberty triggers and, 16–17
 sexual maturation and, 19–21
 somatic development in, 18–25
 timing of puberty and, 21–25
biosocial theories, 8–9
biracial youth, self-esteem in, 217
birth control. *See* contraceptive use

birth order, 248
Black youth. *See also* ethnicity;
  minority youth
 academic achievement and,
  335–337, 339
 adolescent parenthood and, 315,
  318
 adolescent pregnancy and, 312,
  314–316
 clique membership and, 136, 137
 crowd membership and, 134
 dating relationships and,
  280–281
 dropout rate among, 158
 enrolled in higher education,
  176, 177
 ethnic identity in, 229, 230
 ethnic socialization and, 227
 innercity schools and, 158
 obesity among, 35
 pubertal maturation and, 23, 34
 school transitions and, 162, 163
 self-esteem in, 216–218
 sexual initiation and, 294
 in single-parent families, 113
 teacher expectations and,
  170–171
 tracking and, 163–164
 transition to adulthood, 88–89
 violence against Asian students,
  175
Board of Education v. Mergens, 78
body dissatisfaction
 in boys, 39
 eating disorders and, 37–38
 in girls, 19, 32, 36–39
 mass media and, 36–37
 obesity and, 35, 36
body fat, sex differences in, 19
body mass index (BMI), **34**
Boston Marathon bombing case, 2
boys. *See also* gender differences;
  gender-role development; sex
  differences
 body dissatisfaction in, 39
 brain development in, 52
 early vs. late maturation in, 20,
  31–33
 intimacy and, 271, 272
 meaning of sex and, 304
 other-sex friends and, 278
 pubertal maturation in, 25
 romantic relationships and,
  279–280
 self-esteem in, 216
 separation of girls from, 80
 sexual initiation in, 294, 295
 susceptibility to peer influence
  in, 248
 from wealthy communities, 91
brain development
 adolescent behavior and, 60
 biosocial theories and, 9
 brain plasticity and, 54–55
 gender and, 52
 implications for adolescent
  behavior, 2–3
 plasticity and, 54–55
 pubertal maturation and, 25
 research on, 51–52
 social brain and, 58–59

substance use and, 360–361
 susceptibility to peer influence
  and, 247
brain function
 change in adolescence, 55–57
 explanation of, **51**–52
 grey matter and, 53–54
 limbic system and, 57–58
 overview of, 52–53
 white matter and, 54
brain structure
 change in adolescence, 55
 correlation between behavior
  changes and, 60
 explanation of, **51**
*Brown v. Board of Education of
  Topeka,* 167
bulimia, **37**–39
bullies/bullying
 cyberbullying and, 149–150
 outside of schools, 150
 selection versus socialization
  and, 141
 victimization and, 148–150

C

callous-unemotional (CU) traits,
  362–363
caring/compassion, in positive
  youth development, 195
The Catcher in the Rye (Salinger),
  221–222
Catholic schools, 168–169
causation, 60, **199**
character, in positive youth development, 195
charter schools, **157,** 158, 168
childbearing, premarital, 92
child protectionists, **73**
children, of adolescent mothers,
  316–317
chlamydia, **311**
circumcision, 82–83
civic engagement
 explanation of, **253**–254
 research on, 254–255
civil liberties, 64
classroom climate
 characteristics of good, 168–170
 student engagement and, 171–174
 teacher expectations and student
  performance and, 170–171
classroom size, 159–160. *See also*
  schools
cliques
 antisocial activities in, 140
 crowds vs., 130
 explanation of, **128**
 member similarity in, 135–137
 stability of, 141
 structure of, 128–129, 132
cognitive autonomy
 civic engagement and, 253–255
 explanation of, **238,** 248–249
 moral development and, 249–252
 political thinking and, 255–256
 prosocial reasoning and,
  252–253
 religious beliefs and, 256–259

cognitive change
 achievement and, 322
 adolescent relativism and, 47
 adolescent sexuality and, 292
 autonomy and, 237–238
 identity development and,
  209–210
 Internet and, 205
 intimacy and, 262
 thinking about abstract concepts
  as, 45–46
 thinking about possibilities as,
  43–45
 thinking about thinking as,
  45–46
 thinking in multiple dimensions
  as, 46–47
cognitive-developmental view,
  47–48
cognitive transitions, 4–5
cohorts, **79**
collective efficacy, **92**
college education. *See* postsecondary education
Columbine High School shooting,
  175
comic books, 196, 197
Coming of Age in Samoa (Mead),
  85
Common Core, **157**
communities
 girls from wealthy, 91
 violence in, 174–176
community service, 192, 253, 254
comorbidity
 explanation of, **350**
 of externalizing problems,
  350–352
 of internalizing problems, 350
competence, in positive youth
  development, 195
comprehensive high school, **155**
comprehensive sex education,
  318–319
concrete operations period, **47**
condoms, 309–312
conduct disorder, **362**–363
confidence, in positive youth development, 195
conflict
 among friends, 271
 divorce and, 115
 intergenerational, 11
 marital, 115–116
 parent-adolescent, 97–98,
  102–103
connection, in positive youth development, 195
consumers, adolescent, 206–207
continuity of social redefinition
 in contemporary society, 84–85
 current trends in, 87
 in previous eras, 86–87
 in traditional cultures, 85–86
continuous transitions, **84**
contraceptive use
 adolescent pregnancy and, 314
 background of, 309–310
 decisions concerning, 310–311
 right to, 79
 strategies to increase, 311

conventional moral reasoning, **250**
coping, stress and, 378–379
correlation, 60, **199**, 298–299
cortisol, **16**
co-rumination, **271**–272
covert antisocial behavior, **364**
criminal behavior. *See also* delin-
    quency; legal perspective
    adolescents and, 78
    adolescents as victims of, 366
    age and, 365
    explanation of, **364**
    morbidity and mortality rates
        and, 41
    office statistics vs. adolescents'
        reports on, 366–367
    poverty and, 91, 92
criminal justice system, **77**
critical thinking, **156**
cross-sectional studies, **26**
crowds
    adolescent identity and, 133–134
    changes in structure of, 131–132
    cliques vs., 130
    ethnicity and, 134–135
    explanation of, **129**
    nature of, 129–130
    as reference groups, 133–135
    social norms and, 134
    waxing and waning of, 132
cultural capital, **331**
cultural differences. *See also* eth-
    nicity; minority youth; *specific
    groups*
    in academic achievement,
        339–341
    adolescent pregnancy and,
        312–313
    of adolescent work, 185
    in attitude toward pubertal
        events, 30
    bullying rates and, 148
    continuity of adolescent passage
        and, 85–86
    in dating, 280–281
    in expression of intimacy, 274
    family functions and, 100–101
    of leisure, 183–184
    parenting styles and, 106–107
    in physical punishment, 104
    in pubertal maturation, 24, 25
    separation of sexes and, 80
    sexual initiation and, 294–295
    social redefinition in, 82–84
    in use of leisure time, 183–184
    in view of emerging adulthood,
        75
culture
    friendship and teen, 138
    intelligence and, 61–62
custody arrangements, 117
cyberbullying, 149–150

D

date rape, 306–308
dating. *See also* romantic
    relationships
    adolescent development and,
        284–288
    intimacy in, 280–281

partner preferences and, 284
    patterns of, 281–282
    phases of romance in, 283–284
    relationship development and,
        282–284
    role of, 278–279
    statistics related to, 279
    violence and, 286–288
decision making
    behavioral autonomy and,
        243–245
    behavioral decision theory and,
        64–65
deductive reasoning, **44**
de-idealization, **240**
delayed phase preference, **27**
delay of gratification, **323**
delinquency. *See also* antisocial
    behavior; risk taking
    adolescence-limited offenders
        and, 367, 368, 370–371
    biological predisposition for, 369
    early maturation and, 33
    explanation of, **364**
    life-course-persistent offenders
        and, 367–370
    poverty and, 92, 93
    susceptibility to influence
        and, 246
depressed mood, 372
depression
    affluent backgrounds and, 91
    causes of, 377–378
    early maturation and, 33
    electronic media and, 204
    in ethnic minority youth, 229
    explanation of, **372**
    family experiences and, 112
    gender roles and, 373–374
    genetic factors in, 111
    mood, syndrome, and disorder
        and, 372–373
    rejection and, 146
    rumination and, 374
    sensitivity and, 374–375
    sex differences in, 373–374
    stress and, 374
    suicide and, 376
    treatment and prevention of, 378
depressive disorder, 372
depressive symptoms, 372
desegregation, effects of, 167
detachment. *See also* attachment
    emotional autonomy and,
        238–239
    explanation of, **238**, 239
    psychoanalytic theory and,
        238–239
developmental plasticity, **54**
developmental trajectories, **356**
diathesis-stress model, **377**–378
diffusion tensor imaging (DTI),
    51, 52
discontinuous transitions, **84, 85**
discrimination
    ethnic identity and, 228–229
    toward sexual-minority youth,
        308
disengagement. *See* student
    engagement
disordered eating, **36–37**. *See also*
    eating disorders

divided attention, **48**
divorce
    adaptation to, 114–115
    conflict and stress in, 115
    custody following, 116
    effects of, 114
    genetic influences on, 115
    individual differences in effects
        of, 115
    longer-term effects of, 116
    quality of family relationships
        and, 114
    remarriage following, 113,
        118–119
    sleeper effects of, 116
    statistics related to, 112
dopamine, **57, 360**
dropout rate. *See* school dropout
    rate
drugs. *See* substance use/abuse
dual systems theories, 9
dyscalculia, **165**
dysgraphia, **165**
dyslexia, **165**

E

early adolescence, **4**
eating disorders. *See also* obesity
    anorexia nervosa as, 38–39
    binge eating disorder as, 37
    body dissatisfaction and, 37–38
    bulimia as, 38–39
    gender and, 36–39
    mass media influences on, 36–37
    overview of, 36–37
    treatment of, 39
ecological perspective on human
    development, **6**
economic inequality. *See also*
    poverty
    bullying and, 149–150
    effects of, 119
education. *See also* elementary
    schools; middle schools; post-
    secondary education; schools;
    secondary schools
    friendship and attitude toward,
        138
    homeschooling and, 168
    impact of employment on, 188
    in innercities, 158
    reform in, 154–156, 158
    sex, 318–319
educational achievement. *See* aca-
    demic achievement
educational attainment
    academic achievement and,
        338–339
    explanation of, **333**
egocentrism, 45–46
ejaculation, 30
electroencephalography (EEG), **52**
electronic media/electronic media
    use
    adolescent consumer and,
        206–207
    adolescent development and,
        198–199, 203–205
    body image and, 36–37, 206
    cyberbullying and, 149–150

impact of, 198–199
    media saturation and, 197–198
    patterns of, 196–197
    role of, 6
    sexual content and, 198, 199,
        201–202
    sleep patterns and, 28
    substance use and, 202
    violence and, 198, 201–202
    work trends and, 185
elementary schools. *See also*
    schools
    academic achievement in, 339
    explanation of, 160
    intervention programs in, 335
    teachers in, 162
    transition to secondary schools
        from, 161–162
emerging adulthood
    cultural variations in view of,
        74, 75
    explanation of, **4**
    features of, 74–75
    poverty and, 72, 88–89
    psychological development in,
        75–77
    transitional issues in, 87–90
    transition to, 87–90
emotional autonomy
    detachment and, 238–239
    explanation of, **238**
    individuation and, 239
    parenting styles and, 241–243,
        252
    research on, 239–241
emotional perspective, risk-taking
    behavior in, 66–67
employment
    adolescent development and,
        186–189
    cross-cultural variations in, 185
    drop out rate and, 188
    impact on education, 188
    impact on poor youth, 189
    influence of, 6
    poor youth and, 189
    problem behavior and,
        188–189
    responsibility and, 187–188
    transition to, 88
    trends in adolescent, 184–185
    types of, 186
    unemployment and, 189–190
    work environment and, 186
"empty nest" stage, 100
endocrine system. *See also*
    hormones
    adrenarche and, 15–16
    explanation of, **14**
    hormonal feedback loop and,
        14–15
engagement. *See* student
    engagement
environmental factors
    in achievement, 328–343
    in adolescent development, 111
    in homosexuality, 306
    in personality development, 212
epiphysis, **18**
Eriksonian theory, 9, 219, 221
estrogens, **15**, 52, 299, 300

ethnic identity. *See also* identity
  in Black youth, 217
  development of, 226–228
  effects of discrimination on,
    228–230
  explanation of, **225**
  in immigrants, 226, 228
  in multiethnic adolescents, 231
ethnicity. *See also* cultural differ-
    ences; minority youth; *specific
    groups*
  academic achievement and,
    335–339
  adolescent pregnancy and,
    312, 315
  beliefs about abilities and, 337
  clique membership and, 136–137
  crowd membership and, 134–135
  effects of desegregation and, 167
  in expectations for autonomy, 248
  expression of intimacy and, 274
  in home leaving, 87
  parenting styles and, 106–109
  self-esteem and, 216–218
  sexual initiation and, 294–295
  single-parent families and, 113
  substance use and, 355–356
  teacher expectations and,
    170–171
  in timing and tempo of
    puberty, 23
  in transition to adulthood, 88–89
ethnic socialization, **227**
ethnography, **131**
event-related potentials (ERPs), **52**
evidence-based practices, **371**
executive function, **56**
experience sampling method
  (ESM), **190**–191
experimentation, transitory,
  348–349
externalizing problems. *See
    also* antisocial behavior;
    delinquency
  categories of, 362–365
  comorbidity of, 350–352
  explanation of, **350**
  prevention and treatment of, 371
extracurricular activities
  adolescent development and,
    191–193
  neighborhood stressors and, 94
  participation in, 184, 191
  role of, 6
  student engagement and, 174

F

failure, fear of, 323–324
false-self behavior, 211–**212**
families/family relationships. *See
    also* fathers; mothers; parents/
    parenting
  adolescent development and,
    104–105, 121
  adoption and, 120
  autonomy and attachment in, 109
  balance of power in, 101
  behavioral genetics and, 110–112
  causes of conflict in, 97–98,
    102–103

chances within, 6
changing needs and functions in,
  100–101
in changing society, 112–119
delinquency and, 368
divorce and, 112–118
ethnicity and, 108–109
family systems theory and,
  98–99
foster care children and,
  120–121
generation gap and, 96–97
intimacy and, 267–268, 273–275
lesbian and gay, 120
marital conflict in, 115–116
mental health of parents and, 100
midlife stage for parents and,
  99–100
parenting styles and, 105–108
poverty and, 113–114, 119–120
puberty and, 29–30, 101–103
remarriage and, 113, 118–119
roles within, 82
sex differences in, 103–104
sibling relationships in, 109–110
single parenthood and, 112–113
transformations in, 101–103
familism, **101**
family capital, **341**
family relationships
  LGBT youth and, 306
  obesity and, 36
  puberty and, 24, 29–30
family systems theory, **98**
fathers. *See also* families/fam-
    ily relationships; mothers;
    parents/parenting
  adolescent pregnancy and,
    313–315, 317
  adolescent relationships
    with, 104
  divorce and contact with, 116
  intimacy and, 274
  LGBT youth and relationship
    with, 306
  sexual abuse by, 308–309
fear of failure, 323–324
feedback loop, **15**
female genital mutilation, **83**
females. *see* girls
femininity, 233–234
financial issues. *See also* poverty;
    socioeconomic status (SES)
  financial strain as, 119
  for non-college-bound students,
    178–179, 190
firearms, 93
five-factor model, **212**
flow experience, **191**
formal operations period, **47**, 48
foster care, 120–121
free time. *See* leisure/leisure
  activities
Freudian theory, 9
friends/friendship. *See also* cliques;
    crowds; intimacy; peer groups
  achievement and, 331–333
  brain functions and presence
    of, 246
  caring and concern in, 270–271
  changes in nature of, 268

common interests among,
  138–140
conflict resolution and, 271
cross-cultural, 137
cross-ethnic, 167
ethnic segregation and, 135–136
intimacy in, 269–271
jealousy in, 268–269
knowledge about, 269
other-sex, 278
popularity and, 144–145
sex cleavage and, 277–278
similarity between, 140–142
stability of adolescent, 141–142
teen culture and, 138
functional connectivity, **57**
functional magnetic resonance
  imaging (fMRI), **51**
future orientation, **210**

G

gangs, **139**
gateway drugs, **356**. *See also* substance use/abuse
gay and lesbian parents, 120
gender differences. *See also* sex
  differences
  in brain development, 52
  in eating disorders, 36–39
  expectations for autonomy, 248
  identity and, 231–234
gender identity, **231**
gender intensification hypothesis,
  232
gender-role behavior
  explanation of, **231**
  as fluid, 232
gender-role development. *See also*
    sex differences
  depression and, 373–374
  masculinity and femininity and,
    233–234
  nature of, 232
  socialization and, 232–233
generational dissonance, **101**
generation gap, 96–97
genetic factors
  in achievement, 111, 331
  behavioral genetics and, 110–111
  in divorced families, 115
  in homosexuality, 306
  in intelligence, 111, 331
  in obesity, 35
  in personality development, 212
  in pubertal maturation, 23
  siblings and, 111–112
Gen X, 125
Gen Y, 125
Gen Z, 125
gifted students, **164**–165
girls. *See also* gender differences;
    gender-role development; sex
    differences
  aggression in, 146
  attitude to menarche, 30
  bad, 365–366
  body dissatisfaction in, 19, 32,
    36–39
  brain development in, 52

in cliques, 129
early vs. late maturation in,
  31–34
eating disorders in, 36–39
educational attainment of, 326
intimacy and, 271, 272
jealousy and, 268
meaning of sex and, 304–305
other-sex friends and, 278
popularity among, 144
relational aggression and, 146
romantic relationships and,
  279–280
rumination and, 374–375
self-esteem in, 216
sensitivity and, 374–375
separation of boys from, 80
sexual initiation in, 294–296
sexual maturation in, 20–21
in single-parent households, 302
susceptibility to peer influence
  in, 248
from wealthy communities, 91
glands, **14**
globalization, transition to adulthood and, 85–86
goal orientation, **324**
gonadotropin-releasing hormone
  (GnRH) neurons, **14**
gonads, **15**
gonorrhea, **311**
Google, 203
graduated driver licensing, **40**
grandparents, 115, 276
gratification delay, 323
Great Recession, 87, 185
grey matter, 53–54
guns, 93

H

harassment. *See also* victims/
    victimization
  bullying and, 141, 148–150
  sexual, 306–308
  victimization and, 147, 148
Harlem Children's Zone, 158
Hazelwood v. Kuhlmeier, 78
health care, 36, 40–41
height, adolescent growth spurt
  and, 18–19
herpes, **311**
higher education. *see* postsecondary education
high school. *See* secondary schools
Hispanic youth. *See also* ethnicity;
    minority youth
  academic achievement and,
    335–336, 338, 339
  adolescent parenthood and, 315
  adolescent pregnancy and, 312,
    314, 315
  clique membership and, 136, 137
  crowd membership and, 134
  dating relationships and, 281
  drinking among, 143
  dropout rate among, 158
  enrolled in higher education,
    176, 177
  ethnic identity in, 229, 230

Hispanic youth—*Cont.*
  family conflict and, 101
  home leaving and, 87
  innercity schools and, 158
  obesity among, 35
  quinceañera and, 79
  school transitions and, 162
  self-esteem in, 216–218
  sexual initiation and, 294
  in single-parent familes, 113
  teacher expectations and, 170
  timing and tempo of puberty
    in, 23
  transition to adulthood, 88–89
  violence against Asian
    students, 175
historical perspective
  on adolescence, 72–74
  on adolescent passage to adult-
    hood, 86–87
historical theories, 11
HIV/AIDS, **311**–312
Hodgson v. Minnesota, 78
home environment. *See also*
    parents/parenting
  achievement and, 329, 332
  parental style and, 330–331
  parental values and expectations
    and, 329–330
  quality of, 331
home leaving, current trends in, 87
homeschooling, 168
homosexuality. *See also* lesbian,
    gay, bisexual and transgen-
    der (LGBT) youth; sexual
    orientation
  antecedents of, 305–306
  lesbian and gay parents and, 120
hormonal feedback loop, 14–16
hormones
  brain development and, 52
  explanation of, **14**
  hormonal feedback loop and,
    14–16
  HPG axis, 14, 15
  as influence on adolescent devel-
    opment, 17
  sexual activity and, 299–300
hostile attributional bias, **147,**
    369–370
HPG (hypothalamic-pituitary-
    gonadal) axis, **15,** 16
human development
  ecological perspective on, 6
  psychosocial aspect of, 6–7
human papillomavirus (HPV), **311**
Hurricane Katrina, 87
hypothalamus, **15**
hypothetical thinking, 44–45

I

iatrogenic effects, **140**
identity
  as adolescent issue, 209–210
  crowd membership and, 133–134
  ethnicity and, 225–231 (See also
    ethnic identity)
  explanation of, **7**
  gender and, 232–234 (See also
    gender identity)

negative, 222
  personality dimensions and,
    212–213
  self-conceptions and, 210
  self-esteem and, 213–219
  sense of, 210
identity crisis
  Erikson's theoretical framework
    and, 219
  explanation of, 219
  identity vs. diffusion and,
    219–220
  resolution of, 221
  strategy to resolve, 223–224
identity development
  cognitive change and, 209–210
  over time, 224–225
  problems related to, 221–222
  puberty and, 209
  research on, 223–225
  social context of, 220–221
  social roles and, 210
identity diffusion, 219, **221**–222
identity foreclosure, **222**
identity status, approach to deter-
    mine, 223–234
identity vs. identity diffusion
    (Erikson), **219**–220
imaginary audience, **45**
immigrant paradox, **228**
immigrants. *See also* Asian youth;
    Hispanic youth
  academic achievement and,
    337–338
  crown membership and, 136
  ethnic identity in, 226, 228
  expectations for autonomy
    and, 248
  family functions and, 101
indifferent parents
  emotional autonomy and,
    242–243
  explanation of, **106,** 107
individual differences
  in effects of divorce, 115
  in intelligence, 60
  in pubertal maturation, 23
  in religiosity, 259
  in school transitions, 162–163
  in susceptibility to peer influ-
    ence, 247
individuation
  cultural differences and, 241
  emotional autonomy and, 239
  explanation of, **239**
  triggers of, 240–241
indulgent parents
  emotional autonomy and,
    242–243
  explanation of, **105**–106
industrialization, 73, 154
Industrial Revolution, 73
infant attachment, 264–266
influence. *See* susceptibility to
    influence
information-processing perspective
  attention in, 49
  explanation of, **49**
  memory in, 49–50
  metacognition in, 50–51
  nature of, 48–49

organization in, 50
  speed in, 50
initiation ceremonies, **77**
inner-city areas. *See* urban areas
Instagram, 207
instrumental aggression, **144**
intelligence
  academic achievement and, 333
  beliefs about, 326
  culture and, 61–62
  Gardner's theory of multiple, 61
  gender differences and, 325
  genetic factors in, 111, 331
  individual differences in, 60
  IQ and, 60–61
  Sternberg's "triarchic" theory
    of, 61
  types of, 61
intelligence quotient (IQ), 60–61, 333
intergenerational conflict, 11
internalizing problems
  comorbidity of, 352
  depression and, 372–375,
    377–378
  explanation of, **350**
  overview of, 371–372
  prevention and treatment of, 378
  suicide and, 375–377
internal working model, **265**
Internet. *See also* electronic media/
    electronic media use
  adolescent development and,
    203–205
  cognitive change and, 205
  cyberbullying and, 149–150
  pornography and, 200
  product marketing on, 206–207
  sexual content and, 205
  sexual harassment over, 307
  time spent on, 198
Internet addiction, **204**
intimacy. *See also* sexual activity
  as adolescent issue, 262
  changes in display of, 269–271
  cognitive change and, 262
  dating and romantic relationships
    and, 278–280
  explanation of, **7**
  family members as targets of,
    276–277
  in friendship, 268–269
  infant attachment and, 264–266
  other-sex friendships and, 278
  overview of, 262
  parents and peers as targets of,
    273–276
  psychosocial development and,
    288–289
  puberty and, 262
  sex cleavage and, 277–278
  sex differences in, 271–273,
    280, 304
  sexual behavior and, 293
  social roles and, 262
  Sullivan's theory of interpersonal
    development and, 263
  theoretical perspectives on,
    262–268
intuition, risk taking and, 67–68
inventionists, **72,** 73
invulnerability, 65

J

jealousy, 268–269
Jewish youth
  Bar (Bas) Mitzvah ceremonies
    and, 80, 81
  circumcision and, 82–83
  self-esteem in, 218
junior high schools. *See also*
    middle schools; secondary
    schools
  explanation of, **160**
  teachers in, 162
  transition to, 161–162
juvenile justice system, **77**
juvenile offending
  changes over time in, 365–367
  explanation of, **364**

K

KIPP, 158
kisspeptin, **16**

L

late adolescence, **4**
Latino youth. *See* Hispanic youth
laws, 64
learned helplessness, **327**–328
learning disabilities
  explanation of, **164**–165
  strategies for students with,
    165–166
learning theories, 9–10
Leave It to Beaver (TV program), 83
legal perspective
  adolescents as criminal
    defendants and, 78
  inconsistent legal status and,
    78–79
  legal boundaries of adolescence
    and, 77–78
  legal status of adolescents and,
    77–79
leisure/leisure activities. *See also*
    electronic media/electronic
    media use
  adolescent development and,
    195–196, 207
  global variations in, 183–184
  moods and, 190–191
  overview of, 182
  role of, 6
  statistics related to, 182–183
  structured, 191–193
  unstructured, 193–195
leptin, **16,** 25
lesbian, gay, bisexual and transgen-
    der (LGBT) youth
  antecedents of homosexuality
    and, 305–306
  dating and, 284
  explanation of, **284**
  harassment of, 308
  identity development and,
    231–232
  same-sex attraction and, 305
lesbian and gay parents, 120

LGBT youth. *See* lesbian, gay, bisexual and transgender (LGBT) youth; sexual orientation

life-course-persistent offenders, **367**, 368–370

limbic system
  explanation of, **55**
  neurotransmitters and, 57–58

logical thinking, risk taking and, 67–68

long-acting reversible contraception (LARC), 309–310

longitudinal studies, **26**

long-term memory, **49**

M

mainstreaming, **165**

marginality, adolescent, 10–11

marijuana, 353. *See also* substance use/abuse

marriage age, 278–279. *See also* divorce; parents/parenting

masculinity, 233–234

mass media. *See* electronic media/electronic media use; media/media use

mastery motivation, **324**

masturbation, 293, 304

mathematic achievement, in urban schools, 158

Mean Girls (movie), 146

media/media use. *See also* electronic media/electronic media use
  adolescent consumer and, 206–207
  adolescent development and, 198–199, 203–205
  adolescent pregnancy and, 315
  availability of, 197–198
  body dissatisfaction and, 36–37
  body image and, 36–37, 206
  drugs and, 202
  impact of, 198–199
  patterns of, 196–197
  sexual messages and, 198–201
  sleep patterns and, 28
  substance use and, 202
  violence and, 198, 201–202

media practice model, **199**

melatonin, **16,** 28, 29

memory
  autobiographical, 49
  in information-processing perspective, 49–50
  long-term memory, 49
  working memory, 40

menarche, **21,** 30, 71, 72

menstruation. *See* menarche

mental health. *See also* depression
  adolescent parenthood and, 316, 317
  early maturation in girls and, 31–32
  eating disorders and, 39
  in emerging adulthood, 75–77
  ethnic identity and, 227, 229, 230
  genetic factors and, 111
  of parents, 100
  poverty and, 91, 119–120

mentalizing, **62**

mentoring programs, 90

metacognition
  explanation of, **45**
  in information-processing perspective, 50–51

methylphenidate (Ritalin), 166

middle adolescence, **4**

middle schools. *See also* junior high schools; schools; secondary schools
  academic achievement in, 332, 339
  explanation of, **160**
  transition to, 161–162
  violence in, 174

midlife crisis, **99**

midlife stage, 99–100

minority youth. *See also* American Indian/Alaska Native youth; Asian youth; Black youth; ethnicity; Hispanic youth
  academic achievement and, 335–338
  adolescent pregnancy and, 312, 315–316
  as distinct minority in schools, 167
  effects of discrimination on, 228–230
  enrolled in higher education, 176, 177
  expression of intimacy and, 274
  innercity schools and, 158
  parenting styles and, 108–109
  school disengagement in, 162
  self-esteem in, 216–218
  in single-parent families, 113
  teacher expectations and, 170–171
  tracking and, 163–164
  transition to adulthood and, 88–89

Monitoring the Future study, **353**

moods/moodiness. *See also* anxiety; depression
  leisure activities and, 190–191
  puberty and, 27
  student engagement and, 173

moral behavior, moral reasoning and, 251–252

moral development
  explanation of, 249
  moral behavior and, 251–252
  moral reasoning and, 249–251

moral disengagement, **252**

moral reasoning
  assessment of, 249–250
  moral behavior and, 251–252
  parenting styles and, 252
  prosocial behavior and, 253
  stages of, 250–251

mortality, in adolescents, 40–41

mothers. *See also* families/family relationships; fathers; parents/parenting
  adolescent relationships with, 29, 104
  communication between adolescents and divorced, 117–118
  intimacy and, 274

LGBT youth and relationship with, 306
  single-parent, 302

motivation
  achievement, 323–324
  mastery, 324
  performance, 324
  transition to secondary school and, 328

motor vehicle accidents, 40

multidimensional model of racial identity (MMRI), **230**

multidimensional thinking, 46–47

multiethnic, **231**

multiethnic youth, identity development in, 231

multiple intelligences theory (Gardner), 61

multisystemic family therapy, **371**

muscle, sex differences in, 19

music, violent, 201–202

N

National Assessment of Educational Progress (NAEP), 338–339

Native Americans. *See* American Indian/Alaska Native youth

negative emotionality, **352**

negative feedback seeking, 327

negative identity, **222**

neighborhood conditions
  access to resourses and, 94
  adolescent development and, 90–94
  affluent, 91
  collective efficacy and, 92
  stress and, 92–94

"nerds," 131–132

neuroendocrine, **377**

neurons, **52–53**

neuroscientific theories, 9

neurotransmitters, **53,** 57–58, 360

new media, **196**. *See also* electronic media/electronic media use

No Child Left Behind Act (NCLB) (2002), 155–156

noncognitive factors
  achievement motivation and, 323–324
  beliefs about success and failure and, 324–328
  explanation of, **322**

nonshared environmental influences, **111**

non-suicidal self-injury (NSSI), **375–376**

nutrition
  obesity and, 35, 36
  pubertal maturation and, 23, 25

nuturance rights, 64

O

obesity. *See also* eating disorders
  correlates and consequences of, 34–36
  prevention and treatment of, 36

pubertal maturation and, 25
  statistics related to, 34

occupational achievement
  occupational choice and, 346–347
  overview of, 343
  parental and peer influences and, 345–346
  plans for, 343–344
  work values and, 344–345

occupational plans, 343–344

Odd Girl Out (Simmons), 146

online gaming, 198

operant conditioning, 10

opposite-sex friendships, 278

oppositional-defiant disorder, **362**

organismic theories, 9

organization, in information-processing perspective, 50

ovaries, **15**

overt antisocial behavior, **364**

oxytocin, **375**

P

parental demandingness, **105**

parental responsiveness, **105**

parenting styles
  achievement and, 171, 329–331
  authoritarian, 105, 106, 108–109, 242, 247
  authoritative, 105–108, 242, 247–248, 252, 253, 330–331
  behavioral autonomy and, 247–248
  emotional autonomy and, 241–243, 252
  ethnicity in, 106–109
  indifferent, 106, 107, 242–243
  indulgent, 105–106, 242–243
  moral and prosocial reasoning and, 252
  overview of, 105

parents/parenting, 93. *See also* families/family relationships; fathers; mothers; single-parent families
  academic achievement and, 171, 329–331, 335
  adolescent, 315–318
  of adopted youth, 120
  antisocial peer groups and, 139–140
  attachment to, 267–268
  changes in influence of, 245–246
  delinquency and, 368
  extracurricular participation and, 191, 192
  of foster children, 120–121
  generational gap and, 96–97
  identity status and, 224
  immigrant, 101
  intimacy and, 273–276
  lesbian and gay, 120
  mental health of, 100
  midlife crisis and, 99–100
  occupational achievement and, 345–346
  poverty and, 93

parents/parenting—*Cont.*
  puberty and relationship with, 29–30
  real or symbolic separation from, 79–80
  school transitions and, 163
  on sexual activity, 300–302
  as targets of intimacy, 273–275
parochial schools, 167, 168
PATHS (Promoting Alternative Thinking Strategies), 151
peak height velocity, **18**
peer groups. *See also* friends/ friendship
  academic achievement and, 331–333
  achievement and, 322
  antisocial, 138–140
  change in structure of, 130–132
  cliques and, 128–129, 135–137
  common interests and, 138–140
  in contemporary society, 124–125
  crowds and, 129–130, 133–135
  ethnic segregation in, 134–137
  explanation of, **123**
  extracurricular activities and, 192
  family functions and, 100
  gangs as, 139
  harassment and, 147
  importance of, 6
  nature of adolescent, 127–128
  popularity and rejection in, 142–145
  psychosocial development and, 151
  pubertal maturation and, 30
  relational aggression and, 145–147
  risk taking and, 67
  romance and, 130–131
  selection vs. socialization and, 140–142
  sexual behavior and, 302–303
  susceptibility to pressure by, 245–247
  transformation of "nerds" and, **131–132**
  unstructured leisure activities and, 193
  victimization and harassment and, 147–151
  youth culture and, 125–127
peers
  attachment to, 267–268
  occupational achievement and, 345–346
  as targets of intimacy, 273–275
perceived popularity, **142**, 143
performance motivation, **324**
personal fable, **45–46**
personality dimensions, in adolescence, 212–213
pheromones, **24**
physical activity, obesity and, 35–36
physical punishment, cultural differences in, 104
Piagetian theory of cognitive change, 9, 47–48, 249
pituitary gland, **15**
plasticity, **54–55**

platonic relationships, **264**
political behavior, 256
political thinking, 255–256
popularity. *See also* rejection
  aggression and, 143–144
  determinants of, 142–143
  dynamics of, 144–145
  friendship and, 144–145
  helping unpopular teens and, 150–151
  perceived, 142, 143
  rejection and, 145
  sociometric, 142–143
pornography, 200, 205
positive youth development, **195–196**
possibilities, thinking about, 43–45
possible selves, **210**
postconventional moral reasoning, **250–251**
postsecondary education
  characteristics of, 177
  emerging adulthood and, 77
  enrollment growth in, 176
  historical background of, 176
  occupational choice and, 346, 347
  students that do not go on to, 178–179
  transition from high school to, 177–178
poverty
  access to resources and, 94
  adolescent childbearing and, 316
  adolescent employment and, 189
  adolescent parenthood and, 315
  delinquency and, 92, 93
  in families, 113–114, 119–120
  impact of chronic, 119–120
  impact on adolescent development, 91–92
  parenting and, 93
  school reform and, 154–155
  statistics related to, 113
  stress and, 92–94
  tracking and, 163
  transition to adulthood and, 72, 88–89
  urban schools and, 158
power, family relations and, 101
preconventional moral reasoning, **250**
prefrontal cortex, **55**, 57, 58
pregnancy
  adolescent, 312–315
  contraception and, 79, 309–311
  meaning of sex and, 305
  unintended, 312–314
premature affluence, **187**
preoperational period, **47**
preschool intervention programs, 334–335
primary control strategies, **379**
priorities, age differences in, 65–67
private schools, 167, 168
problem behavior syndrome, **351**
Project DARE, 361–362
prosocial behavior, **249**
prosocial reasoning, **252**, 253
protective factors, **359–360**
psychoanalytic theory, 238–239

psychological control, **242**
psychopaths, **362**
psychosocial, 6
psychosocial development
  in adolescence, 6–8
  autonomy and, 237
  in emerging adulthood, 75–77
  intimacy and, 288–289
  peer group and, 151
  schools and, 153, 180
  sexual activity and, 297–298
  social redefinition and, 70–71
psychosocial moratorium, **220–221**
psychosocial problems
  age of onset, 8
  aggression and, 363–364
  antisocial behavior and, 364–365, 367–371
  comorbidity of externalizing, 350–352
  conduct disorder and, 362–363
  depression and, 372–375, 377–378
  externalizing, 362–371
  general principles related to, 348–350
  internalizing, 371–378
  juvenile offending and, 364, 365–367
  nature of, 350
  non-suicidal self-injury and, 375–376
  stress and coping and, 378–379
  substance use and, 352–362
  suicide and, 375–377
puberty
  achievement and, 322
  adolescent sexuality and, 291–292
  autonomy and, 237
  as beginning of adolescence, 71
  body dissatisfaction in, 37–38
  change in stature and body dimensions in, 18–19
  early and late maturation and, 30–34
  eating disorders in, 36–39
  endocrine system in, 14–16
  explanation of, **4**
  family relationships and, 29–30, 101–103
  first ejaculation in, 30
  hormonal influences in, 17
  identity development in, 209
  immediate impact of, 26–30
  impact of specific pubertal events and, 30
  intimacy and, 262
  moodiness in, 27
  obesity and, 25
  overview of, 14
  peer relationships in, 30
  physical manifestations of, 14
  psychological and social impact of, 26–34
  self-esteem in, 26–27, 31
  sexual maturation in, 19–21
  sleep patterns in, 27–29
  timing and tempo of, 21–25
  triggers of, 16–17

Q

Queen Bees and Wannabees (Wiseman), 146
quinceañera, **79**

R

rape
  date, 306–308
  statutory, 71
reactive aggression, **144**
reading achievement, 158
reasoning, prosocial, 252
recapitulation theory, 8–9
reference groups, **133**
rejection. *See also* popularity
  consequences of, 146–147
  determinants of, 142–143
  interventions for, 150–151
  reasons for, 145
  relational aggression and, 145–146
rejection sensitivity, **265**
relational aggression, **145–146**
relativism, 47
religiosity, **258**
religious beliefs
  development of, 257–258
  impact on adolescent development of, 259
  individual differences and, 259
  overview of, 256–257
  patterns of involvement and, 258–259
religious schools, 167
remarriage, 113, 118–119
reminiscence bump, **49**
resilience, **379**
response inhibition, **56**
responsibility, employment and, 187–188
reverse causation, **199**
rights, 64
risk factors
  explanation of, **303**
  poverty as, 113–114
  for substance use, 358–359
  for suicide, 376
risk taking. *See also* adolescent pregnancy; substance use/ abuse; tobacco use
  behavioral decision theory and, 64–65
  emotional and contextual influences on, 66–67
  gangs and, 139
  invulnerability and, 65
  logic and intuition and, 67–68
  moral reasoning and, 251–252
  puberty and, 322
  risky sex and, 309–318
  by sexually abused youth, 308–309
  strategies to reduce, 68
  values and priorities and, 65–67
risky sex
  adolescent parenthood as consequence of, 315–318
  adolescent pregnancy and, 312–315

contraceptive use and, 309–311
sex education to prevent, 318–319
sexually transmitted diseases and, 311–312
Ritalin (methylphenidate), 166
rite of passage, **5**
romantic relationships. *See also* dating; intimacy
in adolescence, 279
nature and significance of, 280–281
peer groups and, 130–131
phases of, 283–284
Roper v. Simmons, 78
routine activity theory, **193**
rumination, 374
rural areas, dating violence and, 286

S

safe sex, 318–319
same-sex attraction, 305. *See also* sexual orientation
Sandy Hook Elementary School shooting, 175
sarcasm, 46–47
SAT (Scholastic Assessment Test) scores, 339
scaffolding, **62**
scarification, **80**
school dropout rate
adolescent pregnancy and, 315
correlates of, 342–343
employment and, 188
historical background of, 341–342
minority youth and, 158
school factors in, 343
strategies to lower, 342–343
unemployment and, 190
school performance, **333**. *See also* academic achievement
school reform
historical background of, 154–155
innercity students and, 158
No Child Left Behind and, 155–156
standards-based, 157
schools. *See also* academic achievement; education; postsecondary education; secondary schools
adolescent development and, 179–180
age grouping in, 160–161
alternatives to public, 167–169
background on, 153–154
bullying outside of, 150
characteristics of good, 179
charter, 157, 158, 168
classroom climate in, 169–170
class size and, 159–160
elementary vs. secondary, 161–162
environment in, 328–329
ethnic composition of, 167
historical background of, 154–155

non-college-bound students and, 178–179, 190
overcrowding in, 160
parochial, 167, 168
private, 167, 168
psychosocial development and, 153, 180
role of, 6
within schools, 159
secondary education and, 153–158
size of, 158–159
start time of, 28–29
student engagement in, 171–174
students with ADHD in, 166
teacher expectations and student performance in, 170–171
tracking in, 163–166
transition from high school to postsecondary, 177–178
transition to secondary, 161–163, 328
urban, 158
schools within schools, **159**
school violence
lethal, 175–176
overview of, 174
strategies to reduce, 175
school vouchers, **157,** 168
science achievement, in urban schools, 158
secondary control strategies, **379**
secondary education system, **153**
secondary schools
academic achievement in, 339
drop rate in, 158, 188, 190, 315, 342–343
elementary schools vs., 161–162
explanation of, **153**
historical background of, 154–155
motivation and, 328
non-college-bound students, 178–179, 190
origins of, 154–155
overcrowding and, 160
transition to, 161–163, 328
transition to postsecondary education from, 177–178
violence in, 174, 175
secondary sex characteristics
explanation of, **20**
pubertal maturation and, 30
secular trend, **25**
secure attachment, **265**
selective attention, **48**
selective serotonin reuptake inhibitors (SSRIs), **378**
self-care, 193–194
self-conceptions
differentiation of, 210–211
explanation of, **210**
false-self behavior and, 211–212
organization and integration of, 211
self-consciousness, 45, 50, 212, **214**
self-control, 93
self-efficacy, **326**–327
self-esteem
body dissatisfaction and, 32, 33
components of, 215–216

consequences of high or low, 218–219
ethnic differences in, 216–218
explanation of, **210**
group differences in, 216–218
influences on, 218
puberty and, 26–27, 31
school transitions and, 161
sex differences in, 216
sexual abuse and, 308
stability and changes in, 213–215
victimization and, 147
self-fulfilling prophecies, 170
self-handicapping, **324**
self-image, 32, 214–215
self-image stabillity, **214**
self-regulation, 369
sensation seeking, **66**
sense of identity, **210**. *See also* identity
sensitivity, 374–375
sensorimotor period, **47**
serotonin, **57**
service learning, **254**
set point, **15**
sex differences. *See also* gender differences
in achievement motivation, 325
in adjustment to remarriage, 118
in brain development, 52
in depression, 373–374
in educational attainment, 326
in family relationships, 103–104
in intimacy, 271–273, 280, 304
in meaning of sex, 304–305
in muscle and fat, 19
in partner preferences, 284
in self-esteem, 216
sex education, 318–319
sex segregation, in cliques, 135–136
sexual abuse
in adolescence, 294–295
date rape and, 306–308
studies of, 308–309
sexual activity
during adolescence, 292–293
contextual influences on, 300
historical trends in, 296
hormonal influences on, 299–300
household composition and, 302
media exposure and, 198–201
parental influences on, 300–302
peer influences on, 302–303
poverty and, 91, 92
psychological development and, 297–299
stages of, 293
start of, 7
substance use and, 297–298
virginity pledges and, 303–304
sexual harassment
date rape and, 306–308
friendship and, 141
sexual-minority youth and, 308
sexual intercourse
ethnicity in age of initiation for, 294–295
prevalence of, 293–294

timing of sexual initiation and, 295
sexuality
as adolescent issue, 291
cognitive change and, 292
electronic media and, 198, 199, 201–202
explanation of, **7**
parent-adolescent communication and, 301–302
puberty and, 291–292
social roles and, 292
sexually transmitted diseases (STDs)
condom use and, 309
explanation of, **311**
protections against, 312
sexual maturation
in boys, 20
in girls, 20–21
overview of, 19–20
sexual-minority youth. *See also* lesbian, gay, bisexual and transgender (LGBT) youth
dating and, 284
harassment of, 308
identity development and, 231–232
sexual orientation
antecedents of homosexuality and, 305–306
explanation of, **231**
fluid nature of, 232
identity development and, 231–232
same-sex attraction and, 305
sexual preditors, 205
sexual socialization, **304**
shared environmental influences, **111**
sibling deidentification, **112**
sibling rivalry, **112**
siblings
behavioral genetics and, 110–111
differences in, 111–112
environmental influences and, 111
intimacy and, 276
relationships between, 109–110
single-parent families. *See also* divorce
adolescent employment and, 189
adolescent sexual activity and, 302
adolescent sexual initiation and, 294
nature of, 112–113
social support and, 115
"sleeper" effects of divorce, 116
sleep patterns
electronic media and, 28
obesity and, 36
puberty and, 27–29
smoking. *See* tobacco use
social brain, 58–59
social capital, **169, 331**
social cognition
explanation of, **62**
laws, civil liberties, and rights and, 64
social conventions and, 63–64
social relationships and, 63
theory of mind and, 62–63

social control theory, **351**
social conventions, **63**–64
socialization
    ethnic, 227
    from family and citizenship roles
        in previous eras, 86–87
    gender-role, 232–234
    intimacy and, 272–273
social learning theory, 10
social networks
    cliques and structure of, 128–129
    communication through, 269
social promotion, **156**
social redefinition
    emphasis on differences between
        sexes and, 80
    explanation of, **70**
    passage of information from
        older generation and, 80
    process of, 79
    psychosocial development and,
        70–71
    separation from parents and, 79
    in traditional cultures, 82–84
social roles
    achievement and, 322
    identity development and, 210
    intimacy and, 262
    sexuality and, 292
social skills, rejection and, 146–147
social support
    adolescent parenthood and, 318
    explanation of, **275**–276
    grandparents and, 115
    single parenthood and, 115
social transitions
    into adulthood, 87–90
    clarity variations in, 81–84
    continuity variations in, 84–87
    dimensions of, 80–81
    explanation of, 5
    neighborhood influences on,
        90–94
socioeconomic status (SES). *See
    also* poverty
    academic achievement and,
        334–335
    occupational achievement and, 345
    political thinking and, 256
sociological theories, 10, 11
sociometric popularity, **142**–143
somatic development
    adolescent growth spurt and, 18–19
    body dissatisfaction and, 19
    sex differences in muscle and fat
        and, 19
South Park (TV program), 47
speed, in information-processing
    perspective, 50
spirituality, **258**
sports, 191–193. *See also* extracur-
    ricular activities
spurious causation, **199**
standards-based reform, **157**–158
Stanford-Binet test, 60
status offense, **77**
statutory rape, **71**
stepparents, 118–119
stereotypes
    of adolescents, 11–12, 162
    scientific study vs., 11–12

stereotype threat, **325**
stimulant medications, 166
"storm and stress" period, 102
stress
    coping and, 378–379
    depression and, 374, 377–378
    diathesis-stress model and,
        377–378
    divorce and, 115
    immigrants and, 101
    neighborhood conditions and,
        92–94
    poverty and, 92–94, 120
    rejection and, 145
student engagement
    explanation of, **171**
    importance of, 171–172
    out-of-school influences on, 172
    school environment and, 328–329
    strategies to enhance, 172–174
    topology of, 172
substance use/abuse
    adolescent brain and, 360–361
    behavioral decision theory and,
        64–65
    causes and consequences of,
        357–360
    changes over time, 354–355
    distinguishing between use and
        abuse, 362
    employment and, 188–189
    ethnic differences in, 355–356
    explanation of, **350**
    media exposure and, 202
    overview of, 352–353
    peer groups and, 140–141
    predictors and consequences of, 358
    prevalence of, 353–354
    prevention and treatment of,
        361–362
    progression of, 356–357
    protective factors and, 359–360
    risk factors for, 358–359
    sexual activity and, 296–297
    statistics related to, 354, 355, 357
success
    attributions for, 327–328
    beliefs about, 324–328
suicidal ideation, **375**
suicide
    prevalence of, 375–376
    risk factors for, 376
    suicide contagion and, 376–377
suicide contagion, **376**–377
suicide risk, genetic factors in, 111
Sullivan's theory of interpersonal
    development, 263, 268
susceptibility to influence
    explanation of, 245
    individual differences in, 247
    parenting and behavioral auton-
        omy and, 247–248
    parents and peers and, 245–247
synapse, **53**–54
synaptic pruning, **53**, 56

T

Tanner stages, **20**
teachers
    classroom climate and, 169–170

extracurricular activities
        and, 192
    in good schools, 179
    junior high vs. elementary, 162
    performance and expectations of
        students, 170–171
    secondary-school, 328
    sexual harassment by, 307
    student engagement and,
        171–174
    violence against, 174
teenagers, **73**–74. *See also*
    adolescence/adolescents
television, 201. *See also* electronic
    media/electronic media use
testes, **15**
testosterone, 52, **299**
theoretical perspectives
    on adolescent thinking, 47
    anthropological theories
        and, 11
    biosocial theories and, 8–9
    historical theories and, 11
    information-processing perspec-
        tive and, 48–51
    on intimacy, 262–268
    learning theories and, 9–10
    nature vs. nurture and, 8
    organismic theories and, 9
    Piagetian theory and, 9,
        47–48
    sociological theories and,
        10–11
theory of mind, **62**–63
tobacco use. *See also* substance
    use/abuse
    employment and, 189
    media exposure and, 202
    methods to reduce, 41
    peer groups and, 140
tracking
    explanation of, **163**
    impact of lower, 164
    pros and cons of, 163–164
    student achievement and, 164
    students at the extremes and,
        164–166
transgender youth, 232
transitory experimentation,
    348–349
triarchic theory of intelligence
    (Sternberg), 61
trichomoniasis, **311**

U

underachievers, **324**
unemployment
    adolescent, 189–190
    educational attainment and,
        178–179
unpopularity. *See* rejection
urban areas
    adolescent employment in, 189
    dating violence and, 286
    education in, 158
U.S. Supreme Court
    legal status of adolescents and,
        78
    school desegregation and, 167
    violent video games and, 202

V

values
    age differences in, 65–67
    parental, 329–330
victims/victimization. *See also*
    harassment
    bullying and, 148–150
    crime, 366
    effects of, 147–148
    interventions for, 150–151
    sexual, 306–309
video games
    effects of, 196
    right to obtain, 79
    violent, 201–202
violence
    dating and, 286–288
    media exposure and, 198,
        201–202
    poverty and, 93–94
    school, 174–176
    sports participation and, 192
viral marketing, **207**
virginity pledges, 303–304
volunteerism, 253, 254

W

Wechsler Adult Intelligence Scale
    (WAIS-III), 60
Wechsler Intelligence Scale for
    Children (WISC-IV), 60
weight, 18–19. *See also* obesity
white matter, 54
White youth. *See also* ethnicity
    academic achievement and, 158
    adolescent pregnancy and, 312
    crowd membership and, 134
    dating relationships and, 281
    drinking among, 142–143
    enrolled in higher education,
        176, 177
    expectations for autonomy in, 248
    obesity among, 35
    self-esteem in, 216
    sexual initiation and, 294
    timing and tempo of puberty
        in, 23
    tracking and, 164
    transition to adulthood, 88, 89
working memory, **49**–50
work values, **344**–345

Y

youth, **74**
youth culture
    effects of, 127
    nature of, 127
    views related to, 125
Youth Internet Safety Survey, 205
YouTube, 203, 206–207

Z

zero tolerance, **175**
zone of proximal development
    (Vygotsky), **61**